STREET ATLAS
Glasgow
and West Central Scotland

First published in 1995 by

Philip's, a division of
Octopus Publishing Group Ltd
2-4 Heron Quays, London E14 4JP

Third colour edition 2005
First impression 2005

ISBN-10   0-540-08835-8 (pocket)
ISBN-13   978-0-540-08835-5 (pocket)

© Philip's 2005

 Ordnance Survey®

This product includes mapping data licensed from
Ordnance Survey® with the permission of the
Controller of Her Majesty's Stationery Office.
© Crown copyright 2005. All rights reserved.
Licence number 100011710.

Printed and bound in Spain
by Cayfosa-Quebecor

Contents

Digital Data

The exceptionally high-quality mapping found in this atlas is available as digital data in TIFF
format, which is easily convertible to other bitmapped (raster) image formats.

The index is also available in digital form as a standard database table. It contains all the details
found in the printed index together with the National Grid reference for the map square in which
each entry is named.

For further information and to discuss your requirements, please contact Philip's on
020 7644 6932 or james.mann@philips-maps.co.uk

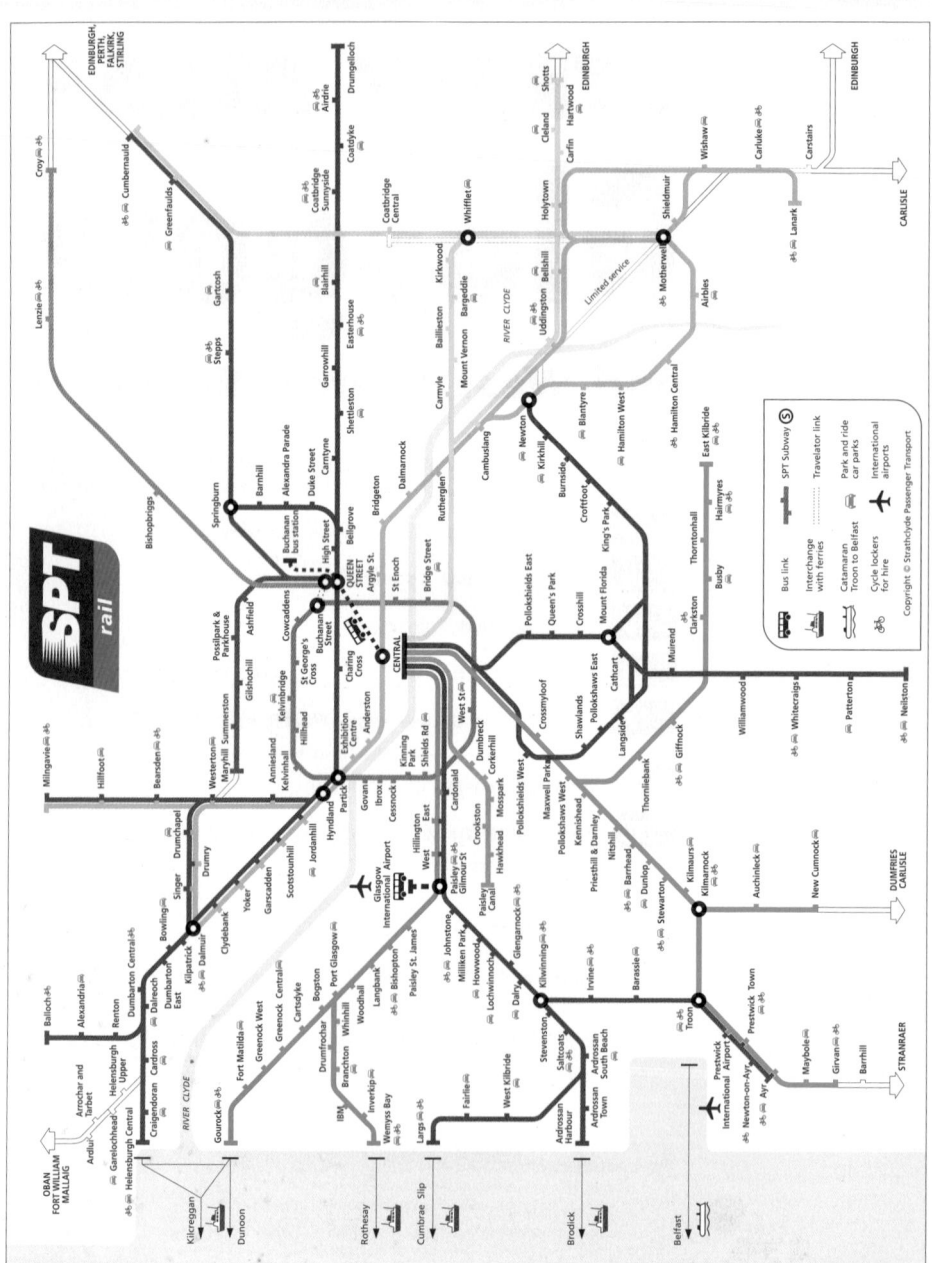

Map reproduced by permission of Strathclyde Passenger Transport

Motorway with junction number (22a)	
Primary route – dual/single carriageway	
A road – dual/single carriageway	
B road – dual/single carriageway	
Minor road – dual/single carriageway	
Other minor road – dual/single carriageway	
Road under construction	
Tunnel, covered road	
Rural track, private road or narrow road in urban area	
Gate or obstruction to traffic (restrictions may not apply at all times or to all vehicles)	
Path, bridleway, byway open to all traffic, road used as a public path	
Pedestrianised area	
DY7 Postcode boundaries	
County and unitary authority boundaries	
Railway, tunnel, railway under construction	
Tramway, tramway under construction	
Miniature railway	
Railway station Walsall	
Private railway station	
Metro station South Shields	
Tram stop, tram stop under construction	
Bus, coach station	

◆	Ambulance station
◆	Coastguard station
◆	Fire station
◆	Police station
+	Accident and Emergency entrance to hospital
H	Hospital
+	Place of worship
i	Information Centre (open all year)
🛒	Shopping Centre
P P&R	Parking, Park and Ride
PO	Post Office
⚊ 🚐	Camping site, caravan site
▶ ✕	Golf course, picnic site
Prim Sch	Important buildings, schools, colleges, universities and hospitals
	Built up area
	Woods
River Medway	Water name
	River, weir, stream
	Canal, lock, tunnel
	Water
	Tidal water
Church	Non-Roman antiquity
ROMAN FORT	Roman antiquity
87	Adjoining page indicators and overlap bands
237	The colour of the arrow and the band indicates the scale of the adjoining or overlapping page (see scales below)

Acad	Academy	Inst	Institute	Recn Gd	Recreation Ground
Allot Gdns	Allotments	Ct	Law Court		
Cemy	Cemetery	L Ctr	Leisure Centre	Resr	Reservoir
C Ctr	Civic Centre	LC	Level Crossing	Ret Pk	Retail Park
CH	Club House	Liby	Library	Sch	School
Coll	College	Mkt	Market	Sh Ctr	Shopping Centre
Crem	Crematorium	Meml	Memorial	TH	Town Hall/House
Ent	Enterprise	Mon	Monument	Trad Est	Trading Estate
Ex H	Exhibition Hall	Mus	Museum	Univ	University
Ind Est	Industrial Estate	Obsy	Observatory	W Twr	Water Tower
IRB Sta	Inshore Rescue Boat Station	Pal	Royal Palace	Wks	Works
		PH	Public House	YH	Youth Hostel

■ The small numbers around the edges of the maps identify the 1 kilometre National Grid lines
■ The dark grey border on the inside edge of some pages indicates that the mapping does not continue onto the adjacent page

Enlarged mapping only

	Railway or bus station building
	Place of interest
	Parkland

The scale of the maps on the pages numbered in blue is 4.2 cm to 1 km • 2⅔ inches to 1 mile • 1: 23810	0 ¼ ½ ¾ 1 mile 0 250m 500m 750m 1 kilometre
The scale of the maps on pages numbered in red is 8.4 cm to 1 km • 5⅓ inches to 1 mile • 1: 11900	0 220 yards 440 yards 660 yards ½ mile 0 125m 250m 375m ½ kilometre

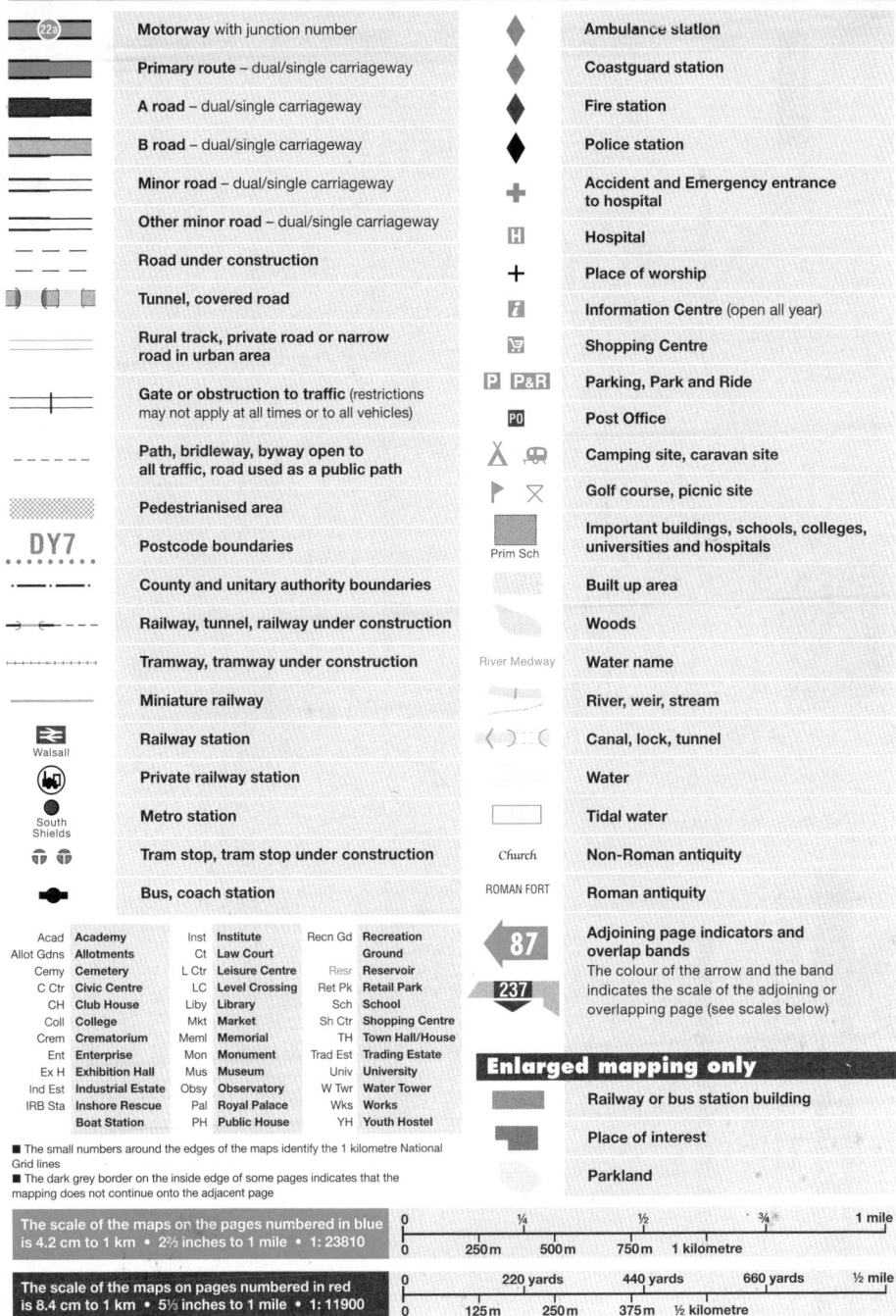

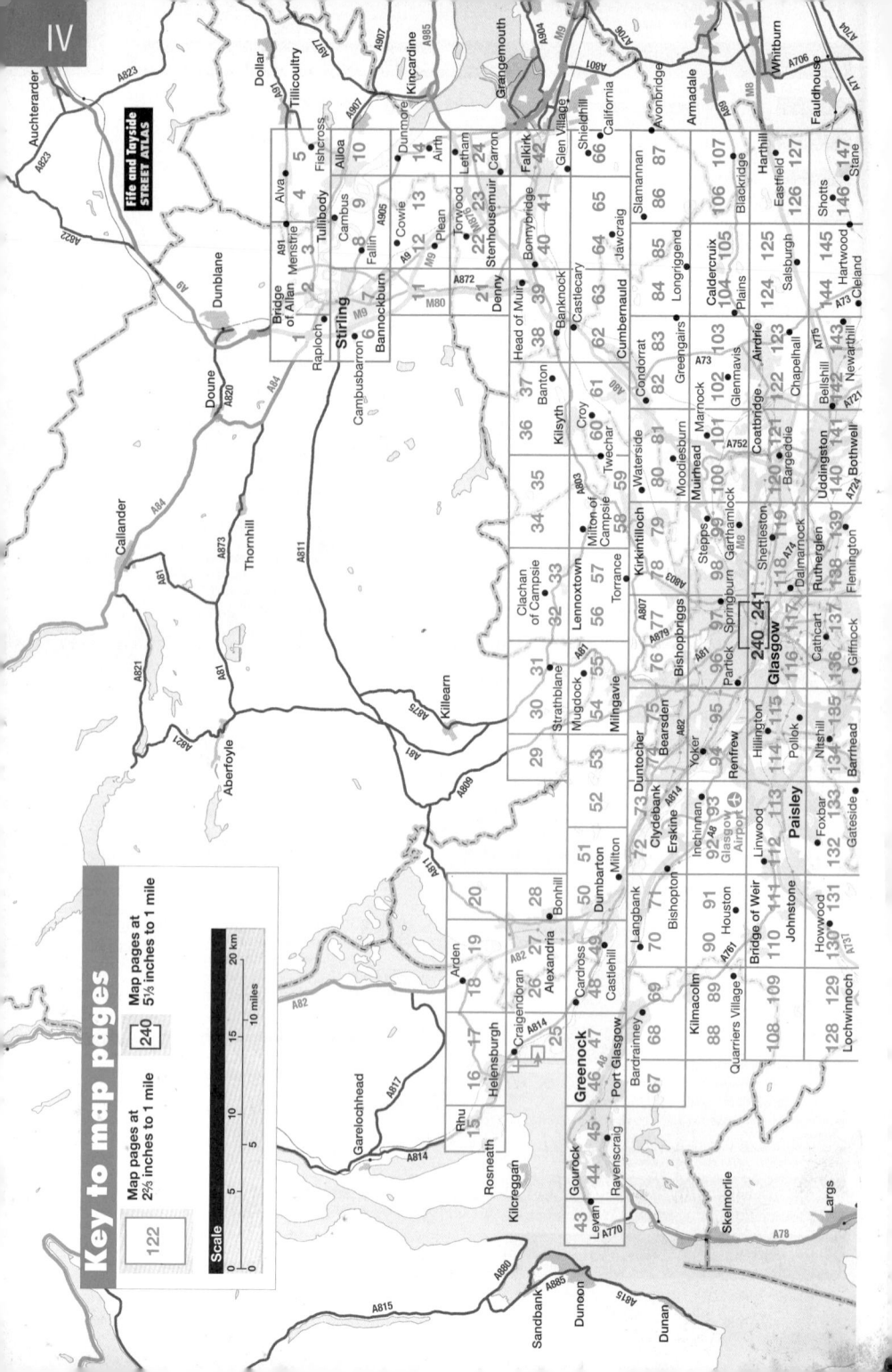

IV

Fife and Tayside
STREET ATLAS

Auchterarder
A823
A823
A822
A9
Dunblane
Doune
A820
A84
A873
Callander
A821
A81
Thornhill
A811
Aberfoyle
A821
A81
A811
Killearn
A875
A809
Garelochhead
A817
Kilcreggan
Rosneath
A814
A880
A885
Sandbank
Dunoon
A815
Dunan
A815

Dollar
Tillicoultry
A977
A907
Fishcross
Alva
Tullibody
Cambus
A91
Menstrie
Bridge of Allan
A9
Raploch
Stirling
M9
Bannockburn
Cambusbarron
Bridge of Allan
M80
A872

Kincardine
A985
Dunmore
Airth
Cowie
Plean
A9
M9
Fallin
Stenhousemuir
Torwood
A905
Denny
M872

Grangemouth
A904
M9
A801
Letham
Carron
Bonnybridge
Banknock
Castlecary
Head of Muir
Banton
Kilsyth
Croy
Twechar
Milton of Campsie
Kirkintilloch
A803
Lennoxtown
Torrance
Milngavie
Strathblane
Mugdock
A81
Clachan of Campsie
A807
Bishopbriggs
A879
A803
Stepps
Muirhead

Glen Village
Falkirk
Shieldhill
California
Avonbridge
M9
A706
Whitburn
Armadale
A89
Fauldhouse
M8
A704
A71
A801
Harthill
Shotts
Stane
A7074
A8
A73
A725
A721

Slamannan
Jawcraig
Longriggend
Greengairs
Plains
Airdrie
Coatbridge
Glenmavis
A73
A752
Marnock
Bargeddie
Bellshill
A75
Newarthill
Cleland
Hartwood
A73
Salsburgh
Caldercrux
Blackridge
Eastfield
Condorrat
Cumbernauld

Waterside
Moodiesburn
Garnkirk
Garnhaven
Springburn
Partick
240 241
Glasgow
Cathcart
Giffnock
Barrhead
Nitshill
Pollok
Hillington
Renfrew
Yoker
Bearsden
Duntocher
Clydebank
Erskine
Inchinnan
A8
Glasgow Airport
Linwood
Paisley
Foxbar
Gateside
A737
Johnstone
Howwood
A761
Houston
Bridge of Weir
Quarriers Village
Kilmacolm
Lochwinnoch
Port Glasgow
Greenock
A8
Gourock
Ravenscraig
Levan
A770
Skelmorlie
Largs
A78

Dumbarton
Milton
Bonhill
Alexandria
A82
Cardross
Castlehill
Langbank
Bishopton
Bardrainney
Arden
Craigendoran
A814
Helensburgh
Rhu
A814

Kirkintilloch
Rutherglen
Dalmarnock
Uddingston
Bothwell
Flemington
Chapelhall

1 2 3 4 5
6 7 8 9 10
11 12 13 14
21 22 23 24
37 38 39 40 41
62 63 64 65 66
82 83 84 85 86 87
102 103 104 105 106 107
122 123 124 125 126 127
142 143 144 145 146 147
140 141
136 137 138 139
116 117 118 119
96 97 98 99 100 101
76 77 78 79 80 81
58 59 60 61
34 35 36
52 53 54 55 56 57
72 73 74 75
90 91 92 93 94 95
110 111 112 113 114 115
130 131 132 133 134 135
108 109
128 129
88 89
67 68 69 70 71
46 47 48 49 50 51
43 44 45
15 16 17 18 19 20
25 26 27 28 29 30 31 32 33

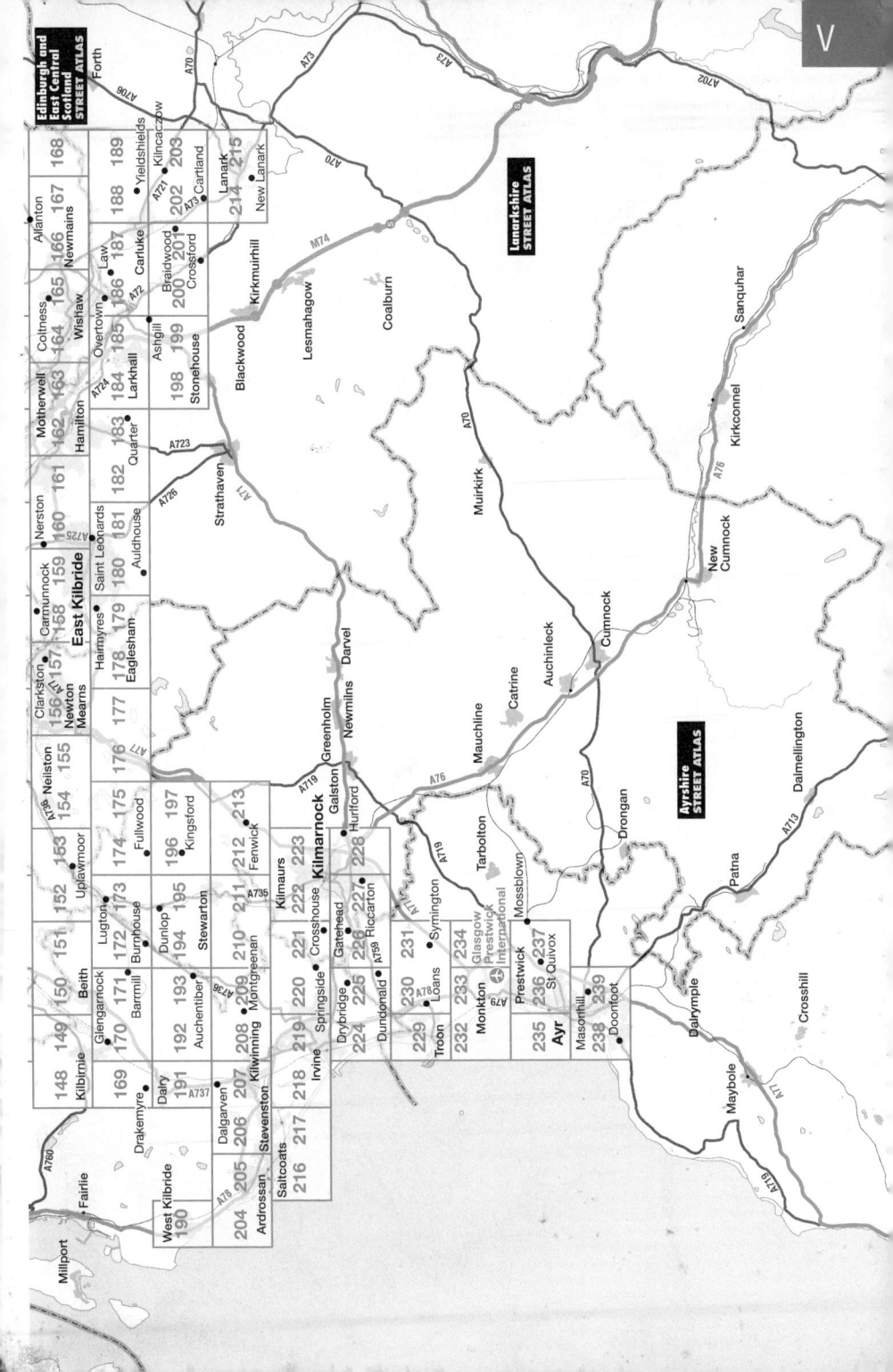

V

Edinburgh and East Central Scotland STREET ATLAS

Lanarkshire STREET ATLAS

Ayrshire STREET ATLAS

Forth
Allanton
168 Newmains
167 166 165 164 163 Wishaw 162 161 160 159 158 157 156 155 154 153 152 151 150 149 148

Coltness
Motherwell Hamilton

Yieldshields
Kilncadzow
189 203 Cartland Lanark
188 202 201 200 Crossford 214 215
187 186 Braidwood New Lanark
185 199 Ashgill
184 198 Stonehouse
183 Larkhall
182 Quarter

Law
Overtown
Carluke
Kirkmuirhill
Blackwood
Lesmahagow
Coalburn
M74
A72
A73

Saint Leonards
Auldhouse
Nerston
East Kilbride
Carnunnock
Clarkston
Newton Mearns
Neilston

Strathaven
Muirkirk
Sanquhar
Kirkconnel
New Cumnock

181 180 179 178 177 176 175 174 173 172 171 170 169
Hairmyres
Eaglesham
Darvel
Newmilns
Greenholm
Galston
Hurlford
Fenwick
Kingsford
Fullwood
Kilmaurs
Kilmarnock
Stewarton
Dunlop
Burnhouse
Barrmill
Auchentiber
Kilwinning
Dalry

Catrine
Mauchline
Tarbolton
Mossblown
Symington
Riccarton
Crosshouse
Gatehead
Dundonald
Loans
Troon
Monkton
Prestwick
Drongan
Patna
Dalmellington
Auchinleck
Cumnock

197 213 223 228 227 226 231 234 237 239
196 195 212 211 222 221 220 230 233 236 238
194 193 210 209 219 218 229 232 235
192 208 207
191

217 216
206 205 204

Glengarnock
Beith
Uplawmoor
Lugton
Montgreenan
Springside
Drybridge
Irvine
Stevenston
Ardrossan
Saltcoats
West Kilbride
Dalgarven
Drakemyre
Kilbirnie
Fairlie
Millport

Glasgow Prestwick International

St Quivox
Ayr
Masonhill
Doonfoot
Dalrymple
Maybole
Crosshill

A70 A73 A706 A71 A719 A76 A77 A78 A713 A723 A724 A725 A726 A735 A736 A737 A759

Route planning

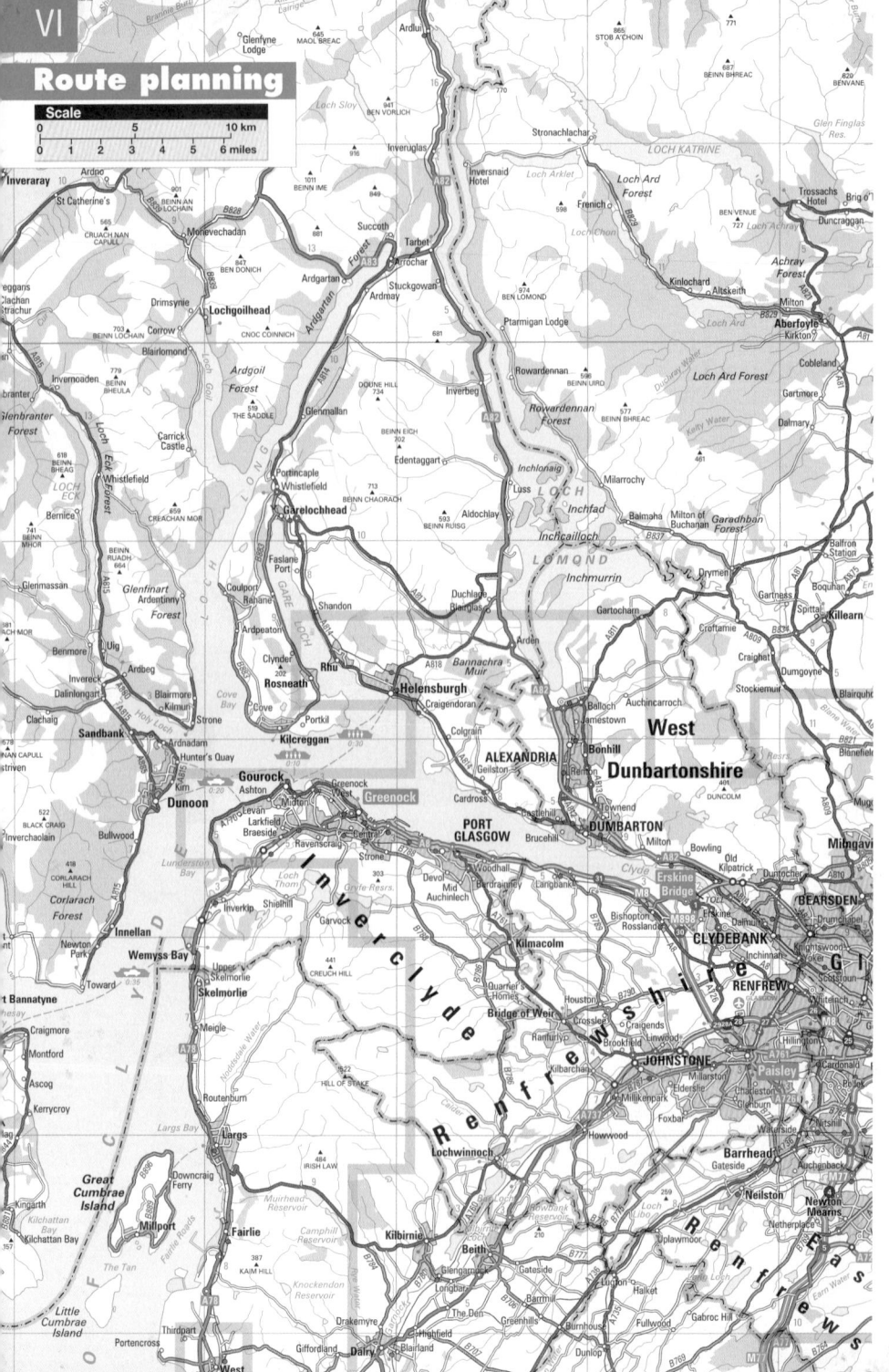

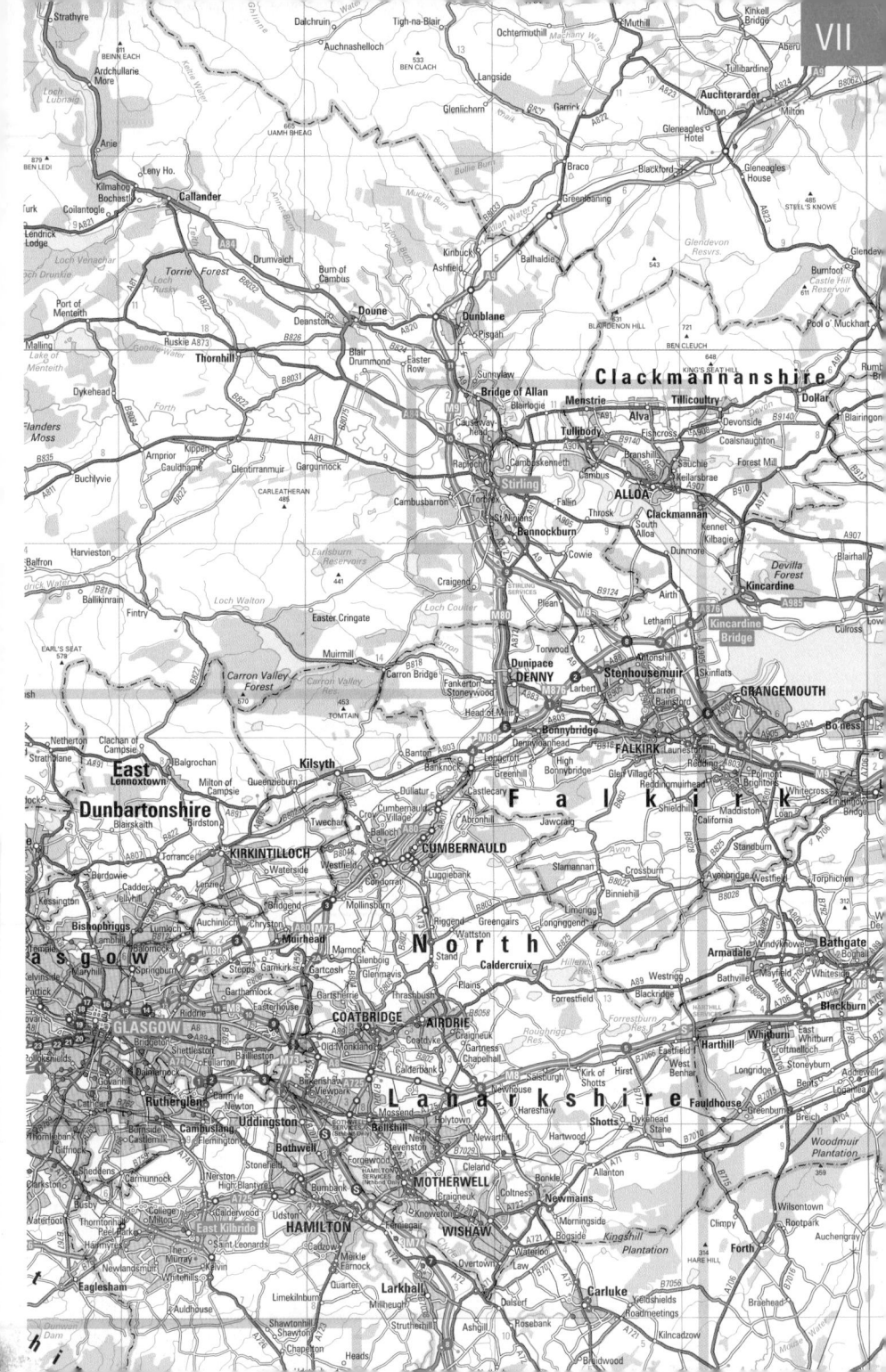

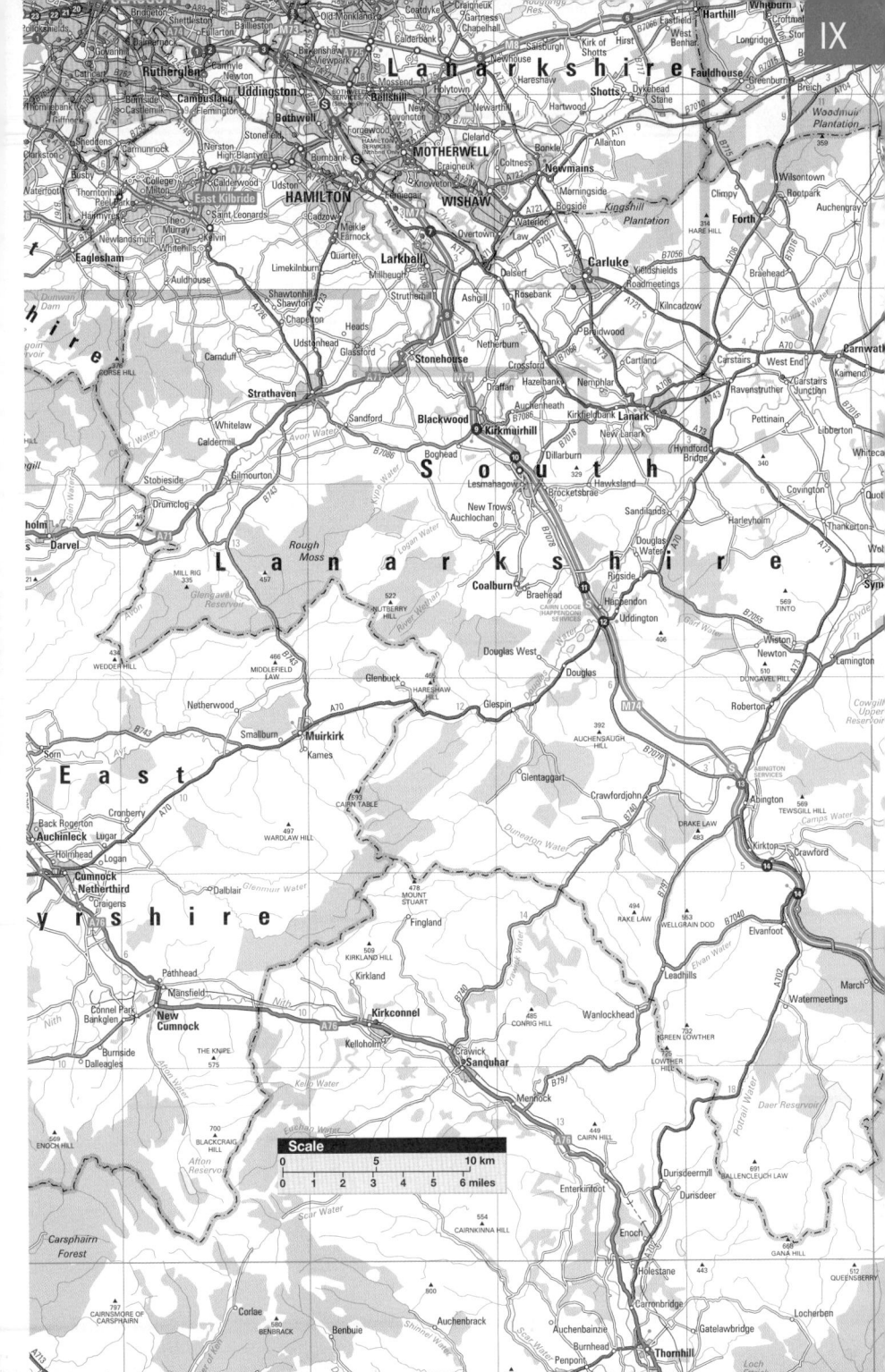

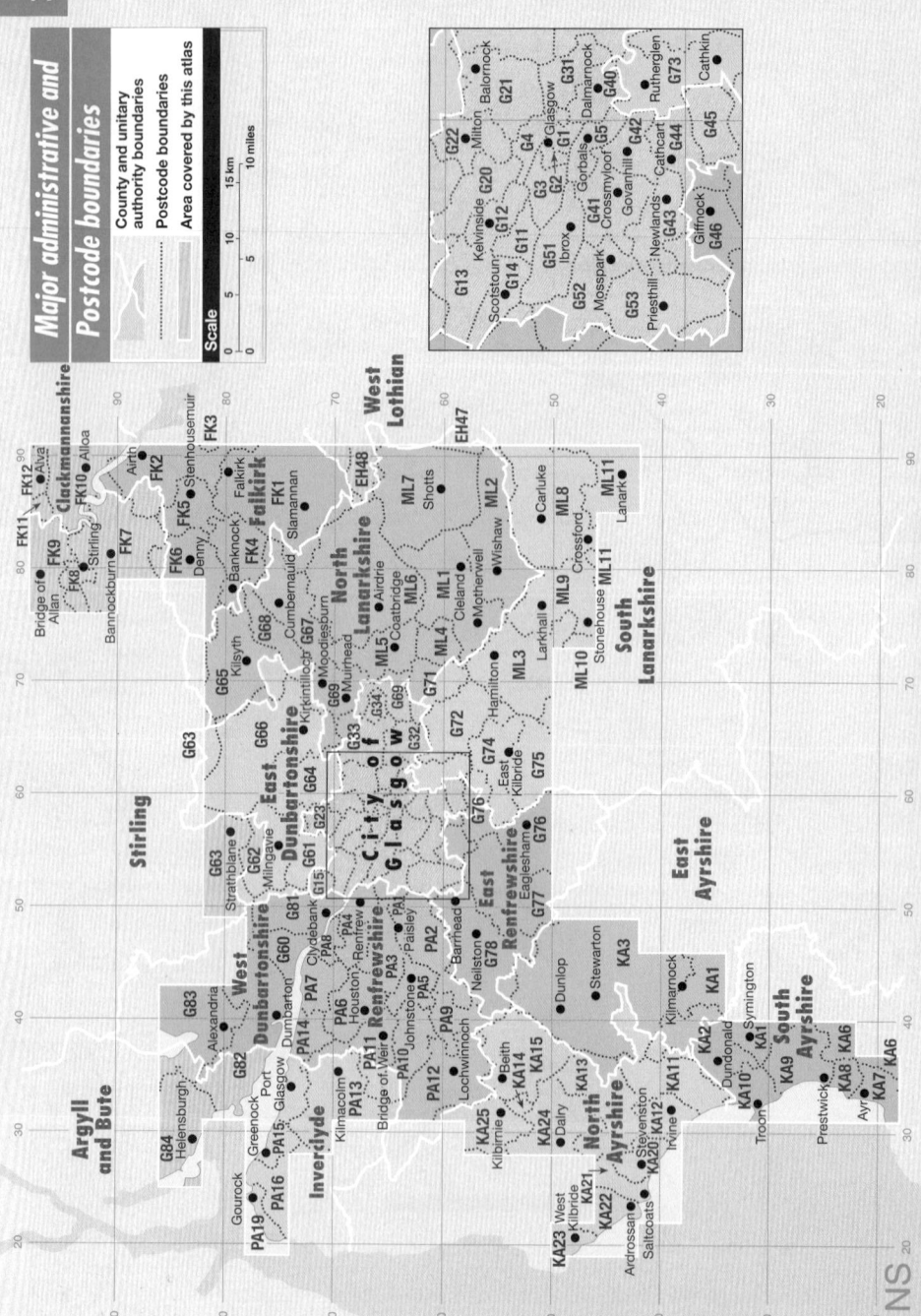

Major administrative and Postcode boundaries

County and unitary authority boundaries

Postcode boundaries

Area covered by this atlas

Scale

0   5   10   15km
0   5   10 miles

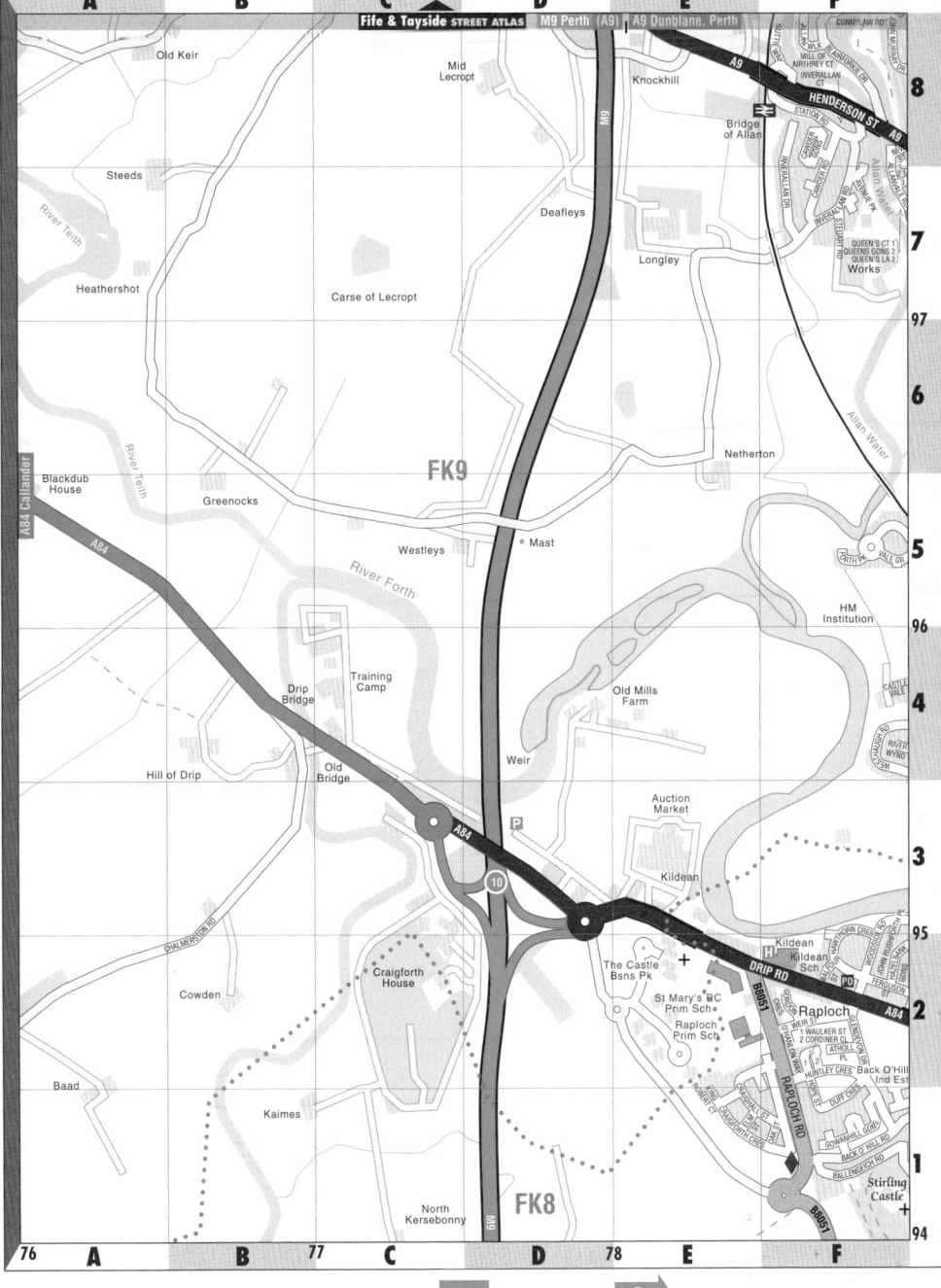

Fife & Tayside STREET ATLAS M9 Perth (A9) A9 Dunblane, Perth

A **B** **C** **D** **E** **F**

8

Old Keir

Mid Lecropt

Knockhill

M9

A9

SUTTIE WAY

MILL OF AIRTHREY CT
INVERALLAN

CUNNINGLAW RD

HENDERSON ST

A9

7

Steeds

Deafleys

Longley

Bridge of Allan

Allan Water

STATION RD

INVERALLAN DR

QUEEN'S CT 1
QUEENS GDNS 2
QUEEN'S LA 2

Works

97

River Teith

Heathershot

Carse of Lecropt

FK9

6

Netherton

Allan Water

River Teith

Blackdub House

A84 Callander

Greenocks

A84

Westleys

River Forth

• Mast

5

TEITH DR

VALE GR

HM Institution

CASTLE VALE

96

Drip Bridge

Training Camp

Old Mills Farm

RIVER WYND

4

Hill of Drip

Old Bridge

Weir

CHALMERSTON RD

P

A84

10

Auction Market

Kildean

3

Craigforth House

Cowden

The Castle Bsns Pk

St Mary's RC Prim Sch

Raploch Prim Sch

Kildean
Kildean Sch

H

DRIP RD

Raploch

BANDS

A84

Back O'Hill Ind Est

95

2

Baad

Kaimes

North Kersebonny

M9

FK8

HUNTLEY CRES

RAPLOCH RD

1 WAULKER ST
2 CORDINER CL
ATHOLL PL

BUFF CRES

BANDS

Stirling Castle

1

94

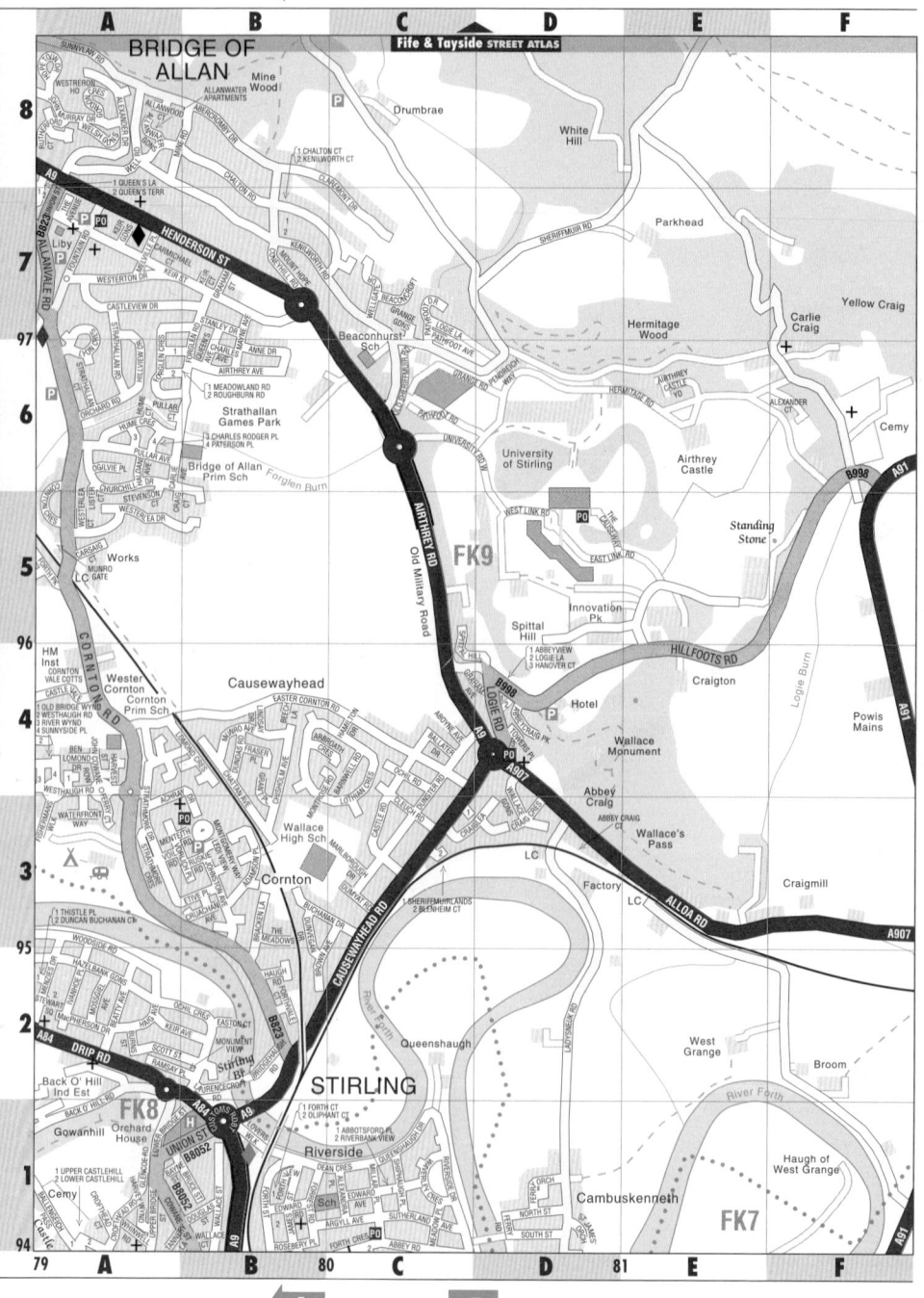

4

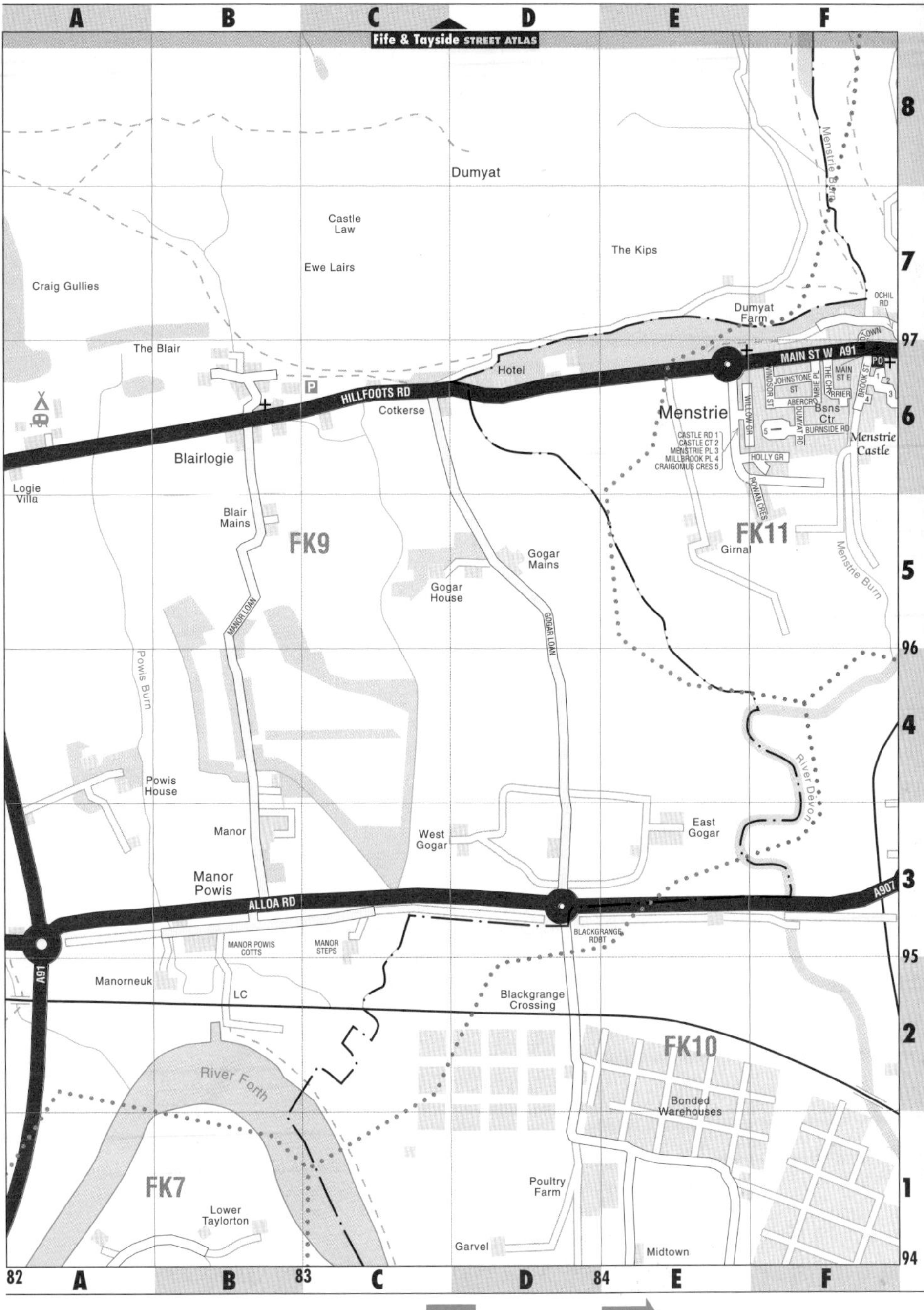
Fife & Tayside STREET ATLAS
A
B
C
D
E
F
8
7
97
6
5
96
4
3
95
2
1
94
82
83
84
Dumyat
Castle Law
Ewe Lairs
Craig Gullies
The Kips
Dumyat Farm
OCHIL RD
The Blair
Hotel
MAIN ST W A91
HILLFOOTS RD
Cotkerse
Menstrie
Menstrie Burn
WINDSOR ST
JOHNSTONE ST
ABERCRO
DUMYAT RD
WILLOW GR
MAIN ST E
THE CRAIGS
Bsns Ctr
BURNSIDE RD
BROOK ST
PO
Menstrie Castle
CASTLE RD 1
CASTLE CT 2
MENSTRIE PL 3
MILLBROOK PL 4
CRAIGOMUS CRES 5
HOLLY GR
ROWAN CRES
Blairlogie
Logie Villa
Blair Mains
FK9
FK11
Girnal
Gogar Mains
Gogar House
MANOR LOAN
GOGAR LOAN
Powis Burn
River Devon
Powis House
Manor
West Gogar
East Gogar
Manor Powis
ALLOA RD
A907
BLACKGRANGE RDBT
MANOR POWIS COTTS
MANOR STEPS
A91
Manorneuk
LC
Blackgrange Crossing
FK10
River Forth
Bonded Warehouses
FK7
Poultry Farm
Lower Taylorton
Garvel
Midtown

8
4

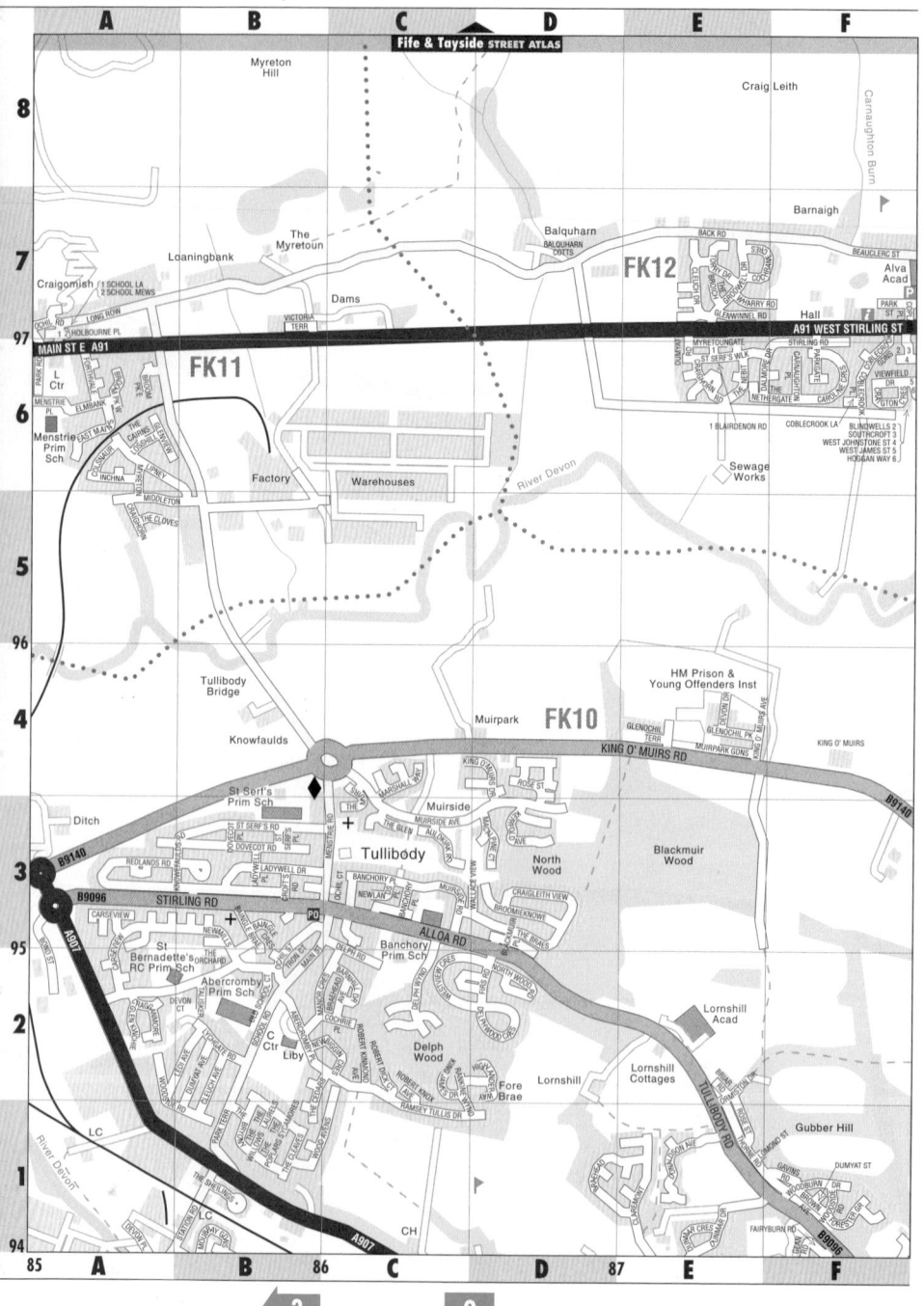

Fife & Tayside STREET ATLAS

8

Myreton
Hill

Craig Leith

Carnaughton Burn

7

Loaningbank

The
Myretoun

Balquharn

Barnaigh

BACK RD

BEAUCLERC ST

FK12

Alva
Acad
P

Craigomish
1 SCHOOL LA
2 SCHOOL MEWS

Dams

97

DOWIE RD
LONG ROW
1 HOLBOURNE PL

VICTORIA
TERR

HARRY RD

GLENWINNEL RD

Hall

PARK
ST

A91 WEST STIRLING ST

MAIN ST E A91

STIRLING RD

FK11

MYRETOUNGATE

ST SERF'S WLK

THE
NETHERGATE

VIEWFIELD
DR

6

Menstrie

L
Ctr

EAST MAINS

ELMBANK

Menstrie
Prim
Sch

THE CAIRNS

INCHNA

LUPIN

MIDDLETON

1 BLAIRDENON RD

COBLECROOK LA

Sewage
Works

BLINKWELLS 2
SOUTHCROFT 3
WEST JOHNSTONE ST 4
WEST JAMES ST 5
HOGGAN WAY 6

Factory

Warehouses

River Devon

5

THE CLOVES

96

Tullibody
Bridge

HM Prison &
Young Offenders Inst

4

Knowfaulds

Muirpark

FK10

KING O' MUIRS RD

GLENOCHIL
TERR

MUIRPARK GDNS

KING O' MUIRS

B9140

St Serf's
Prim Sch

MARSHALL PL

ROSE ST

KING O'MUIRS

Muirside

MUIRSIDE AVE

THE GLEN

Ditch

B9140

REDLANDS RD

ST SERF'S RD

DOVECOT RD

Tullibody

LADYWELL DR

BANCHORY PL

North
Wood

Blackmuir
Wood

CRAIGLEITH VIEW

3

B9096

STIRLING RD

OCHIL CT

BANCHORY

WALLACE VIEW

BROOMIEKNOWE

THE BEILD

95

CARSEVIEW

NEWLANDS

PO

ALLOA RD

A907

St
Bernadette's
RC Prim Sch

2

Abercromby
Prim Sch

DEVON
CT

C
Ctr
Liby

Banchory
Prim Sch

NORTH WOOD

Lornshill
Acad

Delph
Wood

Lornshill

Lornshill
Cottages

Gubber Hill

LC

RAMSAY TULLIS DR

Fore
Brae

DUMYAT ST

TULLIBODY RD

FAIRYBURN RD

B9096

1

River Devon

THE SHIELING

LC

A907

CH

94

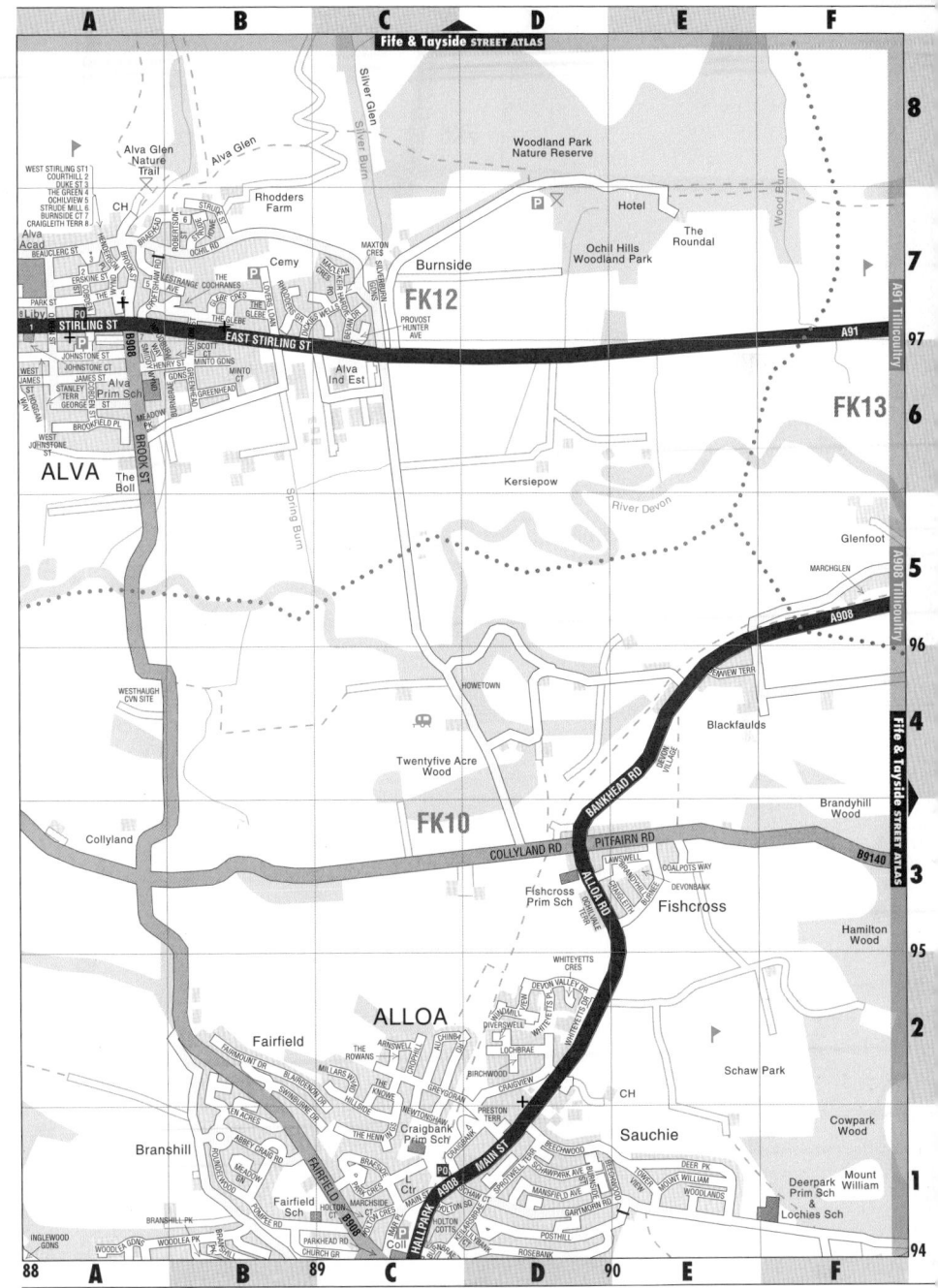

A **B** **C** **D** **E** **F**

8

Woodland Park
Nature Reserve

7

Alva Glen
Nature
Trail

Alva Glen

Rhodders
Farm

WEST STIRLING ST 1
COURTHILL 2
DUKE ST 3
THE GREEN 4
OCHILVIEW 5
STRUDE MILL 6
BURNSIDE CT 7
CRAIGLEITH TERR 8

Silver Glen

Silver Burn

Wood Burn

Hotel

The
Roundal

A91 Tillicoultry

97

Alva
Acad

CH

BEAUCLERC ST

Cemy

Burnside

Ochil Hills
Woodland Park

P ✕

FK12

ERSKINE ST
PARK ST
Libyle
PO

STIRLING ST
P

JOHNSTONE ST
JOHNSTONE CT

WEST
JAMES
ST

STANLEY
TERR
GEORGE ST

WEST
JOHNSTONE
ST

BROOKFIELD PL

B908

BROOK ST

MEADOW

EAST STIRLING ST

SCOTT
CT
MINTO GDNS

MINTO
CT

GREENHEAD

MAXTON
CRES

SILVERBURN

Alva
Ind Est

PROVOST
HUNTER
AVE

A91

97

FK13

6

ALVA

The
Boll

Spring Burn

Kersiepow

River Devon

Glenfoot

MARCHGLEN

A908 Tillicoultry

5

A908

SEAVIEW TERR

96

WESTHAUGH
CVN SITE

HOWETOWN

Twentyfive Acre
Wood

Blackfaulds

BROOK
VILLAGE

Fife & Tayside STREET ATLAS

Brandyhill
Wood

4

Collyland

FK10

COLLYLAND RD

BANKHEAD RD

PITFAIRN RD

LAWSWELL

COALPOTS WAY

DEVONBANK

ALLOA RD

B9140

Hamilton
Wood

3

Fishcross
Prim Sch

Fishcross

95

WHITEYETTS
CRES

DEVON VALLEY DR

WHITE TEES DR

WHITEYETTS DR

ALLOA

THE
ROWANS

ARNSWELL

HILLSIDE

DIVERSWELL

LOCHBRAE

BIRCHWOOD

CRAIGVIEW

PRESTON
TERR

Schaw Park

CH

Cowpark
Wood

2

Fairfield

FAIRMOUNT DR

BEAURSBURN DR

SWINSBURN DR

MILLARS WYND

THE
KNOWE

NEWTONSHAW

THE HENN

Craigbank
Prim Sch

Mount
William

Deerpark
Prim Sch

DEER PK

MOUNT WILLIAM

WOODLANDS

Lochies Sch

1

Branshill

TEN ACRES

ABBEY CRAIG RD

FAIRFIELD

FAIRFIELD RD

Fairfield
Sch

HOLTON

HALLPARK RD

A908

MAIN ST

Sauchie

BEECHWOOD

MANSFIELD AVE

GARTMORN RD

94

BRANSHILL PK

WOODLEA GDNS

WOODLEA PK

CHURCH GR

PARKHEAD GR

Coll

ROSEBANK

POSTHILL

88 **A** **B** 89 **C** **D** 90 **E** **F** 94

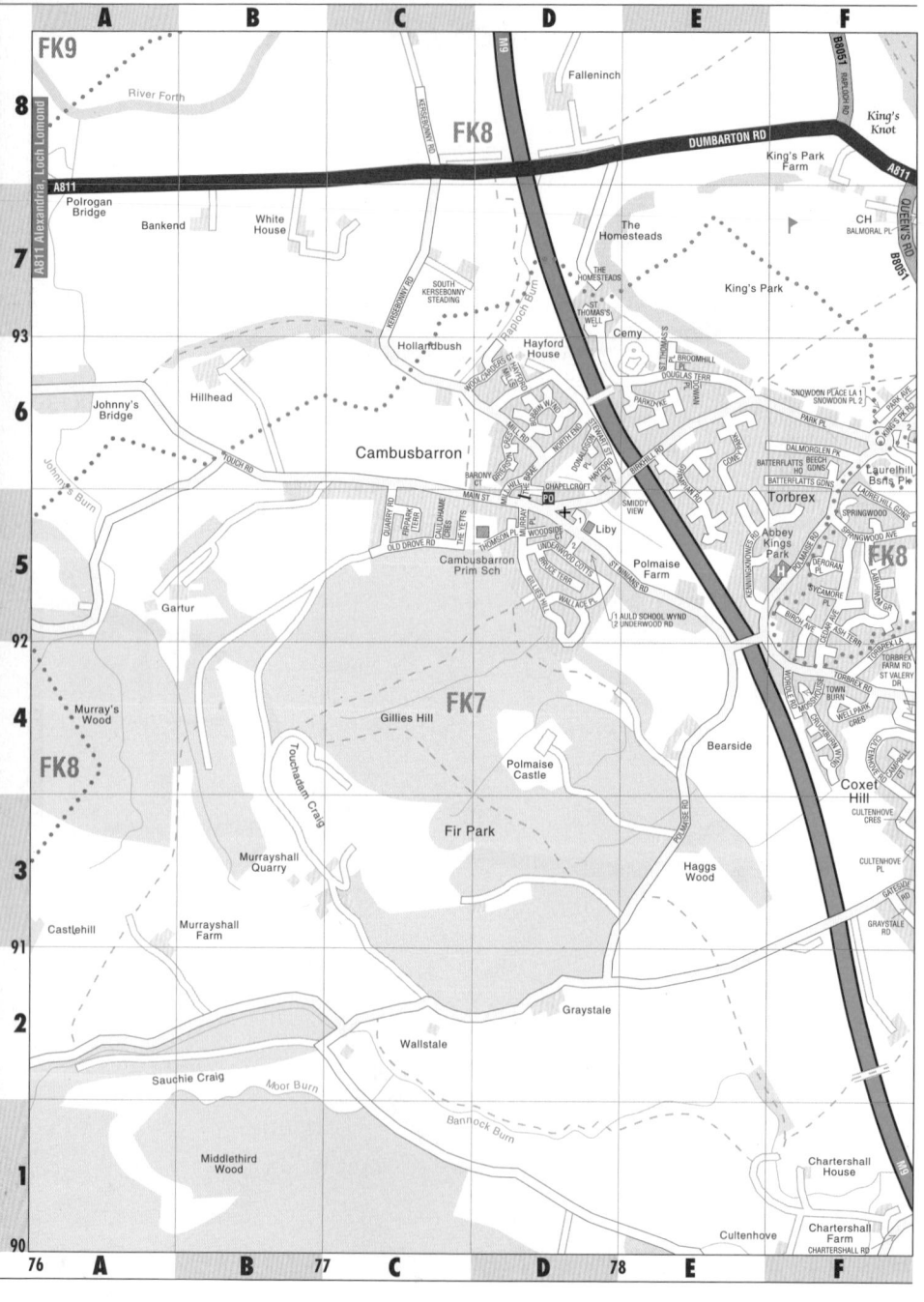

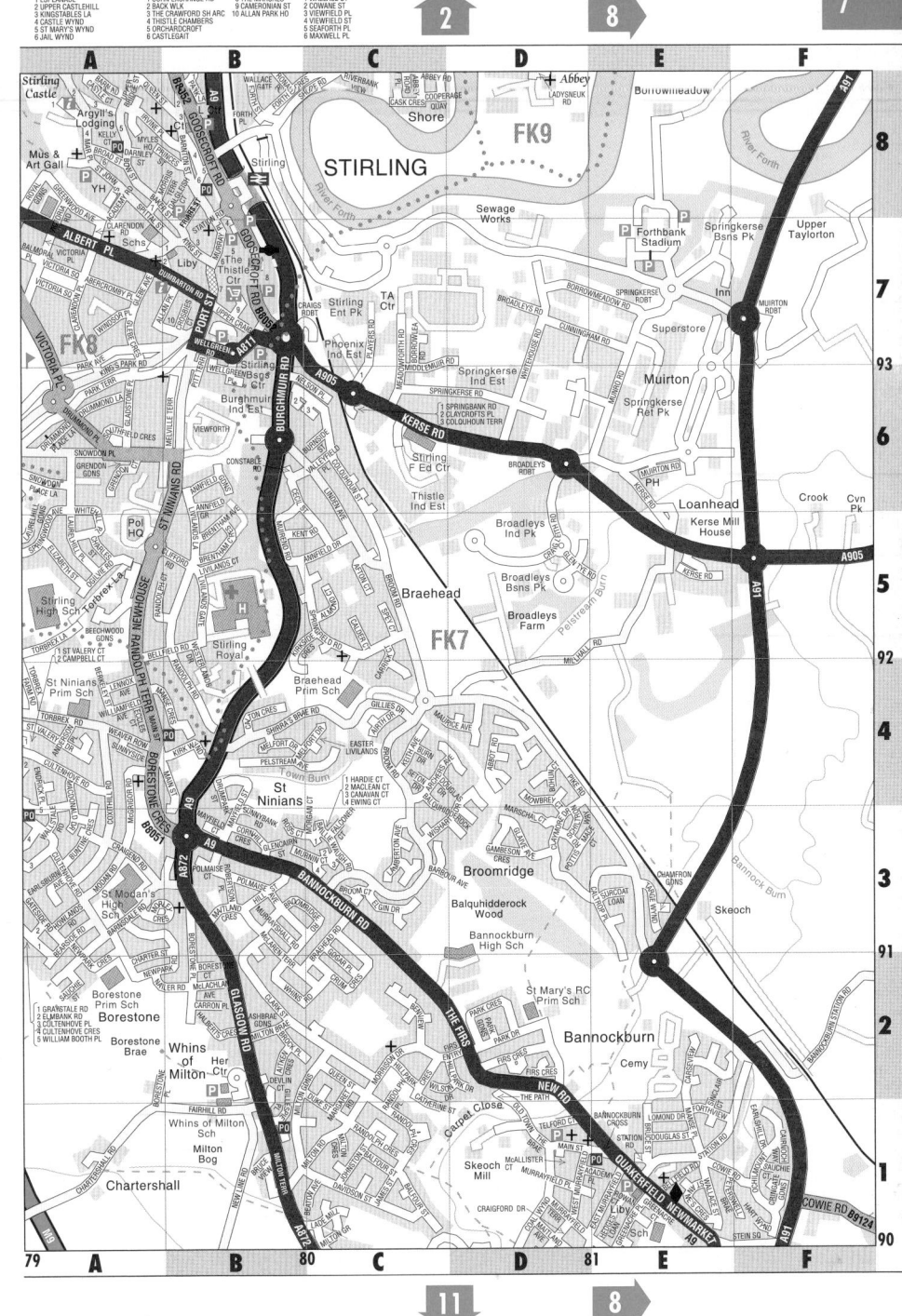

A6
1 ESPLANADE
2 UPPER CASTLEHILL
3 KINGSTABLES LA
4 CASTLE WYND
5 ST MARY'S WYND
6 JAIL WYND

7 BANK ST

B7
1 CORN EXCHANGE RD
2 BACK WLK
3 THE CRAWFORD SH ARC
4 THISTLE CHAMBERS
5 ORCHARDCROFT
6 CASTLEGAIT

7 BASTION WYND
8 THE MARCHES
9 CAMERONIAN ST
10 ALLAN PARK HO

B6
1 WALLACE ST
2 COWANE ST
3 VIEWFIELD PL
4 VIEWFIELD ST
5 SEAFORTH PL
6 MAXWELL PL

A   B   C   D   E   F

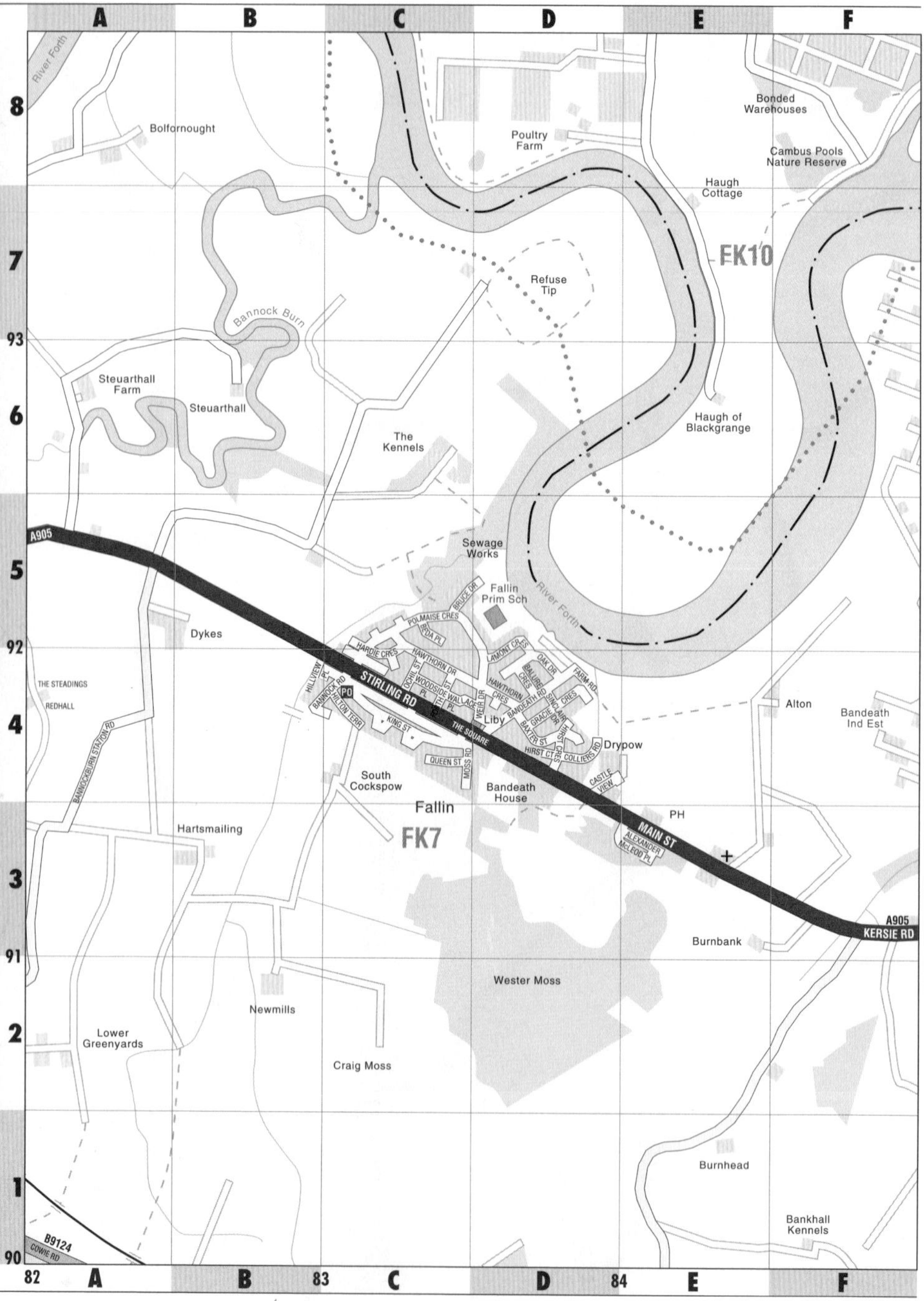

8   Bolfornought   Poultry Farm   Bonded Warehouses

Cambus Pools Nature Reserve

Haugh Cottage

7   Refuse Tip   FK10

93   Bannock Burn

Steuarthall Farm   Steuarthall

6   The Kennels   Haugh of Blackgrange

A905

5   Sewage Works   Fallin Prim Sch   River Forth

Dykes   BRUCE DR   PALMAISE CRES   BOG PL

92   DARDIE CRES   HAWTHORN DR   LAMONT CRES   OAK DR

THE STEADINGS   HILLVIEW   WOODSIDE TERR   WALLACE   HAWTHORN ST   BIRCH RD

REDHALL   STIRLING RD   THE SQUARE   BRAEHEAD RD   Alton   Bandeath Ind Est

BANKNOCKBURN STATION RD   KING ST   HIRST CRES   GRACE CRES

4   Liby   COLLIERS RD

QUEEN ST S   MOSS   Drypow   CASTLE VIEW

South Cockspow   Bandeath House   PH

Fallin   MAIN ST

Hartsmailing   FK7   ALEXANDER McLEOD PL   +

3   A905   KERSIE RD

91   Burnbank

Newmills   Wester Moss

2   Lower Greenyards   Craig Moss

Burnhead

1   Bankhall Kennels

90   B9124   CONIE RD

82   A   B   83   C   D   84   E   F

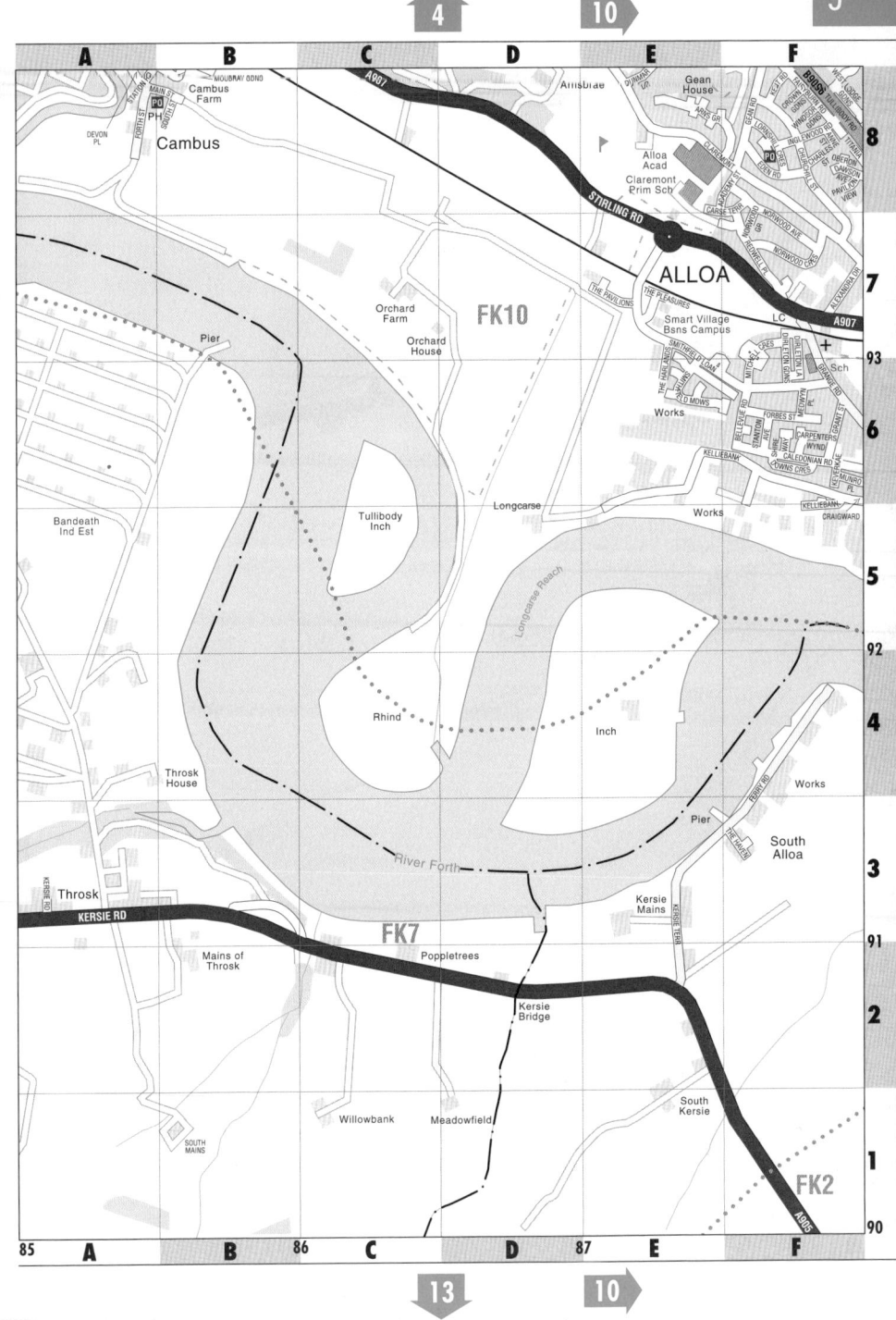

4
10

A B C D E F

8

7

93

6

5

92

4

3

91

2

1

90

85 A 86 B C 86 D 87 E F

13
10

Cambus Farm
Cambus
PO
PH
DEVON PL
MOWBRAY BDND
MAIN ST
FORTH ST
FORTH PL
Amisbrae
Gean House
Alloa Acad
Claremont Prim Sch
STIRLING RD
PO
A907
ALLOA
THE PLEASURES
THE PAVILIONS
LC
A907
Smart Village Bsns Campus
Sch
Works
FK10
Orchard Farm
Orchard House
Pier
KELLIEBANK
KELLIEBANK
CRAIGWARD
Works
Bandeath Ind Est
Tullibody Inch
Longcarse
Longcarse Reach
5
Works
Rhind
Inch
Pier
Works
South Alloa
Throsk House
River Forth
Kersie Mains
KERSIE RD
KERSIE RD
Throsk
FK7
Mains of Throsk
Poppletrees
Kersie Bridge
South Kersie
SOUTH MAINS
Willowbank
Meadowfield
FK2
A905

10

86
1 BURGH MEWS
2 MERCAT WYND
3 STRIPEHEAD
4 UNION ST
5 BREWHOUSE CT
6 WEST VENNEL
7 CANDLERIGGS CT
8 THE CROSS
9 TOWNHEAD APARTMENTS
10 MAPLE CT
11 OLD BRIDGE ST
12 JUNCTION PL
13 BRIDGE TERR

9
5

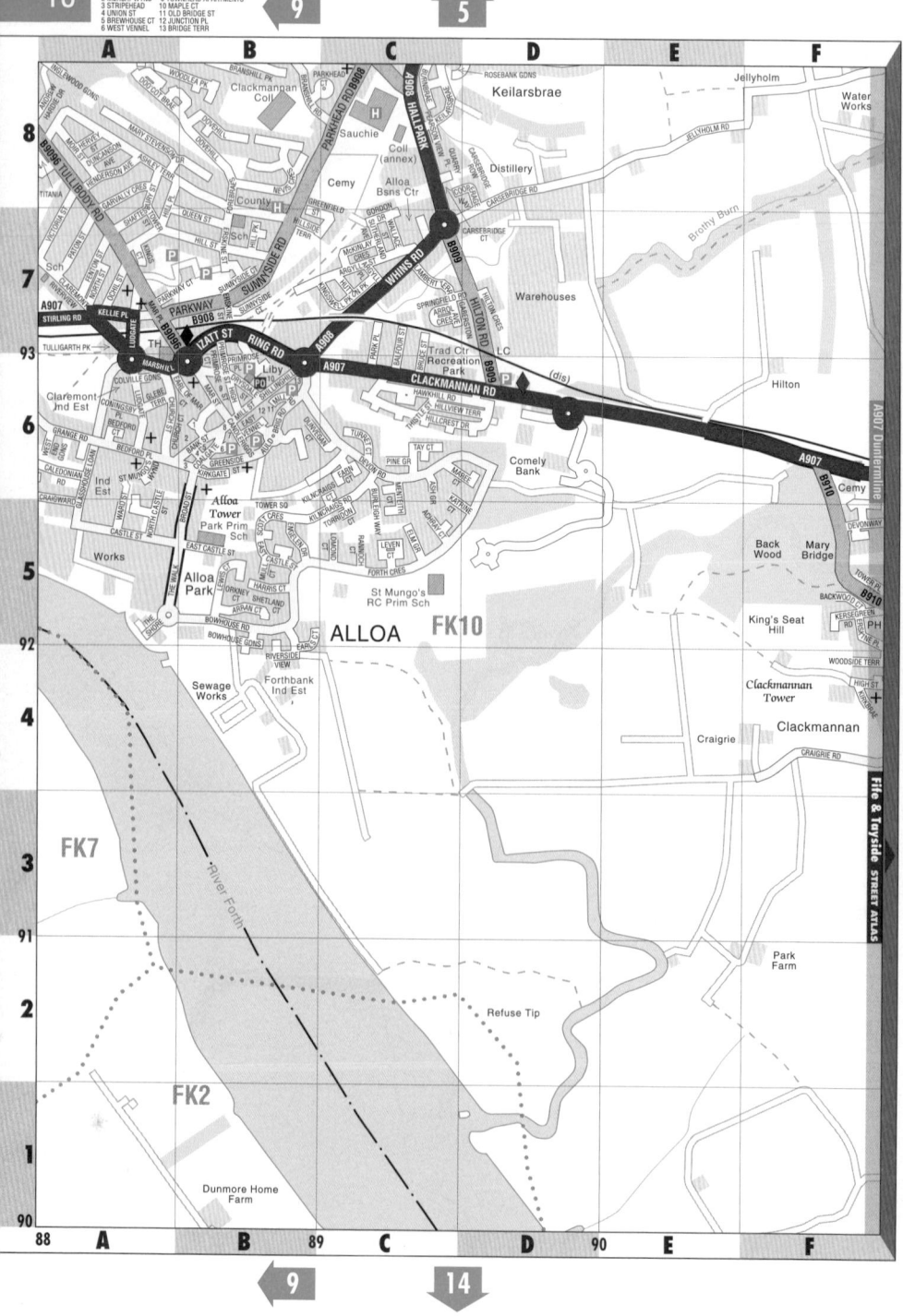

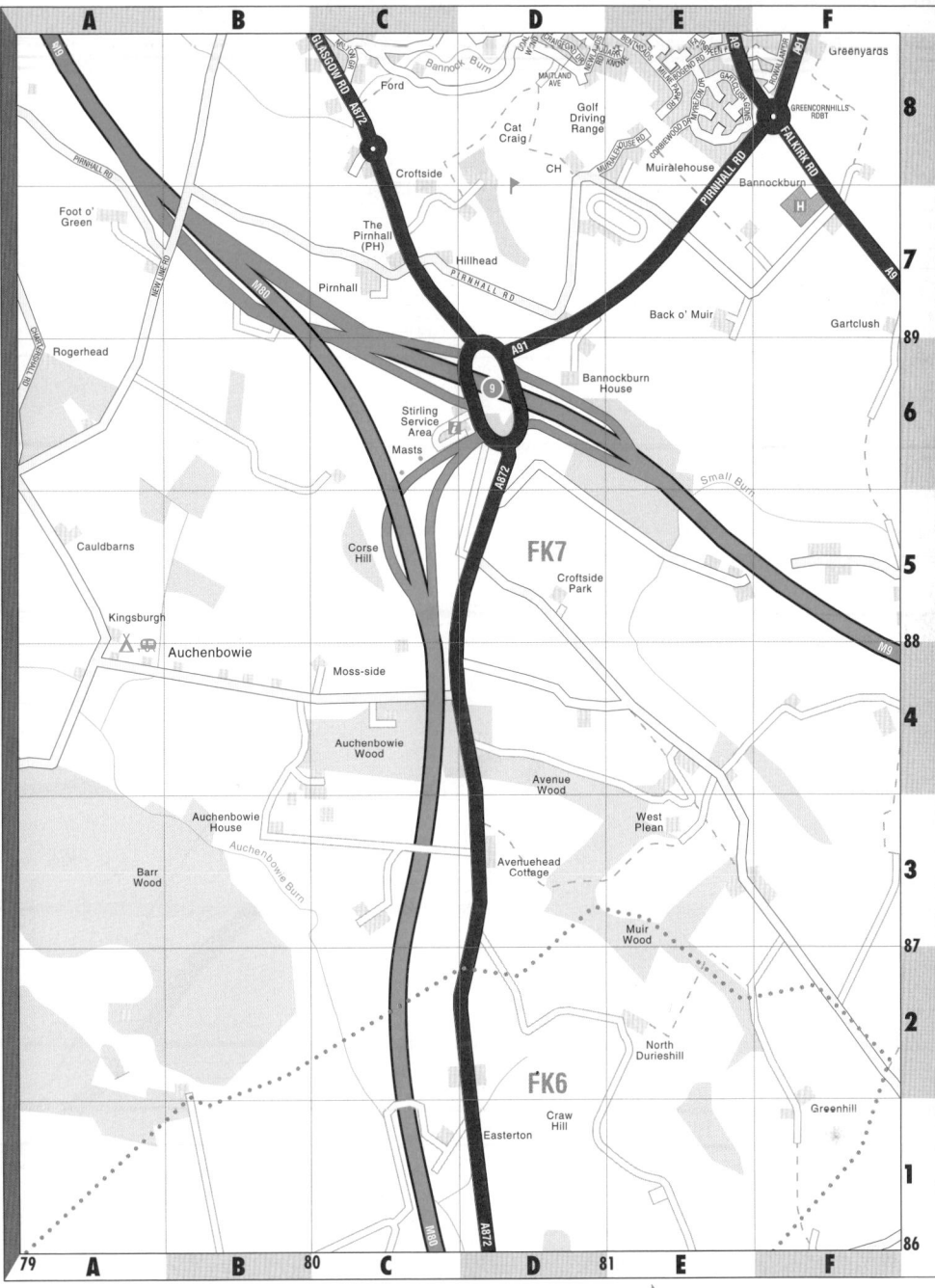

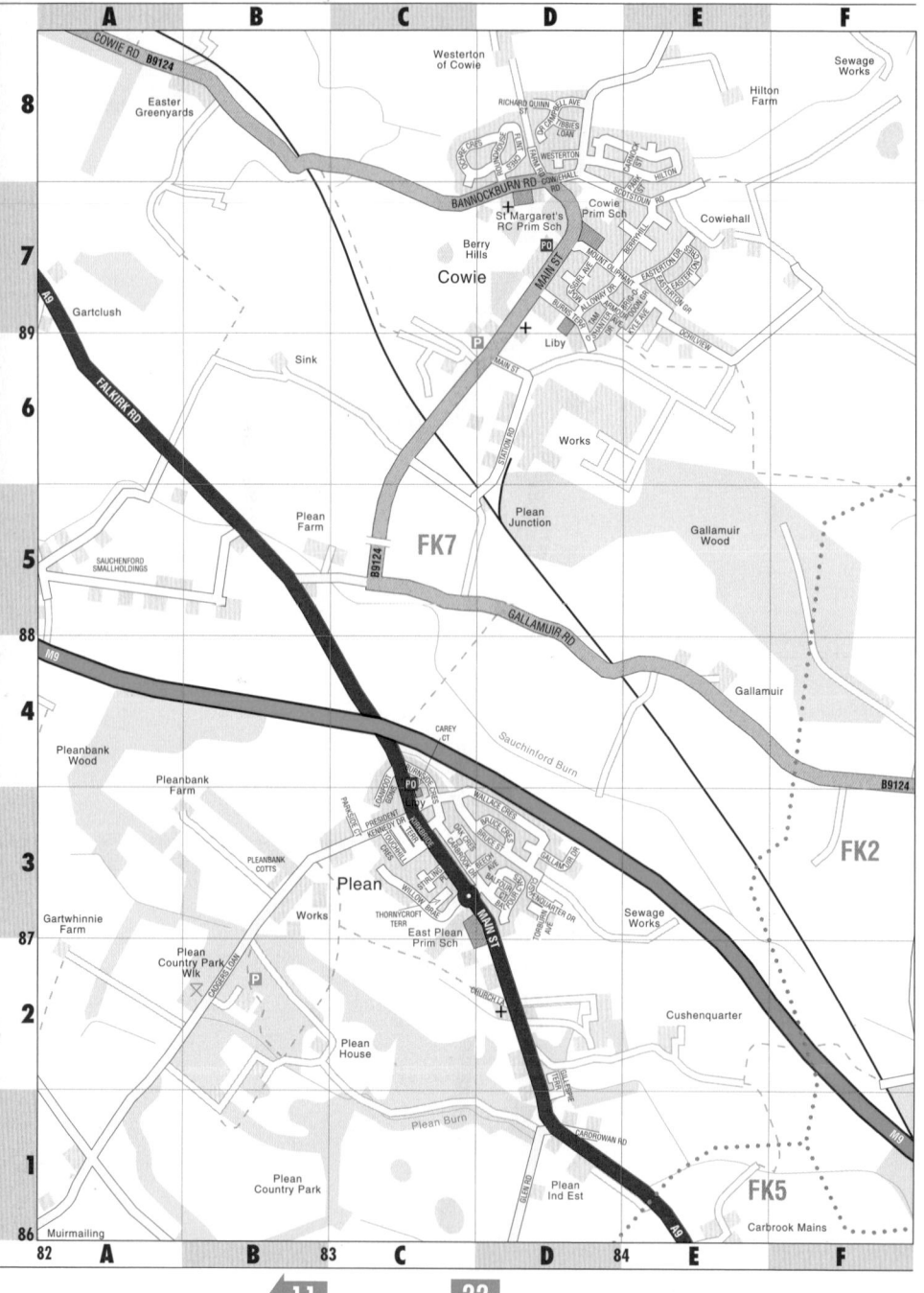

A B C D E F

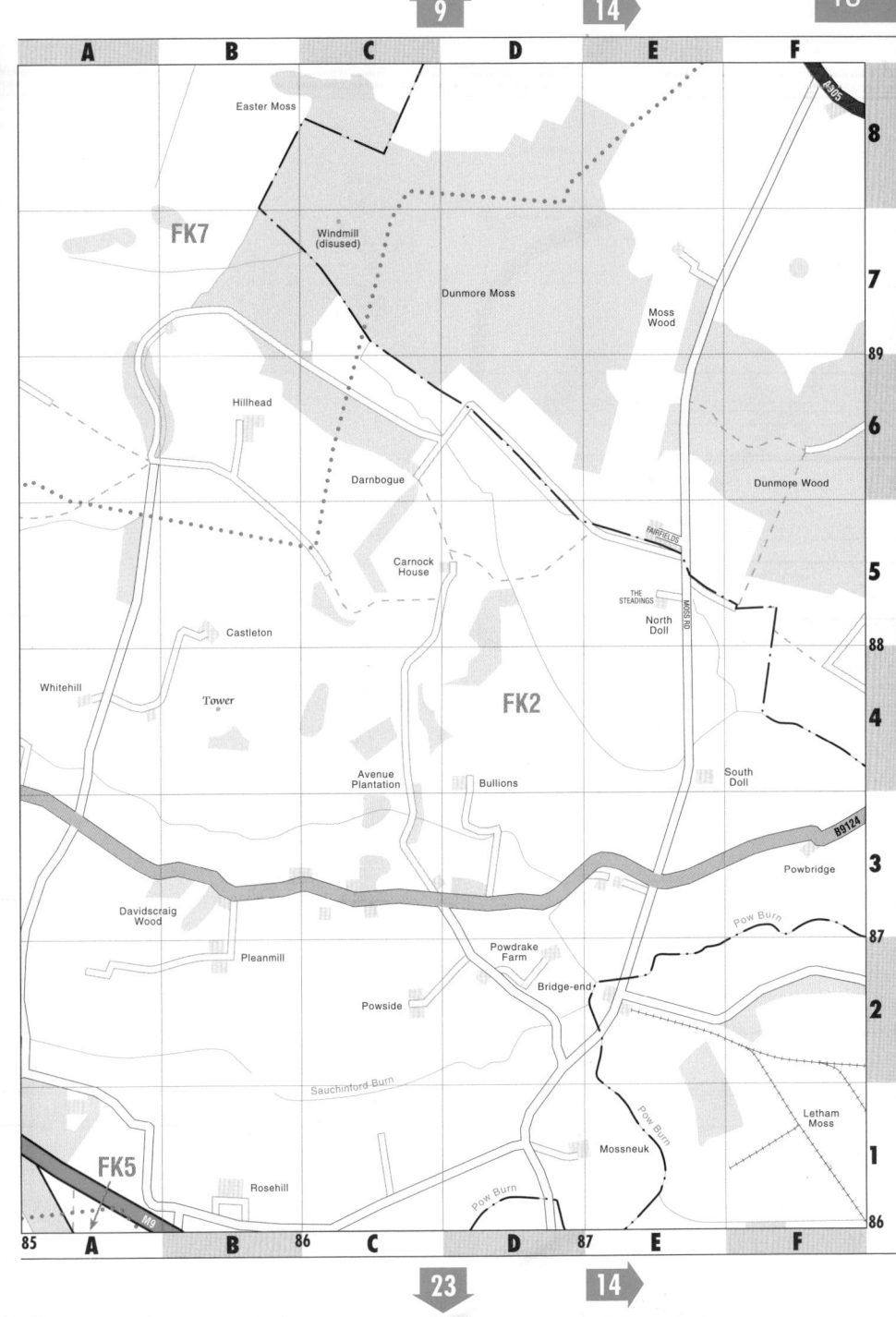

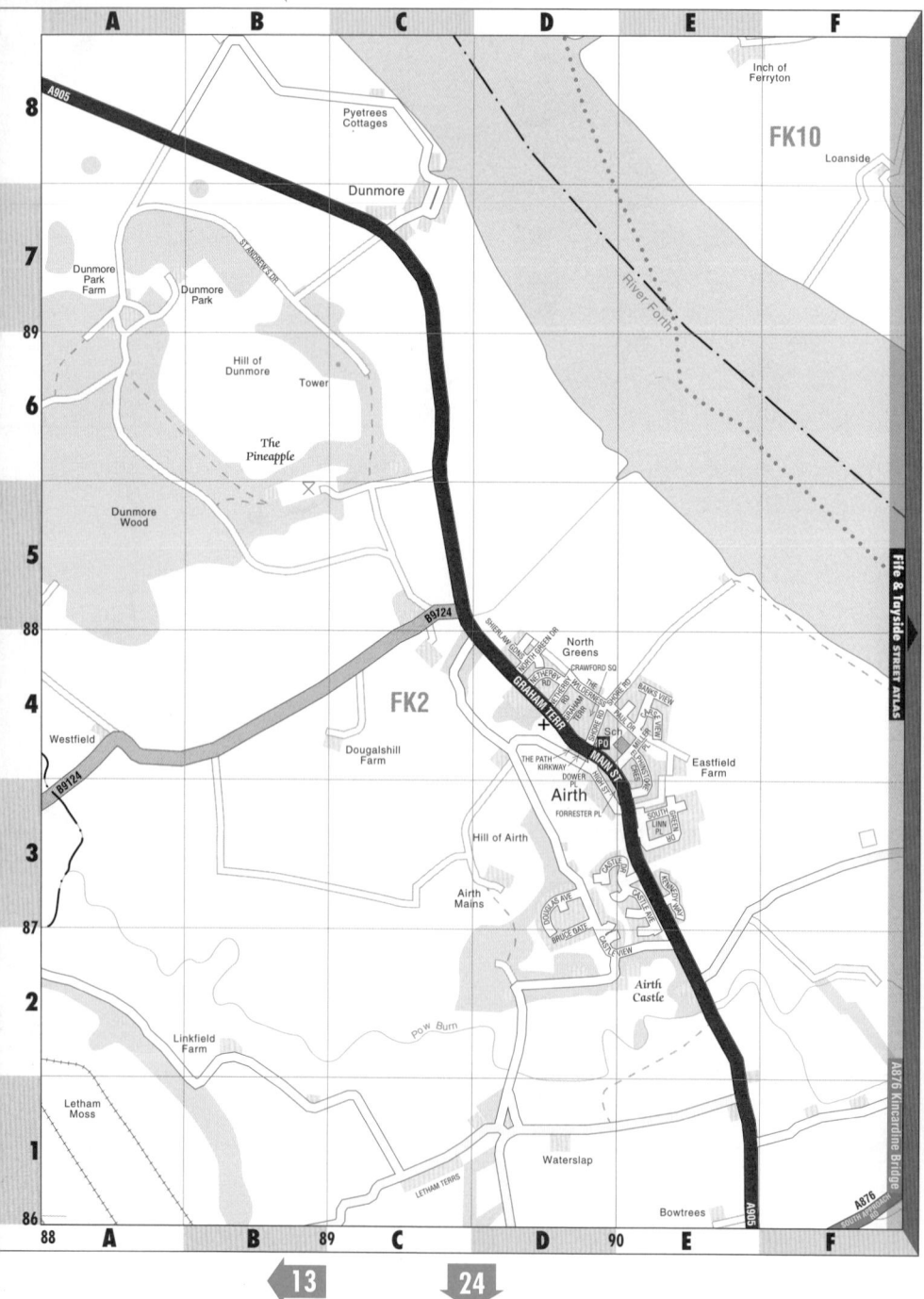

A B C D E F

8

A905

Pyetrees
Cottages

FK10

Inch of
Ferryton

Loanside

Dunmore

7

ST ANDREW'S DR

Dunmore
Park
Farm

Dunmore
Park

89

River Forth

Hill of
Dunmore

Tower

6

The
Pineapple

Dunmore
Wood

5

B9124

SHORLAW

North
Greens

CRAWFORD SQ

88

FK2

GRAHAM TERR

BLACK'S VIEW

4

Westfield

Dougalshill
Farm

Sch
PO

Eastfield
Farm

B9124

THE PATH
KIRKWAY

MAIN ST

DOWER
PL

Airth

FORRESTER PL

3

Hill of Airth

SOUTH
LINN
PL

87

Airth
Mains

DOUGLAS AVE

BRUCE DATE

KINROSS WAY

2

POW Burn

Linkfield
Farm

Airth
Castle

Letham
Moss

1

Waterslap

LETHAM TERRS

86

A905

Bowtrees

A876

SOUTH PL

88 A B 89 C D 90 E F

Fife & Tayside STREET ATLAS

A876 Kincardine Bridge

A · B · C · D · E · F

8

7

85

6

5

84

4

3

83

2

1

82

Croy

Blairvadach

QUEEN'S POINT

Letrualt Farm

ALEXANDER PL

Rhu

ARDENCONNEL MEWS

ARDENCONNEL HO

G84

Pier

Yacht Club Rhu Prim Sch

Liby

HALL RD

CUMBERLAND TERR

SCHOOL RD

MANSE PL

ARDWELL PL

PO

CHURCH PL 1
BRAEHOUSE 2
RHU-ELLEN CT 3
WATERSEDGE CT 4

WOODSTONE CT

Rhu Bay

Gare Loch

STATION

Torr

HIGHLANDMAN'S RD

1 BRAEHEAD PL
2 CALDWELL PL

ROWMORE QUAYS

GLENARIN RD

GARELOCH RD

UPPER TORWOODHILL RD

TORWOODHILL PL
TORWOODHILL

Tor Wood

Marina

A814

RHU RD HIGHER

RHU RD LOWER

DALMORE CRES 1
CUMBERLAND AVE 2
KIDSTON DR 3

Cairndhu Point

Stroul Bay

Jetty

Works

Limekiln Point

Rosneath Prim Sch

HOWIE CRES

Rosneath

THE CLACHAN

PO

Clachan Burn

1 NAVY WAY
2 PRINCESS WAY

CEDAR VIEW

ROSNEATH RD

BB833

Broom Plantation

Pier

Clachan Farm

Clachan Glen

Clachan Burn

Hill of Camsail Plantation

Camsail Wood

Camsail Bay

Rosneath Bay

Creag na Goibhre

Dark Wood

Crane Rock

Castle Point

Castle Bay

ROSNEATH CASTLE CVN PK

BB833

A · B · 26 · C · D · 27 · E · F

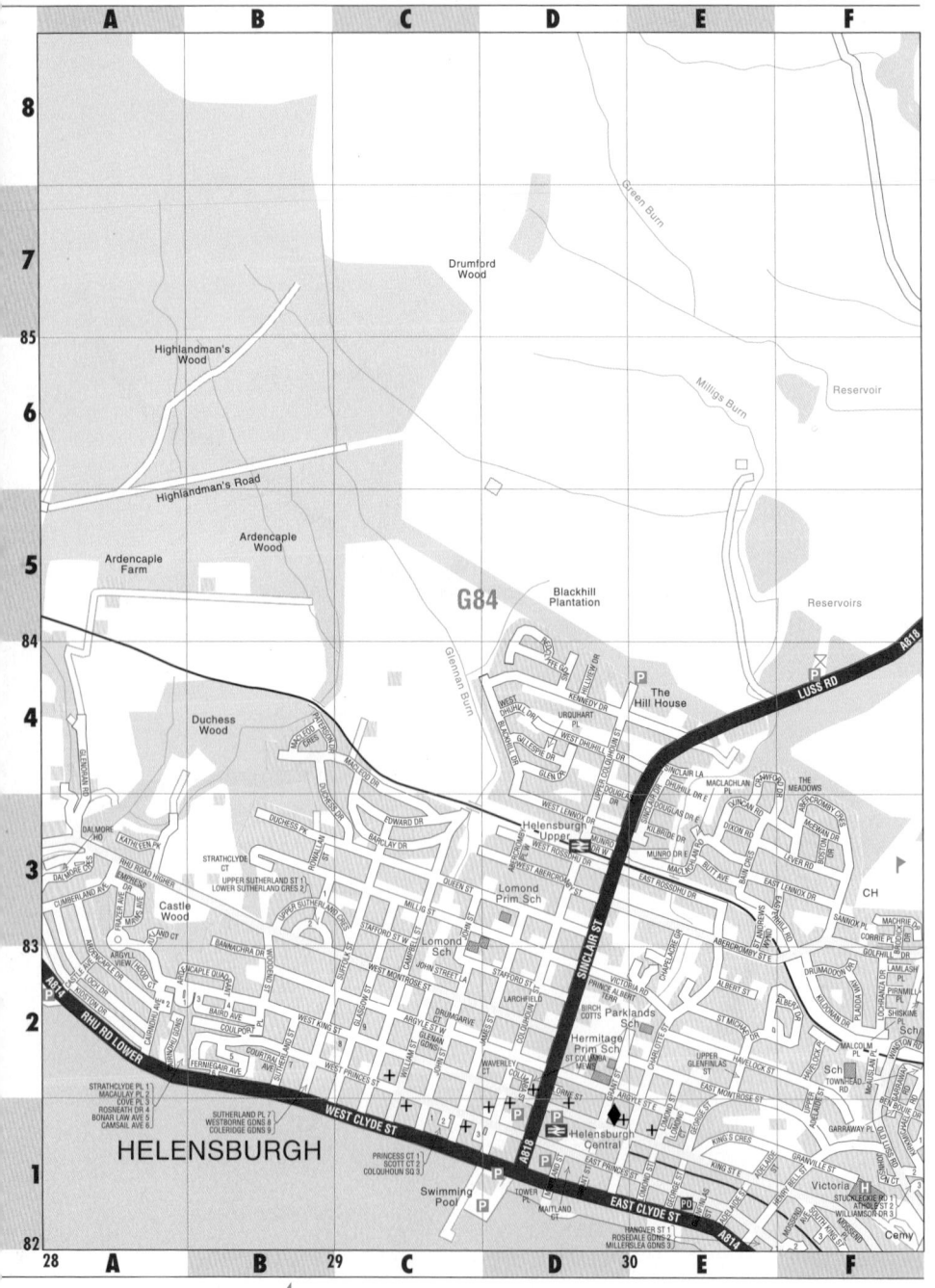

Highfields Muir

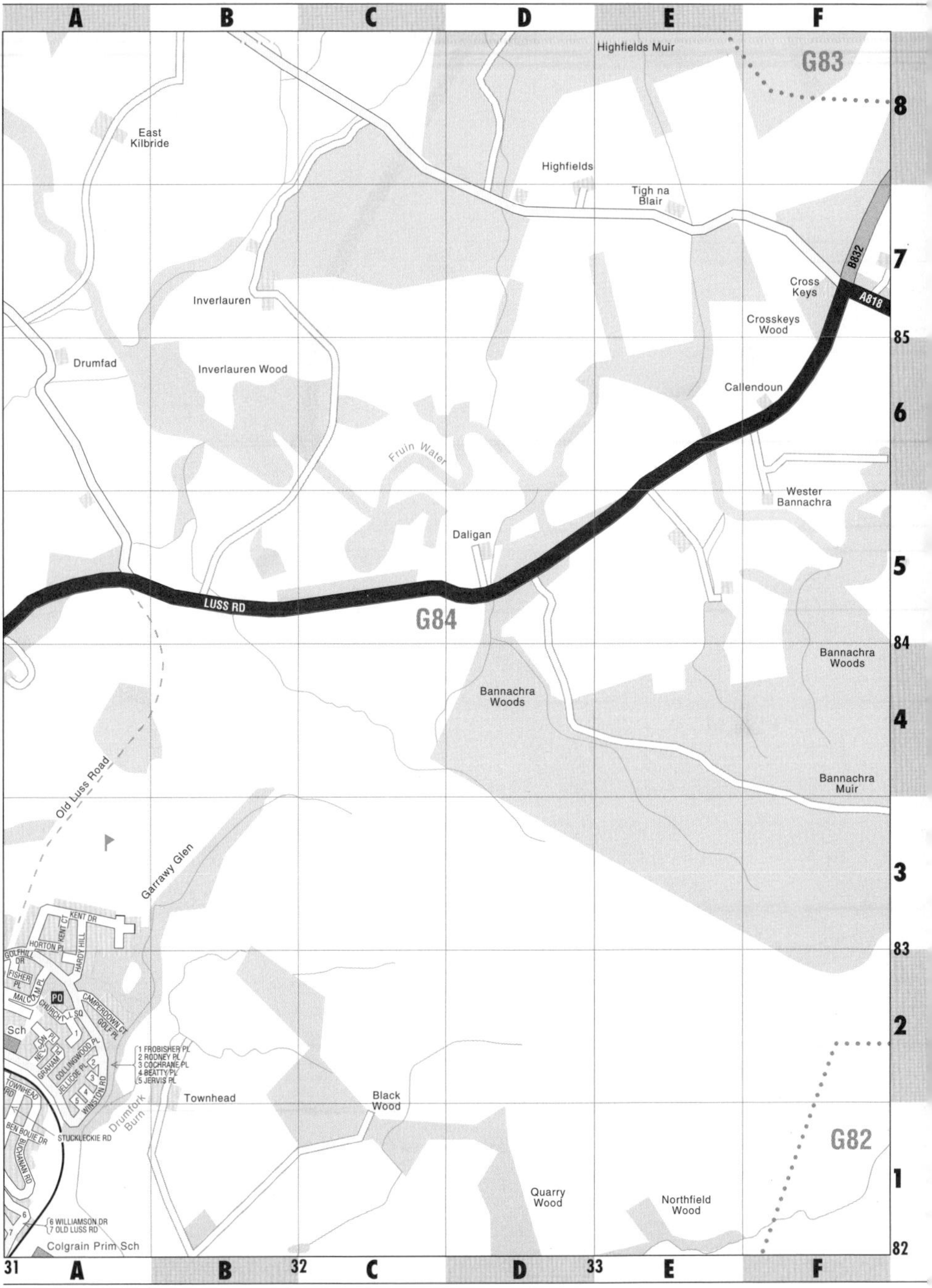

G83

8

East
Kilbride

Highfields

Tigh na
Blair

7

Inverlauren

Cross
Keys

B832

A818

Crosskeys
Wood

85

Drumfad

Inverlauren Wood

Callendoun

6

Fruin Water

Wester
Bannachra

Daligan

5

LUSS RD

G84

84

Bannachra
Woods

Old Luss Road

Bannachra
Woods

4

Garrawy Glen

Bannachra
Muir

3

83

KENT DR
HORTON PL
GOLPHIN
DR
FISHER
PL
MALO
PO
Sch

CAMPBELL
CAMPCROWN CR
GOLF PL

2

1 FROBISHER PL
2 RODNEY PL
3 COCHRANE PL
4 BEATTY PL
5 JERVIS PL

Drumfork
Burn

Townhead

Black
Wood

STUCKLECKIE RD

BEN BOUIE DR

G82

Quarry
Wood

Northfield
Wood

1

6 WILLIAMSON DR
7 OLD LUSS RD

Colgrain Prim Sch

82

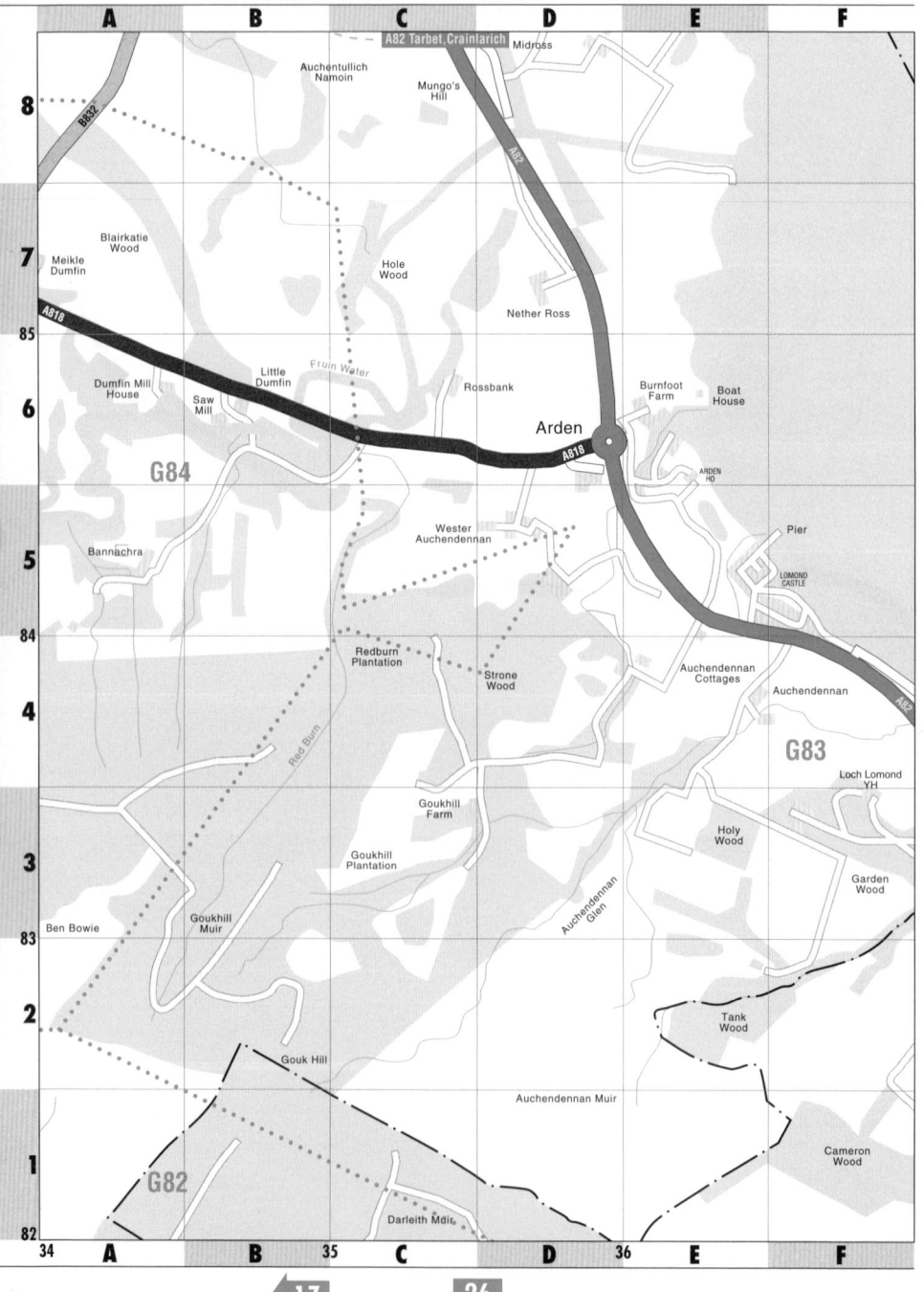

A82 Tarbet, Crainlarich

Midross

Auchentullich
Namoin

Mungo's
Hill

Blairkatie
Wood

Meikle
Dumfin

Hole
Wood

Nether Ross

A818

Little
Dumfin

Fruin Water

Rossbank

Burnfoot
Farm

Boat
House

Dumfin Mill
House

Saw
Mill

Arden

A818

ARDEN
HO

G84

Bannachra

Wester
Auchendennan

Pier

LOMOND
CASTLE

Redburn
Plantation

Strone
Wood

Auchendennan
Cottages

Auchendennan

Red Burn

G83

Loch Lomond
YH

Goukhill
Farm

Holy
Wood

Garden
Wood

Goukhill
Plantation

Auchendennan
Glen

Ben Bowie

Goukhill
Muir

Tank
Wood

Gouk Hill

Auchendennan Muir

Cameron
Wood

G82

Darleith Mdns

	A	B	C	D	E	F	

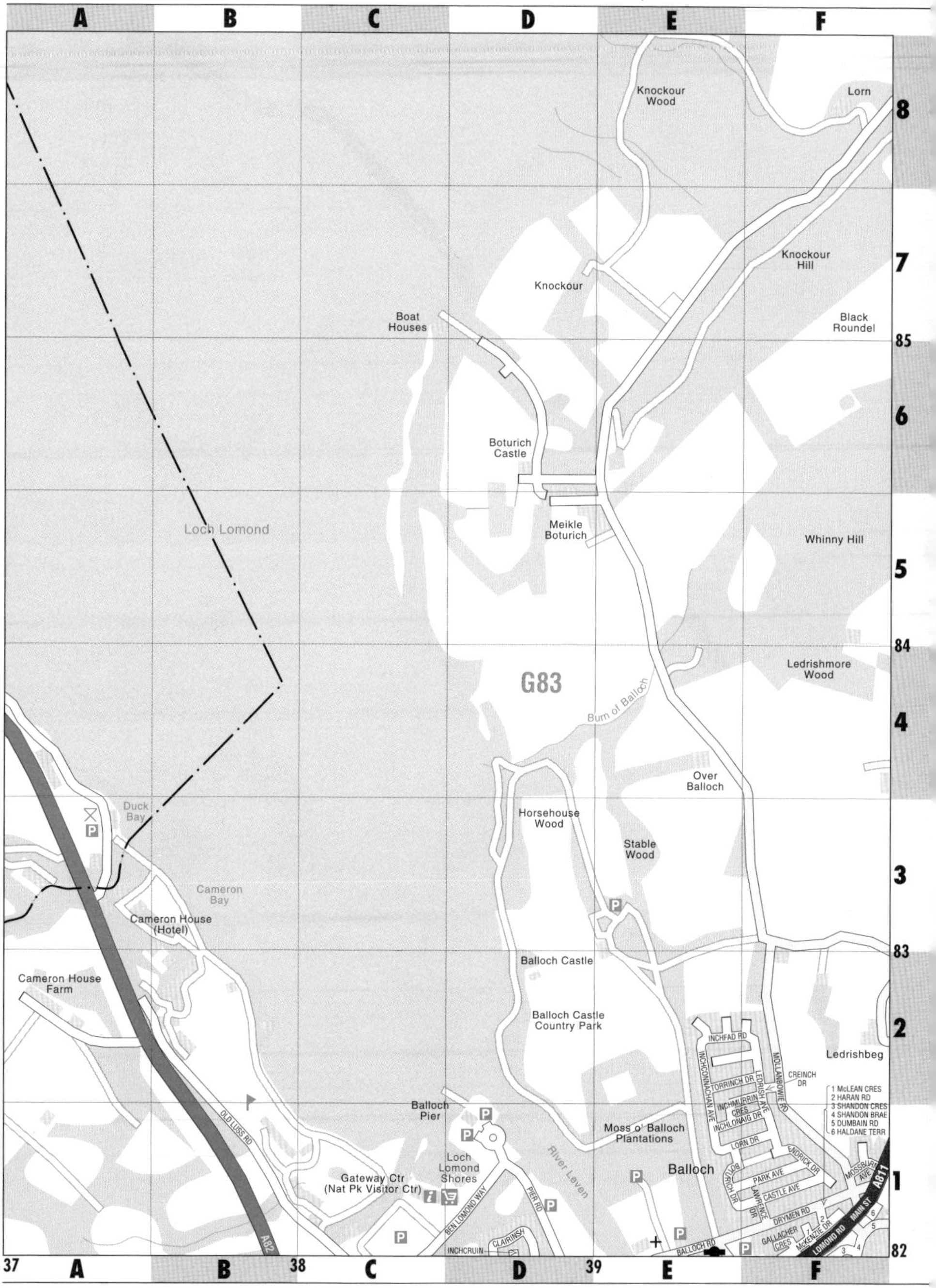

8

Knockour Wood

Lorn

7

Knockour Hill

Knockour

Black Roundel

85

Boat Houses

6

Boturich Castle

Meikle Boturich

Whinny Hill

5

Loch Lomond

Ledrishmore Wood

84

G83

Burn of Balloch

4

Over Balloch

Horsehouse Wood

Stable Wood

Duck Bay

3

Cameron Bay

Cameron House (Hotel)

Balloch Castle

83

Cameron House Farm

Balloch Castle Country Park

2

INCHFAD RD

CREINCH DR

Ledrishbeg

TORRINCH DR

INCHCONNACHAN AVE

INCHMURRIN CRES

INCHLONAIG DR

MOLLANDHUIE RD

1 McLEAN CRES
2 HARAN RD
3 SHANDON CRES
4 SHANDON BRAE
5 DUMBAIN RD
6 HALDANE TERR

Balloch Pier

Balloch

Moss o' Balloch Plantations

CORN DR

LOMOND AVE

MERRICK DR

CASTLE AVE

PARK AVE

Loch Lomond Shores

River Leven

Balloch

DRYMEN RD

1

Gateway Ctr (Nat Pk Visitor Ctr)

OLD LUSS RD

BEN LOMOND WAY

PIER RD

CLAIRINISH

INCHCRUIN

GALLACHER CRES

MERCANTILE DR

BALLOCH RD

LOMOND RD

MARKET

A82

82

37   A   B   38   C   D   39   E   F

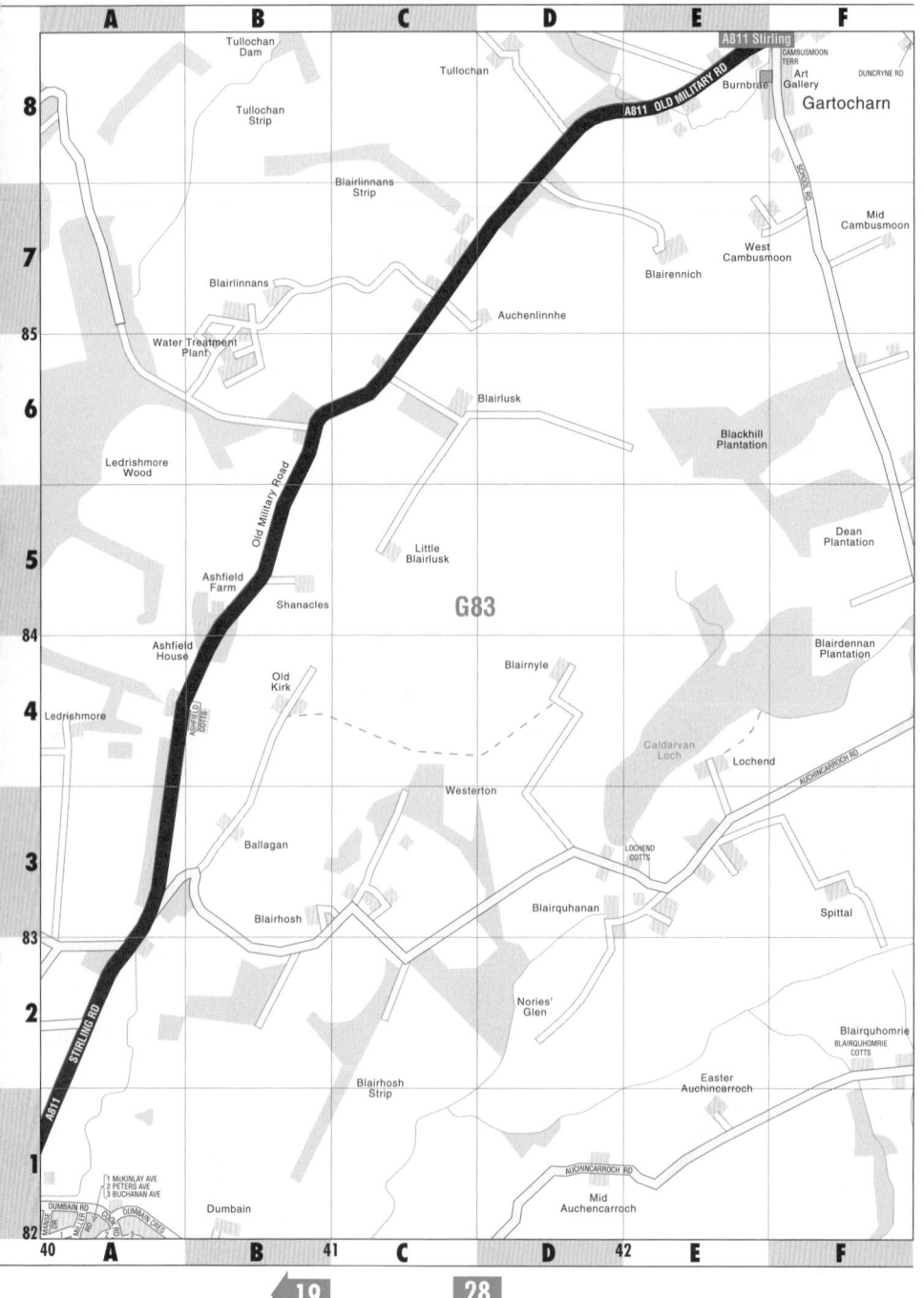

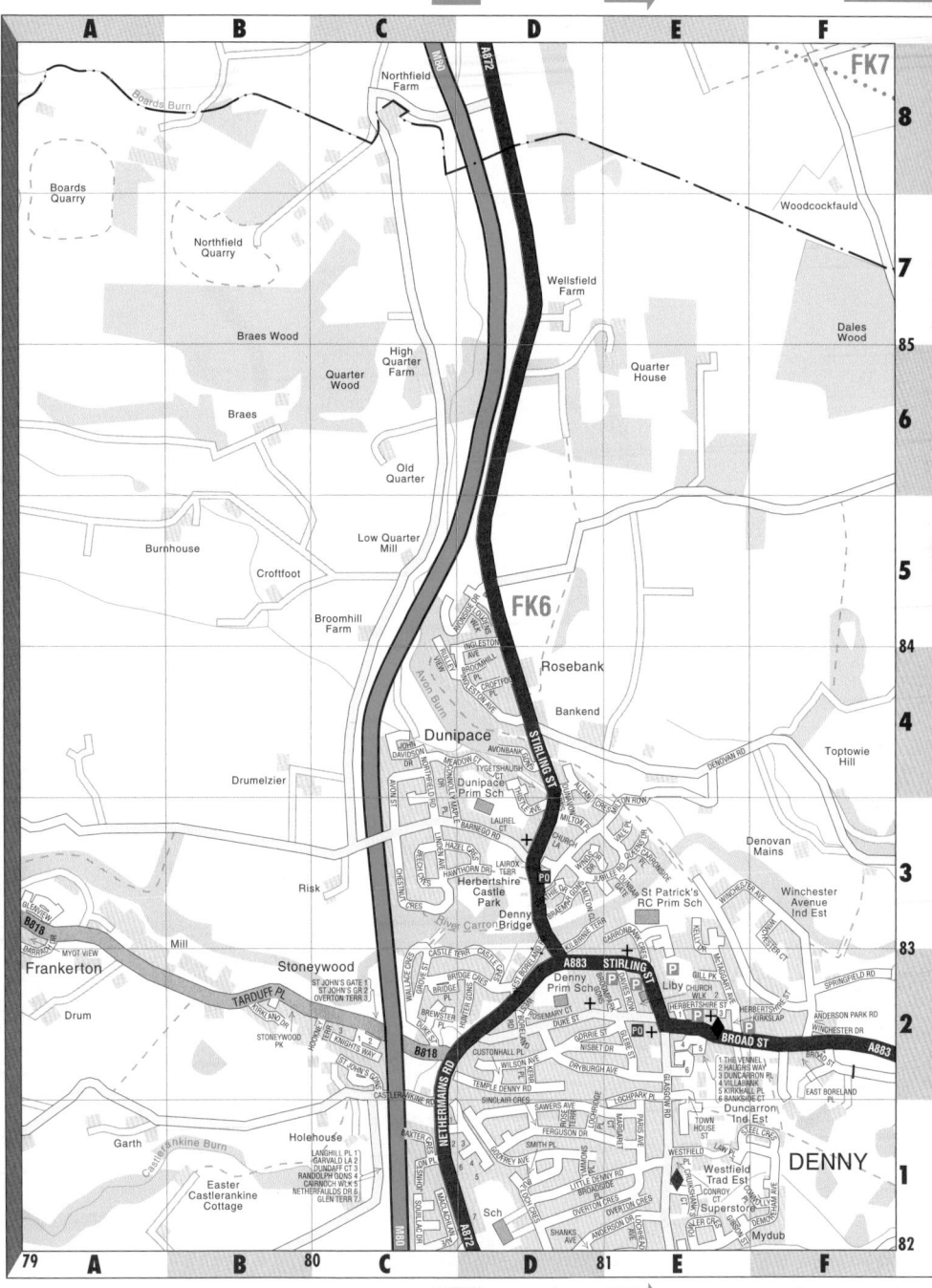

FK7

8

Boards Burn

Northfield
Farm

Boards
Quarry

7

Northfield
Quarry

Woodcockfauld

Wellsfield
Farm

85

Braes Wood

Dales
Wood

High
Quarter
Farm

Quarter
Wood

Quarter
House

6

Braes

Old
Quarter

Burnhouse

Low Quarter
Mill

Croftfoot

5

FK6

84

Broomhill
Farm

Rosebank

Dunipace

Bankend

4

Drumelzier

Dunipace
Prim Sch

Toptowie
Hill

Denovan
Mains

Risk

Herbertshire
Castle
Park

St Patrick's
RC Prim Sch

Winchester
Avenue
Ind Est

3

River Carron

Denny
Bridge

83

Frankerton

Mill

Stoneywood

A883

STIRLING ST

Denny
Prim Sch

Liby

CHURCH

Springfield Rd

Anderson Park Rd

Drum

TARDUFF PL

ST JOHN'S GATE 1
GARVALD LA 2
DUNDAFF CT 3
OVERTON TERR 3

Herbertshire
Kirkslap

B818

BROAD ST

A883

2

Stoneywood
Pk

1 THE VENNEL
2 HAUGHS WAY
3 DUNCARRON PL
4 VILLABANK
5 KIRKHALL PL
6 BANKSIDE CT

EAST BORELAND
PL

Garth

Holehouse

Duncarron
Ind Est

DENNY

Easter
Castlerankine
Cottage

LANGHILL PL 1
GARVALD LA 2
DUNDAFF CT 3
RANDOLPH DDNS 4
CAIRNOCH WLK 5
NETHERFAULDS DR 6
GLEN TERR 7

Westfield
Trad Est

Superstore

Sch

Mydub

1

82

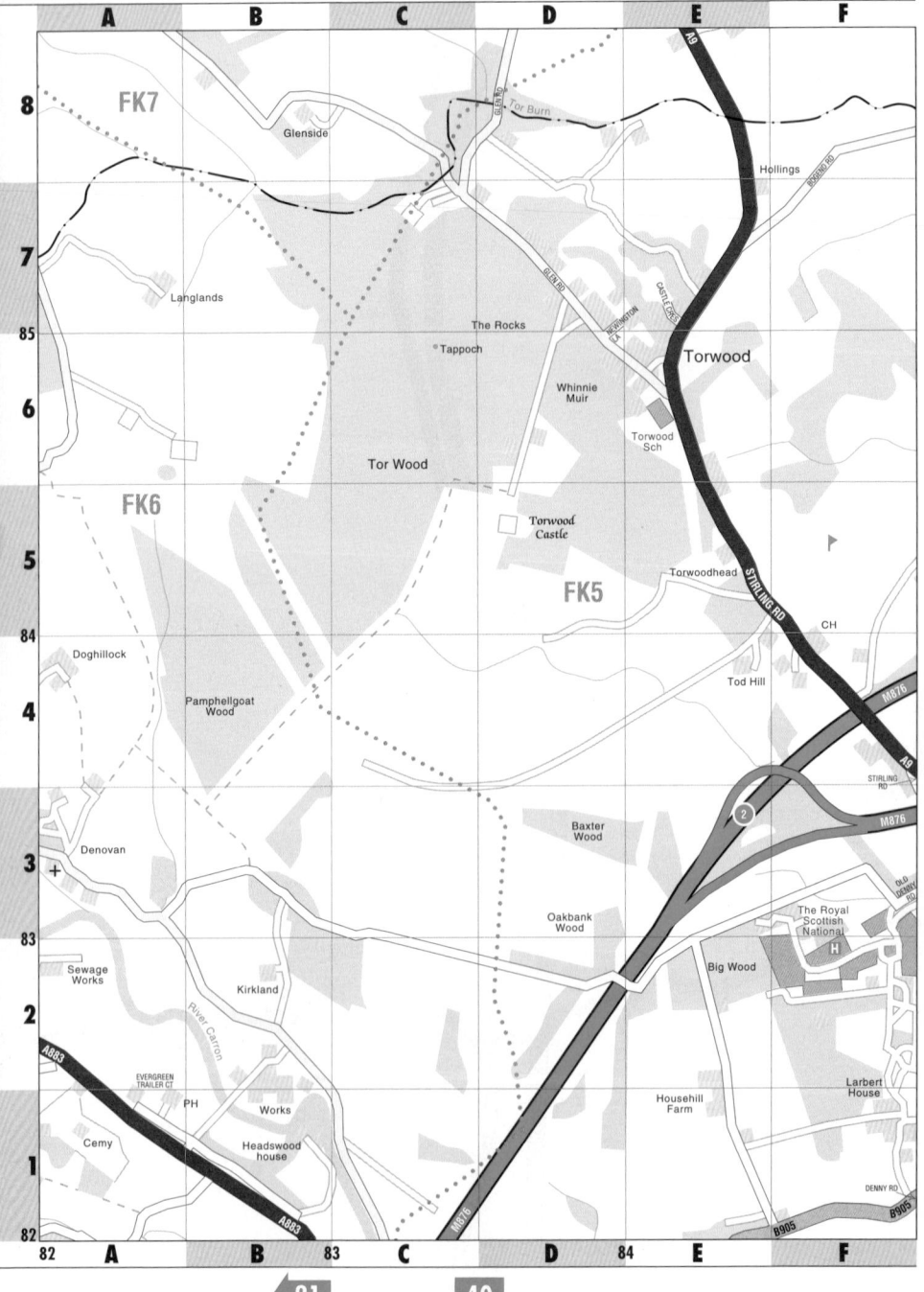

FK7

Glenside

Tor Burn

A9

Hollings

Langlands

The Rocks

Tappoch

Torwood

Whinnie
Muir

Torwood
Sch

Tor Wood

FK6

Torwood
Castle

FK5

Torwoodhead

CH

STIRLING RD

Doghillock

Tod Hill

M876

Pamphellgoat
Wood

STIRLING
RD

A9

2

M876

Denovan

Baxter
Wood

The Royal
Scottish
National

OLD DENNY RD

H

Sewage
Works

Oakbank
Wood

Big Wood

Kirkland

River Carron

A883

EVERGREEN
TRAILER CT

Household
Farm

Larbert
House

PH

Works

Cemy

Headswood
house

DENNY RD

A883

M816

B903

B905

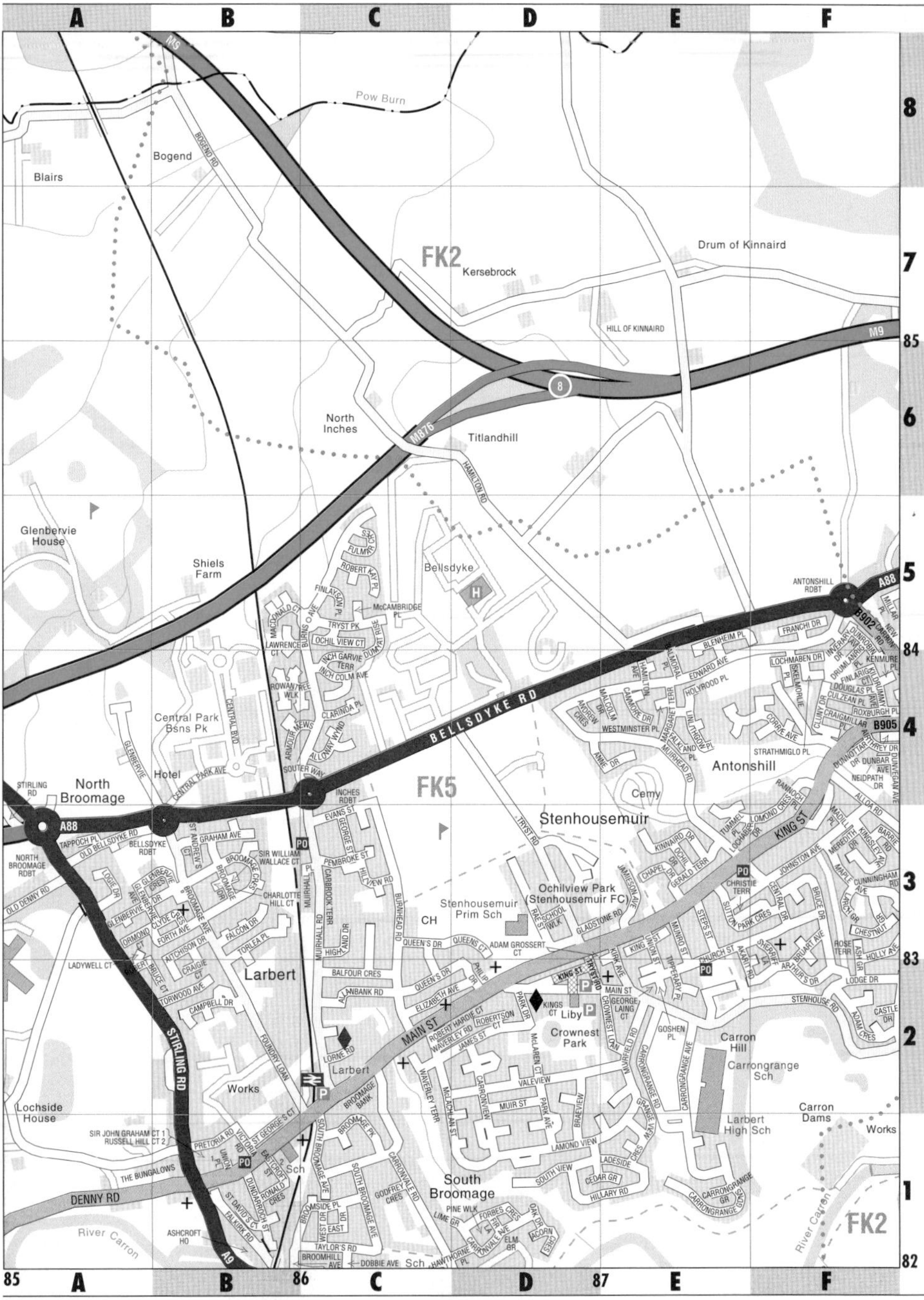

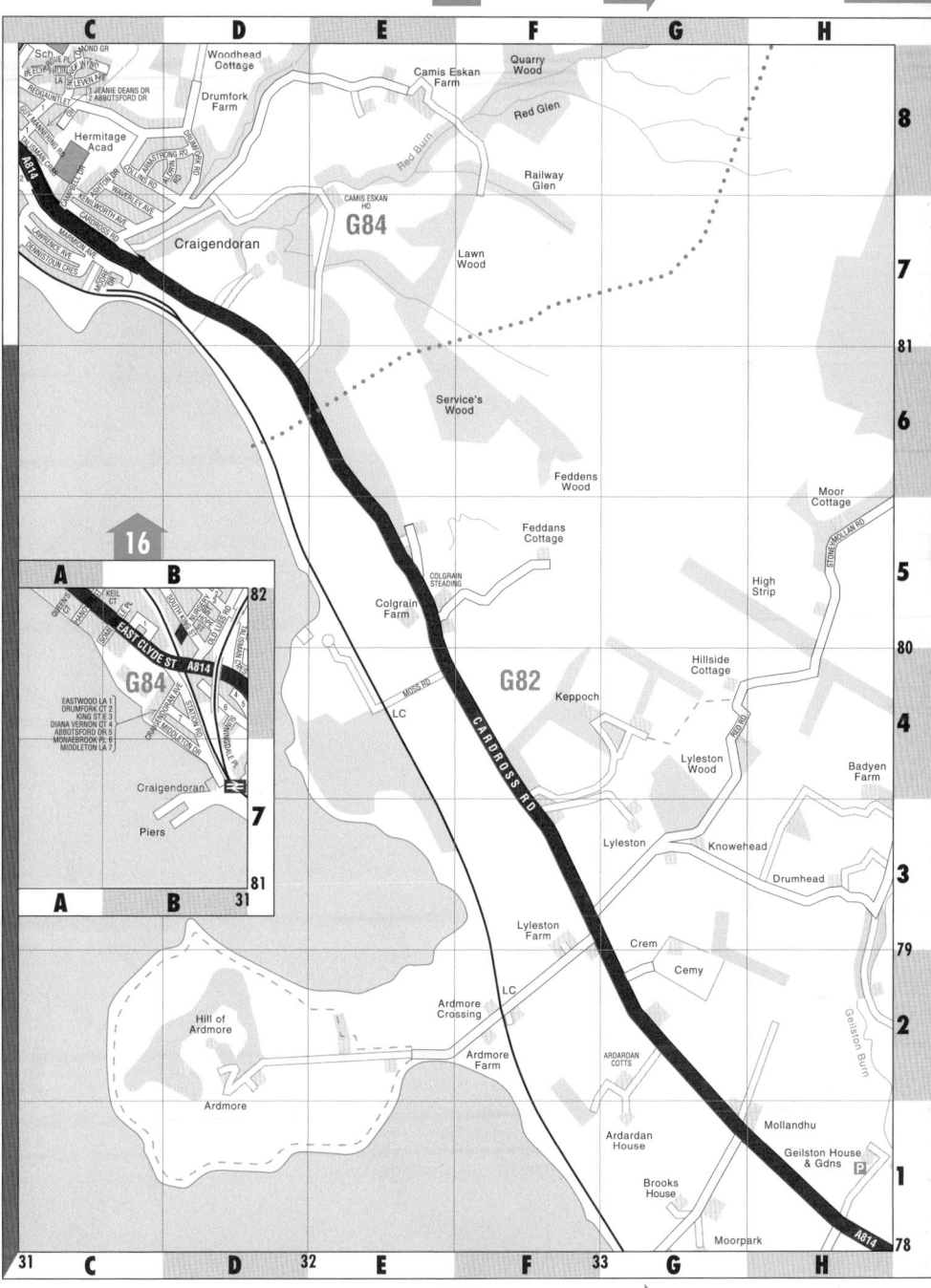

C D E F G H

8

Woodhead
Cottage
Camis Eskan
Farm
Quarry
Wood
Drumfork
Farm
Red Glen

Hermitage
Acad
Railway
Glen

7

CAMIS ESKAN
HO
G84
Craigendoran
Lawn
Wood

81

Service's
Wood

6

Feddens
Wood
Moor
Cottage

Feddans
Cottage

5

High
Strip
COLGRAIN
STEADING
Colgrain
Farm

80

Hillside
Cottage
16
MOSS RD
G82
Keppoch

A B
82
EAST CLYDE ST A814
G84
LC
4

Lyleston
Wood
Badyen
Farm
EASTWOOD LA 1
DRUMFORK CT 2
KING ST E 3
DIANA VERNON CT 4
ABBOTSFORD DR 5
MONAEBROOK PL 6
MIDDLETON LA 7

Craigendoran
Lyleston
Knowehead
Piers
7
Drumhead

81
A B 31
Lyleston
Farm
3
79

Crem
Cemy

Hill of
Ardmore
LC
2

Ardmore
Crossing
ARDARDAN
COTTS
Geilston Burn

Ardmore
Farm

Ardmore
Mollandhu
Geilston House
& Gdns
P
1

ARDARDAN
HOUSE
Brooks
House

Moorpark
A814
78

31 C D 32 E F 33 G H

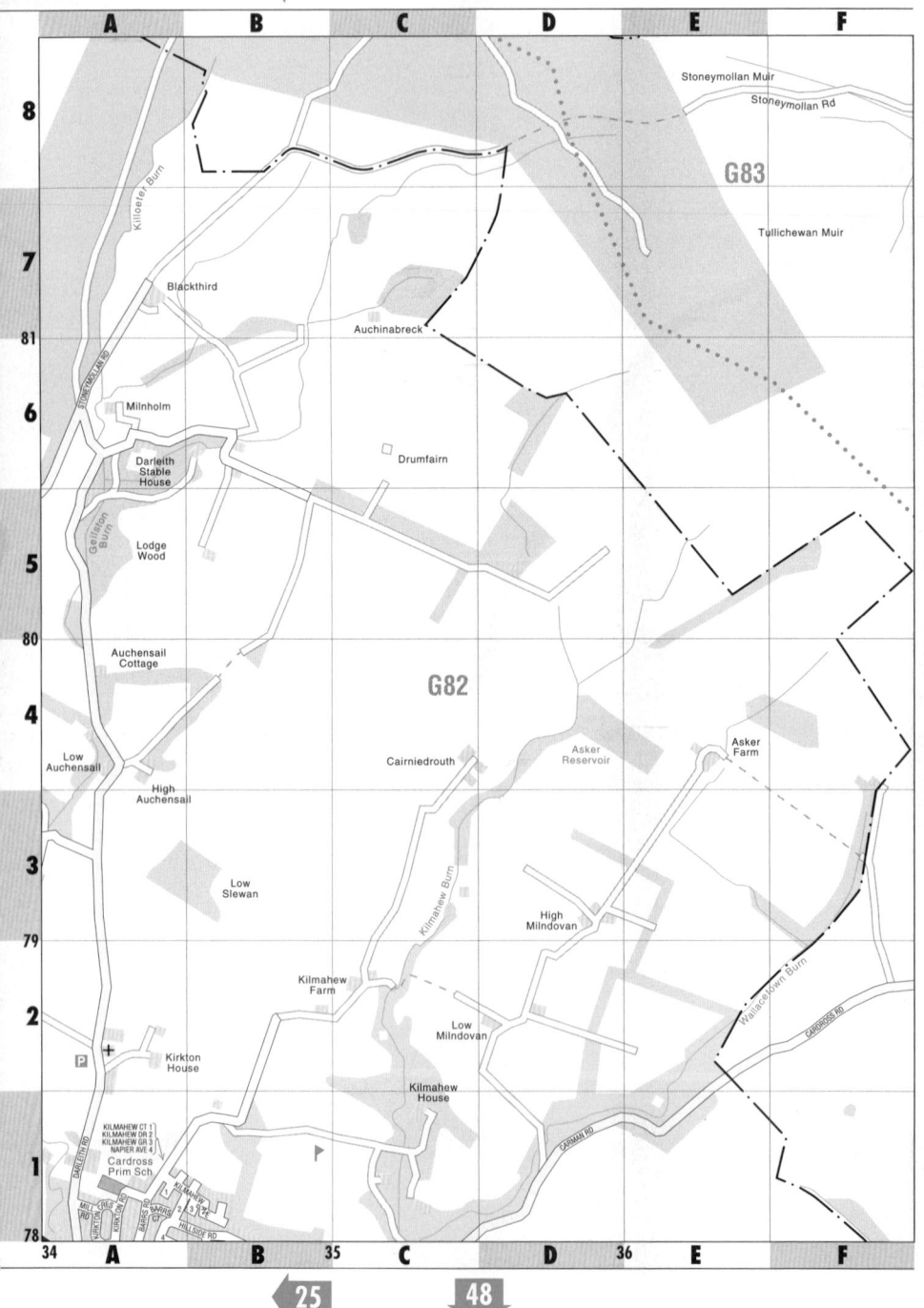

A B C D E F

8

7

81

6

80

5

4

79

3

2

1

78

34 A B 35 C D 36 E F

Stoneymollan Muir
Stoneymollan Rd

G83

Tullichewan Muir

Killoeter Burn

Blackthird

Auchinabreck

STONEYMOLLAN RD

Milnholm

Darleith
Stable
House

Drumfairn

Gelstein Burn

Lodge
Wood

Auchensail
Cottage

G82

Low
Auchensail

Asker
Reservoir

Asker
Farm

High
Auchensail

Cairniedrouth

Low
Slewan

Kilmahew Burn

High
Milndovan

Wallacetown Burn

CARDROSS RD

Kilmahew
Farm

Low
Milndovan

Kirkton
House

Kilmahew
House

KILMAHEW CT 1
KILMAHEW DR 2
KILMAHEW GR 3
NAPIER AVE 4

Cardross
Prim Sch

DARLEITH RD

MILL RD
KIRKTON RD
PEEL RD
BARRS RD
KILMAHEW DR

CARMAN RD

HILLSIDE RD

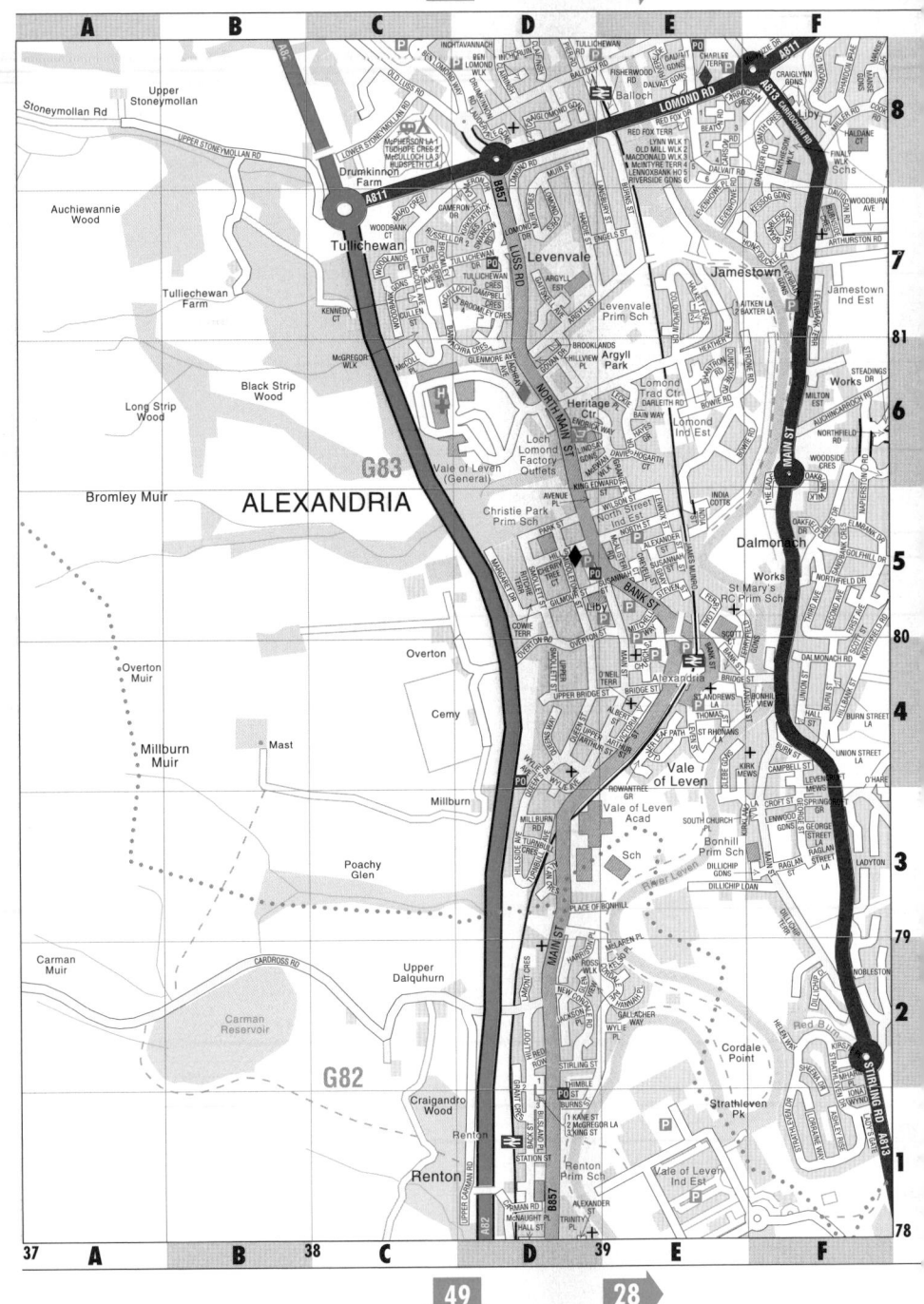

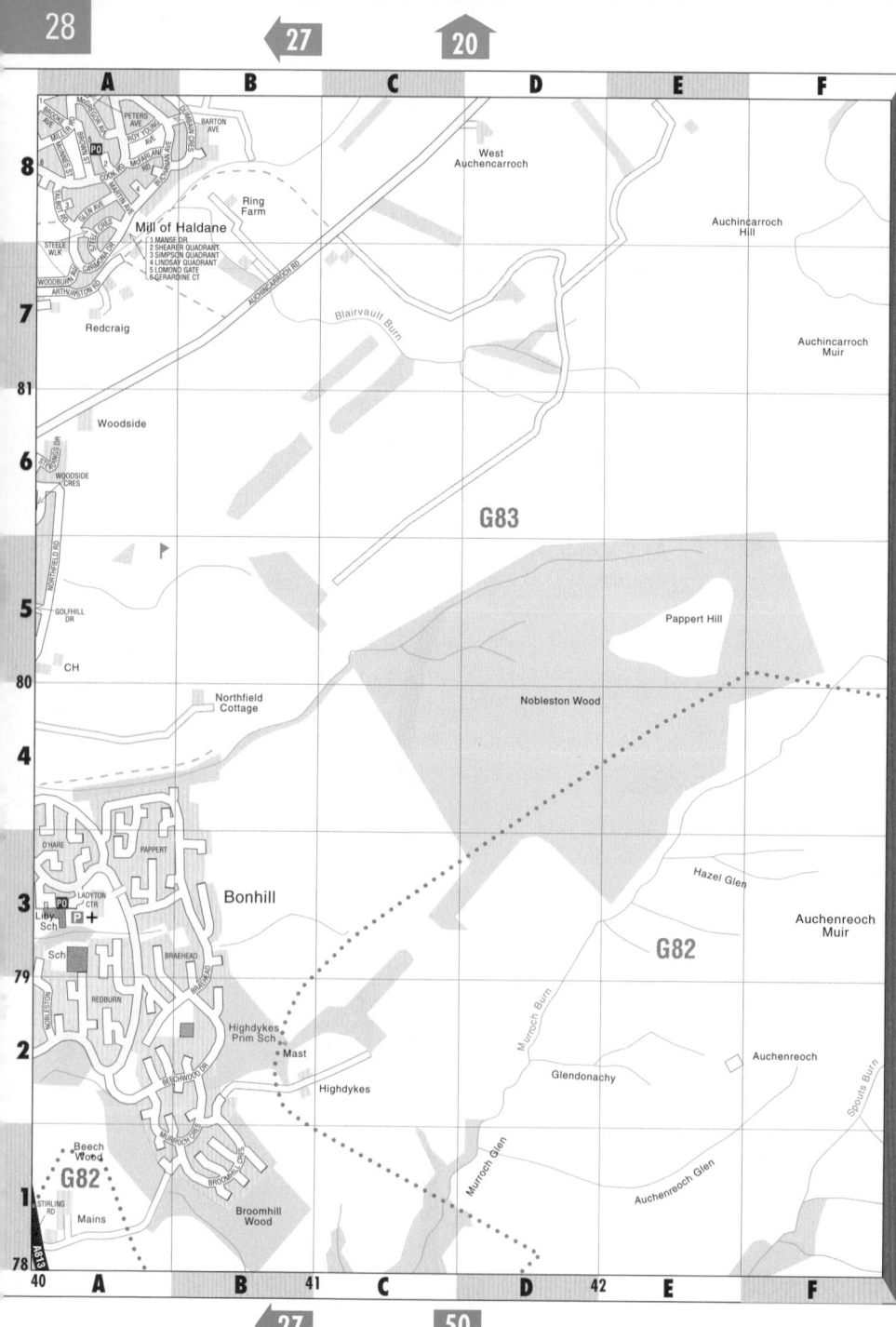

G83

G82

Bonhill

Pappert Hill

Nobleston Wood

Auchenreoch Muir

Mill of Haldane

West Auchencarroch

Auchincarroch Hill

Auchincarroch Muir

Ring Farm

Redcraig

Woodside

Woodside Cres

Golfhill Dr

CH

Northfield Cottage

Blairvault Burn

Pappert

Ladyton Ctr

Liby Sch

Sch

Braehead

Redburn

Highdykes Prim Sch

Mast

Highdykes

Beech Wood

Mains

Broomhill Wood

G82

Stirling Rd

A813

Hazel Glen

Glendonachy

Murroch Burn

Murroch Glen

Auchenreoch

Auchenreoch Glen

Spouts Burn

1 MANSE DR
2 SHEARER QUADRANT
3 SIMPSON QUADRANT
4 LINDSAY QUADRANT
5 LOMOND GATE
6 GERARDINE CT

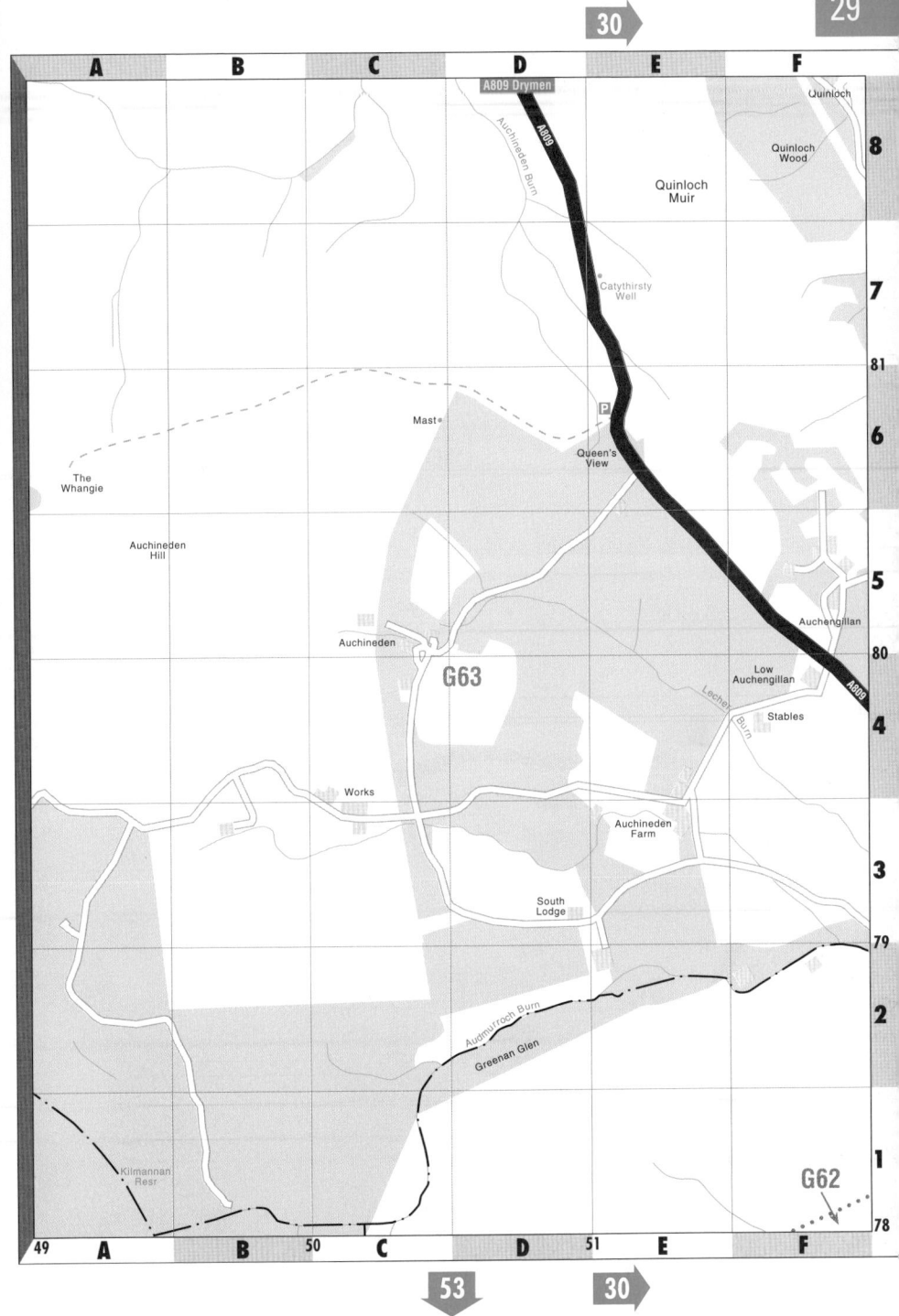

A B C D E F

8

7

81

6

5

80

4

3

79

2

1

78

A809 Drymen

A809

Auchineden Burn

Quinloch

Quinloch
Wood

Quinloch
Muir

Catythirsty
Well

Mast

Queen's
View

The
Whangie

Auchineden
Hill

Auchineden

G63

Auchengillan

Low
Auchengillan

Lecket Burn

Stables

Works

Auchineden
Farm

South
Lodge

Auchmurroch Burn

Greenan Glen

Kilmannan
Resr

G62

49 A B 50 C D 51 E F

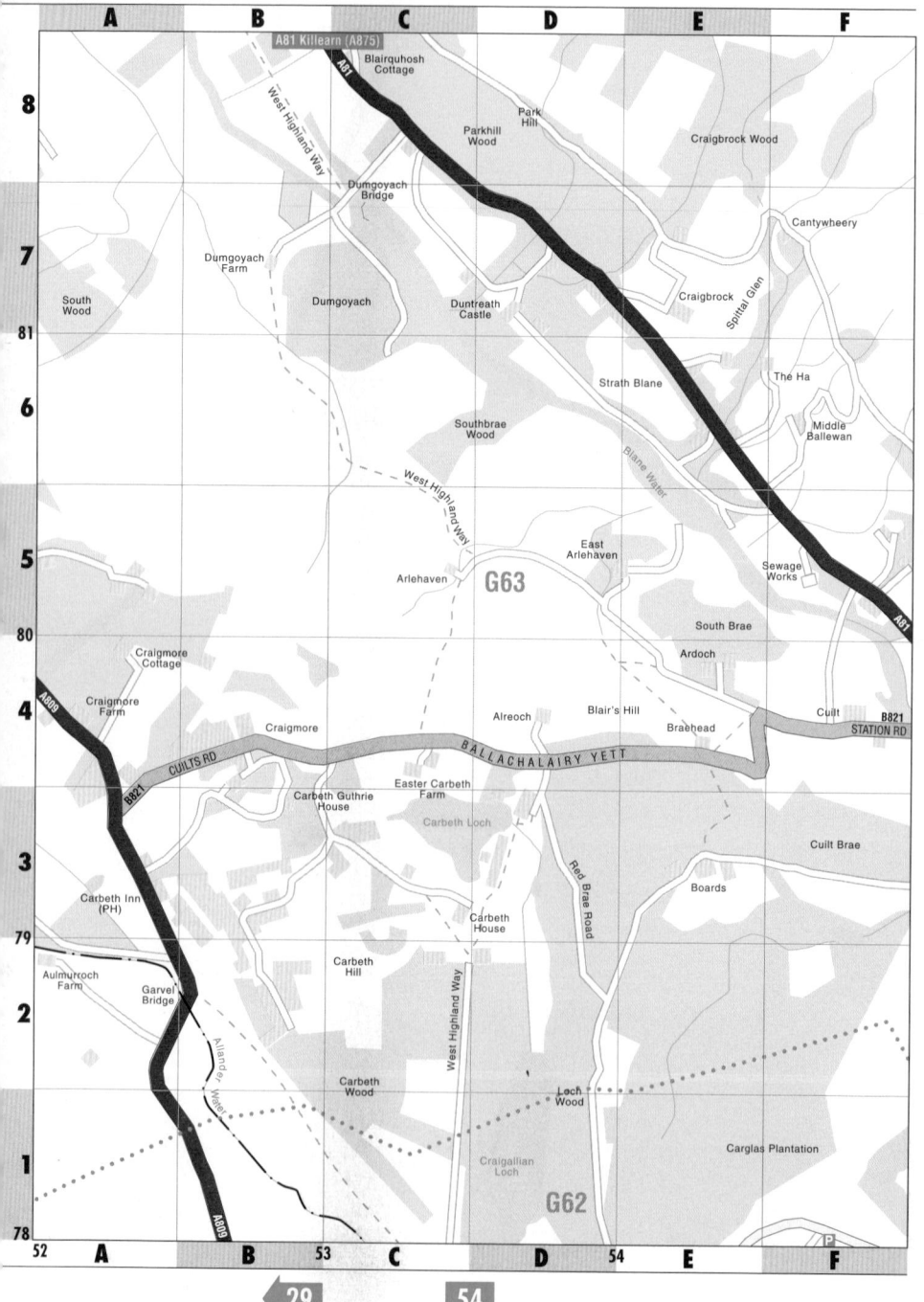

29

A81 Killearn (A875)

Blairquhosh
Cottage

Park
Hill

Parkhill
Wood

Craigbrock Wood

Dumgoyach
Bridge

Cantywheery

Dumgoyach
Farm

West Highland Way

South
Wood

Dumgoyach

Duntreath
Castle

Craigbrock

Spittal Glen

81

The Ha

Strath Blane

6

Southbrae
Wood

Middle
Ballewan

Blane Water

West Highland Way

East
Arlehaven

5

Arlehaven

G63

Sewage
Works

80

South Brae

Ardoch

Craigmore
Cottage

A809

Craigmore
Farm

Alreoch

Blair's Hill

Braehead

Cuilt

B821
STATION RD

Craigmore

BALLACHALAIRY YETT

CUILTS RD

B921

Carbeth Guthrie
House

Easter Carbeth
Farm

Cuilt Brae

Carbeth Loch

Boards

3

Carbeth Inn
(PH)

Red Brae Road

79

Carbeth
House

Aulmurroch
Farm

Carbeth
Hill

2

Garvel
Bridge

West Highland Way

Allander Water

Carbeth
Wood

Loch
Wood

Carglas Plantation

1

Craigallian
Loch

G62

78

A809

52   53   54

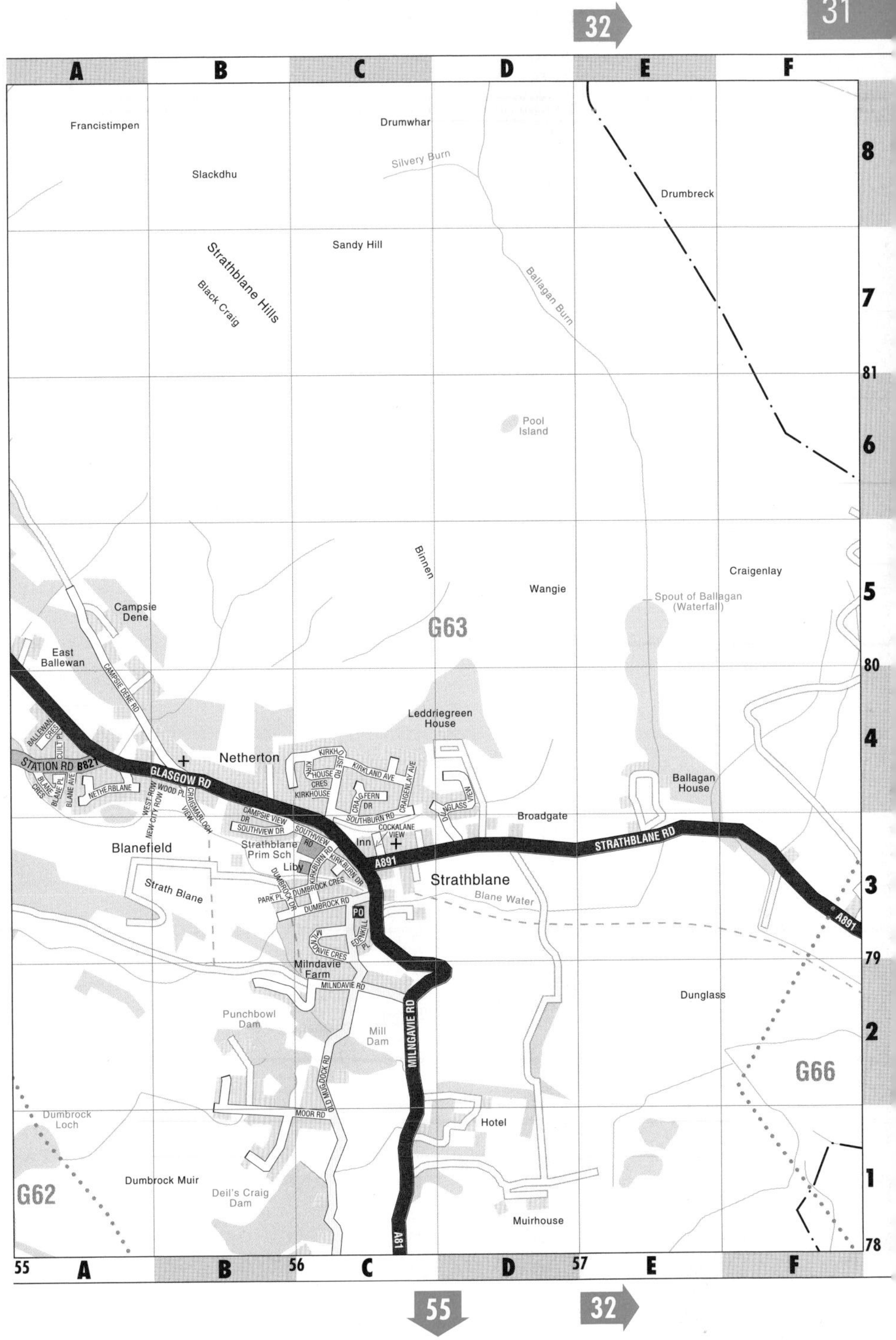
32
A
B
C
D
E
F
Francistimpen
Drumwhar
Silvery Burn
Slackdhu
Drumbreck
Sandy Hill
Strathblane Hills
Black Craig
Ballagan Burn
Pool Island
Binnen
Wangie
Craigenlay
Spout of Ballagan (Waterfall)
G63
Campsie Dene
East Ballewan
CAMPSIE DENE RD
Leddriegreen House
Netherton
STATION RD B821
GLASGOW RD
NETHERBLANE
BALLEWAN CRES
QUILT PL
BLANE PL
BLANE AVE
BLANE CRES
WEST ROW
NEW CITY ROW
WOOD PL
CRAIGMARLOCH VIEW
KIRKHOUSE RD
KIRKLAND AVE
KIRKHOUSE CRES
KIRKHOUSE
CRAIGFERN DR
CRAIGENLAY AVE
SOUTHBURN RD
DUNGLASS VIEW
Ballagan House
Broadgate
CAMPSIE VIEW DR
SOUTHVIEW DR
SOUTHVIEW RD
COCKALANE VIEW
Inn
STRATHBLANE RD
Blanefield
Strathblane Prim Sch
Liby
KIRKBURN RD
KIRKBURN DR
A891
Strathblane
Blane Water
Strath Blane
DUMBROCK DR
DUMBROCK CRES
PARK PL
DUMBROCK RD
PO
EDENKILL PL
MILNDAVIE CRES
Milndavie Farm
MILNDAVIE RD
Dunglass
Punchbowl Dam
Mill Dam
MILNGAVIE RD
OLD MUGDOCK RD
G66
Dumbrock Loch
MOOR RD
Hotel
Dumbrock Muir
Deil's Craig Dam
G62
Muirhouse
A81
8
7
81
6
5
80
4
3
79
2
1
78
55
56
57
55
32

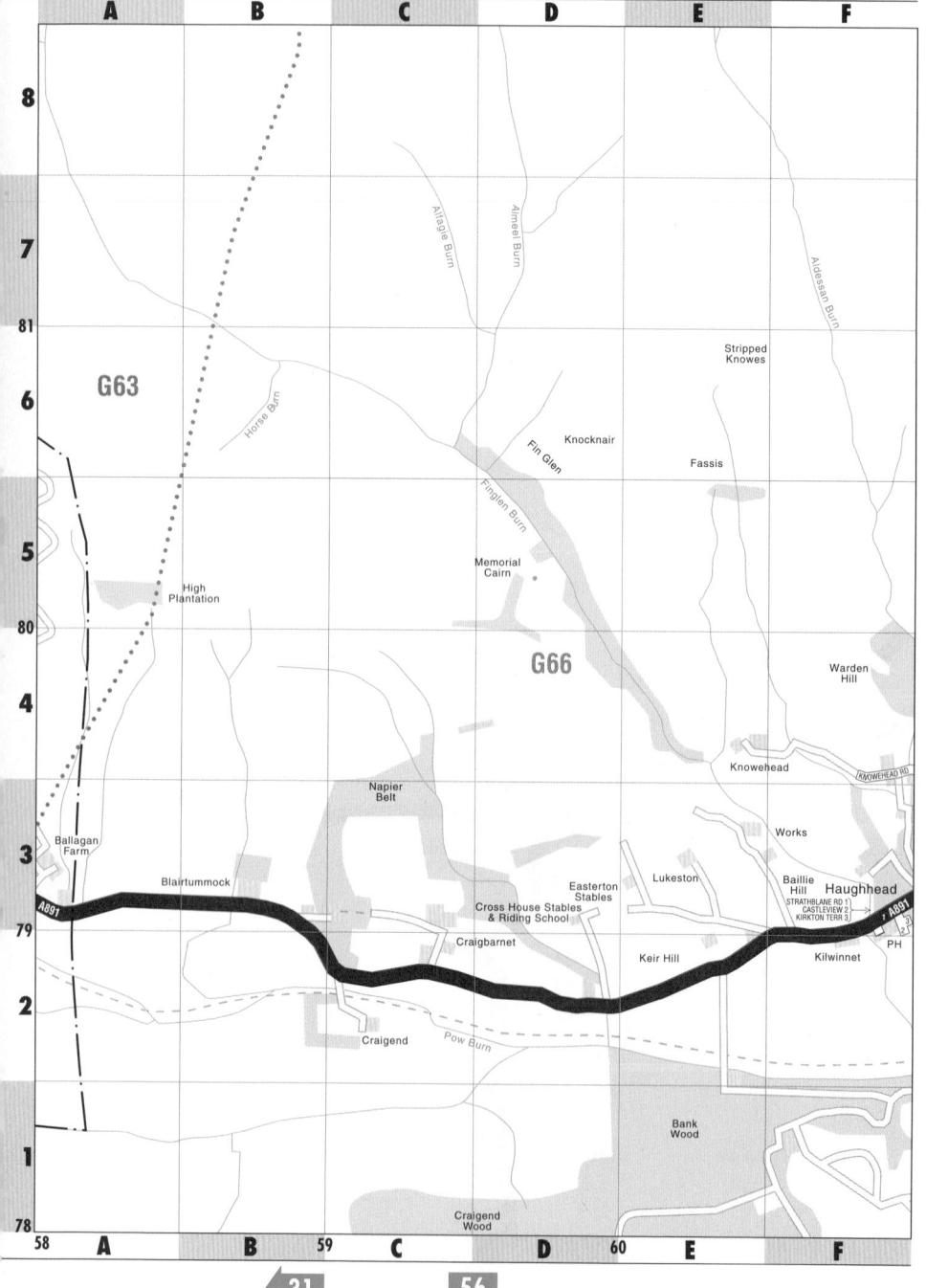

A | B | C | D | E | F

8

7

81

6

G63

5

80

4

3

79

2

1

78

58 | A | B | 59 | C | D | 60 | E | F

Allagie Burn

Almeel Burn

Aldessan Burn

Horse Burn

Stripped
Knowes

Fin Glen

Knocknair

Fassis

Finglen Burn

Memorial
Cairn

High
Plantation

G66

Warden
Hill

Napier
Belt

Knowehead

KNOWEHEAD RD

Works

Ballagan
Farm

A891

Blairtummock

Easterton
Stables

Lukeston

Baillie
Hill

Haughhead

Cross House Stables
& Riding School

STRATHBLANE RD 1
CASTLEVIEW 2
KIRKTON TERR 3

A891

Craigbarnet

Keir Hill

Kilwinnet

PH

Craigend

Pow Burn

Bank
Wood

Craigend
Wood

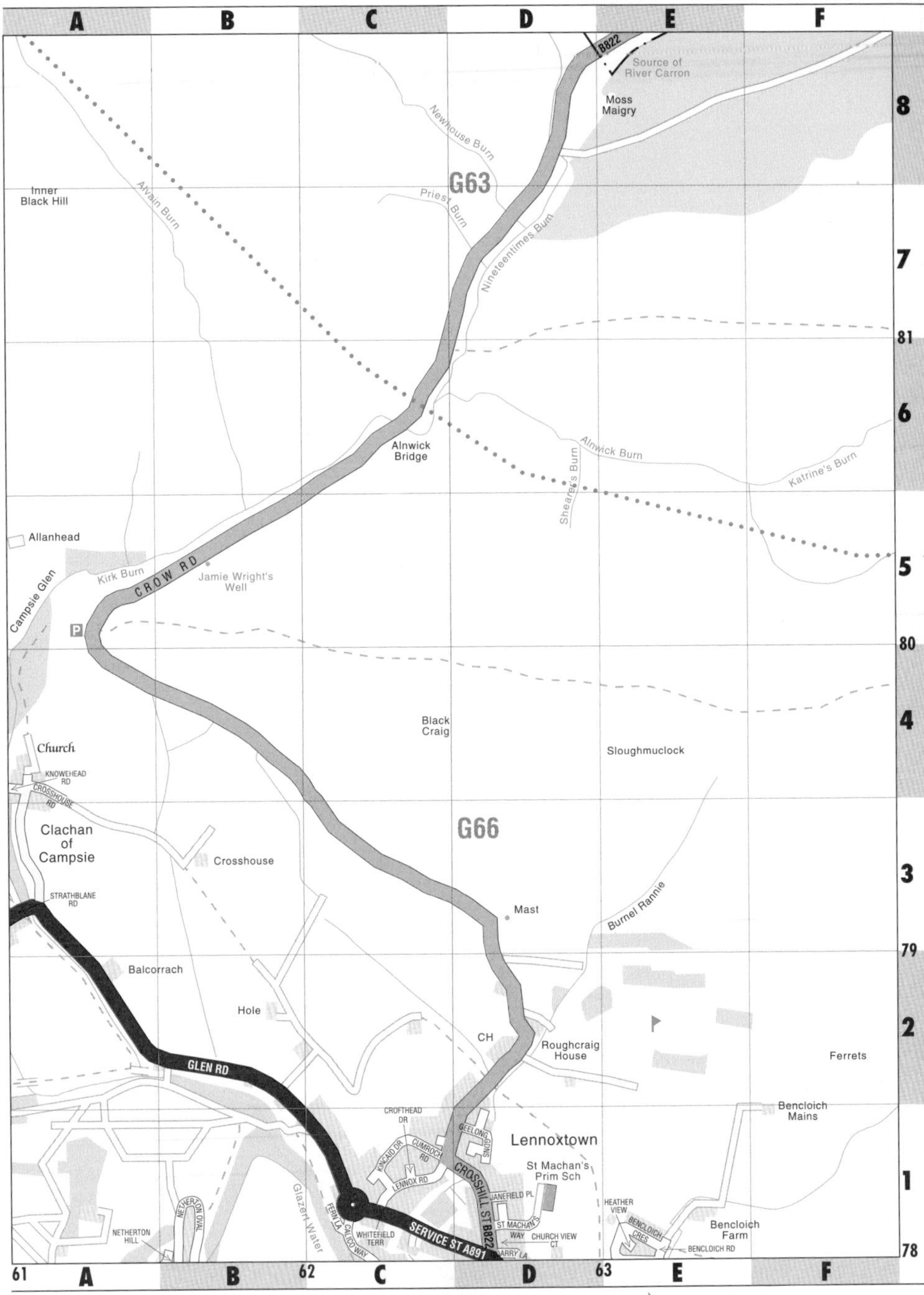

A   B   C   D   E   F

8

7

81

6

5

80

4

3

79

2

1

78

Source of
River Carron

B822

Moss
Maigry

G63

Newhouse Burn

Priest Burn

Nineteentimes Burn

Aldin Burn

Inner
Black Hill

Alnwick
Bridge

Shearna's Burn

Alnwick Burn

Katrine's Burn

Allanhead

Kirk Burn

CROW RD

Jamie Wright's
Well

Campsie Glen

P

Black
Craig

Sloughmuclock

Church

KNOWEHEAD
RD

CROSSHILL
RD

Clachan
of
Campsie

Crosshouse

G66

Burnel Rannie

STRATHBLANE
RD

Balcorrach

Hole

Mast

CH

Roughcraig
House

Ferrets

GLEN RD

CROFTHEAD
DR

BEECLONIC

DIAMOND
RD

ARNOLD ST

LENNOX RD

ANEFIELD PL

Lennoxtown

St Machan's
Prim Sch

CROSSHILL ST B822

ST MACHAN
WAY

CHURCH VIEW
CT

HEATHER
VIEW

BENCLOICH
CRES

Bencloich
Mains

Bencloich
Farm

BENCLOICH RD

NETHERTON
HILL

Glazert Water

NETHERCROSS OVAL

WHITEFIELD
TERR

BENCLOICH RD

SERVICE ST A891

QUARRY LA

61   A   B   62   C   D   63   E   F

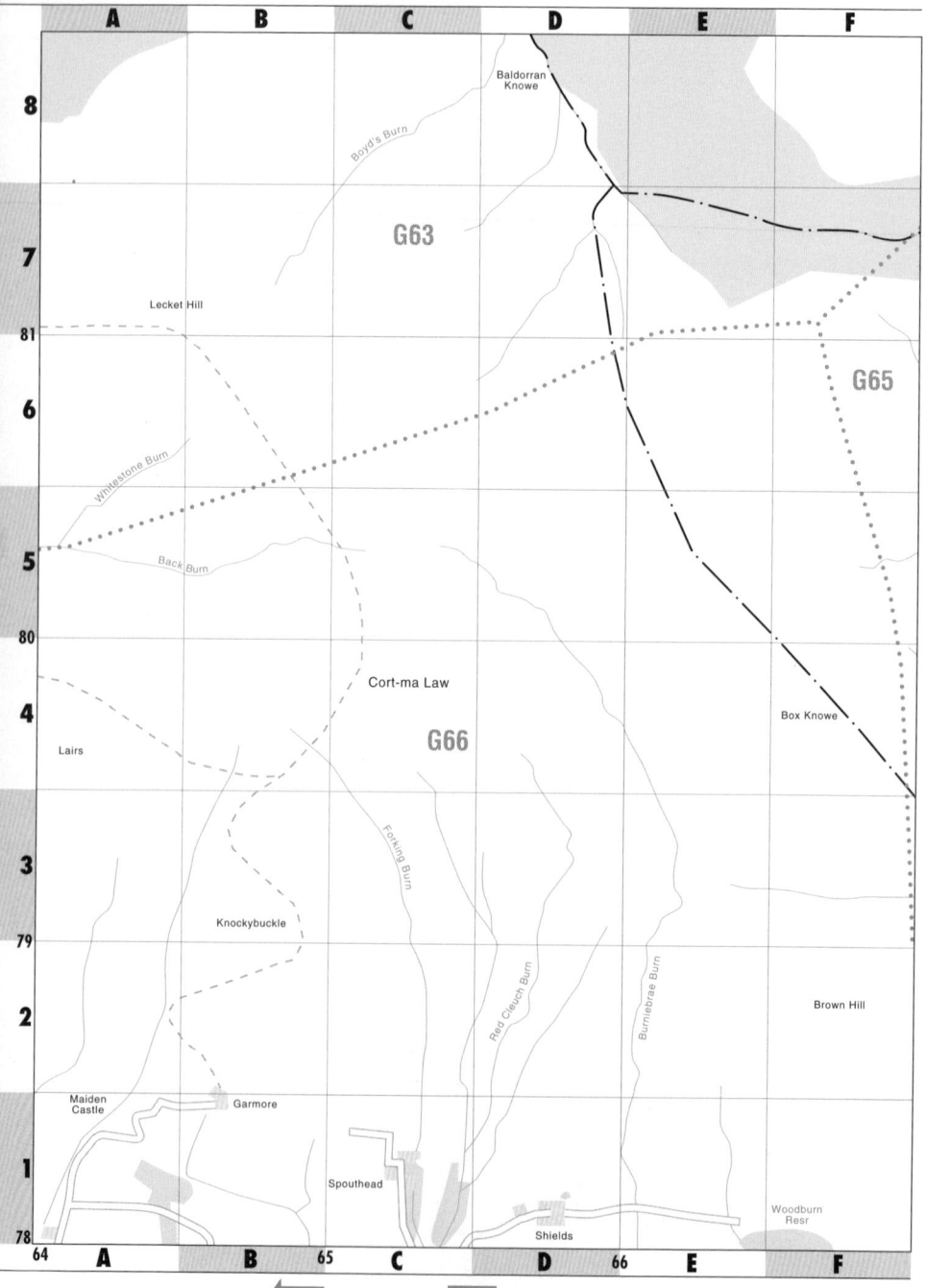

33

8

7

81

6

5

80

4

3

79

2

1

78

A B C D E F

Baldorran Knowe

G63

Lecket Hill

G65

Whitestone Burn

Back Burn

Cort-ma Law

G66

Lairs

Box Knowe

Forking Burn

Knockybuckle

Red Cleuch Burn

Burniebrae Burn

Brown Hill

Maiden Castle

Garmore

Spouthead

Shields

Woodburn Resr

64 A B 65 C D 66 E F

33
58

36

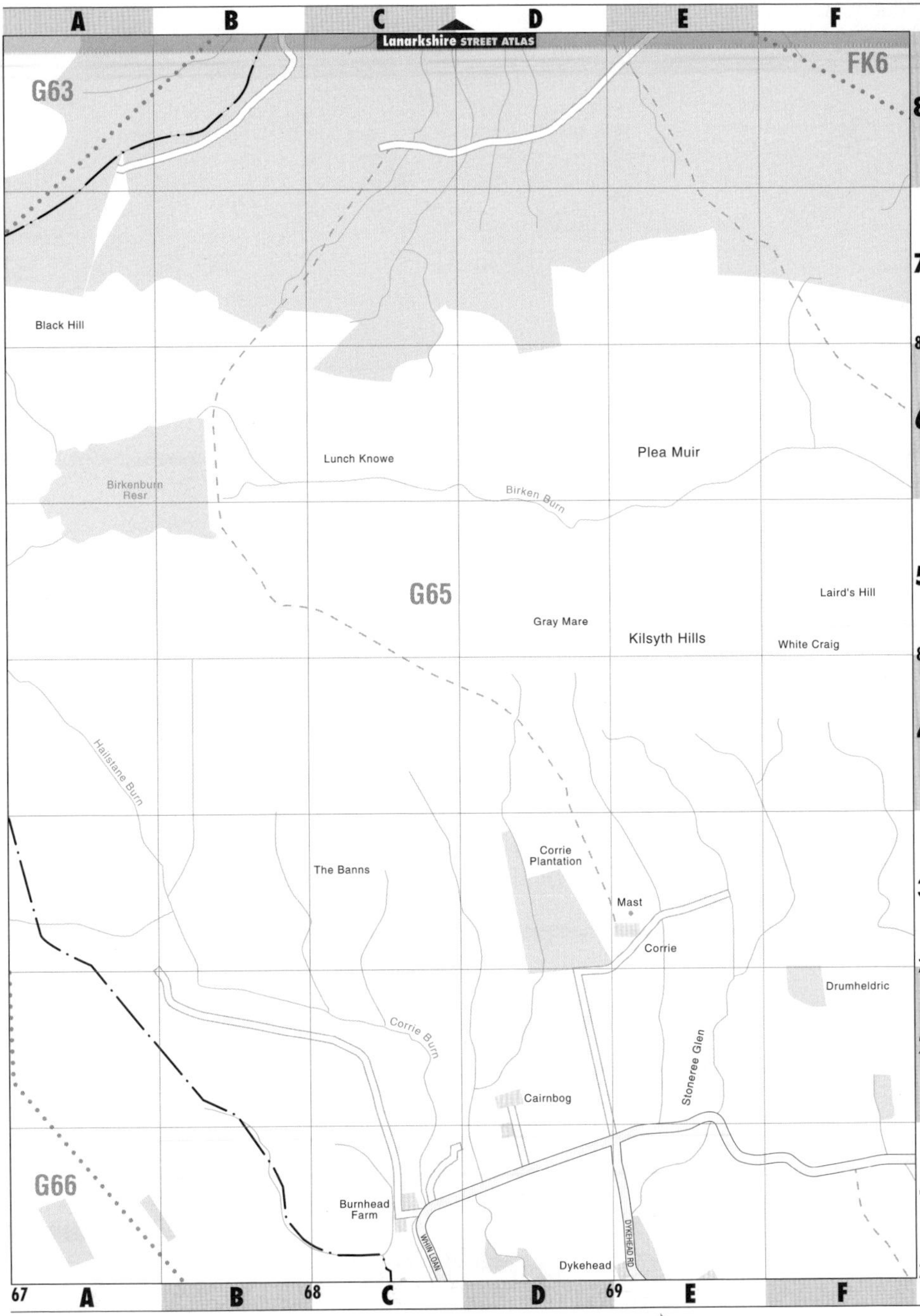
Lanarkshire STREET ATLAS
A
B
C
D
E
F
G63
FK6
Black Hill
Birkenburn Resr
Lunch Knowe
Plea Muir
Birken Burn
G65
Laird's Hill
Gray Mare
Kilsyth Hills
White Craig
Hailstane Burn
Corrie Plantation
The Banns
Mast
Corrie
Drumheldric
Corrie Burn
Stoneree Glen
Cairnbog
G66
Burnhead Farm
WHIN LOAN
DYKEHEAD RD
Dykehead
8
7
81
6
5
80
4
3
79
2
1
78
67
68
69

59
36

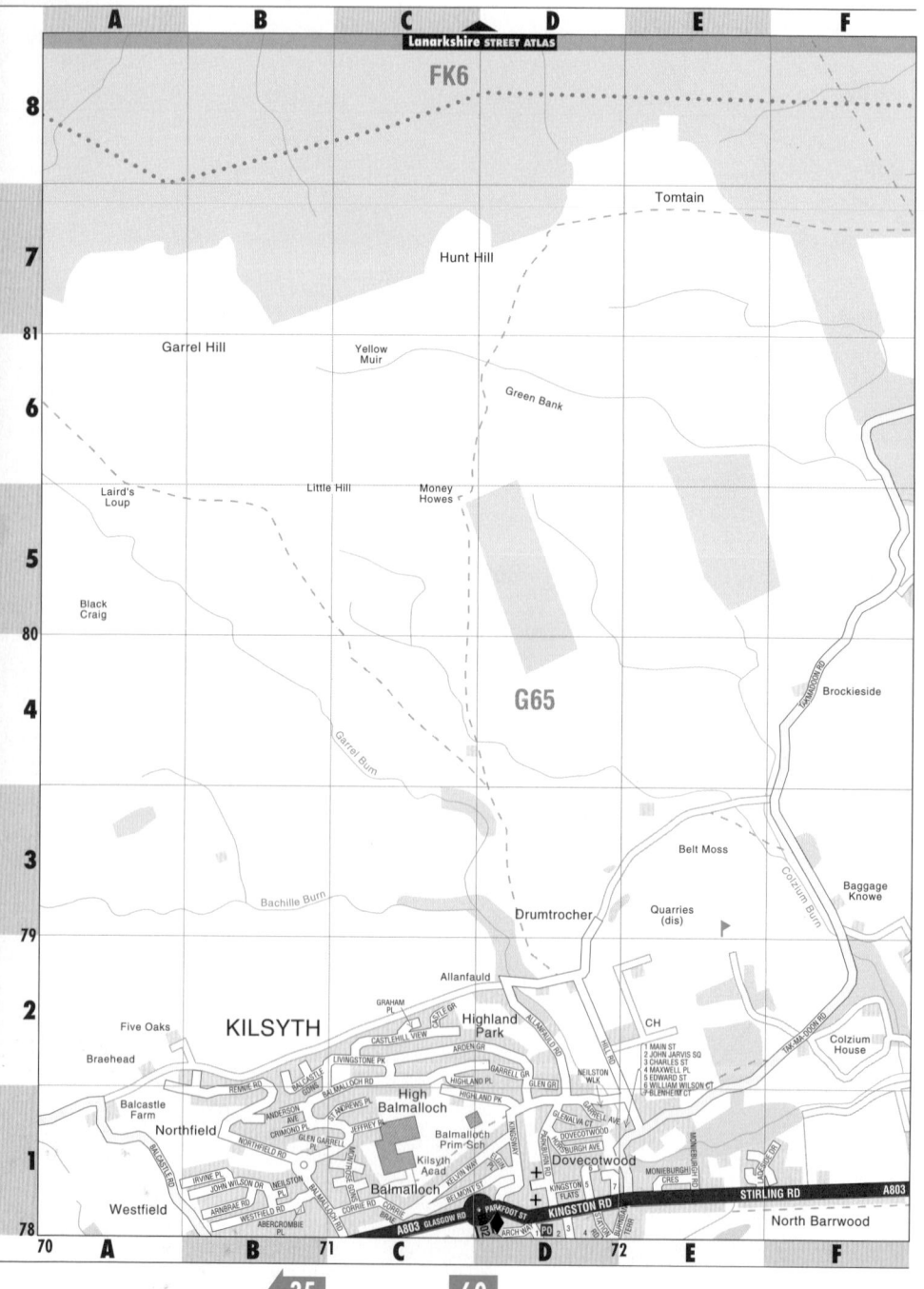

	A	B	C	D	E	F

Lanarkshire STREET ATLAS

FK6

8

Tomtain

7

Hunt Hill

81

Garrel Hill

Yellow Muir

Green Bank

6

Laird's Loup

Little Hill

Money Howes

Black Craig

5

80

G65

4

Garrel Burn

Brockieside

Whassen Rd

3

Belt Moss

Baggage Knowe

Bachille Burn

Colzium Burn

Quarries (dis)

Drumtrocher

79

Allanfauld

2

GRAHAM PL

STE GR

Highland Park

CH

Colzium House

Five Oaks

KILSYTH

CASTLEHILL VIEW

ARDEN GR

GARRELL GR

GLEN GR

1 MAIN ST
2 JOHN JARVIS SQ
3 CHARLES ST
4 MAXWELL PL
5 EDWARD ST
6 WILLIAM WILSON CT
7 BLENHEIM CT

Braehead

LIVINGSTONE PK

Highland PL

NEILSTON WLK

Balcastle Farm

RENNIE RD

BALCASTLE

BAL MALLOCH RD

Highland PK

MONIEBURGH CRES

Northfield

ANDERSON AVE

ST ANDREWS RD

High Balmalloch

CRINMOND PL

GLEN GARREL

JEFFREY PL

GLEN BALMA AVE

DOVECOTWOOD

Balmalloch Prim Sch

GLENBALMA AVE

MONIEBURGH RD

1

IRVINE PL

JOHN WILSON DR

NEILSTON PL

Kilsyth Acad

STIRLING WAY

Dovecotwood

MONIEBURGH CRES

NORTHFIELD RD

ARNBRAE RD

CORBIE RD

BELMONT ST

BALMALLOCH RD

KINGSTON FLATS

Westfield

WESTFIELD RD

ABERCROMBIE PL

Balmalloch

CORBIE WAY

STIRLING RD

A803

78

A803 GLASGOW RD

PARKFOOT ST

KINGSTON RD

PO

North Barrwood

70	A		B	71	C		D	72	E		F

A B C D E F

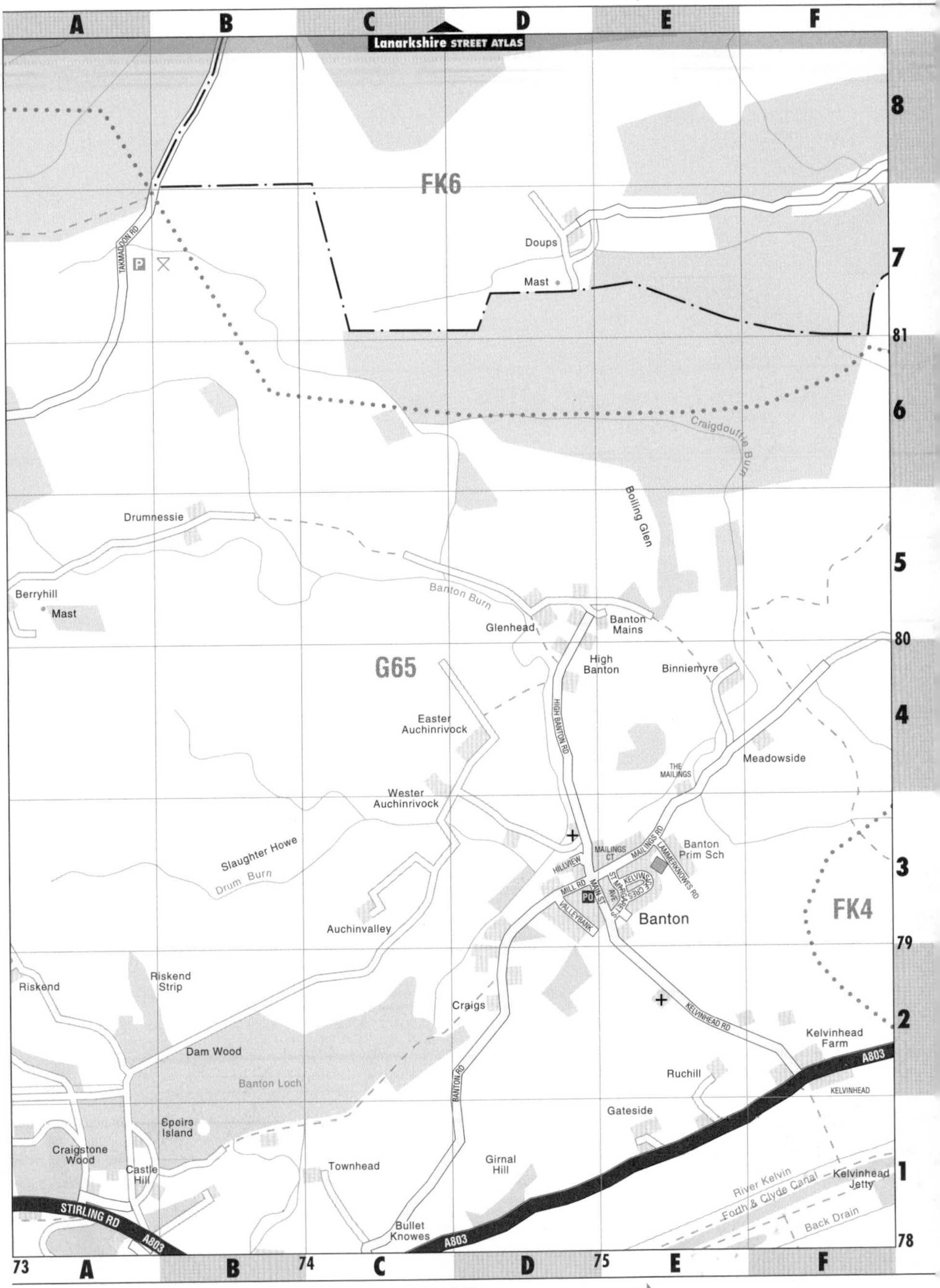

Lanarkshire STREET ATLAS

8

FK6

7

Doups

Mast

81

Craigdouffie Burn

6

Bolling Glen

Drumnessie

Banton Burn

5

Berryhill

Mast

Glenhead

Banton Mains

80

G65

High Banton

Binniemyre

Easter Auchinrivock

4

THE MAILINGS

Meadowside

Wester Auchinrivock

HIGH BANTON RD

Slaughter Howe

Drum Burn

MAILINGS CT

MAILINGS RD

CAMERONS RD

Banton Prim Sch

3

HILLVIEW

MILL RD

KELVIN ...

ALLEYBANK

PO

Banton

FK4

Auchinvalley

BANTON RD

79

Riskend Strip

Riskend

Craigs

KELVINHEAD RD

Kelvinhead Farm

2

A803

Dam Wood

Banton Loch

Ruchill

KELVINHEAD

Epeiro Island

Gateside

River Kelvin

Forth & Clyde Canal

Kelvinhead Jetty

Craigstone Wood

Castle Hill

Townhead

Girnal Hill

1

STIRLING RD

A803

Bullet Knowes

A803

Back Drain

78

37

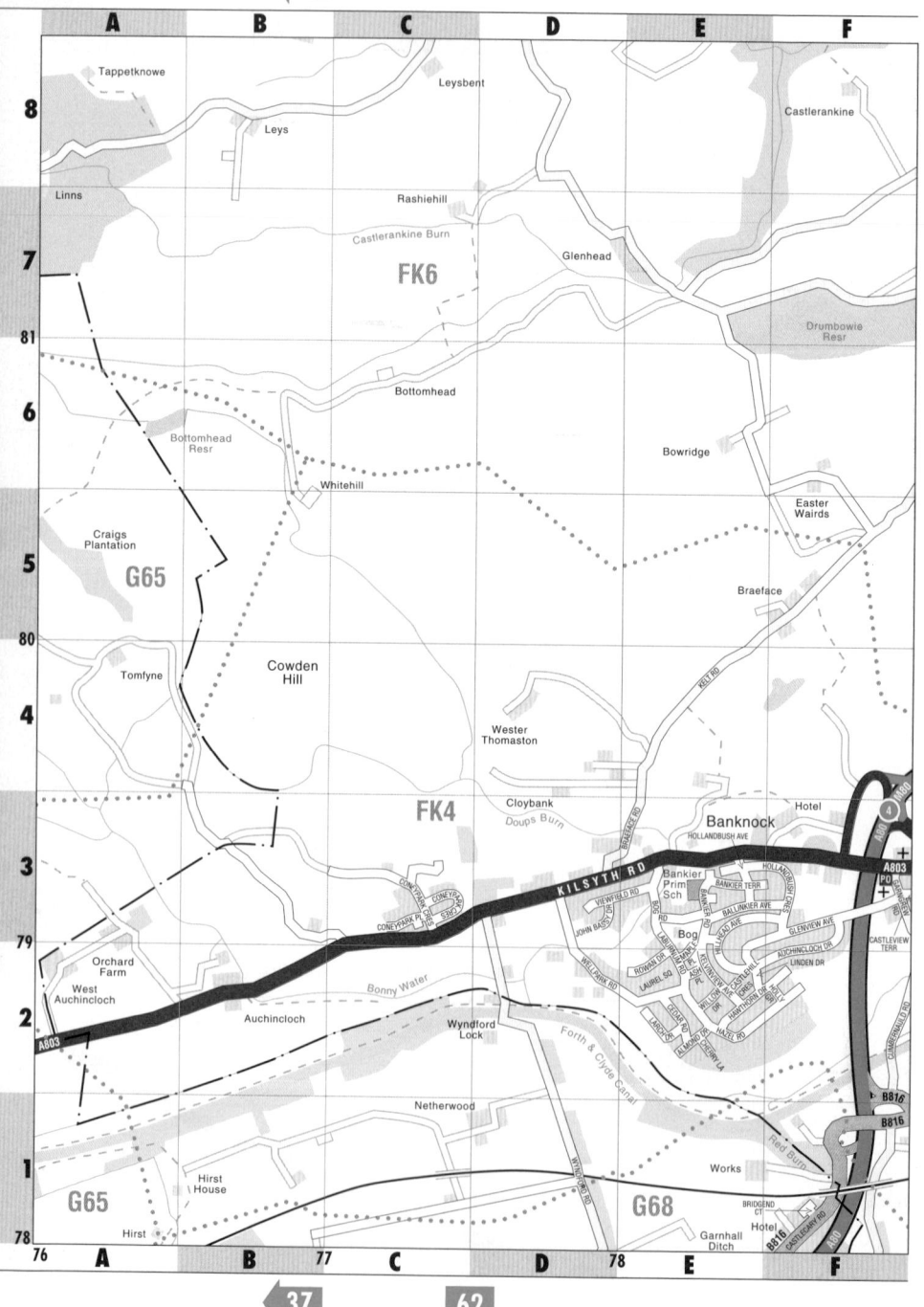

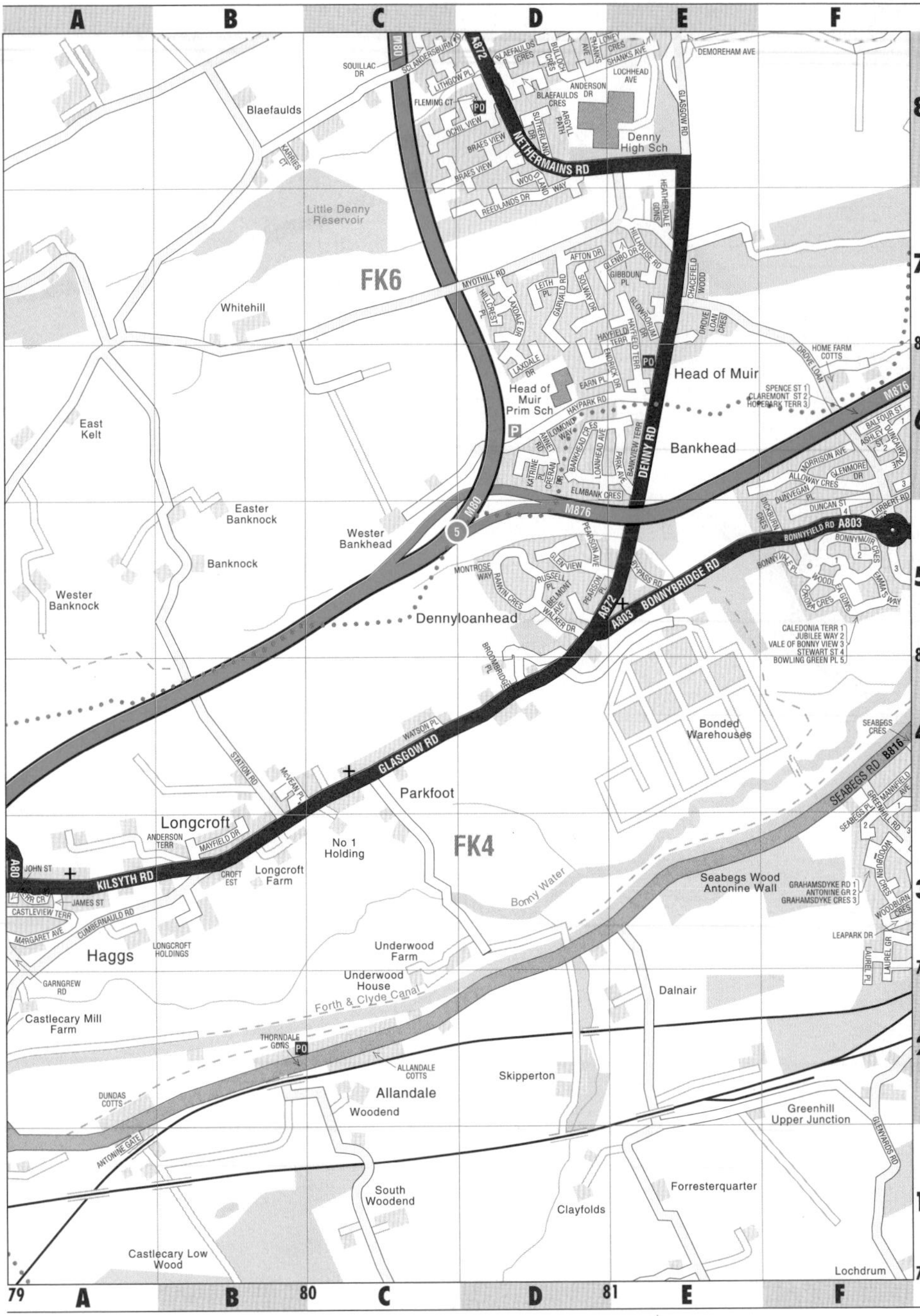

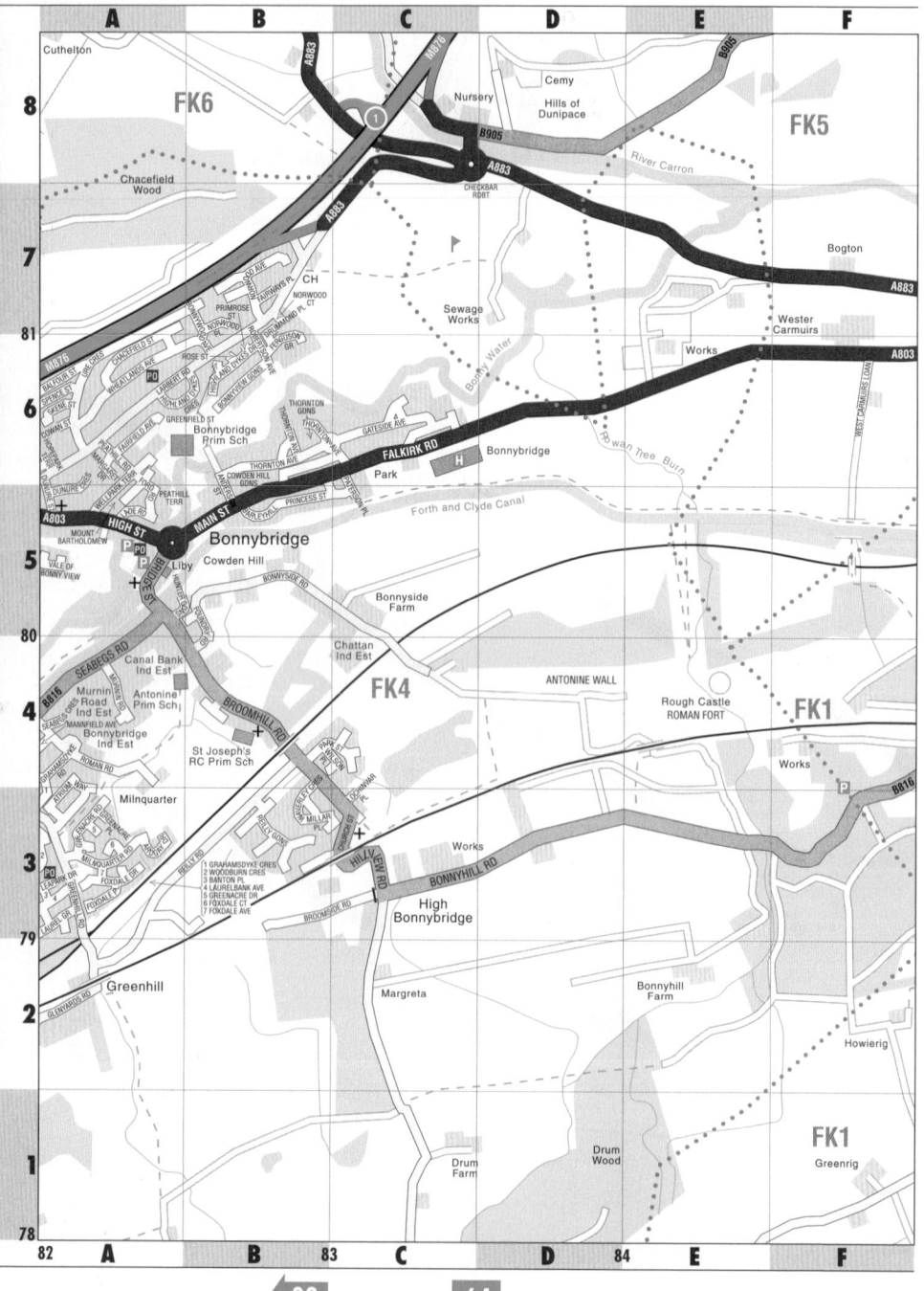

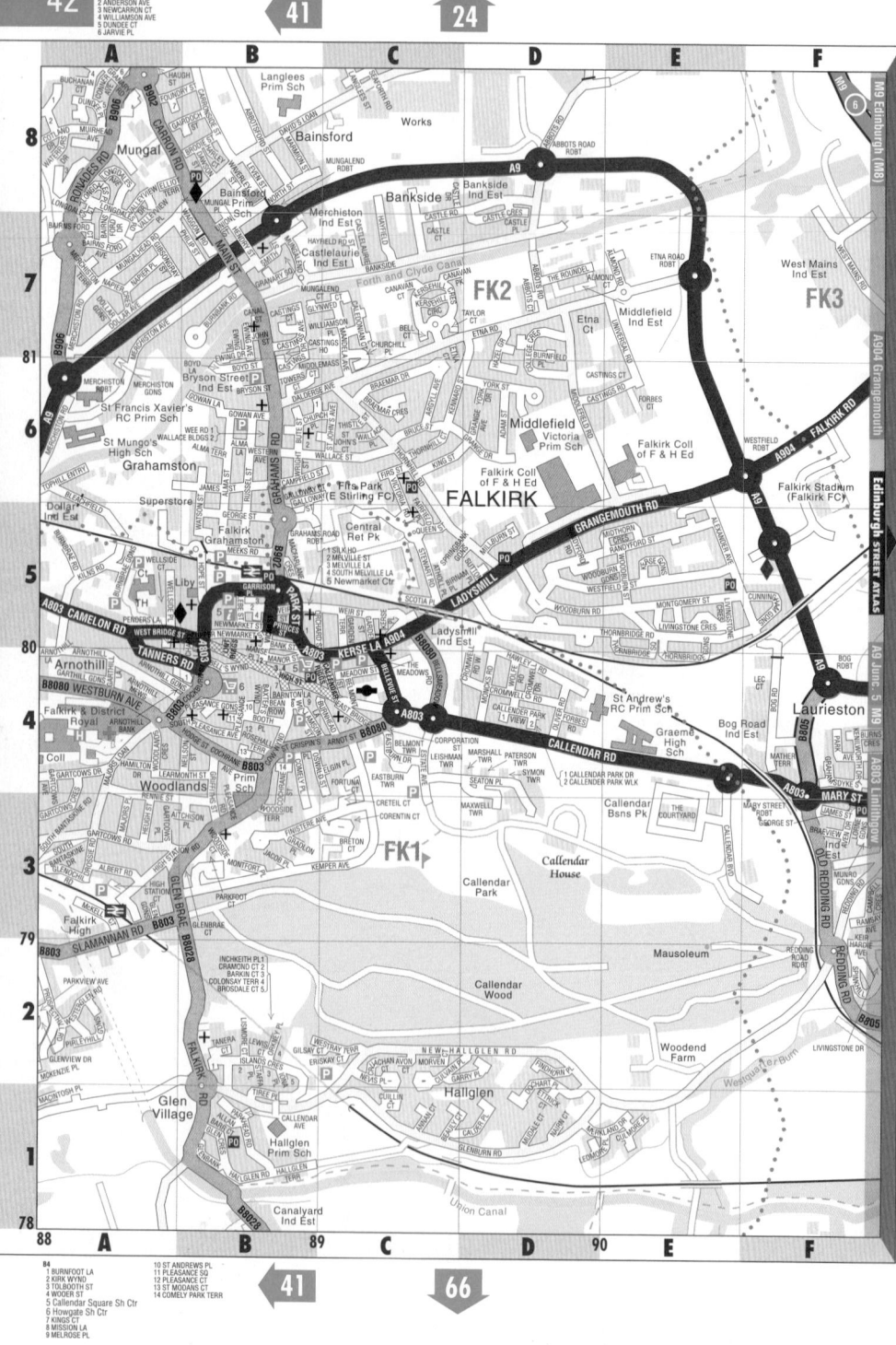

42

A8
1 MULLOCH AVE
2 ANDERSON AVE
3 NEWCARRON CT
4 WILLIAMSON AVE
5 DUNDEE CT
6 JARVIE PL

7 JOHNSTON CT

41

24

FK2

FK3

FALKIRK

FK1

Bainsford

Mungal

Bankside

Middlefield

Grahamston

Ladysmill

Arnothill

Woodlands

Laurieston

Glen Village

Hallglen

Callendar Park

Callendar Wood

Callendar House

Mausoleum

Woodend Farm

B4
1 BURNFOOT LA
2 KIRK WYND
3 TOLBOOTH ST
4 WOOER ST
5 Callendar Square Sh Ctr
6 Howgate Sh Ctr
7 KINGS CT
8 MISSION LA
9 MELROSE PL
10 ST ANDREWS PL
11 PLEASANCE SQ
12 PLEASANCE CT
13 ST MODANS CT
14 COMELY PARK TERR

41

66

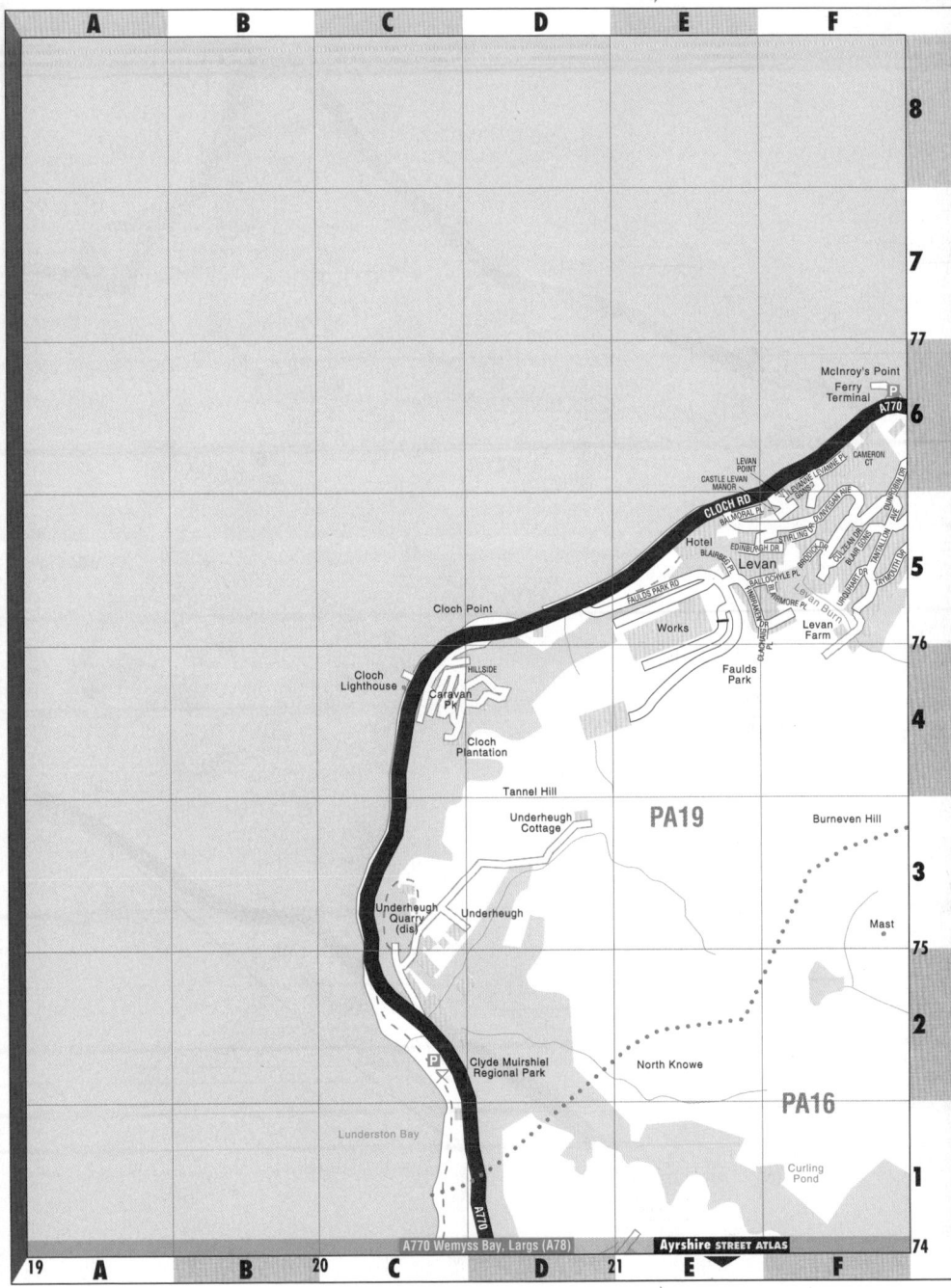

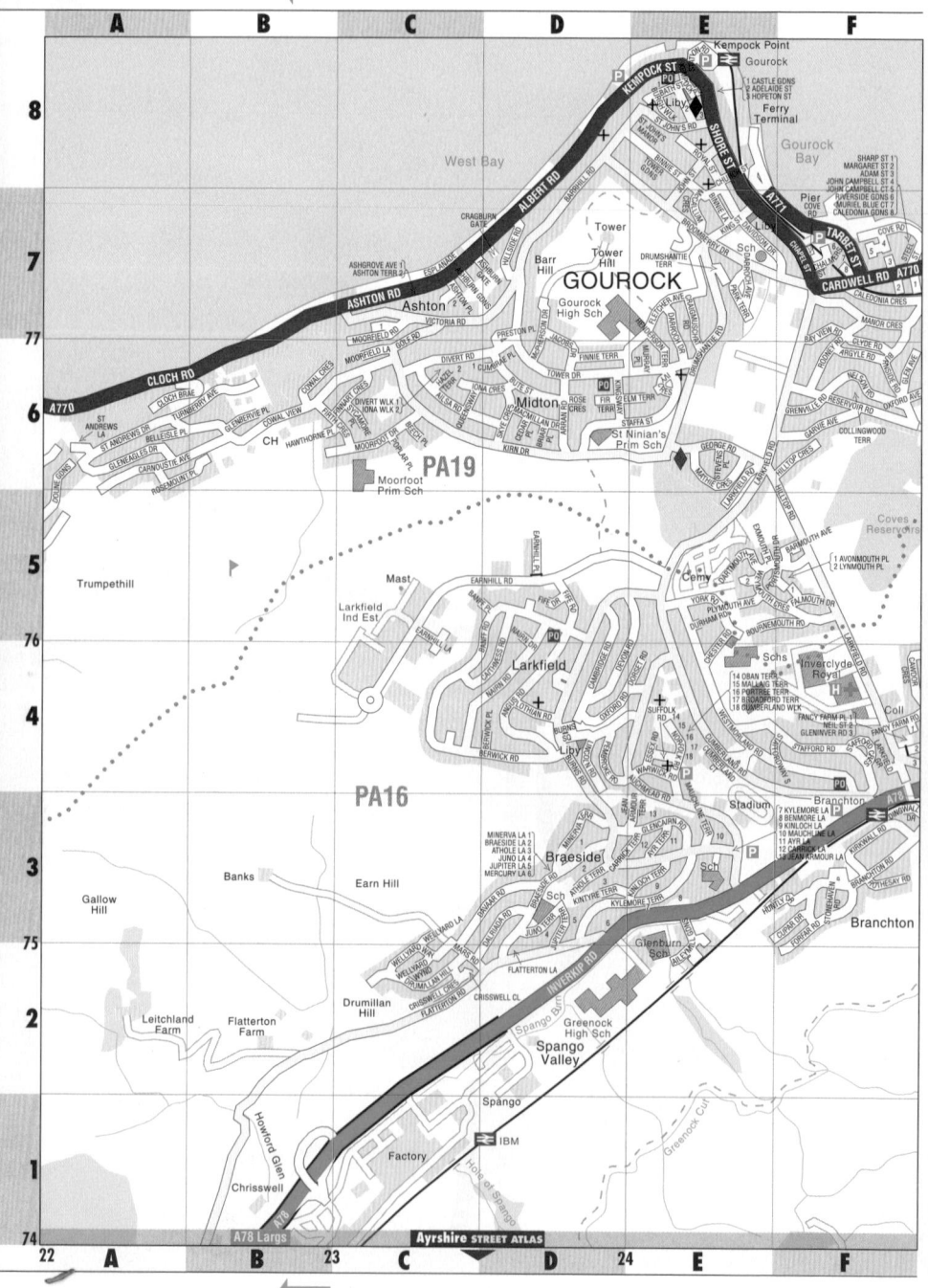

46

7 THE OAK MALL
8 HAMILTON WAY
9 CLYDE SQ
10 CATHCART SQ
11 KILBLAIN ST
12 KILBLAIN CT
13 SIR MICHAEL CT

45

F5
1 WEST BLACKHALL ST
2 WESTBURN BLDGS
3 The Forum
4 CHARLES PL
5 HIGHLAND MARY PL
6 HAMILTON GATE

F4
1 REGENT CT
2 WHINHILL CT
3 ARMADALE CT
4 DEMPSTER CT

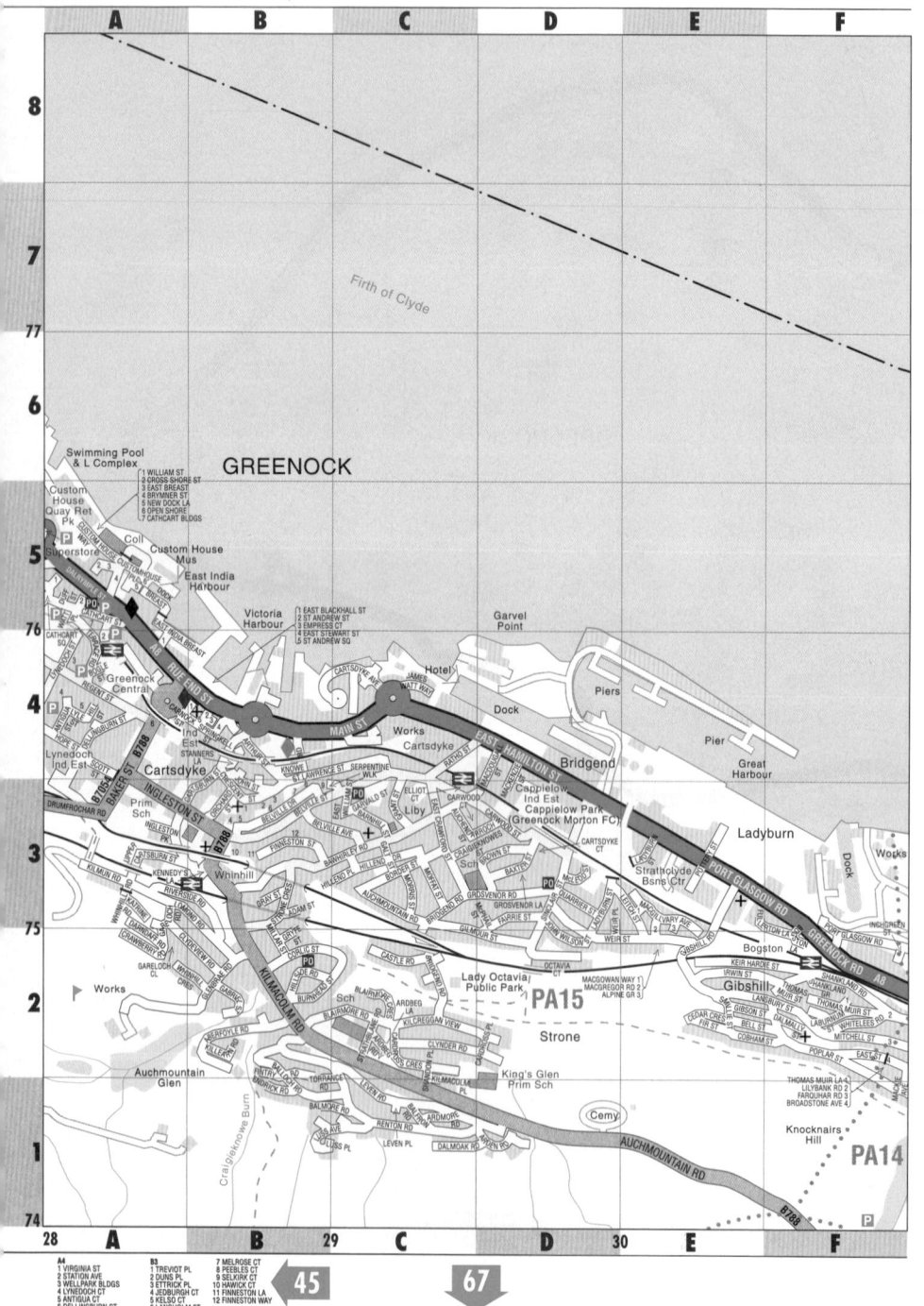

8

7

77

Firth of Clyde

6

Swimming Pool
& L Complex

GREENOCK

Custom
House
Quay Ret
Pk
Superstore

1 WILLIAM ST
2 CROSS SHORE ST
3 EAST BREAST
4 BRYMNER ST
5 NEW DOCK LA
6 OPEN SHORE
7 CATHCART BLDGS

Coll

Custom House
Mus

East India
Harbour

5

Victoria
Harbour

1 EAST BLACKHALL ST
2 ST ANDREW ST
3 EMPRESS ST
4 EAST STEWART ST
5 ST ANDREW SQ

Garvel
Point

76

CATHCART
SQ

Greenock
Central

Hotel
JAMES
WATT WAY

Garvel
Point

Piers

4

Lynedoch
Ind. Est.

MAIN ST

Works
Cartsdyke

EAST HAMILTON RD

Dock

Bridgend

Pier

Great
Harbour

Cartsdyke

Whinhill

Prim
Sch

INGLESTON ST

DRUMFROCHAR RD

LAWRENCE ST
FINNISTON ST

ELLIOT
CT
Liby

CARWOOD

Cappielow
Ind Est
Cappielow Park
(Greenock Morton FC)

CARTSDYKE
CT

Strathclyde
Bsne Ctr

Ladyburn

Works

Dock

3

DALMUIR RD

RIVERSIDE RD

KENNEDY'S

AUCHMOUNTAIN RD

GROSVENOR RD

GROSVENOR LA

LARRIE ST

JOHN WILSON RD

IVARY AVE

GIBSHILL RD

PORT GLASGOW RD

GREENOCK RD A8

75

Works

GARELOCH
CL

CASTLE RD

OCTAVIA
CT

Lady Octavia
Public Park

MACGOWAN WAY 1
MACGREGOR RD 2
ALPINE GR 3

Bogston

Gibshill

KEIR HARDIE ST
IRWIN ST

LANGBURN ST

PA15

2

Works

BLAIRMORE
LA
ARDBEG
LA

KILCREGGAN VIEW

CLYNDER RD

CLYNDER CRES

Strone

King's Glen
Prim Sch

CEDAR CRES
FIR ST

BELL ST

COBHAM ST

POPLAR ST

THOMAS MUIR LA 4
LILYBANK RD 2
FARQUHAR RD 3
BROADSTONE AVE 4

WHITELEES RD

EAST ST

MITCHELL ST

Auchmountain
Glen

Craigielinowe Burn

KILMACOLM RD

BURNSIDE RD

BALMORAL RD

ARDMORE
RD

RENTON RD

LEVEN PL

DALMOAK RD

GLEN RD

Cemy

AUCHMOUNTAIN RD

B788

Knocknairs
Hill

PA14

1

74

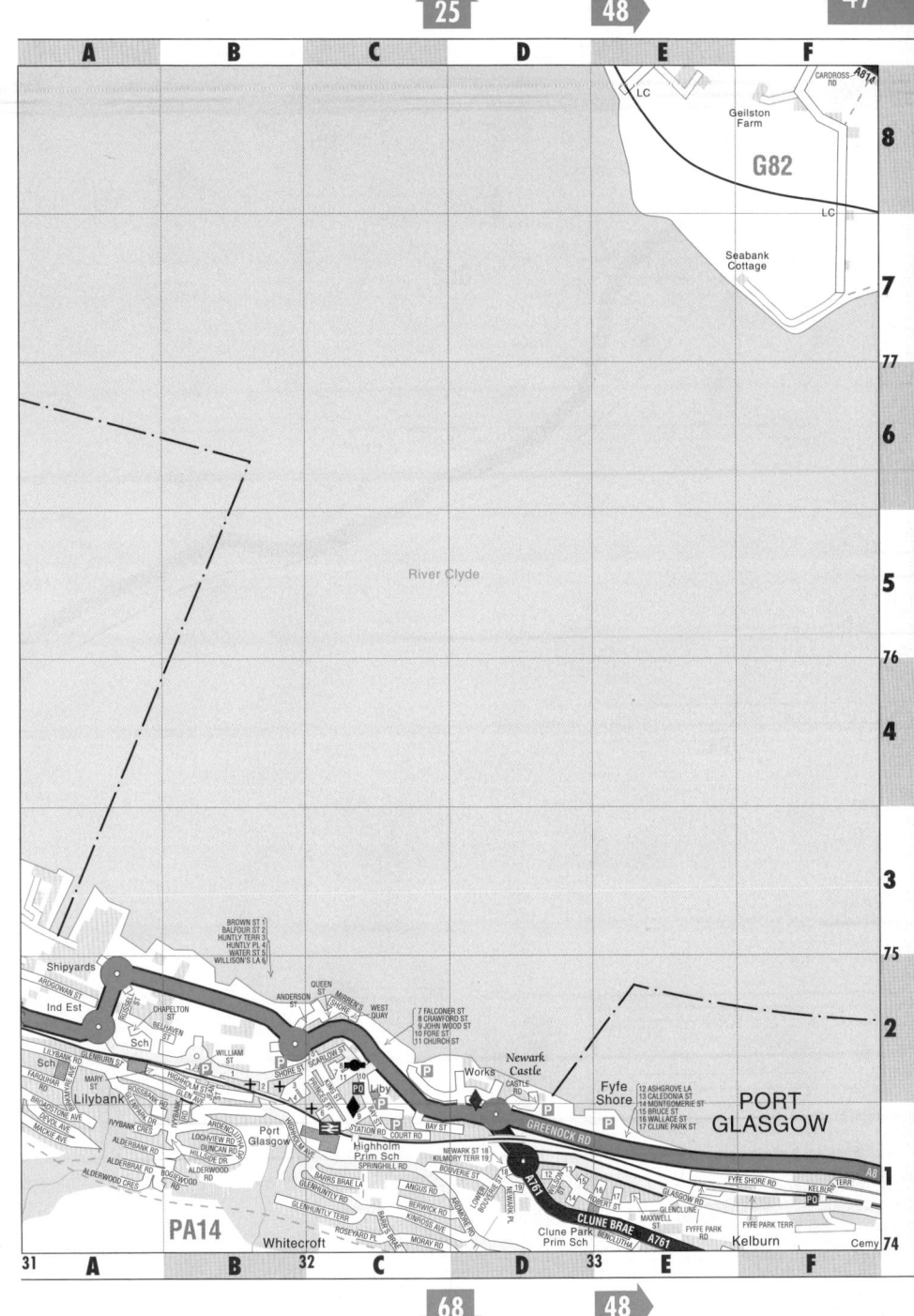

CARDROSS RD A814

LC

Geilston
Farm

G82

8

LC

Seabank
Cottage

7

77

6

River Clyde

5

76

4

3

75

BROWN ST 1
BALFOUR ST 2
HUNTLY TERR 3
HUNTLY PL 4
WATER ST 5
WILLISON'S LA 6

Shipyards

Ind Est

CHAPELTON
ST

BELHAVEN

QUEEN
ST
ANDERSON
ST

MORRIS
ST

WEST
QUAY

7 FALCONER ST
8 CRAWFORD ST
9 JOHN WOOD ST
10 FORE ST
11 CHURCH ST

Newark
Castle

CASTLE
RD

Fyfe
Shore

12 ASHGROVE LA
13 CALEDONIA ST
14 MONTGOMERIE ST
15 BRUCE ST
16 WALLACE ST
17 CLUNE PARK ST

PORT
GLASGOW

2

Sch

LILYBANK
RD

FARQUHAR
RD

MARY
ST

BROADSTONE AVE

DEVOL AVE

MACKIE AVE

GLENBURN ST

ROSSBANK RD

RAILWAY AVE

DUNLOP ST

IVYBANK CRES

ARDENCLUTHA
LOCHVIEW RD
HILLSIDE DR
ALDERWOOD
RD
BOGWOOD
RD

DUNCAN RD

GLEN AVE

WILLIAM
ST

SHORE ST

Lilybank

ALDERBANK RD

ALDERBRAE RD

ALDERWOOD CRES

Port
Glasgow

SCARLOW ST

STATION RD

COURT RD

Libby

Highholm
Prim Sch

BARRS BRAE LA

SPRINGHILL RD

GLENHUNTLY RD

GLENHUNTLY TERR

ROSEYARD PL

BAY ST

KINROSS AVE

BERWICK RD

MORAY RD

Whitecroft

ANGUS RD

Works

NEWARK ST 18
KILMORY TERR 19

ROVERIE ST

ROBERT ST

NEWARK
PL

BONVERIE ST

LOMOND ST

CLUNE BRAE

Clune Park
Prim Sch

A761

BENCLUTHA

GREENOCK RD

GLASGOW RD

MAXWELL
ST

GLENCLUNE

FYFFE PARK

FYFE SHORE RD

KELBURN TERR

FYFFE PARK TERR

Kelburn

Cemy

PD

A8

1

74

PA14

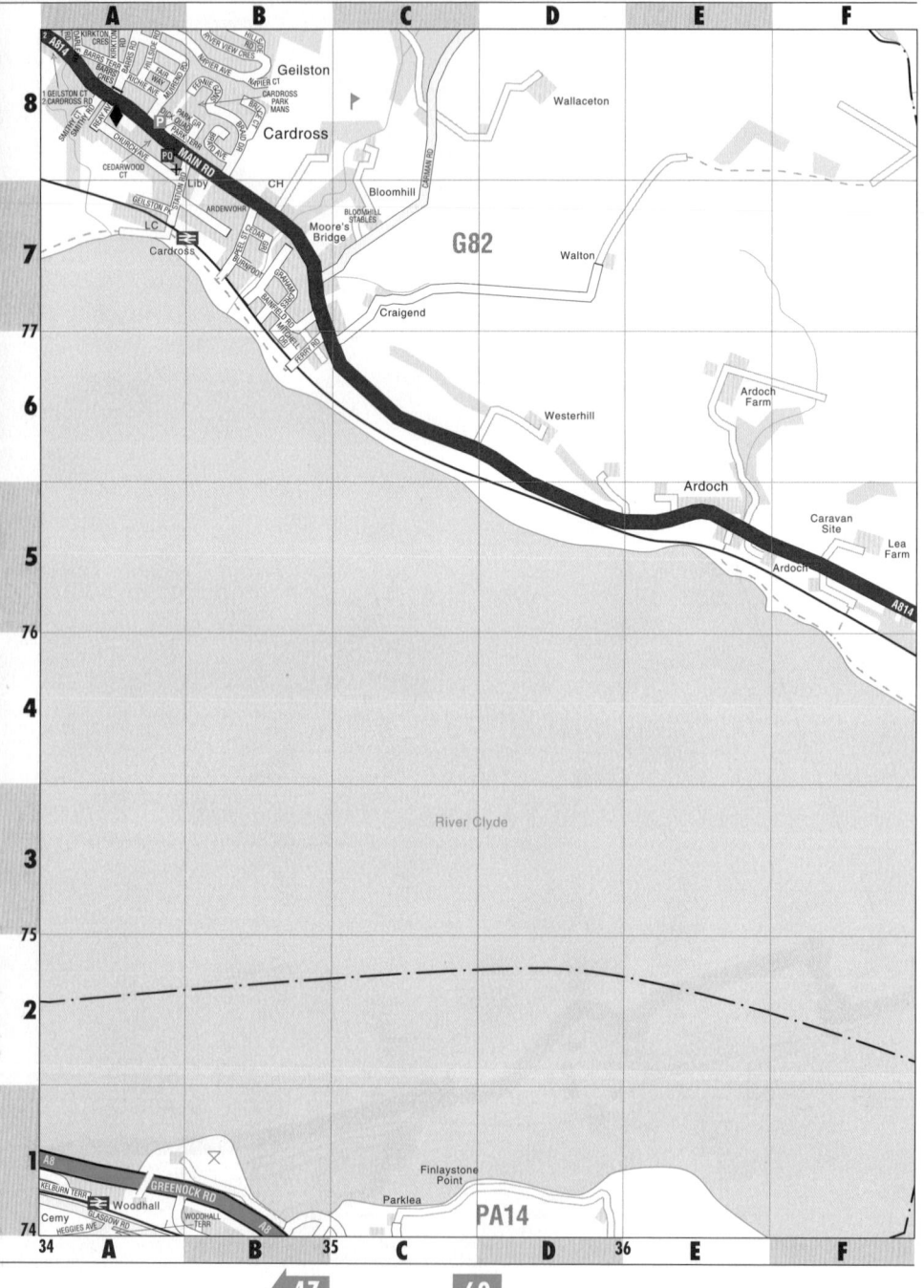

A   B   C   D   E   F

KIRKTON CRES

A814

1 GEILSTON CT
2 CARDROSS RD

Geilston

CARDROSS CT

CARDROSS PARK MANS

8

P

Cardross

PIER VIEW CRES

BARBER AVE

HILL ST

WALLACETON

CEDARWOOD CT

PO

Lilby

CH

MAIN RD

Bloomhill

CARMAN RD

G82

ARDENVOHR

BLOOMHILL STABLES

LC

Moore's Bridge

7

Cardross

Walton

77

Craigend

6

Westerhill

Ardoch Farm

Ardoch

Caravan Site

Lea Farm

5

Ardoch

A814

76

4

River Clyde

3

75

2

1

A8

Finlaystone Point

KELBURN TERR

GREENOCK RD

Woodhall

Parklea

PA14

Cemy

HEGGIES AVE

GLASGOW RD

WOODHALL TERR

A8

74

34   A   B   35   C   D   36   E   F

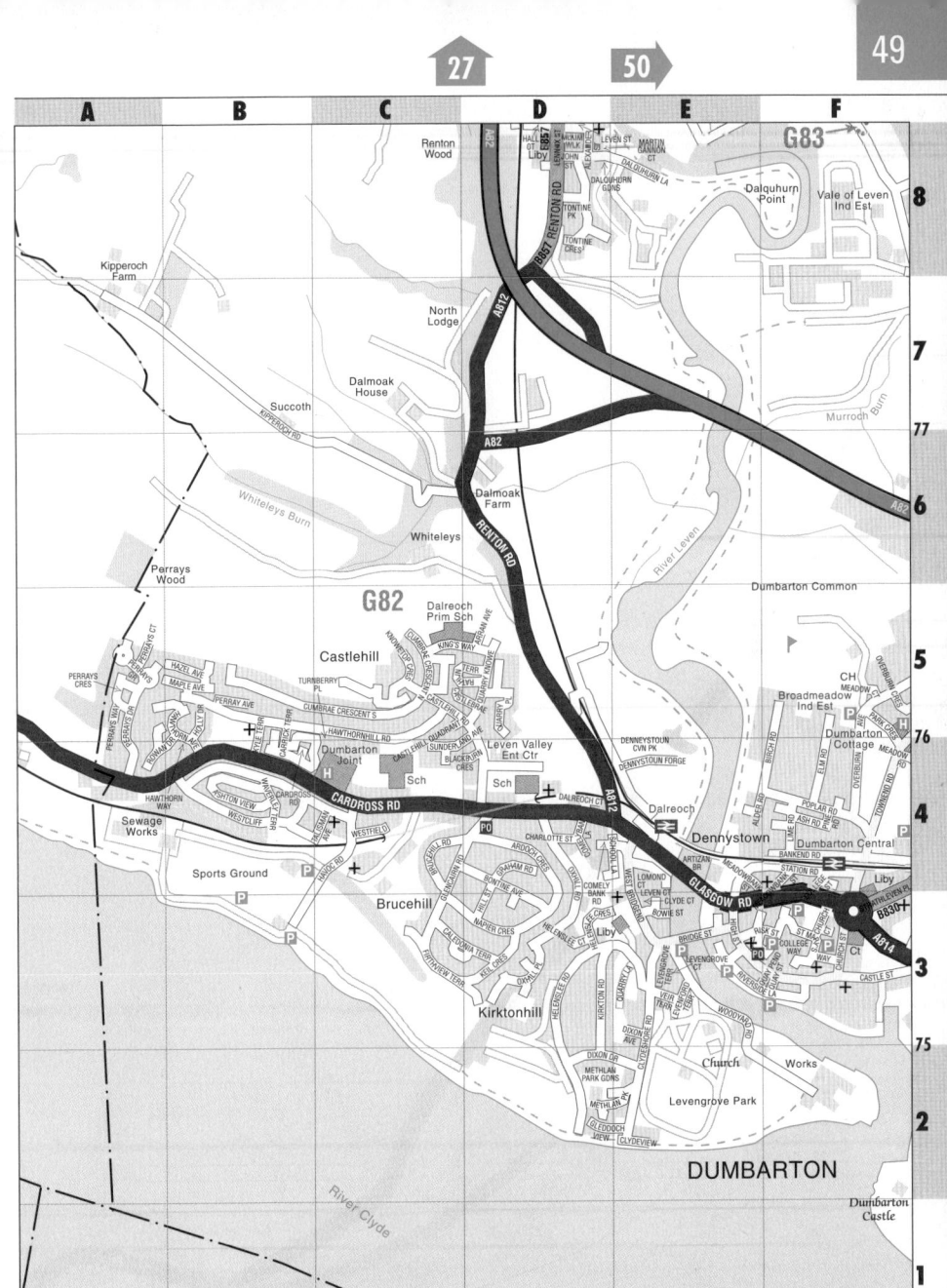

G83

G82

DUMBARTON

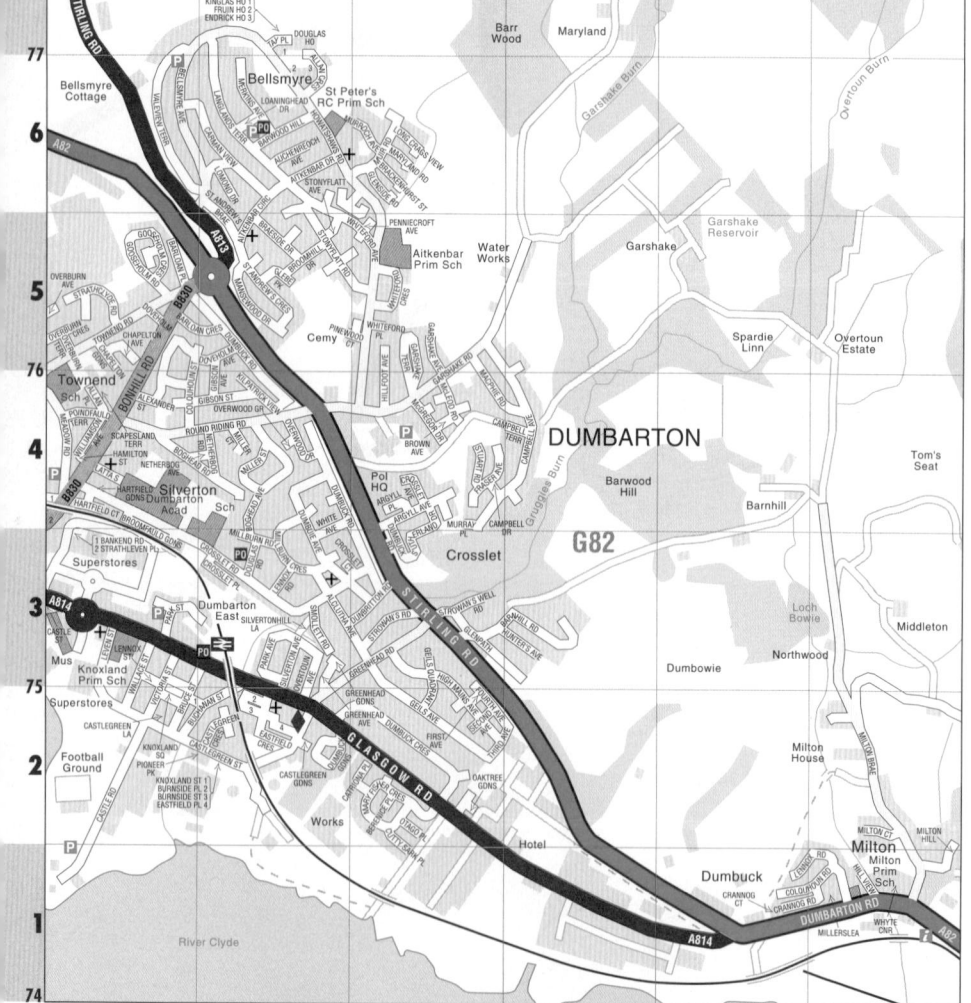

A B C D E F

8

7

77

6

5

76

4

75

3

2

1

74

G83

Murroch

Square Wood

Black Wood

STIRLING RD

A813

Bellsmyre Cottage

Barr Wood

Maryland

Overtoun Burn

Garshake Burn

KINGLAS HO 1
FRUIN HO 2
ENDRICK HO 3

DOUGLAS HO

Bellsmyre

St Peter's RC Prim Sch

LOANINGHEAD DR

PO

A82

A813

B830

LYLE CRAIGS VIEW

Aitkenbar Prim Sch

Water Works

Garshake

Garshake Reservoir

Overburn Ave

PENNIECROFT AVE

Cemy

Whiteford

Pinewood Ave

Spardie Linn

Overtoun Estate

Townend Sch

BONHILL RD

B830

Scapesland Terr

Hamilton St

Silverton

Dumbarton Acad

Sch

PO

Millburn Rd

Crosslet

Brown Ave

Pol HQ

Campbell Dr

DUMBARTON

Barwood Hill

Barnhill

Tom's Seat

G82

Gruggies Burn

STIRLING RD

Superstores

A814

Mus

CASTL

Knoxland Prim Sch

Superstores

Dumbarton East

PO

SILVERTONHILL LA

Lennox

BANKEND RD 1
STRATHLEVEN PL 2

GLASGOW RD

Greenhead Gdns

Greenhead Ave

STRINGHAM'S WELL RD

WHILL RD

HUNTER'S AVE

Dumbowie

Northwood

Loch Bowie

Middleton

Football Ground

Knoxland Sq

Pioneer Pk

KNOXLAND ST 1
BURNSIDE ST 2
BURNSIDE ST 3
EASTFIELD PL 4

Castlegreen Gdns

FIRST AVE

OAKTREE GDNS

Works

Hotel

Dumbuck

CRANNOG CT

Milton House

Milton

Milton Prim Sch

Milton Hill

MILTON BRAE

MILTON RD

COLQUHOUN

A814

DUMBARTON RD

Millerslea

WHYTE CNR

A82

River Clyde

A B C D E F

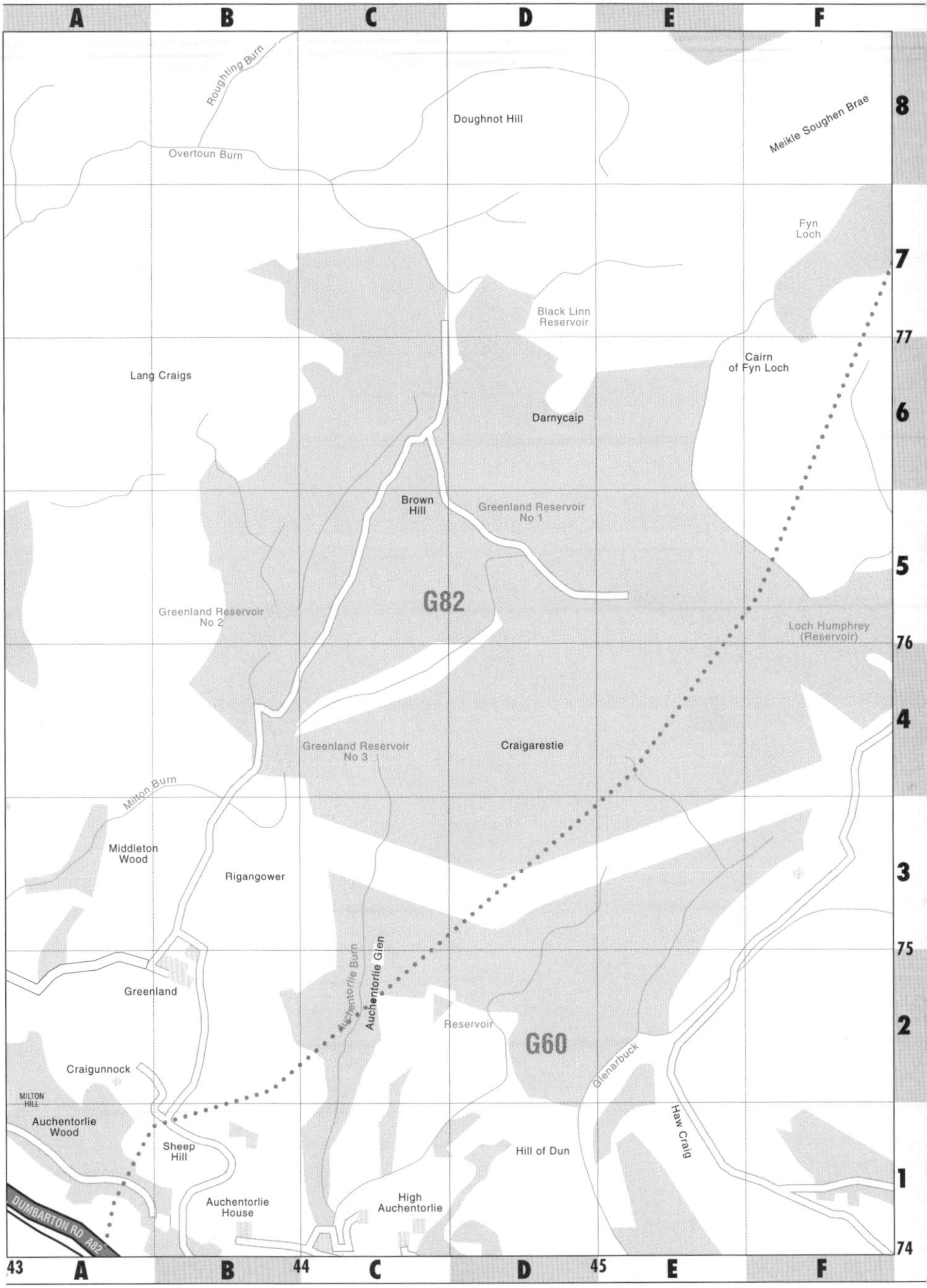

8

Roughling Burn

Doughnot Hill

Meikle Soughen Brae

Overtoun Burn

7

Fyn
Loch

Black Linn
Reservoir

77

Lang Craigs

Cairn
of Fyn Loch

Darnycaip

6

Brown
Hill

Greenland Reservoir
No 1

5

G82

Greenland Reservoir
No 2

Loch Humphrey
(Reservoir)

76

Greenland Reservoir
No 3

Craigarestie

4

Milton Burn

Middleton
Wood

75

Rigangower

Auchentorlie Burn

Auchentorlie Glen

3

Greenland

Reservoir

G60

Glenarbuck

2

Craigunnock

Haw Craig

MILTON
HILL

Auchentorlie
Wood

Hill of Dun

Sheep
Hill

1

DUMBARTON RD A82

Auchentorlie
House

High
Auchentorlie

74

43 A B 44 C D 45 E F

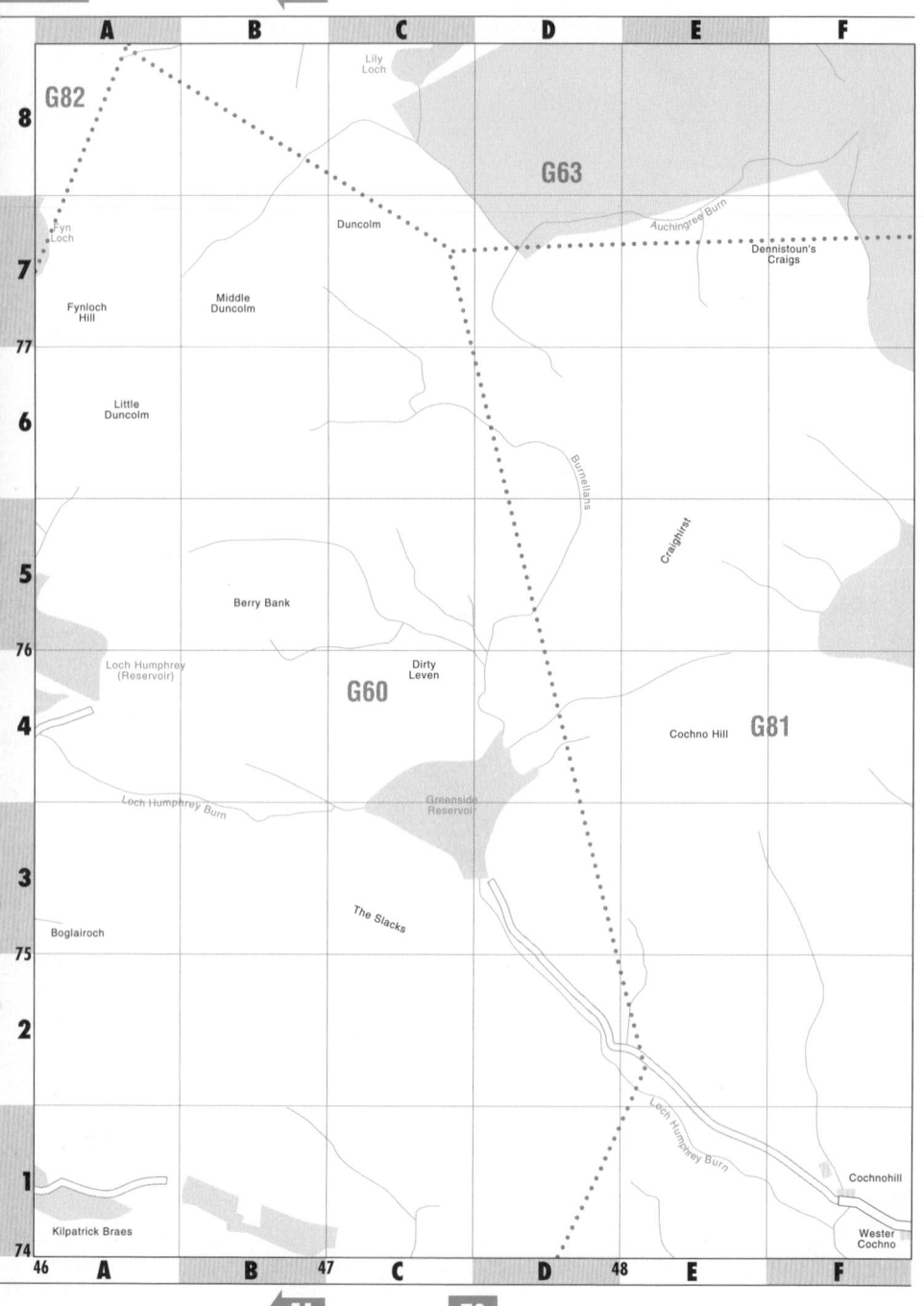

51

73

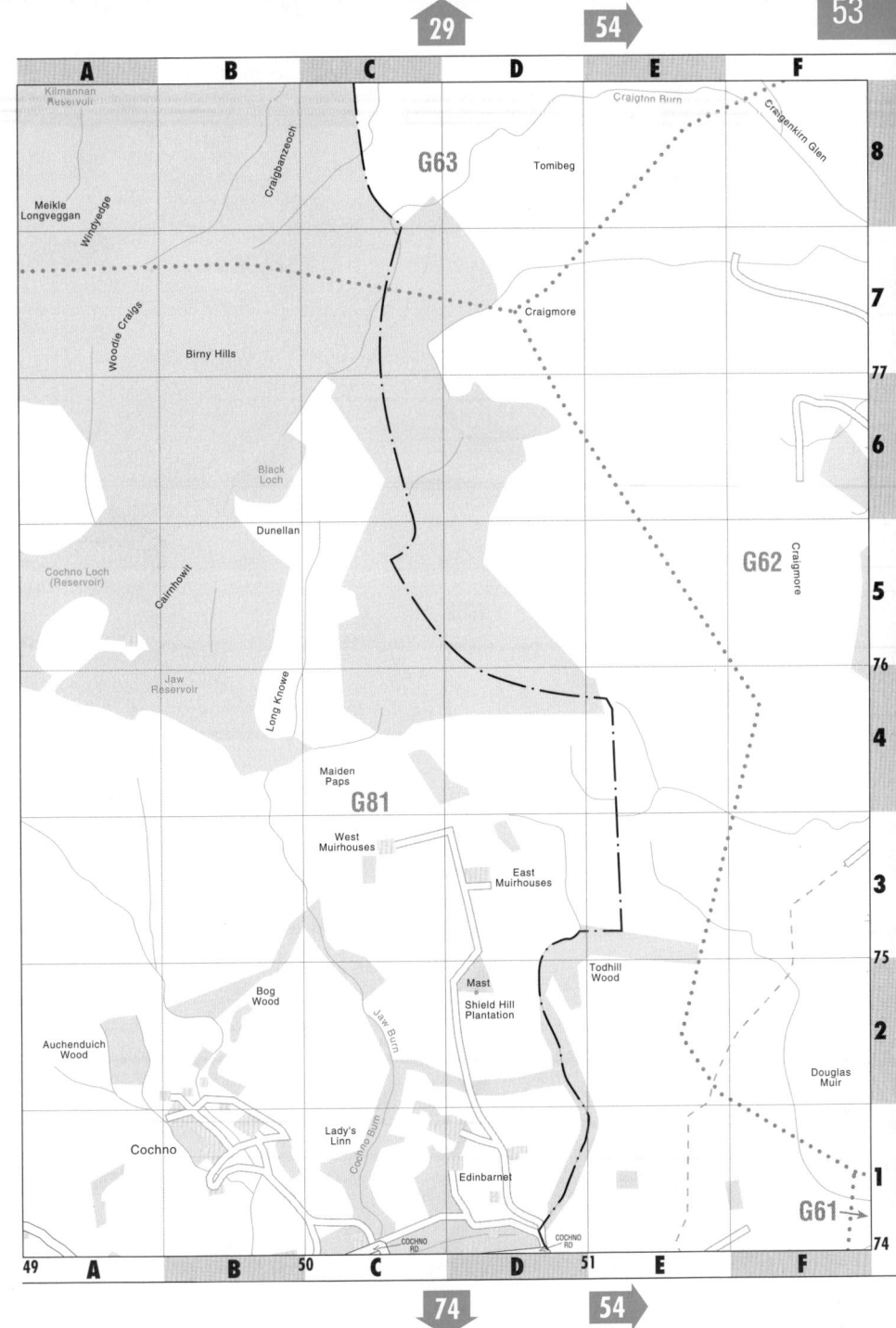

Kilmannan Reservoir

Craigbanzieoch

G63

Craigton Burn

Tomibeg

Craigenkirn Glen

Meikle Longveggan

Windyedge

Woodie Craigs

Birny Hills

Craigmore

77

Black Loch

Dunellan

Cochno Loch (Reservoir)

Cairnhowit

G62

Craigmore

Jaw Reservoir

Long Knowe

76

Maiden Paps

G81

West Muirhouses

East Muirhouses

Bog Wood

Mast

Shield Hill Plantation

Todhill Wood

75

Auchenduich Wood

Jaw Burn

Cochno Burn

Lady's Linn

Edinbarnet

Douglas Muir

Cochno

COCHNO RD.

COCHNO RD.

G61

74

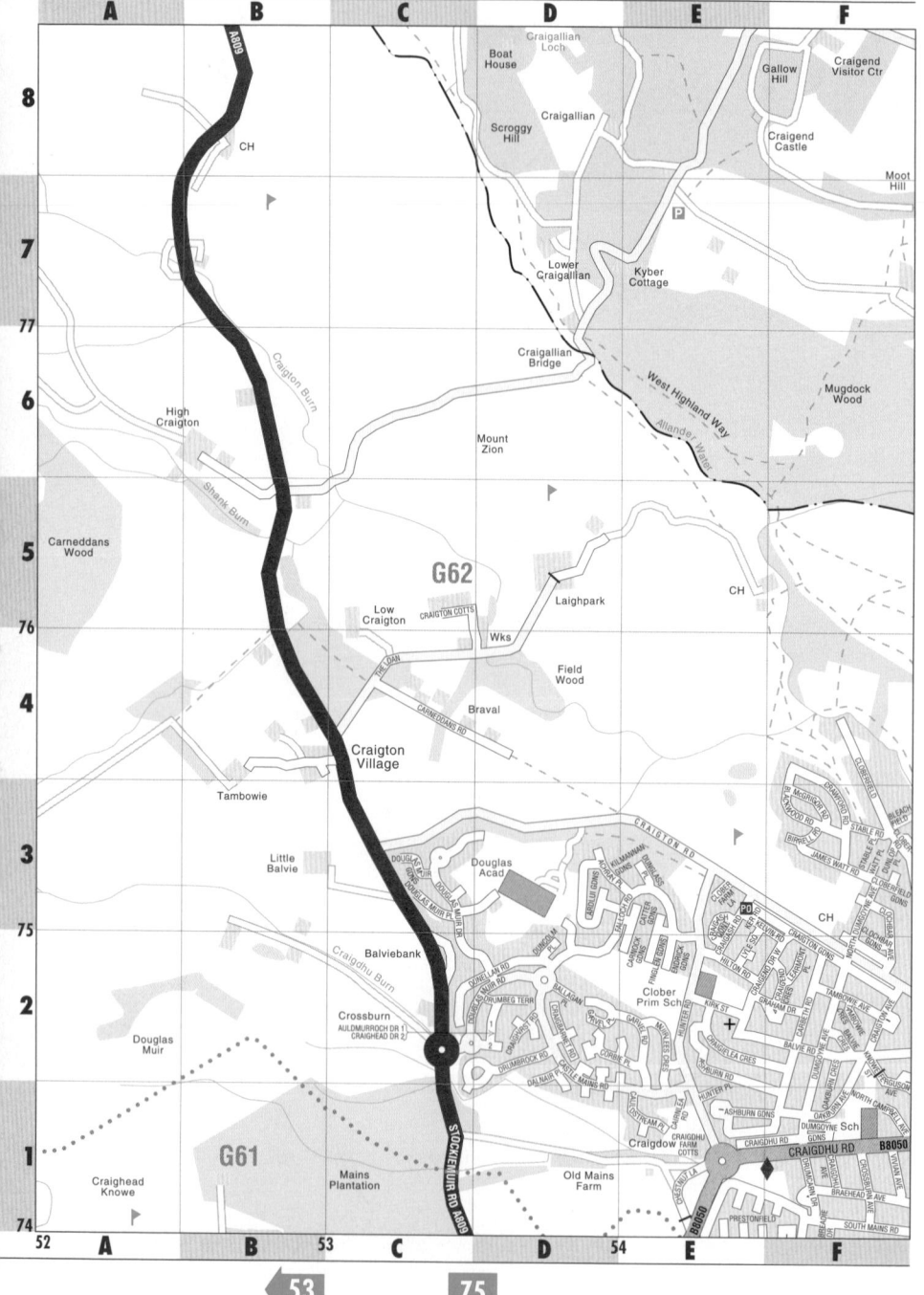

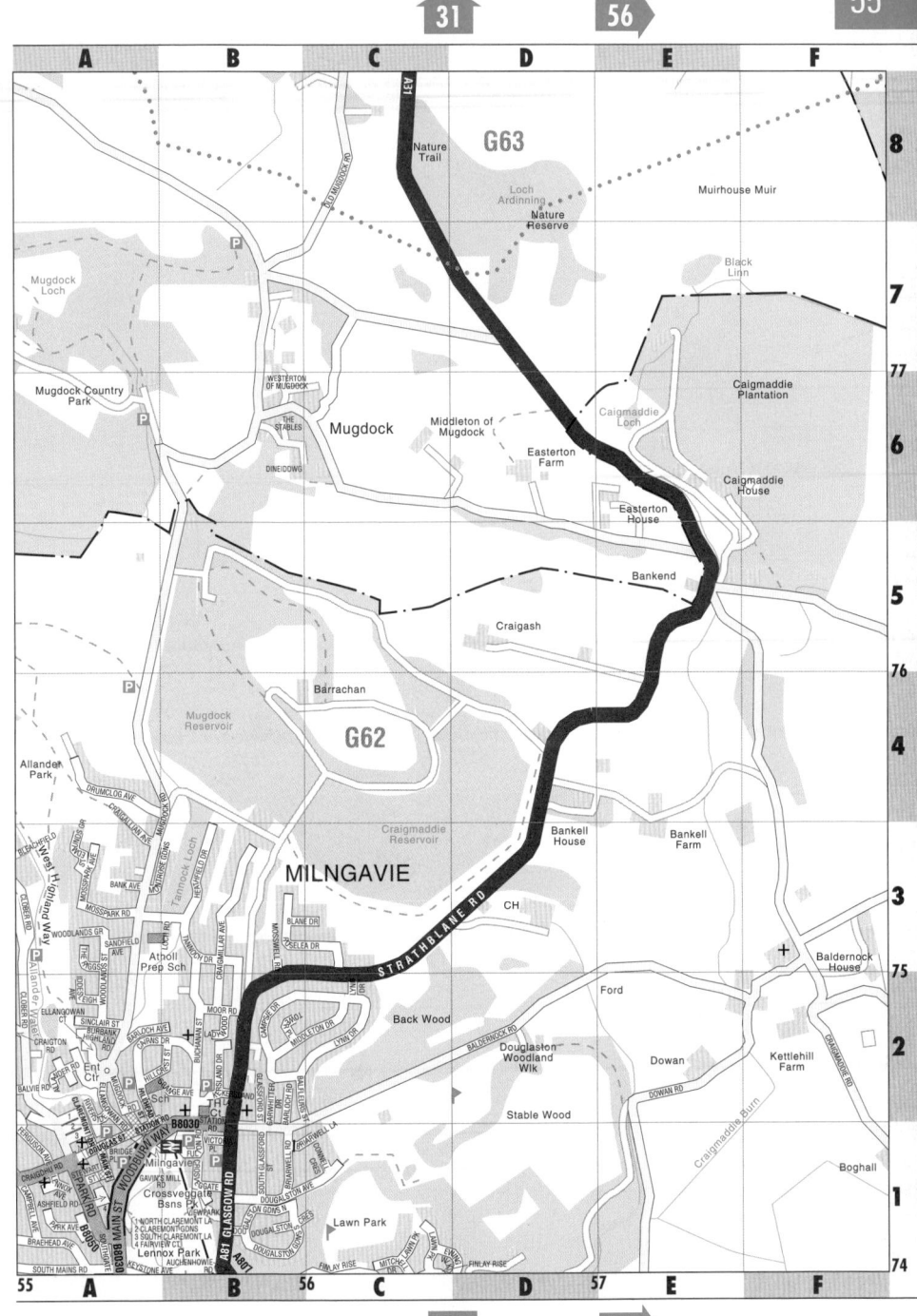

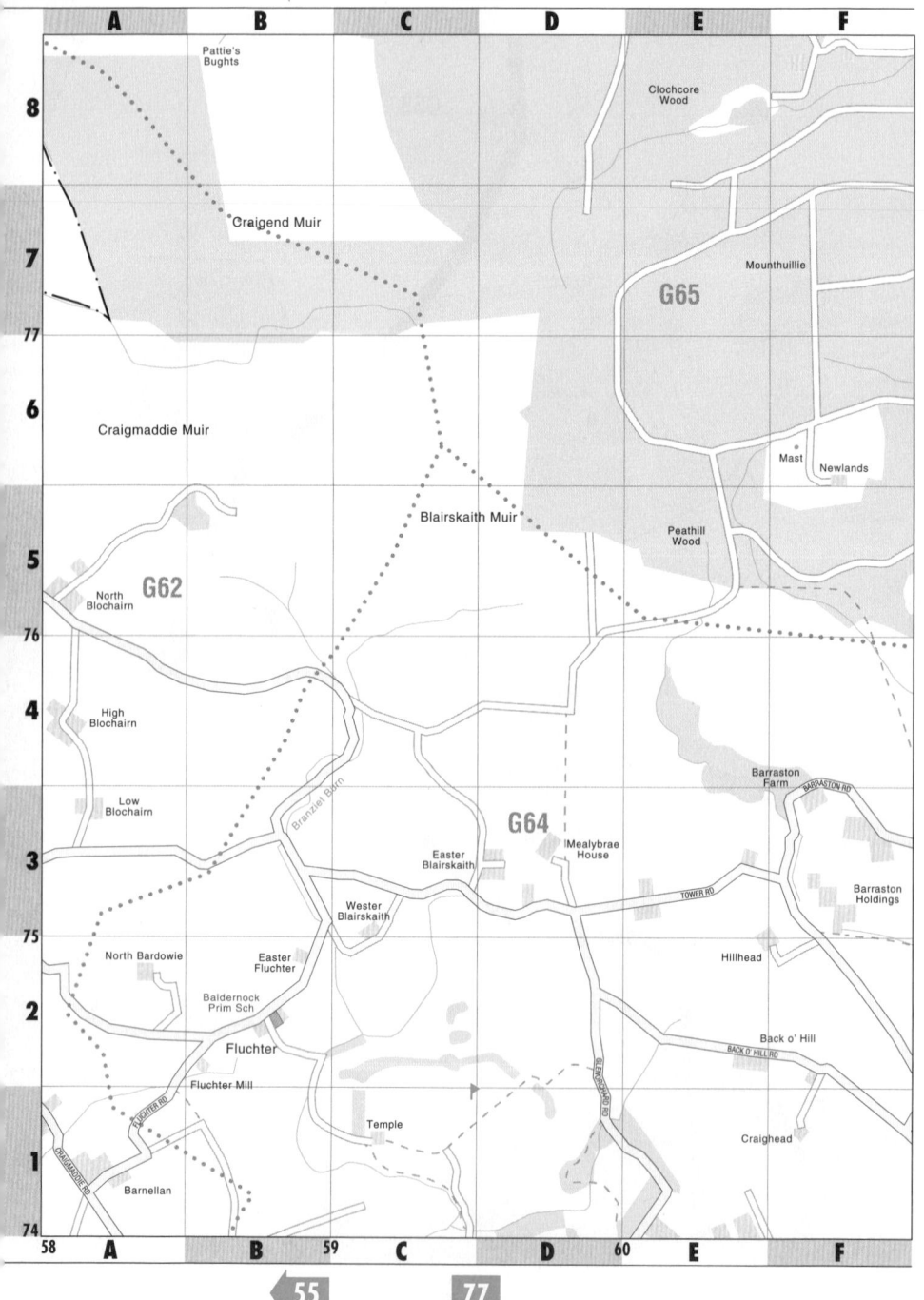

A B C D E F

8

Pattie's
Bughts

Clochcore
Wood

Craigend Muir

Mounthuillie

7

G65

77

6

Craigmaddie Muir

Mast Newlands

Blairskaith Muir

Peathill
Wood

5

North
Blochairn

G62

76

4

High
Blochairn

Barraston
Farm

BARRASTON RD

Low
Blochairn

Branziet Burn

G64

Mealybrae
House

3

Easter
Blairskaith

TOWER RD

Barraston
Holdings

Wester
Blairskaith

75

North Bardowie

Easter
Fluchter

Hillhead

2

Baldernock
Prim Sch

Back o' Hill

BACK O' HILL RD

Fluchter

Fluchter Mill

1

Temple

Craighead

74

Barnellan

CRAIGMADDIE RD

FLUCHTER RD

58 A B 59 C D 60 E F

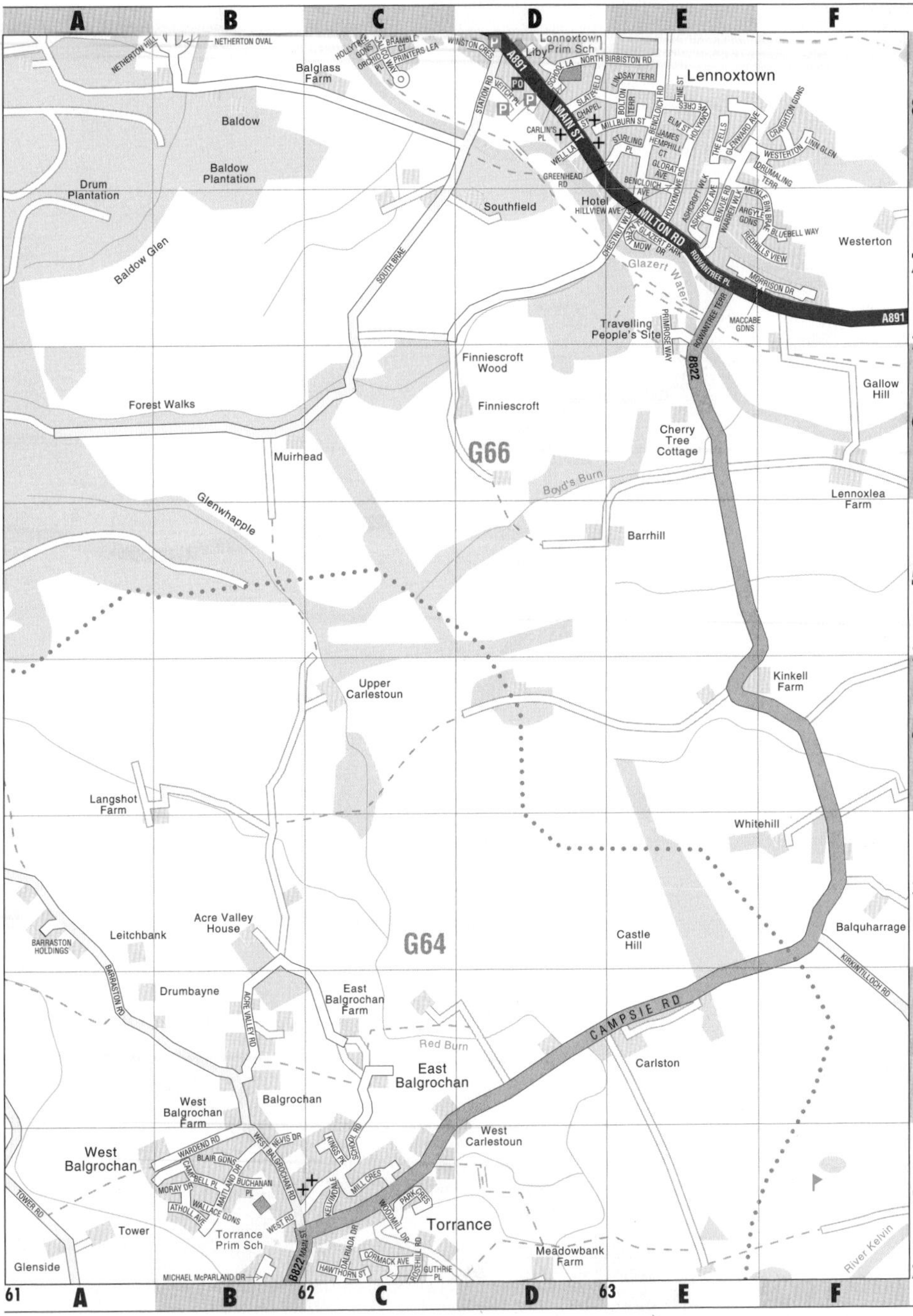

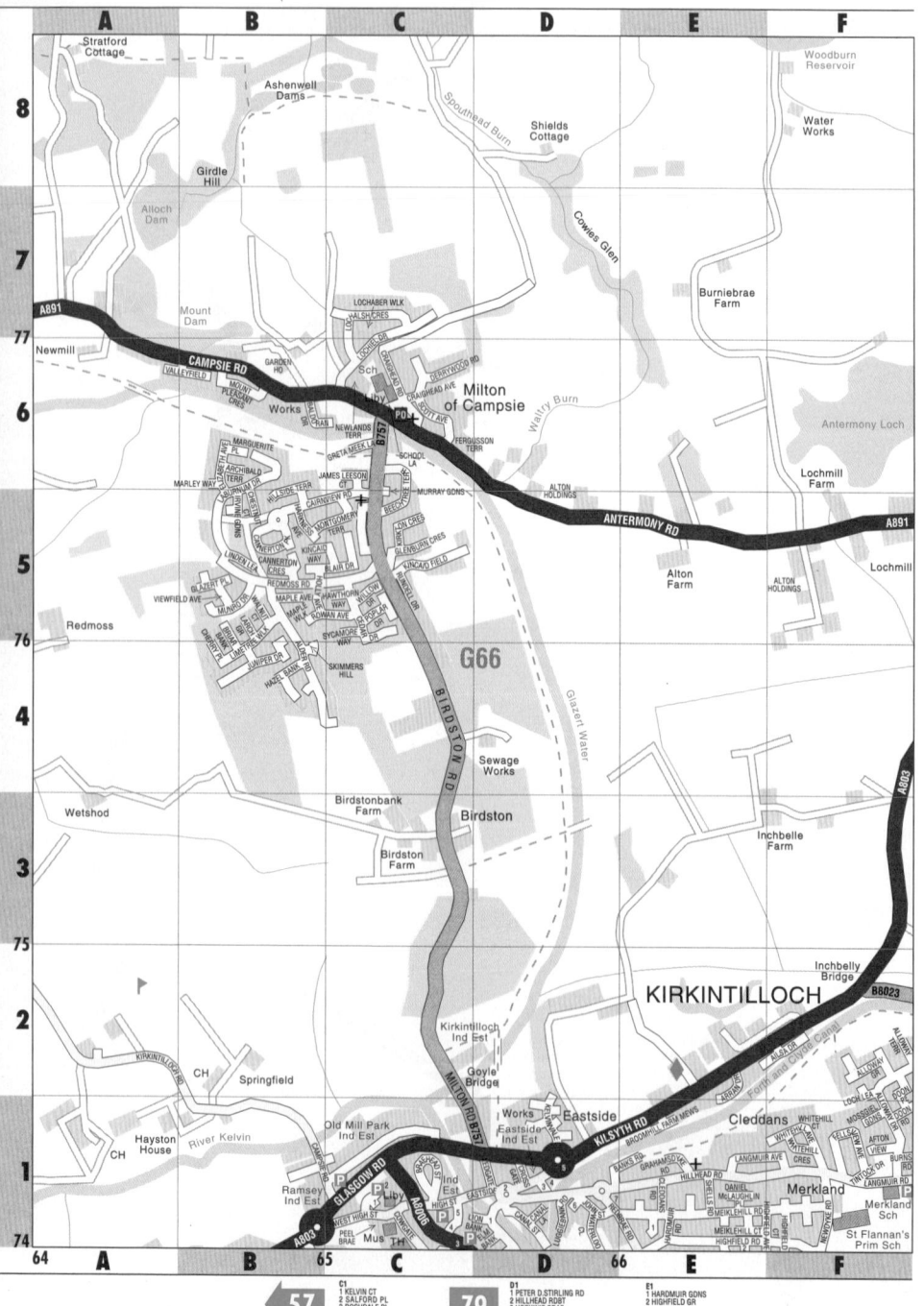

C1
1 KELVIN CT
2 SALFORD PL
3 ROCHDALE PL
4 BROADCROFT
5 BROADCROFT RD

D1
1 PETER D.STIRLING RD
2 HILLHEAD RGBT
3 HOPKIN'S BRAE
4 BROOMHILL CT
5 EASTSIDE RGBT
6 WATERLOO GDNS
7 REDBRAE PL

E1
1 HARDMUIR GDNS
2 HIGHFIELD GR

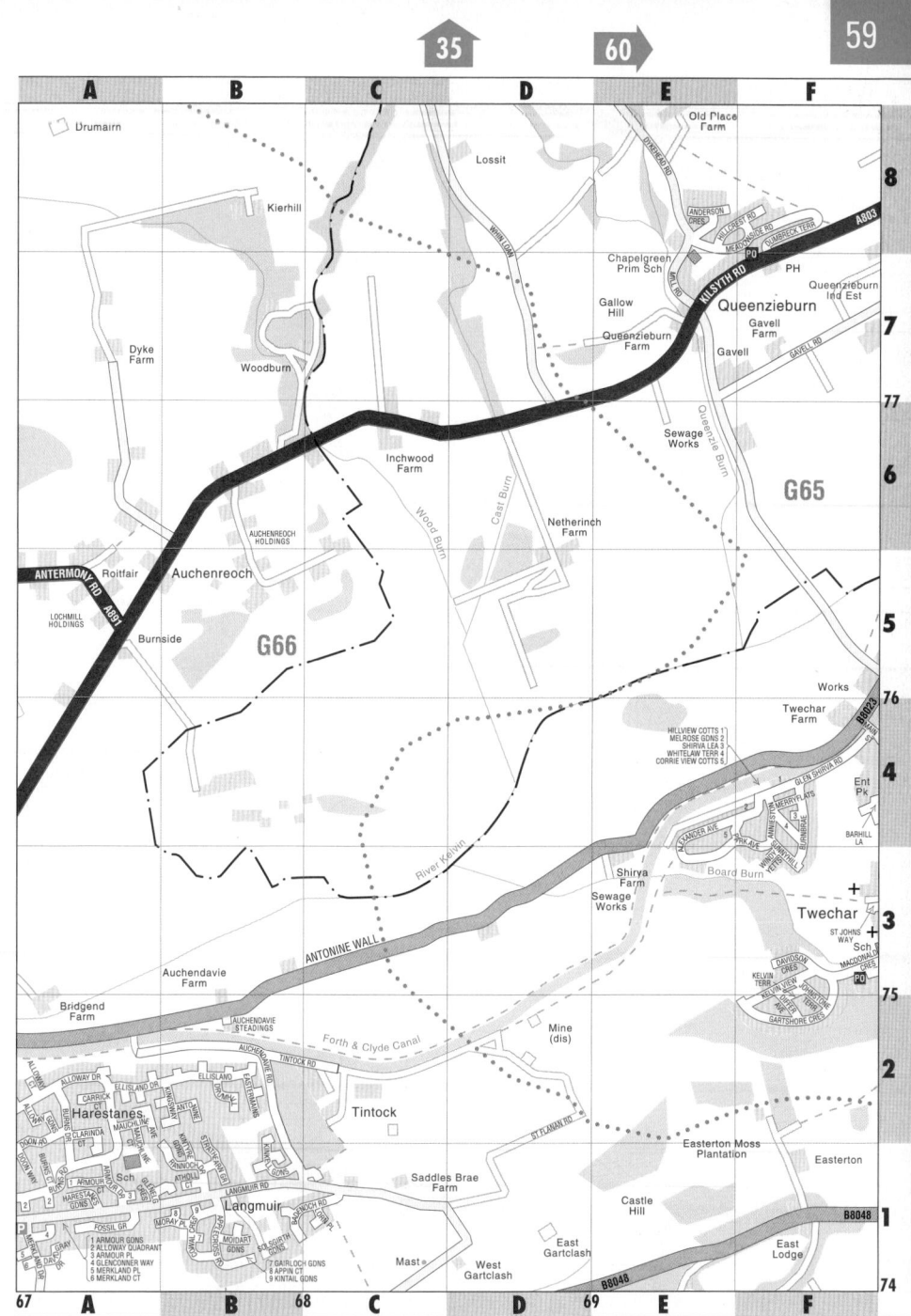

35
60

A B C D E F

8

Drumairn

Old Place
Farm

Lossit

Kierhill

ANDERSON
CRES

A803

Chapelgreen
Prim Sch

KILSYTH RD

Queenzieburn
Ind Est

Gallow
Hill

PH

Queenzieburn

7

Dyke
Farm

Queenzieburn
Farm

Gavell
Farm

Gavell

GAVELL RD

Woodburn

77

Inchwood
Farm

Sewage
Works

G65

6

AUCHENREOCH
HOLDINGS

Netherinch
Farm

Queenzie Burn

ANTERMONY RD

Roitfair

Auchenreoch

A891

LOCHMILL
HOLDINGS

Burnside

G66

5

Works

76

Twechar
Farm

B802?

HILLVIEW COTTS 1
MELROSE GDNS 2
SHIRVA LEA 3
WHITELAW TERR 4
CORRIE VIEW COTTS 5

Ent
Pk

4

River Kelvin

MERRYFLATS

BARHILL
LA

Shirva
Farm

Board Burn

Twechar

3

Sewage
Works

ST JOHNS
WAY

St Johns
Sch

Antonine Wall

DAVIDSON
CRES

MACDONALD
CRES

KELVIN
TERR

PO

Auchendavie
Farm

75

Bridgend
Farm

AUCHENDAVIE
STEADINGS

GARTSHORE CRES

Forth & Clyde Canal

Mine
(dis)

2

ALLOWAY DR

ELLISLAND DR

ELLISLAND

AUCHENDAVIE

TINTOCK RD

Easterton Moss
Plantation

Easterton

CARRICK

MAUCHLINE

ST CANAN RD

Harestanes

CLARINDA
CT

Tintock

B8048

Sch

ARMOUR
CT

HARESTANES
GDNS

LANGMUIR RD

Saddles Brae
Farm

Castle
Hill

East
Lodge

1

FOSSIL GR

1 ARMOUR GDNS
2 ALLOWAY QUADRANT
3 ARMOUR PL
4 GLENCONNER WAY
5 MERKLAND PL
6 MERKLAND CT

MORAY PL

Langmuir

MOIDART
GDNS

7 GAIRLOCH GDNS
8 APPIN CT
9 KINTAIL GDNS

Mast

West
Gartclash

East
Gartclash

B8048

74

67 A 68 B 68 C D 69 E F

80
60

59
36

D8
1 CHARLES ST
2 EAST BURNSIDE ST
3 KING ST LA
4 KING ST
5 MARKET PL
6 MARKET SQ

D8
7 MARKET CL
8 CHURCH LA
9 FINDLAY ST
10 WESTPORT ST
11 WILLIAM ST
12 PARKER PL

13 KEIR HARDIE DR
14 ARRAN VIEW
15 MARKET CT

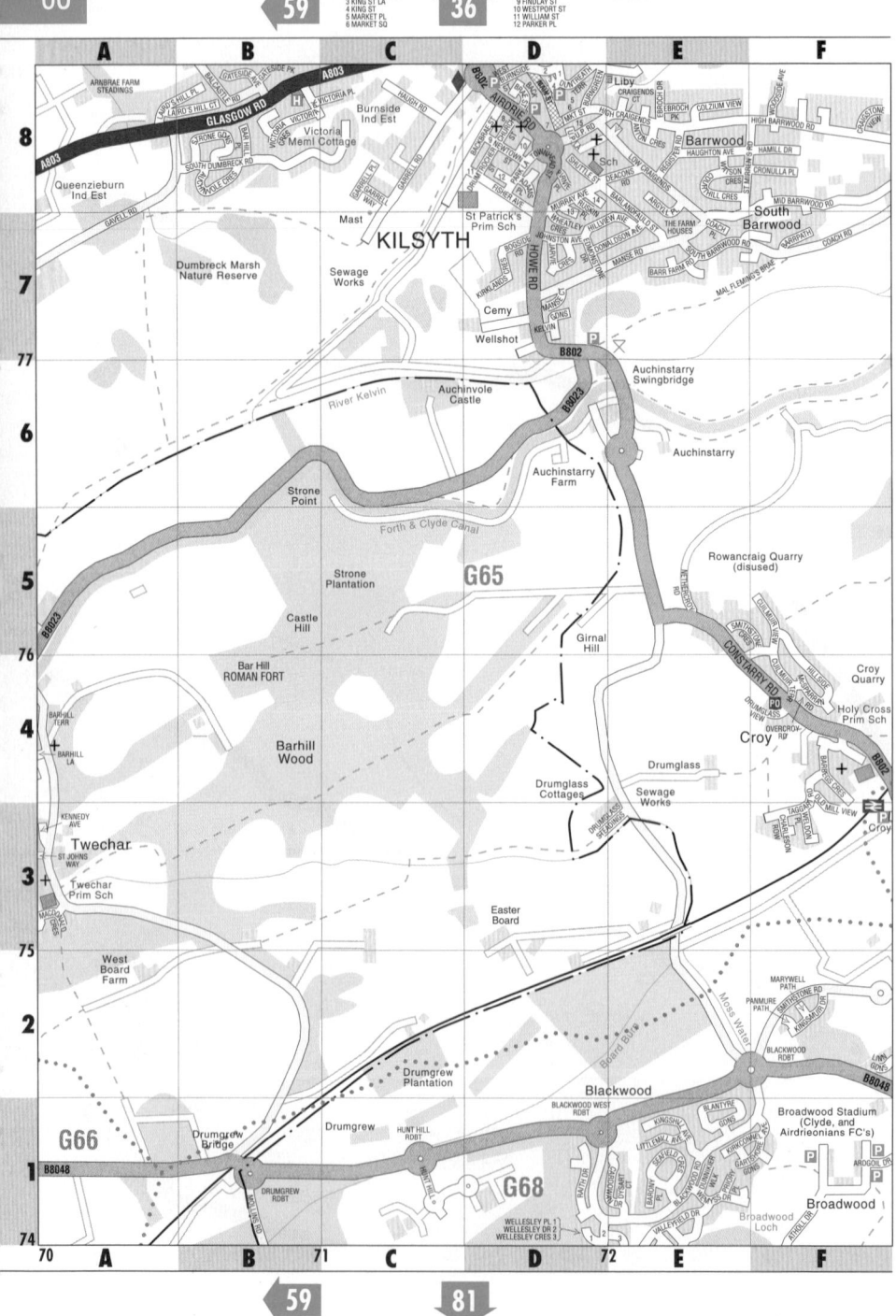

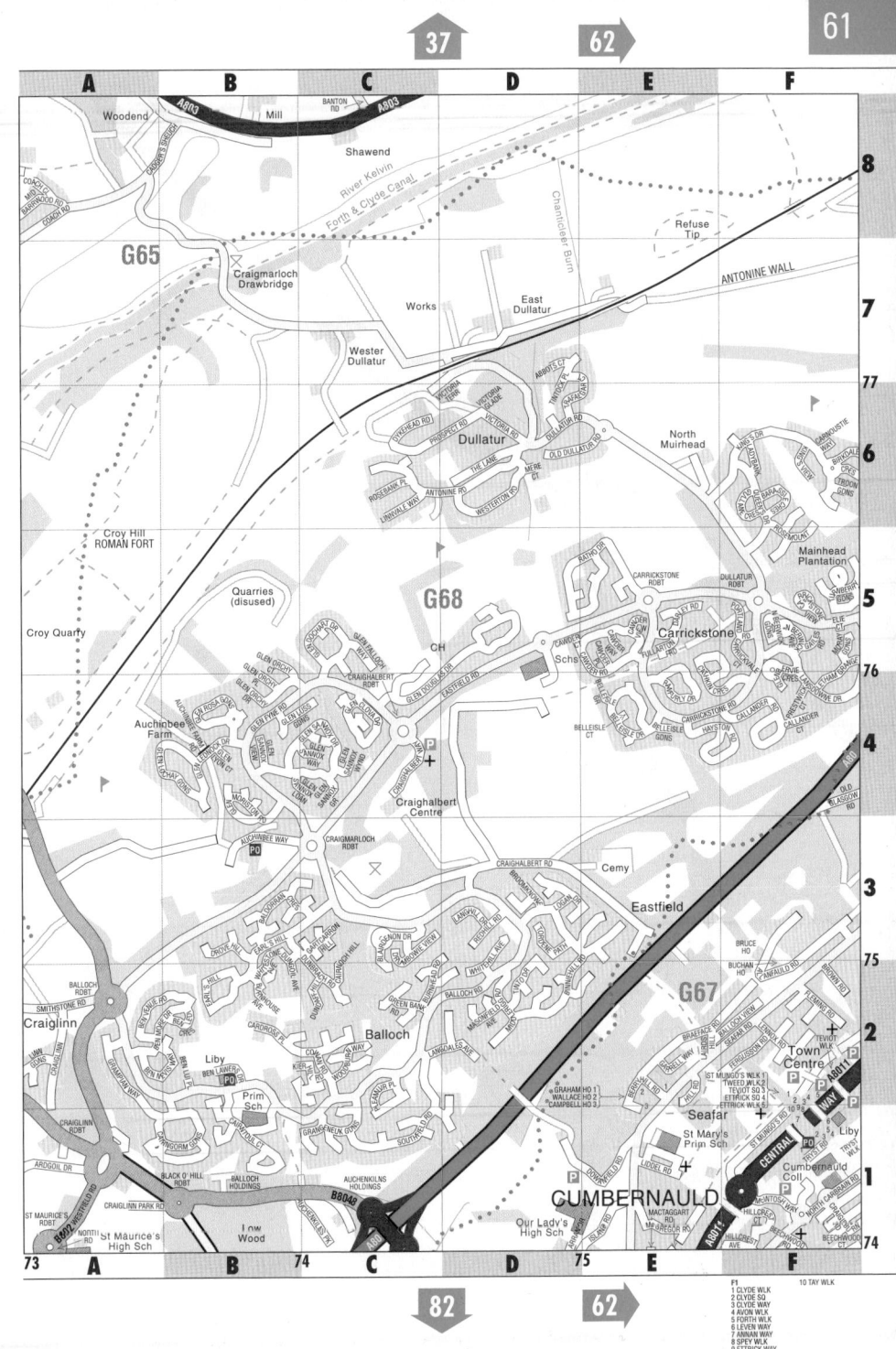

A B C D E F

Woodend

BANTON RD

Mill

Shawend

River Kelvin

Forth & Clyde Canal

Chanticleer Burn

Refuse Tip

G65

ANTONINE WALL

Craigmarloch Drawbridge

Works

East Dullatur

7

Wester Dullatur

77

North Muirhead

6

Dullatur

Croy Hill ROMAN FORT

Mainhead Plantation

Quarries (disused)

G68

CARRICKSTONE RDBT

DULLATUR RDBT

Croy Quarry

5

CH

Carrickstone

Schs

76

Auchinbee Farm

CRAIGHALBERT RDBT

GLEN DOUGLAS DR

EASTFIELD RD

BELLEISLE CT

4

P

Craighalbert Centre

AUCHINBEE WAY

PO

CRAIGMARLOCH RDBT

CRAIGHALBERT RD

Cemy

3

Eastfield

BRUCE HO

BUCHAN HO

75

G67

BALLOCH RDBT

SMITHSTONE RD

Craiglinn

BALLOCH RD

Town Centre

Seafar

2

Liby BEN LAWER PO

Prim Sch

Balloch

GRAHAM HO 1 WALLACE HO 2 CAMPBELL HO 3

ST MUNGO'S WLK 1 TWEED WLK 2 TEVIOT SQ 3 ETTRICK SQ 4 ETTRICK WLK 5

St Mary's Prim Sch

Liby

CRAIGLINN ROBT

ARDGOIL DR

CENTRAL WAY

Cumbernauld Coll

BLACK O' HILL RDBT

BALLOCH HOLDINGS

AUCHENKILNS HOLDINGS

P

1

ST MAURICE'S RDBT

CRAIGLINN PARK RD

Low Wood

B8048

CUMBERNAULD

P

St Maurice's High Sch

Our Lady's High Sch

MACTAGGART RD

HILLCREST

A B C D E F

F1
1 CLYDE WLK
2 CLYDE SQ
3 CLYDE WAY
4 AVON WLK
5 FORTH WLK
6 LEVEN WAY
7 ANNAN WAY
8 SPEY WLK
9 ETTRICK WAY

10 TAY WLK

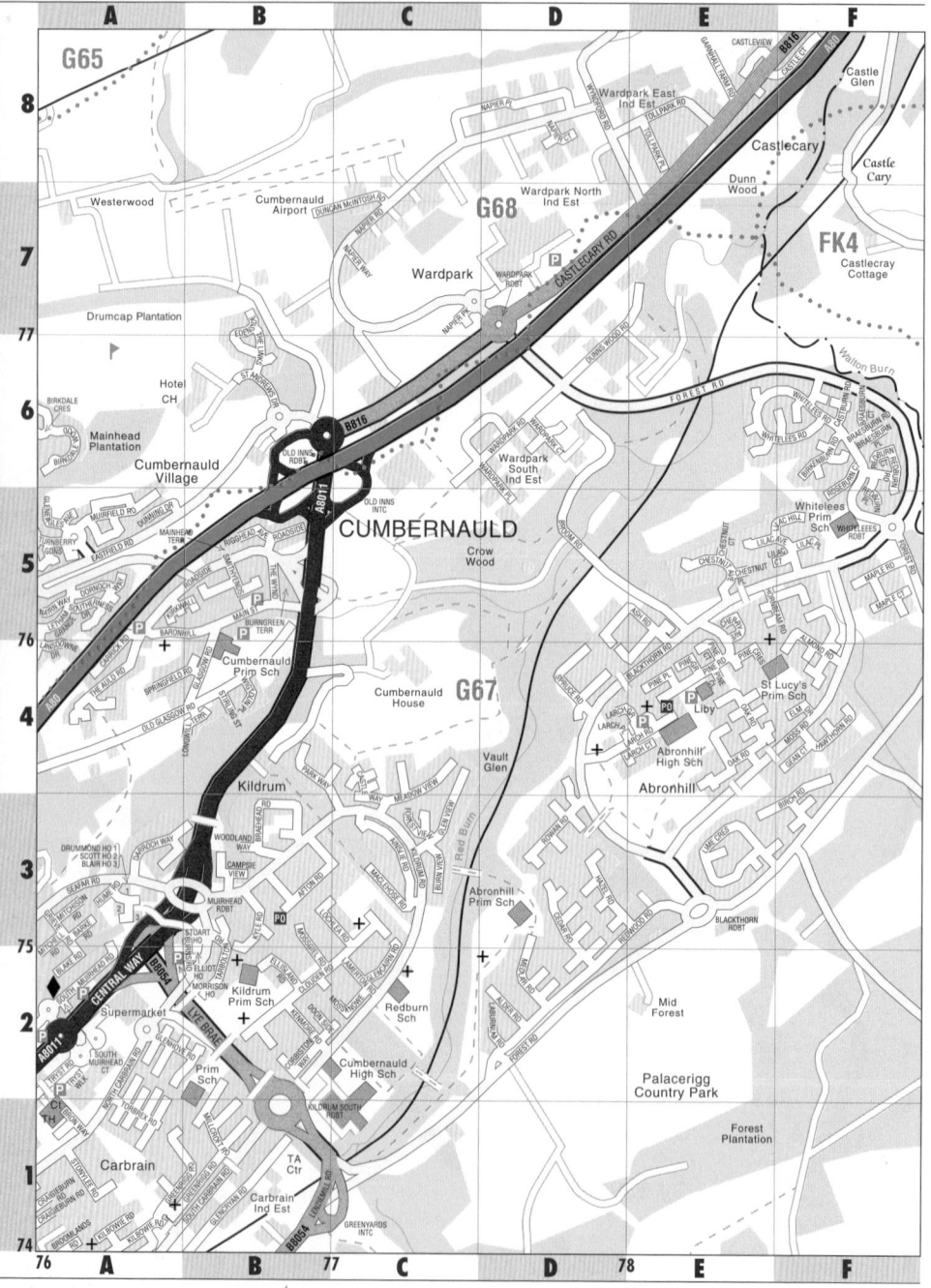

A   B   C   D   E   F

G68

8

Burnhouse
Castlecary
Low Wood
Blackhill
Lochdrum
Wester
Lochgreen
Loch
Green

Skipperton Burn

7

•Mast
Walton
Bandominie
FK4
Castlecary
High Wood
Lochgreen

77

6

Kilt
Farm

5

Kilt Bridge

76

Walton Burn
Graystone Knowe

4

Crowbank
Glenhead
G67
Arns
Old
Shields
Garbethill
House
• Mast

3

75

Garbet

2

Fannyside Muir
Garbethill

FK1

1

74

Easter
Fannyside

A   B   C   D   E   F

8

South Drum

Drum Wood

7   Cadgersloan

FK4

Tippetcraig

Loanfoot

77

6   Beam

5

76   FK1

4   G67

Garbethill Muir

Newcraig
Cottage

3   Wester
Jawcraig

Easter
Jawcraig

Jawcraig
Farm

Jawcraig

75

2   Threaprig

B803

1

Easter
Greenrig

Oakersdykes

Wester Jaw
Cottage

74
82   A   B   83   C   D   84   E   F

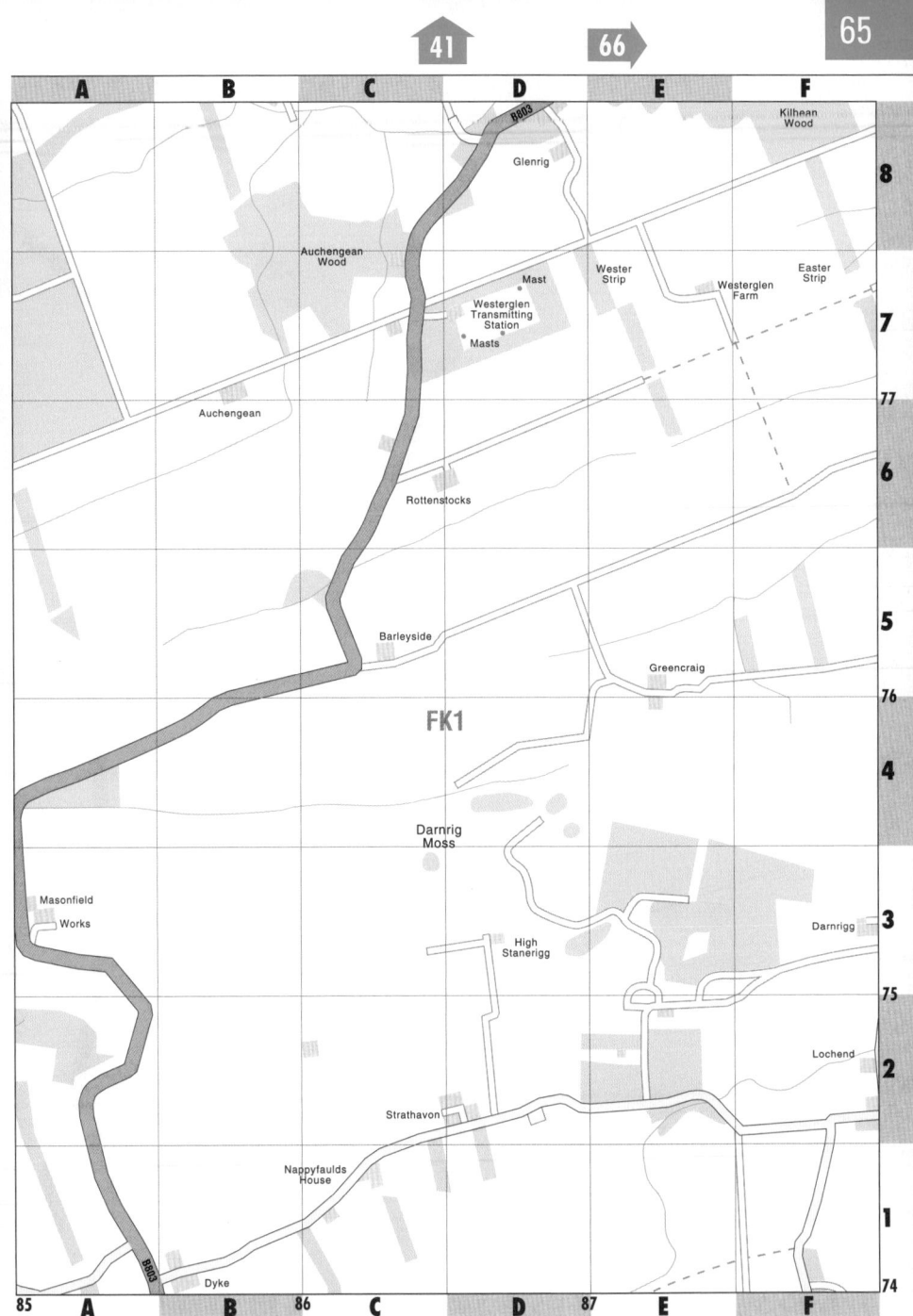

A   B   C   D   E   F

8

B803

Kilhean
Wood

Glenrig

Auchengean
Wood

Mast

Wester
Strip

Westerglen
Farm

Easter
Strip

Westerglen
Transmitting
Station

7

Masts

77

Auchengean

6

Rottenstocks

77

5

Barleyside

Greencraig

76

FK1

4

Darnrig
Moss

3

Masonfield

Works

High
Stanerigg

Darnrigg

75

Lochend

2

Strathavon

Nappyfaulds
House

B803

1

Dyke

74

85   A   B   86   C   D   87   E   F

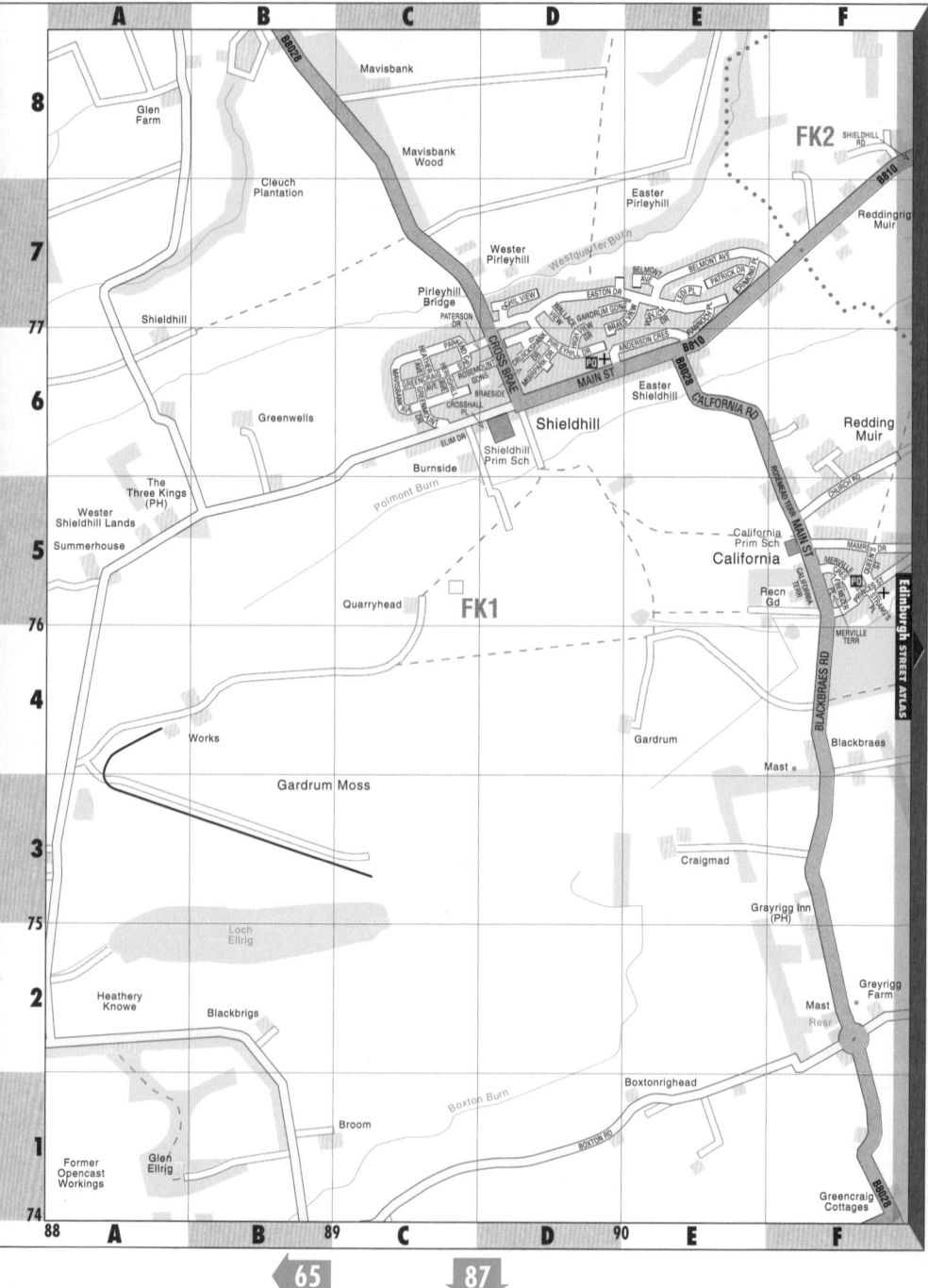

8

7

77

6

5

76

4

3

75

2

1

74

88 A B 89 C D 90 E F

FK2

SHIELDHILL RD

B810

Reddingrig Muir

Glen Farm

Mavisbank

Cleuch Plantation

Mavisbank Wood

Easter Pirleyhill

Westquarter Burn

B8028

CROSS BRAE

Shieldhill

Wester Pirleyhill

BELMONT AVE

BELMONT AVE

PATRICK DR

Pirleyhill Bridge

PATERSON DR

EASTON DR

SAUL VIEW

MELLACK GARDRUM GDNS

BRAES

WARLOCK

ANDERSON CRES

MAIN ST

B810

CALIFORNIA RD

Shieldhill

Easter Shieldhill

Redding Muir

Greenwells

BURNSIDE

Shieldhill Prim Sch

RICHARDSON PEPER

CHURCH RD

MAMRE DR

California Prim Sch

MERVILLE CRES

California

The Three Kings (PH)

Burnside

Polmont Burn

Recn Gd

CALIFORNIA TERR

MERVILLE TERR

Edinburgh STREET ATLAS

Wester Shieldhill Lands

Summerhouse

Quarryhead

FK1

BLACKBRAES RD

Works

Gardrum

Blackbraes

Mast

Gardrum Moss

Craigmad

Grayrigg Inn (PH)

Loch Ellrig

Greyrigg Farm

Heathery Knowe

Blackbrigs

Mast

Resr

Boxton Burn

Boxtonrighead

Broom

BOXTON RD

Former Opencast Workings

Glen Ellrig

Greencraig Cottages

B8028

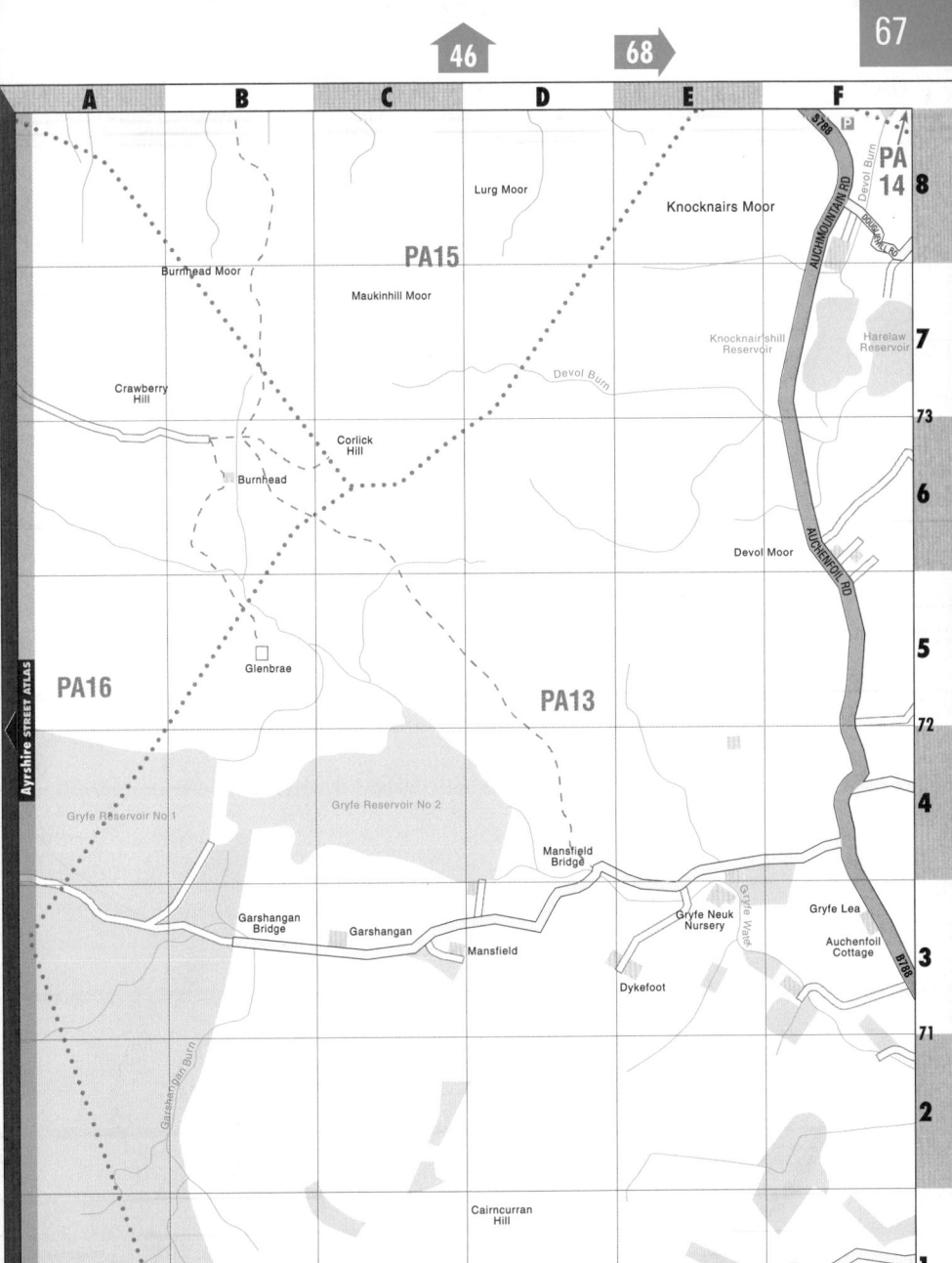

PA15

Lurg Moor

Knocknairs Moor

PA14

Burnhead Moor

Maukinhill Moor

Knocknairshill Reservoir

Harelaw Reservoir

Crawberry Hill

Devol Burn

Corlick Hill

Burnhead

Devol Moor

AUCHENFOIL RD

Glenbrae

PA16

PA13

Gryfe Reservoir No 1

Gryfe Reservoir No 2

Mansfield Bridge

Garshangan Bridge

Garshangan

Mansfield

Gryfe Neuk Nursery

Gryfe Lea

Auchenfoil Cottage

Dykefoot

Garshangan Burn

Cairncurran Hill

Hillside

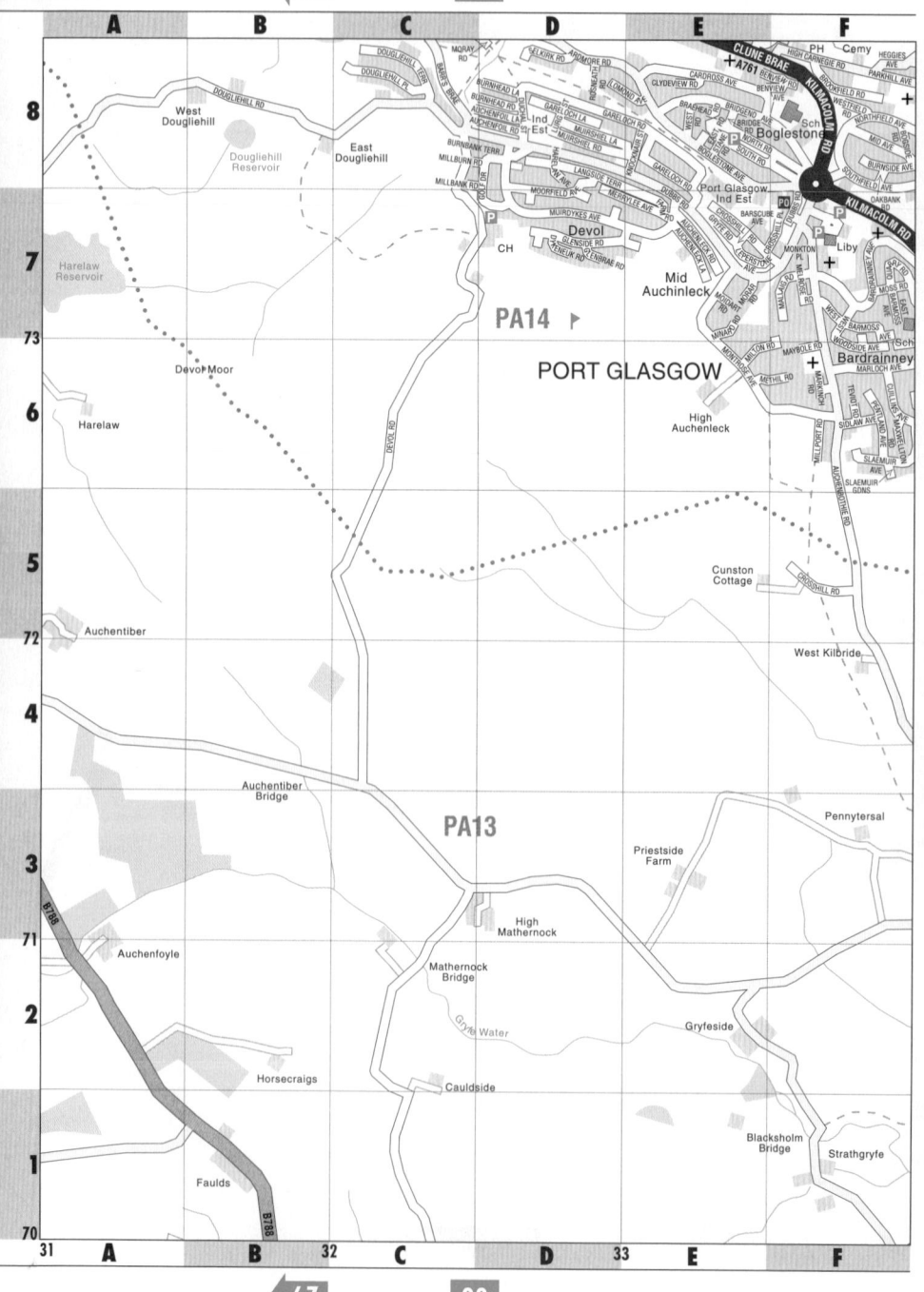

A   B   C   D   E   F

8

West
Dougliehill

Dougliehill
Reservoir

East
Dougliehill

MORAY RD
DOUGLIEHILL TERR

DOUGLIEHILL RD

DOUGLIEHILL PL

SELKIRK RD   ARDMORE RD

CLUNE BRAE
A761   HIGH CARNEGIE RD

PH   Cemy

HEGGIES AVE
PARKHILL AVE

KILMACOLM RD

BRAEHEAD AVE
CLYDEVIEW RD
CARDROSS RD
BRIDGEND

Sch

Boglestone

BROOKFIELD AVE
WESTFIELD RD
NORTHFIELD AVE

MID ZIG

BURNHEAD LA
BURNHEAD TERR
AUCHENFOIL LA
AUCHENFOIL RD
Ind Est

GARELOCH PL
GARELOCH RD
MUIRSHIEL LA
MUIRSHIEL RD

BRIDGE
BENVIEW

BURNSIDE AVE
OAKBANK

7

Harelaw
Reservoir

Devol Moor

MILLBURN RD
MILLBANK TERR
MILLBANK RD
MOORFIELD RD

LANGSIDE TERR
MUIRDYKES AVE
METRYLEE AVE

DUBS

GARELOCH RD

(Port Glasgow
Ind Est)

KILMACOLM RD

73

PA14

PORT GLASGOW

GLENSIDE RD

ENLIR RD GLENBRAE RD

P

CH

Devol

AUCHEN LA

Mid
Auchinleck

MINARY

MILL PORT RD

Bardrainney

MARLOCH AVE

6

Harelaw

High
Auchenleck

SIDLAW AVE

TINTO AVE

CULLEN AVE

PENTLAND RD

SLAEMUIR
AVE

SLAEMUIR
GDNS

5

Cunston
Cottage

CROSSHILL RD

72

Auchentiber

West Kilbride

4

Auchentiber
Bridge

PA13

Pennytersal

3

B788

Auchenfoyle

High
Mathernock

Priestside
Farm

71

Mathernock
Bridge

Gryfe Water

Gryfeside

2

Horsecraigs

Cauldside

1

Blacksholm
Bridge

Strathgryfe

Faulds

B788

70

31   A   B   32   C   D   33   E   F

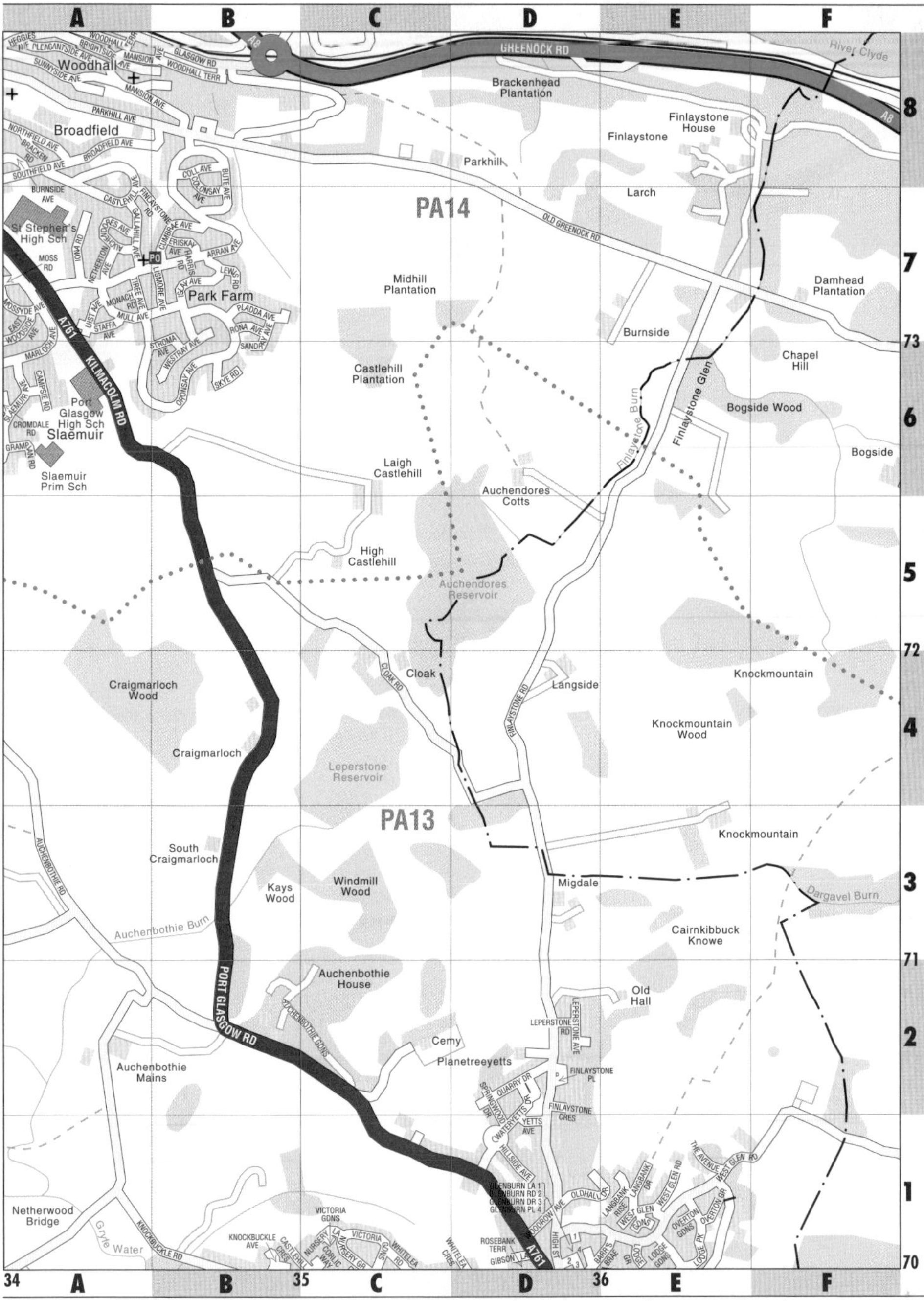

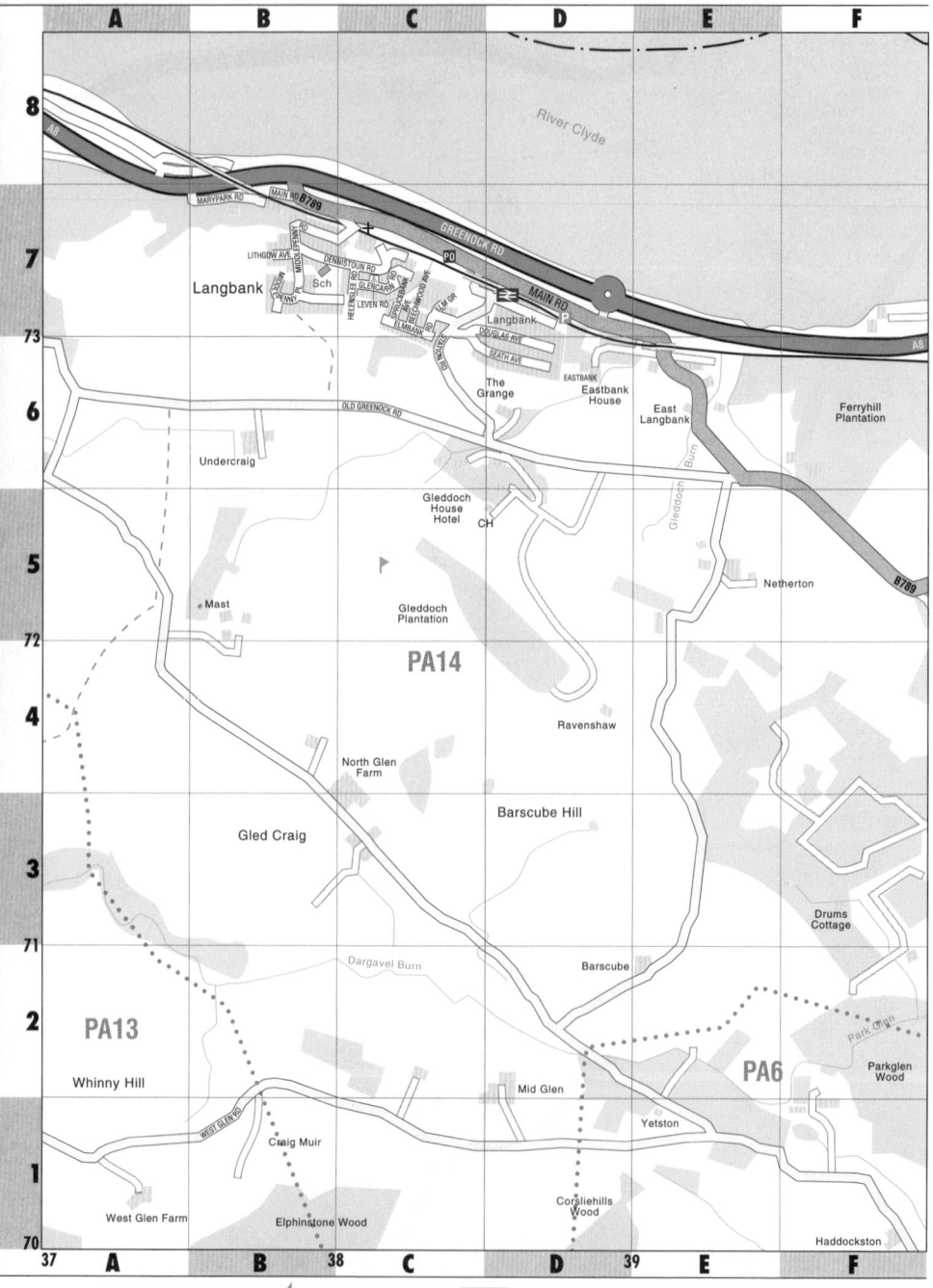

A **B** **C** **D** **E** **F**

River Clyde

MARYPARK RD

MAIN RD B789

GREENOCK RD

Langbank

LITHGOW AVE

DENNISTOUN RD

Sch

LEVEN RD

ELMBANK

MAIN RD

Langbank

DOUGLAS AVE

HEATH AVE

EASTBANK

The Grange

Eastbank House

East Langbank

Ferryhill Plantation

OLD GREENOCK RD

Undercraig

Gleddoch House Hotel

CH

Gleddoch Burn

Netherton

B789

Mast

Gleddoch Plantation

PA14

Ravenshaw

North Glen Farm

Gled Craig

Barscube Hill

Drums Cottage

Dargavel Burn

Barscube

PA13

Whinny Hill

WEST GLEN RD

Craig Muir

Mid Glen

Yetston

PA6

Park Burn

Parkglen Wood

West Glen Farm

Elphinstone Wood

Corsliehills Wood

Haddockston

37 **A** **B** 38 **C** **D** 39 **E** **F**

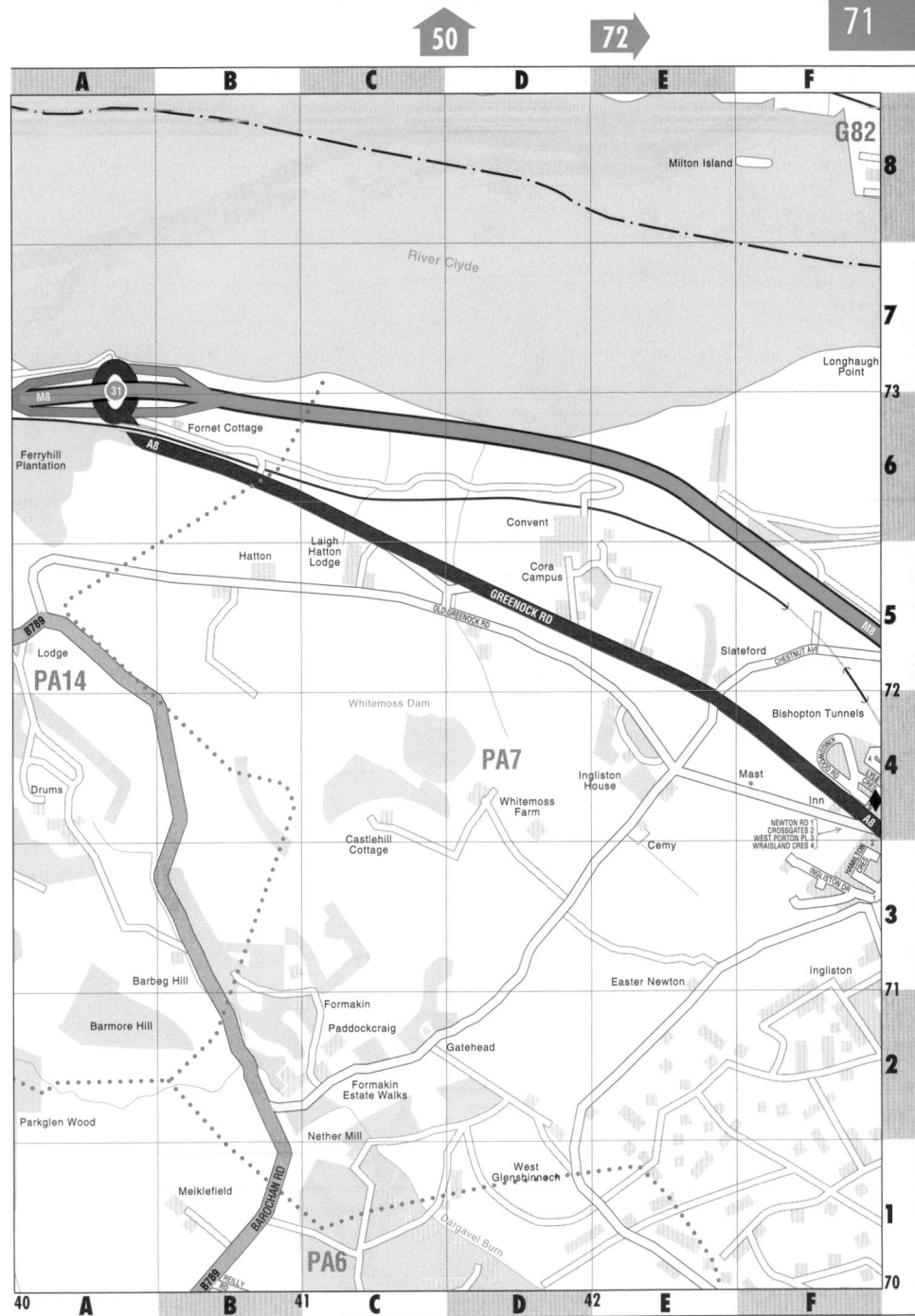

50
72
G82

A B C D E F

8

Milton Island

River Clyde

7

Longhaugh Point

73

M8 31

Fornet Cottage

A8

Ferryhill Plantation

6

Convent

Laigh Hatton Lodge

Hatton

Cora Campus

GREENOCK RD

OLD GREENOCK RD

Slateford

CHESTNUT AVE

5

B789

Lodge

PA14

Whitemoss Dam

PA7

72

Bishopton Tunnels

Drums

Whitemoss Farm

Ingliston House

Mast

Inn

NEWTON RD 1
CROSSGATES 2
WEST PORTON PL 3
WRAISLAND CRES 4.

A8

Castlehill Cottage

Cemy

4

INGLISTON DR

HAMILTON CRES

Barbag Hill

Formakin

Easter Newton

Ingliston

71

Barmore Hill

Paddockcraig

Gatehead

3

Formakin Estate Walks

2

Parkglen Wood

Nether Mill

BAROCHAN RD

West Glenshinnoch

Darpavel Burn

Meiklefield

1

PA6

RELLY RD

B789

70

40 A 41 B C 42 D E F

91
72

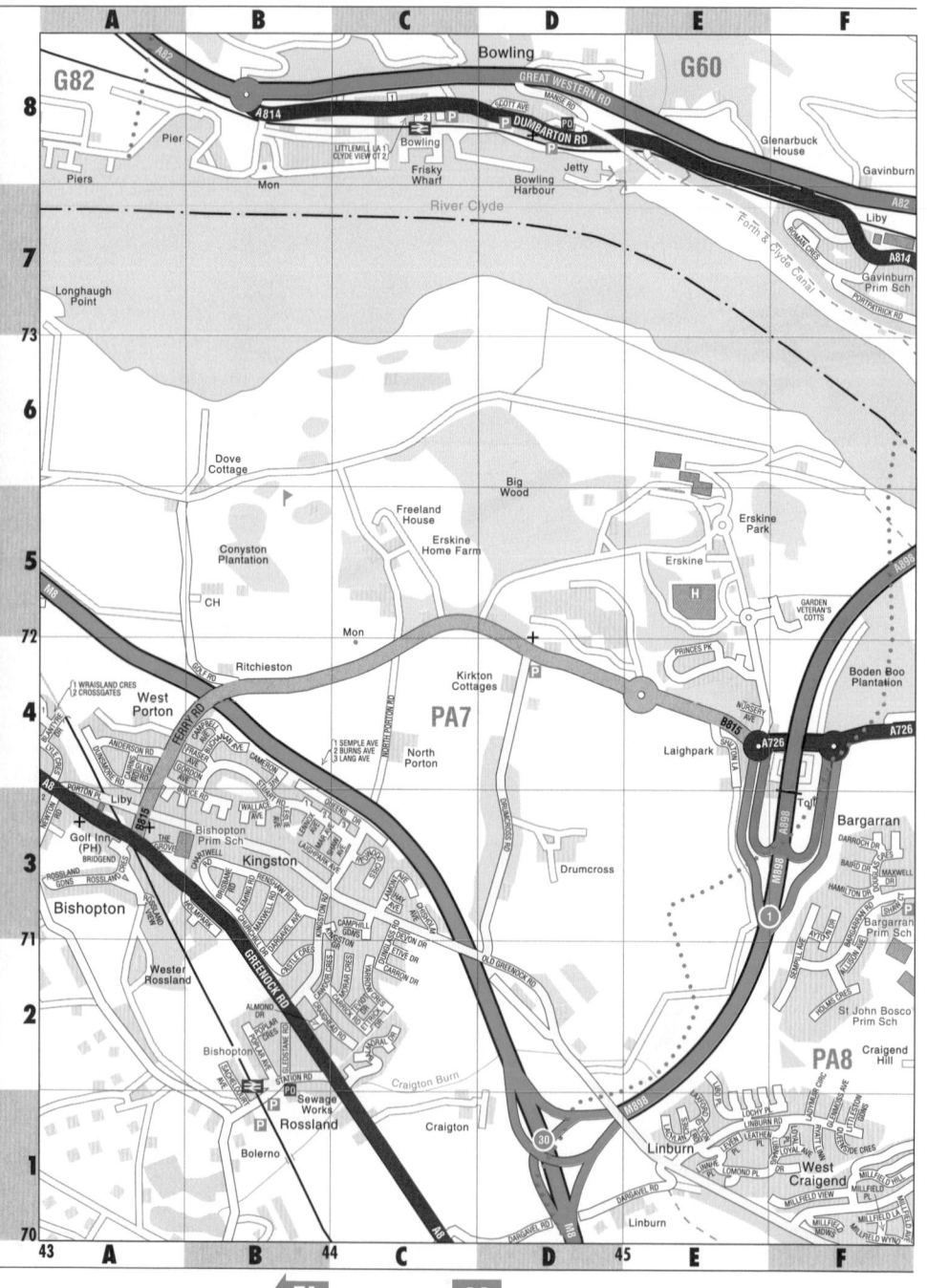

A   B   C   D   E   F

8

Gavinburn Cottages
Craigleith
Resr
Drums
Wester Duntiglennan

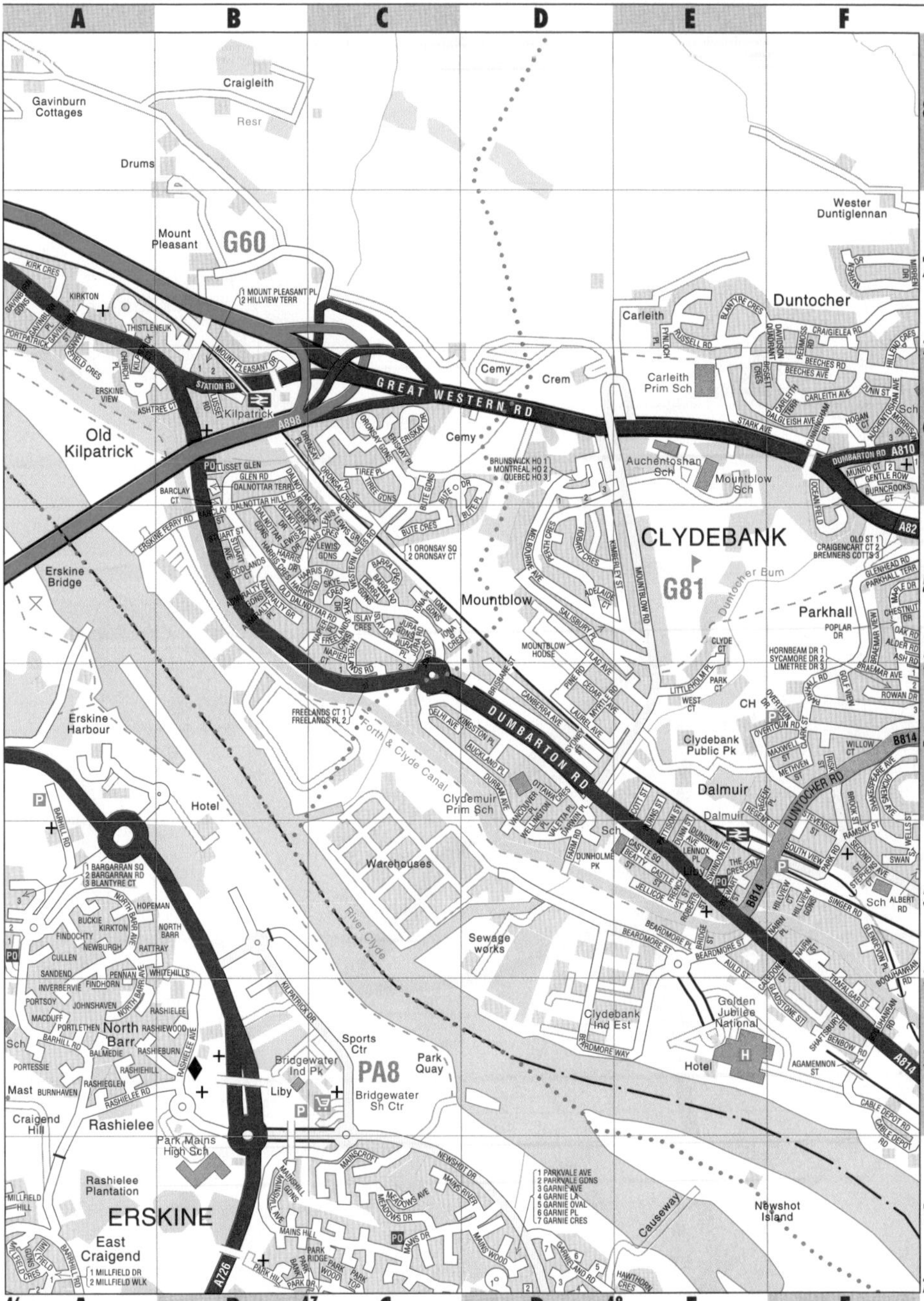

7

Mount Pleasant
G60
KIRK CRES
KIRKTON
THISTLENEUK
PORTPATRICK RD
ERSKINE VIEW
ASHTREE CT
1 MOUNT PLEASANT PL
2 HILLVIEW TERR
Duntocher
Carleith
BLANTYRE CRES
DAVIDSON RD
DUNIBRAE
CRAIGIELEA RD
BEECHES AVE
73

STATION RD
Kilpatrick
A898
GREAT WESTERN RD
Cemy
Crem
Carleith Prim Sch
CARLEITH AVE
DUNN ST
HOGAN CT
6
Old Kilpatrick
Cemy
BRUNSWICK HO 1
MONTREAL HO 2
QUEBEC HO 3
Auchentoshan Sch
Mountblow Sch
DUMBARTON RD
A810
MUNRO DR
GENTLE ROW
BURNCROOKS CT
A82

Erskine Bridge
LUSSET GLEN
GLEN RD
DALNOTTAR TERR
BARCLAY CT
DALNOTTAR HILL RD
TIREE CT
1 ORONSAY SQ
2 ORONSAY CT
BUTE CRES
LEWIS GDNS
ISLAY CRES
CLYDEBANK
G81
Duntocher Burn
Parkhall
POPLAR
OLD ST 1
CRAIGENCART CT 2
BREMNERS COTTS 3
PARKVALE TER
CHESTNUT
OAK
5

Mountblow
MOUNTBLOW RD
Mountblow House
CLYDE CT
HORNBEAM DR 1
SYCAMORE DR 2
LIMETREE DR 3
BRAEMAR AVE
ROWAN DR
72

Erskine Harbour
Hotel
FREELANDS CT 1
FREELANDS PL 2
Forth & Clyde Canal
DELTA AVE
KINGSTON AVE
BUCKLAND ST
CAMBRIDGE AVE
LAUREL AVE
CEDAR AVE
LITTLE HOLM
PARK CT
WEST CT
CH
Clydebank Public Pk
Dalmuir
OVERTON RD
MAXWELL ST
METHVEN ST
WILLOW CT
B814
4

DUMBARTON RD
Clydemuir Prim Sch
Warehouses
River Clyde
DUNHOLME PK
CASTLE RD
LENNOX ST
Sch
THE
DUNTOCHER RD
SINGER RD
RAMSAY ST
SWAN
Sch
ALBERT RD
3
1 BARGARRAN SQ
2 BARGARRAN RD
3 BLANTYRE CT
HOPEMAN
BUCKIE
KIRKTON
NEW BARR
RATTRAY
NEWBURGH
FINDHORN
WHITEHILLS
SANDEND
FINDOCHTY
CULLEN
PENNAN
PORTSOY
JOHNSHAVEN
INVERBERVIE
MACDUFF
PORTLETHEN
RASHIELEE
Sewage works
Clydebank Ind Est
BEARDMORE ST
Golden Jubilee National
AGAMEMNON ST
A814
71

North Barr
RASHIELEE RD
RASHIEWOOD
RASHIEBURN
BALMEDIE
BARHILL RD
RASHIEHILL
Sports Ctr
Bridgewater Ind Pk
Liby
PA8
Park Quay
Bridgewater Sh Ctr
PROMORE WAY
Hotel
H
CABLE DEPOT RD
2

PORTESSIE
Mast
BURNHAVEN
Craigend Hill
Rashielee
MILLFIELD HILL
Park Mains High Sch
A726
Rashielee Plantation
ERSKINE
East Craigend
1 MILLFIELD DR
2 MILLFIELD WLK
MAINS DR
PARK RIDGE DR
PARK DR
NEWSHOT DR
Causeway
HAWTHORN DR
1 PARKVALE AVE
2 PARKVALE GDNS
3 GARNIE AVE
4 GARNIE LN
5 GARNIE OVAL
6 GARNIE PL
7 GARNIE CRES
Newshot Island
1
70

46   A   B   47   C   D   48   E   F

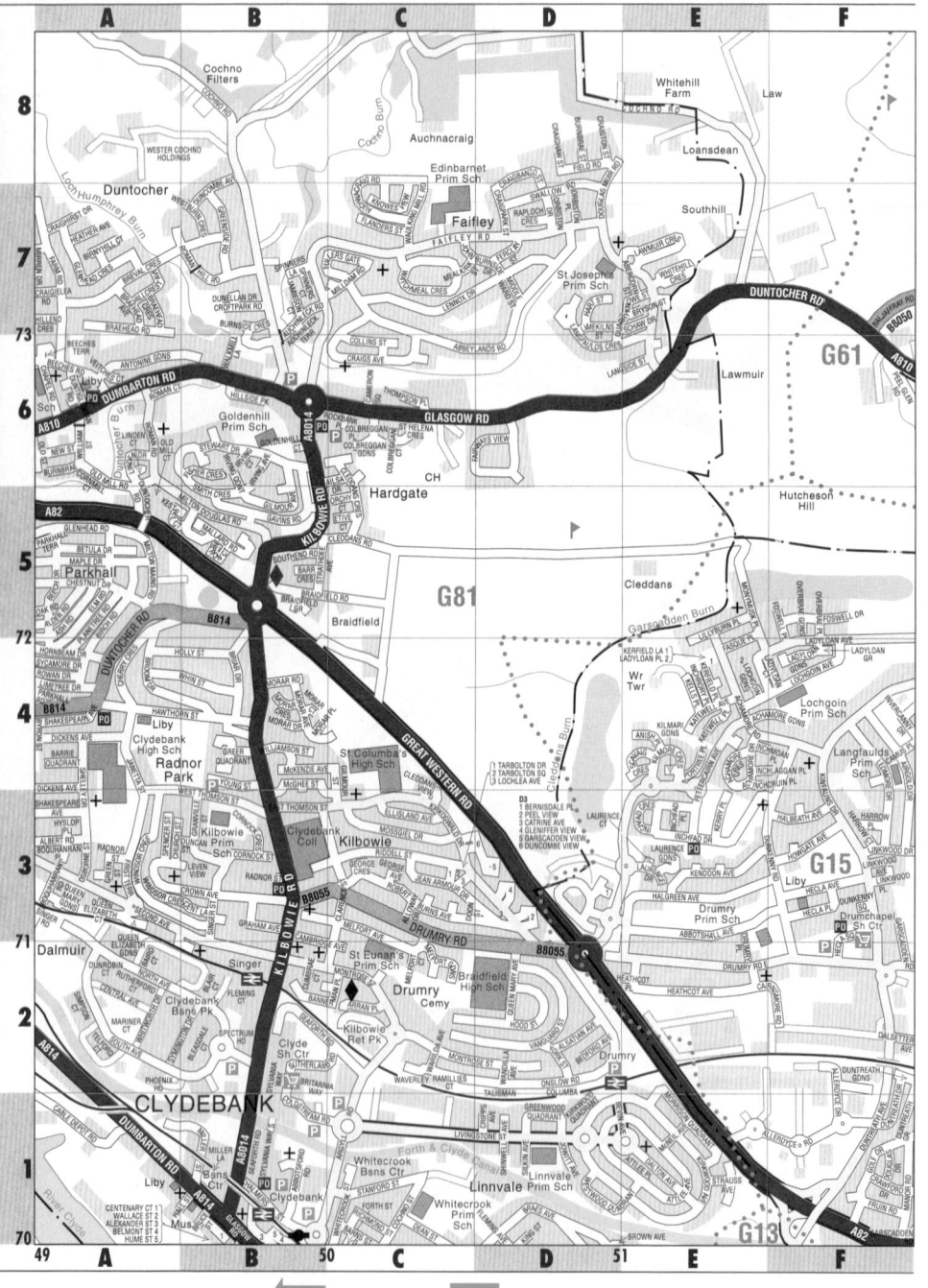

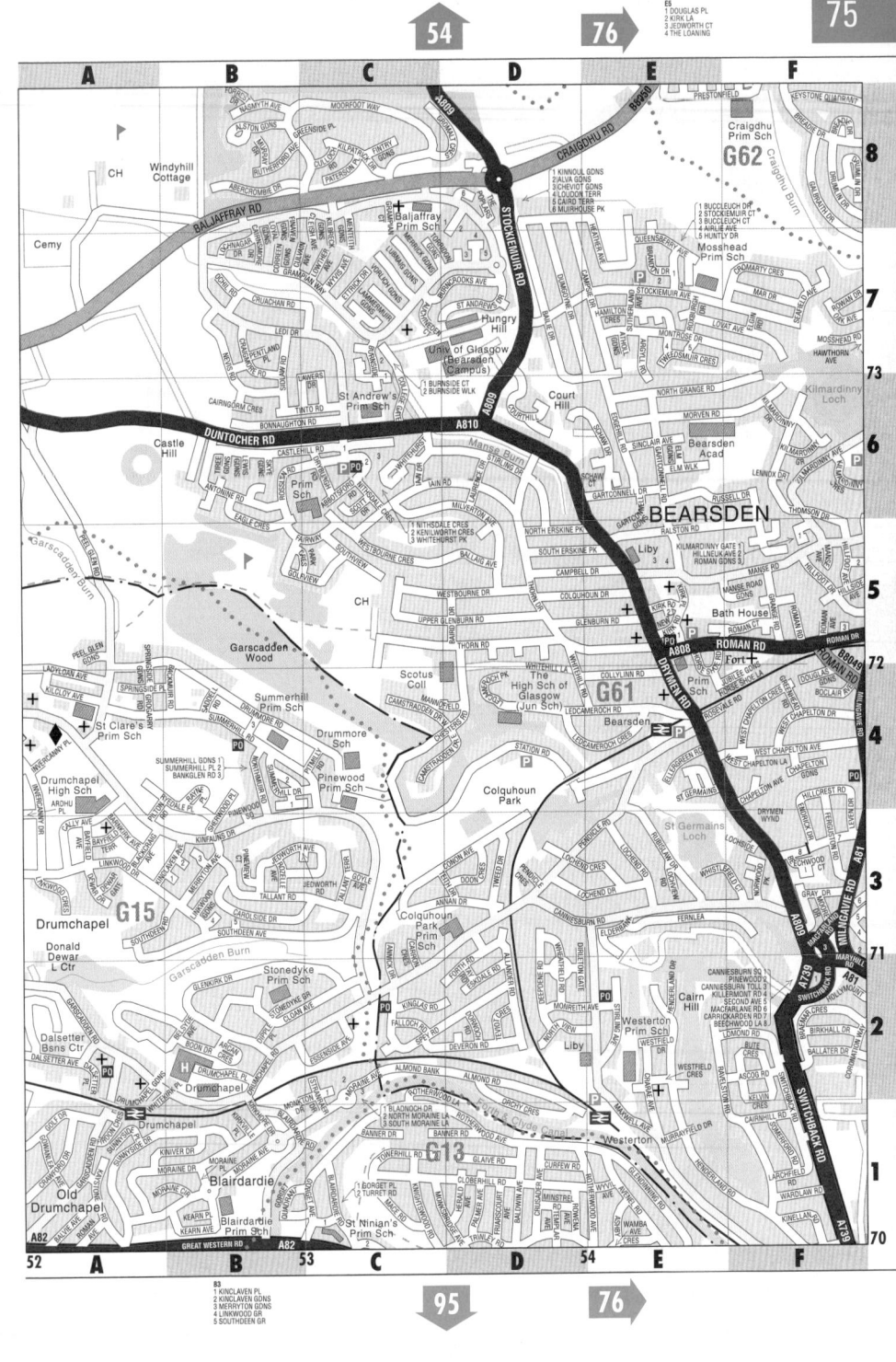

85 E5
1 DOUGLAS PL
2 KIRK LA
3 JEDWORTH CT
4 THE LOANING

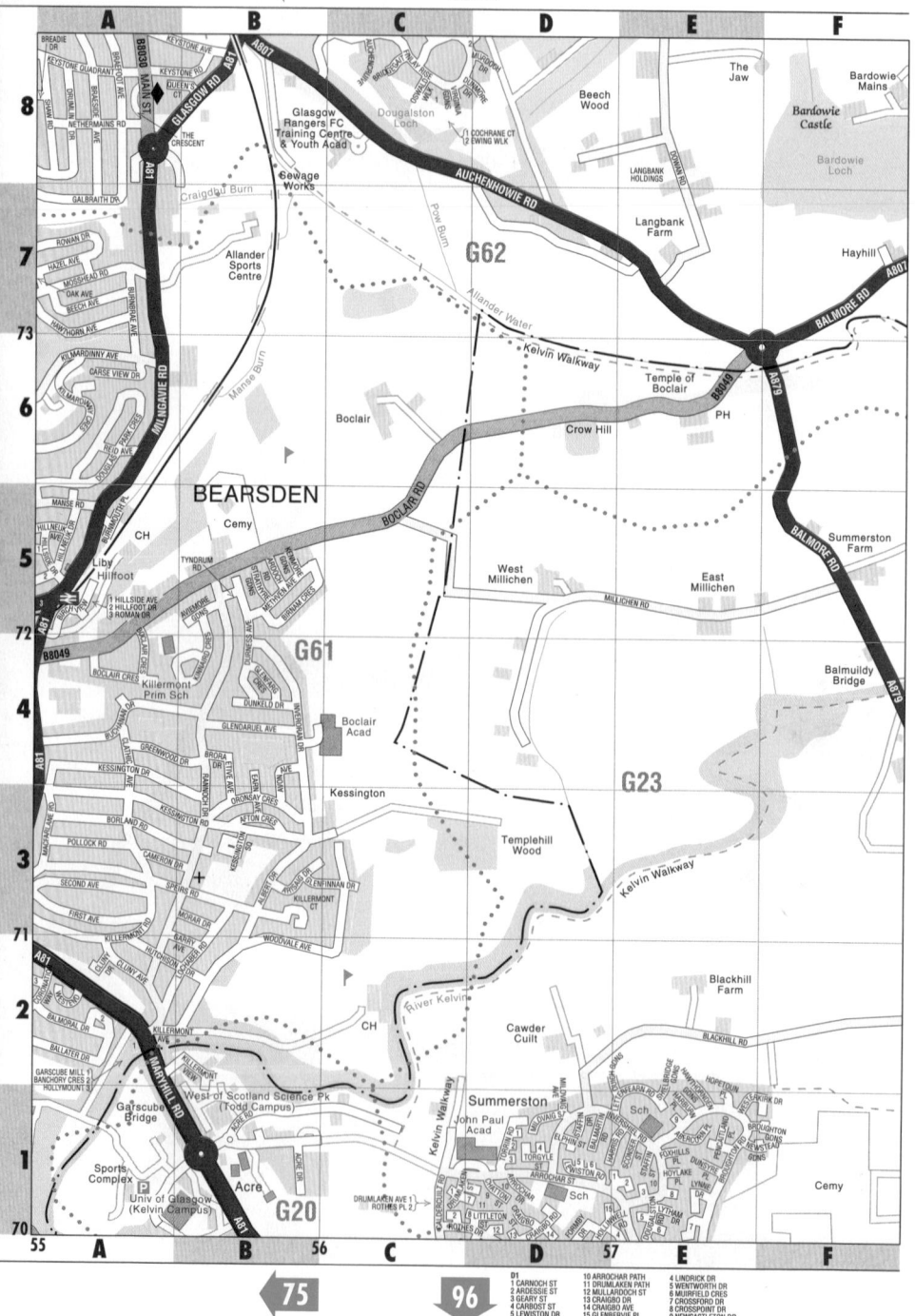

D1
1 CARNOCH ST
2 ARDESSIE ST
3 GEARY ST
4 CARBOST ST
5 LEWISTON DR
6 LEWISTON PL
7 DRUMLAKEN CT
8 LITTLETON DR
9 DRUMLAKEN PL

10 ARROCHAR PATH
11 DRUMLAKEN PATH
12 MULLARDOCH ST
13 CRAIGBO DR
14 CRAIGBO AVE
15 GLENBERVIE PL
E1
1 FORRES ST
2 TOLSTA ST
3 GALLAN AVE

4 LINDRICK DR
5 WENTWORTH DR
6 MUIRFIELD CRES
7 CROSSFORD DR
8 CROSSPOINT DR
9 NEWCASTLETON DR
10 STAFFIN PATH

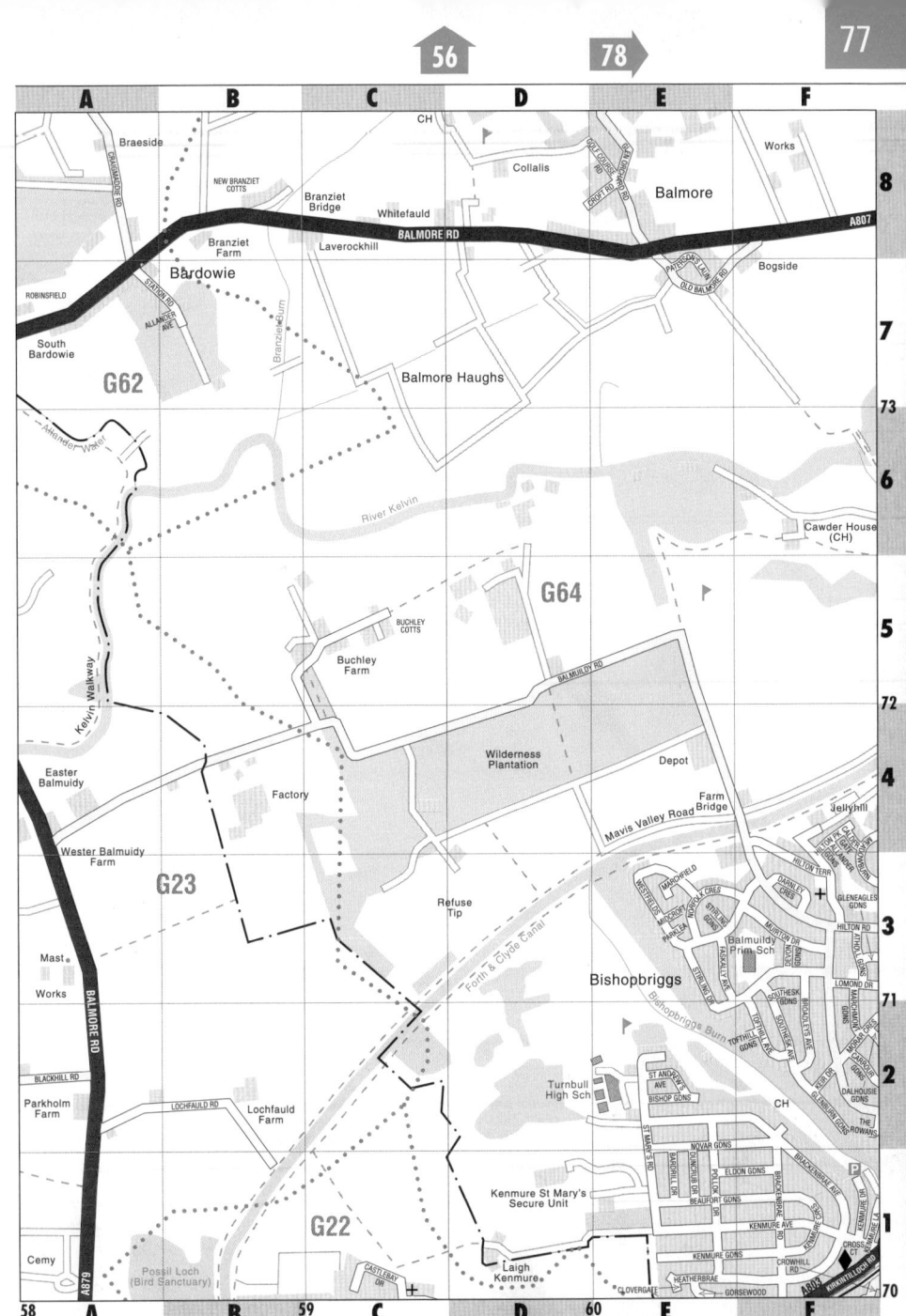

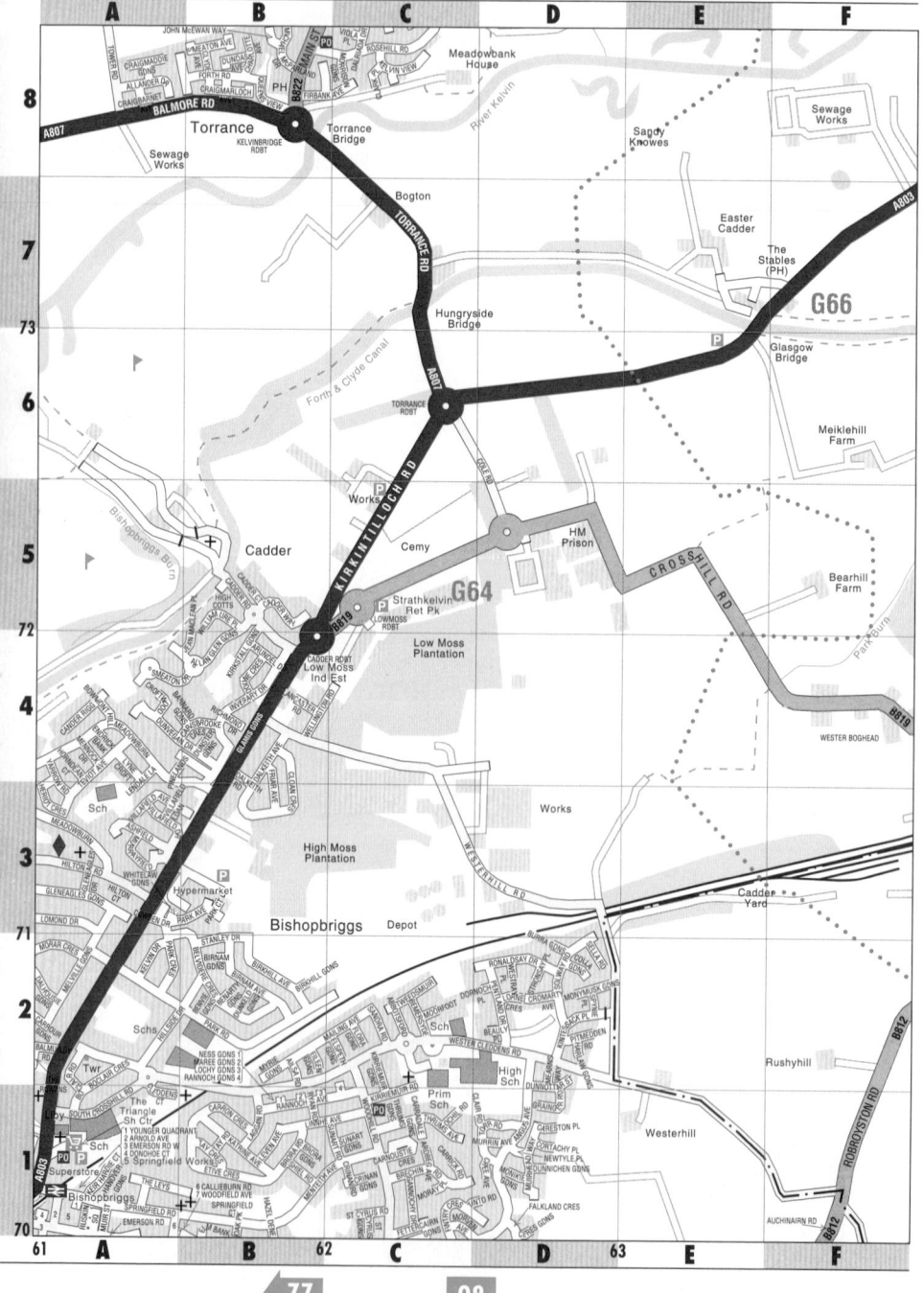

C8
1 YORK PL
2 The Regent Ctr
3 BROADCROFT
4 ROCHDALE PL

58

D8
1 GLENVIEW
2 PETER D.STIRLING RD
3 GLENBURN CT
4 STRATHALLAN GDNS
5 BROOMFIELD WLK
6 BELMONT CT

80

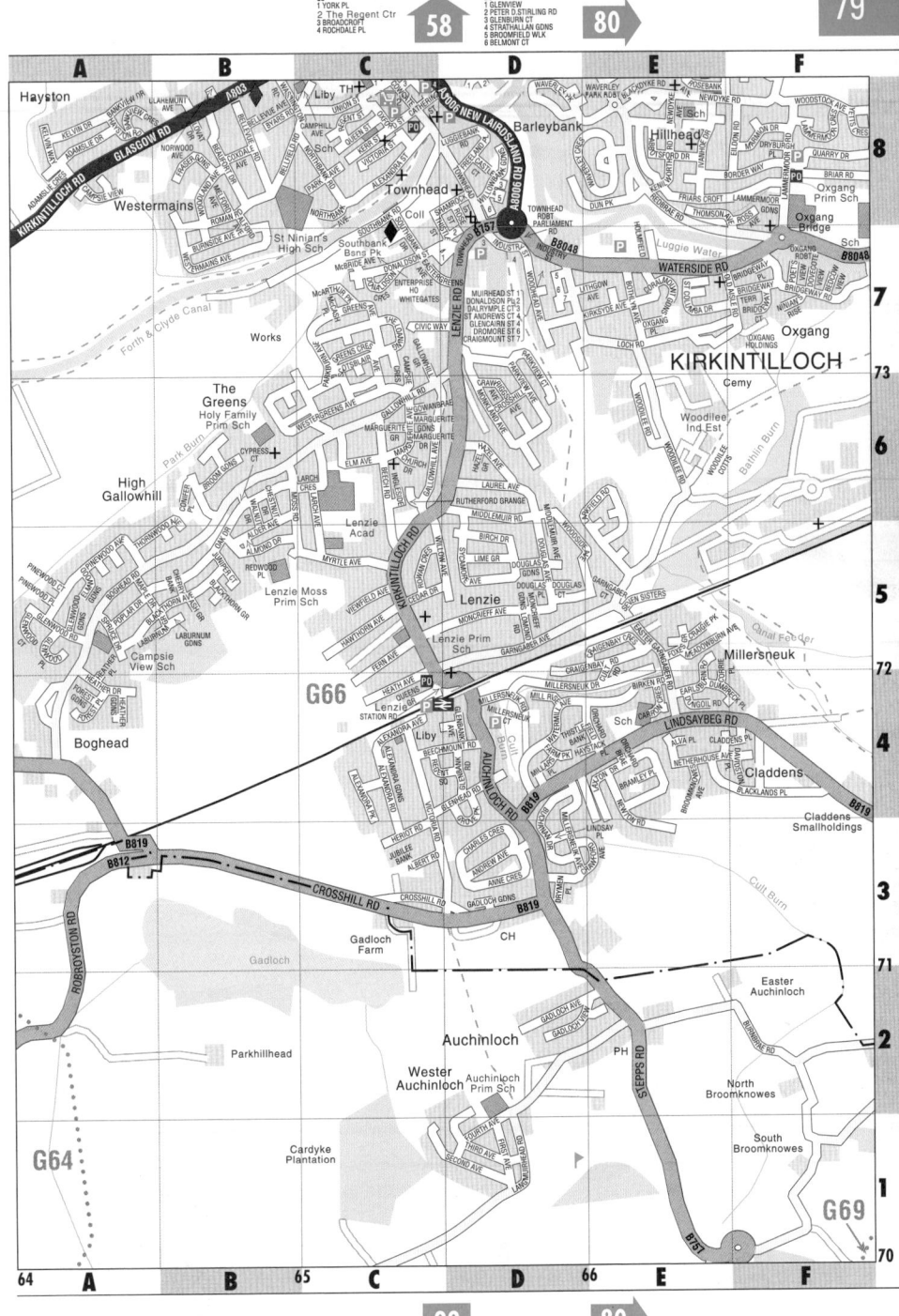

99

80

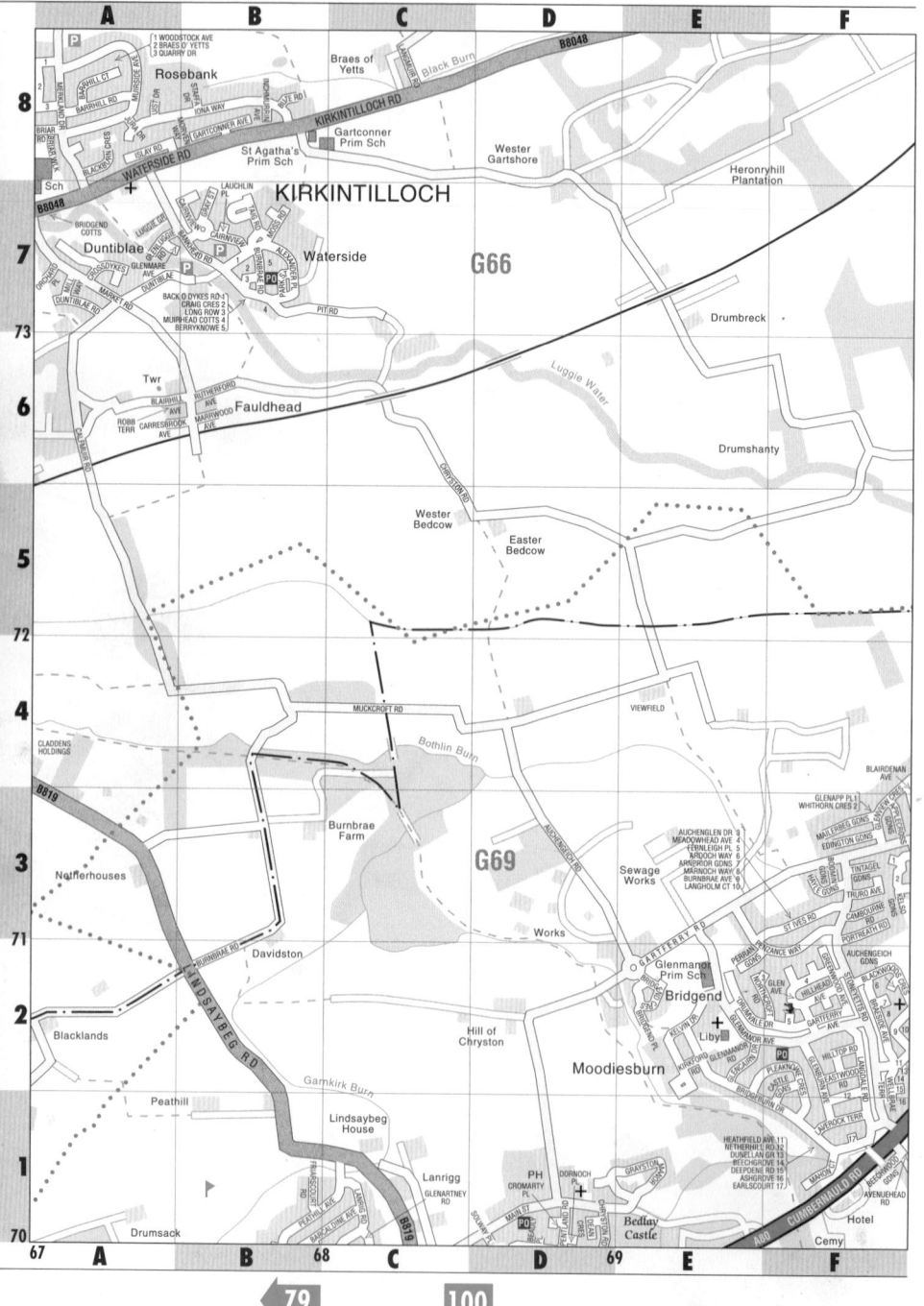

60   82

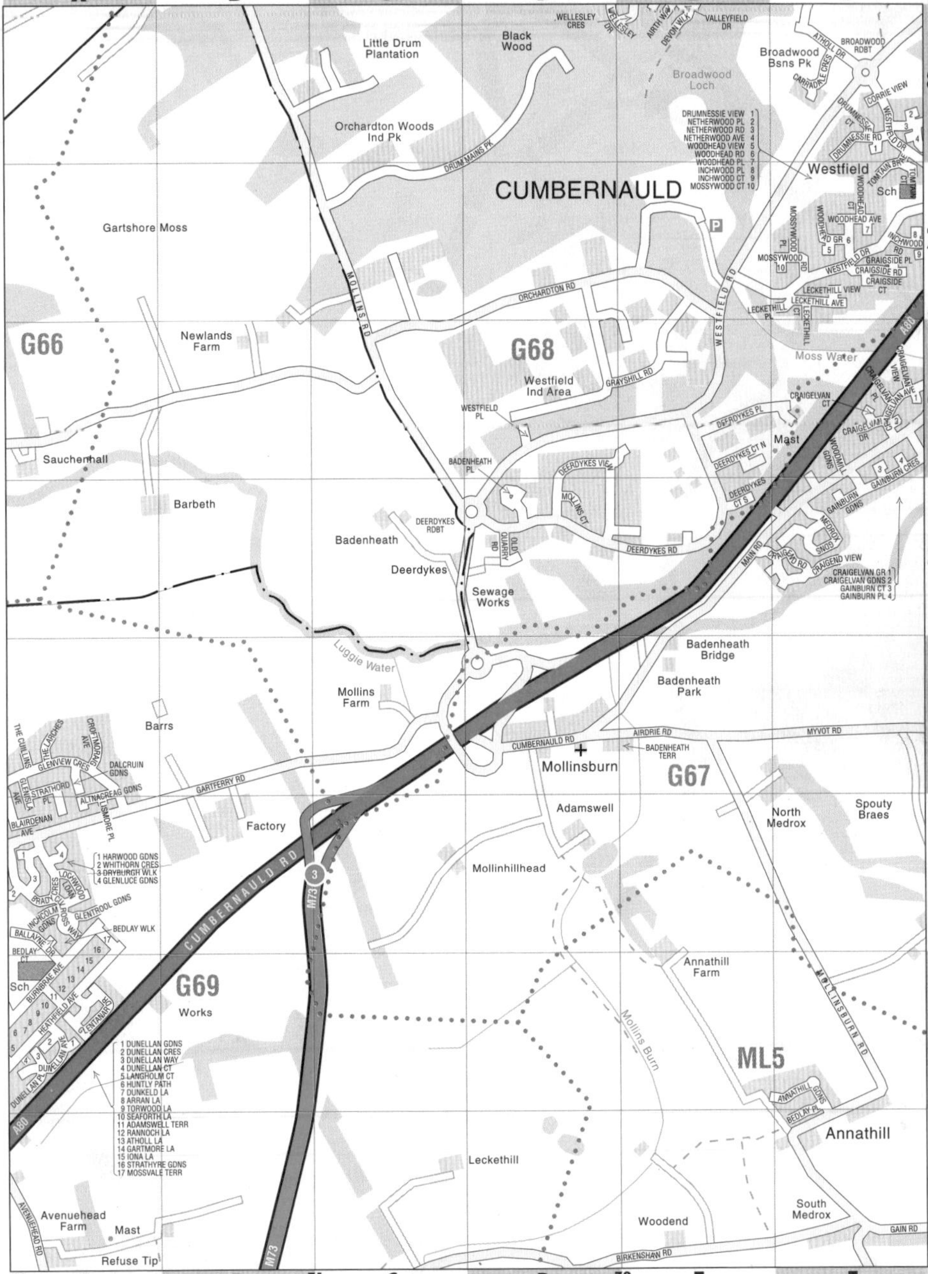

| | A | B | C | D | E | F | |

Wellesley Cres
North Vw
Valleyfield Dr
Little Drum Plantation
Black Wood
Broadwood Bsns Pk
Broadwood Robt
Broadwood Loch
8

Orchardton Woods Ind Pk
DRUMMAINS PK
DRUMNESSIE VIEW 1
NETHERWOOD PL 2
NETHERWOOD RD 3
NETHERWOOD AVE 4
WOODHEAD VIEW 5
WOODHEAD RD 6
WOODHEAD PL 7
INCHWOOD PL 8
INCHWOOD CT 9
MOSSYWOOD CT 10
Westfield
Sch

CUMBERNAULD

Gartshore Moss
MOLLINS RD
ORCHARTON RD
MOSSYWOOD
WOODHEAD AVE
WESTFIELD DR
Mossywood
CRAIGSIDE RD
CRAIGSIDE PL
CRAIGSIDE CT
CRAIGSIDE
LECKETHILL VIEW
LECKETHILL AVE
LECKETHILL
7

G66
Newlands Farm
G68
GRAYSHILL RD
Westfield Ind Area
Moss Water
73

Sauchenhall
WESTFIELD PL
BADENHEATH PL
DEERDYKES VIEW
DEERDYKES PL
DEERDYKES CT N
DEERDYKES
Mast
CRAIGELVAN DR
CRAIGELVAN
GAINBURN GDNS
GAINBURN
6

Barbeth
Badenheath
DEERDYKES ROBT
OLD QUARRY
DEERDYKES RD
Sewage Works
DAGEND VIEW
CRAIGELVAN GR 1
CRAIGELVAN GDNS 2
GAINBURN CT 3
GAINBURN PL 4
5

Deerdykes
72

Luggie Water
Mollins Farm
Badenheath Bridge
Badenheath Park
4

THE GIRLES
ELLENVIEW CRES
DALCRUIN GDNS
ALTNACREAG GDNS
BLAIRDENAN AVE
STROTHFORD
GLENVIEW CRES
ARDMORE PL
Barrs
GARTFERRY RD
CUMBERNAULD RD
AIRDRIE RD
BADENHEATH TERR
MYVOT RD
Mollinsburn
G67
Adamswell
North Medrox
Spouty Braes

1 HARWOOD GDNS
2 WHITHORN CRES
3 DRYBURGH WLK
4 GLENLUCE GDNS
Factory
CUMBERNAULD RD
Mollinhillhead
3

BEDLAY WLK
Sch
G69
Works
Annathill Farm
71

1 DUNELLAN GDNS
2 DUNELLAN CRES
3 DUNELLAN WAY
4 DUNELLAN CT
5 LANGHOLM CT
6 HUNTLY PATH
7 DUNKELD LA
8 ARRAN LA
9 TORWOOD LA
10 SEAFORTH LA
11 ADAMSWELL TERR
12 RANNOCH LA
13 ATHOLL LA
14 GARTMORE LA
15 IONA LA
16 STRATHYRE GDNS
17 MOSSVALE TERR
Mollins Burn
ML5
2

Leckethill
ANNATHILL
BEDLAY PL
Annathill
1

Avenuehead Farm
Mast
M73
Woodend
South Medrox
GAIN RD
70

Refuse Tip
BIRKENSHAW RD

| | A | B | C | D | E | F | |

70   71   72

CUMBERNAULD

CONDORRAT INTC

G68

WESTFIELD RD
St Maurices
High Sch

Low
Wood

GLASGOW RD

1 NETHERWOOD RD
2 NETHERWOOD WAY
3 NETHERWOOD AVE

St Francis
of Assisi
Prim Sch

Libby

Condorrat
Prim Sch

Condorrat

DALSHANNON WAY
TEMPLE COTTS

St Helen's
Prim Sch

Ravenswood
Prim Sch

LANGLANDS-SEAFAR
INTC

SEAFAR RDBT   KENILWORTH
CT

Greenfaulds

Greenfaulds
High Sch

1 AVONHEAD AVE
2 DRUMPELLIER GR

Sch

Woodlands
Prim Sch

Greenfaulds

Sch

Nursery

AUCHENKILNS
HOLDINGS

CHAPELTON RD

North
Myvot

Luggie Water

Dalshannon

CONDORRAT RING RD

MUIRHEAD RD

MYVOT RD

North
Myvot

G67

Garngibboch
House

Wester
Blairlinn

Milncroft

SPAIRDRUM RD

North
Bellstane
Plantation

Blairlinn
Ind Est

South
Myvot

Craigend
Nursery

Wester
Myvot

WESTER MYVOT RD

Gain Burn

Hallbrae

Loanhead

Summerhill

CONDORRAT RD

Summerhill Strips

Shankburn

Shank
Bridge

Bellstane

ML5

Summerfield

GAIN & SHANKBURN RD

Mossywood

The Grain

Douglas Glen

South Bellstane
Plantation

Gain Farm

GAIN RD

Cleddans

Douglas
Plantation

ML6

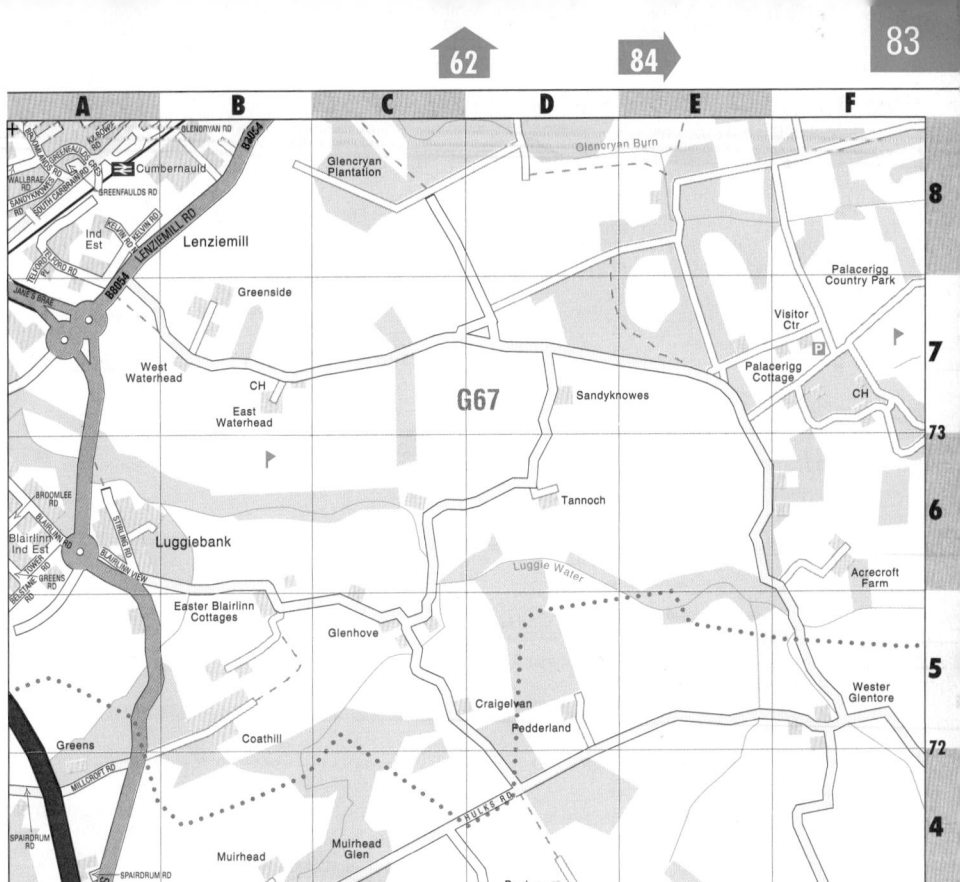

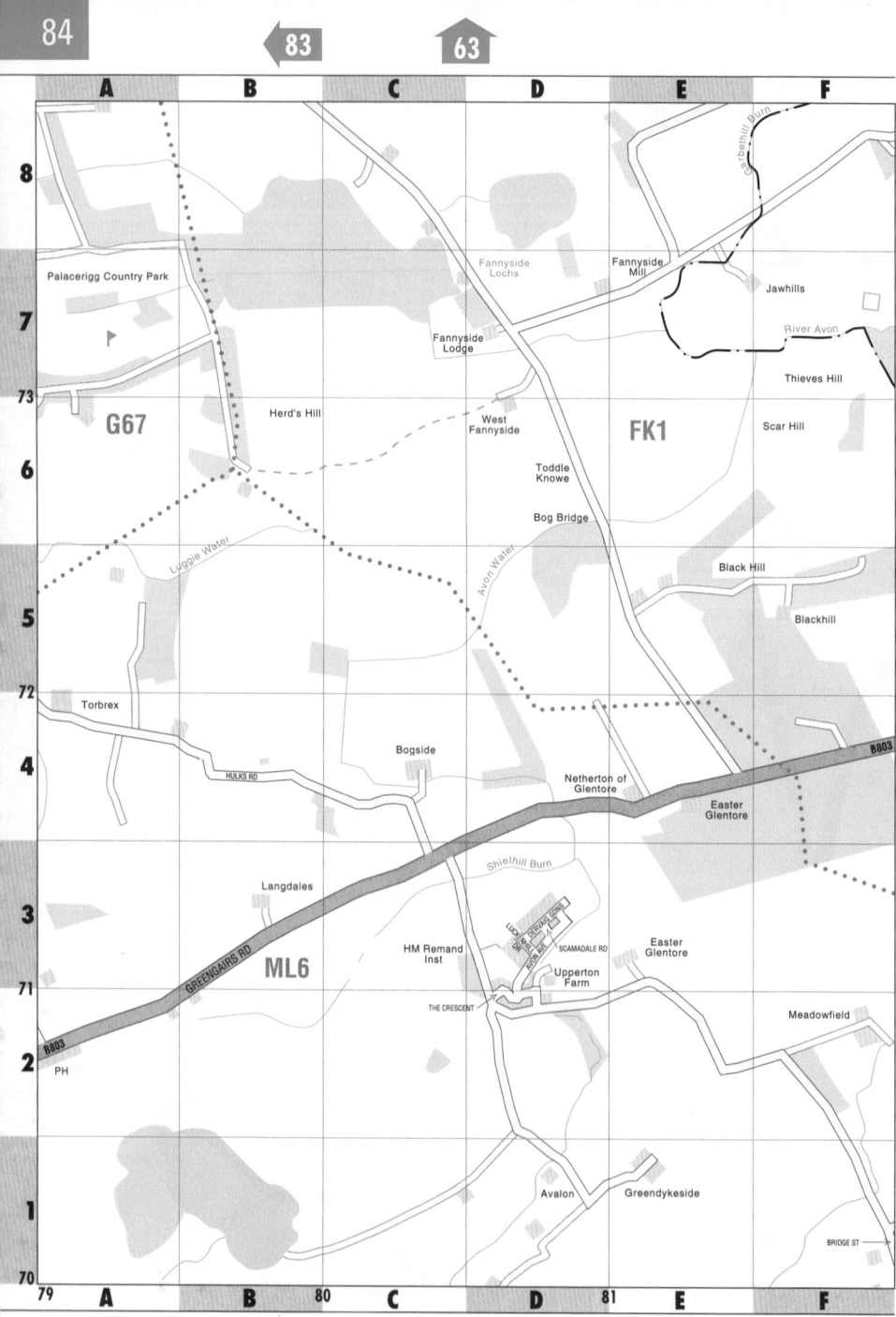

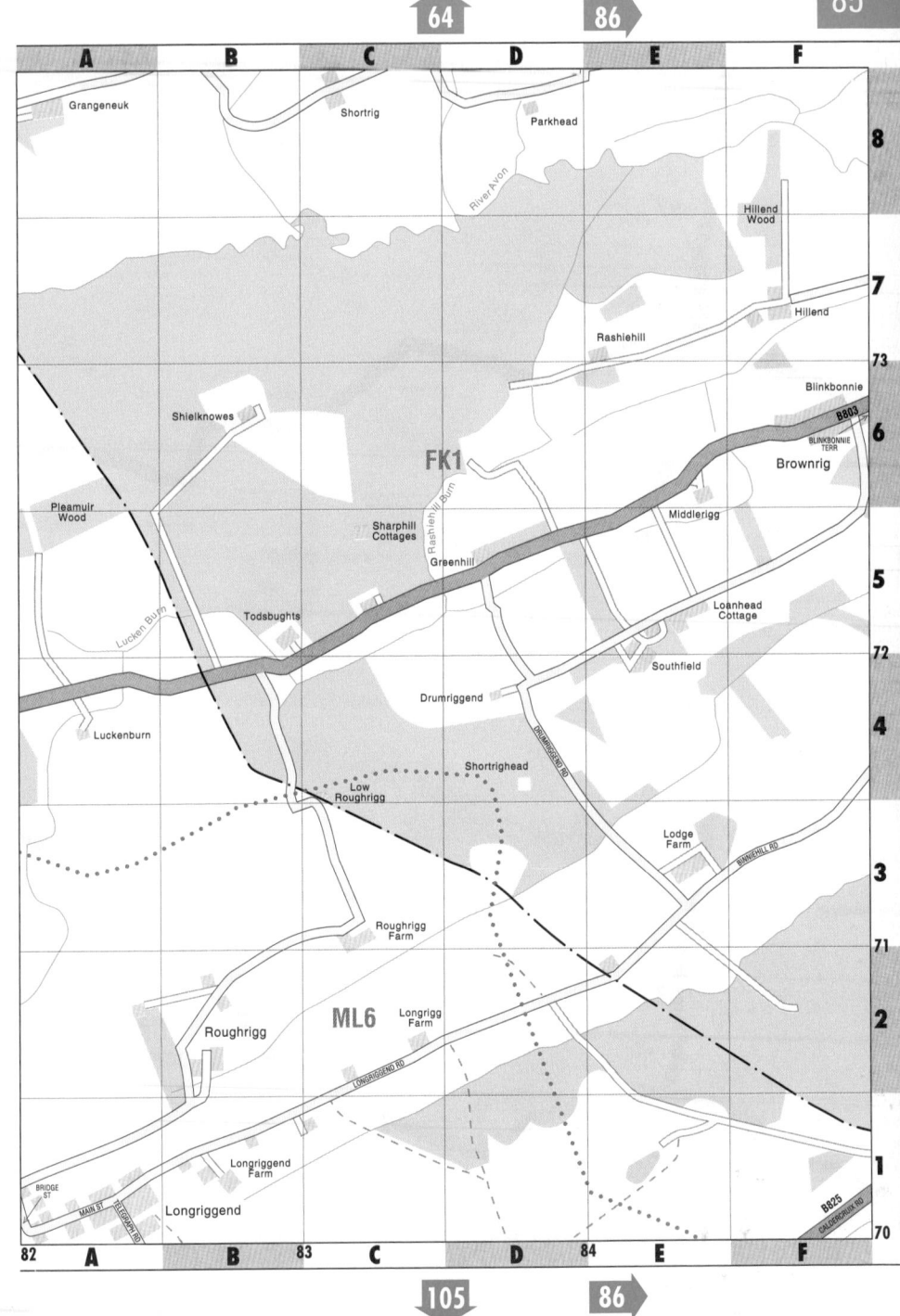

A B C D E F

8

7

73

6

5

72

4

71

2

1

70

Grangeneuk

Shortrig

Parkhead

River Avon

Hillend Wood

Hillend

Rashiehill

Blinkbonnie

B803

BLINKBONNIE TERR

Brownrig

Shielknowes

FK1

Pleamuir Wood

Sharphill Cottages

Rashiehill Burn

Greenhill

Middlerigg

Lucken Burn

Todsbughts

Loanhead Cottage

Southfield

Luckenburn

Drumriggend

DRUMRIGGEND RD

Shortrighead

Low Roughrigg

Lodge Farm

BANNIEHILL RD

Roughrigg Farm

ML6

Roughrigg

Longrigg Farm

LONGRIGGEND RD

Longriggend Farm

BRIDGE ST

MAIN ST

TELEGRAPH RD

Longriggend

B825

CALDERCRUIX RD

A B C D E F

82 83 84

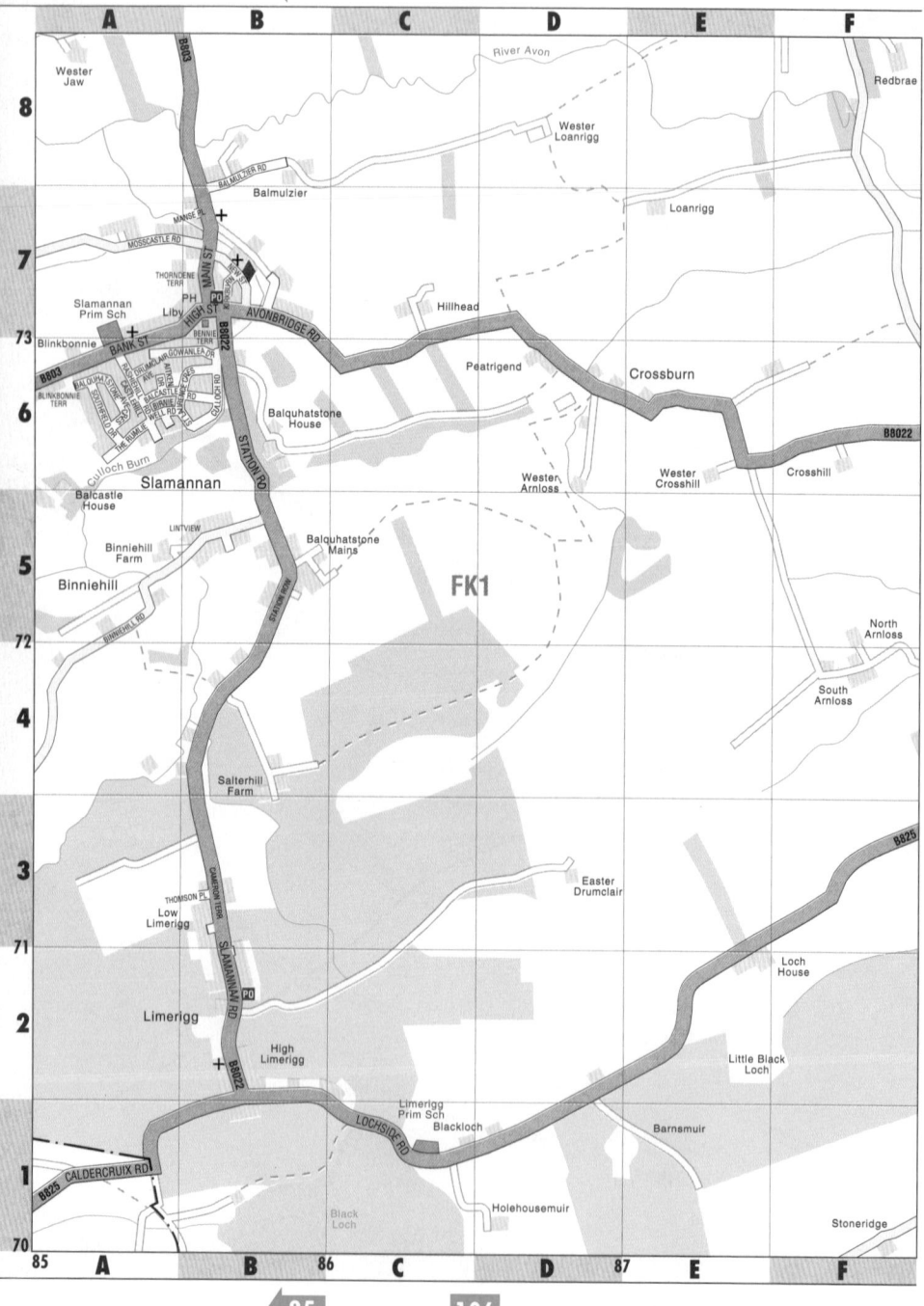

A B C D E F

8

Wester
Jaw

River Avon

Redbrae

Wester
Loanrigg

Loanrigg

7

MANSE PL
MOSSCASTLE RD
BALMULZIER RD
Balmulzier

THORNDENE
TERR

Slamannan
Prim Sch

73

Blinkbonnie

BANK ST
HIGH ST
MAIN'S INN RD
B803
PH
PO
Lib

AVONBRIDGE RD
B8022

Hillhead

Peatrigend

Crossburn

B8022

6

BLINKBONNIE
TERR

B803
BALQUHATSTONE PL
SOUTHFIELD AV
GILMOUR AV
GOWANLEA DR
BENNIE TERR
BALCASTLE RD
CH LLOYD RD
BINNIE
WYND

THE LIME

Culloch Burn

STATION RD

Balquhatstone
House

Wester
Arnloss

Wester
Crosshill

Crosshill

Slamannan

Balcastle
House

LINTVIEW

Binniehill
Farm

Balquhatstone
Mains

FK1

North
Arnloss

5

BINNIEHILL RD

Binniehill

STATION BRAE

South
Arnloss

72

4

Salterhill
Farm

3

B825

THOMSON PL
CAMERON TERR
Low
Limerigg

Easter
Drumclair

Loch
House

71

SLAMANNAN RD
PO

2

Limerigg

High
Limerigg

Little Black
Loch

B8022

Limerigg
Prim Sch
Blackloch

LOCHSIDE RD

Barnsmuir

1

B825
CALDERCRUIX RD

Holehousemuir

Stoneridge

Black
Loch

70

85 A B 86 C D 87 E F

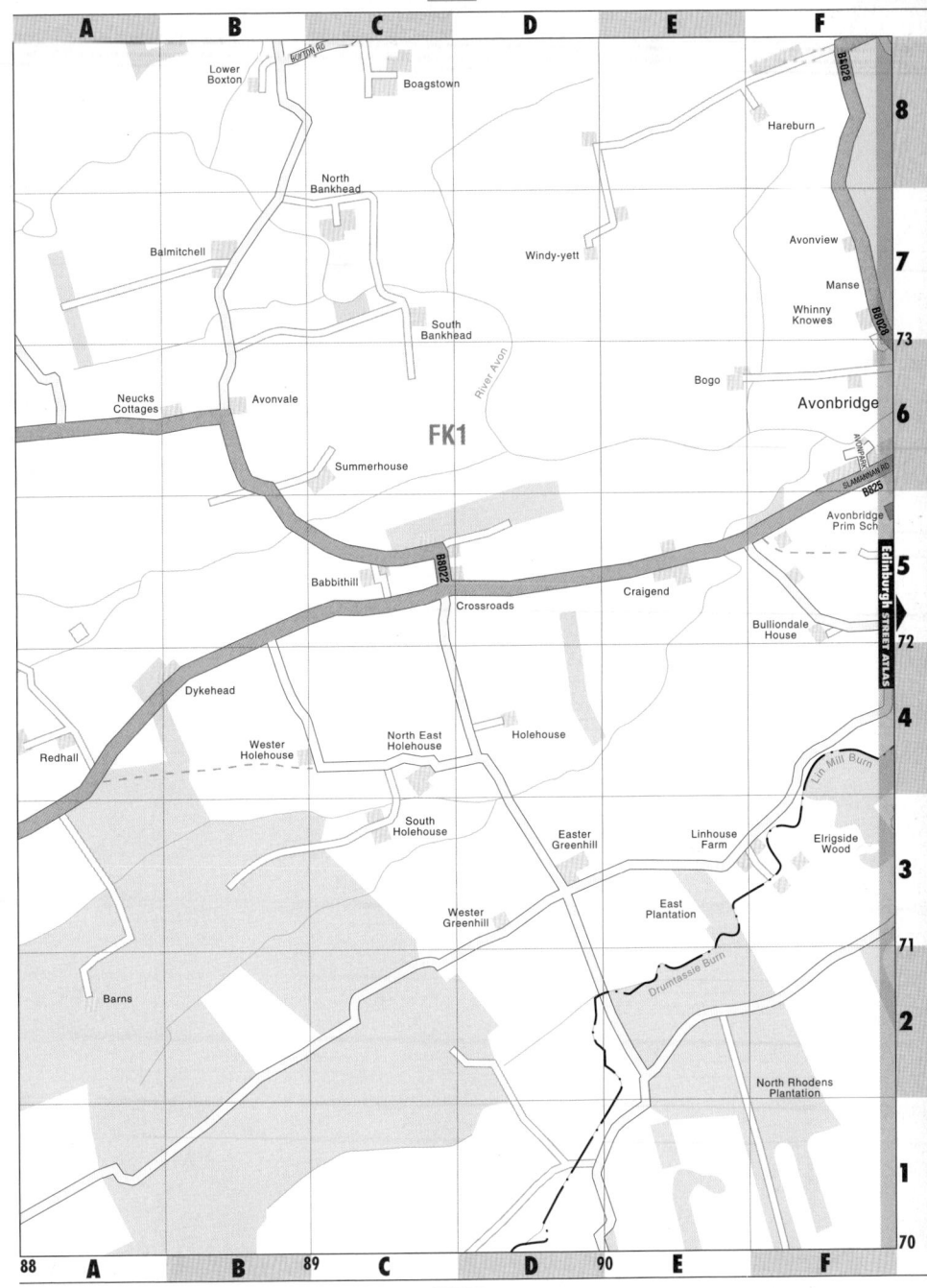

| A | B | C | D | E | F |

Lower Boxton

Boagstown

B8028

Hareburn

8

North Bankhead

Avonview

Balmitchell

Windy-yett

Manse

7

Whinny Knowes

B8028

South Bankhead

73

River Avon

Bogo

Avonbridge

Neucks Cottages

Avonvale

6

FK1

Summerhouse

SLAMANNAN RD

B825

Avonbridge Prim Sch

Babbithill

B8022

Craigend

Edinburgh STREET ATLAS

5

Crossroads

Bulliondale House

72

Dykehead

Holehouse

4

Redhall

Wester Holehouse

North East Holehouse

Lin Mill Burn

South Holehouse

Easter Greenhill

Linhouse Farm

Elrigside Wood

3

Wester Greenhill

East Plantation

71

Barns

Drumtassie Burn

2

North Rhodens Plantation

1

70

| 88 | A | B | 89 | C | D | 90 | E | F |

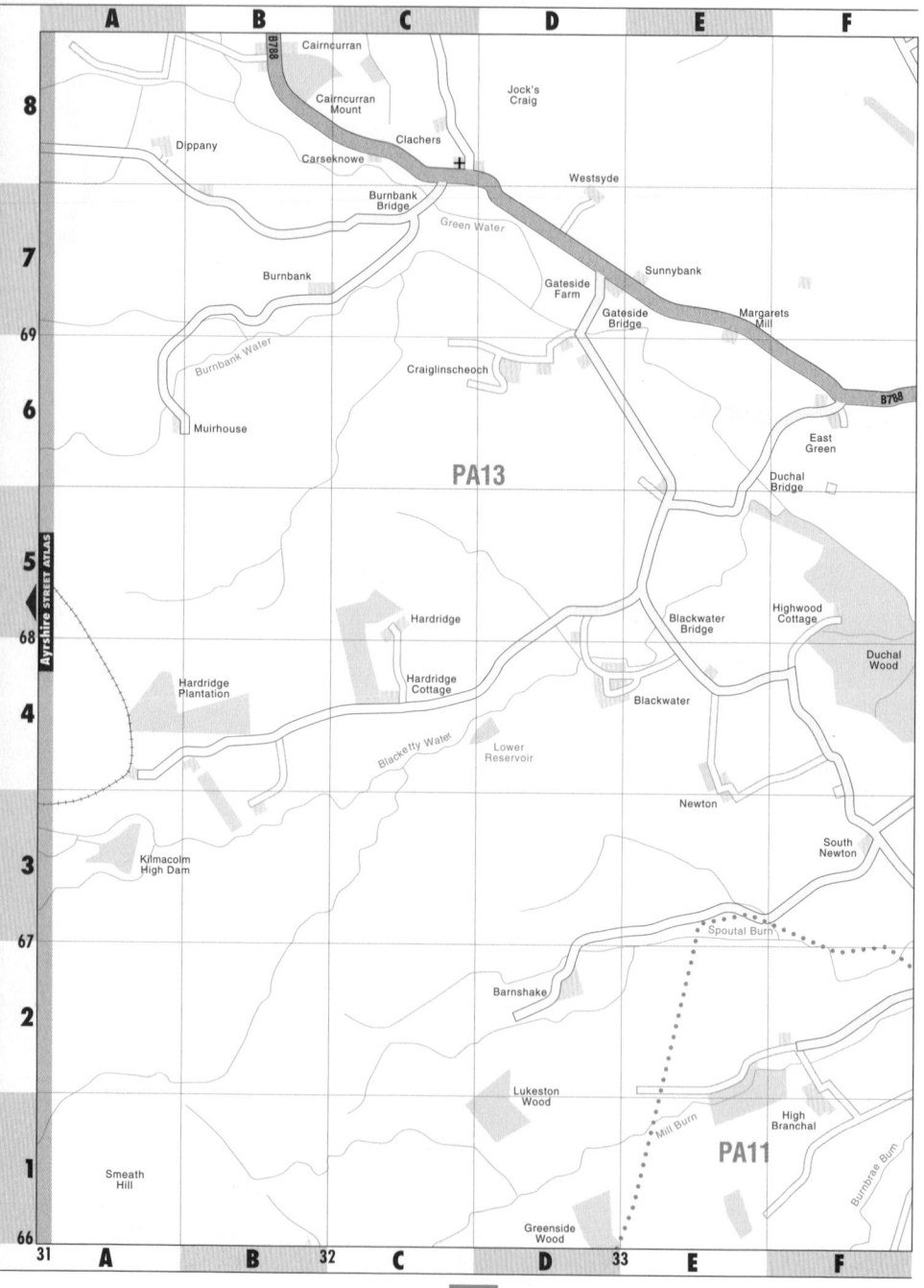

Ayrshire STREET ATLAS

B788

Cairncurran

Cairncurran
Mount

Jock's
Craig

Clachers

Dippany

Carseknowe

Westsyde

Burnbank
Bridge

Green Water

Burnbank

Sunnybank

Burnbank Water

Gateside
Farm

Gateside
Bridge

Margarets
Mill

Craiglinscheoch

B788

Muirhouse

PA13

East
Green

Duchal
Bridge

Blackwater
Bridge

Highwood
Cottage

Hardridge

Duchal
Wood

Hardridge
Plantation

Hardridge
Cottage

Blackwater

Blacketty Water

Lower
Reservoir

Newton

Kilmacolm
High Dam

South
Newton

Spoutal Burn

Barnshake

Lukeston
Wood

High
Branchal

Mill Burn

PA11

Burnbrae Burn

Smeath
Hill

Greenside
Wood

8

7

69

6

5

68

4

3

67

2

1

66

A   B   C   D   E   F

31   32   33

Knockbuckle
Netherwood
Slates

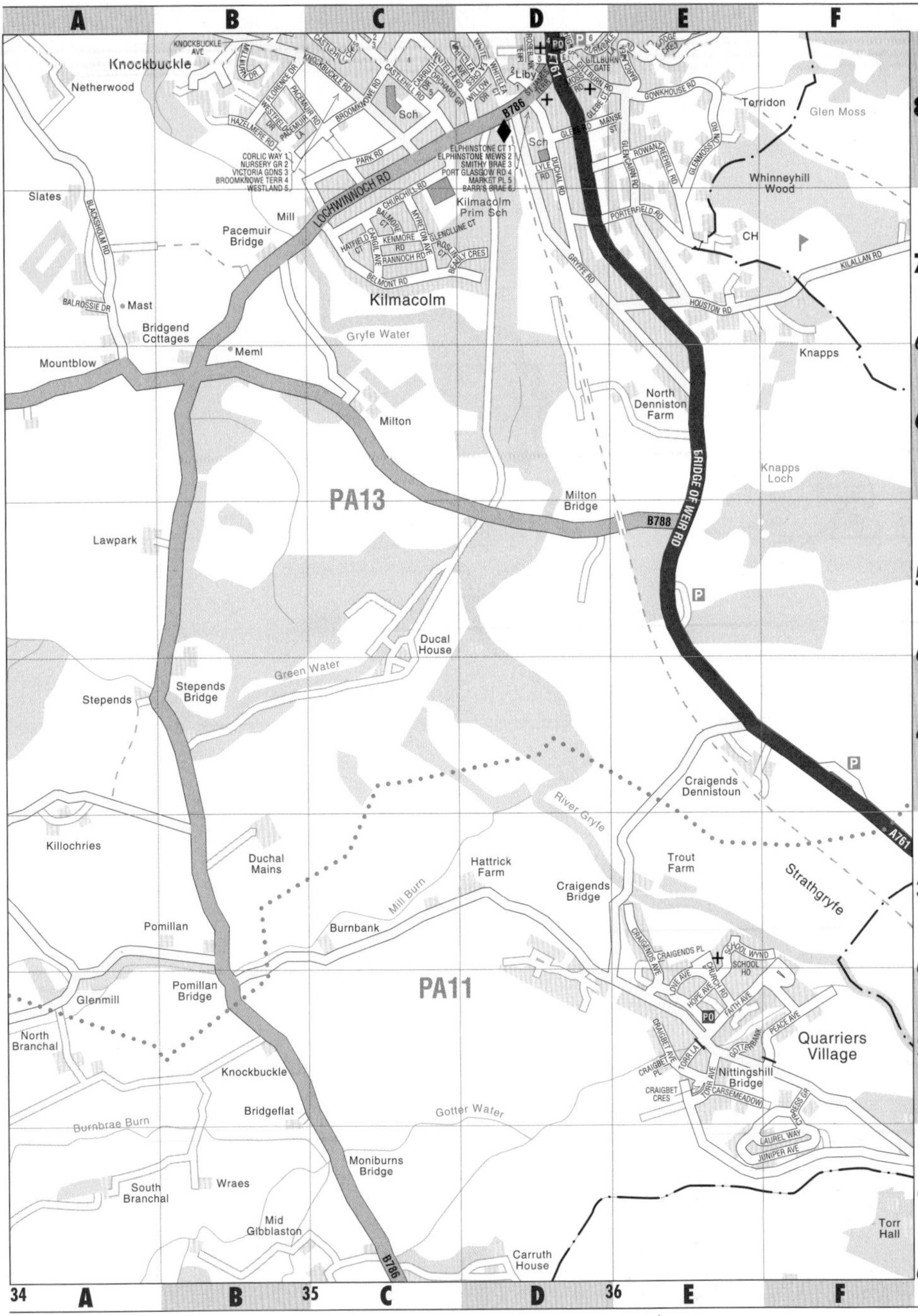

CORLIC WAY 1
NURSERY GR 2
VICTORIA GDNS 3
BROOMKNOWE TERR 4
WESTLAND 5

ELPHINSTONE CT 1
ELPHINSTONE MEWS 2
SMITHY BRAE 3
PORT GLASGOW RD 4
MARKET PL 5
BARR'S BRAE 6

KNOCKBUCKLE AVE

LOCHWINNOCH RD

PARK RD

B788

Sch

Kilmacolm
Prim Sch

Kilmacolm

Lib'y

PO

B761

GOWKHOUSE RD

Torridon
Glen Moss

Whinneyhill
Wood

CH

NILALLAN RD

PORTERFIELD RD

HOUSTON RD

Mill
Pacemuir
Bridge

Bridgend
Cottages

Meml

BALROSSIE DR

Mast

Mountblow

Lawpark

Stepends

Killochries

Pomillan

Glenmill

North
Branchal

South
Branchal

Wraes

Mid
Gibblaston

Knockbuckle

Bridgeflat

Pomillan
Bridge

Duchal
Mains

Stepends
Bridge

Ducal
House

Green Water

Gryfe Water

Milton

Milton
Bridge

PA13

BRIDGE OF WEIR RD

B788

North
Denniston
Farm

Knapps

Knapps
Loch

P

Knaps 69

Craigends
Dennistoun

Strathgryfe

A761

P

Burnbank

Mill Burn

River Gryfe

Hattrick
Farm

Craigends
Bridge

Trout
Farm

PA11

CRAIGENDS PL

SCHOOL RD

CHAPEL WYND

PO

Quarriers
Village

Nittingshill
Bridge

CRAIGBET
CRES

LAUREL WAY

JUNIPER AVE

Burnbrae Burn

Gotter Water

Moniburns
Bridge

Carruth
House

Torr
Hall

B786

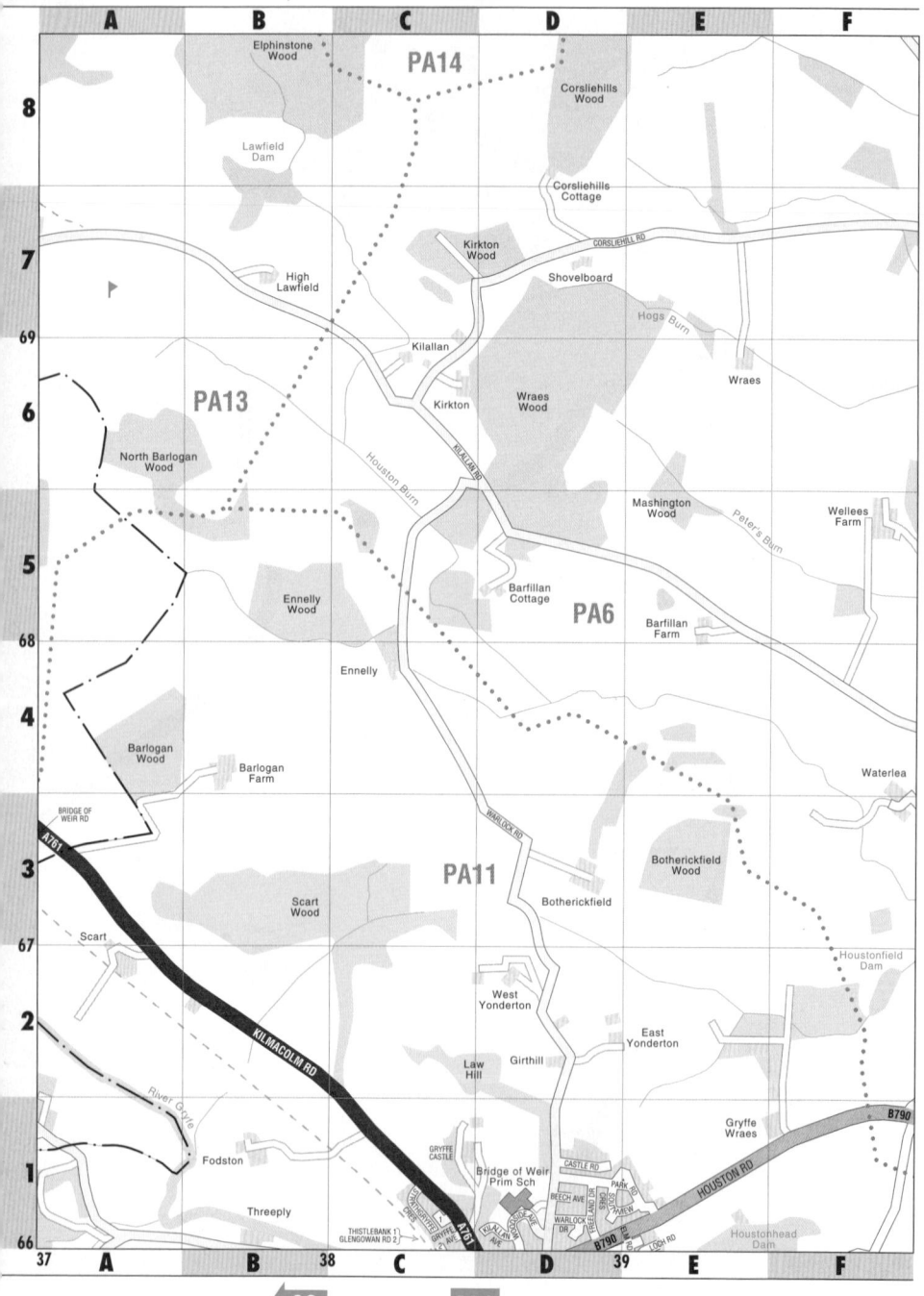

71 92

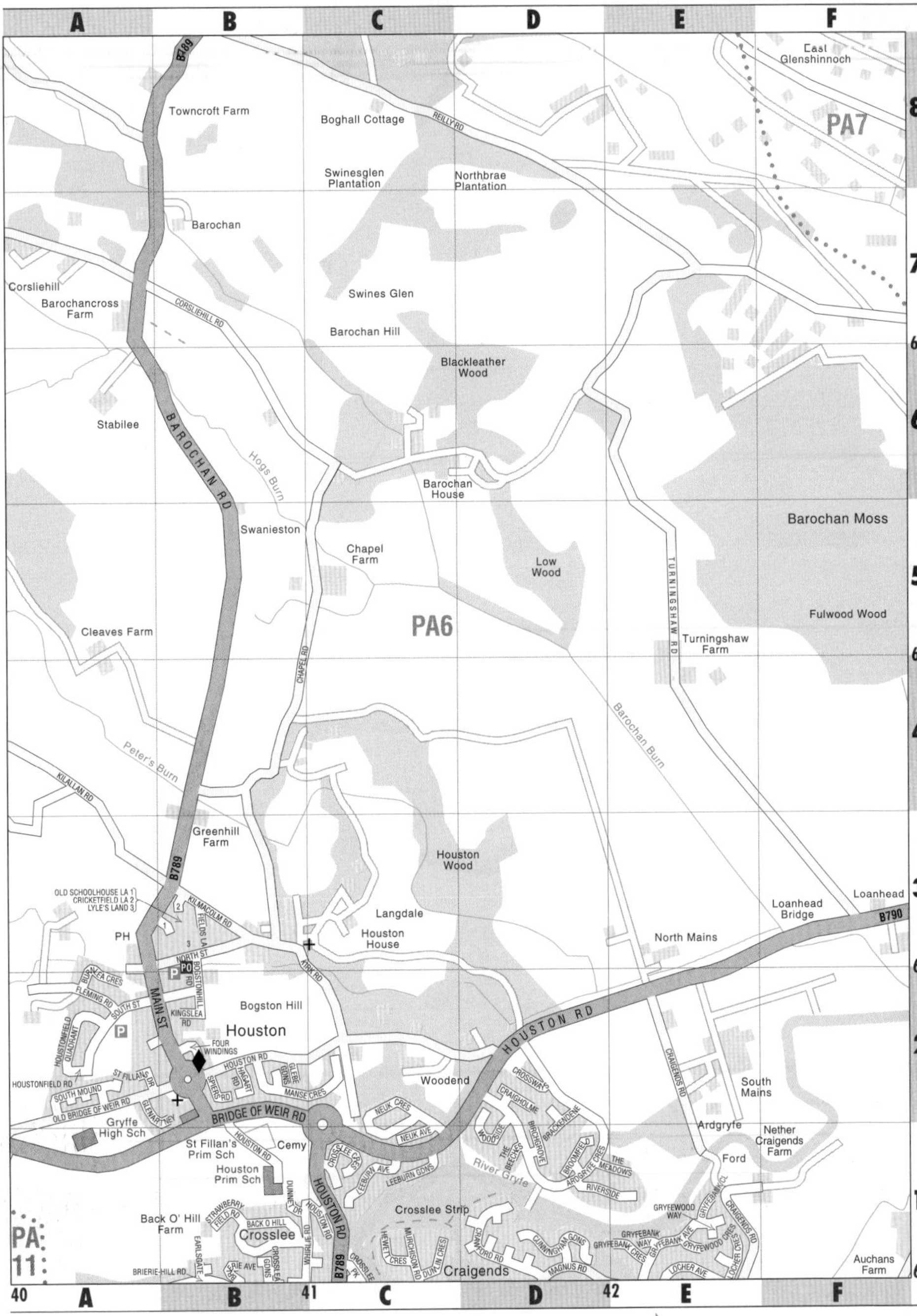

	A	B	C	D	E	F

Towncroft Farm

Boghall Cottage

East Glenshinnoch

PA7

8

Swinesglen Plantation

Northbrae Plantation

Barochan

7

Corsliehill

Barochancross Farm

CORSLIEHILL RD

Swines Glen

Barochan Hill

69

Blackleather Wood

Stabilee

Hogs Burn

Barochan House

6

BAROCHAN RD

Swanieston

Chapel Farm

Low Wood

Barochan Moss

Fulwood Wood

5

PA6

Cleaves Farm

Peter's Burn

TURNINGSHAW RD

Turningshaw Farm

68

KILALLAN RD

Barochan Burn

4

Greenhill Farm

B789

Houston Wood

Langdale

Loanhead Bridge

Loanhead

3

OLD SCHOOLHOUSE LA 1
CRICKETFIELD LA 2
LYLE'S LAND 3

KIRK RD

Houston House

North Mains

B790

67

PH

PO
P

Bogston Hill

Houston

HOUSTON RD

South Mains

2

SOUTH MOUND

Woodend

Ardgryfe

Ford

Nether Craigends Farm

Gryffe High Sch

St Fillan's Prim Sch

BRIDGE OF WEIR RD

Cemy

River Gryfe

1

Houston Prim Sch

Crosslee Strip

GRYFEWOOD WAY

Auchans Farm

66

Back O' Hill Farm

Crosslee

B789

Craigends

PA 11

40	A	B	41	C	D	42	E	F

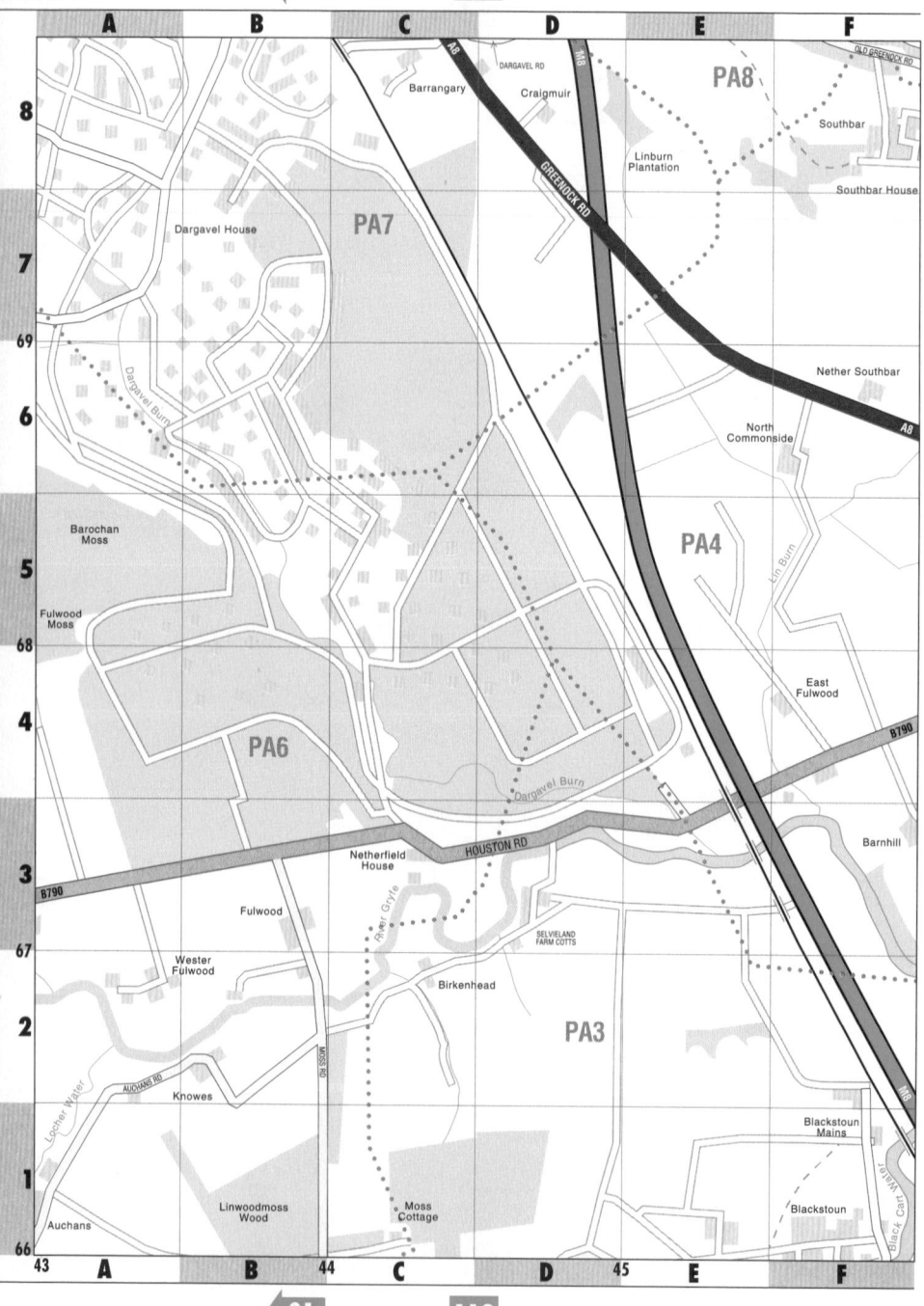

A   B   C   D   E   F

8

DARGAVEL RD

Barrangary   Craigmuir

PA8

Southbar

OLD GREENOCK RD

Southbar House

Dargavel House

PA7

Linburn
Plantation

7

GREENOCK RD

69

Nether Southbar

A8

6

Dargavel Burn

North
Commonside

Barochan
Moss

PA4

Lin Burn

5

Fulwood
Moss

68

East
Fulwood

4

PA6

B790

Dargavel Burn

Barnhill

Netherfield
House

HOUSTON RD

3

B790

River Gryfe

Fulwood

SELVIELAND
FARM COTTS

67

Wester
Fulwood

Birkenhead

PA3

2

MOSS RD

AUCHANS RD

Locher Water

Knowes

Blackstoun
Mains

M8

1

Auchans

Linwoodmoss
Wood

Moss
Cottage

Blackstoun

Black Cart

66

43   A   B   44   C   D   45   E   F

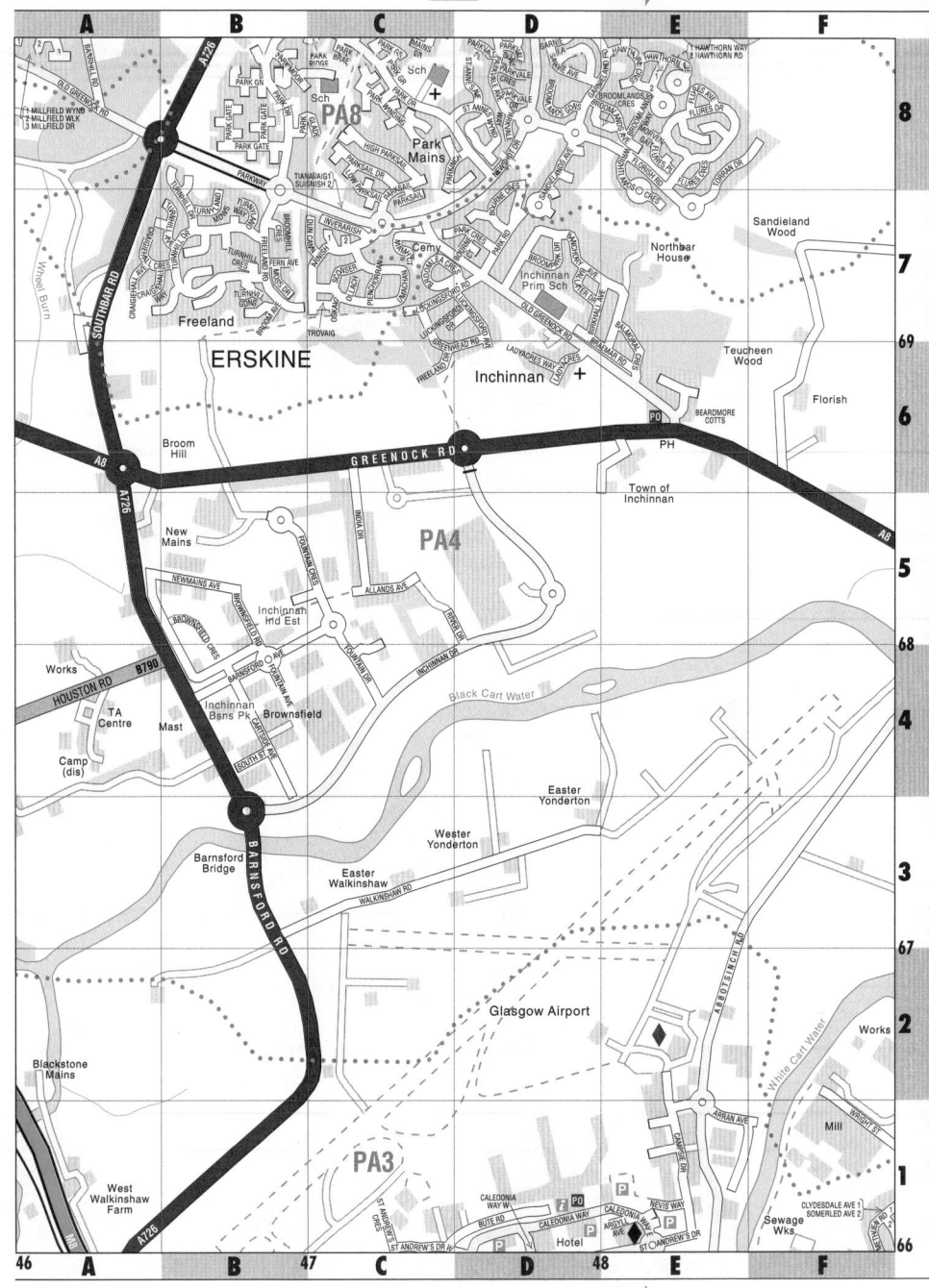

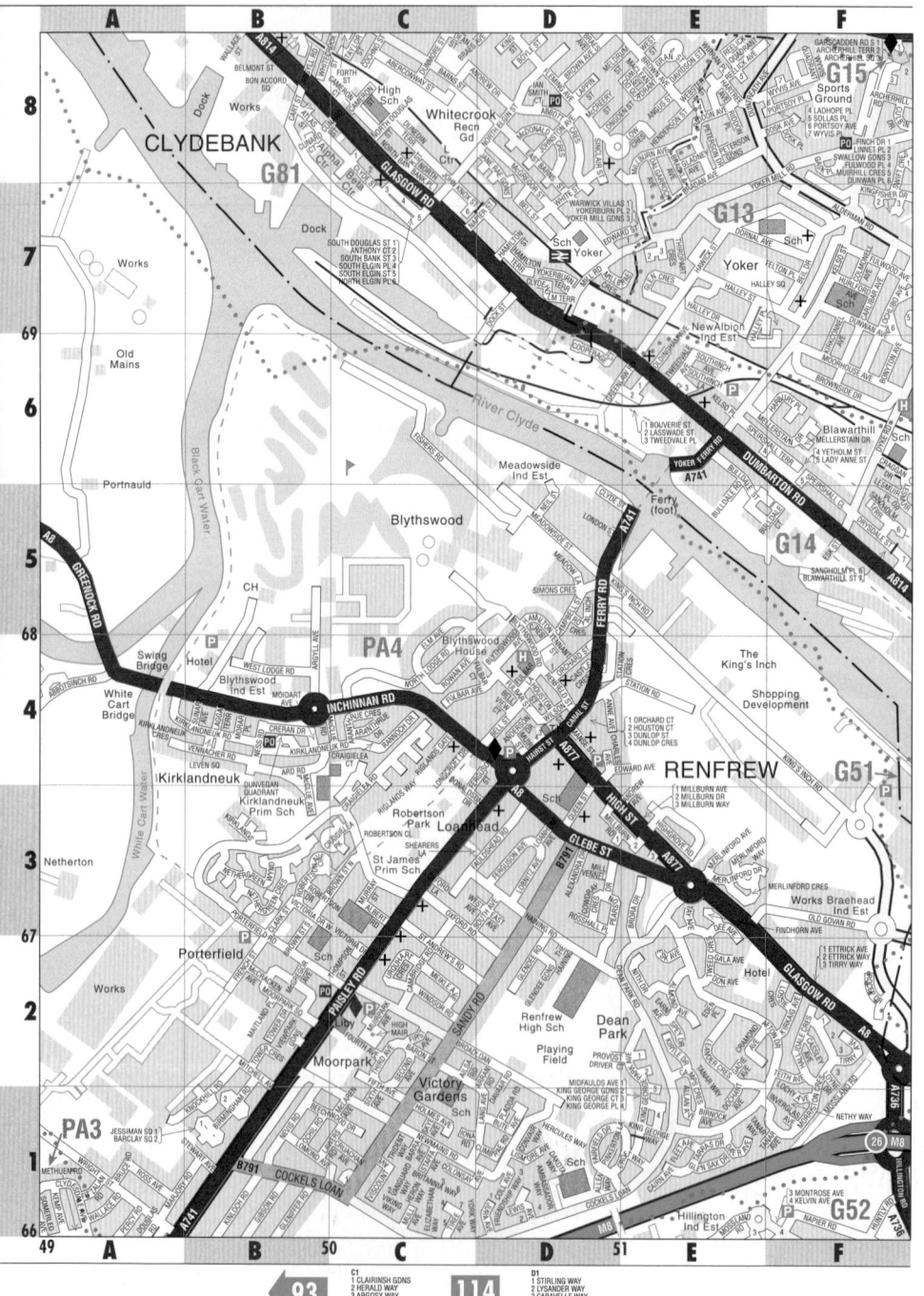

C1
1 CLAIRINSH GDNS
2 HERALD WAY
3 ARGOSSY WAY
4 LANCASTER WAY
5 WELLINGTON WAY
6 ANSON WAY
7 HALIFAX WAY

D1
1 STIRLING WAY
2 LYSANDER WAY
3 CARAVELLE WAY
4 HAMPDEN WAY

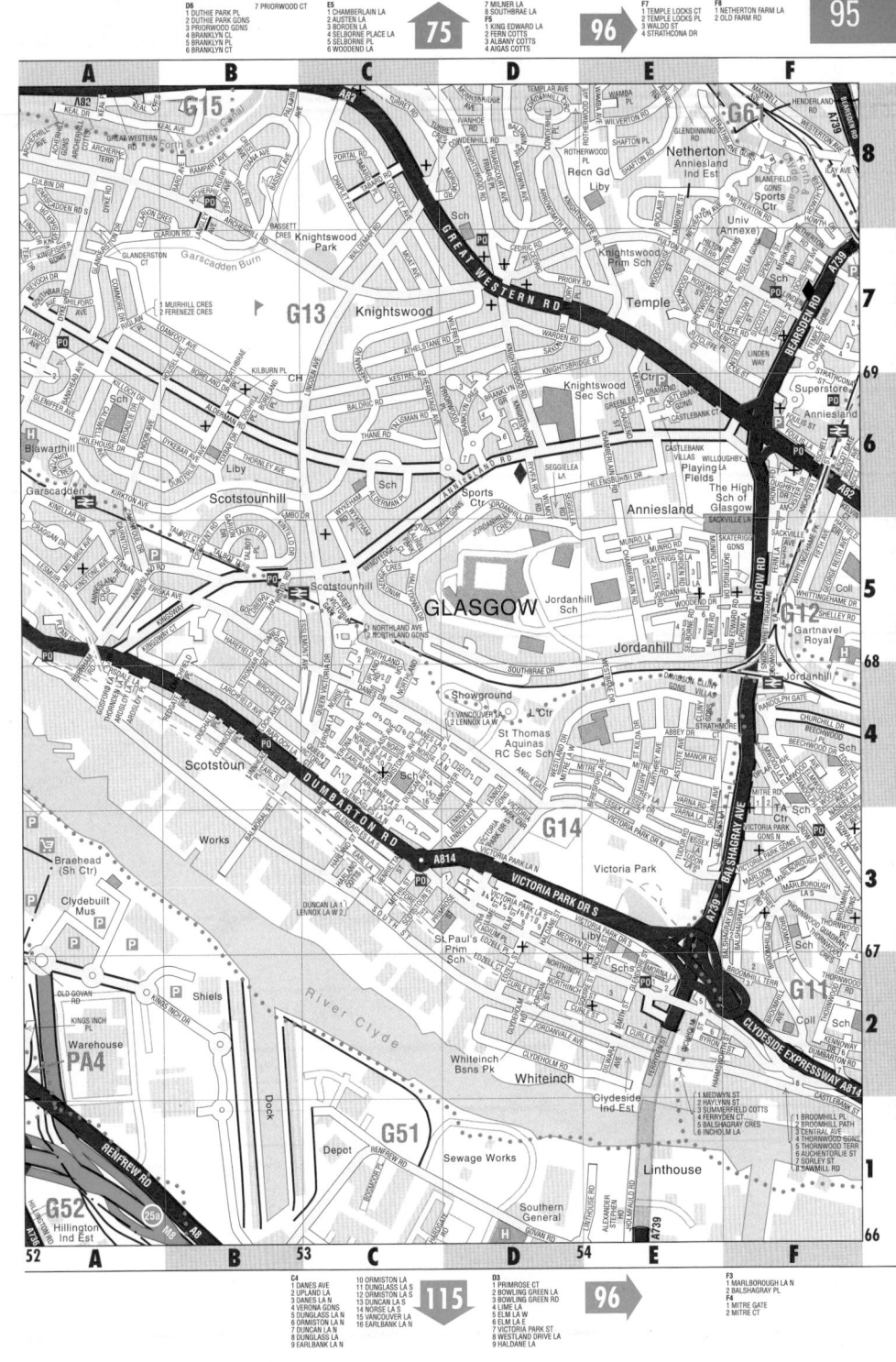

D6
1 DUTHIE PARK PL
2 DUTHIE PARK GDNS
3 PRIORWOOD GDNS
4 BRANKLYN CL
5 BRANKLYN PL
6 BRANKLYN CT

7 PRIORWOOD CT

E5
1 CHAMBERLAIN LA
2 AUSTEN LA
3 BORDEN LA
4 SELBORNE PLACE LA
5 SELBORNE PL
6 WOODEND LA

7 MILNER LA
8 SOUTHBRAE LA
F5
1 KING EDWARD LA
2 FERN COTTS
3 ALBANY COTTS
4 AIGAS COTTS

F7
1 TEMPLE LOCKS CT
2 TEMPLE LOCKS PL
3 WALSD ST
4 STRATHCONA DR

F8
1 NETHERTON FARM LA
2 OLD FARM LA

75

96

95

C4
1 DANES AVE
2 UPLAND LA
3 DANES LA N
4 VERONA GDNS
5 DUNGLASS LA N
6 ORMISTON LA N
7 DUNCAN LA N
8 DUNGLASS LA
9 EARLBANK LA N

10 ORMISTON LA
11 DUNGLASS LA S
12 ORMISTON LA S
13 DUNCAN LA S
14 NORSE LA S
15 VANCOUVER LA
16 EARLBANK LA N

115

D3
1 PRIMROSE CT
2 BOWLING GREEN LA
3 BOWLING GREEN RD
4 LIME LA
5 ELM LA W
6 ELM LA E
7 VICTORIA PARK ST
8 WESTLAND DRIVE LA
9 HALDANE LA

96

F3
1 MARLBOROUGH LA N
2 BALSHAGRAY PL
F4
1 MITRE GATE
2 MITRE CT

A3
1 MONKSCROFT AVE
2 KIRKMICHAEL GDNS
3 KIRKMICHAEL AVE
4 THORNWOOD DR
5 BLAIRATHOLL GDNS
6 TIBBERMORE RD

B3
1 KINGSBOROUGH GATE
2 TURNBERRY AVE
3 HILLSIDE GARDENS LA
4 QUEENSBOROUGH GDNS
5 PRINCES GARDENS LA

B4
1 DEVONSHIRE GDNS
2 DEVONSHIRE GDNS LA
3 WESTBOURNE TERR LA S
C5
1 THORNBRIDGE AVE
2 BELLSHAUGH PL

D5
1 GARRIOCH CRES
2 GARRIOCH QUADRANT
3 WYNDFORD PL
4 DUNBETH PL
5 LATHERON DR
6 INVERSHIN DR

7 KIRKHILL PL
8 GARRIOCH GATE

95   76

For full street detail of the highlighted area see page 240.

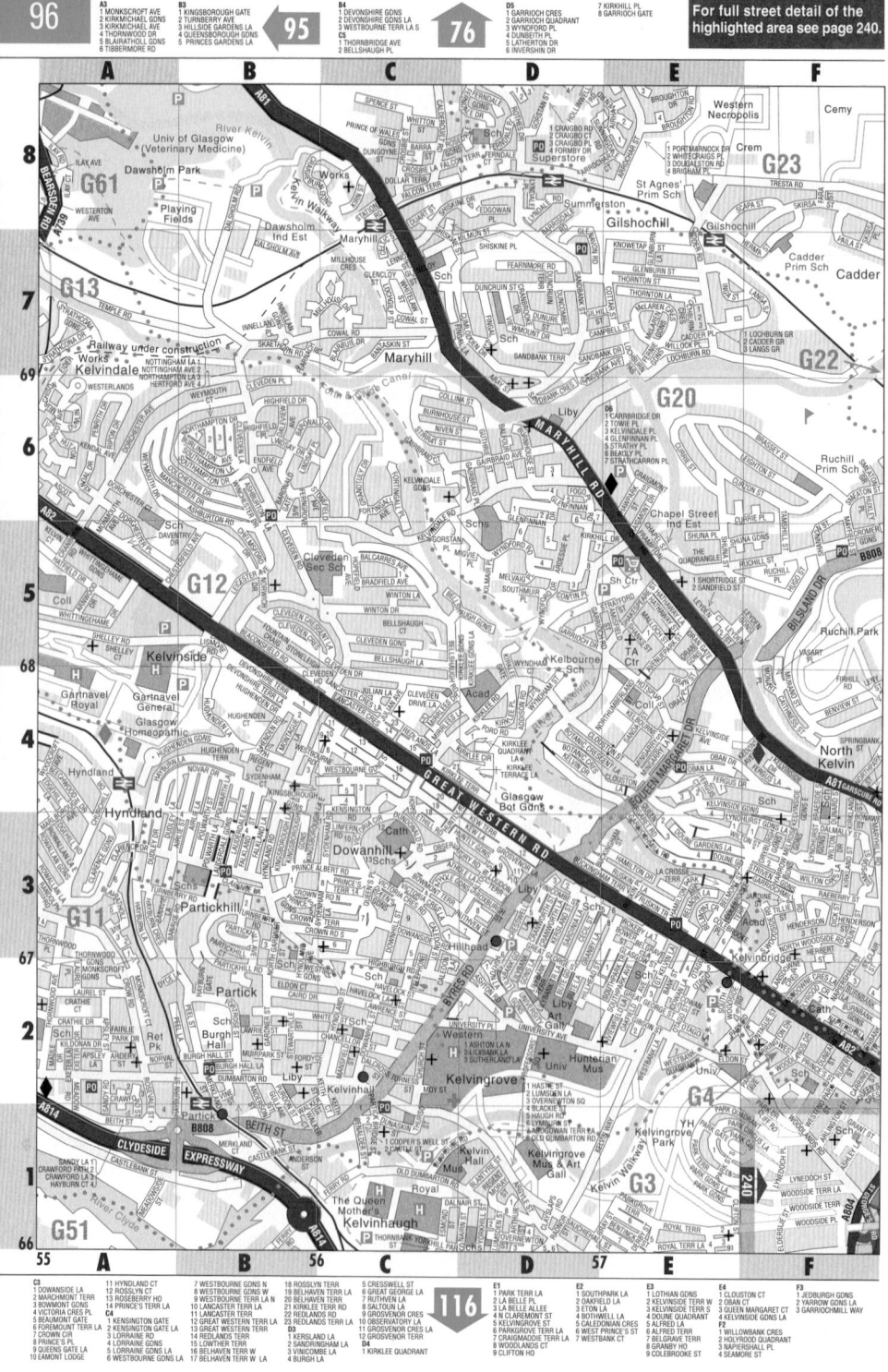

C3
1 DOWANSIDE LA
2 MARCHMONT TERR
3 HYNDLAND GDNS
4 VICTORIA CRES PL
5 BEAUMONT GATE
6 FOREMOUNT TERR LA
7 CROWN CIR
8 PRINCE'S PL
9 QUEENS GATE LA
10 EAMONT LODGE

11 HYNDLAND CT
12 ROSSLYN CT
13 PRINCE'S TERR LA
C4
1 KENSINGTON GATE
2 KENSINGTON GATE LA
3 LORRAINE RD
4 LORRAINE GDNS
5 LORRAINE GDNS LA
6 WESTBOURNE GDNS LA

7 WESTBOURNE GDNS N
8 WESTBOURNE GDNS W
9 WESTBOURNE TERR LA N
10 LANCASTER TERR LA
11 LANCASTER TERR
12 GREAT WESTERN TERR LA
13 GREAT WESTERN TERR
14 REDLANDS TERR
15 LOWTHER TERR
16 BELHAVEN TERR W
17 BELHAVEN TERR W LA

18 ROSSLYN TERR
19 BELHAVEN TERR
20 BELHAVEN TERR LA
21 KIRKLEE TERR RD
22 REDLANDS RD
23 REDLANDS TERR LA
D3
1 KERSLAND LA
2 SANDRINGHAM LA
3 VINICOMBE LA
4 BURGH LA
D4
1 KIRKLEE QUADRANT

5 CRESSWELL ST
6 GREAT GEORGE LA
7 RUTHVEN LA
8 SALTOUN LA
9 GROSVENOR CRES
10 OBSERVATORY LA
11 GROSVENOR CRES LA
12 GROSVENOR TERR
E1
1 PARK TERR LA
2 LA BELLE PL
3 LA BELLE ALLEE
4 N CLAREMONT ST
5 KELVINGROVE ST
6 CALEDONIAN CRES
7 WESTBANK CT

E2
1 SOUTHPARK LA
2 OAKFIELD LA
3 ETON LA
4 BOTHWELL LA
5 PARKGROVE TERR LA
6 WEST PRINCE'S LA
7 WESTBANK CT

E3
1 LOTHIAN GDNS
2 KELVINSIDE TERR W
3 KELVINSIDE TERR S
4 DOUNE QUADRANT
5 ALFRED LA
6 ALFRED TERR
7 BELGRAVE TERR
8 GRANBY HO
9 COLEBROOKE ST

E4
1 CLOUSTON CT
2 OBAN CT
3 QUEEN MARGARET CT
4 KELVINSIDE GDNS LA
F3
1 JEDBURGH GDNS
2 YARROW GDNS LA
3 GARRIOCHMILL WAY

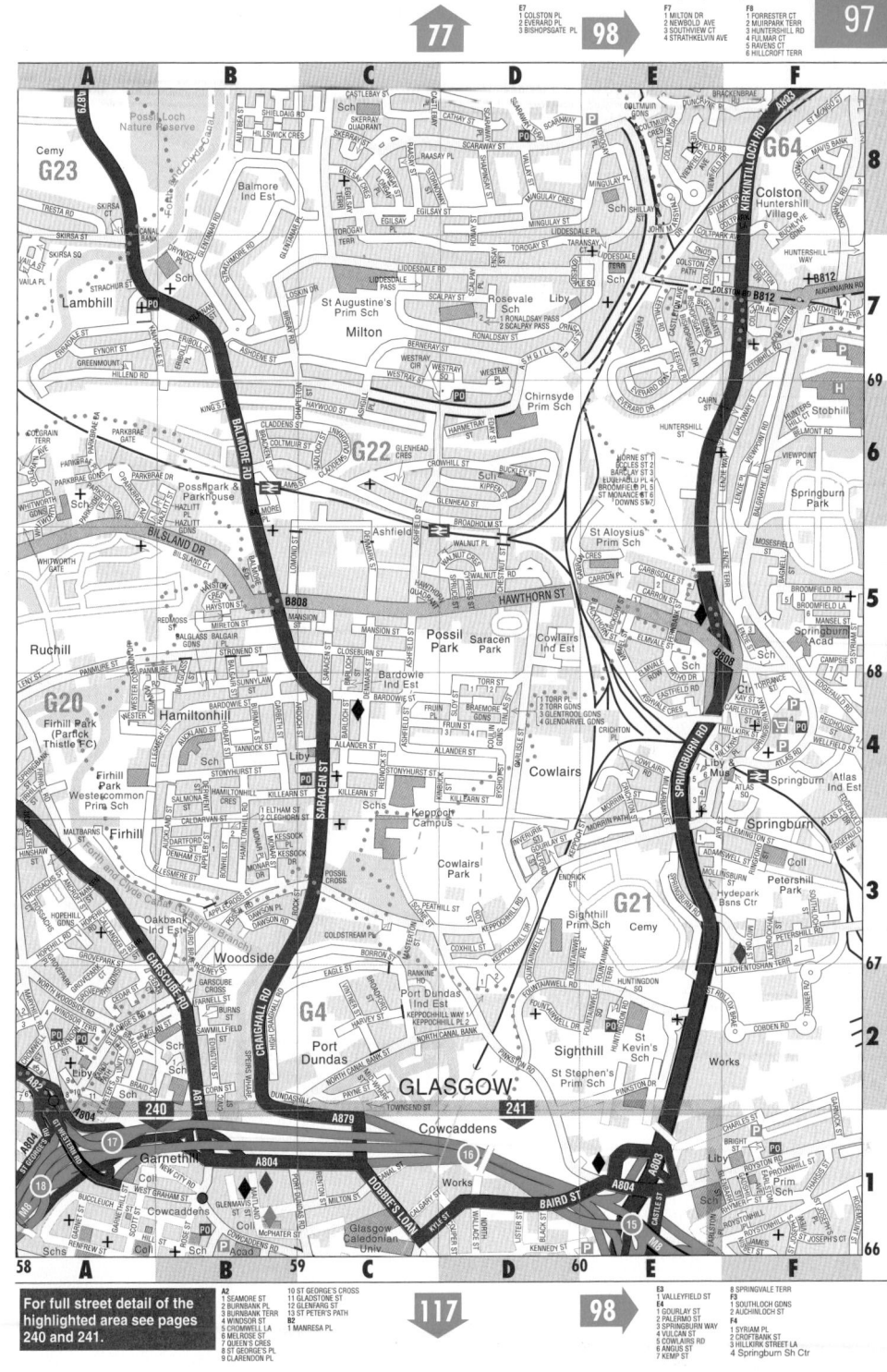

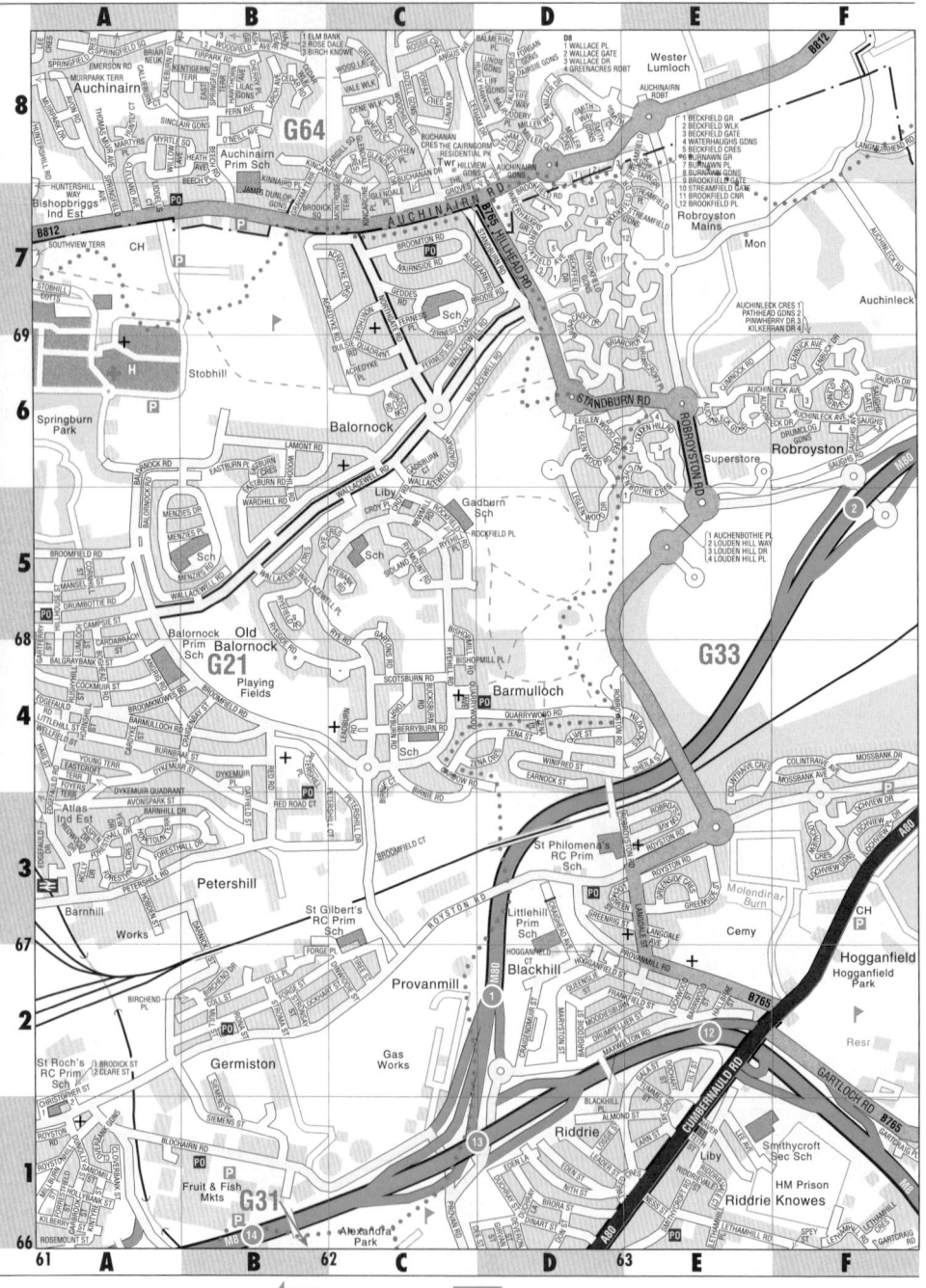

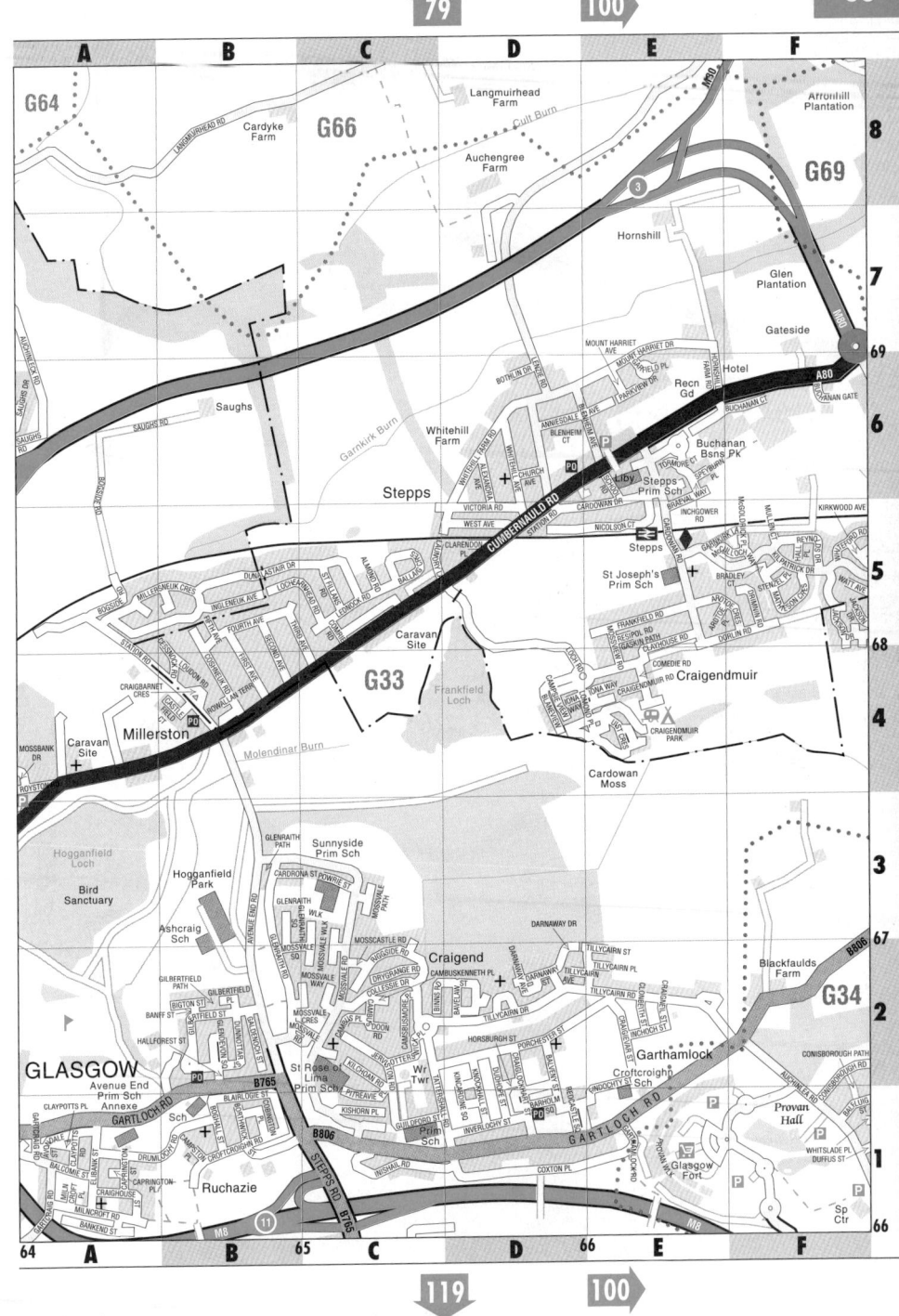

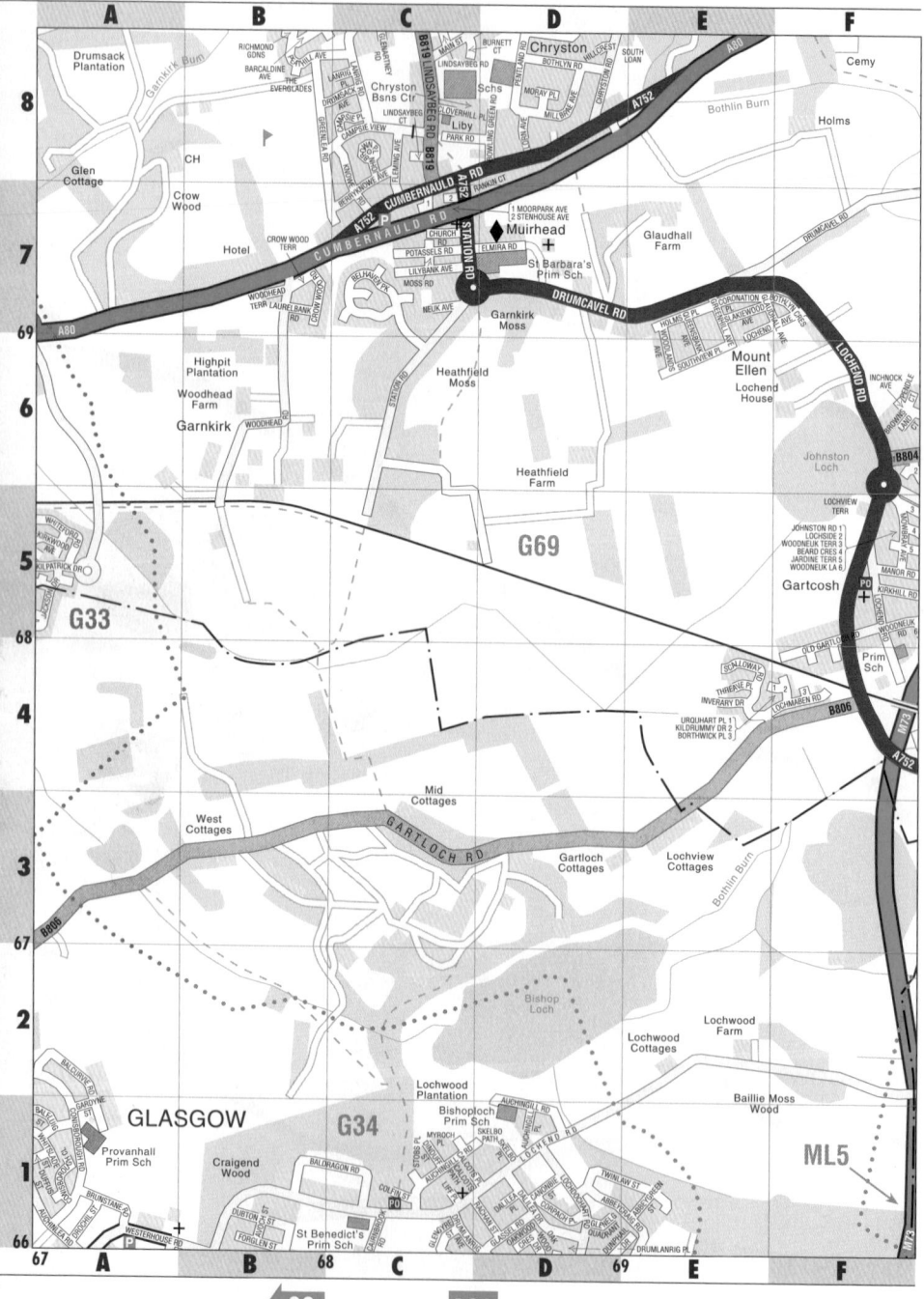

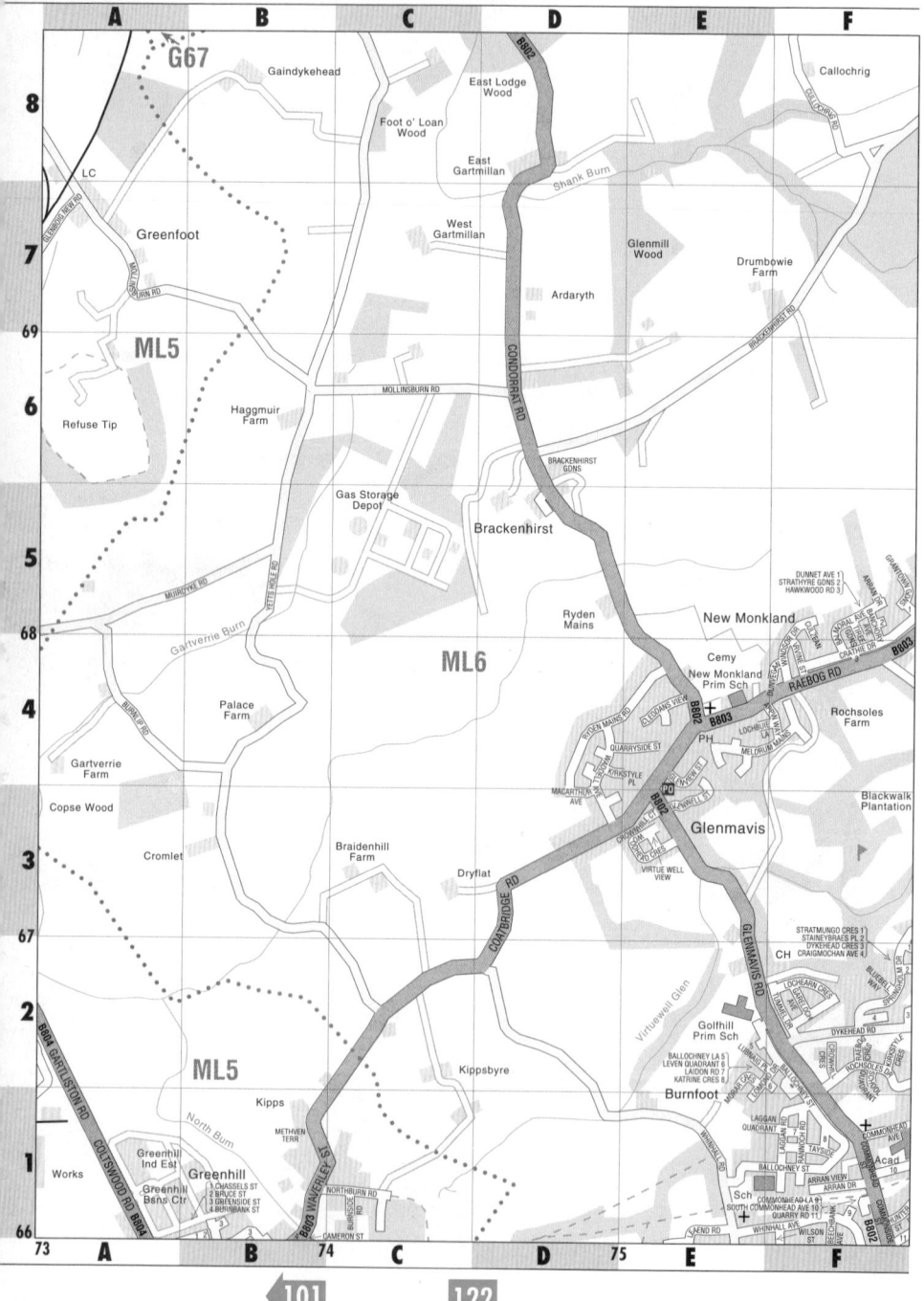

A B C D E F

8

G67

Gaindykehead

East Lodge
Wood

Foot o' Loan
Wood

East
Gartmillan

LC

7 Greenfoot

West
Gartmillan

Shank Burn

Glenmill
Wood

Drumbowie
Farm

Callochrig

69

ML5

Ardaryth

6 Refuse Tip

Haggmuir
Farm

MOLLINSBURN RD

CONDORRAT RD

BRACKENHIRST GDNS

Gas Storage
Depot

5 Brackenhirst

68

MURDYKE RD
YETTS HOLE RD

Gartverrie Burn

Ryden
Mains

New Monkland

ML6

Cemy
New Monkland
Prim Sch

DUNNET AVE 1
STRATHYRE GDNS 2
HAWKWOOD RD 3

RAEBOG RD

4

BURNS RD

Palace
Farm

QUARRYSIDE
PL

B803
B802

PH

PO

Rochsoles
Farm

Gartverrie
Farm

MACARTHUR
AVE

Glenmavis

Blackwalk
Plantation

Copse Wood

3

Cromlet

Braidenhill
Farm

Dryflat

COATBRIDGE RD

VIRTUE WELL
VIEW

STRATMUNGO CRES 1
STAINEYBRAES PL 2
DYKEHEAD CRES 3
CRAIGMOCHAN AVE 4

CH

67

Virtuewell Glen

DYKEHEAD RD

2

ML5

Kippsbyre

GLENMAVIS RD

Golfhill
Prim Sch

BALLOCHNEY LA 5
LEVEN QUADRANT 6
LAIDON RD 7
KATRINE CRES 8

Kipps

North Burn

Methven
Terr

Laggan
Quadrant

Burnfoot

COMMONHEAD
AVE

1

Works

Greenhill
Ind Est

Greenhill
Bsns Ctr

Greenhill

1 CHASSELS ST
2 BRUCE ST
3 GREENSIDE ST
4 BURNBANK ST

B803 WAVERLEY ST

NORTHBURN RD

CAMERON ST

BALLOCHNEY ST

COMMONHEAD LA 9
SOUTH COMMONHEAD AVE 10
QUARRY RD 11

ARRAN VIEW
ARRAN DR

Sch

WHINHALL AVE

WILSON ST

Acad

B802

66

73 A B 74 C D 75 E F

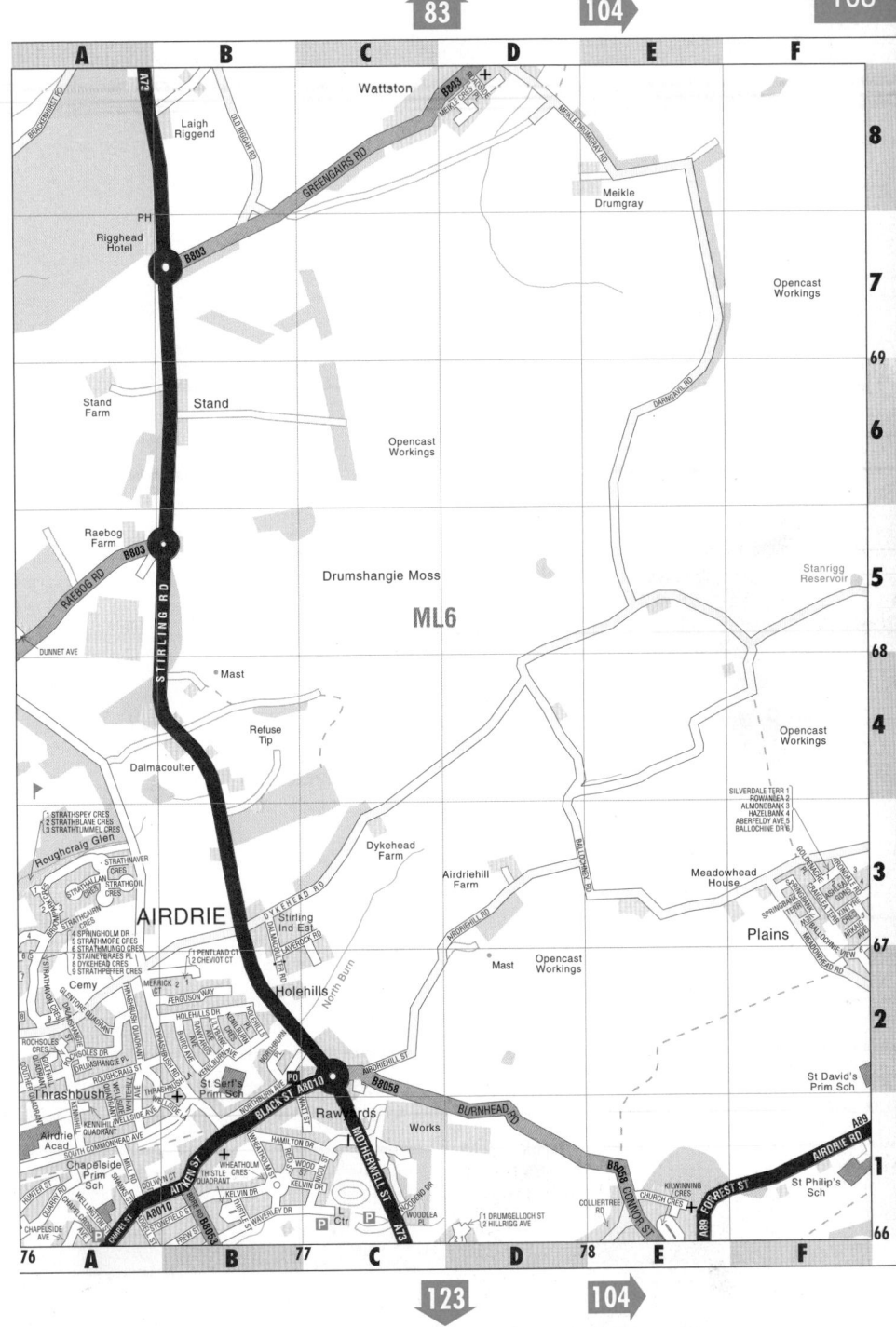

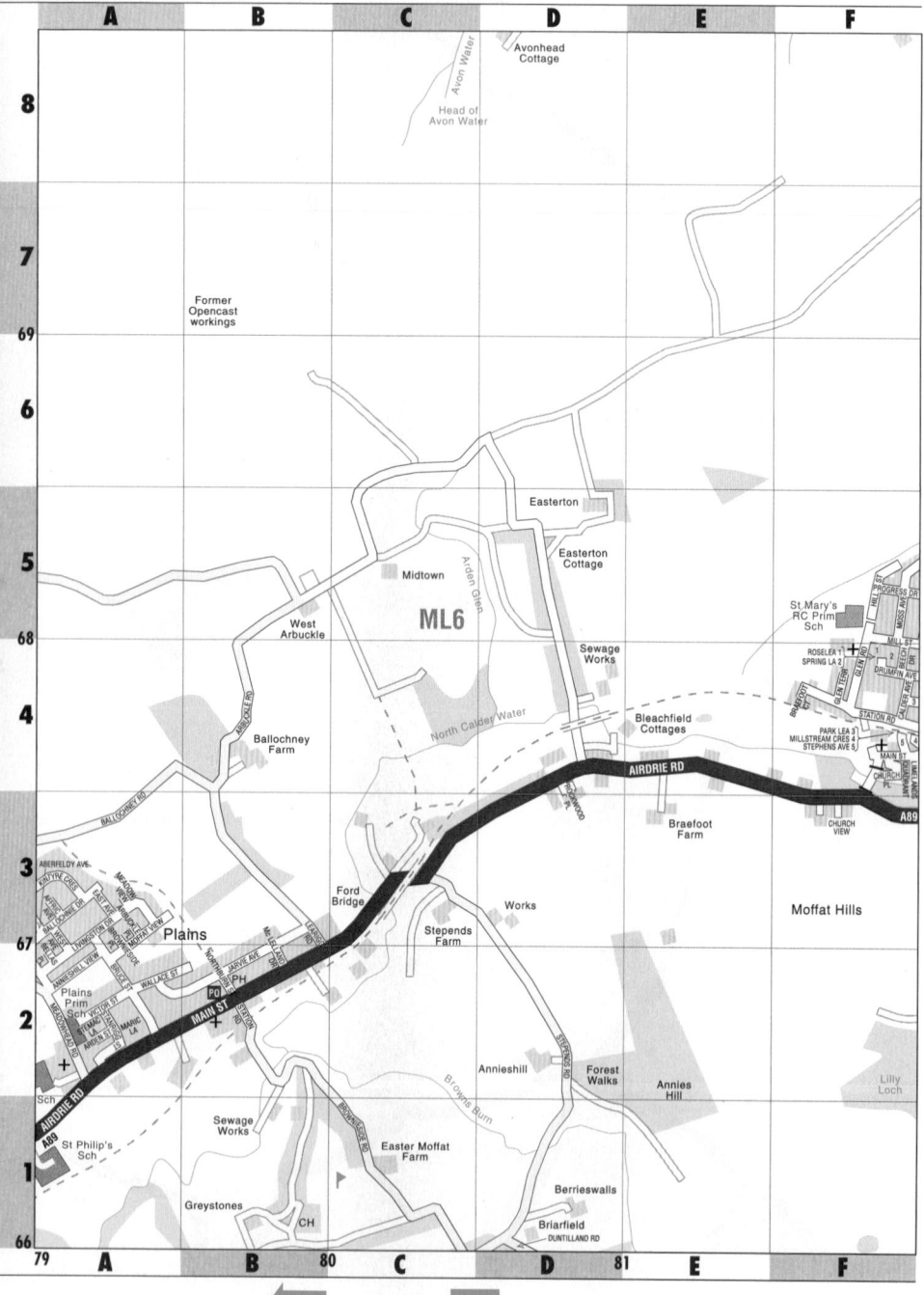

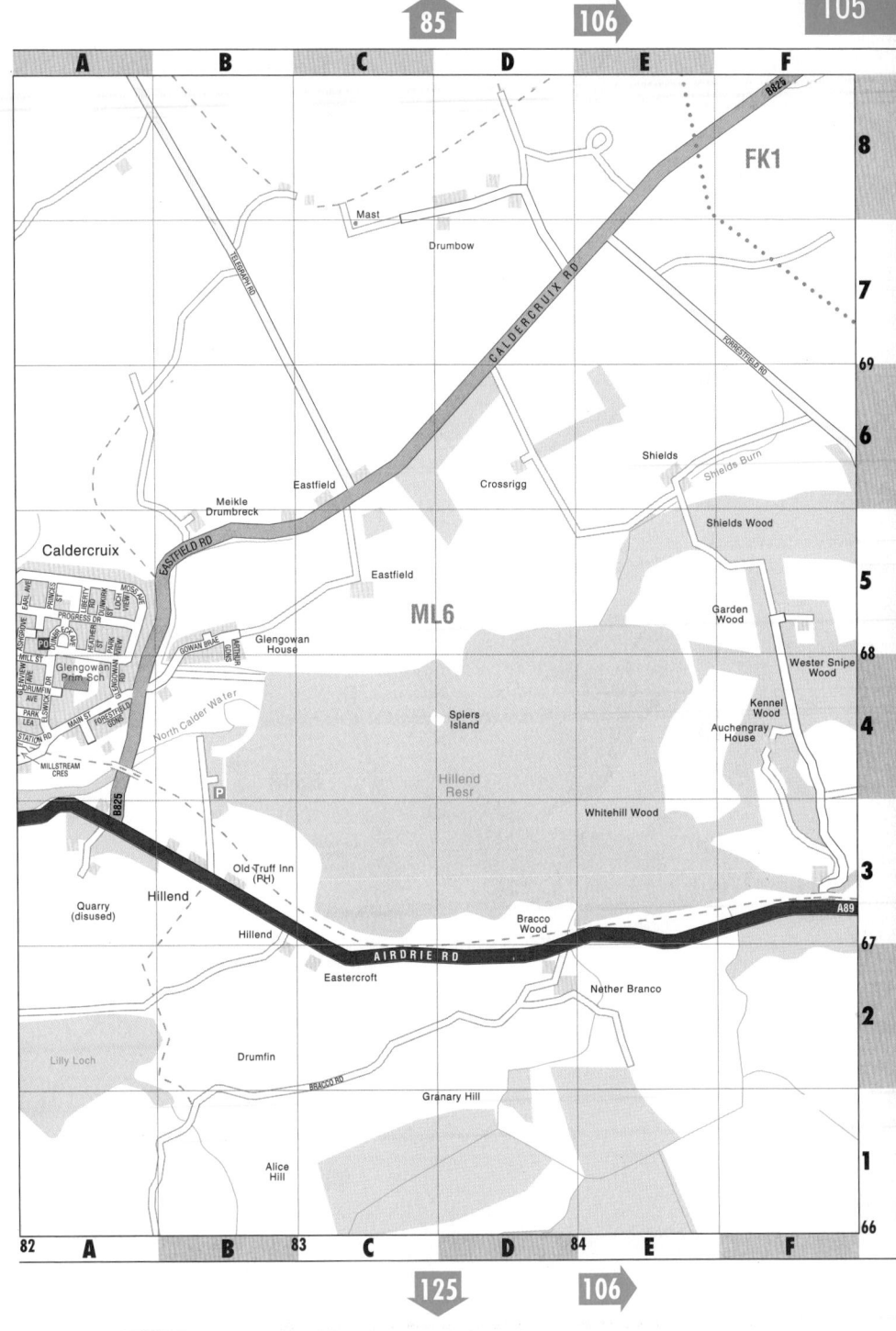

A B C D E F

8
7
69
6
5
68
4
3
67
2
1
66

B825

FK1

Mast

Drumbow

CALDERCRUIX RD

FORRESTFIELD RD

Shields

Shields Burn

Eastfield

Crossrigg

Shields Wood

Meikle
Drumbreck

EASTFIELD RD

Caldercruix

Eastfield

ML6

Garden
Wood

Wester Snipe
Wood

Glengowan
House

GOWAN BRAE

Kennel
Wood

Spiers
Island

Auchengray
House

Glengowan
Prim Sch

North Calder Water

MILLSTREAM
CRES

Hillend
Resr

P

B825

Whitehill Wood

A89

Old Truff Inn
(PH)

Hillend

Quarry
(disused)

Bracco
Wood

Hillend

AIRDRIE RD

67

Eastercroft

Nether Branco

Lilly Loch

Drumfin

BRACCO RD

Granary Hill

Alice
Hill

82 A B 83 C D 84 E F

A · B · C · D · E · F

8

Lochend

Black Loch

7

Lochstank

69

Hillhead

FK1

Easter
Whin

6

Wester
Whin

Whiteside

North Calder Water

Drumtassie Burn

5

Stooprigg
Wood

Drumbeg

68

Easter
Snipe
Wood

Westfield

West Drumbey
Wood

4

Wester
Snipe
Wood

ML6

EH48

Bedlormie

Snipe
Quarry
(dis)

East Fardrum
Wood

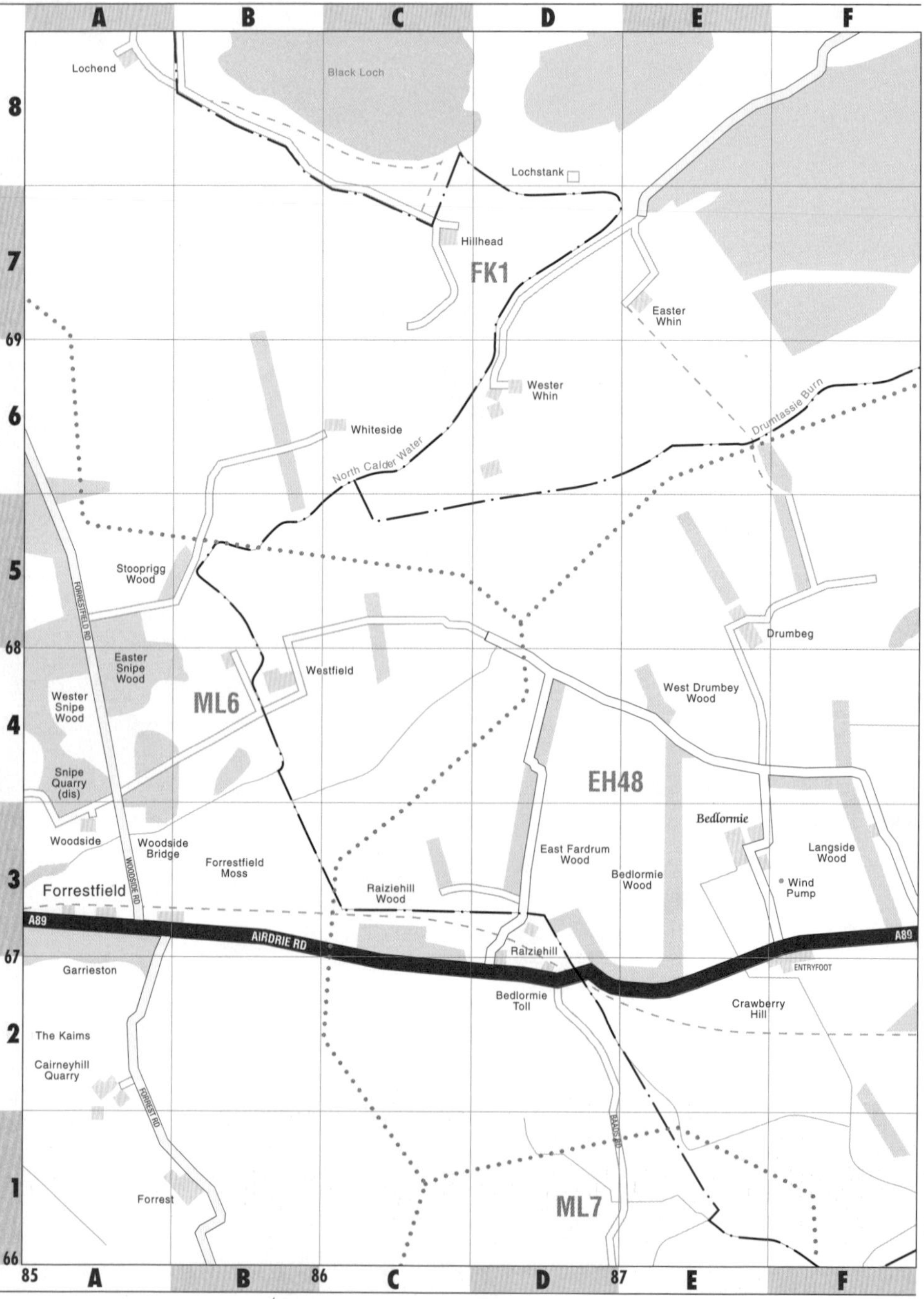

Langside
Wood

3

Woodside

Woodside
Bridge

Forrestfield
Moss

Raiziehill
Wood

Bedlormie
Wood

Wind
Pump

Forrestfield

A89

AIRDRIE RD

A89

67

Garrieston

Raiziehill

ENTRYFOOT

Bedlormie
Toll

Crawberry
Hill

2

The Kaims

Cairneyhill
Quarry

1

Forrest

ML7

66

85 · A · B · 86 · C · D · 87 · E · F

FORREST RD

WOODSIDE RD

FORRESTFIELD RD

BANKS RD

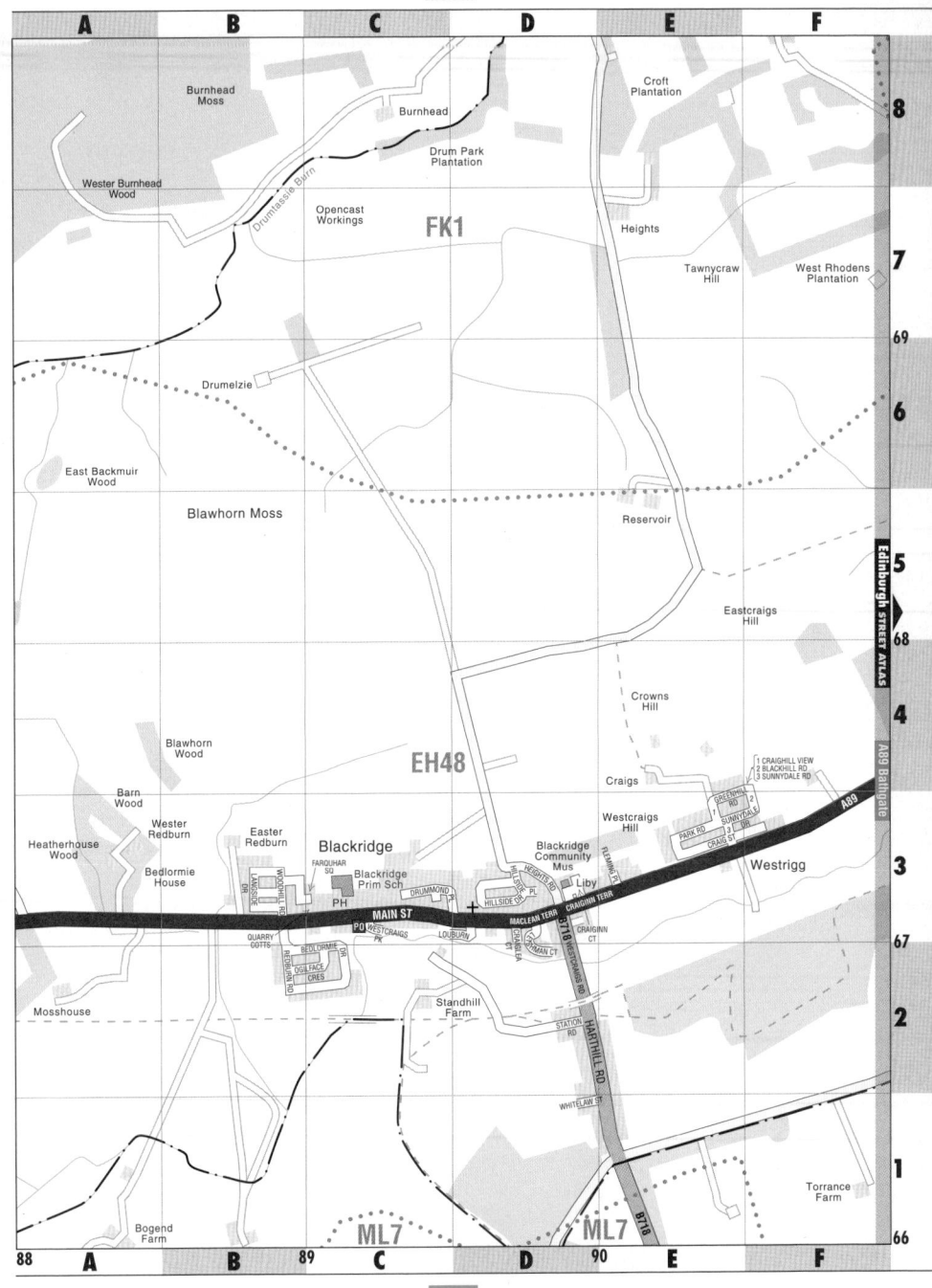

87

127

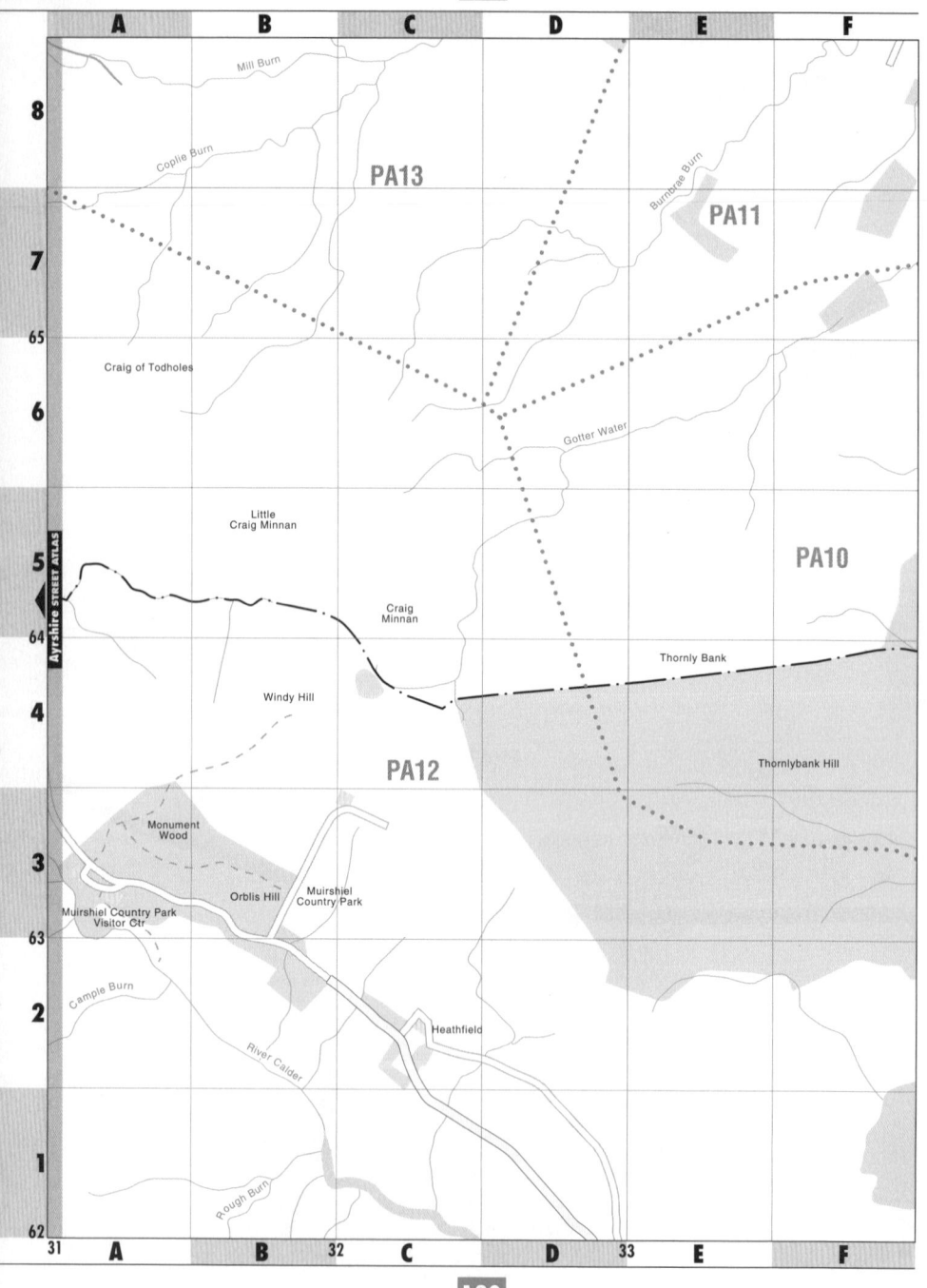

PA13

PA11

Burnbrae Burn

Mill Burn

Coplie Burn

Craig of Todholes

Gotter Water

Little
Craig Minnan

PA10

Craig
Minnan

Thornly Bank

Windy Hill

PA12

Thornlybank Hill

Monument
Wood

Orblis Hill

Muirshiel
Country Park

Muirshiel Country Park
Visitor Ctr

Cample Burn

Heathfield

River Calder

Rough Burn

Ayrshire STREET ATLAS

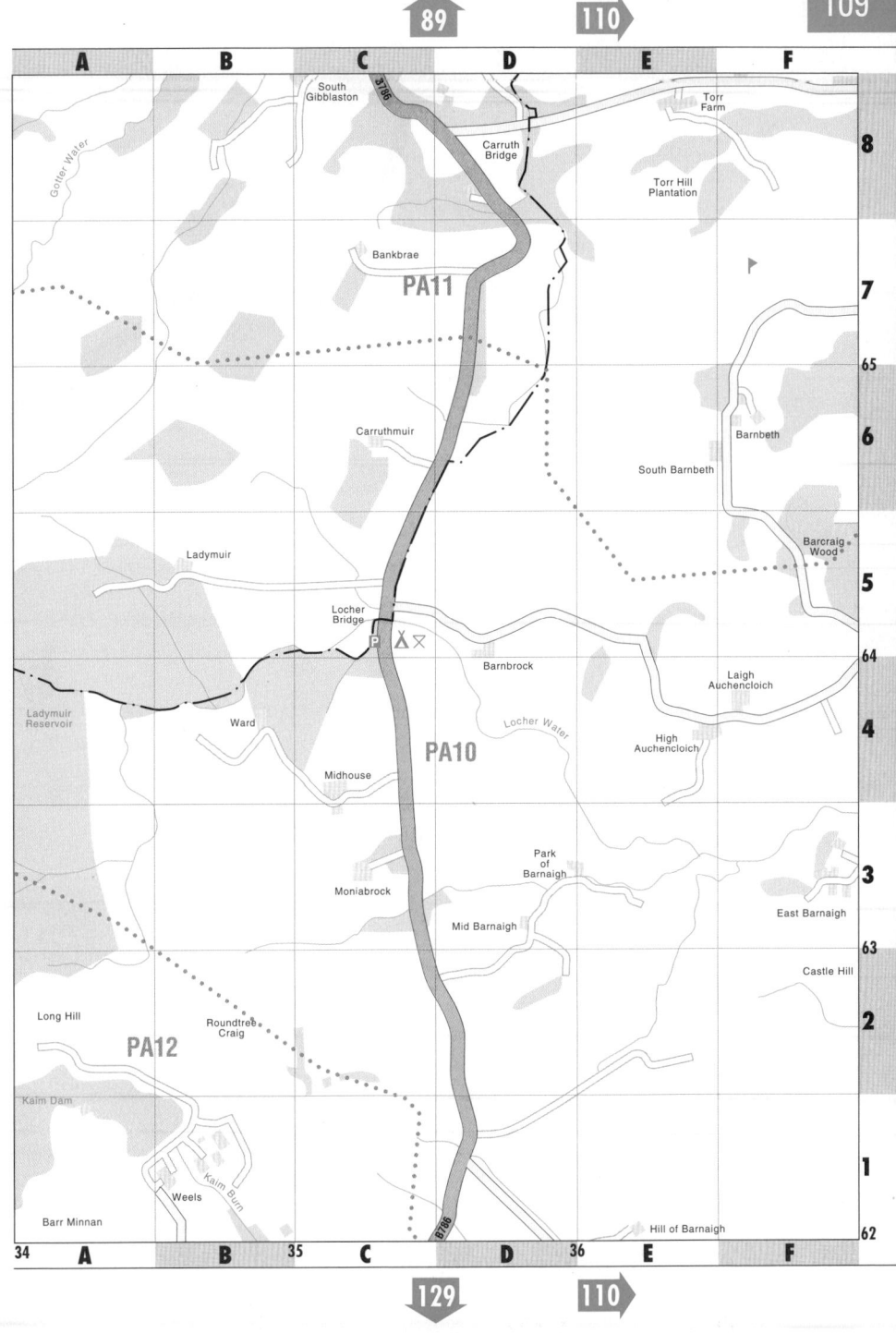

89   110

| A | B | C | D | E | F |

South Gibblaston

B786

Carruth Bridge

Torr Farm

8

Torr Hill Plantation

Bankbrae

PA11

7

65

Carruthmuir

Barnbeth

6

South Barnbeth

Ladymuir

Barcraig Wood

5

Locher Bridge

P

64

Barnbrock

Laigh Auchencloich

Ladymuir Reservoir

Ward

Locher Water

High Auchencloich

4

Midhouse

PA10

Park of Barnaigh

3

Moniabrock

East Barnaigh

Mid Barnaigh

63

Castle Hill

Long Hill

Roundtree Craig

2

PA12

Kaim Dam

Kaim Burn

1

Weels

B786

Barr Minnan

Hill of Barnaigh

62

| 34 | A | B | 35 | C | D | 36 | E | F |

129   110

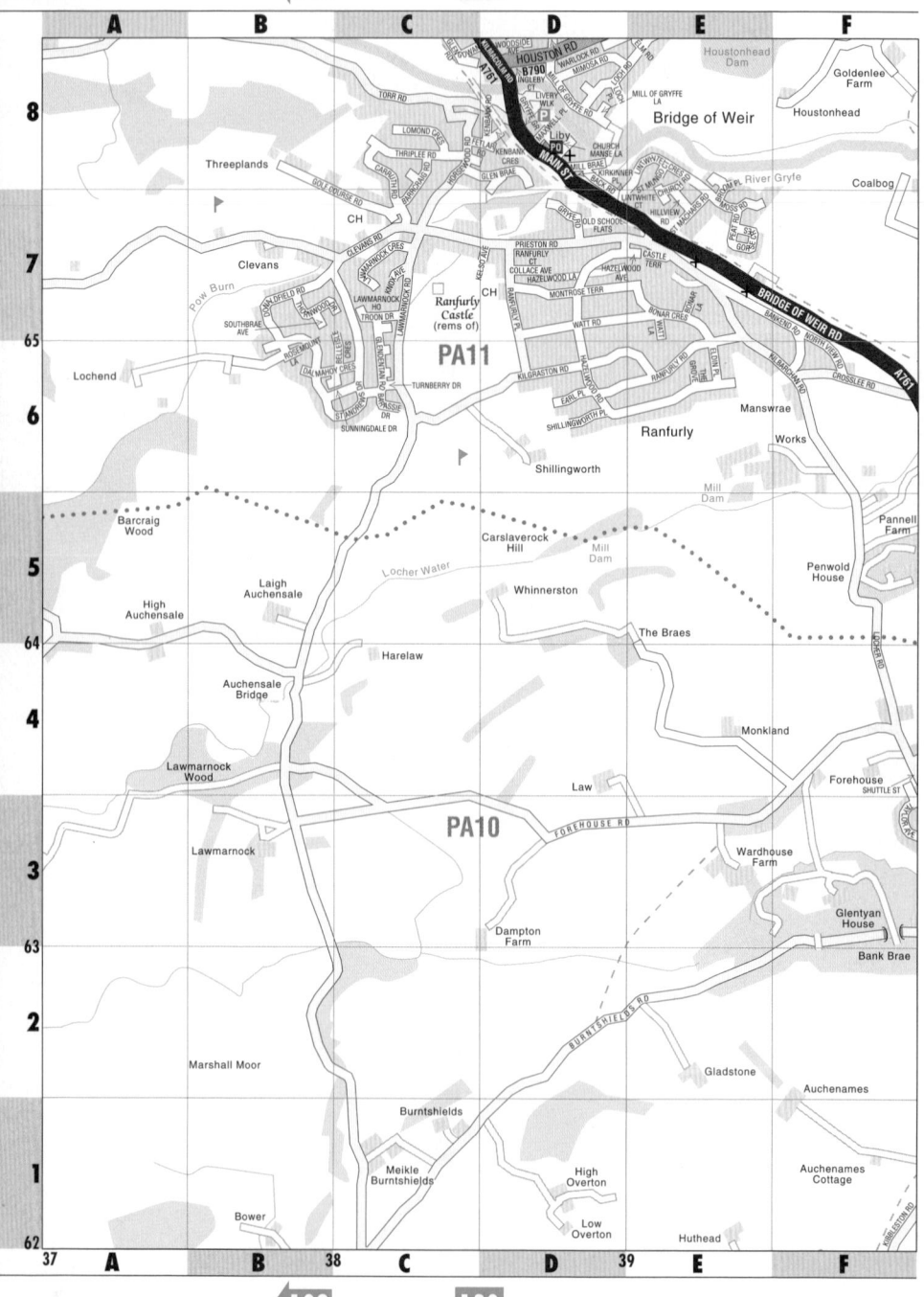

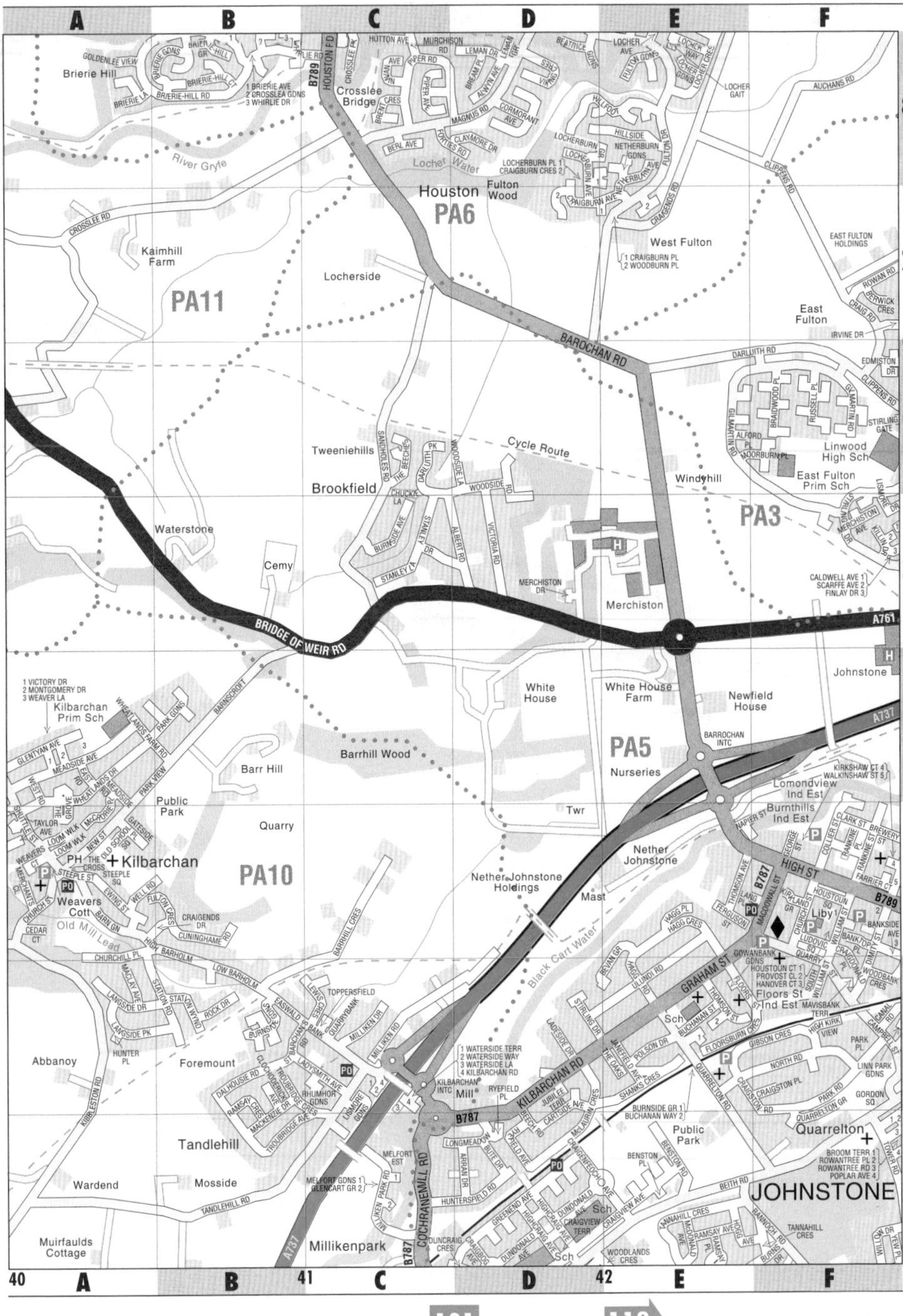

111
92

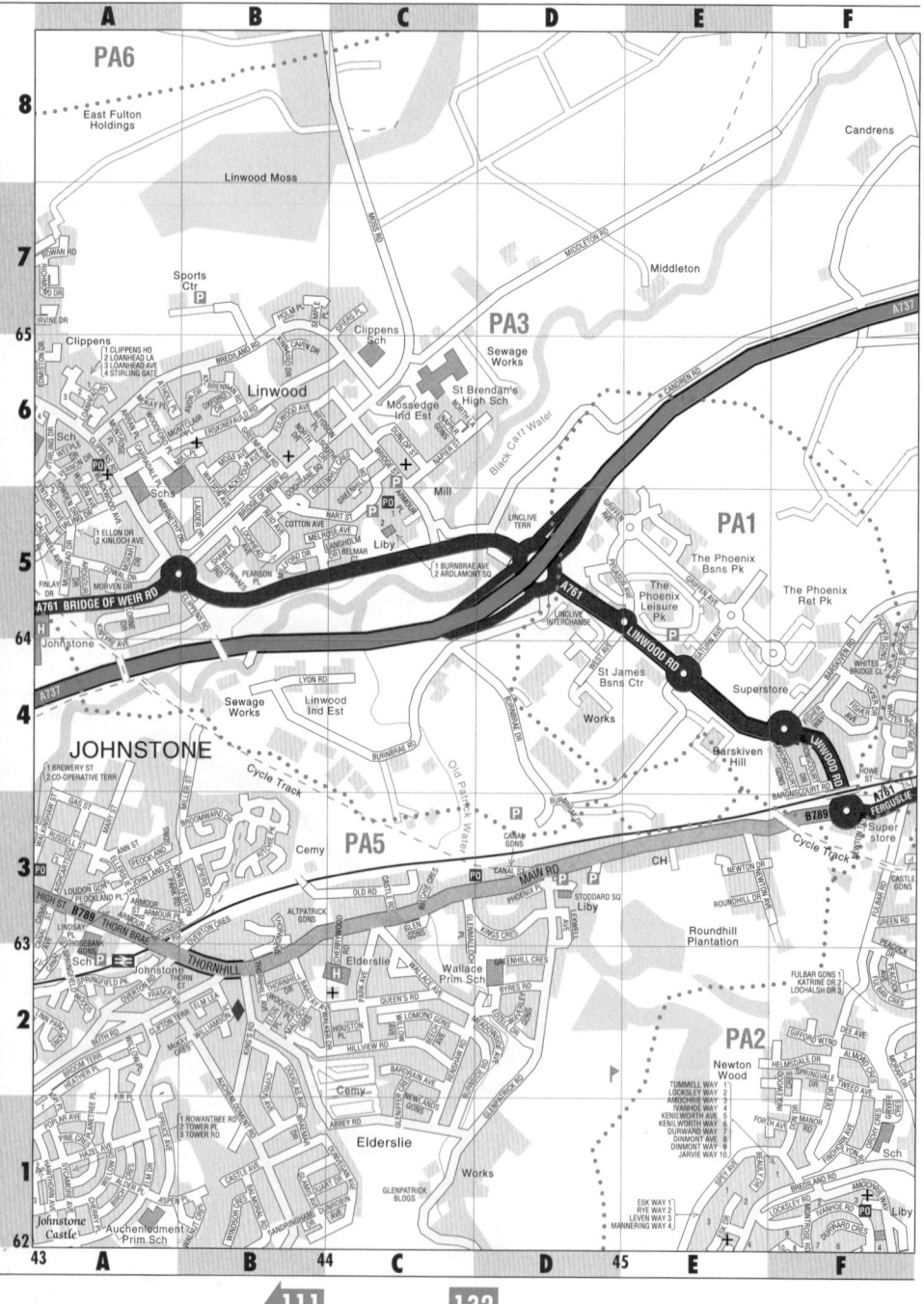

ES
1 MONCRIEFF ST
2 STONEY BRAE
3 BACK SNEDDON ST
4 MAXWELL ST
5 MEETINGHOUSE LA
6 COUNTY SQ

7 COUNTY PL
8 CENTRAL WAY
9 DYERS WYND
FS
1 BRICK LA
2 WALLNEUK
3 EAST BUCHANAN MEWS

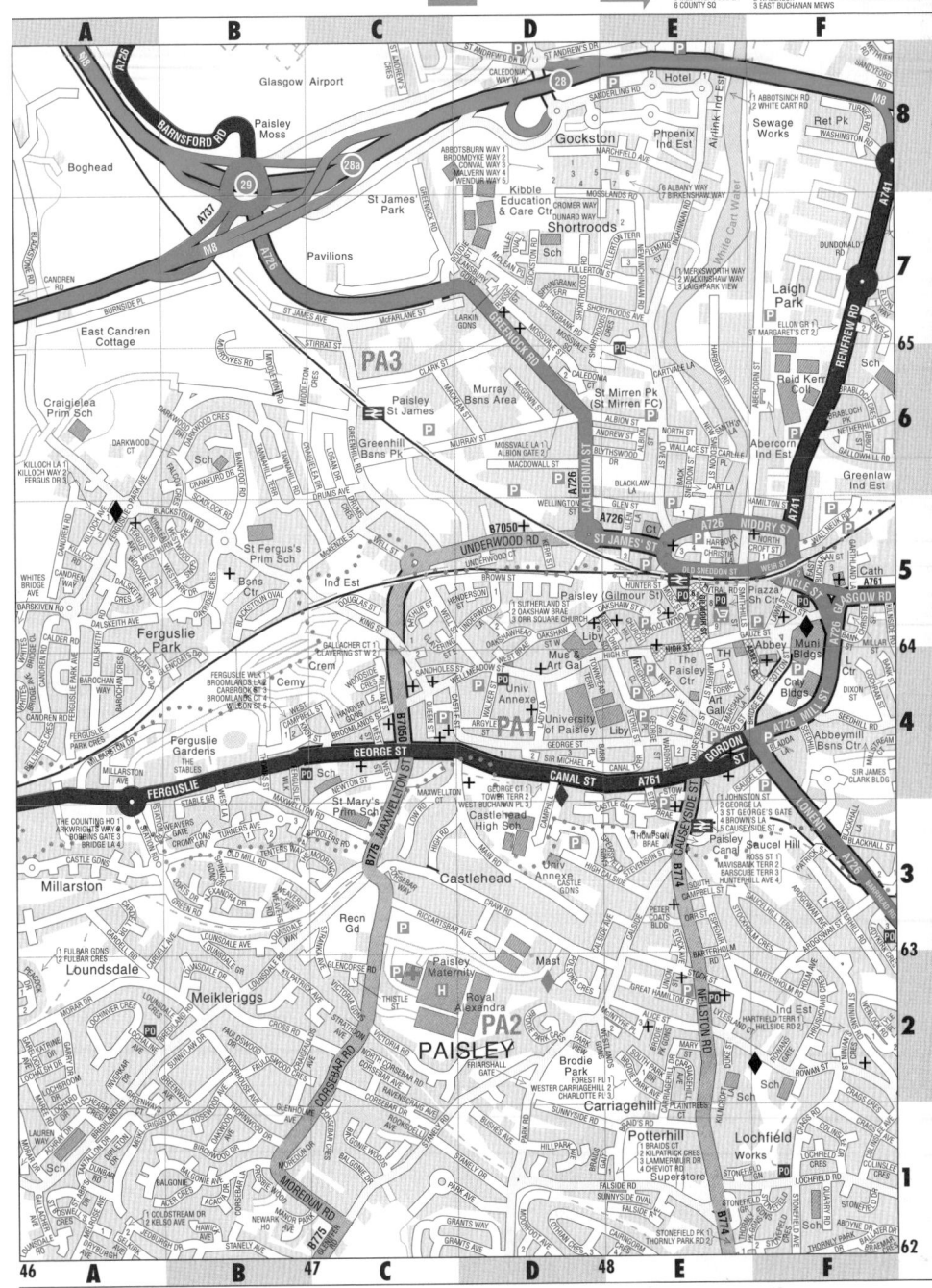

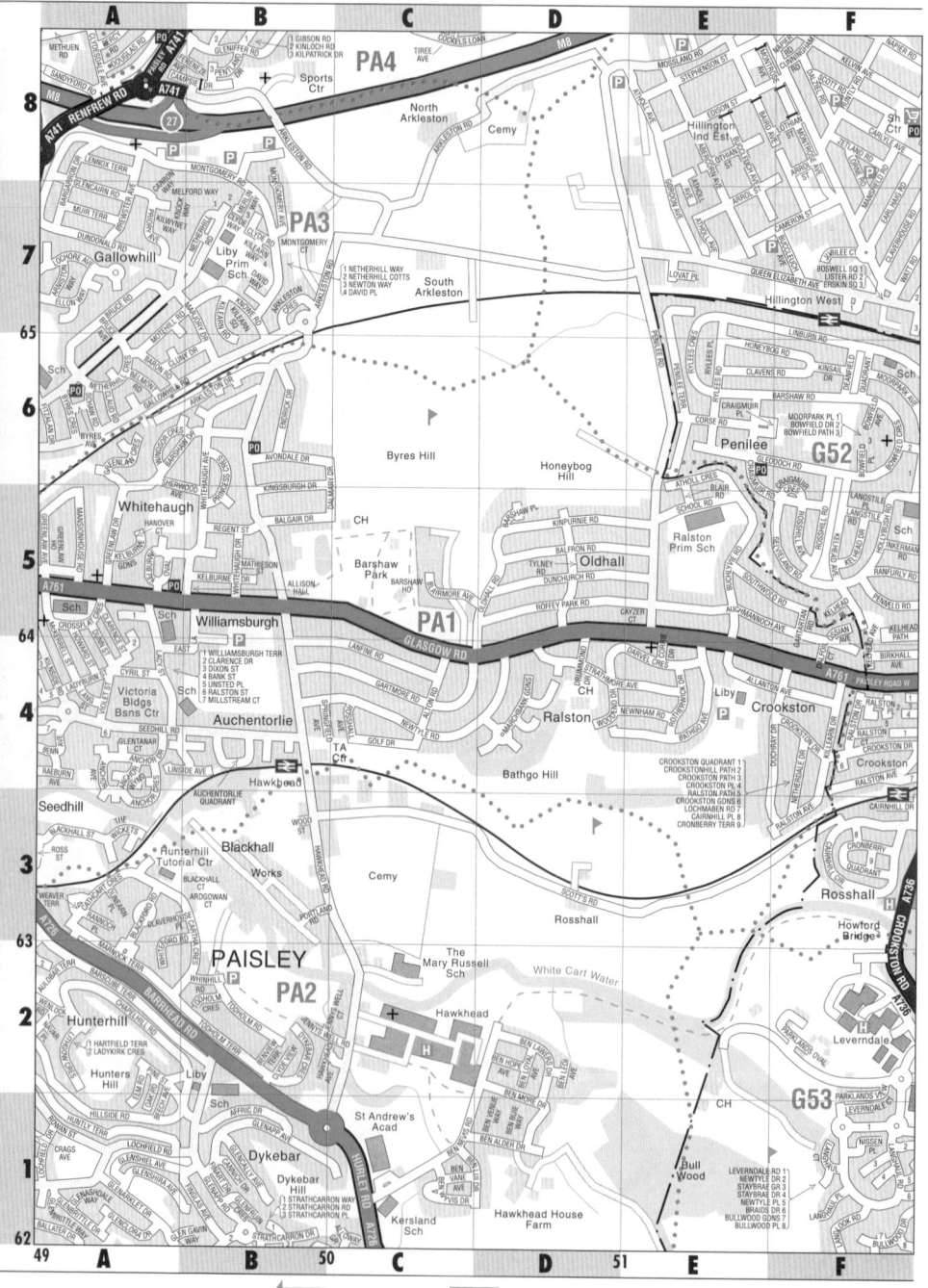

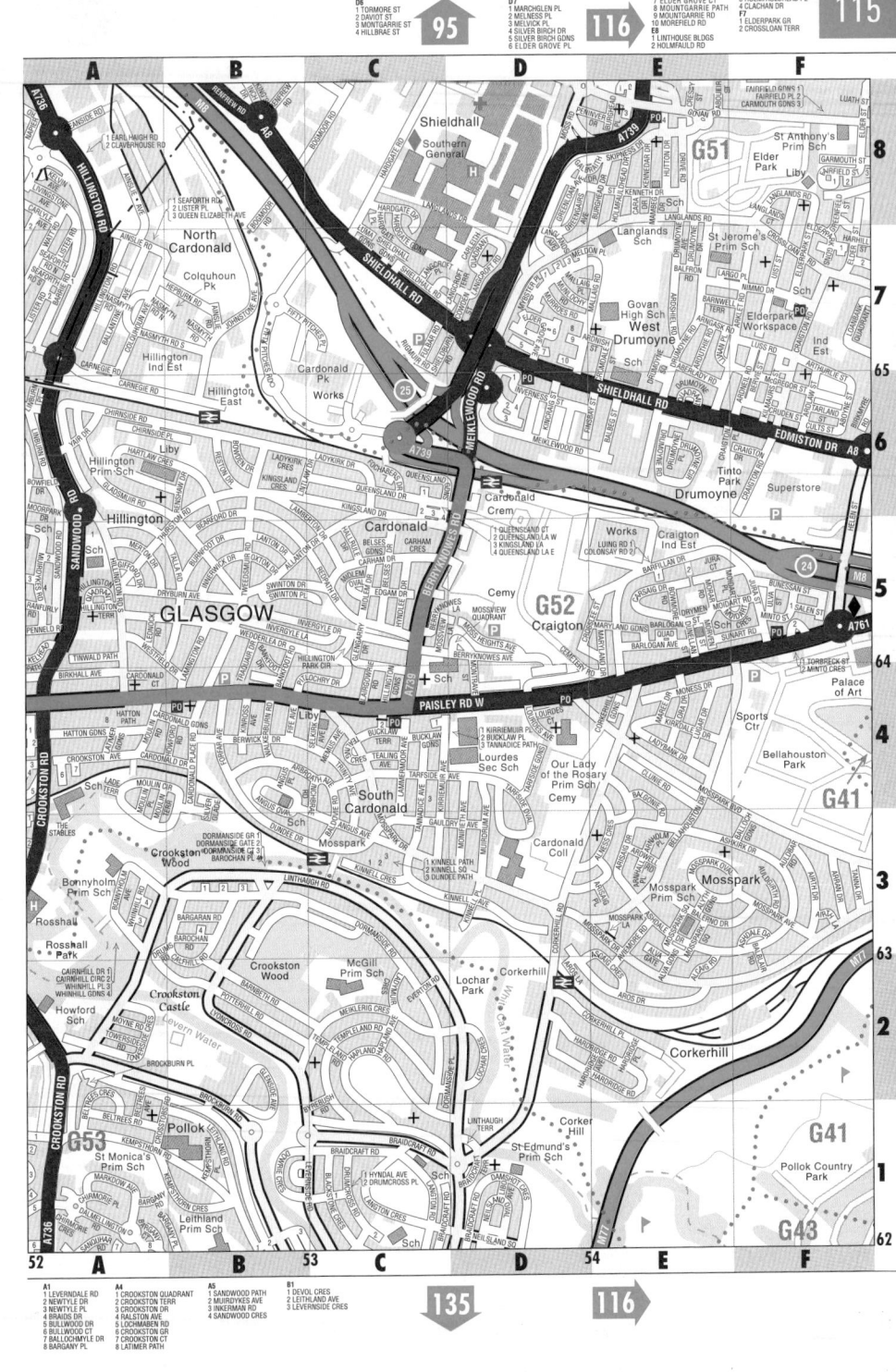

A8
1 HARMONY ROW
2 WARDROP ST
3 GARMOUTH CT
4 GARMOUTH GDNS
D5
1 CLIFFORD PL

2 LANGSHOT ST
3 PLANTATION PARK GDNS

115

E6
1 EAGLESHAM CT
2 EAGLESHAM PL
3 MIDDLESEX GDNS

96

E8
1 CLIFTON PL
2 FITZROY PL
3 WESTMINSTER TERR
4 DERBY TERRACE LA
5 CORUNNA ST
6 Stobcross Bsns Pk

7 HOULDSWORTH LA
8 Clydeway Ind Est
9 FINNIESTON SQ
10 MINERVA CT

For full street detail of the
highlighted area see page 240.

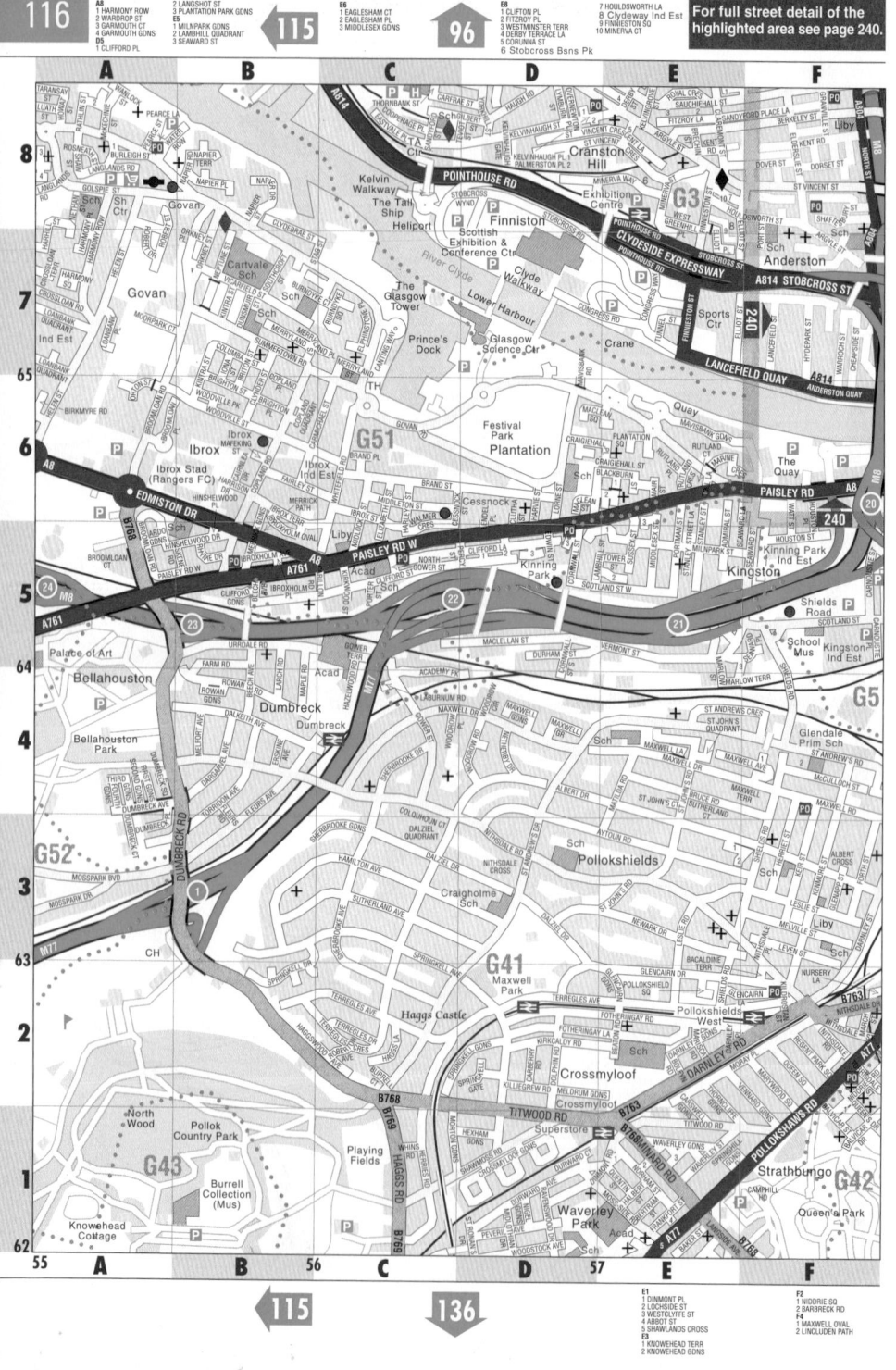

E1
1 DINMONT PL
2 LOCHSIDE ST
3 WESTCLYFFE ST
4 ABBOT ST
5 SHAWLANDS CROSS
E3
1 KNOWEHEAD TERR
2 KNOWEHEAD GDNS

F2
1 NIDDRIE SQ
2 BARBRECK RD
F4
1 MAXWELL OVAL
2 LINCLUDEN PATH

For full street detail of the highlighted area see pages 240 and 241.

B5					
1 LANGBANK ST	7 STIRLINGFAULD PL	F5		2 MILLROAD GDNS	3 CARDROSS CT
2 KILBARCHAN ST		1 FORBES DR		E5	3 SETON TERR
3 COLVILLE ST		2 REDAN ST		1 ABERCROMBY ST	4 OAKLEY TERR
4 HERBERTSON ST		3 OLYMPIA ST		2 GRAIGNESTOCK PL	5 CLAYTON TERR
5 S PORTLAND ST		4 Bridgeton Bsns Ctr		3 MONTEITH PL	6 BROOMPARK ST
6 BEDFORD LA		F6		F7	7 BROOMPARK LA
		1 ABERCROMBY SQ		1 McINTOSH CT	8 BROOMPARK CIR

97 **118** **117**

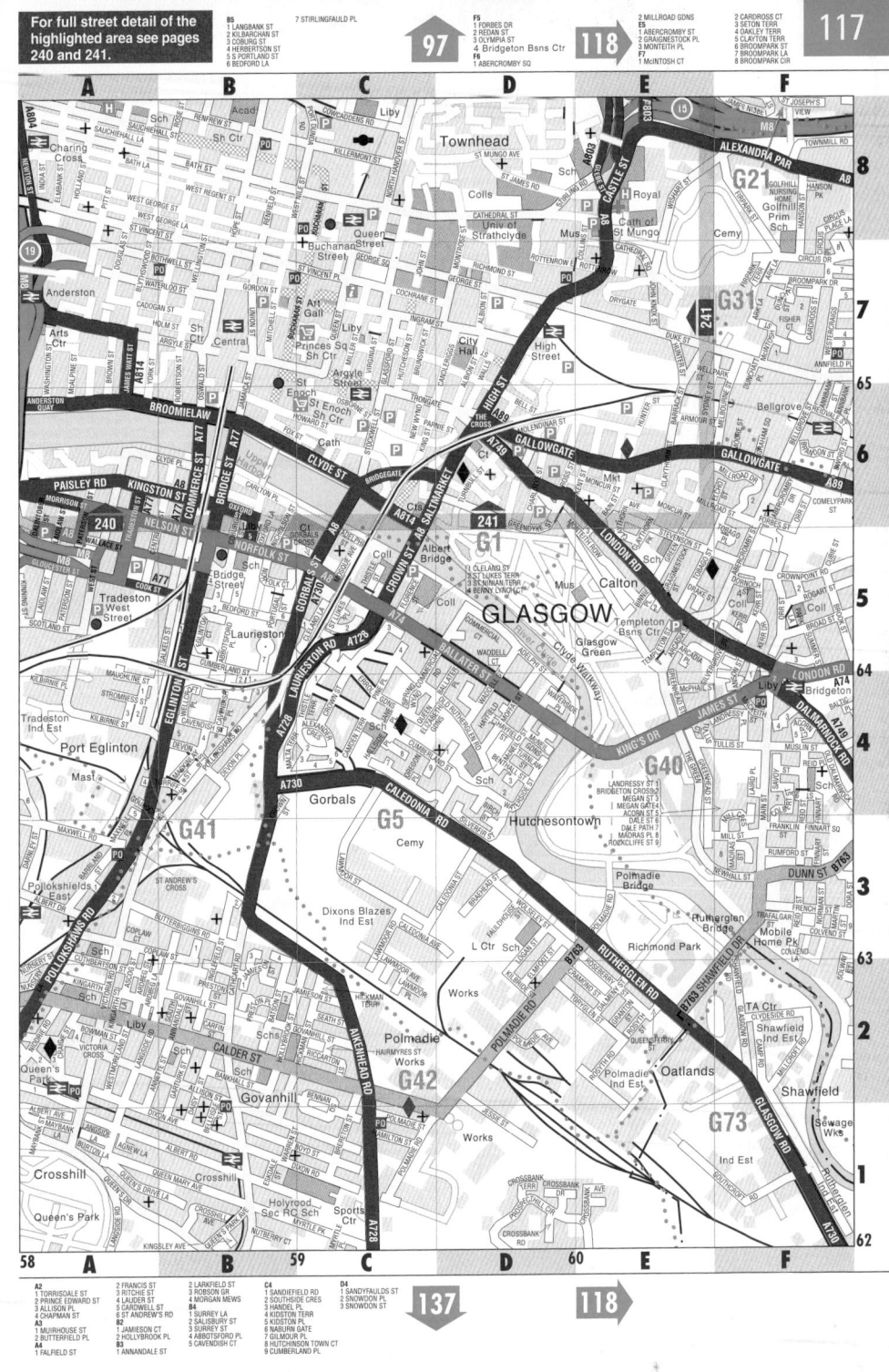

A2	2 FRANCIS ST	2 LARKFIELD ST	C4	D4
1 TORRISDALE ST	3 RITCHIE ST	3 ROBSON GR	1 SANDIEFIELD RD	5 SANDYFAULDS ST
2 PRINCE EDWARD ST	4 LAUDER ST	4 MORGAN MEWS	2 SOUTHSIDE CRES	6 SNOWDON PL
3 ALLISON PL	5 CARDWELL ST	B4	3 HANDEL PL	7 SNOWDON ST
4 CHAPMAN ST	6 ST ANDREW'S RD	1 SURREY LA	4 KIDSTON TERR	
A3	B2	2 SALISBURY ST	5 KIDSTON PL	
1 MUIRHOUSE ST	1 JAMIESON ST	3 SURREY ST	6 NARUIN GATE	
2 BUTTERFIELD PL	2 HOLLYBROOK PL	7 ABBOTSFORD PL	7 GILMOUR PL	
A4	B3	8 CAVENDISH CT	8 HUTCHINSON TOWN CT	
1 FALFIELD ST	3 ANNANDALE ST		9 CUMBERLAND PL	

117
98

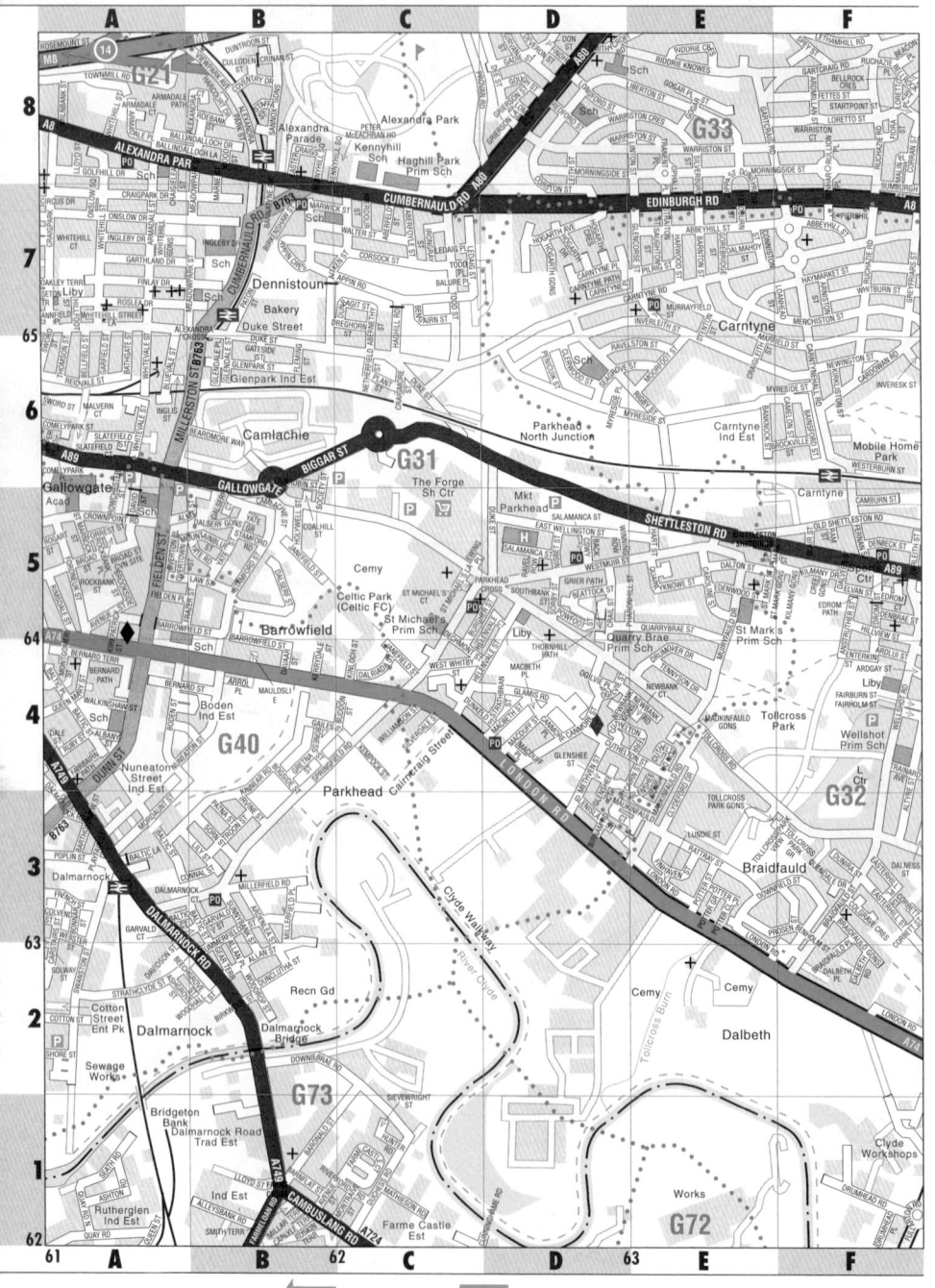

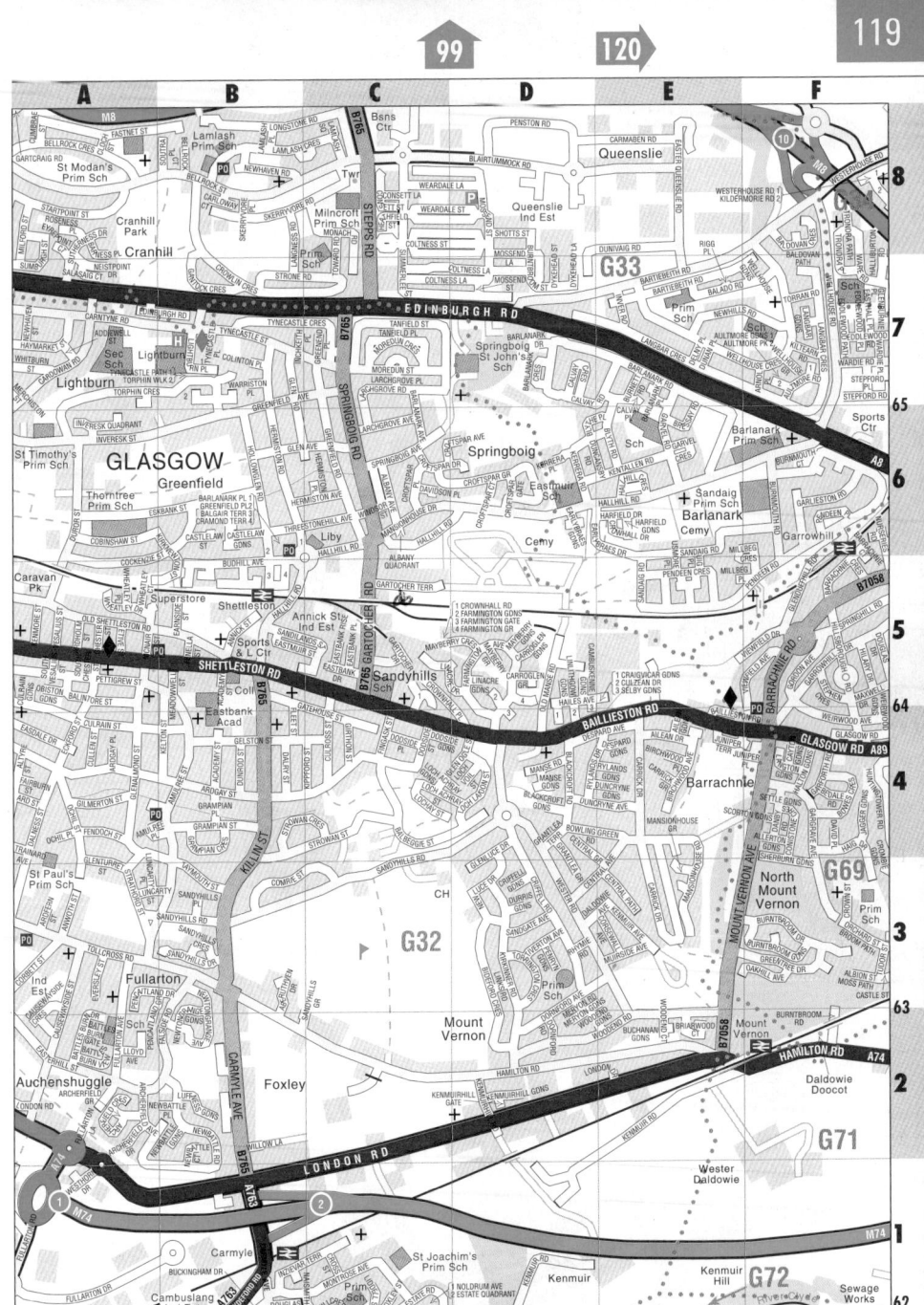

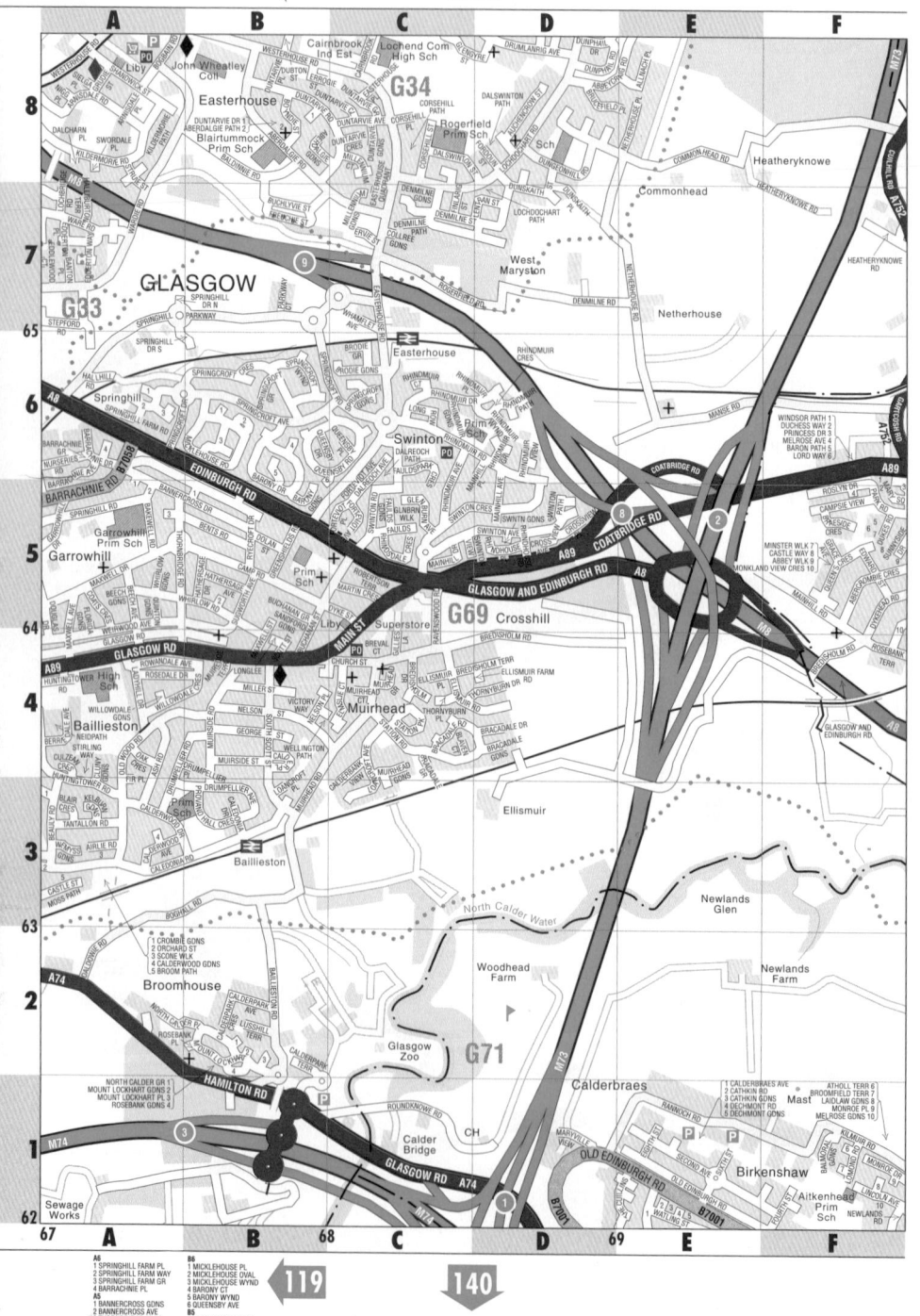

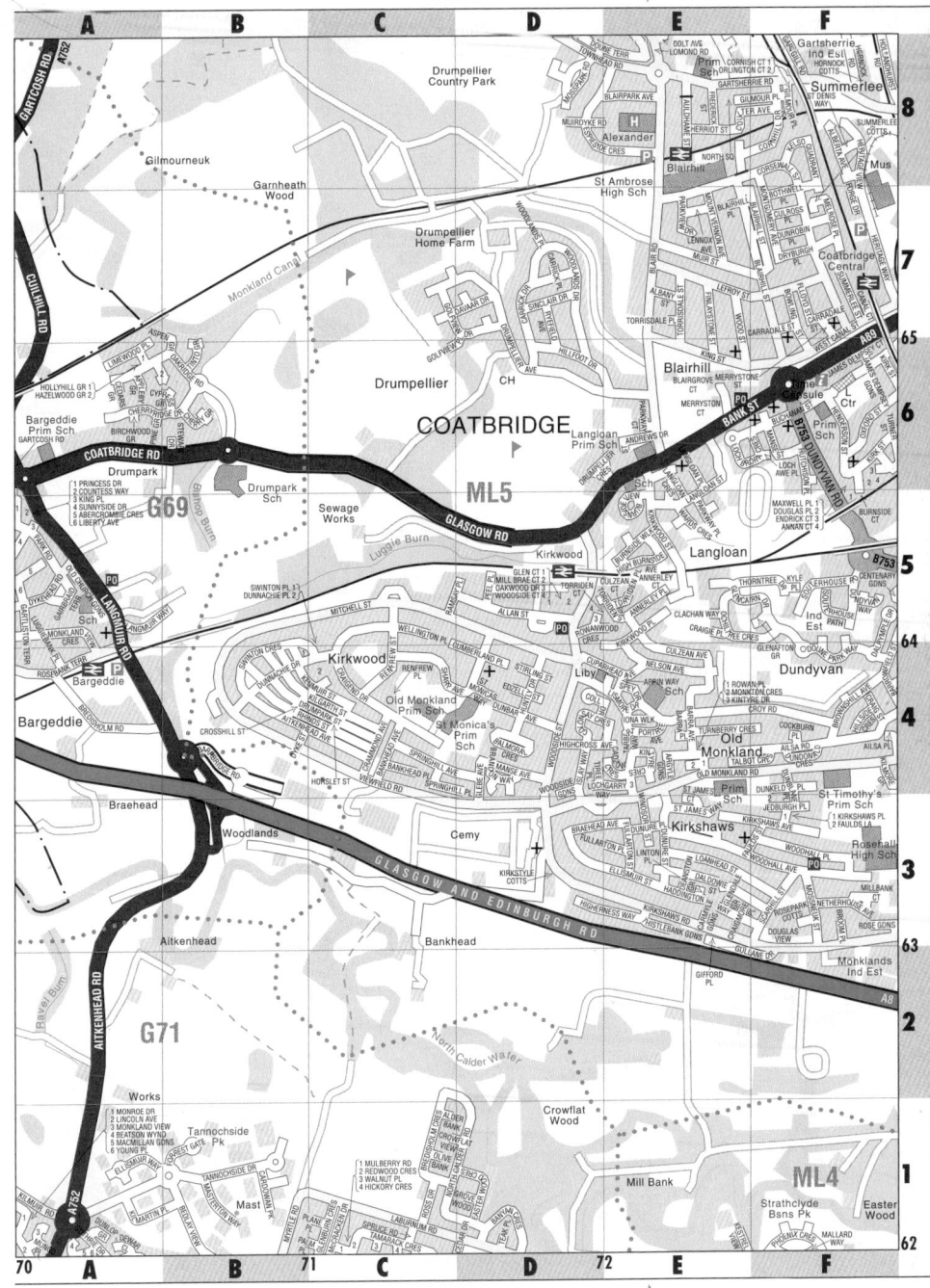

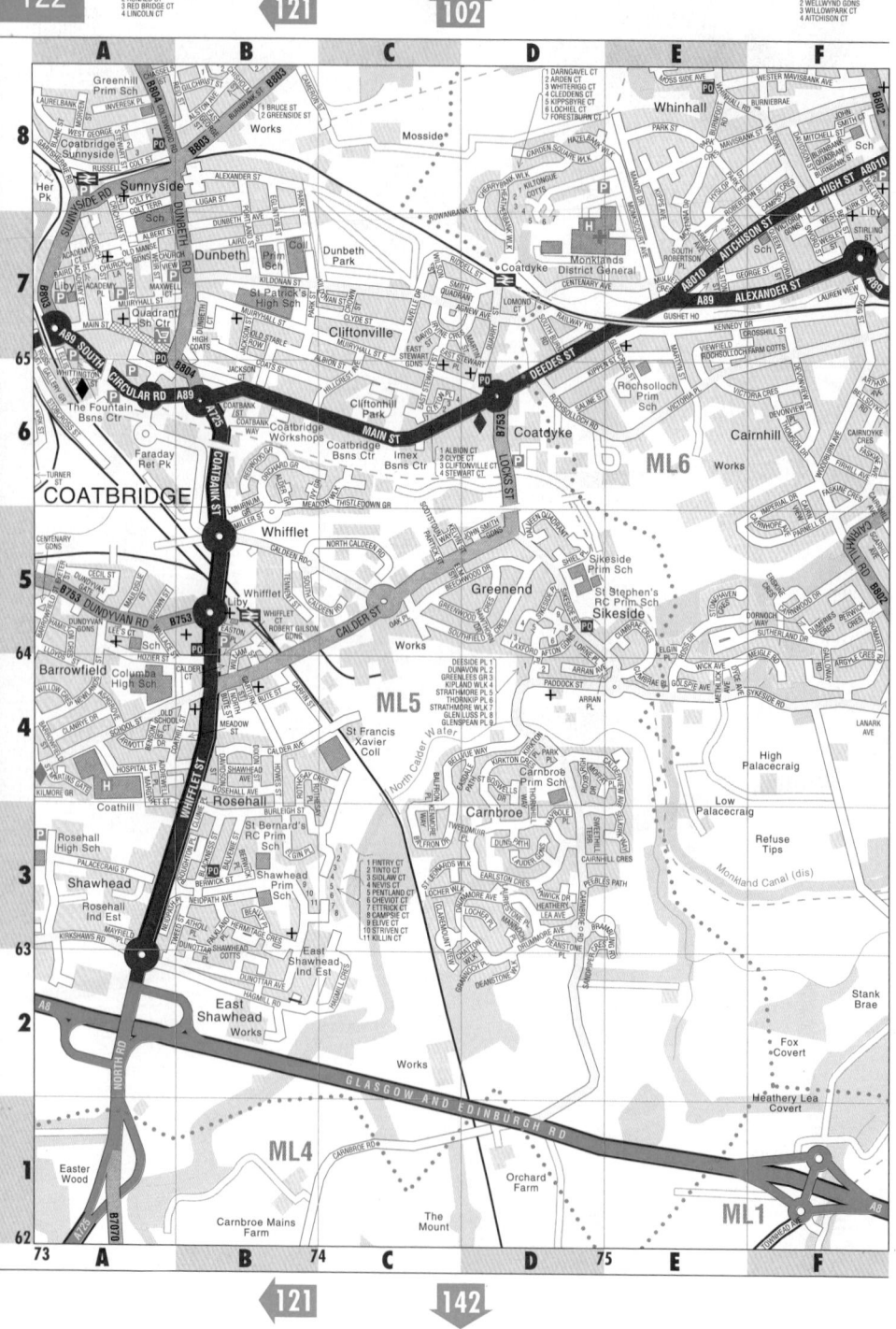

A8
1 COLTSWOOD CT
2 RONALD ST
3 RED BRIDGE CT
4 LINCOLN CT

F8
1 NORTH BRIDGE ST
2 WELLWYND GDNS
3 WILLOWPARK CT
4 AITCHISON CT

121

102

121

142

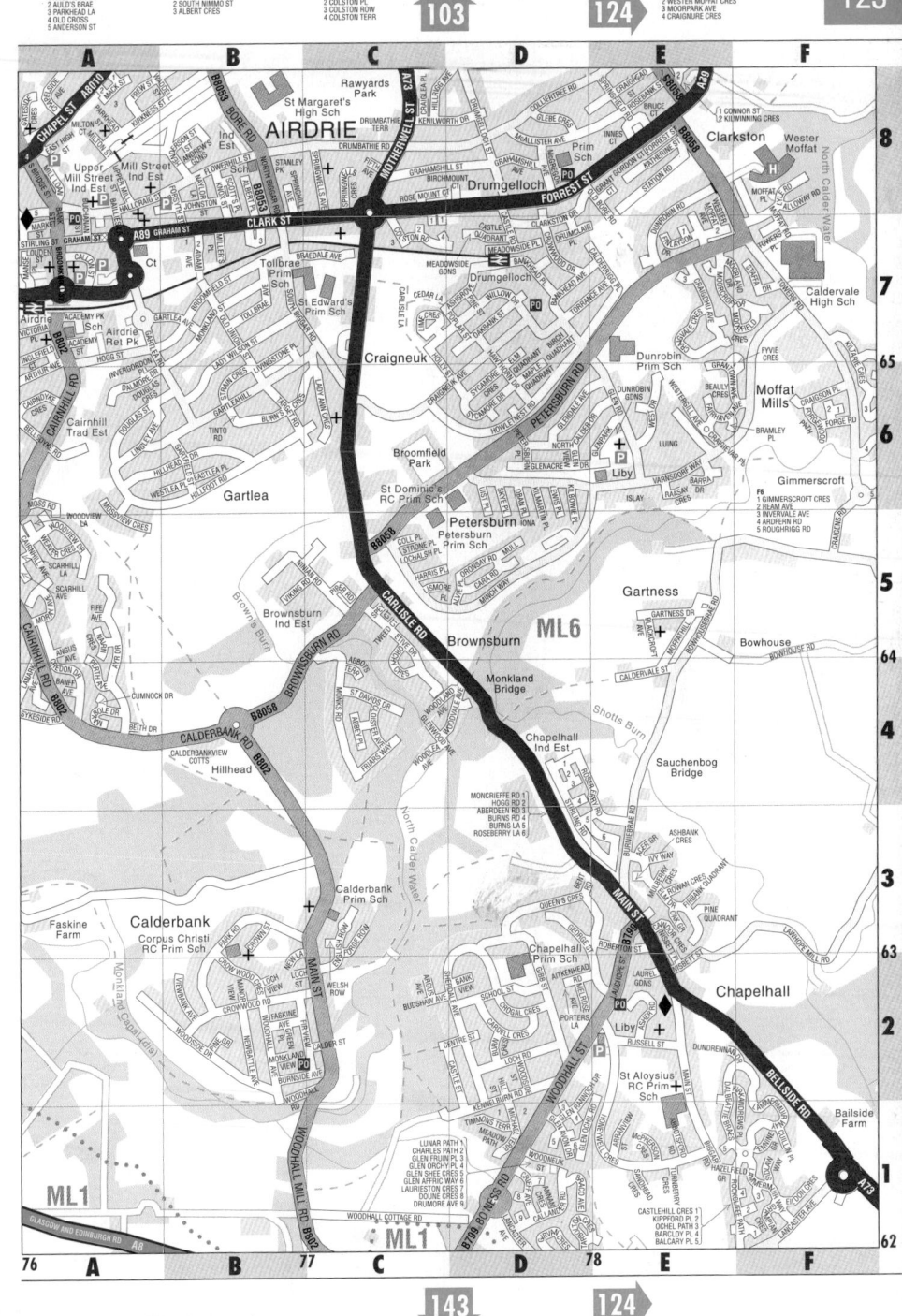

A8
1 ANDERSON LA
2 AULD'S BRAE
3 PARKHEAD LA
4 OLD CROSS
5 ANDERSON ST

B7
1 GARTLEA GDNS
2 SOUTH NIMMO ST
3 ALBERT CRES

C7
1 KINGSTON AVE
2 COLSTON PL
3 COLSTON ROW
4 COLSTON TERR

E7
1 FINLAYSON QUADRANT
2 WESTER MOFFAT CRES
3 MOORPARK AVE
4 CRAIGNURE CRES

AIRDRIE

Rawyards Park

St Margaret's High Sch

Drumgelloch

FORREST ST

Clarkston

Wester Moffat

Caldervale High Sch

Craigneuk

Broomfield Park

St Dominic's RC Prim Sch

Dunrobin Prim Sch

Moffat Mills

Gartlea

Petersburn

Petersburn Prim Sch

Gimmerscroft

F6
1 GIMMERSCROFT CRES
2 REAM AVE
3 INVERVALE AVE
4 ARDFERN RD
5 ROUGHRIGG RD

Brownsburn Ind Est

Brownsburn

Monkland Bridge

ML6

Gartness

Bowhouse

Calderbank Prim Sch

Chapelhall Ind Est

Sauchenbog Bridge

Hillhead

Faskine Farm

Calderbank

Corpus Christi RC Prim Sch

MONCRIEFFE RD 1
HOGG RD 2
ABERDEEN RD 3
BURNS RD 4
BURNS LA 5
ROSEBERRY LA 6

Chapelhall Prim Sch

Chapelhall

Bailside Farm

St Aloysius RC Prim Sch

LUNAR PATH 1
CHARLES PATH 2
GLEN FRUIN PL 3
GLEN ORCHY PL 4
GLEN SHEE CRES 5
GLEN AFFRIC WAY 6
LAURIESTON CRES 7
DOUNE CRES 8
DRUMORE AVE 9

CASTLEHILL CRES 1
KIPFORD PL 2
OCHEL PATH 3
BARCLOY PL 4
BALCARY PL 5

ML1

ML1

GLASGOW AND EDINBURGH RD

WOODHALL COTTAGE RD

123
104

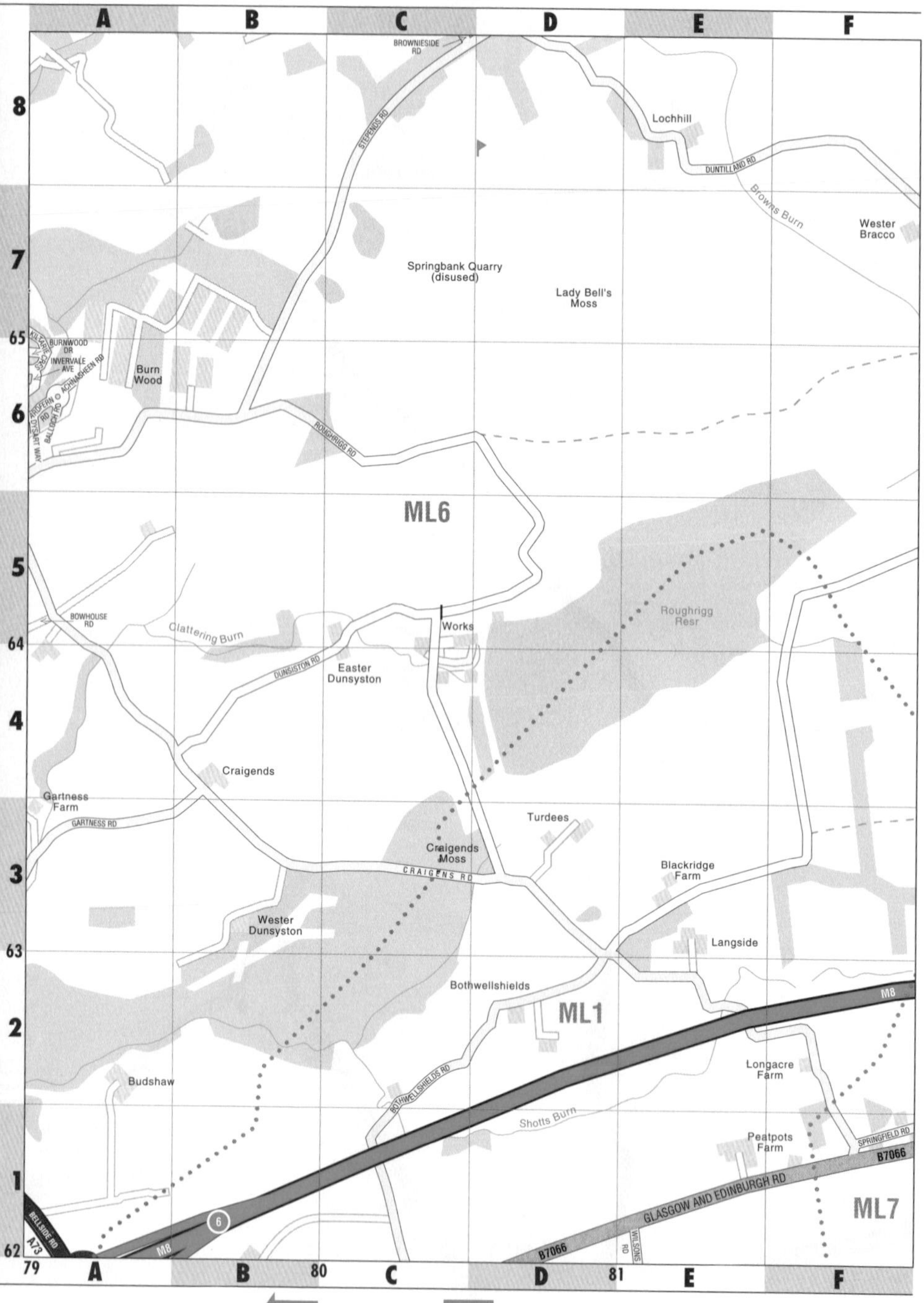

A B C D E F

8

7

BROWNIESIDE RD

STEPENDS RD

Lochhill

DUNTILLAND RD

Browns Burn

Wester Bracco

Springbank Quarry (disused)

Lady Bell's Moss

65

BURNWOOD DR
INVERVALE AVE
ACHARNGREEN RD
BALLOCH RD
STEWART WAY

Burn Wood

6

ROUGHRIGG RD

ML6

5

BOWHOUSE RD

Clattering Burn

Roughrigg Resr

64

DUNSYSTON RD

Easter Dunsyston

Works

4

Craigends

Gartness Farm

GARTNESS RD

Turdees

Craigends Moss

CRAIGENS RD

Blackridge Farm

3

Wester Dunsyston

Langside

63

Bothwellshields

M8

2

ML1

Budshaw

ROTHWELLSHIELDS RD

Longacre Farm

Shotts Burn

Peatpots Farm

SPRINGFIELD RD

B7066

1

A73
BELLSIDE RD

6

M8

GLASGOW AND EDINBURGH RD

ML7

62

79   A   B   80   C   81   D   E   81   F

B7066

WILSONS RD

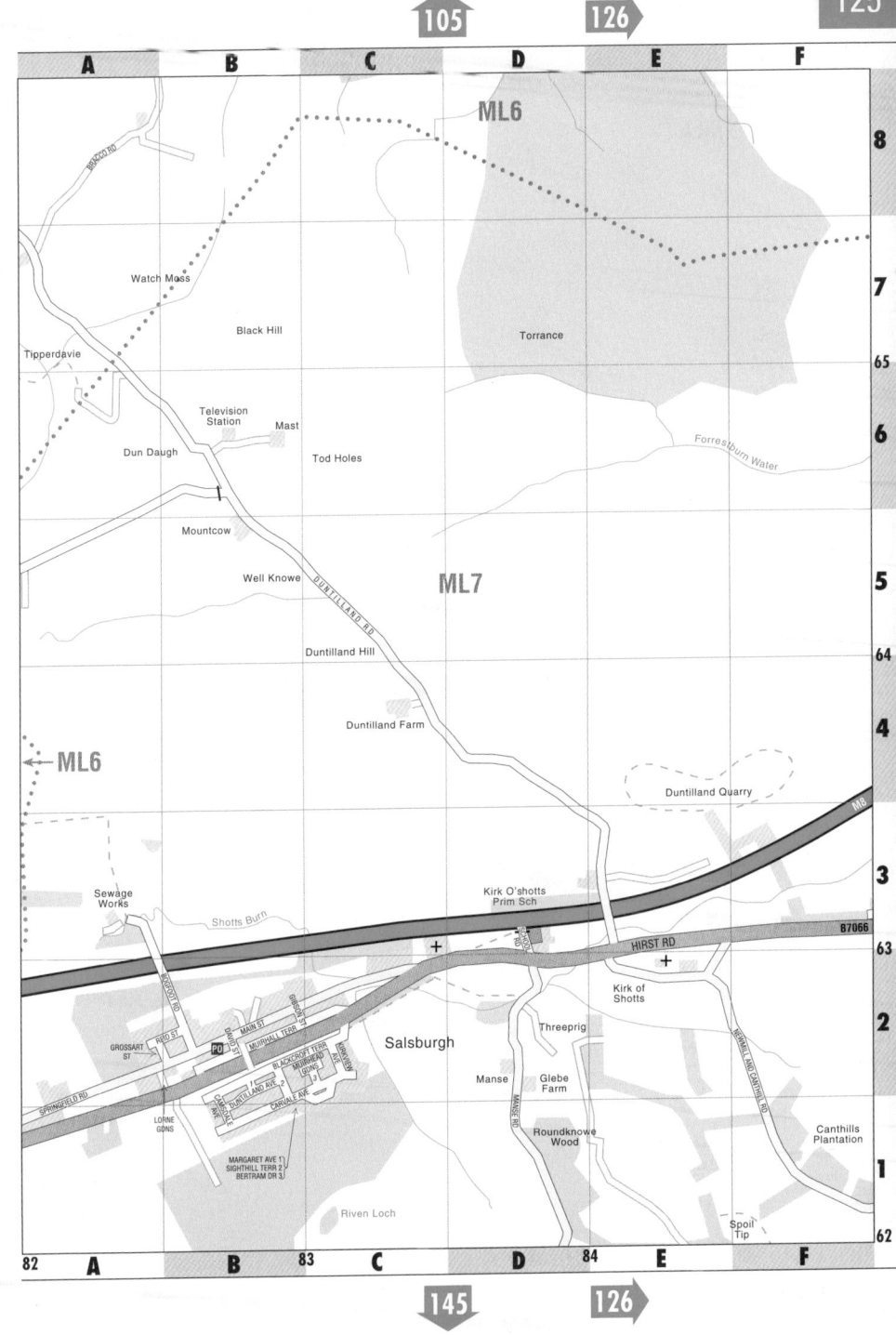

105
126

A   B   C   D   E   F

8

ML6

7

Watch Mass

65

Black Hill

Torrance

Tipperdavie

6

Forrestburn Water

Television
Station   Mast

Dun Daugh

Tod Holes

Mountcow

ML7

Well Knowe

DUNTILLAND RD

5

64

Duntilland Hill

4

Duntilland Farm

Duntilland Quarry

M8

← ML6

Sewage
Works

Kirk O'shotts
Prim Sch

3

63

B7066

Shotts Burn

HIRST RD

+

Kirk of
Shotts

+

2

Salsburgh

Threeprig

GROSSART
ST   MAIN ST

PO

MURRELL TERR

BLACKCROFT TERR

CARLUKE AVE

Manse

Glebe
Farm

SPRINGFIELD RD

LORNE
GDNS

MARGARET AVE 1
SIGHTHILL TERR 2
BERTRAM DR 3

Roundknowe
Wood

Canthills
Plantation

1

Riven Loch

Spoil
Tip

62

82   A   B   83   C   D   84   E   F

145
126

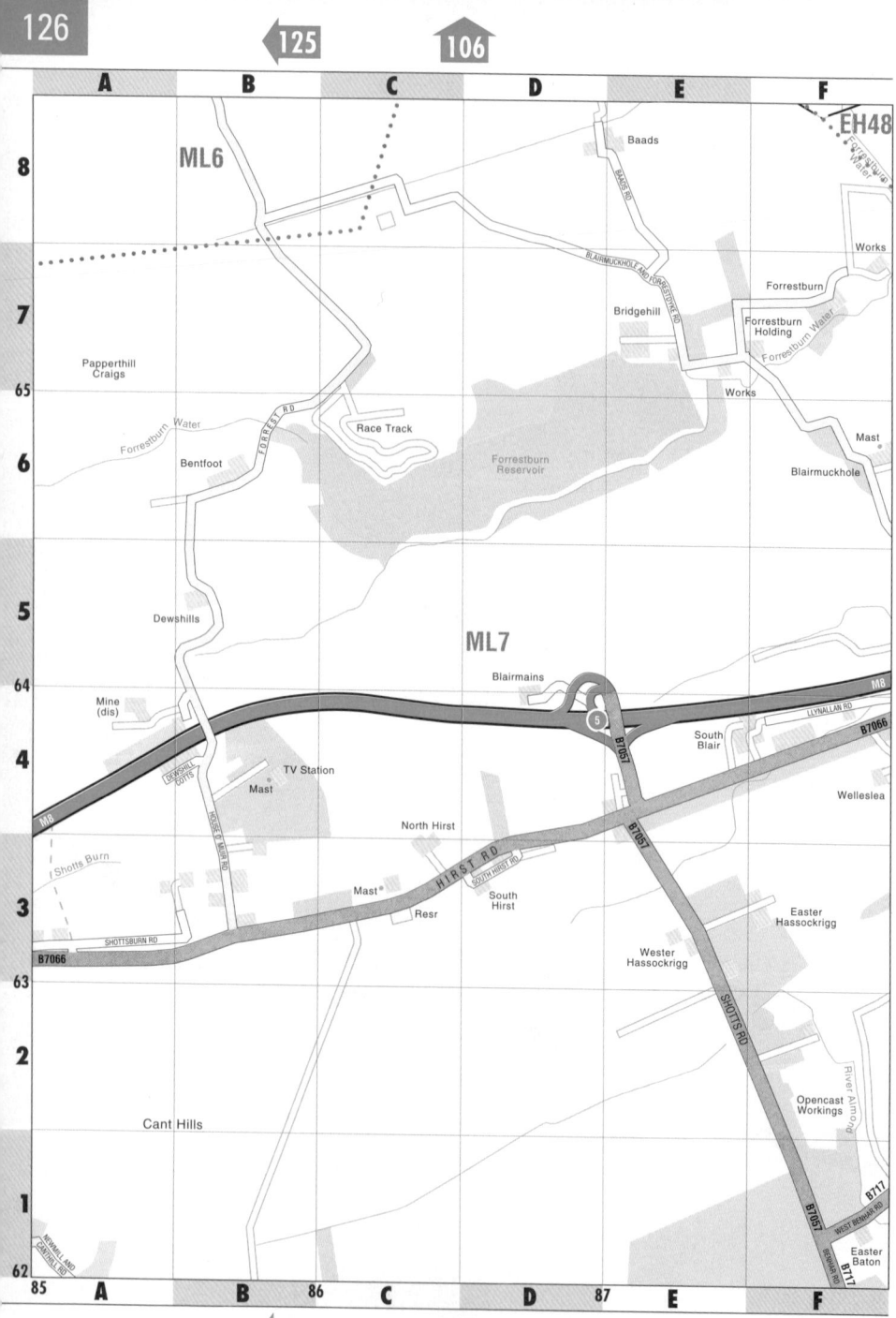

EH48

ML6

8

Baads

BAADS RD

7

Forrestburn

Bridgehill

Forrestburn
Holding

BLAIRMUCKHOLE AND FORRESTONE RD

Forrestburn Water

Papperthill
Craigs

Works

65

Works

Forrestburn Water

Race Track

FORREST RD

Bentfoot

Mast

6

Forrestburn
Reservoir

Blairmuckhole

Dewshills

5

ML7

Blairmains

M8

64

Mine
(dis)

5

B7057

South
Blair

LLYNALLAN RD

B7066

4

LOCKHILL
COTTS

TV Station

Mast

ROSIE'S MUIR RD

Welleslea

M8

North Hirst

HIRST RD

B7057

Shotts Burn

SOUTH HIRST RD

Easter
Hassockrigg

3

Mast

South
Hirst

Resr

SHOTTS RD

63

SHOTTSBURN RD

Wester
Hassockrigg

B7066

River Almond

2

Cant Hills

Opencast
Workings

B717

1

B7057

WEST BENHAR RD

62

NEWMILL AND
CANTSE RD

Easter
Baton

BENHAR RD

B717

108

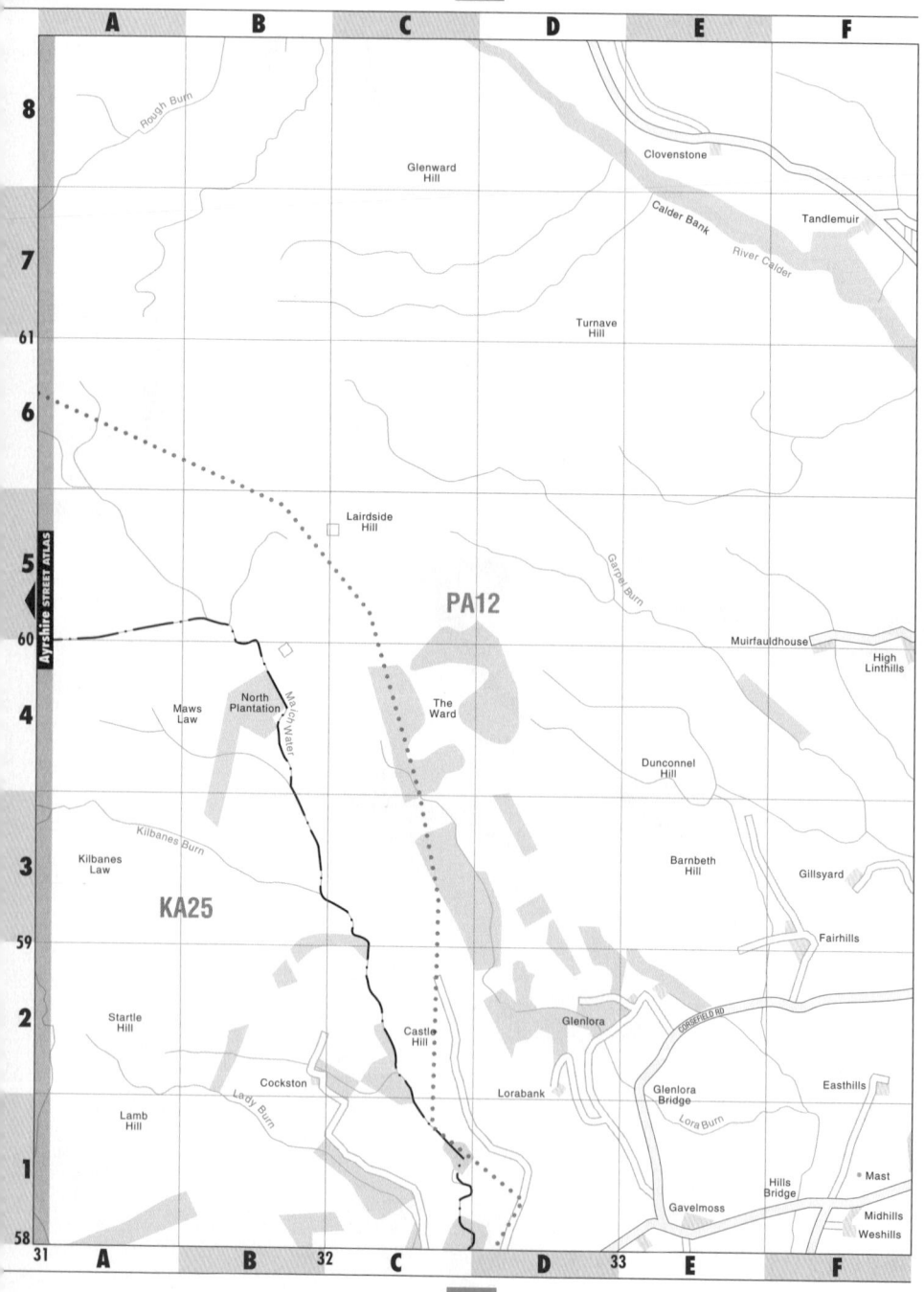

Ayrshire STREET ATLAS

149

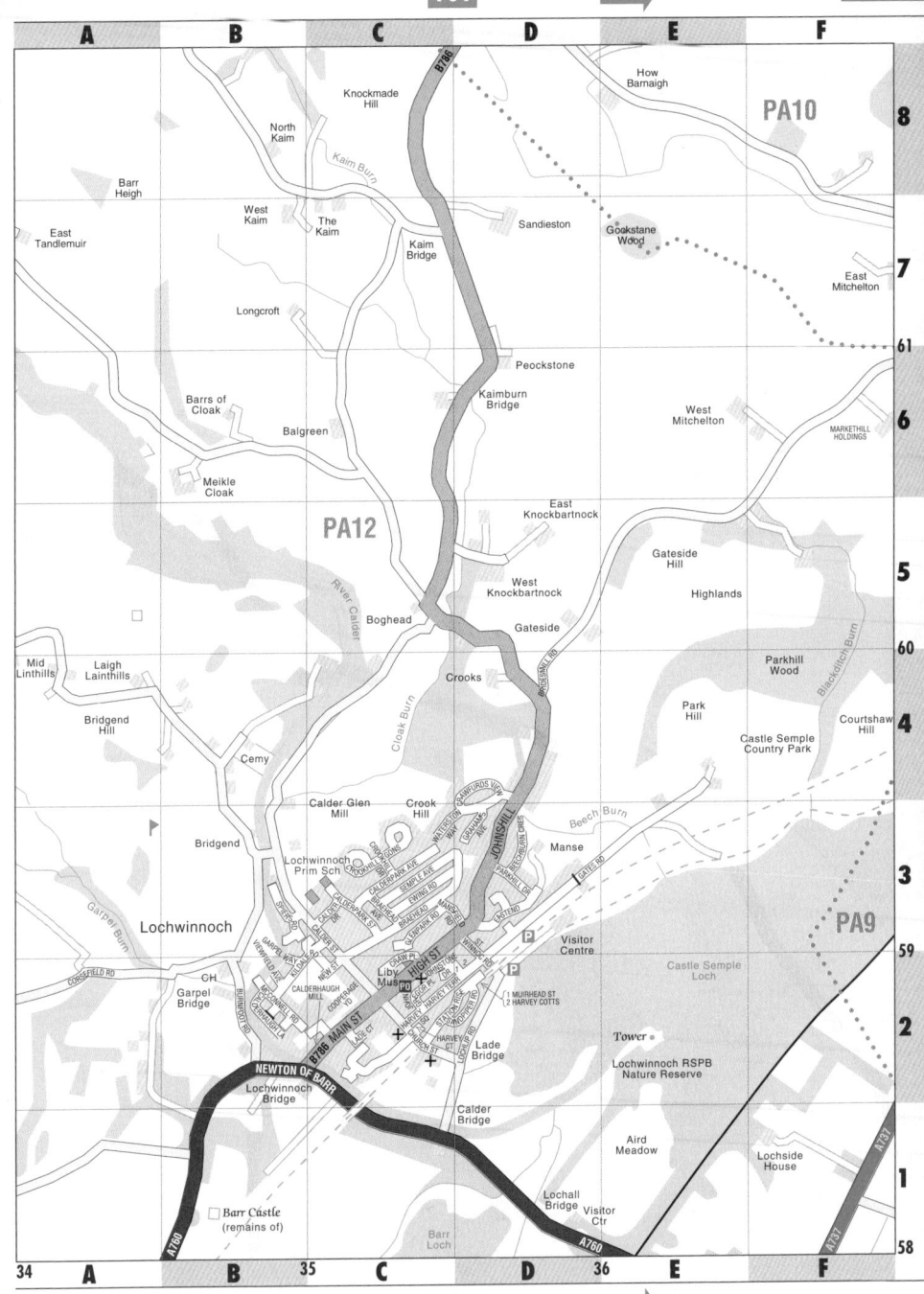

PA10

PA12

PA9

Knockmade
Hill

North
Kaim

Barr
Heigh

East
Tandlemuir

West
Kaim

The
Kaim

Longcroft

Kaim
Bridge

How
Barnaigh

Sandieston

Gookstane
Wood

East
Mitchelton

Peockstone

Kaimburn
Bridge

Barrs of
Cloak

Balgreen

West
Mitchelton

MARKETHILL
HOLDINGS

Meikle
Cloak

East
Knockbartnock

Gateside
Hill

Highlands

West
Knockbartnock

Boghead

Gateside

Crooks

Parkhill
Wood

Mid
Linthills

Laigh
Lainthills

Park
Hill

Courtshaw
Hill

Bridgend
Hill

Castle Semple
Country Park

Cemy

Calder Glen
Mill

Crook
Hill

Manse

Bridgend

Lochwinnoch
Prim Sch

Lochwinnoch

Beech Burn

Visitor
Centre

Castle Semple
Loch

GH
Garpel
Bridge

Calderhaugh
Mill

Liby
Mus

PO

HIGH ST

1 Muirhead St
2 Harvey Cotts

Tower

Lochwinnoch RSPB
Nature Reserve

Lade
Bridge

NEWTON OF BARR

Lochwinnoch
Bridge

Calder
Bridge

Aird
Meadow

Lochside
House

Barr Castle
(remains of)

Lochall
Bridge

Visitor
Ctr

Barr
Loch

River Calder

Kaim Burn

Cloak Burn

Garpel Burn

Blackditch Burn

B786

A760

A737

BRIDGEND RD

KINGSFIELD RD

BURNFOOT RD

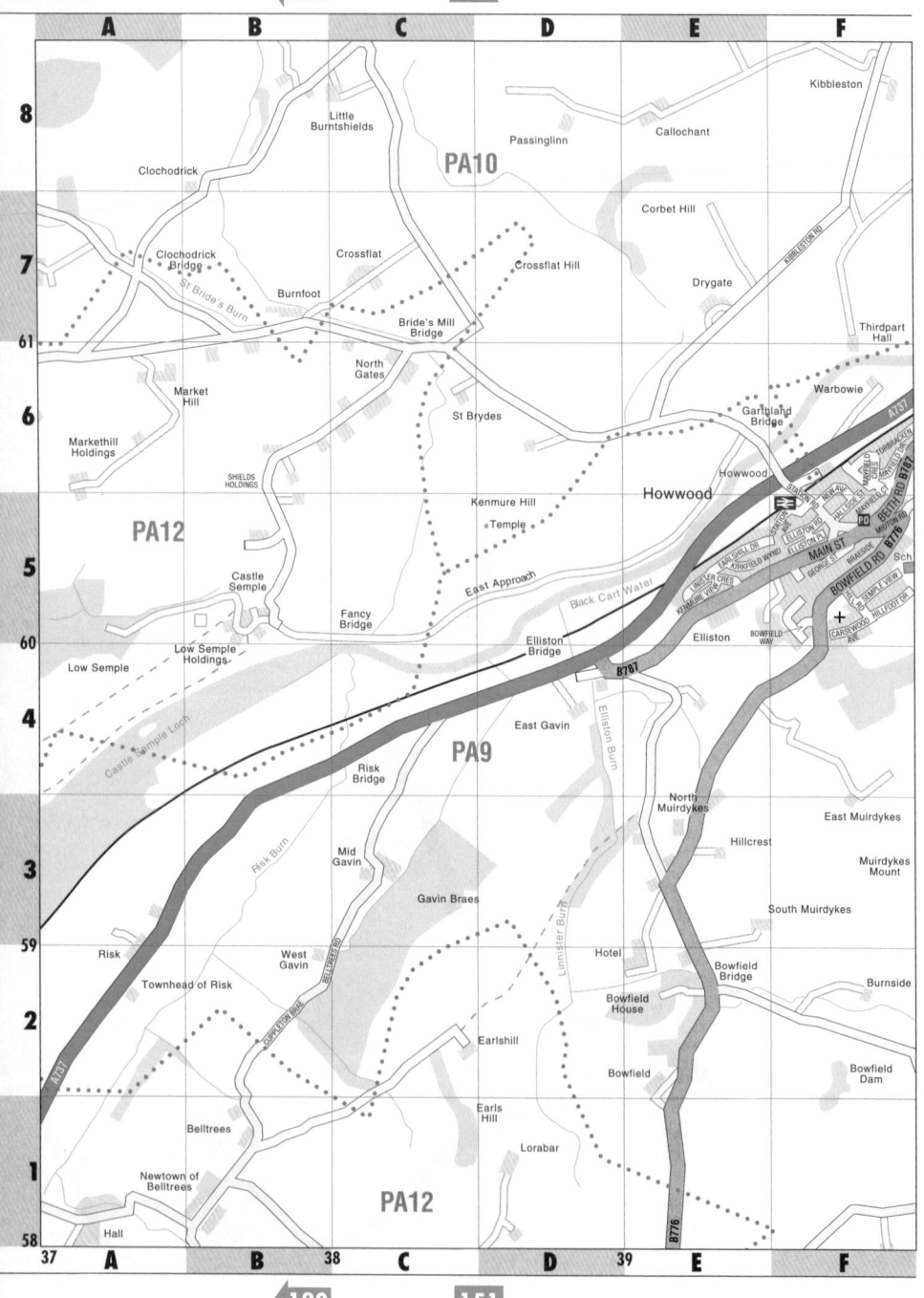

PA10

PA12

PA9

Kibbleston

Little
Burntshields

Passinglinn

Callochant

Clochodrick

Corbet Hill

Clochodrick
Bridge

Crossflat

Crossflat Hill

Drygate

St Bride's Burn

Burnfoot

Bride's Mill
Bridge

Thirdpart
Hall

North
Gates

Warbowie

Market
Hill

Gartbland
Bridge

Markethill
Holdings

St Brydes

Howwood

Howwood

SHIELDS
HOLDINGS

Kenmure Hill

MAIN ST

Temple

BOWFIELD RD

BT61

B776

Castle
Semple

East Approach

Black Cart Water

Sch

Fancy
Bridge

Elliston
Bridge

Elliston

BOWFIELD
WAY

CARSEWOOD
AVE

Low Semple
Holdings

BT61

Low Semple

East Gavin

Elliston Burn

Risk
Bridge

North
Muirdykes

East Muirdykes

Risk Burn

Mid
Gavin

Gavin Braes

Hillcrest

Muirdykes
Mount

Lunnister Burn

South Muirdykes

Risk

West
Gavin

Hotel

Bowfield
Bridge

Burnside

Townhead of Risk

Bowfield
House

Earlshill

Bowfield

Bowfield
Dam

Belltrees

Earls
Hill

Lorabar

Newtown of
Belltrees

PA12

Hall

B776

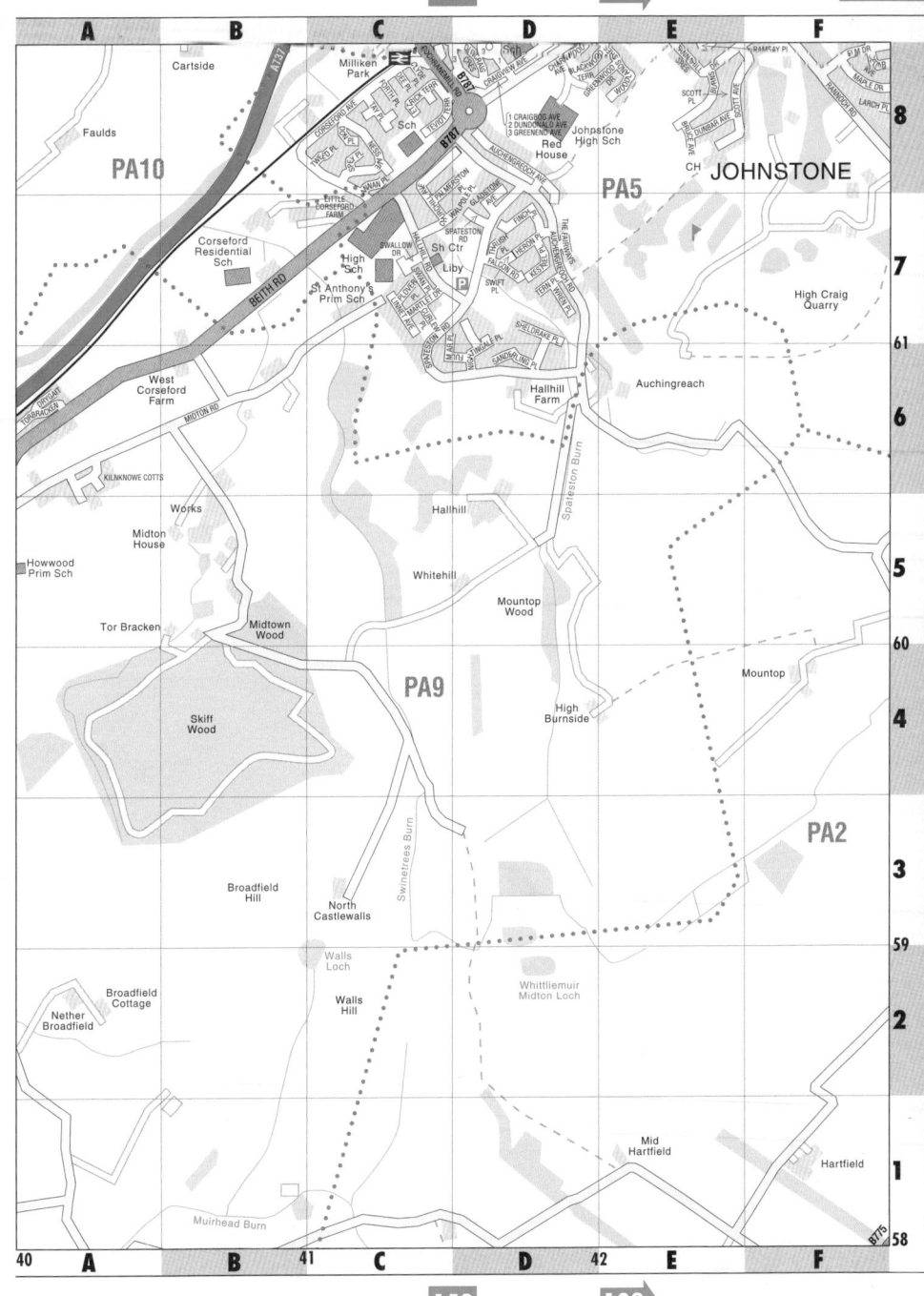

JOHNSTONE

PA10

Cartside
Faulds
Milliken Park
Corseford Residential Sch
Johnstone High Sch
Red House
PA5

High Craig Quarry

West Corseford Farm
KILNKNOWE COTTS
Works
Midton House
Howwood Prim Sch
Tor Bracken
Midtown Wood

Hallhill Farm
Auchingreach

PA9

Hallhill
Whitehill
Mountop Wood
Mountop

High Burnside

Skiff Wood

Broadfield Hill
North Castlewalls
Swinetrees Burn
Spateston Burn

PA2

Walls Loch
Broadfield Cottage
Nether Broadfield
Walls Hill
Whittliemuir Midton Loch

Mid Hartfield
Hartfield

Muirhead Burn

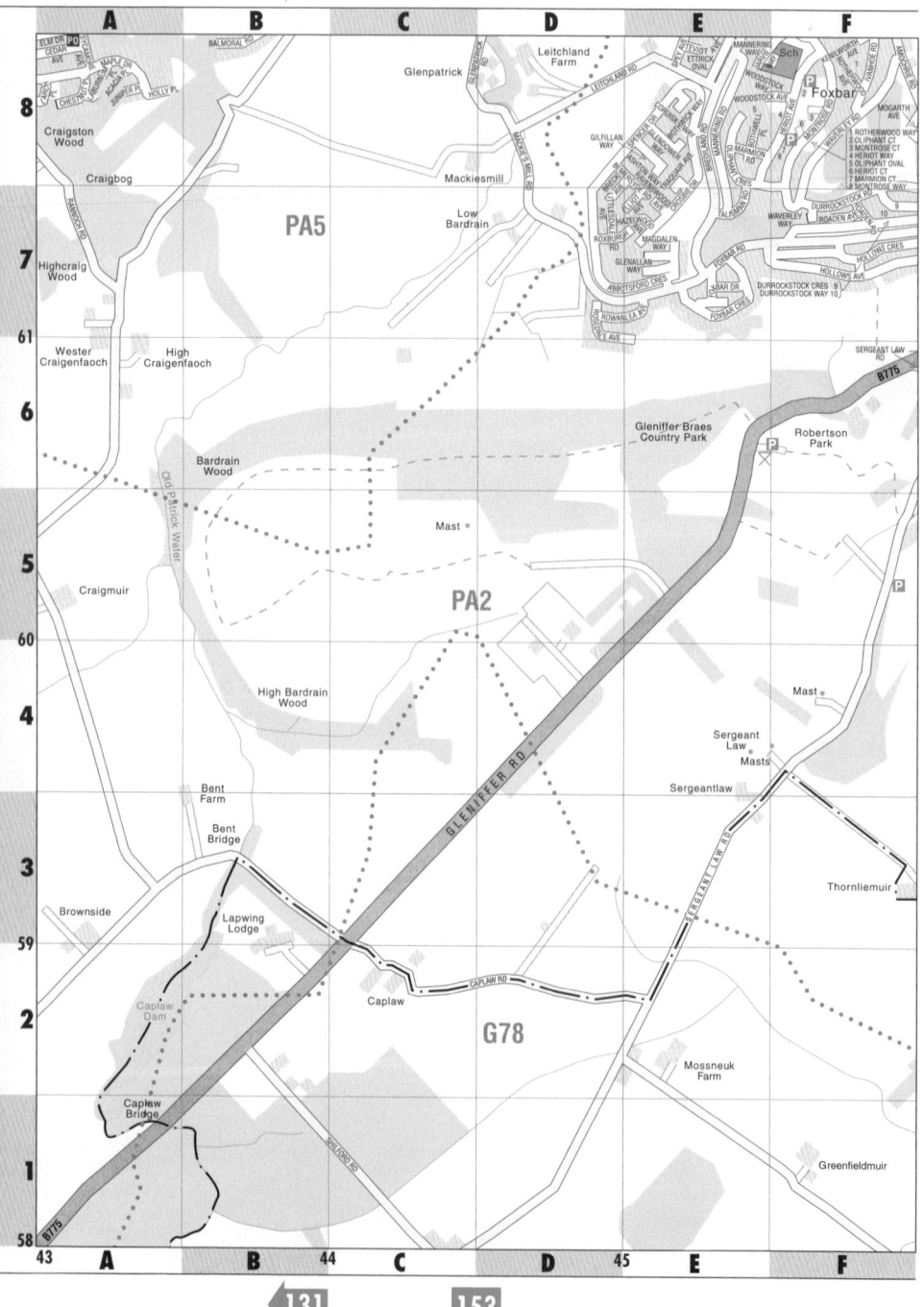

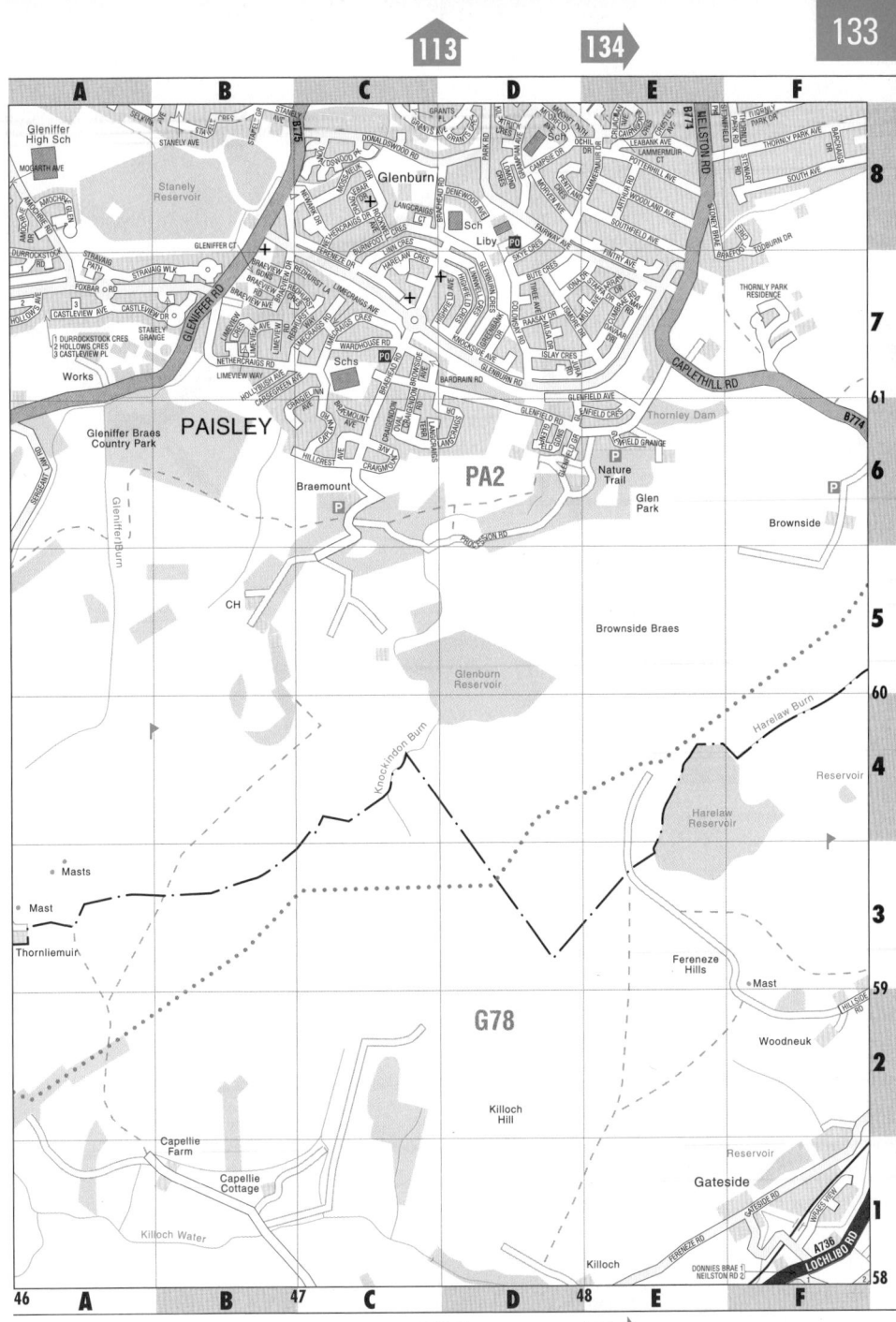

113
134
154
134

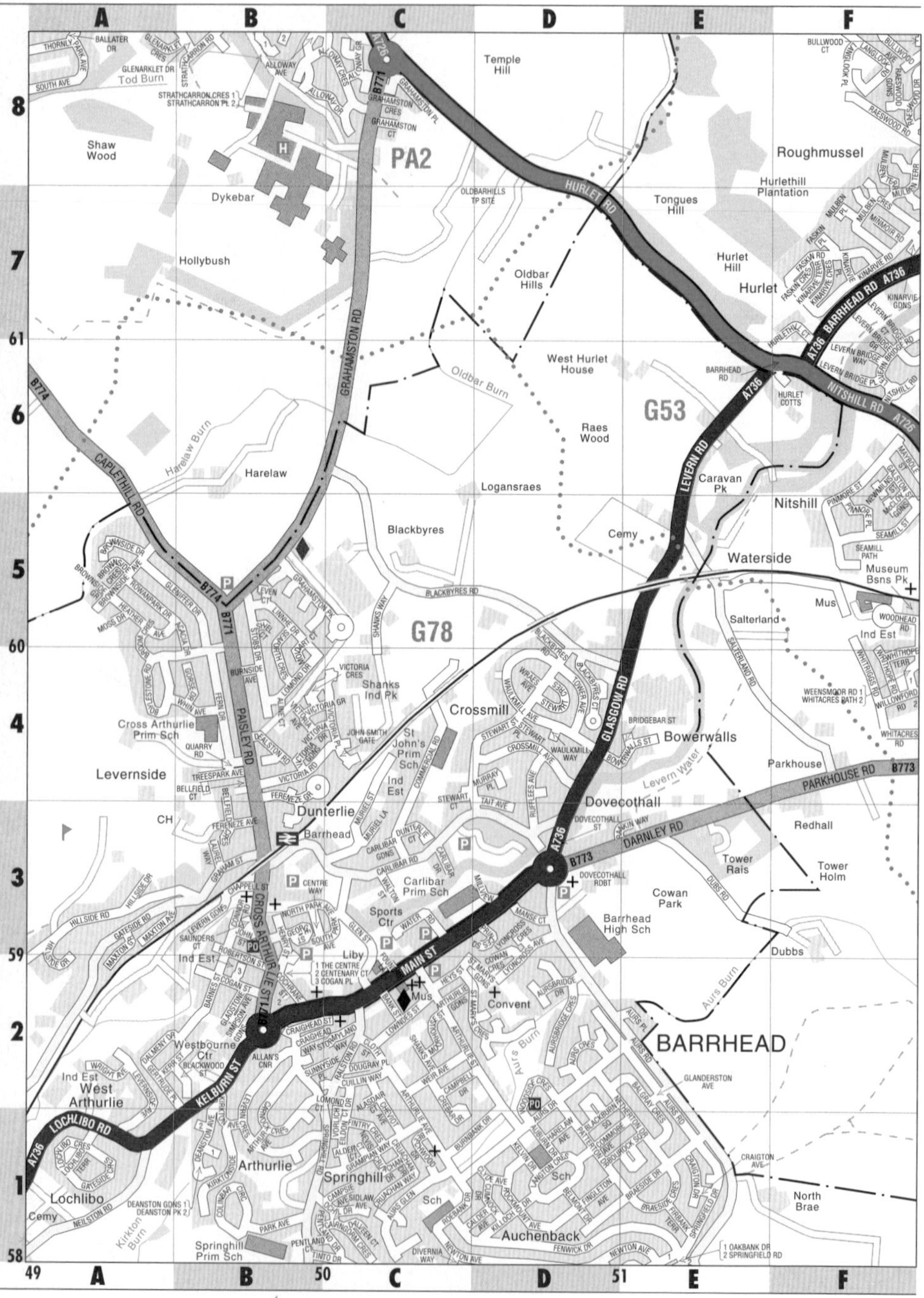

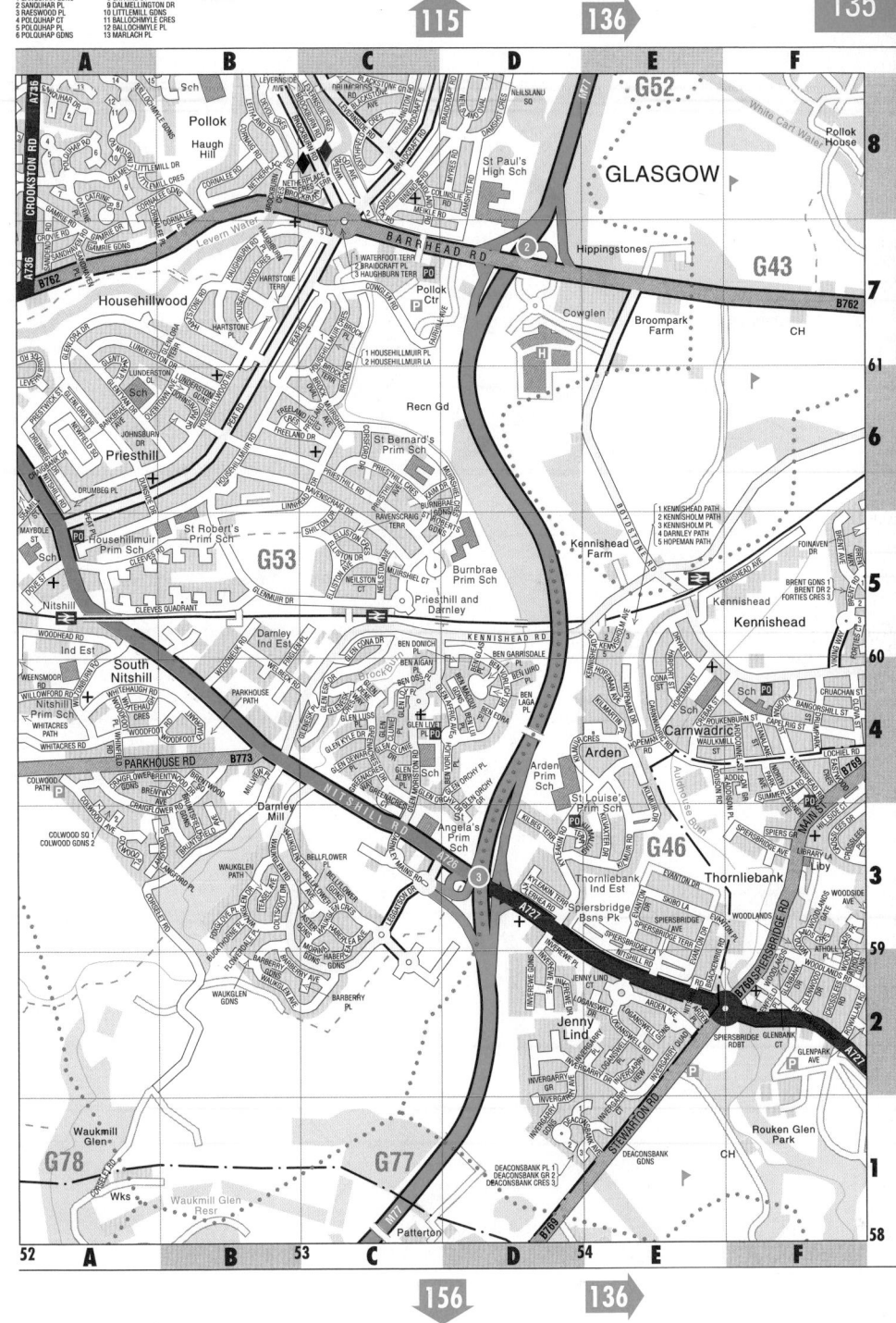

A8
1 SANQUHAR GDNS
2 SANQUHAR PL
3 RAESWOOD DR
4 POLQUHAP CT
5 POLQUHAP PL
6 POLQUHAP GDNS

7 CATRINE GDNS
8 CATRINE CT
9 DALMELLINGTON DR
10 LITTLEMILL GDNS
11 BALLOCHMYLE CRES
12 BALLOCHMYLE PL
13 MARLACH PL

14 BALLOCHMYLE DR
15 BARGANY PL

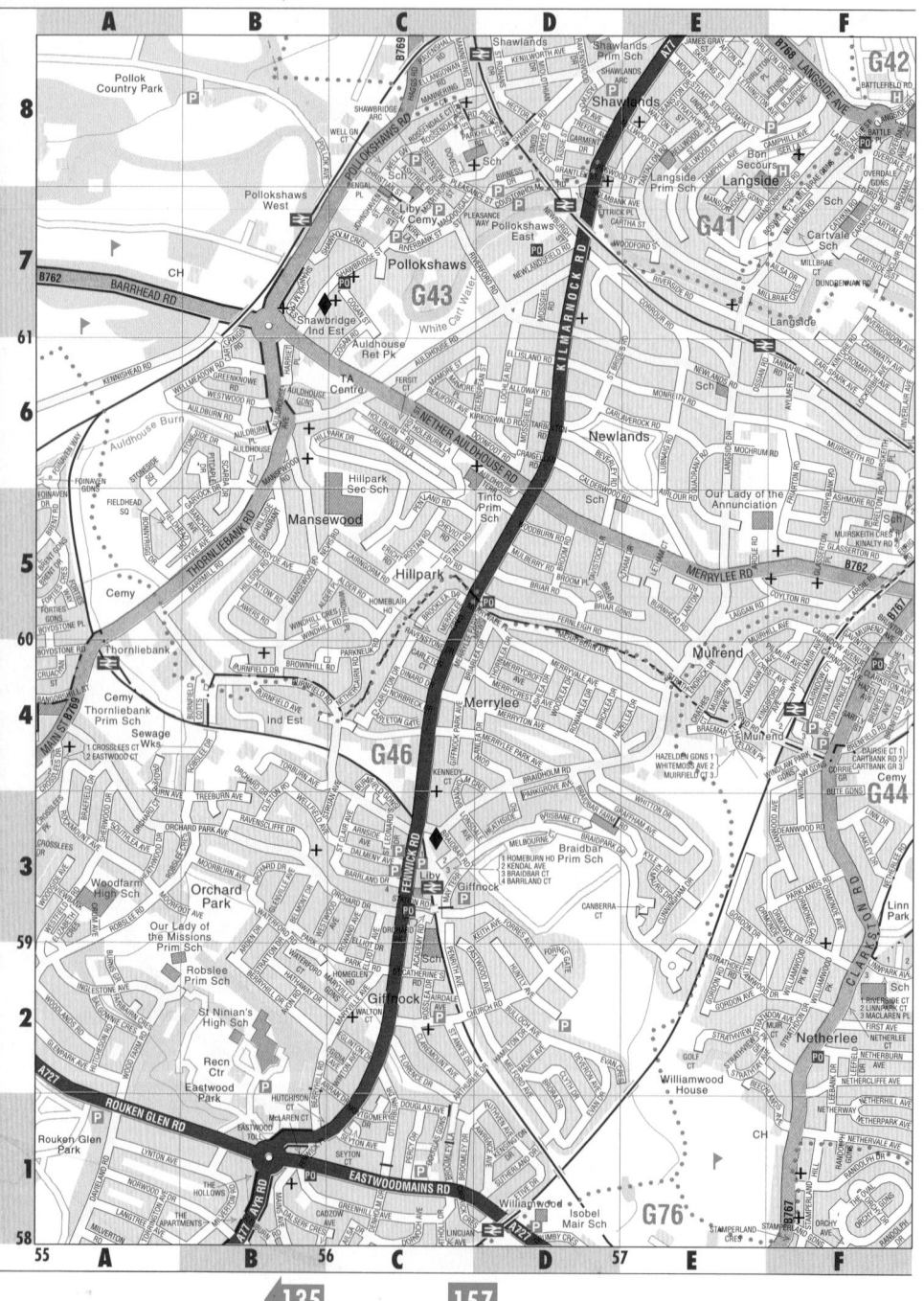

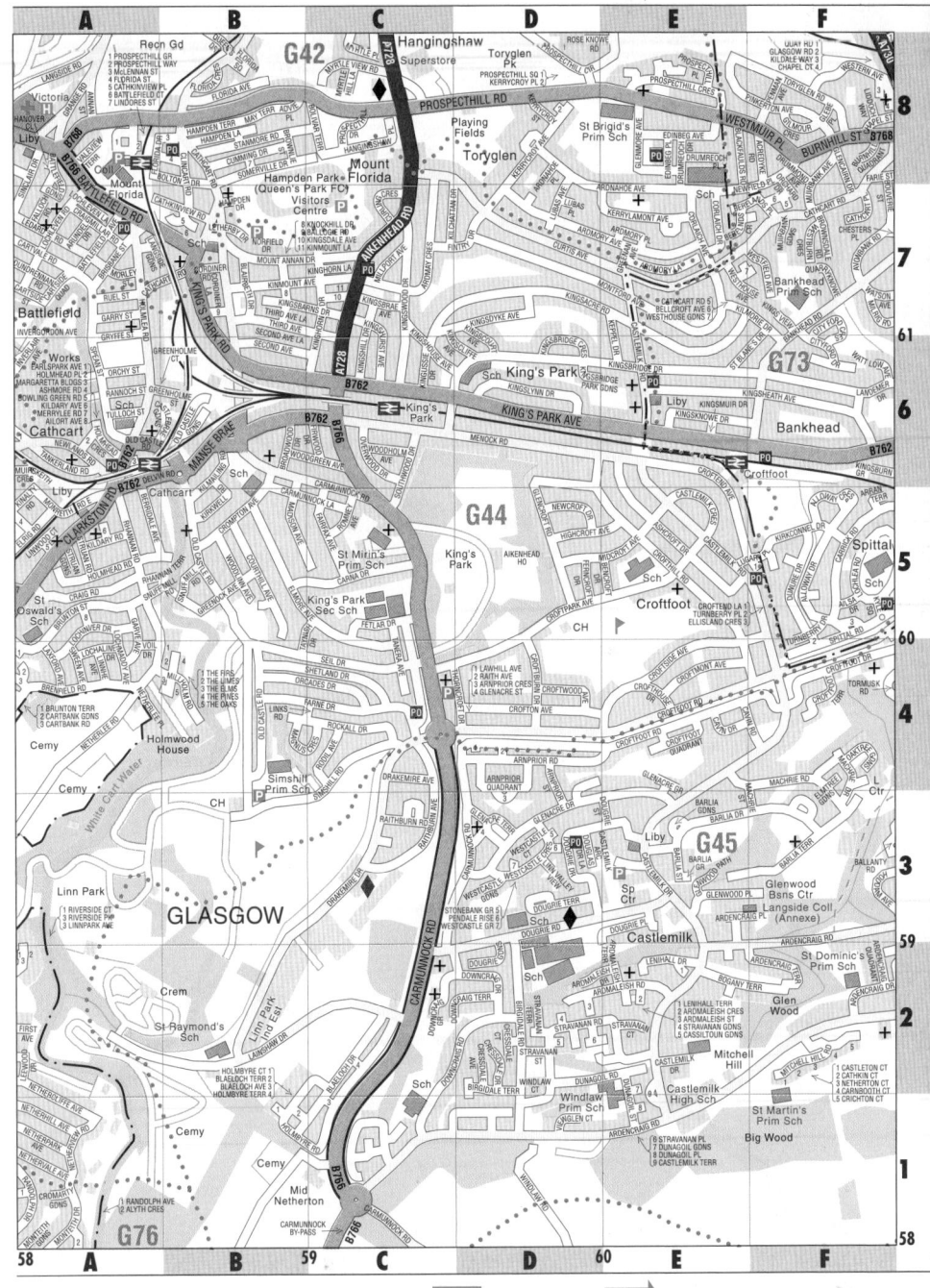

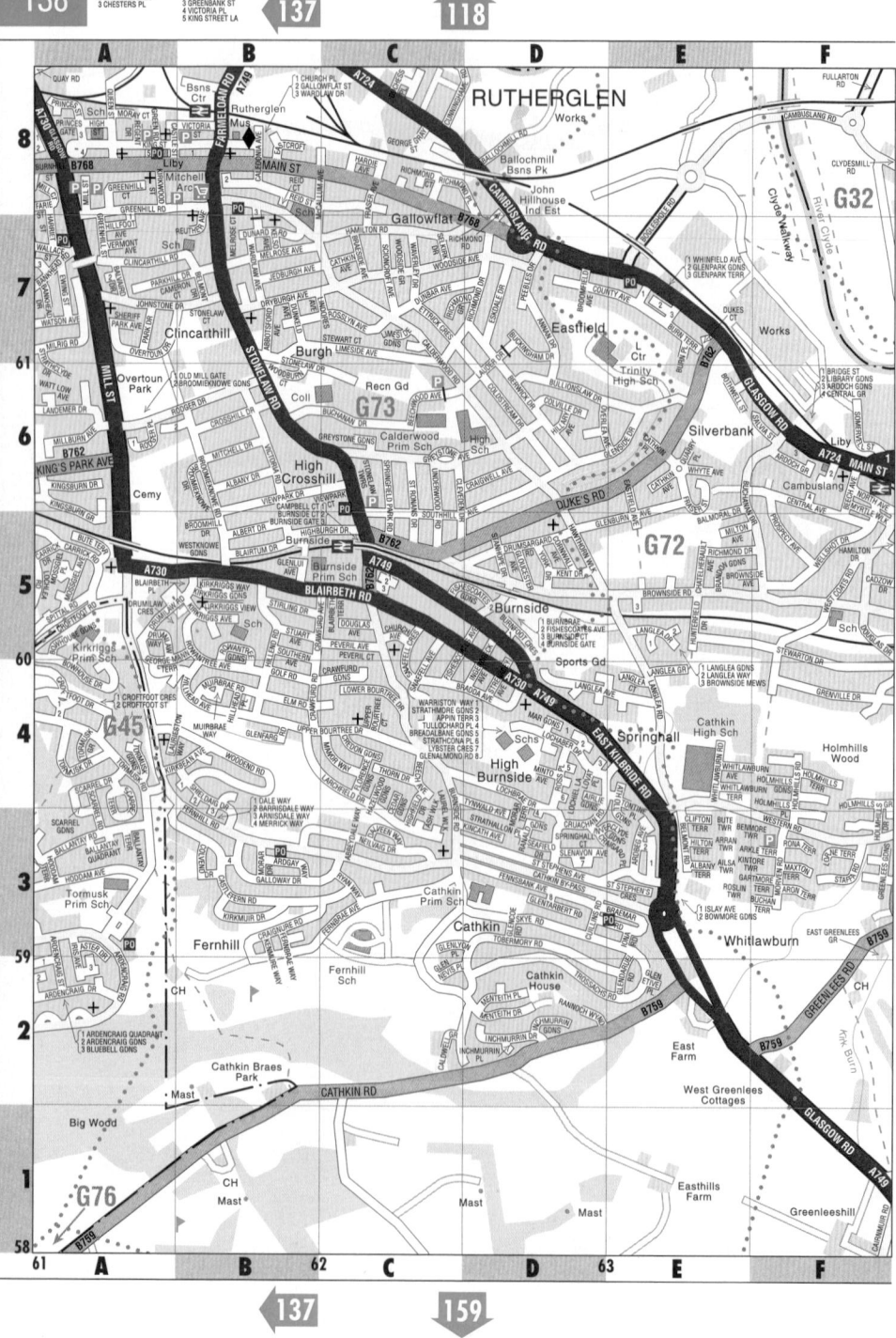

138

A7
1 MACDONALD ST
2 BALVAIRD CRES
3 CHESTERS PL

A8
1 WESTERN AVE
2 CHAPEL ST
3 GREENBANK ST
4 VICTORIA PL
5 KING STREET LA

137   118

RUTHERGLEN

Bsns Ctr
Rutherglen Mus

QUAY RD
Sch
MORAY CT
VICTORIA AVE

Liby
Mitchell Arc

MAIN ST

Gallowflat

Ballochmill Bsns Pk

John Hillhouse Ind Est

Works

G32

FULLARTON RD
CAMBUSLANG RD
CLYDESMILL RD

River Clyde

Clyde Walkway

Clincarthill
Overtoun Park
OLD MILL GATE
Burgh
Recn Gd

G73

Calderwood Prim Sch

Eastfield

L Ctr

Trinity High Sch

Silverbank

Cambuslang

MAIN ST
Liby

WHINFIELD AVE
GLENPARK GDNS
GLENPARK TERR

BRIDGE ST
LIBRARY GDNS
ADDON GDNS
CENTRAL DR

KING'S PARK AVE

High Crosshill

Cemy

Burnside Gate

Burnside

Burnside Prim Sch

DUKE'S RD

G72

BROWNSIDE AV

Sch

BLAIRBETH RD

Kirkriggs Prim Sch

G45

Muirbrae Way

Tormusk Prim Sch

CROFTFOOT CRES
CROFTFOOT ST

Fernhill

Warriston Way
Strathmore Gdns
Appin Terr
Tullochard Pl
Breadalbane Gdns
Strathcona Pl
Glister Cres
Glenalmond Rd

High Burnside

Springhall

Cathkin High Sch

Holmhills Wood

EAST KILBRIDE RD

Cathkin Prim Sch

Cathkin

Cathkin House

Sports Gd

LANGLEA AV

LANGLEA GDNS
LANGLEA WAY
LANGLEA MEWS

Whitlawburn

EAST GREENLEES GR

B759

ARDENCRAIG QUADRANT
ARDENCRAIG GDNS
BLUEBELL GDNS

Fernhill Sch

Cathkin Braes Park

Mast

CATHKIN RD

East Farm

West Greenlees Cottages

GREENLEES RD

B759

GLASGOW RD

CH

Kirk Burn

Big Wood

G76

Mast

CH   Mast

Mast

Mast

Easthills Farm

Greenleeshill

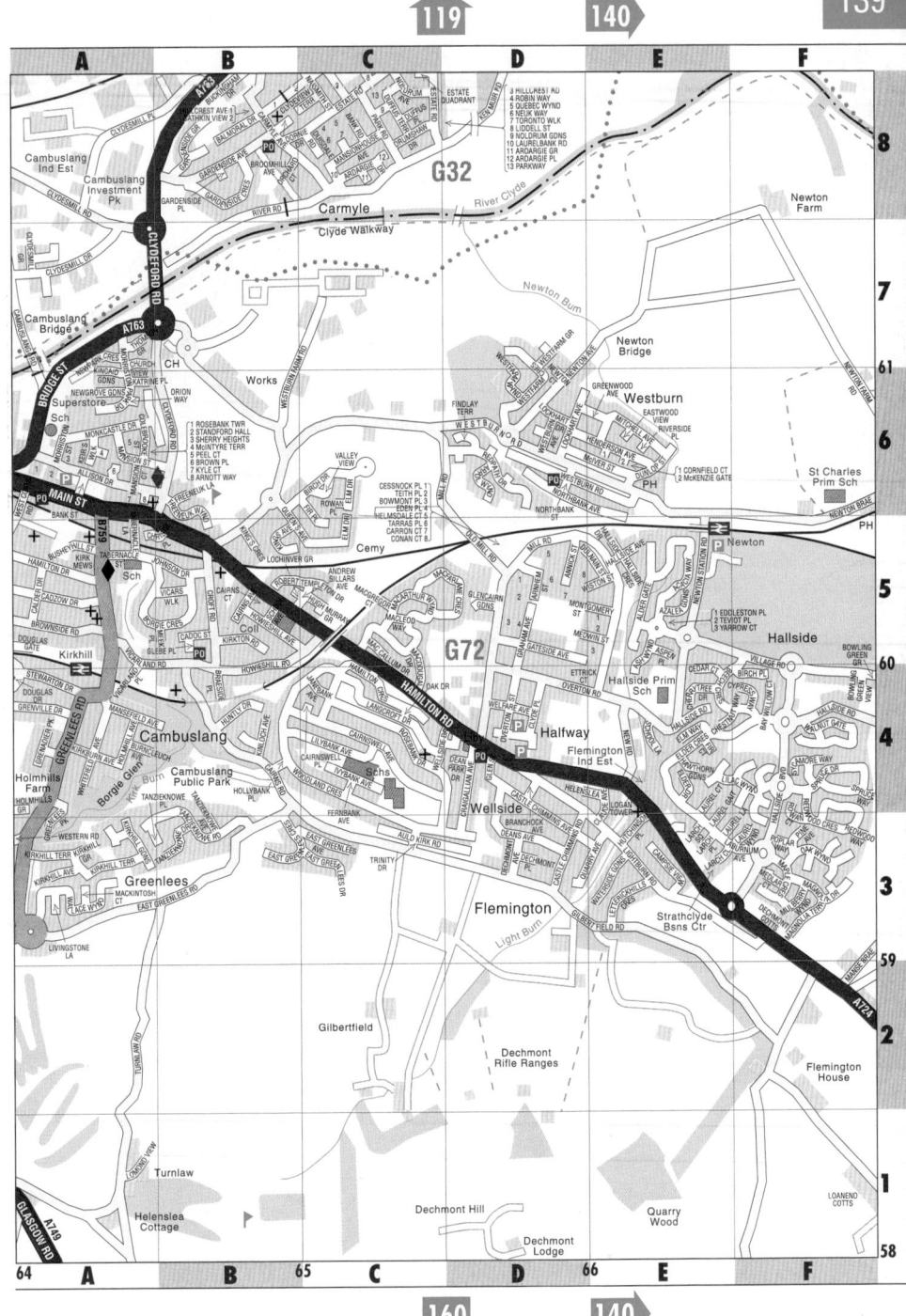

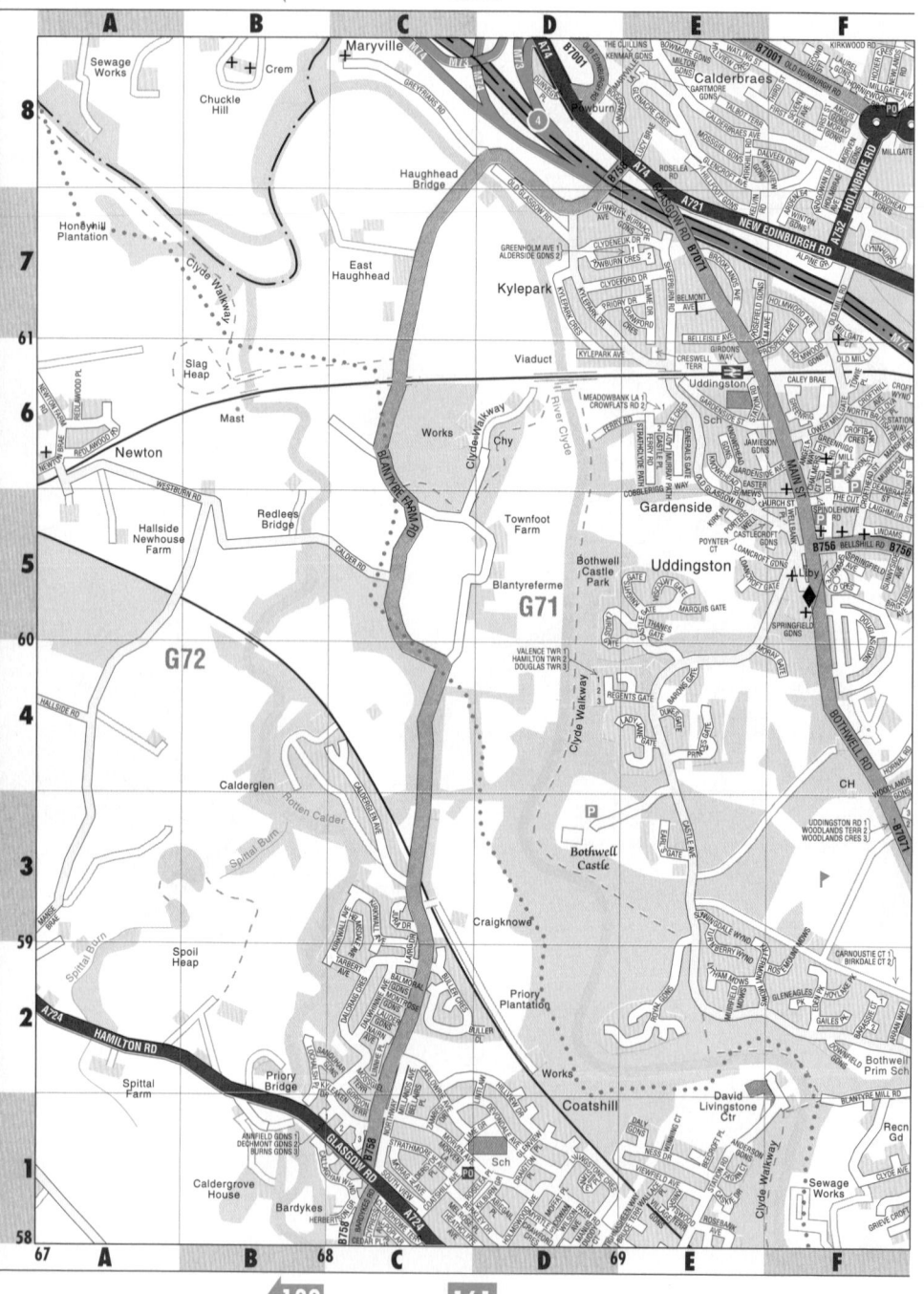

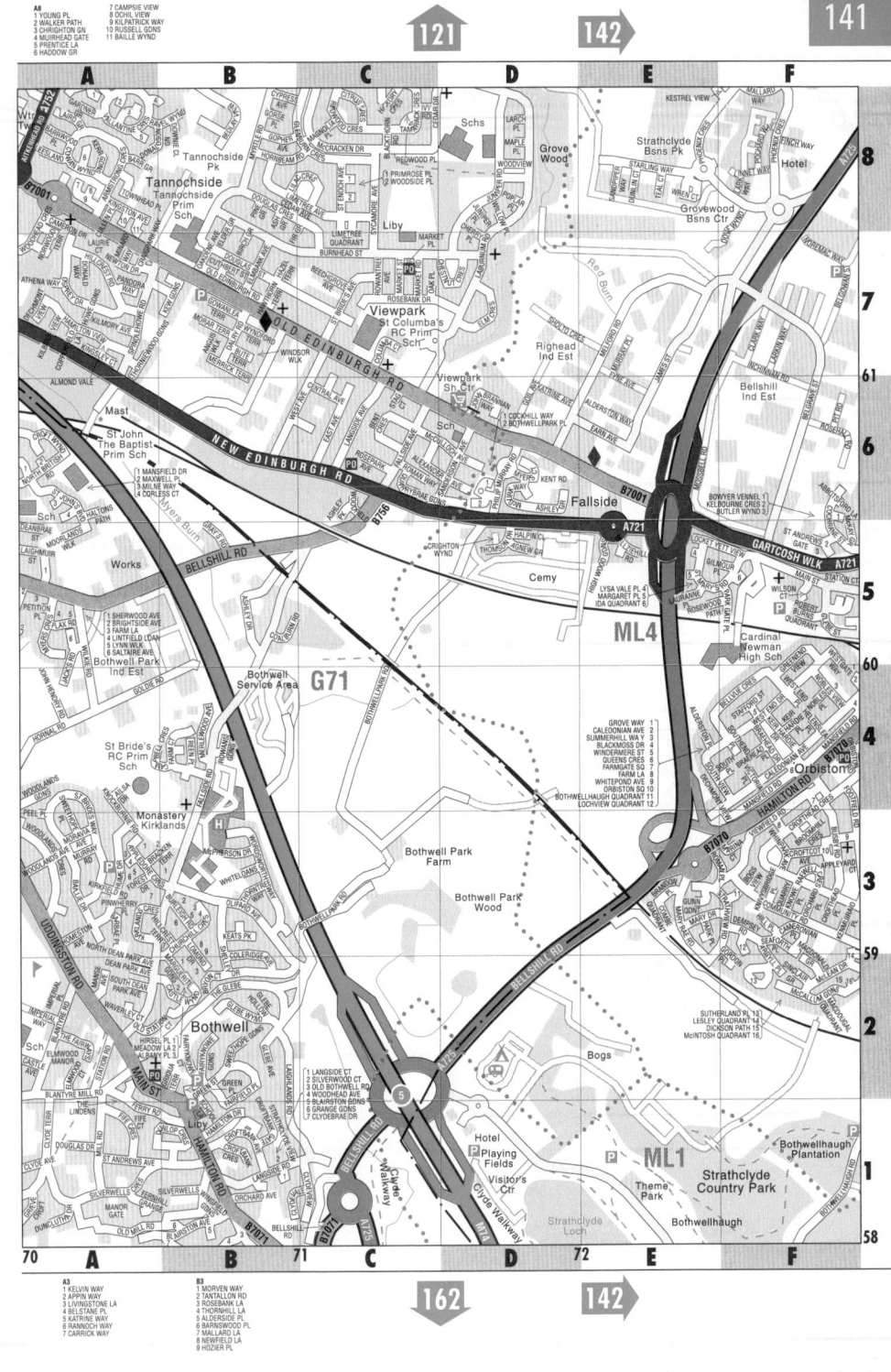

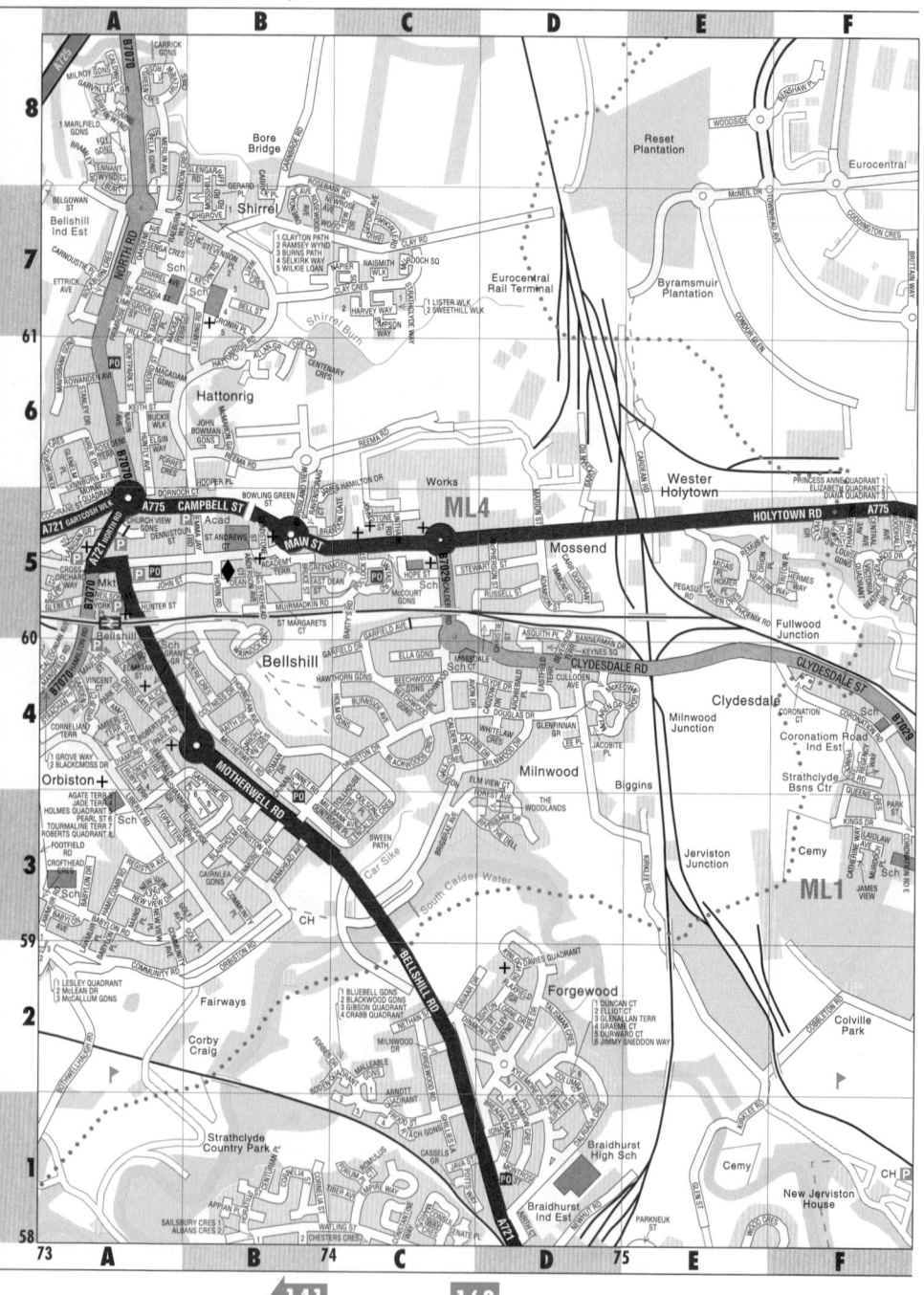

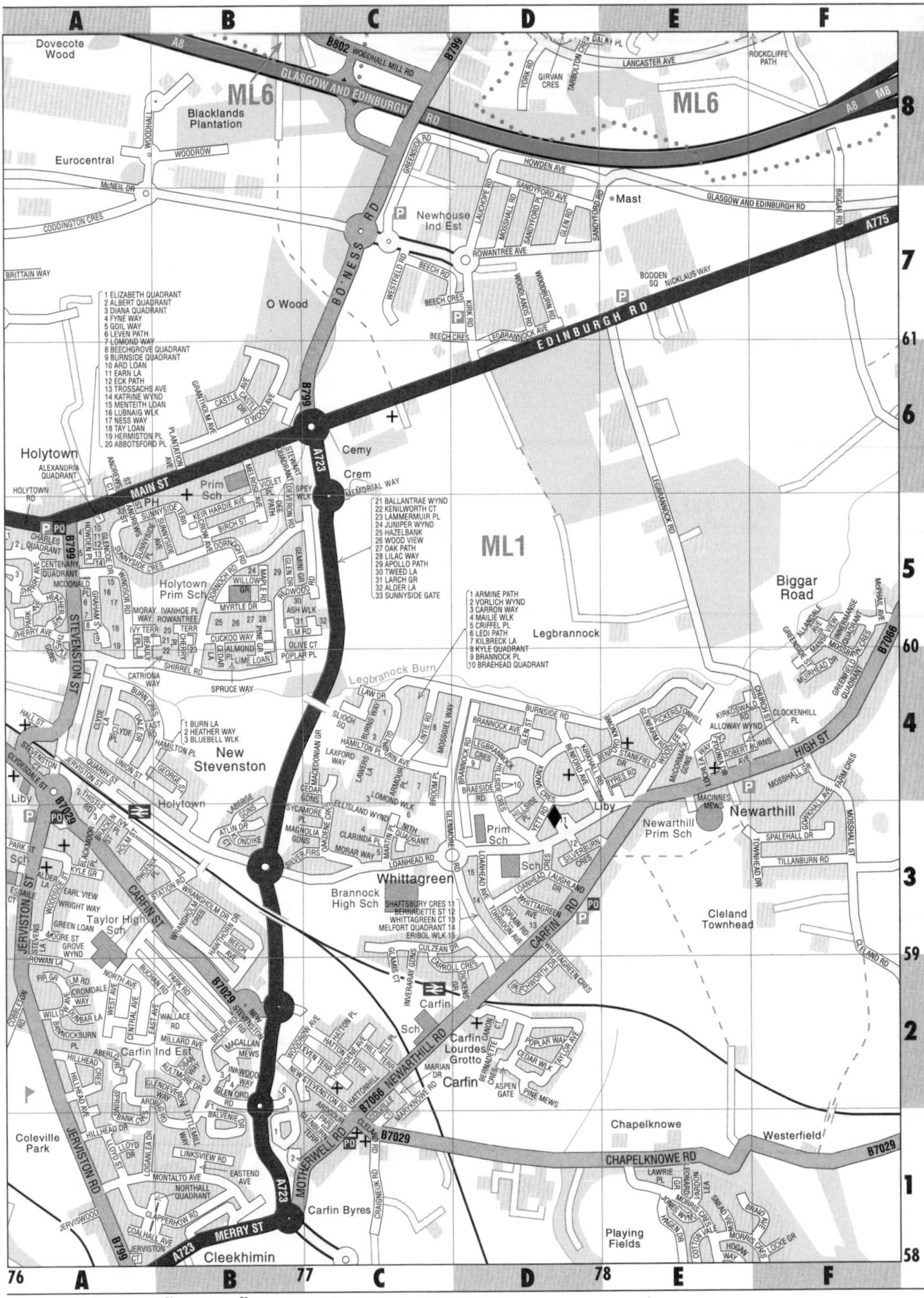

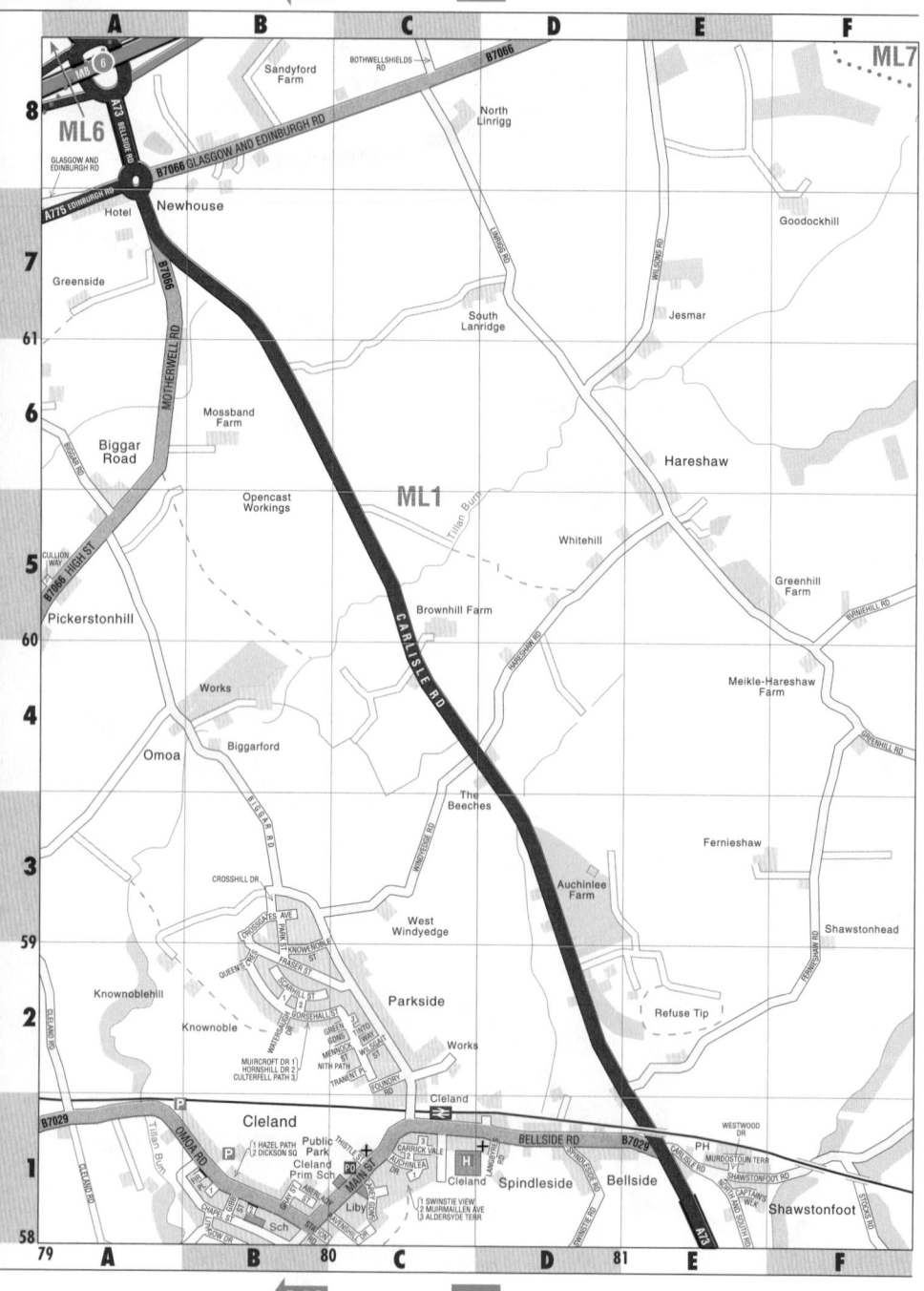

ML7

ML6

8

GLASGOW AND
EDINBURGH RD

A775 EDINBURGH RD

A73 BELLSIDE RD

B7066 GLASGOW AND EDINBURGH RD

B7066

Sandyford
Farm

BOTHWELLSHIELDS
RD

North
Linrigg

Goodockhill

Hotel

Newhouse

7

Greenside

61

B7066

MOTHERWELL RD

LINRIGG RD

WILSONS RD

South
Lanridge

Jesmar

6

BIGGAR RD

Biggar
Road

Mossband
Farm

Hareshaw

ML1

Opencast
Workings

Trillan Burn

Whitehill

5

CULLION
WAY

B7066 HIGH ST

Brownhill Farm

CARLISLE RD

KAPESDHUN RD

Greenhill
Farm

BROWNHILL RD

Pickerstonhill

60

Works

Meikle-Hareshaw
Farm

4

Omoa

Biggarford

BISSAR RD

GREENHILL RD

3

CROSSHILL DR

The
Beeches

WINDYEDGE RD

Auchinlee
Farm

Fernieshaw

Shawstonhead

FERNIESHAW RD

59

CROSSGATES AVE

PARK RD

KNOWNOBLE
ST

FRASER ST

West
Windyedge

Knownoblehill

QUEEN'S CT

SCAHILL

GORSEHALL ST

Parkside

2

Knownoble

WATERSIDE
DR

GREEN
GOONS

MENNOCK
PL

NITH PATH

WELLGATE

ASCENSION PL

TRANENT PL

Works

Refuse Tip

MUIRCROFT DR 1
HORNSHILL DR 2
CULTERFELL PATH 3

FOUNDRY
RD

Cleland

WESTWOOD
DR

1

B7029

OMOA RD

CLELAND RD

Trillan Burn

Cleland

P

THISTLE ST

Public
Park

MAIN ST

3
CARRICK VALE
2 AUCHINLEA
DR

BELLSIDE RD

B7029

CARLISLE RD

A73

PH

MURDOSTOUN TERR

SHAWSTONFOOT RD

CAPTAINS WLK

STOCK RD

1 HAZEL PATH
2 DICKSON SQ

P

Cleland
Prim Sch

RD

H
Cleland

LAMBIE ST

Spindleside

Bellside

Shawstonfoot

Liby

1 SWINSTIE VIEW
2 MUIRMAILLEN AVE
3 ALDERSYDE TERR

Sch

58

79

A

B

80

C

D

81

E

F

A B C D E F

8

7

61

6

ML7

5

60

4

ML1

Mast

3

59

2

Hill of
Murdostoun

1

58

82 A B 83 C D 84 E F

Spoil Tip
Well Hill
Westfield
Fortissat View
Roughdike
Mains
Jersay
Law's Castle
Tillan Burn
Pell Hill
Pellhill Wood
Mine (dis)
Muirhouse
Heatherhead Plantation
Hareshaw Moss
Home Farm
Hartwood
Penty
Penty Wood
Newmill Cottage
Big Wood
Newmill Wood
Muiredge Wood
Shawstonfoot Rd

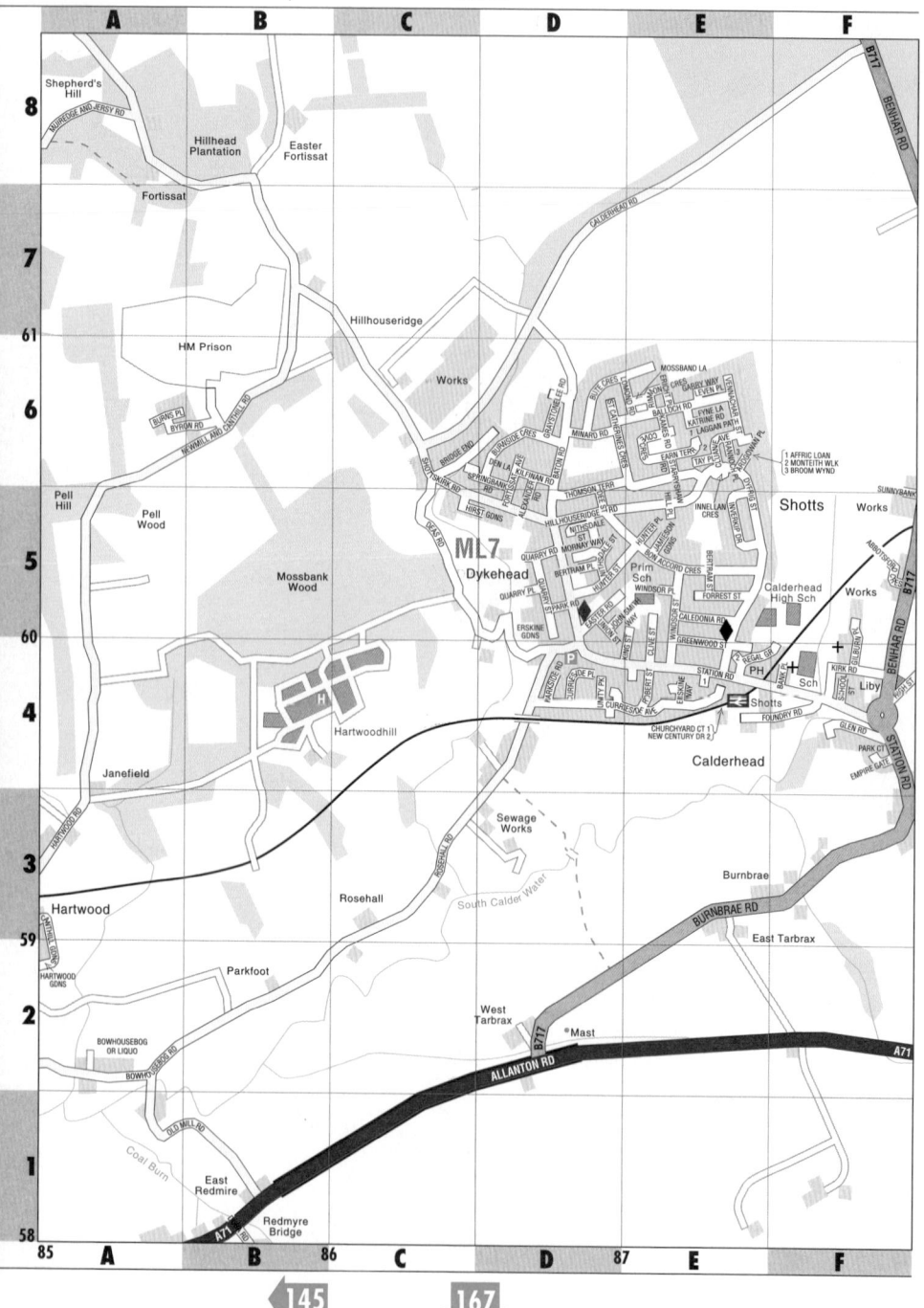

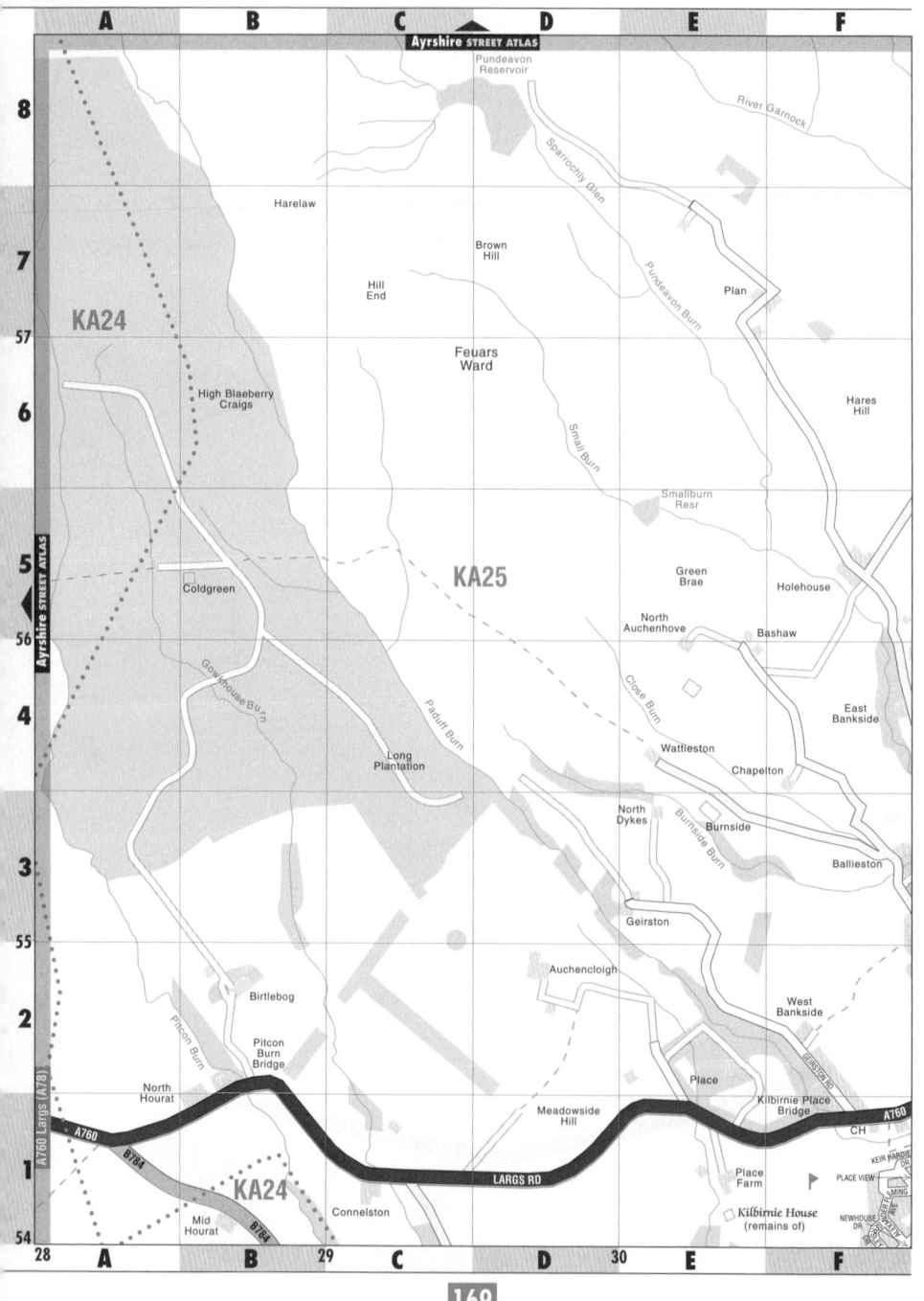

KA24

KA25

KA24

Pundeavon
Reservoir

River Garnock

Harelaw

Brown
Hill

Hill
End

Sparrochly Glen

Pundeavon Burn

Plan

Feuars
Ward

High Blaeberry
Craigs

Small Burn

Hares
Hill

Smallburn
Resr

Coldgreen

Gowkhouse Burn

Green
Brae

Holehouse

North
Auchenhove

Bashaw

Paduff Burn

Close Burn

East
Bankside

Long
Plantation

Wattieston

Chapelton

North
Dykes

Burnside

Burnside Burn

Ballieston

Geirston

Birtlebog

Auchencloigh

West
Bankside

Pitcon Burn

Pitcon
Burn
Bridge

North
Hourat

Place

Kilbirnie Place
Bridge

A760

A760 Largs (A78)

A760

B784

Meadowside
Hill

LARGS RD

CH

Place
Farm

PLACE VIEW

KEIR HARDIE DR

Mid
Hourat

B784

Connelston

Kilbirnie House
(remains of)

NEWHOUSE
DR

Ayrshire STREET ATLAS

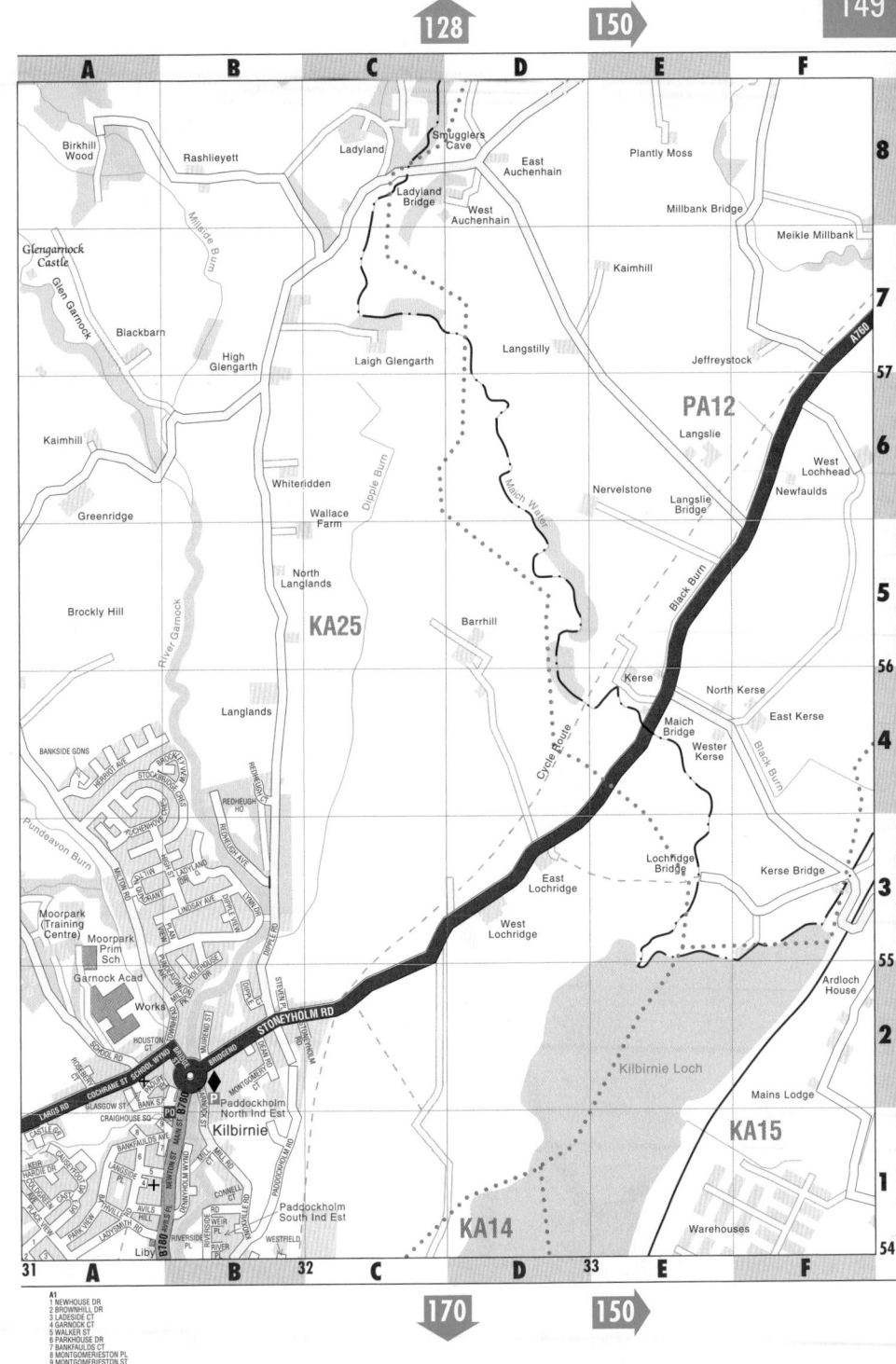

8
7
57
6
5
56
4
55
3
2
1
54

A | B | C | D | E | F

Birkhill Wood
Rashlieyett
Ladyland
Smugglers Cave
East Auchenhain
Plantly Moss

Ladyland Bridge
West Auchenhain
Millbank Bridge
Meikle Millbank

Glengarnock Castle
Kaimhill

Blackbarn
High Glengarth
Laigh Glengarth
Langstilly
Jeffreystock

PA12

Kaimhill
Whiteridden
Langslie

Greenridge
Wallace Farm
Nervelstone
Langslie Bridge
West Lochhead
Newfaulds

North Langlands
Barrhill

Brockly Hill
KA25

Langlands
Kerse
North Kerse
East Kerse

Maich Bridge
Wester Kerse

Cycle Route

Lochridge Bridge
Kerse Bridge

East Lochridge
West Lochridge

Ardloch House

Moorpark (Training Centre)
Moorpark Prim Sch
Garnock Acad
Works

Kilbirnie Loch

Mains Lodge

Paddockholm North Ind Est
Kilbirnie
KA15

Paddockholm South Ind Est
Paddockholm

KA14

Warehouses

Liby

31 A | B 32 C | D 33 E | F

A1
1 NEWHOUSE DR
2 BROWNHILL DR
3 LADESIDE CT
4 GARNOCK CT
5 WALKER ST
6 PARKHOUSE DR
7 BANKFAULDS CT
8 MONTGOMERIESTON PL
9 MONTGOMERIESTON ST

149
129

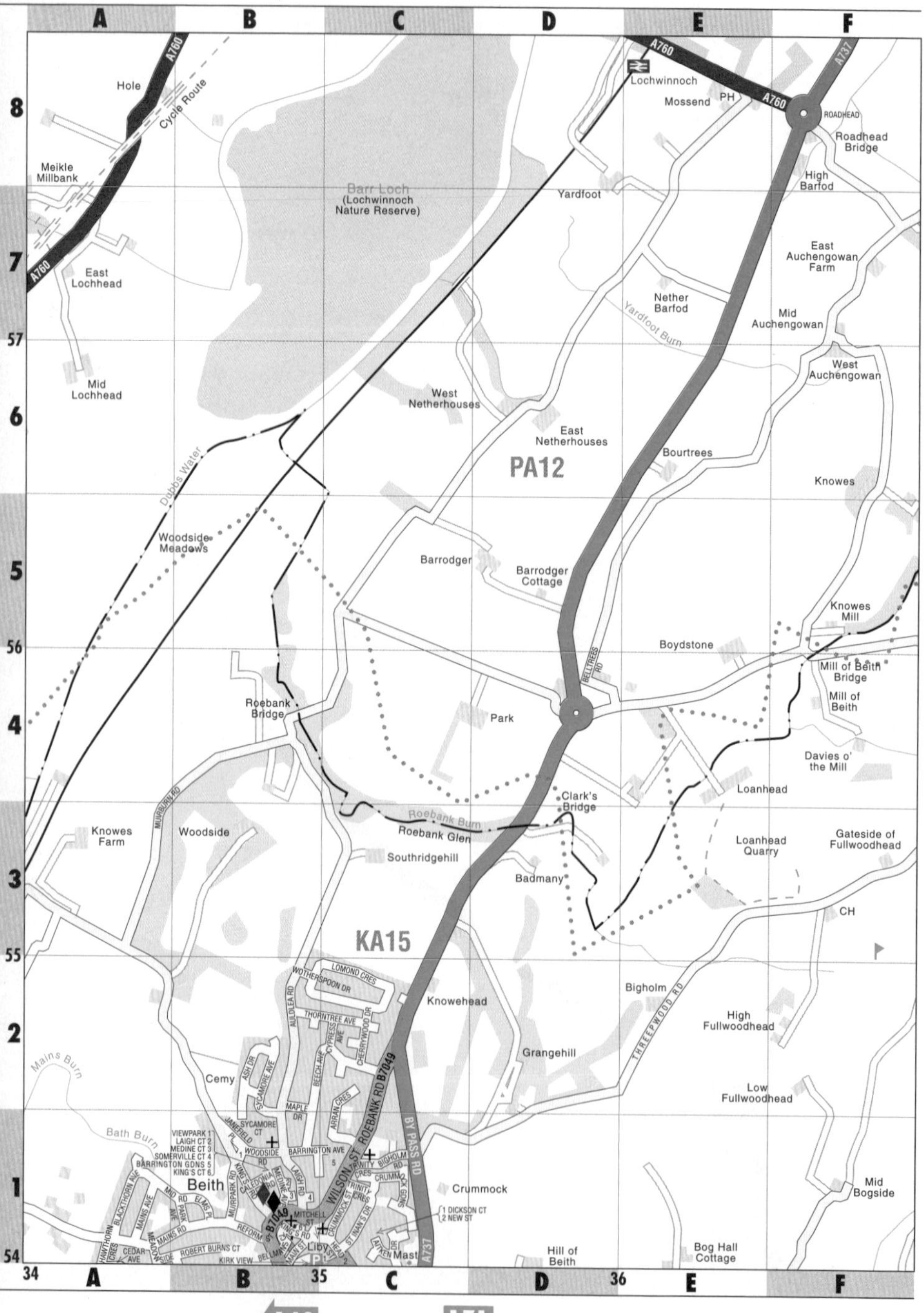
A
B
C
D
E
F
8
7
57
6
5
56
4
3
55
2
1
54
34
35
36
A760
A737
Cycle Route
Hole
Meikle
Millbank
East
Lochhead
Mid
Lochhead
Barr Loch
(Lochwinnoch
Nature Reserve)
Lochwinnoch
Mossend
PH
ROADHEAD
Roadhead
Bridge
High
Barfod
Yardfoot
East
Auchengowan
Farm
Nether
Barfod
Yardfoot Burn
Mid
Auchengowan
West
Auchengowan
West
Netherhouses
East
Netherhouses
Bourtrees
PA12
Knowes
Dubbs Water
Woodside
Meadows
Barrodger
Barrodger
Cottage
Knowes
Mill
Boydstone
Mill of Beith
Bridge
Mill of
Beith
BELLTREES RD
Roebank
Bridge
Park
Davies o'
the Mill
Loanhead
Clark's
Bridge
Roebank Burn
Roebank Glen
MURRBURN RD
Knowes
Farm
Woodside
Southridgehill
Loanhead
Quarry
Gateside of
Fullwoodhead
Badmany
CH
KA15
LOMOND CRES
WOTHERSPOON DR
Knowehead
Bigholm
THREEPWOOD RD
High
Fullwoodhead
Mains Burn
AULDLEA RD
THORNTREE AVE
CYPRESS AVE
CHERRYWOOD DR
BEECH AVE
ASH DR
SYCAMORE AVE
Cemy
Grangehill
MAPLE DR
ARRAN CRES
ROEBANK RD B7049
BY PASS RD
Low
Fullwoodhead
Bath Burn
VIEWPARK 1
LAIGH CT 2
MEDINE CT 3
SOMERVILLE CT 4
BARRINGTON GDNS 5
KING'S CT 6
SYCAMORE CT
JANEFIELD PL
WOODSIDE RD
BARRINGTON AVE
TRINITY
BIGHOLM
Beith
WILSON ST
CRUMMOCK
Crummock
Mid
Bogside
1 DICKSON CT
2 NEW ST
MITCHELL ST
B7049
HAWTHORN CRES
BLACKTHORN AVE
MAINS AVE
CEDAR AVE
MAINS RD
ROBERT BURNS CT
REFORM
KIRK VIEW
MURRPARK RD
Liby
Mast
AITKEN DR
Hill of
Beith
Bog Hall
Cottage
P

149
171

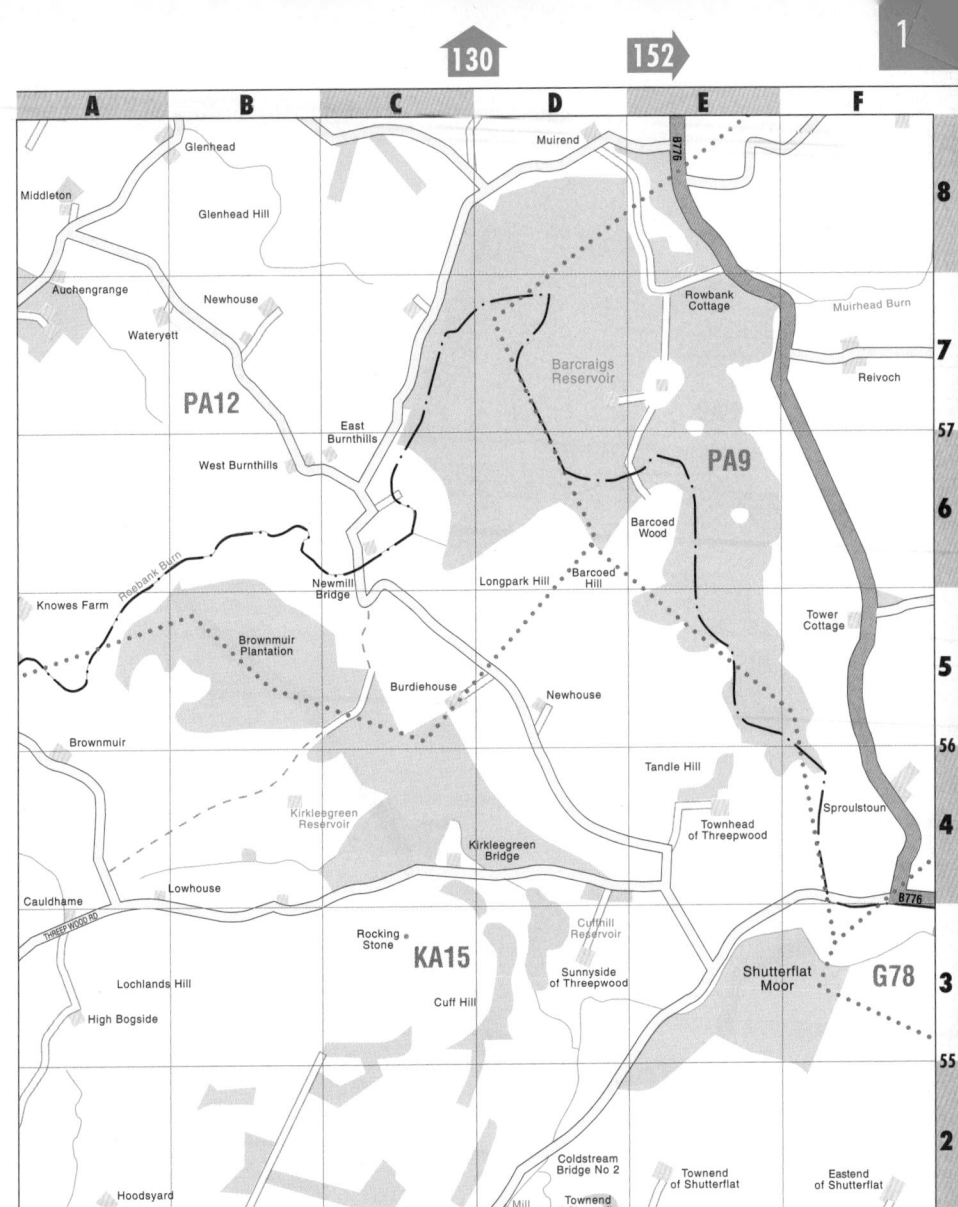

130
152
172
152

A B C D E F

Middleton
Glenhead
Glenhead Hill

Auchengrange
Newhouse
Wateryett

Muirend

Rowbank
Cottage
Muirhead Burn

Reivoch

PA12

Barcraigs
Reservoir

PA9

East
Burnthills

West Burnthills

Barcoed
Wood

Knowes Farm

Roebank Burn

Newmill
Bridge

Longpark Hill

Barcoed
Hill

Barcoed
Wood

Tower
Cottage

Brownmuir
Plantation

Burdiehouse

Newhouse

Brownmuir

Kirkleegreen
Reservoir

Tandle Hill

Townhead
of Threepwood

Sproulstoun

B776

Cauldhame

Lowhouse

THREEP WOOD RD

Kirkleegreen
Bridge

Rocking
Stone

KA15

Cuthill
Reservoir

Sunnyside
of Threepwood

Shutterflat
Moor

G78

Lochlands Hill

High Bogside

Cuff Hill

Hoodsyard

Cuff

Bottoms

Coldstream
Bridge No 2

Mill
Dam

Townend
of Threepwood

Coldstream
Mill

Coldstream
Farm

Coldstream
Bridge No1

Brownhill
of Shutterflat

Townend
of Shutterflat

Eastend
of Shutterflat

Shutterflat

8
7
57
6
57
6
5
56
4
56
4
3
55
2
1
54

37 38 39

A B C D E F

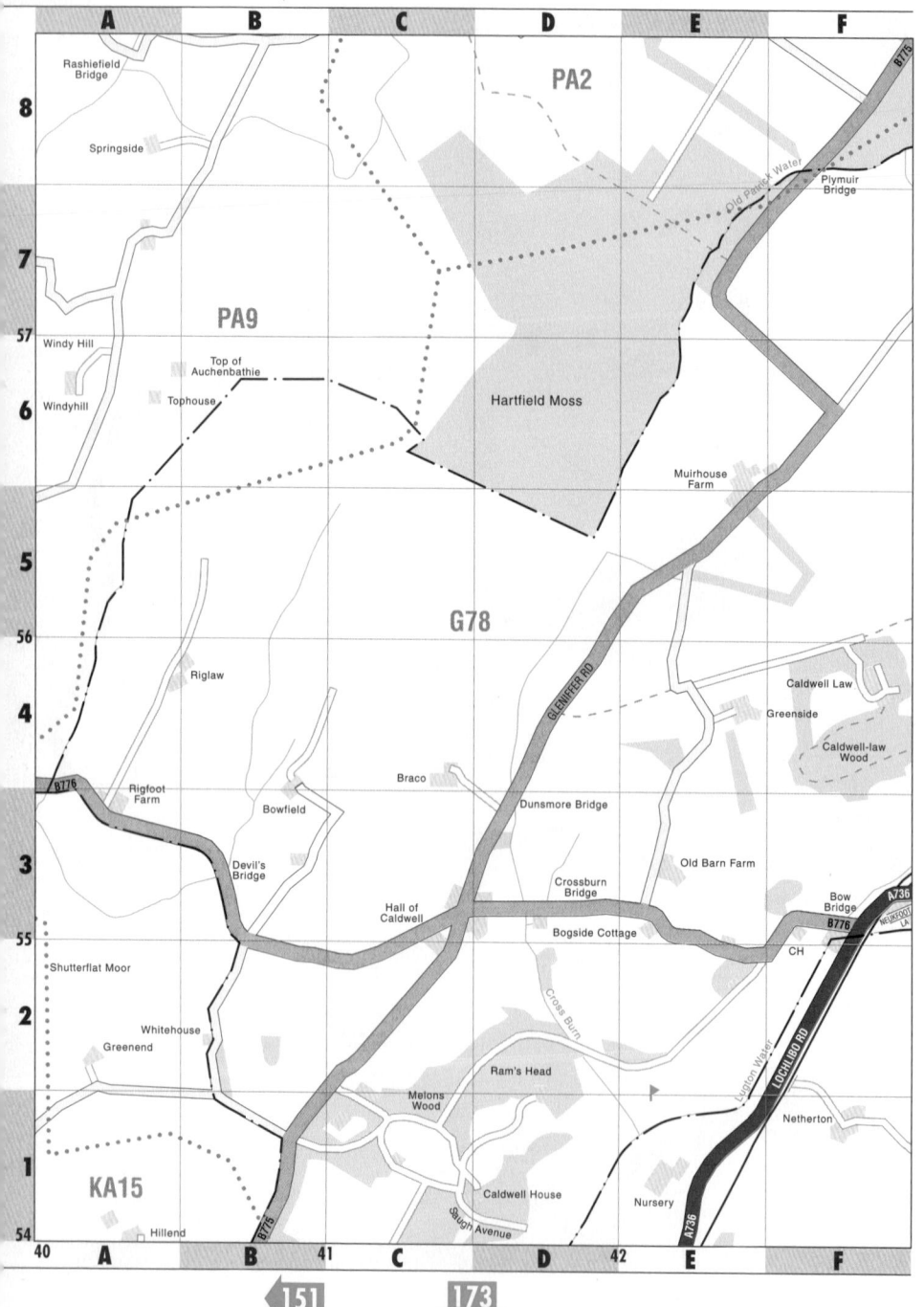

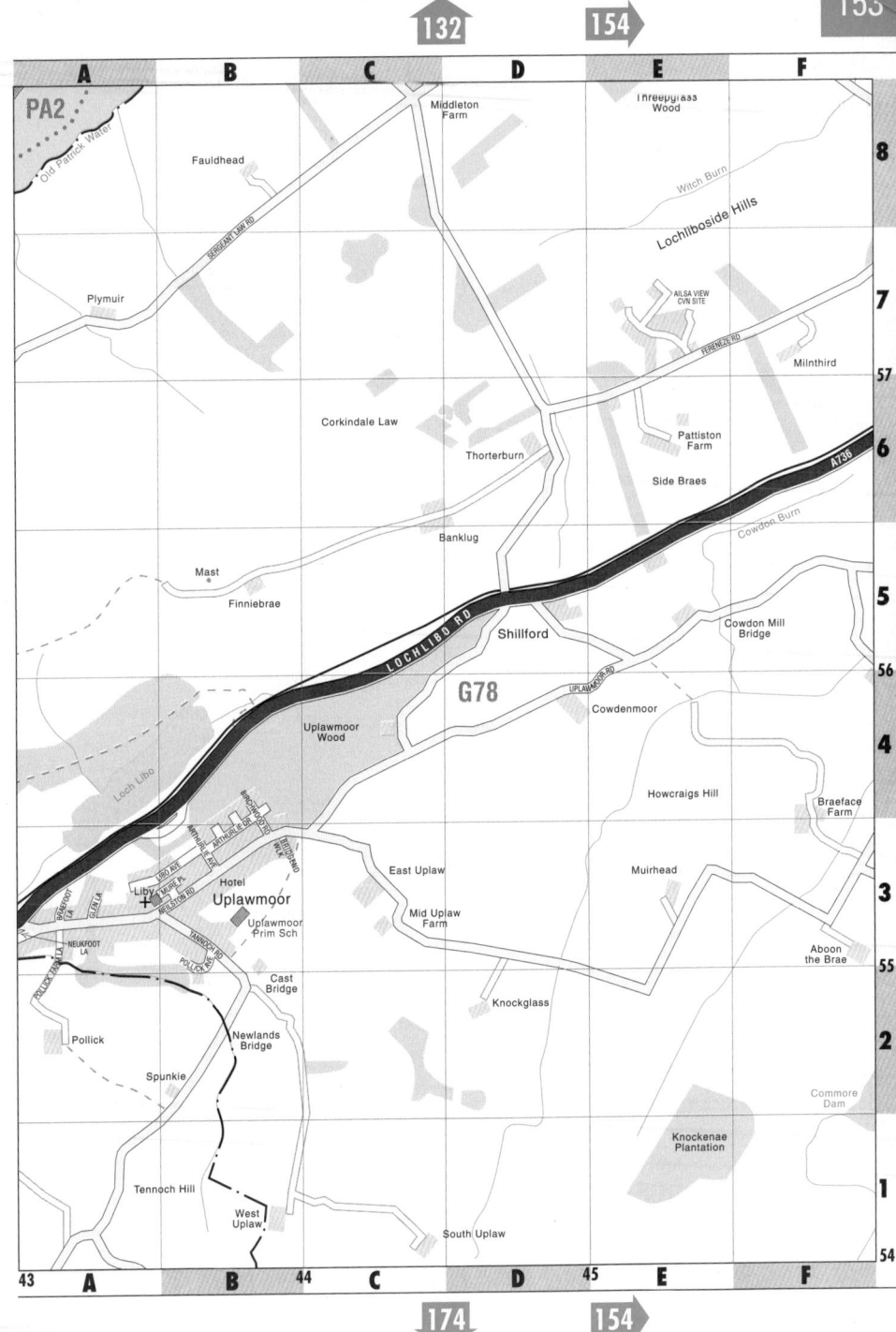

A B C D E F

PA2

Old Patrick Water

Fauldhead

Middleton
Farm

Threepgrass
Wood

8

Witch Burn

Lochliboside Hills

Plymuir

SERGEANT LAW RD

AILSA VIEW
CVN SITE

7

FERENEZE RD

Milnthird

57

Corkindale Law

Thorterburn

Pattiston
Farm

A736

6

Side Braes

Banklug

Cowdon Burn

Mast

Finniebrae

LOCHLIBO RD

Shillford

Cowdon Mill
Bridge

5

G78

UPLAWMOOR RD

Cowdenmoor

56

Uplawmoor
Wood

4

Loch Libo

Howcraigs Hill

Braeface
Farm

BIRCHFIELD RD

ARTHURLIE DR

TEITIERBAND WALK

East Uplaw

Muirhead

Libo

Hotel

LIBO AVE

MAURE PL

NEILSTON RD

Uplawmoor

Uplawmoor
Prim Sch

Mid Uplaw
Farm

3

BRAEFOOT LA

GLEN LA

NEUKFOOT
LA

HANNOCK RD

POLLICK RD

Aboon
the Brae

55

POLLICK VIEW LA

Cast
Bridge

Knockglass

Pollick

Newlands
Bridge

2

Spunkie

Commore
Dam

Knockenae
Plantation

Tennoch Hill

1

West
Uplaw

South Uplaw

54

43 A B 44 C D 45 E F

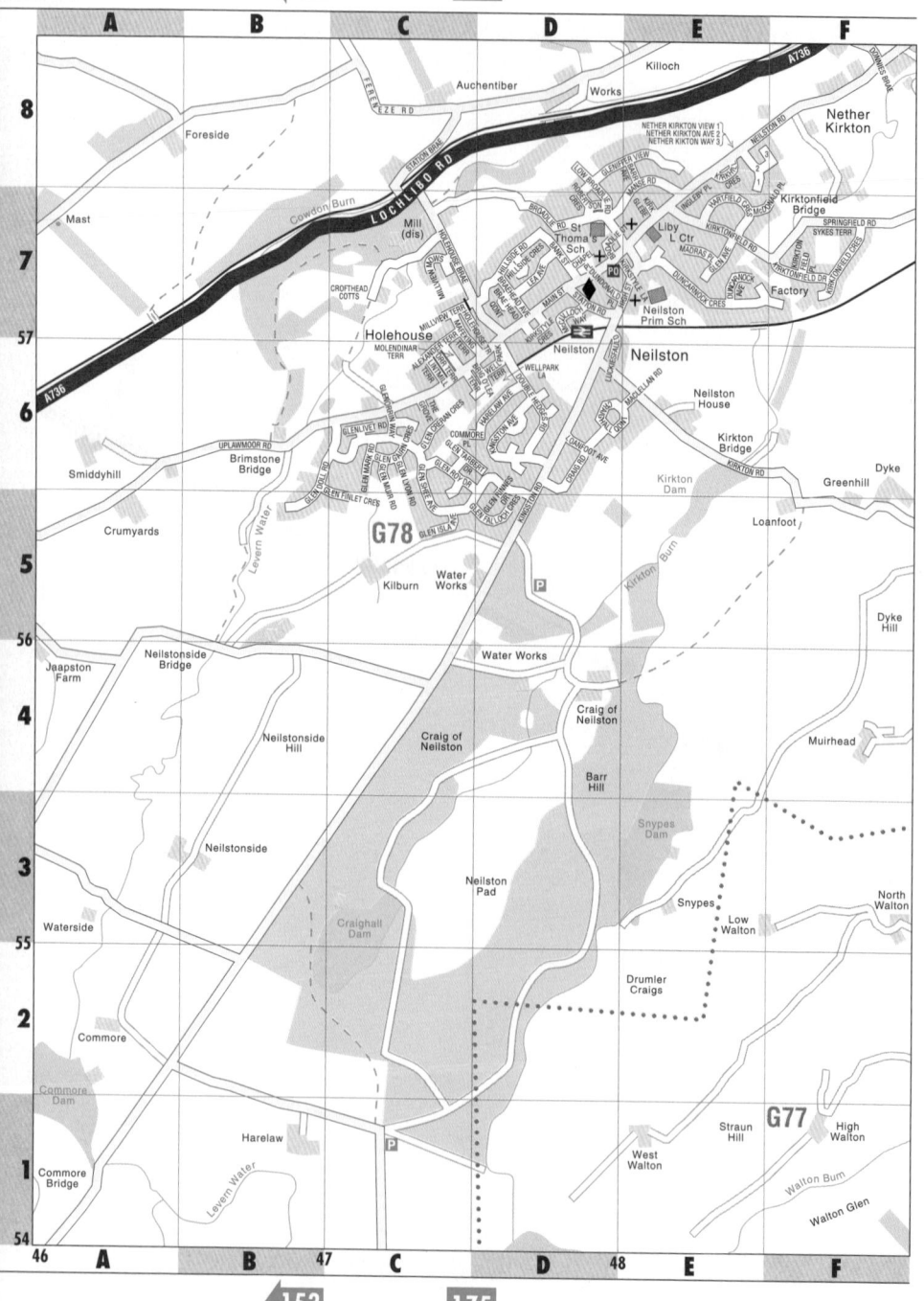

134
156

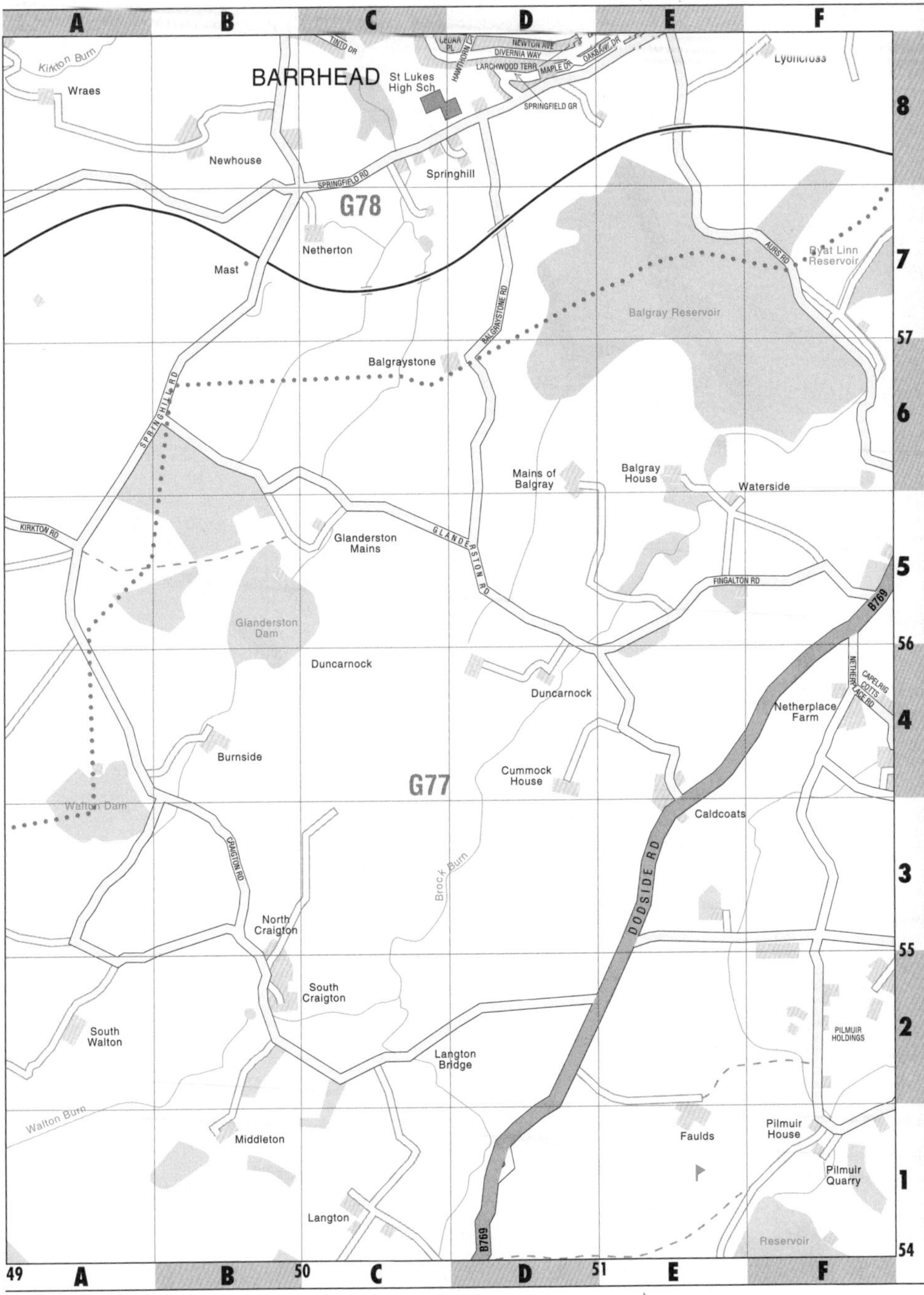
A
B
C
D
E
F
8
7
57
6
5
56
4
3
55
2
1
54
49
50
51
BARRHEAD
Kirkton Burn
Wraes
Newhouse
St Lukes
High Sch
TINTO DR
CEDAR PL
HAWTHORN CT
NEWTON AVE
DIVERNIA WAY
LARCHWOOD TERR
MAPLE DR
OAKBANK DR
SPRINGFIELD GR
Lyoncross
SPRINGFIELD RD
Springhill
G78
Netherton
Mast
AURS RD
Ryat Linn
Reservoir
Balgray Reservoir
BALGRAYSTONE RD
Balgraystone
SPRINGHILL RD
Mains of
Balgray
Balgray
House
Waterside
KIRKTON RD
Glanderston
Mains
GLANDERSTON RD
FINGALTON RD
B769
Glanderston
Dam
Duncarnock
Duncarnock
NETHERPLACE RD
CAPELRIG COTTS
Netherplace
Farm
Burnside
Cummock
House
G77
Walton Dam
Caldcoats
CRAIGTON RD
Brock Burn
DODSIDE RD
North
Craigton
South
Craigton
South
Walton
PILMUIR
HOLDINGS
Langton
Bridge
Walton Burn
Middleton
Faulds
Pilmuir
House
Pilmuir
Quarry
Langton
B769
Reservoir

176
156

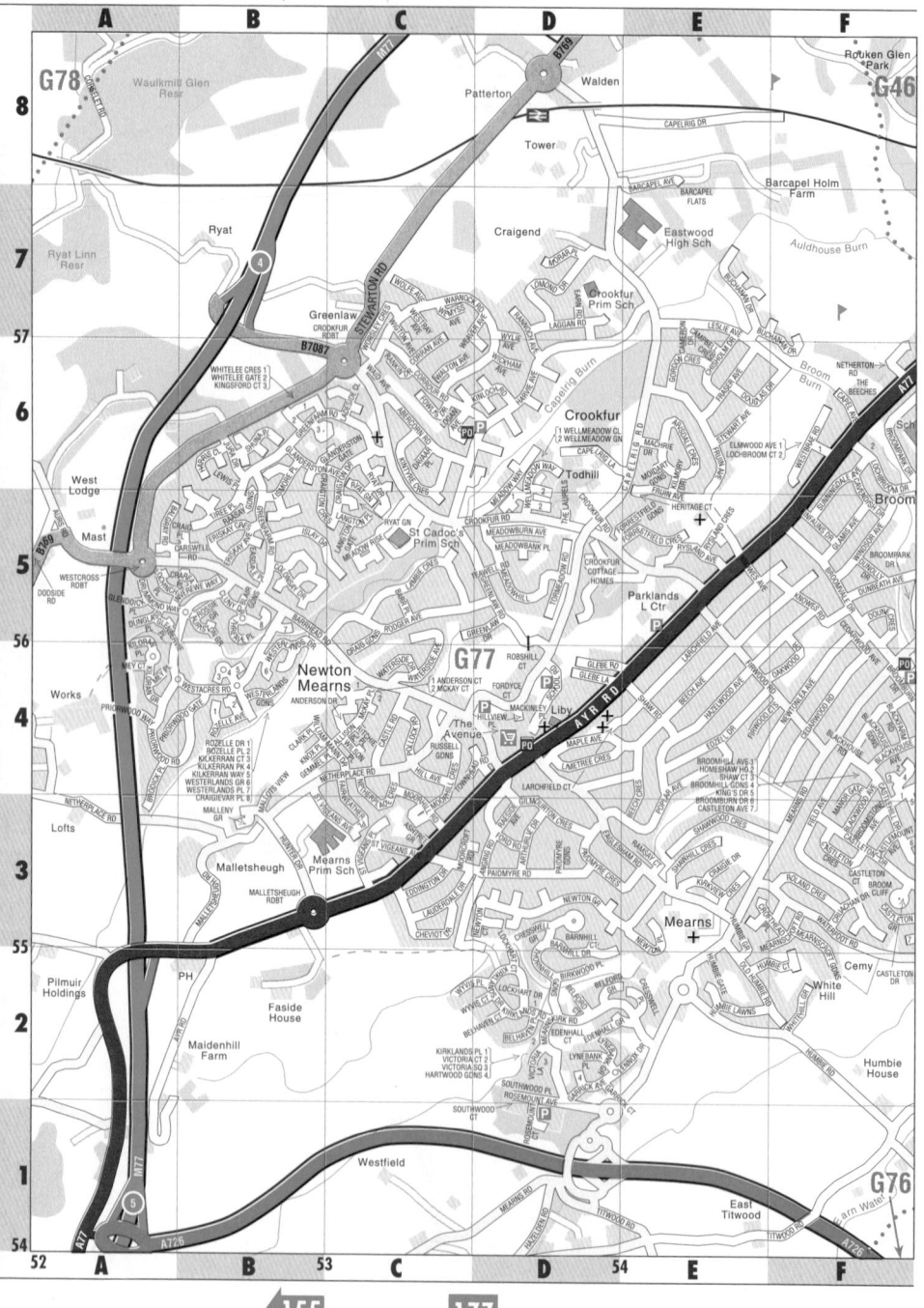

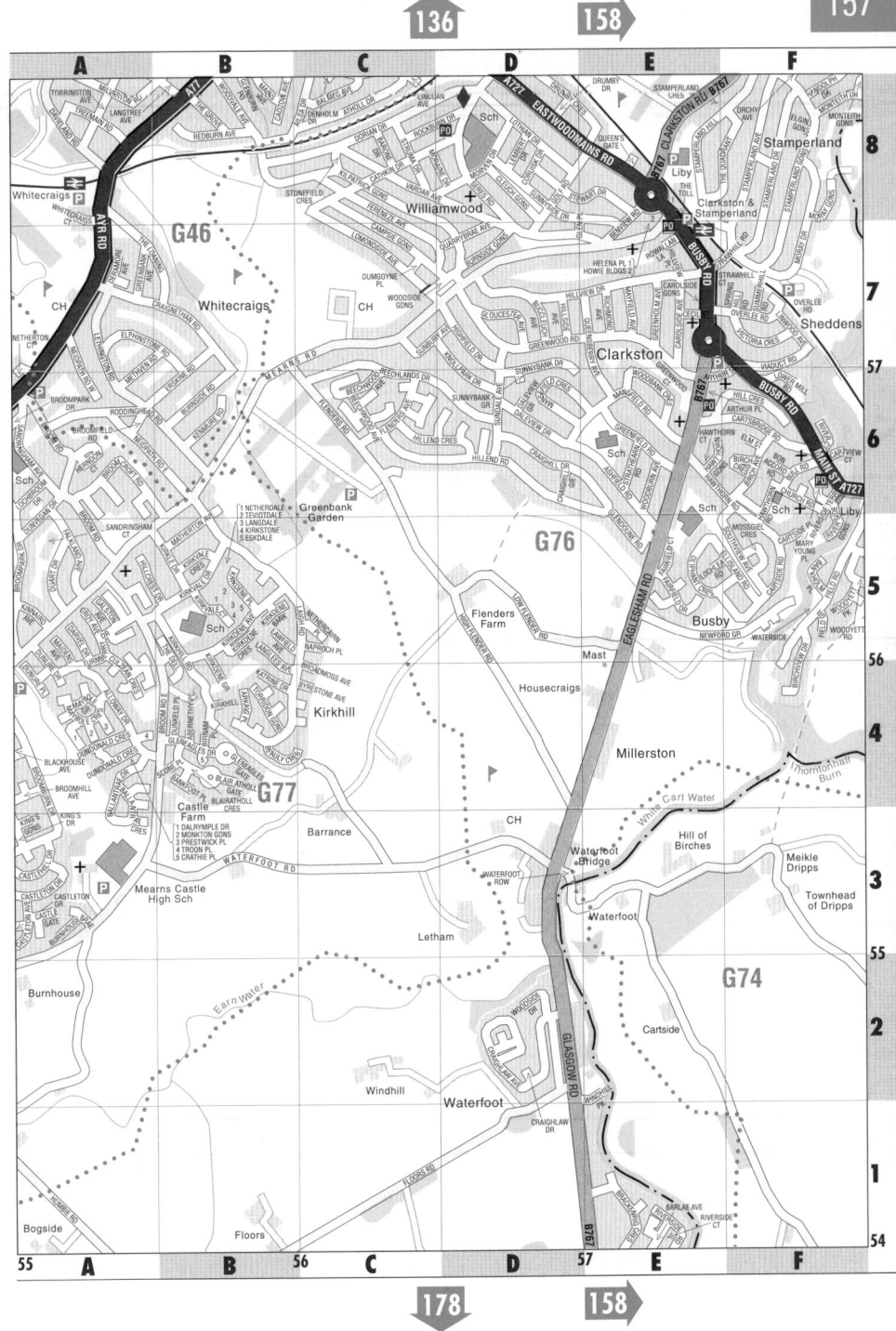

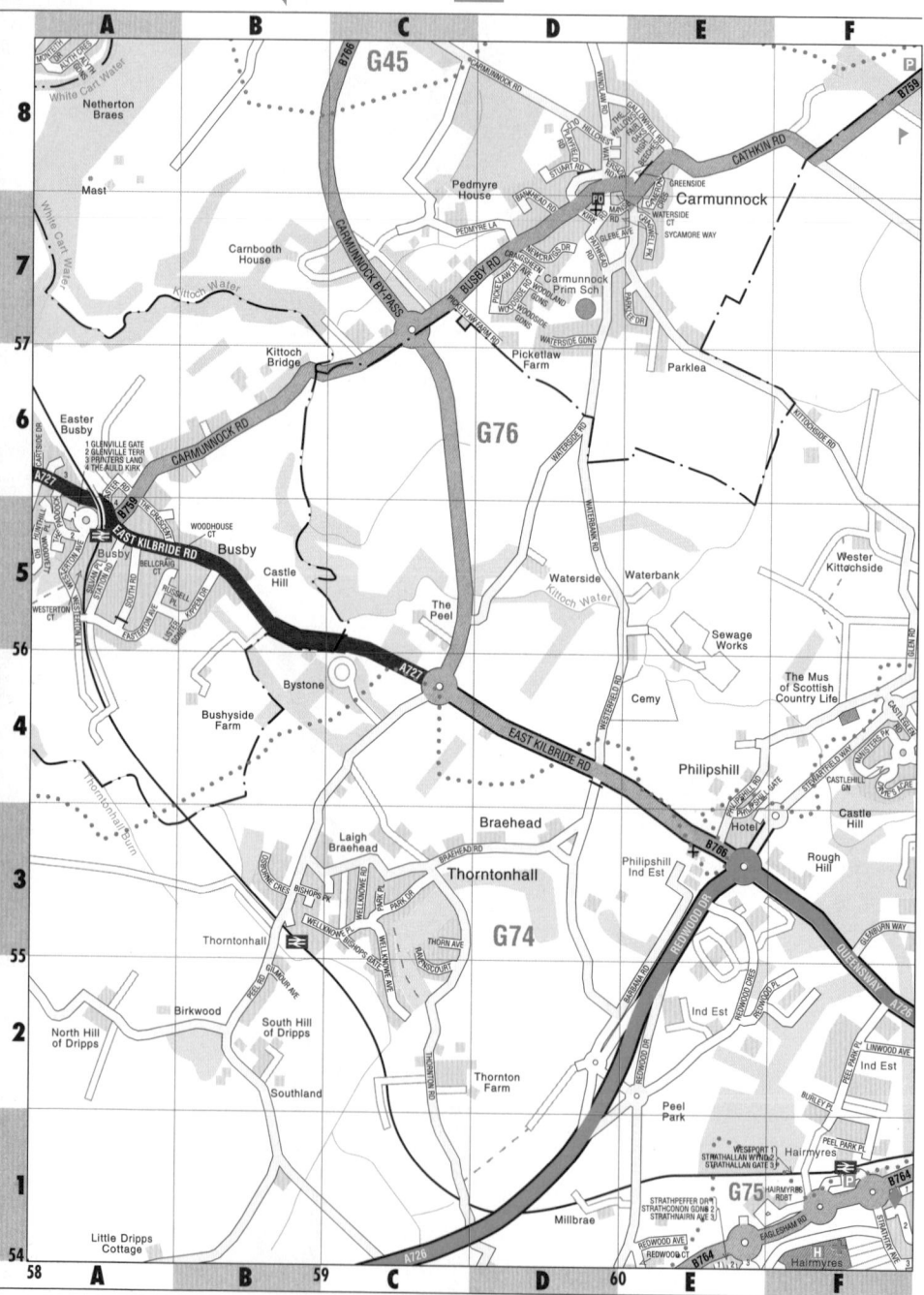

157
137

G45

White Cart Water

Netherton Braes

Mast

Carnbooth House

White Cart Water

Kittoch Water

B766

CARMUNNOCK BYPASS

Kittoch Bridge

CARMUNNOCK RD

PEDMYRE LA

Pedmyre House

Easter Busby

1 GLENVILLE GATE
2 GLENVILLE TERR
3 PRINTERS LAND
4 THE AULD KIRK

CARMUNNOCK RD

EAST KILBRIDE RD

Busby

WOODHOUSE CT

Busby

BELLCRAIG CT

WESTERTON CT

Castle Hill

The Peel

Bystone

Bushyside Farm

Thorntonhall Burn

A727

EAST KILBRIDE RD

Waterside

Kittoch Water

Waterbank

Sewage Works

Cemy

Wester Kittochside

The Mus of Scottish Country Life

Carmunnock

CATHKIN RD

B759

Greenside

WATERSIDE CT

SYCAMORE WAY

Carmunnock Prim Sch

Picketlaw Farm

Parklea

G76

WATERSIDE RD

WATERBANK RD

Philipshill

Braehead

Thorntonhall

Laigh Braehead

BISHOPS PK

G74

Thorntonhall

WELLKNOWE

THORN AVE

Birkwood

South Hill of Dripps

North Hill of Dripps

Southland

THORNTON RD

Thornton Farm

BRAEHEAD RD

Philipshill Ind Est

B766

Castle Hill

Rough Hill

CASTLEHILL GN

Hotel

REDWOOD DR

REDWOOD CRES

Peel Park

Ind Est

QUEENSWAY

A726

GLENBURN WAY

Ind Est

LINWOOD AVE

PEEL PARK PL

BURLEY PL

Hairmyres

G75

STRATHPEFFER DR
STRATHCONON GDNS
STRATHNAIRN AVE

WR ESPORT
STRATHALLAN WYND
STRATHALLAN GATE

Millbrae

REDWOOD AVE
REDWOOD CT

B764

EAGLESHAM RD

B764

Hairmyres

B766

Little Dripps Cottage

157
179

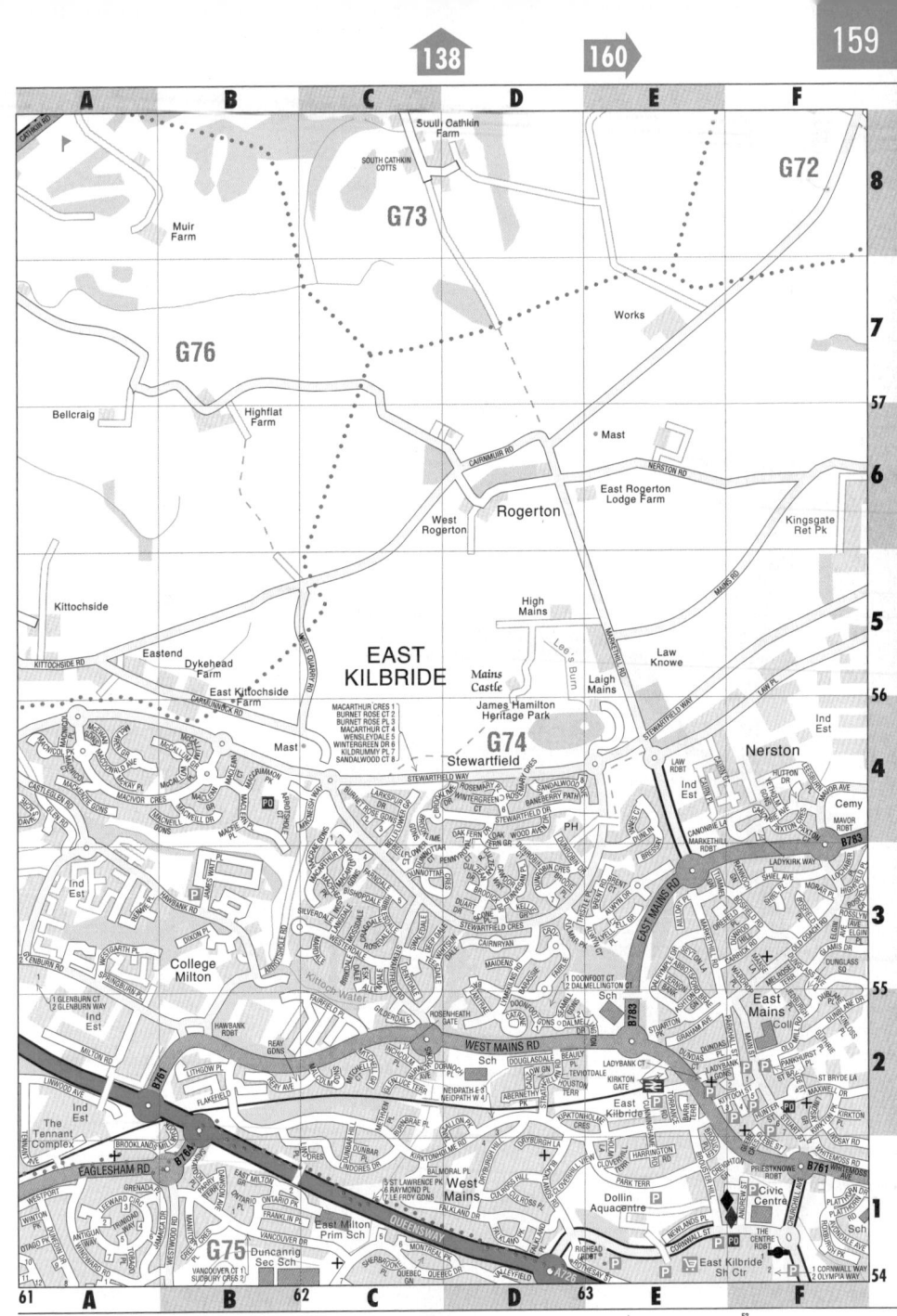

A1
1 NASSAU PL
2 MONTEGO GN
3 TRINIDAD GN
4 DOMINICA GN
5 BARBADOS GN
6 BAHAMAS WAY
7 WATLING PL
8 AUCKLAND PK
9 HAVELOCK PK
10 STRATHALLAN WYND
11 STRATHALLAN GATE
12 STRATHALLAN AVE

F2
1 WEAVERS CT
2 LADYBANK PL
3 MONTGOMERY PL
4 MONTGOMERY ST
5 KITTOCH PL
6 ELIZABETH CT
7 WELLBECK HO

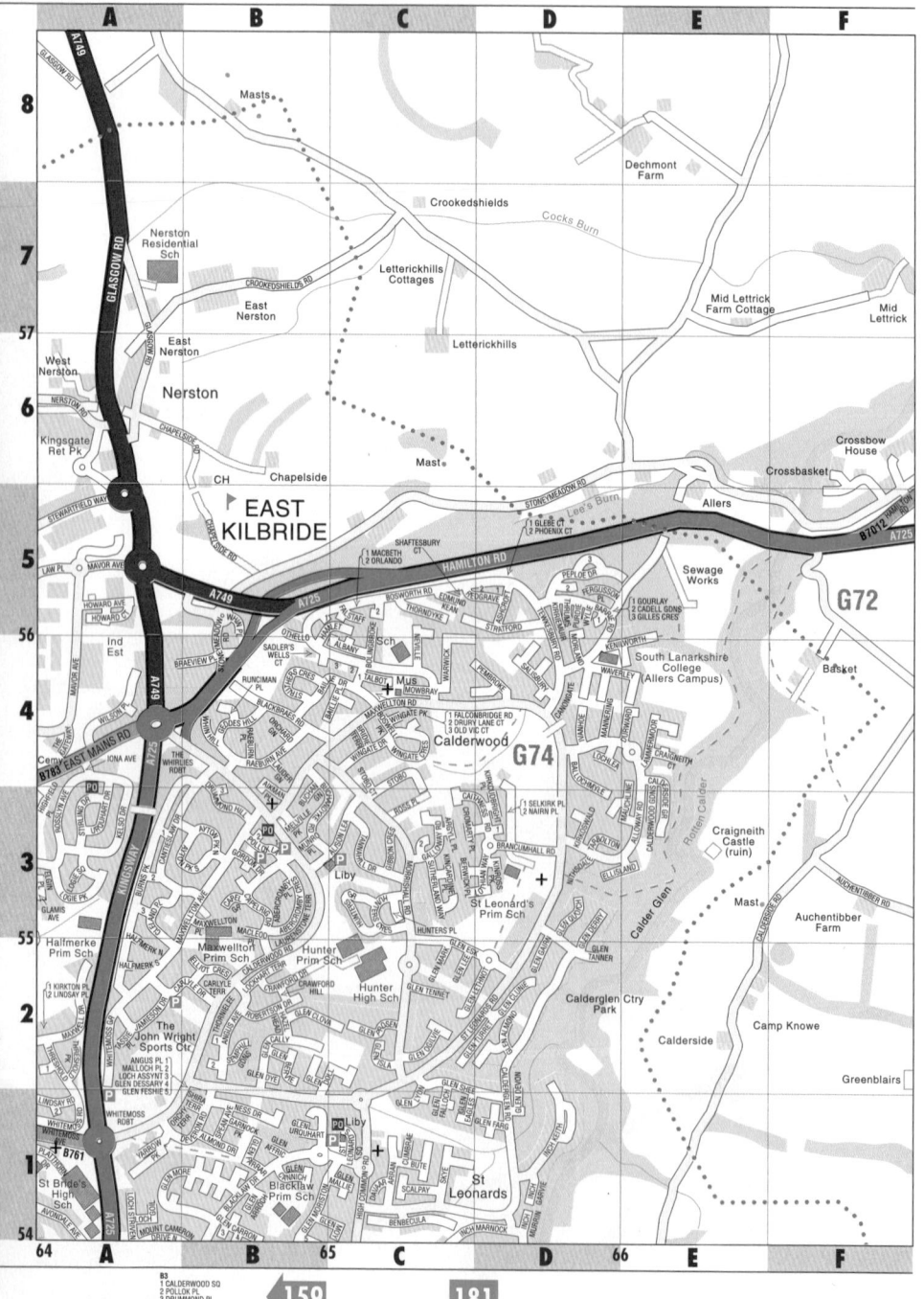

EAST KILBRIDE

B3
1 CALDERWOOD SQ
2 POLLOK PL
3 DRUMMOND PL
A3
1 SCOTT HILL
2 ETTRICK HILL
3 RAMSAY HILL

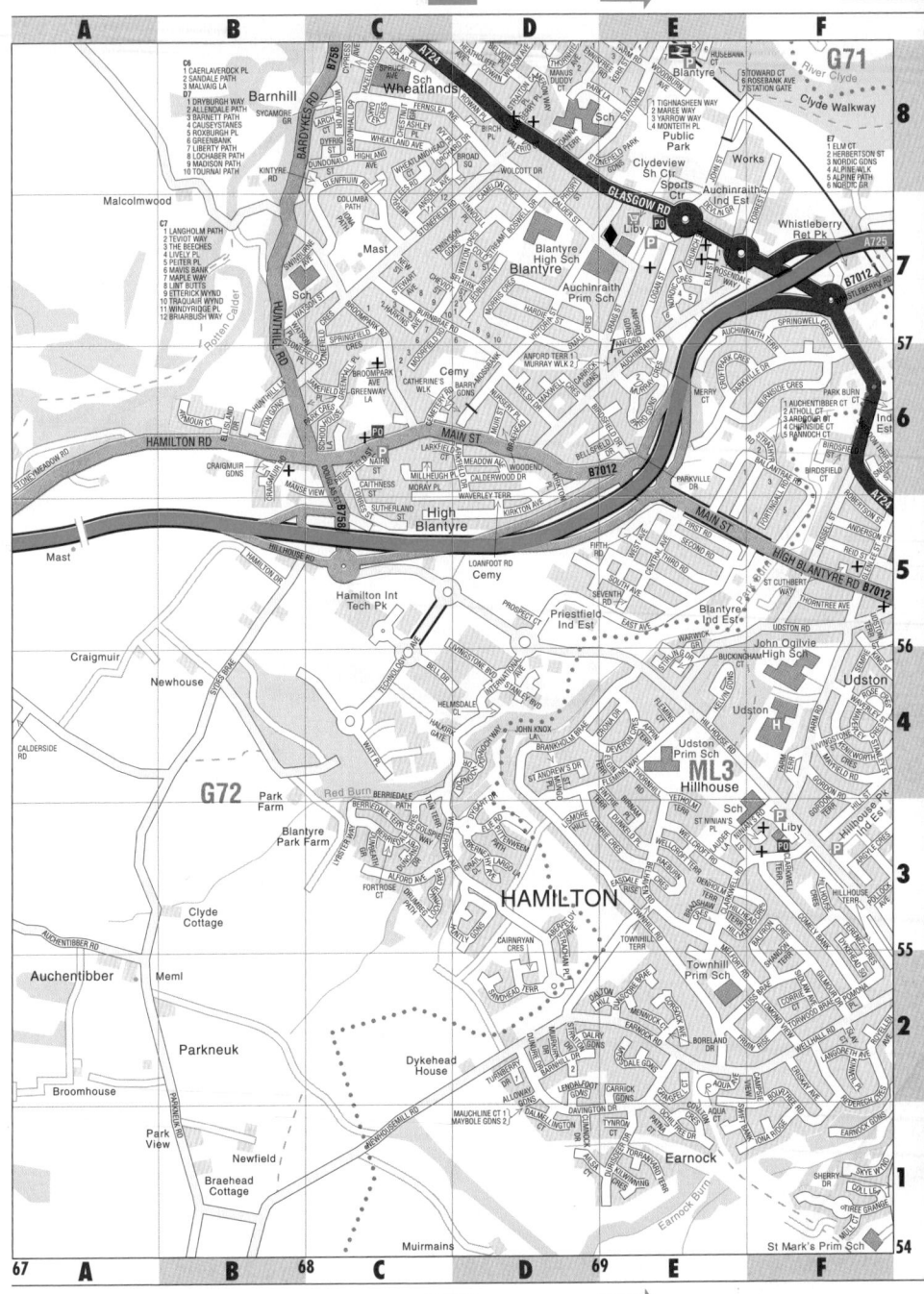

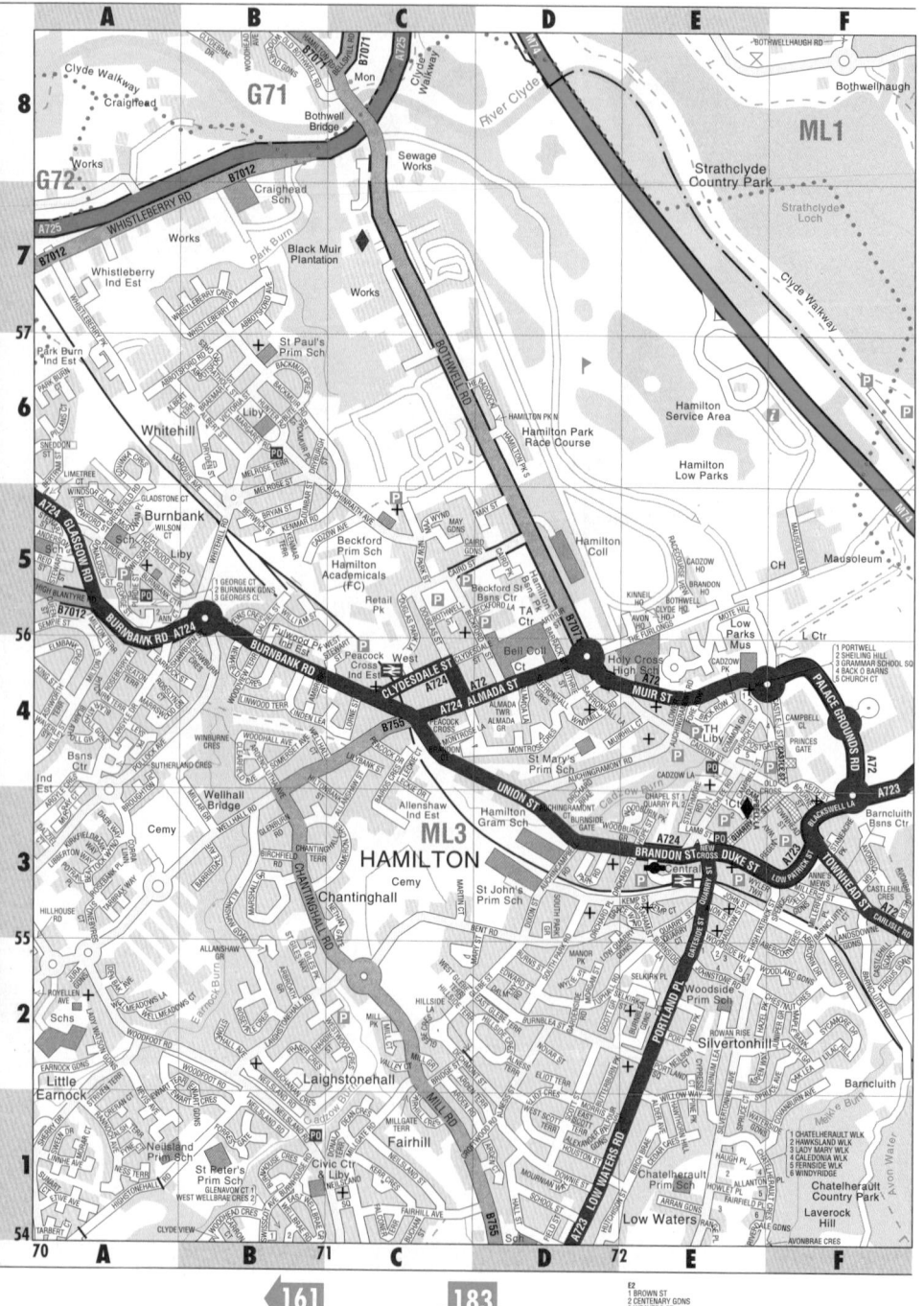

E2
1 BROWN ST
2 CENTENARY GDNS
3 WEAVERS CT
4 WOODSIDE CT
5 WOODSIDE AVE
6 CARLTON ST
7 HILTON CT

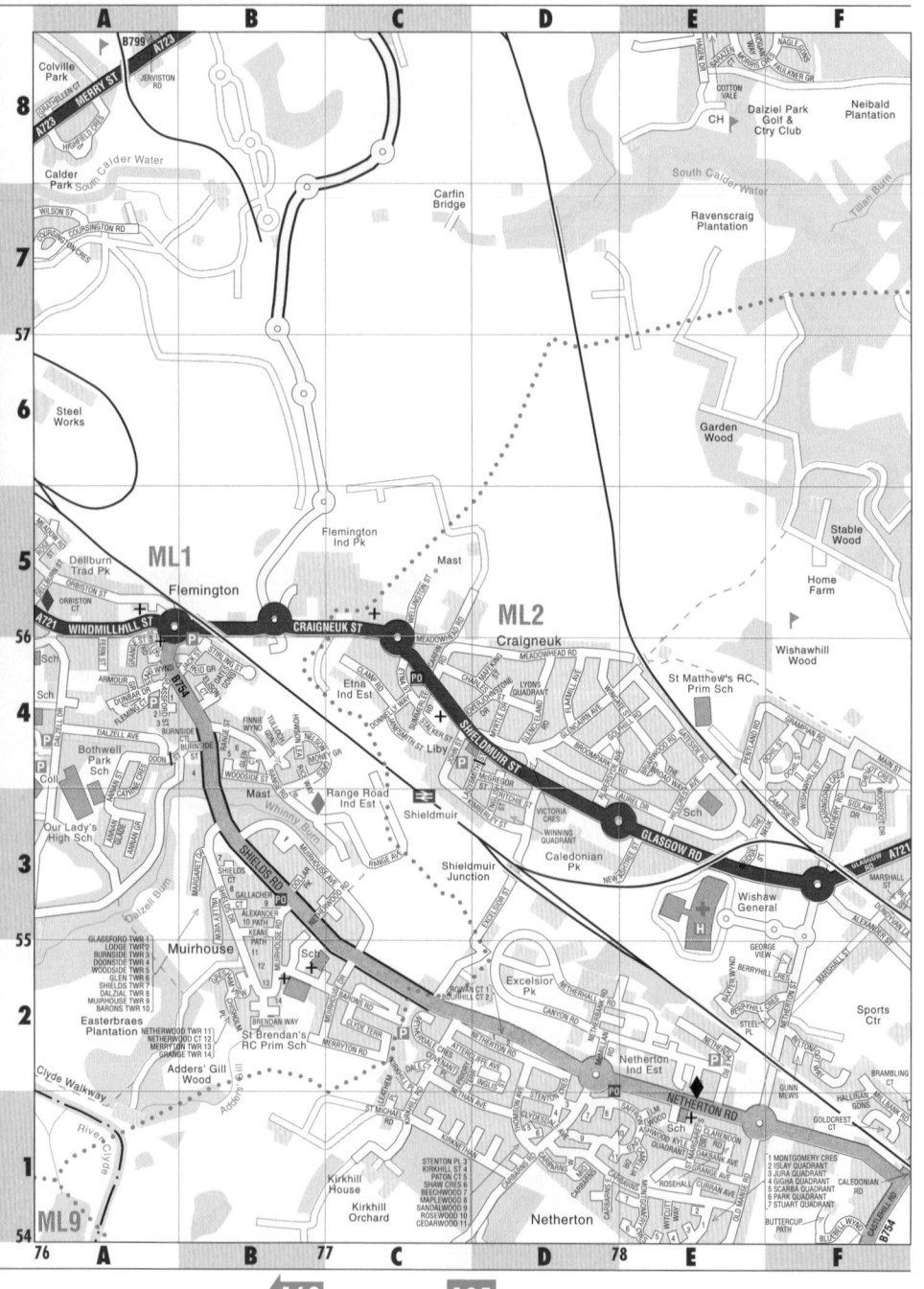

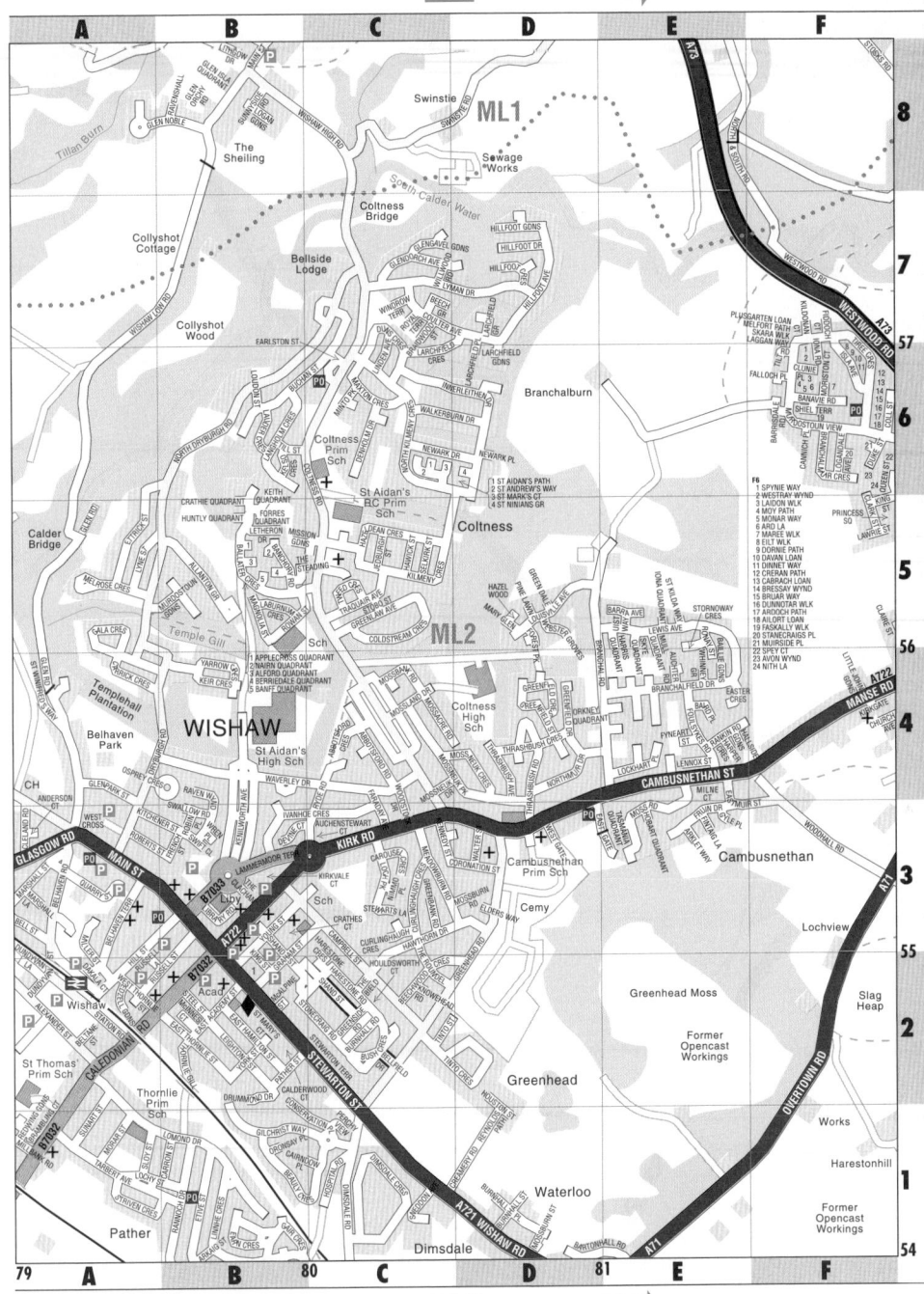

B2
1 Wishaw Bsns Ctr

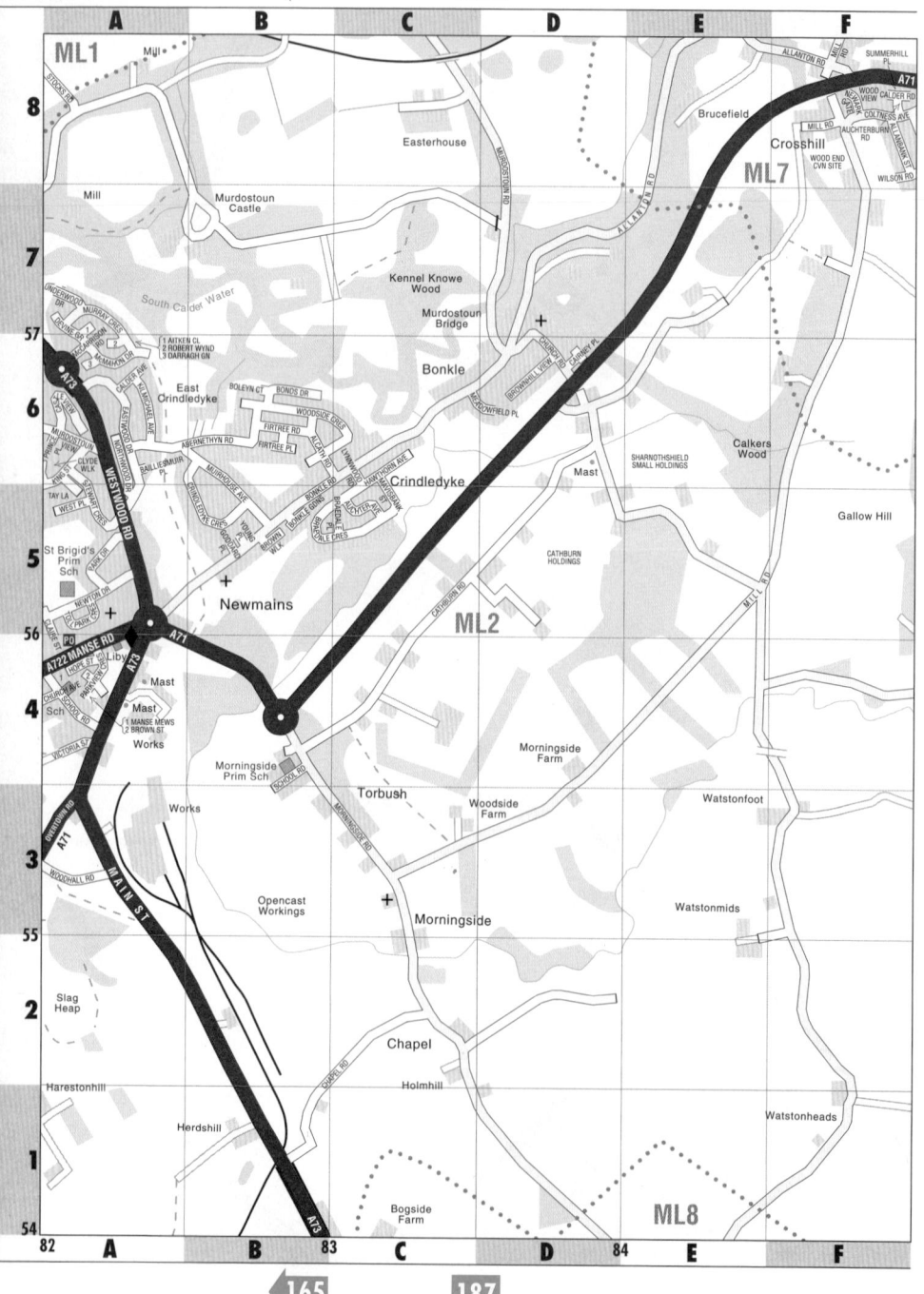

A B C D E F

COLTNESS AVE
P PO
ALLANTON RD A71
Damside (PH)
Allanton Prim Sch
KIRK PATH
HAWTHORN PL
Allanton
REDMILL CRES
WHITFIELD TERR
Coal Burn

ML7

Hartfield

Netherhall

Opencast Workings

Blackhall Farm

Newark Plantation

Upper Daviesdykes

DURA RD

Kirkhall

ML2

Lower Daviesdykes

Lodge Hill

Winterhill

Dura

Brow Farm

Mountpleasant

Sunnyside

Auchterhead

Summerside

Kingshill

Auchter Water

ML8

8

7

57

6

5

56

4

3

55

2

1

54

85 A B 86 C D 87 E F

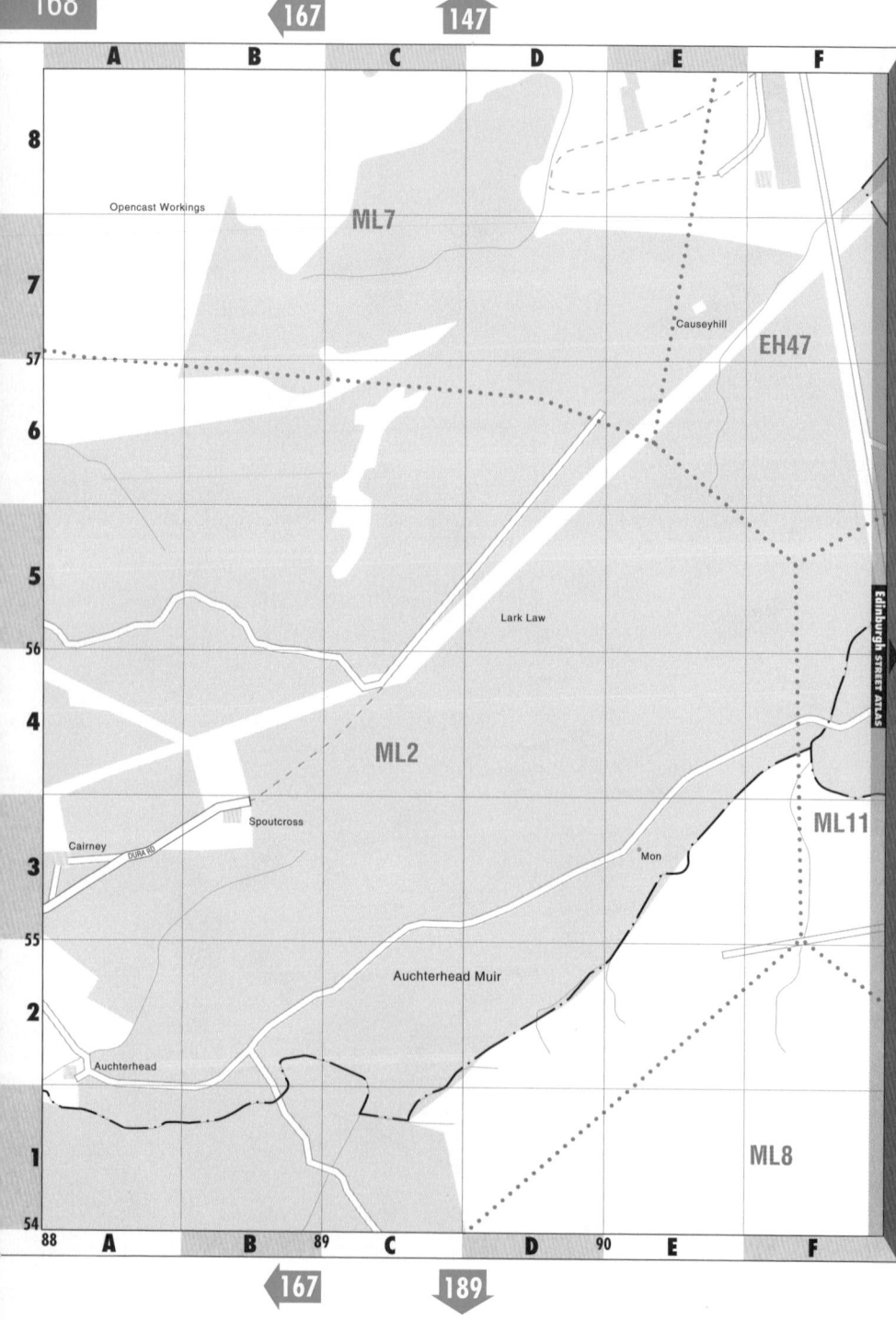

A B C D E F

8

Opencast Workings

ML7

7

Causeyhill

57

EH47

6

5

Lark Law

56

4

ML2

ML11

Spoutcross

Cairney

DURA RD

Mon

3

55

Auchterhead Muir

2

Auchterhead

1

ML8

54

88 A B 89 C D 90 E F

Edinburgh STREET ATLAS

148
170

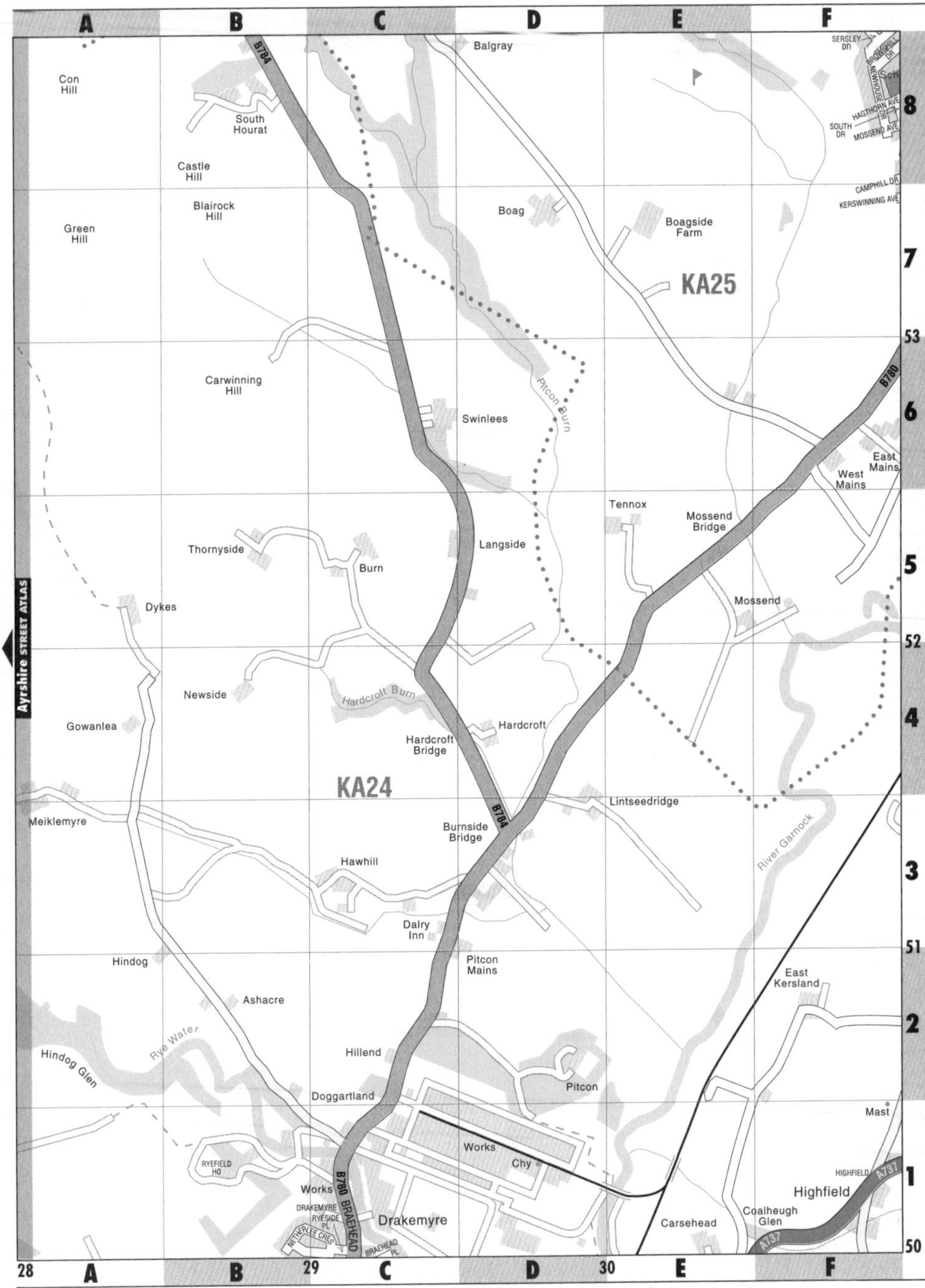

Con
Hill

South
Hourat

Castle
Hill

Balgray

SERSLEY
DR

HAGTHORN AVE
NORTHCRAIG
AVE

SOUTH
DR

MOSSEND AVE

CAMPHILL DR

KERSWINNING AVE

Green
Hill

Blairock
Hill

Boag

Boagside
Farm

KA25

Ayrshire STREET ATLAS

Carwinning
Hill

Swinlees

Pitcon Burn

East
Mains

West
Mains

B780

Thornyside

Burn

Langside

Tennox

Mossend
Bridge

Mossend

Dykes

Newside

Hardcroft Burn

Hardcroft

KA24

Hardcroft
Bridge

Gowanlea

Meiklemyre

Hawhill

Burnside
Bridge

B784

Lintseedridge

River Garnock

Hindog

Ashacre

Dalry
Inn

Pitcon
Mains

East
Kersland

Hindog Glen

Rye Water

Hillend

Doggartland

Pitcon

Mast

RYEFIELD
RD

Works

DRAKEMYRE
RYESIDE
PL

HETHERLEE CRES

B780 BRAEHEAD

Works

Drakemyre

BRAEHEAD PL

Works

Chy

Carsehead

Coalheugh
Glen

HIGHFIELD

Highfield

A737

A737

191
170

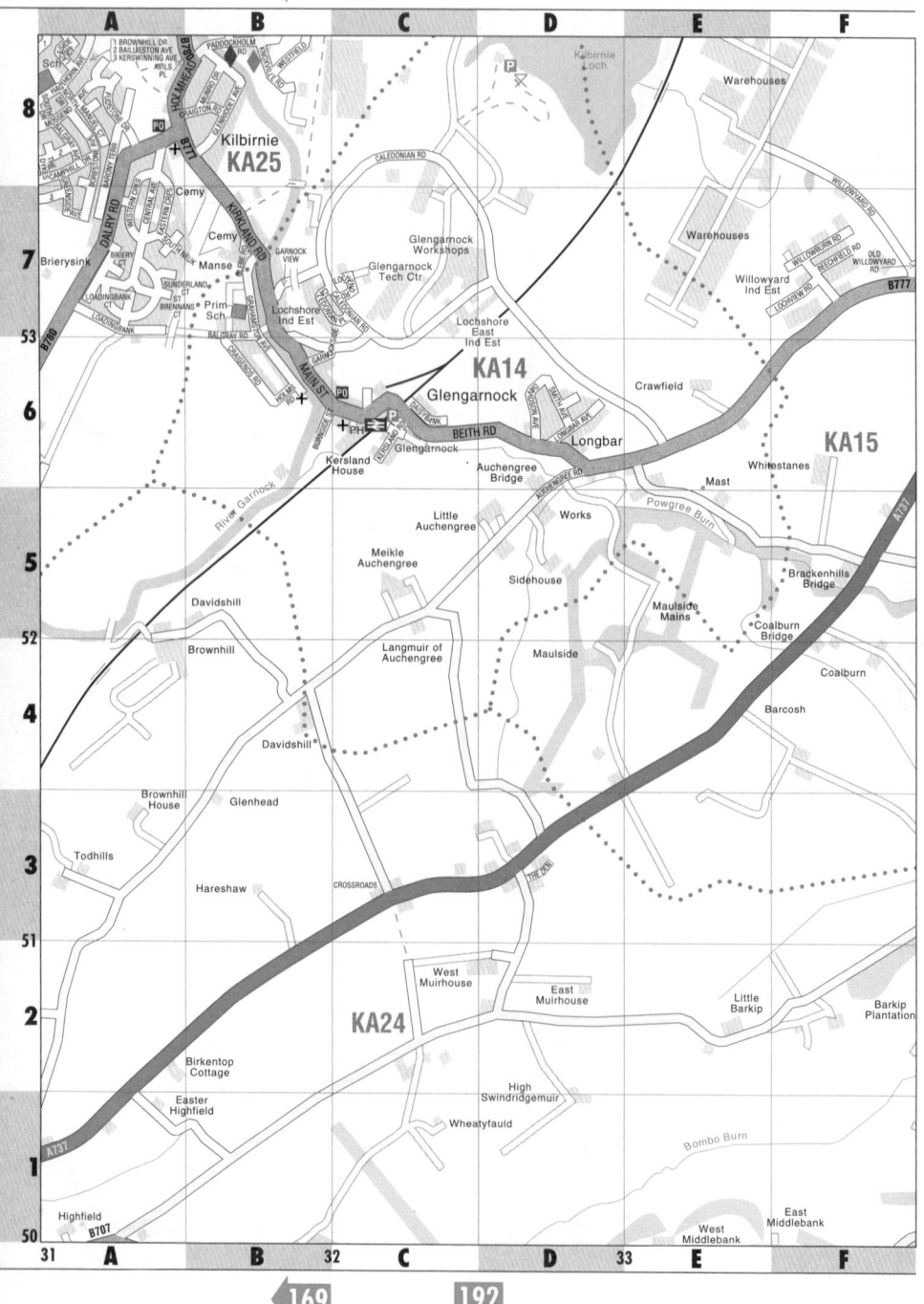

150
172

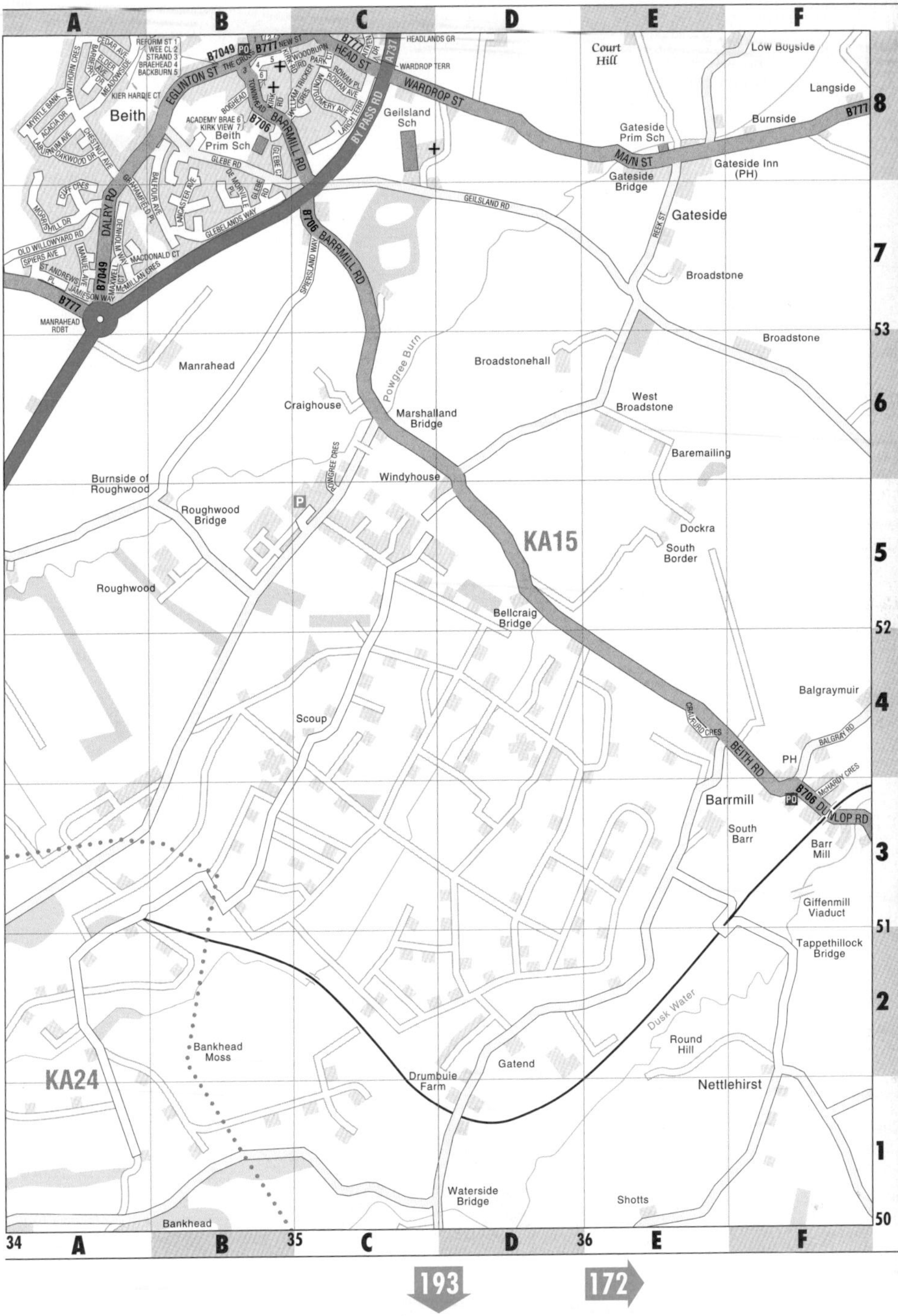
A
B
C
D
E
F
Court Hill
Low Boyside
Langside
Burnside
B777
8
HEADLANDS GR
WARDROP TERR
WARDROP ST
REFORM ST 1
WEE CL 2
STRAND 3
BRAEHEAD 4
BACKBURN 5
B7049
PO
B777
NEW ST
HEAD ST
A737
EGLINTON ST
THE CROSS
WOODBURN
KIRKLAND
ROWAN PL
ROWAN AVE
MONTGOMERY AVE
LARCH TERR
WILLIAM TRICKER CRES
TOWNHEAD
BOGHEAD
KIER HARDIE CT
CEDAR AVE
BARBERRY DR
ELDER AVE
MEADOWSIDE
HAWTHORN CRES
MYRTLE BANK
ACACIA DR
LABURNUM AVE
CHESTNUT AVE
OAKWOOD DR
Beith
ACADEMY BRAE 6
KIRK VIEW 7
B706
BARRMILL RD
BY PASS RD
Beith Prim Sch
Geilsland Sch
GLEBE RD
GLEBE CT
DE MORVILLE PL
GLEBE RD
BALFOUR AVE
LANCASTER AVE
GRAHAMFIELD PL
CUFF CRES
MORISHILL DR
DALRY RD
GLEBELANDS WAY
Gateside Prim Sch
MAIN ST
Gateside Inn (PH)
Gateside Bridge
GEILSLAND RD
REEK ST
Gateside
OLD WILLOWYARD RD
SPIERS AVE
MANUEL AVE
DENHOLM WAY
MACDONALD CT
ST ANDREWS PL
MAXWELL CT
McMILLAN CRES
JAMIESON WAY
B777
SPIERSLAND WAY
B706 BARRMILL RD
7
Broadstone
MANRAHEAD RDBT
53
Broadstone
Manrahead
Powgree Burn
Broadstonehall
West Broadstone
Craighouse
Marshalland Bridge
6
Baremailing
POWGREE CRES
Windyhouse
Burnside of Roughwood
Roughwood Bridge
P
Dockra
KA15
South Border
5
Roughwood
Bellcraig Bridge
52
Balgraymuir
4
Scoup
CRAUFURD CRES
BEITH RD
BALGRAY RD
PH
McHARDY CRES
Barrmill
B706
PO
DUNLOP RD
South Barr
Barr Mill
3
Giffenmill Viaduct
51
Tappethillock Bridge
2
Dusk Water
Bankhead Moss
Round Hill
KA24
Gatend
Drumbuie Farm
Nettlehirst
1
Waterside Bridge
Shotts
Bankhead
50
34
35
36

193
172

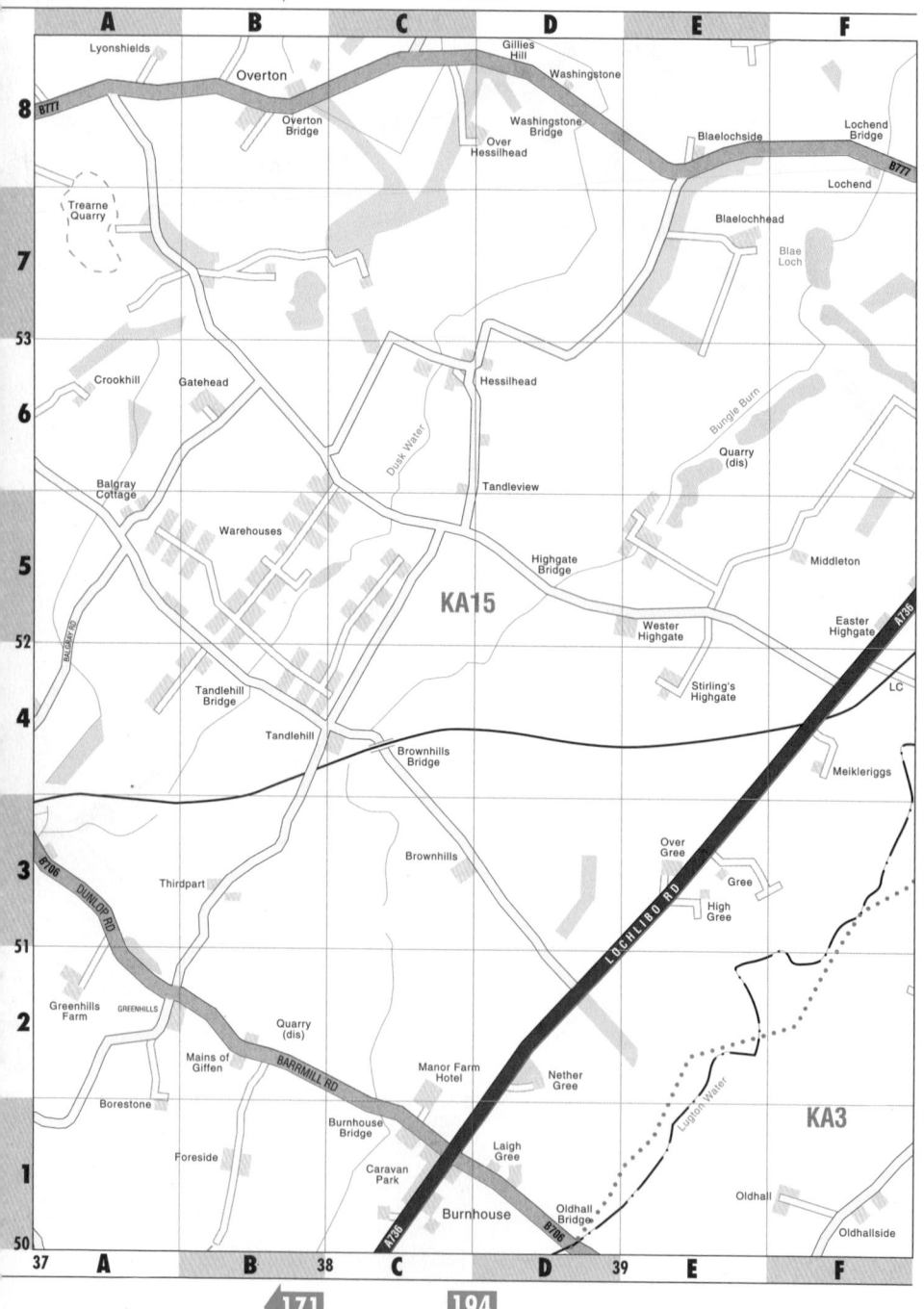

8 B777

Lyonshields

Overton

Overton
Bridge

Over
Hessilhead

Gillies
Hill

Washingstone

Washingstone
Bridge

Blaelochside

Lochend
Bridge

Lochend

B777

7 Trearne
Quarry

Blaelochhead

Blae
Loch

53

6 Crookhill

Gatehead

Hessilhead

Dusk Water

Bungle Burn

Quarry
(dis)

Balgray
Cottage

Warehouses

Tandleview

Tandlehill
Bridge

Highgate
Bridge

Middleton

KA15

5

52

Wester
Highgate

Easter
Highgate

A736

BALGRAY RD

4 Tandlehill

Brownhills
Bridge

Stirling's
Highgate

LC

Meikleriggs

3 B706

DUNLOP RD

Thirdpart

Brownhills

Over
Gree

Gree

High
Gree

LOCHLIBO RD

51

2 B706

Greenhills
Farm

GREENHILLS

Mains of
Giffen

BARRMILL RD

Quarry
(dis)

Manor Farm
Hotel

Nether
Gree

Lugton Water

KA3

Borestone

1 Foreside

Burnhouse
Bridge

Caravan
Park

Laigh
Gree

Burnhouse

A736

B706

Oldhall
Bridge

Oldhall

Oldhallside

50

37 A **38** B C **39** D E F

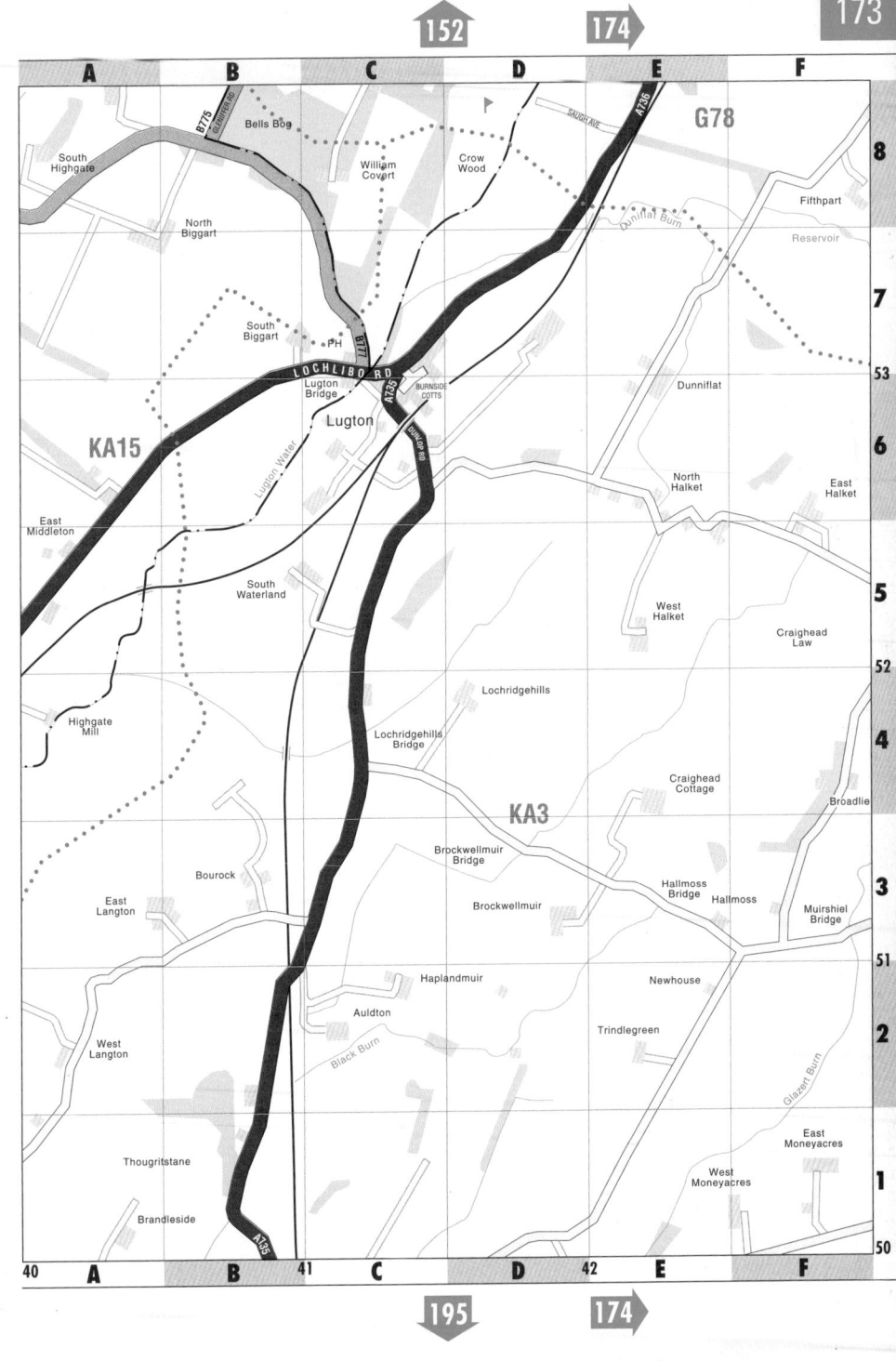

A B C D E F

G78

8

South
Highgate

Bells Bog

William
Covert

Crow
Wood

Fifthpart

Reservoir

North
Biggart

Dunniflat Burn

Dunniflat

53

7

South
Biggart

PH

LOCHLIBO RD

Lugton
Bridge

BURNSIDE
COTTS

Lugton

KA15

Lugton Water

DUNLOP RD

North
Halket

East
Halket

6

East
Middleton

South
Waterland

West
Halket

Craighead
Law

5

52

Highgate
Mill

Lochridgehills

Lochridgehills
Bridge

Craighead
Cottage

Broadlie

4

Bourock

Brockwellmuir
Bridge

KA3

Hallmoss
Bridge

Hallmoss

Muirshiel
Bridge

3

East
Langton

Brockwellmuir

51

West
Langton

Haplandmuir

Auldton

Black Burn

Newhouse

Trindlegreen

Glazert Burn

2

Thougritstane

A735

West
Moneyacres

East
Moneyacres

1

Brandleside

50

40 A B 41 C D 42 E F

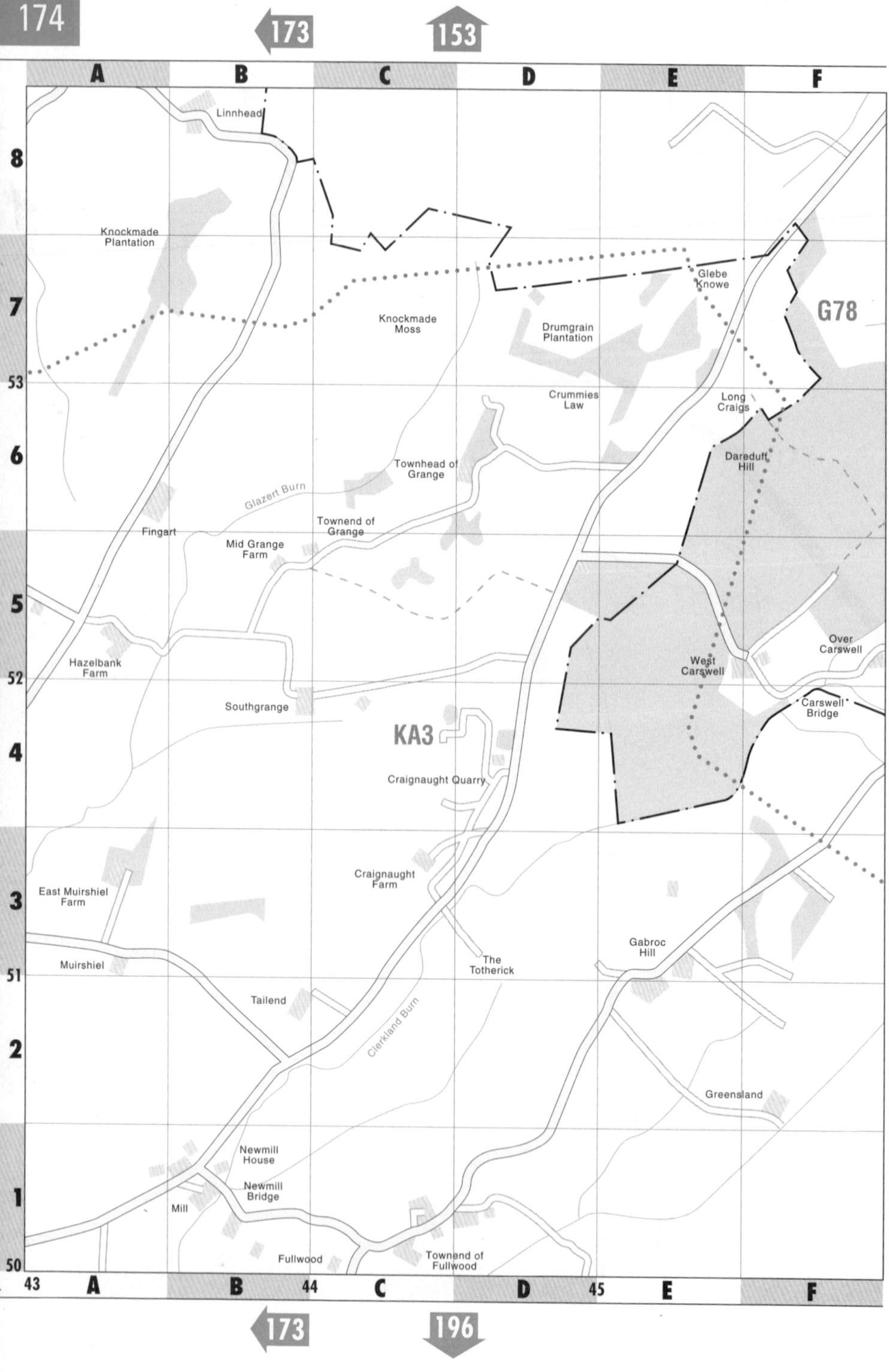

A **B** **C** **D** **E** **F**

8

Linnhead

Knockmade
Plantation

7

Knockmade
Moss

Drumgrain
Plantation

Glebe
Knowe

G78

53

Crummies
Law

Long
Craigs

6

Townhead of
Grange

Dareduff
Hill

Glazert Burn

Fingart

Townend of
Grange

Mid Grange
Farm

Over
Carswell

5

West
Carswell

Hazelbank
Farm

52

Carswell
Bridge

Southgrange

KA3

4

Craignaught Quarry

3

Craignaught
Farm

East Muirshiel
Farm

Gabroc
Hill

51

Muirshiel

The
Totherick

Tailend

Clerkland Burn

2

Greensland

Newmill
House

1

Newmill
Bridge

Mill

50

Fullwood

Townend of
Fullwood

43 **A** **B** 44 **C** **D** 45 **E** **F**

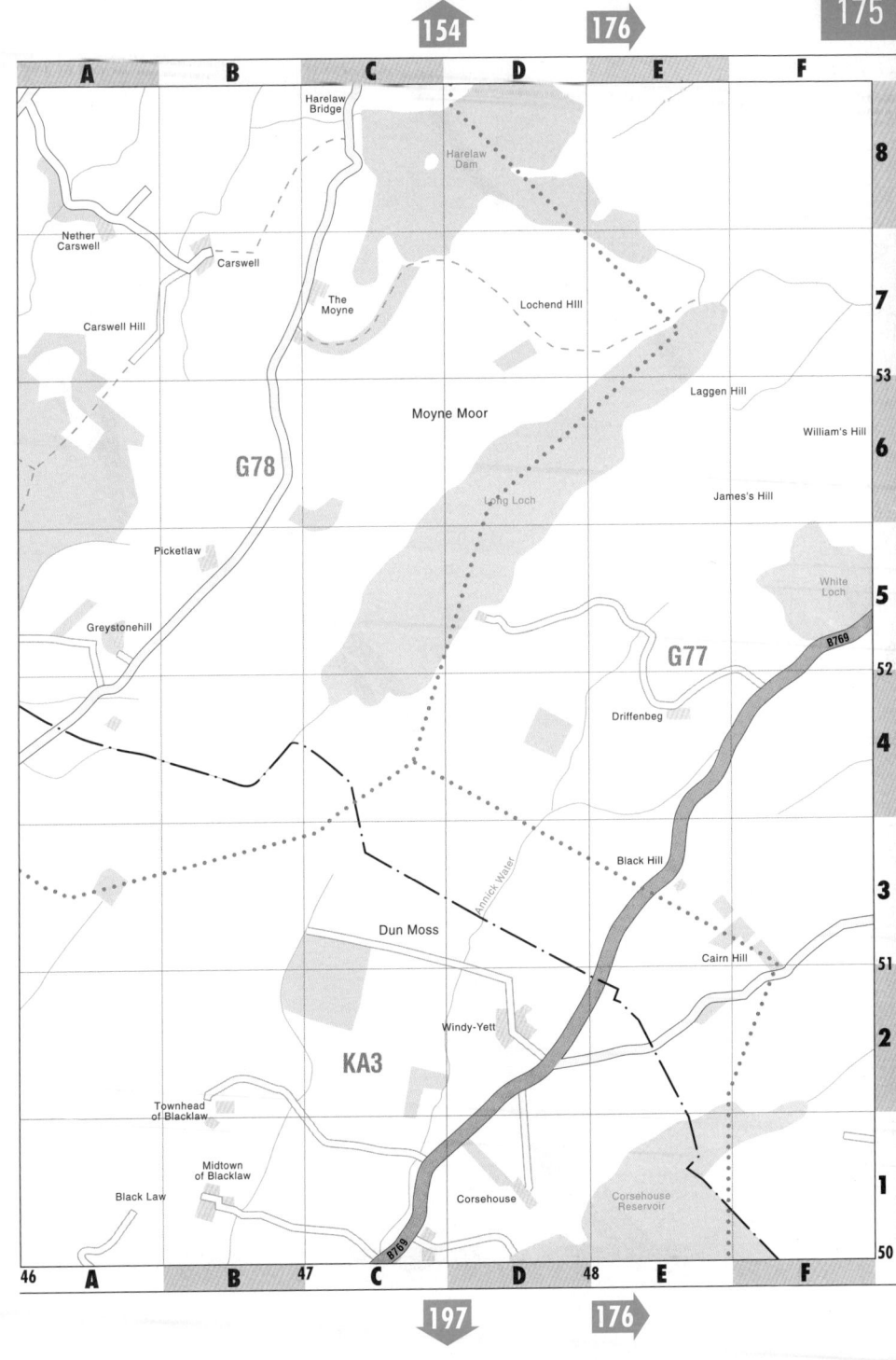

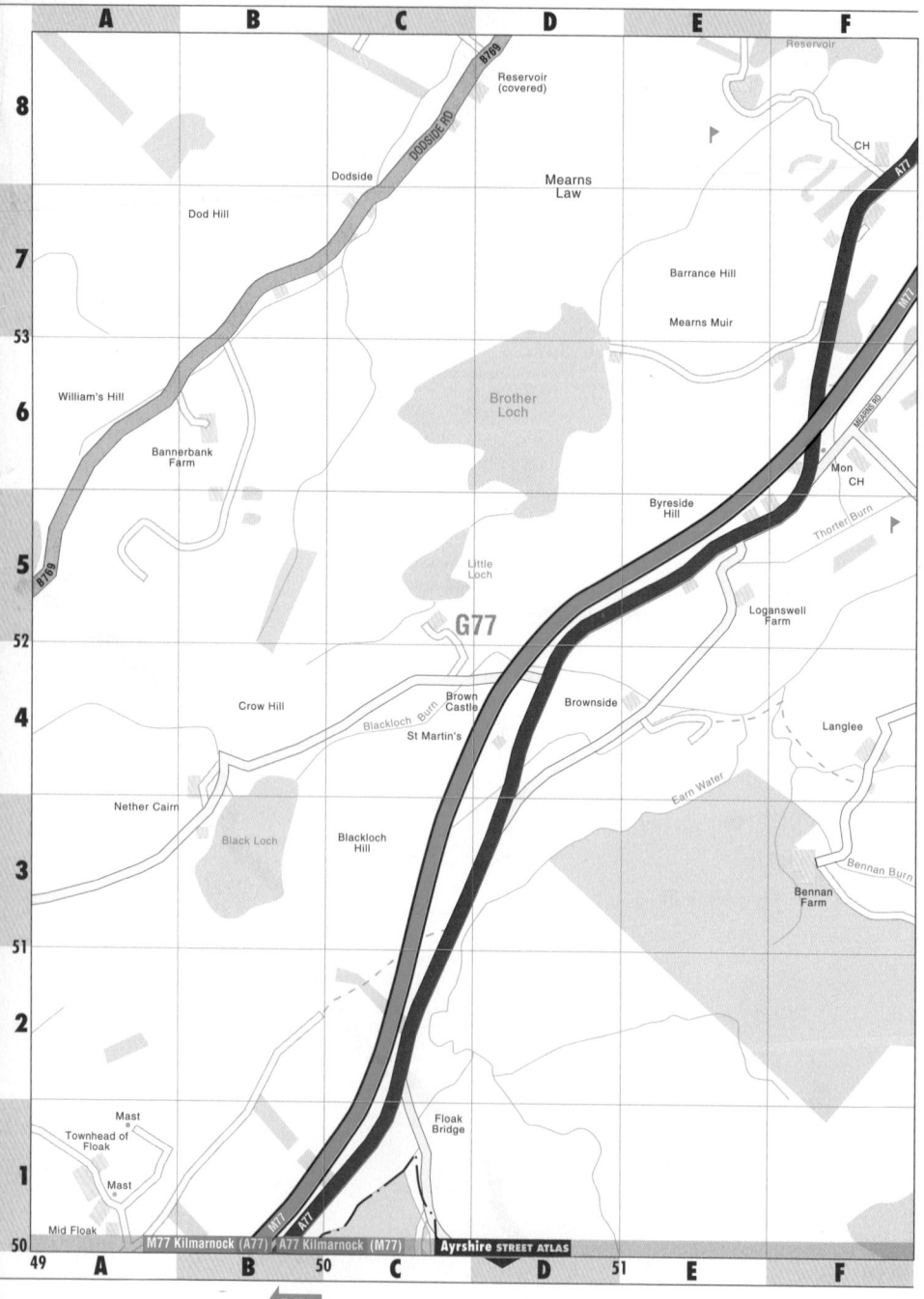

Reservoir

Reservoir
(covered)

B769

DODSIDE RD

Dodside

Dod Hill

CH

A77

Mearns
Law

Barrance Hill

M77

Mearns Muir

MEARNS RD

William's Hill

Brother
Loch

Bannerbank
Farm

Byreside
Hill

Mon
CH

Thorter Burn

B769

Little
Loch

Loganswell
Farm

G77

Crow Hill

Brown
Castle

Blackloch Burn

St Martin's

Brownside

Langlee

Nether Cairn

Black Loch

Blackloch
Hill

Earn Water

Bennan Burn

Bennan
Farm

Mast

Townhead of
Floak

Mast

Floak
Bridge

Mid Floak

M77

A77

M77 Kilmarnock (A77) / A77 Kilmarnock (M77)

Ayrshire STREET ATLAS

A77

Crook

Nursery

HAZELDEN RD

Hazeldean
House

TITWOOD RD

West
Titwood

A726

8

Harelea
Hill

MEARNS RD

Mast

Star and
Garter

Hazeldenhill

Hazelden
Mains

7

Broadlees

Earn Water

53

Fauldside Hill

Blackhouse
Farm

Bonnyton
Moor

6

Thorter Burn

G77

North
Moorhouse

Long
Wood

BONNYTON MOOR RD

Muirshield
Bridge

5

KIRKTON MOOR RD

52

East
Moorhouse

G76

Boshee Hill

4

Water
Works

South
Moorhouse

3

Bennan Burn

Lochcraig Reservoir

51

Boat
House

B764

2

Rieve Hill

Melowther

Bennan Loch

Ballageich Hill

B764

1

50

177
157

A | B | C | D | E | F

Bogside

A726

8

Bonnyton

BONNYTON MOOR RD

FLOORS RD

Brackenrig Burn

B767

KIRKHILL RD
BARLIA AVE
PICKERSTON RD

Stoneside

White Cart Water

G74

7

Castlehill
House

RUMBLE RD

Low
Borland

GLASGOW RD

A726

53

Castlehill
Wood

Castlehill

Crosslees

Holehouse

HOLEHOUSE RD

6

Crosslees
Wood

Borland Burn

Mid
Borland

CORNBRAE RD
POLNOON CRES

Cemy

CH

High
Borland

Resr

Eaglesham

B764

LYNN DR
ALEXANDER AVE

5

Liby

1 MANSEVIEW TERR
2 BORLAND CRES

EAGLESHAM RD

P

52

G76

KIRKTON PL

GILMOUR ST
B767

Park
Cres

POLNOON
DR

CHEAPSIDE ST

KIRKTON MOOR RD

PH

Common

MONTGOMERY SQ

4

North
Kirktonmoor

ALNWICK DR

MOOR RD

MONTGOMERY ST

MONTGOMERY CT 1
KIRKTON CT 2

Eaglesham
Prim Sch

EGLINTON
WLK

South
Kirktonmoor

Sewage
Works

Brownmuir
Holding

3

Picketlaw
Reservoir

Mast

Picketlaw

Low Hill

51

High Dam

High Hill

B764

2

West
Revoch

East
Revoch

Park
Farm

Woodhouse

En Ench Burn

1

55 A | B 56 C | D 57 E | F

50

177

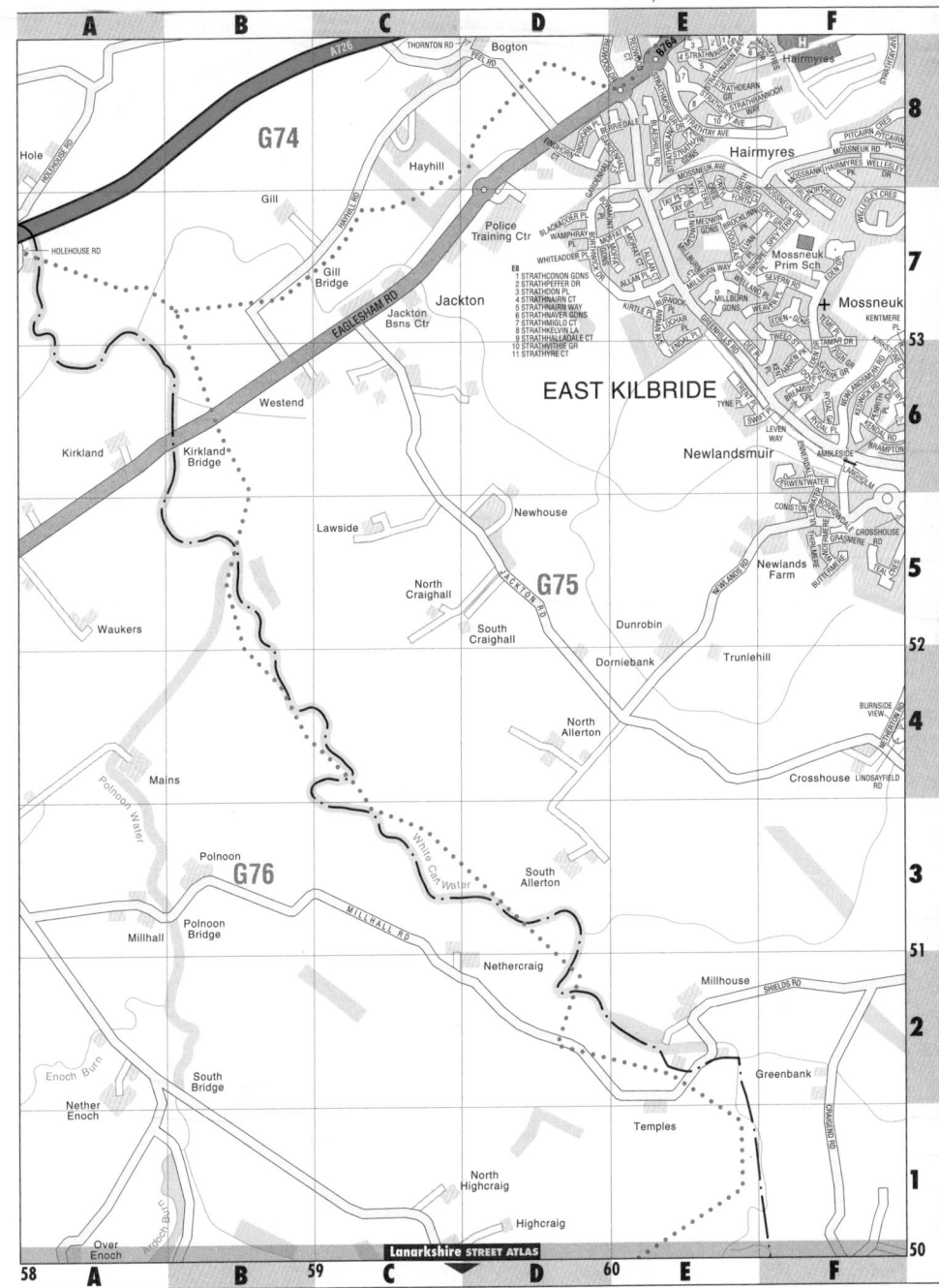

158

180

A B C D E F

G74

Hole
Hole

HOLEHOUSE RD

Gill

Gill
Bridge

THORNTON RD
PEEL RD

Bogton
Hayhill

A726

EAGLESHAM RD

Jackton
Bsns Ctr

Jackton

Police
Training Ctr

Westend

Kirkland

Kirkland
Bridge

Lawside

North
Craighall

Newhouse

South
Craighall

Waukers

Mains

G76

Polnoon
Bridge

Polnoon

Millhall

MILLHALL RD

South
Bridge

Nether
Enoch

Enoch Burn

Polnoon Water

White Cart Water

JACKTON RD

G75

Dunrobin

Dorniebank

North
Allerton

South
Allerton

Nethercraig

Over
Enoch

Ardoch Burn

North
Highcraig

Highcraig

Temples

Millhouse

SHIELDS RD

Greenbank

Crosshouse

EAST KILBRIDE

Hairmyres

Hairmyres

Mossneuk
Prim Sch

Mossneuk

Newlandsmuir

Newlands
Farm

Trunlehill

BURNSIDE
VIEW

LINDSAYFIELD
RD

CRAIGEND RD

B764

E8
1 STRATHCONON GDNS
2 STRATHPEFFER DR
3 STRATHDON PL
4 STRATHNAIRN CT
5 STRATHNAIRN WAY
6 STRATHNAVER GDNS
7 STRATHMIGLO CT
8 STRATHKELVIN LA
9 STRATHHALLADALE CT
10 STRATHVITHIE GR
11 STRATHYRE CT

Lanarkshire STREET ATLAS

58 59 60

50
1
2
3
4
52
5
6
53
7
8

180

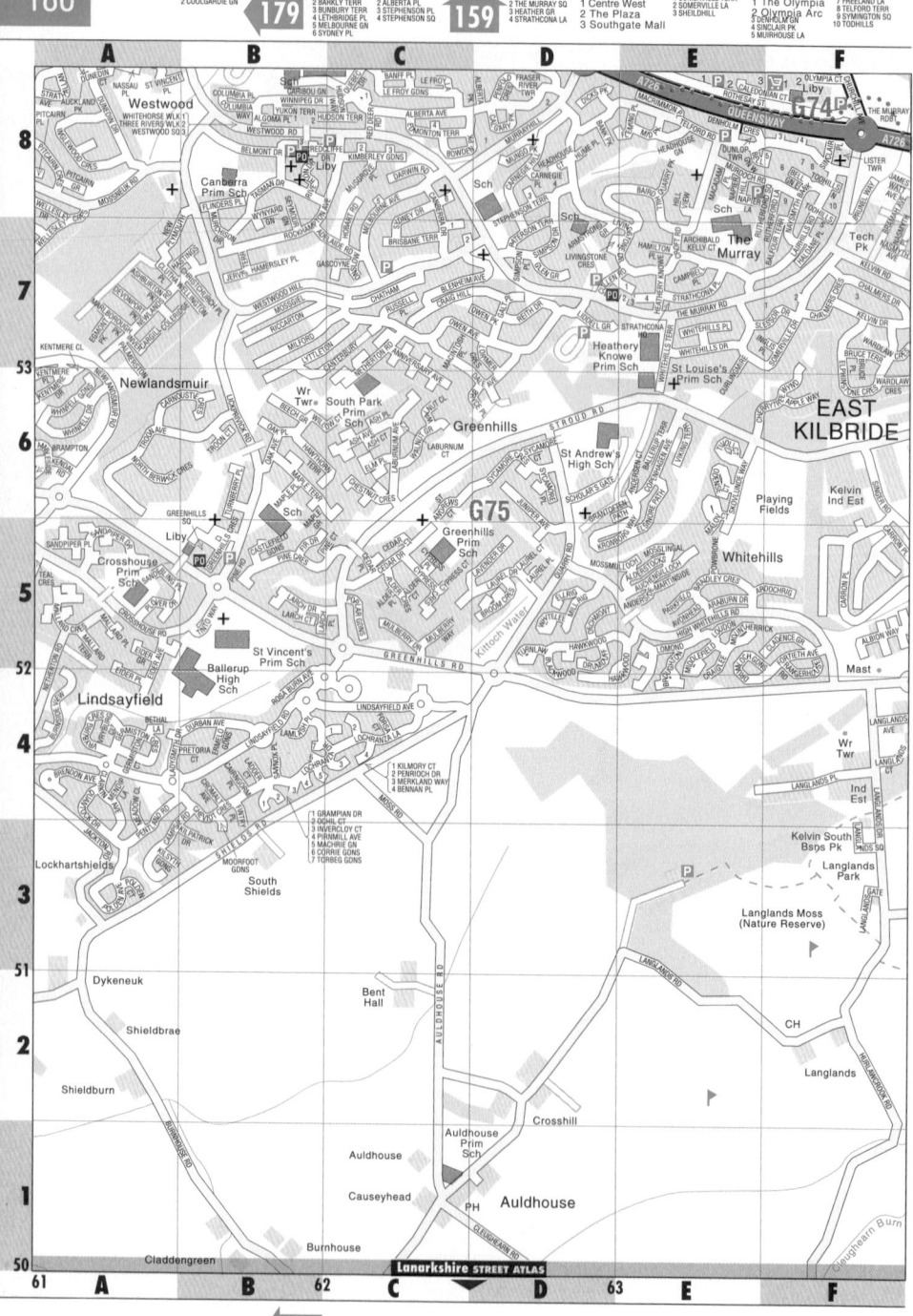

C7
1 COOLGARDIE PL
2 COOLGARDIE GN

179

C8
1 ALBERTA CRES
2 BARKLY TERR
3 BUNBURY TERR
4 LETHBRIDGE PL
5 MELBOURNE GN
6 SYDNEY PL

D8
1 CALGARY PL
2 ALBERTA PL
3 STEPHENSON PL
4 STEPHENSON SQ

159

E7
1 CULLEN LA
2 THE MURRAY SQ
3 HEATHER GR
4 STRATHCONA LA

E8
1 Centre West
2 The Plaza
3 Southgate Mall

F7
1 SOMERVILLE TERR
2 SOMERVILLE LA
3 SHEILDHILL

F8
1 The Olympia
2 Olympia Arc

6 HENRY BELL GN
7 FREELAND LA
8 TELFORD TERR
9 SYMINGTON SQ
10 TODHILLS

179

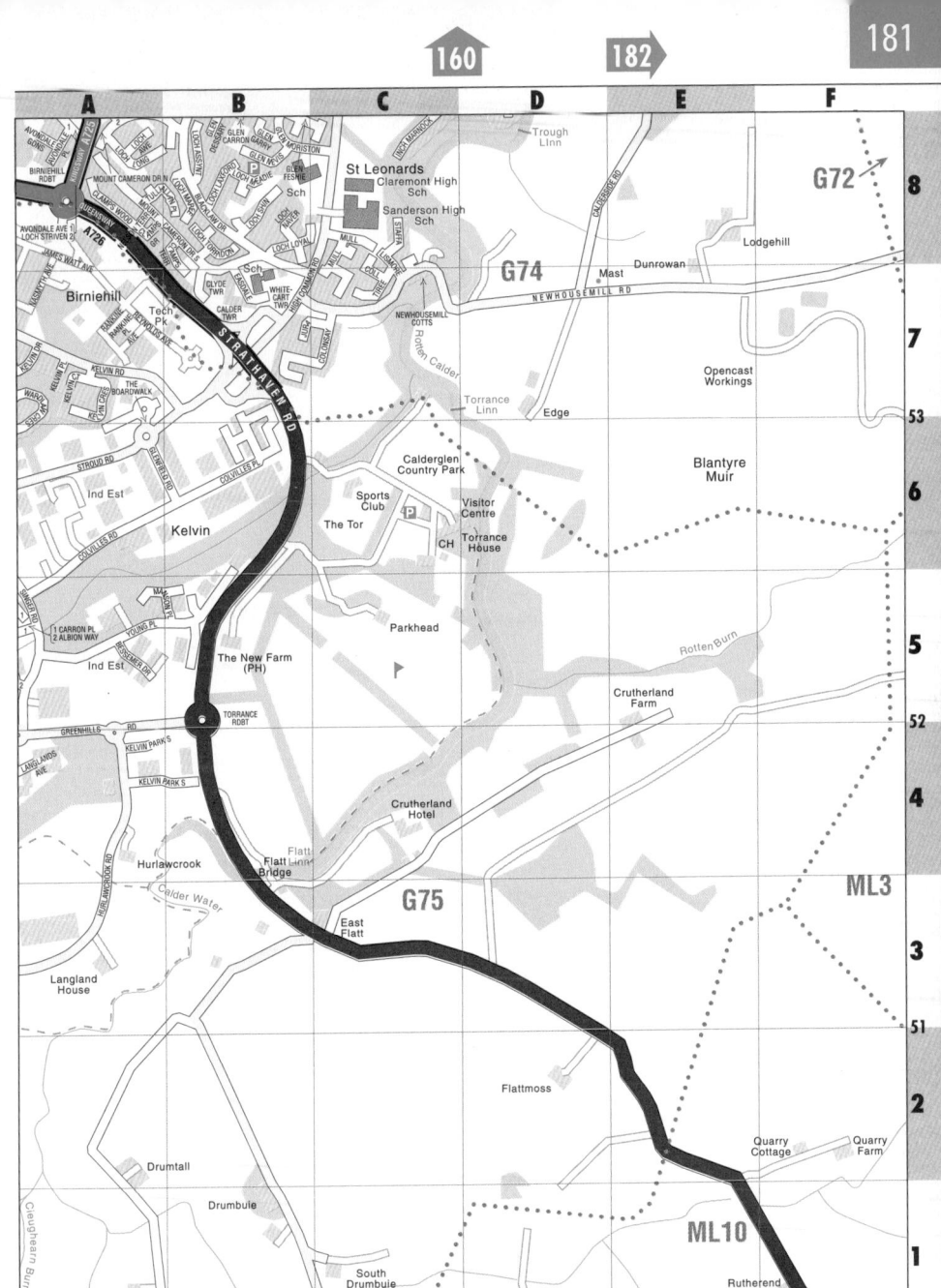

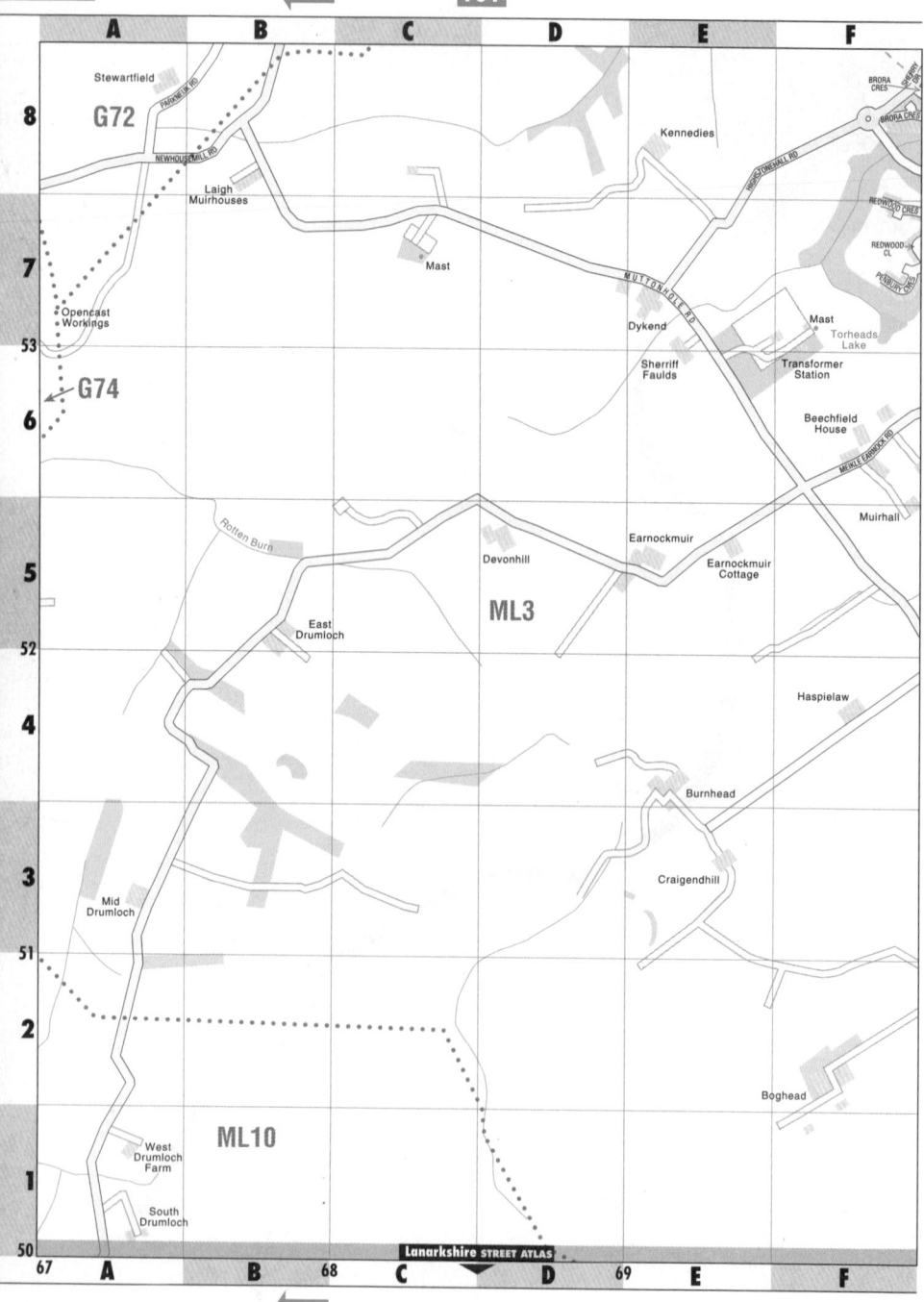

A   B   C   D   E   F

Stewartfield

PARKHEAD RD

G72

8

NEWHOUSEMILL RD

BRORA CRES

BRORA CRES

Kennedies

HIGH TOWNHALL RD

REDWOOD CRES

Laigh
Muirhouses

REDWOOD
CL

7

Mast

MUTTONHOLE RD

FASBURY CRES

Opencast
Workings

53

Dykend

Mast

Torheads
Lake

G74

Sherriff
Faulds

Transformer
Station

6

Beechfield
House

MEIKLE EARNOCK RD

Muirhall

Rotten Burn

Earnockmuir

5

Devonhill

Earnockmuir
Cottage

ML3

52

East
Drumloch

Haspielaw

4

Burnhead

3

Mid
Drumloch

Craigendhill

51

2

Boghead

ML10

West
Drumloch
Farm

1

South
Drumloch

50

67   A   B   68   C   D   69   E   F

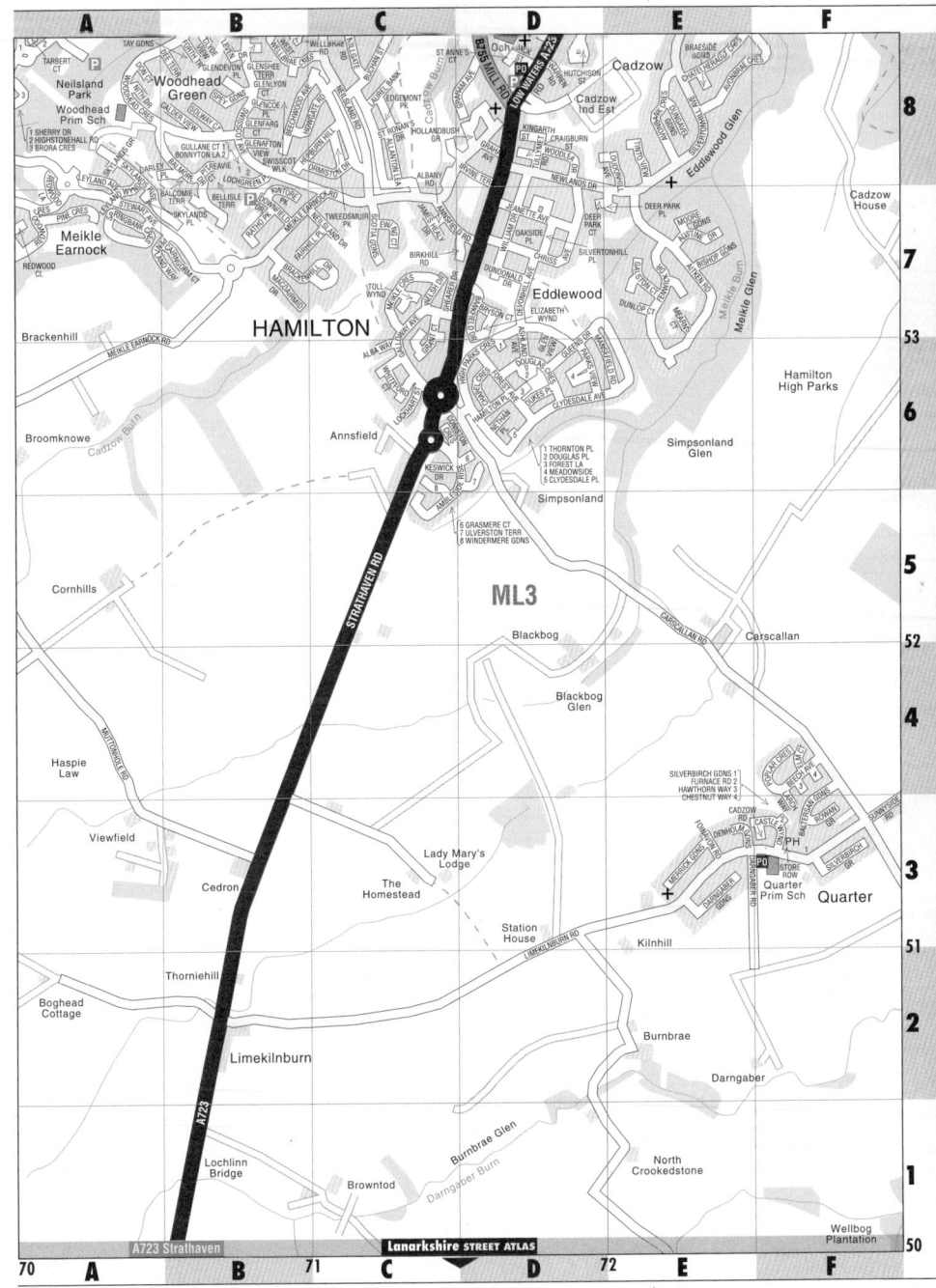

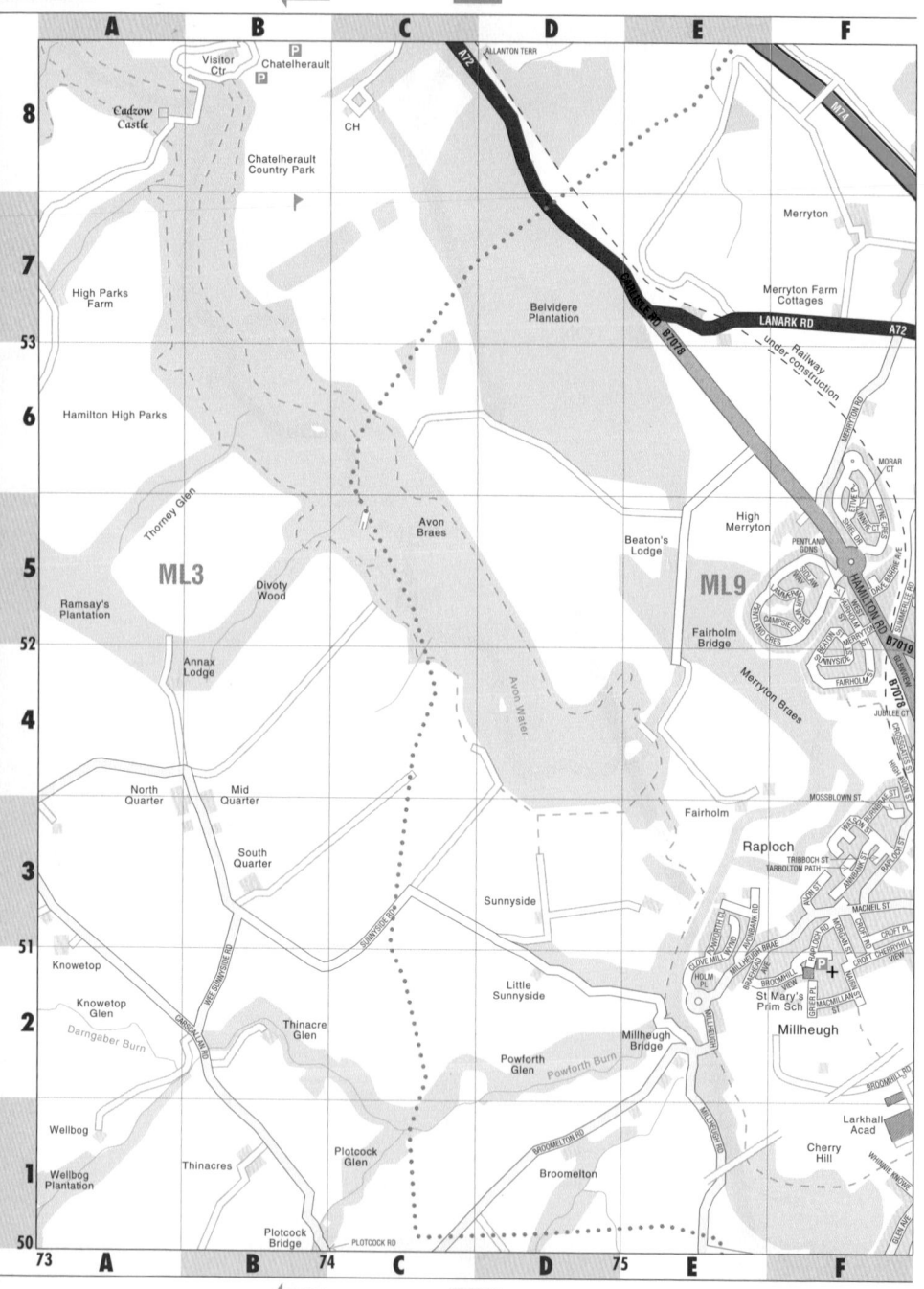

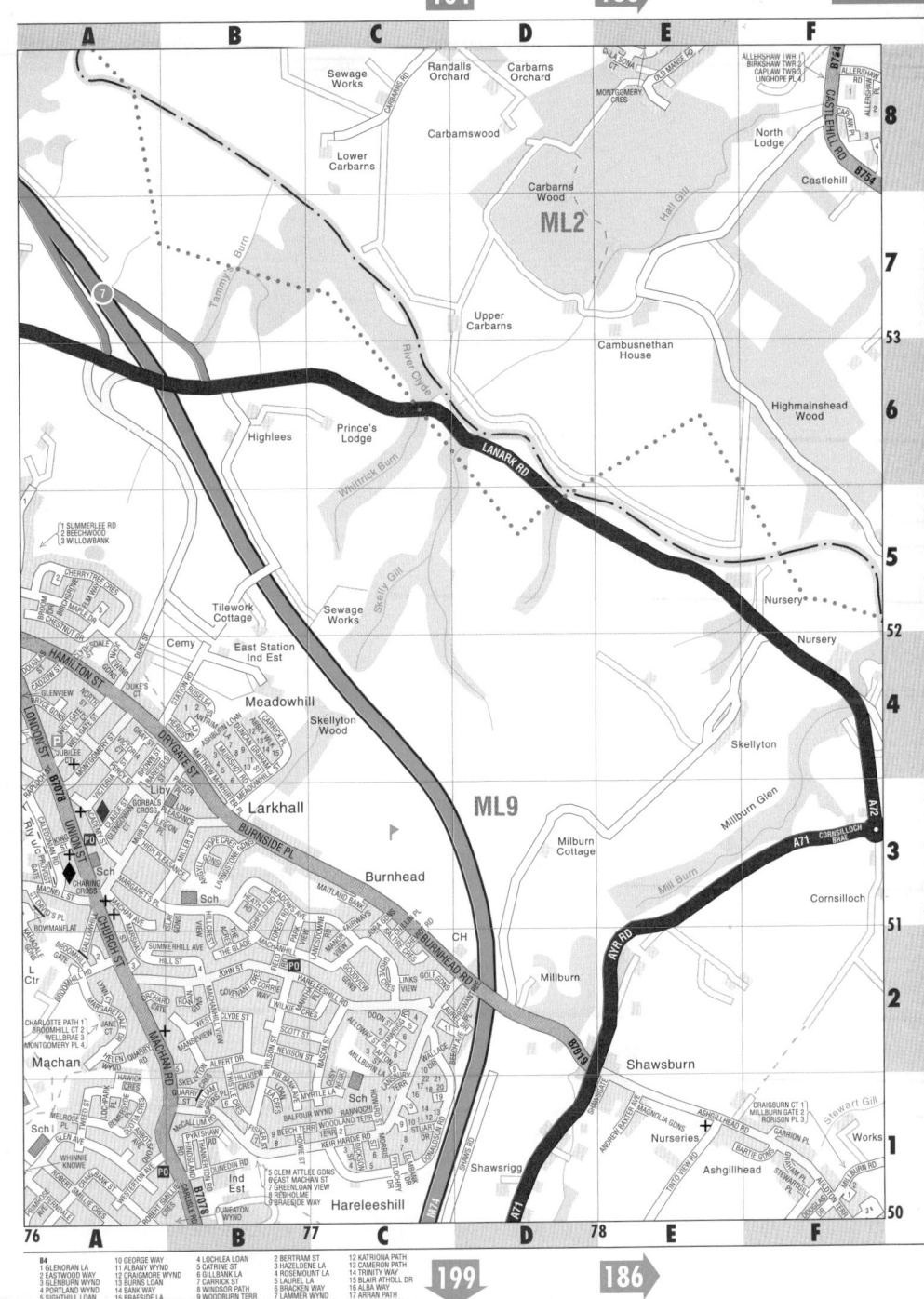

A B C D E F

8
7
53
6
5
52
4
3
51
2
1
50

Sewage Works

Randalls Orchard

Carbarns Orchard

MONTGOMERY CRES

Carbarnswood

Lower Carbarns

Carbarns Wood

ML2

ALLERSHAW (WH 1
BIRKSHAW TWR 2
CAPLAW TWS 3
LINGHOPE PL 4

ALLERSHAW
RD

CASTLEHILL RD

North Lodge

Castlehill

Hall Gill

Upper Carbarns

Cambusnethan House

Highmainshead Wood

Highlees

Prince's Lodge

LANARK RD

1 SUMMERLEE RD
2 BEECHWOOD
3 WILLOWBANK

Whittrick Burn

River Clyde

Tammy Burn

Nursery

Nursery

Tilework Cottage

Sewage Works

Skelly Gill

Cemy

East Station Ind Est

Meadowhill

Skellyton Wood

Skellyton

HAMILTON ST

Larkhall

BURNSIDE PL

ML9

Millburn Glen

A72

A71 CORNSILLOCH BRAE

Cornsilloch

Burnhead

Milburn Cottage

Mill Burn

CH

Millburn

Machan

MACHAN RD

BURNHEAD RD

Shawsburn

CRAIGBURN CT 1
MILLBURN GATE 2
RONISON PL 3

Stewart Gill

Nurseries

Works

Ashgillhead

Ind Est

Hareleeshill

Shawsrigg

A71

AYR RD

B7018

Shawsrigg

Ashgillhead

76 A B 77 C D 78 E F

B4
1 GLENORAN LA
2 EASTWOOD WAY
3 GLENBURN WYND
4 PORTLAND WYND
5 SIGHTHILL LOAN
6 PARKNOOK WAY
7 LOMOND WLK
8 HOZIER LOAN
9 CRAIGIE LA

10 GEORGE WAY
11 ALBANY WYND
12 CRAIGAMORE WYND
13 BURNS LOAN
14 BANK WAY
15 BRAESIDE LA
C2
1 LOANING
2 LOVAT PATH
3 BALMORAL PATH

4 LOCHLEA LOAN
5 CATRINE ST
6 GILLBANK LA
7 CARRICK ST
8 WINDSOR PATH
9 WOODBURN TERR
10 MAXWELL PATH
11 HAWTHORN GDNS
C1
1 MOSSGIEL LA

2 BERTRAM ST
3 HAZELDENE LA
4 ROSEMOUNT LA
5 LAUREL LA
6 BRACKEN WAY
7 LAMMER WYND
8 CAMERONIAN WAY
9 GLEN FRUIN DR
10 ST ANDREWS PATH
11 LAWRIE WAY

12 KATRIONA PATH
13 CAMERON PATH
14 TRINITY WAY
15 BLAIR ATHOLL DR
16 ALBA WAY
17 ARRAN PATH
18 DALSERF PATH
19 BANNOCKBURN DR
20 LOCHNAGAR WAY
21 FLEMING WAY

22 BRUCE'S LOAN

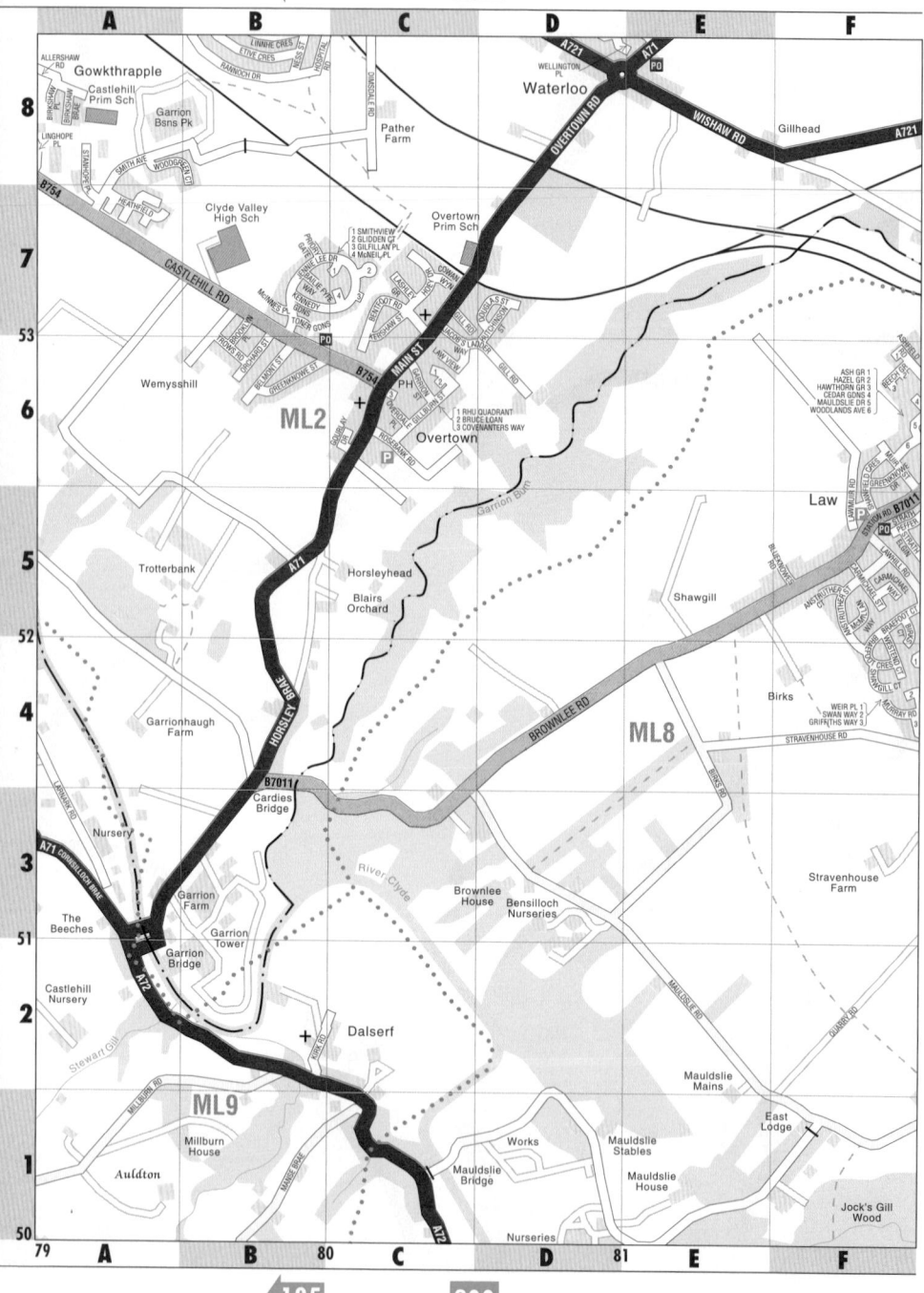

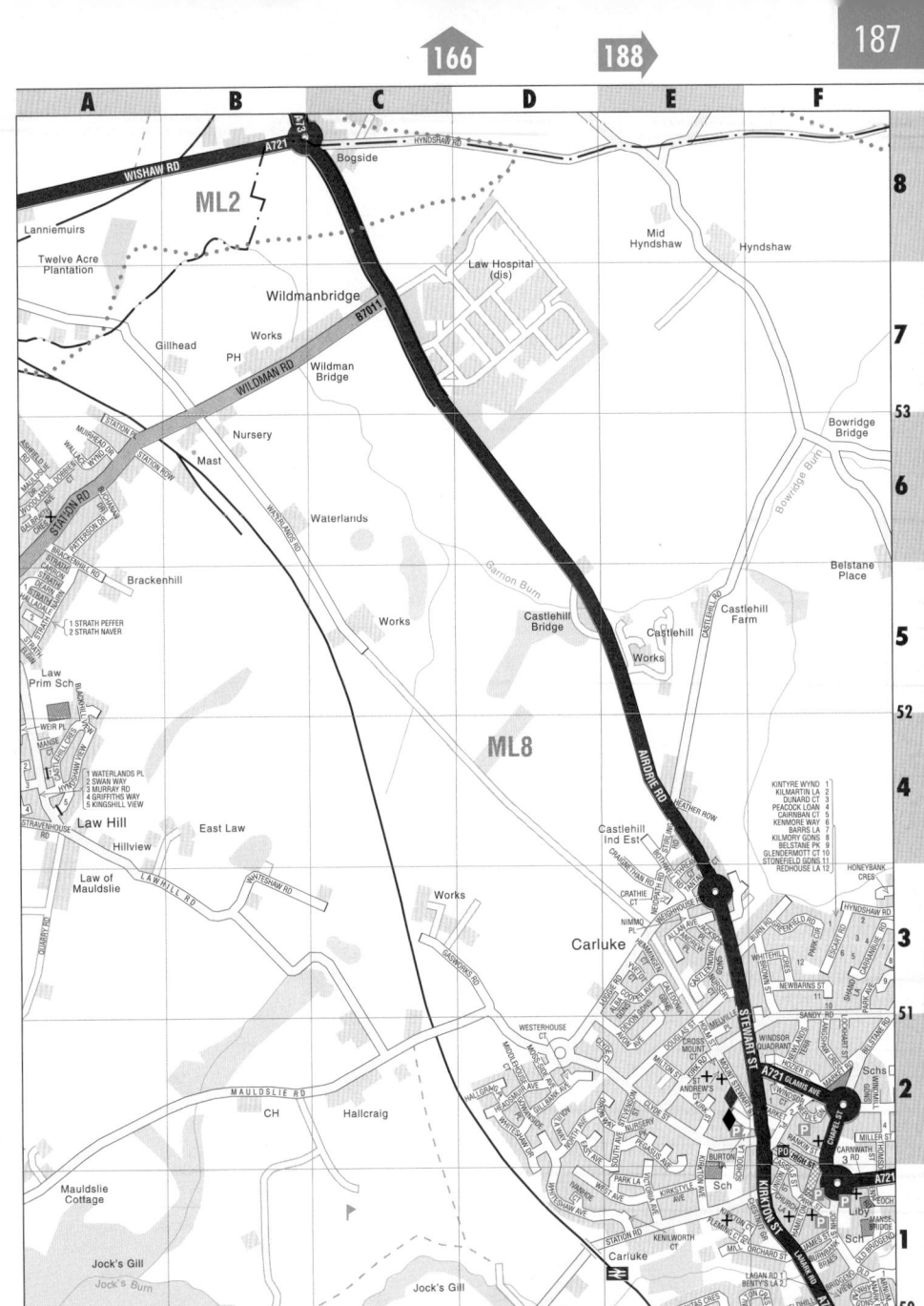

F2
1 STEWART PL
2 MARKET RD
3 Rankin Gate Ctr
4 GREENBANK TERR

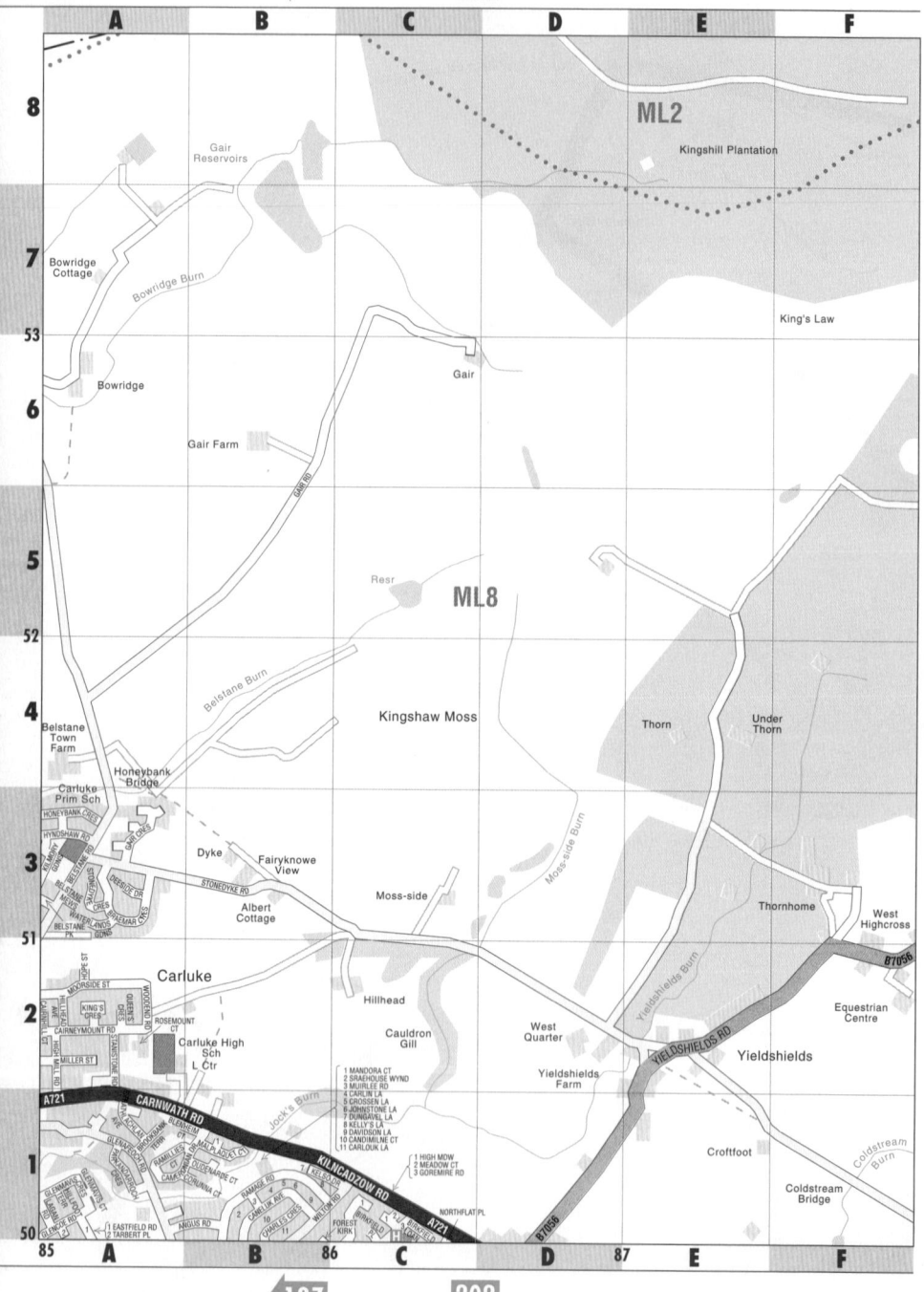

A   B   C   D   E   F

8

ML2

Kingshill Plantation

7   Bowridge
Cottage

Bowridge Burn

King's Law

53

Gair

Bowridge

6

Gair Farm

5

ML8

Resr

52

4   Belstane Burn

Belstane
Town
Farm

Kingshaw Moss

Thorn   Under
Thorn

Honeybank
Bridge

Carluke
Prim Sch

HONEYBANK CRES

HYNDSHAW AVE

Dyke   Fairyknowe
View

CRESSET DR

STONEDYKE RD

Moss-side Burn

3

Albert
Cottage

Moss-side

Thornhome   West
Highcross

BRAEMAR CROS

STONEDYKE RD

BELSTANE
PK

B7056

51

Carluke

MOORSIDE ST

WOODEND RD

Hillhead

Cauldron
Gill

West
Quarter

Yieldshields Burn

Equestrian
Centre

YIELDSHIELDS RD

Yieldshields

2   KING'S
CRES   QUEEN'S

ROSEMOUNT
CT

Carluke High
Sch
L Ctr

MILLER ST

CAIRNEYMOUNT RD

Yieldshields
Farm

1 MANDORA CT
2 SRAEHOUSE WYND
3 MUIRLEE RD
4 CARLIN LA
5 CROSSEN LA
6 JOHNSTONE LA
7 DUNDAGEL LA
8 KELLY'S LA
9 DAVIDSON LA
10 CANDIMILNE CT
11 CARLOUK LA

A721

CARNWATH RD

Jock's Burn

Croftfoot   Coldstream
Burn

1   KILNCADZOW RD

1 EASTFIELD RD
2 TARBERT PL

1 HIGH MDW
2 MEADOW CT
3 GOREMIRE RD

ANGUS RD

FOREST
KIRK

NORTHFLAT PL

A721

Coldstream
Bridge

B7056

50

85   A   B   86   C   D   87   E   F

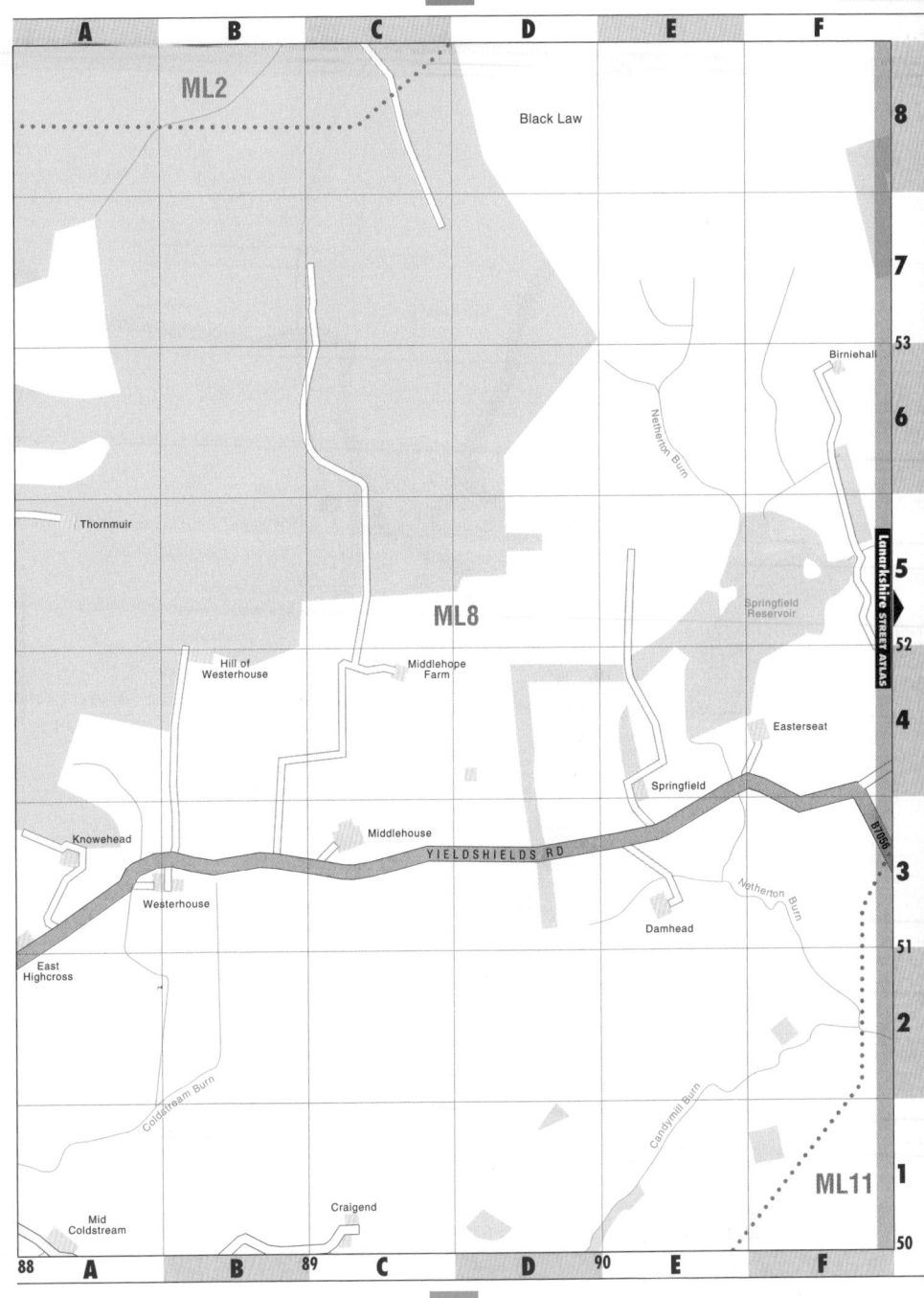

A   B   C   D   E   F

ML2

Black Law

8

7

53

Birniehall

6

Netherton Burn

Thornmuir

Springfield
Reservoir

Lanarkshire STREET ATLAS

5

52

ML8

Hill of
Westerhouse

Middlehope
Farm

4

Easterseat

Springfield

B7056

Knowehead

Middlehouse

YIELDSHIELDS RD

3

Westerhouse

Netherton Burn

Damhead

51

East
Highcross

2

Coldstream Burn

Candymill Burn

ML11

1

Mid
Coldstream

Craigend

50

88   A   B   89   C   D   90   E   F

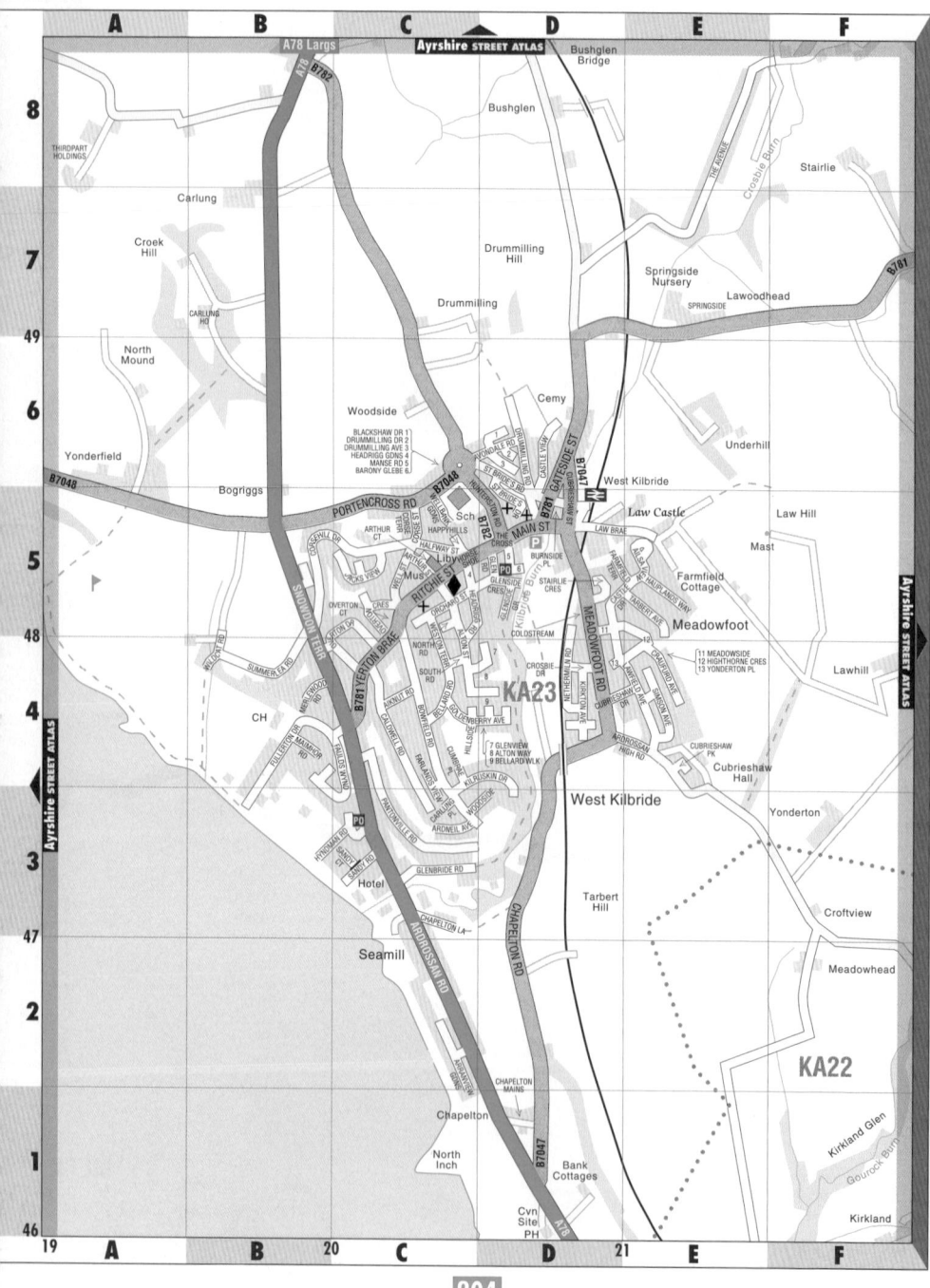

A78 Largs

Bushglen
Bridge

Bushglen

Thirdpart
Holdings

Carlung

Stairlie

Crosbie Burn

THE AVENUE

Croek
Hill

Drummilling
Hill

Drummilling

Springside
Nursery

Lawoodhead

SPRINGSIDE

B781

North
Mound

Woodside

Cemy

BLACKSHAW DR 1
DRUMMILLING DR 2
DRUMMILLING AVE 3
HEADRIGG GDNS 4
MANSE RD 5
BARONY GLEBE 6

Underhill

Yonderfield

GATESIDE ST

West Kilbride

Law Hill

Bogriggs

B7048

PORTENCROSS RD

B7048

ST BRIDE'S RD

Law Castle

LAW BRAE

Mast

Sch

Arthur
CT

HAPPYHILLS

MAIN ST

Farmfield
Cottage

Libwynd

Mus

RITCHIE ST

BURNSIDE
PL

GLENSIDE
CRES

STAIRLIE
CRES

Meadowfoot

MEADOWFOOT RD

COLDSTREAM

11 MEADOWSIDE
12 HIGHTHORNE CRES
13 YONDERTON PL

CROSBIE
DR

Lawhill

CH

SUMMER EADS

B781 YERTON BRAE

KA23

CUBRIESHAW HIGH RD

Cubrieshaw
PK

Cubrieshaw
Hall

West Kilbride

Yonderton

7 GLENVIEW
8 ALTON WAY
9 BELLARD WLK

PO

ARDROSSAN RD

ARDMEIL AVE

Croftview

GLENBRIDE RD

CHAPELTON RD

Tarbert
Hill

Hotel

CHAPELTON LA

Meadowhead

Seamill

CHAPELTON
MAINS

KA22

Chapelton

North
Inch

B7047

Bank
Cottages

Kirkland Glen

Gourock Burn

Cvn
Site
PH

A78

Kirkland

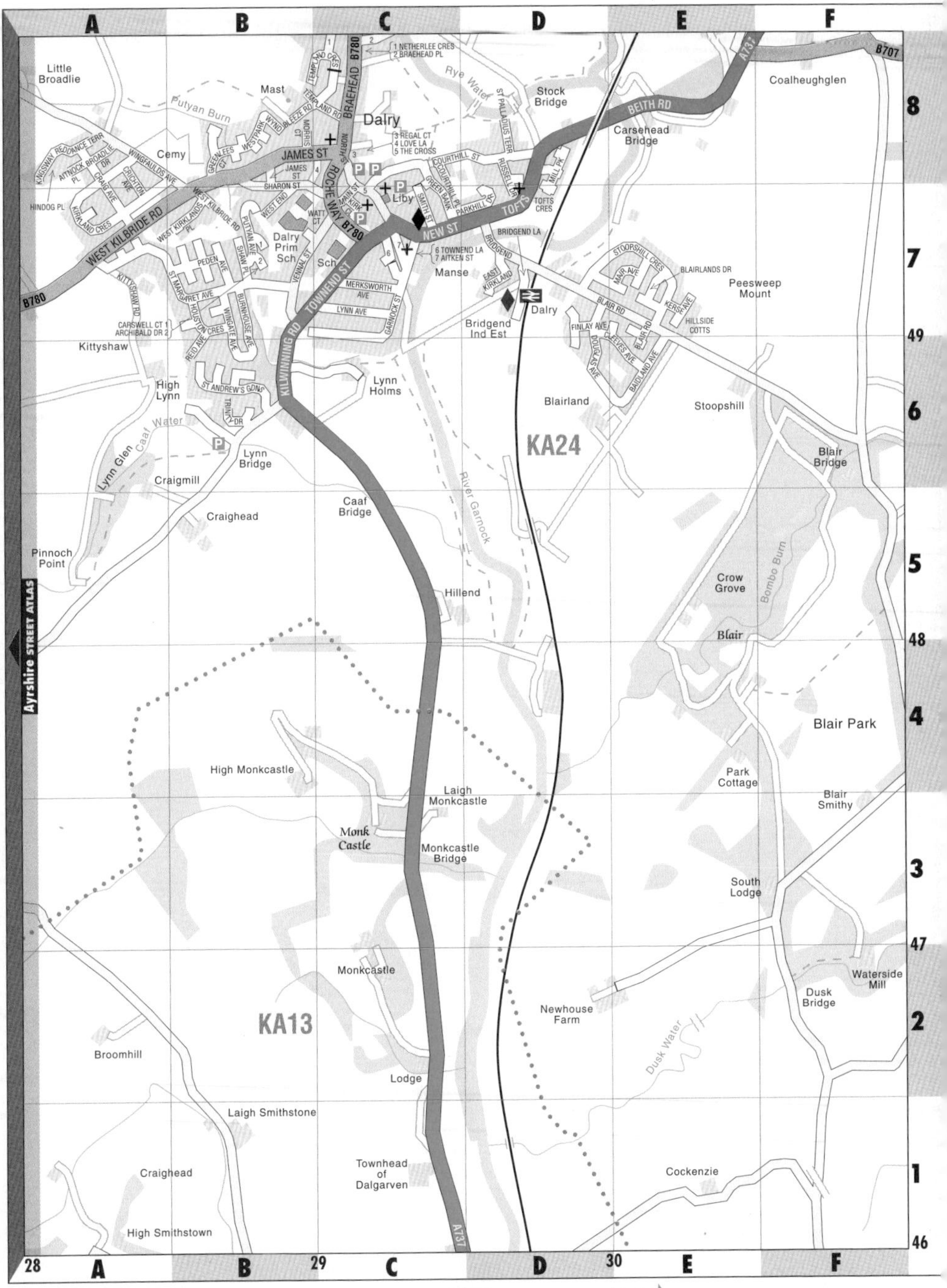

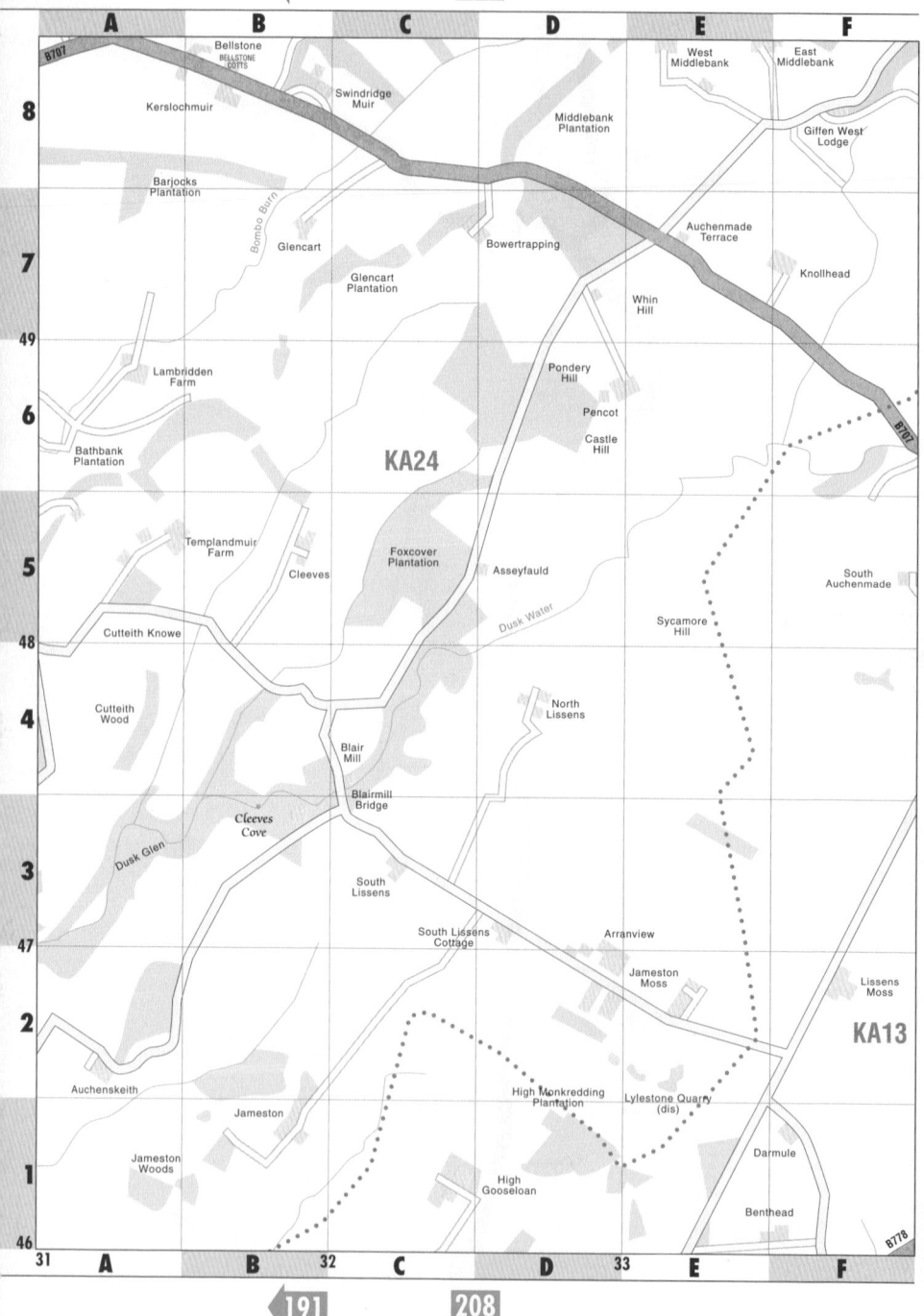

| | A | B | C | D | E | F |

B707

8

Bellstone
BELLSTONE COTTS

Kerslochmuir

Swindridge
Muir

West
Middlebank

East
Middlebank

Giffen West
Lodge

Barjocks
Plantation

Middlebank
Plantation

7

Glencart

Glencart
Plantation

Bombo Burn

Bowertrapping

Auchenmade
Terrace

Knollhead

49

Whin
Hill

Lambridden
Farm

6

Bathbank
Plantation

KA24

Pondery
Hill

Pencot

Castle
Hill

B707

Templandmuir
Farm

Cleeves

Foxcover
Plantation

Asseyfauld

5

South
Auchenmade

Cutteith Knowe

Dusk Water

Sycamore
Hill

48

Cutteith
Wood

4

North
Lissens

Blair
Mill

Blairmill
Bridge

Cleeves
Cove

Dusk Glen

3

South
Lissens

47

South Lissens
Cottage

Arranview

Jameston
Moss

Lissens
Moss

2

Auchenskeith

Jameston

High Monkredding
Plantation

Lylestone Quarry
(dis)

KA13

Jameston
Woods

1

High
Gooseloan

Darmule

Benthead

B778

46

31

A

B

32

C

D

33

E

F

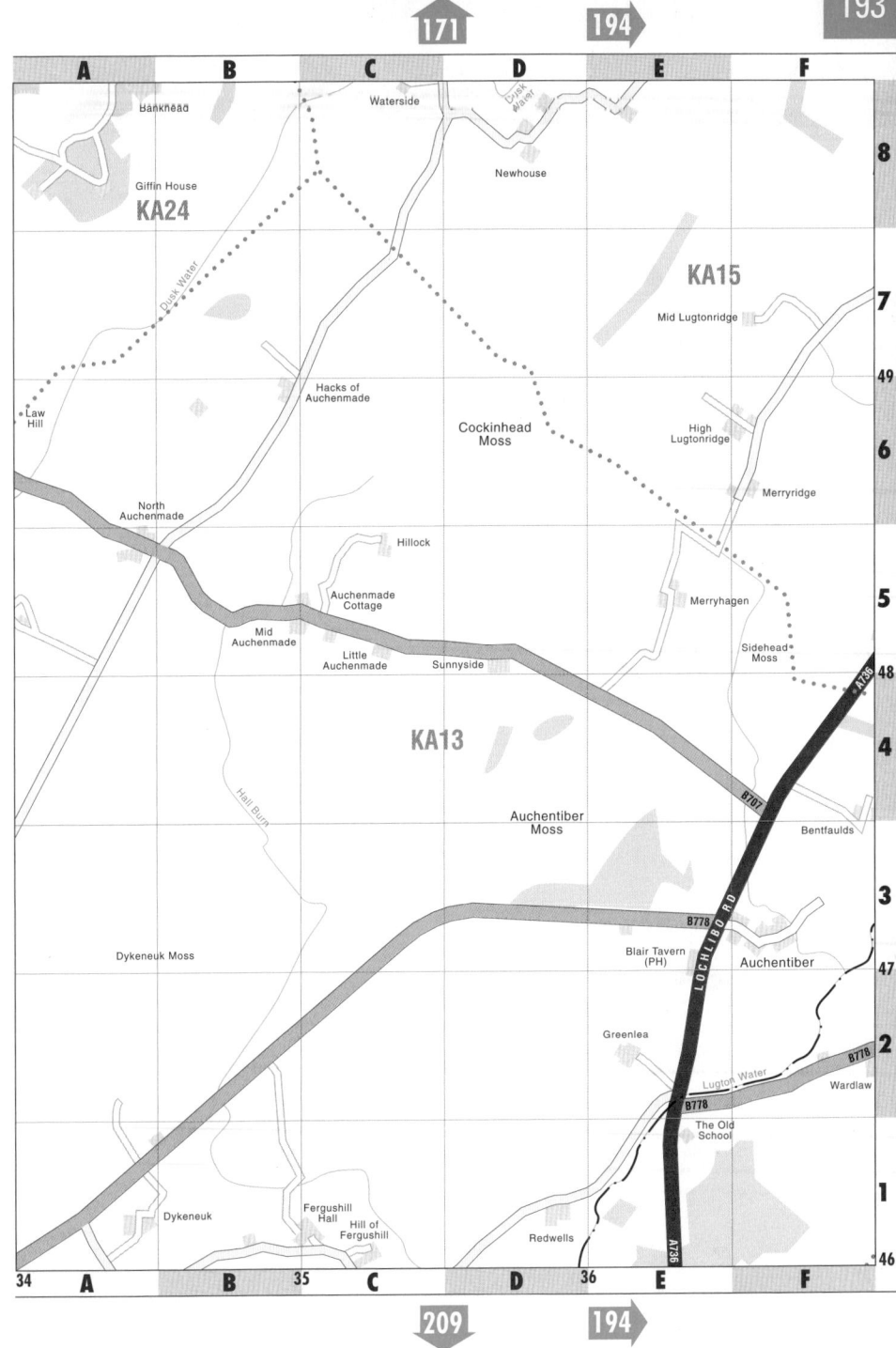

A B C D E F

8

Bankhead

Waterside

Duck Water

Newhouse

Giffin House

KA24

KA15

Mid Lugtonridge

7

49

Hacks of Auchenmade

Law Hill

Cockinhead Moss

High Lugtonridge

6

North Auchenmade

Merryridge

Hillock

Auchenmade Cottage

Merryhagen

5

Mid Auchenmade

Little Auchenmade

Sunnyside

Sidehead Moss

48

KA13

4

Hall Burn

Auchentiber Moss

B707

Bentfaulds

3

B778

LOCHLIBO RD

Dykeneuk Moss

Blair Tavern (PH)

Auchentiber

47

Greenlea

2

Lugton Water

B778

Wardlaw

B778

The Old School

1

Dykeneuk

Fergushill Hall

Hill of Fergushill

Redwells

A736

46

34 A B 35 C D 36 E F

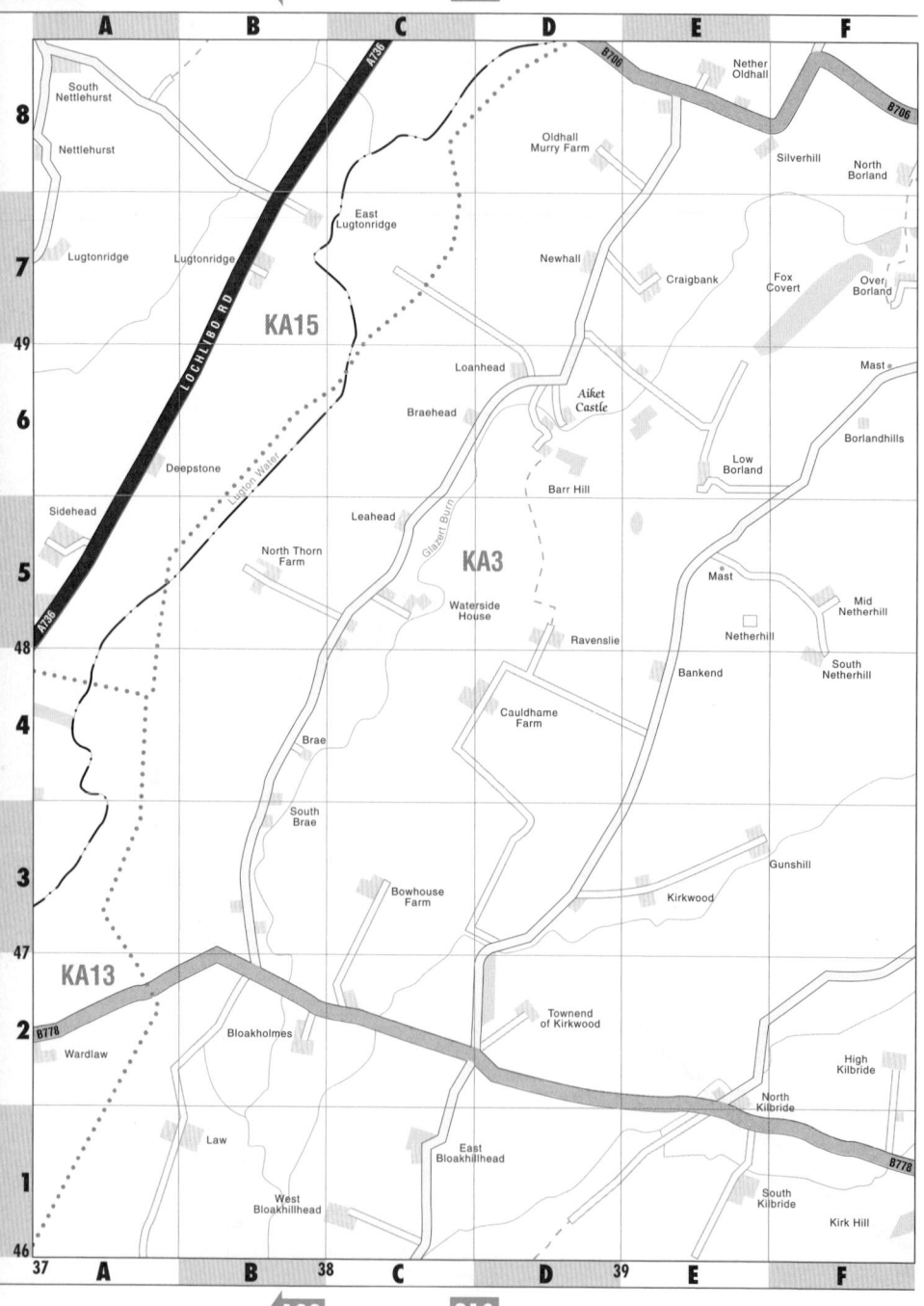

173
196
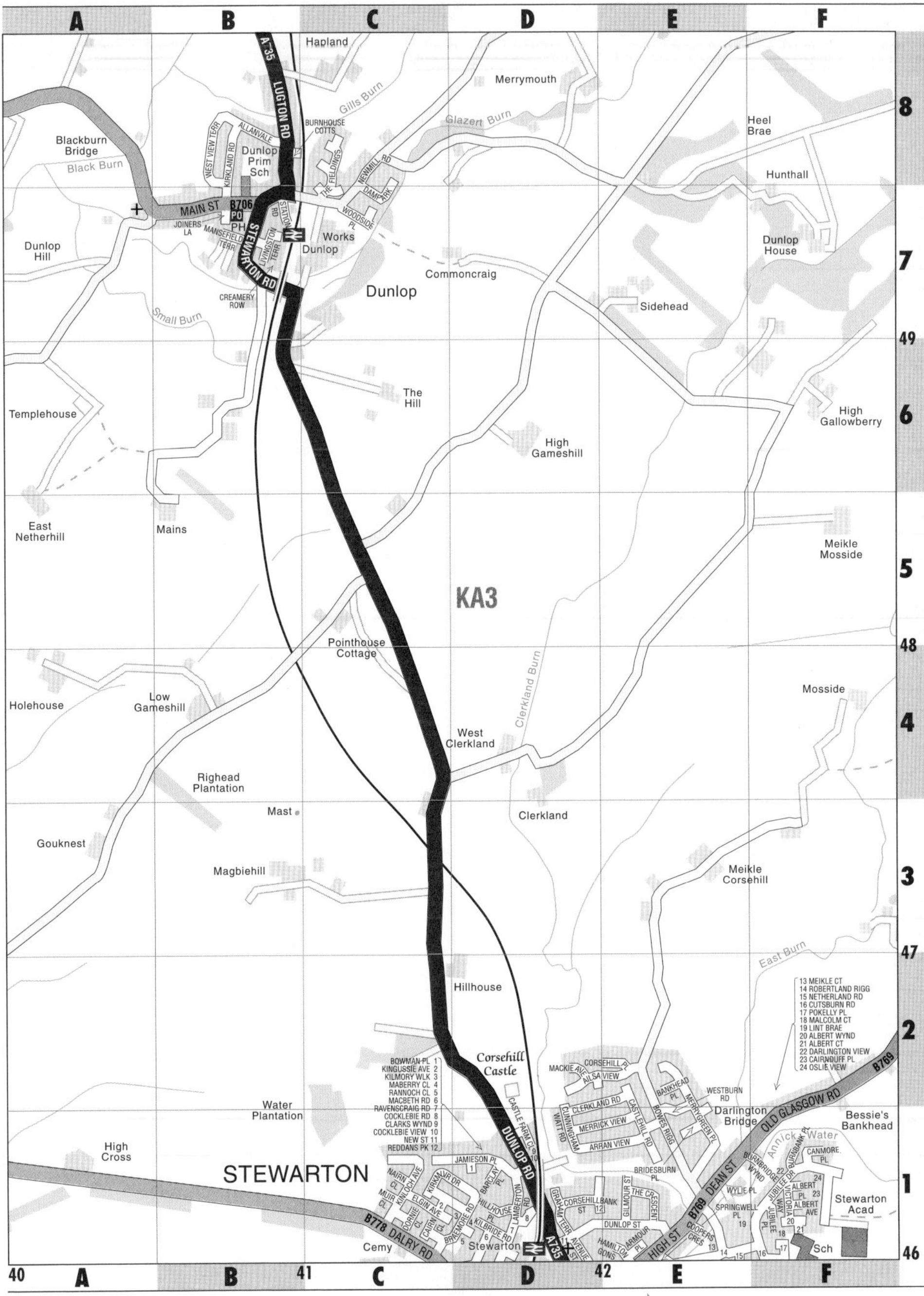
A
B
C
D
E
F
8
7
49
6
5
48
4
3
47
2
1
46
40
41
42
Hapland
Merrymouth
Gills Burn
Glazert Burn
Heel Brae
Hunthall
A735
LUGTON RD
BURNHOUSE COTTS
THE FIELDINGS
NEWMILL RD
DAMPARK
WOODSIDE PL
WEST VIEW TERR
ALLANVALE
KIRKLAND RD
Dunlop Prim Sch
Blackburn Bridge
Black Burn
MAIN ST
B706
PO
PH
JOINERS LA
MANSEFIELD TERR
STEWARTON RD
LIVINGSTON TERR
STATION RD
Works
Dunlop
Dunlop Hill
Dunlop House
Commoncraig
CREAMERY ROW
Small Burn
Sidehead
The Hill
Templehouse
High Gameshill
High Gallowberry
East Netherhill
Mains
Meikle Mosside
KA3
Pointhouse Cottage
Holehouse
Low Gameshill
Mosside
Clerkland Burn
West Clerkland
Righead Plantation
Mast
Clerkland
Gouknest
Magbiehill
Meikle Corsehill
East Burn
Hillhouse
Corsehill Castle
Water Plantation
High Cross
STEWARTON
Cemy
B778 DALRY RD
BOWMAN PL 1
KINGUSSIE AVE 2
KILMORY WLK 3
MABERRY CL 4
RANNOCH CL 5
MACBETH RD 6
RAVENSCRAIG RD 7
COCKLEBIE RD 8
CLARKS WYND 9
COCKLEBIE VIEW 10
NEW ST 11
REDDANS PK 12
13 MEIKLE CT
14 ROBERTLAND RIGG
15 NETHERLAND RD
16 CUTSBURN RD
17 POKELLY PL
18 MALCOLM CT
19 LINT BRAE
20 ALBERT WYND
21 ALBERT CT
22 DARLINGTON VIEW
23 CAIRNDUFF PL
24 OSLIE VIEW
CASTLE FARM CL
DUNLOP RD
JAMIESON PL
NAIRN CL
KINLOCH AVE
KIRKMUIR DR
BARCLAY PL
MUIR CL
ELGIN AVE
DORNIE CL
CAIRN GL
BRAEMORE RD
HILLHOUSE PL
KILBRIDE RD
LAMBERTON RD
Stewarton
A735
MACKIE AVE
CORSEHILL PL
AILSA VIEW
CLERKLAND RD
CUNNINGHAM
WATT RD
MERRICK VIEW
ARRAN VIEW
CASTLEHILL RD
BOWES RIGG
BANKHEAD PL
MERRYGREEN PL
WESTBURN RD
Darlington Bridge
OLD GLASGOW RD
B769
Bessie's Bankhead
BRIDESBURN PL
GRAHAM TERR
AVENUE ST
CORSEHILLBANK ST
GILMOUR ST
THE CRESCENT
DUNLOP ST
HAMILTON GDNS
ARMOUR PL
HIGH ST
B769 DEAN ST
COOPERS CRES
BURNBRIDGE WYND
WYLIE PL
SPRINGWELL PL
JUBILEE PL
JUBILEE DR
VICTORIA WAY
BURNBANK PL
ALBERT PL
ALBERT AVE
CANMORE PL
Annick Water
Stewarton Acad
Sch
211
196

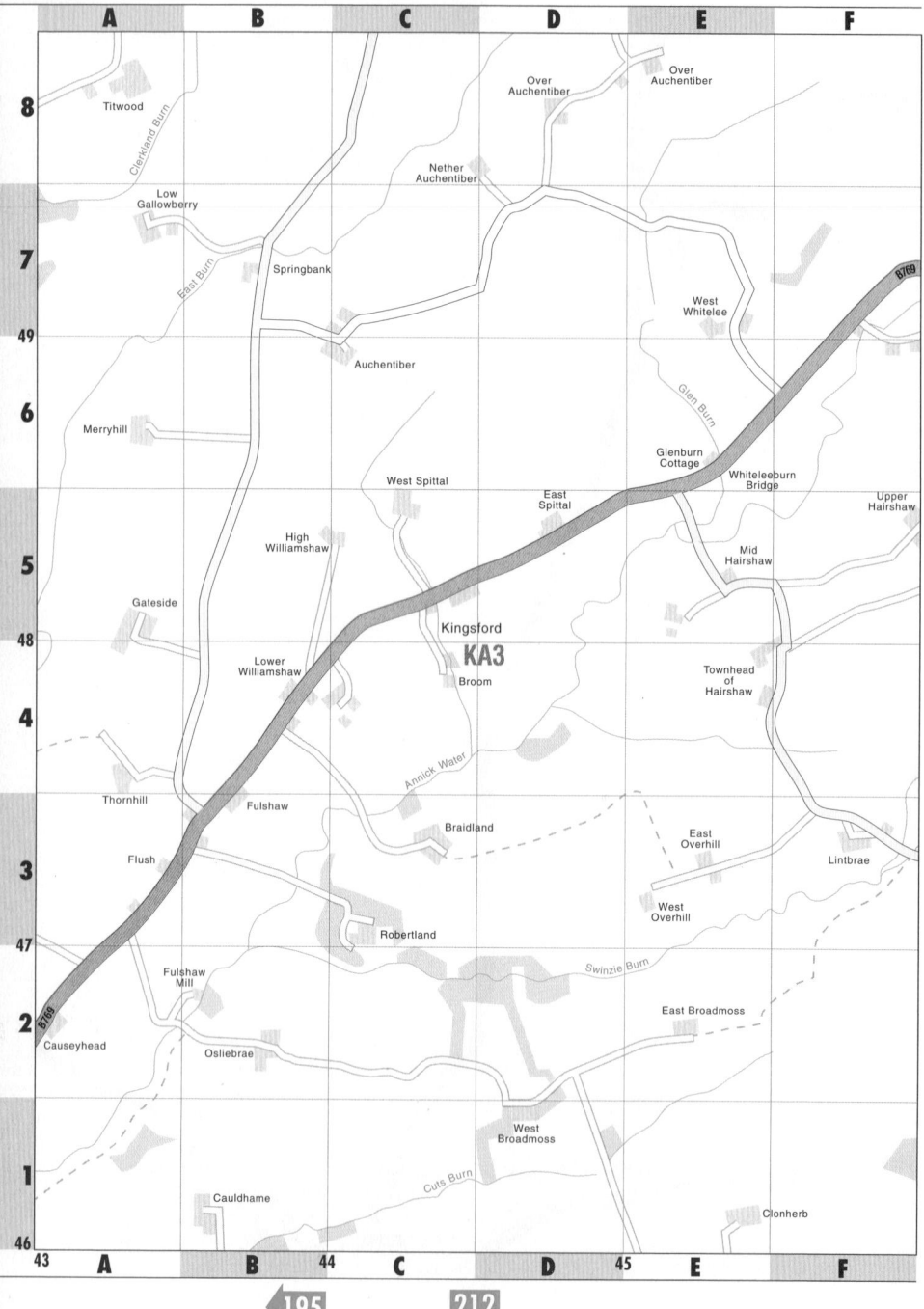

196

195

174

195

212

A B C D E F

8

7

49

6

5

48

4

3

47

2

1

46

43 A B 44 C D 45 E F

Titwood

Clerkland Burn

Low Gallowberry

East Burn

Springbank

Auchentiber

Merryhill

Nether Auchentiber

Over Auchentiber

Over Auchentiber

West Whitelee

B769

Glen Burn

Glenburn Cottage

Whiteleeburn Bridge

Upper Hairshaw

West Spittal

East Spittal

High Williamshaw

Mid Hairshaw

Gateside

Lower Williamshaw

Kingsford

KA3

Broom

Townhead of Hairshaw

Thornhill

Fulshaw

Annick Water

Braidland

East Overhill

Lintbrae

Flush

West Overhill

Robertland

Swinzie Burn

Fulshaw Mill

B769

Causeyhead

Osliebrae

East Broadmoss

West Broadmoss

Cauldhame

Cuts Burn

Clonherb

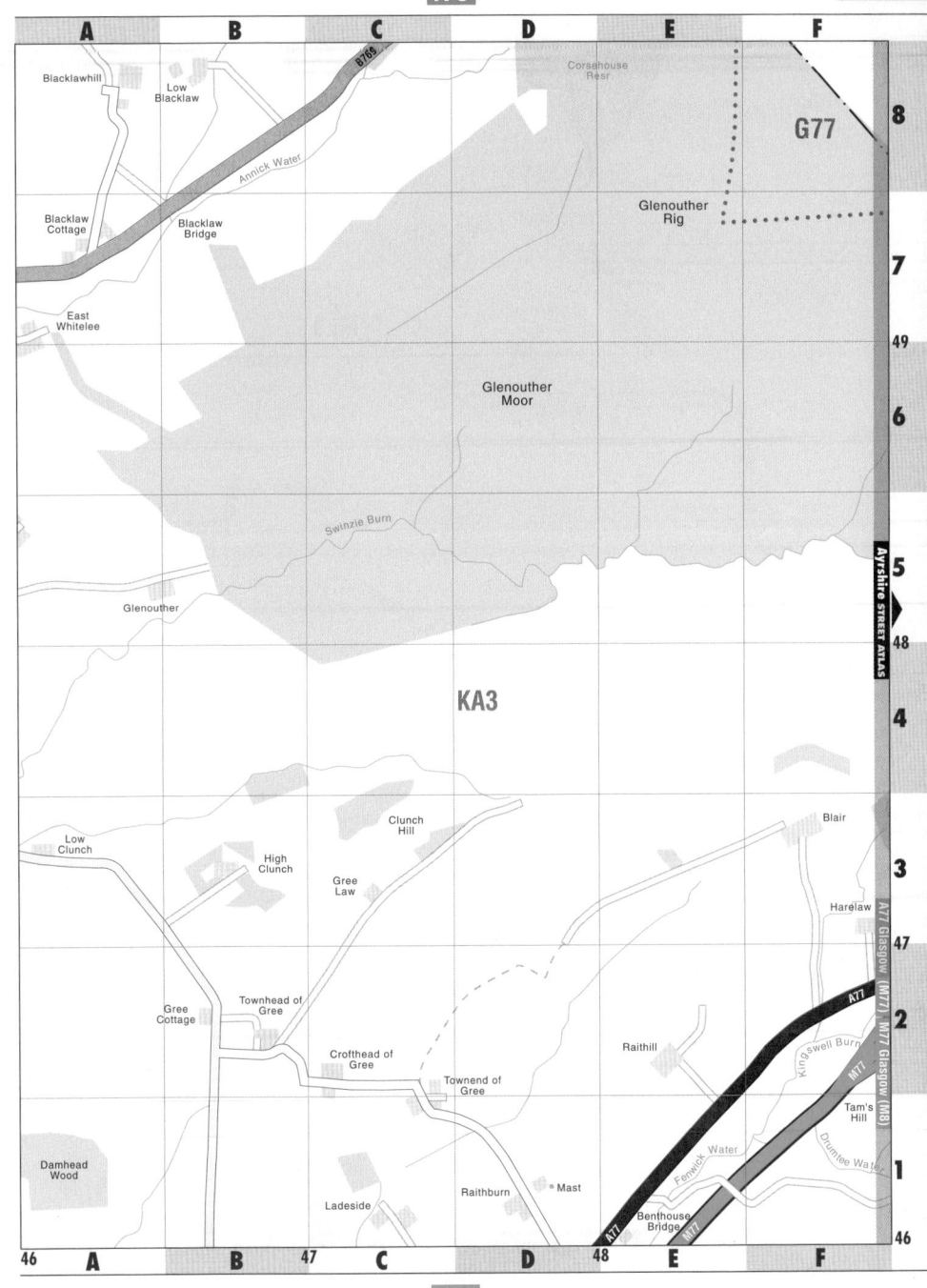

A **B** **C** **D** **E** **F**

Blacklawhill

Low
Blacklaw

B769

Corsehouse
Resr

G77

8

Annick Water

Glenouther
Rig

Blacklaw
Cottage

Blacklaw
Bridge

7

49

East
Whitelee

Glenouther
Moor

6

Swinzie Burn

5
Ayrshire STREET ATLAS
48

Glenouther

KA3

4

Clunch
Hill

Blair

Low
Clunch

High
Clunch

Gree
Law

3

Harelaw

47

A77 Glasgow (M77)

Townhead of
Gree

A77

M77 Glasgow (M8)

2

Gree
Cottage

Crofthead of
Gree

Raithill

Kingswell Burn

M77

Townend of
Gree

Tam's
Hill

Damhead
Wood

Mast

Fenwick Water

Drumtee Water

1

Ladeside

Raithburn

A77

Benthouse
Bridge

M77

46

46
A **47** **B** **C** **D** **48** **E** **F**

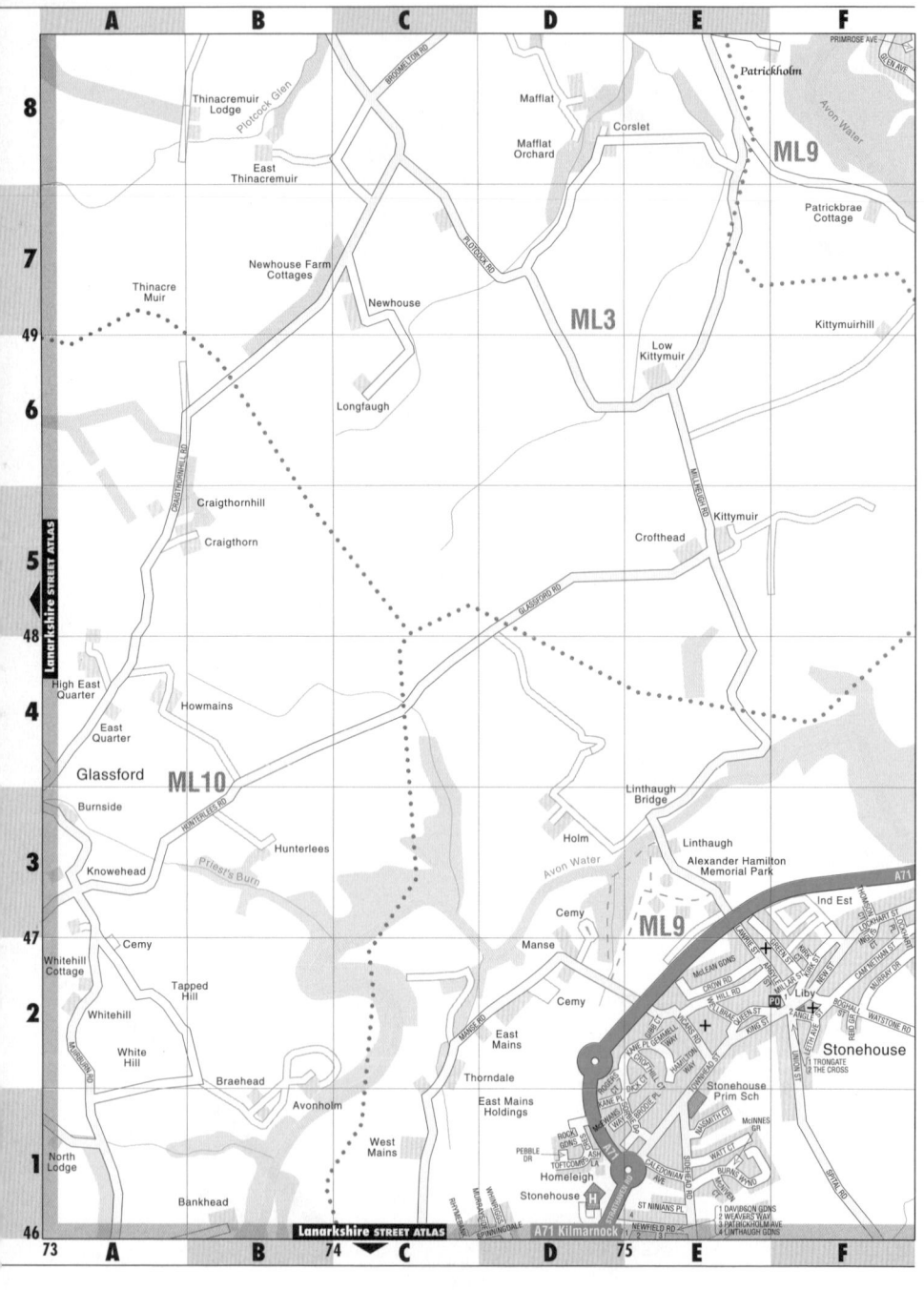

ML9

ML3

ML10

ML9

Stonehouse

A71 Kilmarnock

A B C D E F

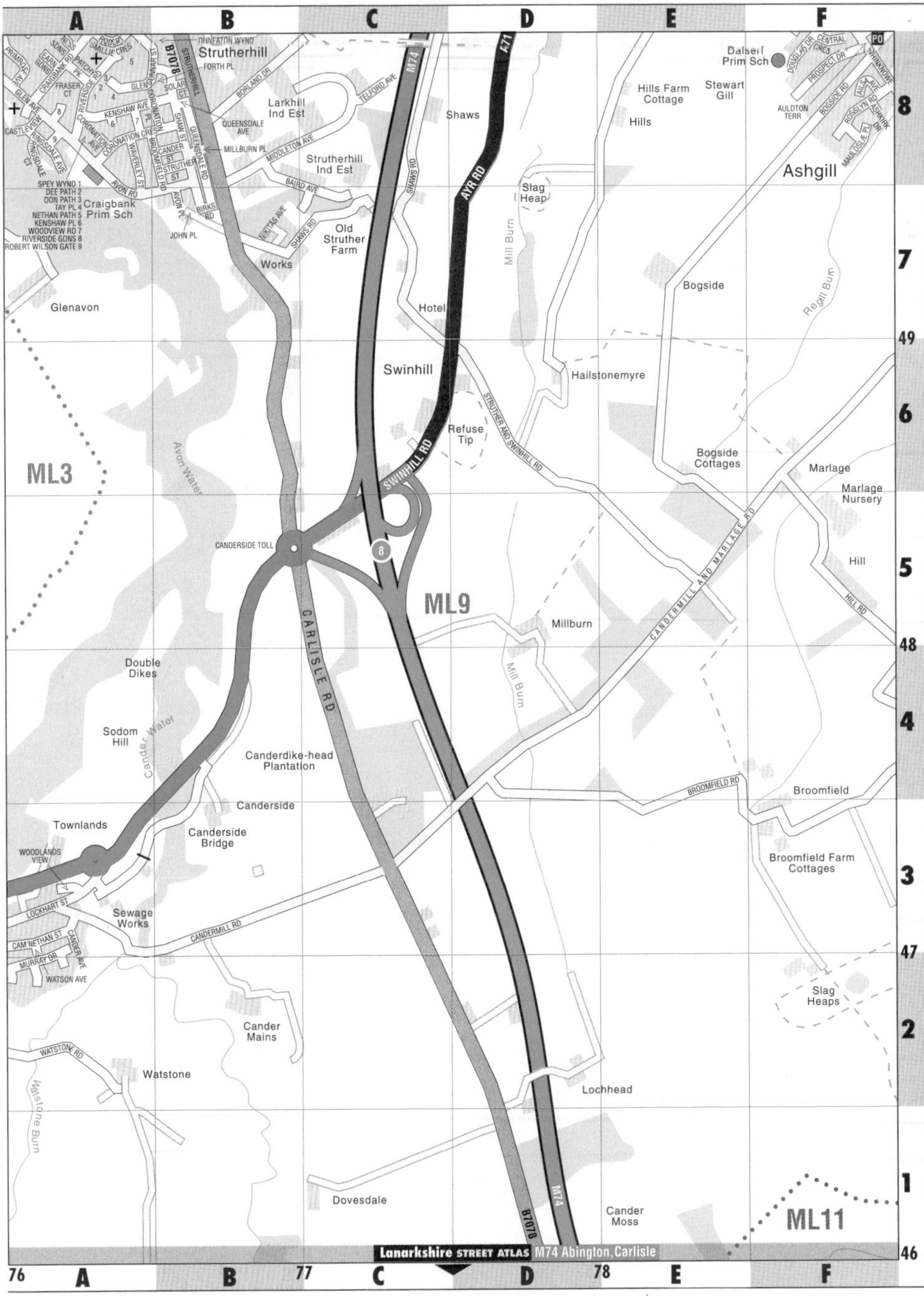

Strutherhill
FORTH PL
DINNEATON WYND
BELLIE CRES
FRASER ST
GLEN ST
CHRYSTAL AVE
RIVERSIDE
KENSHAW AVE
FOUNDATION CRES
CLANCER
BEVERLEY ST
WEBSTER ST
STRUTHER ST
AXON RD
BAIRD AVE
BIRSLE
BURNS RD

Larkhill
Ind Est
QUEENSDALE AVE
MILLBURN PL
MIDDLETON AVE

Shaws

Dalserf
Prim Sch

Hills Farm
Cottage
Stewart
Gill
AULDTON TERR
Hills

PROSPECT RD
CENTRAL

Ashgill

CASTLE
SPEY WYND 1
DEE PATH 2
TAY PL 4
DON PATH 3
NETHAN PATH 5
KENSHAW PL 6
WOODVIEW RD 7
RIVERSIDE GDNS 8
ROBERT WILSON GATE 9

Craigbank
Prim Sch

JOHN PL

VICTORIA AVE
SPRING RD

Strutherhill
Ind Est

Old
Struther
Farm

Works

Hotel

Stag
Heap

Mill Burn

8

Glenavon

Swinhill

Hailstonemyre

Bogside

Regil Burn

7
49

ML3

Avon Water

SWINHILL RD

Refuse
Tip

Bogside
Cottages

Marlage

Marlage
Nursery

6

CANDERSIDE TOLL

8

ML9

Millburn

Hill

CANDERMILL AND MARLAGE RD

HILL RD

5
48

CARLISLE RD

Double
Dikes

Cander Water

Sodom
Hill

Canderdike-head
Plantation

Canderside

Mill Burn

Broomfield

BROOMFIELD RD

Broomfield Farm
Cottages

4

Townlands

WOODLANDS VIEW
LOCKHART ST

Canderside
Bridge

Sewage
Works

CANDERMILL RD

CAM NETHAN ST
MURRAY DR
CASTERNE
WATSON AVE

Slag
Heaps

3
47

WATSTON RD

Watstone

Watstone Burn

Cander
Mains

Lochhead

Dovesdale

M74
B7078

Cander
Moss

ML11

2
1
46

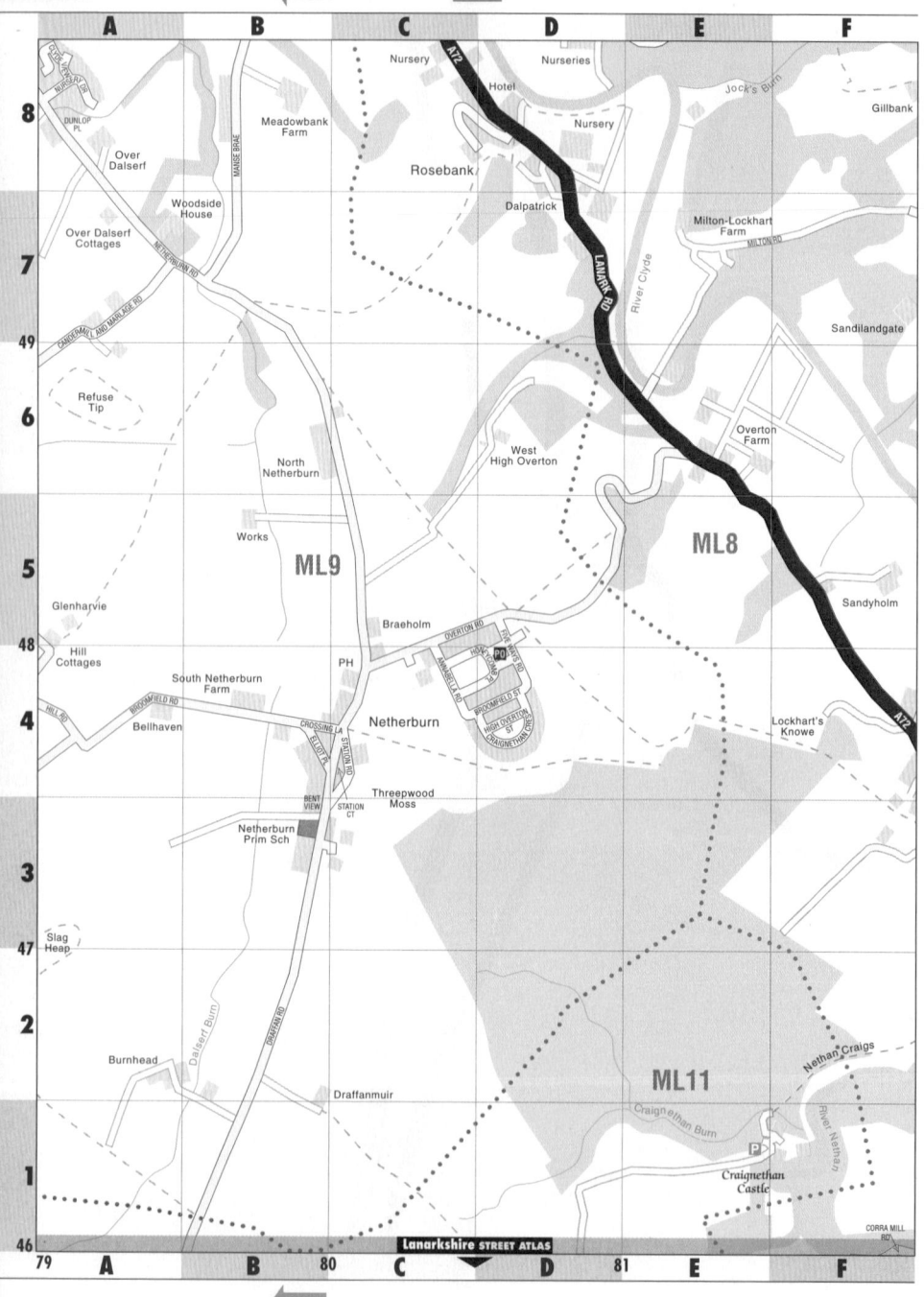

Nursery
Nurseries
Hotel
Nursery
Gillbank
Jock's Burn

DUNLOP PL
Over Dalserf
Meadowbank Farm
Rosebank
Dalpatrick
Milton-Lockhart Farm
MILTON RD

MANSE BRAE

Woodside House
Over Dalserf Cottages
NETHERBURN RD

LANARK RD

River Clyde

Sandilandgate

CANDERHALL AND MARRIAGE RD

Refuse Tip

North Netherburn

West High Overton

Overton Farm

Glenharvie

Works

Braeholm

ML9

ML8

Sandyholm

Hill Cottages

South Netherburn Farm

PH

OVERTON RD

PO

AMBERLY RD

BRICKFIELD RD

HILL RD

Bellhaven

CROSSING LA

STATION RD

Netherburn

Lockhart's Knowe

A72

HIGH OVERTON ST

CRAIGNETHAN DR

BENT VIEW

STATION CT

Threepwood Moss

Netherburn Prim Sch

Slag Heap

Burnhead

DALSERF BURN

SKELLERN RD

Draffanmuir

ML11

Nethan Craigs

Craignethan Burn

River Nethan

P

Craignethan Castle

CORRA MILL RD

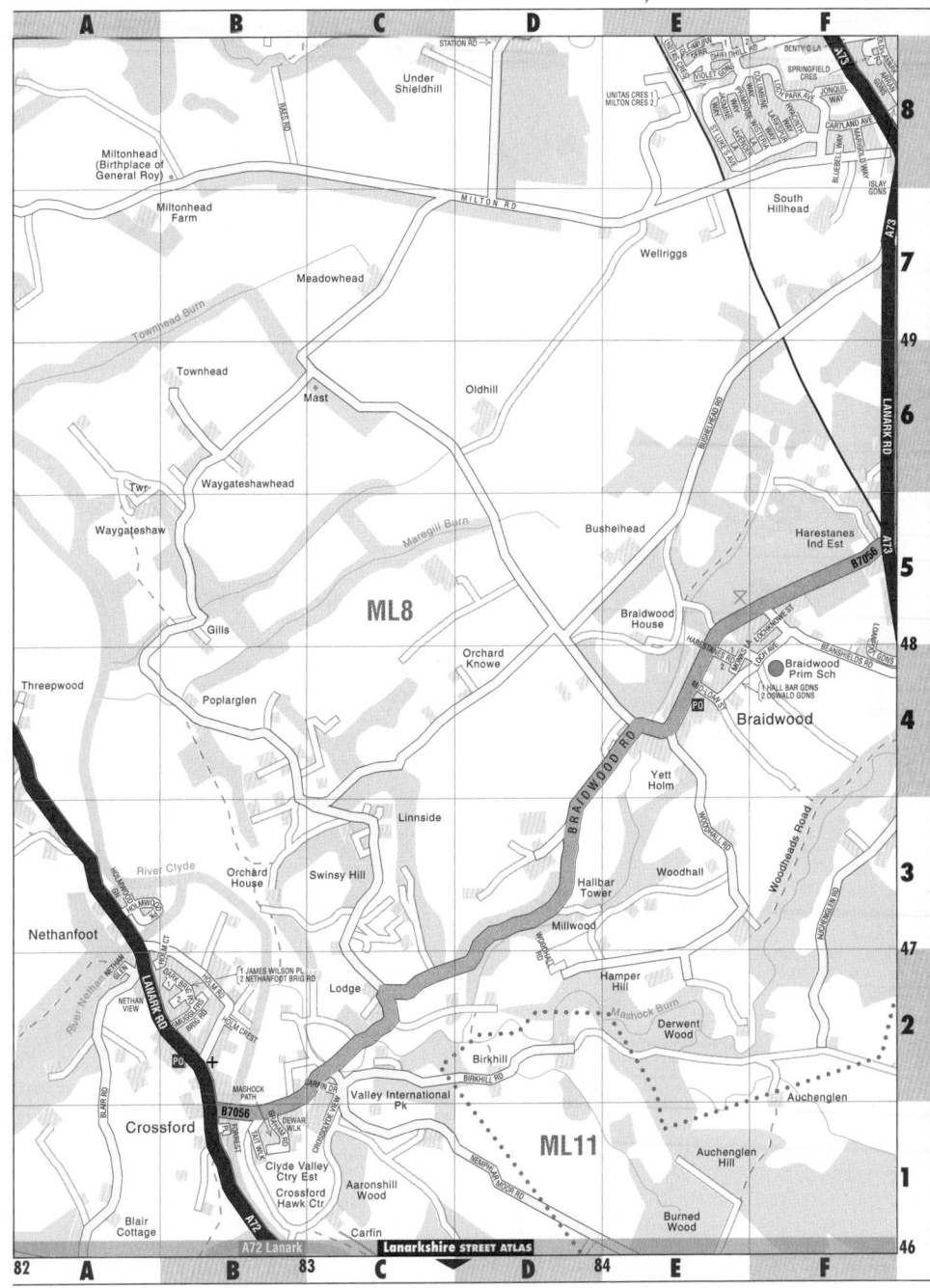

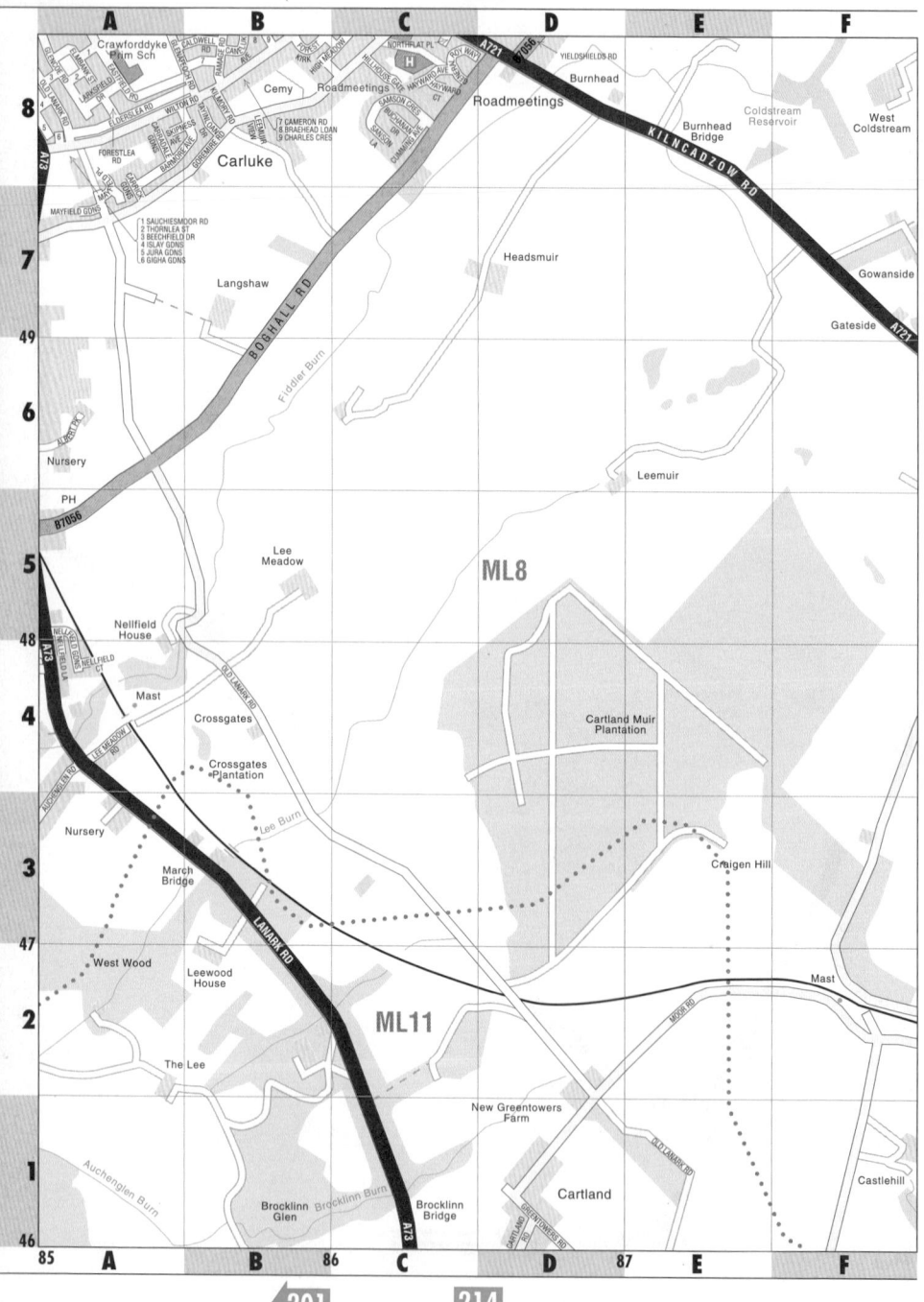

A   B   C   D   E   F

8

Crawforddyke
Prim Sch

Cemy   Roadmeetings

7 CAMERON RD
8 BRAEHEAD LOAN
9 CHARLES CRES

Carluke

NORTHFLAT PL

A721

Roadmeetings

YIELDSHIELDS RD

Burnhead

Burnhead
Bridge

Burnhead Bridge

KILNCADZOW RD

Coldstream
Reservoir

West
Coldstream

1 SAUCHIESMOOR RD
2 THORNLEA ST
3 BEECHFIELD DR
4 ISLAY GDNS
5 JURA GDNS
6 GIGHA GDNS

MAYFIELD GDNS

FORESTLEA
RD

7

Langshaw

Headsmuir

Gowanside

BOSHALL RD

49

Gateside

A721

Fiddler Burn

6

Nursery

Leemuir

PH

B7056

Lee
Meadow

ML8

5

Nellfield
House

48

A73

Hellfield

Mast

OLD LANARK RD

4

Crossgates

Crossgates
Plantation

Cartland Muir
Plantation

ROCKFIELD RD

Lee Burn

Nursery

3

March
Bridge

Craigen Hill

LANARK RD

47

West Wood

Leewood
House

Mast

MOOR RD

2

ML11

The Lee

OLD LANARK RD

New Greentowers
Farm

1

Auchenglen Burn

Castlehill

Brocklinn
Glen

Brocklinn Burn

A73

Brocklinn
Bridge

Cartland

CARTLAND RD

GREENTOWERS RD

46

85   A   B   86   C   D   87   E   F

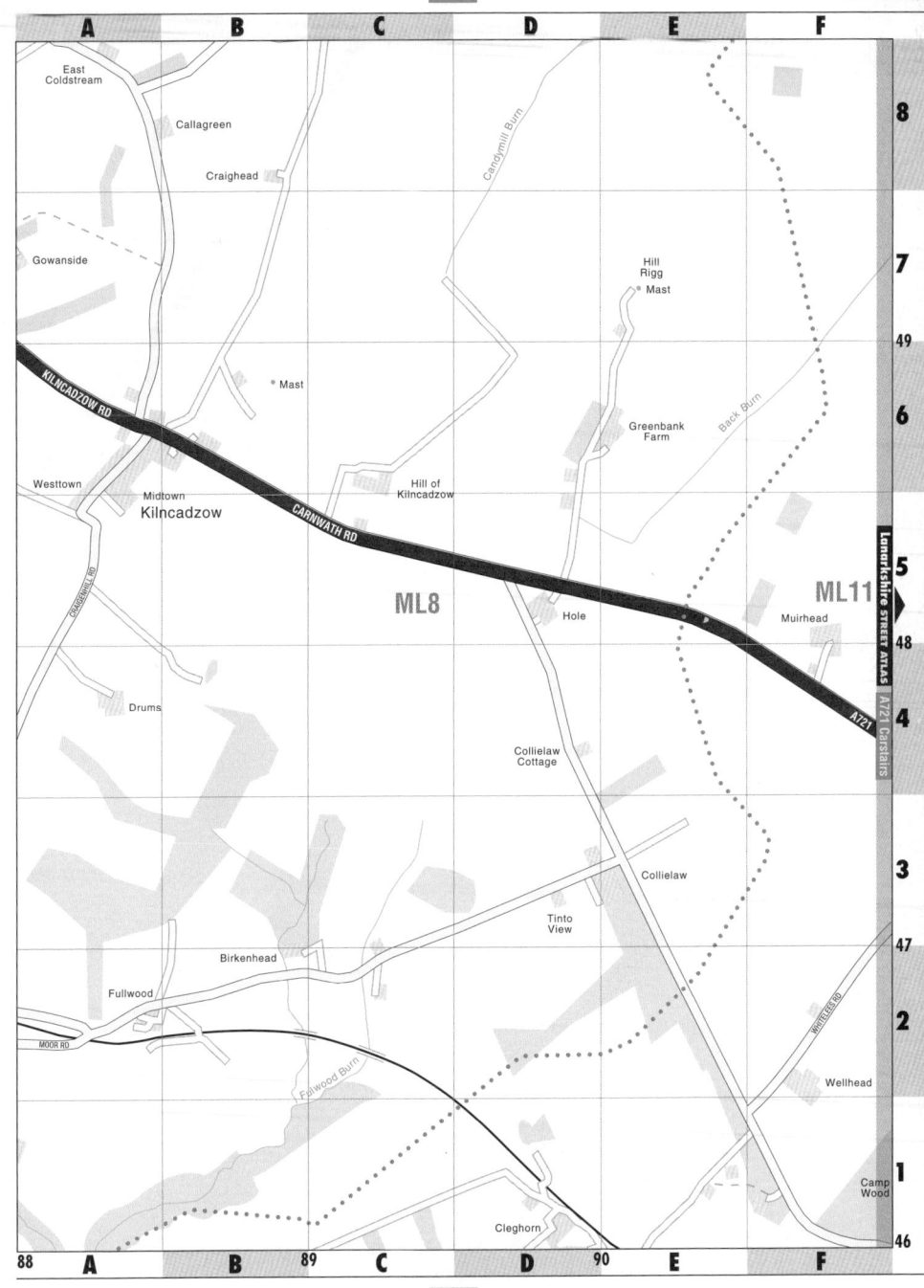

189

A B C D E F

8

East
Coldstream

Callagreen

Craighead

7

Candymill Burn

Gowanside

49

Hill
Rigg
Mast

Mast

6

KILNCADZOW RD

Greenbank
Farm

Back Burn

Westtown

Midtown
Kilncadzow

CARNWATH RD

Hill of
Kilncadzow

5

CANDYMILL RD

ML8

Hole

ML11

Muirhead

Lanarkshire STREET ATLAS

48

Drums

Collielaw
Cottage

A721 Carstairs

4

3

Collielaw

Tinto
View

Birkenhead

47

Fullwood

WHITELEES RD

2

MOOR RD

Wellhead

Fallwood Burn

Camp
Wood

1

Cleghorn

46

88 A B 89 C D 90 E F

215

190

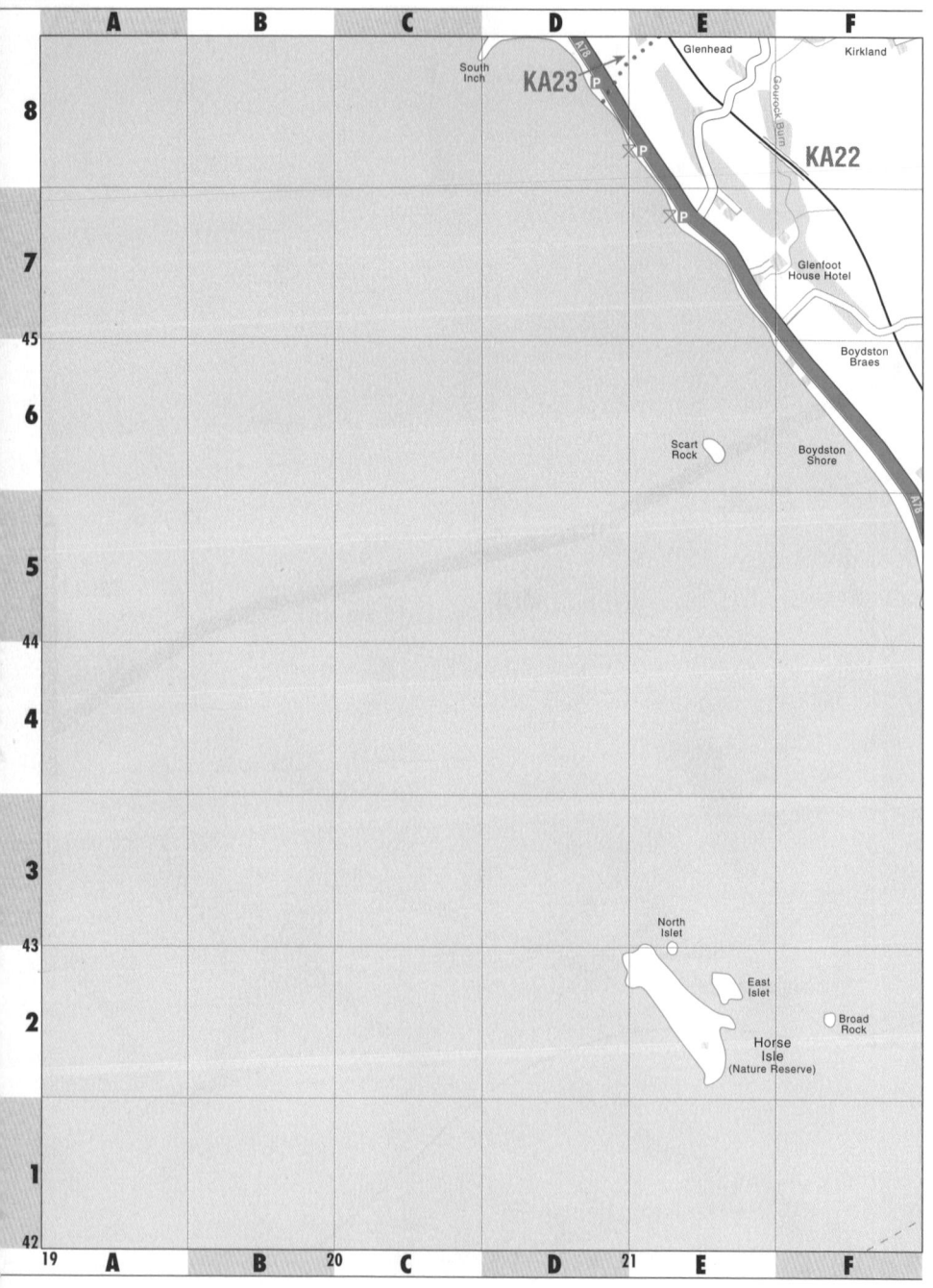

South
Inch

KA23

Glenhead

Kirkland

KA22

Glenfoot
House Hotel

Boydston
Braes

Scart
Rock

Boydston
Shore

North
Islet

East
Islet

Broad
Rock

Horse
Isle
(Nature Reserve)

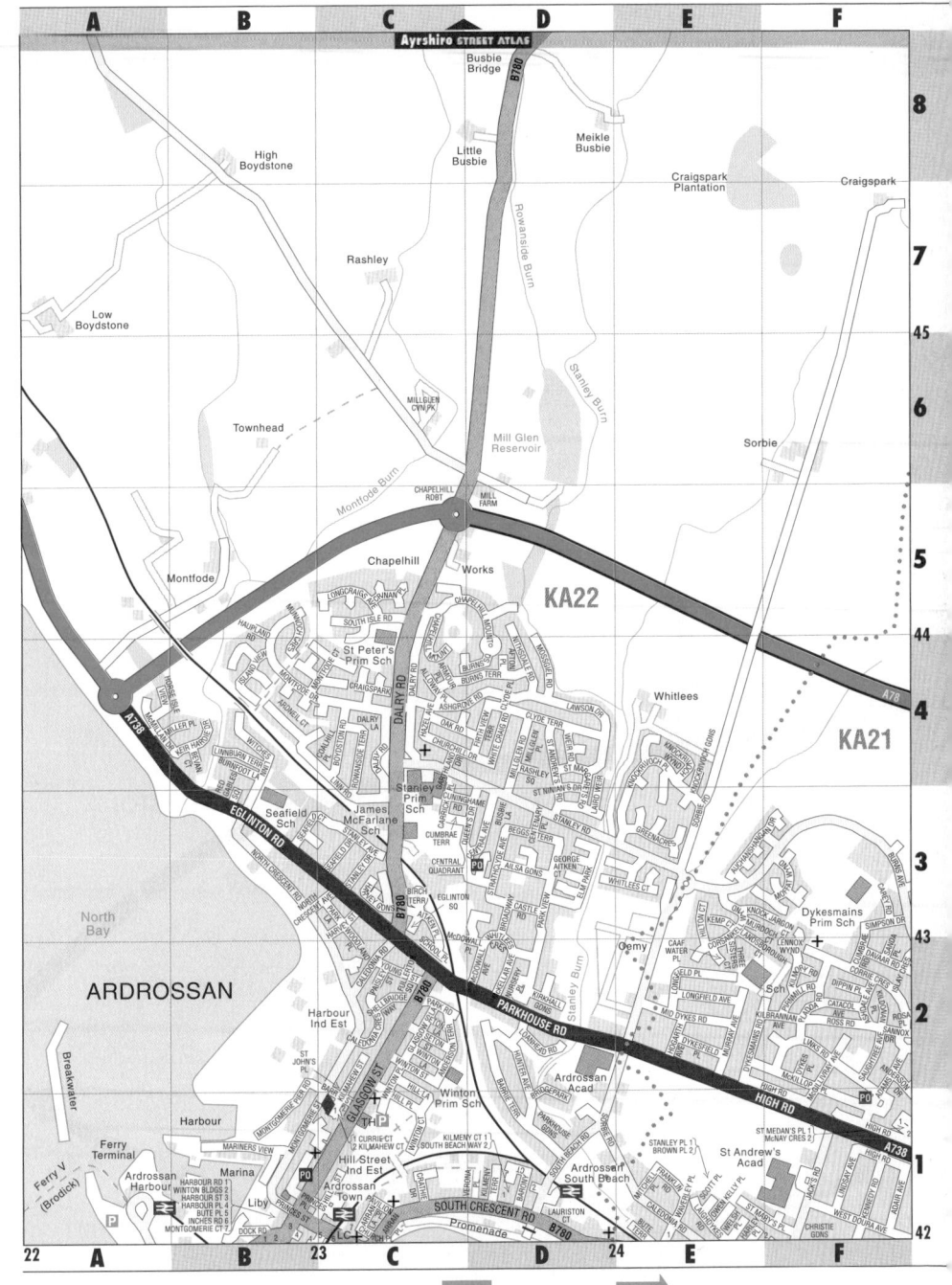

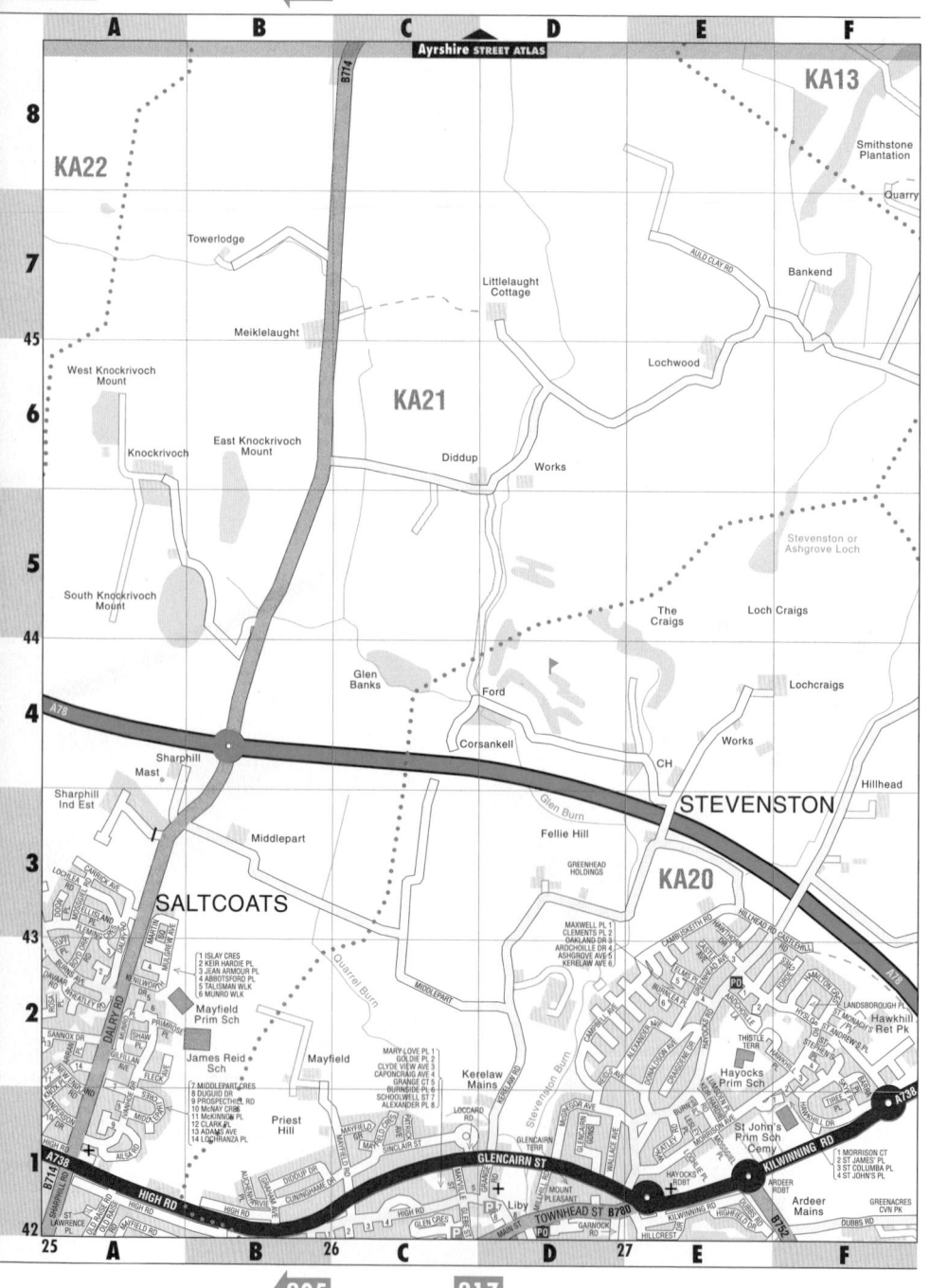

Ayrshire STREET ATLAS

KA13

KA22

Smithstone
Plantation

Quarry

Towerlodge

Littlelaught
Cottage

Bankend

AULD CLAY RD

Meiklelaught

Lochwood

West Knockrivoch
Mount

KA21

East Knockrivoch
Mount

Knockrivoch

Diddup

Works

Stevenston or
Ashgrove Loch

South Knockrivoch
Mount

The
Craigs

Loch Craigs

Glen
Banks

Ford

Lochcraigs

A78

Corsankell

Works

Sharphill
Mast

CH

Hillhead

Sharphill
Ind Est

STEVENSTON

Middlepart

Fellie Hill

Glen Burn

GREENHEAD
HOLDINGS

KA20

SALTCOATS

MAXWELL PL 1
CLEMENTS PL 2
OAKLAND DR 3
ARDCHOILLE DR 4
ASHGROVE AVE 5
KERELAW AVE 6

1 ISLAY CRES
2 KEIR HARDIE PL
3 JEAN ARMOUR PL
4 ABBOTSFORD PL
5 TALISMAN WLK
6 MUNRO WLK

Mayfield
Prim Sch

PO

Mayfield

MARY LOVE PL 1
GOLDIE PL 2
CLYDE VIEW AVE 3
CAPONCRAIG AVE 4
GRANGE CT 5
BURNSIDE PL 6
SCHOOLWELL ST 7
ALEXANDER PL 8

Kerelaw
Mains

Hayocks
Prim Sch

Hawkhill
Ret Pk

James Reid
Sch

7 MIDDLEPART CRES
8 DUGUID DR
9 PROSPECTHILL RD
10 McNAY CRIB
11 McKINNON PL
12 CLARK PL
13 ADAMS AVE
14 LOCHRANZA PL

Priest
Hill

LOCCARD
RD

St John's
Prim Sch

Cemy

1 MORRISON CT
2 ST JAMES' PL
3 ST COLUMBA PL
4 ST JOHN'S PL

GLENCAIRN
TERR

Ardeer
Mains

GREENACRES
CVN PK

GLENCAIRN ST

ROBT

KILWINNING RD

HIGH RD

TOWNHEAD ST

B780

Liby

HILLCREST

207
192

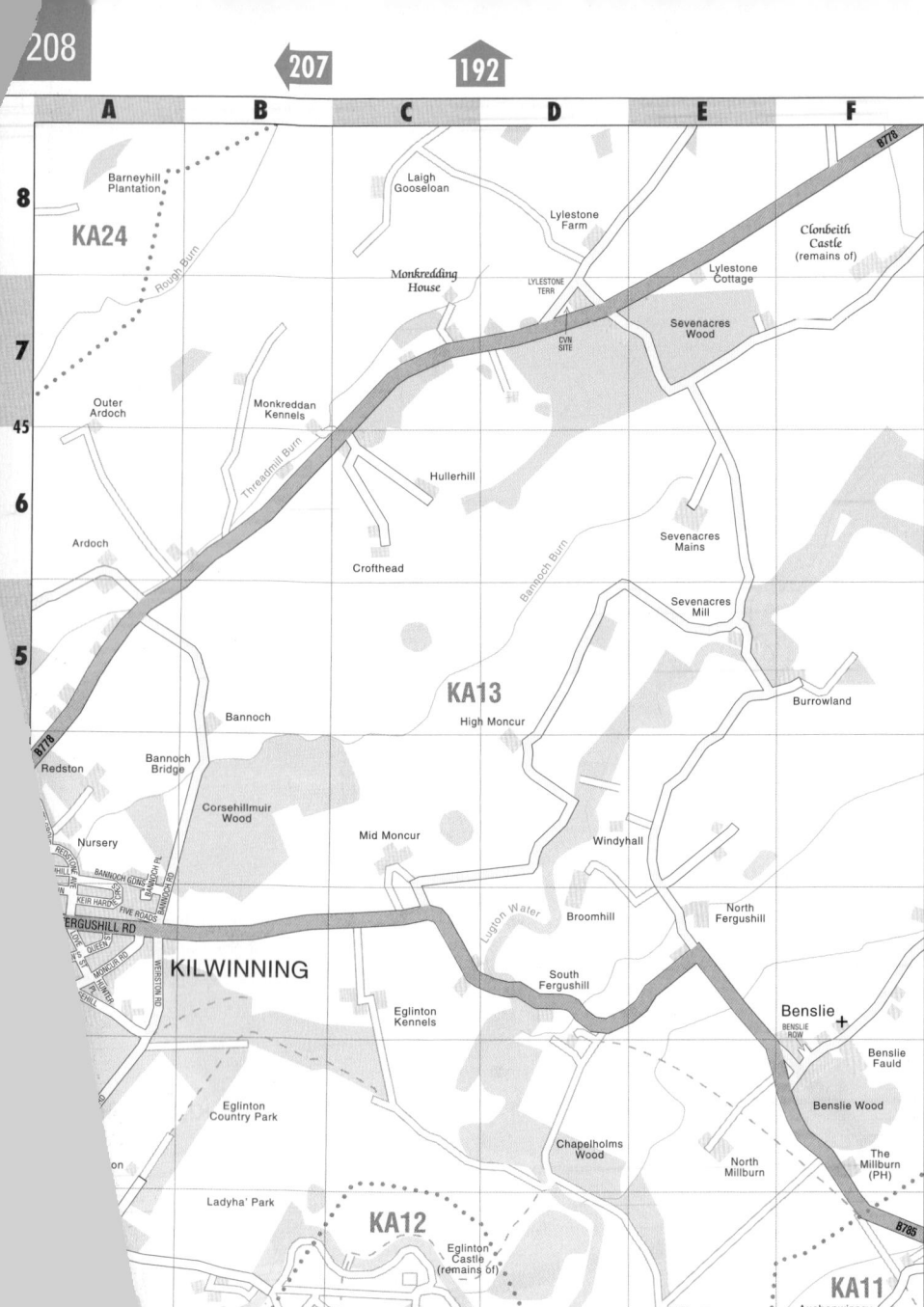

KA24

Barneyhill
Plantation

Laigh
Gooseloan

Lylestone
Farm

Clonbeith
Castle
(remains of)

Monkredding
House

LYLESTONE
TERR

Lylestone
Cottage

Sevenacres
Wood

CVN
SITE

Outer
Ardoch

Monkreddan
Kennels

Hullerhill

Ardoch

Sevenacres
Mains

Crofthead

Sevenacres
Mill

KA13

Bannoch

High Moncur

Burrowland

Redston

Bannoch
Bridge

Corsehillmuir
Wood

Nursery

Mid Moncur

Windyhall

BANNOCH GDNS

LANNOCH PL

LANNOCH RD

KEIR HARDIE

FIVE ROADS

FERGUSHILL RD

Lugton Water

Broomhill

North
Fergushill

KILWINNING

South
Fergushill

Benslie

BENSLIE
ROW

Benslie
Fauld

Eglinton
Kennels

Benslie Wood

Eglinton
Country Park

Chapelholms
Wood

North
Millburn

The
Millburn
(PH)

Ladyha' Park

KA12

KA11

Auchenwinsey

Eglinton
Castle
(remains of)

Millburn
Lodge

Factory

B785

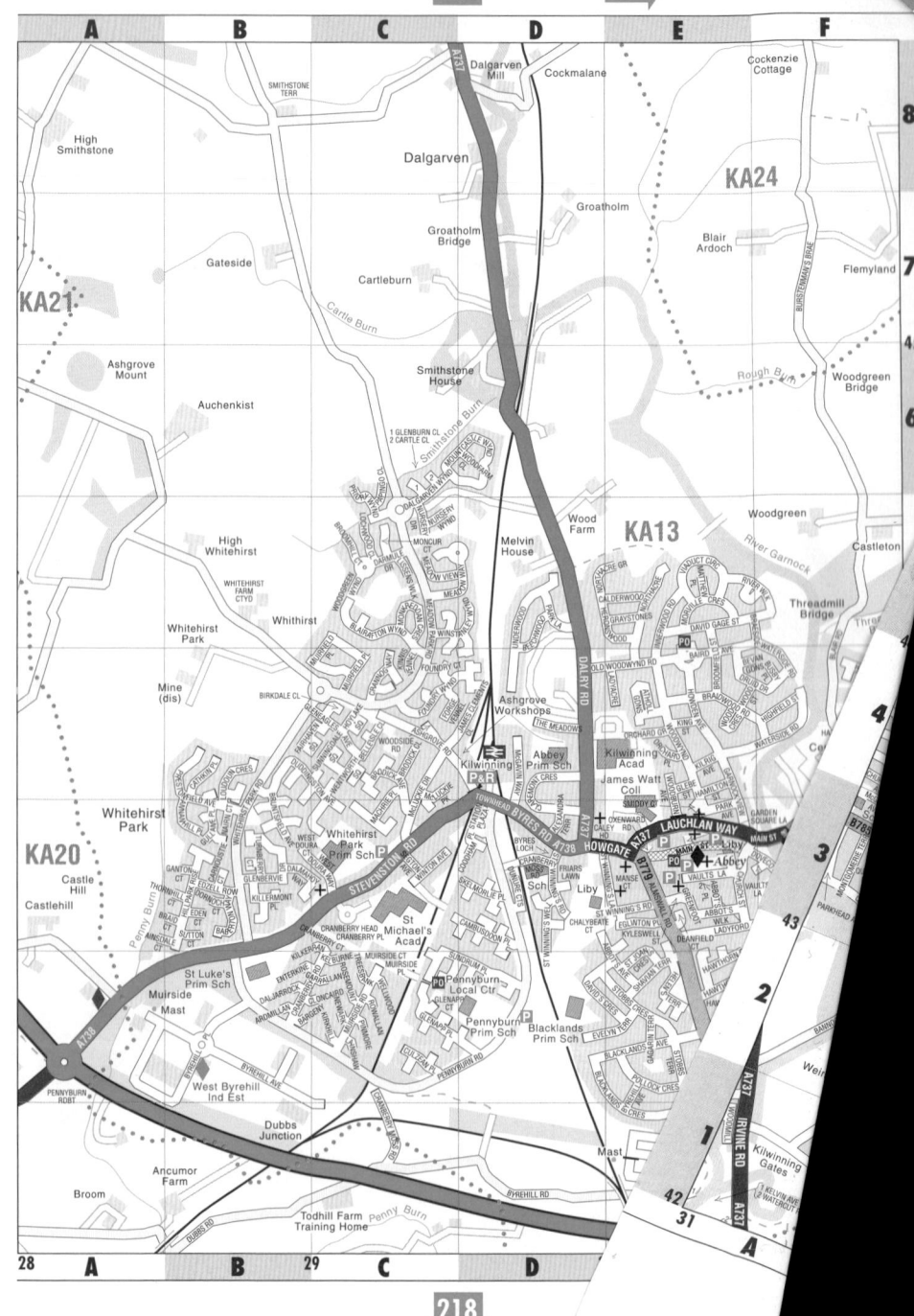

A   B   C   D   E   F

8

SMITHSTONE
TERR

High
Smithstone

Dalgarven Mill
Cockmalane

Cockenzie
Cottage

KA24

Dalgarven

Groatholm

Groatholm
Bridge

Blair
Ardoch

Flemyland

Gateside

Cartleburn

KA21

Cartle Burn

45

Ashgrove
Mount

Smithstone
House

Rough Burn

Woodgreen
Bridge

Auchenkist

6

1 GLENBURN CL
2 CARTLE CL

Smithstone Burn

High
Whitehirst

Melvin
House

Wood
Farm

Woodgreen

KA13

River Garnock

Castleton

WHITEHIRST
FARM
CTYD

Whithirst

Whitehirst
Park

Threadmill
Bridge

Thre

4

Mine
(dis)

BIRKDALE CL

Ashgrove
Workshops

Whitehirst
Park

KA20

Whitehirst
Park
Prim Sch

Castle
Hill
Castlehill

WOODSIDE
RD

Abbey
Prim Sch

Kilwinning
PAR

Kilwinning
Acad

James Watt
Coll

4

43

3

LAUCHLAN WAY

HOWGATE

Abbey

STEVENSTON RD

St
Michael's
Acad

Liby

St Luke's
Prim Sch

Muirside
Mast

Pennyburn
Local Ctr

Pennyburn
Prim Sch

Blacklands
Prim Sch

2

West Byrehill
Ind Est

PENNYBURN
RDBT

IRVINE RD

Weir

1

Kilwinning
Gates

Dubbs
Junction

Mast

42
31

Ancumor
Farm

Broom

Todhill Farm
Training Home

Penny Burn

BYREHILL RD

A

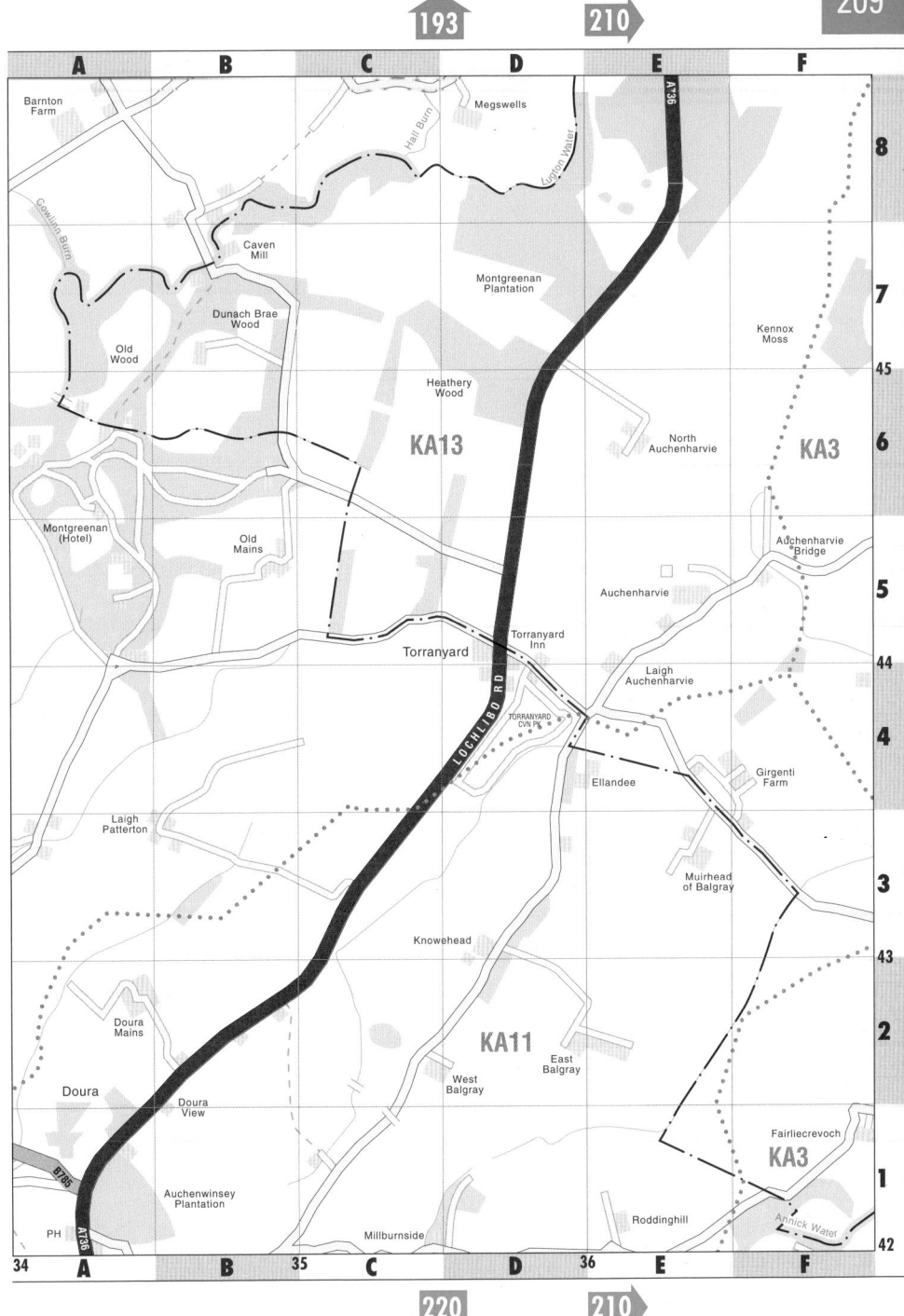

A B C D E F

Barnton Farm

Megswells

Hall Burn

Logan Water

8

Cowling Burn

Caven Mill

Montgreenan Plantation

7

Dunach Brae Wood

Kennox Moss

Old Wood

45

Heathery Wood

KA13

North Auchenharvie

KA3

6

Montgreenan (Hotel)

Old Mains

Auchenharvie Bridge

Auchenharvie

5

Torranyard Inn

Torranyard

Laigh Auchenharvie

44

LOCHLIBO RD

TORRANYARD CVN PK

Girgenti Farm

4

Ellandee

Laigh Patterton

Muirhead of Balgray

3

Knowehead

43

Doura Mains

KA11

2

Doura

East Balgray

West Balgray

Doura View

Fairliecrevoch

KA3

1

AT85

Auchenwinsey Plantation

Roddinghill

Annick Water

PH

AT36

Millburnside

42

34 A 35 B C 36 D E F

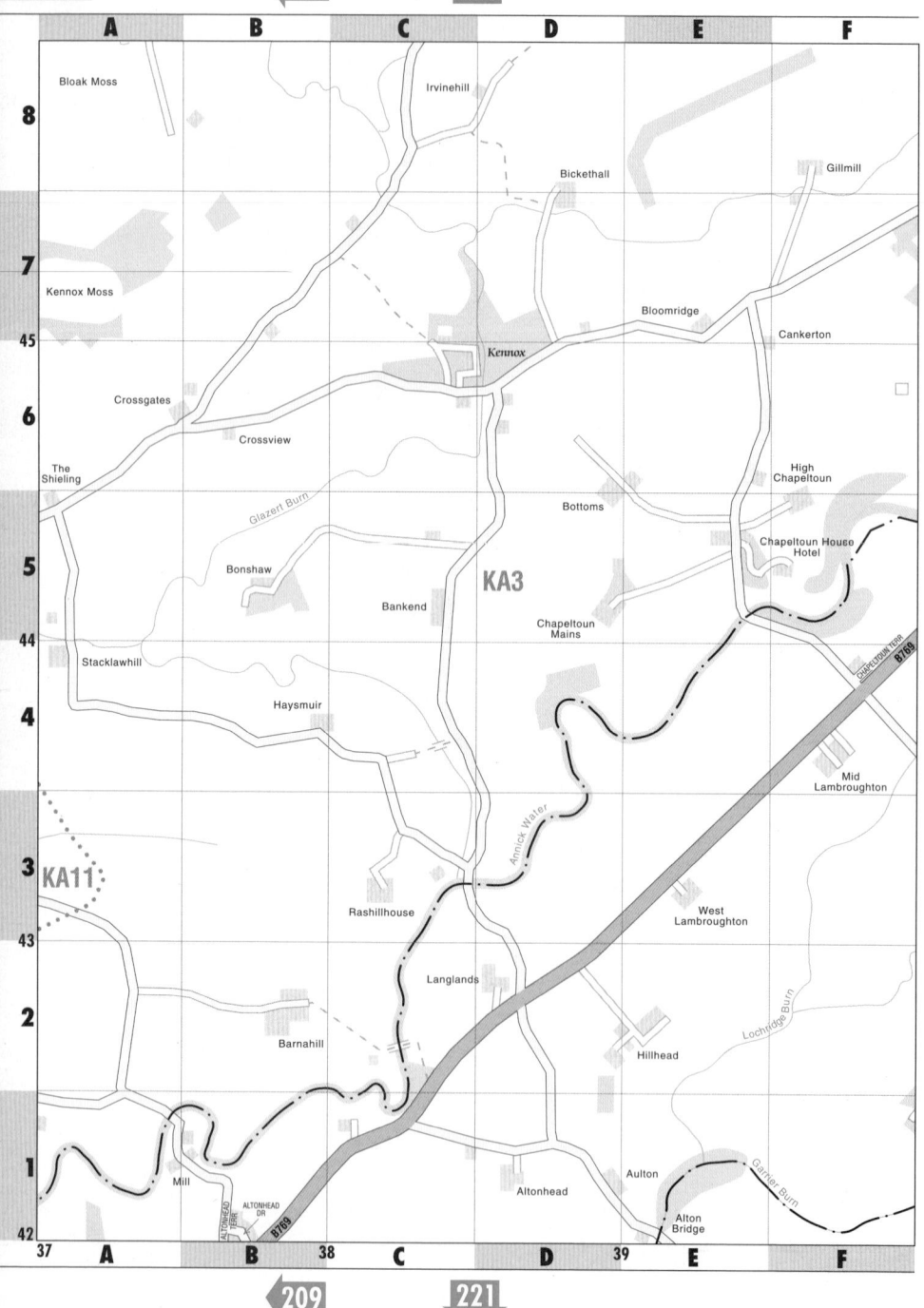

A   B   C   D   E   F

8   Bloak Moss   Irvinehill

                                        Bickethall   Gillmill

7
     Kennox Moss   Bloomridge
45   Cankerton
                                    Kennox
6   Crossgates
          Crossview
     The   High
     Shieling   Bottoms   Chapeltoun
                    Glazert Burn
                                                              Chapeltoun House
5   Bonshaw   Hotel
                              Bankend   KA3
44   Chapeltoun
     Stacklawhill   Mains
4   Haysmuir
                                                                    Mid
                                                                    Lambroughton
                              Annick Water
3   KA11   Rashillhouse   West
                                                      Lambroughton
43
                         Langlands
2   Barnahill   Hillhead   Lochridge Burn

                              CHAPELTOUN TIDR B769

                    Mill   Garnier Burn
1   ALTONHEAD   Aulton
42   ALTONHEAD DR B769   Altonhead   Alton
     37   A   B   38   C   D   39   E   F   Bridge

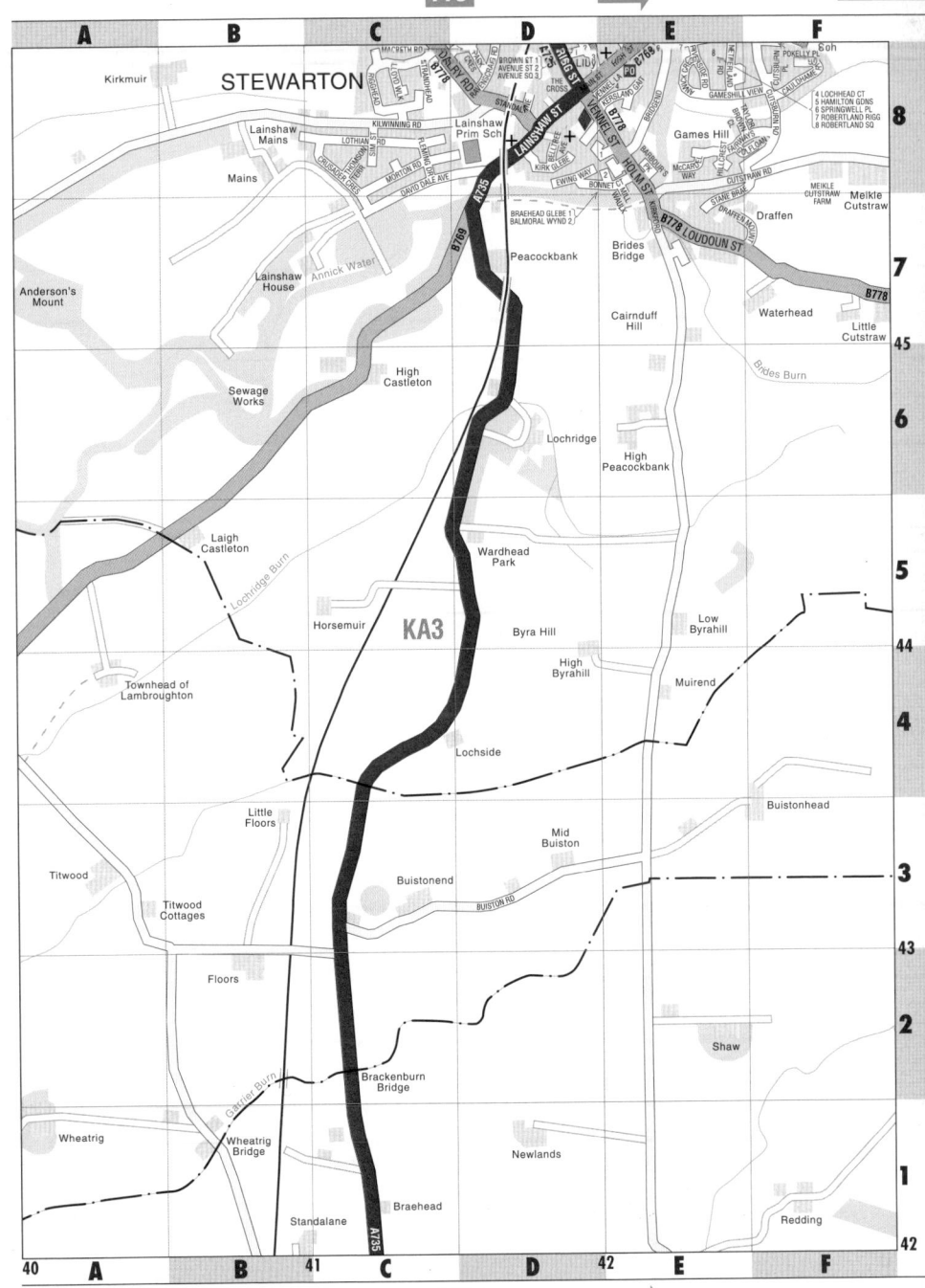

A B C D E F

STEWARTON

Kirkmuir

Lainshaw
Mains

Mains

Lainshaw
Prim Sch

4 LOCHHEAD CT
5 HAMILTON GDNS
6 SPRINGWELL PL
7 ROBERTLAND RIGG
8 ROBERTLAND SQ

Games Hill

Game Shill View

GAMESHILL VIEW

THE
CROSS

KILWINNING RD

MACBETH RD

BROWN ST 1
AVENUE ST 2
AVENUE SQ 3

STANDALE

KIRK GLEBE

EWING WAY

BONNET END

MEIKLE
CUTSTRAW
FARM

Meikle
Cutstraw

Draffen

BRAEHEAD GLEBE 1
BALMORAL WYND 2

Anderson's
Mount

Lainshaw
House

Annick Water

Peacockbank

Brides
Bridge

B778 LOUDOUN ST

B778

Waterhead

Little
Cutstraw

Cairnduff
Hill

Brides Burn

7

45

Sewage
Works

High
Castleton

Lochridge

High
Peacockbank

6

Laigh
Castleton

Lochridge Burn

Wardhead
Park

Low
Byrahill

5

Horsemuir

KA3

Byra Hill

High
Byrahill

Muirend

44

Townhead of
Lambroughton

Lochside

4

Little
Floors

Mid
Buiston

Buistonhead

Titwood

Titwood
Cottages

Buistonend

BUISTON RD

3

43

Floors

Shaw

2

Wheatrig

Gottrier Burn

Wheatrig
Bridge

Brackenburn
Bridge

Newlands

Redding

1

Standalane

A735

Braehead

42

40 A B 41 C D 42 E F

211
196

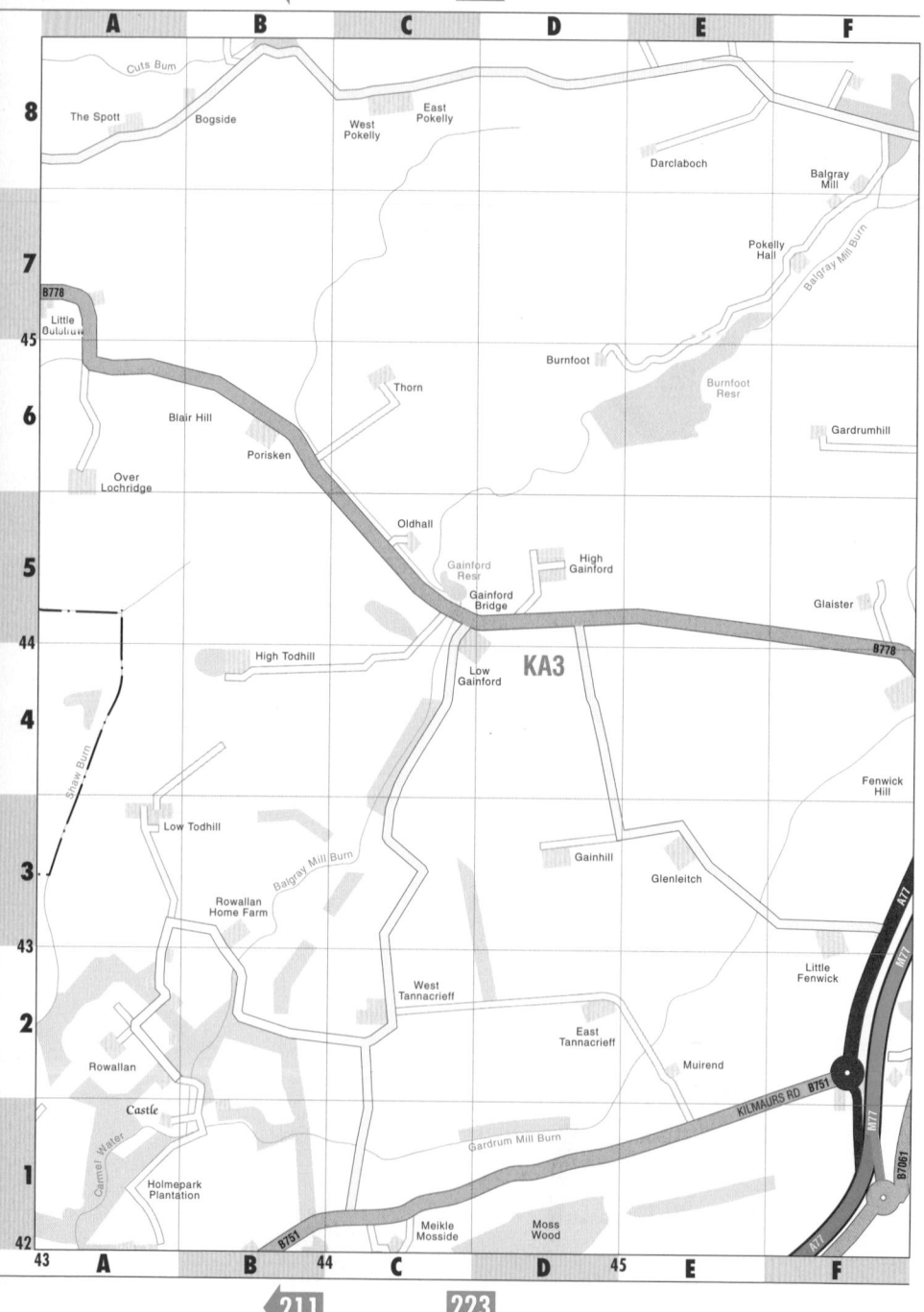

211
223

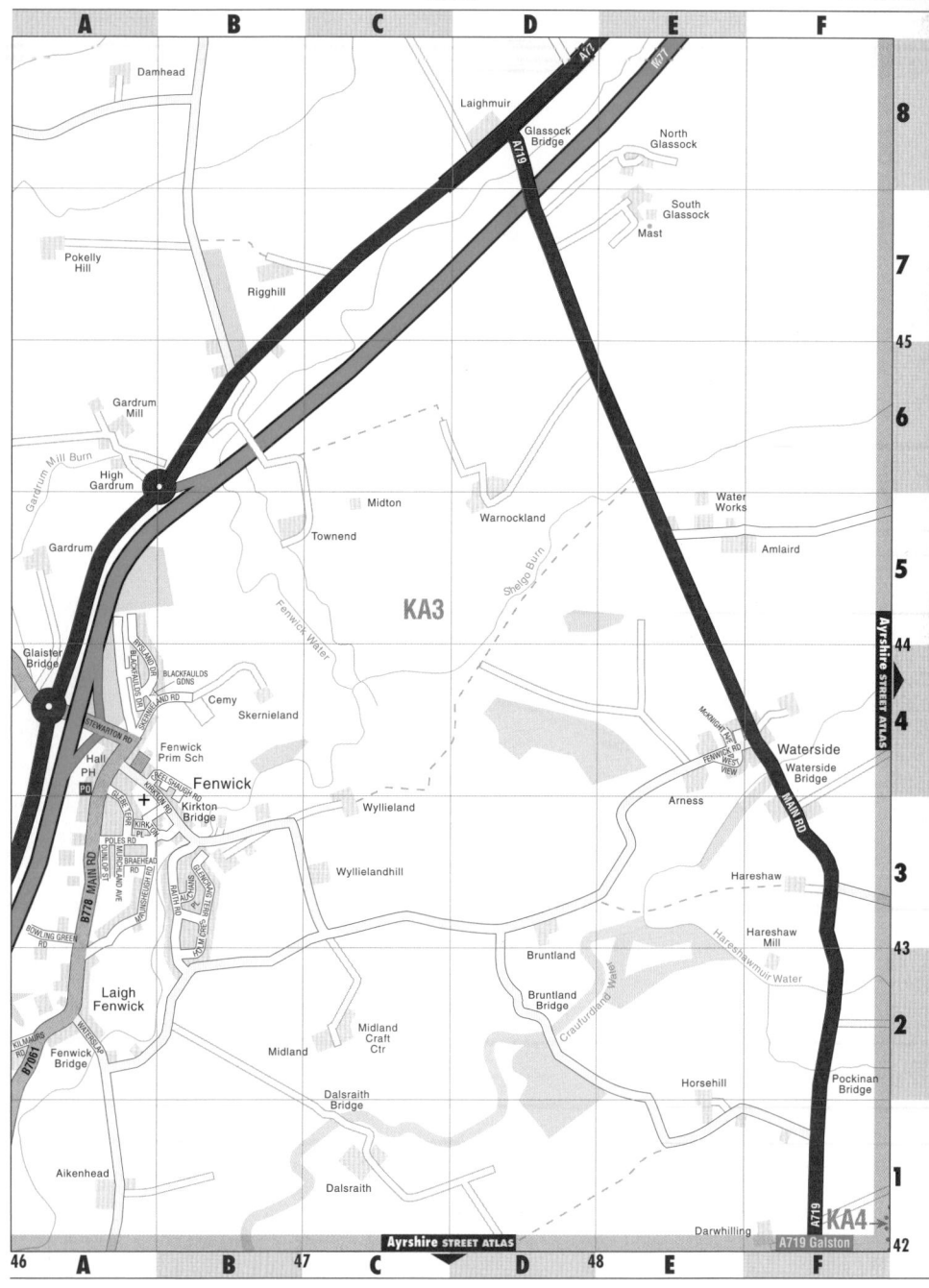

A B C D E F

8
7
45
6
5
44
4
3
43
2
1
42

Damhead

Laighmuir

Glassock
Bridge

North
Glassock

South
Glassock

Mast

Pokelly
Hill

Rigghill

Gardrum
Mill

Gardrum Mill Burn

High
Gardrum

Gardrum

Midton

Townend

Warnockland

Water
Works

Amlaird

Shielgo Burn

KA3

Fenwick Water

Glaister
Bridge

BLACKFAULDS
GDNS

BLACKFAULDS RD

Cemy

Skernieland

STEWARTON RD

Waterside

MCKNIGHT ACT

FENWICK RD
FENWICK WEST
VIEW

Waterside
Bridge

Hall
PH
PO

Fenwick
Prim Sch

Fenwick

Kirkton
Bridge

Wyllieland

Arness

MAIN RD

MAIN RD

BT78

Wyllielandhill

Hareshaw

Hareshaw
Mill

BRAEHEAD

DUNLOP ST

POLES RD

Laigh
Fenwick

BOWLING
GREEN RD

WATERSIDE RD

Bruntland

Bruntland
Bridge

Craufurdland Water

Hareshawmuir Water

KILMARNOCK RD

BT061

Fenwick
Bridge

Midland

Midland
Craft
Ctr

Horsehill

Pockinan
Bridge

Aikenhead

Dalsraith
Bridge

Dalsraith

Darwhilling

A719

KA4

A719 Galston

Ayrshire STREET ATLAS

46 A B 47 C D 48 E F

202

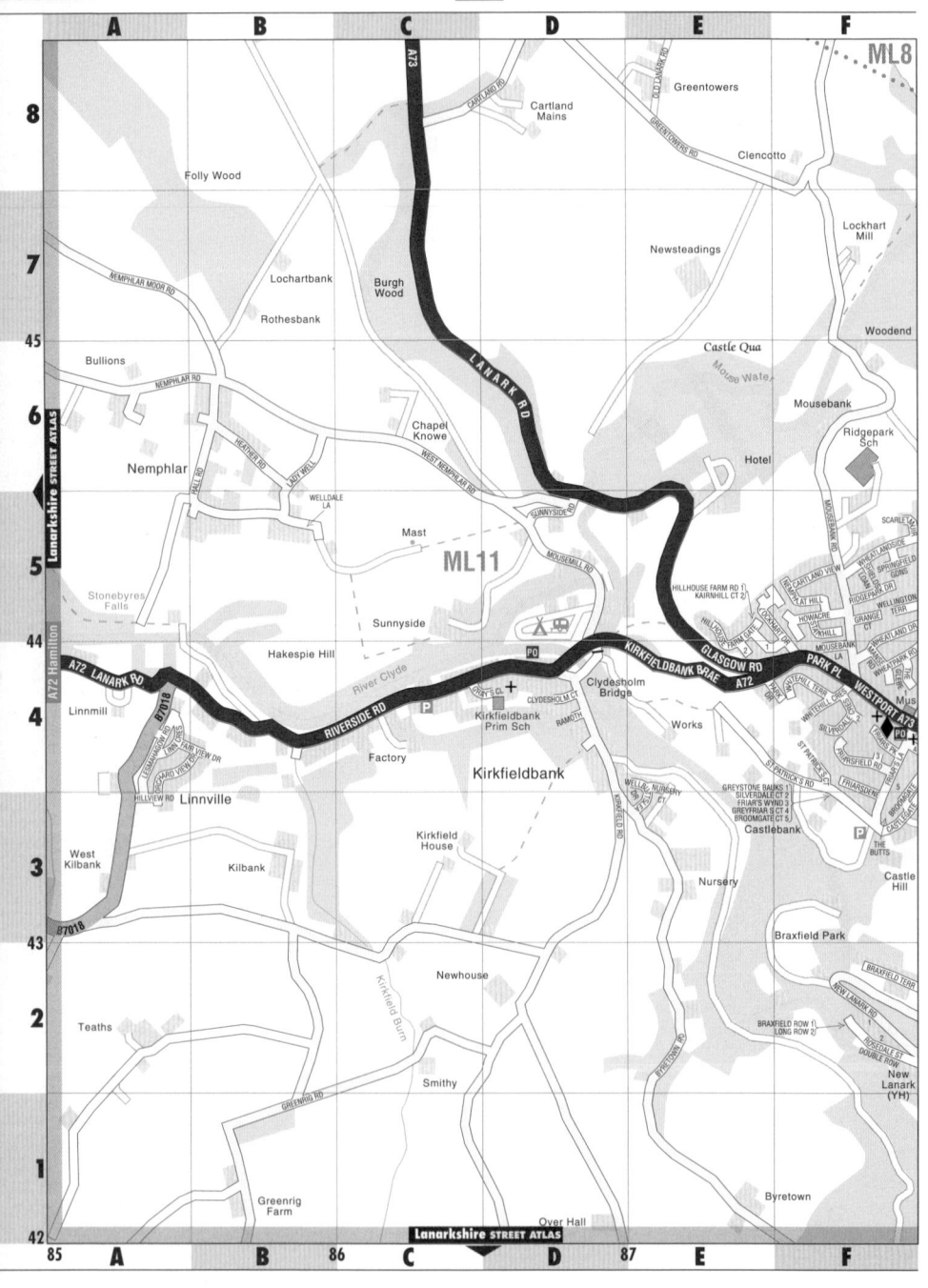

ML8

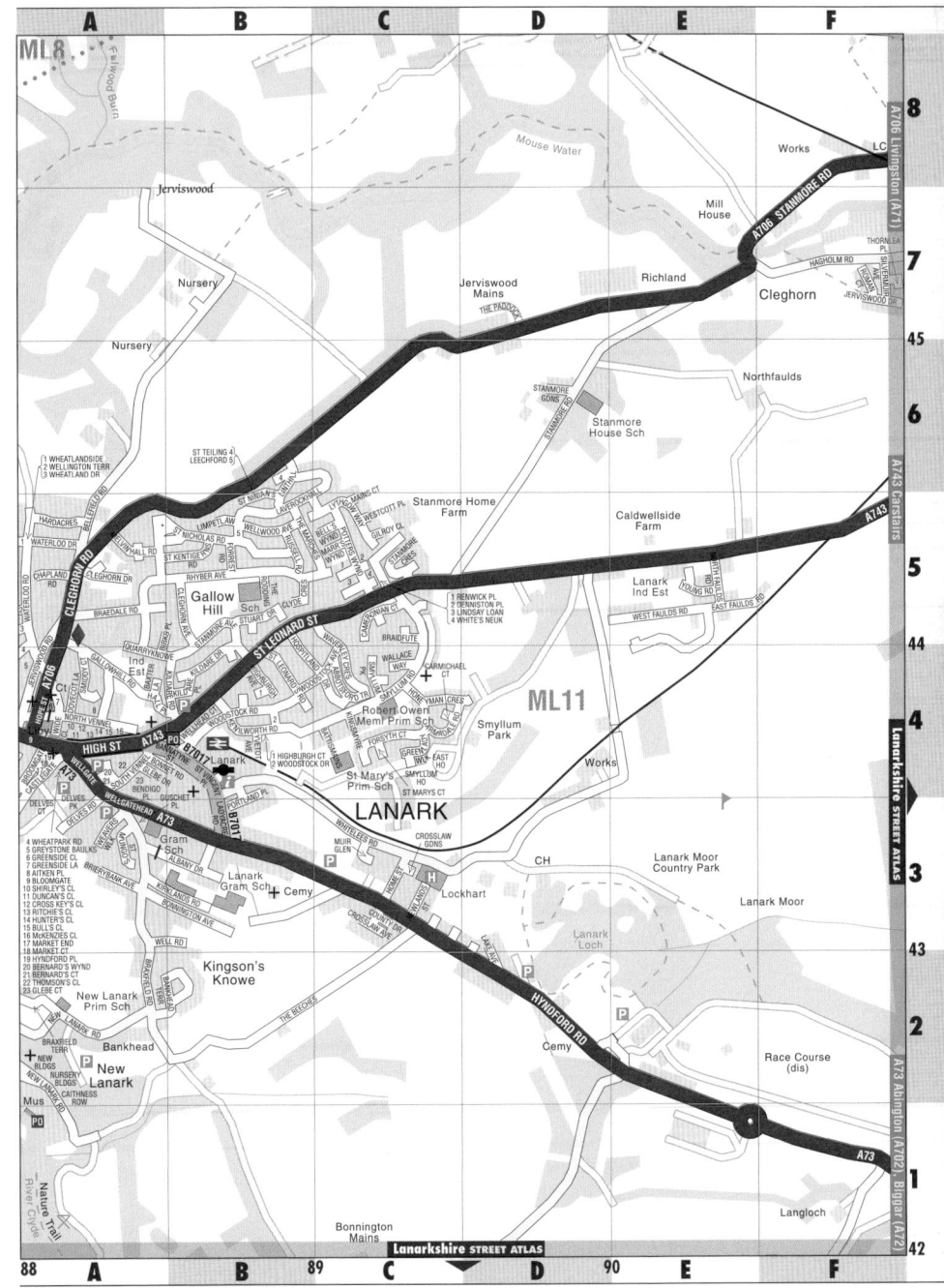

205

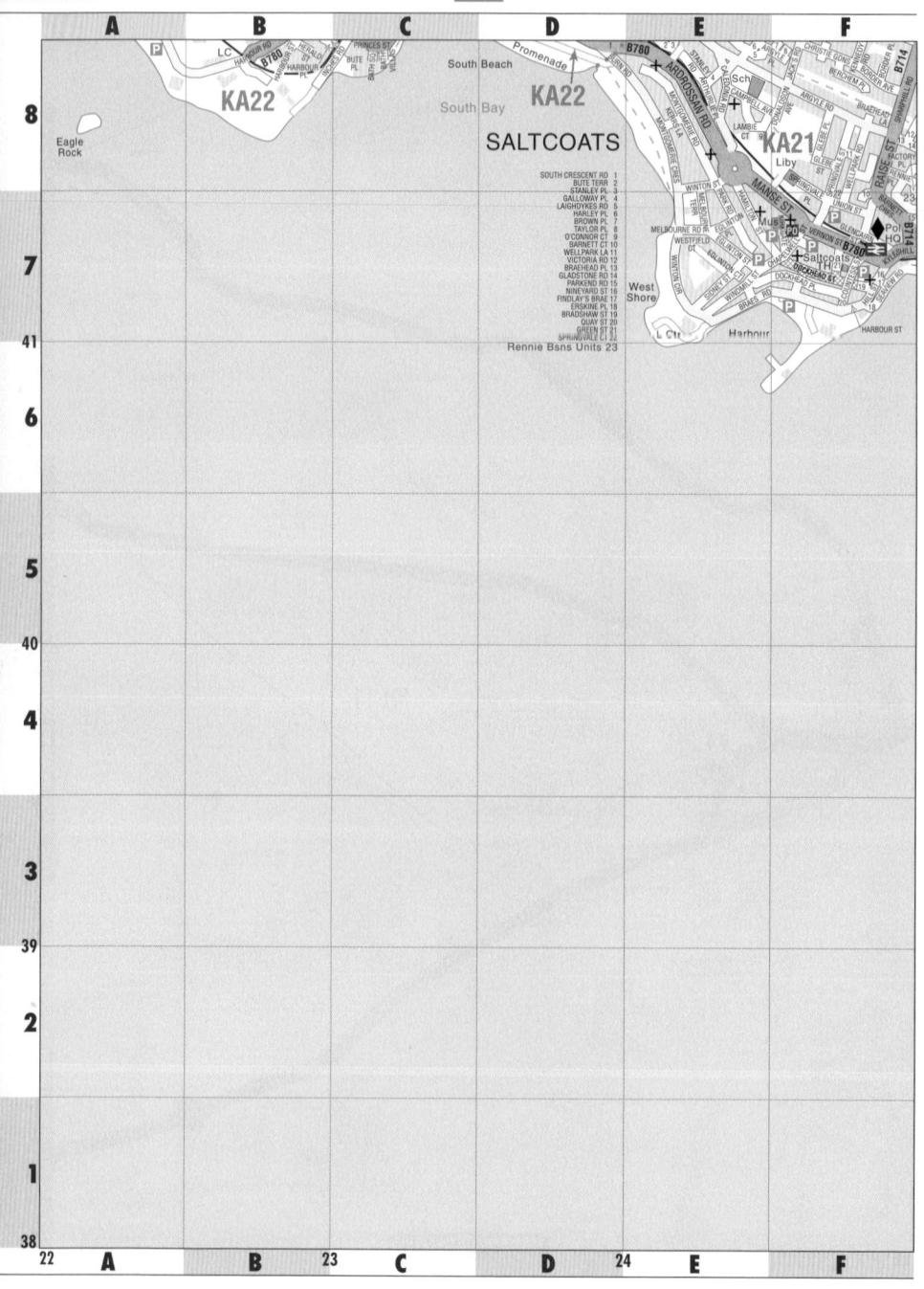

KA22

KA22

South Beach

South Bay

SALTCOATS

KA21

Liby

Eagle
Rock

SOUTH CRESCENT RD   1
BUTE TERR   2
STANLEY PL   3
GALLOWAY PL   4
LAIGHDYKES RD   5
HARLEY PL   6
BROWN PL   7
TAYLOR PL   8
O'CONNOR CT   9
BARNETT CT 10
WELLPARK LA 11
VICTORIA RD 12
BRAEHEAD PL 13
GLADSTONE RD 14
PARKEND RD 15
NINEYARD ST 16
FINDLAY'S BRAE 17
ERSKINE PL 18
BRADSHAW ST 19
QUAY ST 20
GREEN ST 21
SPRINGVALE CT 22
Rennie Bsns Units 23

West
Shore

Saltcoats

Harbour

HARBOUR ST

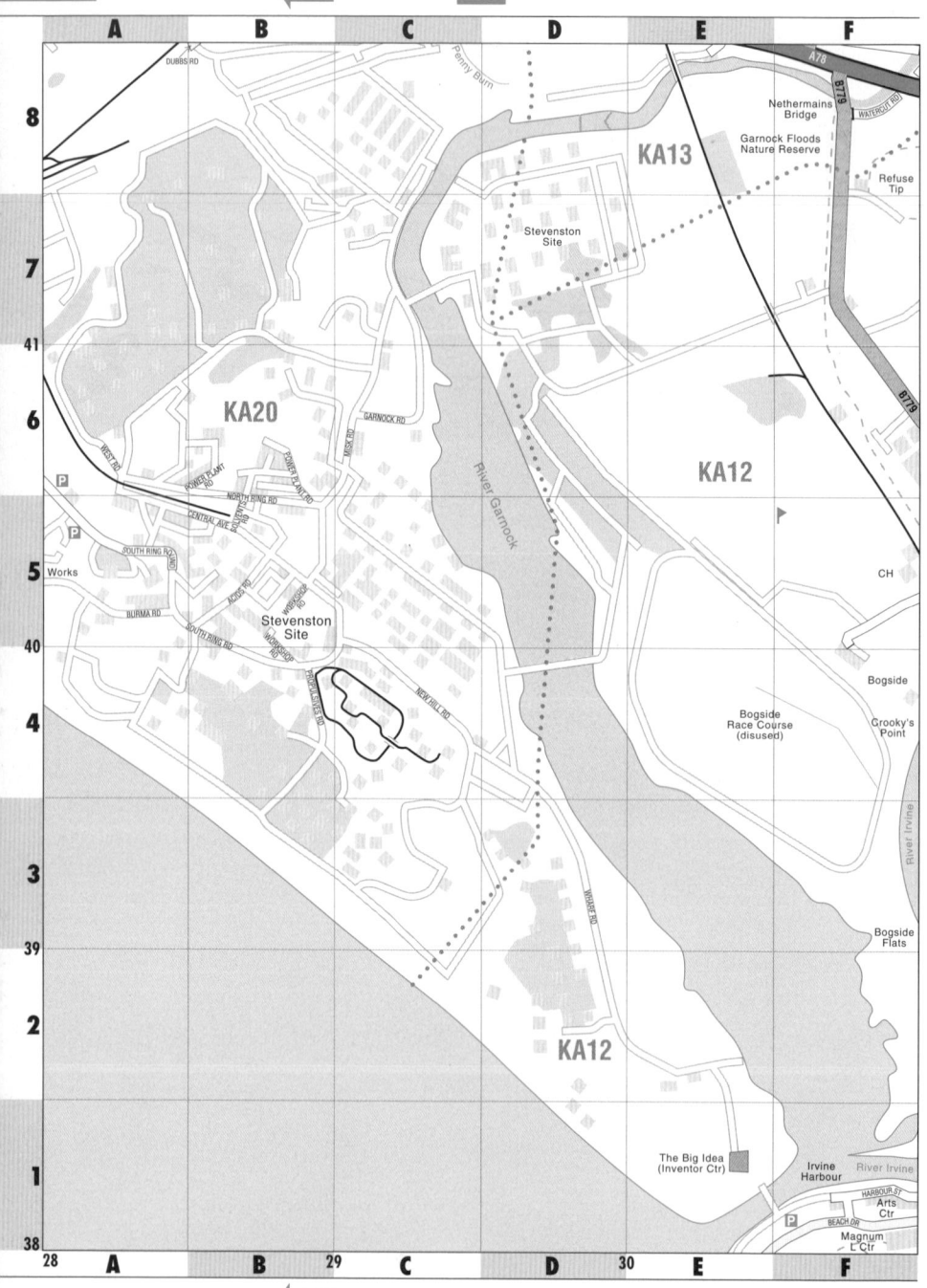

217
207

A B C D E F

KA13
KA13
KA13
KA11
KA12

Eglinton Country Park • Visitor Ctr
Belvidere Hill
Old Wood
Eglinton Country Park
Draught Burn
B7080
LONG DR
LONG DR
CARNMOUNT RD A736
Dykehead
REDBURN RDBT
REDBURN CVN PK
Hotel
FAIRWAYS
EGLINTON INTC
Works
WEST RD
EAST RD
Redburn Ind Est
The Circle
Morven Lodge
HILL INTC
A736
A736
CH
KIDSNEUK
Ayrshire Central
Castlepark Prim Sch
RANNOCH PL
SHIEL PL
LEVEN PL
LOMOND PL
MORAY PL
Stanecastle
Cemy
Red Burn
SANDY RD B779
KILWINNING RD
Irvine Royal Acad
Towns Moor
RAVENSCROFT
FLEMING TERR
DICKSON DR
PO
TERR
GIRDLE TOLL
PO
B769
MIDDLETON RD
B7080
FENCEDYKE WAY
CORSERINE WAY
LONG CR
Weir
IRVINE
HEATHFIELD RD
John Galt Prim Sch
MANSON RD A736
STANECASTLE INTC
St Mark's Prim Sch
TOWERLANDS RD
ARKWRIGHT
TOWERLANDS INTC
Woodlands Prim Sch
MARRESS RD
A737
A736
Mc CLURE GDNS
EGLINTON GDNS
ARRANVIEW
Kilmarnock Coll (Irvine Campus)
BANK ST
North Newmoor Ind Est
ARKWRIGHT WAY
LEWIS WYND
BROOMLANDS RDBT
Works
BOYLE ST
CHURCH ST
VICTORIA RDBT
FULLARTON RD
Irvine Ctr
Liby
BRIDGEGATE
AFTON CT
B7081
Mus
TOWNHEAD
Glebe Prim Sch
Cemy
South Newmoor Ind Est
WHITTLE PL
MACADAM PL
ST KILDA BANK
Scottish Maritime Mus
MONTGOMERY PL
LINTHOUSE VENNEL
Irvine
Riverway Ret Pk
PO
FULLARTON RDBT
Scottish Maritime Mus
Fullarton
MERRYVALE RDBT
AVR RD A737
A71
A736
Hotel
ANNICK RD
Annick Water
ANNICK RD
TELFORD PL
MACKINTOSH PL
Newmoor RDBT
B7081
B7080
B7061
LONG DR
GULLILAND PL
MILGARHOLM RDBT
WARRIX INTC
A71
Works
PORTLAND RD
L Ctr

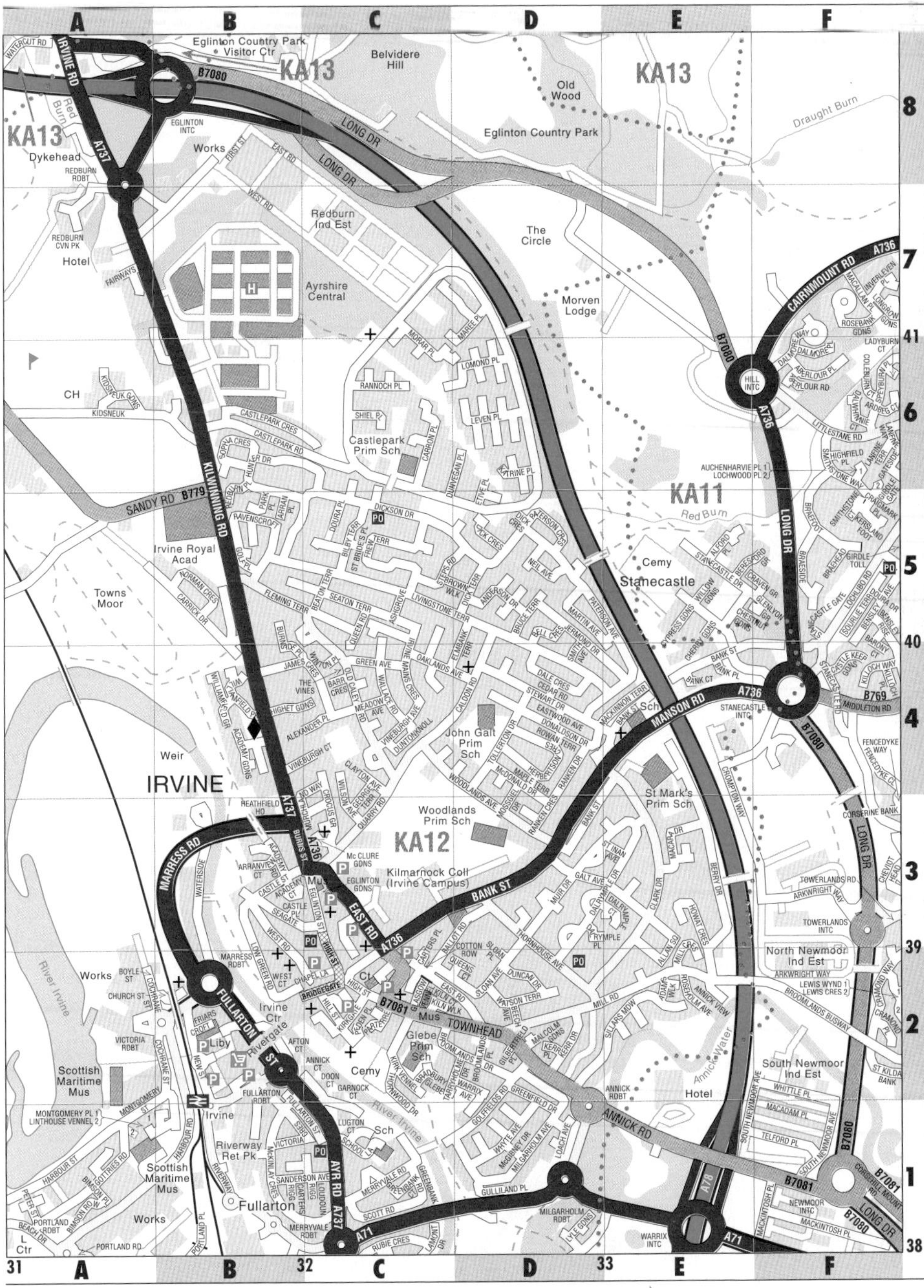

31 A B 32 C D 33 E F 38

8 41 7 6 5 40 4 3 39 2 1

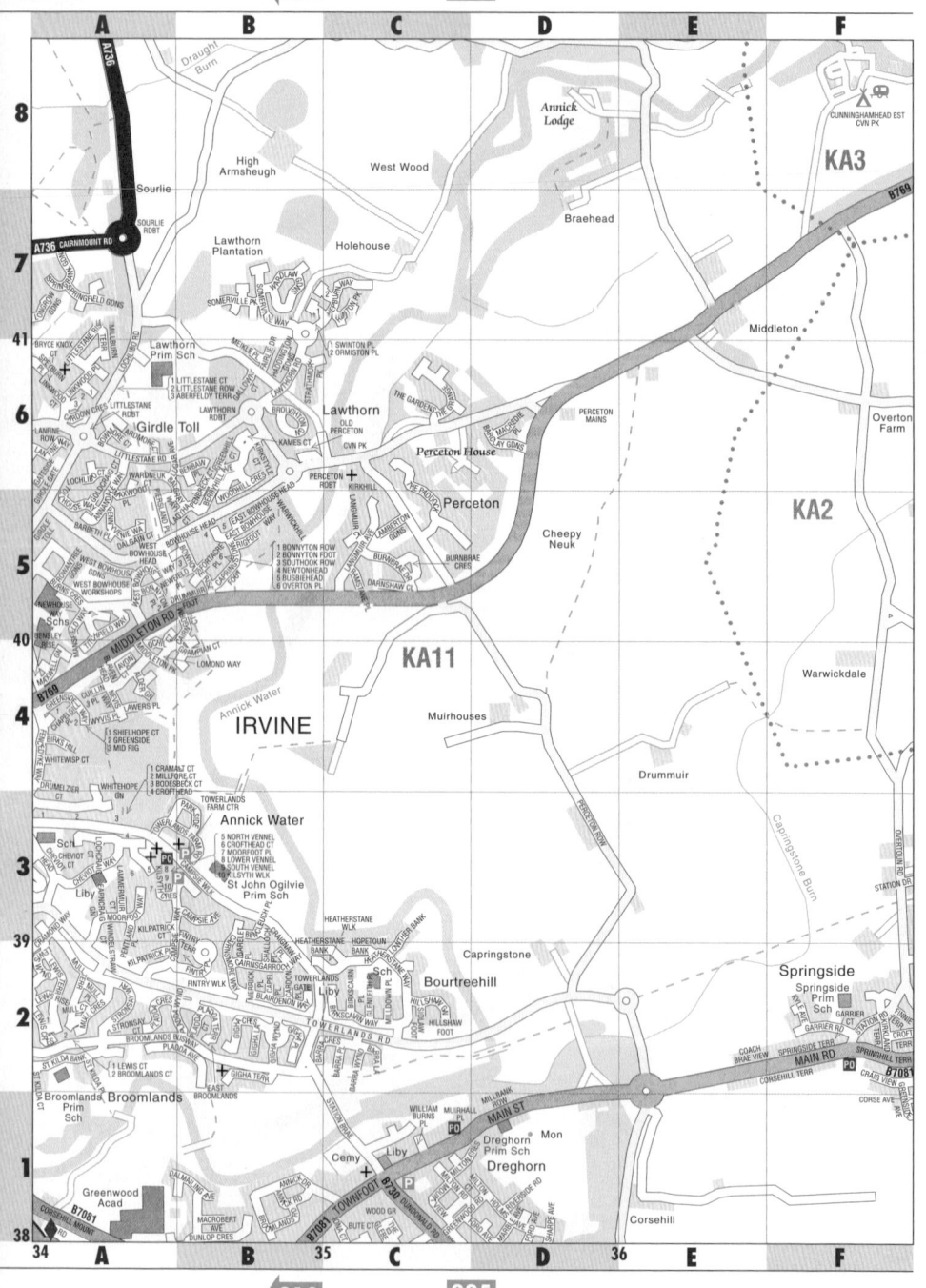

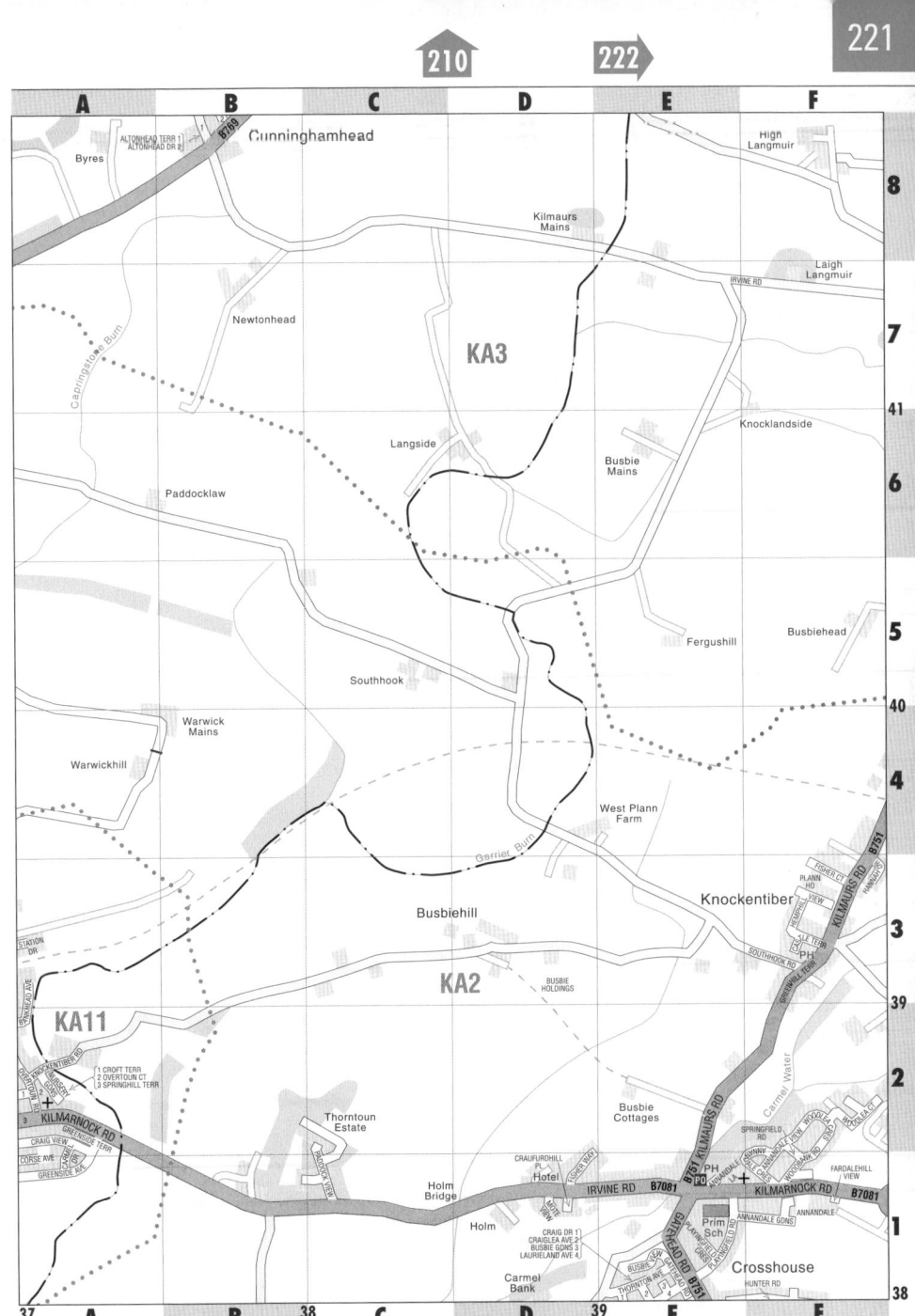

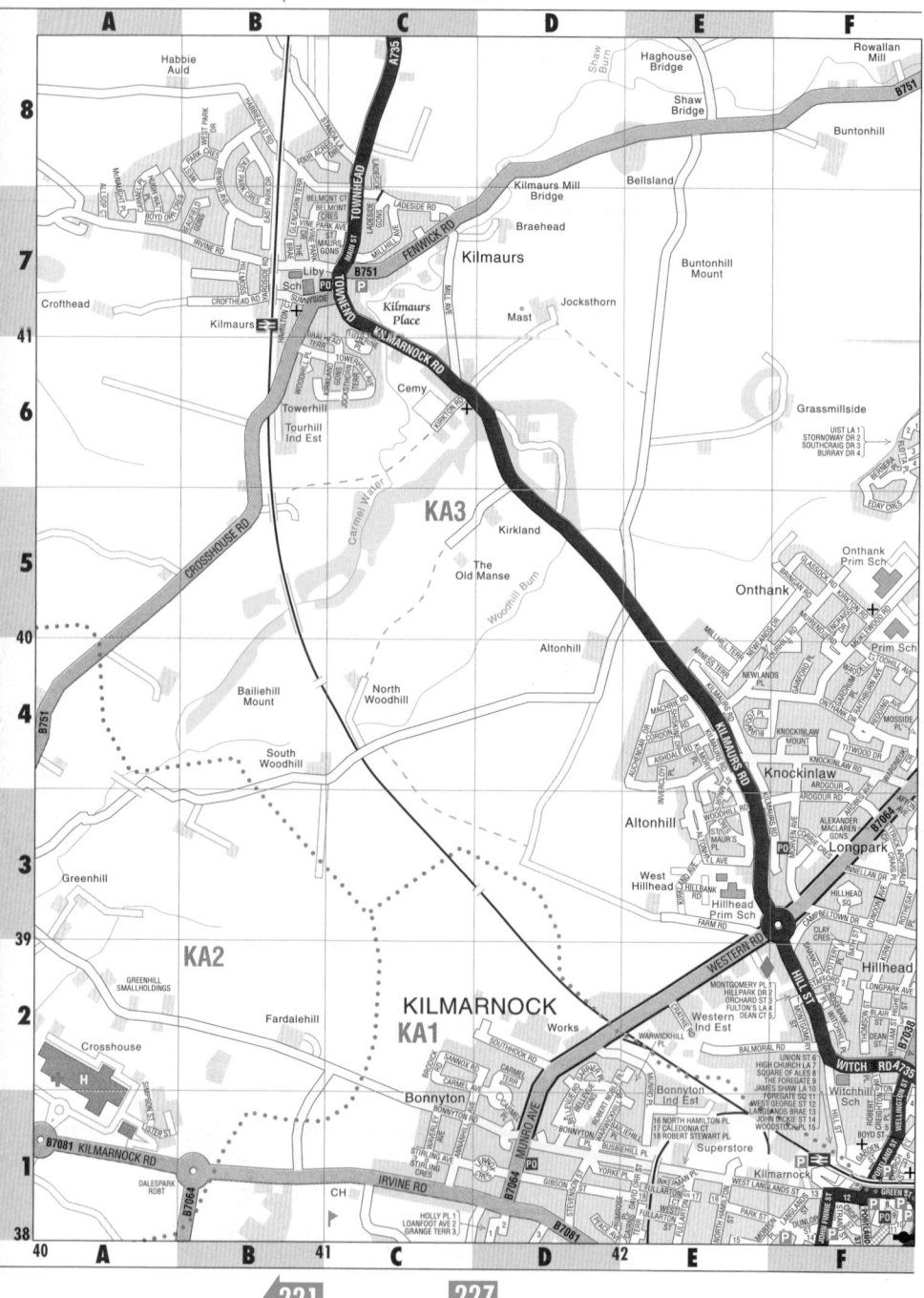

Habbie
Auld

Rowallan
Mill

Haghouse
Bridge

Shaw Burn

Shaw
Bridge

Buntonhill

B751

A735

8

TOWNHEAD

BELMONT CT
BELMONT
CRES

LADESIDE RD

MAIN ST

Kilmaurs Mill
Bridge

Bellsland

FENWICK RD

Braehead

7

B751

Kilmaurs

Buntonhill
Mount

Crofthead

CROFTHEAD RD

Sch

Liby

P

Kilmaurs
Place

KILMARNOCK RD

Mast

Jocksthorn

41

Kilmaurs

Grassmillside

UIST LA 1
STORNOWAY DR 2
SOUTHCRAIG DR 3
BURRAY DR 4

6

Towerhill

Tourhill
Ind Est

Cemy

EUROPE RD

Carmel Water

KA3

Kirkland

EDAY CRES

5

CROSSHOUSE RD

The
Old Manse

Woodhill Burn

Onthank
Prim Sch

Onthank

Prim Sch

40

Altonhill

MILLHILL TER

4

B751

Bailiehill
Mount

North
Woodhill

KILMAURS RD

Knocklaw
Mount

TITWOOD DR

Knocklaw

ARGOGUR

3

Greenhill

South
Woodhill

West
Hillhead

Altonhill

Hillhead
Prim Sch

ALEXANDER
MACLAREN
GDNS

B7038

Longpark

Hillhead
SQ

CLAY
CRES

39

KA2

GREENHILL
SMALLHOLDINGS

WESTERN RD

HILL ST

LONGPARK AVE

Hillhead

2

Crosshouse

H

Fardalehill

KILMARNOCK
KA1

Works

Western
Ind Est

MONTGOMERY PL 3
HILLPARK DR 2
ORCHARD ST 3
FULTON'S LA 4

WARWICKHILL
PL

BALMORAL RD

WITCH RD
A735

Witchhill
Sch

1

B7081 KILMARNOCK RD

DALESPARK
RDBT

B7064

Bonnyton
Ind Est

Bonnyton

MUNRO AVE

SOUTHHOOK RD

CARMEL
TERR

16 NORTH HAMILTON PL
17 CALEDONIA CT
18 ROBERT STEWART PL

Superstore

Kilmarnock

P

CH

IRVINE RD

B7081

STIRLING AVE
STIRLING

GIBSON ST

WEST LANGLANDS ST

GREEN ST

P

P

PO

38

40   A   B   41   C   D   42   E   F

HOLLY PL 1
LOANFOOT AVE 2
GRANGE TERR 3

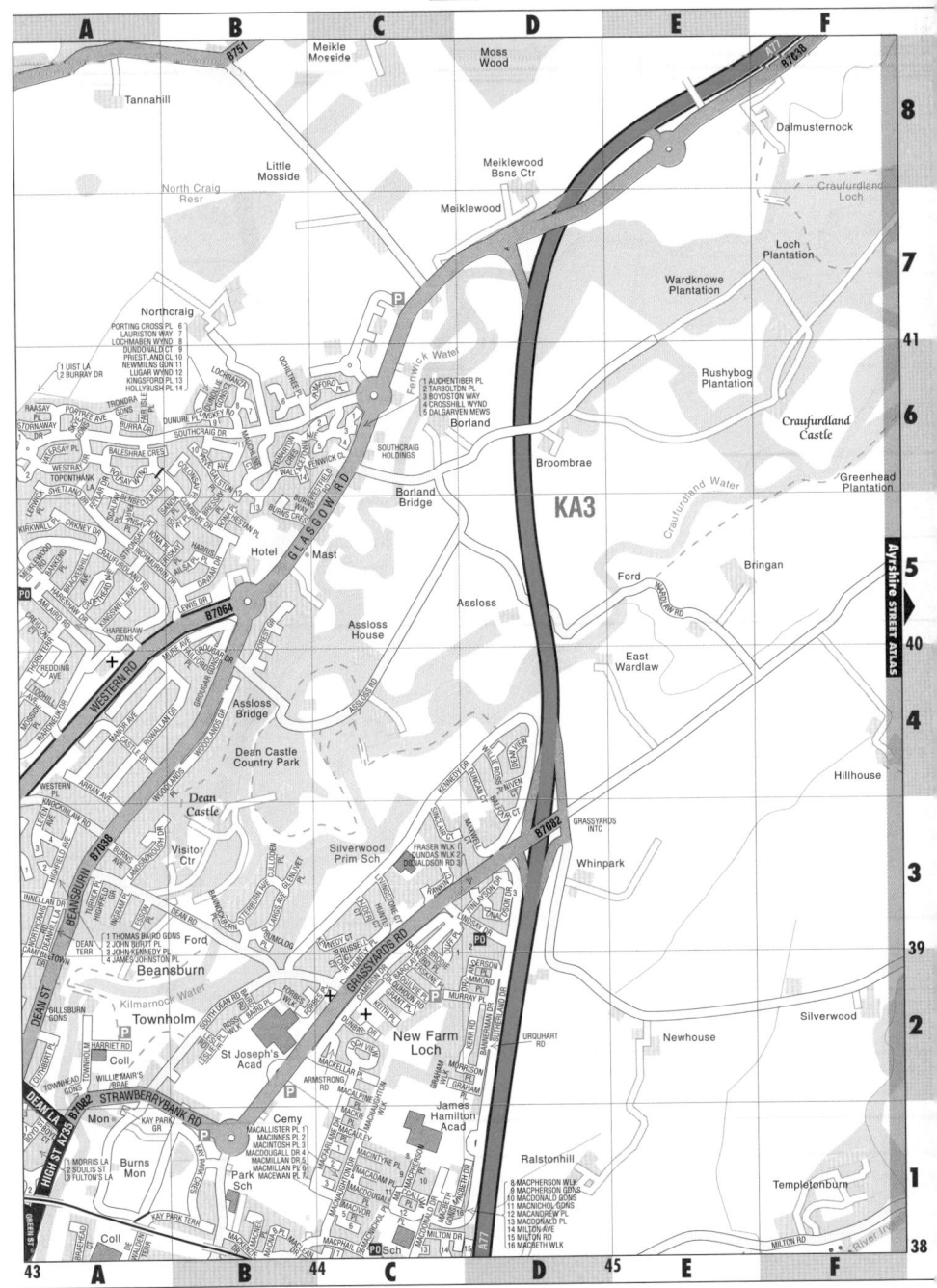

219

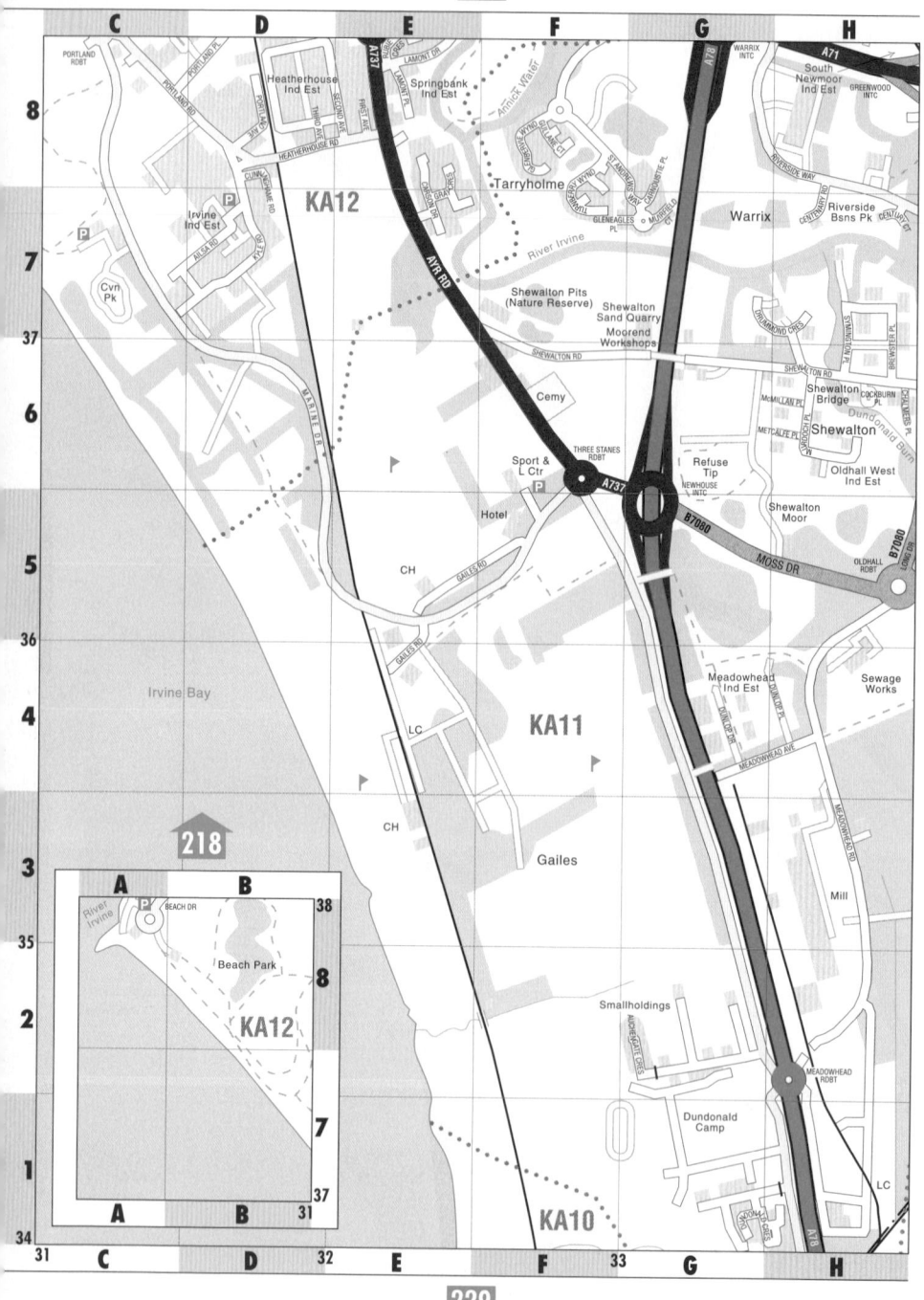

218
229

C D E F G H

PORTLAND RDBT
PORTLAND PL
Heatherhouse Ind Est
Springbank Ind Est
Arnick Whatf
South Newmoor Ind Est
WARRIX INTC
A71
GREENWOOD INTC

KA12
Tarryholme
Warrix
Riverside Bsns Pk

Irvine Ind Est
GLENEAGLES PL
River Irvine

Cvn Pk
Shewalton Pits (Nature Reserve)
Shewalton Sand Quarry
Moorend Workshops

SHEWALTON RD
Shewalton Bridge
COCKBURN PL
Dundonald Burn
Shewalton
McMILLAN PL
METCALFE PL
Oldhall West Ind Est

Cemy
AYR RD

Three Stanes RDBT
A737
Sport & L Ctr
Refuse Tip
NEWHOUSE INTC
Shewalton Moor

Hotel
B7080
MOSS DR
OLDHALL RDBT

CH
GAILES RD
Irvine Bay

KA11

LC
Meadowhead Ind Est
Sewage Works

MEADOWHEAD AVE

CH
Gailes

Mill

River Irvine
BEACH DR
P
38
8
Beach Park
KA12
7
Smallholdings
MEADOWHEAD RDBT
37
A B
31
34
31

Dundonald Camp
KA10
LC

C D 32 E F 33 G H

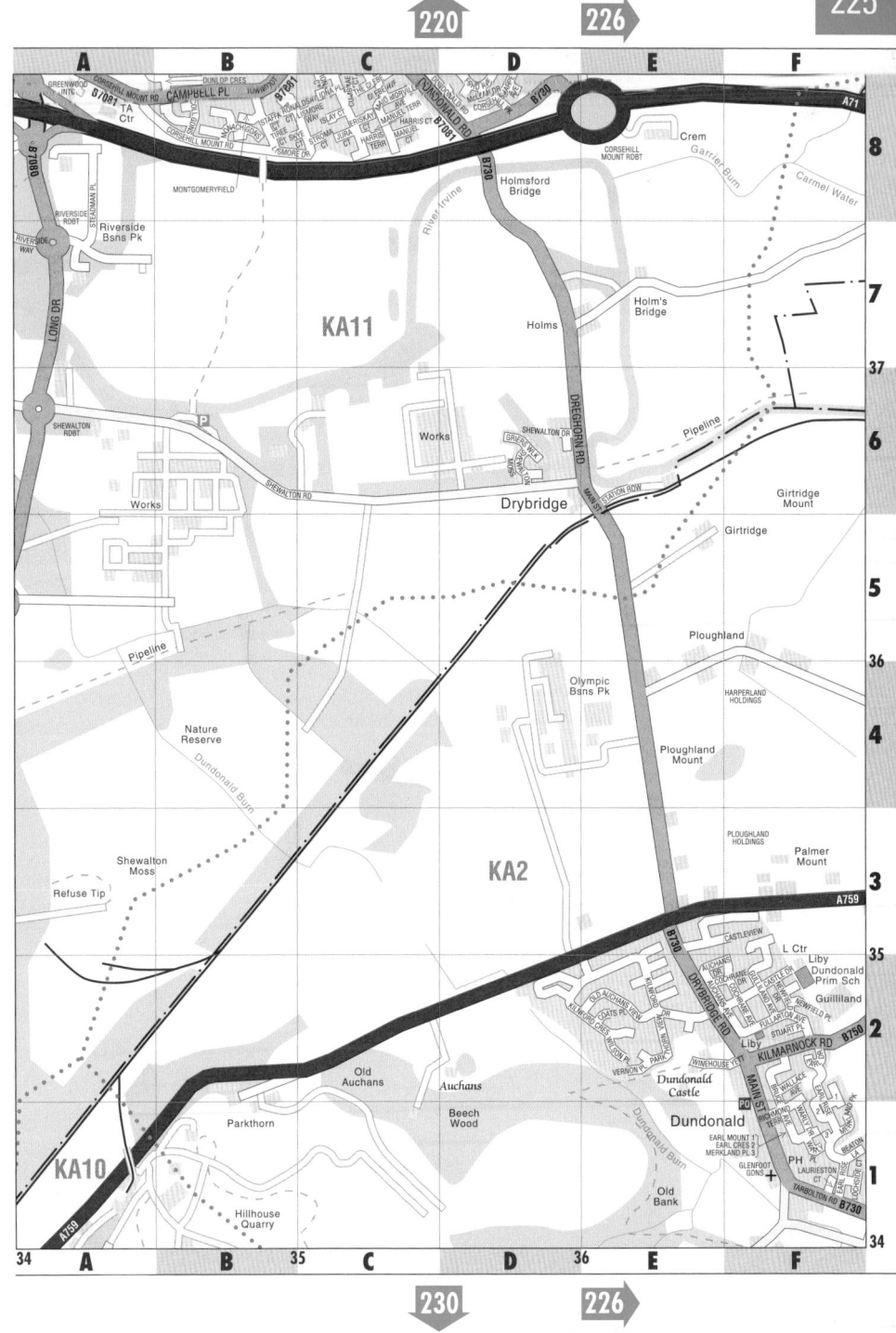

220
226
230
226

A71

CORSEHILL MOUNT RD
CAMPBELL PL
DUNLOP CRES
B7081
TUNWOOD
TURNBERRY
DUNDONALD RD
CORSEHILL
B7081
B730

GREENWOOD INTC
B7081
TA Ctr
B7080

MONTGOMERYFIELD

Crem
CORSEHILL MOUNT ROBT

Garnier Burn
Carmel Water

RIVERSIDE ROBT
STEADMAN PL
Riverside Bsns Pk

RIVERSIDE WAY

Holmsford Bridge

River Irvine

LONG DR

KA11

Holm's Bridge

Holms

SHEWALTON ROBT

P

Works

GREEN WK
SHEWALTON DR

Pipeline

Girtridge Mount

Works

SHEWALTON RD

DREGHORN RD

Drybridge

MAIN ST
STATION ROW

Girtridge

Pipeline

Ploughland

Nature Reserve

Dundonald Burn

Olympic Bsns Pk

HARPERLAND HOLDINGS

Ploughland Mount

Shewalton Moss

KA2

PLOUGHLAND HOLDINGS

Palmer Mount

Refuse Tip

A759

Old Auchans

Auchans

CASTLEVIEW
B730
L Ctr
Liby
Dundonald Prim Sch
Guilliland

DRYBRIDGE RD

B750

Liby
KILMARNOCK RD

Parkthorn

Beech Wood

Dundonald Castle

Dundonald

Dundonald Burn

WINEHOUSE

MAIN ST
PO
PH

EARL MOUNT
EARL CRES
MERKLAND PL

B730

KA10

Old Bank

GLENFOOT GDNS

LAURIESTON RD
TARBOLTON RD
B730

Hillhouse Quarry

A759

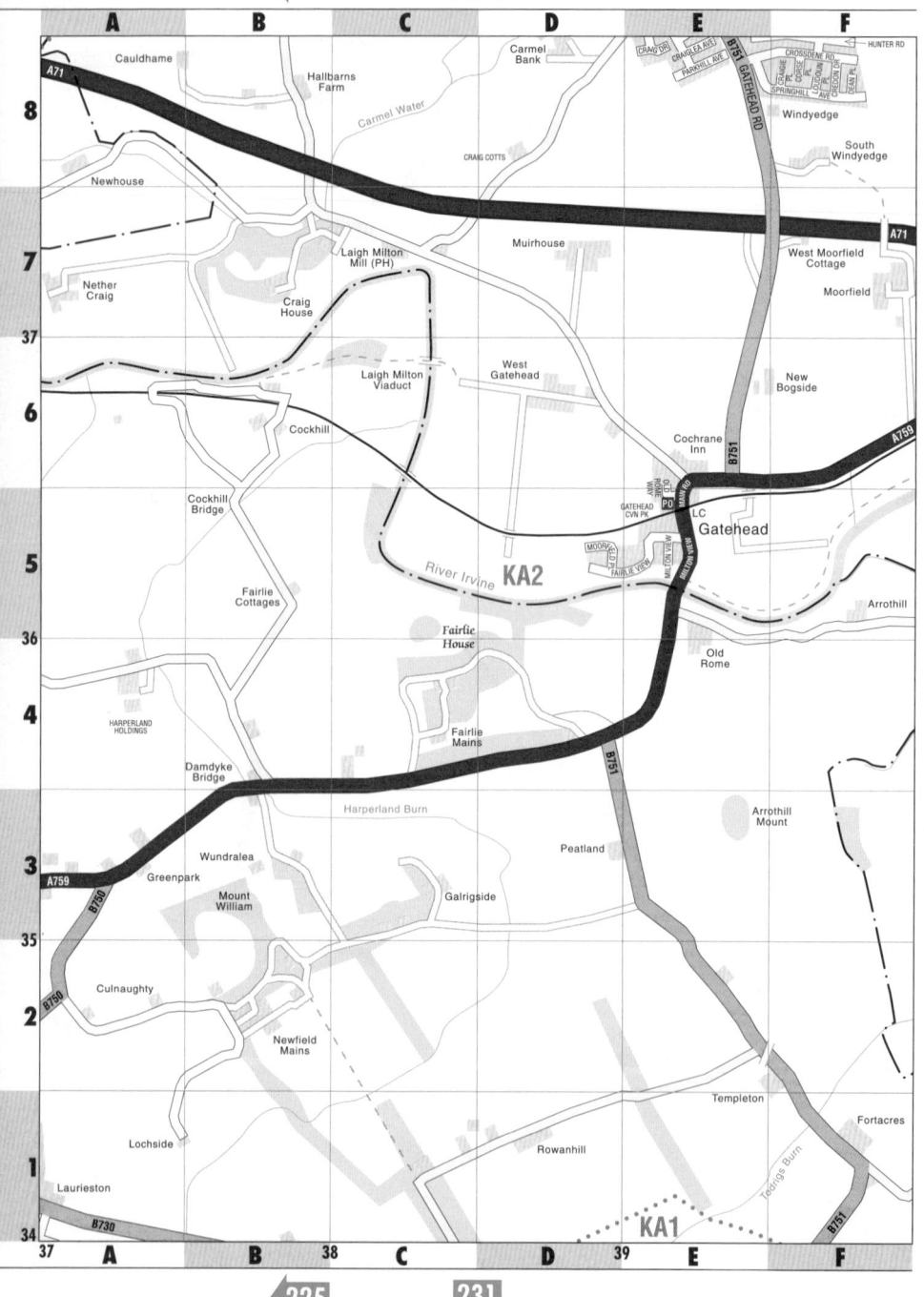

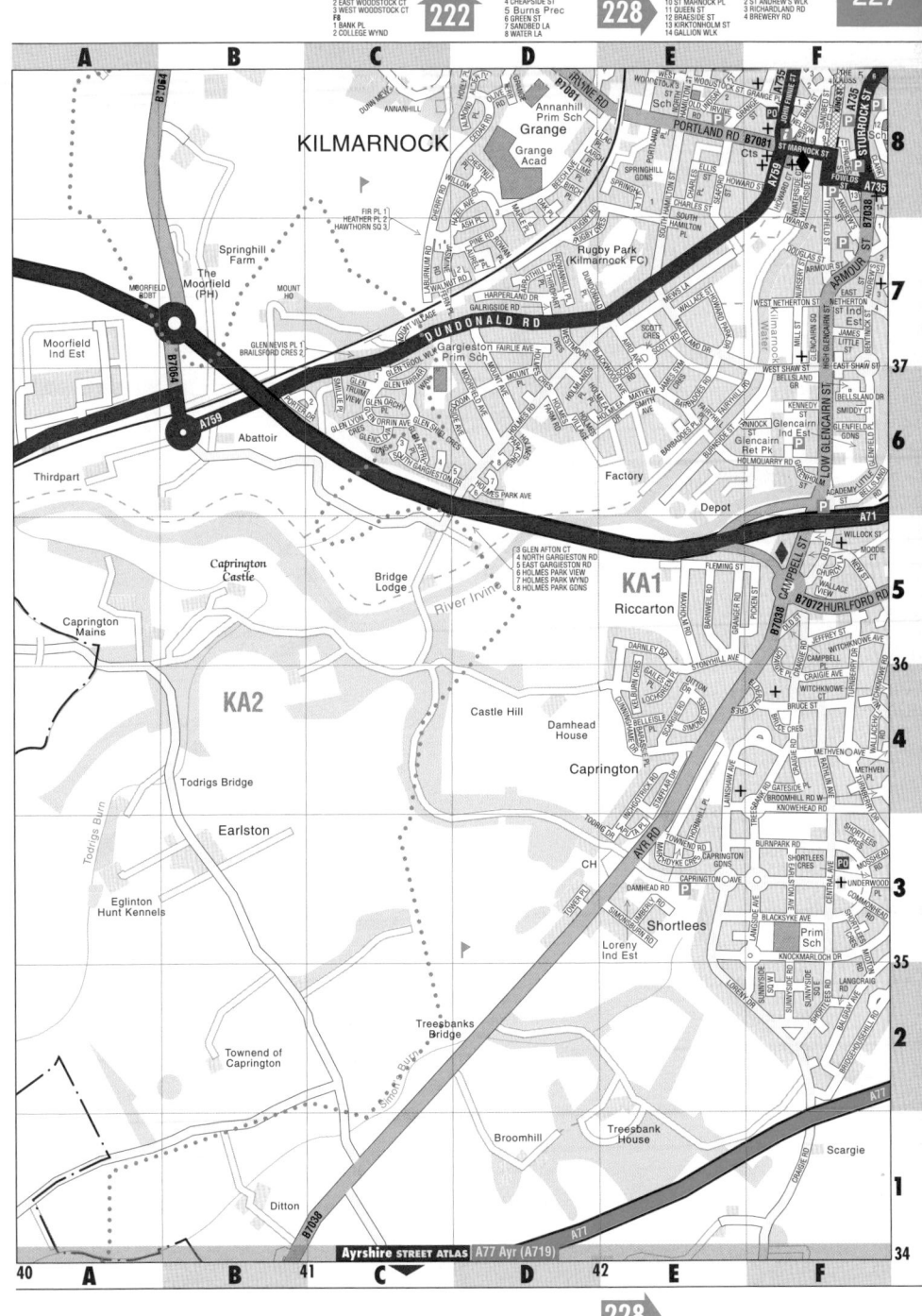

E8
1 SOUTH HAMILTON CT
2 EAST WOODSTOCK CT
3 WEST WOODSTOCK CT
F8
1 BANK PL
2 COLLEGE WYND

F8
3 LOW CHURCH LA
4 CHEAPSIDE ST
5 Burns Prec
6 GREEN ST
7 SANDBED LA
8 WATER LA

F8
9 BRIDGE LA
10 ST MARNOCK PL
11 QUEEN ST
12 BRAESIDE ST
13 KIRKTONHOLM ST
14 GALLION WLK

F7
1 KIRKTONHOLM PL
2 ST ANDREW'S WLK
3 RICHARDLAND RD
4 BREWERY RD

222

228

228

KILMARNOCK

KA1

KA2

A8
1 ACADAEMY APARTMENTS
2 GLEBE CT
3 MITCHELL CT

227

223

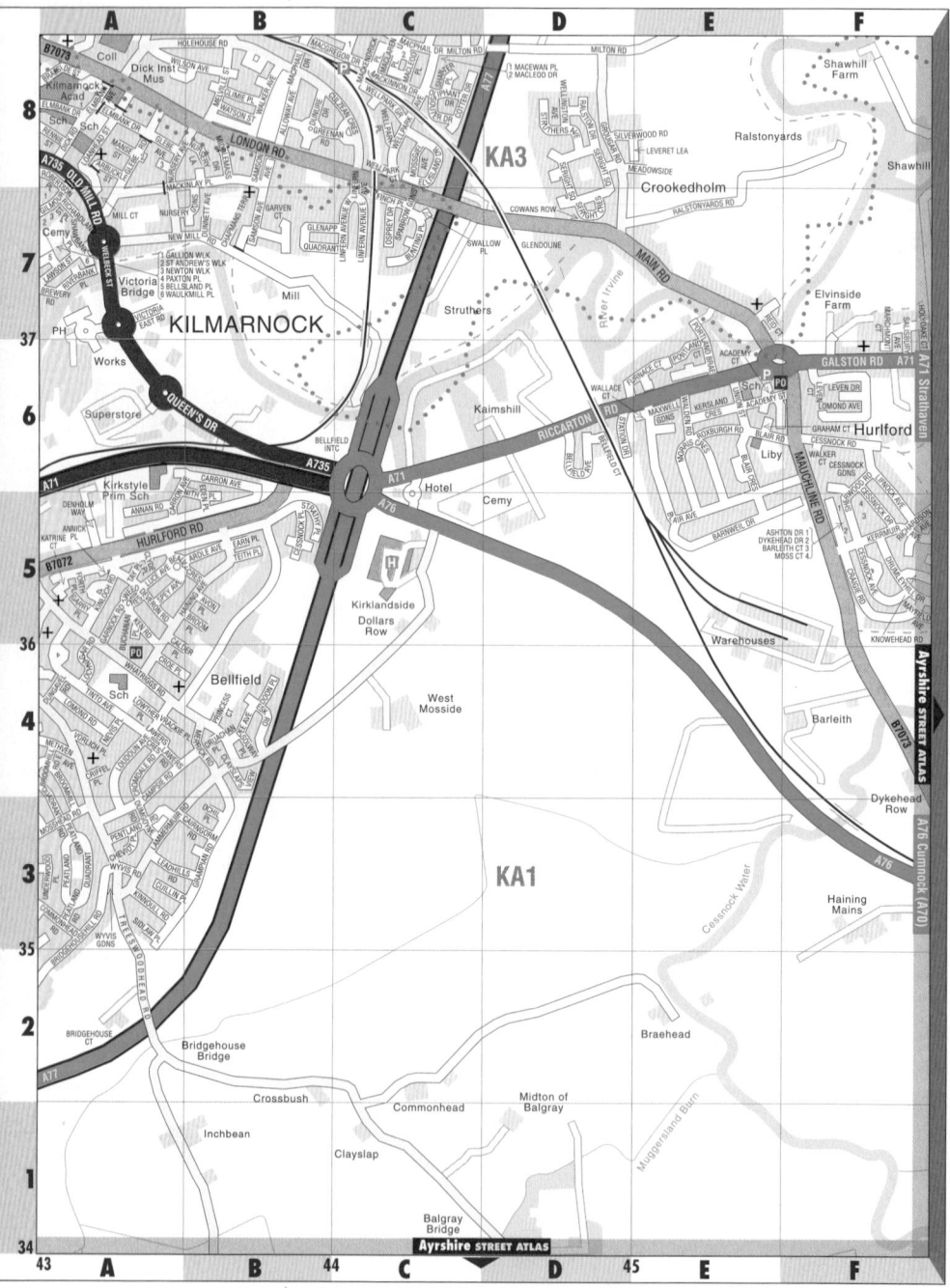

KA3

Crookedholm

Shawhill
Farm

Ralstonyards

Shawhill

Elvinside
Farm

KILMARNOCK

Victoria
Bridge

Struthers

River Irvine

Kaimshill

Hurlford

Works

Superstore

QUEEN'S DR

BELLFIELD
INTC

GALSTON RD

Liby

Hotel

Cemy

Kirkstyle
Prim Sch

HURLFORD RD

Warehouses

Kirklandside
Dollars
Row

West
Mosside

Bellfield

Barleith

Dykehead
Row

KA1

Haining
Mains

Bridgehouse
Bridge

Crossbush

Commonhead

Midton of
Balgray

Braehead

Inchbean

Clayslap

Cessnock Water

Muggersland Burn

Balgray
Bridge

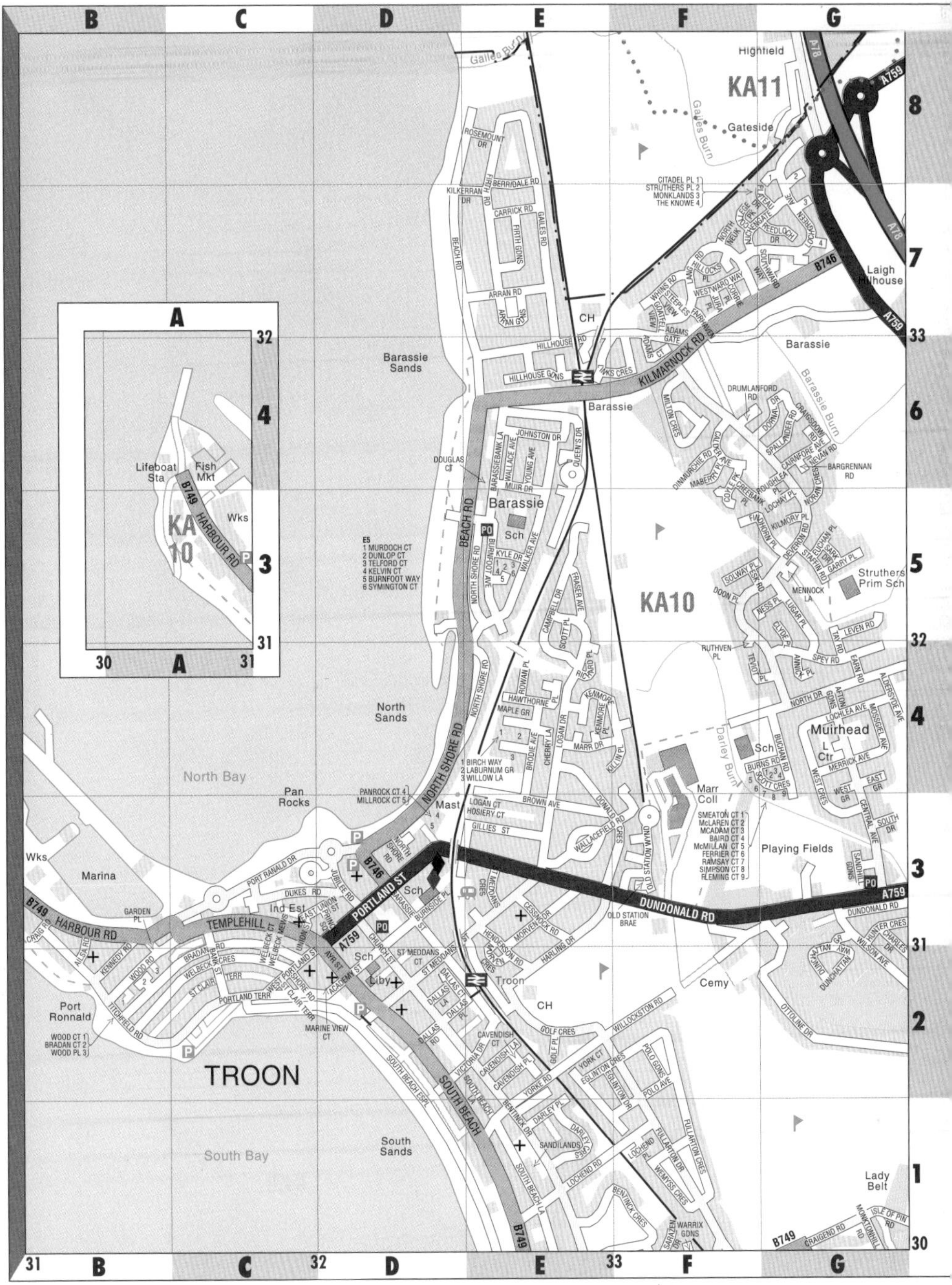

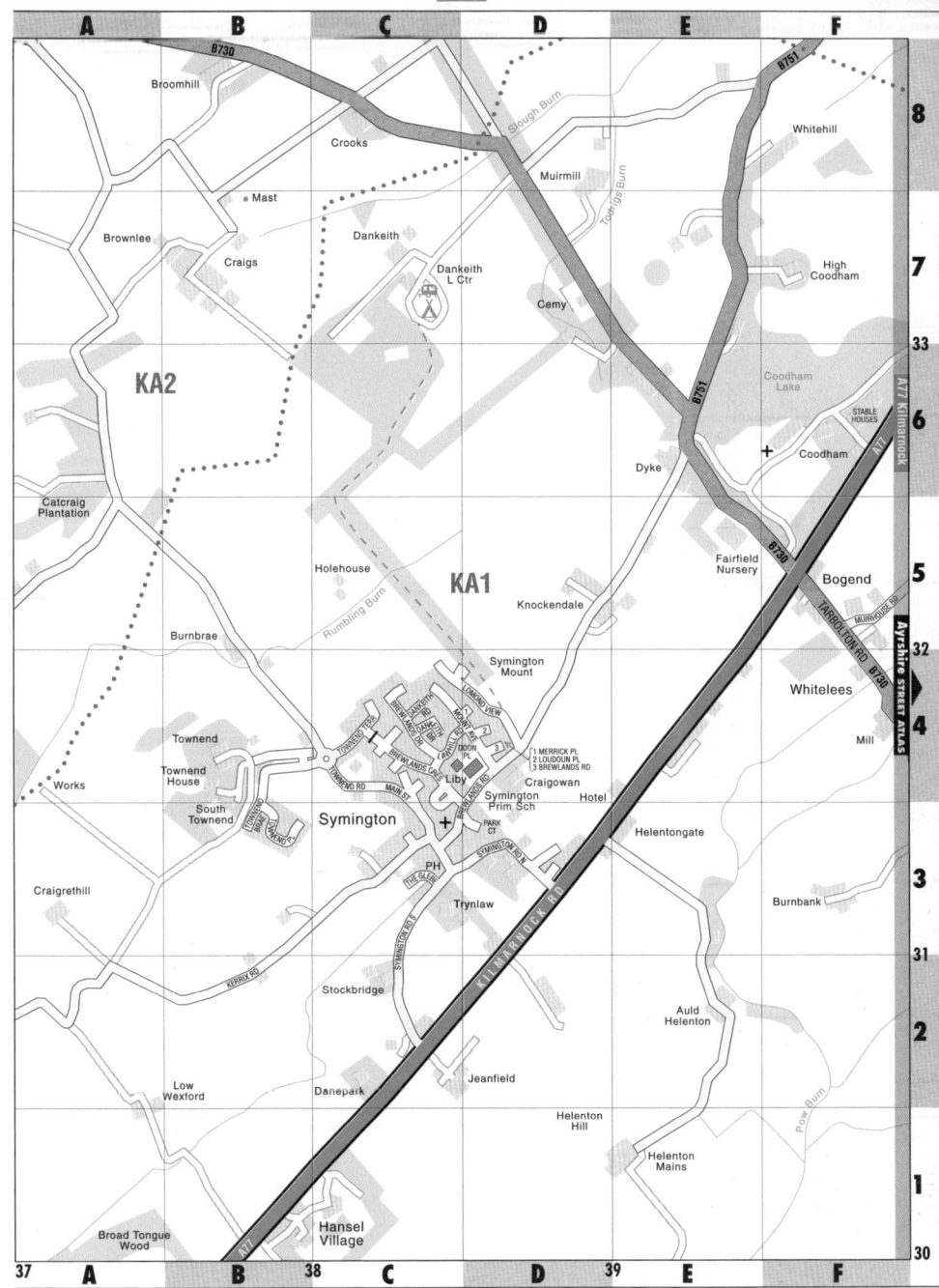

229

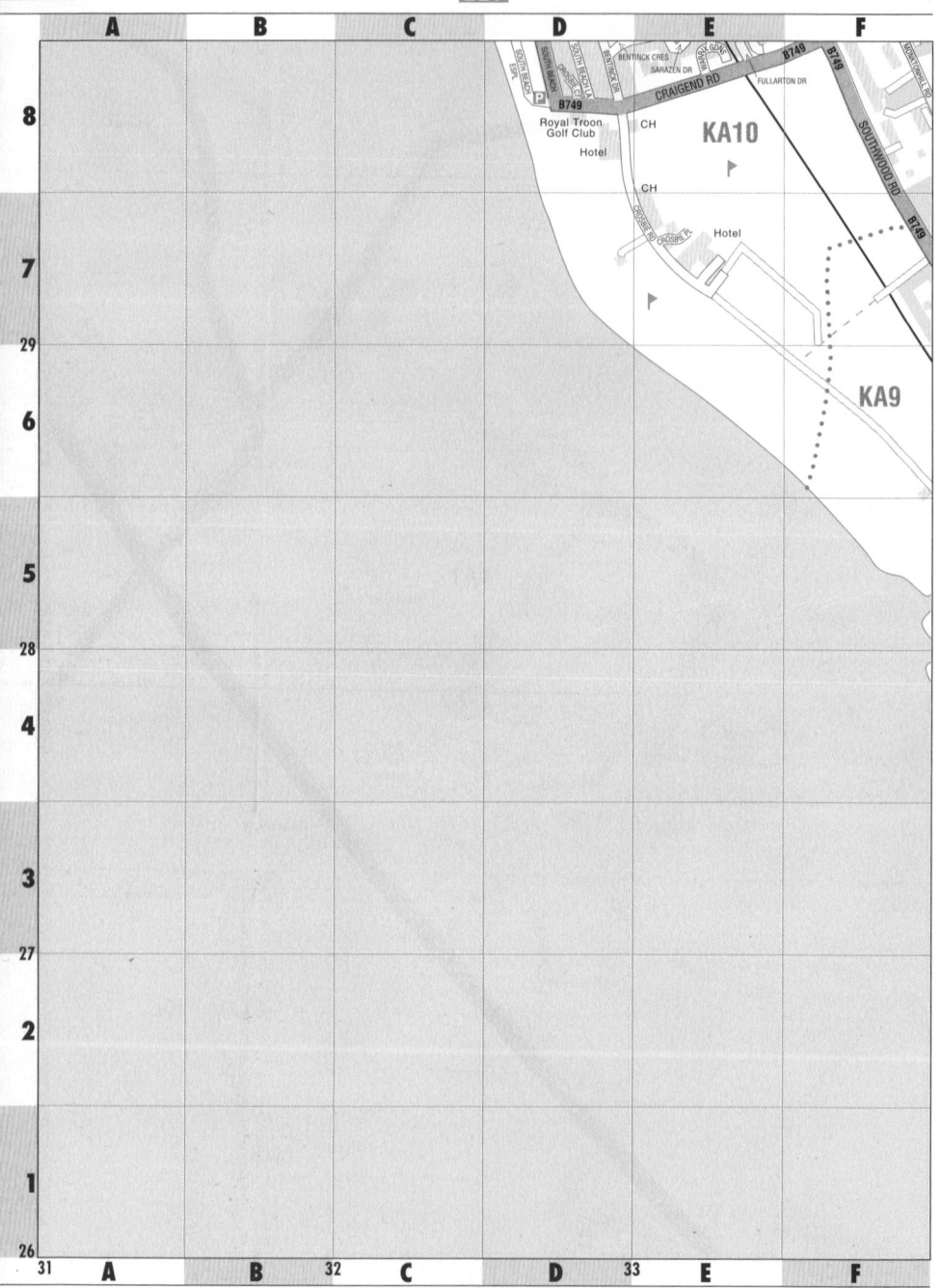

KA10

KA9

Royal Troon
Golf Club

Hotel

CH

CH

Hotel

CRAIGEND RD

BENTINCK CRES

SARAZEN DR

FULLARTON DR

B749

B749

B749

B749

SOUTH BEACH

SOUTH BEACH LA

BENTINCK DR

MAX GDNS

CROSBIE RD

CROSBIE PL

SOUTHWOOD RD

MONKTON RD

235

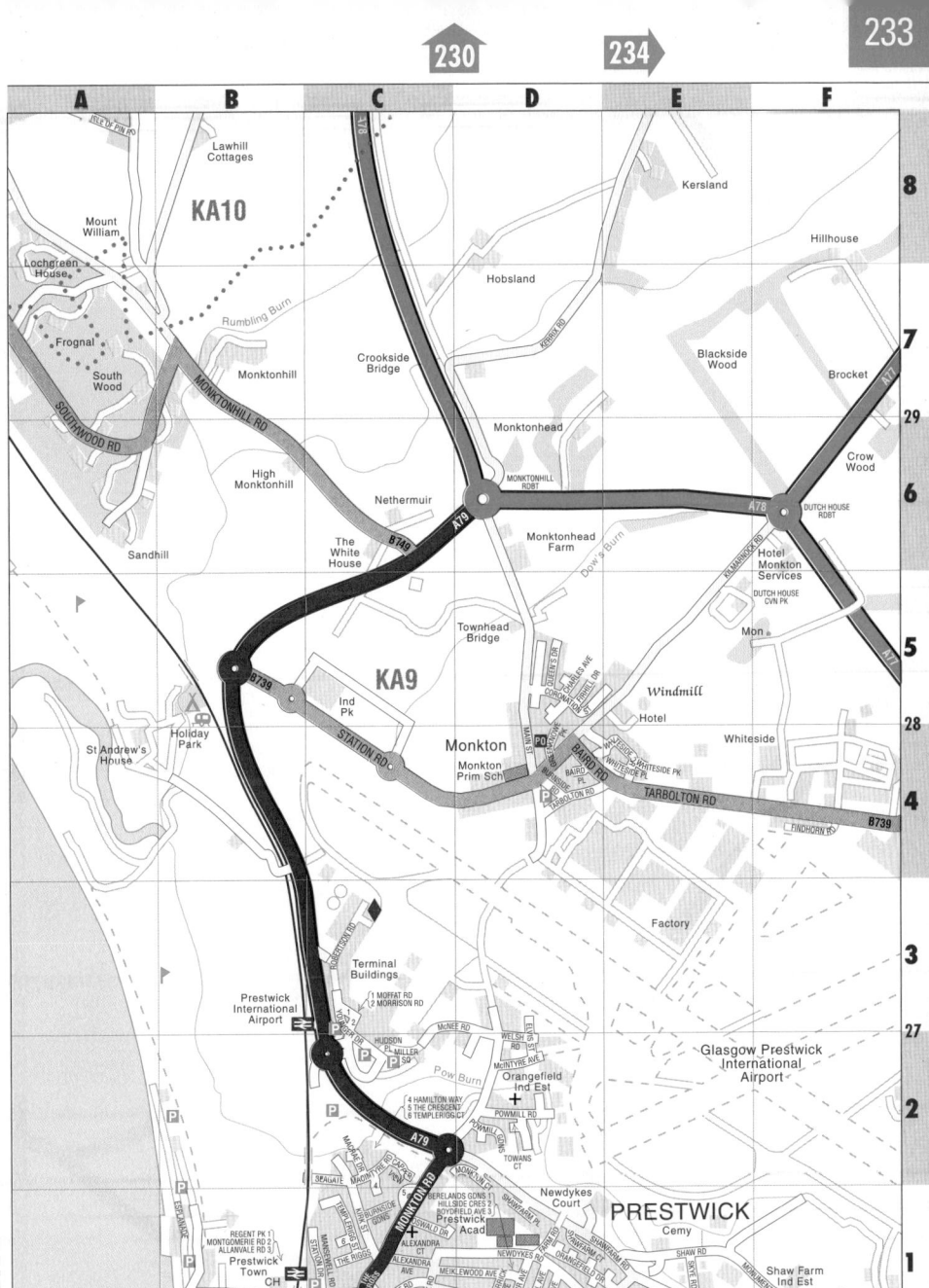

230
234
236
234

A **B** **C** **D** **E** **F**

8
7
29
6
5
28
4
3
27
2
1
26

34   35   36

Lawhill
Cottages

KA10

Mount
William

Lochgreen
House

Frognal

South
Wood

Hobsland

Kersland

Hillhouse

Crookside
Bridge

Monktonhill

SOUTHWOOD RD

MONKTONHILL RD

Rumbling Burn

Blackside
Wood

Brocket

Monktonhead

Crow
Wood

High
Monktonhill

Sandhill

Nethermuir

The
White
House

MONKTONHILL
RDBT

DUTCH HOUSE
RDBT

B740

A79

Monktonhead
Farm

Dow's Burn

Hotel
Monkton
Services

DUTCH HOUSE
CVN PK

KILMARNOCK RD

St Andrew's
House

Holiday
Park

B739

Ind
Pk

KA9

STATION RD

Townhead
Bridge

CHARLES DR

QUEEN'S DR

MAIN ST

Monkton

Monkton
Prim Schl

BAIRD RD

PO

Bairo
St

Windmill

Hotel

Mon

Whiteside

WHITESIDE PK

WHITESIDE PL

WHITE PARK-WHITESIDE RD

TARBOLTON RD

B739

FINDHORN RD

TARBOLTON RD

Factory

ROBERTSON RD

Terminal
Buildings

1 MOFFAT RD
2 MORRISON RD

Prestwick
International
Airport

HUDSON
RD

MILLER
RD

McNEE RD

WELSH
RD

McINTYRE RD

Pow Burn

Orangefield
Ind Est

4 HAMILTON WAY
5 THE CRESCENT
6 TEMPLERIGG CT

POWMILL RD

POWMILL
GDNS

TOWANS
CT

Glasgow Prestwick
International
Airport

MONKTON RD

A79

SEAGATE

MACRAE CT

ESPLANADE

P

ANDAYRE RD

SEABANK RD

LINKS RD

REGENT PK 1
MONTGOMERIE RD 2
ALLANVALE RD 3

Prestwick
Town
CH

STATION RD

STATION RD

MAIN ST

A79

BOYDFIELD RD

MORRIS RD

THE RIDGE

ALEXANDRA
CT

ALEXANDRA
AVE

MEIKLEWOOD AVE

GRANGE RD

SERELANDS GDNS
HILLSIDE CRES 2
BOYDFIELD AVE 3

Prestwick
Acad

NEWDYKES RD

Newdykes
Court

PRESTWICK

SHAW RD

SKYE RD

Cemy

Shaw Farm
Ind Est

GLENBURN
RD

Mon

MONKWOOD PL

LANGCROFT AVE

BLACKFORD RD

MANSION AVE

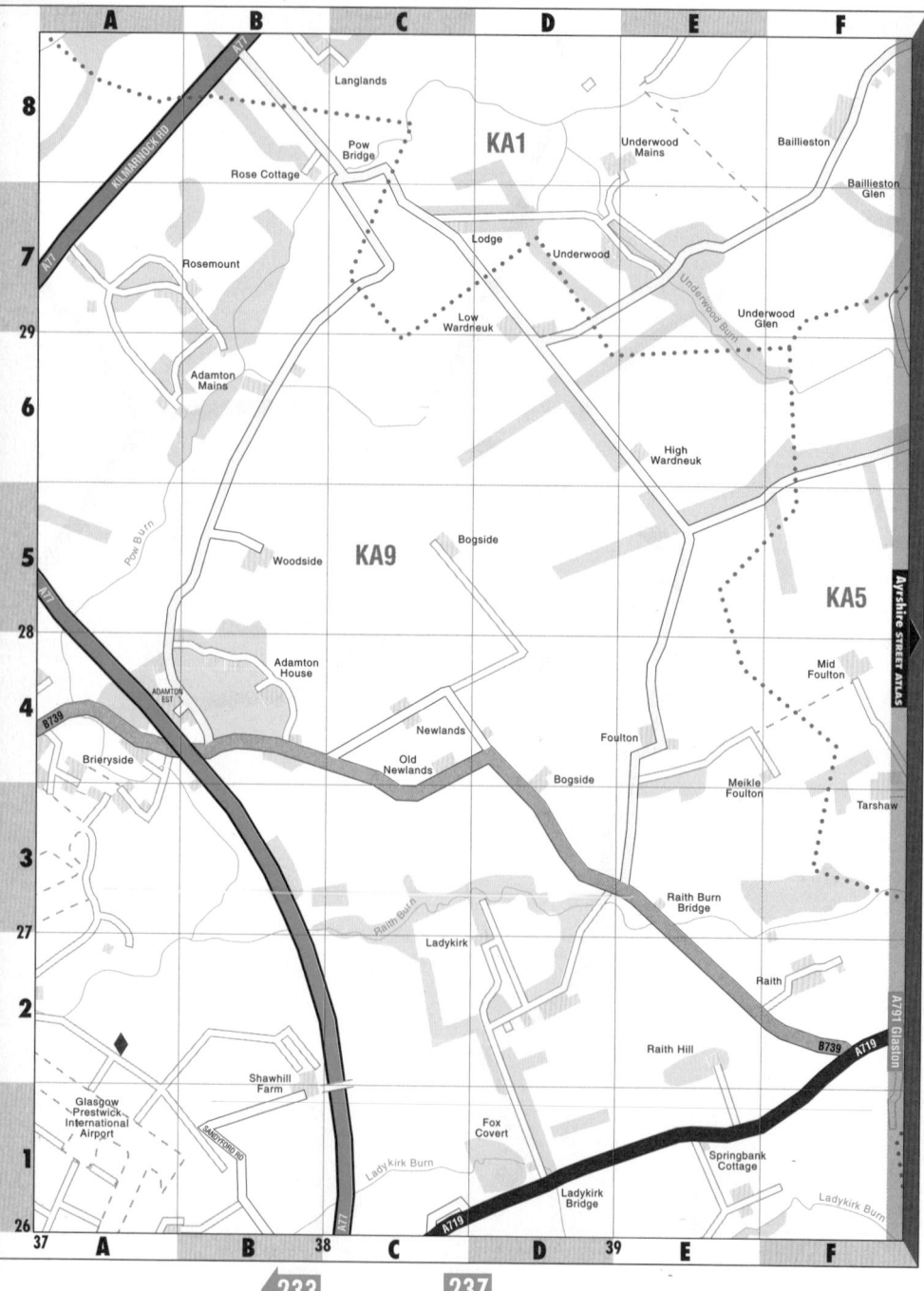

A B C D E F

8

KA1

Langlands

Pow Bridge

Rose Cottage

Underwood Mains

Baillieston

Baillieston Glen

7

Rosemount

Lodge

Underwood

Underwood Burn

Underwood Glen

29

Low Wardneuk

6

Adamton Mains

High Wardneuk

KILMARNOCK RD

A77

Pow Burn

5

Woodside

KA9

Bogside

KA5

A77

28

Adamton House

Mid Foulton

Ayrshire STREET ATLAS

4

ADAMTON EST

B739

Newlands

Old Newlands

Bogside

Foulton

Meikle Foulton

Tarshaw

Brieryside

3

Raith Burn

Ladykirk

Raith Burn Bridge

Raith

27

2

Shawhill Farm

SANDFORD RD

A771

Raith Hill

B739

A719 Glaston

Glasgow Prestwick International Airport

Fox Covert

Springbank Cottage

1

Ladykirk Burn

A719

Ladykirk Bridge

Ladykirk Burn

26

37 A B 38 C A719 D 39 E F

8

7

25

6

5

24

4

F2
1 TAYLGR CT
2 SALTFIELD LA
3 HALLS VENNAL
4 Green Street La Bsns Pk

3

23

North
Breakwater

KA8

Dock

2

South
Pier

CHURCHILL
TWR

E1
1 BRUCE CRES
2 QUEEN'S TERR LA
3 MARLBOROUGH CT
4 BUCHAN CT
5 TRANCHARD CT
6 ROWALLAN CT
7 DONNINI CT

Citadel
L Ctr

10

Liby

AYR
KA7

SEABANK
RD

Ayr
Acad

B748

1

22

F1
1 ALLISON ST
2 GARDEN ST
3 GEORGE ST
4 STRATHAYR PL
5 SANDGATE
6 ST JOHN ST
7 CATHCART ST
8 ACADEMY ST

9 BOAT VENNAL
10 North Harbour Ind Est

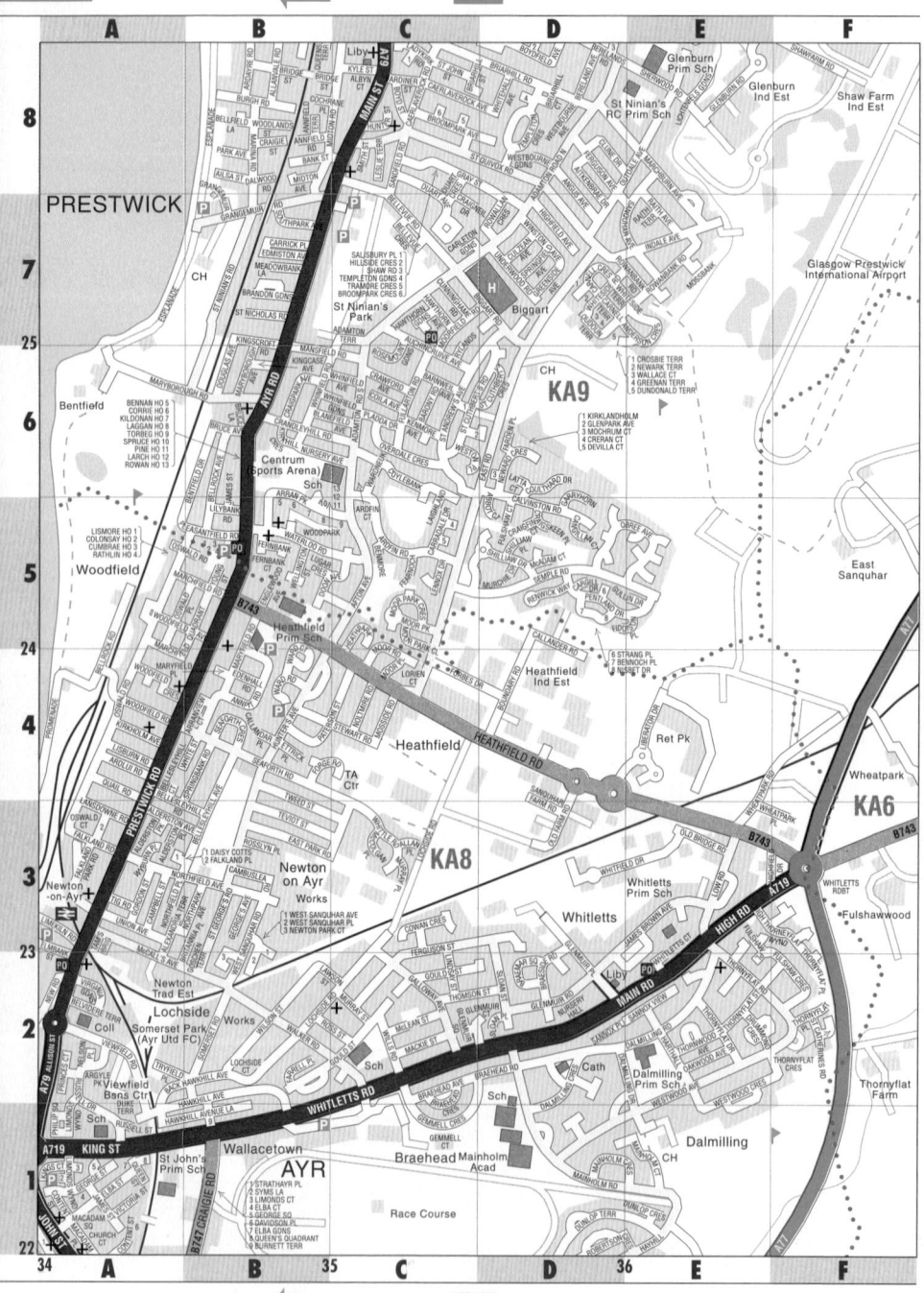

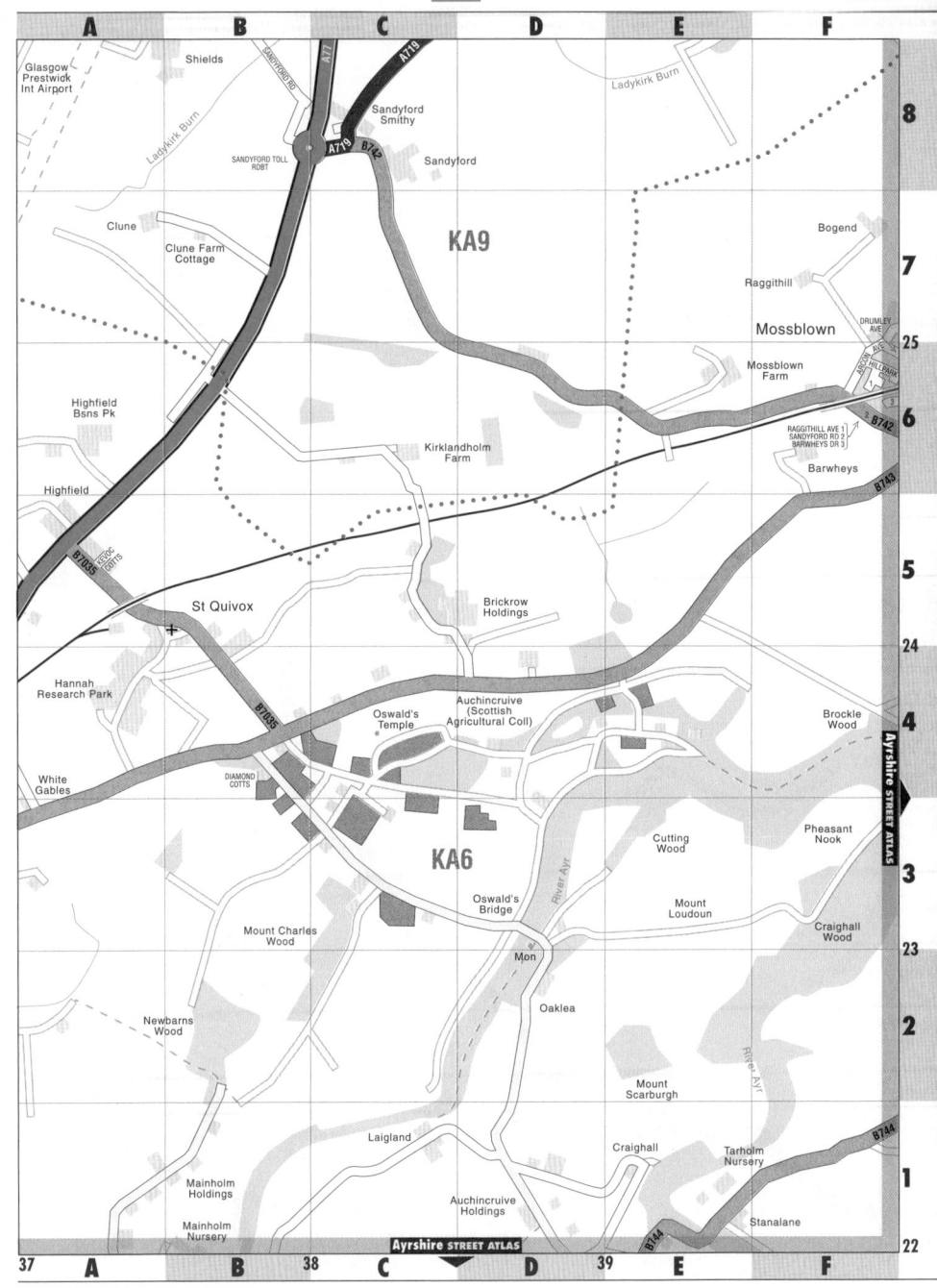

A B C D E F

Glasgow Prestwick Int Airport

Shields

Sandyford Smithy

SANDYFORD TOLL RDBT

Sandyford

Ladykirk Burn

KA9

Bogend

Clune

Clune Farm Cottage

Raggithill

Mossblown

DRUMLEY AVE

25

Mossblown Farm

Highfield Bsns Pk

Kirklandholm Farm

RAGGITHILL AVE 1
SANDYFORD RD 2
BARWHEYS DR 3

B742

6

Highfield

Barwheys

B743

KLEOOC COTTS

5

St Quivox

Brickrow Holdings

24

Hannah Research Park

Auchincruive (Scottish Agricultural Coll)

Brockle Wood

4

Oswald's Temple

White Gables

DIAMOND COTTS

Ayrshire STREET ATLAS

Pheasant Nook

Cutting Wood

KA6

Oswald's Bridge

Mount Loudoun

Craighall Wood

3

23

Mount Charles Wood

Mon

River Ayr

Oaklea

Newbarns Wood

2

Mount Scarburgh

River Ayr

Laigland

Mainholm Holdings

Craighall

Tarholm Nursery

B744

Auchincruive Holdings

B744

Stanalane

1

22

Mainholm Nursery

37 A B 38 C D 39 E F

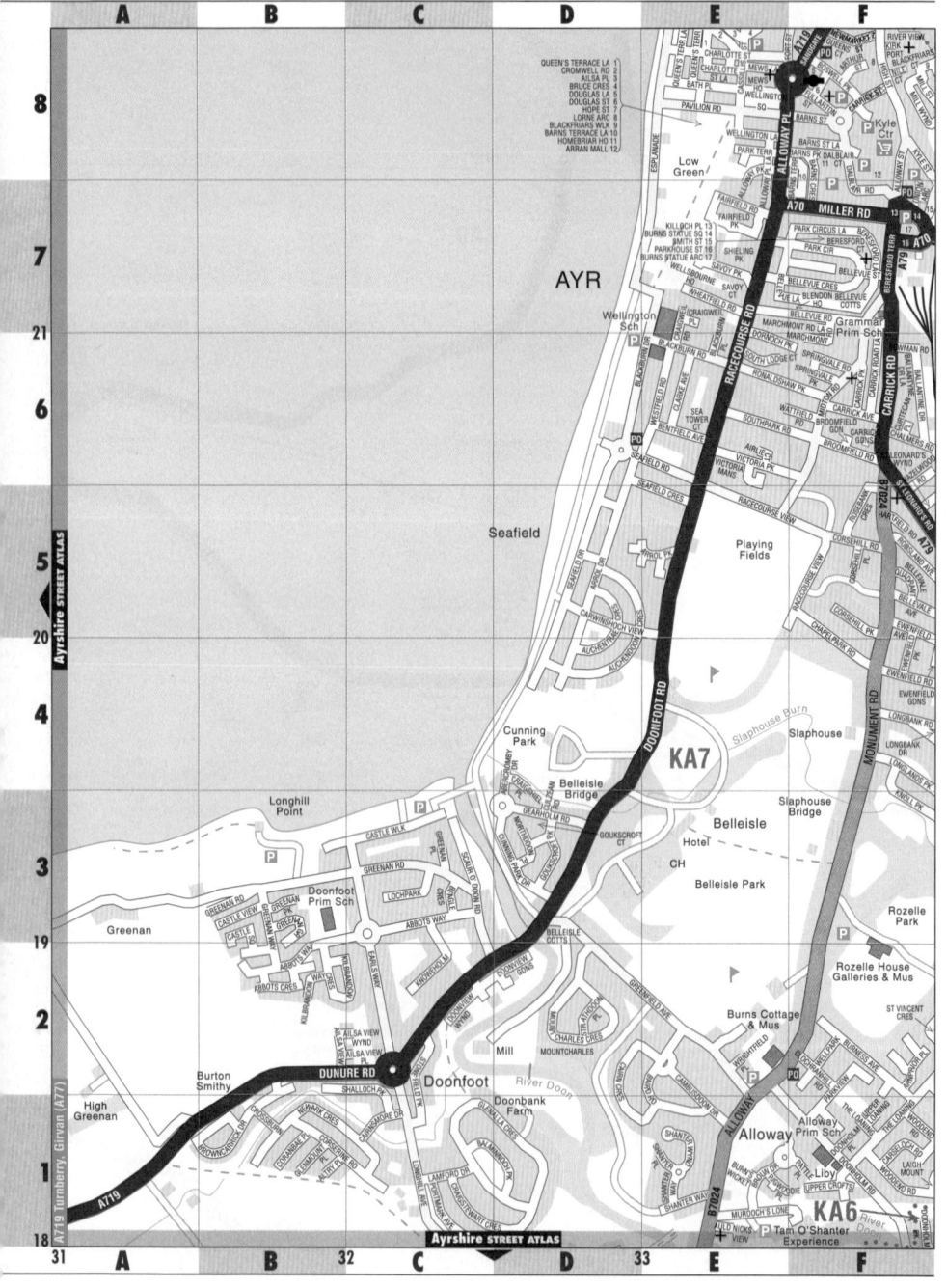

AYR

KA7

KA6

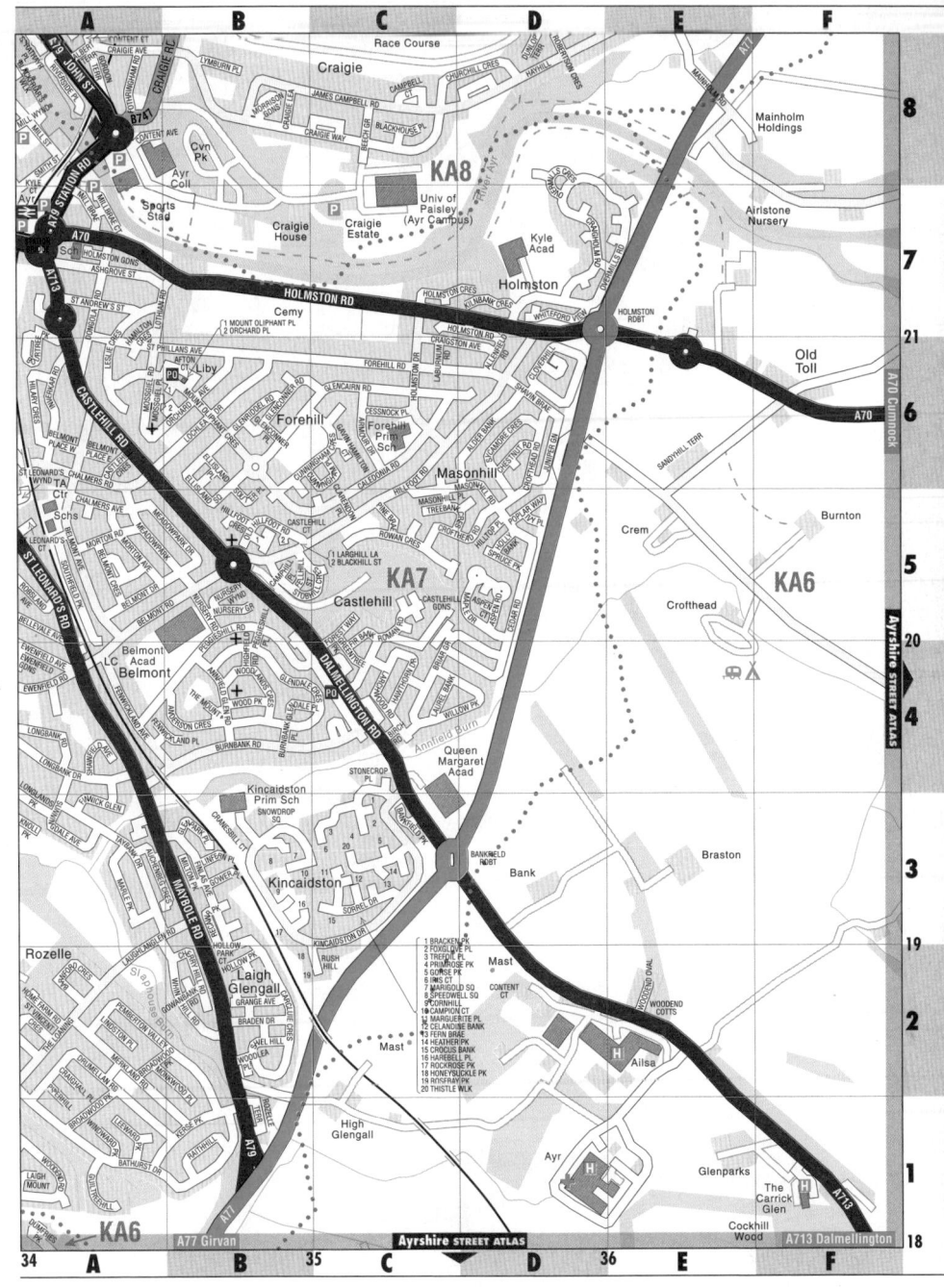

KA8

KA7

KA6

KA6

1 BRACKEN PK
2 FOXGLOVE PL
3 TREFOIL CT
4 PRIMROSE PK
5 GORSE PK
6 IRIS CT
7 MARIGOLD SQ
8 SPEEDWELL SQ
9 CORNHILL
10 CAMPION CT
11 MARGUERITE PL
12 CELANDINE BANK
13 FERN BRAE
14 HEATHER PK
15 CROCUS BANK
16 HAREBELL PL
17 ROCKROSE PK
18 HONEYSUCKLE PK
19 RYEGRASS PK
20 THISTLE WLK

1 MOUNT OLIPHANT PL
2 ORCHARD PL

1 LARGHILL LA
2 BLACKHILL ST

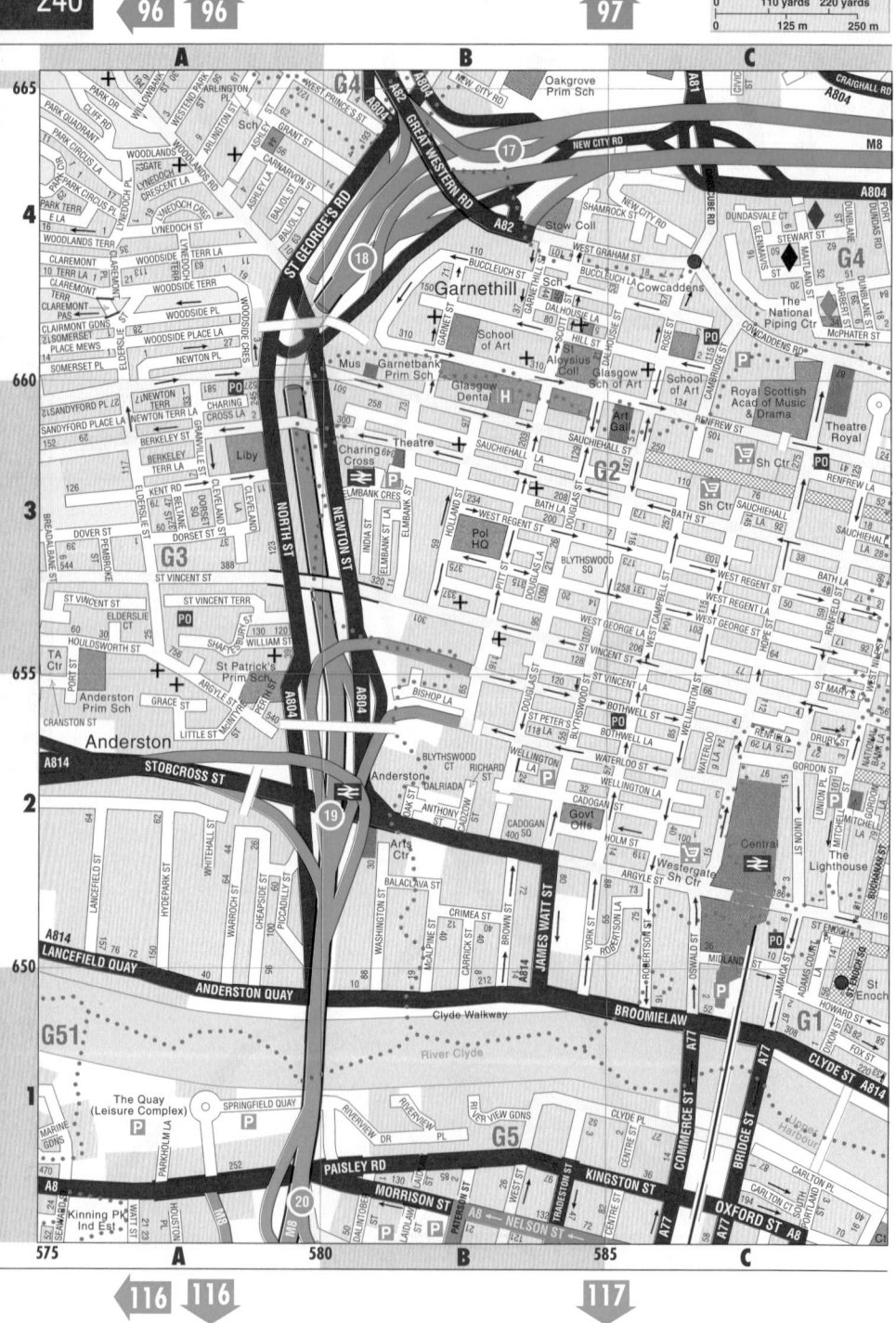

A   B   C

665

+ PARK DR
CLIFF RD
WILLOWBANK ST
WESTERN PARK
ARLINGTON
WEST PRINCES ST
G4
A804
A804
OAKGROVE
Oakgrove Prim Sch
NEW CITY RD
CIVIC ST
CRAIGHALL RD
A804
M8

PARK CIRCUS LA
PARK QUADRANT
ASHLEY ST
GRANT ST
Sch
ARLINGTON ST
17
NEW CITY RD

PARK CIRCUS PL
WOODLANDS GATE
LYNEDOCH PL
CRESCENT LA
CARNARVON ST
BALGIE LA
A82
STOW COLL
Stow Coll
NEW CITY RD
SHAMROCK ST
DUNDASVALE CT
STEWART ST
DUNBLANE ST
DUNDAS RD
POST
A804

4

PARK TERR LA
LYNEDOCH CRES
ST GEORGE'S RD
18
WEST GRAHAM ST
BUCCLEUCH ST
Sch
BUCCLEUCH LA
Cowcaddens
MALTA
MAITLAND ST
DUNBLANE ST
LAMBERT ST
McPHATER ST
G4

WOODLANDS TERR
CLAREMONT TERR LA
WOODSIDE TERR
WOODSIDE TERR LA
WOODSIDE PL
Garnethill
GARNET ST
DALHOUSIE LA
HILL ST
ROSE ST
COWCADDENS RD
The National Piping Ctr

CLAREMONT TERR
CLAREMONT GDNS
SOMERSET PLACE MEWS
WOODSIDE PLACE LA
NEWTON PL
Mus
Garnetbank Prim Sch
School of Art
ST
Aloysius Coll
Glasgow Sch of Art
School of Art
Royal Scottish Acad of Music & Drama
PO

660

SOMERSET PL
SANDYFORD PL
NEWTON TERR
NEWTON TERR LA
CHARING CROSS LA
Glasgow Dental
H
Art Gal
RENFREW ST
CAMBRIDGE ST
Theatre Royal

SANDYFORD PLACE LA
BERKELEY ST
BERKELEY TERR LA
GRANVILLE ST
Liby
Theatre
Charing Cross
SAUCHIEHALL LA
SAUCHIEHALL ST
SAUCHIEHALL LA
Sh Ctr
PO
RENFREW ST

3

KENT RD
ELDERSLIE ST
CLEVELAND LA
CLEVELAND ST
DOVER ST
DORSET ST
ELMBANK CRES
ELMBANK ST LA
INDIA ST
HOLLAND
WEST REGENT ST
BATH LA
BATH ST
Sh Ctr
SAUCHIEHALL ST
SAUCHIEHALL LA

BREADALBANE ST
PEMBROKE ST
DORSET ST
G3
ST VINCENT ST
Pol HQ
BLYTHSWOOD SQ
WEST REGENT ST
WEST REGENT LA
BATH LA

ST VINCENT ST
ELDERSLIE CT
ST VINCENT TERR
PO
WILLIAM ST
St Patrick's Prim Sch
BISHOP LA
WEST GEORGE ST
WEST GEORGE LA
WEST REGENT LA

HOULDSWORTH ST
SHAFTO
ARGYLE ST
LITTLE ST
PEEL ST
A804
A804
BISHOP LA
ST VINCENT ST
ST VINCENT LA
ST MARY'S
DRURY ST

655

TA Ctr
PORT ST
Anderston Prim Sch
GRACE ST
Anderston
BLYTHSWOOD CT
RICHARD ST
DALRIADA
WELLINGTON LA
ST PETER'S
BOTHWELL ST
PO
BOTHWELL LA
WATERLOO LA
WELLINGTON LA
RENFIELD ST
GORDON ST

CRANSTON ST
Anderston
A814
STOBCROSS ST
Anderston
ANTHONY
CADZOW
CADOGAN SQ
Govt Offs
CADOGAN ST
HOLM ST
Westergate Sh Ctr
UNION ST
MITCHELL LA
MITCHELL ST

2

19
Arts Ctr
BALACLAVA ST
OAK ST
CRIMEA ST
BROWN ST
JAMES WATT ST
ARGYLE ST
ROBERTSON ST
Central
The Lighthouse

WHITEHALL ST
HYDEPARK ST
WARROCH ST
CHEAPSIDE ST
PICCADILLY ST
WASHINGTON ST
McALPINE ST
CARRICK ST
A814
YORK ST
OSWALD ST
MIDLAND
PO
BUCHANAN ST

LANCEFIELD ST
A814
LANCEFIELD QUAY
ANDERSTON QUAY
Clyde Walkway
BROOMIELAW
St Enoch
ST ENOCH SQ
G1

650

G51
River Clyde
A77
A77
CLYDE ST
A814

1

MARINE GDNS
The Quay (Leisure Complex)
P
SPRINGFIELD QUAY
P
PARKHOLM LA
RIVERVIEW DR
RIVERVIEW
RIVER VIEW GDNS
CLYDE PL
CENTRE ST
G5
COMMERCE ST
BRIDGE ST
Jones Harbour

A8
SEAWARD
Kinning Pk Ind Est
M8
20
PAISLEY RD
MORRISON ST
NELSON ST
A8
PAISLEY RD
KINGSTON ST
TRADESTON ST
A77
OXFORD ST
A8
CARLTON PL

575   580   585

A   B   C

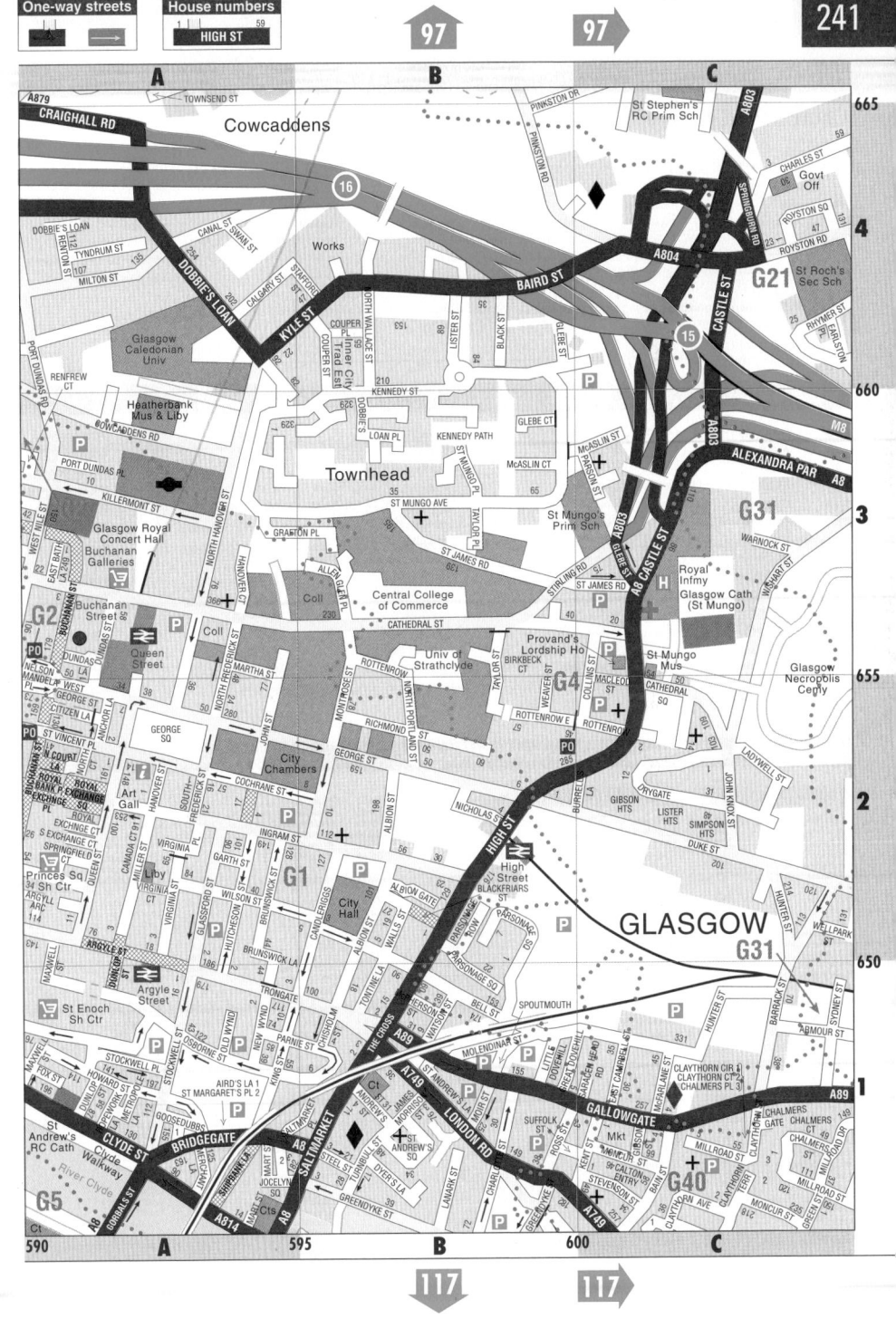

One-way streets
House numbers
1 59
HIGH ST

97 97

665
A879
TOWNSEND ST
CRAIGHALL RD
Cowcaddens
PINKSTON DR
PINKSTON RD
St Stephen's
RC Prim Sch
A803
SPRINGBURN RD
16
CHARLES ST
59
Govt
Off
DOBBIE'S LOAN
CANAL ST
SWAN ST
Works
BAIRD ST
A804
CASTLE ST
ROYSTON SQ
47
ROYSTON RD
4
TYNDRUM ST
RENTON ST
STAFFORD ST
CALGARY ST
COUPER ST
G21
St Roch's
Sec Sch
RHYMER ST
EARLSTON
MILTON ST
KYLE ST
COUPER ST
NORTH WALLACE ST
LISTER ST
BLACK ST
25
GLEBE ST
15
DOBBIE'S LOAN
Glasgow
Caledonian
Univ
RENFREW
CT
PORT DUNDAS RD
Heatherbank
Mus & Liby
COWCADDENS RD
KENNEDY ST
Inner City
Trad Est
KENNEDY PATH
KENNEDY ST
DOBBIE'S
LOAN PL
ST MUNGO PL
GLEBE CT
McASLIN ST
PARSON ST
McASLIN CT
A803
660
ALEXANDRA PAR
A8
M8
PORT DUNDAS PL
10
KILLERMONT ST
Townhead
ST MUNGO AVE
65
35
TAYLOR ST
St Mungo's
Prim Sch
G31
WARNOCK ST
3
Glasgow Royal
Concert Hall
Buchanan
Galleries
GRAFTON PL
ST JAMES RD
STIRLING RD
GLEBE ST
ST JAMES RD
A8 CASTLE ST
Royal
Infmy
Glasgow Cath
(St Mungo)
H
McASLIN ST
G2
Buchanan
Street
PO
DUNDAS
HANOVER CT
ALLEN GLEN PL
Coll
Central College
of Commerce
CATHEDRAL ST
Provand's
Lordship Ho
BIRKBECK
CT
St Mungo
Mus
MACLEOD
CATHEDRAL
SQ
Glasgow
Necropolis
Cemy
655
Queen
Street
NORTH HANOVER ST
NORTH FREDERICK ST
Coll
ROTTENROW
Univ of
Strathclyde
TAYLOR ST
WEAVER ST
COLLINS ST
ROTTENROW
NELSON
MANDELA
PL
GEORGE ST
NORTH PORTLAND ST
RICHMOND ST
ROTTENROW E
G4
ROTTENROW
LADYWELL ST
CITIZEN LA
ST VINCENT PL
GEORGE
SQ
JOHN ST
GEORGE ST
PO
DRYGATE
JOHN KNOX ST
2
IN COURT
LA
ROYAL
BANK PL
EXCHANGE
PL
ROYAL
EXCHANGE
SQ
City
Chambers
COCHRANE ST
HIGH ST
GIBSON
HTS
LISTER
HTS
SIMPSON
HTS
DUKE ST
Art
Gall
FREDERICK ST
INGRAM ST
NICHOLAS ST
BURRELL
HUNTER ST
S EXCHANGE CT
SPRINGFIELD CT
CANADA CT
VIRGINIA ST
GARTH ST
ALBION ST
High
Street
WELLPARK
Princes Sq
34 Sh Ctr
ARGYLL
ARC
114
Liby
VIRGINIA ST
WILSON ST
BLACKFRIARS
ST
GLASGOW
G31
650
MAXWELL
GLASSFORD ST
BRUNSWICK ST
City
Hall
PARSONAGE
ROW
PARSONAGE SQ
HUNTER ST
BARRACK ST
SYDNEY ST
DIXON ST
Argyle
Street
HUTCHESON ST
BRUNSWICK LA
ALBION ST
TRONGATE
CANDLERIGGS
SPOUTMOUTH
St Enoch
Sh Ctr
STOCKWELL PL
STOCKWELL ST
OLD WYND
NEW WYND
KING ST
PARNIE ST
CHISHOLM ST
THE CROSS
A89
BELL'S
JACKSON ST
MOLENDINAR
LITTLE
DOVEHILL
GREAT DOVEHILL
ARMOUR ST
331
1
FOX ST
HOWARD ST
A749
ST ANDREW'S LA
ST ANDREW'S
SQ
ST JAMES
MORRISON
ROSS ST
CAMLACHIE
GALLOWGATE
A89
CHALMERS
GATE CHALMERS
CLAYTHORN CIR
CLAYTHORN CT
CHALMERS PL
St
Andrew's
RC Cath
CLYDE ST
BRIDGEGATE
A8
SALTMARKET
ST
ANDREW'S
SQ
LONDON RD
SUFFOLK
Mkt
CALTON
ENTRY
MILLROAD ST
CHALMERS
G40
MILLROAD ST
G5
Clyde
Walkway
River Clyde
JOCELYN SQ
GREENDYKE ST
A814
LANARK ST
A749
CLAYTHORN AVE
STEVENSON ST
MONCUR ST
GREEN ST
590 595 B 600 C

117 117

Index

Church Rd 6 Beckenham BR2.......... **53** C6

Place name	Location number	Locality, town or village	Postcode	Page and
May be abbreviated on the map	Present when a number indicates the place's position in a crowded area of mapping	Shown when more than one place has the same name	district District for the indexed place	grid square Page number and grid reference for the standard mapping

Public and commercial buildings are highlighted in magenta **Places of interest** are highlighted in blue with a star ★

Abbreviations used in the index

Acad	Academy	Comm	Common	Gd	Ground	L	Leisure	Prom	Promenade
App	Approach	Cott	Cottage	Gdn	Garden	La	Lane	Rd	Road
Arc	Arcade	Cres	Crescent	Gn	Green	Liby	Library	Recn	Recreation
Ave	Avenue	Cswy	Causeway	Gr	Grove	Mdw	Meadow	Ret	Retail
Bglw	Bungalow	Ct	Court	H	Hall	Meml	Memorial	Sh	Shopping
Bldg	Building	Ctr	Centre	Ho	House	Mkt	Market	Sq	Square
Bsns, Bus	Business	Ctry	Country	Hospl	Hospital	Mus	Museum	St	Street
Bvd	Boulevard	Cty	County	HQ	Headquarters	Orch	Orchard	Sta	Station
Cath	Cathedral	Dr	Drive	Hts	Heights	Pal	Palace	Terr	Terrace
Cir	Circus	Dro	Drove	Ind	Industrial	Par	Parade	TH	Town Hall
Cl	Close	Ed	Education	Inst	Institute	Pas	Passage	Univ	University
Cnr	Corner	Emb	Embankment	Int	International	Pk	Park	Wk, Wlk	Walk
Coll	College	Est	Estate	Intc	Interchange	Pl	Place	Wr	Water
Com	Community	Ex	Exhibition	Junc	Junction	Prec	Precinct	Yd	Yard

Index of localities, towns and villages

A

B

C

Bank St *continued*
Paisley PA1 .....113 F5
Prestwick KA9 .....236 B8
Slamannan FK1 .....86 A6
7 Stirling FK8 .....7 A8
Troon KA10 .....229 C2
Bank View ML6 .....123 D2
Bank Way 14 ML9 .....185 B4
Bankbrae Ave G53 .....135 A6
Bankend Pl KA3 .....223 A5
Bankend Rd
Bridge of W PA11 .....110 E7
Dumbarton G82 .....49 F4
Bankend St G33 .....99 A1
Bankfaulds Ave KA25 .....149 A1
Bankfaulds Ct 7 KA25 .....149 A1
Bankfield Dr ML3 .....183 D7
Bankfield Pk KA7 .....239 C3
Bankfield Rdbt KA7 .....239 D3
Bankfoot Dr G52 .....115 B4
Bankfoot Pl G77 .....157 B4
Bankfoot Rd
Glasgow G52 .....115 B4
Paisley PA3 .....113 B6
Bankglen Rd G15 .....75 B4
Bankhall St G42 .....117 B2
Bankhead Ave
Airdrie ML6 .....123 D7
Bellshill ML4 .....142 B3
Coatbridge ML5 .....121 C4
Glasgow G13 .....95 A6
Springside KA11 .....221 A2
Bankhead Cres FK4 .....39 D6
Bankhead Dr G73 .....138 A7
Bankhead Pl Airdrie ML6 .123 D7
Coatbridge ML5 .....121 C4
Stewarton KA3 .....195 E2
Bankhead Prim Sch
Glasgow G13 .....95 A6
Rutherglen G73 .....137 F7
Bankhead Rd
Carmunnock G76 .....158 D7
Fishcross FK10 .....5 D3
Kilwinning KA13 .....207 F3
Kirkintilloch G66 .....80 B7
Rutherglen G73 .....137 F7
Bankhead Terr ML11 .....215 B2
Bankholm Pl G76 .....157 F5
Bankier Prim Sch FK4 .....38 E3
Bankier Rd FK4 .....38 E3
Bankier Terr FK4 .....38 E3
Banknock St G32 .....118 E6
Banks Rd G66 .....58 E1
Banks View FK2 .....14 E4
Bankside FK2 .....42 C7
Bankside Ave PA5 .....111 F3
Bankside Ct FK6 .....21 E2
Bankside Gdns KA25 .....149 A4
Bankside Ind Est FK2 .....42 D8
Banktop Pl PA5 .....111 F3
Bankview Cres G66 .....79 A8
Bankview Dr G66 .....79 A8
Bankview Terr FK4 .....39 E6
Bannachra Cres G83 .....27 D6
Bannachra Dr G84 .....16 B2
Bannatyne Ave G31 .....118 B7
Bannatyne St ML11 .....215 B4
Banner Dr G13 .....75 C1
Banner Rd G13 .....75 D1
Bannercross Ave 2
G69 .....120 A5
Bannercross Dr G69 .....120 A5
Bannercross Gdns 1
G69 .....120 A5
Bannerman Dr
Bellshill ML4 .....142 D5
Kilmarnock KA3 .....223 D2
Bannerman High Sch
G69 .....120 A4
Bannerman Pl G81 .....74 B2
Bannoch Gdns KA13 .....208 A4
Bannoch Pl KA13 .....208 A3
Bannoch Rd
Kilwinning KA13 .....208 A2
Kilwinning KA13 .....208 A3
Bannock Rd FK7 .....8 C4
Bannockburn Cross FK7 .....7 E1
Bannockburn Dr 19
ML9 .....185 C1
Bannockburn Heritage Ctr*
FK7 .....7 B2
Bannockburn High Sch
FK7 .....7 D2
Bannockburn Hospl FK7 ..11 F7
Bannockburn Pl
Kilmarnock KA3 .....223 B3
Motherwell ML1 .....143 A2
Bannockburn Prim Sch
FK7 .....7 E1
Bannockburn Rd
Cowie FK7 .....12 C8
Stirling FK7 .....7 C3
Bannockburn St PA16 .....45 C3
Bannockburn Station Rd
Bannockburn FK7 .....7 F2
Fallin FK7 .....8 A4
Bantaskin Prim Sch FK1 ..41 E4
Bantaskin St G20 .....96 C7
Bantaskine Dr FK1 .....41 F4
Bantaskine Gdns FK1 .....41 E3
Bantaskine Rd FK1 .....41 F4
Bantaskine St FK1 .....41 E3
Banton Pl
Bonnybridge FK4 .....40 A3
Glasgow G33 .....120 A7
Banton Prim Sch G65 .....37 E3
Banton Rd G65 .....37 D2
Banyan Cres G71 .....121 D1
Bar Hill Pl G65 .....60 B8
Bar Hill Roman Fort*
G65 .....60 B4
Barassie G74 .....159 D3
Barassie Cres G68 .....61 F6
Barassie Ct G71 .....140 F2
Barassie Dr PA11 .....110 C6
Barassie Pl KA1 .....227 E4
Barassie Prim Sch KA10 .229 E5
Barassie St KA10 .....229 D3
Barassie Sta KA10 .....229 E6
Barassiebank La KA10 ...229 E6
Barbadoes Pl KA1 .....227 E6
Barbadoes Rd KA1 .....227 E6
Barbados Gn 5 G75 .....159 A1
Barbae Pl G71 .....141 A3
Barbana Rd G74 .....158 E2
Barbegs Cres G65 .....60 F4
Barberry Ave G53 .....135 B2
Barberry Dr KA15 .....171 A8
Barberry Gdns G53 .....135 B2
Barberry Pl G53 .....135 C2
Barbeth Gdns G67 .....82 B6
Barbeth Pl
Cumbernauld G67 .....82 B6
Irvine KA11 .....220 A5
Barbeth Rd G67 .....82 B6
Barbeth Way G67 .....82 A6
Barbour Ave FK7 .....7 C3
Barbour's Pk KA3 .....211 E8
Barbreck Rd 7 G42 .....116 F2
Barcaldine Ave G69 .....80 B1
Barcaldine Terr G41 .....116 F2
Barcapel Ave G77 .....156 E8
Barcapel Flats G77 .....156 E7
Barclaven Rd PA13 .....89 E8
Barclay Ave PA5 .....112 B2
Barclay Ct G60 .....73 B6
Barclay Dr
Helensburgh G84 .....16 C3
Kilmarnock KA3 .....223 C2
Barclay Gdns KA11 .....220 D6
Barclay Pl KA3 .....195 D1
Barclay Rd ML1 .....163 B6
Barclay Sq PA4 .....94 B1
Barclay St Glasgow G21 ....97 F5
Old Kilpatrick G60 .....73 B5
Barcloy Pl ML6 .....123 F1
Barcraigs Dr PA2 .....133 F8
Bard Ave G13 .....95 B8
Bardowie Ind Est G22 .....97 C4
Bardowie St Glasgow G22 .97 B4
Glasgow G22 .....97 C4
Bardrain Ave PA5 .....112 C2
Bardrain Rd PA2 .....133 C7
Bardrainney Ave PA14 .....68 F7
Bardrill Dr G64 .....77 E1
Bardykes Rd
Blantyre G72 .....140 C1
Hamilton G72 .....161 B8
Barefield St ML9 .....185 A4
Barfillan Dr G52 .....115 E5
Bargany Ct G53 .....115 A1
Bargany Pl
8 Glasgow G53 .....115 A1
Glasgow G53 .....115 B1
Bargany Rd G53 .....115 A1
Bargaran Rd G53 .....115 B3
Bargarran Prim Sch PA8 ..72 F2
Bargarran Rd PA8 .....72 F3
Bargarran Sq PA8 .....73 A3
Bargarron Dr PA3 .....114 A8
Barge Ct G84 .....15 D5
Bargeddie Prim Sch
G69 .....121 A6
Bargeddie St G33 .....98 D2
Bargeddie Sta G69 .....121 A4
Bargeny KA13 .....207 B2
Bargrennan Rd KA10 .....229 G6
Barhill La G65 .....59 F4
Barhill Rd PA8 .....73 A2
Barhill Terr G65 .....60 A4
Barholm Sq G33 .....99 D1
Barke Rd G67 .....62 A3
Barkin Ct FK1 .....42 B2
Barkly Terr 2 G75 .....180 C8
Barlae Ave G76 .....178 E8
Barlanark Ave G32 .....119 C6
Barlanark Cres G33 .....119 D7
Barlanark Dr G33 .....119 D7
Barlanark Pl
Glasgow G33 .....119 E7
Glasgow,Greenfield G32 ...119 B6
Barlanark Prim Sch
G33 .....119 F6
Barlanark Rd G33 .....119 E7
Barlandfauld St G65 .....60 E7
Barleith Ct KA1 .....228 F5
Barleyhill FK4 .....40 B5
Barlia Dr G45 .....137 E3
Barlia Gdns G45 .....137 E3
Barlia Gr G45 .....137 E3
Barlia St G45 .....137 E3
Barlia Terr G45 .....137 F3
Barloan Cres G82 .....50 A5
Barloan Pl G82 .....50 A5
Barloch Ave G62 .....55 A2
Barloch Rd G62 .....55 B2
Barloch St Glasgow G22 ...97 C4
Glasgow G22 .....97 C5
Barlogan Ave G52 .....115 E5
Barlogan Quadrant G52 .115 E5
Barmore Ave ML8 .....202 A8
Barmouth Ave PA19 .....44 F5
Barmulloch Prim Sch
G21 .....98 C4
Barmulloch Rd G21 .....98 B4
Barn Gn PA10 .....111 A3
Barn Rd FK8 .....7 A8
Barnard Gdns G64 .....78 B4
Barnbeth Rd G53 .....115 B2
Barncluith Ave ML3 .....163 A2
Barncluith Bsns Ctr
ML3 .....162 F3
Barncluith Ct ML3 .....162 F3
Barncluith Rd ML3 .....162 F2
Barnego Rd FK6 .....21 D3
Barnes St G78 .....134 B2
Barness Pl G33 .....119 A8
Barnett Cres KA21 .....216 F7
Barnett Ct KA21 .....216 F7
Barnett Path 3 G72 .....161 D7
Barnflat St G73 .....118 B1
Barnford Cres KA7 .....239 A2
Barnhill Ct G77 .....156 D3
Barnhill Dr Glasgow G21 ..98 A3
Hamilton ML3 .....161 D2
Newton Mearns G77 .....156 D2
Tullibody FK10 .....4 C2
Barnhill Rd G82 .....50 D3
Barnhill St PA15 .....46 C3
Barnhill Sta G21 .....98 A3
Barnkirk Ave G15 .....75 A3
Barns Cres KA7 .....238 F8
Barns Pk KA7 .....238 F8
Barns St Ayr KA7 .....238 F8
Clydebank G81 .....94 C8
Barns Street La KA7 .....238 F8
Barns Terr KA7 .....238 F8
Barns Terrace La KA7 ...238 F8
Barnscroft PA5,PA10 .....111 B4
Barnsdale Rd FK7 .....7 A3
Barnsford Ave PA4 .....93 B4
Barnsford Rd
Inchinnan PA4 .....93 B3
Paisley PA3 .....113 B8
Barnswood Pl 6 G71 .....141 B3
Barnton La FK1 .....42 B4
Barnton St Glasgow G32 ..118 E7
Stirling FK8 .....7 B8
Barnweil Ave KA9 .....236 C6
Barnweil Dr KA1 .....228 E5
Barnweil Rd KA1 .....227 E5
Barnwell Rd FK9 .....2 C4
Barnwell Terr G51 .....115 E7
Barochan Cres PA3 .....113 A4
Barochan Pl G53 .....115 B3
Barochan Rd
Bellshill ML4 .....142 D6
Brookfield PA3,PA6,PA10,
PA11 .....111 D6
Glasgow G53 .....115 B3
Houston PA6 .....91 B6
Barochan Way PA3 .....113 A4
Baron Ct ML3 .....163 A2
Baron Path G69 .....120 F5
Baron Rd PA3 .....114 A6
Baron St PA4 .....94 C2
Baron's Haugh Nature
Reserve* ML1 .....163 E2
Baronald Dr G12 .....96 B6
Baronald Gate G12 .....96 B6
Baronald St G73 .....118 B1
Barone Dr G76 .....157 C8
Baronhall Dr G72 .....161 C8
Baronhill G67 .....62 B5
Barons Gate G71 .....140 E4
Barons Rd ML1 .....164 C2
Barons Twr ML1 .....164 B3
Baronscourt Dr PA1 .....112 F4
Baronscourt Gdns PA1 ..112 F4
Baronscourt Rd PA1 .....112 F4
Barony Ct
Ardrossan KA22 .....205 D1
Cambusbarron FK7 .....6 D6
4 Glasgow G69 .....120 B6
Irvine KA11 .....219 F5
Barony Dr G69 .....120 B5
Barony Gdns G69 .....120 B5
Barony Glebe KA23 .....190 D5
Barony Pl G68 .....60 E1
Barony Rd KA9 .....236 C6
Barony Terr KA25 .....170 A8
Barony Wynd 5 G69 .....120 B6
Barr Ave G78 .....154 E8
Barr Cres Clydebank G81 ..74 B5
Irvine KA12 .....219 C4
Barr Farm Rd G65 .....60 E7
Barr Gr G71 .....141 A8
Barr Pl
Newton Mearns G77 .....156 C5
Paisley PA1 .....113 D4
Barr St Ardrossan KA22 ...205 C1
Glasgow G20 .....97 A3
Motherwell ML1 .....163 E8
Barr Terr G74 .....159 E2
Barr's Brae
Kilmacolm PA13 .....69 D1
Port Glasgow PA14 .....68 C8
Barra Ave
Coatbridge ML5 .....121 E4
Renfrew PA4 .....94 C1
Wishaw ML2 .....165 E5
Barra Cres Irvine KA11 ...220 C2
Old Kilpatrick G60 .....73 C5
Barra Dr ML6 .....123 E6
Barra Gdns G60 .....73 C5
Barra La KA11 .....220 C2
Barra Pl Coatbridge ML5 ..121 E4
Irvine KA11 .....220 C2
Stenhousemuir FK5 .....24 A4
Stevenston KA20 .....206 F2
Barra Rd G60 .....73 C5
Barra St G20 .....96 C8
Barra Wynd KA11 .....220 C2
Barrachnie Ave G69 .....120 A6
Barrachnie Cres G69 .....119 F5
Barrachnie Ct G69 .....119 F6
Barrachnie Dr G69 .....120 A5
Barrachnie Gr G69 .....120 A6
Barrachnie Pl 4 G69 .....120 A6
Barrachnie Rd G69 .....119 F5
Barrack St Glasgow G4 ...241 C1
Hamilton ML3 .....162 D4
Barras Mkt G4 .....241 C1
Barraston Holdings G64 ..57 A3
Barraston Rd Fluchter G64 .56 F4
Torrance G64 .....57 A2
Barrbridge Rd ML5 .....121 B4
Barrcraig Rd PA11 .....110 C8
Barrhead High Sch G78 .134 D3
Barrhead Mus G78 .....134 C2
Barrhead Rd
Glasgow G43,G53 .....135 C7
Newton Mearns G77 .....156 B5
Paisley PA2 .....114 A2
Barrhead Sta G78 .....134 B3
Barrhill Cres PA10 .....111 C3
Barrhill Ct G66 .....80 A8
Barrhill Rd Erskine PA8 ....73 A2
Gourock PA19 .....44 D8
Kirkintilloch G66 .....80 A8
Barrie Quadrant G81 .....74 A4
Barrie Rd
East Kilbride G74 .....160 D5
Glasgow G52 .....115 A7
Stenhousemuir FK5 .....23 F3
Barrie St ML1 .....163 E6
Barrie Terr KA22 .....205 D1
Barriedale Ave ML3 .....162 B3
Barrington Ave KA15 .....150 B1
Barrington Dr G4 .....96 F2
Barrington Gdns KA15 ..150 C1
Barrisdale Rd
Glasgow G20 .....96 D8
Wishaw ML2 .....165 F6
Barrisdale Way G73 .....138 B4
Barrland Ct G46 .....136 C3
Barrland Dr G46 .....136 C3
Barrland St G41 .....117 A3
Barrmill Rd Beith KA15 ...171 C8
Burnhouse KA15 .....172 B2
Glasgow G43 .....136 B5
Barrochan Intc PA5 .....111 E4
Barrowfield Prim Sch
G40 .....118 A5
Barrowfield St
Coatbridge ML5 .....121 F4
Glasgow G40 .....118 A5
Barrpath G65 .....60 F7
Barrs Brae La PA14 .....47 C1
Barrs Cres G82 .....48 A8
Barrs Ct G82 .....26 A1
Barrs La ML8 .....187 F3
Barrs Rd G82 .....48 A8
Barrs Terr G82 .....48 A8
Barrwood Pl G71 .....141 A8
Barrwood St G33 .....98 E2
Barry Gdns G72 .....161 D6
Barsail Prim Sch PA8 .....93 C8
Barscube Ave PA14 .....68 E7
Barscube Terr PA2 .....114 A2
Barshaw Dr PA1 .....114 A6
Barshaw Ho PA1 .....114 C5
Barshaw Pl PA1 .....114 D5
Barshaw Rd G52 .....114 F6
Barskiven Rd PA1 .....112 F4
Barterholm Rd PA2 .....113 F2
Bartholomew St G40 .....118 A3
Bartie Gdns ML9 .....185 F1
Bartiebeith Rd G33 .....119 E7
Bartlands Pl G76 .....178 F4
Barton Ave G83 .....28 A8
Bartonhall Rd ML2 .....165 D1
Bartonholm Terr KA13 ...207 F1
Barty's Rd ML4 .....142 C5
Barwheys Dr KA6 .....237 F6
Barwood Hill G82 .....50 B6
Bassett Ave G13 .....95 B8
Bassett Cres G13 .....95 B8
Bastion Wynd 7 FK8 .....7 B7
Bath La G2 .....240 B3
Bath Pl KA7 .....238 E8
Bath Sq KA22 .....216 C8
Bath St Glasgow G2 .....240 C3
Gourock PA19 .....44 E8
Kilmarnock KA3 .....222 F3
Bath Villas KA22 .....216 C8
Bathgate St G31 .....118 A6
Bathgo Ave PA1 .....114 E4
Bathurst Dr KA7 .....239 A1
Bathville Rd KA25 .....149 A1
Baton Rd ML7 .....146 D6
Batson St G42 .....117 B2
Batterflatts Gdns FK7 .....6 F6
Batterflatts Ho FK7 .....6 F6
Battery Park Ave PA16 .....45 B8
Battery Park Dr PA16 .....45 B8
Battismains ML11 .....215 C4
Battle Pl G42 .....136 F8
Battlefield Ave G42 .....137 A7
Battlefield Ct G42 .....137 B7
Battlefield Gdns G42 .....137 A8
Battlefield Prim Sch
G42 .....136 F7
Battlefield Rd G42 .....137 A7
Battles Burn Dr G32 .....119 A2
Battles Burn Gate G32 ..119 A2
Battles Burn View G32 ..119 A2
Bavelaw St G33 .....99 D2
Bawhirley Rd PA15 .....46 C3
Baxter Cres FK6 .....21 C1
Baxter La Alexandria G83 ..27 E7
Lanark ML11 .....215 A4
Baxter St Fallin FK7 .....8 D4
Greenock PA15 .....46 D3
Baxter Wynd ML2 .....164 E2
Baxter's Wynd FK1 .....42 B4
Bay St PA14 .....47 C1
Bay View Rd PA19 .....44 F7
Bay Willow Ct G72 .....139 F4
Bayfield Ave G15 .....75 A3
Bayfield Terr G15 .....75 A3
Bayne St FK8 .....2 A1
Beach Dr KA12 .....218 F1
Beach Rd Troon KA10 .....229 D7
Troon KA10 .....229 E5
Beacon Pl G33 .....118 F8
Beaconcroft FK9 .....2 C7
Beaconhurst Sch FK9 .....2 C6
Beaconsfield Rd G12 .....96 B5
Beagle Cres KA7 .....238 C3
Bean Row FK1 .....42 B4
Beansburn KA3 .....223 A3
Beanshields Rd ML8 .....201 F4
Beard Cres G69 .....101 A5
Beardmore Cotts PA4 .....93 E6
Beardmore Pl G81 .....73 E3
Beardmore St G81 .....73 E3
Beardmore Way
Clydebank G81 .....73 D2
Glasgow G31 .....118 B6
Bearford Dr G52 .....115 B6
Bearhope St PA15 .....45 F5
Bearsden Acad G61 .....75 E6
Bearsden Bath Ho* G61 ..75 F5
Bearsden Prim Sch G61 ..75 E5
Bearsden Rd
Bearsden G61 .....95 F7
Bearsden G61 .....95 F8
Bearsden Sta G61 .....75 E4
Bearside Rd FK7 .....7 A3
Beaton Ave FK7 .....7 C1
Beaton La KA2 .....225 F1
Beaton Rd Balloch G83 .....27 E8
Glasgow G41 .....116 E2
Beaton St ML9 .....184 F5
Beaton Terr KA12 .....219 C5
Beatrice Dr ML1 .....142 F5
Beatrice Gdns PA6 .....111 D8
Beatson Wynd G71 .....121 A1
Beattie Ct KA20 .....217 D7
Beattock St G31 .....118 D5
Beattock Wynd ML3 .....162 A3
Beatty Ave FK8 .....2 A2
Beatty Pl G84 .....17 A2
Beatty St G81 .....73 E3
Beauclerc St FK12 .....5 A7
Beaufield Gdns KA3 .....222 B7
Beaufort Ave G43 .....136 C6
Beaufort Dr Falkirk FK2 ...24 A3
Kirkintilloch G66 .....79 B8
Beaufort Gdns G64 .....77 E1
Beauly Cres Airdrie ML6 ..123 E6
Kilmacolm PA13 .....89 D7
Kilmarnock KA1 .....228 A5
Newton Mearns G77 .....157 B4
Wishaw ML2 .....165 B1
Beauly Ct FK1 .....42 C1
Beauly Dr PA2 .....112 E1
Beauly Pl
Bishopbriggs G64 .....78 D2
Chryston G69 .....80 D1
Coatbridge ML5 .....122 B3
East Kilbride G74 .....159 D2
6 Glasgow G20 .....96 D6
Motherwell ML1 .....143 A5
Beauly Rd G69 .....120 A3
Beaumont Dr FK2 .....24 B2
Beaumont Gate 5 G12 .....96 C3
Beckfield Cres G33 .....98 D7
Beckfield Dr G33 .....98 D7
Beckfield Gate G33 .....98 D7
Beckfield Gr G33 .....98 D7
Beckfield Wlk G33 .....98 D7
Beckford La ML3 .....162 D5
Beckford Prim Sch ML3 .162 C5
Beckford St ML3 .....162 D5
Beckford St Bsns Ctr
ML3 .....162 D5
Beda Pl FK7 .....8 C5
Bedale Rd G69 .....119 F4
Bedcow View G66 .....79 F7
Bedford Ave G81 .....74 D2
Bedford Ct FK10 .....10 A6
Bedford La 6 G5 .....117 B5
Bedford Pl FK10 .....10 A6
Bedford St Glasgow G5 .....117 B5
Greenock PA16 .....45 D7
Bedlay Ct G69 .....81 A3
Bedlay Pl ML5 .....81 F1
Bedlay View G71 .....141 B8
Bedlay Wlk G69 .....81 A3
Bedlormie Dr EH48 .....107 C2
Beech Ave Bearsden G61 ..76 A7
Beith KA15 .....150 B2
Bridge Of W PA11 .....90 D1
Cambuslang G72 .....138 F6
Elderslie PA5 .....112 C2
Glasgow,Dumbreck G41 ...116 B4
Glasgow,Garrowhill G69 ...120 A5
Glasgow,Ibrox G41 .....116 B5
Irvine KA12 .....219 D2
Kilmarnock KA1 .....227 D8
Larkhall ML9 .....185 D2
Motherwell ML1 .....143 B3
Newton Mearns G77 .....156 E4
Paisley PA2 .....114 A1
Plean FK7 .....12 C3

Birkhall Ave
Glasgow G52 115 A4
Inchinnan PA4 93 D7
Birkhall Dr G61 75 F2
Birkhill Ave G64 78 B2
Birkhill Gdns G64 78 B2
Birkhill Rd
Crossford ML8,ML11 201 D2
Hamilton ML3 183 D7
Stirling FK7 6 E6
Birkmyre Ave PA14 47 A2
Birks Ct ML8 186 F5
Birks Hill KA11 220 A4
Birks Pl ML11 215 A5
Birks Rd Larkhall ML9 199 B7
Law ML8 186 E3
Birkscairn Pl KA11 220 C2
Birkscairn Way KA11 220 C2
Birkshaw Brae ML2 186 A8
Birkshaw Pl ML2 186 A8
Birkshaw Twr ML2 185 F8
Birkwood Pl G77 156 D2
Birkwood St G40 118 B2
Birmingham Rd PA4 94 B1
Birnam Ave G64 78 B2
Birnam Cres G61 76 B5
Birnam Ct FK2 24 C1
Birnam Gdns G64 78 B2
Birnam Pl Falkirk FK2 42 C5
Hamilton ML3 161 E3
Newton Mearns G77 157 B4
Birnam Rd G31 118 D3
Birness Dr G43 136 D7
Birnie Ct G21 98 C4
Birnie Rd G21 98 C3
Birnie Well Rd FK1 86 A6
Birniehill Rd ML1 145 A5
Birniehill Rdbt G74 181 A8
Birnock Ave PA4 94 E1
Birnyhill Ct G81 74 A7
Birrell Rd G62 54 F3
Birrens Rd ML1 163 C8
Birsay Rd G22 97 B7
Bishop Gdns
Bishopbriggs G64 77 E2
Hamilton ML3 183 E7
Bishop La G2 240 B2
Bishopbriggs High Sch
G64 78 A1
Bishopbriggs Ind Est
G21 98 A7
Bishopbriggs Sta G64 78 A1
Bishopdale G74 159 C3
Bishoploch Prim Sch
G34 100 D1
Bishopmill Pl G21 98 C4
Bishopmill Rd G21 98 C4
Bishops Gate G74 158 C3
Bishops Pk G74 158 B3
Bishopsgate Dr G21 97 E7
Bishopsgate Gdns G21 97 E7
Bishopsgate Pl 3 G21 97 E7
Bishopsgate Rd G21 97 E7
Bishopton Prim Sch PA7 72 A3
Bishopton Sta PA7 72 B2
Bissett Cres G81 73 E6
Black O' Hill Rdbt G68 61 B1
Black St Airdrie ML6 103 B1
Glasgow G4 241 B4
Blackadder Pl G75 179 D7
Blackbog Rd ML6 82 F2
Blackbraes Rd
California FK1 66 F4
East Kilbride G74 160 B4
Blackburn Cres
Dumbarton G82 49 D4
Kirkintilloch G66 80 A8
Blackburn Dr KA7 238 E6
Blackburn Pl KA7 238 E6
Blackburn Rd KA7 238 E6
Blackburn Sq G78 134 D1
Blackburn St G51 116 E6
Blackbyres Ct G78 134 D4
Blackbyres Rd G78 134 C5
Blackcraig Ave G15 75 A3
Blackcroft Ave ML6 123 E5
Blackcroft Gdns G32 119 D4
Blackcroft Rd G32 119 D4
Blackcroft Terr ML7 125 B2
Blackdyke Rd G66 79 E8
Blackfarm Rd G77 156 F4
Blackfaulds Dr KA3 213 A4
Blackfaulds Gdns KA3 213 A4
Blackfaulds Rd G73 137 E8
Blackford Cres KA9 233 E1
Blackford Rd PA2 114 A3
Blackfriars Ct KA7 238 F8
Blackfriars Prim Sch
G5 117 C4
Blackfriars St G1 241 B2
Blackfriars Wlk KA7 238 F8
Blackgrange Rdbt FK9 3 D3
Blackhall Ct PA2 114 B3
Blackhall La PA1 113 F3
Blackhall St Paisley PA1 114 A3
Shotts ML7 147 B3
Blackhill Dr G84 16 D4
Blackhill Pl G33 98 D2
Blackhill Rd
Blackridge EH48 107 F3
Glasgow G23 76 E2
Blackhill St KA7 239 B5
Blackhill View ML8 187 A4
Blackhouse Ave G77 156 F4
Blackhouse Gdns G77 156 F4
Blackhouse Pl KA8 239 C8
Blackhouse Rd G77 156 F4
Blackie St G3 96 D1
Blacklands Ave KA13 207 E2
Blacklands Cres KA13 207 E1
Blacklands Pl G66 79 F4
Blacklands Prim Sch
KA13 207 D2
Blacklands Rd G74 159 D1
Blacklaw Dr G74 181 D8
Blacklaw La PA3 113 E6
Blacklaw Prim Sch G74 160 B1
Blackmill Cres FK2 24 B3
Blackmoor Pl ML1 143 A3
Blackmoss Dr ML4 141 F4
Blackmuir Pl FK10 4 D3
Blackness St ML5 122 B3
Blackridge Community Mus*
EH48 107 C3
Blackridge Prim Sch
EH48 107 C3
Blackshaw Dr KA23 190 D6
Blacksholm Rd PA13 89 A7
Blackstone Ave G53 135 C8
Blackstone Cres G53 115 C1
Blackstone Rd PA3 113 A7
Blackstoun Ave PA3 112 B6
Blackstoun Oval PA3 113 B5
Blackstoun Rd PA3 113 B5
Blackswell La ML3 162 F3
Blacksyke Ave KA1 227 F3
Blackthorn Ave
Beith KA15 150 A1
Kirkintilloch G66 79 B5
Blackthorn Gr G66 79 B5
Blackthorn Rd
Cumbernauld G67 62 E4
Uddingston G71 141 C8
Blackthorn Rdbt G67 62 E3
Blackthorn St G22 97 E5
Blacktongue Farm Rd
ML6 83 E2
Blackwood G75 180 D5
Blackwood Ave
Kilmarnock KA1 227 E6
Linwood PA3 112 A5
Newton Mearns G77 156 F3
Blackwood Gdns ML1 142 C2
Blackwood Rd
Cumbernauld G68 60 E1
Milngavie G62 54 F3
Blackwood Rdbt G68 60 F2
Blackwood St
Barrhead G78 134 B2
Glasgow G13 95 E7
Blackwood Terr PA5 131 D8
Blackwood West Rdbt
G68 60 D1
Blackwoods Cres
Bellshill ML4 142 C4
Moodiesburn G69 80 F2
Bladda La PA1 113 F4
Blades Ct G69 101 A6
Bladnoch Dr G15 75 C2
Blaefaulds Cres FK6 39 D8
Blaeloch Ave G45 137 C1
Blaeloch Dr G45 137 C2
Blaeloch Terr G45 137 B1
Blaeshill Rd G75 179 E8
Blair Athol Wynd 4
ML1 143 B2
Blair Atholl Dr 15 ML9 185 C1
Blair Atholl Gate G77 157 B4
Blair Atholl Gdns ML3 162 A4
Blair Atholl Gr ML3 162 A4
Blair Ave KA1 228 E5
Blair Cres Glasgow G69 120 A3
Hurlford KA1 228 E6
Blair Ct G81 74 B2
Blair Dr G66 58 C5
Blair Gdns Gourock PA19 43 F5
Newton Mearns G77 156 B5
Torrance G64 57 B1
Blair Ho G67 62 A3
Blair Path 5 ML1 163 F5
Blair Rd Coatbridge ML5 121 E7
Crossford ML8 201 A1
Dalry KA24 191 E7
Hurlford KA1 228 E6
Kilwinning KA13 207 F5
Paisley PA1 114 E5
Blair St Glasgow G32 118 F5
Kilmarnock KA3 222 F2
Blair Terr FK5 24 A4
Blairafton Wynd KA13 207 C5
Blairatholl Ave G11 96 A3
Blairatholl Cres G77 157 B4
Blairatholl Gdns 5 G11 96 A3
Blairbeg Pl PA19 43 E5
Blairbeth Dr G44 137 B7
Blairbeth Pl G73 138 A5
Blairbeth Rd G73 138 C5
Blairbeth Terr G73 138 C5
Blairbuie Dr G20 96 C7
Blairdardie Prim Sch
G15 75 B1
Blairdardie Rd
Clydebank G15 75 B1
Glasgow G13 75 C1
Blairdenan Ave G69 81 A3
Blairdenon Cres FK1 41 F3
Blairdenon Dr Alloa FK10 5 B2
Cumbernauld G68 61 C3
Blairdenon Rd FK12 4 E6
Blairdenon Way KA11 220 B2
Blairforkie Dr FK9 1 F8
Blairgowrie Rd G52 115 C4
Blairgrove Ct ML5 121 E6
Blairhall Ave G41 136 F8
Blairhill Ave G66 80 A6
Blairhill Pl ML5 121 E7
Blairhill St ML5 121 F7
Blairhill Sta ML5 121 E8
Blairholm Dr ML4 142 B3
Blairlands Dr KA24 191 E7
Blairlinn Ind Est G67 82 F6
Blairlinn Rd G67 82 F6
Blairlinn View G67 83 A6
Blairlogie St G33 99 B2
Blairmore Ave PA1 114 C5
Blairmore Cres PA15 46 C2
Blairmore Pl PA19 43 F5
Blairmore Rd PA15 46 C2
Blairmuckhole & Forrestdyke
Rd ML7 126 E7
Blairpark Ave ML5 121 E8
Blairquhomrie Cotts G83 20 F2
Blairston Ave G71 141 B1
Blairston Gdns G71 141 B1
Blairtum Dr G73 138 B5
Blairtummock Prim Sch
G34 120 B8
Blairtummock Rd G33 119 D8
Blake Rd G67 62 A2
Blakely Rd KA21 217 B7
Blane Ave G63 31 A4
Blane Cres G63 31 A4
Blane Dr G62 55 B3
Blane Pl G63 31 A4
Blane St ML5 122 A8
Blanefield Ave KA9 236 B6
Blanefield Gdns G13 95 F8
Blaneview G33 99 D4
Blantyre Cres G81 73 E7
Blantyre Ct PA8 73 A3
Blantyre Dr PA7 72 A4
Blantyre Farm Rd G71,
G72 140 C5
Blantyre Gdns G68 60 E1
Blantyre High Sch G72 161 D7
Blantyre Ind Est G72 161 E5
Blantyre Mill Rd G71 141 A2
Blantyre Rd G71 141 A2
Blantyre St G3 96 D1
Blantyre Sta G72 161 E8
Blaven Ct G69 120 C4
Blaven Head KA11 220 A4
Blawarthill Hospl G14 95 A6
Blawarthill St G14 94 F5
Bleachfield Falkirk FK2 42 A5
Milngavie G62 55 A3
Bleasdale Ct G81 74 B2
Bleeze Rd KA24 191 B8
Blendon Ho KA7 238 F7
Blenheim Ave
East Kilbride G75 180 C7
Stepps G33 99 E6
Blenheim Ct Carluke ML8 188 B1
Kilsyth G65 36 D1
Stepps G33 99 C5
Stirling FK9 2 C3
Blenheim Pl FK5 23 E5
Blindwells FK12 4 F6
Blinkbonnie Terr FK1 86 A6
Blinkbonny Rd FK1 41 E4
Blinny Ct ML7 147 A3
Blochairn Rd G21 98 B1
Bloomgate ML11 215 A4
Bloomhill Stables G82 48 C7
Bluebell Gdns
Glasgow G45 138 A2
Motherwell ML1 142 C2
Bluebell Way
Airdrie ML6 102 F2
Carluke ML8 201 F8
Lennoxtown G66 57 F7
Bluebell Wlk ML1 143 A3
Bluebell Wynd ML2 164 F1
Blueknowes Rd ML8 186 F5
Bluevale St G31 118 A6
Blyth Rd G33 119 E6
Blythe Pl G33 119 D6
Blythswood Ave PA4 94 D4
Blythswood Ct G2 240 B2
Blythswood Dr PA3 113 E6
Blythswood Ho Hospl
PA4 94 D4
Blythswood Ind Est PA4 94 B4
Blythswood Rd PA4 94 D4
Blythswood Sq G2 240 B3
Blythswood St G2 240 B2
Bo'ness Rd
Chapelhall ML6 123 D1
Motherwell ML1 143 C7
Boardwalk The G75 181 A7
Boat Vennal 9 KA7 235 F1
Bobbin Wynd FK7 6 D6
Bobbins Gate PA1 113 B3
Boclair Acad G61 76 C4
Boclair Ave G61 75 F4
Boclair Cres
Bearsden G61 76 A4
Bishopbriggs G64 78 A2
Boclair Rd Bearsden G62 76 C5
Bishopbriggs G64 78 A2
Boclair St G13 95 E8
Bodden Sq ML1 143 E7
Boden Ind Est G40 118 B4
Boden Quadrant ML1 142 C2
Boden St G40 118 A4
Bodesbeck Ct KA11 220 A3
Bodmin Gdns G69 80 F3
Bog Rd Banknock FK4 38 E3
Laurieston FK2 42 F4
Bog Rdbt FK2 42 F4
Bog Road Ind Est FK2 42 F4
Bogany Terr G45 137 E2
Bogbain Rd G34 120 A8
Bogend Rd
Bannockburn FK7 11 E8
Larbert FK2 23 B8
Torwood FK5 22 F8
Bogfoot Rd ML7 125 B2
Boggknowe G71 140 D8
Boghall Rd Carluke ML8 202 B7
Glasgow G69 120 B3
Boghall St Glasgow G33 99 B1
Stonehouse ML9 198 F2
Boghead KA15 171 B8
Boghead Ave G82 50 B4
Boghead Rd
Dumbarton G82 50 B4
Glasgow G21 98 A4
Kirkintilloch G66 79 A5
Bogiewood Rd PA14 47 B1
Bogle St PA15 46 A4
Boglemart St KA20 217 C8
Bogleshole Rd G72 138 E7
Boglestone Ave PA14 68 E8
Bogmoor Pl G51 95 C1
Bogmoor Rd G51 115 C8
Bogs View ML4 141 F3
Bogside Rd Ashgill ML9 199 F8
Kilsyth G65 60 D7
Millerston G33 99 A5
Port Glasgow PA14 68 F8
Bogside St G40 118 B4
Bogston La PA15 46 F2
Bogston Sta PA15 46 F2
Bogstonhill Rd PA6 91 B2
Bogton Ave G44 136 F4
Bogton Avenue La G44 136 F4
Bohun Ct FK7 7 D4
Boleyn Ct ML2 166 B6
Boleyn Rd G41 116 E2
Bolingbroke G74 160 C4
Bolivar Terr G42 137 C8
Bolton Dr G42 137 B8
Bolton Terr G66 57 E8
Bon Accord Cres ML7 146 E5
Bon Accord Rd G76 157 F6
Bon Accord Sq G81 94 B8
Bon Secours Hospl G41 136 F8
Bonar Cres PA11 110 E7
Bonar La PA11 110 E7
Bonar Law Ave G84 16 B2
Bonawe St G20 96 F3
Bond St FK10 4 A3
Bonds Dr ML2 166 B6
Boness St G40 118 B4
Bonhill Prim Sch G83 27 F3
Bonhill Rd G82 50 A4
Bonhill St G22 97 B3
Bonhill View G83 27 F4
Bonkle Gdns ML2 166 B5
Bonkle Rd ML2 166 B5
Bonnar St G40 118 A3
Bonnaughton Rd G61 75 B6
Bonnet Ct KA3 211 E8
Bonnet Rd ML11 215 A4
Bonnie Lesley Ct KA20 217 C8
Bonnington Ave ML11 215 B3
Bonnybridge Hospl FK4 40 C6
Bonnybridge Ind Est FK4 40 A4
Bonnybridge Prim Sch
FK4 40 B6
Bonnybridge Rd FK4 39 E5
Bonnyfield Rd FK4 39 F5
Bonnyhill Rd
Bonnybridge FK4 40 D3
Falkirk FK1 41 A4
Bonnyholm Ave G53 115 A3
Bonnyholm Prim Sch
G53 115 A3
Bonnymuir Cres FK4 39 F5
Bonnyrigg Dr G43 136 A5
Bonnyside Rd FK4 40 B5
Bonnyton Dr G76 178 D5
Bonnyton Foot KA11 220 A5
Bonnyton Ind Est KA1 222 E1
Bonnyton La ML3 183 B8
Bonnyton Moor Rd G76 178 A7
Bonnyton Pl Irvine KA11 220 A5
Kilmarnock KA1 222 D1
Bonnyton Rd KA1 222 C1
Bonnyton Row KA11 220 A5
Bonnyvale Pl FK4 39 F5
Bonnyview Gdns FK4 40 B6
Bonnywood Ave FK4 40 B7
Bontine Ave G82 49 D4
Bonyton Ave G13 94 F6
Boon Dr G15 75 B2
Booth Pl FK1 42 B4
Boquhanran Pl G81 74 A3
Boquhanran Rd
Clydebank G81 73 F2
Clydebank G81 74 A3
Borden La 3 G13 95 E5
Borden Rd G13 95 E5
Border Ave KA21 216 F8
Border Pl KA21 216 F8
Border St PA15 46 C3
Border Way G66 79 F8
Bore Rd ML6 123 B8
Boreland Dr Glasgow G13 95 B6
Hamilton ML3 161 E2
Boreland Pl G13 95 B6
Borestone Ave KA25 170 A8
Borestone Cres FK7 7 A4
Borestone Ct FK7 7 B2
Borestone Pl FK7 7 A2
Borestone Prim Sch FK7 7 A2
Borgie Cres G72 139 B5
Borland Cres G76 178 E5
Borland Dr ML9 199 B8
Borland Rd G61 76 A3
Borron St G4 97 C3
Borrowdale G75 179 F5
Borrowlea Rd FK7 7 C7
Borrowmeadow Rd FK7 7 E7
Borthwick Dr G75 179 D7
Borthwick Pl G69 100 F4
Borthwick St G33 99 B1
Bosfield Cnr G74 159 F3
Bosfield Pl G74 159 F3
Bosfield Rd G74 159 F3
Boston Dr G84 16 F3
Boswell Ct G42 136 F7
Boswell Dr G72 161 D7
Boswell Pk Ayr KA7 238 F8
East Kilbride G74 160 C4
Boswell Sq G52 114 F7
Bosworth Rd G74 160 C5
Botanic Cres G20 96 D4
Botanic Crescent La G20 96 D4
Bothkennar Prim Sch
FK2 24 F3
Bothkennar Rd FK2 24 E3
Bothlin Dr G33 99 D6
Bothlyn Ave G66 79 E7
Bothlyn Cres G69 100 F7
Bothlyn Rd G69 100 D8
Bothwell Castle* G72 140 D3
Bothwell Ho ML3 162 E5
Bothwell La Glasgow G2 240 C2
4 Glasgow,Kelvingrove
G12 96 E2
Bothwell Park Ind Est
G71 141 A5
Bothwell Park Sch ML1 164 A4
Bothwell Pl
Coatbridge ML5 121 F7
Paisley PA2 132 E8
Bothwell Prim Sch G71 141 A2
Bothwell Rd
Bothwell G71 140 F4
Carluke ML8 187 E3
Hamilton ML3 162 C6
Bothwell St
Cambuslang G72 138 E6
Glasgow G2 240 C2
Hamilton ML3 162 C5
Bothwellhaugh Quadrant
ML4 141 F3
Bothwellhaugh Rd ML4 142 A2
Bothwellpark Pl ML4 141 D6
Bothwellpark Rd
Bothwell G71 141 C3
Fallside G71,ML4 141 C4
Bothwellshields Rd
ML1 124 C2
Bothwick Way PA2 132 E8
Boturich Dr G83 19 E1
Boundary Rd KA8 236 D4
Bourhill Ct ML2 164 D2
Bourne Cres PA4 93 D7
Bourne Ct PA4 93 D7
Bourne St ML3 162 F3
Bournemouth Rd PA19 44 E5
Bourock Sq G78 134 E1
Bourtree Pk KA7 239 A6
Bourtree Rd ML3 161 F2
Bouverie St Glasgow G14 94 E6
Port Glasgow PA14 47 D1
Rutherglen G73 137 F7
Bow Rd PA16 45 C4
Bow St FK8 7 A8
Bowden Dr G52 115 B6
Bowden Pk G75 180 C8
Bower St G12 96 E3
Bowerwalls St G78 134 E4
Bowes Cres G69 119 F4
Bowes Rigg KA3 195 E1
Bowfield Ave G52 114 F6
Bowfield Cres G52 114 F6
Bowfield Dr G52 115 A6
Bowfield Path G52 114 F6
Bowfield Pl G52 114 F6
Bowfield Rd
Howwood PA9 130 F5
West Kilbride KA23 190 C4
Bowfield Way PA9 130 F5
Bowhouse Dr G45 138 A4
Bowhouse Gdns
Alloa FK10 10 B5
Glasgow G45 138 A5
Bowhouse Head KA11 220 B5
Bowhouse Rd
Airdrie ML6 123 F5
Alloa FK10 10 B5
Bowhouse Rise KA11 220 B5
Bowhousebog or Liquo
ML7 146 A2
Bowhousebog Rd ML7 146 A2
Bowhousebrae Rd ML6 123 E5
Bowie Rd G83 27 E6
Bowie St G82 49 E3
Bowling Green Gr G72 139 F4
Bowling Green La 2
G14 95 D3
Bowling Green Pl FK4 39 F5
Bowling Green Rd
Chryston G69 100 D8
Fenwick KA3 213 A3
Glasgow G44 137 A5
Glasgow,Barrachnie G32 119 D4
3 Glasgow,Whiteinch G14 95 D3
Bowling Green St ML4 142 B5
Bowling Green View
G72 139 F4
Bowling St ML5 121 F7

Bowling Sta G60 72 C8
Bowman Pl KA3 195 D1
Bowman Rd KA7 238 F6
Bowman St G42 117 A2
Bowmanflat ML9 185 A3
Bowmont Gdns 3 G12 96 C3
Bowmont Hill G64 78 A4
Bowmont Pl
Cambuslang G72 139 D5
East Kilbride G75 179 D7
Bowmont Terr G12 96 C3
Bowmore Ct KA11 220 A6
Bowmore Gdns
Rutherglen G73 138 E3
Uddingston G71 140 E8
Bowmore Rd G52 115 E5
Bowmore Wlk ML7 147 A3
Bowyer Vennel ML4 141 F6
Boxton Rd FK1 66 D1
Boyd Ct KA3 223 A1
Boyd Dr ML1 163 B7
Boyd La FK2 42 B6
Boyd Orr Cres KA3 222 A7
Boyd Orr Rd KA21 206 A2
Boyd St Falkirk FK2 42 B6
Glasgow G42 117 C1
Kilmarnock KA3 223 A1
Prestwick KA9 236 C8
Boydfield Ave KA9 236 D8
Boydston Rd KA22 205 C4
Boydston Way KA3 223 C6
Boydstone Pl G46 136 A5
Boydstone Rd
Glasgow G53,G46,G43 135 E5
Thornliebank G46 136 A4
Boyle St Clydebank G81 94 D8
Irvine KA12 219 A2
Boylestone Rd G78 134 A4
Boyndie St G34 120 B8
Brabloch Cres PA3 113 F6
Brabloch Pk PA3 113 F6
Bracadale Dr G69 120 D4
Bracadale Gdns G69 120 D4
Bracadale Gr G69 120 C4
Bracadale Rd G69 120 C4
Bracco Rd ML6 105 C2
Brachelston St PA16 45 D4
Bracken La FK9 2 B3
Bracken Pk KA7 239 C3
Bracken Rd PA14 69 A8
Bracken St Glasgow G22 97 B6
Motherwell ML1 143 A3
Bracken Terr G71 141 A3
Bracken Way 6 ML9 185 C1
Brackenbrae Ave G64 77 F1
Brackenbrae Rd G64 77 F1
Brackendene PA6 91 D2
Brackenhill Ave KA3 223 A5
Brackenhill Dr ML3 183 C7
Brackenhill Rd ML8 187 A6
Brackenhirst Gdns ML6 102 D6
Brackenhirst Rd ML6 102 E7
Brackenhurst St G82 50 C6
Brackenknowe Rd ML6 83 D3
Brackenlees Rd FK2 24 F4
Brackenrig Cres G76 157 E1
Brackenrig Rd G46 135 E2
Brackla Ave G13,G81 94 E8
Braco Ave ML6 123 D1
Bradan Ave G13 94 E7
Bradan Ct KA10 229 B2
Bradan Rd KA10 229 C2
Bradbury Glebe KA12 219 C2
Bradbury St FK2 24 B2
Bradda Ave G73 138 D4
Braden Dr KA7 239 B2
Bradfield Ave G12 96 C5
Bradley Ct G33 99 F5
Bradshaw Cres ML3 161 E3
Bradshaw St KA21 216 F7
Brady Cres G69 81 A3
Brae Head Quadrant
G78 154 D7
Brae The Bannockburn FK7 7 D1
Cambusbarron FK7 6 D6
Kilmaurs KA3 222 B7
Brae View PA16 45 C5
Braedale Ave
Airdrie ML6 123 C7
Motherwell ML1 163 C6
Braedale Cres ML2 166 B5
Braedale Pl ML2 166 C5
Braedale Rd ML11 215 A5
Braeface Rd Banknock FK4 38 E3
Cumbernauld G67 61 E2
Braefield Dr G46 136 A3
Braefoot KA11 219 F5
Braefoot Ave G62 76 A8
Braefoot Cres Law ML8 186 F4
Paisley PA2 133 F8
Braefoot Ct
Caldercruix ML6 104 F4
Law ML8 186 F5
Braefoot La G78 153 A3
Braehead Alexandria G83 28 B3
Alloa FK10 4 D1
Alva FK10 5 A7
Beith KA15 171 B8
Dalry KA24 191 C8
Hamilton G72 161 D6
Irvine KA11 219 F5
Lochwinnoch PA12 129 C3
Braehead (Sh Ctr) G51 95 A3
Braehead Ave Ayr KA8 236 C2
Clydebank G81 74 A7
Braehead Ave *continued*
Coatbridge ML5 121 D3
Larkhall ML9 184 E2
Lochwinnoch PA12 129 C3
Milngavie G62 54 F1
Neilston G78 154 D7
Tullibody FK10 4 C2
Braehead Cres Ayr KA8 236 C2
Clydebank G81 74 A7
Braehead Ct KA3 223 A1
Braehead Dr ML4 141 F4
Braehead Glebe KA3 211 E8
Braehead Ind Est PA4 94 F3
Braehead La KA21 216 F8
Braehead Loan ML8 202 B8
Braehead Pl Bellshill ML4 141 F4
Dalry KA24 191 C8
Rhu G84 15 E5
Saltcoats KA21 216 F8
Braehead Prim Sch
Ayr KA8 236 C2
Dumbarton G82 50 A4
Stirling FK7 7 C4
Braehead Quadrant
ML1 143 D4
Braehead Rd Ayr KA8 236 D2
Clydebank G81 74 A7
Cumbernauld G67 62 B3
Fenwick KA3 213 A3
Paisley PA2 133 C7
Paisley PA2 133 D8
Port Glasgow PA14 68 E8
Stirling FK7 7 C3
Thorntonhall G74 158 C3
Braehead St Glasgow G5 117 D3
Kirkintilloch G66 58 C1
Braehead Terr KA3 222 C6
Braehouse G84 15 D4
Braemar Ave G81 73 F4
Braemar Cres
Bearsden G61 75 F2
Carluke ML8 188 A3
Falkirk FK2 42 C6
Paisley PA2 113 F1
Braemar Ct G44 136 E4
Braemar Dr Elderslie PA5 112 B1
Falkirk FK2 42 C6
Braemar Gdns Denny FK6 21 D3
Greenock PA16 45 E6
Braemar Pl FK5 24 A4
Braemar Rd Inchinnan PA4 93 E6
Rutherglen G73 138 E3
Braemar Sq KA8 236 D2
Braemar St Glasgow G42 136 F7
Hamilton ML3 162 B6
Braemar View G81 73 F5
Braemore Gdns G22 97 D4
Braemore Rd KA3 195 D1
Braemount Ave PA2 133 C6
Braes Ave G81 74 D1
Braes O' Yetts G66 80 A8
Braes Rd KA21 216 E7
Braes The FK10 4 D3
Braes View Denny FK6 39 D8
Shieldhill FK1 66 E7
Braesburn Ct G67 62 F6
Braesburn Pl G67 62 F6
Braesburn Rd G67 62 F6
Braeside Alloa FK10 5 C1
Howwood PA9 130 F5
Irvine KA11 219 F5
Kilwinning KA13 207 E5
Shieldhill FK1 66 D6
Braeside Ave
Milngavie G62 76 A8
Moodiesburn G69 80 F2
Rutherglen G73 138 C7
Braeside Cres
Barrhead G78 134 E1
Coatbridge G69 120 F5
Braeside Dr
Barrhead G78 134 E1
Dumbarton G82 50 B5
Braeside Gdns ML3 183 E8
Braeside La
Greenock PA16 44 D3
15 Larkhall ML9 185 B4
Braeside Pl G72 139 B4
Braeside Rd Ayr KA8 236 D2
Greenock PA16 44 D3
Motherwell ML1 143 D4
Braeside St Glasgow G20 96 F4
Kilmarnock KA1 228 A8
Braeside Way ML9 185 B1
Braeval Way G33 99 E5
Braeview Laurieston FK2 42 F3
Stenhousemuir FK5 23 D2
Braeview Ave PA2 133 B7
Braeview Dr PA2 133 B7
Braeview Gdns PA2 133 B7
Braeview Pl G74 160 B4
Braeview Rd PA2 133 B7
Braid Ave Cardross G82 48 B8
Motherwell ML1 143 F1
Braid Ct KA13 207 B3
Braid Dr G82 48 B8
Braid Sq G4 97 A2
Braid St G4 97 A2
Braid's Rd PA2 113 E1
Braidbar Ct G46 136 C3
Braidbar Farm Rd G46 136 D3
Braidbar Prim Sch G46 136 D3
Braidbar Rd G46 136 C3
Braidcraft Pl G53 135 C8
Braidcraft Rd
Glasgow G53 115 C1
Glasgow G53 115 D1
Braidcraft Terr G53 115 D1
Braidfauld Gdns G32 118 F3
Braidfauld Pl G32 118 F2
Braidfauld St G32 118 F3
Braidfield Gr G81 74 B5
Braidfield High Sch G81 74 D2
Braidfield Rd G81 74 B5
Braidfute ML11 215 C5
Braidholm Cres G46 136 C4
Braidholm Rd G46 136 D4
Braidhurst High Sch
ML1 142 D1
Braidhurst Ind Est ML1 142 D1
Braidhurst St ML1 163 E8
Braidley Cres G75 180 E5
Braidpark Dr G46 136 D3
Braids Ct PA2 113 E1
Braids Dr G53 114 F1
Braids Gait PA2 113 D1
Braidwood Pl PA3 111 F6
Braidwood Prim Sch
ML8 201 F4
Braidwood Rd
Braidwood ML8 201 D4
Kilwinning KA13 207 E4
Braidwood St ML2 165 C7
Brailsford Cres KA2 227 C6
Bramah Ave G75 180 F8
Bramble Ct G66 57 C8
Bramblehedge Path G83 27 F7
Brambling Ct ML2 165 A1
Brambling Rd ML5 122 D3
Bramley Dr ML4 142 A8
Bramley Pl Airdrie ML6 123 E6
Kirkintilloch G66 79 E4
Brampton G75 179 F6
Branchal Rd ML2 165 E4
Branchalfield Dr ML2 165 E4
Branchalmuir Cres ML2 165 F6
Branchline Ind Est
KA10 229 C3
Branchock Ave G72 139 D4
Branchton Rd PA16 44 F3
Branchton Sta PA16 44 F3
Brancumhall Rd G74 160 D3
Brand Pl G51 116 C6
Brand St G51 116 C6
Brandon Arc 1 ML1 163 E6
Brandon Ct
Hamilton ML3 162 C4
Motherwell ML1 163 E6
Brandon Dr G61 75 E7
Brandon Gate ML4 142 B5
Brandon Gdns
Cambuslang G72 138 E5
Prestwick KA9 236 B7
Brandon Ho ML3 162 E5
Brandon Par E ML1 163 E7
Brandon Par S ML1 163 E6
Brandon Pl ML4 141 E3
Brandon St Glasgow G31 117 F6
Hamilton ML3 162 E3
Motherwell ML1 163 F6
Brandon Way ML5 121 D4
Brandyhill FK10 5 E3
Brankholm Brae ML3 161 D4
Branklyn Cl 4 G13 95 D6
Branklyn Cres G13 95 D6
Branklyn Ct 6 G13 95 D6
Branklyn Gr G13 95 D6
Branklyn Pl 5 G13 95 D6
Brannock Ave ML1 143 D4
Brannock High Sch
ML1 143 C3
Brannock Pl ML1 143 D4
Brannock Rd ML1 143 D4
Branshill Pk Alloa FK10 10 B8
Sauchie FK10 5 B1
Branshill Rd FK10 10 B8
Brassey St G20 96 F6
Braxfield Rd ML11 215 A2
Braxfield Row ML11 214 F2
Braxfield Terr ML11 214 F2
Breadalbane Cres ML1 142 D1
Breadalbane Gdns G73 138 D4
Breadalbane St G3 240 A3
Breadie Dr G62 75 F8
Bream Pl PA6 111 D8
Breamish Pl G75 179 F6
Brechin Rd G64 78 C1
Brechin St G3 116 E8
Breck Ave PA2 132 D7
Brediland Prim Sch
PA2 113 A1
Brediland Rd
Linwood PA3 112 B6
Paisley PA2 112 F1
Bredin Way ML1 163 B8
Bredisholm Cres G71 121 C1
Bredisholm Dr G69 120 C4
Bredisholm Rd
Coatbridge G69 120 F4
Coatbridge G69 121 A4
Glasgow G69 120 D4
Bredisholm Terr G69 120 D4
Bremners Cotts G81 73 F6
Brendan Way ML1 164 B2
Brendon Ave G75 180 A4
Brenfield Ave G44 136 F4
Brenfield Dr G44 136 F4
Brenfield Rd G44 136 F4
Brent Ave G46 135 F5
Brent Cres PA6 111 C8
Brent Ct G74 159 E3
Brent Dr Glasgow G46 135 F5
Thornliebank G46 136 A5
Brent Gdns Glasgow G46 135 F5
Thornliebank G46 136 A5
Brent Rd
East Kilbride G74 159 E3
Glasgow G46 135 F5
Thornliebank G46 136 A5
Brent Way G46 135 F5
Brentham Ave FK8 7 B5
Brentham Cres FK8 7 B5
Brentwood Ave G53 135 B4
Brentwood Dr G53 135 B4
Brentwood Sq G53 135 B4
Brereton St G42 117 C1
Breslin Terr ML7 127 C5
Bressay G74 159 E4
Bressay Pl KA3 223 B5
Bressay Rd G33 119 E6
Bressay Wynd 14 ML2 165 F6
Breton Ct FK1 42 C3
Breval Cres G81 74 A7
Breval Ct G69 120 C4
Brewery Rd 4 KA1 227 F7
Brewery St PA5 111 F3
Brewhouse Ct 5 FK10 10 B6
Brewlands Cres KA1 231 C4
Brewlands Dr KA1 231 C4
Brewlands Rd KA1 231 D4
Brewster Ave PA3 114 A7
Brewster Pl Denny FK6 21 C2
Irvine KA11 224 H6
Briar Bank G66 58 B5
Briar Dr G81 74 B4
Briar Gdns G43 136 D5
Briar Gr Ayr KA7 239 C4
Glasgow G43 136 D5
Briar Neuk G64 98 B8
Briar Pl PA19 44 D6
Briar Rd Alloa FK10 4 E2
Glasgow G43 136 D5
Kirkintilloch G66 79 F8
Briar Wlk G66 80 A8
Briarbush Way 12 G72 161 C7
Briarcroft Dr G33 98 D7
Briarcroft Pl G33 98 E6
Briarcroft Rd G33 98 D6
Briarhill Ct KA9 236 D8
Briarhill Rd KA9 236 D8
Briarhill St KA9 236 C8
Briarlea Dr G46 136 C4
Briarwell La G62 55 B1
Briarwell Rd G62 55 B1
Briarwood Ct G32 119 E2
Briarwood Rd ML2 164 E4
Brick La 1 PA3 113 F5
Bridesburn Pl KA3 195 E1
Bridesmill Rd PA12 129 D4
Bridge Cres FK6 21 D2
Bridge End ML7 146 C6
Bridge La
9 Kilmarnock KA1 227 F8
Paisley PA2 113 B3
Bridge of Allan Prim Sch
FK9 2 B6
Bridge of Allan Sta FK9 1 E8
Bridge of Weir Prim Sch
PA11 90 D1
Bridge of Weir Rd
Bridge of W PA11 110 F7
Brookfield PA5,PA11 111 C5
Houston PA6 91 B2
Kilmacolm PA13 89 E6
Linwood PA3 112 B5
Bridge Pl Denny FK6 21 C2
Milngavie G62 55 A1
Shotts ML7 147 A3
Bridge Rd PA14 68 E8
Bridge St Alexandria G83 27 E4
Bonnybridge FK4 40 A5
Cambuslang G72 139 A6
Clydebank G81 73 E3
Dumbarton G82 49 E3
Glasgow G5 240 C1
Hamilton ML3 162 C2
Kilbirnie KA25 149 B2
Linwood PA3 112 C6
Longriggend ML6 84 F1
Paisley PA1 113 F4
Prestwick KA9 236 B8
Wishaw ML2 164 E3
Bridge Street Underground
Sta G5 117 B5
Bridge Terr 13 FK10 10 B6
Bridgebar St G78 134 E4
Bridgeburn Dr G69 80 F1
Bridgeford Ave ML4 142 C7
Bridgegait G62 76 C8
Bridgegate Glasgow G1 241 A1
Irvine KA12 219 C2
Bridgehaugh Rd FK9 2 B2
Bridgehouse Ct KA1 228 A2
Bridgehousehill Rd KA1 228 A3
Bridgend Bishopton PA7 72 A3
Dalry KA24 191 D7
Kilbirnie KA25 149 B2
Kilwinning KA13 207 F3
Stewarton KA3 211 E8
Bridgend Ave PA14 68 E8
Bridgend Cotts G66 80 A7
Bridgend Cres G69 80 E2
Bridgend Ct G68 38 F1
Bridgend Ind Est KA24 191 D7
Bridgend La Dalry KA24 191 D7
Kilwinning KA13 207 F4
Bridgend Pl G69 80 E2
Bridgend Rd PA15 46 C2
Bridgend View ML8 187 F1
Bridgend Wlk G78 153 B3
Bridgepark KA22 205 D2
Bridgeton Bsns Ctr 4
G40 117 F5
Bridgeton Cross G40 117 F4
Bridgeton Sta G40 117 F4
Bridgewater Ind Pk PA8 73 C2
Bridgewater Sh Ctr PA8 73 C2
Bridgeway Ct G66 79 F7
Bridgeway Pl G66 79 F7
Bridgeway Rd G66 79 F7
Bridgeway Terr G66 79 F7
Bridie Terr G74 160 C4
Brierie Ave PA6 91 B1
Brierie Gdns PA6 111 B8
Brierie Hill Ct PA6 111 B8
Brierie La PA6 111 A8
Brierie-Hill Gr PA6 111 B8
Brierie-Hill Rd PA6 111 B8
Briery Ct KA25 170 A7
Brierybank Ave ML11 215 A3
Brig O'lea Terr G78 154 D6
Brig-O-Doon Gr FK7 12 E7
Brigbrae Ave ML4 142 C3
Brigham Pl G23 96 E8
Bright St G21 97 F1
Brighton Pl G51 116 B6
Brighton St G51 116 B6
Brightside Ave
Port Glasgow PA14 69 A8
Uddingston G71 140 F5
Brigside Gdns ML3 163 A2
Bringan Rd KA3 222 F5
Brisbane Ct G46 136 D3
Brisbane Rd PA7 72 B3
Brisbane St
Clydebank G81 73 D4
Glasgow G42 137 A7
Greenock PA16 45 D6
Brisbane Terr G75 180 C7
Britannia Pl KA8 236 B2
Britannia Way
Clydebank G81 74 B2
Renfrew PA4 94 C1
Briton St G51 116 B7
Brittain Way ML1 142 F7
Broad Sq G72 161 D8
Broad St Alloa FK10 10 B5
Denny FK6 21 F2
Glasgow G40 118 A5
Stirling FK8 7 A8
Broad St Cvn Site G40 118 A5
Broad Way The ML2 164 E4
Broadcroft
4 Kirkintilloch G66 58 C1
3 Kirkintilloch G66 79 C8
Broadcroft Rd 5 G66 58 C1
Broadfield Ave PA14 69 A8
Broadford St G4 97 C2
Broadford Terr PA16 44 E4
Broadholm St G22 97 C6
Broadleys Ave G64 77 F2
Broadleys Bsns Pk FK7 7 D5
Broadleys Ind Pk FK7 7 D5
Broadleys Rd FK7 7 D7
Broadleys Rdbt FK7 7 D6
Broadlie Ct G78 154 D7
Broadlie Dr Dalry KA24 191 A8
Glasgow G13 95 A6
Broadlie Rd G78 154 D7
Broadloan PA4 94 C2
Broadmeadow Ind Est
G82 49 F5
Broadmoss Ave G77 157 C4
Broadside Pl FK6 21 D1
Broadstone Ave
Greenock PA14 46 F2
Port Glasgow PA14 47 A1
Broadway KA22 205 D3
Broadwood Bsns Pk G68 81 F8
Broadwood Dr G44 137 B6
Broadwood Pk KA7 239 A1
Broadwood Rdbt G68 81 F8
Broadwood Stad (Clyde, &
Airdrieonians FC's) G68 60 F1
Brock Oval G53 135 C6
Brock Pl Glasgow G53 135 C7
Stirling FK7 7 B2
Brock Rd G53 135 C6
Brock Terr G53 135 C6
Brockburn Cres G53 135 B8
Brockburn Pl G53 115 A2
Brockburn Rd G53 115 B1
Brockburn Terr G53 135 C8
Brockley View KA25 149 B4
Brocklinn Pk G75 179 E7
Brockville St G32 118 F6
Brodick Ave
Kilwinning KA13 207 C4
Motherwell ML1 163 B7
Brodick Cl KA13 207 C4
Brodick Dr
East Kilbride G74 159 D3
Gourock PA19 43 F5
Helensburgh G84 16 F3
Brodick Pl Falkirk FK1 41 C4
Newton Mearns G77 156 A4
Brodick Rd KA1 222 C2
Brodick Sq G64 98 C7
Brodick St G21 98 A1
Brodie Ave KA10 229 E4
Brodie Gdns G69 120 C6
Brodie Gr G69 120 C6
Brodie Park Ave PA2 113 E2
Brodie Park Cres PA2 113 D2
Brodie Park Gdns PA2 113 E2
Brodie Pl
East Kilbride G74 159 D3
Kilmarnock KA3 223 C2
Stonehouse ML9 198 E1
Brodie Rd G21 98 D7
Brodie St FK2 42 B8

Brogan Cres ML1 163 B7
Broich The FK12 4 E7
Bron Way G67 62 A1
Bronte Pl FK5 24 A3
Brook St Alva FK12 5 A6
Alva FK12 5 A7
Clydebank G81 73 F4
Glasgow G40 117 F5
Menstrie FK11 3 F6
Brookbank Terr ML8 188 A1
Brooke Ave G83 28 A8
Brookfield Ave G33 98 D7
Brookfield Cnr G33 98 D7
Brookfield Dr G33 98 D7
Brookfield Gate G33 98 D8
Brookfield Gdns G33 98 D7
Brookfield Pl Alva FK12 5 A6
Glasgow G33 98 E7
Brookfield Rd
Glasgow G33 98 D7
Port Glasgow PA14 68 F8
Brooklands
Alexandria G83 27 D6
East Kilbride G74 159 A1
Brooklands Ave G71 140 E7
Brooklea Dr G46 136 C5
Brooklime Dr G74 159 C4
Brooklime Gdns G74 159 C4
Brooklyn Pl ML2 186 B7
Brookside St G40 118 A5
Broom Ave PA8 93 B7
Broom Cliff G77 156 F3
Broom Cres
Barrhead G78 134 A5
East Kilbride G75 180 D5
Broom Ct FK7 7 C3
Broom Dr Clydebank G81 74 A4
Larkhall ML9 185 A5
Broom Gdns G66 79 B6
Broom Path G69 119 F3
Broom Pl
Bridge of W PA11 110 E7
Coatbridge ML5 121 F3
Glasgow G43 136 D5
Kilmarnock KA1 228 B5
Motherwell ML1 143 C4
Broom Rd
Cumbernauld G67 62 D5
Glasgow G43 136 D5
Newton Mearns G77 157 A6
Rosneath G84 15 B3
Stirling FK7 7 C4
Broom Rd E G77 157 B4
Broom Terr PA5 112 A2
Broom Wynd ML7 146 E6
Broomage Ave FK5 23 B3
Broomage Bank FK5 23 C2
Broomage Cres FK5 23 B3
Broomage Dr FK5 23 B3
Broomage Pk FK5 23 C1
Broomberry Dr PA19 44 E7
Broomburn Dr G77 157 A4
Broomcroft Rd G46 157 A6
Broomdyke Way PA3 113 D8
Broomelton Rd ML3, ML9 184 D1
Broomfauld Gdns G82 50 A3
Broomfield PA6 91 D1
Broomfield Ave
Cambuslang G72 138 D7
Newton Mearns G77 156 F3
Broomfield Ct G21 98 C3
Broomfield Gdn KA7 238 F6
Broomfield Gdns G84 15 C7
Broomfield La G21 97 F5
Broomfield Pl G21 97 F5
Broomfield Rd Ayr KA7 238 F6
Glasgow G21 98 B4
Larkhall ML9 199 B8
Netherburn ML9 199 E4
Rutherglen G46 157 A6
Broomfield St
Airdrie ML6 123 B7
Kilwinning KA13 207 E4
Netherburn ML9 200 D4
Broomfield Terr G71 120 F1
Broomfield Wlk 5 G66 79 D8
Broomgate ML11 215 A4
Broomgate Ct ML11 214 F4
Broomhill Ave
Glasgow G32 139 B8
Glasgow,Whiteinch G11 95 F2
Larbert FK5 41 C8
Newton Mearns G77 156 F4
Broomhill Cres
Bellshill ML4 141 F3
Bonhill G83 28 B1
Erskine PA8 93 B7
Broomhill Ct
Greenock PA15 45 E4
Kilwinning KA13 207 C5
4 Kirkintilloch G66 58 D1
Larkhall ML9 185 A2
Broomhill Dr
Dumbarton G82 50 B5
Glasgow G11 95 F3
Rutherglen G73 138 B5
Broomhill Farm Mews G66 58 E1
Broomhill Gate ML9 185 A2
Broomhill Gdns
Glasgow G11 95 F3
Newton Mearns G77 156 F4
Broomhill La G11 95 F3
Broomhill Path G11 95 F2
Broomhill Pl Denny FK6 21 D4
Glasgow G11 95 F2
Stirling FK7 6 E6
Broomhill Prim Sch G11 95 F4
Broomhill Prim Sch Annexe G11 95 F4
Broomhill Quadrant KA1 228 A4
Broomhill Rd
Bonnybridge FK4 40 B4
Larkhall ML9 185 A2
Broomhill Rd E KA1 228 A4
Broomhill Road W KA1 227 F4
Broomhill St
Greenock PA15 45 E4
Harthill ML7 127 C5
Broomhill Terr G11 95 F2
Broomhill View ML9 184 F2
Broomhill Way PA15 45 E4
Broomieknowe FK10 4 D3
Broomieknowe Dr G73 138 B6
Broomieknowe Gdns G73 138 B6
Broomieknowe Rd G73 138 B6
Broomielaw G1,G2 240 C1
Broomknoll St ML6 123 A7
Broomknowe G68 61 D3
Broomknowe Rd PA13 89 C8
Broomknowe Terr PA13 89 C8
Broomknowes Ave G66 79 E4
Broomknowes Rd G21 98 A4
Broomlands Ave PA8 93 E8
Broomlands Busway KA11 220 A2
Broomlands Cres PA8 93 E8
Broomlands Ct
Irvine KA11 220 A2
Paisley PA1 113 C4
Broomlands Dr KA12 219 D2
Broomlands Gdns PA8 93 D8
Broomlands La PA1 113 B4
Broomlands Pl KA12 219 D2
Broomlands Prim Sch KA11 220 A2
Broomlands Rd
Cumbernauld G67 83 A8
Irvine KA11 220 B1
Broomlands St PA1 113 C4
Broomlands Way PA8 93 E8
Broomlea Cres PA4 93 D7
Broomlea Sch G11 95 F3
Broomlee Rd G67 82 F6
Broomley Cres G83 27 D7
Broomley Dr G46 136 C1
Broomley La G46 136 C1
Broomloan Ct G51 116 A5
Broomloan Pl G51 116 B6
Broomloan Rd
Glasgow G51 116 A5
Glasgow G51 116 A6
Broompark Ave
Hamilton G72 161 C6
Prestwick KA9 236 C8
Broompark Cir 8 G31 117 F7
Broompark Cres
Airdrie ML6 103 A3
Prestwick KA9 236 C8
Broompark Dr
Glasgow G31 117 F7
Inchinnan PA4 93 D7
Newton Mearns G77 157 A5
Broompark E FK11 4 A6
Broompark Gdns FK6 21 E2
Broompark La 7 G31 117 F7
Broompark Rd
Hamilton G72 161 C7
Wishaw ML2 164 D4
Broompark St 6 G31 117 F7
Broompark W FK11 4 A6
Broomridge Pl FK4 39 D4
Broomridge Rd FK7 7 B3
Broomside Cres ML1 163 E4
Broomside Pl FK5 23 C1
Broomside Rd FK4 40 B3
Broomside St ML1 163 E4
Broomstone Ave G77 156 F3
Broomton Rd G21 98 C7
Broomvale Dr G77 156 F5
Broomward Dr PA5 112 B3
Brora Cres ML3 182 F8
Brora Dr Bearsden G61 76 B4
Glasgow G46 136 D2
Renfrew PA4 94 E3
Brora Gdns G64 78 B1
Brora Rd G64 78 B1
Brora St G33 98 D1
Brosdale Ct FK1 42 B2
Brougham St PA16 45 E7
Broughton G75 180 E5
Broughton Dr G23 96 E8
Broughton Gdns G23 76 F1
Broughton Gn KA11 220 B6
Broughton Pl
Coatbridge ML5 122 B3
Hamilton ML3 162 A3
Broughton Rd G23 76 E1
Broun Dr KA7 238 E1
Brouster Hill G74 159 E1
Brouster Pl G74 159 E1
Brown Ave Alloa FK10 4 F1
Clydebank G81 94 E8
Dumbarton G82 50 C4
Stirling FK9 2 B2
Troon KA10 229 E3
Brown Pl
Cambuslang G72 139 A6
Saltcoats KA21 205 F1
Brown Rd G67 61 F2
Brown St Balloch G83 28 A8
Carluke ML8 187 F3
Coatbridge ML5 122 A5
Brown St *continued*
Falkirk FK1 41 D5
Glasgow G2 240 B2
Greenock PA15 46 D3
1 Hamilton ML3 162 E2
Larkhall ML9 185 A4
Motherwell ML1 163 F8
Paisley PA1 113 D5
Port Glasgow PA14 47 B2
Shotts ML7 147 B3
Stewarton KA3 211 D8
Wishaw ML2 166 A4
Brown St N PA4 94 C3
Brown St S PA4 94 B3
Brown Wlk Irvine KA12 219 D5
Wishaw ML2 166 B5
Brown's La PA1 113 E4
Browncarrick Dr KA7 238 B1
Brownhill Dr KA25 169 F8
Brownhill Rd G43 136 B4
Brownhill View ML2 166 D6
Brownieknowe Pl FK2 41 F8
Brownieside Pl ML6 104 A3
Brownieside Rd ML6 104 C1
Brownlee Rd ML8 186 D4
Brownlie St G42 137 B8
Brownmuir Ave G76 178 F4
Brownsburn Ind Est ML6 123 B5
Brownsburn Rd ML6 123 C5
Brownsdale Rd G73 137 F7
Brownsfield Cres PA4 93 B5
Brownsfield Rd PA4 93 B5
Brownshill Ave ML5 121 F4
Brownside Ave
Barrhead G78 134 A5
Cambuslang G72 138 E5
Brownside Cres G78 134 A5
Brownside Dr
Barrhead G78 134 A5
Glasgow G13 94 F6
Brownside Gr G78 134 A5
Brownside Mews G72 138 E5
Brownside Rd G72,G73 138 E5
Brownsland Ct G69 100 F6
Browside Ave PA2 133 C7
Bruar Way 15 ML2 165 F6
Bruart Ave FK5 23 F3
Bruce Ave
Dundonald KA2 225 F1
Johnstone PA5 131 E8
Motherwell ML1 163 D7
Paisley PA3 114 A7
Prestwick KA9 236 B6
Bruce Cres 1 Ayr KA7 235 E1
Falkirk FK2 24 B3
Kilmarnock KA1 227 F4
Plean FK7 12 D3
Bruce Ct Airdrie ML6 123 E8
Cardross G82 48 B8
Bruce Dr Fallin FK7 8 C5
Stenhousemuir FK5 23 F3
Bruce Gate FK2 14 D2
Bruce Ho G67 61 F3
Bruce La KA9 236 B6
Bruce Loan ML2 186 C6
Bruce Pl G75 180 F7
Bruce Rd Bishopton PA7 72 B3
Glasgow G41 116 E4
Motherwell ML1 143 B2
Paisley PA3 114 A7
Renfrew PA4 94 A1
Bruce St Alloa FK10 10 C7
Bannockburn FK7 7 E1
Bellshill ML4 142 B5
Clydebank G81 74 B1
Coatbridge ML5 122 B8
Dumbarton G82 50 A2
Falkirk FK2 42 C6
Greenock PA15 45 E5
Kilmarnock KA1 227 F4
Plains ML6 104 A2
Plean FK7 12 D3
Port Glasgow PA14 47 D1
Stirling FK8 2 B1
Bruce Terr Blantyre G72 140 E1
Cambusbarron FK7 6 D5
East Kilbride G75 180 F7
Irvine KA12 219 D5
Bruce View FK7 7 B1
Bruce's Loan 22 ML9 185 C1
Brucefield Pl G34 120 D8
Brucehill Rd G82 49 C4
Brunel Way G75 180 F8
Brunstane Rd G34 100 A1
Brunswick Ho G81 73 D6
Brunswick La G1 241 A2
Brunswick St G1 241 A2
Brunton St G44 137 A5
Brunton Terr G44 137 A4
Bruntsfield Ave
Glasgow G53 135 B3
Kilwinning KA13 207 B3
Bruntsfield Gdns G53 135 B3
Bryan St ML3 162 B5
Bryce Ave FK2 24 B2
Bryce Gdns ML9 185 A4
Bryce Knox Ct KA11 220 A6
Bryce Pl G75 180 D6
Brydson Pl PA3 112 B6
Brymner St PA15 46 A5
Bryon Ct G71 141 B2
Bryony The FK10 4 B1
Bryson Ct ML3 183 D7
Bryson St Clydebank G81 74 E2
Falkirk FK2 42 B6
Bryson Street Ind Est FK2 42 B6
Buccleuch Ave
Clarkston G76 157 D7
Glasgow G52 114 E8
Glasgow G52 114 F7
Buccleuch Ct G61 75 E7
Buccleuch Dr G61 75 E7
Buccleuch La G3 240 B4
Buccleuch St G3 240 B4
Buccleugh St PA15 45 F5
Buchan Ct 4 KA7 235 E1
Buchan Gn G74 160 B3
Buchan Ho G67 61 F2
Buchan Rd
Motherwell ML1 143 B2
Troon KA10 229 G4
Buchan St Hamilton ML3 183 C8
Wishaw ML2 165 B6
Buchan Terr G72 138 F3
Buchanan Ave
Balloch G83 28 A8
Bishopton PA7 72 B4
Buchanan Bsns Pk G33 99 E6
Buchanan Cres
Bishopbriggs G64 98 C7
Hamilton ML3 162 B2
Buchanan Ct Falkirk FK2 42 A8
Stepps G33 99 F6
Buchanan Dr
Bearsden G61 76 A4
Bishopbriggs G64 98 C8
Cambuslang G72 138 E6
Carluke ML8 202 C8
Kirkintilloch G66 79 D3
Law ML8 187 A6
Newton Mearns G77 156 E7
Rutherglen G73 138 C6
Stirling FK9 2 B3
Buchanan Galleries G1 241 A3
Buchanan Gate G33 99 F6
Buchanan Gdns G32 119 E2
Buchanan Gr G69 120 B5
Buchanan Pl
Kilmarnock KA1 228 A5
Torrance G64 57 B1
Buchanan Rd G84 17 A1
Buchanan St Airdrie ML6 123 A7
Coatbridge ML5 121 F6
Dumbarton G82 50 B2
Glasgow G1 240 C2
Glasgow G1 241 A3
Glasgow,Muirhead G69 120 B4
Greenock PA16 45 B4
Johnstone PA5 111 E2
Milngavie G62 55 B2
Buchanan Street Underground Sta G1 241 A3
Buchanan Way PA5 111 E2
Buchandyke Rd G74 160 B3
Buchley Cotts G64 77 C5
Buchlyvie Gdns G64 97 F8
Buchlyvie Rd PA1 114 E5
Buchlyvie St G34 120 B7
Buckie PA8 73 A3
Buckie Wlk ML4 142 A6
Buckingham Ct ML3 161 E4
Buckingham Dr
Glasgow G32 139 B8
Rutherglen G73 138 D7
Buckingham St G12 96 D3
Buckingham Terr G12 96 D3
Bucklaw Gdns G52 115 C4
Bucklaw Pl G52 115 C4
Bucklaw Terr G52 115 C4
Buckley St G22 97 D6
Bucksburn Rd G21 98 C4
Buckthorne Pl G53 135 B3
Buddon St G31 118 C4
Budhill Ave G32 119 B5
Budshaw Ave ML6 123 C2
Buiston Rd KA3 211 D3
Bull Rd G76 157 F6
Bull's Cl ML11 215 A4
Bulldale Ct G14 94 F5
Bulldale Rd G14 94 E5
Bulldale St G14 94 E6
Buller Cl G72 140 D2
Buller Cres G72 140 C2
Bullionslaw Dr G73 138 D6
Bulloch Ave G46 136 D2
Bulloch Cres FK6 21 D1
Bullwood Ave G53 134 F8
Bullwood Ct 6 G53 115 A1
Bullwood Dr G53 114 F1
Bullwood Gdns G53 114 F1
Bullwood Pl G53 114 F1
Bunbury Terr 3 G75 180 C8
Bunessan St G52 115 F5
Bungalows The FK5 23 B1
Bunhouse Rd G3 96 C1
Buntine Cres FK7 7 A3
Bunting Pl KA1 228 C7
Burbank G62 55 A2
Burder Pk FK2 24 A2
Burgh Hall La G11 96 B2
Burgh Hall St G11 96 B2
Burgh La 4 G12 96 D3
Burgh Mews 1 FK10 10 B6
Burgh Prim Sch G73 138 A8
Burgh Rd KA9 236 B8
Burgh Wlk PA19 44 E8
Burghead Dr G51 115 E8
Burghead Pl G51 115 E8
Burgher St G31 118 C5
Burghmuir Ind Est FK8 7 B6
Burghmuir Rd FK7 7 B6
Burleigh Rd G71 141 B3
Burleigh St
Coatbridge ML5 122 B3
Burleigh St *continued*
Glasgow G51 116 A8
Burleigh Way FK10 10 C6
Burley Pl G74 158 F2
Burlington Ave G12 96 B6
Burma Rd KA20 218 A5
Burmola St G22 97 B4
Burn Cres
Chapelhall ML6 123 D2
Motherwell ML1 143 B4
Burn Dr FK7 7 C4
Burn La ML1 143 A4
Burn Pl G72 138 E7
Burn Rd Carluke ML8 187 F3
Saltcoats KA21 216 D8
Burn St G83 27 F4
Burn Street La G83 27 F4
Burn Terr G72 138 E7
Burn View G67 62 C3
Burn's Cres ML6 123 B6
Burn's Pl KA20 206 E1
Burnacre Gdns G71 140 E7
Burnawn Gdns G33 98 D7
Burnawn Gr G33 98 D7
Burnawn Pl G33 98 D7
Burnbank Braes ML8 187 F1
Burnbank Ctr ML3 162 A5
Burnbank Dr G78 134 D1
Burnbank Gdns
Hamilton ML3 162 A5
Glasgow G20 96 F2
Burnbank La G20 96 F2
Burnbank Pl Ayr KA7 239 B4
2 Glasgow G20 97 A2
Stewarton KA3 195 F1
Burnbank Quadrant ML6 122 F8
Burnbank Rd Ayr KA7 239 B4
Falkirk FK2 42 B7
Hamilton ML3 162 B4
Burnbank St Airdrie ML6 122 F8
Coatbridge ML5 122 B8
Stevenston KA20 217 D8
Burnbank Terr
Glasgow G20 96 F2
Kilsyth G65 36 D1
Port Glasgow PA14 68 D8
Burnblea Gdns ML3 162 E2
Burnblea St ML3 162 D2
Burnbrae Alloa FK10 10 C8
Clydebank G81 74 A6
Sauchie FK10 5 C1
Twechar G65 59 F4
Burnbrae Ave
Bearsden G61 76 A7
Linwood PA3 112 C5
Moodiesburn G69 81 A2
Burnbrae Cres KA11 220 C5
Burnbrae Dr
Linwood PA3 112 D4
Perceton KA11 220 C5
Rutherglen G73 138 D5
Burnbrae Gdns Alva FK12 5 B6
Falkirk FK1 42 A5
Glasgow G53 135 D6
Burnbrae Pl G74 159 C2
Burnbrae Prim Sch G53 135 D5
Burnbrae Rd Falkirk FK1 42 A5
Hamilton G72 161 C7
Harthill ML7 127 F6
Kirkintilloch G66 80 B2
Kirkintilloch,Auchinloch G66 79 F2
Kirkintilloch,Waterside G66 80 B7
Linwood PA3 112 C4
Shotts ML7 146 E3
Burnbrae St
Clydebank G81 74 D8
Glasgow G21 98 A4
Larkhall ML9 184 F3
Burnbridge Wynd KA3 195 F1
Burncleuch Ave G72 139 A4
Burncrooks Ave
Bearsden G61 75 D7
East Kilbride G74 159 C2
Burncrooks Ct G81 73 F6
Burndale La PA13 89 D8
Burndyke Ct G51 116 C7
Burndyke Sq G51 116 C7
Burnee FK10 5 E3
Burness Ave KA7 238 F2
Burnet Rose Ct G74 159 C4
Burnet Rose Gdns G74 159 C4
Burnet Rose Pl G74 159 C4
Burnett Ct G69 100 C8
Burnett Rd G33 119 E7
Burnett Terr KA8 236 B1
Burnfield Ave G46 136 B4
Burnfield Cotts G46 136 B4
Burnfield Dr G43 136 B4
Burnfield Gdns G46 136 C4
Burnfield Pl FK2 42 D7
Burnfield Rd G46 136 B4
Burnfoot G82 48 B7
Burnfoot Ave KA10 229 E5
Burnfoot Cres
Paisley PA2 133 C8
Rutherglen G73 138 D5
Burnfoot Dr G52 115 B5
Burnfoot La
Ardrossan KA22 205 B4
1 Falkirk FK1 42 B4
Burnfoot Pl KA3 222 E4
Burnfoot Rd Airdrie ML6 122 E8
Lochwinnoch PA12 129 B2
Burnfoot Way 5 KA10 229 E5

Burngreen G65 60 D8
Burngreen Terr G67 62 B5
Burnhall Pl ML2 165 D1
Burnhall Rd ML2 165 C2
Burnhall St ML2 165 D1
Burnham Rd G14 95 A4
Burnhaven PA8 73 A2
Burnhead La Falkirk FK1 42 C4
Port Glasgow PA14 68 D8
Burnhead Prim Sch G71 141 D8
Burnhead Rd
Airdrie ML6 103 D1
Cumbernauld G68 61 C2
Glasgow G43 136 E5
Larkhall ML9 185 C2
Port Glasgow PA14 68 D8
Stenhousemuir FK5 23 C3
Burnhead St
Greenock PA15 46 B2
Uddingston G71 141 C7
Burnhill Quadrant G73 137 F8
Burnhill St G73 137 F8
Burnhouse Ave
Cumbernauld G68 61 B2
Dalry KA24 191 B7
Burnhouse Brae G77 157 A3
Burnhouse Cotts KA3 195 B8
Burnhouse Cres ML3 162 B1
Burnhouse Rd
East Kilbride G75 180 A1
Hamilton ML3 162 B1
Burnhouse St
Glasgow G20 96 C6
Glasgow G20 96 D6
Burniebrae ML6 122 F8
Burniebrae Rd ML6 123 E3
Burnlea Cres PA6 91 A3
Burnlea Pl KA20 206 E2
Burnlip Rd ML6 102 A4
Burnmouth Ct G33 119 F6
Burnmouth Pl G61 76 A5
Burnmouth Rd G33 119 F6
Burnock Pl G75 179 E7
Burnpark Ave G71 140 D7
Burnpark Rd KA1 227 F3
Burns Ave Bishopton PA7 72 B3
Kilmarnock KA3 223 A3
Saltcoats KA21 205 F3
Stenhousemuir FK5 23 C5
Burns Cottage & Mus* KA7 238 E2
Burns Cres Harthill ML7 127 F6
Irvine KA11 220 A5
Kilmarnock KA3 223 B5
Laurieston FK2 42 F4
Burns Ct G66 59 A1
Burns Dr Johnstone PA5 131 E8
Kirkintilloch G66 59 A2
Burns Gdns G72 140 C1
Burns Gr G46 136 A2
Burns La ML6 123 D3
Burns Loan 13 ML9 185 B4
Burns Mon* KA3 223 A1
Burns Path ML4 142 B7
Burns Pk G74 160 A3
Burns Pl Kilwinning KA13 207 F3
Shotts ML7 146 A6
Burns Prec 5 KA1 227 F8
Burns Rd Chapelhall ML6 123 D4
Cumbernauld G67 62 B2
Greenock PA16 44 D4
Kirkintilloch G66 59 A1
Troon KA10 229 G4
Burns Sq Ardrossan KA22 205 D4
Greenock PA16 44 D4
Burns St Alexandria G83 27 E7
Clydebank G81 73 E4
Glasgow G4 97 B2
Hamilton ML3 162 D2
Irvine KA12 219 B3
Renton G82 27 D1
Stirling FK8 2 A2
Burns Statue Arc KA7 238 F7
Burns Statue Sq KA7 238 F7
Burns Terr
Ardrossan KA22 205 D4
Cowie FK7 12 D7
Burns Way
Kilmarnock KA3 223 B5
Motherwell ML1 143 C4
Burns Wynd ML9 198 E1
Burns' Wicket KA7 238 E1
Burnside G61 75 C7
Burnside Ave
Barrhead G78 134 B4
Bellshill ML4 142 C4
Brookfield PA5 111 C5
Calderbank ML6 123 B2
Kirkintilloch G66 79 B7
Port Glasgow PA14 68 F8
Burnside Cotts KA3 173 C6
Burnside Cres Balloch G83 27 F7
Clydebank G81 74 B7
Hamilton G72 161 F6
Plean FK7 12 C4
Shotts ML7 146 D6
Burnside Ct Alva FK12 5 A7
Bearsden G61 75 C7
Coatbridge ML5 121 F5
Falkirk,Camelon FK1 41 E5
Motherwell ML1 164 B4
Rutherglen G73 138 C5
Burnside Gate
Hamilton ML3 162 D3
Burnside Gate *continued*
Rutherglen G73 138 C5
Burnside Gdns
Clarkston G76 157 D7
Johnstone PA10 111 B2
Prestwick KA9 233 C1
Burnside Gr PA5 111 E2
Burnside Ind Est G65 60 C8
Burnside La ML3 162 E2
Burnside Pl
Dumbarton G82 50 B2
Falkirk FK2 24 B3
Irvine KA12 219 B4
Larkhall ML9 185 B3
Paisley PA3 113 A7
Stevenston KA20 206 D1
Troon KA10 229 D3
West Kilbride KA23 190 D5
Burnside Prim Sch G73 138 B5
Burnside Quadrant ML1 143 A5
Burnside Rd
Elderslie PA5 112 D2
Glenmavis ML5 102 C1
Gourock PA19 44 F6
Menstrie FK11 3 F6
Monkton KA9 233 D4
Motherwell ML1 143 D4
Rutherglen G46 157 B6
Rutherglen,High Burnside G73 138 C4
Burnside St Alloa FK10 5 D1
Dumbarton G82 50 B2
Glengarnock KA14 170 B6
Kilmarnock KA1 227 E6
Motherwell ML1 164 B4
Stirling FK7 7 C6
Burnside Sta G73 138 C5
Burnside Terr FK1 41 E5
Burnside Twr ML1 164 B3
Burnside View
Coatbridge ML5 121 E5
East Kilbride G75 180 A4
Burnside Wlk
Bearsden G61 75 C7
Coatbridge ML5 121 E5
Burntbroom Dr G69 119 F3
Burntbroom Gdns G69 119 F3
Burntbroom Rd G69 119 F2
Burntbroom St G33 119 D7
Burnthills Ind Est PA5 111 F3
Burntshields Rd PA10 110 D2
Burnwood Dr ML6 124 A6
Burra Gdns G64 78 D2
Burray Dr KA3 223 A6
Burrell Collection (Mus)* G43 116 B1
Burrell Ct G41 116 C2
Burrell's La G4 241 C2
Burrelton Rd G43 136 F5
Burstenman's Brae KA13,KA24 207 F7
Burte Ct ML4 142 A7
Burton La Carluke ML8 187 E2
Glasgow G42 117 A1
Busbie Gdns KA2 221 E1
Busbie Holdings KA2 221 D3
Busbie La KA22 205 D3
Busbie View KA2 221 E1
Busbiehead KA11 220 B5
Busbiehill Pl KA1 222 D1
Busby Pl KA13 207 F4
Busby Prim Sch G76 157 F6
Busby Rd Bellshill ML4 141 F3
Carmunnock G76 158 C7
Clarkston G76 157 E7
Busby Sta G76 158 A5
Bush Cres ML2 165 C2
Bushelhead Rd ML8 201 E6
Bushes Ave PA2 113 D1
Bushes Prim Sch PA2 133 D8
Busheyhill St G72 139 A5
Bute G74 160 C1
Bute Ave Motherwell ML1 163 C7
Port Glasgow PA14 69 B8
Renfrew PA4 94 D1
Bute Cres Bearsden G61 75 F2
Old Kilpatrick G60 73 C5
Paisley PA2 133 D7
Shotts ML7 146 D6
Bute Ct Irvine KA11 220 C1
Stevenston KA20 217 C8
Bute Dr Johnstone PA5 111 D1
Old Kilpatrick G60 73 C6
Bute Gdns Glasgow G44 136 F4
Glasgow,Kelvingrove G12 96 D2
Old Kilpatrick G60 73 C6
Bute La G12 96 D2
Bute Pl Ardrossan KA22 205 C1
Old Kilpatrick G60 73 D5
Bute Rd Kirkintilloch G66 80 B8
Renfrew PA3 93 D1
Bute St Coatbridge ML5 122 B4
Falkirk FK2 42 B6
Gourock PA19 44 D6
Hamilton ML3 162 B6
Bute Terr Rutherglen G73 138 A5
Saltcoats KA21 205 E1
Uddingston G71 141 B7
Bute Twr G72 138 E3
Butler Wynd ML4 141 F5
Butt Ave G84 16 E3
Butterbiggins Rd G42 117 B3
Butterburnpark St ML3 162 D2
Buttercup Path ML2 164 F1
Butterfield Pl 2 G41 117 A3
Buttermere G75 179 F5
Butts The ML11 214 F3
Buttsley Ct ML11 214 E4
By Pass Rd KA15 150 C1
By-Pass Rd FK4 39 E5
Byars Rd G66 79 B8
Byrebush Rd G53 115 C1
Byrehill Ave KA13 207 B2
Byrehill Pl KA13 207 B2
Byrehill Rd KA13,KA20 207 D1
Byres Ave PA3 114 A6
Byres Cres PA3 114 A6
Byres Loch KA13 207 D3
Byres Rd Elderslie PA5 112 D2
Glasgow G12 96 C2
Kilwinning KA13 207 D3
Motherwell ML1 143 E4
Byresknowe La 2 ML1 143 B1
Byrestone Ave G77 157 C4
Byretown Rd ML11 214 E2
Byron Rd ML7 146 B6
Byron St Clydebank G81 74 A4
Glasgow G11 95 F2
Byshot St G22 97 D4

C

Caaf Water Pl KA21 205 E2
Cable Depot Rd G81 73 F2
Cables Dr G83 27 F5
Cabrach Loan 13 ML2 165 F6
Cadder Ct G64 78 B5
Cadder Gr G20 96 E7
Cadder Pl G20 96 E7
Cadder Prim Sch G23 96 F7
Cadder Rd
Bishopbriggs G64 78 B5
Glasgow G23 96 E7
Cadder Rdbt G64 78 B4
Cadder Way G64 78 B5
Caddlehill St PA16 45 D5
Cadell Dr FK2 24 A5
Cadell Gdns G74 160 D5
Cadger's Sheuch G68 61 B8
Cadgers Loan FK7 12 B2
Cadoc St G72 139 B5
Cadogan Sq G2 240 B2
Cadogan St G2 240 B2
Cadzow Ave
Hamilton ML3 162 C5
Rutherglen G46 157 B8
Cadzow Cres ML5 121 E4
Cadzow Dr Bellshill ML4 142 D4
Cambuslang G72 139 A5
Cadzow Gn G74 159 D2
Cadzow Ho ML3 162 E5
Cadzow Ind Est ML3 183 D8
Cadzow La ML3 162 E4
Cadzow Pk ML3 162 E4
Cadzow Rd ML3 183 F3
Cadzow St Glasgow G2 240 B2
Hamilton ML3 162 E4
Larkhall ML9 185 A4
Motherwell ML1 163 D6
Caerlaverock Ave KA9 236 C8
Caerlaverock Pl 1 G72 161 C6
Caerlaverock Rd KA9 236 C8
Caird Ave PA16 45 C7
Caird Dr G11 96 B2
Caird Gdns ML3 162 D5
Caird Pk ML3 162 D5
Caird St ML3 162 C5
Caird Terr G61 75 D7
Cairn Ave PA4 94 E1
Cairn Cl KA3 195 C1
Cairn Cres KA7 238 D2
Cairn Ct East Kilbride G74 159 E4
2 Motherwell ML1 163 F5
Cairn Dr PA3 112 B6
Cairn Pl G74 159 E4
Cairn St G21 97 F6
Cairn View ML6 122 F6
Cairnban Ct ML8 187 F3
Cairnbrook Ind Est G34 120 C8
Cairnbrook Rd G34 120 C8
Cairncurran Ct PA15 45 E3
Cairndhu Ave G84 16 A2
Cairndhu Gdns G84 16 A2
Cairndow Ave G44 136 F4
Cairndow Avenue La G44 136 F4
Cairndow Ct G44 136 F4
Cairndow Pl ML2 165 C1
Cairnduff Pl KA3 195 F1
Cairndyke Cres ML6 123 A6
Cairney Pl ML2 166 D6
Cairneymount Rd ML8 188 A2
Cairnfore Ave KA10 229 G6
Cairngorm Cres
Barrhead G78 134 C1
Bearsden G61 75 B6
Paisley PA2 113 E1
Wishaw ML2 164 F3
Cairngorm Ct
Greenock PA16 45 B5
Hamilton ML3 183 B7
Irvine KA11 220 B5
Cairngorm Gdns G68 61 B1
Cairngorm Pl G75 180 B4
Cairngorm Rd
Glasgow G43 136 C5
Kilmarnock KA1 228 B3
Cairngorm Residential Pk The G64 98 C8
Cairnhill Ave ML6 123 A5
Cairnhill Cir G53 114 F3
Cairnhill Cres ML5 122 D3
Cairnhill Ct ML8 188 A2
Cairnhill Dr G53 114 F3
Cairnhill Pl G53 114 F3
Cairnhill Rd Airdrie ML6 123 A6
Bearsden G61 75 F1
Cairnhill Trad Est ML6 123 A6
Cairnhope Ave ML6 122 F5
Cairnlea Dr G51 116 B6
Cairnlea Gdns ML4 142 B3
Cairnlea Rd G62 54 E1
Cairnmount Rd KA11 219 F7
Cairnmuir Rd G74 159 D6
Cairnoch Hill G68 61 C2
Cairnoch Way FK7 7 F1
Cairnoch Wlk FK6 21 D1
Cairnryan G74 159 D3
Cairnryan Cres G72 161 D2
Cairns Ave G72 139 B5
Cairns Ct G72 139 B5
Cairns Dr G62 55 A2
Cairns Prim Sch G72 139 C4
Cairns Rd Bishopton PA7 72 A4
Cambuslang G72 139 B4
Cairns St ML1 163 E6
Cairns Terr KA1 222 E1
Cairns The FK11 4 A6
Cairnsgarroch Way KA11 220 B2
Cairnsmore Dr
Bearsden G61 75 B7
Doonfoot KA7 238 C1
Cairnsmore Rd G15 74 F2
Cairnsmore Way KA11 220 B2
Cairnswell Ave G72 139 C4
Cairnswell Pl G72 139 C4
Cairntoul Ct G68 61 B1
Cairntoul Dr G14 95 A5
Cairntoul Pl G14 95 A5
Cairnview G66 80 B7
Cairnview Rd G66 58 C5
Cairnwood Dr ML6 122 F5
Caithness Rd
East Kilbride G74 160 D3
Greenock PA16 44 D4
Caithness Row ML11 215 A2
Caithness St Glasgow G20 96 F4
Hamilton G72 161 C6
Cala Sona Ct ML2 185 E8
Calcots Path G34 100 C1
Calcots Pl G34 100 D1
Caldarvan St G22 97 B3
Caldeen Rd ML5 122 B5
Calder Ave Barrhead G78 134 D1
Caldercruix ML6 104 F4
Coatbridge ML5 122 B4
Troon KA10 229 F6
Wishaw ML2 166 A6
Calder Ct Coatbridge ML5 122 B4
Stirling FK7 7 C5
Calder Dr Bellshill ML4 142 C4
Cambuslang G72 139 A5
Lochwinnoch PA12 129 C3
Shotts ML7 147 B4
Calder Gate G64 77 F4
Calder Pl Falkirk FK1 42 D1
Glasgow G69 120 B4
Kilmarnock KA1 228 A5
Calder Prim Sch ML1 163 F7
Calder Rd Bellshill ML4 142 C4
Paisley PA3 113 A5
Shotts ML7 166 F8
Uddingston G71,G72 140 C5
Calder St
Calderbank ML6 123 C2
Coatbridge ML5 122 C5
Glasgow G42 117 B2
Hamilton G72 161 D7
Lochwinnoch PA12 129 C3
Calder Twr
East Kilbride G74 181 B7
6 Motherwell ML1 163 E5
Calder View ML3 183 B8
Calderbank Prim Sch ML6 123 C3
Calderbank Rd ML6 123 B4
Calderbank Terr ML1 163 F7
Calderbank View G69 120 C4
Calderbankview Cotts ML6 123 B4
Calderbraes Ave G71 140 E8
Caldercruix Rd ML6 105 D7
Caldercuilt Prim Sch G23 76 E1
Caldercuilt Rd G20 96 C8
Calderglen Ave G72 140 C3
Calderglen Ctry Pk* G75 181 C6
Calderglen Ctry Pk Visitor Ctr* G75 181 C6
Calderglen Rd G74 160 D1
Caldergrove ML1 163 E8
Calderhaugh La PA12 129 B2
Calderhaugh Mill PA12 129 C2
Calderhead High Sch ML7 146 F5
Calderhead Rd ML7 146 D7
Calderpark Ave
Glasgow G71 120 B2
Lochwinnoch PA12 129 C3
Calderpark Cres G71 120 B2
Calderpark St PA12 129 C3
Calderpark Terr G71 120 B2
Calderrigg Pl ML6 123 E7
Calderside Gr G74 160 E3
Calderside Rd G72,G74 160 E3
Caldervale High Sch ML6 123 F7
Caldervale St ML6 123 E4
Calderview ML1 163 F7
Calderview Ave ML5 122 E4
Calderwood KA13 207 E5
Calderwood Ave G69 120 A3
Calderwood Ct ML2 165 B2
Calderwood Dr
Glasgow G69 120 A3
Hamilton G72 161 D6
Calderwood Gdns
East Kilbride G74 160 E3
Glasgow G69 120 A3
Calderwood Lodge Prim Sch G43 136 E5
Calderwood Prim Sch G73 138 C6
Calderwood Rd
East Kilbride G74 160 B2
Glasgow G43 136 D6
Rutherglen G73 138 C7
Calderwood Sq 1 G74 160 B3
Caldon Rd KA12 219 D4
Caldwell Ave
Glasgow G13 95 A6
Linwood PA3 112 A5
Caldwell Gr Bellshill ML4 142 A8
Rutherglen G73 138 C2
Caldwell Pl G84 15 E5
Caldwell Quadrant ML1 163 C5
Caldwell Rd
Carluke ML8 202 B8
West Kilbride KA23 190 C4
Caledon La G12 96 C2
Caledon St G12 96 C3
Caledonia Ave
Glasgow G5 117 C3
Rutherglen G73 138 B8
Caledonia Cres
Ardrossan KA22 205 C2
Gourock PA19 44 F7
Gourock PA19 45 A7
Caledonia Ct
Kilmarnock KA1 222 E1
Paisley PA3 113 D6
Caledonia Dr
Glasgow G69 120 B3
Motherwell ML1 143 E4
Caledonia Gdns
Carluke ML8 187 E3
Gourock PA19 44 F7
Caledonia Prim Sch
Glasgow G69 120 A3
Saltcoats KA21 216 E8
Caledonia Rd
Ardrossan KA22 205 C2
Ayr KA7 239 C6
Beith KA15 150 B1
Glasgow G69 120 A3
Glasgow,Gorbals G5 117 C4
Saltcoats KA21 205 E1
Shotts ML7 146 E5
Caledonia St
Clydebank G81 73 F3
Glasgow G5 117 D3
Paisley PA3 113 D6
Port Glasgow PA14 47 D1
Caledonia Terr
Bonnybridge FK4 39 F5
Dumbarton G82 49 D3
Caledonia Way PA3 93 D1
Caledonia Way E PA3 93 E1
Caledonia Way W PA3 93 D1
Caledonia Wlk ML3 162 E1
Caledonian Ave
Bellshill ML4 141 F4
Stonehouse ML9 198 E1
Caledonian Cres 5 G12 96 E2
Caledonian Ct
East Kilbride G75 180 E8
Falkirk FK2 42 C7
Caledonian Pk ML2 164 D3
Caledonian Pl KA14 170 B7
Caledonian Rd Alloa FK10 9 F6
Glengarnock KA14 170 C7
Larkhall ML9 185 A3
Stevenston KA20 217 E7
Wishaw ML2 165 A2
Caley Brae G71 140 F6
Caley Ct KA20 217 D7
Caley Ho KA13 207 B2
Calfhill Rd G53 115 B2
Calfmuir Rd G66 80 A6
Calgary Pk G75 180 D8
Calgary Pl 1 G75 180 D8
Calgary St G4 241 A4
Calico Way G66 33 C1
California Prim Sch FK1 66 F5
California Rd FK1 66 E6
California Terr FK1 66 F5
Callaghan Wynd G72 140 C1
Callandar Pl KA8 236 B4
Callander Ct G68 61 F4
Callander Dr FK5 41 C8
Callander Rd Ayr KA8 236 D5
Chapelhall ML6 123 D1
Cumbernauld G68 61 F4
Callander St G20 97 A3
Callendar Ave FK1 42 B1
Callendar Bsns Pk FK1 42 E3
Callendar Bvd FK1 42 E3
Callendar Ho* FK1 42 D3
Callendar Park Dr FK1 42 D4
Callendar Rd FK1 42 D4
Callendar Riggs FK1 42 C4
Callendar Square Sh Ctr 5 FK1 42 B4
Callender Park View FK1 42 D4
Callender Park Wlk FK1 42 D4
Callieburn Ct G64 98 A8
Callieburn Rd G64 98 A8
Callon St ML6 123 A7
Cally Ave G15 75 A3

256 Car – Cha

Carrick Rd *continued*
East Kilbride G74 ....159 F3
Rutherglen G73 ....137 F5
Troon KA10 ....229 E7
Rutherglen G73 ....138 A5
Carrick Road La KA7 ....238 F6
Carrick St Ayr KA7 ......238 F8
Glasgow G2 ....240 B2
7 Larkhall ML9 ....185 C2
Carrick Terr
Dumbarton G82 ....49 B4
Greenock PA16 ....44 E3
Carrick Vale ML1 ....144 C1
Carrick View ML5 ....101 E6
Carrick Way 7 G71 .....141 A3
Carrickarden Rd G61 .....75 F3
Carrickstone Rd G68 .....61 E4
Carrickstone Rdbt G68 ...61 E5
Carrickstone View G68 ...61 F5
Carrickvale Ct G68 ....61 F5
Carrington St G4 ....96 F2
Carrochan Cres G83 ......27 F8
Carrochan Rd G83 ....27 F8
Carroglen Gdns G32 ....119 D5
Carroglen Gr G32 ....119 D5
Carroll Cres ML1 ....143 D2
Carron Ave KA1 ....228 B6
Carron Cres Bearsden G61 .75 C3
Bishopbriggs G64 ....78 B1
Glasgow G22 ....97 D5
Kirkintilloch G66 ....79 E4
Carron Ct
Cambuslang G72 ....139 D5
Hamilton ML3 ....162 B1
Carron Dr PA7 ....72 C2
Carron Pl
Coatbridge ML5 ....101 D1
East Kilbride G75 ....180 F5
Glasgow G22 ....97 E5
Irvine KA12 ....219 C6
Stirling FK7 ....7 B2
Carron Prim Sch FK2 ....24 A2
Carron Rd Falkirk FK2 .....24 A1
Falkirk FK2 ....42 A8
Carron Rdbt FK2 ....24 A2
Carron St Glasgow G22 ....97 E5
Wishaw ML2 ....165 B1
Carron Way
Motherwell ML1 ....143 C4
Paisley PA3 ....114 A7
Carronbank Ave FK2 .....24 B2
Carronbank Cres FK6 .....21 E3
Carronbank Ct FK2 ....24 B2
Carrongrange Ave FK5 ...23 E2
Carrongrange Gdns FK5 ..23 E1
Carrongrange Gr FK5 ....23 E1
Carrongrange Rd FK5 ....23 E2
Carrongrange Sch FK5 ...23 E2
Carrongrove Ave FK2 ....24 A2
Carrongrove Bsns Pk
FK2 ....24 A2
Carrongrove Rd FK2 .....24 A2
Carronhall Ave FK2 ......24 C4
Carronlea Dr FK2 ....24 A2
Carronshore Prim Sch
FK2 ....24 C4
Carronshore Rd FK2 .....24 B2
Carronside Pl FK6 ....21 E3
Carronside St FK2 ....42 B8
Carronvale Ave FK5 ......23 D1
Carronvale Rd
Larbert FK5 ....41 D8
Stenhousemuir FK5 ....23 C1
Carronview FK5 ....23 D2
Carrour Gdns G64 ....77 F2
Carruth Dr PA13 ....89 C8
Carruth Rd PA11 ....110 C8
Carsaig Ct FK9 ....2 A5
Carsaig Dr G52 ....115 E5
Carsaig Loan ML5 ....101 C6
Carscallan Rd ML3 ......183 E5
Carse Terr FK10 ....9 F8
Carse View FK2 ....14 E4
Carse View Dr G61 ....76 A6
Carsebridge Ct FK10 ......10 C8
Carsebridge Rd FK10 .....10 D8
Carsebridge Row FK10 ...10 D8
Carsegreen Ave PA2 ....133 B7
Carseloch Rd KA7 ....238 F1
Carsemeadow PA11 ....89 E2
Carseview Bannockburn FK7 .7 E2
Tullibody FK10 ....4 A3
Carsewood Ave PA9 .....130 F5
Carson Dr KA12 ....224 E7
Carson Rd G83 ....27 E8
Carstairs St G40 ....118 A2
Carswell Ct KA24 ....191 B7
Carswell Gdns G41 .....116 E2
Carswell Rd G77 ....156 B5
Cart La PA3 ....113 E6
Cart St G81 ....94 B8
Cartbank Gdns G44 .....137 A4
Cartbank Gr G44 ....136 F4
Cartbank Rd G44 ....137 A4
Cartcraigs Rd G43 ......136 B6
Carters Pl KA12 ....219 C2
Carters Rigg KA12 ......219 B1
Cartha Cres PA2 ....114 B3
Cartha St G41 ....136 E7
Cartland Ave ML8 ....201 F8
Cartland Rd ML11 ....214 D8
Cartland View ML11 .....214 F5
Cartle Cl KA13 ....207 C6
Cartsbridge Rd G76 .....157 F6
Cartsburn St PA15 ....46 B3
Cartsdyke Ave PA15 ......46 C4
Cartsdyke Ct PA15 ....46 D3
Cartsdyke Sta PA15 ......46 C4
Cartside Ave
Inchinnan PA4 ....93 B4
Johnstone PA5 ....111 D1
Cartside Dr G76 ....158 A6
Cartside Pl G76 ....157 F5
Cartside Quadrant G42 .137 A7
Cartside Rd G76 ....157 F5
Cartside St G42 ....136 F7
Cartvale La PA3 ....113 E6
Cartvale Rd G42 ....136 F7
Cartvale Sch
Glasgow,Govan G51 .....116 B7
Glasgow,Langside G42 ...136 F7
Cartview Ct G76 ....157 F6
Carvale Ave ML7 ....125 B2
Carwinshoch View KA7 ..238 D5
Carwood Ct PA15 ....46 C3
Carwood St PA15 ....46 D3
Cask Cres FK8 ....7 C8
Caskie Dr G72 ....140 E1
Cassels Gr ML1 ....142 C1
Cassels St Carluke ML8 ..187 F1
Motherwell ML1 ....163 E8
Cassillis St KA7 ....238 E8
Cassiltoun Gdns G45 ....137 D2
Cassley Ave PA4 ....94 F2
Castburn Rd G67 ....62 F6
Castings Ave FK2 ....42 B7
Castings Ct Falkirk FK2 ...42 B7
Falkirk,Middlefield FK2 ....42 E6
Castings Dr FK2 ....42 B6
Castings Ho FK2 ....42 B7
Castings Rd FK2 ....42 E6
Castle Ave Airth FK2 ......14 E3
Balloch G83 ....19 F1
Bothwell G71 ....140 E3
Elderslie PA5 ....112 B1
Falkirk FK2 ....24 C3
Helensburgh G84 ....16 A2
Motherwell ML1 ....143 B6
Stevenston KA20 ....206 E2
Castle Bsns Pk The FK9 ....1 E2
Castle Chimmins Ave
G72 ....139 D4
Castle Chimmins Rd
G72 ....139 D3
Castle Cres Bishopton PA7 .72 B2
Denny FK6 ....21 D2
Falkirk FK2 ....42 D7
Torwood FK5 ....22 E7
Castle Ct Cumbernauld G68 .62 F8
Falkirk FK2 ....42 C7
Kirkintilloch G66 ....79 D8
Menstrie FK11 ....3 F6
Stirling FK8 ....7 A8
Castle Dr Airth FK2 ....14 E3
Dundonald KA2 ....225 F2
Falkirk FK2 ....42 C8
Kilbirnie KA25 ....149 A1
Kilmarnock KA3 ....223 A4
Motherwell ML1 ....143 B6
Stenhousemuir FK5 ....23 F2
West Kilbride KA23 .....190 D5
Castle Farm Cl KA3 .....195 D1
Castle Gait PA1 ....113 E3
Castle Gate
Newton Mearns G77 .....157 A3
Uddingston G71 ....140 E5
Castle Gdns Gourock PA19 .44 E8
Moodiesburn G69 ....80 F2
Paisley PA2 ....113 A3
Paisley,Castlehead PA2 ...113 D3
Castle Gr Kilbirnie KA25 ..149 A1
Kilsyth G65 ....36 C2
Castle Keep Gdns KA11 ..219 F4
Castle Levan Manor
PA19 ....43 F5
Castle Mains Rd G62 .....54 D2
Castle Pl Falkirk FK2 ......42 D7
Irvine KA12 ....219 B3
Uddingston G71 ....140 E6
Castle Quadrant ML6 ....123 D7
Castle Rd Airdrie ML6 ....123 D7
Ardrossan KA22 ....205 D3
Bridge Of W PA11 ....90 D1
Dumbarton G82 ....50 A2
Elderslie PA5 ....112 C3
Falkirk FK2 ....42 C8
Greenock PA15 ....46 C2
Menstrie FK11 ....3 F6
Newton Mearns G77 .....156 C4
Port Glasgow PA14 ....47 D1
Stirling FK9 ....2 C3
Castle Semple Ctry Pk*
PA12 ....129 E3
Castle Semple Loch Visitor
Ctr* PA12 ....129 D3
Castle Sq Clydebank G81 ..73 E3
Doonfoot KA7 ....238 B3
Castle St Alloa FK10 ......10 A5
Chapelhall ML6 ....123 D2
Clydebank G81 ....73 E3
Dumbarton G82 ....49 F3
Glasgow G4 ....241 C3
Glasgow,Baillieston G69 ..120 A3
Glasgow,Kelvinhaugh G11 ..96 C1
Hamilton ML3 ....162 F4
Irvine KA12 ....219 B3
Paisley PA1 ....113 C4
Rutherglen G73 ....138 A8
Castle Terr
Bridge of W PA11 ....110 E7
Denny FK6 ....21 C2
Knockentiber KA2 ....221 F3
Castle Vale FK9 ....2 A4
Castle View Airth FK2 .....14 D2
Doonfoot KA7 ....238 B3
Fallin FK7 ....8 D4
West Kilbride KA23 .....190 D6
Wishaw ML2 ....166 A6
Castle Way
Coatbridge G69 ....120 F5
Cumbernauld G67 ....62 C4
Castle Wlk KA7 ....238 C3
Castle Wynd
Bothwell G71 ....141 B2
Quarter ML3 ....183 F3
4 Stirling FK8 ....7 A8
Castlebank Ct G13 ....95 E6
Castlebank Gdns G13 ....95 E6
Castlebank St
Glasgow G11 ....96 A1
Glasgow G11 ....96 B1
Castlebank Villas G13 ....95 E6
Castlebay Dr G22 ....77 C1
Castlebay Pl G22 ....97 C8
Castlebay St G22 ....97 C8
Castlebrae G82 ....49 D5
Castlebrae Gdns G44 ....137 B6
Castlecary Rd G67,G68 ....62 D7
Castlecroft Gdns G71 ....140 F5
Castlefern Rd G73 ....138 B3
Castlefield Ct G33 ....99 B4
Castlefield Gdns G75 ....180 B5
Castlefield Prim Sch
G75 ....180 B6
Castlegait 6 FK8 ....7 B7
Castlegate ML11 ....215 A4
Castleglen Rd G74 ......159 A4
Castlegreen Cres G82 ....50 B2
Castlegreen Gdns G82 ....50 B2
Castlegreen La G82 ......50 A2
Castlegreen St G82 ....50 B2
Castlehead High Sch
PA1 ....113 D3
Castlehill Ave
Port Glasgow PA14 ....69 A7
Slamannan FK1 ....86 A6
Castlehill Cres Ayr KA7 ..239 A6
Banknock FK4 ....38 E2
Chapelhall ML6 ....123 F1
Hamilton ML3 ....162 F3
Hamilton,Allanton ML3 ...163 D1
Kilmacolm PA13 ....89 C8
Law ML8 ....187 A4
Renfrew PA4 ....94 D4
Castlehill Ct KA7 ....239 B5
Castlehill Dr G77 ....156 F3
Castlehill Gdns Ayr KA7 ..239 C5
Hamilton ML3 ....162 F2
Castlehill Gn G74 ....158 F4
Castlehill Ind Est ML8 ...187 E4
Castlehill Prim Sch
Bearsden G61 ....75 C6
Wishaw ML2 ....186 A8
Castlehill Quadrant G82 ..49 C5
Castlehill Rd Ayr KA7 ....239 A6
Bearsden G61 ....75 C6
Carluke ML8 ....187 E5
Dumbarton G82 ....49 C5
Kilmacolm PA13 ....89 C8
Overtown ML2 ....186 B7
Stevenston KA20 ....206 F2
Stewarton KA3 ....195 E1
Castlehill View G65 ......36 C2
Castleknowe Gdns ML8 ..187 E3
Castlelaurie Ind Est FK2 ..42 C7
Castlelaurie St FK2 ....42 C7
Castlelaw Gdns G32 .....119 B6
Castlelaw St G32 ....119 B6
Castlemilk Arc G45 ......137 D3
Castlemilk Cres G44 .....137 E5
Castlemilk Dr G45 ....137 E3
Castlemilk High Sch
G45 ....137 E2
Castlemilk Rd
Glasgow,Croftfoot G44 ...137 E5
Glasgow,King's Park G44 .137 E6
Castlemilk Terr G45 .....137 E1
Castlemount Ave G77 ....156 F3
Castlepark Cres KA12 ...219 B6
Castlepark Prim Sch
KA12 ....219 C6
Castlepark Rd KA12 .....219 B6
Castlerankine Rd FK6 ....21 C2
Castleton Ave
Bishopbriggs G64 ....97 E7
Newton Mearns G77 .....157 A3
Castleton Cres G77 ......156 F3
Castleton Ct
Glasgow G45 ....137 F2
Newton Mearns G77 .....156 F3
Castleton Dr G77 ....156 F3
Castleton Gr G77 ....156 F3
Castleton Prim Sch
G45 ....137 D3
Castleview
Clachan of C G66 ....32 F3
Cumbernauld G68 ....62 E8
Dundonald KA2 ....225 F3
Larkhall ML9 ....199 A8
Castleview Ave PA2 .....133 A7
Castleview Dr
Bridge of A FK9 ....2 A7
Paisley PA2 ....133 A7
Castleview Pl PA2 ....133 A7
Castleview Terr FK4 .....39 A3
Catacol Ave KA21 ....205 F2
Cathay St G22 ....97 C8
Cathburn Holdings ML2 .166 D5
Cathburn Rd ML2 ....166 C5
Cathcart Bldgs PA15 .....46 A5
Cathcart Cres PA2 ......114 A3
Cathcart Pl G73 ....137 F7
Cathcart Rd
Glasgow,Govanhill G42 ...117 B2
Glasgow,Mount Florida
G42 ....137 B8
Cathcart Sq PA15 ....46 A5
Cathcart St 7 Ayr KA7 ...235 F1
Greenock PA15 ....46 A5
Cathcart Sta G44 ....137 A6
Cathedral Prim Sch
ML1 ....163 E7
Cathedral Sq G4 ....241 C2
Cathedral St G1,G4 ......241 B3
Catherine Pl KA3 ....222 C6
Catherine St
Bannockburn FK7 ....7 C1
Kirkintilloch G66 ....79 C8
Motherwell ML1 ....163 E4
Catherine Way ML1 .....142 F3
Catherine's Wlk G72 ....161 D6
Cathkin Ave
Cambuslang G72 ....138 E6
Rutherglen G73 ....138 C7
Cathkin By-Pass G73 ...138 D3
Cathkin Cres G68 ....61 E4
Cathkin Ct G45 ....137 F2
Cathkin Dr G76 ....157 C8
Cathkin Gdns G71 ......120 E1
Cathkin High Sch G72 ...138 E4
Cathkin Pl
Cambuslang G72 ....138 E6
Kilwinning KA13 ....207 B4
Cathkin Prim Sch G73 ..138 D3
Cathkin Rd
Carmunnock G76 ....158 F8
Glasgow G42 ....136 F7
Rutherglen G73 ....138 C2
Uddingston G71 ....120 E1
Cathkin View G32 ....139 B8
Cathkinview Pl G42 .....137 B7
Cathkinview Rd G42 .....137 B7
Catrine G74 ....159 D2
Catrine Ave 3 G81 ....74 D3
Catrine Cres ML1 ....164 A4
Catrine Ct 8 G53 ....135 A8
Catrine Gdns 7 G53 .....135 A8
Catrine Pl G53 ....135 A8
Catrine Rd G53 ....135 A8
Catrine St 5 ML9 ....185 C2
Catriona Pl G82 ....50 C2
Catriona Way ML1 ......143 B4
Catter Gdns G62 ....54 E3
Cauldhame Cres FK7 ......6 C5
Cauldhame Rigg KA3 ....211 F8
Cauldstream Pl G62 ......54 E1
Causeway The FK9 ....2 D5
Causewayhead Rd FK9 ....2 C3
Causewayside Cres G32 .119 A2
Causewayside St G32 ...119 A2
Causeyfoot Dr KA25 .....149 A1
Causeyside St PA1 ......113 E4
Causeystanes 4 G72 ....161 D7
Cavendish Ct
5 Glasgow G5 ....117 B4
Troon KA10 ....229 E2
Cavendish Dr G77 ....156 F5
Cavendish La KA10 .....229 E2
Cavendish Pl
Glasgow G5 ....117 B4
Troon KA10 ....229 E2
Cavendish St G5 ....117 B4
Cavin Dr G45 ....137 E4
Cavin Rd G45 ....137 F4
Cawder Ct G68 ....61 D5
Cawder Gdns FK9 ....1 F8
Cawder Pl G68 ....61 E5
Cawder Rd Bridge of A FK9 ..1 F7
Cumbernauld G68 ....61 E5
Cawder View G68 ....61 E5
Cawder Way G68 ....61 E5
Cawdor Cres
Bishopton PA7 ....72 B2
Chapelhall ML6 ....123 E3
Greenock PA16 ....45 A4
Cawdor Pl PA16 ....45 A4
Cawdor Way G74 ....159 D3
Cayton Gdns G69 ....119 F4
Cayzer Ct PA1 ....114 E5
Cecil St Clarkston G76 ...157 E7
Coatbridge ML5 ....122 A5
Glasgow G12 ....96 D3
Stirling FK7 ....7 B6
Cedar Ave Beith KA15 ....171 A8
Clydebank G81 ....73 D4
Johnstone PA5 ....132 A8
Stirling FK8 ....6 F5
Uddingston G71 ....141 B8
Cedar Cres Greenock PA15 .46 E2
Hamilton ML3 ....162 E1
Cedar Ct Cambuslang G72 .139 E4
East Kilbride G75 ....180 C5
Glasgow G20 ....97 A2
Kilbarchan PA10 ....111 A3
Cedar Dr
East Kilbride G75 ....180 C5
Kirkintilloch G66 ....79 C5
Milton Of C G66 ....58 C5
Uddingston G71 ....141 C8
Cedar Gdns Law ML8 ....186 F6
Motherwell ML1 ....143 C4
Rutherglen G73 ....138 C4
Cedar Gr Cardross G82 ....48 B7
Stenhousemuir FK5 ....23 D1
Cedar La Airdrie ML6 ....123 C7
Motherwell ML1 ....143 B4
Cedar Pl Barrhead G78 ...155 D8
Blantyre G72 ....140 C1
East Kilbride G75 ....180 C5
Cedar Pl *continued*
Gourock PA19 ....44 D6
Cedar Rd Ayr KA7 ....239 D5
Banknock FK4 ....38 E2
Bishopbriggs G64 ....98 B8
Cumbernauld G67 ....62 D3
Irvine KA12 ....219 D4
Kilmarnock KA1 ....227 D8
Cedar St G20 ....97 A2
Cedar View G84 ....15 A3
Cedar Wlk
Bishopbriggs G64 ....98 B8
Motherwell ML1 ....143 D2
Cedar Wynd ML7 ....147 B4
Cedars Gr G69 ....121 A6
Cedars The FK10 ....4 B2
Cedarwood ML2 ....164 D1
Cedarwood Ave G77 .....156 F5
Cedarwood Ct G82 ....48 A8
Cedarwood Rd G77 ......156 F4
Cedric Pl G13 ....95 D7
Cedric Rd G13 ....95 D7
Celandine Bank KA7 ....239 C3
Celtic Pk (Celtic FC)*
G40 ....118 C5
Celtic St G20 ....96 C7
Cemetery Rd
Glasgow G52 ....115 E4
Hamilton G72 ....161 C6
Shotts ML7 ....147 B4
Centenary Ave ML6 .....122 D7
Centenary Cres ML4 ....142 B6
Centenary Ct
Barrhead G78 ....134 B2
Clydebank G81 ....74 B1
Centenary Gdns
Coatbridge ML5 ....122 A5
2 Hamilton ML3 ....162 E2
Centenary Pl KA22 ......205 D3
Centenary Quadrant
ML1 ....143 A5
Centenary Rd KA11 .....224 H7
Central Ave
Ardrossan KA22 ....205 D3
Cambuslang G72 ....138 F6
Clydebank G81 ....74 A2
Glasgow G11 ....95 F2
Glasgow,North Mount Vernon
G32 ....119 E3
Hamilton G72 ....161 E5
Kilbirnie KA25 ....170 A7
Kilmarnock KA1 ....227 F3
Motherwell ML1 ....143 A2
Motherwell,Holytown ML1 .142 F5
Stevenston KA20 ....218 B5
Troon KA10 ....229 G3
Uddingston G71 ....141 C6
Central Bvd FK5 ....23 B4
Central College of Commerce
G1,G4 ....241 B3
Central Cres ML9 ....199 F8
Central Dr FK5 ....23 F3
Central Gr
Cambuslang G72 ....138 F6
Glasgow G32 ....119 D4
Central Park Ave FK5 ....23 B4
Central Park Bsns Pk
FK5 ....23 B4
Central Path G32 ....119 E3
Central Quadrant KA22 .205 C3
Central Rd PA1 ....113 E5
Central Ret Pk FK1 ....42 C5
Central Sta Glasgow G2 ..240 C2
Hamilton ML3 ....162 E3
Central Way
Cumbernauld G67 ....61 F1
8 Paisley PA1 ....113 E5
Centre Rdbt The G74 ....159 F1
Centre St Chapelhall ML6 .123 D2
Glasgow G5 ....240 C1
Glenboig ML5 ....101 C6
Centre W 1 G74 ....180 E8
Centre Way G78 ....134 B3
Centrum (Sports Arena)
KA9 ....236 B6
Centurion Pl ML1 ....142 B1
Centurion Way FK2 ......41 D6
Century Ct KA11 ....224 H7
Ceres Gdns G64 ....78 D1
Cessnock Ave KA1 ......228 F5
Cessnock Dr KA1 ....228 F5
Cessnock Gdns KA1 .....228 F6
Cessnock Pl Ayr KA7 ....239 C6
Cambuslang G72 ....139 D5
Kilmarnock KA1 ....228 B5
Cessnock Rd
Hurlford KA1 ....228 F6
Millerston G33 ....99 B4
Troon KA10 ....229 E3
Cessnock St G51 ....116 C6
Cessnock Underground Sta
G51 ....116 C6
Chacefield St FK4 ....40 A6
Chacefield Wood FK6 ....39 E7
Chalmers Ave KA7 ......239 A5
Chalmers Cres G75 .....180 F7
Chalmers Ct
Glasgow G40 ....241 C1
Uddingston G71 ....140 F6
Chalmers Dr G75 ....180 F7
Chalmers Gate G40 .....241 C1
Chalmers Pl
Glasgow G40 ....241 C1
Irvine KA11 ....224 H6
Chalmers Rd KA7 ....239 A6
Chalmers St
Clydebank G81 ....74 B1
Glasgow G40 ....241 C1

Chalmers St *continued*
Gourock PA19 ....44 F7
Chalmerston Rd FK9 ....1 B3
Chalton Ct FK9 ....2 B7
Chalton Rd FK9 ....2 B7
Chalybeate Ct KA13 ....207 D3
Chamberlain La 1 G13 ....95 E5
Chamberlain Rd
Glasgow,Anniesland G13 ....95 E6
Glasgow,Jordanhill G13 ....95 E5
Chambers Dr FK2 ....24 B2
Chamfron Gdns FK7 ....7 E3
Chancellor St G11 ....96 C2
Chantinghall Rd ML3 ....162 B3
Chantinghall Terr ML3 ....162 B3
Chapel Cres Falkirk FK2 ....24 B3
Hamilton ML3 ....183 D6
Chapel Ct G73 ....137 F8
Chapel Dr FK5 ....23 E3
Chapel La Falkirk FK1 ....42 B5
Irvine KA12 ....219 C2
Chapel Pl G78 ....154 D7
Chapel Rd Clydebank G81 ....74 A6
Houston PA6 ....91 B4
Wishaw ML2 ....166 C2
Chapel St Airdrie ML6 ....123 A8
Carluke ML8 ....187 F2
Cleland ML1 ....144 B1
Glasgow G20 ....96 E5
Gourock PA19 ....44 F7
Hamilton ML3 ....162 E3
Lennoxtown G66 ....57 D8
Rutherglen G73 ....137 F8
Chapel Street Ind Est
G20 ....96 E5
Chapelacre Gr G84 ....16 E2
Chapelcroft FK7 ....6 D6
Chapelcross Ave ML6 ....103 A1
Chapelgill Pl KA11 ....220 A4
Chapelgreen Prim Sch
G65 ....59 E7
Chapelhall Ind Est ML6 ....123 D4
Chapelhall Prim Sch
ML6 ....123 D2
Chapelhill Mount KA22 ....205 D5
Chapelhill Rd PA2 ....114 A2
Chapelhill Rdbt KA22 ....205 C5
Chapelknowe Rd ML1 ....143 E1
Chapelpark Rd KA7 ....238 F4
Chapelside Ave ML6 ....123 A8
Chapelside Prim Sch
ML6 ....103 A1
Chapelside Rd
East Kilbride G74 ....160 B5
Nerston G74 ....160 A6
Chapelton Ave
Bearsden G61 ....75 F4
Dumbarton G82 ....50 A5
Chapelton Gdns
Bearsden G61 ....75 F4
Dumbarton G82 ....50 A5
Chapelton La KA23 ....190 C3
Chapelton Mains KA23 ....190 D1
Chapelton Rd
Cumbernauld G67 ....82 D6
West Kilbride KA23 ....190 D2
Chapelton St PA14 ....47 A2
Chapeltoun Terr KA3 ....210 F4
Chapelwell St KA21 ....216 F7
Chapland Rd ML11 ....215 A5
Chaplet Ave G13 ....95 C8
Chapman Ave ML5 ....101 C6
Chapman St 4 G42 ....117 A2
Chapmans Terr KA1 ....228 B7
Chappell St G78 ....134 B3
Charing Cross ML9 ....185 A3
Charing Cross La G3 ....240 A3
Charing Cross Sta G2 ....240 B3
Charles Ave Bridge of A FK9 ....2 B6
Monkton KA9 ....233 D5
Renfrew PA4 ....94 D4
Charles Cres
Carluke ML8 ....188 B1
Kirkintilloch G66 ....79 D3
Charles Dr Larbert FK5 ....41 C8
Troon KA10 ....230 A2
Charles Path ML6 ....123 D1
Charles Pl
4 Greenock PA15 ....45 F5
Kilmarnock KA1 ....227 E8
Charles Quadrant ML1 ....143 A5
Charles Rodger Pl FK9 ....2 A6
Charles St Alloa FK10 ....9 F8
Glasgow G21 ....97 F1
Kilmarnock KA1 ....227 E8
Kilsyth G65 ....36 D1
Shotts ML7 ....147 B4
Stirling FK8 ....7 A5
Wishaw ML2 ....164 D4
Charles Terr G83 ....27 E8
Charleson Row G65 ....60 F3
Charlotte Ave G64 ....78 B8
Charlotte Hill Ct FK5 ....23 B3
Charlotte Path ML9 ....185 A2
Charlotte Pl PA2 ....113 E2
Charlotte St Ayr KA7 ....238 E8
Dumbarton G82 ....49 D4
Glasgow G1 ....241 B1
Helensburgh G84 ....16 E2
Shotts ML7 ....147 A3
Charlotte Street La KA7 ....238 E8
Charnwood Ave PA5 ....131 D8
Charrier The FK11 ....3 F6
Charter St FK7 ....7 A3
Chartershall Rd
Bannockburn FK7 ....11 A6
Stirling FK7 ....7 A1
Chartwell Rd PA7 ....72 B3
Chassels St ML5 ....122 A8
Chateau Gr ML3 ....183 A2
Chatelherault Ave G72 ....138 E5
Chatelherault Country Pk*
ML3 ....184 B8
Chatelherault Country Pk
Visitor Ctr* ML3 ....184 B8
Chatelherault Cres ML3 ....162 F1
Chatelherault Prim Sch
ML3 ....162 E1
Chatelherault Wlk ML3 ....162 E1
Chatham G75 ....180 C7
Chattan Ave FK9 ....2 B4
Chattan Ind Est FK4 ....40 C4
Chatton St G23 ....76 D1
Chatton Wlk ML5 ....122 D3
Cheapside St
Eaglesham G76 ....178 F5
Glasgow G3 ....240 A2
4 Kilmarnock KA1 ....227 F8
Checkbar Rdbt FK5 ....40 C7
Chelmsford Dr G12 ....96 B5
Cherry Ave G67 ....62 E5
Cherry Bank G66 ....79 B5
Cherry Cres G81 ....74 A4
Cherry Gdns KA11 ....219 E5
Cherry Gr G69 ....121 B6
Cherry Hill Rd KA7 ....239 B2
Cherry La Banknock FK4 ....38 E2
Troon KA10 ....229 E4
Cherry Pl
Bishopbriggs G64 ....98 B8
Johnstone PA5 ....112 A1
Milton Of C G66 ....58 B4
Motherwell ML1 ....143 B5
Uddingston G71 ....141 D7
Cherry Rd KA1 ....227 C8
Cherry Tree Ct G83 ....27 D5
Cherry Wlk ML1 ....163 E3
Cherrybank Rd G43 ....136 F5
Cherrybank Wlk ML6 ....122 D8
Cherryhill View ML9 ....184 F3
Cherryridge Dr G69 ....121 A6
Cherrytree Cres ML9 ....185 A5
Cherrytree Dr G72 ....139 E4
Cherrytree Wynd G75 ....180 F6
Cherrywood Dr KA15 ....150 C2
Cherrywood Rd PA5 ....112 C2
Chester Rd PA16 ....44 E4
Chester St G32 ....119 A5
Chesterfield Ave G12 ....96 B5
Chesters Cres ML1 ....163 C8
Chesters Pl 3 G73 ....138 A7
Chesters Rd G61 ....75 D4
Chestnut Ave Beith KA15 ....171 A8
Bishopton PA7 ....71 F5
Cumbernauld G67 ....62 E5
Chestnut Cres Denny FK6 ....21 C3
East Kilbride G75 ....180 C6
Hamilton ML3 ....162 F2
Uddingston G71 ....141 D7
Chestnut Ct
Cumbernauld G67 ....62 E5
Milton Of C G66 ....58 B5
Chestnut Dr
Clydebank G81 ....74 A5
Kirkintilloch G66 ....79 B6
Chestnut Gdns KA11 ....219 E5
Chestnut Gr Carluke ML8 ....187 F1
Glenboig G69 ....101 C6
Hamilton G72 ....161 C8
Larkhall ML9 ....185 A5
Motherwell ML1 ....163 D4
Stenhousemuir FK5 ....23 F3
Chestnut La G62 ....54 E1
Chestnut Pl
Cumbernauld G67 ....62 E5
Johnstone PA5 ....132 A8
Kilmarnock KA1 ....227 D8
Chestnut Rd KA7 ....239 D6
Chestnut St G22 ....97 D5
Chestnut Way
Cambuslang G72 ....139 E4
Quarter ML3 ....183 F4
Chestnut Wlk G66 ....57 E7
Cheviot Ave G78 ....134 C1
Cheviot Cres
East Kilbride G75 ....180 B4
Wishaw ML2 ....164 F4
Cheviot Ct Airdrie ML6 ....103 B2
Coatbridge ML5 ....122 C3
Irvine KA11 ....220 A3
Cheviot Dr G77 ....156 C3
Cheviot Gdns G61 ....75 D7
Cheviot Head
Irvine KA11 ....219 F3
Irvine,Bourtreehill KA11 ....220 A3
Cheviot Pl KA1 ....228 A3
Cheviot Rd Glasgow G43 ....136 C5
Hamilton ML3 ....162 F2
Larkhall ML9 ....185 C2
Paisley PA2 ....113 E1
Cheviot St G72 ....161 C7
Cheviot Way KA11 ....220 A3
Chirmorie Cres G53 ....115 A1
Chirmorie Pl G53 ....115 A1
Chirnside Ct G72 ....161 F5
Chirnside Pl G52 ....115 B6
Chirnside Rd G52 ....115 A6
Chirnsyde Prim Sch G22 ....97 D6
Chisholm Ave
Bishopton PA7 ....72 C3
Stirling FK9 ....2 B4
Chisholm Dr G77 ....156 E6
Chisholm Pl ML1 ....164 B2
Chisholm St
Coatbridge ML5 ....122 B8
Glasgow G1 ....241 B1
Chrighton Gn 3 G71 ....141 A8
Chriss Ave ML3 ....183 D7
Christ the King Prim Sch
ML1 ....143 B6
Christchurch Pl G75 ....180 B7
Christian St G43 ....136 C8
Christie Gdns KA21 ....216 F8
Christie La PA3 ....113 E5
Christie Park Prim Sch
G83 ....27 D5
Christie Pl G72 ....139 B5
Christie St Bellshill ML4 ....142 D5
Paisley PA1 ....113 F5
Christie Terr FK5 ....23 E3
Christopher St G21 ....98 A1
Chromars Pl PA15 ....45 E3
Chryston Bsns Ctr G69 ....100 C8
Chryston High Sch G69 ....100 C8
Chryston Prim Sch G69 ....100 D8
Chryston Rd
Chryston G69 ....100 D8
Kirkintilloch G69,G66 ....80 C5
Chuckie La PA5 ....111 C6
Church Ave Cardross G82 ....48 A8
Rutherglen G73 ....138 C5
Stepps G33 ....99 D6
Wishaw ML2 ....166 A4
Church Cres ML6 ....103 E1
Church Ct Alloa FK10 ....10 A6
Ayr KA8 ....236 A1
Dumbarton G82 ....49 F3
Hamilton ML3 ....162 E4
Church Dr G66 ....79 C6
Church Gr FK10 ....5 C1
Church Hill PA1 ....113 E5
Church La Carluke ML8 ....187 F1
Coatbridge ML5 ....122 A7
Denny FK6 ....21 D3
Kilmarnock KA1 ....227 F5
8 Kilsyth G65 ....60 D8
Plean FK7 ....12 D2
Church Manse La PA11 ....110 D8
Church Pl
Ardrossan KA22 ....205 C1
Caldercruix ML6 ....104 F4
Falkirk FK2 ....42 B6
Old Kilpatrick G60 ....73 A6
Rhu G84 ....15 D4
Rutherglen G73 ....138 B8
Church Rd
Bridge of W PA11 ....110 E8
California FK1 ....66 F5
Clarkston G76 ....157 F6
Glasgow G46 ....136 D2
Muirhead G69 ....100 C7
Quarriers Village PA11 ....89 E2
Rhu G84 ....15 D5
Wishaw ML2 ....166 D6
Church St Alexandria G83 ....27 E4
Alloa FK10 ....10 A6
Bonnybridge FK4 ....40 C3
Clydebank G81 ....74 A3
Coatbridge ML5 ....122 A7
Dumbarton G82 ....49 F3
Falkirk FK2 ....24 C2
Glasgow,Kelvingrove G11 ....96 C2
Glasgow,Muirhead G69 ....120 C4
Gourock PA19 ....44 E8
Hamilton ML3 ....162 E4
Hamilton,Blantyre G72 ....161 E7
Harthill ML7 ....127 C5
Irvine KA12 ....219 B2
Johnstone PA5 ....111 F3
Kilbarchan PA10 ....111 A3
Kilmarnock KA3 ....222 F1
Kilsyth G65 ....60 D8
Kilwinning KA13 ....207 E3
Larkhall ML9 ....185 A2
Lochwinnoch PA12 ....129 C2
Motherwell ML1 ....143 F4
Port Glasgow PA14 ....47 C2
Stenhousemuir FK5 ....23 E3
Troon KA10 ....229 D2
Uddingston G71 ....140 F5
Church View
Caldercruix ML6 ....104 F3
Cambuslang G72 ....139 A7
Coatbridge ML5 ....122 A7
Church View Ct G66 ....33 D1
Church View Gdns ML4 ....142 A5
Church Wlk FK6 ....21 E2
Churchhill Ave KA13 ....208 A4
Churchill Ave
East Kilbride G74 ....159 F1
Johnstone PA5 ....131 C7
Churchill Cres Ayr KA8 ....239 D8
Bothwell G71 ....141 B3
Churchill Dr
Ardrossan KA22 ....205 D4
Bishopton PA7 ....72 B3
Bridge of A FK9 ....2 A6
Glasgow G11 ....96 A4
Churchill Pl Falkirk FK2 ....42 C7
Kilbarchan PA10 ....111 A3
Churchill Rd PA13 ....89 C7
Churchill Sq G84 ....17 A2
Churchill St FK10 ....9 F8
Churchill Twr KA7 ....235 E2
Churchyard Ct ML7 ....146 E4
Circus Dr G31 ....117 F7
Circus Pl G31 ....117 F8
Circus Place La G31 ....117 F8
Citadel L Ctr KA7 ....235 E1
Citadel Pl Ayr KA7 ....235 E1
Motherwell ML1 ....163 C8
Citadel Way KA10 ....229 C8
Citizen La G1 ....241 A2
Citrus Cres G71 ....141 C8
Cityford Cres G73 ....137 F7
Cityford Dr G73 ....137 F6
Civic Sq 4 ML1 ....163 F5
Civic St G4 ....97 B2
Civic Way G66 ....79 C7
Clachaig Pl PA19 ....43 F5
Clachan Dr 4 G51 ....115 F8
Clachan Rd G84 ....15 A3
Clachan The
Rosneath G84 ....15 A3
Wishaw ML2 ....165 B3
Clachan Way ML5 ....121 E5
Clackmannan Coll (annex)
FK10 ....10 C8
Clackmannan Coll of F Ed
FK10 ....10 B8
Clackmannan County Hospl
FK10 ....10 B8
Clackmannan Rd FK10 ....10 D6
Clackmannan Twr*
FK10 ....10 F4
Claddens Holdings G66 ....80 A4
Claddens Pl G66 ....79 E4
Claddens Quadrant G22 ....97 C6
Claddens St G22 ....97 B6
Cladence Gr G75 ....180 F5
Clair Rd G64 ....78 D1
Claire St ML2 ....166 A5
Clairinsh G83 ....27 D8
Clairinsh Gdns 1 PA4 ....94 C1
Clairmont Gdns G3 ....240 A4
Clamp Rd ML2 ....164 C4
Clamps Gr G74 ....181 A8
Clamps Terr G74 ....181 B8
Clamps Wood G74 ....181 A8
Clanranald Pl FK1 ....41 F1
Clanrye Dr ML5 ....122 A4
Clapperhow Rd ML1 ....143 B1
Clare St G21 ....98 A2
Claremont FK10 ....9 F8
Claremont Ave G66 ....79 B8
Claremont Cres KA13 ....207 D4
Claremont Dr
Bridge of A FK9 ....2 C7
Milngavie G62 ....55 A2
Claremont Gdns G62 ....55 A1
Claremont High Sch
G74 ....181 C8
Claremont Ind Est FK10 ....10 A6
Claremont Pas G3 ....240 A4
Claremont Pl G3 ....240 A4
Claremont Prim Sch FK10 ....9 E8
Claremont St
Bonnybridge FK4 ....39 F6
Glasgow G3 ....116 E8
Claremont Terr G3 ....240 A4
Claremont Terrace La
G3 ....240 A4
Claremount Ave G46 ....136 C2
Claremount View ML5 ....122 C3
Clarence Dr Glasgow G12 ....96 A3
Paisley PA1 ....114 A4
Clarence Gdns G11 ....96 A3
Clarence La G12 ....96 B3
Clarence St
Clydebank G81 ....74 C3
Greenock PA15 ....45 F6
Paisley PA1 ....114 A5
Clarendon Pl Ayr KA7 ....239 C5
9 Glasgow G20 ....97 A2
Stepps G33 ....99 D5
Stirling FK8 ....7 A7
Clarendon Rd Stirling FK8 ....7 A7
Wishaw ML2 ....164 E1
Clarendon St G20 ....97 A2
Clarinda Ave FK1 ....41 B5
Clarinda Ct G66 ....59 A2
Clarinda Pl
Motherwell ML1 ....143 C3
Stenhousemuir FK5 ....23 C4
Clarion Cres G13 ....95 A8
Clarion Rd G13 ....95 B7
Clark Cres KA20 ....217 D7
Clark Dr KA12 ....219 E3
Clark Pl
Newton Mearns G77 ....156 B4
Saltcoats KA21 ....206 A2
Torrance G64 ....78 C8
Clark St Airdrie ML6 ....123 B7
Clydebank G81 ....73 F4
Johnstone PA5 ....111 F3
Kilmarnock KA1 ....227 F8
Paisley PA3 ....113 C6
Renfrew PA4 ....94 B3
Stirling FK7 ....7 B2
Wishaw ML2 ....165 F5
Clark Way ML4 ....141 F7
Clarke Ave KA7 ....238 E6
Clarkin Ave G75 ....180 A4
Clarkston & Stamperland Sta
G76 ....157 E7
Clarkston Ave G44 ....136 F4
Clarkston Dr ML6 ....123 D7
Clarkston Prim Sch
ML6 ....123 D8
Clarkston Rd
Clarkston G76 ....157 E8
Glasgow G44,G76 ....136 F3
Clarkwell Rd ML3 ....161 E3
Clarkwell Terr ML3 ....161 F3
Clathic Ave G61 ....76 A4
Claud Rd PA3 ....114 A6
Claude Ave G72 ....139 E4
Claude St ML9 ....185 A3
Clavens Rd G52 ....114 E6
Claverhouse Pl PA2 ....114 B3
Claverhouse Rd G52 ....114 F7
Clavering St E PA1 ....113 C5
Clavering St W PA1 ....113 C4
Clay Cres Bellshill ML4 ....142 C7
Kilmarnock KA3 ....222 F2
Clay Ct ML1 ....163 F4
Clay Rd ML4 ....142 C7
Claycrofts Pl FK7 ....7 B6
Clayhouse Rd G33 ....99 E5
Claymore Dr
Houston PA6 ....111 D8
Stirling FK7 ....7 D3
Claypotts Pl G33 ....99 A1
Claypotts Rd G33 ....99 A1
Clayslaps Rd G3 ....96 D1
Clayslaps View KA1 ....228 B4
Claythorn Ave G40 ....241 C1
Claythorn Cir G40 ....241 C1
Claythorn Ct G40 ....241 C1
Claythorn Pk G40 ....117 E5
Claythorn St G40 ....241 C1
Claythorn Terr G40 ....241 C1
Clayton Ave KA12 ....219 C4
Clayton Path ML4 ....142 B7
Clayton Terr 5 G31 ....117 F7
Clearfield Ave ML3 ....162 B4
Cleaves The FK10 ....4 B1
Cleddans Cres G81 ....74 C5
Cleddans Rd
Clydebank G81 ....74 C5
Kirkintilloch G66 ....58 E1
Cleddans View
Clydebank G81 ....74 C4
Glenmavis ML6 ....102 E4
Cleddens Ct Airdrie ML6 ....122 D8
Bishopbriggs G64 ....78 A1
Cleeves Ave KA24 ....191 E6
Cleeves Quadrant G53 ....135 B5
Cleeves Rd G53 ....135 A5
Cleghorn Ave ML11 ....215 B5
Cleghorn Dr ML11 ....215 A5
Cleghorn Rd ML11 ....215 A5
Cleghorn St G22 ....97 B3
Cleish Ave G61 ....75 C8
Cleland Hospl ML1 ....144 C1
Cleland La G5 ....117 C5
Cleland Pl G74 ....160 A3
Cleland Prim Sch ML1 ....144 C1
Cleland Rd Cleland ML1 ....144 A2
Wishaw ML2 ....165 A3
Cleland St G5 ....117 C5
Cleland Sta ML1 ....144 C1
Clelland Ave G64 ....98 A8
Clem Attlee Gdns ML9 ....185 B2
Clements Pl KA20 ....206 E2
Clerkland Rd KA3 ....195 D2
Clerwood St G32 ....118 D6
Cleuch Ave FK10 ....4 B2
Cleuch Dr FK12 ....4 E7
Cleuch Gdns G76 ....157 D8
Cleuch Rd FK9 ....2 C3
Cleughearn Rd G75 ....180 D1
Clevans Rd PA11 ....110 C7
Cleveden Cres G12 ....96 B5
Cleveden Crescent La
G12 ....96 B5
Cleveden Dr Glasgow G12 ....96 C4
Rutherglen G73 ....138 C6
Cleveden Drive La G12 ....96 C4
Cleveden Gdns G12 ....96 C5
Cleveden Ho G12 ....96 C4
Cleveden La G12 ....96 B6
Cleveden Pl G12 ....96 B6
Cleveden Rd G12 ....96 B5
Cleveden Sec Sch G12 ....96 C5
Cleveland La G3 ....240 A3
Cleveland St G3 ....240 A3
Cliff Rd G3 ....240 A4
Clifford Gdns G51 ....116 B5
Clifford La G51 ....116 D5
Clifford Pl 3 G51 ....116 D5
Clifford Rd FK8 ....7 B5
Clifford St G51 ....116 C5
Clifton Ho 9 G3 ....96 E1
Clifton Pl Coatbridge ML5 ....122 C6
1 Glasgow G3 ....116 E8
Clifton Rd G46 ....136 B3
Clifton St G3 ....96 E1
Clifton Terr
Cambuslang G72 ....138 E3
Johnstone PA5 ....112 A2
Cliftonville Ct ML5 ....122 C6
Climie Pl KA3 ....228 B8
Clincart Rd G42 ....137 B8
Clincarthill Rd G73 ....138 A7
Clippens Ho PA3 ....112 A6
Clippens Rd
Houston PA3,PA6 ....111 F8
Linwood PA3 ....112 A6
Clippens Sch PA3 ....112 C6
Clive St ML7 ....146 E5
Cloak Rd PA13 ....69 C4
Cloan Ave G15 ....75 B2
Cloan Cres G64 ....78 B3
Clober Farm La G62 ....54 E3
Clober Prim Sch G62 ....54 E2
Clober Rd G62 ....55 A2
Cloberfield G62 ....54 F4
Cloberfield Gdns G62 ....54 F3
Cloberhill Rd G13 ....75 D1
Cloch Brae PA19 ....44 A6
Cloch Rd PA19 ....43 E5
Cloch St G33 ....119 A8
Clochbar Ave G62 ....54 F3
Clochbar Gdns G62 ....54 F2
Clochoderick Ave PA10 ....111 B2
Clochranhill Rd KA7 ....238 F2

Corona Cres FK4 ... 39 F5
Coronation Ave ML9 ... 199 A8
Coronation Cres ML9 ... 199 A8
Coronation Ct ML1 ... 142 F4
Coronation Pl
Larkhall ML9 ... 199 B8
Mount Ellen G69 ... 100 E7
Skinflats FK2 ... 24 F3
Coronation Rd ML1 ... 142 F4
Coronation Rd E ML1 ... 142 F3
Coronation Road Ind Est
ML1 ... 142 F4
Coronation St
Monkton KA9 ... 233 D5
Wishaw ML2 ... 165 D3
Coronation Way G61 ... 76 A2
Corpach Pl G34 ... 100 D1
Corporation St FK1 ... 42 C4
Corpus Christi RC Prim Sch
Airdrie ML6 ... 123 B3
Glasgow G13 ... 95 C6
Corra Linn ML3 ... 162 A3
Corran Ave G77 ... 156 C6
Corran St G33 ... 118 F8
Correen Gdns G61 ... 75 B7
Corrie Ave FK5 ... 23 F4
Corrie Brae G65 ... 36 C1
Corrie Cres
Kilmarnock KA3 ... 222 F3
Saltcoats KA21 ... 205 F2
Corrie Ct ML3 ... 161 F2
Corrie Dr
Motherwell ML1 ... 163 B7
Paisley PA1 ... 114 E4
Corrie Gdns G75 ... 180 B4
Corrie Gr G44 ... 136 F4
Corrie Ho KA9 ... 236 B5
Corrie Pl Falkirk FK1 ... 41 C4
Helensburgh G84 ... 16 F3
Kirkintilloch G66 ... 79 E4
Troon KA10 ... 229 F7
Corrie Rd G65 ... 36 C1
Corrie View G68 ... 81 F8
Corrie View Cotts G65 ... 59 E4
Corrie Way ML9 ... 185 B2
Corrour Rd Glasgow G43 ... 136 E7
Newton Mearns G77 ... 156 C6
Corsankell Wynd KA21 ... 205 E3
Corse Ave KA11 ... 221 A1
Corse Pl KA2 ... 226 F8
Corse Rd G52 ... 114 E6
Corse St KA23 ... 190 C5
Corse Terr KA23 ... 190 C5
Corsebar Ave PA2 ... 113 C2
Corsebar Cres PA2 ... 113 C1
Corsebar Dr PA2 ... 113 C2
Corsebar La PA2 ... 113 B1
Corsebar Rd PA2 ... 113 C2
Corsebar Way PA2 ... 113 C3
Corsefield Rd PA12 ... 128 E2
Corseford Ave PA5 ... 131 C8
Corseford Residential Sch
PA10 ... 131 B7
Corsehill KA13 ... 208 A3
Corsehill Dr KA23 ... 190 B5
Corsehill Mount Rd
KA11 ... 220 A1
Corsehill Mount Rdbt
KA11 ... 225 E8
Corsehill Path G34 ... 120 C8
Corsehill Pk Ayr KA7 ... 238 F5
Irvine KA11 ... 225 D8
Corsehill Pl Ayr KA7 ... 238 F5
Glasgow G34 ... 120 C8
Stewarton KA3 ... 195 E2
Corsehill Prim Sch
KA13 ... 207 F3
Corsehill Rd KA7 ... 238 F5
Corsehill St G34 ... 120 C8
Corsehill Terr KA11 ... 220 F2
Corsehillbank St KA3 ... 195 D1
Corselet Rd
Glasgow G53 ... 135 A3
Glasgow G78,G53 ... 135 A1
Corserine Bank KA11 ... 219 F3
Corserine Rd KA7 ... 238 B1
Corsewall Ave G32 ... 119 E3
Corsewall St ML5 ... 121 F8
Corsford Dr G53 ... 135 C6
Corsliehill Rd PA6 ... 90 D7
Corsock Ave ML3 ... 161 E2
Corsock St G31 ... 118 C7
Corston St G33 ... 118 D7
Cortachy Ave FK2 ... 24 A3
Cortachy Pl G64 ... 78 D1
Coruisk Dr G76 ... 157 D8
Coruisk Way PA2 ... 132 E8
Corunna Ct ML8 ... 188 B1
Corunna St 5 G3 ... 116 E8
Coshneuk Rd G33 ... 99 B4
Cosy Neuk ML9 ... 185 C1
Cotland Dr FK2 ... 41 F8
Cottage Cres FK1 ... 41 E5
Cottar St G20 ... 96 E7
Cotter Dr KA3 ... 228 C8
Cotton Ave PA3 ... 112 B5
Cotton Row KA12 ... 219 C2
Cotton St Glasgow G40 ... 118 A2
Paisley PA1 ... 113 F4
Cotton Street Ent Pk
G40 ... 118 A2
Cotton Vale ML1 ... 143 E1
Coulin Gdns G22 ... 97 D4
Coulport Pl G84 ... 16 B2
Coulter Ave
Coatbridge ML5 ... 121 E8
Wishaw ML2 ... 165 C7
Coulthard Dr KA9 ... 236 D6
Countess St KA21 ... 216 F7
Countess Way G69 ... 121 A5
Counting Ho The PA1 ... 113 B3
County Ave G72 ... 138 E7
County Dr ML11 ... 215 C3
County Pl 7 PA1 ... 113 E5
County Sq 6 PA1 ... 113 E5
Couper Pl G4 ... 241 B4
Couper St G4 ... 241 B4
Coursington Cres ML1 ... 164 A7
Coursington Gdns ML1 ... 163 F7
Coursington Pl ML1 ... 163 F7
Coursington Rd ML1 ... 164 A7
Coursington Twr ML1 ... 163 F7
Court Hill G84 ... 15 A3
Court Rd PA14 ... 47 C1
Courthill Alva FK12 ... 5 A7
Bearsden G61 ... 75 D6
Courthill Ave G44 ... 137 B5
Courthill Cres G65 ... 60 E8
Courthill Pl KA24 ... 191 C8
Courthill St KA24 ... 191 C8
Courtrai Ave G84 ... 16 B2
Courtyard The FK1 ... 42 E3
Coustonholm Rd G43 ... 136 D8
Couther Quadrant ML6 ... 103 A2
Covanburn Ave ML3 ... 162 F1
Cove Cres ML7 ... 146 E6
Cove Pl G84 ... 16 B2
Cove Rd PA19 ... 44 F7
Covenant Cres ML9 ... 185 B2
Covenant Pl ML2 ... 164 C2
Covenanter Rd ML7 ... 127 D4
Covenanters Way ML2 ... 186 C6
Coventry Dr G31 ... 118 B8
Cow Wynd FK1 ... 42 B4
Cowal Cres Gourock PA19 ... 44 B6
Kirkintilloch G66 ... 59 B1
Cowal Dr PA3 ... 112 A5
Cowal Rd Glasgow G20 ... 96 C7
Glasgow G20 ... 96 C7
Cowal St G20 ... 96 C7
Cowal View PA19 ... 44 B6
Cowan Cres Ayr KA8 ... 236 C3
Barrhead G78 ... 134 D3
Cowan La G12 ... 96 E2
Cowan Rd G68 ... 61 C2
Cowan St Bonnybridge FK4 ... 40 A6
Glasgow G12 ... 96 E2
Cowan Wilson Ave
Blantyre G72 ... 140 D1
Hamilton G72 ... 161 D8
Cowan Wynd
Overtown ML2 ... 186 C7
Uddingston G71 ... 141 A8
Cowane St Stirling FK8 ... 2 B1
2 Stirling FK8 ... 7 B8
Cowans Row KA3 ... 228 D7
Cowcaddens Rd G2,G3,
G4 ... 240 C4
Cowcaddens Underground
Sta G4 ... 240 C4
Cowden Dr G64 ... 78 A3
Cowden Hill Gdns FK4 ... 40 B6
Cowden St G51 ... 115 D7
Cowdenhill Circ G13 ... 95 D8
Cowdenhill Pl G13 ... 95 D8
Cowdenhill Rd G13 ... 95 D8
Cowdray Cres PA4 ... 94 D3
Cowgate G66 ... 79 C8
Cowglen Hospl G53 ... 135 D7
Cowglen Rd G53 ... 135 C7
Cowie Prim Sch FK7 ... 12 D7
Cowie Rd Bannockburn FK7 ... 7 E1
Cowie FK7 ... 12 A8
Cowie Terr G83 ... 27 D5
Cowiehall Rd FK7 ... 12 D8
Cowlairs Ind Est G22 ... 97 D5
Cowlairs Rd 5 G21 ... 97 E4
Coxdale Ave G66 ... 79 B8
Coxhill St G21 ... 97 D3
Coxithill Rd FK7 ... 7 A3
Coxton Pl G33 ... 99 D1
Coyle Pk KA10 ... 229 F6
Coylebank KA9 ... 236 C6
Coylton Cres ML3 ... 161 E1
Coylton Rd G43 ... 136 F5
Crabb Quadrant ML1 ... 142 C1
Cragburn Gate PA19 ... 44 D7
Cragdale G74 ... 159 C3
Craggan Dr G14 ... 95 A5
Cragganmore FK10 ... 4 A2
Crags Ave PA2 ... 113 F1
Crags Cres PA2 ... 113 F2
Crags Rd PA2 ... 113 F1
Cragwell Pk G76 ... 158 E7
Craig Ave Alexandria G83 ... 27 C7
Dalry KA24 ... 191 A8
Craig Cotts KA2 ... 226 D8
Craig Cres
Kirkintilloch G66 ... 80 B7
Stirling FK9 ... 2 D3
Craig Ct FK9 ... 2 A5
Craig Dr KA2 ... 226 E8
Craig Gdns G77 ... 156 C5
Craig Hill G75 ... 180 C7
Craig Leith Rd FK7 ... 7 D6
Craig Pl G77 ... 156 B5
Craig Rd Glasgow G44 ... 137 A5
Linwood PA3 ... 111 F7
Neilston G78 ... 154 D6
Troon KA10 ... 229 B3
Craig St Airdrie ML6 ... 122 F7
Blackridge EH48 ... 107 E3
Coatbridge ML5 ... 121 F4
Hamilton G72 ... 161 E7
Craig View KA11 ... 221 A2
Craigallian Ave
Cambuslang G72 ... 139 D4
Milngavie G62 ... 55 A3
Craiganour La G43 ... 136 C6
Craigard Pl G73 ... 138 D3
Craigash Quadrant G62 ... 54 E3
Craigash Rd G62 ... 54 E3
Craigbank FK10 ... 5 C1
Craigbank Cres G76 ... 178 E6
Craigbank Dr G53 ... 135 A6
Craigbank Gr G76 ... 178 E6
Craigbank Prim Sch
Alloa FK10 ... 5 C1
Larkhall ML9 ... 199 A8
Craigbank Rd ML9 ... 199 A8
Craigbank St ML9 ... 185 A1
Craigbanzo St G81 ... 74 D8
Craigbarnet Ave G64 ... 78 A8
Craigbarnet Cres G33 ... 99 B4
Craigbarnet Rd G62 ... 54 D2
Craigbet Ave PA11 ... 89 E2
Craigbet Cres PA11 ... 89 E2
Craigbet Pl PA11 ... 89 E2
Craigbo Ave 14 G23 ... 76 D1
Craigbo Ct G23 ... 96 D8
Craigbo Dr 13 G23 ... 76 D1
Craigbo Pl G23 ... 96 D8
Craigbo Rd G23 ... 76 D1
Craigbo St G23 ... 76 D1
Craigbog Ave PA5 ... 131 D8
Craigburn Ave PA6 ... 111 D7
Craigburn Cres PA6 ... 111 D7
Craigburn Ct Ashgill ML9 ... 185 F1
Falkirk FK1 ... 41 F2
Craigburn Pl PA6 ... 111 E7
Craigburn St ML3 ... 183 D8
Craigdene Dr KA20 ... 206 E2
Craigdhu Ave
Airdrie ML6 ... 123 E7
Milngavie G62 ... 54 F1
Craigdhu Farm Cotts
G62 ... 54 E1
Craigdhu Prim Sch G62 ... 75 F8
Craigdhu Rd
Bearsden G61 ... 75 E8
Milngavie G62 ... 54 F1
Craigdonald Pl PA5 ... 111 F3
Craigellan Rd G43 ... 136 D6
Craigelvan Ave G67 ... 81 F6
Craigelvan Ct G67 ... 81 F6
Craigelvan Dr G67 ... 81 F6
Craigelvan Gdns G67 ... 81 F6
Craigelvan Gr G67 ... 81 F6
Craigelvan Pl G67 ... 81 F6
Craigelvan View G67 ... 81 F6
Craigenbay Cres G66 ... 79 E5
Craigenbay Rd G66 ... 79 E5
Craigenbay St G21 ... 98 B4
Craigencart Ct G81 ... 73 F6
Craigend Cres G62 ... 54 F2
Craigend Dr ML5 ... 121 C4
Craigend Dr W G62 ... 54 F2
Craigend Pl G13 ... 95 E6
Craigend Rd
Cumbernauld G67 ... 81 F5
East Kilbride G75 ... 179 F1
Stirling FK7 ... 7 A3
Troon KA10 ... 232 E8
Craigend St G13 ... 95 E6
Craigend View G67 ... 81 F5
Craigend Visitor Ctr*
G62 ... 54 F8
Craigendmuir Pk G33 ... 99 E4
Craigendmuir Rd G33 ... 99 E4
Craigendmuir St G33 ... 98 D2
Craigendon Oval PA2 ... 133 C6
Craigendon Rd PA2 ... 133 C6
Craigendoran Ave G84 ... 25 B8
Craigendoran Sta G84 ... 25 B7
Craigends Ave PA11 ... 89 E3
Craigends Ct G65 ... 60 E8
Craigends Dr PA10 ... 111 B3
Craigends Pl PA11 ... 89 E3
Craigends Rd
Glengarnock KA14 ... 170 B6
Houston PA6 ... 111 E7
Houston PA6 ... 91 E2
Craigenfeoch Ave PA5 ... 111 D1
Craigenhill Rd ML8 ... 203 A5
Craigenlay Ave G63 ... 31 C4
Craigens Rd ML1,ML6 ... 124 C3
Craigfaulds Ave PA2 ... 113 B2
Craigfell Ct ML3 ... 161 E2
Craigfern Dr G63 ... 31 C4
Craigfin Ct KA9 ... 236 D5
Craigflower Gdns G53 ... 135 A4
Craigflower Rd G53 ... 135 B3
Craigford Dr FK7 ... 7 D1
Craigforth Cres FK8 ... 1 F1
Craighalbert Rd G68 ... 61 D3
Craighalbert Rdbt G68 ... 61 C4
Craighalbert Way G68 ... 61 C4
Craighall Pl KA7 ... 239 A2
Craighall Quadrant G78 ... 154 D6
Craighall Rd G4 ... 97 B2
Craighall St FK8 ... 1 E1
Craighaw St G81 ... 74 D8
Craighead Ave
Glasgow G33 ... 98 D3
Milton Of C G66 ... 58 C6
Craighead Dr G62 ... 54 D2
Craighead Prim Sch G66 ... 58 C6
Craighead Rd
Bishopton PA7 ... 72 B2
Milton Of C G66 ... 58 C6
Craighead Sch ML3 ... 162 B7
Craighead St Airdrie ML6 ... 123 E8
Barrhead G78 ... 134 B2
Craighead Way G78 ... 134 B2
Craighill Dr G76 ... 157 D6
Craighill Gr G76 ... 157 D6
Craighill View EH48 ... 107 E3
Craighirst Dr G81 ... 74 A7
Craighirst Rd G62 ... 54 D2
Craighlaw Ave G76 ... 157 D2
Craighlaw Dr G76 ... 157 D2
Craigholm Rd KA7 ... 239 D7
Craigholme PA6 ... 91 D2
Craigholme Sch G41 ... 116 D3
Craighorn FK11 ... 4 A5
Craighorn Dr FK1 ... 41 E2
Craighorn Rd FK12 ... 4 E6
Craighouse Sq KA25 ... 149 B1
Craighouse St G33 ... 99 A1
Craighton Gdns G66 ... 57 F8
Craigie Ave Ayr KA8 ... 239 A8
Kilmarnock KA1 ... 227 F4
Craigie Ct FK5 ... 23 B2
Craigie Dr G77 ... 156 E3
Craigie Est* KA8 ... 239 C7
Craigie La 9 ML9 ... 185 B4
Craigie Lea KA8 ... 239 B8
Craigie Pk G66 ... 79 E5
Craigie Pl
Coatbridge ML5 ... 121 E5
Crosshouse KA2 ... 226 F8
Kilmarnock KA1 ... 227 F4
Craigie Rd Ayr KA8 ... 236 B1
Hurlford KA1 ... 228 F5
Kilmarnock KA1 ... 227 F1
Craigie St Glasgow G42 ... 117 A2
Prestwick KA9 ... 236 B8
Craigie Way KA8 ... 239 C8
Craigiebar Dr PA2 ... 133 C8
Craigieburn Gdns G20 ... 96 B8
Craigieburn Rd G67 ... 61 F1
Craigiehall Ave PA8 ... 93 A7
Craigiehall Cres PA8 ... 93 A7
Craigiehall Pl G51 ... 116 D6
Craigiehall St G51 ... 116 E6
Craigiehall Way PA8 ... 93 A7
Craigieknowes St PA15 ... 46 C3
Craigielea Cres G62 ... 54 E2
Craigielea Ct PA4 ... 94 C4
Craigielea Dr PA3 ... 113 C6
Craigielea Pk PA4 ... 94 C3
Craigielea Prim Sch
PA3 ... 113 A6
Craigielea Rd
Duntocher G81 ... 73 F7
Renfrew PA4 ... 94 C3
Craigielea St G31 ... 118 A8
Craigielinn Ave PA2 ... 133 C7
Craigievar Ave FK2 ... 24 A3
Craigievar Pl Airdrie ML6 ... 123 E6
Newton Mearns G77 ... 156 B5
Craigievar St G33 ... 99 E2
Craiginn Ct EH48 ... 107 D3
Craiginn Terr EH48 ... 107 D3
Craiglea FK9 ... 2 C3
Craiglea Ave KA2 ... 226 E8
Craiglea Ct EH48 ... 107 D3
Craiglea Pl ML6 ... 123 C8
Craiglea Terr ML6 ... 103 F3
Craiglee G75 ... 180 E5
Craigleith FK10 ... 5 E3
Craigleith Ave FK1 ... 41 E2
Craigleith St G32 ... 118 E6
Craigleith Terr FK12 ... 5 A7
Craigleith View FK10 ... 4 D3
Craiglinn G68 ... 61 A2
Craiglinn Park Rd G68 ... 61 A1
Craiglinn Rdbt G68 ... 61 A1
Craiglockhart St G33 ... 99 D1
Craiglomond Gdns G83 ... 27 D8
Craiglynn Gdns G83 ... 27 F8
Craigmaddie Gdns G64 ... 78 A8
Craigmaddie Rd G62 ... 56 A1
Craigmaddie Terrace La 7
G3 ... 96 E1
Craigmark Pl KA11 ... 219 F5
Craigmarloch Ave G64 ... 78 B8
Craigmarloch Rdbt G68 ... 61 C3
Craigmarloch View G63 ... 31 B4
Craigmillar Ave G62 ... 55 B3
Craigmillar Pl FK5 ... 23 F4
Craigmillar Rd G42 ... 137 A7
Craigmochan Ave ML6 ... 102 F2
Craigmont Dr G20 ... 96 E6
Craigmont St G20 ... 96 E6
Craigmore Pl ML5 ... 121 E3
Craigmore Rd G61 ... 75 B7
Craigmore St G31 ... 118 C6
Craigmore Wynd 12
ML9 ... 185 B4
Craigmount Ave PA2 ... 133 C6
Craigmount St G66 ... 79 D7
Craigmuir Cres G52 ... 114 F6
Craigmuir Gdns G72 ... 161 B6
Craigmuir Pl G52 ... 114 E6
Craigmuir Rd
Glasgow G52 ... 114 E6
Hamilton G72 ... 161 B6
Craigmuschat Rd PA19 ... 44 E7
Craignaw Pl KA11 ... 220 B2
Craigneil Dr KA9 ... 236 C7
Craigneil St G33 ... 99 E2
Craigneith Ct G74 ... 160 E4
Craignethan Castle*
ML9 ... 200 F1
Craignethan Cres ML9 ... 200 D4
Craignethan Rd
Carluke ML8 ... 187 E3
Rutherglen G46 ... 157 B7
Craigneuk Ave ML6 ... 123 C6
Craigneuk Rd ML1 ... 143 C1
Craigneuk St ML2 ... 164 C5
Craignure Cres 4 ML6 ... 123 E7
Craignure Rd G73 ... 138 B3
Craigomus Cres FK11 ... 3 F6
Craigpark G31 ... 118 A7
Craigpark Ave KA9 ... 236 B6
Craigpark Dr G31 ... 118 A7
Craigpark Sch KA7 ... 239 A5
Craigpark St G81 ... 74 D7
Craigpark Way G71 ... 141 A7
Craigrie Rd FK10 ... 10 F4
Craigs Ave G81 ... 74 C6
Craigs Pl KA21 ... 217 B8
Craigs Rdbt FK7 ... 7 B7
Craigs The PA16 ... 45 C7
Craigsdow Rd KA10 ... 229 G6
Craigsheen Ave G76 ... 158 D7
Craigshiel Pl KA7 ... 238 D4
Craigside Ct G68 ... 81 F7
Craigside Rd G68 ... 81 F7
Craigskeen Pl KA9 ... 236 D5
Craigson Pl ML6 ... 123 F6
Craigspark KA22 ... 205 C4
Craigstewart Cres KA7 ... 238 C1
Craigston Ave KA7 ... 239 C6
Craigston Pl PA5 ... 111 F2
Craigston Rd PA5 ... 111 F2
Craigstone View G65 ... 60 F8
Craigthornhill Rd ML3,
ML10 ... 198 A6
Craigton Ave
Barrhead G78 ... 134 E1
Milngavie G62 ... 54 F2
Craigton Cotts G62 ... 54 C5
Craigton Cres Alva FK12 ... 4 F6
Newton Mearns G77 ... 156 B5
Craigton Dr
Barrhead G78 ... 134 E1
Glasgow G51 ... 115 F6
Newton Mearns G77 ... 156 C6
Craigton Gdns G62 ... 54 F2
Craigton Ind Est G52 ... 115 E5
Craigton Pl Blantyre G72 ... 140 D1
Glasgow G51 ... 115 E6
Craigton Prim Sch G52 ... 115 E5
Craigton Rd
Glasgow,Drumoyne G51 ... 115 F6
Glasgow,West Drumoyne
G51 ... 115 F7
Kilbirnie KA25 ... 170 B8
Milngavie G62 ... 54 E3
Neilston G77 ... 155 B3
Craigton St G81 ... 74 D8
Craigvale Cres ML6 ... 123 E7
Craigvicar Gdns G32 ... 119 D4
Craigview FK10 ... 5 D2
Craigview Ave PA5 ... 111 E1
Craigview Rd ML1 ... 163 F8
Craigview Terr PA5 ... 111 D1
Craigward FK10 ... 10 A6
Craigweil Pl KA7 ... 238 E7
Craigweil Rd KA7 ... 238 E7
Craigwell Ave G73 ... 138 D6
Craiksland Pl KA10 ... 230 A4
Crail Cl G72 ... 161 D3
Crail St G31 ... 118 D5
Cramalt Ct KA11 ... 220 A3
Crammond Ave ML5 ... 121 C4
Cramond Ave PA4 ... 94 E2
Cramond Ct FK1 ... 42 B2
Cramond Pl KA11 ... 219 F2
Cramond St G5 ... 117 E2
Cramond Terr G32 ... 119 B5
Cramond Way KA11 ... 219 F2
Cranberry Ct KA13 ... 207 C3
Cranberry Head KA13 ... 207 C3
Cranberry Moss Rd
Kilwinning KA13 ... 207 D3
Kilwinning KA13,KA20 ... 207 C1
Cranberry Pl KA13 ... 207 C3
Cranberry Rd KA13 ... 207 B2
Cranborne Rd G12 ... 96 A5
Cranbrooke Dr G20 ... 96 D7
Crandleyhill Rd KA9 ... 236 B6
Cranesbill Ct KA7 ... 239 B3
Crannog Ct G82 ... 50 E1
Crannog Rd G82 ... 50 F1
Crannog Way KA13 ... 207 C4
Cranston St G3 ... 240 A2
Cranworth La G12 ... 96 D3
Cranworth St G12 ... 96 D3
Crarae Ave G61 ... 75 E2
Crarae Pl G77 ... 156 B5
Crathes Ave FK5 ... 24 A4
Crathes Ct Glasgow G44 ... 136 E4
Wishaw ML2 ... 165 B3
Crathie Ct Carluke ML8 ... 187 E3
Glasgow G11 ... 96 A2
Crathie Dr
Ardrossan KA22 ... 205 C1
Denny FK6 ... 21 D3
Glasgow G11 ... 96 A2
Glenmavis ML6 ... 102 F4
Crathie Pl G77 ... 157 B4
Crathie Quadrant ML2 ... 165 B5
Crathie Rd KA3 ... 222 E2
Craufurd Ave KA23 ... 190 E4
Craufurd Cres KA15 ... 171 E4
Craufurdhill Pl KA2 ... 221 D1
Craufurdland Rd KA3 ... 223 A5
Craven Gr KA11 ... 219 F5
Craw Pl PA12 ... 129 C2
Craw Rd PA2 ... 113 D3
Crawberry Rd PA15 ... 46 A2

Cunningair Dr ML1 163 E4
Cunningham Cres KA7 239 C6
Cunningham Dr
Duntocher G81 73 F6
Glasgow G46 136 E3
Harthill ML7 127 D5
Cunningham Gdns
Falkirk FK2 42 F5
Houston PA6 91 D1
Cunningham Pl KA7 239 C6
Cunningham Rd
Glasgow G52 114 F8
Stenhousemuir FK5 24 A3
Stirling FK7 7 D7
Cunningham St ML1 163 D6
Cunningham Watt Rd KA3 195 D1
Cunninghame Cres KA21 217 A8
Cunninghame Dr KA1 227 E4
Cunninghame Rd
East Kilbride G74 159 E1
Irvine KA12 224 D8
Prestwick KA9 236 C7
Rutherglen G73 138 C8
Saltcoats KA21 217 A8
Cunninghamhead Est Cvn Pk KA3 220 F8
Cupar Dr PA16 44 F3
Cuparhead Ave ML5 121 E4
Cuppleton Brae PA9, PA12 130 B2
Curfew Rd G13 75 D1
Curle St Glasgow G14 95 D2
Glasgow G14 95 E2
Curlew Cres PA16 45 B4
Curlew La PA16 45 B4
Curlew Pl PA5 131 C7
Curling Cres G44 137 C7
Curlinghaugh Cres ML2 165 C3
Curlingmire G75 180 E7
Curran Ave ML2 164 E1
Currie Ct KA22 205 C1
Currie Pl G20 96 F6
Currie St G20 96 E6
Currieside Ave ML7 146 E4
Currieside Pl ML7 146 D4
Curtecan Pl KA7 238 F6
Curtis Ave G44 137 D7
Curzon St G20 96 F6
Cushenquarter Dr FK7 12 D3
Custom House Mus* PA15 46 A5
Custom House Quay Ret Pk PA15 46 A5
Custom House Way PA15 46 A5
Customhouse Pl PA15 46 A5
Customs Rdbt FK8 2 B1
Custonhall Pl FK6 21 D2
Cut The G71 140 F5
Cuthbert Pl KA3 223 A2
Cuthbert St G71 141 B7
Cuthbertson Prim Sch G42 117 A3
Cuthbertson St G42 117 A2
Cuthelton Dr G31 118 E4
Cuthelton St G31 118 D4
Cuthelton Terr G31 118 D4
Cutsburn Pl KA3 211 F8
Cutsburn Rd KA3 211 F8
Cutstraw Rd KA3 211 F8
Cutty Sark Pl G82 50 C2
Cuttyfield Pl FK2 24 C3
Cypress Ave Beith KA15 150 C2
Blantyre G72 140 C1
Uddingston G71 141 B8
Cypress Cres G75 180 C5
Cypress Ct
East Kilbride G75 180 C5
Hamilton ML3 162 E2
Kirkintilloch G66 79 B6
Cypress Gdns KA11 219 E5
Cypress Gr
Coatbridge G69 121 B6
Quarriers Village PA11 89 F2
Cypress Pl G75 180 C5
Cypress St G22 97 D5
Cypress Way G72 139 F4
Cyprus Ave PA5 112 B2
Cyril St PA1 114 A4

D

Daer Ave PA4 94 E1
Daer Way ML3 162 A3
Daffodil Way ML1 163 E8
Daintree Terr FK1 41 E5
Dairsie Ct G44 136 F4
Dairsie Gdns G64 98 D8
Dairsie House Sch G43 136 E6
Dairsie St G44 136 F4
Daisy Cotts KA8 236 A3
Daisy St G42 117 B2
Daisybank KA14 170 C6
Dakala Ct ML2 165 A2
Dakota Way PA4 94 D1
Dalbeattie Braes ML6 123 E1
Dalbeth Pl G32 118 F2
Dalbeth Rd G32 118 F2
Dalblair Ct KA7 238 F8
Dalblair Rd KA7 238 F7
Dalcharn Pl G34 120 A8
Dalcraig Cres G72 140 C2
Dalcross St G11 96 C2
Dalcruin Gdns G69 81 A4
Dalderse Ave FK2 42 B6
Daldowie Ave G32 119 D3
Daldowie Doocot* G69 119 F2
Daldowie Rd G71 120 A2
Daldowie St ML5 121 E3
Dale Ave G75 180 D6
Dale Cres KA12 219 D4
Dale Ct ML2 164 C2
Dale Dr ML1 143 A4
Dale Path G40 117 F4
Dale St Glasgow G40 117 F4
Glasgow G40 118 A4
Dale Way G73 138 B4
Dalespark Rdbt KA2 222 A1
Daleview Ave G12 96 B6
Daleview Dr G76 157 D6
Daleview Gr G76 157 D6
Dalfoil Ct PA1 114 F4
Dalgain Ct KA11 220 A5
Dalgarroch Ave G81 94 E8
Dalgarven Mews KA3 223 C6
Dalgarven Mill* KA13 207 D8
Dalgarven Wynd KA13 207 C6
Dalgleish Ave G81 73 F6
Dalgleish Ct FK8 7 B8
Dalhousie Gdns G64 78 A2
Dalhousie La G3 240 B4
Dalhousie Rd PA10 111 B2
Dalhousie St G3 240 C4
Dalilea Dr G34 100 D1
Dalilea Pl G34 100 D1
Dalintober St G5 240 B1
Daljarrock KA13 207 B2
Dalkeith Ave
Bishopbriggs G64 78 B4
Glasgow G41 116 B4
Dalkeith Rd G64 78 B4
Dallas Ct KA10 229 D2
Dallas La KA10 229 D2
Dallas Pl KA10 229 D2
Dallas Rd KA10 229 D2
Dalmacoulter Rd ML6 103 B3
Dalmahoy Cres PA11 110 C6
Dalmahoy St G32 118 E7
Dalmahoy Way KA13 207 B3
Dalmailing Ave KA11 220 B1
Dalmally St Glasgow G20 96 F3
Greenock PA15 46 F2
Dalmarnock Ct G40 118 B3
Dalmarnock Prim Sch G40 118 A4
Dalmarnock Rd G40 118 A3
Dalmarnock Road Trad Est G73 118 B1
Dalmarnock Sta G40 118 A3
Dalmary Dr PA1 114 B5
Dalmellington Ct
East Kilbride G74 159 D2
Hamilton ML3 161 D1
Dalmellington Dr
East Kilbride G74 159 D2
9 Glasgow G53 135 A8
Dalmellington Rd
Ayr KA7 239 C4
Glasgow G53 115 A1
Glasgow G53 135 A8
Dalmeny Ave G46 136 C3
Dalmeny Dr G78 134 A2
Dalmeny Rd ML3 162 D2
Dalmeny St G5 117 E2
Dalmilling Cres KA8 236 D2
Dalmilling Dr KA8 236 E2
Dalmilling Prim Sch KA8 236 E2
Dalmilling Rd KA8 236 E2
Dalmoak Rd PA15 46 C1
Dalmonach Rd G83 27 F4
Dalmore Cres G84 16 A3
Dalmore Dr Airdrie ML6 123 A6
Alva FK12 4 E6
Dalmore Ho G84 16 A3
Dalmore Pl KA11 219 F6
Dalmore Way KA11 219 F6
Dalmorglen Pk FK7 6 F6
Dalmuir Sta G81 73 E3
Dalnair Pl G62 54 D2
Dalnair St G3 96 D1
Dalness St G32 119 A4
Dalnottar Ave G60 73 B6
Dalnottar Dr G60 73 B5
Dalnottar Gdns G60 73 B5
Dalnottar Hill Rd G60 73 B6
Dalnottar Terr G60 73 B6
Dalquhurn Gdns G82 49 D8
Dalquhurn La
Dumbarton G82 49 E8
Renton G82 49 E8
Dalreoch Ave G69 120 C6
Dalreoch Ct G82 49 D4
Dalreoch Path G69 120 C5
Dalreoch Prim Sch G82 49 C5
Dalreoch Sta G82 49 E4
Dalriada G2 240 B2
Dalriada Cres ML1 142 D1
Dalriada Dr G64 78 C8
Dalriada Rd PA16 44 D3
Dalriada St G40 118 C4
Dalry Gdns ML3 161 D2
Dalry La KA22 205 C4
Dalry Pl ML6 143 D8
Dalry Prim Sch KA24 191 B7
Dalry Rd Ardrossan KA22 205 C4
Beith KA15 171 A7
Kilbirnie KA25 170 A7
Kilwinning KA13 207 D4
Saltcoats KA21 206 A2
Stewarton KA3 211 C8
Uddingston G71 141 B7
Dalry St G32 119 B4
Dalry Sta KA24 191 D7
Dalrymple Ct
Irvine KA12 219 E3
Kirkintilloch G66 79 D7
Dalrymple Dr
Coatbridge ML5 121 F5
East Kilbride G74 159 F3
Irvine KA12 219 E3
Newton Mearns G77 157 A4
Dalrymple Pl KA12 219 D3
Dalrymple St
Greenock PA15 45 F6
Greenock PA15 46 A5
Dalserf Cres G46 136 B1
Dalserf Ct G31 118 B5
Dalserf Gdns G31 118 B5
Dalserf Path 18 ML9 185 C1
Dalserf Prim Sch ML9 199 F8
Dalserf St G31 118 B5
Dalsetter Ave G15 75 A2
Dalsetter Bsns Ctr G15 75 A2
Dalsetter Pl G15 75 A2
Dalshannon Pl G67 82 A7
Dalshannon Rd G67 82 B7
Dalshannon View G67 82 B7
Dalshannon Way G67 82 A7
Dalsholm Ave G20 96 A8
Dalsholm Rd G20 96 B8
Dalskeith Ave PA3 113 A5
Dalskeith Cres PA3 113 A5
Dalskeith Rd PA3 113 A5
Dalswinton Path G34 120 D8
Dalswinton St G34 120 C8
Dalton Ave G81 74 E1
Dalton Hill ML3 161 E2
Dalton St G31 118 E5
Dalvait Ct G83 27 F8
Dalvait Gdns G83 27 E8
Dalvait Rd G83 27 E8
Dalveen Ct G78 134 C1
Dalveen Dr G71 140 F8
Dalveen Quadrant ML5 122 D5
Dalveen St G32 118 F5
Dalveen Way G73 138 C3
Dalwhinnie Ave G72 140 C2
Dalwhinnie Ct KA11 219 F6
Dalwood Rd KA9 236 B8
Daly Gdns G72 140 E1
Dalzell Ave ML1 164 A4
Dalzell Dr ML1 164 A4
Dalzell Pk* ML1 163 F3
Dalziel Ct ML3 162 A3
Dalziel Dr Glasgow G41 116 C3
Glasgow G41 116 D3
Dalziel High Sch ML1 163 D6
Dalziel Quadrant G41 116 C3
Dalziel Rd G52 114 F8
Dalziel St Hamilton ML3 162 B5
Motherwell ML1 163 F7
Dalziel Twr ML1 164 B3
Damhead Rd KA1 227 E3
Dampark KA3 195 C7
Damshot Cres G53 115 D1
Damshot Rd G53 135 D8
Damside KA8 235 F2
Danby Rd G69 119 F4
Danes Ave 1 G14 95 C4
Danes Cres G14 95 B5
Danes Dr G14 95 C4
Danes La N 3 G14 95 C4
Danes La S G14 95 C4
Daniel McLaughlin Pl G66 58 E1
Dankeith Dr KA1 231 C4
Dankeith Rd KA1 231 C4
Darg Rd KA20 217 D8
Dargarvel Ave G41 116 B4
Dargavel Ave PA7 72 B3
Dargavel Rd
Bishopton PA7 72 D1
Erskine PA8 72 E1
Dark Brig Rd ML8 201 B2
Darkwood Cres PA3 113 B6
Darkwood Ct PA3 113 B6
Darkwood Dr PA3 113 B6
Darleith Rd
Alexandria G83 27 E6
Cardross G82 26 A1
Darleith St G32 118 F5
Darley Cres KA10 229 E1
Darley Pl Hamilton ML3 183 B8
Troon KA10 229 E1
Darley Rd G68 61 E5
Darlington View KA3 195 F1
Darluith Pk PA5 111 C6
Darluith Rd PA3 111 F6
Darmeid Pl ML7 167 B8
Darmule Dr KA13 207 C5
Darnaway Ave G33 99 D2
Darnaway Dr G33 99 D2
Darnaway St G33 99 D2
Darndaff Rd PA15 46 A2
Darngaber Gdns ML3 183 E3
Darngaber Rd ML3 183 E3
Darngavel Ct ML6 122 D8
Darngavil Rd ML6 103 E6
Darnick St G21 98 B2
Darnley Cres G64 77 F3
Darnley Dr KA1 227 E5
Darnley Gdns G41 116 E2
Darnley Ind Est G53 135 B5
Darnley Mains Rd G53 135 C3
Darnley Path G46 135 E5
Darnley Pl G41 116 E2
Darnley Prim Sch G53 135 C3
Darnley Rd Barrhead G78 134 E3
Glasgow G41 116 E2
Darnley St Glasgow G41 116 F3
Stirling FK8 7 A8
Darnshaw Cl KA11 220 C5
Darrach Dr FK6 21 A2
Darragh Gn ML2 166 A6
Darroch Ave PA19 44 E7
Darroch Dr Erskine PA8 72 F3
Gourock PA19 44 E7
Darroch Way G67 62 A3
Dartford St G22 97 B3
Dartmouth Ave PA19 44 E5
Darvel Ave KA3 223 B6
Darvel Cres PA1 114 E4
Darvel Dr G77 157 A5
Darwin Pl G81 73 D4
Darwin Rd G75 180 C8
Davaar G74 160 C1
Davaar Dr
Coatbridge ML5 121 D7
Kilmarnock KA3 223 B5
Motherwell ML1 142 C2
Paisley PA2 133 E7
Davaar Pl Falkirk FK1 41 C4
Newton Mearns G77 156 C6
Davaar Rd Greenock PA16 44 D3
Renfrew PA4 94 D2
Saltcoats KA21 205 F2
Davaar St G40 118 B4
Davan Loan 10 ML2 165 F6
Dave Barrie Ave ML9 184 F5
Daventry Dr G12 96 A5
Davey St PA16 45 C5
David Dale Ave KA3 211 C8
David Gage St KA13 207 E5
David Gray Dr G66 59 A1
David Livingstone Ctr* G72 140 E2
David Livingstone Meml Prim Sch G72 140 D1
David Orr St KA1 222 E1
David Pl Glasgow G69 119 F4
Paisley PA3 114 B7
David St Coatbridge ML5 122 C7
Glasgow G40 118 A5
Salsburgh ML7 125 B2
David Way PA3 114 B7
David's Cres KA13 207 D2
David's Loan FK2 24 D1
Davidson Ave KA14 170 D6
Davidson Cres G65 59 F3
Davidson Dr PA19 44 E7
Davidson Gdns
Glasgow G14 95 E4
Stonehouse ML9 198 E1
Davidson La ML8 188 B1
Davidson Pl Ayr KA8 236 A1
Glasgow G32 119 C6
Davidson Quadrant G81 73 F7
Davidson Rd G83 27 F7
Davidson St Airdrie ML6 122 F8
Bannockburn FK7 7 C1
Clydebank G81 94 E8
Coatbridge ML5 122 B4
Glasgow G40 118 A2
Davidston Pl G66 79 F4
Davie's Acre G74 158 F4
Davieland Rd G46 136 A1
Davies Dr G83 27 E6
Davies Quadrant ML1 142 D2
Davies Row FK6 21 E2
Davington Dr ML3 161 D1
Daviot St 2 G51 115 D6
Dawsholm Ind Est G20 96 B7
Dawson Ave Alloa FK10 9 F8
East Kilbride G75 159 B1
Dawson Pl G4 97 B3
Dawson Rd G4 97 B3
Dawson St FK2 42 B8
De Morville Pl KA15 171 B7
De Walden Terr KA3 223 A1
Deacons Rd G65 60 E8
Deaconsbank Ave G46 135 E1
Deaconsbank Cres G46 135 D1
Deaconsbank Gdns G46 135 E1
Deaconsbank Gr G46 135 D1
Deaconsbank Pl G46 135 D1
Dealston Rd G78 134 B4
Dean Castle* KA3 223 B3
Dean Castle Ctry Pk* KA3 223 B4
Dean Cres Chryston G69 80 D1
Hamilton ML3 162 C1
Stirling FK8 2 C1
Dean Ct KA3 222 F1
Dean La KA3 223 A1
Dean Park Ave G71 141 A2
Dean Park Dr G72 139 D4
Dean Park Rd PA4 94 E2
Dean Pl KA2 226 F8
Dean Rd Kilbirnie KA25 149 B2
Kilmarnock KA3 223 B3
Dean St Bellshill ML4 142 B5
Clydebank G81 74 C1
Kilmarnock KA3 223 A2
Stewarton KA3 195 E1
Dean Terr KA3 223 A3
Dean View KA3 223 D4
Deanbrae St G71 140 F6
Deanfield Ct KA13 207 E3
Deanfield Quadrant G52 114 F6
Deanhill La KA3 223 A3
Deans Ave G72 139 D3
Deanside Rd G52 115 A8
Deanston Ave G78 134 B1
Deanston Dr G41 136 E8
Deanston Gdns G78 134 B1
Deanston Gr ML5 121 E3
Deanston Pk G78 134 B1
Deanstone Pl ML5 122 D3
Deanstone Wlk ML5 122 D2
Deanwood Ave G44 136 F3
Deanwood Rd G44 136 F3
Deas Rd ML7 146 C5
Dechmont G75 180 D5
Dechmont Ave
Cambuslang G72 139 D3
Motherwell ML1 163 C7
Dechmont Cotts G72 139 F3
Dechmont Gdns
Blantyre G72 140 C1
Uddingston G71 120 E1
Dechmont Pl G72 139 D3
Dechmont Rd G71 120 E1
Dechmont St
Glasgow G31 118 C4
Hamilton ML3 162 C2
Dechmont View
Bellshill ML4 141 F3
Uddingston G71 141 A7
Dee Ave Kilmarnock KA1 228 B4
Paisley PA2 112 F2
Renfrew PA4 94 E3
Dee Dr PA2 112 F2
Dee Path Larkhall ML9 199 A8
Motherwell ML1 143 B5
Dee Pl East Kilbride G75 179 E6
Johnstone PA5 131 C8
Dee St Coatbridge ML5 101 D2
Glasgow G33 118 D8
Greenock PA16 45 B5
Shotts ML7 146 D5
Dee Terr ML3 183 B8
Deedes St ML6 122 D6
Deep Dale G74 159 C3
Deepdene Rd
Bearsden G61 75 D2
Moodiesburn G69 80 F2
Deer Park Ave KA20 217 E7
Deer Park Ct ML3 183 D7
Deer Park Pl ML3 183 E7
Deer Path ML7 127 E5
Deer Pk FK10 5 E1
Deerdykes Ct N G68 81 E6
Deerdykes Ct S G68 81 E5
Deerdykes Pl G68 81 E6
Deerdykes Rd G67,G68 81 E5
Deerdykes Rdbt G68 81 C5
Deerdykes View G68 81 D6
Deerpark Prim Sch FK10 5 F1
Deeside Dr ML8 188 A3
Deeside Pl ML5 122 D4
Delfie Dr PA16 45 B4
Delhi Ave G81 73 C4
Dell The Bellshill ML4 142 D3
Newton Mearns G77 157 B5
Dellburn St ML1 164 A5
Dellburn Trad Pk ML1 164 A5
Dellingburn St 6 PA15 46 A4
Delny Pl G33 119 E7
Delph Rd FK10 4 C2
Delph Wynd FK10 4 C2
Delphwood Cres FK10 4 D2
Delves Ct ML11 215 A4
Delves Pk ML11 215 A4
Delves Rd ML11 215 A3
Delvin Rd G44 137 A6
Demoreham Ave FK6 21 F1
Dempsey Rd ML4 141 F3
Dempster Ct 4 PA15 45 F4
Dempster St PA15 45 E4
Den Bak Ave ML3 162 A2
Den La ML7 146 D6
Den The KA24 170 D3
Denbeck St G32 118 F5
Denbrae St G32 118 F5
Dene Wlk G64 98 C8
Denewood Ave PA2 133 D8
Denham St G22 97 B3
Denholm Cres G75 180 E8
Denholm Dr
Glasgow G46 136 C1
Wishaw ML2 165 C6
Denholm Gdns
Greenock PA16 45 C5
Quarter ML3 183 E3
Denholm Gn 3 G75 180 F8
Denholm St PA16 45 D5
Denholm Terr
Greenock PA16 45 D5
Hamilton ML3 161 E3
Denholm Way
Beith KA15 171 A7
Kilmarnock KA1 228 A5
Denmark St Glasgow G22 97 C4
Glasgow G22 97 C5
Denmilne Gdns G34 120 C7
Denmilne Path G34 120 C7
Denmilne Rd G34 120 D7
Denmilne St G34 120 C7
Denneystoun Cvn Pk G82 49 E4
Denniston Pl ML11 215 C5
Dennistoun Cres G84 25 C7
Dennistoun Rd PA14 70 C7
Dennistoun St ML4 142 B5
Denny High Sch FK6 39 E8
Denny Prim Sch FK6 21 D2
Denny Rd Denny FK4 39 E6
Larbert FK5 23 A1
Denny Tank Mus* G82 50 A3
Dennyholm Wynd KA25 149 B1
Dennystoun Forge G82 49 E4
Denovan Rd FK6 21 E4
Dentdale G74 159 C3
Deramore Ave G46 157 A7

Drumpellier Cres ML5 121 D6
Drumpellier Ct G67 82 C7
Drumpellier Ctry Pk* ML5 121 D8
Drumpellier Gdns G67 82 C7
Drumpellier Gr G67 82 C7
Drumpellier Pl
Cumbernauld G67 82 C7
Glasgow G69 120 B4
Drumpellier Rd G69 120 A4
Drumpellier St G33 98 D2
Drumreoch Dr G42 137 E8
Drumreoch Pl G42 137 E8
Drumriggend Rd FK1 85 D4
Drumry Pl G15 74 E2
Drumry Prim Sch G15 74 E3
Drumry Rd G81 74 C3
Drumry Rd E G15 74 E2
Drumry Sta G81 74 D2
Drums Ave PA3 113 C6
Drums Cres PA3 113 C5
Drums Rd G53 115 A3
Drums Terr PA16 45 B8
Drums The PA16 45 B8
Drumsack Ave G69 100 C8
Drumsargard Rd G73 138 D5
Drumshangie Pl ML6 103 A2
Drumshangie St ML6 103 A2
Drumshantie Rd PA19 44 E6
Drumshantie Terr PA19 44 E7
Drumshaw Dr G32 139 C8
Drumslea Pl PA16 45 C8
Drumtrocher St G65 60 D8
Drumvale Dr G69 80 E2
Drury Lane Ct G74 160 C4
Drury St G2 240 C2
Dryad St G46 135 E5
Drybridge Rd KA2 225 E2
Dryburgh Ave Denny FK6 21 D2
Paisley PA2 113 A1
Rutherglen G73 138 B7
Dryburgh Gdns G20 96 F3
Dryburgh Hill G74 159 D1
Dryburgh La G74 159 D1
Dryburgh Pl
Coatbridge ML5 121 F7
Kirkintilloch G66 79 F8
Dryburgh Rd
Bearsden G61 75 C6
Wishaw ML2 165 B4
Dryburgh St ML3 162 B6
Dryburgh Way 1 G72 161 D7
Dryburgh Wlk G69 81 A3
Dryburn Ave G52 115 B5
Dryden St ML3 162 B6
Drygait PA9 131 A6
Drygate G4 241 C2
Drygate St ML9 185 B4
Drygrange Rd G33 99 C2
Drymen Pl G66 79 D3
Drymen Rd Balloch G83 19 F1
Bearsden G61 75 E5
Drymen St G52 115 E5
Drymen Wynd G61 75 F3
Drynoch Pl G22 97 B7
Drysdale St Alloa FK10 10 B6
Glasgow G14 94 F5
Duart Ave KA9 236 C8
Duart Cres KA9 236 C8
Duart Dr
East Kilbride G74 159 D3
Elderslie PA5 112 C1
Newton Mearns G77 157 A5
Duart St G20 96 C8
Dubbs Rd
Kilwinning KA20 207 B1
Port Glasgow PA14 68 E7
Port Glasgow PA14 68 F7
Stevenston KA20 206 E1
Stevenston KA20 206 F1
Dubs Rd G78 134 E3
Dubton St G34 100 B1
Duchal Rd PA13 89 D8
Duchal St PA14 68 D8
Duchall Pl G14 95 B4
Duchess Ct ML3 163 A2
Duchess Dr G84 16 B3
Duchess Pk G84 16 B3
Duchess Pl G73 138 C8
Duchess Rd G73 118 C1
Duchess Way G69 120 F5
Duchray Dr PA1 114 F4
Duchray La G33 98 D1
Duchray St G33 98 D1
Duddingston Ave KA13 207 B4
Dudhope St G33 99 D2
Dudley Dr
Coatbridge ML5 101 C2
Glasgow G12 96 A3
Dudley La G12 96 A3
Duff Cres FK8 1 F1
Duff Pl Kilmarnock KA3 223 C3
Saltcoats KA21 206 A2
Duff St PA15 46 A5
Duffus Pl G32 139 C8
Duffus St G34 100 A1
Duffus Terr G32 139 C8
Duguid Dr KA21 206 A1
Duich Gdns G23 76 E1
Duisdale Rd G32 139 C8
Duke St Alva FK12 5 A7
Bannockburn FK7 7 C1
Denny FK6 21 C2
Glasgow G4 241 C2
Glasgow,Barrowfield G31 118 D5
Glasgow,Dennistoun G31 118 B6
Hamilton ML3 162 E3
Larkhall ML9 185 A4
Duke St *continued*
Motherwell ML1 163 E8
Paisley PA2 113 E2
Wishaw ML2 165 F6
Duke Street Sta G31 118 B7
Duke Terr KA8 236 A1
Duke's Ct ML9 185 A4
Duke's Rd G72,G73 138 D6
Dukes Ct G72 138 E7
Dukes Gate G71 140 E4
Dukes Pl ML3 183 D6
Dukes Rd Coatbridge G69 120 F5
Troon KA10 229 C3
Dullatur Rd G68 61 D6
Dullatur Rdbt G68 61 F5
Dulnain St G72 139 E5
Dulsie Rd G21 98 C6
Dumbain Cres G83 28 B8
Dumbain Rd G83 20 A1
Dumbarton Acad G82 50 A4
Dumbarton Castle* G82 49 F2
Dumbarton Central Sta G82 49 F4
Dumbarton Cottage Hospl G82 49 F5
Dumbarton East Sta G82 50 B3
Dumbarton Joint Hospl G82 49 C4
Dumbarton Rd
Bowling G60 72 D8
Cambusbarron FK8 6 E8
Clydebank G60,G81 73 D4
Clydebank,Duntocher G81 74 A6
Glasgow G11 95 F2
Glasgow G14 94 E6
Glasgow,Partick G11 96 B2
Milton G82 50 F1
Stirling FK8 7 B7
Dumbreck Ave G41 116 A4
Dumbreck Ct G41 116 A3
Dumbreck Marsh Nature Reserve* G65 60 B7
Dumbreck Pl
Glasgow G41 116 A3
Kirkintilloch G66 79 E4
Dumbreck Rd G41 116 B3
Dumbreck Sq G41 116 A4
Dumbreck Sta G41 116 C4
Dumbreck Terr G65 59 F8
Dumbrock Cres G63 31 C3
Dumbrock Dr G63 31 B3
Dumbrock Rd
Milngavie G62 54 D2
Strathblane G63 31 C3
Dumbuck Cres G82 50 C2
Dumbuck Gdns G82 50 B2
Dumbuck Rd
Dumbarton G82 50 B4
Dumbarton G82 50 B5
Dumbuie Ave G82 50 B3
Dumfries Cres ML6 122 F5
Dumfries Pk KA6 239 A1
Dumgoyne Ave G62 54 F2
Dumgoyne Dr G61 75 D7
Dumgoyne Gdns G62 54 F1
Dumgoyne Pl G76 157 C7
Dumgoyne Rd KA1 228 A3
Dumyat Ave FK10 4 B2
Dumyat Dr FK1 41 E3
Dumyat Rd Alva FK12 4 E6
Menstrie FK11 3 F6
Stirling FK9 2 C3
Dumyat Rise FK5 23 C5
Dumyat St FK10 4 F1
Dun Cann PA4 93 C7
Dun Pk G66 79 E8
Dunagoil Gdns G45 137 E2
Dunagoil Pl G45 137 E1
Dunagoil Rd G45 137 D2
Dunagoil St G45 137 E1
Dunalastair Dr G33 99 B5
Dunan Pl G33 119 E7
Dunard Ct ML8 187 F3
Dunard Prim Sch G20 96 F4
Dunard Rd G73 138 B7
Dunard St G20 96 F4
Dunard Way PA3 113 D7
Dunaskin St G11 96 C1
Dunavon Gdns FK6 21 D4
Dunavon Pl ML5 122 D4
Dunbar Ave
Coatbridge ML5 121 D4
Johnstone PA5 131 E8
Rutherglen G73 138 C7
Stenhousemuir FK5 23 F4
Dunbar Dr
Kilmarnock KA3 223 C2
Motherwell ML1 164 A4
Dunbar Gate FK6 21 E3
Dunbar Hill G74 159 C1
Dunbar La ML1 143 A2
Dunbar Pl G74 159 C1
Dunbar Rd PA2 113 A1
Dunbar St ML3 162 B5
Dunbeath Ave G77 156 F5
Dunbeath Gr G72 161 C3
Dunbeith Pl 4 G20 96 D5
Dunbeth Ave ML5 122 B7
Dunbeth Ct ML5 122 B7
Dunbeth Rd ML5 122 B7
Dunblane Dr G74 159 F2
Dunblane Pl
Coatbridge ML5 121 F4
East Kilbride G74 159 F2
Dunblane St G4 240 C4
Dunbrach Rd G68 61 C2
Dunbreck Ave ML6 105 A5
Dunbritton Rd G82 50 C3
Duncairn Ave FK4 39 F6
Duncan Ave Falkirk FK2 24 B3
Glasgow G14 95 C4
Duncan Buchanan Ct FK8 2 A2
Duncan Ct
Kilmarnock KA3 223 D4
Motherwell ML1 142 D1
Duncan Dr KA12 219 D2
Duncan Graham St ML9 185 B4
Duncan La G14 95 C3
Duncan La N 7 G14 95 C4
Duncan La S 13 G14 95 C4
Duncan McIntosh Rd G68 62 C7
Duncan Rd
Helensburgh G84 16 E3
Port Glasgow PA14 47 B1
Duncan St
Bonnybridge FK4 39 F5
Clydebank G81 74 B3
Greenock PA15 45 E5
Duncan's Cl ML11 215 A4
Duncanrig Sec Sch G75 159 B1
Duncansby Dr G72 161 C3
Duncansby Rd G33 119 D6
Duncanson Ave FK10 10 A8
Duncarnock Ave G78 154 E7
Duncarnock Cres G78 154 E7
Duncarron Ind Est FK6 21 F1
Duncarron Pl FK6 21 E2
Dunchattan Gr KA10 229 G2
Dunchattan Pl G31 117 F7
Dunchattan St G31 117 F7
Dunchattan Way KA10 229 G2
Dunchurch Rd PA1 114 D5
Dunclutha Dr G71 141 A1
Dunclutha St G40 118 B2
Duncolm Pl G62 54 D2
Duncombe Ave G81 74 B7
Duncombe St G20 96 D7
Duncombe View 6 G81 74 D3
Duncraig Cres PA5 131 D8
Duncrub Dr G64 77 E1
Duncruin St G20 96 D7
Duncruin Terr G20 96 D7
Duncryne Ave G32 119 E4
Duncryne Gdns G32 119 E4
Duncryne Pl G64 97 E8
Duncryne Rd
Alexandria G83 27 E6
Gartocharn G83 20 F8
Dundaff Ct FK6 21 D1
Dundaff Hill G68 61 C2
Dundarroch St FK5 23 B1
Dundas Ave G64 78 B8
Dundas Cotts FK4 39 A2
Dundas Ct G74 159 E2
Dundas La G1 241 A3
Dundas Pl G74 159 E2
Dundas Rd FK9 2 B4
Dundas St G1 241 A3
Dundas Wlk KA3 223 D3
Dundashill G4 97 B2
Dundasvale Ct G4 240 C4
Dundee Ct 5 FK2 42 A8
Dundee Dr G52 115 B3
Dundee Path G52 115 C3
Dundee Pl FK2 42 A8
Dundonald Ave PA5 111 D1
Dundonald Castle* KA2 225 E2
Dundonald Cres
Coatbridge ML5 121 F4
Irvine KA11 224 H1
Newton Mearns G77 157 A4
Dundonald Ct KA3 223 B6
Dundonald Dr ML3 183 D7
Dundonald Pl
Kilmarnock KA1 227 D7
Neilston G78 154 D7
Dundonald Prim Sch KA2 225 F2
Dundonald Rd
Glasgow G12 96 C3
Irvine KA11 225 C8
Kilmarnock KA1,KA2 227 D7
Paisley PA3 114 A7
Troon KA10 229 F3
Dundonald St G72 161 C8
Dundonald Terr KA9 236 D7
Dundrennan Dr ML6 123 E2
Dundrennan Rd G42 136 F7
Dundyvan Gate ML5 122 A5
Dundyvan Gdns ML5 122 A5
Dundyvan Ind Est ML5 121 F5
Dundyvan La ML2 165 A2
Dundyvan Rd ML5 121 F5
Dundyvan St ML2 165 A2
Dundyvan Way ML5 121 F5
Dunearn Pl PA2 114 A3
Dunearn St G4 96 F2
Duneaton Wynd ML9 185 B1
Dunedin Ct G75 180 A8
Dunedin Dr G75 180 A8
Dunedin Rd ML9 185 B1
Dunedin Terr G81 94 C8
Dunellan Ave G69 81 A2
Dunellan Cres G69 81 A2
Dunellan Ct G69 81 A2
Dunellan Dr G81 74 B7
Dunellan Gdns G69 81 A2
Dunellan Gr G69 80 F2
Dunellan Pl G69 81 A2
Dunellan Rd G62 54 D2
Dunellan St G52 115 E5
Dunellan Way G69 81 A2
Dungavel Gdns ML3 183 E8
Dungavel La ML8 188 B1
Dungavel Rd KA1 228 A4
Dungeonhill Rd G34 120 D8
Dunglass Ave
East Kilbride G74 159 F3
Glasgow G14 95 C4
Dunglass La 8 G14 95 C4
Dunglass La N 5 G14 95 C4
Dunglass La S 11 G14 95 C4
Dunglass Pl Milngavie G62 54 E3
Newton Mearns G77 156 A5
Dunglass Rd PA7 72 C2
Dunglass Sq G74 159 F3
Dunglass View G63 31 D4
Dungoil Ave G68 61 B3
Dungoil Rd G66 79 E4
Dungourney Dr PA16 45 D7
Dungoyne St G20 96 C8
Dunholme Pk G81 73 D3
Dunipace Prim Sch FK6 21 D3
Dunira St G32 118 F3
Dunivaig Rd G33 119 E8
Dunkeld Ave G73 138 B7
Dunkeld Dr G61 76 B4
Dunkeld Gdns G64 78 B2
Dunkeld La G69 81 A2
Dunkeld Pl
Coatbridge ML5 121 F4
Falkirk FK2 24 C1
Hamilton ML3 161 E3
Newton Mearns G77 157 B4
Dunkeld St G31 118 C4
Dunkenny Rd G15 74 F3
Dunkenny Sq G15 74 F3
Dunkirk St ML6 105 A5
Dunlin East Kilbride G74 159 E4
Glasgow G12 96 A6
Dunlin Cres PA6 91 C1
Dunlin Ct ML4 141 E8
Dunlop Cres Ayr KA8 236 E1
Bothwell G71 141 B1
Irvine KA11 220 B1
Renfrew PA4 94 D4
Dunlop Ct Hamilton ML3 183 E7
2 Troon KA10 229 E5
Dunlop Dr KA11 224 G4
Dunlop Gr G71 121 A1
Dunlop Halt KA3 195 B7
Dunlop Pl Ashgill ML9 200 A8
Irvine KA11 224 H4
Milngavie G62 54 F3
Dunlop Prim Sch KA3 195 B8
Dunlop Rd Barrmill KA15 172 A3
Lugton KA3 173 C6
Stewarton KA3 195 D1
Dunlop St
Cambuslang G72 139 E6
Fenwick KA3 213 A3
Glasgow G1 241 A1
Greenock PA16 45 D3
Kilmarnock KA1 222 F1
Linwood PA3 112 C6
Renfrew PA4 94 D4
Stewarton KA3 195 E1
Dunlop Terr KA8 236 D1
Dunlop Twr G75 180 E8
Dunmar Cres FK10 4 E1
Dunmar Dr FK10 4 E1
Dunmore Dr G62 76 D8
Dunmore St G81 94 C8
Dunn Mews KA1 227 C8
Dunn St Clydebank G81 73 E3
Duntocher G81 73 F6
Glasgow G40 118 A4
Greenock PA15 45 E4
Paisley PA1 114 A4
Dunn Terr ML7 127 F6
Dunnachie Dr ML5 121 B4
Dunnachie Pl ML5 121 C4
Dunnet Ave ML6 102 F5
Dunnet Dr PA6 91 B1
Dunnett Ave KA1 228 B7
Dunnichen Gdns G64 78 D1
Dunnikier Wlk G68 60 E1
Dunning Dr G68 62 A5
Dunning Pl FK2 24 C1
Dunnotar Wlk 16 ML2 165 F6
Dunnottar Cres G74 159 D3
Dunnottar Ct G74 159 C3
Dunnottar Dr FK5 23 F4
Dunnottar St
Bishopbriggs G64 78 D2
Glasgow G33 99 B2
Dunns Wood Rd G67 62 D6
Dunollie Gdns KA3 223 B6
Dunolly Dr G77 156 F5
Dunolly St G21 98 A1
Dunoon Ave KA3 222 F3
Dunottar Ave ML5 122 B2
Dunottar Pl ML5 122 B3
Dunphail Dr G34 100 D1
Dunphail Rd G34 120 D8
Dunragit St G31 118 C7
Dunrobin Ave
Elderslie PA5 112 C1
Stenhousemuir FK5 23 F5
Dunrobin Cres G74 159 D3
Dunrobin Ct
Clydebank G81 74 A2
East Kilbride G74 159 D3
Dunrobin Dr
East Kilbride G74 159 D3
Gourock PA19 43 F6
Dunrobin Gdns ML6 123 E6
Dunrobin Pl ML5 121 F7
Dunrobin Prim Sch ML6 123 E7
Dunrobin Rd ML6 123 E7
Dunrobin St G31 118 B6
Dunrod Hill G74 159 F3
Dunrod St G32 119 B4
Duns Cres ML2 165 C7
Duns Path ML5 122 D3
Duns Pl 2 PA15 46 B3
Dunscore Brae ML3 161 E2
Dunside Dr G53 135 A6
Dunsiston Rd ML6 124 B4
Dunskaith Pl G34 120 D7
Dunskaith St G34 120 D7
Dunskey Rd KA3 223 B6
Dunsmore Rd PA7 72 A4
Dunsmuir St G51 116 B7
Dunster Gdns G64 78 B4
Dunster Rd FK9 2 C3
Dunswin Ave G81 73 E3
Dunsyre Pl G23 76 E1
Dunsyre St G33 118 E8
Duntarvie Ave G34 120 C8
Duntarvie Cl G34 120 C8
Duntarvie Cres G34 120 C8
Duntarvie Dr G34 120 B8
Duntarvie Gdns G34 120 C8
Duntarvie Gr G34 120 C8
Duntarvie Pl G34 120 B8
Duntarvie Rd G34 120 B8
Dunterlie Ave G13 95 B6
Dunterlie Ct G78 134 C3
Duntiblae G66 80 A7
Duntiblae Rd G66 80 A7
Duntiglennan Rd G81 74 A6
Duntilland Ave ML7 125 B2
Duntilland Rd
Airdrie ML6 124 E8
Salsburgh ML7 125 C5
Duntocher Rd
Bearsden G61 75 B6
Clydebank G81 74 A4
Clydebank,Parkhall G81 74 A5
Duntonknoll KA12 219 C4
Duntreath Ave
Clydebank G15 74 F1
Glasgow G13 94 E8
Duntreath Dr G15 74 F1
Duntreath Gdns G15 74 F2
Duntreath Gr G15 74 F1
Duntreath Terr G65 60 D8
Duntroon Pl ML4 142 B3
Duntroon St G31 118 B8
Dunure Cres FK4 40 A5
Dunure Cts KA13 207 D3
Dunure Dr Hamilton ML3 161 D2
Kilmarnock KA3 228 B8
Newton Mearns G77 157 A5
Rutherglen G73 137 F5
Dunure Pl
Coatbridge ML5 121 E3
Kilmarnock KA3 223 B6
Newton Mearns G77 157 A4
Dunure Rd KA7 238 B2
Dunure St
Bonnybridge FK4 40 A5
Coatbridge ML5 121 E3
Glasgow G20 96 D7
Dunvegan ML6 102 F4
Dunvegan Ave
Coatbridge ML5 101 D1
Elderslie PA5 112 C1
Gourock PA19 43 F5
Stenhousemuir FK5 23 F4
Dunvegan Ct FK10 10 B6
Dunvegan Dr
Bishopbriggs G64 78 A4
Falkirk FK2 24 C1
Newton Mearns G77 157 A5
Stirling FK9 2 B3
Dunvegan Pl
Bonnybridge FK4 39 F6
East Kilbride G74 159 D3
Irvine KA12 219 D6
Uddingston G71 140 D8
Dunvegan Quadrant PA4 94 B4
Dunwan Ave G13 94 F7
Dunwan Pl G13 94 F7
Dura Rd ML2,ML7 167 C5
Durban Ave
Clydebank G81 73 D4
East Kilbride G75 180 B4
Durham Rd PA16 44 E5
Durham St G41 116 D5
Durisdeer Dr ML3 161 E1
Durness Ave G61 76 B4
Duror St G32 119 A6
Durris Gdns G32 119 D3
Durrockstock Cres PA2 132 F7
Durrockstock Rd PA2 132 F7
Durrockstock Way PA2 132 F7
Durward G74 160 E4
Durward Ave G41 116 D1
Durward Cres PA2 112 F1
Durward Ct Glasgow G41 116 D1
Motherwell ML1 142 D1
Durward Way PA2 112 F1
Dutch House Cvn Pk KA9 233 E5
Dutch House Rdbt KA9 233 F6
Duthie Park Gdns 2 G13 95 D6
Duthie Park Pl 1 G13 95 D6
Duthie Rd PA19 45 A7
Dyce Ave ML6 122 E4
Dyce La G11 96 A2
Dyer's La G1 241 B1
Dyers' Wynd 9 PA1 113 E5
Dyfrig St Hamilton G72 161 C8
Shotts ML7 146 E5

Elm Cres G71 141 D7
Elm Ct 1 Hamilton G72 161 E7
Quarter ML3 183 F4
Elm Dr Cambuslang G72 139 C6
Chapelhall ML6 123 E3
Cumbernauld G67 62 F4
Johnstone PA5 112 A1
Elm Gdns Bearsden G61 75 E6
Troon KA10 230 A2
Elm Gr Alloa FK10 10 C5
Langbank PA14 70 C7
Stenhousemuir FK5 23 D1
Elm La E 6 G14 95 D3
Elm La W 5 G14 95 D3
Elm Lea PA5 112 B2
Elm Pk KA22 205 D3
Elm Pl G75 180 C6
Elm Quadrant ML6 123 D7
Elm Rd Bridge of W PA11 110 E8
Clydebank G81 74 A5
Dumbarton G82 49 F4
Motherwell,Carfin ML1 143 A2
Motherwell,Holytown ML1 143 B5
Paisley PA2 114 A2
Rutherglen G73 138 B4
Elm St Clarkston G76 157 F6
Coatbridge ML5 122 C5
Glasgow G14 95 D3
Hamilton G72 161 E7
Lennoxtown G66 57 E8
Motherwell ML1 163 D7
Stirling FK8 1 E1
Elm Terr PA19 44 E6
Elm View Ct ML4 142 D4
Elm Way Cambuslang G72 139 E4
Larkhall ML9 185 A5
Elm Wlk G61 75 E6
Elmbank FK11 4 A6
Elmbank Ave
Kilmarnock KA1 228 A8
Uddingston G71 141 B7
Elmbank Cres Denny FK4 39 D6
Glasgow G2 240 B3
Hamilton ML3 162 A4
Elmbank Dr
Alexandria G83 27 F5
Kilmarnock KA1 228 A8
Larkhall ML9 185 C1
Elmbank Rd
Langbank PA14 70 C7
Stirling FK7 7 A3
Elmbank St Ayr KA8 236 A3
Bellshill ML4 142 A4
Carluke ML8 202 A8
Glasgow G2 240 B3
Elmbank Street La G2 240 B3
Elmbank Terr KA12 219 D4
Elmfoot St G5 117 D2
Elmhurst ML1 163 D4
Elmira Rd G69 100 D7
Elmore Ave G44 137 B5
Elms Pl Beith KA15 150 B1
Stevenston KA20 206 E2
Elms The G44 137 B4
Elmslie Ct G69 120 C4
Elmtree Gdns G45 137 F4
Elmvale Prim Sch G22 97 E5
Elmvale Row G21 97 E5
Elmvale St G21 97 E5
Elmwood ML2 164 E1
Elmwood Ave
Glasgow G11 95 F4
Newton Mearns G77 156 F6
Elmwood Ct G71 141 A2
Elmwood Gdns G66 79 A5
Elmwood La G11 95 F4
Elmwood Manor G71 141 A2
Elmwood Rd ML7 147 B2
Elphin St G23 76 D1
Elphinstone Cres
Airth FK2 14 E4
East Kilbride G75 180 F6
Elphinstone Ct PA13 89 D8
Elphinstone Mews PA13 89 D8
Elphinstone Pl G51 116 C7
Elphinstone Rd G46 157 A7
Elrig Rd G44 137 A5
Elsinore Path G75 180 E6
Elspeth Gdns G64 78 C2
Elswick Dr ML6 105 A4
Eltham St G22 97 B3
Elvan Ct ML1 163 D6
Elvan Pl G75 179 E7
Elvan St Glasgow G32 118 F5
Motherwell ML1 163 D6
Elvan Twr 4 ML1 163 E5
Elvis St KA9 233 D2
Embo Dr G13 95 B6
Emerald Terr ML4 142 A4
Emerson Rd G64 78 A1
Emerson Rd W G64 78 A1
Emily Dr ML1 163 E4
Emma Jay Rd ML4 142 B5
Emma's Way FK4 39 F5
Empire Gate ML7 146 F4
Empire Way ML1 142 C1
Empress Ct PA15 46 B4
Empress Dr G84 16 A3
Empress Rd G84 15 D5
Endfield Ave G12 96 B6
Endrick Bank G64 78 A4
Endrick Ct ML5 121 F6
Endrick Dr Balloch G83 19 F1
Bearsden G61 75 F3
Denny FK6 39 E6
Paisley PA1 114 B6
Endrick Gdns G62 54 E2
Endrick Ho G82 50 B6
Endrick Pl FK7 7 A4
Endrick Rd PA15 46 B1
Endrick St G21 97 D3
Endrick Way G83 27 E6
Endrick Wynd G84 25 C8
Engelen Dr FK10 10 B5
Engels St G83 27 E7
Englewood Ave KA8 236 B5
English Row ML6 123 C3
English St ML2 164 D3
Ennerdale G75 179 F6
Ennisfree Rd G72 161 D8
Ensay St G22 97 D7
Enterkin St G32 118 F4
Enterkine KA13 207 B2
Enterprise Ho
Kirkintilloch G66 79 C7
Motherwell ML1 163 F7
Entryfoot EH48 106 F2
Eribol Wlk ML1 143 D3
Eriboll Pl G22 97 B7
Eriboll St G22 97 B7
Ericht Pl ML7 146 E6
Ericht Rd G43 136 C5
Eriska Ave G14 95 B5
Eriskay Ave
Hamilton ML3 161 F2
Newton Mearns G77 156 B5
Port Glasgow PA14 69 B7
Eriskay Cres G77 156 B5
Eriskay Ct Falkirk FK1 42 C2
Irvine KA11 225 C8
Eriskay Dr G60 73 C6
Eriskay Pl
Kilmarnock KA3 223 B5
Old Kilpatrick G60 73 C6
Ermelo Gdns G75 180 B4
Erradale St G22 97 A7
Errogie St G34 120 B8
Errol Gdns G5 117 C4
Erskine Ave G41 116 B4
Erskine Cres ML6 122 F5
Erskine Ferry Rd G60 73 B5
Erskine Gdns ML7 146 D5
Erskine Hospl PA7 72 E5
Erskine Pl
Clackmannan FK10 10 F5
Kilmarnock KA3 223 C2
Saltcoats KA21 216 F7
Erskine Rd G46 157 B6
Erskine Sq G52 114 F7
Erskine St Alloa FK10 10 B7
Alva FK12 5 A7
Erskine View G60 73 A6
Erskine Way ML7 146 E4
Erskinefauld Rd PA3 112 B6
Ervie St G34 120 C7
Escart Rd ML8 187 F3
Esdaile Ct ML1 143 A3
Esk Ave PA4 94 E2
Esk Dale G74 159 C3
Esk Dr PA2 112 E1
Esk Rd Kilmarnock KA1 228 B4
Troon KA10 229 F5
Esk St G14 94 F5
Esk Way PA2 112 E1
Eskbank St G32 119 B6
Eskdale G77 157 B5
Eskdale Dr G73 138 D7
Eskdale Rd G61 75 D2
Eskdale St G42 117 B1
Esmond St G3 96 C1
Espedair St PA2 113 E3
Espieside Cres ML5 121 D8
Esplanade Ayr KA7 238 E8
Gourock PA19 44 C7
Greenock PA16 45 D8
Prestwick KA9 236 B8
1 Stirling FK8 7 A8
Essenside Ave G15 75 C2
Essex Dr G14 95 E4
Essex La G14 95 E3
Essex Rd PA16 44 E4
Esslemont Ave G14 95 C5
Esson Pl KA3 223 A3
Estate Ave FK1 42 C4
Estate Quadrant G32 139 C8
Estate Rd G32 139 C8
Etive Ave Bearsden G61 76 B4
Hamilton ML3 162 A1
Etive Cres
Bishopbriggs G64 78 B1
Cumbernauld G67 82 B6
Etive Ct Clydebank G81 74 C5
Cumbernauld G67 82 B6
Etive Dr Airdrie ML6 123 C5
Bishopton PA7 72 C2
Cumbernauld G67 82 B6
Glasgow G46 136 D1
Etive Pl Cumbernauld G67 82 C6
Irvine KA12 219 D5
Larkhall ML9 184 F5
Stirling FK9 2 B3
Etive St Glasgow G32 119 A5
Wishaw ML2 165 B1
Etive Wlk ML7 147 B3
Etna Ct FK2 42 D7
Etna Ind Est ML2 164 C4
Etna Rd FK2 42 D7
Etna Road Rdbt FK2 42 E7
Etna St ML2 164 C4
Eton La 3 G12 96 E2
Etterick Wynd 9 G72 161 C7
Ettrick Ave
Hattonrig ML4 142 A7
Renfrew PA4 94 F2
Ettrick Cres
Kilmarnock KA3 222 F3
Ettrick Cres *continued*
Rutherglen G73 138 C7
Ettrick Ct
Cambuslang G72 139 D4
Coatbridge ML5 122 C3
Falkirk FK1 42 D1
Ettrick Dr Bearsden G61 75 C7
Bishopton PA7 72 C2
Ettrick Hill 2 G74 160 A3
Ettrick Oval PA2 132 E8
Ettrick Pl Ayr KA8 236 B4
Glasgow G43 136 D7
3 Greenock PA15 46 B3
Ettrick Sq G67 61 F2
Ettrick St ML2 165 A5
Ettrick Terr PA5 131 C8
Ettrick Way
9 Cumbernauld G67 61 F1
Renfrew PA4 94 F2
Ettrick Wlk G67 61 F2
Euchan Pl KA10 229 G5
Eurocentral ML4 142 F8
Eurocentral Rail Terminal ML1 142 D7
Evan Cres G46 136 D2
Evan Dr G46 136 D2
Evans St FK5 23 C3
Evanton Dr G46 135 E3
Evanton Pl G46 135 E3
Evelyn Terr KA13 207 E2
Everard Ct G21 97 E7
Everard Dr G21 97 E6
Everard Pl 2 G21 97 E7
Everard Quadrant G21 97 E7
Everglades The G69 100 B8
Evergreen Trailer Ct FK6 22 A2
Eversley St G32 119 A3
Everton Rd G53 115 C2
Ewart Cres ML3 162 B1
Ewart Gdns ML3 162 B1
Ewart Terr ML3 162 A2
Ewenfield Ave KA7 239 A4
Ewenfield Gdns KA7 239 A4
Ewenfield Pk KA7 238 F4
Ewenfield Rd KA7 239 A4
Ewing Ave FK2 42 B7
Ewing Ct Hamilton ML3 183 C7
Stirling FK7 7 C3
Ewing Dr FK2 42 B7
Ewing Pl Falkirk FK2 42 B7
Glasgow G31 118 C5
Ewing Rd PA12 129 C3
Ewing St Kilbarchan PA10 111 A3
Rutherglen G73 138 A7
Ewing Way KA3 211 D8
Ewing Wlk G62 55 C1
Excelsior Pk ML2 164 D2
Excelsior St ML1,ML2 164 D3
Exchange Pl G1 241 A2
Exeter Dr G11 96 A2
Exeter La G11 96 A2
Exeter St ML5 122 A5
Exhibition Centre Sta G3 116 E8
Exmouth Pl PA19 44 E5
Eynort St G22 97 A7
Eyrepoint Ct G33 119 A8

F

Factory Pl KA21 216 F8
Factory Rd ML1 163 E5
Fagan Ct G72 140 E1
Faifley Rd G81 74 C7
Failford Pl KA3 223 B4
Fair Isle Pl KA3 223 A6
Fair Oaks G76 158 E8
Fair View Dr ML11 214 A4
Fair Way G82 48 A8
Fairbairn Cres G46 136 A2
Fairbairn Path G40 118 A4
Fairburn St G32 118 F4
Fairfax Ave G44 137 C5
Fairfield FK10 5 C1
Fairfield Ave FK4 40 A6
Fairfield Ct G76 157 E5
Fairfield Dr
Clarkston G76 157 E5
Renfrew PA4 94 D1
Fairfield Gdns G51 115 F8
Fairfield Pk KA7 238 F7
Fairfield Pl Bothwell G71 141 B2
East Kilbride G74 159 C2
Falkirk FK2 42 C5
Glasgow G51 115 F8
Hamilton ML3 162 E1
Fairfield Rd Ayr KA7 238 E7
Sauchie FK10 5 C1
Fairfield Sch FK10 5 B1
Fairfield St G51 115 F8
Fairfields FK2 13 E5
Fairford Dr G67 82 D7
Fairgreen Pl FK7 11 E8
Fairhaven KA10 229 F7
Fairhaven Ave ML6 123 E6
Fairhaven Rd G23 96 E8
Fairhaven Sq KA13 207 B4
Fairhill Ave Glasgow G53 135 C7
Hamilton ML3 162 C1
Fairhill Cres ML3 162 C1
Fairhill Pl ML3 183 C7
Fairhill Rd FK7 7 B1
Fairholm Ave ML3 163 D1
Fairholm St Glasgow G32 118 F4
Larkhall ML9 184 F4
Fairley St G51 116 B6
Fairlie G74 159 D3
Fairlie Ave KA1 227 D7
Fairlie Dr Falkirk FK1 41 D5
Irvine KA11 220 B6
Fairlie Gdns FK1 41 D5
Fairlie Park Dr G11 96 A2
Fairlie St FK1 41 C5
Fairlie View KA2 226 E5
Fairmount Dr FK10 5 B2
Fairrie St PA15 46 D3
Fairview Ct G62 55 A1
Fairway G61 75 C5
Fairway Ave PA2 133 D8
Fairways Irvine KA12 219 A7
Larkhall ML9 185 C3
Stewarton KA3 211 E8
Fairways Pl FK4 40 B7
Fairways The
Bothwell G71 141 A2
Johnstone PA5 131 D7
Fairways View G81 74 D6
Fairweather Pl G77 156 C3
Fairyburn Rd FK10 9 F8
Fairyhill Pl KA1 227 E6
Fairyhill Rd KA1 227 E6
Fairyknowe Ct G71 141 B2
Fairyknowe Gdns G71 141 B2
Faith Ave PA11 89 E2
Falcon Cres
Greenock PA16 45 A6
Paisley PA3 113 B6
Falcon Dr FK5 23 B3
Falcon La PA16 45 A5
Falcon Rd PA5 131 D7
Falcon Terr G20 96 C8
Falcon Terrace La G20 96 C8
Falconbridge Rd G74 160 C4
Falconer Ct FK7 7 C3
Falconer St PA14 47 C2
Falconer Terr ML3 162 C1
Falfield St 1 G5 117 A4
Falkirk & District Royal Infmy FK1 42 A4
Falkirk Coll of F & H Ed Ctr FK2 42 E6
Falkirk Grahamston Sta FK1 42 B5
Falkirk High Sch FK1 41 E4
Falkirk High Sta FK1 42 A3
Falkirk Rd
Bannockburn FK7 11 F8
Bonnybridge FK4 40 C6
Cowie FK7 12 A6
Falkirk FK2,FK3 42 F6
Falkirk,Glen Village FK1 42 B1
Larbert FK5 23 B1
Larbert FK5 41 C8
Falkirk Stadium (Falkirk FC) FK2 42 F6
Falkirk Wheel (Rotating Boat Lift)* FK1 41 A5
Falkland Ave G77 157 A5
Falkland Cres G64 98 D8
Falkland Dr G74 159 D1
Falkland La G12 96 B3
Falkland Park Rd KA8 236 A3
Falkland Pk G74 159 D1
Falkland Pl Ayr KA8 236 A3
Coatbridge ML5 122 B3
East Kilbride G74 159 D1
Stenhousemuir FK5 23 E4
Falkland Rd KA8 236 A3
Falkland St G12 96 B3
Fallin Prim Sch FK7 8 D5
Falloch Pl ML2 165 F6
Falloch Rd Bearsden G61 75 C2
Glasgow G42 137 A7
Milngavie G62 54 E3
Fallside Ave G71 141 C6
Fallside Rd G71 141 B4
Fallside Sec Sch G71 141 D6
Falmouth Dr PA19 44 F5
Falside Ave PA2 113 E1
Falside Rd Glasgow G32 119 B2
Paisley PA2 113 E1
Falstaff G74 160 C5
Fancy Farm Pl PA16 44 F4
Fancy Farm Rd PA16 45 A4
Fara St G23 96 F8
Faraday Ave ML2 165 C3
Faraday Ret Pk ML5 122 A6
Faransay Pl KA3 223 A5
Fardalehill View KA2 221 F1
Farden Pl KA9 236 D6
Farie St G73 137 F8
Farlands View KA23 190 C4
Farm Cres ML1 143 F4
Farm Ct G71 141 B4
Farm Houses The G65 60 E7
Farm La ML4 141 F3
Farm Pk G66 79 D4
Farm Rd Blantyre G72 140 D1
Clydebank G81 73 D3
Clydebank,Duntocher G81 74 A7
Cowie FK7 12 D8
Fallin FK7 8 D4
Glasgow G41 116 B5
Hamilton ML3 161 F4
Kilmarnock KA3 222 E3
Port Glasgow PA14 68 E7
Prestwick KA9 233 D1
Farm St Falkirk FK2 24 A1
Motherwell ML1 163 D7
Farm Terr ML3 161 F4
Farme Castle Ct G73 118 C1
Farme Castle Est G73 118 C1
Farme Cross G73 118 B1
Farmeloan Rd G73 138 B8
Farmfield Terr KA23 190 D5
Farmgate Sq ML4 141 F4
Farmington Ave G32 119 D5
Farmington Gate G32 119 D4
Farmington Gdns G32 119 D5
Farmington Gr G32 119 D5
Farndale G74 159 C3
Farne Dr G44 137 C4
Farnell St G4 97 B2
Farquhar Rd
Greenock PA14 46 F2
Port Glasgow PA14 47 A2
Farquhar Sq EH48 107 C3
Farquharson Way FK1 41 F1
Farrell Pl KA8 236 B2
Farrier Ct PA5 111 F3
Faskally Ave G64 77 E3
Faskally Wlk 19 ML2 165 F6
Faskin Cres G53 134 F7
Faskin Pl G53 134 F7
Faskin Rd G53 134 F7
Faskine Ave Airdrie ML6 122 F6
Calderbank ML6 123 B2
Faskine Cres ML6 122 F6
Fasque Pl G15 74 E4
Fastnet St G33 119 A8
Fauldhouse St G5 117 D3
Faulds G69 120 C5
Faulds Gdns G69 120 C5
Faulds La ML5 121 F3
Faulds Park Rd PA19 43 E5
Faulds St ML5 121 F3
Faulds Wynd KA23 190 C4
Fauldshead Rd PA4 94 D3
Fauldspark Cres G69 120 C6
Fauldswood Cres PA2 113 B2
Fauldswood Dr PA2 113 B2
Faulkner Gr ML1 164 F8
Fearnach Pl G20 96 B7
Fearnan Pl PA16 45 A4
Fearnmore Rd G20 96 D7
Fearnoch KA9 236 C5
Fellhill St KA7 239 B5
Fells The G66 57 E8
Fellsview Ave G66 58 F1
Felton Pl G13 94 F7
Fencedyke Cl KA11 219 F4
Fencedyke Prim Sch KA11 220 A3
Fencedyke Way KA11 220 A4
Fendoch St G32 119 A4
Fenella St G32 119 B5
Fennsbank Ave G73 138 D3
Fenton St FK10 10 A7
Fenwick Cl KA3 223 C6
Fenwick Dr
Barrhead G78 134 D1
Hamilton ML3 183 E7
Fenwick Pl G46 136 B1
Fenwick Prim Sch KA3 213 A4
Fenwick Rd Glasgow G46 136 C3
Kilmaurs KA3 222 C7
Waterside KA3 213 E4
Fenwickland Ave KA7 239 A4
Fenwickland Pl KA7 239 B4
Ferclay St G81 74 D7
Fereneze Ave
Barrhead G78 134 B3
Clarkston G76 157 C8
Paisley PA4 114 A8
Fereneze Cres
Glasgow G13 95 A7
Hamilton ML3 161 F3
Fereneze Dr PA2 133 C7
Fereneze Gr G78 134 B4
Fereneze Rd G78 154 C8
Fergus Ave PA3 113 A5
Fergus Ct G20 96 E4
Fergus Dr Glasgow G20 96 E4
Greenock PA16 45 A4
Paisley PA3 113 A5
Fergus Gdns ML3 162 F2
Fergus La G20 96 F4
Fergus Pl PA16 45 A4
Fergus Rd PA16 45 A4
Fergushill Rd KA13 208 A3
Ferguslie PA1 113 B4
Ferguslie Park Ave PA3 113 A5
Ferguslie Park Cres PA3 113 A4
Ferguslie Prim Sch PA3 113 B6
Ferguslie Wlk PA1 113 B4
Ferguson Ave
Milngavie G62 55 A1
Prestwick KA9 236 D8
Renfrew PA4 94 D3
Ferguson Dr Denny FK6 21 D1
Motherwell ML1 163 E3
Stenhousemuir FK2 24 A5
Ferguson Gr FK4 40 B6
Ferguson St Ayr KA8 236 C3
Johnstone PA5 111 E3
Renfrew PA4 94 D3
Stirling FK8 1 F2
Ferguson Way ML6 103 B2
Fergusson Pl G74 160 D5
Fergusson Rd G67 61 F2
Fergusson Terr G66 58 C5
Ferguston Rd G61 75 F3
Fern Ave Bishopbriggs G64 98 B8
Erskine PA8 93 B7
Kirkintilloch G66 79 C5
Fern Brae KA7 239 C3
Fern Cotts 2 G13 95 F5
Fern Dr G78 134 B4
Fern Gr G69 101 A6

Fern La Glasgow G13 ... 95 F5
Lennoxtown G66 ... 33 C1
Fern Lea Gr FK2 ... 24 C3
Fern Pl KA1 ... 227 C7
Fern St ML1 ... 164 A4
Fernan St G32 ... 118 F5
Fernbank KA9 ... 236 B5
Fernbank Ave G72 ... 139 C4
Fernbank Ct KA9 ... 236 B5
Fernbank St G22 ... 97 E5
Fernbrae Ave G73 ... 138 C3
Fernbrae Way G73 ... 138 B3
Ferncroft Dr G44 ... 137 D5
Ferndale ML9 ... 185 A1
Ferndale Ct G23 ... 96 D8
Ferndale Dr G23 ... 96 D8
Ferndale Gdns G23 ... 96 D8
Ferndale Pl G23 ... 96 D8
Ferness Oval G21 ... 98 C7
Ferness Pl G21 ... 98 C7
Ferness Rd G21 ... 98 C6
Ferngrove Ave G12 ... 96 B6
Fernhill Grange G71 ... 141 A1
Fernhill Rd G73 ... 138 B3
Fernhill Sch G73 ... 138 C3
Fernie Gdns Cardross G82 ... 48 B8
Glasgow G20 ... 96 E7
Ferniegair Ave G84 ... 16 B2
Fernieshaw Rd ML1 ... 144 F2
Fernlea G61 ... 75 E3
Fernleigh Pl G69 ... 80 F2
Fernleigh Rd G43 ... 136 D5
Fernside Wlk ML3 ... 162 E1
Fernslea Ave G72 ... 161 C8
Ferrier Ct KA10 ... 229 F4
Ferry Ct FK9 ... 2 A3
Ferry Loan G83 ... 27 E5
Ferry Orch FK9 ... 2 D1
Ferry Rd Bishopton PA7 ... 72 B4
Bothwell G71 ... 141 A1
Cardross G82 ... 48 B6
Glasgow G3 ... 96 B1
Glasgow G3 ... 96 C1
Renfrew PA4 ... 94 D5
Rosneath G84 ... 15 B3
South Alloa FK7 ... 9 F4
Stirling FK9 ... 2 D1
Uddingston G71 ... 140 D6
Ferryden Ct G14 ... 95 E2
Ferryden St G14 ... 95 E2
Ferryfield Gdns G83 ... 27 F4
Fersit Ct G43 ... 136 C6
Fersit St G43 ... 136 C6
Fetlar Dr Glasgow G44 ... 137 C5
Kilmarnock KA3 ... 223 A6
Fetlar Rd PA11 ... 110 D8
Fettercairn Ave G15 ... 74 E4
Fettercairn Gdns G64 ... 78 C1
Fettes St G33 ... 118 F8
Fiddison Pl KA9 ... 236 E5
Fiddoch Ct ML2 ... 165 F7
Fidra St G33 ... 118 F8
Field Gr G76 ... 157 F5
Field Rd Clarkston G76 ... 157 F5
Clydebank G81 ... 74 D8
Larkhall ML9 ... 185 B2
Field St ML3 ... 162 D1
Fielden Pl G40 ... 118 A5
Fielden St G40 ... 118 A5
Fieldhead Dr G43 ... 136 A5
Fieldhead Sq G43 ... 136 A5
Fieldings The KA3 ... 195 C8
Fields La PA6 ... 91 B3
Fife Ave Airdrie ML6 ... 123 A5
Glasgow G52 ... 115 B4
Fife Cres G71 ... 141 A1
Fife Ct G71 ... 141 A1
Fife Dr Greenock PA16 ... 44 D5
Motherwell ML1 ... 142 D2
Fife Rd PA16 ... 44 D5
Fife Way G64 ... 98 D8
Fifth Ave Airdrie ML6 ... 123 C8
Glasgow G12 ... 95 F5
Millerston G33 ... 99 B5
Renfrew PA4 ... 94 C1
Fifth Rd G72 ... 161 E5
Fifty Pitches Pl G51 ... 115 C7
Fifty Pitches Rd G52 ... 115 B7
Finaly Wlk G83 ... 27 F8
Finart Dr PA2 ... 114 B1
Finaven Gdns G61 ... 75 B8
Finbraken Dr PA19 ... 43 E5
Finch Dr G13 ... 95 A8
Finch Pl Johnstone PA5 ... 131 D7
Kilmarnock KA1 ... 228 C7
Finch Rd PA16 ... 45 B5
Finch Way ML4 ... 141 F8
Findhorn PA8 ... 73 A2
Findhorn Ave
Paisley PA2 ... 112 F1
Renfrew PA4 ... 94 E3
Findhorn Ct G75 ... 179 D8
Findhorn Pl
East Kilbride G75 ... 179 D8
Falkirk FK1 ... 42 D2
Troon KA10 ... 229 G5
Findhorn Rd KA9 ... 233 F4
Findhorn St G33 ... 118 D8
Findlay Ct ML1 ... 163 D8
Findlay St 9 Kilsyth G65 ... 60 D8
Motherwell ML1 ... 163 F5
Findlay Terr G72 ... 139 D6
Findlay's Brae KA21 ... 216 F7
Findochty PA8 ... 73 A3
Findochty St G33 ... 99 E2
Fingal La G20 ... 96 C7
Fingal St G20 ... 96 D7
Fingalton Rd G77 ... 155 E5
Fingask St G32 ... 119 C4
Finglas Ave PA2 ... 114 B1
Finglen Gdns G62 ... 54 E2
Finglen Pl G53 ... 135 B5
Fingleton Ave G78 ... 134 D1
Finhaven St G32 ... 118 E3
Finistere Ave FK1 ... 42 B3
Finlarig Ct FK5 ... 23 F4
Finlarig St G34 ... 120 C7
Finlas Ave KA7 ... 239 B3
Finlas St G22 ... 97 D4
Finlay Ave KA24 ... 191 D7
Finlay Dr Glasgow G31 ... 118 A7
Linwood PA3 ... 111 F5
Finlay Rise G62 ... 76 C8
Finlayson Dr Airdrie ML6 ... 123 E7
Kilmarnock KA3 ... 223 D3
Finlayson Pl FK5 ... 23 C5
Finlayson Quadrant 1
ML6 ... 123 E7
Finlaystone* PA14 ... 69 E8
Finlaystone Cres PA13 ... 69 D2
Finlaystone Pl PA13 ... 69 D2
Finlaystone Rd
Kilmacolm PA13 ... 69 D4
Port Glasgow PA14 ... 69 A7
Finlaystone St ML5 ... 121 E7
Finnart Cres PA19 ... 44 C6
Finnart Rd PA16 ... 45 D6
Finnart Sq G40 ... 117 F3
Finnart St Glasgow G40 ... 117 F3
Glasgow G40 ... 117 F4
Greenock PA16 ... 45 D6
Finneston La 11 PA15 ... 46 B3
Finneston St PA15 ... 46 B3
Finneston Way 12 PA15 ... 46 B3
Finnick Glen KA7 ... 239 A3
Finnie Terr Gourock PA19 ... 44 D6
Springside KA11 ... 220 F2
Finnie Wynd ML1 ... 164 B4
Finnieston Sq 9 G3 ... 116 E8
Finnieston St
Glasgow G3 ... 116 E7
Glasgow G3 ... 116 E8
Finsbay St G51 ... 115 E6
Fintaig La ML2 ... 165 E3
Fintrie Terr ML3 ... 161 E4
Fintry Ave PA2 ... 133 E7
Fintry Cres Barrhead G78 ... 134 C1
Bishopbriggs G64 ... 78 C1
Fintry Ct ML5 ... 122 C3
Fintry Dr G44 ... 137 D7
Fintry Gdns G61 ... 75 C8
Fintry Pl
East Kilbride G75 ... 180 B4
Irvine KA11 ... 220 B2
Fintry Rd PA15 ... 46 B2
Fintry Terr KA11 ... 220 B3
Fintry Wlk KA11 ... 220 B2
Fir Bank KA7 ... 239 C5
Fir Bank Ave ML9 ... 185 B1
Fir Ct G72 ... 139 E4
Fir Dr G75 ... 180 B5
Fir Gr Motherwell ML1 ... 143 A2
Uddingston G71 ... 141 C8
Fir La FK5 ... 23 D1
Fir Park St ML1 ... 163 F4
Fir Pk (Motherwell FC)
ML1 ... 163 F4
Fir Pl Cambuslang G72 ... 139 C6
Cleland ML1 ... 144 B1
Glasgow G69 ... 120 A3
Johnstone PA5 ... 112 A1
Kilmarnock KA1 ... 227 C7
Fir St PA15 ... 46 E2
Fir Terr PA19 ... 44 D6
Fir View ML6 ... 123 B2
Firbank Ave G64 ... 78 B8
Firbank Quadrant ML6 ... 123 E3
Firbank Terr G78 ... 134 E1
Firdon Cres G15 ... 75 A1
Firhill Ave ML6 ... 122 F6
Firhill Dr KA9 ... 233 D5
Firhill Pk (Partick Thistle FC)
G20 ... 97 A4
Firhill Rd G20 ... 97 A4
Firhill St G20 ... 97 A4
Firlee G75 ... 179 F7
Firpark Rd G64 ... 98 B8
Firpark Sch ML1 ... 163 F4
Firpark St G31 ... 117 F8
Firpark Terr
Cambusbarron FK7 ... 6 C5
Glasgow G31 ... 117 F7
Firs Cres FK7 ... 7 D2
Firs Entry FK7 ... 7 D2
Firs Pk (East Stirlingshire
FC) FK2 ... 42 C6
Firs Rd FK10 ... 4 D2
Firs St FK2 ... 42 C6
Firs The Bannockburn FK7 ... 7 D2
Glasgow G44 ... 137 B4
First Ave Alexandria G83 ... 27 F5
Auchinloch G66 ... 79 D1
Bearsden G61 ... 76 A3
Dumbarton G82 ... 50 C2
Glasgow G44 ... 136 F2
Irvine KA12 ... 224 E8
Millerston G33 ... 99 B4
Renfrew PA4 ... 94 C2
Stevenston KA20 ... 217 F7
Uddingston G71 ... 140 F8
First Gdns G41 ... 116 A4
First Rd G72 ... 161 E5
First St Irvine KA12 ... 219 B8
First St *continued*
Uddingston G71 ... 140 F8
First Terr G81 ... 74 A3
Firth Cres PA19 ... 44 C6
Firth Gdns KA10 ... 229 E7
Firth Rd KA10 ... 229 E7
Firth View Terr KA22 ... 205 D4
Firthview Terr G82 ... 49 C3
Firtree Pl ML2 ... 166 B6
Firtree Rd ML2 ... 166 B6
Firwood Cts G77 ... 156 E4
Firwood Dr G44 ... 137 C6
Firwood Rd G77 ... 156 E4
Fischer Gdns PA1 ... 112 F5
Fishcross Prim Sch FK10 ... 5 D3
Fisher Ave Kilsyth G65 ... 60 D8
Paisley PA1 ... 112 F4
Fisher Cres G81 ... 74 B6
Fisher Ct Glasgow G31 ... 117 F7
Knockentiber KA2 ... 221 F3
Fisher Dr PA1 ... 112 F4
Fisher Pl G84 ... 17 A2
Fisher St ML9 ... 185 B1
Fisher Way
Crosshouse KA2 ... 221 D1
Paisley PA1 ... 112 F4
Fishermans Wlk FK9 ... 2 A3
Fishers Rd PA4 ... 94 C6
Fisherwood Rd G83 ... 27 E8
Fishescoates Ave G73 ... 138 C4
Fishescoates Gdns G73 ... 138 D5
Fitzalan Dr PA3 ... 114 A6
Fitzalan Rd PA4 ... 94 A1
Fitzroy La G3 ... 116 E8
Fitzroy Pl 2 G3 ... 116 E8
Five Roads KA13 ... 208 A3
Five Ways Rd ML9 ... 200 D4
Flakefield G74 ... 159 B2
Flanders St G81 ... 74 C7
Flanigan Gr ML4 ... 142 A5
Flatterton La PA16 ... 44 D2
Flatterton Rd PA16 ... 44 C2
Flax Mill Rd ML7 ... 127 F5
Flax Rd G71 ... 141 A5
Flaxfield Gr ML1 ... 142 D2
Flaxmill Ave ML2 ... 164 D4
Fleck Ave KA21 ... 206 A2
Fleet Ave PA4 ... 94 E1
Fleet St G32 ... 119 B4
Fleming Ave
Chryston G69 ... 100 C8
Clydebank G81 ... 94 D8
Fleming Cres KA21 ... 206 A3
Fleming Ct Carluke ML8 ... 187 E1
Clydebank G81 ... 74 B2
Denny FK6 ... 39 D8
Hamilton ML3 ... 161 E4
Motherwell ML1 ... 164 A4
Troon KA10 ... 229 G4
Fleming Dr
Stenhousemuir FK5 ... 24 A3
Stewarton KA3 ... 211 C8
Fleming Gdns FK1 ... 41 E6
Fleming Pl
Blackridge EH48 ... 107 E3
East Kilbride G75 ... 180 E8
Fleming Rd Bellshill ML4 ... 142 B7
Bishopton PA7 ... 72 B3
Cumbernauld G67 ... 61 F2
Houston PA6 ... 91 A2
Fleming St Glasgow G31 ... 118 B6
Kilmarnock KA1 ... 227 E5
Paisley PA3 ... 113 E7
Fleming Terr KA12 ... 219 B5
Fleming Way
Hamilton ML3 ... 161 E4
21 Larkhall ML9 ... 185 C1
Flemington Ind Est G72 ... 139 E4
Flemington Ind Pk ML1 ... 164 C5
Flemington St G21 ... 97 F3
Flenders Ave G76 ... 157 C6
Flenders Rd G76 ... 157 C6
Fletcher Ave PA19 ... 44 E7
Fleurs Ave G41 ... 116 B4
Fleurs Rd G41 ... 116 B4
Flinders Pl G75 ... 180 B8
Flint Cres FK7 ... 12 D8
Flloyd St ML5 ... 121 F7
Floors Rd G76 ... 157 C1
Floors St PA5 ... 111 F2
Floors Street Ind Est
PA5 ... 111 F2
Floorsburn Cres PA5 ... 111 E2
Flora Gdns G64 ... 78 C2
Florence Dr
Glasgow G46 ... 136 C2
Kilmacolm PA13 ... 89 B8
Florence Gdns G73 ... 138 C4
Florence St Glasgow G5 ... 117 C5
Greenock PA16 ... 45 B4
Florida Ave G42 ... 137 B8
Florida Cres G42 ... 137 B8
Florida Dr G42 ... 137 A8
Florida Gdns G69 ... 120 A5
Florida Sq G42 ... 137 B8
Florida St G42 ... 137 B8
Florish Rd PA8 ... 93 E8
Flotta Pl KA3 ... 222 F6
Flowerdale Pl G53 ... 135 B3
Flowerhill Ind Est ML6 ... 123 B8
Flowerhill St ML6 ... 123 B8
Fluchter Rd G64 ... 56 A1
Flures Ave PA8 ... 93 E8
Flures Cres PA8 ... 93 E8
Flures Dr PA8 ... 93 E8
Flures Pl PA8 ... 93 E8
Fochabers Dr G52 ... 115 C6
Fogo Pl G20 ... 96 D6
Foinaven Dr G46 ... 136 A5
Foinaven Gdns G46 ... 136 A6
Foinaven Way G46 ... 136 A6
Foinavon Rd ML3 ... 183 E3
Footfield Rd ML4 ... 141 F3
Forbes Cres FK5 ... 23 D1
Forbes Ct FK2 ... 42 E6
Forbes Dr Ayr KA8 ... 236 C4
1 Glasgow G40 ... 117 F5
Motherwell ML1 ... 142 C2
Forbes Pl Kilmarnock KA3 ... 223 B2
Paisley PA1 ... 113 E4
Forbes Rd FK1 ... 42 D4
Forbes St Alloa FK10 ... 9 F6
Glasgow G40 ... 117 F6
Forbes Wlk KA3 ... 223 B2
Ford Ave KA11 ... 225 D8
Ford Rd Bonnybridge FK4 ... 40 A5
Glasgow G12 ... 96 D4
Newton Mearns G77 ... 156 D3
Fordbank Prim Sch
PA5 ... 131 C8
Forde Cres KA20 ... 206 F2
Fordneuk St G40 ... 118 A5
Fordoun St G34 ... 120 D8
Fordyce Ct G77 ... 156 D4
Fordyce Gdns FK1 ... 41 E4
Fordyce St G11 ... 96 C2
Fore Row ML3 ... 162 E4
Fore St Glasgow G14 ... 95 C3
Port Glasgow PA14 ... 47 C2
Forebraes FK10 ... 10 B7
Foregate Sq KA1 ... 222 F1
Foregate The KA1 ... 222 F1
Forehill Prim Sch KA7 ... 239 C6
Forehill Rd KA7 ... 239 C6
Forehouse Rd PA10 ... 110 D3
Foremount Terrace La 6
G12 ... 96 C3
Forest Ave Bellshill ML4 ... 142 D3
Hamilton ML3 ... 183 D6
Forest Dr G71 ... 141 A3
Forest Gdns G66 ... 79 A4
Forest Gr KA3 ... 223 B5
Forest Kirk ML8 ... 202 B8
Forest La ML3 ... 183 D6
Forest Pk ML2 ... 165 D5
Forest Pl Kirkintilloch G66 ... 79 A4
Paisley PA2 ... 113 E2
Forest Rd
Cumbernauld G67 ... 62 D2
Cumbernauld G67 ... 62 E6
Larkhall ML9 ... 185 B3
Forest View G67 ... 62 C3
Forest Way KA7 ... 239 C5
Forestburn Ct ML6 ... 122 D7
Forester Gr FK10 ... 4 F1
Forestfield Gdns ML6 ... 105 A4
Foresthall Cres G21 ... 98 A3
Foresthall Dr G21 ... 98 A3
Forestlea Rd ML8 ... 202 A8
Forfar Ave G52 ... 115 B4
Forfar Cres G64 ... 98 C8
Forfar Rd PA16 ... 44 F3
Forgan Gdns G64 ... 98 D8
Forge Dr ML5 ... 121 F7
Forge Pl G21 ... 98 B2
Forge Rd Airdrie ML6 ... 123 F6
Ayr KA8 ... 236 B4
Forge Row ML6 ... 123 C3
Forge Sh Ctr The G31 ... 118 C5
Forge St G21 ... 98 B2
Forge Vennel KA13 ... 207 C4
Forgewood Path ML6 ... 123 F6
Forgewood Rd ML1 ... 142 C2
Forglen Cres FK9 ... 2 A6
Forglen Rd FK9 ... 2 B6
Forglen St G34 ... 100 B1
Formakin Estate Walks*
PA7 ... 71 C2
Formby Dr G23 ... 76 D1
Forres Ave G46 ... 136 D3
Forres Cres ML4 ... 142 A6
Forres Gate G46 ... 136 D2
Forres Quadrant ML2 ... 165 B5
Forres St 1 Glasgow G23 ... 76 E1
Hamilton G72 ... 161 C5
Forrest Dr G61 ... 75 B8
Forrest Gate
Hamilton ML3 ... 162 B1
Motherwell G71 ... 121 B1
Forrest Pl Crossford ML8 ... 201 B1
Harthill ML7 ... 127 E5
Forrest Rd
Forrestfield ML6 ... 106 A1
Lanark ML11 ... 215 B5
Salsburgh ML6,ML7 ... 126 B6
Stirling FK8 ... 2 B1
Forrest St Airdrie ML6 ... 123 D8
Airdrie,Clarkston ML6 ... 123 E8
Glasgow G40 ... 118 A5
Hamilton G72 ... 161 F7
Shotts ML7 ... 146 E5
Forrester Ct 1 G64 ... 97 F8
Forrester Pl FK2 ... 14 D3
Forrestfield Cres G77 ... 156 E5
Forrestfield Gdns G77 ... 156 E5
Forrestfield Rd ML6 ... 105 F7
Forrestfield St G21 ... 98 A1
Forsa Ct G75 ... 180 C4
Forsyth Ct ML11 ... 215 C4
Forsyth Gr PA16 ... 45 D6
Forsyth St Airdrie ML6 ... 123 B8
Greenock PA16 ... 45 D6
Fort Matilda Pl PA16 ... 45 B7
Fort Matilda Sta PA16 ... 45 B8
Fort Matilda Terr PA16 ... 45 B7
Fort St Ayr KA7 ... 235 F1
Fort St *continued*
Motherwell ML1 ... 163 B8
Fortacre Pl KA11 ... 220 B5
Forteviot Ave G69 ... 120 C5
Forteviot Pl G69 ... 120 C5
Forth Ave Larbert FK5 ... 23 B3
Paisley PA2 ... 112 F1
Forth Cres Alloa FK10 ... 10 C5
East Kilbride G75 ... 179 E7
Stirling FK8 ... 7 B8
Forth Ct East Kilbride G75 ... 179 E7
Stirling FK8 ... 2 B1
Forth Gr G75 ... 179 E8
Forth Pk Bridge of A FK9 ... 2 A5
Stirling FK9 ... 1 F5
Forth Pl Johnstone PA5 ... 131 C8
Kilmarnock KA1 ... 228 A5
Larkhall ML9 ... 199 B8
Stirling FK8 ... 7 B8
Forth Rd Bearsden G61 ... 75 D2
Torrance G64 ... 78 B8
Forth St Cambus FK10 ... 9 A8
Clydebank G81 ... 94 C8
Fallin FK7 ... 8 C4
Glasgow G41 ... 116 F3
Greenock PA16 ... 45 B5
Stirling FK8 ... 2 B1
Forth Terr ML3 ... 183 B8
Forth Valley Coll of Nursing
& Midwifery FK1 ... 42 A4
Forth View FK8 ... 2 B1
Forth Wlk 5 G67 ... 61 F1
Forthbank Ind Est FK10 ... 10 B4
Forthvale FK11 ... 4 A6
Forthvale Ct FK9 ... 2 B2
Forthview FK7 ... 7 E1
Forthview Ct FK1 ... 41 F2
Forties Cres G46 ... 136 A5
Forties Ct G46 ... 135 F5
Forties Gdns G46 ... 136 A5
Forties Rd PA6 ... 111 C8
Forties Way G46 ... 136 A5
Fortieth Ave G75 ... 180 F5
Fortingall Ave G12 ... 96 C6
Fortingall Pl G12 ... 96 C6
Fortingall Rd G72 ... 161 F5
Fortissat Ave ML7 ... 146 D6
Fortrose Ct G72 ... 161 C3
Fortrose St G11 ... 96 B2
Fortuna Ct FK1 ... 42 C4
Forum Pl ML1 ... 142 C1
Forum The (Sh Ctr) 3
PA15 ... 45 F5
Fossil Gr G66 ... 59 A1
Foswell Dr G15 ... 74 F5
Foswell Pl G15 ... 74 F5
Fotheringay La G41 ... 116 D2
Fotheringay Rd G41 ... 116 E2
Fothringham Rd KA8 ... 239 A8
Foulburn Rd ML7 ... 145 D2
Foulis La G13 ... 95 F6
Foulis St G13 ... 95 F6
Foulsykes Rd ML2 ... 165 E4
Foundry Ct KA13 ... 207 C4
Foundry La G78 ... 134 C2
Foundry Loan FK5 ... 23 B2
Foundry Rd
Bonnybridge FK4 ... 40 B5
Cleland ML1 ... 144 C2
Shotts ML7 ... 146 F4
Foundry St FK2 ... 42 A8
Foundry Wynd KA13 ... 207 C4
Fountain Ave PA4 ... 93 B4
Fountain Bsns Ctr The
ML5 ... 122 A6
Fountain Craig G12 ... 96 B5
Fountain Cres PA4 ... 93 C5
Fountain Dr PA4 ... 93 C4
Fountain Rd FK9 ... 2 A7
Fountainwell Ave G21 ... 97 D3
Fountainwell Dr G21 ... 97 D2
Fountainwell Pl G21 ... 97 D3
Fountainwell Rd G21 ... 97 D2
Fountainwell Sq G21 ... 97 E2
Fountainwell Terr G21 ... 97 E2
Four Acres Dr KA3 ... 222 B8
Four Windings PA6 ... 91 B2
Fourth Ave
Auchinloch G66 ... 79 D1
Dumbarton G82 ... 50 D2
Millerston G33 ... 99 B5
Renfrew PA4 ... 94 C2
Fourth Gdns G41 ... 116 A4
Fourth St G71 ... 120 F1
Fowlds St KA1 ... 227 F8
Fowler Cres FK6 ... 21 E1
Fowlis Dr G77 ... 156 C6
Fox Gr ML1 ... 163 B7
Fox St Glasgow G1 ... 240 C1
Greenock PA16 ... 45 D7
Foxbar Cres PA2 ... 132 E7
Foxbar Dr Glasgow G13 ... 95 B6
Paisley PA2 ... 132 E7
Foxbar Rd PA2 ... 132 E7
Foxdale Ave FK4 ... 40 A3
Foxdale Ct FK4 ... 40 A3
Foxdale Dr FK4 ... 40 A3
Foxdale Pl FK4 ... 40 A3
Foxes Gr G66 ... 79 E5
Foxglove Pl Ayr KA7 ... 239 C3
Glasgow G53 ... 135 B3
Foxhills Pl G23 ... 76 E1
Foxley St G32 ... 119 C1
Foy Gdns ML4 ... 142 A8
Foyers Terr G21 ... 98 A4
Frampton Ho G20 ... 96 E5
Franchi Dr FK5 ... 23 F5
Francis St 2 G5 ... 117 A4

270 Gra – Hal

Grahams Rd FK1 42 B6
Grahams Road Rdbt FK1 42 B5
Grahamsdyke Cres FK4 40 A3
Grahamsdyke Rd
Bonnybridge FK4 40 A4
Kirkintilloch G66 58 E1
Grahamsdyke St FK2 42 F4
Grahamshill Ave ML6 123 D8
Grahamshill St ML6 123 C8
Grahamston Ave KA14 170 B7
Grahamston Cres PA2 134 C8
Grahamston Ct PA2 134 C8
Grahamston Pk G78 134 B5
Grahamston Pl PA2 134 C8
Grahamston Rd G78 134 C6
Graignestock Pl 2 G40 117 E5
Graignestock St G40 117 E5
Graigside Pl G68 81 F7
Grainger Rd G64 78 D1
Grammar Prim Sch KA7 238 F7
Grammar School Sq
ML3 162 E4
Grampian Ave PA2 133 D8
Grampian Cres
Chapelhall ML6 123 F1
Glasgow G32 119 B4
Grampian Ct
Bearsden G61 75 C8
Greenock PA16 45 B5
Irvine KA11 220 B4
Grampian Dr G75 180 B4
Grampian Pl G32 119 B4
Grampian Rd
Kilmarnock KA1 228 B3
Port Glasgow PA14 69 A6
Stirling FK7 6 E6
Wishaw ML2 164 F4
Grampian St G32 119 B4
Grampian Way
Barrhead G78 134 C1
Bearsden G61 75 C7
Cumbernauld G68 61 A2
Gran St G81 94 E8
Granary Rd FK2 42 A8
Granary Sq FK2 42 B7
Granby Ho 8 G12 96 E3
Granby La G12 96 D3
Grandtuly Dr G12 96 C6
Grange Acad KA1 227 D8
Grange Ave Ayr KA7 239 B2
Falkirk FK2 42 D6
Milngavie G62 55 B2
Wishaw ML2 164 E1
Grange Ct Lanark ML11 214 F5
Stevenston KA20 206 C1
Grange Dr FK2 42 D6
Grange Gdns
Bothwell G71 141 B1
Bridge of A FK9 2 C7
Grange Pl Alexandria G83 27 E5
Kilmarnock KA1 227 F8
Grange Rd Alloa FK10 9 F6
Bearsden G61 75 F5
Bridge of A FK9 2 C6
Glasgow G42 137 A8
Stevenston KA20 206 D1
Grange St
Kilmarnock KA1 227 F8
Motherwell ML1 164 A4
Grange Terr KA1 227 D8
Grange The KA11 220 C6
Grange Twr ML1 164 B2
Grange View FK5 23 E1
Grangemouth Rd FK2 42 E5
Grangemuir Ct KA9 236 B7
Grangemuir Rd KA9 236 B7
Grangeneuk Gdns G68 61 C1
Granger Rd Balloch G83 27 F8
Kilmarnock KA1 227 E5
Grannoch Pl ML5 122 D2
Grant Cres G82 27 D1
Grant Ct Airdrie ML6 123 E8
Hamilton ML3 183 C7
Grant Gr ML4 142 A4
Grant Pl Kilmarnock KA3 223 C2
Stirling FK9 2 B4
Grant St Alloa FK10 9 F6
Glasgow G3 240 A4
Greenock PA15 46 C3
Helensburgh G84 16 D1
Helensburgh G84 16 D2
Grantholm Ave ML1 143 B6
Grantlea Gr G32 119 D4
Grantlea Terr G32 119 D4
Grantley Gdns G41 136 D8
Grantley St G41 136 D8
Grantofften Path G75 180 E6
Granton St G5 117 E2
Grantown Ave ML6 123 E6
Grantown Gdns ML6 102 F5
Grants Ave PA2 113 D1
Grants Cres PA2 133 D8
Grants Pl PA2 133 C8
Grants Way PA2 113 D1
Granville St
Clydebank G81 74 B3
Glasgow G3 240 A3
Helensburgh G84 16 F1
Grasmere G75 179 F5
Grasmere Ct ML3 183 D6
Grassyards Intc KA3 223 D3
Grassyards Rd KA3 223 C2
Grathellen Ct ML1 164 A8
Gray Cres KA12 224 E8
Gray Dr G61 75 F3
Gray St Alexandria G83 27 E5
Cleland ML1 144 B1
Glasgow G3 96 E1
Greenock PA15 46 B3
Kirkintilloch G66 80 B7
Larkhall ML9 185 A4
Prestwick KA9 236 C8
Shotts ML7 147 A4
Gray's Cl ML11 214 C4
Gray's Rd G71 141 B5
Grayshill Rd G68 81 E6
Graystale Rd FK7 7 A3
Grayston Manor G69 80 E1
Graystonelee Rd ML7 146 D6
Graystones KA13 207 E5
Great Dovehill G1,G4 241 B1
Great George La 6 G12 96 D3
Great George St
Glasgow G12 96 D3
Glasgow G12 96 E2
Great Hamilton St PA2 113 E2
Great Kelvin La G12 96 E2
Great Western Rd
Bowling G60 72 D8
Clydebank G81 74 C4
Glasgow,Dowanhill G4,G12 96 D3
Glasgow,Knightswood G15 95 D7
Great Western Terr 13
G12 96 C4
Great Western Terrace La 12
G12 96 C4
Green Ave KA12 219 C4
Green Bank KA24 191 C7
Green Bank Rd G68 61 C2
Green Dale ML2 165 D5
Green Gdns ML1 144 C2
Green Loan ML1 143 A3
Green Pl Bothwell G71 141 B2
Calderbank ML6 123 B2
Green Rd Paisley PA2 113 B3
Rutherglen G73 138 A8
Green St Ayr KA8 235 F2
Bothwell G71 141 B2
Clydebank G81 74 A3
Glasgow G40 117 E5
Kilmarnock KA1 222 F1
6 Kilmarnock KA1 227 F8
Saltcoats KA21 216 F7
Stonehouse ML9 198 F2
Green Street La Ayr KA8 235 F1
Ayr KA8 235 F2
Green Street Lane Bsns Pk 4
KA8 235 F2
Green The Alva FK12 5 A7
Glasgow G40 117 E4
Greenacre Ct FK7 7 E1
Greenacre Dr FK4 40 A3
Greenacre Pl
Bannockburn FK7 7 E1
Bonnybridge FK4 40 A3
Greenacre Rd FK4 40 A3
Greenacres
Ardrossan KA22 205 E3
Motherwell ML1 163 C5
Greenacres Ct G53 135 C4
Greenacres Cvn Pk
KA20 206 F1
Greenacres Dr G53 135 C4
Greenacres Rdbt 4 G64 98 D8
Greenacres View ML1 163 C5
Greenacres Way G53 135 C4
Greenan Ave G42 137 E7
Greenan Gr KA7 238 B3
Greenan Pk KA7 238 B3
Greenan Pl KA7 238 C3
Greenan Rd
Doonfoot KA7 238 C3
Kilmarnock KA3 228 B8
Greenan Terr KA9 236 D7
Greenan Way KA7 238 B3
Greenbank 6 G72 161 D7
Greenbank Ave G46 157 A7
Greenbank Ct Falkirk FK1 41 D4
Irvine KA12 219 C1
Greenbank Dr PA2 133 D7
Greenbank Gdn* G76 157 C6
Greenbank Mews PA16 45 D5
Greenbank Pl FK1 41 D4
Greenbank Rd Falkirk FK1 41 D3
Irvine KA12 219 C1
Wishaw ML2 165 C3
Greenbank St 3 G73 138 A8
Greenbank Terr 4 ML8 187 F2
Greencornhills Rdbt FK7 11 F8
Greencraig Ave FK1 66 C6
Greendyke St G1 241 B1
Greenend Ave PA5 111 D1
Greenend Pl G32 119 C7
Greenend View ML4 141 F5
Greenfarm Rd
Linwood PA3 112 B6
Newton Mearns G77 156 B6
Greenfaulds Cres G67 83 A8
Greenfaulds High Sch
G67 82 D7
Greenfaulds Rd
Cumbernauld G67 82 E7
Cumbernauld G67 83 A8
Greenfaulds Sta G67 82 F7
Greenfield Ave
Alloway KA7 238 E2
Glasgow G32 119 B7
Greenfield Cres ML2 165 D4
Greenfield Dr
Irvine KA12 219 D2
Wishaw ML2 165 D4
Greenfield Pl G32 119 B6
Greenfield Prim Sch
G51 115 F7
Greenfield Quadrant
ML1 143 F4
Greenfield Rd
Carluke ML8 187 F3
Clarkston G76 157 E6
Glasgow G32 119 C6
Hamilton ML3 162 A5
Greenfield St Alloa FK10 10 B7
Bonnybridge FK4 40 B6
Glasgow G51 115 F7
Wishaw ML2 165 D4
Greenfoot KA13 207 E3
Greengairs Ave G51 115 D8
Greengairs Prim Sch
ML6 83 E2
Greengairs Rd ML6 83 E1
Greenhall Pl G72 161 C6
Greenhead FK12 5 B6
Greenhead Ave
Dumbarton G82 50 B3
Stevenston KA20 206 E2
Greenhead Gdns G82 50 B3
Greenhead Holdings
KA20 206 D3
Greenhead Rd
Bearsden G61 75 F4
Dumbarton G82 50 C3
Inchinnan PA4 93 C6
Lennoxtown G66 57 E8
Wishaw ML2 165 D2
Greenhead St G40 117 E4
Greenhill G64 98 C8
Greenhill Ave
Glasgow G46 136 C1
Mount Ellen G69 100 E7
Greenhill Bsns Ctr ML5 102 A1
Greenhill Bsns Pk PA3 113 C6
Greenhill Cres
Elderslie PA5 112 D2
Linwood PA3 112 C6
Greenhill Ct Irvine KA11 220 B6
Rutherglen G73 138 A8
Greenhill Dr PA3 112 C6
Greenhill Ind Est ML5 102 A1
Greenhill Prim Sch ML5 122 A8
Greenhill Rd
Blackridge EH48 107 E3
Bonnybridge FK4 40 A3
Cleland ML1 144 F3
Paisley PA3 113 C6
Rutherglen G73 138 A8
Greenhill Smallholdings
KA2 222 A2
Greenhill St G73 138 A7
Greenhill Terr KA2 221 F3
Greenhills KA15 172 A2
Greenhills Cres G75 180 B5
Greenhills Prim Sch
G75 180 C5
Greenhills Rd G75 180 C5
Greenhills Sq G75 180 B5
Greenholm Ave
Clarkston G76 157 E7
Uddingston G71 140 E7
Greenholm St KA1 227 F6
Greenholme Ct G44 137 B7
Greenholme St G44 137 B6
Greenhorn's Well Ave
FK1 41 F3
Greenhorn's Well Cres
FK1 41 F3
Greenhorn's Well Dr FK1 41 F3
Greenknowe Dr ML8 186 F6
Greenknowe Pk KA9 233 D4
Greenknowe Rd G43 136 B6
Greenknowe St ML2 186 B6
Greenlady Wlk ML11 215 C4
Greenlaw Ave
Paisley PA1 114 A5
Wishaw ML2 165 C5
Greenlaw Cres PA1 114 A6
Greenlaw Dr
Newton Mearns G77 156 D5
Paisley PA1 114 A5
Greenlaw Ho PA1 114 A5
Greenlaw Ind Est PA3 113 F6
Greenlaw Rd Glasgow G14 94 E6
Newton Mearns G77 156 D5
Greenlea Rd G69 100 B8
Greenlea St G13 95 E6
Greenlees Ct KA24 191 B8
Greenlees Gdns G72 138 F3
Greenlees Gr ML5 122 D5
Greenlees Pk G72 139 A4
Greenlees Rd G72 139 A4
Greenloan Ave G51 115 D8
Greenloan View ML9 185 B1
Greenmoss Pl ML4 142 C5
Greenmount G22 97 A7
Greenmount Dr FK1 66 C6
Greenock Acad PA16 45 D7
Greenock Ave G44 137 B5
Greenock Central Sta
PA15 46 A4
Greenock High Sch PA16 44 D2
Greenock Rd
Bishopton PA7 71 D5
Greenock PA15 46 F2
Inchinnan PA4 93 C6
Langbank PA14 70 C7
Paisley PA3 113 D7
Port Glasgow PA14 47 D1
Renfrew PA4 94 A5
Greenock West Sta PA15 45 E5
Greenrig G71 140 F6
Greenrig Rd ML11 214 B1
Greenrig St G33 98 D3
Greenrigg Cotts ML7 127 F5
Greenrigg Prim Sch
ML7 127 F6
Greenrigg Rd G67 62 B1
Greenrigg St G71 140 F6
Greens Ave G66 79 C7
Greens Cres G66 79 C7
Greens Rd G67 82 F6
Greenshields Rd G69 120 B5
Greenside
Carmunnock G76 158 E8
Irvine KA11 220 A4
Greenside Ave
Kilbirnie KA25 170 A7
Prestwick KA9 236 D7
Springside KA11 221 A1
Greenside Cl ML11 215 A4
Greenside Cres G33 98 E3
Greenside La ML11 215 A4
Greenside Pl G61 75 C8
Greenside Rd
Clydebank G81 74 B7
Motherwell ML1 143 C8
Wishaw ML2 165 C2
Greenside St Alloa FK10 10 B6
Coatbridge ML5 122 B8
Glasgow G33 98 E3
Motherwell ML1 143 F4
Greenside Terr KA11 221 A2
Greenside Way KA11 220 A4
Greentowers Rd ML11 214 E8
Greentree Dr G69 119 F3
Greentree Pk KA7 239 C4
Greenview Sch G22 97 D6
Greenview St G43 136 C8
Greenway La G72 161 C5
Greenways Ave PA2 113 B2
Greenways Ct PA2 113 A2
Greenwood Acad KA11 220 C1
Greenwood Ave
Cambuslang G72 139 E6
Moodiesburn G69 80 F2
Stirling FK8 7 A8
Greenwood Cres ML5 122 D5
Greenwood Ct G76 157 E6
Greenwood Dr
Bearsden G61 76 A4
Johnstone PA5 131 E8
Greenwood Intc KA11 225 A8
Greenwood Quadrant
G81 74 D1
Greenwood Rd
Clarkston G76 157 D7
Irvine KA11 220 C1
Greenwood St ML7 146 E5
Greenyards Intc G67 62 C1
Greer Quadrant G81 74 B4
Grenada Pl G75 159 B1
Grenadier Gdns ML1 163 D4
Grenadier Pk G72 139 A4
Grendon Ct FK8 7 A6
Grendon Gdns FK8 7 A6
Grenville Ct FK1 41 F4
Grenville Dr G72 138 F4
Grenville Rd PA19 44 F6
Gresham View ML1 164 B2
Greta Meek La G66 58 C6
Gretna St G40 118 B4
Grey Pl PA15 45 F6
Greyfriars Ct ML11 214 F4
Greyfriars Rd G71 140 C8
Greyfriars St G32 118 F7
Greygoran FK10 5 C2
Greystone Ave G73 138 C6
Greystone Bauks ML11 214 F4
Greystone Baulks ML11 214 A4
Greystone Gdns G73 138 C6
Greywood St G13 95 E7
Grier Path G31 118 D5
Grier Pl ML9 184 F2
Griers Wlk KA11 225 D6
Grierson Cres FK7 6 D6
Grierson La G33 118 D8
Grierson St G33 118 D8
Grieve Croft G71 140 F1
Grieve Rd
Cumbernauld G67 62 A3
Greenock PA16 45 B5
Griffen Ave PA1 112 E5
Griffin Dock Rd KA8 235 E2
Griffin Pl ML4 142 A8
Griffiths St FK1 42 B4
Griffiths Way ML8 186 F4
Griqua Terr G71 141 B2
Grodwell Dr FK12 4 E7
Grogarry Rd G15 75 A4
Grossart St ML7 125 A2
Grosvenor Cres 9 G12 96 D3
Grosvenor Crescent La 11
G12 96 D3
Grosvenor La
Glasgow G12 96 D3
Greenock PA15 46 D3
Grosvenor Rd PA15 46 D3
Grosvenor Terr 12 G12 96 D3
Grougar Dr KA3 223 B4
Grougar Gdns KA3 223 B4
Grougar Rd KA3 228 D8
Grove Cres Falkirk FK2 24 A2
Larkhall ML9 185 C2
Grove Pk G66 79 D4
Grove St FK6 21 C2
Grove The Bishopton PA7 72 A3
Bridge of W PA11 110 E6
Kilbarchan PA10 111 A3
Neilston G78 154 C6
Rutherglen G46 157 B8
Grove Way ML4 141 F4
Grove Wood G71 121 D1
Grove Wynd ML1 143 A3
Groveburn Ave G46 136 A4
Grovepark Ct G20 97 A2
Grovepark Gdns G20 97 A2
Grovepark St G20 97 A3
Groves The G64 98 C7
Grovewood Bsns Ctr
ML4 141 E8
Grudie St G34 120 A8
Gryfe Rd
Bridge of W PA11 110 D7
Port Glasgow PA14 68 E7
Gryfe St PA15 46 B2
Gryfebank Ave PA6 91 E1
Gryfebank Cl PA6 91 E1
Gryfebank Cres PA6 91 E1
Gryfebank Way PA6 91 E1
Gryfewood Cres PA6 91 E1
Gryfewood Way PA6 91 E1
Gryffe Ave PA11 90 C1
Gryffe Castle PA11 90 C1
Gryffe Cres PA2 112 F1
Gryffe Gr PA11 110 D8
Gryffe High Sch PA6 91 A1
Gryffe Rd PA13 89 D7
Gryffe St G44 137 A7
Guildford St G33 99 C1
Guiltreehill KA7 239 A1
Gullane Cres G68 61 F6
Gullane Ct Hamilton ML3 183 B7
Irvine KA11 224 F8
Gullane Dr ML5 121 F2
Gullane Pl KA13 207 B3
Gullane St G11 96 B1
Gulliland Ave KA2 225 F2
Gulliland Pl KA12 219 D1
Gullin Dr KA9 236 E5
Gunn Mews ML2 164 F2
Gunn Quadrant ML4 141 E3
Gushet Ho ML6 122 E7
Gushet Pl ML11 214 A3
Guthrie Ct ML1 163 C6
Guthrie Dr G71 121 A1
Guthrie Pl
East Kilbride G74 159 F2
Rhu G84 15 D4
Torrance G64 57 C1
Guthrie Rd KA21 217 A8
Guthrie St Glasgow G20 96 D6
Hamilton ML3 162 D4
Guy Mannering Rd G84 25 C8
Gyle Pl ML2 165 E3

H

Habbieauld Rd KA3 222 B8
Haberlea Ave G53 135 C3
Haberlea Gdns G53 135 C2
Haddington Gdns KA11 220 B6
Haddington Way ML5 121 E3
Haddow Gr 6 G71 141 A8
Haddow St ML3 162 E3
Hadrian Terr ML1 163 C8
Hagart Rd PA6 91 B2
Hagen Dr ML1 143 E1
Hagg Cres PA5 111 E3
Hagg Pl PA5 111 E3
Hagg Rd PA5 111 E2
Haggs La G41 116 C2
Haggs Rd G41 116 C1
Haggswood Ave G41 116 C2
Haghill Park Prim Sch
G31 118 C8
Haghill Prim Sch G31 118 B7
Haghill Rd G31 118 C7
Hagholm Rd ML11 215 F7
Hagmill Cres ML5 122 C2
Hagmill Rd ML5 122 B2
Hagthorn Ave KA25 170 A8
Haig Ave FK8 2 A2
Haig Dr G69 119 F4
Haig St Glasgow G21 98 A4
Greenock PA15 45 F6
Hailes Ave G32 119 D5
Haining Ave KA1 228 B5
Haining Rd PA4 94 D3
Haining The PA4 94 D2
Hairmyres G75 158 F1
Hairmyres Dr G75 179 F8
Hairmyres Hospl G75 179 F8
Hairmyres La G75 158 E1
Hairmyres Pk G75 179 F8
Hairmyres Rdbt G75 158 F1
Hairmyres St G42 117 C2
Hairmyres Sta G75 158 F1
Hairst St PA4 94 D4
Halbeath Ave G15 74 F3
Halbert St G41 116 E1
Halberts Cres FK7 7 B2
Haldane Ave FK9 2 A6
Haldane Ct G83 27 F8
Haldane La 9 G14 95 D3
Haldane Pl G75 180 F7
Haldane Prim Sch G83 27 F8
Haldane St G14 95 D3
Haldane Terr G83 19 F1
Halfmerk N G74 160 A2
Halfmerk S G74 160 A2
Halfmerke Prim Sch
G74 160 A3
Halfway St KA23 190 C5
Halgreen Ave G15 74 E3
Halidon Ave G67 82 F7
Halifax Way 7 PA4 94 C1
Halket Cres FK2 24 C2

Halkett Cres G83 27 E7
Halkett Pl KA21 217 A8
Halkirk Gate G72 161 C4
Hall Bar Gdns ML8 201 E4
Hall La KA10 230 B4
Hall Pl Lanark ML11 215 A4
Stepps G33 99 F6
Hall Rd Nemphlar ML11 214 B6
Rhu G84 15 D5
Hall St Alexandria G83 27 F4
Clydebank G81 74 B1
Hamilton ML3 162 D1
Motherwell ML1 143 A4
Renton G82 49 D8
Hallbrae St G33 98 E2
Hallcraig St ML6 123 A8
Halley Dr G13 94 E7
Halley Pl G13 94 E7
Halley Sq G13 94 F7
Halley St G13 94 E7
Hallforest St G33 99 B2
Hallglen Prim Sch FK1 42 B1
Hallglen Rd FK1 42 B1
Hallglen Terr FK1 42 B1
Hallgraig Pl ML8 187 D2
Hallhill Cres G33 119 E6
Hallhill Rd
Glasgow,Barlanark G32 119 E6
Glasgow,Barlanark G33 119 E6
Glasgow,Garrowhill G69 120 A6
Glasgow,Greenfield G32 119 B5
Johnstone PA5 131 C7
Halliburton Rd G33 119 F7
Halliburton Terr G34 120 A7
Hallidale Cres PA4 94 F2
Hallinan Gdns ML2 164 F1
Hallpark Alloa FK10 10 C8
Sauchie FK10 5 C1
Hallrule Dr G52 115 C5
Halls Vennal 3 KA8 235 F2
Hallside Ave G72 139 E5
Hallside Bvd G72 139 F4
Hallside Cres G72 139 E5
Hallside Dr G72 139 E5
Hallside Gdns ML2 165 E4
Hallside Pl G5 117 C4
Hallside Prim Sch G72 139 E4
Hallside Rd
Cambuslang G72 139 E4
Cambuslang G72 139 F4
Hallside St PA9 130 F5
Hallydown Dr G13 95 C5
Halpin Cl ML4 141 D5
Halton Gdns G69 119 F4
Haltons Path G71 141 A6
Hamersley Pl G75 180 B7
Hamilcomb Rd ML4 142 A3
Hamill Dr G65 60 F8
Hamilton Academicals (FC) ML3 162 C5
Hamilton Ave
Glasgow G41 116 C3
Stenhousemuir FK5 23 E4
Hamilton Bsns Pk ML3 162 D5
Hamilton Coll ML3 162 D5
Hamilton Cres Ayr KA7 239 A7
Bearsden G61 75 E7
Bishopton PA7 71 F3
Cambuslang G72 139 C4
Coatbridge ML5 122 A5
Renfrew PA4 94 D5
Stevenston KA20 206 F2
Hamilton Ct KA3 222 B7
Hamilton Dr Airdrie ML6 103 B1
Bothwell G71 141 B1
Cambuslang G72 139 A5
Erskine PA8 72 F3
Falkirk FK1 42 A4
Glasgow G12 96 E3
Glasgow,Giffnock G46 136 D2
Hamilton G72 161 B5
Motherwell ML1 163 F4
Stirling FK9 2 C4
Hamilton Gate 6 PA15 45 F5
Hamilton Gdns KA3 195 E1
Hamilton Gram Sch ML3 162 D3
Hamilton Int Tech Pk G72 161 C5
Hamilton Mausoleum* ML3 162 F5
Hamilton Park Ave G12 96 E3
Hamilton Pk N ML3 162 D6
Hamilton Pk S ML3 162 D6
Hamilton Pl
East Kilbride G75 180 F7
Hamilton ML3 183 D6
Motherwell ML1 143 B4
Motherwell,Whittagreen ML1 143 C4
Hamilton Rd
Bellshill ML4 141 F4
Bothwell G71 141 B1
Cambuslang G72 139 C4
East Kilbride G74 160 C5
Glasgow G32 119 D2
Hamilton G72 161 B6
Larkhall ML9 184 F5
Motherwell ML1 163 D6
Rutherglen G73 138 C7
Stenhousemuir FK5 23 D6
Hamilton Sch for the Deaf ML3 162 A2
Hamilton St Carluke ML8 187 F1
Clydebank G81 94 D7
Dumbarton G82 50 A4
Falkirk FK1 41 D6
Glasgow G42 117 C1
Hamilton St *continued*
Kilwinning KA13 207 E4
Larkhall ML9 185 A4
Paisley PA3 113 F5
Saltcoats KA21 216 E7
Hamilton Terr G81 94 D7
Hamilton Twr G71 140 D4
Hamilton View G71 141 A7
Hamilton Way
8 Greenock PA15 45 F5
Prestwick KA9 233 C2
Stonehouse ML9 198 E2
Hamiltonhill Cres G22 97 B4
Hamiltonhill Rd G22 97 B3
Hamlet G74 160 B5
Hampden Dr G42 137 B7
Hampden La G42 137 B8
Hampden Park Visitors Ctr* G42 137 C7
Hampden Pk (Queen's Park FC)* G42 137 B7
Hampden Terr G42 137 B8
Hampden Way 4 PA4 94 D1
Handel Pl 3 G5 117 C4
Hangingshaw Pl G42 137 C8
Hannah Dr KA2 221 F3
Hannah Pl G82 27 E2
Hanover Cl G42 137 A8
Hanover Ct Glasgow G1 241 A3
Johnstone PA5 111 F3
Paisley PA1 114 A5
Stirling FK9 2 D4
Hanover Gdns
Bishopbriggs G64 78 A1
Paisley PA1 113 C4
Hanover St Glasgow G1 241 A2
Helensburgh G84 25 A8
Hanson Pk G31 117 F8
Hanson St G31 117 F8
Hapland Ave G53 115 C2
Hapland Rd G53 115 C2
Happyhills KA23 190 C5
Haran Rd G83 19 F1
Harbour Ind Est KA22 205 C2
Harbour La PA3 113 E5
Harbour Pl KA22 205 B1
Harbour Rd
Ardrossan KA22 216 B8
Irvine KA12 219 B1
Paisley PA3 113 E6
Troon KA10 229 B3
Harbour St
Ardrossan KA22 216 B8
Irvine KA12 219 A1
Saltcoats KA21 216 F7
Harburn Pl G23 76 E1
Harbury Pl G14 94 F6
Harcourt Dr G31 118 B8
Hardacres ML11 215 A5
Hardgate Dr G51 115 C8
Hardgate Gdns G51 115 C7
Hardgate Pl G51 115 C8
Hardgate Rd G51 115 C8
Hardie Ave G73 138 C8
Hardie Cres FK7 8 C4
Hardie Ct FK7 7 C3
Hardie St Alexandria G83 27 D7
Hamilton,Blantyre G72 161 D7
Hamilton,Laighstonehall ML3 162 B2
Motherwell ML1 163 E8
Hardmuir Gdns 1 G66 58 E1
Hardmuir Rd G66 58 E1
Hardridge Ave G52 115 E2
Hardridge Pl G52 115 E2
Hardridge Rd G52 115 E2
Hardwood Ct PA16 45 E7
Hardy Hill G84 17 A2
Harebell Pl KA7 239 B3
Harefield Dr G14 95 B5
Harelaw Ave
Barrhead G78 134 D1
Glasgow G44 136 E4
Neilston G78 154 D6
Port Glasgow PA14 68 D8
Harelaw Cres PA2 133 C7
Hareleeshill Prim Sch ML9 185 C1
Hareleeshill Rd ML9 185 C2
Hareshaw Dr KA3 223 A5
Hareshaw Gdns KA3 223 A5
Hareshaw Rd ML1 144 D5
Harestanes Gdns G66 59 A1
Harestanes Ind Est ML8 201 F5
Harestanes Prim Sch G66 59 A1
Harestanes Rd ML8 201 E4
Harestone Cres ML2 165 C2
Harestone Rd ML2 165 C2
Harfield Dr G33 119 E6
Harfield Gdns G33 119 E6
Harhill St G51 116 A8
Harkins Ave G72 161 C7
Harkness Ave G66 58 B5
Harland Cotts G14 95 C3
Harland St G14 95 C3
Harlands The FK10 9 E7
Harlaw Gdns G64 78 D2
Harley Ct FK2 42 B8
Harley Pl KA21 205 E1
Harley St G51 116 C6
Harling Dr KA10 229 E2
Harmetray St G22 97 D6
Harmony Pl G51 116 A7
Harmony Row 1 G51 116 A8
Harmony Sq G51 116 A7
Harmsworth St G11 95 F2
Harper Cres ML2 165 E4
Harperland Dr KA1 227 D7
Harperland Holdings KA2 226 A4
Harport St G46 135 E4
Harrier Way PA16 45 B4
Harriet Pl G43 136 B6
Harriet Rd KA3 223 A2
Harriet St G73 138 A7
Harrington Rd G74 159 E1
Harris Cl G77 156 B6
Harris Cres G60 73 B5
Harris Ct Alloa FK10 10 B5
Irvine KA11 225 C8
Harris Dr G60 73 B5
Harris Gdns G60 73 C5
Harris Pl Airdrie ML6 123 C5
Kilmarnock KA3 223 B5
Harris Quadrant ML2 165 E5
Harris Rd Glasgow G23 76 E1
Old Kilpatrick G60 73 C5
Port Glasgow PA14 69 B7
Harris Terr KA11 225 C8
Harrison Dr G51 116 B6
Harrison Pl Falkirk FK1 41 F5
Renton G82 27 D2
Harrow Ct G15 74 F3
Harrow Pl G15 74 F3
Hart St Clydebank G81 74 D7
Glasgow G31 118 E5
Linwood PA3 112 C5
Hart Wynd FK7 7 F1
Hartfield Cres G78 154 E7
Hartfield Ct G82 50 A4
Hartfield Gdns G82 50 A4
Hartfield Rd KA7 238 F5
Hartfield Terr
Paisley PA2 113 F2
Paisley PA2 114 A2
Shotts ML7 167 B8
Harthall KA8 236 E2
Harthill Ind Est ML7 127 D5
Harthill Rd EH48 107 D2
Hartlaw Cres G52 115 A6
Hartree Ave G13 94 E8
Hartstone Pl G53 135 B7
Hartstone Rd G53 135 B7
Hartstone Terr G53 135 B7
Hartwood Gdns
Hartwood ML7 146 A2
Newton Mearns G77 156 D2
Hartwood Rd
Hartwood ML7 145 F2
Shotts ML7 146 A3
Hartwoodhill Hospl ML7 146 C4
Harvest Dr ML1 163 D4
Harvest St FK9 2 A4
Harvey Cotts PA12 129 D2
Harvey Ct PA12 129 C2
Harvey Gdns KA22 205 C3
Harvey Sq PA12 129 C2
Harvey St
Ardrossan KA22 205 C3
Glasgow G4 97 C2
Harvey Terr PA12 129 C2
Harvey Way ML4 142 C7
Harvey Wynd FK8 2 A1
Harvie Ave G77 156 D6
Harvie St G51 116 D6
Harwood Gdns G69 81 A3
Harwood St G32 118 E7
Hastie St G3 96 D1
Hastings G75 180 B7
Hatfield Ct PA13 89 C7
Hatfield Dr G12 96 A5
Hathaway Dr G46 136 B2
Hathaway La G20 96 E5
Hathaway St G20 96 E5
Hathersage Ave G69 120 B5
Hathersage Dr G69 120 B5
Hathersage Gdns 2 G69 120 B5
Hatton Gdns G52 115 A4
Hatton Path G52 115 A4
Hatton Pl ML1 143 C2
Hatton Terr ML1 143 C2
Hattonhill ML1 143 C2
Hattonrigg Rd ML4 142 B6
Haugh Gdns FK2 24 B1
Haugh Pl ML3 162 E1
Haugh Rd Glasgow G3 116 D8
Kilsyth G65 60 C8
Stirling FK9 2 B2
Haugh St FK2 24 B1
Haughburn Pl G53 135 B7
Haughburn Rd G53 135 B7
Haughburn Terr G53 135 C7
Haughs Way FK6 21 E2
Haughton Ave G65 60 E8
Haughview Rd ML1 163 B6
Haupland Rd KA22 205 B5
Hauplands Way KA23 190 E5
Havelock La G11 96 C2
Havelock Pk 9 G75 159 A1
Havelock Pl G84 16 F2
Havelock St Glasgow G11 96 C2
Helensburgh G84 16 E2
Haven Pk G75 179 F6
Haven The FK7 9 F3
Havoc Rd G82 49 C4
Hawbank Rd G74 159 B3
Hawbank Rdbt G74 159 B2
Hawick Ave PA2 113 B1
Hawick Cres ML9 185 A2
Hawick Ct 10 PA15 46 B3
Hawick Dr ML5 122 D3
Hawick St Glasgow G13 94 E7
Wishaw ML2 165 C5
Hawkhead Ave PA2 114 B2
Hawkhead Hospl PA2 114 C2
Hawkhead Rd PA2 114 B3
Hawkhead Sta PA1 114 B4
Hawkhill Ave KA8 236 B2
Hawkhill Avenue La KA8 236 B2
Hawkhill Dr KA20 206 F1
Hawkhill Pl KA20 206 F2
Hawkhill Rd FK10 10 C6
Hawkhill Ret Pk KA20 206 F2
Hawksland Wlk ML3 162 E1
Hawkwood G75 180 D5
Hawkwood Rd ML6 102 F4
Hawley Rd FK1 42 D4
Hawthorn Ave
Bearsden G61 76 A7
Bishopbriggs G64 98 B8
Dumbarton G82 49 B5
Erskine PA8 93 E8
Johnstone PA5 112 A1
Kirkintilloch G66 79 C5
Prestwick KA9 236 C7
Wishaw ML2 166 C6
Hawthorn Cres
Beith KA15 171 A8
Erskine PA8 93 E8
Fallin FK7 8 D4
Stirling FK8 1 F2
Hawthorn Ct
Clarkston G76 157 E6
Kilwinning KA13 207 E2
Hawthorn Dr
Airdrie ML6 123 D6
Ayr KA7 239 C4
Banknock FK4 38 E2
Barrhead G78 155 D8
Coatbridge ML5 122 D5
Denny FK6 21 D3
Falkirk FK1 41 E4
Fallin FK7 8 C4
Harthill ML7 127 E6
Motherwell ML1 143 B3
Shotts ML7 147 C4
Stevenston KA20 206 E3
Wishaw ML2 165 C3
Hawthorn Gdns
Bellshill ML4 142 C4
Cambuslang G72 139 E4
Clarkston G76 157 E6
11 Larkhall ML9 185 C2
Prestwick KA9 236 C7
Hawthorn Gr ML8 186 F6
Hawthorn Hill ML3 162 E1
Hawthorn Pl
Kilwinning KA13 207 E2
Shotts ML7 167 A8
Troon KA10 229 E4
Hawthorn Prim Sch (Keppoch Campus) G22 97 C3
Hawthorn Quadrant G22 97 C5
Hawthorn Rd
Clarkston G76 157 E6
Cumbernauld G67 62 F4
Erskine PA8 93 E8
Hawthorn Sq KA1 227 D8
Hawthorn St
Clydebank G81 74 A4
Glasgow G22 97 D5
Torrance G64 57 C1
Hawthorn Terr
East Kilbride G75 180 B6
Uddingston G71 141 B7
Hawthorn Way
Dumbarton G82 49 B4
Erskine PA8 93 E8
Milton Of C G66 58 C5
Quarter ML3 183 F4
Hawthorn Wlk G72 138 D5
Hawthornden Gdns G23 76 E1
Hawthorne Pl
Gourock PA19 44 B6
Stenhousemuir FK5 23 D1
Hawthornhill Rd G82 49 C5
Hay Ave PA7 72 C3
Hay St PA15 45 F4
Hayburn Cres G11 96 A3
Hayburn Ct G11 96 A1
Hayburn Gate G11 96 B2
Hayburn La Glasgow G11 96 A3
Glasgow G11 96 A4
Hayburn St G11 96 B2
Hayes Gr G83 27 E6
Hayfield FK2 42 C7
Hayfield Ct G5 117 D4
Hayfield Rd FK2 42 C7
Hayfield St G5 117 D4
Hayfield Terr FK6 39 E7
Hayford Mills FK7 6 D6
Hayford Pl FK7 6 D6
Hayhill KA8 239 D8
Hayhill Rd G74 179 C7
Hayle Gdns G69 80 F3
Haylynn St G14 95 E2
Haymarket St G32 118 F7
Hayocks Prim Sch KA20 206 E2
Hayocks Rd KA20 206 E2
Hayocks Rdbt KA20 206 E1
Haypark Rd FK6 39 D6
Haysholm Sch KA12 219 E4
Haystack Pl G66 79 E4
Hayston Cres G22 97 B5
Hayston Rd
Cumbernauld G68 61 E4
Kirkintilloch G66 79 A8
Hayston St G22 97 B5
Hayward Ave ML8 202 C8
Hayward Ct ML8 202 C8
Haywood St G22 97 C6
Hazel Ave
Ardrossan KA22 205 C4
Bearsden G61 76 A7
Dumbarton G82 49 B5
Glasgow G44 136 F4
Johnstone PA5 112 A1
Kilmarnock KA1 227 D7
Kirkintilloch G66 79 D6
Hazel Bank G66 58 B4
Hazel Cres FK6 21 D3
Hazel Dene G64 98 B8
Hazel Gdns ML1 163 E3
Hazel Gr Falkirk FK2 42 D7
Kirkintilloch G66 79 D6
Law ML8 186 F6
Shotts ML7 147 B4
Hazel Path ML1 144 B1
Hazel Pk ML3 162 E2
Hazel Rd Banknock FK4 38 E2
Cumbernauld G67 62 D3
Hazel Terr Gourock PA19 44 C6
Uddingston G71 141 B7
Hazel Wood ML2 165 D5
Hazelbank
Motherwell ML1 143 B5
Plains ML6 103 F3
Hazelbank Gdns FK8 2 A2
Hazelbank Wlk ML6 122 D8
Hazeldean Cres ML2 165 C5
Hazelden Gdns G44 136 E4
Hazelden Pk G44 136 E4
Hazelden Rd G77 177 C7
Hazeldene La 3 ML9 185 C1
Hazeldene Pk KA13 207 F4
Hazelfield Gr ML6 123 E1
Hazelgrove KA13 208 A4
Hazelhead G74 160 B2
Hazellea Dr G46 136 E4
Hazelmere Rd PA13 89 B8
Hazelton ML1 163 D5
Hazelwood Ave
Bridge of W PA11 110 E7
Newton Mearns G77 156 E4
Paisley PA2 132 E7
Hazelwood Dr G72 161 C8
Hazelwood Gdns G73 138 C4
Hazelwood Gr G69 121 A6
Hazelwood La PA11 110 D7
Hazelwood Rd Ayr KA7 238 F6
Bridge of W PA11 110 D6
Glasgow G41 116 C4
Hazlitt Gdns G20 97 A6
Hazlitt Pl G20 97 B6
Hazlitt St G20 97 B6
Head of Muir Prim Sch FK6 39 D6
Head St KA15 171 C8
Headhouse Ct G75 180 D8
Headhouse Gn G75 180 E8
Headlands Gr KA15 171 C8
Headlesscross Rd EH47 147 F2
Headrigg Gdns KA23 190 C5
Headrigg Rd KA23 190 C5
Headsmuir Ave ML8 187 D2
Heath Ave
Bishopbriggs G64 98 B8
Kirkintilloch G66 79 C4
Heath Rd ML9 185 B3
Heathcliffe Ave G72 140 C1
Heathcot Ave G15 74 E2
Heathcot Pl G15 74 E2
Heather Ave
Alexandria G83 27 E6
Barrhead G78 134 A5
Bearsden G61 75 E7
Clydebank G81 74 A7
Motherwell ML1 143 A5
Shieldhill FK1 66 C6
Heather Dr G66 79 A4
Heather Gdns G66 79 A4
Heather Gr 3 G75 180 E7
Heather Pk KA7 239 C3
Heather Pl
Johnstone PA5 112 A2
Kilmarnock KA1 227 D7
Kirkintilloch G66 79 A4
Heather Rd ML11 214 B6
Heather Row ML8 187 E4
Heather St ML6 105 A5
Heather View G66 33 E1
Heather Way ML1 143 A4
Heatherbank Wlk ML6 122 D7
Heatherbrae G64 77 E1
Heatherdale Gdns FK6 39 E7
Heatherhouse Ind Est KA12 224 D8
Heatherhouse Rd KA12 224 D8
Heatherstane Bank KA11 220 C2
Heatherstane Way KA11 220 C2
Heatherstane Wlk KA11 220 C2
Heathery Knowe G75 180 E7
Heathery Knowe Prim Sch G75 180 E7
Heathery Lea Ave ML5 122 D3
Heathery Rd ML2 164 F3
Heatheryknowe Rd
Coatbridge G69 120 F7
Glasgow G69 120 F7
Heathfield ML2 186 A7
Heathfield Ave G69 81 A2
Heathfield Dr G62 55 B3
Heathfield Ho KA12 219 B3

Hogarth Ave
Glasgow G32 ...118 D7
Saltcoats KA21 ...205 E2
Hogarth Cres G32 ...118 D7
Hogarth Ct G83 ...27 E6
Hogarth Dr G32 ...118 D7
Hogarth Gdns G32 ...118 D7
Hogg Ave PA5 ...111 E1
Hogg Rd ML6 ...123 D4
Hogg St ML6 ...123 A7
Hoggan Way FK12 ...4 F6
Hogganfield Ct G33 ...98 D2
Hogganfield St G33 ...98 D2
Holbourne Pl FK11 ...4 A7
Hole Farm Rd PA15,PA16 ..45 D3
Holeburn La G43 ...136 C6
Holeburn Rd G43 ...136 C6
Holehills Dr ML6 ...103 B2
Holehills Pl ML6 ...103 B2
Holehouse Brae G78 ...154 C7
Holehouse Dr
Glasgow G13 ...95 A6
Kilbirnie KA25 ...149 B3
Holehouse Rd
Eaglesham G76 ...178 F6
Kilmarnock KA3 ...228 B8
Holehouse Terr G78 ...154 C7
Holland St G2 ...240 B3
Hollandbush Ave FK4 ...38 E3
Hollandbush Cres FK4 ...38 F3
Hollandbush Gr ML3 ...183 D8
Hollandhurst Rd ML5 ...101 F1
Hollinwell Rd G23 ...76 D1
Hollow Park Ct KA7 ...239 B2
Hollow Pk KA7 ...239 B2
Hollowglen Rd G32 ...119 B6
Hollows Ave PA2 ...132 F7
Hollows Cres PA2 ...132 F7
Hollows The G46 ...136 B1
Holly Ave Milton Of C G66 ..58 B5
Stenhousemuir FK5 ...23 F3
Holly Bank KA7 ...239 D5
Holly Dr Dumbarton G82 ...49 B5
Glasgow G21 ...98 A3
Holly Gr Banknock FK4 ...38 F2
Bellshill ML4 ...142 F5
Menstrie FK11 ...3 F6
Holly Pl Johnstone PA5 ...132 A8
Kilmarnock KA1 ...222 D1
Holly St Airdrie ML6 ...123 C6
Clydebank G81 ...74 B4
Hollybank Pl G72 ...139 B4
Hollybank St G21 ...98 A1
Hollybrook Pl 2 G42 ...117 B2
Hollybrook Sch G42 ...117 B2
Hollybrook St G42 ...117 B2
Hollybush Ave PA2 ...133 B7
Hollybush Pl KA3 ...223 B6
Hollybush Rd G52 ...114 F5
Hollyhill Gr G69 ...121 A6
Hollymount G61 ...75 F2
Hollytree Gdns G66 ...57 C7
Holm Ave Paisley PA2 ...113 F2
Uddingston G71 ...140 E7
Holm Cres KA3 ...213 B3
Holm Crest ML8 ...201 B2
Holm Ct ML8 ...201 B2
Holm Gdns ML4 ...142 C4
Holm La G74 ...159 E1
Holm Pl Larkhall ML9 ...184 E2
Linwood PA3 ...112 B7
Holm Rd ML8 ...201 B2
Holm St Carluke ML8 ...187 E2
Glasgow G2 ...240 C2
Motherwell ML1 ...143 A3
Stewarton KA3 ...211 E8
Holmbank Ave G41 ...136 D7
Holmbrae Ave G71 ...140 F7
Holmbrae Rd G71 ...140 F8
Holmbyre Ct G45 ...137 B1
Holmbyre Rd G45 ...137 B1
Holmbyre Terr G45 ...137 C2
Holmes Ave PA4 ...94 C1
Holmes Cres KA1 ...227 D6
Holmes Farm Rd KA1 ...227 D6
Holmes Park Ave KA1 ...227 D6
Holmes Park Cres KA1 ...227 D6
Holmes Park Gdns KA1 ...227 D6
Holmes Park View KA1 ...227 D6
Holmes Park Wynd KA1 ...227 D6
Holmes Quadrant ML4 ...142 B4
Holmes Rd KA1 ...227 D6
Holmes Village KA1 ...227 D6
Holmfauld Rd G51 ...95 E1
Holmfauldhead Dr G51 ...115 E8
Holmfauldhead Pl 3
G51 ...115 E8
Holmfield G66 ...79 E7
Holmhead KA25 ...170 A8
Holmhead Cres G44 ...137 A6
Holmhead Pl G44 ...137 A6
Holmhead Rd G44 ...137 A5
Holmhill Ave G72 ...139 A4
Holmhills Dr G72 ...138 F3
Holmhills Gdns G72 ...138 F4
Holmhills Gr G72 ...138 F4
Holmhills Pl G72 ...138 F4
Holmhills Rd G72 ...138 F4
Holmhills Terr G72 ...138 F4
Holmlands Pl KA1 ...227 D6
Holmlea Dr KA1 ...227 E6
Holmlea Pl KA1 ...227 E6
Holmlea Prim Sch G44 ...137 A6
Holmlea Rd G44 ...137 A7
Holmpark PA7 ...72 B3
Holmquarry Rd KA1 ...227 F6
Holms Ave KA11 ...220 D1
Holms Cres PA8 ...72 F2
Holms Pl G69 ...100 E7
Holms Rd KA14 ...170 B6
Holmscroft Ave PA15 ...45 E4
Holmscroft St PA15 ...45 E5
Holmscroft Way PA15 ...45 E4
Holmston Cres KA7 ...239 C7
Holmston Dr KA7 ...239 C6
Holmston Gdns KA7 ...239 A7
Holmston Prim Sch
KA7 ...239 A7
Holmston Rd KA7 ...239 C7
Holmston Rdbt KA7 ...239 E7
Holmswood Ave G72 ...140 D1
Holmwood Ave G71 ...140 F7
Holmwood Gdns G71 ...140 F6
Holmwood Gn ML8 ...201 A3
Holmwood Ho* G44 ...137 B4
Holmwood Pk ML8 ...201 A3
Holton Cotts FK10 ...5 C1
Holton Cres FK10 ...5 C1
Holton Ct FK10 ...5 C1
Holton Sq FK10 ...5 C1
Holy Cross High Sch
ML3 ...162 E4
Holy Cross Prim Sch
Croy G65 ...60 F4
Glasgow G42 ...117 B2
Holy Family Prim Sch
G66 ...79 B6
Holy Family RC Prim Sch
ML4 ...142 C5
Holyknowe Cres G66 ...57 E8
Holyknowe Rd G66 ...57 E7
Holyoake Ct KA1 ...228 F7
Holyrood Cres G20 ...96 F2
Holyrood Pl FK5 ...23 E4
Holyrood Quadrant 2
G20 ...96 F2
Holyrood Sec Sch G42 ...117 C1
Holyrood St ML3 ...162 A5
Holytown Prim Sch
ML1 ...143 B5
Holytown Rd ML1 ...142 E5
Holytown Sta ML1 ...143 A3
Holywell St G31 ...118 B5
Home Farm Cotts FK6 ...39 F6
Home Farm Rd Ayr KA7 ...239 A2
Hartwood ML7 ...145 F3
Home St ML11 ...215 C3
Homeblair Ho G46 ...136 C5
Homebriar Ho KA7 ...238 F8
Homeburn Ho G46 ...136 C3
Homeglen Ho G46 ...136 C2
Homer Pl ML4 ...142 E5
Homeshaw Ho G77 ...156 F4
Homesteads The FK8 ...6 D7
Homeston Ave G71 ...141 A3
Honeybank Cres ML8 ...188 A3
Honeybog Rd G52 ...114 E6
Honeycomb Pl ML9 ...200 D4
Honeyman Cres ML11 ...215 C4
Honeysuckle La G83 ...27 B7
Honeysuckle Pk KA7 ...239 B2
Honeywell Cres ML6 ...123 E1
Hood Ct G84 ...16 A2
Hood St Clydebank G81 ...74 D2
Greenock PA15 ...45 F6
Hookney Terr FK6 ...21 C2
Hooper Pl ML4 ...142 B5
Hope Ave PA11 ...89 E2
Hope Cres ML9 ...185 B3
Hope St Ayr KA7 ...238 F8
Bellshill ML4 ...142 C5
Carluke ML8 ...188 A2
Falkirk FK1 ...42 B5
Glasgow G2 ...240 C3
Greenock PA15 ...45 F4
Hamilton ML3 ...162 E3
Helensburgh G84 ...25 B8
Lanark ML11 ...215 A4
Motherwell ML1 ...163 E7
Stirling FK8 ...1 F1
Wishaw ML2 ...166 A4
Hopefield Ave G12 ...96 C5
Hopehill Gdns G20 ...97 A3
Hopehill Rd G20 ...97 A3
Hopeman PA8 ...73 A3
Hopeman Ave G46 ...135 E4
Hopeman Dr G46 ...135 E4
Hopeman Path G46 ...135 E5
Hopeman Rd G46 ...135 E4
Hopeman St G46 ...135 E4
Hopepark Terr FK4 ...39 F6
Hopeton St PA19 ...44 E8
Hopetoun Bank KA11 ...220 C2
Hopetoun Dr FK9 ...2 A8
Hopetoun Pl G23 ...76 E1
Hopetoun Terr G21 ...98 A3
Hopkin's Brae 3 G66 ...58 D1
Horatius St ML1 ...142 B1
Hornal Rd G71 ...141 A4
Hornbeam Dr G81 ...74 A4
Hornbeam Rd
Cumbernauld G67 ...62 E5
Uddingston G71 ...141 B8
Horndean Ct G64 ...78 A4
Horne St G22 ...97 E5
Hornock Cotts ML5 ...121 F8
Hornock Rd ML5 ...101 F1
Hornshill Dr ML1 ...144 B2
Hornshill Farm Rd G33 ...99 E6
Hornshill St G21 ...98 A4
Horsburgh Ave G65 ...36 D1
Horsburgh St G33 ...99 D2
Horse Isle View KA22 ...205 A4
Horse Shoe KA23 ...190 C5
Horse Shoe La G61 ...75 F4
Horse Shoe Rd G61 ...75 E4
Horsewood Rd PA11 ...110 C8
Horslet St ML5 ...121 C4
Horslethill Rd G12 ...96 C3
Horsley Brae ML2 ...186 B4
Horton Pl G84 ...17 A3
Hosiery Ct KA10 ...229 E3
Hospital Rd Wishaw ML2 ...165 C1
Wishaw ML2 ...186 B8
Hospital St ML5 ...122 A4
Hospitland Dr ML11 ...215 C4
Hotspur St G20 ...96 E4
Houldsworth Cres ML7 ...167 A8
Houldsworth Ct ML2 ...165 C2
Houldsworth La 7 G3 ...116 E8
Houldsworth St G3 ...240 A3
House O' Muir Rd ML7 ...126 B3
Househillmuir Cres
G53 ...135 C7
Househillmuir La G53 ...135 C7
Househillmuir Pl G53 ...135 C7
Househillmuir Prim Sch
G53 ...135 A5
Househillmuir Rd G53 ...135 B6
Househillwood Cres
G53 ...135 B7
Househillwood Rd G53 ...135 B6
Housel Ave G13 ...95 B7
Houston Cres KA24 ...191 B7
Houston Ct
Kilbirnie KA25 ...149 A2
Renfrew PA4 ...94 D4
Houston Pl Elderslie PA5 ...112 C2
Glasgow G5 ...240 A1
Houston Prim Sch PA6 ...91 B1
Houston Rd
Bridge Of W PA11 ...90 E1
Houston PA6 ...91 B1
Houston PA6 ...91 B2
Houston PA6 ...91 D2
Inchinnan PA3,PA4,PA6 ...92 D3
Kilmacolm PA11 ...89 E7
Linwood PA3 ...91 C1
Houston St Glasgow G5 ...116 F5
Greenock PA16 ...45 E6
Hamilton ML3 ...162 D1
Renfrew PA4 ...94 D4
Wishaw ML2 ...165 D2
Houston Terr G74 ...159 D2
Houstonfield Quadrant
PA6 ...91 A2
Houstonfield Rd PA6 ...91 A2
Houstoun Ct PA5 ...111 F3
Houstoun Sq PA5 ...111 F3
Howacre ML11 ...214 F5
Howard Ave G74 ...160 A5
Howard Ct
East Kilbride G74 ...160 A5
Kilmarnock KA1 ...227 F8
Howard Park Dr KA1 ...227 E7
Howard St Falkirk FK1 ...41 F4
Glasgow G1 ...241 A1
Kilmarnock KA1 ...227 F8
Larkhall ML9 ...185 C1
Paisley PA1 ...114 A4
Howat Cres KA12 ...219 E3
Howat St G51 ...116 A8
Howatshaws Rd G82 ...50 B6
Howburn Cres ML7 ...127 E6
Howburn Rd ML7 ...127 D6
Howden Ave
Kilwinning KA13 ...207 E4
Motherwell ML1 ...143 D8
Howden Dr PA3 ...112 A5
Howden Pl ML1 ...143 A5
Howe Gdns G71 ...141 A7
Howe Rd G65 ...60 D7
Howe St PA1 ...112 F4
Howes St ML5 ...122 B4
Howetown FK10 ...5 D4
Howford Rd G52 ...115 B4
Howford Sch G53 ...115 A2
Howgate KA13 ...207 D3
Howgate Ave G15 ...74 F3
Howgate Rd ML3 ...183 C8
Howgate Sh Ctr 6 FK1 ...42 B4
Howie Bldgs G76 ...157 E8
Howie Cres G84 ...15 A3
Howie St ML9 ...185 B1
Howie's Pl FK1 ...41 B4
Howieshill Ave G72 ...139 B5
Howieshill Rd G72 ...139 B5
Howlands Rd FK7 ...7 A3
Howlet Pl ML3 ...162 E1
Howletnest Rd ML6 ...123 D6
Howson Lea ML1 ...164 B4
Howson View ML1 ...163 B7
Howth Dr G13 ...95 F8
Howth Terr G13 ...95 F8
Howwood Prim Sch
PA9 ...131 A5
Howwood Sta PA9 ...130 F5
Hoylake Pk G71 ...140 F2
Hoylake Pl G23 ...76 E1
Hoylake Sq KA13 ...207 C4
Hozier Cres G71 ...140 F8
Hozier Loan 8 ML9 ...185 B4
Hozier Pl 9 G71 ...141 B3
Hozier St Carluke ML8 ...187 F2
Coatbridge ML5 ...122 A4
Hudson Pl KA9 ...233 C2
Hudson Terr G75 ...180 C8
Hudson Way G75 ...180 C8
Hudspeth Ct G83 ...27 D7
Hugh Murray Gr G72 ...139 C5
Hugh Watt Pl KA3 ...222 A7
Hughenden Ct G12 ...96 B4
Hughenden Dr G12 ...96 B4
Hughenden Gdns G12 ...96 B4
Hughenden La G12 ...96 B4
Hughenden Rd G12 ...96 B4
Hughenden Terr G12 ...96 B4
Hugo St G20 ...96 F5
Hulks Rd Greengairs ML6 ...83 D4
Greengairs ML6 ...84 B4
Humbie Ct G77 ...156 F2
Humbie Gate G77 ...156 E2
Humbie Gr G77 ...156 E3
Humbie Lawns G77 ...156 E2
Humbie Rd
Eaglesham G76 ...178 C7
Newton Mearns G77 ...156 F2
Hume Cres FK9 ...2 A6
Hume Ct FK9 ...2 A6
Hume Dr Bothwell G71 ...141 A3
Uddingston G71 ...140 E7
Hume Pl G75 ...180 D8
Hume Rd G67 ...62 A3
Hume St G81 ...74 B1
Hunt Hill G68 ...60 C1
Hunt Hill Rdbt G68 ...60 C1
Hunter Ave KA22 ...205 D2
Hunter Cres KA10 ...230 A2
Hunter Dr Irvine KA12 ...219 B6
Newton Mearns G77 ...156 B3
Hunter Gdns
Bonnybridge FK4 ...40 A5
Denny FK6 ...21 D2
Hunter High Sch G74 ...160 C2
Hunter House Mus*
G74 ...160 C4
Hunter Pl
Kilbarchan PA10 ...111 A2
Kilwinning KA13 ...208 A3
Milngavie G62 ...54 E1
Shotts ML7 ...146 E5
Stenhousemuir FK2 ...24 A4
Hunter Prim Sch G74 ...160 C2
Hunter Rd
Crosshouse KA2 ...221 F1
Hamilton ML3 ...162 B6
Milngavie G62 ...54 E2
Rutherglen G73 ...118 C1
Hunter St Airdrie ML6 ...103 A1
Bellshill ML4 ...142 A5
East Kilbride G74 ...159 F2
Glasgow G4 ...241 C2
Paisley PA1 ...113 E5
Prestwick KA9 ...236 C8
Shotts ML7 ...146 D5
Hunter's Ave Ayr KA8 ...236 B4
Dumbarton G82 ...50 B3
Hunter's Cl ML11 ...215 A4
Hunterfield Dr G72 ...138 E5
Hunterhill Ave PA2 ...113 F3
Hunterhill Rd PA2 ...113 F3
Hunterhill Tutorial Ctr
PA2 ...114 A3
Hunterian Mus* G12 ...96 D2
Hunterlees Rd ML10 ...198 B3
Hunters Cres G74 ...160 C3
Hunters Gr G74 ...160 C3
Hunters Hill Ct G21 ...97 F6
Hunters Pl
East Kilbride G74 ...160 C3
Greenock PA15 ...45 F5
Huntersfield Rd PA5 ...111 D1
Huntershill Rd G64 ...98 A8
Huntershill St G21 ...97 E6
Huntershill Village G64 ...97 F8
Huntershill Way G64 ...97 F7
Hunterston Rd KA23 ...190 D5
Hunthill La G72 ...161 B6
Hunthill Pl G76 ...158 A5
Hunthill Rd G72 ...161 B7
Hunting Lodge Gdns
ML3 ...163 A2
Huntingdon Rd G21 ...97 E2
Huntingdon Sq G21 ...97 E2
Huntingtower Rd
Baillieston G69 ...119 F4
Glasgow G69 ...120 A3
Huntly Ave Bellshill ML4 ...142 A6
Glasgow G46 ...136 D2
Huntly Cres FK8 ...1 F2
Huntly Ct
Bishopbriggs G64 ...98 A8
Kilmarnock KA3 ...223 C3
Huntly Dr Bearsden G61 ...75 E7
Cambuslang G72 ...139 B4
Coatbridge ML5 ...121 D4
Greenock PA16 ...44 F3
Huntly Gdns Glasgow G12 ...96 D3
Hamilton G72 ...161 D3
Huntly Path G69 ...81 A2
Huntly Pl Kilmarnock KA3 ...223 C2
Port Glasgow PA14 ...47 B2
Huntly Quadrant ML2 ...165 B5
Huntly Rd
Glasgow (Hillington Ind Est)
G52 ...94 F1
Glasgow,Dowanhill G12 ...96 C3
Glasgow,Hillington G52 ...114 F8
Huntly Terr Paisley PA2 ...114 A1
Port Glasgow PA14 ...47 B2
Shotts ML7 ...147 B3
Hurlawcrook Rd G75 ...180 F2
Hurlet Cotts G53 ...134 F6
Hurlet Rd PA2,G53 ...134 D7
Hurlethill Ct G53 ...134 F7
Hurlford Ave G13 ...94 F7
Hurlford Prim Sch KA1 ...228 E6
Hurlford Rd KA1 ...228 A5
Hurly Hawkin G64 ...98 D8
Hurworth St FK1 ...41 F3
Hutcheson Rd G46 ...136 A2
Hutcheson St G1 ...241 A2
Hutchesons' Gram Sch
Glasgow G42 ...117 A2
Glasgow,Crossmyloof G41 ...116 E2
Hutchinson Pl G72 ...139 E3
Hutchinson St ML2 ...186 D7
Hutchinson Town Ct 8
G5 ...117 C4
Hutchison Ct G46 ...136 B1
Hutchison Dr G61 ...76 A2
Hutchison Pl ML5 ...121 F6
Hutchison St ML3 ...162 D1
Hutton G12 ...96 A6
Hutton Ave PA6 ...111 C8
Hutton Dr
East Kilbride G74 ...159 F4
Glasgow G51 ...115 E8
Hutton Pk FK10 ...10 C7
Huxley Pl G20 ...96 F6
Hyacinth Way ML8 ...201 F8
Hydepark Bsns Ctr G21 ...97 E3
Hydepark St G3 ...240 A2
Hyndal Ave G53 ...115 C1
Hyndford Pl ML11 ...215 A4
Hyndford Rd ML11 ...215 D2
Hyndland Ave G11 ...96 B2
Hyndland Ct 11 G12 ...96 C3
Hyndland Prim Sch G11 ...96 B2
Hyndland Rd G12 ...96 B3
Hyndland Sec Sch G12 ...96 B3
Hyndland St G11 ...96 C2
Hyndland Sta G12 ...96 A4
Hyndlee Dr G52 ...115 C5
Hyndman Rd KA23 ...190 C3
Hyndshaw Rd
Carluke ML8 ...188 A3
Law ML8 ...187 C8
Hyndshaw View ML8 ...187 A4
Hyslop Pl G81 ...74 A3
Hyslop Rd KA20 ...206 F2
Hyslop St ML6 ...122 E8

I

Iain Dr G61 ...75 C6
Iain Rd G61 ...75 C6
Ian Smith Ct G81 ...94 D8
IBM Sta PA16 ...44 D1
Ibrox Ind Est G51 ...116 C6
Ibrox Prim Sch G51 ...116 B5
Ibrox St G51 ...116 C6
Ibrox Stad (Rangers FC)
G51 ...116 B6
Ibrox Terr G51 ...116 B6
Ibrox Underground Sta
G51 ...116 B6
Ibroxholm Ave G51 ...116 B5
Ibroxholm Oval G51 ...116 B5
Ibroxholm Pl G51 ...116 B5
Ida Quadrant ML4 ...141 F5
Iddesleigh Ave G62 ...55 A2
Ilay Ave Bearsden G61 ...95 F8
Glasgow G61 ...96 A8
Ilay Ct G61 ...96 A8
Ilay Rd G61 ...96 A8
Imex Bsns Ctr ML5 ...122 C6
Imlach Pl ML1 ...163 D5
Imperial Dr ML6 ...122 F6
Imperial Pl G71 ...141 A2
Imperial Way G71 ...141 A2
Inch Colm Ave FK5 ...23 C4
Inch Garve G74 ...160 D1
Inch Garvie Terr FK5 ...23 C4
Inch Keith G74 ...160 D1
Inch Marnock G74 ...160 D1
Inch Murrin G74 ...160 D1
Inchbrae Rd G52 ...115 C4
Inchcolm Gdns G69 ...81 A3
Inchcolm Pl G74 ...159 C2
Inchconnachan Ave G83 ...19 E2
Inchcruin G83 ...27 D8
Inchcruin Pl G15 ...74 E4
Inches Rd KA22 ...216 B8
Inches Rdbt FK5 ...23 C4
Inchfad Cres G15 ...74 E3
Inchfad Dr G15 ...74 E3
Inchfad Pl G15 ...74 E3
Inchfad Rd G83 ...19 E2
Inchgotrick Rd KA1 ...227 E4
Inchgower Gr G84 ...15 D5
Inchgower Rd G33 ...99 E6
Inchgreen St PA14 ...46 F2
Inchholm La G11 ...95 E2
Inchholm St G11 ...95 E2
Inchinnan Bsns Pk PA4 ...93 B4
Inchinnan Dr PA4 ...93 C4
Inchinnan Ind Est PA4 ...93 B5
Inchinnan Prim Sch PA4 ...93 D7
Inchinnan Rd
Bellshill ML4 ...141 F7
Paisley PA3 ...113 E7
Renfrew PA4 ...94 C4
Inchkeith Pl Falkirk FK1 ...42 B2
Glasgow G32 ...119 B7
Inchlagan Pl G15 ...74 E4
Inchlee St G14 ...95 E3
Inchlonaig Dr G83 ...19 E1
Inchmoan Pl G15 ...74 E4
Inchmurrin Ave G66 ...80 B8
Inchmurrin Cres G83 ...19 E2
Inchmurrin Dr
Kilmarnock KA3 ...223 A5
Rutherglen G73 ...138 D2
Inchmurrin Gdns G73 ...138 D2
Inchmurrin Pl G73 ...138 D2

Jura Quadrant ML2 ... 164 E1
Jura Rd Old Kilpatrick G60 ... 73 C5
Paisley PA2 ... 133 D7
Jura St Glasgow G52 ... 115 F5
Greenock PA16 ... 45 C4
Jura Wynd ML5 ... 101 C6
Jutland Ct G84 ... 16 A3

K

Kaim Dr G53 ... 135 C6
Kairnhill Ct ML11 ... 214 E4
Kames Ct KA11 ... 220 B6
Kames Rd ML7 ... 146 E6
Kane Pl ML9 ... 198 D1
Kane St G82 ... 27 D2
Karadale Gdns ML9 ... 185 A2
Karries Ct FK6 ... 39 B8
Katewell Ave G15 ... 74 E4
Katewell Pl G15 ... 74 E4
Katherine St ML6 ... 123 E8
Kathleen Pk G84 ... 16 A3
Katrine Ave
Bishopbriggs G64 ... 78 B1
Uddingston ML4 ... 141 D6
Katrine Cres ML6 ... 102 F1
Katrine Ct Alloa FK10 ... 10 C5
Kilmarnock KA1 ... 228 A5
Katrine Dr
Newton Mearns G77 ... 157 B4
Paisley PA2 ... 113 A2
Katrine Pl
Cambuslang G72 ... 139 A6
Coatbridge ML5 ... 101 D1
Denny FK6 ... 39 D6
Irvine KA12 ... 219 D6
Katrine Rd Greenock PA15 ... 46 A3
Shotts ML7 ... 146 E6
Katrine Way 5 G71 ... 141 A3
Katrine Wynd ML1 ... 143 A5
Katriona Path 12 ML9 ... 185 C1
Kay Gdns ML1 ... 163 B6
Kay Park Cres KA3 ... 223 B1
Kay Park Gr KA3 ... 223 A1
Kay Park Terr KA3 ... 223 B1
Kay St G21 ... 97 F4
Kaystone Rd G15 ... 75 A1
Keal Ave G15 ... 95 B8
Keal Cres G15 ... 95 A8
Keal Dr G15 ... 95 A8
Keal Pl G15 ... 95 A8
Keane Path ML1 ... 164 B3
Kearn Ave G15 ... 75 B1
Kearn Pl G15 ... 75 B1
Keats Pk G71 ... 141 B3
Keil Cres G82 ... 49 D3
Keil Ct G84 ... 25 B8
Keilarsbrae Alloa FK10 ... 5 C1
Sauchie FK10 ... 10 C8
Keir Ave FK8 ... 2 A2
Keir Cres ML2 ... 165 B4
Keir Ct FK9 ... 2 A7
Keir Dr G64 ... 77 F2
Keir Gdns FK9 ... 2 A7
Keir Hardie Ave
Laurieston FK2 ... 42 F3
Motherwell ML1 ... 143 B5
Keir Hardie Cres KA13 ... 208 A3
Keir Hardie Ct G64 ... 78 A1
Keir Hardie Dr
Ardrossan KA22 ... 205 B4
Bellshill ML4 ... 141 F4
Kilbirnie KA25 ... 149 A1
13 Kilsyth G65 ... 60 D8
Keir Hardie Meml Prim Sch
ML1 ... 143 D3
Keir Hardie Pl
Bellshill ML4 ... 141 F4
Saltcoats KA21 ... 206 A2
Keir Hardie Rd Alva FK12 ... 5 C7
Larkhall ML9 ... 185 C1
Stevenston KA20 ... 206 E1
Keir Hardie St PA15 ... 46 E2
Keir St Bridge of A FK9 ... 2 A7
Glasgow G41 ... 116 F3
Keir's Wlk G72 ... 139 A6
Keirfold Ave FK10 ... 4 D3
Keith Ave Glasgow G46 ... 136 D3
Stirling FK7 ... 7 C4
Keith Ct G11 ... 96 C1
Keith Pl KA3 ... 223 C2
Keith Quadrant ML2 ... 165 B5
Keith St Bellshill ML4 ... 142 A6
Glasgow G11 ... 96 C2
Hamilton ML3 ... 162 F4
Kelbourne Cres ML4 ... 141 F5
Kelbourne Sch G20 ... 96 E4
Kelbourne St G20 ... 96 E4
Kelburn Cres KA1 ... 227 E4
Kelburn St G78 ... 134 B2
Kelburn Terr PA14 ... 48 A1
Kelburne KA13 ... 207 C2
Kelburne Dr PA1 ... 114 B5
Kelburne Gdns
Glasgow G69 ... 120 A3
Paisley PA1 ... 114 A5
Kelburne Oval PA1 ... 114 A5
Kelhead Ave G52 ... 114 F4
Kelhead Dr G52 ... 114 F5
Kelhead Path G52 ... 114 F5
Kelhead Pl G52 ... 114 F5
Kellie Gr G74 ... 159 D3
Kellie Pl FK10 ... 10 A7
Kelliebank FK10 ... 9 E6
Kells Pl G15 ... 74 E4
Kelly Ct FK8 ... 7 A8
Kelly Dr FK6 ... 21 E3
Kelly St Greenock PA16 ... 45 D5
Greenock PA16 ... 45 E6
Kelly's La ML8 ... 188 B1
Kelso Ave
Bridge of W PA11 ... 110 D7
Paisley PA2 ... 113 A1
Rutherglen G73 ... 130 D7
Kelso Cres ML2 ... 165 B6
Kelso Ct 5 PA15 ... 46 B3
Kelso Dr Carluke ML8 ... 188 C1
East Kilbride G74 ... 160 A3
Kelso Gdns G69 ... 80 F3
Kelso Pl Glasgow G14 ... 94 E6
Renton G82 ... 27 E2
Kelso Quadrant ML5 ... 121 F8
Kelso St G13 ... 94 F7
Kelt Rd FK4 ... 38 E4
Kelton St G32 ... 119 B4
Kelvin Ave Glasgow G52 ... 114 F8
Glasgow G52 ... 115 A8
Glasgow (Hillington Ind Est)
G52 ... 94 F1
Kilwinning KA13 ... 207 F1
Kelvin Cres Bearsden G61 ... 75 F2
East Kilbride G75 ... 181 A7
Kelvin Ct
East Kilbride G75 ... 181 A7
Glasgow G12 ... 96 A5
1 Kirkintilloch G66 ... 58 C1
4 Troon KA10 ... 229 E5
Kelvin Dr Airdrie ML6 ... 103 B1
Barrhead G78 ... 134 D1
Bishopbriggs G64 ... 78 A2
East Kilbride G75 ... 180 F7
Glasgow G20 ... 96 D4
Kirkintilloch G66 ... 79 A8
Moodiesburn G69 ... 80 E2
Shotts ML7 ... 147 B4
Kelvin Gdns
Hamilton ML3 ... 161 E4
Kilsyth G65 ... 60 D7
Kelvin Hall G3 ... 96 C1
Kelvin Pk S G75 ... 181 A4
Kelvin Pl G75 ... 181 A7
Kelvin Rd Bellshill ML4 ... 142 B7
Cumbernauld G67 ... 83 A8
East Kilbride G75 ... 181 A7
Milngavie G62 ... 54 E3
Uddingston G71 ... 140 E7
Kelvin Rd N G67 ... 83 A8
Kelvin Sch G3 ... 96 D1
Kelvin South Bsns Pk
G75 ... 180 F3
Kelvin St ML5 ... 122 C5
Kelvin Terr G65 ... 59 F3
Kelvin View Torrance G64 ... 78 C8
Twechar G65 ... 59 F3
Kelvin Way
1 Bothwell G71 ... 141 A3
Glasgow G3,G12 ... 96 E1
Kilsyth G65 ... 36 C1
Kirkintilloch G66 ... 79 A8
Kelvinbridge Rdbt G64 ... 78 B8
Kelvinbridge Underground
Sta G4 ... 96 E2
Kelvindale G64 ... 57 C1
Kelvindale Gdns G20 ... 96 D6
Kelvindale Pl 3 G20 ... 96 D6
Kelvindale Prim Sch G12 ... 96 A5
Kelvindale Rd G12,G20 ... 96 C5
Kelvingrove Mus & Art Gall*
G3 ... 96 D1
Kelvingrove St G3 ... 116 E8
Kelvinhall Underground Sta
G11 ... 96 C2
Kelvinhaugh Gate G3 ... 116 D8
Kelvinhaugh Pl G3 ... 116 D8
Kelvinhaugh Prim Sch
G3 ... 116 C8
Kelvinhaugh St G3 ... 116 D8
Kelvinhead G65 ... 37 F2
Kelvinhead Rd G65 ... 37 E2
Kelvinside Acad G12 ... 96 D4
Kelvinside Ave
Glasgow G20 ... 96 E4
Glasgow G20 ... 96 F4
Kelvinside Cres G65 ... 37 E3
Kelvinside Dr G20 ... 96 F4
Kelvinside Gardens La 4
G20 ... 96 E4
Kelvinside Gdns G20 ... 96 E4
Kelvinside Gdns E G20 ... 96 F4
Kelvinside Terr S 3 G20 ... 96 E3
Kelvinside Terr W 2
G20 ... 96 E3
Kelvinvale G66 ... 58 D1
Kelvinview Ave FK4 ... 38 E2
Kemp Ave PA3 ... 94 A1
Kemp Ct Hamilton ML3 ... 162 E3
Saltcoats KA21 ... 205 E3
Kemp St 7 Glasgow G21 ... 97 E4
Hamilton ML3 ... 162 E3
Kemper Ave FK1 ... 42 C3
Kempock Pl PA19 ... 44 E8
Kempock St
Glasgow G40 ... 118 C4
Gourock PA19 ... 44 E8
Kempsthorn Cres G53 ... 115 B1
Kempsthorn Path G53 ... 115 B1
Kempsthorn Rd G53 ... 115 A1
Ken Rd KA1 ... 228 A5
Kenbank Cres PA11 ... 110 D8
Kenbank Rd PA11 ... 110 D8
Kendal Ave Glasgow G12 ... 96 A6
Glasgow,Giffnock G46 ... 136 C3
Kendal Dr G12 ... 96 A6
Kendal Rd G75 ... 179 F6
Kendoon Ave G15 ... 74 E3
Kenilburn Ave ML6 ... 103 B2
Kenilburn Cres ML6 ... 103 B2
Kenilworth G74 ... 160 E4
Kenilworth Ave
Glasgow G41 ... 136 D8
Helensburgh G84 ... 25 C7
Paisley PA2 ... 132 F8
Wishaw ML2 ... 165 B3
Kenilworth Cres
Bearsden G61 ... 75 C6
Bellshill ML4 ... 142 A6
Greenock PA16 ... 45 D3
Hamilton ML3 ... 161 F4
Kenilworth Ct
Bridge of A FK9 ... 2 B7
Carluke ML8 ... 187 E1
Cumbernauld G67 ... 82 E8
Motherwell ML1 ... 143 A5
Kenilworth Dr
Airdrie ML6 ... 123 D8
Laurieston FK2 ... 42 F4
Saltcoats KA21 ... 206 A2
Kenilworth Rd
Bridge of A FK9 ... 2 B7
Kirkintilloch G66 ... 79 E8
Lanark ML11 ... 215 B4
Kenilworth Way PA2 ... 112 F1
Kenmar Gdns G71 ... 140 E8
Kenmar Rd ML3 ... 162 B5
Kenmar Terr ML3 ... 162 B5
Kenmore KA10 ... 229 E4
Kenmore Ave KA9 ... 236 C6
Kenmore Dr PA16 ... 45 A4
Kenmore Gdns G61 ... 76 B5
Kenmore Pl
Greenock PA16 ... 45 A4
Troon KA10 ... 229 E4
Kenmore Rd
Cumbernauld G67 ... 62 B2
Kilmacolm PA13 ... 89 C7
Kenmore St G32 ... 119 A5
Kenmore Way
Carluke ML8 ... 187 F3
Coatbridge ML5 ... 122 C3
Kenmuir Ave G32 ... 119 E3
Kenmuir Rd
Glasgow,Carmyle G32 ... 139 D8
Glasgow,Mount Vernon
G32 ... 119 E2
Kenmuir St
Coatbridge ML5 ... 121 C4
Falkirk FK1 ... 41 A5
Kenmuiraid Pl ML4 ... 141 F3
Kenmuirhill Gate G32 ... 119 D2
Kenmuirhill Gdns G32 ... 119 D2
Kenmuirhill Rd G32 ... 119 D2
Kenmure Ave G64 ... 77 F1
Kenmure Cres G64 ... 77 F1
Kenmure Dr G64 ... 77 F1
Kenmure Gdns G64 ... 77 E1
Kenmure La G64 ... 77 F1
Kenmure Pl FK5 ... 23 F4
Kenmure Rd G46 ... 157 B6
Kenmure St G41 ... 116 F3
Kenmure View PA9 ... 130 E5
Kenmure Way G73 ... 138 B3
Kennard St FK2 ... 42 C6
Kennedar Dr G51 ... 115 E8
Kennedy Ave G65 ... 60 A3
Kennedy Ct
Alexandria G83 ... 27 C7
Glasgow G46 ... 136 C4
Kilmarnock KA3 ... 223 C3
Kennedy Dr Airdrie ML6 ... 122 E7
Helensburgh G84 ... 16 D4
Kilmarnock KA3 ... 223 C4
Kennedy Gdns ML2 ... 186 B7
Kennedy Path G4 ... 241 B3
Kennedy Rd
Saltcoats KA21 ... 205 F1
Troon KA10 ... 229 B2
Kennedy St Glasgow G4 ... 241 B3
Kilmarnock KA1 ... 227 F6
Wishaw ML2 ... 165 C3
Kennedy Way FK2 ... 14 E3
Kennedy's La PA15 ... 46 B3
Kennelburn Rd ML6 ... 123 D2
Kenneth Rd ML1 ... 163 C5
Kennihill ML6 ... 103 A1
Kennihill Quadrant ML6 ... 103 A1
Kenningknowes Rd FK7 ... 6 E5
Kennishead Ave G46 ... 135 F5
Kennishead Path G46 ... 135 E5
Kennishead Pl G46 ... 135 E5
Kennishead Rd
Glasgow G43,G46 ... 136 A6
Glasgow G53,G46,G43 ... 135 D5
Kennishead Sta G46 ... 135 E5
Kennisholm Ave G46 ... 135 E5
Kennisholm Path G46 ... 135 E5
Kennisholm Pl G46 ... 135 E5
Kennoway Dr G11 ... 95 F2
Kennyhill Sch G31 ... 118 C8
Kennyhill Sq G31 ... 118 B8
Kenshaw Ave ML9 ... 199 A8
Kenshaw Pl ML9 ... 199 A8
Kensington Dr G46 ... 136 D1
Kensington Gate 1 G12 ... 96 C4
Kensington Gate La 2
G12 ... 96 C4
Kensington Rd G12 ... 96 C4
Kent Ct G84 ... 17 A3
Kent Dr Helensburgh G84 ... 17 A3
Rutherglen G73 ... 138 D5
Kent Pl G75 ... 179 F6
Kent Rd Alloa FK10 ... 9 F8
Bellshill ML4 ... 141 D6
Glasgow G3 ... 116 E8
Kent Rd *continued*
Glasgow G3 ... 240 A3
Stirling FK7 ... 7 B5
Kent St G40 ... 241 C1
Kentallen Rd G33 ... 119 E6
Kentigern Terr G64 ... 98 B8
Kentmere Cl G75 ... 180 A6
Kentmere Dr G75 ... 180 A6
Kentmere Pl G75 ... 180 A6
Keppel Dr G44 ... 137 E6
Keppoch St G21 ... 97 D3
Keppochhill Dr G21 ... 97 D3
Keppochhill Rd G22 ... 97 D3
Keppock Pl FK1 ... 41 F1
Ker Rd G62 ... 54 E3
Ker St PA15 ... 45 F6
Kerelaw Ave KA20 ... 206 E2
Kerelaw Rd KA20 ... 206 D2
Kerfield La G15 ... 74 E4
Kerfield Pl G15 ... 74 E4
Kerr Ave KA21 ... 217 A8
Kerr Cres Haggs FK4 ... 39 A3
Hamilton ML3 ... 162 C1
Kerr Dr Glasgow G40 ... 117 F5
Irvine KA12 ... 219 D2
Motherwell ML1 ... 163 C6
Kerr Gdns G71 ... 141 A8
Kerr Grieve Ct 5 ML1 ... 163 E5
Kerr Pl Denny FK6 ... 21 D2
Glasgow G40 ... 117 F5
Irvine KA12 ... 219 D2
Kerr Rd KA3 ... 223 D2
Kerr St Barrhead G78 ... 134 B2
Glasgow G40 ... 117 F5
Hamilton G72 ... 161 E8
Kirkintilloch G66 ... 79 C8
Paisley PA3 ... 113 D5
Kerrera Pl G33 ... 119 D6
Kerrera Rd G33 ... 119 D6
Kerrix Rd Monkton KA9 ... 233 D7
Symington KA9,KA1 ... 230 F1
Kerrmuir Ave KA1 ... 228 F5
Kerrs La KA21 ... 216 E8
Kerry Pl G15 ... 74 E3
Kerrycroy Ave G42 ... 137 D8
Kerrycroy Pl G42 ... 137 D8
Kerrycroy St G42 ... 137 D8
Kerrydale St G40 ... 118 B4
Kerrylamont Ave G42 ... 137 E7
Kerse Ave KA24 ... 191 E7
Kerse Gdns FK2 ... 42 E5
Kerse La FK1 ... 42 C4
Kerse Pk KA7 ... 239 B1
Kerse Pl FK1 ... 42 C5
Kerse Rd Stirling FK7 ... 7 C6
Stirling,Loanhead FK7 ... 7 E5
Kersebonny Rd FK7 ... 6 C7
Kersegreen Rd FK10 ... 10 F5
Kersehill Circ FK2 ... 42 C7
Kersehill Cres FK2 ... 42 C7
Kershaw St ML2 ... 186 C7
Kersie Rd FK7 ... 9 A3
Kersie Terr FK7 ... 9 E3
Kersland Cres KA1 ... 228 E6
Kersland Dr G62 ... 55 B2
Kersland Foot KA11 ... 219 F5
Kersland Gait KA3 ... 211 E8
Kersland La
1 Glasgow G12 ... 96 D3
Milngavie G62 ... 55 B2
Kersland Rd KA14 ... 170 C6
Kersland Sch PA2 ... 114 C1
Kersland St G12 ... 96 D3
Kerswinning Ave KA25 ... 170 A7
Kessington Dr G61 ... 76 A4
Kessington Rd G61 ... 76 B3
Kessington Sq G61 ... 76 B3
Kessock Dr G22 ... 97 B3
Kessock Pl G22 ... 97 B3
Kessog Gdns G83 ... 27 F7
Kestrel Cres PA16 ... 45 A5
Kestrel Ct G81 ... 74 A5
Kestrel Pl Greenock PA16 ... 45 A5
Johnstone PA5 ... 131 D7
Kestrel Rd G13 ... 95 C6
Kestrel View
Bellshill ML4 ... 141 E8
Motherwell ML4 ... 121 E1
Keswick Dr ML3 ... 183 C6
Keswick Rd G75 ... 179 F6
Kethers La ML1 ... 163 C7
Kethers St ML1 ... 163 C6
Keverkae FK10 ... 9 F6
Kevoc Cotts KA6 ... 237 A5
Kew Gdns G71 ... 141 B7
Kew La G12 ... 96 D3
Kew Terr G12 ... 96 D3
Keynes Sq ML4 ... 142 D4
Keystone Ave G62 ... 76 B8
Keystone Quadrant G62 ... 76 A8
Keystone Rd G62 ... 76 B8
Kibble Education & Care Ctr
PA3 ... 113 D7
Kibbleston Rd PA10 ... 130 F7
Kidsneuk KA12 ... 219 A6
Kidsneuk Gdns KA12 ... 219 A6
Kidston Dr G84 ... 16 A2
Kidston Pl 5 G5 ... 117 C4
Kidston Terr 4 G5 ... 117 C4
Kier Ct FK9 ... 2 B7
Kier Hardie Ct KA15 ... 171 A8
Kierhill Rd G68 ... 61 C2
Kilallan Ave PA11 ... 90 D1
Kilallan Rd PA6 ... 90 C6
Kilbarchan Intc PA10 ... 111 C2
Kilbarchan Prim Sch
PA10 ... 111 A4
Kilbarchan Rd
Bridge of W PA11 ... 110 F6
Johnstone PA10 ... 111 C2
Johnstone PA5 ... 111 D2
Kilbarchan St 2 G5 ... 117 B5
Kilbean Dr FK1 ... 41 E2
Kilbeg Terr G46 ... 135 D3
Kilberry St G21 ... 98 A1
Kilbirnie Pl G5 ... 117 A4
Kilbirnie St G5 ... 117 A4
Kilbirnie Terr FK6 ... 21 D3
Kilblain Ct 12 PA15 ... 45 F5
Kilblain St 11 PA15 ... 45 F5
Kilbowie Pl ML6 ... 123 D6
Kilbowie Prim Sch G81 ... 74 B3
Kilbowie Rd
Clydebank G81 ... 74 B3
Clydebank,Hardgate G81 ... 74 B5
Cumbernauld G67 ... 62 A1
Kilbowie Ret Pk G81 ... 74 C2
Kilbrandon Cres KA7 ... 238 B2
Kilbrandon Way KA7 ... 238 B2
Kilbrannan Ave KA21 ... 205 F2
Kilbrannan Dr PA16 ... 45 B3
Kilbreck Gdns G61 ... 75 C8
Kilbreck La ML1 ... 143 C3
Kilbrennan Dr Falkirk FK1 ... 41 B4
Motherwell ML1 ... 163 B7
Kilbrennan Rd PA3 ... 112 B6
Kilbride Dr G84 ... 16 E3
Kilbride Rd KA3 ... 195 D1
Kilbride St G5 ... 117 D2
Kilbride View G71 ... 141 A7
Kilburn Gr G72 ... 140 D1
Kilburn Pl G13 ... 95 B6
Kilchattan Dr G44 ... 137 C7
Kilchoan Rd G33 ... 99 C2
Kilcloy Ave G15 ... 75 A4
Kilcreggan View PA15 ... 46 C2
Kildale Rd PA12 ... 129 B2
Kildale Way G73 ... 137 F8
Kildare Dr ML11 ... 215 B4
Kildare Pl ML11 ... 215 B4
Kildare Rd ML11 ... 215 B4
Kildary Ave G44 ... 137 A5
Kildary Rd G44 ... 137 A5
Kildean Hospl FK8 ... 1 F2
Kildean Sch FK8 ... 1 F2
Kildermorie Path G34 ... 120 A8
Kildermorie Rd G34 ... 120 A8
Kildonan Ct ML2 ... 165 F7
Kildonan Dr Glasgow G11 ... 96 A2
Helensburgh G84 ... 16 F2
Kildonan Ho KA9 ... 236 B5
Kildonan Pl
Motherwell ML1 ... 163 C7
Saltcoats KA21 ... 205 F2
Kildonan St ML5 ... 122 B7
Kildrostan St G41 ... 116 F2
Kildrum Prim Sch G67 ... 62 B2
Kildrum Rd G67 ... 62 C3
Kildrum South Rdbt G67 ... 62 B1
Kildrummy Ave FK5 ... 23 F4
Kildrummy Dr G69 ... 100 F4
Kildrummy Pl G74 ... 159 D3
Kilearn Rd PA3 ... 114 B7
Kilearn Sq PA3 ... 114 B7
Kilearn Way PA3 ... 114 B7
Kilfinan Rd ML7 ... 146 D6
Kilfinan St G22 ... 97 B7
Kilgarth St ML5 ... 121 C4
Kilgraston Rd PA11 ... 110 D6
Kilkerran KA13 ... 207 C3
Kilkerran Ct G77 ... 156 B4
Kilkerran Dr Glasgow G33 ... 98 F6
Troon KA10 ... 229 E7
Kilkerran Pk G77 ... 156 B4
Kilkerran Way G77 ... 156 B4
Killearn Dr PA1 ... 114 F4
Killearn Rd PA15 ... 46 B2
Killearn St
Glasgow G21,G22 ... 97 D4
Glasgow G22 ... 97 C4
Killermont Ave G61 ... 76 A2
Killermont Ct G61 ... 76 B3
Killermont Mdws G71 ... 140 E2
Killermont Pl KA13 ... 207 B3
Killermont Prim Sch G61 ... 76 A4
Killermont Rd G61 ... 76 A2
Killermont St G1 ... 241 A3
Killermont View G20 ... 76 B2
Killiegrew Rd G41 ... 116 D2
Killin Ct ML5 ... 122 B3
Killin Dr PA3 ... 111 F5
Killin Pl Greenock PA16 ... 45 A4
Troon KA10 ... 229 F4
Killin St G32 ... 119 B4
Killoch Ave PA3 ... 113 A5
Killoch Dr Barrhead G78 ... 134 D1
Glasgow G13 ... 95 A6
Killoch La PA3 ... 113 A5
Killoch Pl Ayr KA7 ... 238 F7
Irvine KA11 ... 219 F4
Killoch Rd PA3 ... 113 A5
Killoch Way Irvine KA11 ... 219 F4
Paisley PA3 ... 113 A5
Killochend Dr PA15 ... 45 E3
Kilmacolm Pl PA15 ... 46 C2
Kilmacolm Prim Sch
PA13 ... 89 C7
Kilmacolm Rd
Bridge Of W PA11 ... 90 B2
Greenock PA15 ... 46 B2
Houston PA6 ... 91 B3
Port Glasgow PA14 ... 69 A6

Kilmahew Ave G82 ....26 B1
Kilmahew Ct
Ardrossan KA22 ....205 C1
Cardross G82 ....26 A1
Kilmahew Dr G82 ....26 A1
Kilmahew Gr G82 ....26 B1
Kilmahew St KA22 ......205 C2
Kilmailing Rd G44 ......137 B6
Kilmair Pl G20 ....96 D5
Kilmaluag Terr G46 .....135 D3
Kilmannan Gdns G62 .....54 E3
Kilmany Dr G32 ....118 F5
Kilmany Gdns G32 ....118 F5
Kilmardinny Ave G61 .....75 F6
Kilmardinny Cres G61 ....76 A6
Kilmardinny Dr G61 ......75 F6
Kilmardinny Gate G61 ....75 F5
Kilmardinny Gr G61 ......75 F6
Kilmari Gdns G15 ....74 E4
Kilmarnock Acad KA1 ...228 A8
Kilmarnock Coll KA3 ....228 A8
Kilmarnock Coll (Irvine
Campus) KA12 ....219 C3
Kilmarnock Coll of Sporting
Excellence KA3 ....223 A2
Kilmarnock Rd
Crosshouse KA2 ....221 F1
Dundonald KA2 ....225 F2
Glasgow G43 ....136 D7
Kilmaurs KA3 ....222 C6
Monkton KA9 ....233 E6
Prestwick KA1,KA9 ....234 A8
Springside KA11 ....221 A2
Symington KA1 ....231 D3
Troon KA10 ....229 F6
Kilmarnock Sta KA1 .....222 F1
Kilmartin La ML8 ....187 F3
Kilmartin Pl Airdrie ML6 .123 D6
Glasgow G46 ....135 E4
Motherwell G71 ....121 A1
Kilmaurs Dr G46 ....136 E3
Kilmaurs Prim Sch KA3 .222 B7
Kilmaurs Rd
Crosshouse KA2 ....221 E2
Fenwick KA3 ....213 A2
Fenwick KA3 ....212 F2
Kilmarnock KA3 ....222 E4
Knockentiber KA2 ....221 F3
Kilmaurs St G51 ....115 F6
Kilmaurs Sta KA3 ....222 B7
Kilmeny Cres ML2 ....165 C5
Kilmeny Ct KA22 ....205 D1
Kilmeny Terr KA22 ......205 D1
Kilmichael Ave ML2 .....166 A6
Kilmore Cres G15 ....74 E4
Kilmore Gr ML5 ....121 F4
Kilmorie Dr G73 ....137 F7
Kilmory Ave G71 ....141 A7
Kilmory Ct
East Kilbride G75 ....180 C4
Falkirk FK1 ....41 C4
Kilmory Dr G77 ....156 E6
Kilmory Gdns ML8 ....188 A3
Kilmory Pl
Kilmarnock KA3 ....222 E4
Troon KA10 ....229 G5
Kilmory Rd Carluke ML8 ..202 B8
Saltcoats KA21 ....205 F2
Kilmory Terr PA14 ....47 D1
Kilmory Wlk KA3 ....195 D1
Kilmuir Cres G46 ....135 D4
Kilmuir Dr G46 ....135 E3
Kilmuir Rd Glasgow G46 ..135 E3
Uddingston G71 ....120 F1
Kilmun Rd PA15 ....46 A3
Kilmun St G20 ....96 D7
Kiln Ct KA12 ....219 C2
Kiln Wlk KA12 ....219 C2
Kilnbank Cres KA7 ......239 D7
Kilnburn Rd ML1 ....163 C7
Kilncadzow Rd ML8 .....202 E8
Kilncraigs Ct FK10 ....10 C5
Kilncraigs Rd FK10 ......10 C6
Kilncroft La PA2 ....113 E2
Kilnford Cres KA2 ......225 D2
Kilnford Dr KA2 ....225 E2
Kilnknowe Cotts PA9 ....131 A6
Kilns Pl FK2 ....41 F6
Kilns Rd FK1 ....42 A5
Kilnside Rd PA1 ....114 A4
Kilnwell Quadrant ML1 .163 D7
Kiloran Gr G77 ....156 A4
Kiloran Pl G77 ....156 A4
Kiloran St G46 ....135 F4
Kilpatrick Ave PA2 ......113 B2
Kilpatrick Cres PA2 .....133 D8
Kilpatrick Ct Irvine KA11 .220 A3
Old Kilpatrick G60 ....73 A6
Kilpatrick Dr
Bearsden G61 ....75 C8
East Kilbride G75 ....180 B3
Erskine PA8 ....73 B2
Paisley PA4 ....114 B8
Stepps G33 ....99 F5
Kilpatrick Gdns G76 ....157 C8
Kilpatrick Pl KA11 ......220 A2
Kilpatrick Sta G60 ....73 B6
Kilpatrick View G82 .....50 B4
Kilpatrick Way 9 G71 ...141 A8
Kilrig Ave KA13 ....207 E4
Kilruskin Dr KA23 ......190 D4
Kilsyth Acad G65 ....36 C1
Kilsyth Cres KA11 ......220 A3
Kilsyth Gdns G75 ....180 A3
Kilsyth Prim Sch G65 ....60 D8
Kilsyth Rd Banknock FK4 ...38 D3
Kirkintilloch G66 ....58 E1
Queenzieburn G65,G66 .....59 E7
Kilsyth Wlk KA11 ....220 A3
Kiltarie Cres ML6 ....123 F6
Kiltearn Rd G33 ....119 F7
Kiltongue Cotts ML6 ....122 D8
Kilvaxter Dr G46 ....135 E3
Kilwinning Abbey*
KA13 ....207 E3
Kilwinning Acad KA13 ...207 E4
Kilwinning Cres
Airdrie ML6 ....103 E1
Hamilton ML3 ....161 E1
Kilwinning Rd
Dalry KA24 ....191 B6
Irvine KA12 ....219 B5
Stevenston KA20 ....206 F1
Stewarton KA3 ....211 C8
Kilwinning Sta KA13 ....207 D4
Kilwynet Way PA3 ....114 A7
Kimberley Gdns G75 ....180 C8
Kimberley St
Clydebank G81 ....73 E5
Wishaw ML2 ....164 D3
Kinalty Rd G44 ....137 A5
Kinarvie Cres G53 ......134 F7
Kinarvie Gdns G53 ......134 F7
Kinarvie Pl G53 ....134 F7
Kinarvie Rd G53 ....134 F7
Kinarvie Terr G53 ......134 F7
Kinbuck St G22 ....97 D4
Kincaid Dr G66 ....33 C1
Kincaid Field G66 ....58 C5
Kincaid Gdns G72 ......139 A6
Kincaid St PA16 ....45 B8
Kincaid Way G66 ....58 B5
Kincaidston Dr KA7 .....239 C3
Kincaidston Prim Sch
KA7 ....239 B3
Kincardine Dr G64 ......98 C8
Kincardine Pl
Bishopbriggs G64 ....98 C7
East Kilbride G74 ....160 C3
Kincardine Rd FK2 ....24 C3
Kincardine Sq G33 ......99 D1
Kincath Ave G73 ....138 D3
Kinclaven Ave G15 ....75 B3
Kinclaven Gdns 2 G15 ...75 B3
Kinclaven Pl 1 G15 ......75 B3
Kincraig St G51 ....115 D6
Kinellan Rd G61 ....75 F1
Kinellar Dr G14 ....95 A6
Kinfauns Dr
Clydebank G15 ....75 B3
Newton Mearns G77 .....156 F5
King Ct ML1 ....163 D7
King Edward La 1 G13 ...95 F5
King Edward Rd G13 .....95 F5
King Edward St G83 .....27 E6
King George Ct PA4 ......94 E1
King George Gdns PA4 ...94 E2
King George Park Ave
PA4 ....94 E2
King George Pl PA4 .....94 E1
King George Way PA4 ....94 E1
King James Dr FK10 ....4 C2
King O' Muirs FK10 ....4 F4
King O' Muirs Ave FK10 ....4 E4
King O' Muirs Rd FK10 .....4 E4
King O'Muirs Dr FK10 ......4 D4
King Pl G69 ....121 A5
King Robert Ct FK8 ....1 E1
King St Ayr KA8 ....235 F1
Ayr KA8 ....236 A1
Clydebank G81 ....94 D8
Coatbridge ML5 ....121 E6
Falkirk FK2 ....42 C6
Fallin FK7 ....8 C4
Glasgow G1 ....241 A1
Gourock PA19 ....44 E7
Greenock PA15 ....45 F5
Hamilton ML3 ....162 A4
Kilmarnock KA1 ....227 F8
4 Kilsyth G65 ....60 D8
Kilwinning KA13 ....207 E4
Larkhall ML9 ....185 A3
Paisley PA1 ....113 C5
Port Glasgow PA14 ....47 C2
Renton G82 ....27 D1
Rutherglen G73 ....138 A8
Shotts ML7 ....146 E4
Stenhousemuir FK5 ....23 D2
Stenhousemuir FK5 ....23 E3
Stenhousemuir FK5 ....23 F3
Stirling FK8 ....7 B7
Stonehouse ML9 ....198 E2
Wishaw ML2 ....165 B2
Wishaw,Newmains ML2 ...166 A6
King St E G84 ....16 E1
King Street La
3 Kilsyth G65 ....60 D8
5 Rutherglen G73 ....138 A8
King's Cres
Cambuslang G72 ....139 B5
Carluke ML8 ....188 A2
Helensburgh G84 ....16 E1
King's Ct KA15 ....150 B1
King's Dr Cumbernauld G68 .61 F6
Glasgow G40 ....117 E4
Newton Mearns G77 .....157 A3
King's Gdns G77 ....157 A3
King's Glen Prim Sch
PA15 ....46 D2
King's Inch Rd PA4,G51 ...94 F4
King's Knot* FK8 ....6 F8
King's Park Ave G44 ....137 D6
King's Park Prim Sch
G44 ....137 D6
King's Park Rd
Glasgow G44 ....137 B7
Stirling FK8 ....7 A7
King's Park Sec Sch
G44 ....137 C5
King's Park Sta G44 ....137 C6
King's Pl G22 ....97 B6
King's Rd Beith KA15 ....150 B1
Elderslie PA5 ....112 B2
King's View G68 ....61 F6
King's Way G82 ....49 C5
Kingarth La G42 ....117 A2
Kingarth St Glasgow G42 .117 A2
Hamilton ML3 ....183 D8
Kingcase Ave KA9 ......236 B6
Kingcase Prim Sch KA9 .236 B6
Kingfisher Dr G13 ....94 F7
Kingfisher Gdns G13 ....95 A7
Kinghorn Dr G44 ....137 C7
Kinghorn La G44 ....137 C7
Kinglas Ho G82 ....50 B7
Kinglas Rd G61 ....75 C2
Kings Ave G72 ....139 B5
Kings Cres
Cambuslang G72 ....139 B5
Elderslie PA5 ....112 D3
Kings Ct Alloa FK10 ......10 A7
Ayr KA8 ....236 A1
7 Falkirk FK1 ....42 B4
Stenhousemuir FK5 ....23 D2
Kings Dr ML1 ....142 F3
Kings Inch Dr G51 ....95 B2
Kings Inch Pl G51 ....95 A2
Kings Myre ML11 ....215 C4
Kings Pk G64 ....57 C1
Kings View G73 ....137 F7
Kingsacre Rd G44 ......137 D7
Kingsbarns Dr G44 .....137 B7
Kingsborough Gate 1
G12 ....96 B3
Kingsborough Gdns G12 .96 B4
Kingsborough La G12 ....96 B3
Kingsborough La E G12 ..96 B3
Kingsbrae Ave G44 .....137 C7
Kingsbridge Cres G44 ..137 D6
Kingsbridge Dr G44 ....137 E6
Kingsbridge Park Gdns
G44 ....137 D6
Kingsburgh Dr PA1 .....114 B6
Kingsburn Dr G73 ......138 A6
Kingsburn Gr G73 ......138 A6
Kingscliffe Ave G44 ....137 D6
Kingscourt Ave G44 ....137 D6
Kingscroft Rd KA9 .....236 B7
Kingsdale Ave G44 .....137 C7
Kingsdyke Ave G44 .....137 D7
Kingseat Pl FK1 ....41 F3
Kingsford Ave G44 .....136 E4
Kingsford Ct G77 ......156 C6
Kingsford Pl KA3 ....223 B5
Kingsgate Ret Pk G74 ..160 A6
Kingsheath Ave G73 ....137 F6
Kingshill Ave G68 ....60 E1
Kingshill Dr G44 ....137 C6
Kingshill Rd ML7 ....167 A8
Kingshill View ML8 .....187 A4
Kingshouse Ave G44 ...137 C6
Kingshurst Ave G44 ....137 C6
Kingsknowe Dr G73 .....137 E6
Kingsland Cres G52 ....115 B6
Kingsland Dr G52 ......115 C6
Kingsland La G52 ......115 C6
Kingslea Rd PA6 ....91 B2
Kingsley Ave
Glasgow G42 ....117 B1
Stenhousemuir FK5 ....23 F3
Kingsley Ct G71 ....141 A7
Kingslynn Dr G44 ....137 D6
Kingsmuir Dr
Cumbernauld G68 ....60 F2
Rutherglen G73 ....137 E6
Kingstables La 3 FK8 ......7 A8
Kingston Ave
1 Airdrie ML6 ....123 C7
Neilston G78 ....154 D6
Uddingston G71 ....141 A8
Kingston Flats G65 ......36 D1
Kingston Gr PA7 ....72 B3
Kingston Ind Est G5 ....116 F5
Kingston Pl G81 ....73 D4
Kingston Rd
Bishopton PA7 ....72 B3
Kilsyth G65 ....36 D1
Neilston G78 ....154 D5
Kingston St G5 ....240 C1
Kingsway Dalry KA24 ....191 A8
East Kilbride G74 ....160 A3
Glasgow G14 ....95 B5
Gourock PA19 ....44 D6
Kilsyth G65 ....36 D1
Kirkintilloch G66 ....59 B2
Kingsway Ct G14 ....95 A5
Kingswell Ave KA3 .....223 A5
Kingswell Pk FK10 ....10 C7
Kingswood Dr G44 .....137 C7
Kingswood Rd PA7 ....71 F4
Kingussie Ave KA3 ......195 C1
Kingussie Dr G44 ......137 C6
Kiniver Dr G15 ....75 B1
Kinkell Gdns G66 ....59 B1
Kinloch Ave
Cambuslang G72 ....139 B4
Linwood PA3 ....112 A5
Stewarton KA3 ....195 C1
Kinloch Dr ML1 ....142 D2
Kinloch La PA16 ....44 E3
Kinloch Rd
Kilmarnock KA1 ....228 A5
Newton Mearns G77 .....156 D6
Renfrew PA4 ....94 B1
Kinloch St G40 ....118 C4
Kinloch Terr PA16 ....44 E3
Kinloss Pl G74 ....159 F2
Kinmount Ave G44 ......137 B7
Kinmount La G44 ....137 C7
Kinnaird Ave Falkirk FK2 ..24 B3
Newton Mearns G77 .....157 A5
Kinnaird Cres G61 ....76 B4
Kinnaird Dr Linwood PA3 .112 B6
Stenhousemuir FK5 ....23 E3
Kinnaird Pl G64 ....98 B7
Kinnear Rd G40 ....118 B4
Kinneil Ho ML3 ....162 E5
Kinneil Pl ML3 ....161 F2
Kinnell Ave G52 ....115 D3
Kinnell Cres G52 ....115 C3
Kinnell Path G52 ....115 C3
Kinnell Pl G52 ....115 D3
Kinnell Sq G52 ....115 C3
Kinnier Rd KA21 ....217 A8
Kinning Park Ind Est
G5 ....116 F5
Kinning Park Underground
Sta G41 ....116 D5
Kinning St G5 ....117 A5
Kinnis Vennel KA13 .....207 C4
Kinnoul Gdns G61 ....75 D8
Kinnoull Pl G72 ....161 D7
Kinnoull Rd KA1 ....228 A3
Kinpurnie Rd PA1 ....114 D5
Kinross Ave
Glasgow G52 ....115 B4
Port Glasgow PA14 ....47 C1
Kinross Pk G74 ....160 D3
Kinsail Dr G52 ....114 F6
Kinstone Ave G14 ....95 A5
Kintail Gdns G66 ....59 B1
Kintessack Pl G64 ....78 D2
Kintillo Dr G13 ....95 B5
Kintore Pk ML3 ....183 B7
Kintore Rd G43 ....136 F6
Kintore Twr G72 ....138 E3
Kintra St G51 ....116 B7
Kintyre Ave PA3 ....112 A4
Kintyre Cres
Coatbridge ML5 ....121 E4
Newton Mearns G77 .....156 C6
Plains ML6 ....104 A3
Kintyre Dr ML5 ....121 E4
Kintyre Gdns G66 ....59 B1
Kintyre Pl FK1 ....41 C4
Kintyre Rd G72 ....161 C8
Kintyre St G21 ....98 A1
Kintyre Terr PA16 ....44 D3
Kintyre Wynd ML8 ......187 F3
Kipland Wlk ML5 ....122 D5
Kippen Dr G76 ....158 B5
Kippen St Airdrie ML6 ...122 E7
Glasgow G22 ....97 D6
Kipperoch Rd G82 ....49 B7
Kippford Pl ML6 ....123 F1
Kippford St G32 ....119 C4
Kipps Ave ML6 ....122 E8
Kippsbyre Ct ML6 ......122 D7
Kirk Ave FK5 ....23 E2
Kirk Cl KA24 ....191 C7
Kirk Cres G60 ....73 A7
Kirk Ct ML9 ....198 F2
Kirk Glebe Neilston G78 ..154 E7
Stewarton KA3 ....211 D8
Kirk La 2 Bearsden G61 ...75 E5
Glasgow G43 ....136 C7
Kirk Mews Alexandria G83 .27 F4
Cambuslang G72 ....139 A5
Kirk O'shotts Prim Sch
ML7 ....125 D3
Kirk Path ML7 ....167 A8
Kirk Pl Bearsden G61 .....75 E5
Cumbernauld G67 ....82 A7
Uddingston G71 ....140 E5
Kirk Port KA7 ....238 F8
Kirk Rd Bearsden G61 .....75 E5
Beith KA15 ....171 B8
Carluke ML8 ....187 E2
Carmunnock G76 ....158 D7
Dalserf ML9 ....186 B2
Houston PA6 ....91 C2
Motherwell ML1 ....143 D7
Shotts ML7 ....146 F4
Wishaw ML2 ....165 C3
Kirk St Carluke ML8 .....187 E2
Coatbridge ML5 ....121 F6
Milngavie G62 ....54 E2
Motherwell ML1 ....163 E7
Prestwick KA9 ....233 C1
Stonehouse ML9 ....198 F2
Kirk Vennel KA12 ....219 C2
Kirk View KA15 ....150 B1
Kirk Wynd
Eaglesham G76 ....178 E4
2 Falkirk FK1 ....42 B4
Stirling FK7 ....7 B4
Kirkaig Ave PA4 ....94 F2
Kirkandrews Pl ML6 .....123 F2
Kirkbean Ave G73 ....138 B4
Kirkbrae FK10 ....10 F4
Kirkbride Terr FK7 ....12 C3
Kirkburn FK1 ....86 B7
Kirkburn Ave G72 ....139 A4
Kirkburn Dr G63 ....31 C3
Kirkburn Rd G63 ....31 C3
Kirkcaldy Rd G41 ......116 D2
Kirkconnel Ave
Cumbernauld G68 ....60 F1
Kirkconnel Ave *continued*
Glasgow G13 ....94 F6
Kirkconnel Dr G73 ......137 F5
Kirkcudbright Pl G74 ...160 D3
Kirkdale Dr G52 ....115 E4
Kirkdene Ave G77 ......157 B5
Kirkdene Bank G77 .....157 B5
Kirkdene Cres G77 .....157 B5
Kirkdene Gr G77 ....157 B4
Kirkdene Pl G77 ....157 B5
Kirkfield Rd
Bothwell G71 ....141 A3
Kirkfieldbank ML11 ....214 D3
Kirkfield Wynd PA9 .....130 E5
Kirkfieldbank Brae
ML11 ....214 E4
Kirkfieldbank Prim Sch
ML11 ....214 D4
Kirkfieldbank Way ML3 .162 A3
Kirkford KA3 ....211 E7
Kirkford Rd G69 ....80 E2
Kirkgate Alloa FK10 ......10 B6
Irvine KA12 ....219 C2
Saltcoats KA21 ....216 F7
Wishaw ML2 ....165 F4
Kirkhall Gdns KA22 .....205 D2
Kirkhall Pl FK6 ....21 E2
Kirkhall Rd ML1 ....143 D4
Kirkhill Irvine KA11 .....220 C6
Kilwinning KA13 ....207 C2
Kirkhill Ave G72 ....139 A3
Kirkhill Cres
Neilston G78 ....154 E8
Prestwick KA9 ....236 B6
Kirkhill Dr G20 ....96 D5
Kirkhill Gate G77 ....157 B4
Kirkhill Gdns G72 ......139 A3
Kirkhill Gr G72 ....139 A3
Kirkhill Pl 7 Glasgow G20 .96 D5
Wishaw ML2 ....164 C2
Kirkhill Prim Sch G77 ..157 B6
Kirkhill Rd Gartcosh G69 .100 F5
Newton Mearns G77 .....157 B5
Uddingston G71 ....140 E8
Wishaw ML2 ....164 C1
Kirkhill St ML2 ....164 D1
Kirkhill Sta G72 ....139 A5
Kirkhill Terr G72 ....139 A3
Kirkholm Ave KA8 ......236 A4
Kirkhope Dr G15 ....75 B1
Kirkhouse G63 ....31 C4
Kirkhouse Cres G63 ......31 C4
Kirkhouse Rd G63 ....31 C4
Kirkinner Pl PA11 ....110 D8
Kirkinner Rd G32 ....119 D3
Kirkintilloch High Sch
G66 ....80 A7
Kirkintilloch Ind Est G66 .58 C2
Kirkintilloch Rd
Bishopbriggs G64 ....78 C5
Kirkintilloch G66 ....58 A2
Kirkintilloch,Waterside G66 .80 C8
Lenzie G66 ....79 C5
Kirkland Ave
Kilmarnock KA3 ....222 E3
Strathblane G63 ....31 C4
Kirkland Cres KA24 .....191 A7
Kirkland Dr FK6 ....21 B2
Kirkland Gdns KA3 .....222 C6
Kirkland Gr PA5 ....111 F3
Kirkland La G83 ....27 F3
Kirkland Rd Dunlop KA3 .195 B8
Glengarnock KA14,KA25 ...170 B7
Kirkland St Glasgow G20 ..96 F3
Motherwell ML1 ....163 D7
Kirkland Terr KA11 .....220 F2
Kirklandholm KA9 ......236 C6
Kirklandneuk Cres PA4 ...94 A4
Kirklandneuk Prim Sch
PA4 ....94 B3
Kirklandneuk Rd PA4 ....94 B4
Kirklands PA4 ....94 B3
Kirklands Cres
Bothwell G71 ....141 A3
Kilsyth G65 ....60 D7
Kirklands Dr G77 ....156 D2
Kirklands Hospl G71 ....141 B3
Kirklands Pl G77 ....156 D2
Kirklands Rd
Lanark ML11 ....215 B3
Newton Mearns G77 .....156 D2
Kirklandside Hospl KA1 .228 C5
Kirkle Dr G77 ....157 B5
Kirklea Gdns PA3 ....113 A5
Kirklee Cir G12 ....96 D4
Kirklee Gardens La G12 ..96 D4
Kirklee Gate G12 ....96 D5
Kirklee Gdns G12 ....96 C5
Kirklee Pl G12 ....96 D4
Kirklee Quadrant 1 G12 .96 D4
Kirklee Quadrant La G12 .96 D4
Kirklee Rd Glasgow G12 ..96 D4
Motherwell ML1,ML4 .....142 E3
Kirklee Terr G12 ....96 C4
Kirklee Terrace La G12 ..96 D4
Kirklee Terrace Rd 21
G12 ....96 C4
Kirkliston St G32 ....118 F6
Kirkmichael Ave 3 G11 ..96 A3
Kirkmichael Gdns 2
G11 ....96 A3
Kirkmichael Rd G84 .....16 F1
Kirkmuir Dr
Rutherglen G73 ....138 B3
Stewarton KA3 ....195 C1
Kirkness St ML6 ....123 A8
Kirknethan ML2 ....164 C1
Kirknewton St G32 .....119 B6

Lochinver Cres
Hamilton G72 .161 C3
Paisley PA2 .113 A2
Lochinver Dr G44 .137 A5
Lochinver Gr G72 .139 B5
Lochknowe St ML8 .201 F5
Lochlands Ave FK1 .41 B8
Lochlands Bsns Pk FK5 .41 B8
Lochlands Ind Est FK5 .41 A8
Lochlands Loan FK1 .41 B7
Lochlea G74 .160 D4
Lochlea Ave
Clydebank G81 .74 C3
Troon KA10 .229 G4
Lochlea Dr KA7 .239 B6
Lochlea Rd
Clarkston G76 .157 E5
Cumbernauld G67 .62 C3
Glasgow G43 .136 D6
Rutherglen G73 .137 F5
Saltcoats KA21 .206 A3
Lochlea Way ML1 .143 E4
Lochlee Loan 4 ML9 .185 C2
Lochleven La G42 .137 A7
Lochleven Rd G42 .137 A7
Lochlibo Ave G13 .94 F7
Lochlibo Cres G78 .134 A1
Lochlibo Ct KA11 .220 A6
Lochlibo Rd
Barrhead G78 .134 A1
Burnhouse KA15 .172 E3
Burnhouse,Auchentiber KA13 .193 E3
Irvine KA11 .220 A6
Lugton KA15,KA3 .173 C7
Neilston G78 .154 C7
Torranyard KA11,KA13 .209 D4
Uplawmoor G78 .153 C5
Lochlibo Terr G78 .134 A1
Lochlie Pl KA20 .206 E1
Lochlip Rd PA12 .129 D2
Lochmaben Dr FK5 .23 F4
Lochmaben Rd
Gartcosh G69 .100 F4
5 Glasgow G52 .115 A4
Lochmaben Wynd KA3 .223 B6
Lochmaddy Ave G44 .137 A4
Lochmill Holdings G66 .59 A5
Lochnagar Dr G61 .75 B7
Lochnagar Rd KA1 .228 A4
Lochnagar Way 20 ML9 .185 C1
Lochore Ave PA3 .114 A7
Lochpark KA7 .238 C3
Lochpark Pl Denny FK6 .21 E2
Larkhall ML9 .185 A1
Lochranza Ct
Kilmarnock KA3 .223 B6
2 Motherwell ML1 .143 B2
Lochranza Dr
East Kilbride G75 .180 B4
Helensburgh G84 .16 F2
Lochranza La G75 .180 C4
Lochranza Pl KA21 .206 A2
Lochridge Pl FK6 .21 D1
Lochshore East Ind Est KA14 .170 D7
Lochshore Ind Est KA25 .170 B7
Lochside Bearsden G61 .75 F3
Gartcosh G69 .100 F6
Lochside Ct Ayr KA8 .236 A1
Dundonald KA2 .225 F1
Lochside Rd Ayr KA8 .236 B2
Ayr KA8 .236 C3
Slamannan FK1 .86 C1
Lochside St 2 G41 .116 E1
Lochview Ave PA19 .45 A7
Lochview Cres G33 .98 F3
Lochview Dr G33 .98 F4
Lochview Gdns G33 .98 F3
Lochview Pl G33 .98 F3
Lochview Quadrant ML4 .141 F3
Lochview Rd
Bearsden G61 .75 E3
Beith KA15 .170 F7
Coatbridge ML5 .101 C1
Port Glasgow PA14 .47 B1
Lochview Terr G69 .100 F5
Lochwinnoch Community Mus* PA12 .129 C2
Lochwinnoch Prim Sch PA12 .129 C3
Lochwinnoch Rd PA13 .89 C7
Lochwinnoch RSPB Nature Reserve* PA12 .129 E1
Lochwinnoch Sta PA12 .150 E8
Lochwood Cl KA13 .207 C5
Lochwood Loan G69 .81 A3
Lochwood Pl KA11 .219 F6
Lochwood St G33 .98 E2
Lochy Ave PA4 .94 F1
Lochy Gdns G64 .78 B1
Lochy Pl PA8 .72 F1
Lochy St ML2 .165 A1
Lock Sixteen FK1 .41 D5
Locke Gr ML1 .143 F1
Lockerbie Ave G43 .136 F6
Locket Yett View ML4 .141 E5
Lockhart Ave G72 .139 D6
Lockhart Ct G77 .156 D2
Lockhart Dr
Cambuslang G72 .139 D6
Lanark ML11 .214 E5
Newton Mearns G77 .156 D2
Lockhart Hospl ML11 .215 C3
Lockhart Pl
Stonehouse ML9 .198 F3
Wishaw ML2 .165 E4
Lockhart St Carluke ML8 .187 F2
Glasgow G21 .98 B2
Hamilton ML3 .183 C6
Stonehouse ML9 .199 A3
Lockhart Terr G74 .160 B2
Locks St ML5 .122 D6
Locksley Ave
Cumbernauld G67 .82 E7
Glasgow G13 .95 C8
Locksley Cres G67 .82 E6
Locksley Ct G67 .82 E6
Locksley Pl G67 .82 E6
Locksley Rd
Cumbernauld G67 .82 E6
Paisley PA2 .112 F1
Locksley Way PA2 .112 F1
Lodge Cres PA13 .89 E8
Lodge Dr FK5 .23 F2
Lodge Gdns PA13 .69 E1
Lodge Gr PA13 .69 E1
Lodge Pk PA13 .69 E1
Lodge Twr ML1 .164 B3
Logan Ave G77 .156 C6
Logan Ct KA10 .229 E3
Logan Dr
Cumbernauld G68 .61 D3
Paisley PA3 .113 C6
Troon KA10 .229 E4
Logan Gdns ML1 .165 B8
Logan St Glasgow G5 .117 D3
Hamilton G72 .161 E7
Logan Twr G72 .139 E4
Logandale Ave ML2 .165 F6
Loganlea Dr ML1 .143 A1
Logans Prim Sch ML1 .163 B7
Logans Rd ML1 .163 C8
Loganswell Dr G46 .135 E2
Loganswell Gdns G46 .135 E2
Loganswell Pl G46 .135 E2
Loganswell Rd G46 .135 E2
Logie Dr FK5 .23 A3
Logie La Bridge of A FK9 .2 C7
Stirling FK9 .2 D4
Logie Pk G74 .160 A3
Logie Rd FK9 .2 D4
Logie Sq G74 .160 A3
Lomax St G33 .118 D8
Lomond G75 .180 E5
Lomond Ave
Hurlford KA1 .228 F6
Port Glasgow PA14 .68 E8
Renfrew PA4 .94 B1
Lomond Castle G83 .18 F5
Lomond Cres
Alexandria G83 .27 D7
Beith KA15 .150 C2
Bridge of W PA11 .110 C8
Cumbernauld G67 .82 C7
Paisley PA2 .133 D8
Stenhousemuir FK5 .23 F3
Stirling FK9 .2 B4
Lomond Ct Alloa FK10 .10 C5
Barrhead G78 .134 C2
Coatbridge ML5 .122 D7
Cumbernauld G67 .82 C7
Dumbarton G82 .49 E4
Helensburgh G84 .16 E1
Lomond Dr Airdrie ML6 .102 F2
Alexandria G83 .27 D7
Bannockburn FK7 .7 E1
Barrhead G78 .134 B4
Bishopbriggs G64 .78 A3
Bothwell G71 .141 B3
Cumbernauld G67 .82 B7
Dumbarton G82 .50 B6
Falkirk FK2 .24 C1
Newton Mearns G77 .156 D7
Wishaw ML2 .165 B1
Lomond Gate G83 .28 A8
Lomond Gdns PA5 .112 C2
Lomond Gr
Cumbernauld G67 .82 C7
Helensburgh G84 .25 C8
Lomond Ind Est G83 .27 E6
Lomond Pl
Coatbridge ML5 .101 E1
Cumbernauld G67 .82 B7
Erskine PA8 .72 E1
Irvine KA12 .219 D6
Stepps G33 .99 E4
Lomond Prim Sch G84 .16 D3
Lomond Rd
Alexandria G83 .27 D8
Balloch G83 .27 E8
Bearsden G61 .75 F2
Coatbridge ML5 .101 D2
Greenock PA15 .46 B3
Kilmarnock KA1 .228 A4
Kirkintilloch G66 .79 D5
Shotts ML7 .146 E6
Uddingston G71 .120 F1
Lomond Sch G84 .16 C3
Lomond St Alloa FK10 .4 E1
Glasgow G22 .97 B5
Helensburgh G84 .16 E1
Lomond Trad Ctr G83 .27 E6
Lomond View
Cambuslang G72 .139 A1
Cumbernauld G67 .82 C7
Hamilton ML3 .161 F2
Symington KA1 .231 D4
Lomond Way Denny FK6 .39 D6
Irvine KA11 .220 A4
Motherwell ML1 .143 A5
Lomond Wlk
7 Larkhall ML9 .185 B4
Motherwell ML1 .143 C4
Lomondside Ave G76 .157 C7
Lomondview Ind Est PA5 .111 F3
London Dr G32 .119 E2
London Rd Glasgow G31 .118 D4
Kilmarnock KA3 .228 B8
London St Larkhall ML9 .185 A4
Renfrew PA4 .94 D5
Lonend PA1 .113 F3
Loney Cres FK6 .39 E8
Long Calderwood Prim Sch G74 .160 C4
Long Crags View G82 .50 C6
Long Dr Irvine KA11,KA12 .219 F5
Irvine,Shewalton KA11 .225 A7
Long Row Glasgow G69 .120 C6
Kirkintilloch G66 .80 B7
Lanark ML11 .214 F2
Menstrie FK11 .4 A7
Longay Pl G22 .97 C8
Longay St G22 .97 C8
Longbank Dr KA7 .239 A4
Longbank Rd KA7 .239 A4
Longbar Ave KA14 .170 D6
Longcraigs Ave KA22 .205 C5
Longcroft Dr PA4 .94 C4
Longcroft Holdings FK4 .39 B3
Longdales Ave FK2 .42 A8
Longdales Ct FK2 .42 A8
Longdales Pl FK2 .42 A8
Longdales Rd FK2 .42 A8
Longden St G81 .94 D8
Longdyke Pl FK2 .24 C4
Longfield Ave KA21 .205 E2
Longfield Pl KA21 .205 E2
Longford Ave KA13 .207 E1
Longford St G33 .118 D8
Longhill Ave KA7 .238 C1
Longlands Pk KA7 .238 F4
Longlee G69 .120 B4
Longmeadow PA5 .111 D1
Longmorn Pl 1 ML1 .143 B2
Longpark Ave KA3 .222 F2
Longriggend Rd ML6 .85 C2
Longrow Gdns KA11 .219 F7
Longstone Rd G33 .119 B8
Longwill Terr G67 .62 B4
Lonsdale Ave G46 .136 D3
Loom Wlk PA10 .111 A3
Lora Dr G52 .115 E4
Lord Way G69 .120 F5
Loreny Dr KA1 .227 E2
Loreny Ind Est KA1 .227 E3
Loretto Pl G33 .118 F8
Loretto St G33 .118 F8
Lorien Ct KA8 .236 C4
Lorimar Pl FK2 .24 B2
Lorimer Cres G75 .180 D7
Lorn Ave G69 .100 D8
Lorn Dr G83 .19 F1
Lorn Pl G66 .59 C1
Lorne Arc KA7 .238 F8
Lorne Cres G64 .78 D2
Lorne Dr Linwood PA3 .112 A5
Motherwell ML1 .142 D2
Lorne Gdns Laurieston FK2 .42 F3
Salsburgh ML7 .125 A2
Lorne Pl ML5 .122 D5
Lorne Rd Glasgow G52 .114 F8
Stenhousemuir FK5 .23 C2
Lorne St Glasgow G51 .116 D6
Hamilton ML3 .162 C4
Helensburgh G84 .16 D2
Lorne Street Prim Sch G51 .116 D6
Lorne Terr G72 .138 F3
Lornshill Acad FK10 .4 E2
Lornshill Cres FK10 .9 F8
Lorraine Gardens La 5 G12 .96 C4
Lorraine Gdns 4 G12 .96 C4
Lorraine Rd 3 G12 .96 C4
Lorraine Way G83 .27 F1
Loskin Dr G22 .97 B7
Losshill FK11 .4 A6
Lossie Cres PA4 .94 F2
Lossie St G33 .98 D1
Lothian Cres Paisley PA2 .113 D1
Stirling FK9 .2 C3
Lothian Dr G76 .157 D8
Lothian Gdns 1 G20 .96 E3
Lothian Rd Ayr KA7 .239 A7
Greenock PA16 .44 D4
Stewarton KA3 .211 C8
Lothian St Glasgow G52 .114 E8
Glasgow G52 .114 F8
Lothian Way G74 .160 D3
Louburn EH48 .107 D3
Louden Hill Dr G33 .98 E6
Louden Hill Pl G33 .98 E6
Louden Hill Rd G33 .98 E6
Louden Hill Way G33 .98 E6
Louden St ML6 .123 A7
Loudens Wlk FK6 .21 D5
Loudon G75 .180 E5
Loudon Gdns PA5 .112 A3
Loudon Rd G33 .99 B4
Loudon St ML2 .165 B6
Loudon Terr
Bearsden G61 .75 D7
Glasgow G12 .96 D3
Loudonhill Ave ML3 .183 E8
Loudoun Ave KA1 .228 A4
Loudoun Cres KA13 .207 B4
Loudoun Pl
Crosshouse KA2 .226 F8
Symington KA1 .231 D4
Loudoun Rigg KA12 .219 C1
Loudoun St KA3 .211 E7
Loudoun Terr KA9 .236 D7
Loudoun-Montgomery Prim Sch KA12 .219 C1
Louise Gdns ML1 .142 F5
Louisville Ave ML2 .165 D5
Lounsdale Ave PA2 .113 B3
Lounsdale Cres PA2 .113 B2
Lounsdale Dr PA2 .113 B2
Lounsdale Gr PA2 .113 B3
Lounsdale Ho PA2 .113 A1
Lounsdale Pl G14 .95 B4
Lounsdale Rd PA2 .113 B2
Lounsdale Way PA2 .113 B3
Lourdes Ave G52 .115 D4
Lourdes Ct G52 .115 D4
Lourdes Prim Sch G52 .115 C5
Lourdes Sec Sch G52 .115 D4
Lovat Ave G61 .75 F7
Lovat Dr G66 .79 B8
Lovat Path 2 ML9 .185 C2
Lovat Pl Glasgow G52 .114 E7
Rutherglen G73 .138 D4
Love Ave PA11 .89 E2
Love Dr ML4 .142 B6
Love La KA24 .191 C8
Love St Kilwinning KA13 .208 A3
Paisley PA3 .113 E6
Lovers Loan FK12 .5 B7
Lovers Wlk FK8 .2 B1
Low Barholm PA10 .111 B2
Low Broadlie Rd G78 .154 D7
Low Church La 3 KA1 .227 F8
Low Craigends G65 .60 E8
Low Cres G81 .94 E8
Low Flender Rd G76 .157 D5
Low Glencairn St KA1 .227 F6
Low Green Rd KA12 .219 B2
Low Moss Ind Est G64 .78 B4
Low Parks Mus* ML3 .162 E4
Low Parksail PA8 .93 C7
Low Patrick St ML3 .162 F3
Low Pleasance ML9 .185 B3
Low Quarry Gdns ML3 .162 D2
Low Rd Ayr KA8 .236 E3
Paisley PA2 .113 C3
Low Waters Rd ML3 .162 D1
Lower Auchingramont Rd ML3 .162 E4
Lower Bourtree Dr G73 .138 C4
Lower Bouverie St PA14 .47 D1
Lower Bridge St FK8 .2 A1
Lower Castlehill FK8 .2 A1
Lower Mill Rd G76 .157 F6
Lower Millgate G71 .140 F6
Lower Stoneymollan Rd G83 .27 C8
Lower Sutherland Cres G84 .16 B3
Lower Vennel KA11 .220 A3
Lowmoss Rdbt G64 .78 C5
Lowndes St G78 .134 C2
Lowther Ave G61 .75 C7
Lowther Bank KA11 .220 C2
Lowther Pl KA1 .228 A4
Lowther Terr 15 G12 .96 C4
Loyal Ave PA8 .72 F1
Loyal Gdns G61 .75 B8
Loyal Pl PA8 .72 F1
Loyne Dr PA4 .94 F2
Luath St G51 .116 A8
Lubas Ave G42 .137 D7
Lubas Pl G42 .137 D7
Lubnaig Dr PA8 .72 E1
Lubnaig Gdns G61 .75 C7
Lubnaig Pl ML6 .102 E2
Lubnaig Rd G43 .136 E6
Lubnaig Wlk ML1 .143 A5
Luce Ave KA1 .228 A5
Luckenhill Dr ML6 .84 D3
Luckiesfauld G78 .154 D7
Luckingsford Ave PA4 .93 D7
Luckingsford Dr PA4 .93 D7
Luckingsford Rd PA4 .93 C7
Lucy Brae G71 .140 E8
Ludgate FK10 .10 A6
Ludovic Sq PA5 .111 F3
Luffness Gdns G32 .119 B2
Lugar Ave KA11 .220 A6
Lugar Cres KA9 .236 B5
Lugar Dr G52 .115 E4
Lugar Pl Glasgow G44 .137 F5
Troon KA10 .229 G5
Lugar St ML5 .122 B8
Lugar Wynd KA3 .223 B6
Luggie Gr G66 .80 A7
Luggie Rd ML8 .187 E3
Luggie View G67 .82 A6
Luggiebank Pl G69 .121 A4
Luggiebank Rd
Kirkintilloch,Eastside G66 .58 D1
Kirkintilloch,Townhead G66 .79 D8
Lugton Ct KA12 .219 C1
Lugton Rd KA3 .195 B8
Luing ML6 .123 E6
Luing Rd G52 .115 E5
Luma Gdns G51 .115 C7
Lumloch St G21 .98 A4
Lumsden La G3 .96 D1
Lumsden Pl KA20 .206 E1
Lumsden St G3 .96 D1
Lunan Dr G64 .98 C8
Lunan Pl G51 .115 E7
Lunar Path ML6 .123 D1
Luncarty Pl G32 .119 A3
Luncarty St G32 .119 A3
Lunderston Cl G53 .135 B6
Lunderston Dr G53 .135 A7
Lunderston Gdns G53 .135 B6
Lundholm Rd KA20 .217 E7
Lundie Gdns G64 .98 D8
Lundie St G32 .118 E3
Lurg St PA14 .68 D8
Luss Ave PA15 .46 B1
Luss Brae ML3 .161 F2
Luss Pl PA15 .46 B1
Luss Rd Alexandria G83 .27 D7
Glasgow G51 .115 F7
Helensburgh G84 .17 B5
Lusset Glen G60 .73 B6
Lusset Rd G60 .73 B6
Lusshill Terr G71 .120 B2
Lybster Cres G73 .138 D3
Lybster Way G72 .161 C3
Lychgate Rd FK10 .4 B2
Lye Brae G67 .62 B2
Lyell Gr G74 .159 E3
Lyell Pl G74 .159 E3
Lyle Cres PA7 .72 A4
Lyle Gdns KA12 .219 D1
Lyle Gr PA16 .45 B7
Lyle Pl Greenock PA16 .45 A7
Paisley PA2 .113 F2
Lyle Rd Airdrie ML6 .123 F8
Greenock PA16 .45 B7
Kilmacolm PA13 .89 D8
Lyle Sq G62 .54 E2
Lyle St Greenock PA15 .46 A4
Greenock,Central PA15 .45 F4
Lyle's Land PA6 .91 B3
Lylefoot Cres PA16 .45 B8
Lylefoot Pl PA16 .45 B7
Lylesland Ct PA2 .113 E2
Lylestone Terr KA13 .208 D7
Lyman Dr ML2 .165 C7
Lymburn Pl KA8 .239 B8
Lymburn St G3 .116 D8
Lymekilns Rd G74 .159 D3
Lyndale Pl G20 .96 D8
Lyndale Rd G20 .96 D8
Lyndhurst Gardens La G20 .96 F3
Lyndhurst Gdns G20 .96 F3
Lyne Croft G64 .78 A4
Lyne St ML2 .165 A5
Lynebank Gr G77 .156 D2
Lynebank Pl G77 .156 D2
Lynedoch Cres G3 .240 A4
Lynedoch Ct 4 PA15 .46 A4
Lynedoch Ind Est PA15 .46 A4
Lynedoch Pl G3 .240 A4
Lynedoch St Glasgow G3 .240 A4
Greenock PA15 .45 F4
Lynedoch Terr G3 .240 A4
Lynmouth Pl PA19 .44 E5
Lynn Ave KA24 .191 C7
Lynn Ct ML9 .185 A2
Lynn Dr Eaglesham G76 .178 E6
Kilbirnie KA25 .149 B3
Milngavie G62 .55 C2
Lynn Wlk Balloch G83 .27 E8
Bothwell G71 .141 A5
Lynnburn Ave ML4 .142 A6
Lynne Dr G23 .76 E1
Lynnhurst G71 .140 F7
Lynnwood Rd ML2 .166 C6
Lynton Ave G46 .136 A1
Lyon Cres FK9 .2 A6
Lyon Rd Erskine PA8 .72 E1
Linwood PA3 .112 B4
Paisley PA2 .112 F1
Lyoncross Ave G78 .134 D3
Lyoncross Cres G78 .134 D3
Lyoncross Rd G53 .115 B2
Lyons Quadrant ML2 .164 D4
Lysa Vale Pl ML4 .141 E5
Lysander Way 2 PA4 .94 D1
Lytham Dr G23 .76 E1
Lytham Mdws G71 .140 E2
Lythgow Way ML11 .215 C5
Lyttleton G75 .180 B7

M

Mabel St ML1 .163 E5
Maberry Cl KA3 .195 D1
Maberry Pl KA10 .229 F6
MacAdam Gdns ML4 .142 A6
MacAdam Pl Ayr KA8 .236 A1
East Kilbride G75 .180 E8
Falkirk FK1 .41 D6
Irvine KA11 .219 F1
Kilmarnock KA3 .223 C1
MacAdam Sq KA8 .236 A1
MacAllan Mews ML1 .143 B2
MacAllan Pl KA11 .219 F7
MacAllister Pl KA3 .223 C1
MacAlpine Ct FK10 .4 D3
MacAlpine Pl KA3 .223 C2
MacAndrew Pl KA3 .223 C1
Macara Dr KA12 .219 E3
MacArthur Ave ML6 .102 D3
MacArthur Cres G74 .159 C4
MacArthur Ct G74 .159 C3
MacArthur Dr G74 .159 C3
MacArthur Gdns G74 .159 C3
MacArthur Wynd G72 .139 C5
MacAulay Pl G84 .16 A2
MacAuley Pl KA3 .223 C1
MacBeth G74 .160 B5
MacBeth Dr KA3 .223 C1

MacBeth Gdns KA3 223 C1
MacBeth Pl G31 118 D4
MacBeth Rd
Greenock PA16 45 A5
Stewarton KA3 195 D1
MacBeth St G31 118 D4
MacBeth Wlk KA3 223 C1
MacCabe Gdns G66 57 F7
MacCallum Dr G72 139 C5
MacCallum Pl KA3 223 C1
MacCrimmon Pk G74 159 B4
MacDairmid Dr ML3 183 B7
MacDonald Ave G74 159 A4
MacDonald Cres G65 60 A3
MacDonald Ct
Beith KA15 171 A7
Larbert FK5 23 B5
MacDonald Dr
Kilmarnock KA3 223 C1
Stirling FK7 7 A4
MacDonald Gdns KA3 223 C1
MacDonald Gr ML4 141 F2
MacDonald Pl KA3 223 C1
MacDonald St
3 Motherwell ML1 163 F5
1 Rutherglen G73 138 A7
MacDonald Wlk G83 27 E8
MacDougal Dr G72 139 C5
MacDougal Quadrant
ML4 141 F2
MacDougall Dr KA3 223 C1
MacDougall Pl KA3 223 C1
MacDougall St
Glasgow G43 136 C7
Greenock PA15 46 D4
MacDowall St
Johnstone PA5 111 F3
Paisley PA3 113 D6
MacDuff PA8 73 A2
MacDuff Pl G31 118 D4
MacDuff St G31 118 D4
Mace Ct FK7 7 D3
Mace Rd G13 75 C1
Macedonian Gr ML1 143 C4
MacEwan Pl KA3 228 C8
MacFarland Rd G61 75 F3
MacFarlane Cres
Cambuslang G72 139 C5
Falkirk FK1 42 B5
MacFarlane Dr KA3 223 C1
MacFarlane Rd G61 76 A3
MacFie Pl G74 159 B4
MacGillvary Ave PA15 46 E3
MacGowan Way PA15 46 E3
MacGregor Ct G72 139 C5
MacGregor Dr KA3 228 C8
MacGregor Rd PA15 46 E3
Machan Ave ML9 185 A3
Machan Rd ML9 185 B1
Machanhill ML9 185 B2
Machanhill Prim Sch
ML9 185 B3
Machanhill View ML9 185 B2
Machrie Ct FK1 41 C4
Machrie Dr Glasgow G45 137 F4
Helensburgh G84 16 F3
Newton Mearns G77 156 E6
Machrie Gn G75 180 B4
Machrie Pl KA13 207 C3
Machrie Rd Glasgow G45 137 F4
Kilmarnock KA3 222 E4
Machrie St Glasgow G45 137 F3
Motherwell ML1 163 B7
MacInnes Mews ML1 143 E4
MacInnes Pl KA3 223 C1
Macintosh Pl
East Kilbride G75 180 C7
Falkirk FK1 42 A1
Kilmarnock KA3 223 C1
MacIntyre Pl KA3 223 C1
MacIntyre Rd KA9 233 C2
MacIvor Cres G74 159 A4
MacIvor Pl KA3 223 C1
Mack St ML6 123 A8
MacKean St PA3 113 D6
MacKeith St G40 117 F4
MacKellar Pl KA3 223 C2
MacKendrick Pl KA3 228 C8
MacKenzie Dr
Johnstone PA10 111 B1
Kilmarnock KA3 223 B1
MacKenzie Gdns G74 159 A4
MacKenzie Pl FK1 41 F2
MacKenzie St PA15 46 D4
MacKenzie Terr ML4 142 A7
MacKie Ave
Greenock PA14 46 F1
Port Glasgow PA14 47 A1
Stewarton KA3 195 D2
MacKie Pl KA3 223 C1
MacKie St KA8 236 C2
MacKie's Mill Rd PA5 132 D8
MacKinlay Pl KA1 228 B8
MacKinlay St G5 117 B4
MacKinley Pl G77 156 D4
MacKinnon Dr KA3 228 C8
MacKinnon Terr KA12 219 E4
MacKintosh Ct G72 139 A3
MacKintosh Pl KA11 219 F1
Maclachlan Ave FK6 21 C1
Maclachlan Pl G84 16 E3
Maclachlan Rd G84 16 E3
MacLaren Ct KA10 229 G4
MacLaren Pl
Kilmarnock KA3 228 C8
Netherlee G44 136 F2
MacLaren Terr FK2 24 A2
Maclay Ave PA10 111 A2
MacLean Cres FK12 5 C7
MacLean Ct
East Kilbride G74 159 B4
Stirling FK7 7 C3
MacLean Dr KA3 223 B1
MacLean Gr G74 159 B4
MacLean Pl G74 159 B4
MacLean Sq G51 116 E6
MacLean St
Clydebank G81 94 E8
Glasgow G51 116 D6
MacLean Terr EH48 107 C3
MacLehose Ct PA16 45 E7
MacLehose Rd G67 62 C3
MacLellan Rd G78 154 E6
MacLellan St G41 116 D5
MacLeod Cres G84 16 B4
MacLeod Dr
Helensburgh G84 16 C4
Kilmarnock KA3 228 C8
MacLeod Pl
East Kilbride G74 160 B3
Kilmarnock KA3 228 C8
MacLeod St G4 241 C2
MacLeod Way G72 139 C5
MacMillan Dr
Gourock PA19 44 D6
Kilmarnock KA3 223 C1
MacMillan Gdns G71 121 A1
MacMillan Pl KA3 223 C1
MacMillan St ML9 184 F2
MacNab Pl KA3 223 B1
MacNaughton Dr KA3 223 C1
MacNaughton Wlk KA3 223 C1
MacNeil Pl KA3 223 B1
MacNeil St ML9 184 F3
MacNeill Dr G74 159 B4
MacNeill Gdns G74 159 B4
MacNeish Way G74 159 C4
MacNichol Gdns KA3 223 C1
MacNichol Pl KA3 223 C1
MacNicol Ct G74 159 A4
MacNicol Pk G74 159 A4
MacNicol Pl G74 159 A4
Macphail Dr KA3 223 C1
Macpherson Dr FK8 2 A2
Macpherson Gdns KA3 223 C1
Macpherson Pk G74 159 C3
Macpherson Pl
Falkirk FK1 41 F2
Kilmarnock KA3 223 C1
Macpherson Wlk KA3 223 C1
Macphie Rd G82 50 C4
Macrae Dr KA9 233 C2
Macrae Gdns G74 159 C3
Macredie Pl KA11 220 D6
Macrimmon Pl G75 180 E8
MacRobert Ave KA11 220 B1
MacTaggart Rd G67 82 E8
Madeira La PA16 45 D7
Madeira St PA16 45 D7
Madill Pl FK5 23 F3
Madison Ave G44 137 B5
Madison Path 9 G72 161 D7
Madras Pl Glasgow G40 117 F3
Neilston G78 154 E7
Madras St G40 117 F3
Mafeking St
Glasgow G51 116 B6
Wishaw ML2 164 D4
Mafeking Terr G78 154 C7
Magdalen Way PA2 132 E7
Maggie Wood's Loan
Falkirk FK1 41 F4
Falkirk FK1 41 F5
Magna St ML1 163 B8
Magnolia Dr G72 139 F3
Magnolia Gdns
Ashgill ML9 185 E1
Motherwell ML1 143 C3
Magnolia Pl G71 141 C8
Magnolia St ML2 165 B5
Magnolia Terr G72 139 F3
Magnum L Ctr* KA12 218 F1
Magnus Cres G44 137 B4
Magnus Rd PA6 111 D8
Mahon Ct G69 80 F1
Maid Morville Ave KA11 225 C8
Maidens G74 159 D3
Maidens Ave G77 157 A5
Maidland Rd G53 135 C8
Mailerbeg Gdns G69 80 F3
Mailie Wlk ML1 143 C3
Mailing Ave G64 78 C2
Mailings Ct G65 37 E3
Mailings Rd G65 37 E3
Mailings The G65 37 E4
Maimhor Rd KA23 190 B4
Main Rd Ayr KA8 236 E2
Cardross G82 48 A8
Crookedholm KA3 228 E7
Cumbernauld,Condorrat
G67 82 A7
Cumbernauld,Mollinsburn
G67 81 E5
Elderslie PA5 112 D3
Fenwick KA3 213 A3
Gatehead KA2 226 E5
Langbank PA14 70 D7
Paisley PA2 113 D3
Rosneath G84 15 A3
Springside KA11 220 F2
Waterside KA3 213 F3
Main St Airth FK2 14 D4
Alexandria G83 27 E4
Alexandria,Dalmonach G83 27 E5
Alloa FK10 5 D1
Ayr KA8 235 F1
Main St *continued*
Balloch G83 19 F1
Bannockburn FK7 7 D1
Banton G65 37 D3
Barrhead G78 134 C2
Beith KA15 150 B1
Bellshill ML4 141 F5
Bellshill ML4 142 B5
Blackridge EH48 107 C3
Bonhill G83 27 F3
Bonhill,Dalmonach G83 27 F6
Bonnybridge FK4 40 B5
Bothwell G71 141 A2
Bridge of W PA11 110 D8
Calderbank ML6 123 C2
Caldercruix ML6 105 A4
California FK1 66 F5
Cambus FK10 9 B8
Cambusbarron FK7 6 D5
Cambuslang G72 139 A6
Chapelhall ML6 123 E3
Chryston G69 80 D1
Clarkston G76 157 F6
Cleland ML1 144 C1
Coatbridge ML5 122 A7
Coatbridge,Cliftonville
ML5 122 C6
Cowie FK7 12 D7
Cumbernauld G67 62 B5
Dalry KA24 191 C7
Drybridge KA11 225 E6
Dundonald KA2 225 F2
Dunlop KA3 195 B7
East Kilbride G74 159 F2
Falkirk,Bainsford FK2 42 B7
Falkirk,Camelon FK1 41 E5
Falkirk,Carronshore FK2 24 C3
Fallin FK7 8 E3
Gateside KA15 171 E8
Glasgow G40 117 F4
Glasgow,Muirhead G69 120 C4
Glasgow,Thornliebank G46 135 F3
Glenboig ML5 101 E6
Glengarnock KA14 170 B6
Greenock PA15 46 C4
Hamilton G72 161 D6
Hamilton G72 161 E5
Houston PA6 91 B2
Howwood PA9 130 F5
Irvine KA11 220 D1
Kilbirnie KA25 149 B1
Kilmaurs KA3 222 C7
Kilsyth G65 36 D1
Kilsyth G65 60 D8
Kilwinning KA13 207 E3
Lennoxtown G66 57 D8
Lochwinnoch PA12 129 C2
Longriggend ML6 85 A1
Milngavie G62 76 A8
Monkton KA9 233 D4
Motherwell ML1 143 B6
Neilston G78 154 D7
Overtown ML2 186 C6
Plains ML6 104 B2
Plean FK7 12 D3
Prestwick KA9 236 C8
Renton G82 27 D2
Rutherglen G73 138 B8
Salsburgh ML7 125 B2
Shieldhill FK1 66 D6
Shotts ML7 147 A3
Slamannan FK1 86 B7
Stenhousemuir FK5 23 C2
Stenhousemuir FK5 23 E2
Stevenston KA20 206 D1
Stewarton KA3 211 D8
Stirling FK7 7 B4
Symington KA1 231 C4
Thornliebank G46 136 A4
Torrance G64 78 B8
Troon KA10 230 A4
Tullibody FK10 4 B2
Twechar G65 59 F4
Uddingston G71 140 F5
West Kilbride KA23 190 D5
Wishaw ML2 164 F4
Wishaw ML2 165 A3
Wishaw,Newmains ML2 166 A3
Main St E FK11 4 A6
Main St W FK11 3 F6
Mainhead Terr G67 62 B5
Mainhill Ave G69 120 D5
Mainhill Dr G69 120 C5
Mainhill Pl G69 120 D6
Mainhill Rd G69 120 F5
Mainholm Acad KA8 236 D1
Mainholm Cres KA8 236 D1
Mainholm Ct KA8 236 E1
Mainholm Rd
Ayr KA6,KA8 239 E8
Ayr,Braehead KA8 236 D1
Mains Ave Beith KA15 150 A1
Glasgow G46 136 B1
Helensburgh G84 16 A3
Mains Ct ML11 215 C5
Mains Dr PA8 73 C1
Mains Hill PA8 73 B1
Mains Pl ML4 142 A3
Mains Rd Beith KA15 150 A1
East Kilbride G74 159 F5
Harthill ML7 127 E5
Mains River PA8 73 C1
Mains Wood PA8 73 D1
Mainscroft PA8 73 C1
Mainshill Ave PA8 73 B1
Mainshill Gdns PA8 73 B1
Mair Ave KA24 191 E7
Mair St G51 116 E6
Maitland Ave FK7 7 D1
Maitland Bank ML9 185 C3
Maitland Cres FK7 7 B3
Maitland Ct G84 16 D1
Maitland Dr G64 57 B1
Maitland Pl PA4 94 B2
Maitland St Glasgow G4 240 C4
Helensburgh G84 16 D1
Majors Loan FK1 42 A4
Majors Pl FK1 42 A3
Mal Fleming's Brae G65 60 F7
Malcolm Ct KA3 195 F1
Malcolm Dr FK5 23 E4
Malcolm Gdns
East Kilbride G74 159 C2
Irvine KA12 219 D2
Malcolm Pl G84 17 A2
Malcolm St ML1 163 C6
Malin Pl G33 118 F8
Mallaig Pl G51 115 D7
Mallaig Rd Glasgow G51 115 E7
Port Glasgow PA14 68 F7
Mallaig Terr PA16 44 E4
Mallard Cres
East Kilbride G75 180 A5
Greenock PA16 45 A6
Mallard La
7 Bothwell G71 141 B3
Greenock PA16 45 A6
Mallard Pl G75 180 A5
Mallard Rd G81 74 B5
Mallard Terr G75 180 A5
Mallard Way ML4 141 F8
Malleable Gdns ML1 142 C2
Malleny Gr G77 156 B3
Malletsheugh Rd G77 156 B3
Malletsheugh Rdbt G77 156 B3
Malloch Cres PA5 112 B2
Malloch Pl G74 160 B2
Malloch St G20 96 E5
Mallot's View G77 156 B4
Malov Ct G75 180 E6
Malplaquet Ct ML8 188 B1
Malta Terr G5 117 B4
Maltbarns St G20 97 A3
Malvaig La 8 G72 161 C6
Malvern Ct G31 118 A6
Malvern Way PA3 113 D8
Mambeg Dr G51 115 E8
Mamore Pl G43 136 C6
Mamore St G43 136 C6
Mamre Dr FK1 66 F5
Manchester Dr G12 96 E6
Mandela Ave FK2 42 C7
Mandora Ct ML8 188 B1
Manitoba Cres G75 159 B1
Mannering G74 160 D4
Mannering Ct G41 136 C8
Mannering Rd
Glasgow G41 136 C8
Paisley PA2 132 E8
Mannering Way PA2 112 E1
Mannfield Ave FK4 39 F4
Mannoch Pl ML5 122 D3
Mannofield G61 75 D4
Manor Ave KA3 223 A4
Manor Cres Gourock PA19 44 F7
Tullibody FK10 4 B2
Manor Dr ML6 122 E8
Manor Gate
Bothwell G71 141 B1
Newton Mearns G77 156 F4
Manor Loan FK9 3 B5
Manor Park Ave PA2 113 B1
Manor Pk ML3 162 D2
Manor Powis Cotts FK9 3 B3
Manor Rd Clydebank G15 74 F1
Gartcosh G69 100 F5
Glasgow G14 95 E4
Paisley PA2 112 F1
Manor St FK1 42 B4
Manor Stps FK9 3 C3
Manor View
Calderbank ML6 123 B2
Larkhall ML9 185 C2
Manor Way G73 138 C4
Manrahead Rdbt KA15 171 A7
Manresa Pl 1 G4 97 B2
Manse Ave Bearsden G61 75 F5
Bothwell G71 141 A2
Coatbridge ML5 121 D4
Manse Brae Ashgill ML9 200 B8
Cambuslang G72 139 F2
Dalserf ML9 186 B1
Glasgow G44 137 B6
Rhu G84 15 D5
Manse Bridge ML8 187 F1
Manse Cres Houston PA6 91 B2
Stirling FK7 7 B4
Manse Ct Barrhead G78 134 D3
Kilsyth G65 60 D7
Kilwinning KA13 207 E3
Law ML8 187 A4
Manse Dr G83 27 F8
Manse Garden's G83 27 F8
Manse Gdns Balloch G83 27 E7
Glasgow G32 119 D4
Manse La G74 159 F3
Manse Mews ML2 166 A4
Manse Pl Airdrie ML6 123 A7
Bannockburn FK7 7 E1
Falkirk FK1 42 B4
Rhu G84 15 D5
Slamannan FK1 86 B7
Manse Rd Bearsden G61 75 F5
Bowling G60 72 D8
Carmunnock G76 158 D7
Glasgow,Barrachnie G32 119 D4
Manse Rd *continued*
Glasgow,Easterhouse G69 120 E6
Kilsyth G65 60 E7
Lanark ML11 214 F4
Motherwell ML1 163 F4
Neilston G78 154 E8
Salsburgh ML7 125 D1
Shotts ML7 147 A3
Stonehouse ML9 198 C2
West Kilbride KA23 190 D5
Wishaw ML2 166 A4
Manse Road Gdns G61 75 F5
Manse St Coatbridge ML5 121 F6
Kilmacolm PA13 89 D8
Kilmarnock KA1 228 A8
Renfrew PA4 94 D4
Saltcoats KA21 216 F7
Manse View
Hamilton G72 161 C6
Motherwell ML1 143 F5
Mansefield Ave G72 139 A4
Mansefield Cres
Clarkston G76 157 D6
Old Kilpatrick G60 73 A6
Mansefield Rd
Clarkston G76 157 E6
Quarter ML3 183 E6
Mansefield Terr KA3 195 B7
Mansel St G21 98 A5
Manseview ML9 185 B2
Manseview Terr G76 178 E5
Mansewell Rd KA9 233 C1
Mansewood Dr G82 50 B5
Mansewood Rd G43 136 B5
Mansfield Ave FK10 5 D1
Mansfield Dr G71 141 A6
Mansfield Rd
Bellshill ML4 141 F4
Glasgow G52 114 F8
Lochwinnoch PA12 129 C3
Prestwick KA9 236 B6
Mansfield St G11 96 C2
Mansfield Way KA11 220 A5
Mansion Ave PA14 69 A8
Mansion Ct G72 139 A6
Mansion St
Cambuslang G72 139 A6
Glasgow G22 97 B5
Glasgow G22 97 C5
Mansionhouse Ave G32 139 C8
Mansionhouse Dr G32 119 C6
Mansionhouse Gdns
G41 136 E7
Mansionhouse Gr G32 119 E3
Mansionhouse Rd
Falkirk FK1 41 D5
Glasgow G32 119 E3
Glasgow,Langside G41 136 E7
Paisley PA1 114 A5
Manson Ave KA9 233 D1
Manson Pl G75 181 B5
Manson Rd KA12 219 E4
Manuel Ave KA15 171 A7
Manuel Ct Irvine KA11 225 C8
Kilbirnie KA25 170 A8
Manuel Terr KA11 225 C8
Manus Duddy Ct
Blantyre G72 140 D1
Hamilton G72 161 D8
Maple Ave Dumbarton G82 49 B5
Milton Of C G66 58 B5
Newton Mearns G77 156 D4
Stenhousemuir FK5 23 F3
Maple Bank ML3 162 F2
Maple Cres G72 139 F3
Maple Ct 10 Alloa FK10 10 B6
Cumbernauld G67 62 F5
Maple Dr Ayr KA7 239 D5
Barrhead G78 155 D8
Beith KA15 150 B2
Clydebank G81 74 A5
Johnstone PA5 132 A8
Kirkintilloch G66 79 A5
Larkhall ML9 185 A5
Maple Gr
East Kilbride G75 180 B6
Troon KA10 229 E4
Maple Pl Banknock FK4 38 E2
Denny FK6 21 C3
East Kilbride G75 180 B6
Kilmarnock KA1 227 D7
Uddingston G71 141 D8
Maple Quadrant ML6 123 D6
Maple Rd
Cumbernauld G67 62 F5
Glasgow G41 116 B4
Greenock PA16 45 B3
Motherwell ML1 143 B5
Maple Terr
East Kilbride G75 180 B6
Irvine KA12 219 D4
Maple Way 7 G72 161 C7
Maple Wlk G66 58 B5
Maplewood ML2 164 D1
Mar Ave PA7 72 B3
Mar Dr G61 75 F7
Mar Gdns G73 138 D4
Mar Pl Alloa FK10 10 A7
Alloa,Sauchie FK10 5 C1
Stirling FK8 7 A8
Mar St FK10 10 B6
Marble Ave KA11 220 D1
March St G41 116 F2
Marchbank Gdns PA1 114 D4
Marchburn Ave KA9 236 E8

Marchdyke Cres KA1 ....227 E3
Marches The
Lanark ML11 ....215 B5
8 Stirling FK8 ....7 B7
Marchfield G64 ....77 E3
Marchfield Ave PA3 .....113 E8
Marchfield Quadrant
KA8 ....236 B5
Marchfield Rd KA8 ......236 B5
Marchglen FK13 ....5 F5
Marchglen Pl 1 G51 ....115 D7
Marchmont Ct KA1 ......228 F7
Marchmont Gdns G64 ....77 F2
Marchmont Rd KA7 .....238 F6
Marchmont Road La
KA7 ....238 F7
Marchmont Terr 2 G12 ...96 C3
Marchside Ct FK10 ....5 C1
Mardale G74 ....159 C3
Maree Ct FK10 ....10 C6
Maree Dr
Cumbernauld G67 ....82 B7
Glasgow G52 ....115 E4
Maree Gdns G64 ....78 B1
Maree Pl KA12 ....219 D7
Maree Rd PA2 ....113 A2
Maree Way G72 ....161 D8
Maree Wlk 7 ML2 ......165 F6
Marfield St G32 ....118 F8
Margaret Ave Haggs FK4 ..39 A3
Salsburgh ML7 ....125 B2
Margaret Ct FK6 ....21 E1
Margaret Dr
Alexandria G83 ....27 D5
Bonnybridge FK4 ....40 A6
Motherwell ML1 ....164 B3
Margaret Pl ML4 ....141 E5
Margaret Rd
Bannockburn FK7 ....7 C2
Hamilton ML3 ....162 B6
Margaret St
Coatbridge ML5 ....122 A4
Gourock PA19 ....44 F7
Greenock PA16 ....45 D7
Margaret Terr FK5 ....23 E4
Margaret's Pl ML9 ......185 A3
Margaretta Bldgs G44 ..137 A6
Margaretvale Dr ML9 ...185 A2
Marguerite Ave G66 ......79 C6
Marguerite Dr G66 ....79 C6
Marguerite Gdns
Bothwell G71 ....141 B2
Kirkintilloch G66 ....79 C6
Marguerite Gr G66 ....79 C6
Marguerite Pl Ayr KA7 ..239 C3
Milton Of C G66 ....58 B6
Marian Dr ML1 ....143 C2
Maric La ML6 ....104 A2
Marigold Ave ML1 ......163 E8
Marigold Sq KA7 ....239 B3
Marigold Way ML8 ......201 F8
Marina Ct ML4 ....141 F3
Marina Rd KA9 ....236 B8
Marine Cres G51 ....116 E6
Marine Dr KA11,KA12 ...224 D6
Marine Gdns G51 ....240 A1
Marine View Ct KA10 ...229 D2
Mariner Ave FK1 ....41 B5
Mariner Ct G81 ....74 A2
Mariner Dr FK1 ....41 B5
Mariner Gdns FK1 ....41 C6
Mariner Rd FK1 ....41 C5
Mariner St FK1 ....41 B5
Mariners View KA22 .....205 B1
Marion St ML4 ....142 D5
Mariscat Rd G41 ....116 E2
Marius Cres ML1 ....142 C1
Marjory Dr PA3 ....114 B7
Marjory Rd PA4 ....94 A1
Markdow Ave G53 ......115 A1
Market Cl 7 G65 ....60 D8
Market Ct 15 Kilsyth G65 ..60 D8
Lanark ML11 ....215 A4
Market End ML11 ....215 A4
Market Pl Carluke ML8 ..187 F2
Kilmacolm PA13 ....89 D8
5 Kilsyth G65 ....60 D8
Uddingston G71 ....141 C7
Market Rd
2 Carluke ML8 ....187 F2
Kirkintilloch G66 ....80 A7
Uddingston G71 ....141 C7
Market Sq 6 G65 ....60 D8
Market St Airdrie ML6 ...123 A7
Kilsyth G65 ....60 D8
Uddingston G71 ....141 C7
Markethill Rd
East Kilbride G74 ....159 E5
East Kilbride,East Mains
G74 ....159 E3
Markethill Rdbt G74 ....159 E3
Markinch Rd PA14 ....68 F6
Marlach Pl 18 G53 ......135 A8
Marlborough Ave G11 ....95 F3
Marlborough Ct 3 KA7 .235 E1
Marlborough Dr FK9 ......2 C3
Marlborough La N 1
G11 ....95 F3
Marlborough La S G11 ...95 F3
Marlborough Pk G75 ...180 A7
Marldon La G11 ....95 F3
Marle Pk KA7 ....239 A3
Marley Way G66 ....58 B6
Marlfield Gdns ML4 .....142 A8
Marloch Ave PA14 ....69 A6
Marlow St G41 ....116 E5
Marlow Terr G41 ....116 E4
Marmion Ave G84 ....25 C7
Marmion Cres ML1 .....142 D1
Marmion Ct PA2 ....132 F8
Marmion Dr G66 ....79 F8
Marmion Pl G67 ....82 E7
Marmion Rd
Cumbernauld G67 ....82 E7
Paisley PA2 ....132 E8
Marmion St FK2 ....42 B8
Marne St G31 ....118 B8
Marnoch Dr ML5 ....101 D6
Marnoch Way G69 ....80 F2
Marnock Terr PA2 ......114 A2
Marquis Ave ML3 ....162 B6
Marquis Gate G71 ......140 E5
Marr Coll KA10 ....229 F4
Marr Dr KA10 ....229 E4
Marr's Wynd ML11 .....215 C5
Marress Rd KA12 ....219 B3
Marress Rdbt KA12 .....219 B2
Marrs Wynd ML11 ......215 C5
Marrswood Gn ML3 ....162 A4
Marrwood Ave G66 ....80 B6
Mars Rd PA16 ....44 C2
Marschal Ct FK7 ....7 D3
Marshall Gr ML3 ....162 B3
Marshall La ML2 ....165 A3
Marshall Rd ML1 ....143 D7
Marshall St Larkhall ML9 .185 A2
Wishaw ML2 ....164 F2
Wishaw ML2 ....165 A3
Marshall Twr FK1 ....42 D4
Marshall Way FK10 ....4 C4
Marshall's La PA1 ......113 E4
Marshill FK10 ....10 A6
Marsmount Rd KA9 .....233 F1
Mart St G1 ....241 A1
Martha Pl ML9 ....185 B2
Martha St G1 ....241 A3
Martin Ave Balloch G83 ...28 A8
Irvine KA12 ....219 D5
Martin Cres G69 ....120 C5
Martin Ct ML3 ....162 C3
Martin Gannon Ct G82 ...49 D8
Martin Pl ML1 ....143 C3
Martin Sq KA21 ....206 A2
Martin St Coatbridge ML5 .122 D7
Glasgow G40 ....117 F3
Martinside G75 ....180 E5
Martlet Dr PA5 ....131 C7
Martyn St ML6 ....122 E6
Martyrs Pl G64 ....98 A8
Marwick St G31 ....118 B7
Mary Dr ML4 ....141 E3
Mary Fisher Cres G82 ....50 C2
Mary Glen ML2 ....165 D5
Mary Love Pl KA20 .....206 B1
Mary Rae Rd ML4 ....141 E3
Mary Russell Sch The
PA2 ....114 C2
Mary Sq G69 ....120 F5
Mary St Greenock PA16 ...45 C4
Hamilton ML3 ....162 D2
Johnstone PA5 ....112 A3
Laurieston FK2 ....42 F4
Paisley PA2 ....113 E2
Port Glasgow PA14 ....47 A2
Mary Stevenson Dr FK10 .10 A8
Mary Street Rdbt FK2 ....42 F3
Mary Young Pl G76 .....157 F6
Maryborough Ave KA9 ..236 B6
Maryborough Rd KA9 ...236 A6
Maryfield Pl Ayr KA8 ....236 B4
Falkirk FK1 ....41 B4
Maryfield Rd KA8 ....236 B4
Maryhill Prim Sch G20 ...96 D7
Maryhill Rd
Bearsden G61,G20 ....76 A1
Glasgow G20 ....97 A2
Glasgow,Maryhill G20 ....96 D6
Maryhill Sta G20 ....96 C8
Maryknowe Rd ML1 ....143 C2
Maryland Dr G52 ....115 E5
Maryland Gdns G52 ....115 E5
Maryland Rd G82 ....50 C6
Marypark Rd PA14 ....70 B7
Maryston St G33 ....98 D2
Maryville Ave G46 .....136 C2
Maryville Gdns G46 ....136 C2
Maryville La G71 ....140 E8
Maryville View G71 .....120 D1
Marywell Path G68 ....60 F2
Marywood Sq G41 ......116 F2
Mashock Path ML8 .....201 B1
Mason Ct ML1 ....163 E6
Mason La ML1 ....163 E6
Mason St Larkhall ML9 ..185 C2
Motherwell ML1 ....163 E6
Masonfield Ave G68 .....61 D2
Masonhill Pl KA7 ....239 C5
Masonhill Rd KA7 ......239 D6
Masterton St G21 ....97 C3
Masterton Way G71 .....121 B1
Mather Terr FK2 ....42 F4
Matherton Ave G77 .....157 B5
Matheson Wlk G83 ....27 E7
Mathew Smith Ave KA1 .227 E6
Mathie Cres PA19 ....44 E6
Mathieson Cres G33 .....99 F5
Mathieson Rd G73 ......118 C1
Mathieson St PA1 ......114 B5
Mathieson Wlk G83 ......27 F8
Matilda Rd G41 ....116 E4
Matthew McWhirter Pl
ML9 ....185 B4
Matthew Pl KA13 ....207 E5
Mauchline G74 ....160 E3
Mauchline Ave G66 ......59 A2
Mauchline Ct
Hamilton ML3 ....161 D2
Kilmarnock KA3 ....223 B6
Kirkintilloch G66 ....59 A2
Mauchline La PA16 ......44 E3
Mauchline Rd KA1 .....228 F6
Mauchline St G5 ....117 A4
Mauchline Terr PA16 ....44 E3
Maukinfauld Ct G32 ....118 D3
Maukinfauld Gdns G31 .118 E4
Maukinfauld Rd G32 ...118 E3
Mauldslie Dr ML8 ......187 A6
Mauldslie Pl ML9 ....199 F8
Mauldslie Rd ML8 ......187 B2
Mauldslie St
Bellshill ML4 ....142 A4
Coatbridge ML5 ....122 A5
Glasgow G40 ....118 B4
Maule Dr G11 ....96 A2
Maunsheugh Rd KA3 ...213 A3
Maurice Ave FK7 ....7 D4
Mausoleum Dr ML3 ....162 F5
Mavis Bank
Bishopbriggs G64 ....97 F8
6 Hamilton G72 ....161 C7
Mavis Rd PA16 ....45 B4
Mavisbank Ave FK1 ......66 C6
Mavisbank Gdns
Bellshill ML4 ....142 A6
Glasgow G51 ....116 E6
Mavisbank Rd G51 .....116 D6
Mavisbank Sch ML6 ....122 F8
Mavisbank St
Airdrie ML6 ....122 E8
Wishaw ML2 ....166 C5
Mavisbank Terr
Johnstone PA5 ....111 F2
Paisley PA1 ....113 F3
Mavor Ave G74 ....160 A4
Mavor Rdbt G74 ....159 F4
Maxholm Rd KA1 ......227 E5
Maxton Ave G78 ....134 A3
Maxton Cres Alva FK12 ....5 C7
Wishaw ML2 ....165 C6
Maxton Gr G78 ....134 A3
Maxton Terr G72 ....138 F3
Maxwell Ave
Bearsden G61 ....75 E1
Glasgow G69 ....120 A5
Glasgow,Pollokshields G41 .116 F4
Maxwell Cres G72 ......161 D6
Maxwell Ct Beith KA15 ..171 A7
Coatbridge ML5 ....122 A7
Kilmarnock KA3 ....223 D3
Maxwell Dr
East Kilbride G74 ....160 A2
Erskine PA8 ....72 F3
Glasgow,Garrowhill G69 ..120 A5
Glasgow,Pollokshields
G41 ....116 C4
Glasgow,Pollokshields
G41 ....116 E4
Maxwell Gdns
Glasgow G41 ....116 D4
Hurlford KA1 ....228 E6
Maxwell Gn KA11 ......220 A4
Maxwell Gr G41 ....116 D4
Maxwell La G41 ....116 E4
Maxwell Oval 2 G41 ...116 F4
Maxwell Park Sta G41 ..116 D2
Maxwell Path 10 ML9 ..185 C2
Maxwell Pl
Bridge of W PA11 ....110 D8
Coatbridge ML5 ....121 F5
Glasgow G41 ....117 A3
Kilsyth G65 ....36 D1
Stevenston KA20 ....206 E2
6 Stirling FK8 ....7 B8
Uddingston G71 ....141 A6
Maxwell Rd Bishopton PA7 .72 B3
Glasgow G41 ....116 F4
Maxwell St Clydebank G81 .73 F4
Glasgow G1 ....241 A1
Glasgow,Muirhead G69 ..120 B4
4 Paisley PA3 ....113 E5
Port Glasgow PA14 ....47 E1
Maxwell Terr G41 ......116 F4
Maxwell Twr FK1 ....42 D3
Maxwellton Ave G74 ...160 B3
Maxwellton Ct PA2 .....113 C4
Maxwellton Pl G74 .....160 B3
Maxwellton Prim Sch
G74 ....160 B3
Maxwellton Rd
East Kilbride G74 ....160 C4
Paisley PA1 ....113 B3
Port Glasgow PA14 ....68 F6
Maxwellton St PA1,PA2 .113 C3
Maxwelton Rd G33 ......98 D2
Maxwood Pl KA11 ......220 A5
May Gdns ML3 ....162 C5
May Rd PA2 ....133 E7
May St ML3 ....162 D5
May Terr Glasgow G46 ...137 B8
Glasgow,Merrylee G46 ..136 C3
May Wynd ML3 ....162 C5
Maybank La G42 ....117 A1
Maybank St G42 ....117 A1
Mayberry Cres G32 ....119 D5
Mayberry Gdns G32 ...119 D5
Mayberry Gr G32 ......119 D5
Mayberry Pl G72 ....161 D8
Maybole Cres G77 .....157 A4
Maybole Dr ML6 ....123 A4
Maybole Gdns ML3 ....161 D2
Maybole Gr G77 ....157 A4
Maybole Pl ML5 ....122 D3
Maybole Rd Ayr KA7 ....239 B3
Port Glasgow PA14 ....68 F6
Maybole St G53 ....134 F6
Mayfield Ave G76 ......157 E7
Mayfield Cres
Howwood PA9 ....130 F6
Stevenston KA20 ....206 C1
Mayfield Ct
Howwood PA9 ....130 F6
Stirling FK7 ....7 B3
Mayfield Dr
Howwood PA9 ....130 F6
Longcroft FK4 ....39 B3
Mayfield Gdns ML8 ....202 A7
Mayfield Gr KA20 ......206 C1
Mayfield Mews FK1 ......41 F4
Mayfield Pl Carluke ML8 ..202 A7
Coatbridge ML5 ....122 A3
Saltcoats KA21 ....217 A8
Mayfield Prim Sch
KA21 ....206 A2
Mayfield Rd
Hamilton ML3 ....161 F4
Saltcoats KA21 ....217 A8
Stevenston KA20 ....206 C1
Mayfield St Glasgow G20 ..96 F5
Stirling FK7 ....7 B4
Mayne Ave FK9 ....2 B6
Mayville St KA20 ....206 C1
McAdam Ct
Prestwick KA9 ....236 D5
Troon KA10 ....229 G4
McAlister Rd G83 ....27 E5
McAllister Ave ML6 ....123 D8
McAllister Ct FK7 ....7 D1
McAlpine St Glasgow G2 .240 B2
Wishaw ML2 ....165 B2
McArdle Ave ML1 ......163 B7
McArthur Pk G66 ....79 C7
McArthur St G43 ....136 C7
McAslin Ct G4 ....241 B3
McAslin St G4 ....241 C3
McAuslan Pl G84 ....16 F2
McBride Ave G66 ....79 C7
McCall's Ave KA8 ......236 A2
McCallum Ave G73 ....138 B8
McCallum Cres PA19 ....44 E7
McCallum Ct G74 ......159 B4
McCallum Gdns ML4 ...141 F2
McCallum Gr G74 ......159 B4
McCallum Pl G74 ......159 B4
McCallum Rd ML9 .....185 B1
McCambridge Pl FK5 ....23 C5
McCardel Way KA3 ....211 E8
McCarrison Rd ML2 ...166 A6
McCash Pl G66 ....79 C7
McCloy Gdns G53 .....134 F5
McClue Ave PA4 ....94 B3
McClue Rd PA4 ....94 C4
McClure Gdns KA12 ...219 C3
McClurg Ct 3 ML1 ....163 E5
McColgan Pl KA8 ......236 C3
McColl Ave G83 ....27 C7
McColl Pl G83 ....27 C6
McConnell Rd PA12 ...129 B2
McCormack Gdns ML1 ..143 E4
McCourt Gdns ML4 ....142 C5
McCracken Ave PA4 ....94 B2
McCracken Dr G71 ....141 C8
McCreery St G81 ....94 D8
McCrorie Pl PA10 .....111 A3
McCulloch Ave G71 ...141 D6
McCulloch La G83 ....27 D7
McCulloch St G41 .....116 F4
McCulloch Way
Neilston G78 ....154 D7
Stepps G33 ....99 F5
McDonald Ave PA5 ....111 E1
McDonald Cres G81 .....94 D8
McDonald Dr KA12 ....219 D4
McDonald Pl
Motherwell ML1 ....143 A5
Neilston G78 ....154 E7
McDowall Ave KA22 ...205 D2
McDowall Pl KA22 ....205 D2
McEwan Dr G84 ....16 F3
McEwan Gdns G74 ....159 A4
McEwan Wlk G83 ....27 E6
McEwans Way ML9 ....198 D1
McFarlane Rd G83 ......28 A8
McFarlane St
Glasgow G4 ....241 C1
Paisley PA3 ....113 C7
McGavin Ave KA13 ....208 A3
McGavin Way KA13 ...207 D4
McGhee Pl FK1 ....41 F2
McGhee St G81 ....74 B4
McGibney Dr KA12 ...219 D1
McGill Prim Sch G53 ..115 C2
McGillivray Ave KA21 ..205 F2
McGoldrick Pl G33 ......99 F5
McGowan Pl ML3 .....162 A5
McGown St PA3 ....113 D6
McGregor Ave
Airdrie ML6 ....123 D8
Balloch G83 ....28 A8
Renfrew PA4 ....94 B2
Stevenston KA20 ......206 D1
McGregor Dr G82 ....50 C4
McGregor La G82 ....27 D2
McGregor Path ML5 ...101 C6
McGregor Rd G67 ....61 E1
McGregor St
Clydebank G81 ....94 D8
Glasgow G51 ....115 F6
Wishaw ML2 ....164 D4
McGregor Wlk G83 .....27 C7
McGrigor Rd
Milngavie G62 ....54 F3
Stirling FK7 ....7 A4
McGurk Way ML4 .....141 D6
McHardy Cres KA15 ...171 F3
McInnes Ct ML2 ....165 B2
McInnes Gr ML9 ....198 E1
McInnes Pl ML2 ....186 B7
McInnes St G83 ....28 A8
McIntosh Ct 1 G31 ...117 F7
McIntosh Quadrant ML4 .141 F2
McIntosh St G31 ......117 F7
McIntosh Way
Cumbernauld G67 ....61 F1
Motherwell ML1 ....163 C5
McIntyre Ave KA9 .....233 D2
McIntyre Pl PA2 ....113 E2
McIntyre St G3 ....240 A2
McIntyre Terr Balloch G83 ..27 E7
Cambuslang G72 ....139 A6
McIsaac Rd KA21 ......217 A7
McIver St G72 ....139 E6
McKay Cres PA5 ....112 B2
McKay Ct G77 ....156 C3
McKay Gr ML4 ....141 F5
McKay Pl
East Kilbride G74 ....159 A4
Newton Mearns G77 ....156 C4
McKechnie St G51 ....116 A8
McKell Ct FK1 ....42 A3
McKellar Ave KA22 ...205 D2
McKenna Dr ML6 ......122 E7
McKenzie Ave G81 ......74 B4
McKenzie Dr G83 ....19 F1
McKenzie Gate G72 ...139 E6
McKenzie Pl FK1 ....42 A2
McKenzie St PA3 ......113 C5
McKenzie's Cl ML11 ..215 A4
McKeown Gdns ML4 ..142 D4
McKerrell St PA1 .....114 A5
McKillop Pl KA21 .....205 F2
McKim Wlk G82 ....49 D8
McKinlay Ave G83 ......20 A1
McKinlay Cres Alloa FK10 .10 C7
Irvine KA12 ....219 B1
McKinnon Pl KA21 ....206 A2
McKnight Ave KA3 ....213 E4
McLachlan Ave FK7 ......7 B2
McLachlan St FK5 ....23 C2
McLaren Ave PA4 ....94 C1
McLaren Cres G20 ......96 E7
McLaren Ct Glasgow G46 .136 B1
Stenhousemuir FK5 ......23 D2
Troon KA10 ....229 G4
McLaren Dr ML4 ......142 D4
McLaren Gdns G20 ......96 E7
McLaren Gr G74 ......159 A4
McLaren Pl G82 ....27 E2
McLaren Terr FK7 ....7 B3
McLauchlan View ML7 ..127 F6
McLaurin Cres PA5 ...111 D1
McLean Cres G83 ....19 F1
McLean Dr Bellshill ML4 ..141 F2
Irvine KA11 ....225 D8
McLean Gdns ML9 ....198 E2
McLean Mus & Art Gall*
PA16 ....45 E6
McLean Pl PA3 ....113 D7
McLean St KA8 ....236 C2
McLees La ML1 ....163 B7
McLellan Galleries*
G3 ....240 C3
McLelland Dr
Kilmarnock KA1 ....227 E7
Plains ML6 ....104 B2
McLennan St G42 ....137 B8
McLeod Rd G82 ....50 C4
McLeod St PA15 ....46 D3
McLuckie Dr KA13 ....207 C4
McLuckie Pk KA13 ....207 C4
McMahon Dr ML2 .....166 A6
McMahon Gr ML4 .....142 B6
McMillan Cres KA15 ..171 A7
McMillan Ct KA10 ....229 F4
McMillan Dr KA22 ....205 A4
McMillan Pl KA11 .....224 H6
McMillan Rd ML2 .....164 D2
McMillan Way ML8 ...186 F5
McNab Gdns FK1 ....41 F2
McNair St G32 ....119 A5
McNaught Pl
Kilmaurs KA3 ....222 A7
Renton G82 ....27 D1
McNay Cres KA21 ....206 A1
McNee Rd KA9 ....233 C3
McNeil Ave G81 ....74 E1
McNeil Dr ML1 ....143 A8
McNeil Gdns G5 ......117 D4
McNeil Pl ML2 ....186 C7
McNeil St G5 ....117 D4
McNeill Ave KA9 .....233 D1
McNiven Ct ML9 ......198 E1
McPhail Ave ML1 .....143 F5
McPhail St Glasgow G40 .117 E4
Greenock PA15 ....46 D3
McPhater St G4 ....240 C4
McPherson Cres ML6 ..123 E1
McPherson Dr
Bothwell G71 ....141 B3
Gourock PA19 ....44 D7
McPherson La G83 ......27 D7
McPherson St
Bellshill ML4 ....142 D5
Glasgow G1 ....241 B1
McShannon Gr ML4 ...142 A3
McSparran Rd G65 .....60 F4
McTaggart Ave FK6 .....21 E2
McVean Pl FK4 ....39 B4

Meadow Ave
Hamilton G72 161 D6
Irvine KA12 219 C4
Meadow Cl G75 180 A4
Meadow Ct Carluke ML8 188 C1
Denny FK6 21 D4
Dumbarton G82 49 F5
Meadow Gn FK10 5 B1
Meadow La Bothwell G71 141 B2
Renfrew PA4 94 D5
Meadow Park Rd KA13 207 C5
Meadow Path ML6 123 D1
Meadow Pk FK12 5 A6
Meadow Pl FK8 2 C1
Meadow Rd
Dumbarton G82 50 A4
Glasgow G11 96 A2
Motherwell ML1 163 F5
Meadow Rise G77 156 C5
Meadow St
Coatbridge ML5 122 B4
Falkirk FK1 42 C4
Meadow View
Cumbernauld G67 62 C4
Kilwinning KA13 207 C5
Plains ML6 104 A3
Meadow Way
Kilwinning KA13 207 D5
Newton Mearns G77 156 D6
Meadow Wlk ML5 122 C6
Meadowbank La
Prestwick KA9 236 B7
Uddingston G71 140 E6
Meadowbank Pl G77 156 D5
Meadowbank St G82 49 E4
Meadowburn
Bishopbriggs G64 78 A3
Bishopbriggs G64 78 A4
Meadowburn Ave
Kirkintilloch G66 79 E5
Newton Mearns G77 156 D5
Meadowburn Prim Sch
G64 78 A3
Meadowburn Rd ML2 165 C3
Meadowfield Pl ML2 166 C6
Meadowfoot Rd KA23 190 D4
Meadowforth Rd FK7 7 C7
Meadowhead Ave
Irvine KA11 224 G4
Moodiesburn G69 80 F2
Meadowhead Ind Est
KA11 224 G4
Meadowhead Rd
Irvine KA11 224 H3
Plains ML6 103 F2
Wishaw ML2 164 C4
Meadowhead Rdbt
KA11 224 H2
Meadowhill G77 156 D5
Meadowhill St ML9 185 B4
Meadowland Rd FK9 2 A6
Meadowpark KA7 239 A5
Meadowpark Dr KA7 239 B5
Meadowpark St G31 118 B7
Meadows Ave Erskine PA8 73 C1
Larkhall ML9 185 B3
Meadows Dr PA8 73 C1
Meadows The Falkirk FK1 42 C4
Falkirk,Carronshore FK2 24 B2
Helensburgh G84 16 F4
Houston PA6 91 E1
Kilwinning KA13 207 D4
Stirling FK9 2 B3
Meadowside Beith KA15 171 A8
Crookedholm KA3 228 E8
Hamilton ML3 183 D6
West Kilbride KA23 190 D5
Meadowside Ave PA5 112 D2
Meadowside Gdns ML6 123 D7
Meadowside Ind Est PA4 94 D6
Meadowside Pl ML6 123 D7
Meadowside Rd G65 59 F8
Meadowside St
Glasgow G11 96 A1
Renfrew PA4 94 D5
Meadowwell St G32 119 B5
Meadside Ave PA10 111 A4
Meadside Rd PA10 111 A4
Mealkirk St G81 74 C7
Mearns Castle High Sch
G77 157 A3
Mearns Ct ML3 183 E7
Mearns Prim Sch G77 156 B3
Mearns Rd
Motherwell ML1 163 C8
Newton Mearns,Mearns
G77 156 D1
Newton Mearns,Whitecraigs
G77 157 B7
Mearns St Greenock PA15 45 F4
Greenock PA15 45 F5
Mearns Terr PA15 45 F4
Mearns Way G64 78 D2
Mearnscroft Gdns G77 156 F3
Mearnscroft Rd G77 156 F3
Mearnskirk Rd G77 156 D2
Medine Ave KA15 150 B1
Medine Ct KA15 150 B1
Medlar Ct G72 139 F3
Medlar Rd G67 62 D2
Medrox Gdns G67 81 F5
Medwin Ct G75 179 E7
Medwin Gdns G75 179 E7
Medwin St G72 139 E5
Medwyn Pl FK10 9 F6
Medwyn St Glasgow G14 95 D3
Glasgow G14 95 E2
Meek Pl G72 139 B5
Meeks Rd FK2 42 B5
Meetinghouse La 5
PA1 113 E5
Megan Gate G40 117 F4
Megan St G40 117 F4
Meigle Rd ML6 122 F5
Meikle Ave PA4 94 C2
Meikle Bin Brae G66 57 F7
Meikle Cres
Greengairs ML6 103 D8
Hamilton ML3 183 C7
Meikle Ct KA3 195 E1
Meikle Cutstraw Farm
KA3 211 F8
Meikle Drumgray Rd
ML6 103 E8
Meikle Earnock Rd ML3 183 B7
Meikle Pl KA11 220 B6
Meikle Rd G53 135 C8
Meiklehill Ct G66 58 E1
Meiklehill Rd G66 58 E1
Meiklerig Cres G53 115 C2
Meikleriggs Dr PA2 113 A1
Meiklewood Ave KA9 233 D1
Meiklewood Bsns Ctr
KA3 223 D8
Meiklewood Rd
Glasgow G51 115 D6
Kilmarnock KA3 222 F5
Melbourne Ave
Clydebank G81 73 D5
East Kilbride G75 180 C8
Melbourne Ct G46 136 D3
Melbourne Gn 5 G75 180 C8
Melbourne Rd KA21 216 E7
Melbourne St G31 117 F6
Melbourne Terr KA21 216 E7
Meldon Pl G51 115 D7
Meldrum Gdns G41 116 D2
Meldrum Mains ML6 102 E4
Meldrum St G81 94 D8
Melford Ave
Glasgow G46 136 D2
Kirkintilloch G66 79 B8
Shotts ML7 147 B3
Melford Rd ML4 141 E7
Melford Way PA3 114 B7
Melfort Ave
Clydebank G81 74 C3
Glasgow G41 116 B4
Melfort Ct G81 74 C2
Melfort Dr FK7 7 C4
Melfort Est PA10 111 C1
Melfort Gdns
Clydebank G81 74 C2
Johnstone PA10 111 C1
Melfort Path ML2 165 F7
Melfort Quadrant ML1 143 D3
Melfort Rd ML3 161 E2
Mellerstain Dr G14 94 F6
Mellerstain Gr G14 94 F6
Mellock Gdns FK1 41 E2
Melness Pl 2 G51 115 D7
Melrose Ave
Chapelhall ML6 123 D2
Coatbridge G69 120 F6
Linwood PA3 112 B5
Motherwell ML1 143 B6
Paisley PA2 113 A1
Rutherglen G73 138 B7
Melrose Cres ML2 165 A5
Melrose Ct
7 Greenock PA15 46 B3
Rutherglen G73 138 B7
Melrose Gdns
Glasgow G20 96 F3
Twechar G65 59 F4
Uddingston G71 120 F1
Melrose Pl Blantyre G72 140 C1
Coatbridge ML5 121 F7
9 Falkirk FK1 42 B4
Larkhall ML9 185 A1
Melrose Rd
Cumbernauld G67 82 E7
Port Glasgow PA14 68 F7
Melrose St 6 Glasgow G4 97 A2
Hamilton ML3 162 B5
Melrose Terr
East Kilbride G74 159 F3
Hamilton ML3 162 B6
Melvaig Pl G20 96 D5
Melvick Pl 3 G51 115 D7
Melville Cres ML1 163 F6
Melville Ct G1 241 A1
Melville Dr ML1 163 F6
Melville Gdns G64 78 A2
Melville La FK1 42 B5
Melville Pk G74 160 B3
Melville Pl Bridge of A FK9 2 A7
Carluke ML8 187 E2
Melville St Falkirk FK1 42 B5
Glasgow G41 116 F3
Kilmarnock KA3 228 B8
Melville Terr FK8 7 B6
Melvinhall Rd ML11 215 A5
Memel St G21 97 E5
Memorial Way ML1 143 C6
Memus Ave G52 115 C4
Mendip La G75 180 A4
Mennock Ct ML3 161 E2
Mennock Dr G64 78 A4
Mennock La KA10 229 G5
Mennock St ML1 144 C2
Menock Rd G44 137 D6
Menstrie Bsns Ctr FK11 3 F6
Menstrie Castle* FK11 3 F6
Menstrie Pl FK10 4 A6
Menstrie Prim Sch FK11 4 A6
Menstrie Rd FK10 4 C3
Menteith Ave G64 78 B1
Menteith Ct Alloa FK10 10 C6
Motherwell ML1 163 F6
Menteith Dr G73 138 D2
Menteith Gdns G61 75 C8
Menteith Loan ML1 143 A5
Menteith Pl G73 138 D2
Menteith Rd
Motherwell ML1 163 E7
Stirling FK9 2 A3
Menzies Dr Glasgow G21 98 B5
Stirling FK8 2 A2
Menzies Pl G21 98 B5
Menzies Rd G21 98 A5
Mercat Wynd 2 FK10 10 B6
Merchant La G1 241 A1
Merchants Cl PA10 111 A3
Merchiston Ave
Falkirk FK2 42 A7
Linwood PA3 111 F5
Merchiston Dr PA5 111 D5
Merchiston Gdns FK2 42 A6
Merchiston Hospl PA5 111 E5
Merchiston Ind Est FK2 42 C8
Merchiston Rd
Falkirk,Grahamston FK2 42 A6
Falkirk,Mungal FK2 42 A7
Merchiston Rdbt FK2 42 A6
Merchiston St G32 118 F7
Merchiston Terr FK2 42 A7
Mercury La PA16 44 D3
Mere Ct G68 61 D6
Meredith Dr FK5 23 F3
Merino Rd PA15 45 E3
Merkins Ave G82 50 B6
Merkland Ct Glasgow G11 96 B1
Kirkintilloch G66 59 A1
Merkland Dr Falkirk FK1 42 E1
Kirkintilloch G66 80 A8
Merkland Pk KA2 225 F1
Merkland Pl
Dundonald KA2 225 F1
Kirkintilloch G66 59 A1
Merkland Rd Ayr KA7 239 A2
Coatbridge ML5 101 C2
Merkland Sch G66 58 F1
Merkland St G11 96 B2
Merkland Way G75 180 C4
Merksworth Ave KA24 191 C7
Merksworth Way PA3 113 E7
Merlewood Ave G71 141 B4
Merlewood Rd KA23 190 B4
Merlin Ave Bellshill ML4 142 A8
Greenock PA16 45 B6
Merlin La PA16 45 A6
Merlin Way PA3 114 B7
Merlinford Ave PA4 94 E3
Merlinford Cres PA4 94 E3
Merlinford Dr PA4 94 E3
Merlinford Way PA4 94 E3
Merrick Ave
Prestwick KA9 233 D1
Troon KA10 229 G4
Merrick Ct ML6 103 A2
Merrick Gdns
Bearsden G61 75 C7
Glasgow G51 116 B5
Quarter ML3 183 E3
Merrick Path G51 116 B5
Merrick Pl Irvine KA11 220 B2
Symington KA1 231 D4
Merrick Rd KA1 228 B4
Merrick Terr G71 141 B7
Merrick View KA3 195 E1
Merrick Way G73 138 B3
Merry Ct G72 161 E6
Merry St ML1 163 F7
Merryburn Ave G46 136 D4
Merrycrest Ave G46 136 D4
Merrycroft Ave G46 136 D4
Merryflats G65 59 F4
Merrygreen Pl KA3 195 E1
Merryland Pl G51 116 C7
Merryland St
Glasgow G51 116 B7
Glasgow G51 116 C7
Merrylee Ave PA14 68 E7
Merrylee Cres G46 136 C5
Merrylee Park Ave G46 136 D4
Merrylee Park Mews
G46 136 C5
Merrylee Prim Sch G44 136 F5
Merrylee Rd G44 136 E5
Merrylees Rd G72 161 C7
Merryston Ct ML5 121 E6
Merrystone St ML5 121 F7
Merryton Ave
Clydebank G15 75 B3
Glasgow,Merrylee G46 136 D4
Merryton Gdns 3 G15 75 B3
Merryton Rd
Larkhall ML9 184 F6
Motherwell ML1 164 C2
Merryton St ML9 184 F5
Merryton Twr ML1 164 B2
Merryvale Ave G46 136 D4
Merryvale Pl G46 136 D5
Merryvale Rd KA12 219 C1
Merryvale Rdbt KA12 219 C1
Merton Dr G52 115 A5
Merville Cres FK1 66 F5
Merville Terr FK1 66 F5
Meryon Gdns G32 119 D2
Meryon Rd G32 119 D3
Metcalfe Pl KA11 224 H6
Methil Rd PA14 68 F6
Methil St G14 95 C3
Methlan Park Gdns G82 49 D2
Methlan Pk G82 49 E2
Methlick Ave ML6 122 E4
Methuen Rd Paisley PA3 113 F8
Renfrew PA3 93 F1
Methven Ave
Bearsden G61 76 B5
Kilmarnock KA1 227 F4
Methven Pl
East Kilbride G74 159 C2
Kilmarnock KA1 227 F4
Methven Rd G46 157 A7
Methven St Clydebank G81 73 F4
Glasgow G31 118 D4
Methven Terr ML5 102 B1
Metropole La G1 241 A1
Mews Ho KA7 238 E8
Mews La Ayr KA7 238 E8
Greenock PA16 45 C8
Kilmarnock KA1 227 E7
Paisley PA3 113 F7
Mey Ct G77 156 A4
Mey Pl G77 156 A4
Mharie Pl G83 27 F2
Michael McParland Dr
G64 78 B8
Michael Terr ML6 123 D1
Micklehouse Oval 2
G69 120 B6
Micklehouse Pl 1 G69 120 B6
Micklehouse Rd G69 120 B6
Micklehouse Wynd 3
G69 120 B6
Mid Ave PA14 68 F8
Mid Barrwood Rd G65 60 F8
Mid Carbarns ML2 164 D1
Mid Dykes Rd KA21 205 E2
Mid Pk G75 180 E8
Mid Rd Beith KA15 150 B1
Cumbernauld G67 82 F6
Eaglesham G76 178 E4
Mid Rig KA11 220 A4
Mid-Loan St ML8 201 E4
Mid-Wharf St G4 97 C2
Midas Pl ML4 142 E5
Midcroft G64 77 E3
Midcroft Ave G44 137 E5
Middle Ward St G81 74 D7
Middlefield G75 180 E5
Middlefield Ind Est FK2 42 D7
Middlefield Rd FK2 42 D6
Middlefield Residential Sch
G11 96 B3
Middlehouse Ct ML8 187 D2
Middlemass Ct FK2 42 B6
Middlemass Dr KA1 228 B8
Middlemuir Ave G66 79 D5
Middlemuir Rd
Kirkintilloch G66 79 D6
Stirling FK7 7 C6
Middlepart KA20 206 C2
Middlepart Cres KA21 206 A1
Middlepenny Pl PA14 70 B7
Middlepenny Rd PA14 70 B7
Middlerigg Rd G68 61 D2
Middlesex Gdns 3 G41 116 E6
Middlesex St G41 116 E5
Middleton FK11 4 A5
Middleton Ave ML9 199 B8
Middleton Cres PA3 113 B6
Middleton Dr
Helensburgh G84 25 B8
Milngavie G62 55 C2
Middleton La G84 25 B8
Middleton Pk KA11 220 A4
Middleton Rd
Irvine KA11 220 A4
Linwood PA3 112 D7
Paisley PA3 113 B6
Middleton St
Alexandria G83 27 D5
Glasgow G51 116 C6
Midfaulds Ave PA4 94 E2
Midland Craft Ctr*
KA3 213 C2
Midland St G1 240 C2
Midlem Dr G52 115 C5
Midlem Oval G52 115 C5
Midlock St G51 116 C6
Midlothian Dr
Glasgow G41 116 D1
Glasgow G41 136 D8
Midthorn Cres FK2 42 E5
Midton Ave KA9 236 B8
Midton Rd Ayr KA7 238 F6
Howwood PA9 131 B6
Kilmarnock KA1 227 F2
Prestwick KA9 236 C8
Midton St G21 97 F3
Midtown FK11 3 F6
Migvie Pl G20 96 D5
Milford G75 180 B7
Milford St G33 119 A8
Milgarholm Ave KA12 219 D1
Milgarholm Rdbt KA12 219 D1
Mill Ave KA3 222 C7
Mill Brae Ayr KA7 239 A7
Bridge of W PA11 110 D8
Mill Brae Ct ML5 121 D5
Mill Cres Glasgow G40 117 F4
Irvine KA12 219 E3
Torrance G64 57 C1
Mill Ct Falkirk FK2 24 B3
Hamilton ML3 162 C2
Kilbirnie KA25 149 B1
Kilmarnock KA1 228 A7
Rutherglen G73 138 A8
Mill Farm KA22 205 D5
Mill Gr ML3 162 C2
Mill Hill FK7 6 D6
Mill Loan ML6 123 A8
Mill Of Airthrey Ct FK9 1 F8
Mill of Gryffe Rd PA11 110 D8
Mill Pk Dalry KA24 191 D8
Hamilton ML3 162 C2
Mill Pl Linwood PA3 112 A6
Uddingston G71 140 F6
Mill Rd Airdrie ML6 103 A1
Alloa FK10 10 B6
Banton G65 37 D3
Bothwell G71 141 A1
Cambusbarron FK7 6 D6
Cambuslang G72 139 D5
Cardross G82 26 A1
Carluke ML8 187 E1
Clydebank G81 94 D7
Falkirk FK2 24 B3
Hamilton ML3 162 C1
Harthill ML7 127 F5
Hartwood ML7 145 F1
Irvine KA12 219 E2
Kilbirnie KA25 149 B1
Motherwell ML1 163 F8
Queenzieburn G65 59 E7
Shotts ML7 166 F8
Wattston ML6 83 B1
Wishaw ML2 166 E5
Mill Rig G75 180 D5
Mill Rise G66 79 D4
Mill St Alloa FK10 10 B6
Ayr KA7 239 A8
Caldercruix ML6 104 F5
Glasgow G40 117 F3
Greenock PA15 45 E4
Kilmarnock KA1 227 F7
Paisley PA1 113 F4
Rutherglen G73 138 A6
Mill Street Ind Est ML6 123 A8
Mill Vennel PA4 94 D3
Mill Waulk KA3 211 E8
Mill Way G66 80 A7
Mill Wynd KA7 238 F8
Millands Ave G72 140 C2
Millar Gr ML3 162 B3
Millar Pl Bonnybridge FK4 40 B3
Stenhousemuir FK2 24 A5
Stirling FK8 2 C1
Millar Rd KA21 217 A8
Millar St Greenock PA15 46 B2
Paisley PA1 113 F5
Stonehouse ML9 198 F2
Millar Terr G73 118 B1
Millarbank St G21 97 E4
Millard Ave ML1 143 B2
Millars Pl G66 79 D4
Millars Wynd FK10 5 C2
Millarston Ave PA1 113 A4
Millarston Dr PA1 113 A4
Millbank Ave ML4 142 C3
Millbank Ct ML5 121 F3
Millbank Rd
Port Glasgow PA14 68 C8
Wishaw ML2 164 F1
Millbank Row KA11 220 D1
Millbeg Cres G33 119 F5
Millbeg Pl G33 119 F5
Millbrae Ave G69 100 D8
Millbrae Cres
Clydebank G81 94 D7
Glasgow G42 136 F7
Millbrae Ct Ayr KA7 239 A7
Glasgow G42 136 F7
Millbrae Gdns G42 136 F7
Millbrae Rd G42 136 F7
Millbrix Ave G14 95 A5
Millbrook G74 159 B1
Millbrook Pl FK11 3 F6
Millburn Ave
Clydebank G81 94 E8
Renfrew PA4 94 E3
Rutherglen G73 138 A6
Millburn Cres G82 50 B3
Millburn Ct G75 179 E7
Millburn Dr
Kilmacolm PA13 89 B8
Renfrew PA4 94 E3
Millburn Gate ML9 185 F1
Millburn Gdns G75 179 E7
Millburn La ML9 185 C2
Millburn Pl ML9 199 B8
Millburn Rd
Alexandria G83 27 D3
Ashgill ML9 186 A1
Dumbarton G82 50 B3
Port Glasgow PA14 68 C8
Renfrew PA4 94 D3
Millburn St Falkirk FK2 42 D5
Glasgow G21 98 A1
Lennoxtown G66 57 E8
Motherwell ML1 163 E7
Millburn Terr KA11 220 A6
Millburn Way
East Kilbride G75 179 E7
Renfrew PA4 94 E3
Millcroft Rd
Cumbernauld G67 82 E4
Cumbernauld G67 83 A4
Cumbernauld,Carbrain G67 62 B1
Rutherglen G73 117 F2
Milldam Rd G81 74 C7
Milldown Pl KA11 220 C2
Millennium Ct G34 120 C8
Millennium Gdns G34 120 C7

Miller Cl G64 .....98 D8
Miller Ct G82 .....50 B4
Miller Dr G64 .....98 D8
Miller Gdns G64 .....98 D8
Miller La G81 .....74 B1
Miller Pl Airth FK2 .....14 E4
Ardrossan KA22 .....205 B4
Harthill ML7 .....127 F6
Miller Rd Ayr KA7 .....238 F7
Balloch G83 .....27 F8
Balloch G83 .....28 A8
Miller Sq KA9 .....233 C2
Miller St Carluke ML8 .....188 A2
Clydebank G81 .....74 B1
Coatbridge ML5 .....122 B5
Dumbarton G82 .....50 B4
Glasgow G1 .....241 A2
Glasgow,Muirhead G69 .....120 B4
Hamilton ML3 .....162 F3
Harthill ML7 .....127 E6
Johnstone PA5 .....112 B3
Larkhall ML9 .....185 B3
Wishaw ML2 .....165 A3
Miller Wlk G64 .....98 D8
Miller's Pl ML6 .....123 B7
Millerfield Pl
Glasgow G40 .....118 B3
Hamilton ML3 .....162 F3
Millerfield Rd G40 .....118 B3
Millerslea G82 .....50 F1
Millerslea Gdns G84 .....16 F1
Millersneuk Ave G66 .....79 D3
Millersneuk Cres G33 .....99 B5
Millersneuk Ct G66 .....79 D4
Millersneuk Dr G66 .....79 D4
Millersneuk Prim Sch
G66 .....79 E4
Millersneuk Rd G66 .....79 D4
Millerston St G31 .....118 B6
Millfield Ave Erskine PA8 .....72 F1
Motherwell ML1 .....163 F8
Millfield Cres PA8 .....73 A1
Millfield Dr PA8 .....73 A1
Millfield Gdns PA8 .....73 A1
Millfield Hill PA8 .....72 F1
Millfield La PA8 .....72 F1
Millfield Mdws PA8 .....72 F1
Millfield Pl PA8 .....72 F1
Millfield View PA8 .....72 F1
Millfield Wlk PA8 .....73 A1
Millfield Wynd PA8 .....72 F1
Millflats St FK2 .....24 A1
Millford Dr PA3 .....112 B5
Millfore Ct KA11 .....220 A3
Millgate G71 .....140 F8
Millgate Ave G71 .....140 F8
Millgate Ct G71 .....140 F7
Millgate Rd ML3 .....162 C1
Millgate Terr ML3 .....162 C1
Millglen Cvn Pk KA22 .....205 C6
Millglen Pl KA22 .....205 D4
Millglen Rd KA22 .....205 D4
Millhall Rd
Eaglesham G76 .....179 C3
Stirling FK7 .....7 D5
Millheugh ML9 .....184 E2
Millheugh Brae ML9 .....184 E2
Millheugh Pl G72 .....161 C6
Millheugh Rd ML3 .....198 E5
Millhill Ave KA3 .....222 C7
Millhill Rd KA20 .....206 D1
Millhill Terr KA3 .....222 E4
Millholm Rd G44 .....137 B4
Millhouse Cres G20 .....96 C7
Millhouse Dr G20 .....96 C7
Millichen Rd G23 .....76 E5
Millig St G84 .....16 C3
Milliken Dr PA10 .....111 C2
Milliken Park Rd PA10 .....111 C1
Milliken Park Sta PA5 .....131 C8
Milliken Rd PA10 .....111 C2
Millport Ave G44 .....137 C7
Millport Rd PA14 .....68 F6
Millroad Dr G40 .....241 C1
Millroad Gdns 2 G40 .....117 F6
Millroad St G40 .....117 F6
Millrock Ct KA10 .....229 D3
Millstream Cres ML6 .....105 A4
Millstream Ct PA1 .....113 F4
Millview G78 .....134 D3
Millview Mdws G78 .....154 C7
Millview Pl G53 .....135 B4
Millview Terr G78 .....154 C7
Millwood St G41 .....136 E8
Milnbank St G31 .....118 A8
Milncroft Pl G33 .....99 A1
Milncroft Prim Sch G33 .....119 C8
Milncroft Rd G33 .....99 A1
Milndavie Cres G63 .....31 C3
Milndavie Rd G63 .....31 C2
Milne Ct ML2 .....165 E4
Milne Park Rd FK7 .....11 E8
Milne Way G71 .....141 A6
Milner La 7 G13 .....95 E5
Milner Rd G13 .....95 E5
Milngavie Ent Ctr G62 .....55 A2
Milngavie Prim Sch G62 .....55 A2
Milngavie Rd
Bearsden G61 .....76 A6
Strathblane G63 .....31 C2
Milngavie Sta G62 .....55 B1
Milnpark Gdns 4 G41 .....116 E5
Milnpark St G41 .....116 E5
Milnquarter Rd FK4 .....40 A3
Milnwood Dr
Bellshill ML4 .....142 D4
Motherwell ML1 .....142 C2
Milovaig Ave G23 .....76 D1
Milovaig St G23 .....76 D1
Milrig Rd G73 .....137 F7
Milroy Gdns ML4 .....142 A8
Milton Ave
Cambuslang G72 .....138 E5
Kilmarnock KA3 .....223 C1
Milton Brae Milton G82 .....50 F2
Stirling FK7 .....7 B2
Milton Cl FK6 .....21 D3
Milton Cres
Bannockburn FK7 .....7 C1
Carluke ML8 .....187 F1
Irvine KA11 .....220 C1
Troon KA10 .....229 F6
Milton Ct Airdrie ML6 .....123 A8
Irvine KA11 .....220 D1
Milton G82 .....50 F2
Milton Douglas Rd G81 .....74 B5
Milton Dr
1 Bishopbriggs G64 .....97 F7
Kilmarnock KA3 .....223 C1
Milton Est G83 .....27 F6
Milton Gdns Stirling FK7 .....7 B1
Uddingston G71 .....140 E8
Milton Gr FK7 .....7 C1
Milton Hill G82 .....50 F1
Milton Mains Rd G81 .....74 A5
Milton Pk Ayr KA7 .....239 B3
Kilbirnie KA25 .....149 B2
Milton Pl FK6 .....21 D3
Milton Prim Sch G82 .....50 F1
Milton Quadrant KA25 .....149 A3
Milton Rd Bannockburn FK7 .....7 C1
Carluke ML8 .....201 D7
East Kilbride G74 .....159 A2
Irvine KA11 .....220 C1
Kilbirnie KA25 .....149 A3
Kilmarnock KA3 .....228 C8
Kilmarnock KA3 .....228 D8
Kirkintilloch G66 .....58 C1
Lennoxtown G66 .....57 E7
Port Glasgow PA14 .....68 E6
Milton Row FK6 .....21 E3
Milton Sch G22 .....97 E7
Milton St Airdrie ML6 .....123 A8
Carluke ML8 .....187 E2
Glasgow G4 .....241 A4
Hamilton ML3 .....162 A4
Motherwell ML1 .....163 E8
Milton Terr
Hamilton ML3 .....162 A5
Stirling FK7 .....7 B1
Milton View KA2 .....226 E5
Miltonbank Prim Sch
G22 .....97 C8
Milverton Ave G61 .....75 D6
Milverton Rd
Glasgow G46 .....136 B1
Rutherglen G46 .....157 A8
Mimosa Rd PA11 .....110 D8
Minard Rd Glasgow G41 .....116 E1
Port Glasgow PA14 .....68 E7
Shotts ML7 .....146 D6
Minard Way G71 .....141 A7
Minch Way ML6 .....123 D5
Mincher Cres ML1 .....163 E4
Mine Rd FK9 .....2 A8
Minella Gdns ML4 .....142 A8
Minerva Ct 10 G3 .....116 E8
Minerva La PA16 .....44 D3
Minerva St G3 .....116 E8
Minerva Terr PA16 .....44 D3
Minerva Way G3 .....116 E8
Mingarry La G20 .....96 E4
Mingarry St G20 .....96 E4
Mingulay Cres G22 .....97 D8
Mingulay Pl G22 .....97 E8
Mingulay St G22 .....97 D8
Ministers Pk G74 .....158 F4
Minmoir Rd G53 .....134 F7
Minster Wlk G69 .....120 F5
Minstrel Rd G13 .....75 D1
Minthill Pl ML7 .....127 D5
Minto Ave G73 .....138 D4
Minto Cres G52 .....115 F5
Minto Ct FK12 .....5 B6
Minto Gdns FK12 .....5 B6
Minto Pk ML2 .....165 C6
Minto St Glasgow G52 .....115 F5
Greenock PA16 .....45 D4
Mireton St G22 .....97 B5
Mirren Dr G81 .....73 F7
Mirren's Shore PA14 .....47 C2
Mirrlees Dr G12 .....96 C4
Mirrlees La G12 .....96 C4
Misk Knowes KA20 .....217 E6
Misk Rd KA20 .....218 C6
Mission Gdns ML2 .....165 C5
Mission La 8 FK1 .....42 B4
Mitchell Arc G73 .....138 B8
Mitchell Ave
Cambuslang G72 .....139 E6
Renfrew PA4 .....94 B2
Mitchell Cres FK10 .....9 F7
Mitchell Ct
East Kilbride G74 .....159 C2
3 Kilmarnock KA1 .....228 A8
Mitchell Dr Cardross G82 .....48 B6
Milngavie G62 .....55 C1
Rutherglen G73 .....138 B6
Mitchell Gr G74 .....159 C2
Mitchell Hill Rd G45 .....137 F2
Mitchell La G1 .....240 C2
Mitchell Pl Falkirk FK1 .....41 E1
Mitchell Pl *continued*
Saltcoats KA21 .....205 E1
Mitchell Rd G67 .....62 A3
Mitchell St Airdrie ML6 .....122 F8
Beith KA15 .....150 B1
Coatbridge ML5 .....121 C5
Glasgow G1 .....240 C2
Greenock PA15 .....46 F2
Mitchell Way G83 .....27 E5
Mitchison Rd G67 .....62 A3
Mitre Ct 2 G11 .....95 F4
Mitre Gate 1 G11 .....95 F4
Mitre La G14 .....95 E4
Mitre La W G14 .....95 D4
Mitre Rd Glasgow G11 .....95 F4
Glasgow G14 .....95 E4
Moat Ave G13 .....95 C7
Mochrum Ct KA9 .....236 D6
Mochrum Rd G43 .....136 E6
Modan Rd FK7 .....7 A3
Moffat Ave FK2 .....24 C3
Moffat Ct G75 .....179 E7
Moffat Gdns G75 .....179 E7
Moffat Pl Airdrie ML6 .....123 F8
Blantyre G72 .....140 D1
Coatbridge ML5 .....122 E4
East Kilbride G75 .....179 E7
Moffat Rd Airdrie ML6 .....123 F7
Prestwick KA9 .....233 C3
Moffat St Glasgow G5 .....117 D4
Greenock PA15 .....46 C3
Moffat View ML6 .....104 A3
Moffat Wynd KA21 .....205 F3
Moffathill ML6 .....123 E5
Mogarth Ave PA2 .....132 F8
Moidart Ave PA4 .....94 B4
Moidart Cres G52 .....115 F5
Moidart Ct G78 .....134 B4
Moidart Gdns
Kirkintilloch G66 .....59 B1
Newton Mearns G77 .....156 E6
Moidart Pl G52 .....115 F5
Moidart Rd Glasgow G52 .....115 E5
Port Glasgow PA14 .....68 E7
Moir St Alloa FK10 .....10 A8
Glasgow G1 .....241 B1
Molendinar St G1 .....241 B1
Molendinar Terr G78 .....154 C6
Mollanbowie Rd G83 .....19 F2
Mollins Ct G68 .....81 D5
Mollins Rd G68 .....81 C7
Mollinsburn Rd
Annathill G67,ML5 .....81 F2
Glenboig ML5,ML6 .....101 F8
Glenmavis ML6 .....102 C6
Mollinsburn St G21 .....97 E3
Mollison Ave ML7 .....127 E6
Monach Gdns KA11 .....225 B8
Monach Rd Glasgow G33 .....119 C8
Port Glasgow PA14 .....69 A7
Monaebrook Pl G84 .....25 B8
Monar Dr G22 .....97 B3
Monar Pl G22 .....97 B3
Monar St G22 .....97 B3
Monar Way 5 ML2 .....165 F6
Monart Pl G20 .....96 F4
Moncks Rd FK1 .....42 D4
Moncreiff Gdns G66 .....79 D5
Moncrieff Ave G66 .....79 D5
Moncrieff St 1 PA3 .....113 E5
Moncrieffe Rd ML6 .....123 D4
Moncur Ct KA13 .....207 C5
Moncur Rd KA13 .....208 A3
Moncur St G40 .....241 C1
Moness Dr G52 .....115 E4
Money Gr ML1 .....164 B4
Monieburgh Cres G65 .....36 E1
Monieburgh Rd G65 .....36 E1
Monifieth Ave G52 .....115 D3
Monikie Gdns G64 .....78 D1
Monkcastle Dr G72 .....139 A6
Monkland Ave G66 .....79 D6
Monkland St ML6 .....123 B7
Monkland Terr ML5 .....101 D6
Monkland View
Calderbank ML6 .....123 B2
Uddingston G71 .....121 A1
Monkland View Cres
G69 .....121 A5
Monklands KA10 .....229 G7
Monklands District General
Hospl ML6 .....122 D7
Monklands Ind Est ML5 .....121 F2
Monkreddan Cres KA13 .....207 C5
Monks La ML8 .....201 E4
Monks Rd ML6 .....123 C4
Monksbridge Ave G13 .....75 D1
Monkscourt Ave ML6 .....122 E7
Monkscroft Ave 1 G11 .....96 A3
Monkscroft Ct G11 .....96 A2
Monkscroft Gdns G11 .....96 A2
Monkton Cres ML5 .....121 E4
Monkton Ct KA9 .....233 D2
Monkton Dr G15 .....75 C2
Monkton Gdns G77 .....157 A4
Monkton Pl PA14 .....68 F7
Monkton Prim Sch KA9 .....233 D4
Monkton Rd KA9 .....233 C1
Monktonhill Rd
Monkton KA9 .....233 B7
Troon KA10 .....232 F8
Monktonhill Rdbt KA9 .....233 D6
Monkwood Pl KA7 .....239 B2
Monmouth Ave G12 .....96 A5
Monreith Ave G61 .....75 D2
Monreith Rd G43 .....136 E6
Monreith Rd E G44 .....137 A5
Monroe Dr G71 .....120 F1
Monroe Pl G71 .....120 F1
Montague La G12 .....96 B4
Montague St G4 .....96 F2
Montalto Ave ML1 .....143 B1
Montclair Pl PA3 .....112 B6
Montego Gn 2 G75 .....159 A1
Monteith Dr G76 .....158 A8
Monteith Gdns G76 .....157 F8
Monteith Pl
3 Glasgow G40 .....117 E5
Hamilton G72 .....161 E8
Monteith Row G40 .....117 E5
Monteith Wlk ML7 .....146 E6
Montfode Ct KA22 .....205 B4
Montfode Dr KA22 .....205 B4
Montford Ave G44 .....137 E7
Montfort Pl FK1 .....42 B3
Montgarrie St 3 G51 .....115 D6
Montgomerie Cres
KA21 .....216 E8
Montgomerie Ct KA22 .....205 C1
Montgomerie Pier Rd
KA22 .....205 B1
Montgomerie Rd
Prestwick KA9 .....233 B1
Saltcoats KA21 .....216 E8
Montgomerie St
Ardrossan KA22 .....205 C1
Port Glasgow PA14 .....47 D1
Montgomerie Terr
Ayr KA7 .....235 E1
Kilwinning KA13 .....208 A3
Montgomerieston Pl 8
KA25 .....149 A1
Montgomerieston St 9
KA25 .....149 A1
Montgomery Ave
Beith KA15 .....171 C8
Coatbridge ML5 .....121 F7
Paisley PA3 .....114 B7
Montgomery Cres
Falkirk FK2 .....24 B2
Wishaw ML2 .....185 E8
Montgomery Ct
Eaglesham G76 .....178 E3
Kilbirnie KA25 .....149 B2
Paisley PA3 .....114 B7
Montgomery Dr
Falkirk FK2 .....24 B2
Glasgow G46 .....136 C1
Kilbarchan PA10 .....111 A4
Montgomery Pl
3 East Kilbride G74 .....159 F2
Falkirk FK2 .....24 B2
Irvine KA12 .....219 A1
Kilmarnock KA3 .....222 F2
Larkhall ML9 .....185 B2
Montgomery Rd PA3 .....114 B8
Montgomery Sq G76 .....178 E4
Montgomery St
Cambuslang G72 .....139 E5
Eaglesham G76 .....178 E4
4 East Kilbride G74 .....159 F2
Falkirk FK2 .....42 E5
Glasgow G40 .....118 A4
Irvine KA12 .....219 A1
Kilmarnock KA3 .....222 F2
Larkhall ML9 .....185 A4
Montgomery Terr G66 .....58 C5
Montgomery Way FK9 .....2 B3
Montgomery Well FK2 .....24 B2
Montgomeryfield KA11 .....225 B8
Montgreenan View
KA13 .....207 F3
Montraive St G73 .....118 C1
Montrave St G52 .....115 D4
Montreal Ho G81 .....73 D6
Montreal Pk G75 .....159 C1
Montrose Ave
Glasgow G52 .....114 E8
Glasgow G52 .....114 F8
Glasgow (Hillington Ind Est)
G52 .....94 E1
Glasgow,Carmyle G32 .....119 C1
Port Glasgow PA14 .....68 E6
Montrose Cres ML3 .....162 D4
Montrose Ct PA2 .....132 F8
Montrose Dr G61 .....75 E7
Montrose Gdns
Blantyre G72 .....140 C2
Kilsyth G65 .....36 C1
Milngavie G62 .....55 A3
Montrose La ML3 .....162 C4
Montrose Pl PA3 .....112 A6
Montrose Rd Paisley PA2 .....132 F8
Stirling FK9 .....2 C4
Montrose St
Clydebank G81 .....74 C2
Glasgow G1 .....241 B2
Motherwell ML1 .....142 D1
Montrose Terr
Bishopbriggs G64 .....98 C7
Bridge of W PA11 .....110 D7
Montrose Way
Bonnybridge FK4 .....39 D5
Paisley PA2 .....132 F8
Monument Cres KA9 .....233 F1
Monument Rd KA7 .....238 F4
Monument View FK8 .....2 B2
Monymusk Gdns G64 .....78 D2
Monymusk Pl G15 .....74 E5
Moodie Ct KA1 .....227 F5
Moodiesburn St G33 .....98 E2
Moor Park Cres KA9 .....236 C5
Moor Park Pl KA9 .....236 C5
Moor Pk KA9 .....236 C5
Moor Pl KA8 .....236 C4
Moor Rd Ayr KA8 .....236 C4
Moor Rd *continued*
Cartland ML8,ML11 .....202 E2
Eaglesham G76 .....178 D4
Milngavie G62 .....55 B2
Strathblane G63 .....31 C1
Moorburn Ave G46 .....136 B3
Moorburn Pl PA3 .....111 F6
Moorcroft Dr ML6 .....123 E7
Moorcroft Rd G77 .....156 C3
Moore Dr Bearsden G61 .....75 F3
Helensburgh G84 .....25 C7
Moore Gdns ML3 .....183 E7
Moore St
Glasgow G31,G40 .....117 F6
Motherwell ML1 .....143 A3
Moorend Workshops
KA11 .....224 G7
Moorfield Ave
Kilmarnock KA1 .....227 D6
Port Glasgow PA14 .....68 D7
Moorfield Cres ML6 .....123 F7
Moorfield Ind Est KA2 .....227 A7
Moorfield La PA19 .....44 C6
Moorfield Pl KA2 .....226 D5
Moorfield Rd
Gourock PA19 .....44 C7
Hamilton G72 .....161 C6
Prestwick KA9 .....236 C7
Moorfield Rdbt KA1 .....227 A7
Moorfoot G64 .....78 C2
Moorfoot Ave
Glasgow G46 .....136 A3
Paisley PA2 .....113 D1
Moorfoot Dr
Gourock PA19 .....44 C6
Wishaw ML2 .....164 F3
Moorfoot Gdns G75 .....180 B3
Moorfoot Path PA2 .....133 D8
Moorfoot Pl KA11 .....220 A3
Moorfoot Prim Sch PA19 .....44 C6
Moorfoot St G32 .....118 E6
Moorfoot Way
Bearsden G61 .....75 C8
Irvine KA11 .....220 A3
Moorhill Cres G77 .....156 C4
Moorhill Rd G77 .....156 C3
Moorhouse Ave
Glasgow G13 .....94 F6
Paisley PA2 .....113 B2
Moorhouse St G78 .....134 C2
Moorings The PA2 .....113 C3
Moorland Dr ML6 .....123 E7
Moorlands Wlk G71 .....141 A5
Moorpark Ave
3 Airdrie ML6 .....123 E7
Glasgow G52 .....114 F6
Muirhead G69 .....100 C7
Moorpark Ct G51 .....116 A7
Moorpark Dr G52 .....115 A6
Moorpark Ind Est KA20 .....217 D7
Moorpark Pl
Glasgow G52 .....114 F6
Stevenston KA20 .....217 D7
Moorpark Prim Sch
Kilbirnie KA25 .....149 A3
Renfrew PA4 .....94 B2
Moorpark Rd E KA20 .....217 D8
Moorpark Rd W KA20 .....217 D7
Moorpark Sq PA4 .....94 B2
Moorside St ML8 .....188 A2
Morag Ave G72 .....140 C1
Moraine Ave G15 .....75 B1
Moraine Cir G15 .....75 B1
Moraine Dr
Clarkston G76 .....157 D8
Clydebank G15 .....75 B1
Moraine Pl G15 .....75 B1
Morar Ave G81 .....74 B4
Morar Cres Airdrie ML6 .....102 E2
Bishopbriggs G64 .....77 F2
Bishopton PA7 .....72 C2
Clydebank G81 .....74 B4
Coatbridge ML5 .....101 D1
Morar Ct Clydebank G81 .....74 B4
Cumbernauld G67 .....82 B8
Hamilton ML3 .....162 A1
Larkhall ML9 .....184 F5
Morar Dr Bearsden G61 .....76 B3
Clydebank G81 .....74 B4
Cumbernauld G67 .....82 B8
Falkirk FK2 .....24 C1
Linwood PA3 .....112 A5
Paisley PA2 .....113 A2
Rutherglen G73 .....138 B3
Morar Pl Clydebank G81 .....74 B4
East Kilbride G74 .....159 F3
Irvine KA12 .....219 C6
Newton Mearns G77 .....156 D7
Renfrew PA4 .....94 B4
Morar Rd Clydebank G81 .....74 B4
Glasgow G52 .....115 E5
Port Glasgow PA14 .....68 E7
Morar St ML2 .....165 A1
Morar Terr
Rutherglen G73 .....138 D4
Uddingston G71 .....141 B7
Morar Way
Motherwell ML1 .....143 C3
Shotts ML7 .....147 B3
Moravia Ave G71 .....141 A3
Moray Ave ML6 .....123 A5
Moray Ct G73 .....138 A8
Moray Dr Clarkston G76 .....157 F7
Torrance G64 .....57 B1
Moray Gate G71 .....140 F4
Moray Gdns
Clarkston G76 .....157 F8
Cumbernauld G68 .....61 F5

...

Old Hillfoot Rd KA7 .....239 B5
Old Humbie Rd G77 .....156 E2
Old Inns Intc G67 .....62 C5
Old Inns Rdbt G68 .....62 B6
Old Inverkip Rd PA16 .....45 C4
Old Irvine Rd KA1 .....227 E8
Old Lanark Rd
Braidwood ML8,ML11 .....202 B4
Carluke ML8 .....201 F8
Cartland ML11 .....202 E1
Old Largs Rd PA15,PA16 .....45 E2
Old Loans Rd KA10 .....230 A4
Old Luss Rd Balloch G83 .....19 B1
Helensburgh G84 .....16 F1
Old Manse Gdns ML5 .....122 A7
Old Manse Rd
Glasgow G32 .....119 D5
Wishaw ML2 .....164 E1
Old Military Rd G83 .....20 E8
Old Mill Ct G81 .....74 A5
Old Mill Gate G73 .....138 A6
Old Mill La G71 .....140 F7
Old Mill Park Ind Est
G66 .....58 C1
Old Mill Rd Bothwell G71 .....141 B1
Cambuslang G72 .....139 D5
Clydebank G81 .....74 A6
East Kilbride G74 .....159 F2
Hartwood ML7 .....146 B1
Kilmarnock KA1 .....228 A7
Paisley PA1,PA2 .....113 B3
Uddingston G71 .....140 F7
Old Mill View G65 .....60 F3
Old Mill Wlk G83 .....27 E7
Old Monkland Prim Sch
ML5 .....121 C4
Old Monkland Rd ML5 .....121 E4
Old Mugdock Rd G63 .....31 C2
Old Perceton KA11 .....220 B6
Old Playfield Rd G76 .....158 D8
Old Quarry Rd
Cumbernauld G68 .....81 D5
Stevenston KA20 .....217 D8
Old Raise Rd KA21 .....206 A1
Old Rd PA5 .....112 C3
Old Redding Rd FK2 .....42 F3
Old Rome Way KA2 .....226 E5
Old Rutherglen Rd G5 .....117 D4
Old School Ct
Coatbridge ML5 .....122 A4
Tullibody FK10 .....4 B2
Old School Flats PA11 .....110 D8
Old School Sq PA10 .....111 A3
Old Schoolhouse La PA6 .....91 B3
Old Sheriffmuir Rd FK9 .....2 C6
Old Shettleston Rd G32 .....119 A5
Old Sneddon St PA3 .....113 E5
Old St Duntocher G81 .....73 F6
Kilmarnock KA1 .....227 F5
Old Stable Row ML5 .....122 B7
Old Station Brae KA10 .....229 F3
Old Station Ct G71 .....141 A2
Old Station Wynd KA10 .....229 F3
Old Town FK7 .....7 D1
Old Union St ML6 .....123 B7
Old Vic Ct G74 .....160 C4
Old Willowyard Rd
KA15 .....171 A7
Old Wood Rd G69 .....120 A4
Old Woodwynd Rd
KA13 .....207 E4
Old Wynd G1 .....241 A1
Oldbarhills TP Site PA2 .....134 D8
Oldhall Dr PA13 .....69 D1
Oldhall Rd PA1 .....114 D5
Oldhall Rdbt KA11 .....224 H5
Oldhall West Ind Est
KA11 .....224 H6
Olifard Ave G71 .....141 B3
Oliphant Cres
Clarkston G76 .....157 E5
Paisley PA2 .....132 E8
Oliphant Ct Paisley PA2 .....132 F8
Stirling FK8 .....2 B1
Oliphant Dr KA3 .....228 C8
Oliphant Oval PA2 .....132 E8
Olive Bank G71 .....121 C1
Olive Ct ML1 .....143 B5
Olive Rd KA1 .....227 D8
Olive St G33 .....98 D4
Oliver Rd FK1 .....42 D4
Ollach PA8 .....93 C7
Olympia Arc 2 G74 .....180 F8
Olympia Ct G75 .....180 F8
Olympia St 3 G40 .....117 F5
Olympia The 1 G74 .....180 F8
Olympia Way G74 .....159 F1
Olympic Bsns Pk KA2 .....225 D4
Omoa Rd ML1 .....144 B1
Onich Pl ML7 .....147 B3
Onslow G75 .....180 C7
Onslow Dr G31 .....118 A7
Onslow Rd G81 .....74 D2
Onslow Sq G31 .....118 A7
Ontario Pk G75 .....159 B1
Ontario Pl G75 .....159 B1
Onthank Dr KA3 .....222 F4
Onthank Prim Sch KA3 .....222 F5
Onyx St ML4 .....142 A4
Open Shore PA15 .....46 A5
Oran Gate G20 .....96 E5
Oran Gdns G20 .....96 E5
Oran Pl G20 .....96 E4
Oran St G20 .....96 E4
Orangefield PA15 .....45 E5
Orangefield Dr KA9 .....233 D1
Orangefield Ind Est
KA9 .....233 D2
Orangefield La PA15 .....45 E5
Orbiston Ct ML1 .....164 A5
Orbiston Dr Bellshill ML4 .....142 C4
Clydebank G81 .....74 D7
Orbiston Pl G81 .....74 D7
Orbiston Rd Bellshill ML4 .....141 F4
Bellshill ML4 .....142 B2
Orbiston Sq ML4 .....141 F3
Orbiston St ML1 .....163 F5
Orcades Dr G44 .....137 C4
Orchard Ave Ayr KA7 .....239 B6
Bothwell G71 .....141 B1
Orchard Brae
Hamilton ML3 .....162 D4
Kirkintilloch G66 .....79 E4
Orchard Ct Glasgow G32 .....139 B8
Glasgow,Orchard Pk G46 .....136 A3
Renfrew PA4 .....94 D4
Orchard Dr Glasgow G46 .....136 B3
Hamilton G72 .....161 D8
Rutherglen G73 .....137 F7
Orchard Field G66 .....79 E4
Orchard Gate ML9 .....185 A2
Orchard Gn G74 .....160 B4
Orchard Gr
Coatbridge ML5 .....122 B6
Glasgow G46 .....136 B4
Kilmacolm PA13 .....89 C8
Kilwinning KA13 .....207 E4
Orchard House Hospl FK8 .....2 A1
Orchard Park Ave G46 .....136 B3
Orchard Pk G46 .....136 C3
Orchard Pl Ayr KA7 .....239 B6
Bellshill ML4 .....141 F3
Hamilton ML3 .....162 D3
Kilwinning KA13 .....207 E4
Kirkintilloch G66 .....80 A7
Orchard Rd FK9 .....2 A6
Orchard St Carluke ML8 .....187 F1
Falkirk FK1 .....42 B5
Glasgow G69 .....119 F3
Greenock PA15 .....46 B3
Hamilton ML3 .....162 E3
Kilmarnock KA3 .....222 F2
Motherwell ML1 .....163 D7
Overtown ML2 .....186 B6
Paisley PA1 .....113 E4
Renfrew PA4 .....94 D4
West Kilbride KA23 .....190 C5
Orchard The FK10 .....4 B2
Orchard View Dr ML11 .....214 A4
Orchardcroft 5 FK8 .....7 B7
Orchardton Rd G68 .....81 D7
Orchardton Woods Ind Pk
G68 .....81 C8
Orchid Pl G66 .....57 C8
Orchy Ave Clarkston G76 .....157 F8
Glasgow G76 .....136 F1
Orchy Cres Airdrie ML6 .....123 C4
Bearsden G61 .....75 D1
Paisley PA2 .....112 F1
Orchy Ct G81 .....74 C5
Orchy Dr G76 .....136 F1
Orchy Gdns G76 .....136 F1
Orchy St G44 .....137 A6
Orchy Terr G74 .....160 A1
Orefield Pl G74 .....159 E3
Oregon Pl G5 .....117 C4
Orion Pl ML4 .....142 E5
Orion Way
Cambuslang G72 .....139 A6
Carluke ML8 .....187 D2
Orkney Ct FK10 .....10 B5
Orkney Dr KA3 .....223 A5
Orkney Pl Falkirk FK1 .....42 B2
Glasgow G51 .....116 B7
Orkney Quadrant ML2 .....165 D4
Orkney St G51 .....116 B7
Orlando G74 .....160 C5
Orleans Ave G14 .....95 E4
Orleans La G14 .....95 E3
Orlington Ct ML5 .....121 F8
Ormiston Ave G14 .....95 C4
Ormiston Dr Alloa FK10 .....4 E2
Hamilton ML3 .....183 C8
Ormiston La 10 G14 .....95 C4
Ormiston La N 6 G14 .....95 C4
Ormiston La S 12 G14 .....95 C4
Ormiston Pl KA11 .....220 C7
Ormond Ct FK5 .....23 A3
Ormonde Ave G44 .....136 F3
Ormonde Cres G44 .....136 F3
Ormonde Ct G44 .....136 F3
Ormonde Dr G44 .....136 F3
Ornsay St G22 .....97 D7
Oronsay Ave PA14 .....69 B6
Oronsay Cres
Bearsden G61 .....76 B3
Old Kilpatrick G60 .....73 C6
Oronsay Ct G60 .....73 C6
Oronsay Gdns G60 .....73 C6
Oronsay Pl
Old Kilpatrick G60 .....73 C6
Wishaw ML2 .....165 B1
Oronsay Rd ML6 .....123 D5
Oronsay Sq G60 .....73 C6
Orr Sq PA1 .....113 E5
Orr Square Church PA1 .....113 D5
Orr St Glasgow G40 .....117 F5
Glasgow G40 .....117 F6
Paisley PA2 .....113 E3
Paisley,Castlehead PA1 .....113 E5
Orr Terr Harthill ML7 .....127 C4
Neilston G78 .....154 C6
Orton Pl G51 .....116 A6
Osborne Cres G74 .....158 B3
Osborne Gdns FK1 .....41 F3
Osborne St Clydebank G81 .....74 A3
Falkirk FK1 .....41 F3
Glasgow G1 .....241 A1
Oskaig PA8 .....93 C7
Oslie View KA3 .....195 F1
Osprey Cres ML2 .....165 B4
Osprey Dr
Kilmarnock KA1 .....228 C7
Uddingston G71 .....141 A7
Osprey Rd PA16 .....45 B4
Ossian Ave PA1 .....114 F5
Ossian Rd G43 .....136 E6
Oswald Ct KA8 .....236 A3
Oswald Dr KA9 .....233 C1
Oswald Gdns ML8 .....201 E4
Oswald La KA8 .....235 E2
Oswald Pl KA8 .....236 A5
Oswald Rd KA8 .....236 A4
Oswald St Falkirk FK1 .....42 B4
Glasgow G1 .....240 C2
Oswald Wlk G62 .....76 C8
Otago La G12 .....96 E2
Otago La N G12 .....96 E2
Otago Pk G75 .....159 A1
Otago Pl G82 .....50 C2
Otago St G12 .....96 E2
Othello G74 .....160 B5
Ottawa Cres G81 .....73 D4
Otterburn Ave KA3 .....223 B3
Otterburn Dr G46 .....136 C1
Otterswick Pl G33 .....99 C2
Ottoline Dr KA10 .....229 G2
Oudenarde Ct ML8 .....188 B1
Our Holy Redeemer's RC
Prim Sch G81 .....94 D7
Our Lady & St Francis RC
Prim Sch ML1 .....143 C2
Our Lady & St Joseph's Prim
Sch ML5 .....101 C7
Our Lady & St Patricks High
Sch G82 .....49 C4
Our Lady of Loretto Prim Sch
G81 .....73 E3
Our Lady of Lourdes Prim
Sch G75 .....180 D8
Our Lady of Peace Prim Sch
PA3 .....112 A5
Our Lady of the Annunciation
G43 .....136 E5
Our Lady of the Assumption
Prim Sch G20 .....97 A6
Our Lady of the Missions
Prim Sch G46 .....136 A2
Our Lady of the Rosary Prim
Sch G52 .....115 D4
Our Lady's High Sch
Cumbernauld G67 .....61 D1
Motherwell ML1 .....164 A3
Outdale Ave KA9 .....236 E8
Oval The Glasgow G76 .....136 F1
Glenboig ML5 .....101 C6
Overbrae Gdns G15 .....74 F5
Overbrae Pl G15 .....74 F5
Overburn Ave G82 .....49 F4
Overburn Cres G82 .....49 F5
Overburn Terr G82 .....50 A5
Overcroy Rd G65 .....60 F4
Overdale Ave G42 .....136 F8
Overdale Cres KA9 .....236 C6
Overdale Gdns G42 .....136 F8
Overdale Pl ML2 .....186 C6
Overdale St G42 .....136 F8
Overjohnstone Dr ML2 .....164 D4
Overlea Ave G73 .....138 D6
Overlee Ho G76 .....157 F7
Overlee Rd G76 .....157 F7
Overmills Cres KA7 .....239 D8
Overmills Rd KA7 .....239 E7
Overnewton Pl G3 .....116 D8
Overnewton Sq G3 .....96 D1
Overnewton St G3 .....96 D1
Overton Cres Denny FK6 .....21 D1
Greenock PA15 .....45 D3
Johnstone PA5 .....112 B3
West Kilbride KA23 .....190 C5
Overton Ct KA23 .....190 C5
Overton Dr KA23 .....190 C5
Overton Gdns PA13 .....69 E1
Overton Gr PA13 .....69 E1
Overton Pl Glasgow G31 .....118 A5
Irvine KA11 .....220 B5
Overton Prim Sch PA15,
PA16 .....45 D3
Overton Rd
Alexandria G83 .....27 D4
Cambuslang G72 .....139 D4
Johnstone PA5 .....112 A2
Netherburn ML9 .....200 C5
Overton St Alexandria G83 .....27 E5
Cambuslang G72 .....139 D4
Overton Terr FK6 .....21 C2
Overtoun Ave G82 .....50 B3
Overtoun Ct KA11 .....221 A2
Overtoun Dr
Clydebank G81 .....73 F4
Rutherglen G73 .....138 A7
Overtoun Est* G82 .....50 F5
Overtoun Rd
Clydebank G81 .....73 F4
Springside KA11 .....220 F3
Overtown Ave G53 .....135 B6
Overtown Prim Sch
ML2 .....186 C7
Overtown Rd ML2 .....165 F2
Overtown St G31 .....118 A5
Overwood Dr
Dumbarton G82 .....50 B4
Glasgow G44 .....137 C6
Overwood Gr G82 .....50 B4
Owen Ave G75 .....180 C7
Owen Kelly Pl KA21 .....205 E1
Owen Pk G75 .....180 D7
Owen St ML1 .....163 E8
Owendale Ave ML4 .....142 B7
Oxenward Rd KA13 .....207 E3
Oxford Ave PA19 .....45 A6
Oxford Dr PA3 .....112 B6
Oxford La Glasgow G5 .....117 B5
Renfrew PA4 .....94 C3
Oxford Rd Greenock PA16 .....44 D4
Renfrew PA4 .....94 C3
Oxford St Coatbridge ML5 .....121 F6
Glasgow G5 .....240 C1
Kirkintilloch G66 .....79 C8
Oxgang Holdings G66 .....79 F7
Oxgang Pl G66 .....79 E7
Oxgang Prim Sch G66 .....79 F8
Oxgang Rdbt G66 .....79 F7
Oxhill Pl G82 .....49 D3
Oxhill Rd G82 .....49 D4
Oxton Dr G52 .....115 B5

P

Pacemuir La PA13 .....89 B8
Pacemuir Rd PA13 .....89 B8
Paddock St ML5 .....122 D4
Paddock The
Clarkston G76 .....158 A5
Hamilton ML3 .....162 D6
Lanark ML11 .....214 D7
Perceton KA11 .....220 C5
Paddock View KA2 .....221 C1
Paddockholm North Ind Est
KA25 .....149 B2
Paddockholm Rd KA25 .....149 B1
Paddockholm South Ind Est
KA25 .....149 B1
Paduff Pl KA25 .....149 A2
Paidmyre Cres G77 .....156 D3
Paidmyre Gdns G77 .....156 D3
Paidmyre Rd G77 .....156 D3
Paisley (Gilmour St) Sta
PA3 .....113 E5
Paisley Abbey* PA1 .....113 F4
Paisley Canal Sta PA1 .....113 E3
Paisley Ctr The PA1 .....113 E4
Paisley Gram Sch PA1 .....114 A5
Paisley Maternity Hospl
PA2 .....113 C2
Paisley Mus & Art Gallery*
PA1 .....113 D4
Paisley Rd Barrhead G78 .....134 B4
Glasgow G5 .....240 B1
Renfrew PA4 .....94 C2
Paisley Rd W
Glasgow G51,G52 .....115 D4
Glasgow,Ibrox G52 .....116 A5
Paisley St KA22 .....205 C2
Paisley St James Sta
PA3 .....113 C6
Palace Grounds Rd ML3 .....162 F4
Palace of Art* G41 .....115 F5
Palacecraig St ML5 .....122 A3
Palacerigg Country Pk*
G67 .....83 F7
Paladin Ave G13 .....95 B8
Palermo St 2 G21 .....97 E4
Palladium Pl G14 .....95 D3
Palm Pl G71 .....121 C1
Palmer Ave G13 .....75 D1
Palmerston G75 .....180 A7
Palmerston Pl
Glasgow G3 .....116 D8
Johnstone PA5 .....131 C8
Pandora Way G71 .....141 A7
Pankhurst Pl G74 .....159 F2
Panmure Path G68 .....60 F2
Panmure Pl G22 .....97 B5
Panmure St G20 .....97 A5
Panrock Ct KA10 .....229 D3
Pantonville Rd KA23 .....190 C3
Papermill Rd PA15,PA16 .....45 D2
Papingo Cl KA13 .....207 C6
Pappert G83 .....28 A3
Pardovan Pl FK1 .....41 F6
Paris Ave FK6 .....21 E1
Park Ave Balloch G83 .....19 F1
Barrhead G78 .....134 B1
Beith KA15 .....150 B1
Bishopbriggs G64 .....78 B3
Carluke ML8 .....187 F3
Denny FK4 .....39 E6
Dumbarton G82 .....50 B3
Elderslie PA5 .....112 C2
Glasgow G3 .....96 F2
Greenock PA16 .....45 A7
Kilwinning KA13 .....207 E3
Kirkintilloch G66 .....79 C8
Laurieston FK2 .....42 F4
Milngavie G62 .....55 A1
Motherwell ML1 .....143 A5
Paisley PA2 .....113 D1
Prestwick KA9 .....236 B8
Stenhousemuir FK5 .....23 D1
Stirling FK8 .....7 A6
Twechar G65 .....59 F4
Park Bank PA8 .....73 B1
Park Brae PA8 .....93 C8
Park Burn Ct ML3 .....162 A6
Park Burn Ind Est ML3 .....162 A6
Park Cir Ayr KA7 .....238 F7
Park Cir *continued*
Carluke ML8 .....187 F3
Glasgow G3 .....240 A4
Park Circus La Ayr KA7 .....238 F7
Glasgow G3 .....240 A4
Park Circus Pl G3 .....240 A4
Park Cres Airdrie ML6 .....122 E8
Alloa FK10 .....5 C1
Bannockburn FK7 .....7 D2
Bearsden G61 .....75 C5
Bishopbriggs G64 .....78 A2
Dumbarton G82 .....49 F5
Eaglesham G76 .....178 E5
Falkirk FK2 .....24 A2
Hamilton G72 .....161 C6
Inchinnan PA4 .....93 D7
Stewarton KA3 .....211 D8
Torrance G64 .....57 C1
Park Ct Beith KA15 .....171 C8
Bishopbriggs G64 .....78 B3
Clydebank G81 .....73 E4
Glasgow G46 .....136 B3
Shotts ML7 .....146 F4
Symington KA1 .....231 D3
Park Dr Bannockburn FK7 .....7 D2
Bellshill ML4 .....142 A4
Erskine PA8 .....93 B8
Glasgow G3 .....240 A4
Hamilton ML3 .....163 C1
Lanark ML11 .....214 F4
Rutherglen G73 .....138 A7
Stenhousemuir FK5 .....23 D2
Thorntonhall G74 .....158 C3
Wishaw ML2 .....166 A5
Park Gardens La G3 .....96 E1
Park Gate Erskine PA8 .....93 B8
Glasgow G3 .....96 E1
Park Gate Pl ML4 .....141 F5
Park Gdns Bannockburn FK7 .....7 D2
Glasgow G3 .....96 E1
Kilbarchan PA10 .....111 B4
Park Glade PA8 .....93 B8
Park Gn PA8 .....93 B8
Park Gr Cardross G82 .....48 B8
Erskine PA8 .....93 C8
Park Hill PA8 .....73 B1
Park La Ardrossan KA22 .....205 C3
Carluke ML8 .....187 E1
Glasgow G40 .....117 F5
Hamilton G72 .....161 D8
Kilsyth G65 .....60 D8
Kilwinning KA13 .....207 D5
Stirling FK8 .....7 B8
Park Lea ML6 .....105 A4
Park Mains High Sch
PA8 .....73 B1
Park Moor PA8 .....93 B8
Park Pl Alloa FK10 .....10 C7
Bellshill ML4 .....141 E3
Coatbridge ML5 .....122 D4
Irvine KA12 .....219 B5
Johnstone PA5 .....111 F2
Lanark ML11 .....214 F4
Stirling FK7 .....6 F6
Strathblane G63 .....31 B3
Thorntonhall G74 .....158 C3
Park Prim Sch FK10 .....10 B5
Park Quadrant
Glasgow G3 .....240 A4
Wishaw ML2 .....164 E1
Park Rd Ardrossan KA22 .....205 C2
Bellshill ML4 .....142 A4
Bishopbriggs G64 .....78 B2
Blackridge EH48 .....107 E3
Bridge Of W PA11 .....90 D1
Calderbank ML6 .....123 B3
Chryston G69 .....100 C8
Clydebank G81 .....73 F3
Coatbridge G69 .....121 A5
Falkirk FK2 .....24 A1
Glasgow G4 .....96 E2
Glasgow,Carmyle G32 .....139 C8
Glasgow,Giffnock G46 .....136 C2
Hamilton ML3 .....162 D3
Inchinnan PA4 .....93 D7
Johnstone PA5 .....111 F2
Kilmacolm PA13 .....89 C8
Menstrie FK11 .....4 A6
Milngavie G62 .....55 A1
Motherwell ML1 .....143 B2
Paisley PA2 .....113 D1
Saltcoats KA21 .....216 E7
Shotts ML7 .....146 D5
Park Ridge PA8 .....93 C7
Park Sch KA3 .....223 B1
Park St Airdrie ML6 .....122 E8
Alexandria G83 .....27 D5
Alva FK12 .....5 A7
Bonnybridge FK4 .....40 C4
Carluke ML8 .....187 F1
Cleland ML1 .....144 B3
Coatbridge ML5 .....122 B8
Cowie FK7 .....12 E8
Dumbarton G82 .....50 A3
Falkirk FK1 .....42 B5
Kilmarnock KA1 .....222 E1
Kirkintilloch G66 .....80 B7
Motherwell ML1 .....163 F6
Motherwell,New Stevenston
ML1 .....143 A3
Park St S G3 .....96 E1
Park Terr Ayr KA7 .....238 E8
Cardross G82 .....48 A8
East Kilbride G74 .....159 E1
Glasgow G3 .....96 E1
Gourock PA19 .....44 E7
Stirling FK8 .....7 A6
Tullibody FK10 .....4 B1

Park Terrace East La
G3 .240 A4
Park Terrace La 1 G3 .96 E1
Park Top PA8 .73 C1
Park View
Ardrossan KA22 .205 D3
Caldercruix ML6 .105 A5
Kilbarchan PA10 .111 A4
Kilbirnie KA25 .149 A1
Larkhall ML9 .185 B2
Paisley PA2 .113 D2
Park View Ct FK1 .41 E5
Park Way G67 .62 B4
Park Winding PA8 .93 C8
Park Wood PA8 .73 C1
Parkandarroch Cres
ML8 .188 A1
Parkbrae Ave G20 .97 A6
Parkbrae Dr G20 .97 A6
Parkbrae Gate G20 .97 A6
Parkbrae Gdns G20 .97 A6
Parkbrae La G20 .97 A6
Parkbrae Pl G20 .97 A6
Parkburn Ave G66 .79 C7
Parkburn Rd G65 .36 D1
Parkdyke FK7 .6 E6
Parkend Ave KA21 .217 A7
Parkend Cres FK1 .66 C6
Parkend Gdns KA21 .217 A7
Parkend Rd KA21 .217 A7
Parkend Terr KA21 .217 A7
Parker Pl 12 Kilsyth G65 .60 D8
Larkhall ML9 .185 B4
Parkfield G75 .180 E5
Parkfoot Ct FK1 .42 B3
Parkfoot St G65 .36 D1
Parkgate FK12 .4 F6
Parkgrove Ave G46 .136 D4
Parkgrove Terr G3 .96 E1
Parkgrove Terrace La 6
G3 .96 E1
Parkhall Rd G81 .73 F4
Parkhall St G74 .159 F2
Parkhall Terr G81 .73 F5
Parkhead Ave KA13 .207 F3
Parkhead Cross G31 .118 D5
Parkhead Ct FK10 .10 C8
Parkhead Hospl G31 .118 D5
Parkhead La 3 ML6 .123 A8
Parkhead Rd Alloa FK10 .10 C8
Falkirk FK1 .42 B1
Parkhead St Airdrie ML6 .123 A8
Motherwell ML1 .163 F5
Parkhill Ave
Crosshouse KA2 .226 E8
Port Glasgow PA14 .69 A8
Parkhill Dr Dalry KA24 .191 D7
Lochwinnoch PA12 .129 D3
Rutherglen G73 .138 A7
Parkhill Rd G43 .136 D8
Parkholm La G5 .240 A1
Parkhouse Dr 6 KA25 .149 A1
Parkhouse Gdns KA22 .205 D1
Parkhouse Rd
Ardrossan KA22 .205 D2
Glasgow G53 .135 A4
Parkhouse St KA7 .238 F7
Parkinch PA8 .93 C8
Parklands Oval G53 .114 F2
Parklands Rd G44 .136 F3
Parklands Sch G84 .16 E2
Parklands View G53 .114 F2
Parklea G64 .77 E3
Parklee Dr G76 .158 E7
Parkneuk Rd
Glasgow G43 .136 C4
Hamilton G72 .161 B1
Parkneuk St ML1 .163 E8
Parknook Way 6 ML9 .185 B4
Parks View ML3 .183 D6
Parksail PA8 .93 C7
Parksail Dr PA8 .93 C8
Parkside KA11 .220 B3
Parkside Ct FK7 .12 C3
Parkside Gdns G20 .97 A6
Parkside Pl G20 .97 A6
Parkside Rd
Motherwell ML1 .163 B6
Shotts ML7 .146 D4
Parkthorn View KA2 .225 E2
Parkvale Ave PA8 .93 D8
Parkvale Cres PA8 .93 D8
Parkvale Dr PA8 .93 D8
Parkvale Gdns PA8 .93 D8
Parkvale Pl PA8 .93 D8
Parkvale Way PA8 .93 D8
Parkview KA7 .238 F2
Parkview Ave Falkirk FK1 .41 F2
Kirkintilloch G66 .79 D6
Parkview Cres ML2 .166 A4
Parkview Ct G66 .79 D7
Parkview Dr
Coatbridge ML5 .121 E7
Stepps G33 .99 E6
Parkview Prim Sch G23 .96 D8
Parkville Dr
Hamilton G72 .161 E6
Hamilton G72 .161 F6
Parkville Rd ML4 .142 C7
Parkway Alloa FK10 .10 B7
Erskine PA8 .93 B8
Glasgow G72 .139 C8
Parkway Ct Alloa FK10 .10 A7
Coatbridge ML5 .121 E6
Glasgow G69 .120 B7
Parkway Pl ML5 .121 E5
Parliament Rd G66 .79 D7
Parnell St ML6 .122 F5
Parnie St G1 .241 A1
Parry Terr G75 .159 B1
Parson St G4 .241 C3
Parsonage Row G1 .241 B2
Parsonage Sq G4 .241 B2
Parterre KA12 .219 C2
Partick Bridge St G11 .96 C1
Partick St ML5 .122 C5
Partick Sta (Underground)
G11 .96 B1
Partickhill Ave G11 .96 B3
Partickhill Ct G11 .96 B3
Partickhill Rd G11 .96 B2
Partridge Rd PA16 .45 A6
Patchy Pk ML9 .199 A8
Paterson Ave KA12 .219 E5
Paterson Cres KA12 .219 D5
Paterson Dr
Helensburgh G84 .16 B4
Shieldhill FK1 .66 C6
Paterson Pl Bearsden G61 .75 C8
Bonnybridge FK4 .40 C5
Bridge of A FK9 .2 A6
Paterson St Ayr KA8 .236 B4
Glasgow G5 .240 B1
Motherwell ML1 .163 E8
Paterson Terr G75 .180 D7
Paterson Twr FK1 .42 D4
Paterson's Laun G64 .77 E7
Path The Airth FK2 .14 D4
Bannockburn FK7 .7 D2
Pather St ML2 .165 B2
Pathfoot KA13 .207 F3
Pathfoot Ave FK9 .2 C7
Pathfoot Dr FK9 .2 C7
Pathfoot Rd FK9 .2 C6
Pathfoot View KA13 .207 F3
Pathhead Gdns G33 .98 F6
Pathhead Rd G76 .158 D7
Patna Ct ML3 .161 E1
Patna St G40 .118 B3
Paton Ct ML2 .164 D1
Paton St Alloa FK10 .10 A7
Glasgow G31 .118 B7
Greenock PA16 .45 C5
Patrick Ave KA20 .206 C1
Patrick Dr FK1 .66 E7
Patrick St Greenock PA16 .45 E6
Paisley PA2 .113 F3
Patrickholm Ave ML9 .198 E1
Patterson Dr ML8 .187 A6
Patterton Dr G78 .134 D1
Patterton Sta G77 .156 D8
Pattison St G81 .73 E3
Pattle Pl KA7 .238 F1
Paul Dr FK2 .14 E4
Pavilion Pl KA22 .205 C1
Pavilion Rd KA7 .238 E8
Pavilion View FK10 .9 F8
Pavilions The FK10 .9 E7
Paxstone Cres ML7 .127 E5
Paxstone Dr ML7 .127 E5
Paxton Cres G74 .159 F4
Paxton Ct G74 .159 F4
Paxton Pl KA1 .228 A7
Payne St G4 .97 C2
Peace Ave
Kilmarnock KA1 .222 D1
Quarriers Village PA11 .89 F2
Peacock Ave PA2 .112 F2
Peacock Cross ML3 .162 C4
Peacock Cross Ind Est
ML3 .162 C4
Peacock Dr
Hamilton ML3 .162 C4
Paisley PA2 .112 F2
Peacock Loan ML8 .187 F3
Pearce La G51 .116 A8
Pearce St G51 .116 A8
Pearl St ML4 .142 B3
Pearson Ave FK4 .39 D5
Pearson Dr PA4 .94 D3
Pearson Pl
Bonnybridge FK4 .39 D5
Linwood PA3 .112 B5
Pearson View FK10 .10 C8
Peat Pl G53 .135 A5
Peat Rd Bridge of W PA11 .110 E7
Glasgow G53 .135 B6
Greenock PA15 .45 D3
Peathill Ave G69 .80 B1
Peathill Rd FK4 .40 A6
Peathill St G21 .97 C3
Peathill Terr FK4 .40 A5
Peatland Quadrant KA1 .228 A3
Peatland Rd KA1 .228 A3
Pebble Dr ML9 .198 D1
Peden Ave KA24 .191 B7
Peden Pl KA12 .219 C2
Peden St ML7 .127 C5
Pedmyre La G76 .158 D7
Peebles Ct 8 PA15 .46 B3
Peebles Dr G73 .138 D7
Peebles Path ML5 .122 D3
Peebles St KA8 .235 F2
Peel Ave ML1 .163 E4
Peel Brae G66 .58 C1
Peel Ct G72 .139 A6
Peel Glen Gdns G15 .75 A5
Peel Glen Rd G15,G61 .75 A5
Peel La G11 .96 B2
Peel Park Pl G74 .158 F2
Peel Pl Bothwell G71 .141 A3
Coatbridge ML5 .121 D5
Peel Rd G74 .158 B2
Peel St Cardross G82 .48 B7
Glasgow G11 .96 B2
Peel View 2 G81 .74 D3
Pegasus Ave
Carluke ML8 .187 E2
Paisley PA1 .112 D5
Pegasus Rd ML4 .142 E5
Peggieshill Pl KA7 .239 B5
Peggieshill Rd KA7 .239 B5
Peile La PA16 .45 D6
Peile St PA16 .45 C6
Peiter Pl 5 G72 .161 C7
Pelstream Ave FK7 .7 B4
Pemberton Valley KA7 .239 A2
Pembroke G74 .160 D4
Pembroke Rd PA16 .44 D4
Pembroke St
Glasgow G3 .240 A3
Stenhousemuir FK5 .23 C3
Penbreck Ct KA11 .220 B6
Penbury Cres ML3 .182 F7
Pencaitland Dr G32 .119 A3
Pencaitland Gr G32 .119 A3
Pencaitland Pl G23 .76 E1
Pendale Rise G45 .137 D3
Pendeen Cres G33 .119 E5
Pendeen Pl G33 .119 F6
Pendeen Rd G33 .119 F5
Penders La FK1 .42 A5
Pendicle Cres G61 .75 D3
Pendicle Rd G61 .75 E3
Pendle Ct G69 .100 F6
Pendreich Way FK9 .2 D6
Penfold Cres G75 .180 D8
Penicuik St G32 .118 D6
Penilee Rd G52 .114 E6
Penilee Terr G52 .114 E6
Peninver Dr G51 .115 E8
Penman Ave G73 .137 F8
Pennan PA8 .73 A3
Pennan Pl G14 .95 A5
Penneld Rd G52 .114 F5
Penniecroft Ave G82 .50 C5
Pennine Gr ML6 .123 F1
Pennyburn Local Ctr
KA13 .207 C2
Pennyburn Prim Sch
KA13 .207 D2
Pennyburn Rd KA13 .207 D2
Pennyburn Rdbt KA20 .207 A2
Pennyfern Dr PA16 .45 B3
Pennyfern Rd PA16 .45 B3
Pennyroyal Ct G74 .159 D4
Pennyvenie Way KA11 .220 A5
Penrioch Dr G75 .180 C4
Penrith Ave G46 .136 C2
Penrith Dr G12 .96 A6
Penrith Pl G75 .179 F6
Penryn Gdns G32 .119 D3
Penston Rd G33 .119 D8
Pentland Ave
Linwood PA3 .112 A5
Port Glasgow PA14 .68 F6
Pentland Cres
Larkhall ML9 .184 E5
Paisley PA2 .133 D8
Pentland Ct Airdrie ML6 .103 B2
Barrhead G78 .134 C1
Coatbridge ML5 .122 C3
Greenock PA16 .45 B5
Pentland Dr
Barrhead G78 .134 C1
Bishopbriggs G64 .78 D2
Paisley PA4 .114 B8
Prestwick KA9 .236 D5
Pentland Gdns ML9 .184 F5
Pentland Pl Bearsden G61 .75 B7
Irvine KA11 .220 A3
Pentland Rd
Chryston G69 .100 D8
East Kilbride G75 .180 A3
Glasgow G43 .136 C5
Kilmarnock KA1 .228 A3
Wishaw ML2 .164 E4
Pentland Sch ML5 .101 C1
Pentland Way ML3 .183 A7
Penzance Way G69 .80 F2
Peockland Gdns PA5 .112 A3
Peockland Pl PA5 .112 A3
People's Palace (Mus)*
G40 .117 E5
Peploe Dr G74 .160 D5
Perceton Mains KA11 .220 D6
Perceton Rdbt KA11 .220 B6
Perceton Row KA11 .220 D3
Perchy View ML2 .165 C1
Percy Dr G46 .136 C1
Percy Rd PA4 .94 A1
Percy St Glasgow G51 .116 D5
Larkhall ML9 .185 A4
Perran Gdns G69 .80 E2
Perray Ave G82 .49 B5
Perrays Cres G82 .49 A5
Perrays Ct G82 .49 A5
Perrays Dr G82 .49 A5
Perrays Gr G82 .49 A5
Perrays Way G82 .49 A5
Perth Ave ML6 .123 A4
Perth Cres G81 .73 D5
Perth St G3 .240 A2
Peter Coats Bldg PA2 .113 E3
Peter DStirling Rd 1
G66 .58 D1
Peter McEachran Ho
G31 .118 C8
Peter St KA12 .219 A1
Peters Ave G83 .28 A8
Petersburn Pl ML6 .123 D6
Petersburn Prim Sch
ML6 .123 C6
Petersburn Rd ML6 .123 D6
Petershill Ct G21 .98 C3
Petershill Dr G21 .98 C3
Petershill Pl G21 .98 B4
Petershill Rd G21 .98 A3
Peterson Dr G13 .94 E8
Peterson Gdns G13 .94 E8
Peterswell Brae FK7 .7 E1
Petition Pl G71 .141 A5
Pettigrew St G32 .119 A5
Peveril Ave Glasgow G41 .116 D1
Rutherglen G73 .138 C5
Peveril Ct G73 .138 C5
Pharonhill St G31 .118 D5
Philip Ct ML4 .142 A4
Philip Dr FK5 .23 D2
Philip Murray Rd ML4 .141 D6
Philip Sq KA8 .236 A1
Philip St FK2 .42 B7
Philipshill Gate G74 .158 E3
Philipshill Ind Est G74 .158 E3
Philipshill Rd G76 .158 E4
Phoenix Bsns Pk The
PA1 .112 E5
Phoenix Cres ML4 .141 F8
Phoenix Ct G74 .160 D5
Phoenix Ho G81 .74 A2
Phoenix Ind Est
Paisley PA3 .113 E8
Stirling FK7 .7 C7
Phoenix Leisure Pk The
PA1 .112 E5
Phoenix Pl Elderslie PA5 .112 D3
Motherwell ML1 .143 A3
Phoenix Rd ML4 .142 E5
Phoenix Ret Pk The
PA1 .112 F5
Piazza Sh Ctr PA1 .113 E5
Piccadilly St G3 .240 A2
Picken St KA1 .227 F5
Pickerstonhill ML1 .143 E4
Picketlaw Dr G76 .158 D7
Picketlaw Farm Rd G76 .158 C7
Pienchorran PA4 .93 C7
Pier Rd Balloch G83 .19 D1
Rhu G84 .15 E4
Piershill St G32 .118 F7
Piersland Pl KA11 .220 A5
Pike Rd FK7 .7 D4
Pikeman Rd G13 .95 C7
Pillans Ct ML3 .162 A6
Pilmuir Ave G44 .136 F4
Pilmuir Holdings G77 .155 F2
Pilrig St G32 .118 E7
Pilton Rd G15 .75 A4
Pine Ave G72 .139 F3
Pine Brae KA7 .239 C5
Pine Cl G67 .62 E4
Pine Cres
Cumbernauld G67 .62 E4
East Kilbride G75 .180 B5
Hamilton ML3 .183 A7
Johnstone PA5 .112 A1
Pine Ct Cumbernauld G67 .62 E4
East Kilbride G75 .180 C5
Pine Gr Alloa FK10 .10 C6
Calderbank ML6 .123 B2
Coatbridge G69 .121 A6
Cumbernauld G67 .62 E4
Motherwell ML1 .143 B5
Uddingston G71 .141 B8
Pine Ho East Kilbride G75 .180 B5
Prestwick KA9 .236 C5
Pine Lawn ML2 .165 D5
Pine Mews ML1 .143 D2
Pine Pk ML3 .162 E1
Pine Pl Cumbernauld G67 .62 E4
Glasgow G5 .117 C4
Pine Quadrant ML6 .123 E3
Pine Rd Clydebank G81 .73 D4
Cumbernauld G67 .62 E4
Dumbarton G82 .49 F4
Kilmarnock KA1 .227 D7
Pine St Airdrie ML6 .123 D7
Greenock PA15 .45 E4
Lennoxtown G66 .57 E8
Paisley PA2 .114 A2
Pine Wlk FK5 .23 D1
Pineapple The* FK2 .14 B6
Pinelands G64 .78 A4
Pines The G44 .137 B4
Pineview Ct G15 .75 B3
Pinewood G61 .75 F3
Pinewood Ave G66 .79 A5
Pinewood Ct
Dumbarton G82 .50 C5
Kirkintilloch G66 .79 A5
Pinewood Pl G66 .79 A5
Pinewood Prim Sch G15 .75 C4
Pinewood Sq G15 .75 B3
Pinkerton Ave G73 .137 F8
Pinkerton La PA4 .94 D1
Pinkston Dr G21 .97 E2
Pinkston Rd G4,G21 .97 D2
Pinmore KA13 .207 C2
Pinmore Pl G53 .134 F5
Pinmore St G53 .134 F5
Pinwherry Dr G33 .98 F6
Pinwherry Pl G71 .141 A3
Pioneer Pk G82 .50 A2
Piper Ave PA6 .111 C8
Piper Rd Airdrie ML6 .123 C5
Houston PA6 .111 C8
Piperhill KA7 .239 A2
Pirleyhill Dr FK1 .66 D6
Pirleyhill Gdns FK1 .42 A2
Pirnhall Rd
Bannockburn FK7 .11 D7
Bannockburn FK7 .11 E8
Pirnhall Rd *continued*
Bannockburn,Chartershall
FK7 .11 A8
Pirnie Pl G65 .60 D8
Pirnmill Ave
East Kilbride G75 .180 B4
Motherwell ML1 .163 B7
Pirnmill Pl G84 .16 F2
Pirnmill Rd KA21 .205 F2
Pit Rd Bellshill ML4 .141 F6
Kirkintilloch G66 .80 C7
Pitcairn Cres G75 .179 F8
Pitcairn Gr G75 .180 A8
Pitcairn Pl G75 .179 F8
Pitcairn St G31 .118 E4
Pitcairn Terr ML3 .162 A4
Pitcaple Dr G43 .136 B6
Pitfairn Rd FK10 .5 E3
Pitlochry Dr
Glasgow G52 .115 C4
Larkhall ML9 .185 C1
Pitmedden Rd G64 .78 D2
Pitmilly Rd G15 .75 C4
Pitreavie Ct ML3 .183 B8
Pitreavie Pl G33 .99 C1
Pitt St G2 .240 B3
Pitt Terr FK8 .7 B6
Pittenweem Path G72 .161 D3
Place Of Bonhill G82 .27 D3
Place View KA25 .149 A1
Pladda Ave Irvine KA11 .220 B2
Port Glasgow PA14 .69 B7
Pladda Cres KA11 .220 A2
Pladda Ct KA11 .220 B2
Pladda Dr KA9 .236 C6
Pladda Rd Renfrew PA4 .94 D1
Saltcoats KA21 .205 F2
Pladda St ML1 .163 B7
Pladda Terr KA11 .220 B2
Pladda Way G84 .16 F2
Pladda Wynd KA11 .220 B2
Plains Prim Sch ML6 .104 A2
Plaintrees Ct PA2 .113 E1
Plan View KA25 .149 B3
Plane Pl G71 .121 C1
Planetree Pl PA5 .112 A1
Planetree Rd G81 .74 A5
Plann Ho KA2 .221 F3
Plant St G31 .118 C6
Plantation Ave ML1 .143 B6
Plantation Park Gdns 5
G51 .116 D5
Plantation Sq G51 .116 E6
Plateau Dr KA10 .229 G7
Platthorn Dr G74 .159 F1
Platthorn Rd G74 .159 F1
Players Rd FK7 .7 C7
Playfair St G40 .118 A3
Playingfield Cres KA2 .221 E1
Playingfield Rd KA2 .221 E1
Plaza The 2 G74 .180 E8
Pleaknowe Cres G69 .80 F2
Pleamuir Pl G68 .61 C2
Plean Country Park Wlk*
FK7 .12 B2
Plean Ctry Pk* FK7 .12 B1
Plean Ind Est FK7 .12 D1
Plean St G14 .95 A5
Pleanbank Cotts FK7 .12 B3
Pleasance FK1 .42 B4
Pleasance Ct 12 FK2 .42 B4
Pleasance Gdns FK1 .42 B4
Pleasance Rd FK1 .42 B3
Pleasance Sq 11 FK1 .42 B4
Pleasance St G43 .136 D7
Pleasance Way G43 .136 D7
Pleasantfield Rd KA9 .236 B5
Pleasantside Ave PA14 .69 A8
Pleasures The FK10 .9 E7
Plotcock Rd ML3 .198 D7
Ploughland Holdings
KA2 .225 F3
Plover Dr G75 .180 A5
Plover Pl PA5 .131 C7
Plusgarten Loan ML2 .165 F7
Plymouth Ave PA19 .44 E5
Pochard Way ML4 .141 F8
Poet's View G66 .79 F7
Poindfauld Terr G82 .50 A4
Pointhouse Rd G3 .116 D8
Pokelly Pl KA3 .195 F1
Polbae Cres G76 .178 E5
Polden Ave G75 .180 A3
Polden Ct G75 .180 A3
Poles Rd KA3 .213 A3
Polkemmet Dr ML7 .127 F6
Polkemmet La ML7 .127 F5
Polkemmet Rd ML7 .127 F6
Pollick Ave G78 .153 B3
Pollick Farm La G78 .153 A2
Pollock Ave
Eaglesham G76 .178 E5
Hamilton ML3 .162 A4
Pollock Cres KA13 .207 E2
Pollock Rd Bearsden G61 .76 A3
Newton Mearns G77 .156 C4
Pollock St Bellshill ML4 .142 C5
Motherwell ML1 .163 E7
Pollok Ave G43 .136 B8
Pollok Ctry Pk* G43 .116 B1
Pollok Dr G64 .77 E1
Pollok Ho* G43 .135 F8
Pollok La G74 .160 B3
Pollok Pl 2 G74 .160 B3

Robert Kinmond Ave FK10 4 C2
Robert Knox Ave FK10 4 C2
Robert Noble Pl KA1 222 D2
Robert Owen Meml Prim Sch ML11 215 C4
Robert Smillie Cres ML9 185 A1
Robert Smillie Meml Prim Sch ML9 185 A1
Robert St Glasgow G51 116 A8
Port Glasgow PA14 47 E1
Shotts ML7 146 E4
Robert Stewart Pl KA1 222 E1
Robert Templeton Dr G72 139 B5
Robert W Service Ct KA13 207 E2
Robert Wilson Gate ML9 199 A8
Robert Wynd ML2 166 A6
Robertland Rigg KA3 195 E1
Robertland Sq KA3 211 E8
Roberton Ave G41 116 C2
Roberton St ML6 123 E3
Roberts Quadrant ML4 142 B3
Roberts St Clydebank G81 73 E3
Wishaw ML2 165 A3
Robertson Ave
Bonnybridge FK4 40 B6
Renfrew PA4 94 B3
Robertson Cl PA4 94 C3
Robertson Cres Ayr KA8 236 D1
Neilston G78 154 D7
Saltcoats KA21 217 A7
Robertson Ct FK5 23 D2
Robertson Dr
Bellshill ML4 142 A4
East Kilbride G74 160 B2
Renfrew PA4 94 B3
Robertson La G2 240 C2
Robertson Pl
Kilmarnock KA1 228 A8
Stirling FK7 7 B3
Robertson Rd KA9 233 C3
Robertson St
Airdrie ML6 122 E8
Alva FK12 5 B7
Barrhead G78 134 B2
Glasgow G1,G2 240 C2
Greenock PA16 45 E6
Hamilton ML3 161 F5
Robertson Terr G69 120 C5
Robin Pl ML2 165 B3
Robin Rd PA16 45 B5
Robin Way G72 139 C8
Robinsfield G22 77 A7
Robroyston Ave G33 98 E3
Robroyston Rd
Bishopbriggs G64,G66 78 F1
Glasgow G33 98 E6
Glasgow,Barmulloch G33 98 D4
Glasgow,Blackhill G33 98 E3
Robshill Ct G77 156 D4
Robsland Ave KA7 238 F5
Robslee Cres G46 136 B3
Robslee Dr G46 136 B4
Robslee Prim Sch G46 136 A2
Robslee Rd G46 136 A3
Robson Gr [3] G42 117 B3
Rocep Dr G51 94 F2
Rochdale Pl [4] G66 79 C8
Roche Way KA24 191 C7
Rochsoles Cres ML6 103 A2
Rochsoles Dr ML6 103 A2
Rochsolloch Farm Cotts ML6 122 E7
Rochsolloch Prim Sch ML6 122 E6
Rochsolloch Rd ML6 122 D6
Rock Dr PA10 111 B2
Rock Gdns ML9 198 D1
Rock St G4 97 B3
Rockall Dr G44 137 C4
Rockbank Pl
Clydebank G81 74 C6
Glasgow G40 118 A5
Rockbank St G40 118 A5
Rockburn Cres ML4 142 A7
Rockburn Dr G76 157 D8
Rockcliffe Path ML6 123 F1
Rockcliffe St G40 117 F3
Rockfield Pl G21 98 C5
Rockfield Rd G21 98 C5
Rockhampton Ave G75 180 B7
Rockliffe Path ML6 123 E1
Rockmount Ave
Barrhead G78 134 D1
Glasgow G46 136 A3
Rockrose Pk KA7 239 B3
Rockwell Ave PA2 133 C8
Rockwood Pl ML6 104 D4
Rodding The ML11 215 B5
Roddinghead Rd G46 157 A6
Rodger Ave G77 156 C5
Rodger Dr G73 138 B6
Rodger Pl G73 138 A6
Rodil Ave G44 137 C4
Rodney Pl G84 17 A2
Rodney Rd PA19 44 F6
Rodney St G4 97 B2
Roebank Dr G78 134 C1
Roebank Rd KA15 150 C2
Roebank St G31 118 B8
Roffey Park Rd PA1 114 D5
Rogart St G40 117 F5
Rogerfield Prim Sch G34 120 C8
Rogerfield Rd G34,G69 120 C7
Rogers Ct ML9 198 D2
Rokeby La G12 96 E3
Roland Cres G77 156 F3
Roman Ave Bearsden G61 75 F5
Clydebank G15 75 A1
Roman Cres G60 72 F7
Roman Ct Bearsden G61 75 F5
Cleghorn ML11 215 F7
Clydebank G81 74 A6
Roman Dr Bearsden G61 75 F5
Bellshill ML4 142 B4
Falkirk FK1 41 D5
Roman Gdns G61 75 F5
Roman Hill Rd G81 74 B7
Roman Pl ML4 141 E3
Roman Rd Ayr KA7 239 C5
Bearsden G61 75 F5
Bonnybridge FK4 40 A4
Clydebank G81 74 A6
Kirkintilloch G66 79 B8
Motherwell ML1 163 E7
Roman Way G71 141 C6
Romney Ave G44 137 C5
Romulus Ct ML1 142 C1
Rona Ave PA14 69 B7
Rona Pl KA3 223 B5
Rona St G21 98 B2
Rona Terr G72 138 F3
Ronades Rd FK2 42 A8
Ronald Cres FK5 23 B1
Ronald Pl FK8 7 B8
Ronald St [2] ML5 122 A8
Ronaldsay Ct KA11 225 B8
Ronaldsay Dr G64 78 D2
Ronaldsay Pass G22 97 D7
Ronaldsay Pl G67 82 D8
Ronaldsay St G22 97 D7
Ronaldshaw Pk KA7 238 E6
Ronay St Glasgow G22 97 D8
Wishaw ML2 165 E5
Rook Rd PA16 45 A5
Rooksdell Ave PA2 113 C1
Ropework La G1 241 A1
Rorison Pl ML9 185 F1
Rosa Burn Ave G75 180 B4
Rosa Pl KA21 206 A2
Rose Cres Gourock PA19 44 D6
Hamilton ML3 161 F4
Rose Dale G64 98 B8
Rose Gdns ML5 121 F3
Rose Knowe Rd G42 137 D8
Rose Mount Ct ML6 123 C8
Rose St Alloa FK10 4 E1
Bonnybridge FK4 40 B6
Cumbernauld G67 82 B6
Glasgow G3 240 C4
Greenock PA16 45 C4
Kirkintilloch G66 79 D8
Motherwell ML1 164 A5
Tullibody FK10 4 D4
Rose Terr Denny FK6 21 D1
Stenhousemuir FK5 23 F3
Rosebank FK10 5 D1
Rosebank Ave
Blantyre G72 140 E1
Falkirk FK1 41 F5
Kirkintilloch G66 79 E8
Rosebank Cres KA7 238 F5
Rosebank Ct G72 161 E8
Rosebank Dr
Cambuslang G72 139 C4
Uddingston G71 141 C7
Rosebank Gdns
Alloa FK10 10 C8
Glasgow G71 120 B2
Irvine KA11 219 F7
Johnstone PA5 112 A2
Rosebank La [3] G71 141 B3
Rosebank Pl Dullatur G68 61 C6
Falkirk FK1 41 F5
Glasgow G71 120 B2
Hamilton ML3 162 A3
Kilmarnock KA3 222 F2
Rosebank Rd
Bellshill ML4 142 B8
Overtown ML2 186 C6
Rosebank Rdbt FK1 41 F5
Rosebank St ML6 123 E8
Rosebank Terr
Coatbridge G69 121 A4
Kilmacolm PA13 89 D8
Rosebank Twr G72 139 A6
Rosebay Pk KA7 239 B2
Roseberry Ct [13] G12 96 C3
Roseberry La ML6 123 E3
Roseberry Pl ML3 162 A4
Roseberry Rd ML6 123 E4
Roseberry St G5 117 E2
Rosebery Ct KA25 149 A2
Rosebery Pl FK8 2 B1
Roseburn Ct G67 62 F6
Rosedale G74 159 C3
Rosedale Ave PA2 132 D7
Rosedale Dr G69 120 A4
Rosedale Gdns
Glasgow G20 96 C8
Helensburgh G84 16 F1
Rosedale St ML11 214 F2
Rosedene Terr ML4 142 A6
Rosefield Gdns G71 140 E7
Rosegreen Cres ML4 142 A8
Rosehall Ave ML5 122 B4
Rosehall High Sch ML5 121 F3
Rosehall Ind Est ML5 122 A3
Rosehall Rd Bellshill ML4 141 F6
Rosehall Rd *continued*
Shotts ML7 146 C3
Rosehall Terr Falkirk FK1 42 B4
Wishaw ML2 164 E1
Rosehill Dr G67 82 A6
Rosehill Rd G64 78 C8
Roseholm Ave KA12 219 E2
Roselea ML6 104 F4
Roselea Dr G62 55 B3
Roselea Gdns G13 95 F7
Roselea Pl G72 140 D1
Roselea Rd G71 140 E8
Roselea St ML9 185 B4
Rosemary Cres G74 159 D4
Rosemary Ct FK6 21 D2
Rosemary Pl G74 159 D4
Rosemead Terr FK1 66 F5
Rosemount
Cumbernauld G68 61 F5
Kilwinning KA13 207 C2
Rosemount Ave G77 156 D2
Rosemount Ct
Carluke ML8 188 A2
Newton Mearns G77 156 D1
Rosemount Dr KA10 229 E8
Rosemount Gdns
Prestwick KA9 236 C6
Shieldhill FK1 66 D6
Rosemount La
Bridge of W PA11 110 B6
[4] Larkhall ML9 185 C1
Rosemount Mdws G71 140 F2
Rosemount Pl PA19 44 A6
Rosemount St G21 97 F1
Rosendale Way G72 161 E7
Roseneath Prim Sch G84 15 A3
Roseneath St PA16 45 C8
Roseness Pl G33 119 A8
Rosenheath Gate G74 159 C2
Rosepark Ave G71 141 C6
Rosepark Cotts ML5 121 E3
Rosevale Cres
Bellshill ML4 142 C4
Hamilton ML3 162 B2
Rosevale Rd G61 75 E4
Rosevale Sch G22 97 D7
Rosevale St G11 96 A2
Rosewood ML2 164 D1
Rosewood Ave
Bellshill ML4 142 B7
Paisley PA2 113 B2
Rosewood Path ML4 141 E5
Rosewood St G13 95 E7
Roseyard Pl PA14 47 C1
Roslea Dr G31 118 A7
Roslin Ct PA13 89 C7
Roslin St PA15 45 F6
Roslin Twr G72 138 E3
Roslyn Dr G69 120 F6
Rosneath Castle Cvn Pk G84 15 E1
Rosneath Dr G84 16 B2
Rosneath Rd
Port Glasgow PA14 68 D8
Rosneath G84 15 B2
Rosneath St G51 116 A8
Ross Ave Kirkintilloch G66 79 F8
Renfrew PA4 94 A1
Ross Cres Falkirk FK1 41 C5
Motherwell ML1 163 C5
Ross Ct FK7 7 B3
Ross Dr Airdrie ML6 122 E5
Motherwell,Braedale ML1 163 C5
Motherwell,Tannochside G71 121 C1
Ross Gdns ML1 163 C5
Ross Pl East Kilbride G74 160 C3
Rutherglen G73 138 D4
Ross Rd KA21 205 F2
Ross St Ayr KA8 236 C2
Coatbridge ML5 122 A7
Glasgow G40 241 B1
Paisley PA1 114 A3
Ross Terr ML3 163 C1
Ross Wlk Kilmarnock KA3 223 B2
Renton G82 27 D2
Rossbank Rd PA14 47 A2
Rossendale Ct G43 136 C8
Rossendale Rd G43 136 C8
Rosshall Acad G52 115 A4
Rosshall Ave PA1 114 C4
Rosshall Hospl G52 115 A3
Rosshall Pl PA4 94 D3
Rosshill Ave G52 114 F5
Rosshill Rd G52 114 F5
Rossie Cres G64 98 C8
Rossie Gr G77 156 B5
Rossland Cres PA7 72 A3
Rossland Gdns PA7 72 A3
Rossland View PA7 72 A3
Rosslea Dr G46 136 C2
Rosslyn Ave
East Kilbride G74 160 A3
Rutherglen G73 138 C7
Rosslyn Ct ML3 162 A4
Rosslyn Ho [12] G12 96 C3
Rosslyn Pl KA8 236 B3
Rosslyn Rd Ashgill ML9 199 F8
Bearsden G61 75 B6
Rosslyn Terr [13] G12 96 C4
Rostan Rd G43 136 C5
Rosyth Rd G5 117 E2
Rosyth St G5 117 E2
Rotherwick Dr PA1 114 E4
Rotherwood Ave
Glasgow G13 75 E1
Paisley PA2 132 F8
Rotherwood La G13 75 C2
Rotherwood Pl G13 95 D8
Rotherwood Way PA2 132 F8
Rothes Dr G23 96 D8
Rothes Pl G23 76 C1
Rothesay Cres ML5 122 B4
Rothesay Pl
Coatbridge ML5 122 B4
Kilmarnock KA3 222 F3
Rothesay Rd PA16 44 F3
Rothesay St G75 180 E8
Rottenrow Glasgow G4 241 B3
Glasgow G4 241 C2
Rottenrow E G4 241 B2
Roughburn Rd FK9 2 A6
Roughcraig St ML6 103 A2
Roughlands Cres FK2 24 B3
Roughlands Dr FK2 24 A3
Roughlea Pl KA10 229 G6
Roughrigg Rd ML6 124 C6
Rouken Glen Pk* G46 135 F1
Rouken Glen Rd G46 136 A1
Roukenburn St G46 135 F4
Round Riding Rd G82 50 B4
Roundel The Falkirk FK2 42 D7
Wishaw ML2 165 C2
Roundelwood FK10 5 B1
Roundhill Dr PA5 112 E3
Roundhouse FK7 12 D8
Roundknowe Rd G71 120 C1
Rousay Wynd KA3 223 A6
Rowallan KA13 207 C2
Rowallan Cres KA9 236 D7
Rowallan Ct [6] KA7 235 E1
Rowallan Dr
Bannockburn FK7 11 F8
Kilmarnock KA3 223 A4
Rowallan Gdns G11 96 A3
Rowallan La
Clarkston G76 157 E7
Glasgow G11 96 A3
Rowallan La E G11 96 A3
Rowallan Rd G46 135 F2
Rowallan St G84 16 B3
Rowallan Terr G33 99 B4
Rowan Ave Beith KA15 171 C8
Milton Of C G66 58 C5
Renfrew PA4 94 C4
Rowan Cres Ayr KA7 239 C5
Chapelhall ML6 123 E3
Falkirk FK1 41 A4
Kirkintilloch G66 79 C5
Menstrie FK11 3 F6
Shotts ML7 147 B4
Rowan Ct Bannockburn FK7 7 E1
Cambuslang G72 139 F3
Wishaw ML2 164 D2
Rowan Dr Banknock FK4 38 E2
Bearsden G61 76 A7
Clydebank G81 73 F4
Dumbarton G82 49 A4
Rowan Gdns
Glasgow G41 116 B4
Larkhall ML9 185 B2
Rowan Gr ML3 183 F3
Rowan Ho KA9 236 C6
Rowan La ML1 143 A2
Rowan Pl Beith KA15 171 C8
Cambuslang G72 139 C6
Coatbridge ML5 121 E4
Hamilton G72 161 D8
Kilmarnock KA1 227 D7
Troon KA10 229 E4
Rowan Rd
Cumbernauld G67 62 D3
Glasgow G41 116 B4
Linwood PA3 111 F7
Rowan Rise ML3 162 E2
Rowan St Greenock PA16 45 C5
Paisley PA2 113 F2
Wishaw ML2 165 B5
Rowan Terr KA12 219 D4
Rowanbank Pl ML6 122 D8
Rowanbank Rd KA9 236 E7
Rowand Ave G46 136 C3
Rowandale Ave G69 120 A4
Rowanden Ave ML4 142 A6
Rowanhill Pl KA1 227 D7
Rowanlea ML6 103 F3
Rowanlea Ave PA2 132 E7
Rowanlea Dr G46 136 D4
Rowanpark Dr G78 134 A5
Rowans Gate PA2 113 F2
Rowans Gdns G71 141 B4
Rowans The Alloa FK10 5 C2
Bishopbriggs G64 77 F2
Rowanside Terr KA22 205 C4
Rowantree Ave
Motherwell ML1 143 D7
Rutherglen G73 138 B5
Uddingston G71 141 C7
Rowantree Gdns
Irvine KA11 220 A5
Rutherglen G73 138 B5
Rowantree Gr G83 27 E4
Rowantree Pl
Johnstone PA5 111 F1
Larkhall ML9 185 D2
Lennoxtown G66 57 E7
Rowantree Rd PA5 112 A1
Rowantree Terr
Lennoxtown G66 57 E7
Motherwell ML1 143 B5
Rowantree Wlk FK5 23 B4
Rowantreehill Rd PA13 89 E8
Rowanwood Cres ML5 121 D5
Rowchester St G40 118 A5
Rowena Ave G13 75 D1
Rowmore Quays G84 15 E4
Roxburgh Ave PA15 45 E4
Roxburgh Dr
Bearsden G61 75 E7
Coatbridge ML5 122 D4
Roxburgh Pk G74 159 F1
Roxburgh Pl
[5] Hamilton G72 161 D7
Stenhousemuir FK5 23 F4
Roxburgh Rd
Hurlford KA1 228 E6
Paisley PA2 132 D7
Roxburgh St Glasgow G12 96 D3
Greenock PA15 45 E5
Roxburgh Way PA15 45 E4
Roy St G21 97 D3
Roy Young Ave G83 28 A8
Royal Alexandra Hospl PA2 113 D2
Royal Bank Pl G1 241 A2
Royal Cres G3 116 E8
Royal Ct PA15 45 E5
Royal Dr ML3 163 A2
Royal Exchange Ct G1 241 A2
Royal Exchange Sq G1 241 A2
Royal Gdns Bothwell G71 140 E2
Stirling FK8 7 A8
Royal Highland Fusiliers Regimental Mus* G2 240 B4
Royal Hospl (For Sick Children) G3 96 C1
Royal Inch Cres PA4 94 D5
Royal Infmy Hospl G4 241 C3
Royal Scottish Acad of Music & Drama G2 240 C3
Royal Scottish National Hospl The FK5 22 F3
Royal St PA19 44 E8
Royal Terr Glasgow G3 96 E1
Wishaw ML2 165 C7
Royal Terrace La G3 96 E1
Royal Troon Golf Club* KA10 232 D8
Royellen Ave ML3 161 F2
Royston Prim Sch G21 97 F1
Royston Rd G21,G33 98 C3
Royston Sq G21 241 C4
Roystonhill G21 97 F1
Roystonhill Pl G21 97 F1
Rozelle Ave Clydebank G15 75 B3
Newton Mearns G77 156 B4
Rozelle Dr G77 156 B4
Rozelle House Galleries & Mus* KA7 238 F2
Rozelle Pl G77 156 B4
Rozelle Terr KA7 239 B1
Rubie Cres KA12 219 C1
Rubislaw Dr G61 75 E3
Ruby St G40 118 A4
Ruby Terr ML4 142 A4
Ruchazie Pl G32,G33 118 F8
Ruchazie Rd G33 118 F7
Ruchill Pl G20 96 F5
Ruchill Prim Sch G20 96 F6
Ruchill St G20 96 F5
Rue End St PA15 46 A4
Ruel St G44 137 A7
Rufflees Ave G78 134 D4
Rugby Ave G13 95 B8
Rugby Cres KA1 227 D7
Rugby Pk (Kilmarnock FC) KA1 227 E7
Rugby Rd KA1 227 D7
Rulley View FK6 21 C4
Rullion Pl G33 118 F8
Rumford Pl KA3 223 C6
Rumford St G40 117 F3
Rumlie The FK1 86 A6
Runciman Pl G74 160 B4
Rundell Dr G66 58 C5
Rupert St G4 96 F2
Rush Hill KA7 239 C2
Rushyhill St G21 98 A4
Ruskie Rd FK9 2 B3
Ruskin La G12 96 E3
Ruskin Pl Glasgow G12 96 E3
Kilsyth G65 60 D8
Ruskin Sq G64 78 A1
Ruskin Terr Glasgow G12 96 E3
Rutherglen G73 118 B1
Russel St FK2 42 B6
Russell Colt St ML5 122 A8
Russell Ct KA3 223 C3
Russell Dr Alexandria G83 27 C7
Ayr KA8 236 A2
Bearsden G61 75 F6
Dalry KA24 191 D8
Russell Gdns
Newton Mearns G77 156 C4
[10] Uddingston G71 141 A8
Russell Hill Ct FK5 23 B1
Russell La ML2 165 A2
Russell Pl
Bonnybridge FK4 39 D5
Clarkston G76 158 A5
East Kilbride G75 180 C7
Linwood PA3 111 F6
Russell Rd Duntocher G81 73 E7
Lanark ML11 215 B5
Russell St Ayr KA8 236 A1
Bellshill ML4 142 D5
Chapelhall ML6 123 E2
Hamilton ML3 161 F5
Johnstone PA5 112 A3
Paisley PA3 113 D7
Port Glasgow PA14 47 A2
Wishaw ML2 165 B2
Rutherford Ave
Bearsden G61 75 B8

Rutherford Ave *continued*
Kirkintilloch G66 .80 B6
Rutherford Ct
Bridge of A FK9 .2 A8
Clydebank G81 .74 A2
Rutherford Grange G66 .79 C6
Rutherford La G75 .180 F6
Rutherford Sq G75 .180 F6
Rutherglen Ind Est G73 .118 A1
Rutherglen Rd G5,G73 .117 E2
Rutherglen Sta G73 .138 B8
Ruthven Ave G46 .136 D1
Ruthven La
7 Glasgow G12 .96 D3
Glenboig ML5 .101 C6
Ruthven Pl
Bishopbriggs G64 .98 C8
Troon KA10 .229 F4
Ruthven St G12 .96 D3
Rutland Cres G51 .116 E6
Rutland Ct G51 .116 E6
Rutland Pl G51 .116 E6
Ryan Rd G64 .78 B1
Ryan Way G73 .138 C3
Ryat Dr G77 .156 C6
Ryat Gn G77 .156 C5
Ryatt Linn PA8 .72 F1
Rydal Gr G75 .179 F6
Rydal Pl G75 .179 F6
Ryde Rd ML2 .165 C4
Ryden Mains Rd ML6 .102 D4
Rye Cres G21 .98 B5
Rye Rd G21 .98 C5
Rye Way PA2 .112 E1
Ryebank Rd G21 .98 C5
Ryecroft Dr G69 .120 B5
Ryedale Pl G15 .75 B4
Ryefield Ave
Coatbridge ML5 .121 D7
Johnstone PA5 .111 D1
Ryefield Ho KA24 .169 B1
Ryefield Pl PA5 .111 D1
Ryefield Rd G21 .98 B5
Ryehill Pl G21 .98 C5
Ryehill Rd G21 .98 C4
Ryemount Rd G21 .98 C5
Ryeside Pl KA24 .169 C1
Ryeside Rd G21 .98 B4
Ryewraes Rd PA3 .112 B5
Rylands KA9 .236 C6
Rylands Dr G32 .119 D4
Rylands Gdns G32 .119 E4
Rylees Cres G52 .114 E6
Rylees Pl G52 .114 E6
Rylees Rd G52 .114 E6
Rysland Ave G77 .156 E5
Rysland Cres G77 .156 E5
Rysland Dr KA3 .213 A4
Ryvra Rd G13 .95 D6

S

Sachelcourt Ave PA7 .72 B2
Sackville Ave G13 .95 F5
Sackville La G13 .95 F5
Sacred Heart Prim Sch
Glasgow G40 .117 F4
Greenock PA16 .44 E4
Sacred Heart RC Prim Sch
ML4 .142 A3
Saddell Rd G15 .75 B4
Sadler's Wells Ct G74 .160 B4
Saffron Cres ML2 .164 E1
Saffronhall Cres ML3 .162 D4
Saffronhall La ML3 .162 D4
Sainford Cres FK2 .24 A1
St Abb's Dr PA2 .113 A1
St Agatha's Prim Sch
G66 .80 B8
St Agnes' Prim Sch G23 .96 E8
St Aidan's High Sch
ML2 .165 B4
St Aidan's Path ML2 .165 C6
St Aidan's RC Prim Sch
ML2 .165 C5
St Aidan's Sch G32 .118 D6
St Albert's Prim Sch
G41 .116 E4
St Aloysius Coll G3 .240 B4
St Aloysius' Prim Sch
G22 .97 E5
St Aloysius' RC Prim Sch
ML6 .123 E2
St Ambrose High Sch
ML5 .121 E8
St Ambrose's Prim Sch
G22 .97 E8
St Andrew Sq PA15 .46 B4
St Andrew St PA15 .46 B4
St Andrew's Acad PA2 .114 C1
St Andrew's Acad
KA21 .205 F1
St Andrew's Ave
Bishopbriggs G64 .77 E2
Prestwick KA9 .236 C6
St Andrew's Brae G82 .50 B5
St Andrew's Cres
Dumbarton G82 .50 B5
Paisley PA3 .113 C8
St Andrew's Cross G41 .117 A3
St Andrew's Ct ML8 .187 E1
St Andrew's Ct FK5 .23 B3
St Andrew's Dr Airth FK2 .14 B7
Glasgow G41 .116 D3
Hamilton ML3 .161 D4
Paisley PA3 .113 D8
Renfrew PA3 .93 E1
St Andrew's Dr W
Paisley PA3 .113 D8
Renfrew PA3 .93 C1
St Andrew's Gdns
Airdrie ML6 .123 B8
Dalry KA24 .191 B6
St Andrew's High Sch
Clydebank G81 .94 C8
East Kilbride G75 .180 D6
St Andrew's La G1 .241 B1
St Andrew's Pl KA20 .206 F2
St Andrew's Prim Sch
Airdrie ML6 .102 E1
Cumbernauld G68 .61 D5
St Andrew's RC Cath*
G1 .241 A1
St Andrew's RC Prim Sch
G61 .75 C6
St Andrew's RC Prim Sch
FK1 .42 E4
St Andrew's Rd
Ardrossan KA22 .205 D4
Glasgow G41 .116 F4
Renfrew PA4 .94 C2
St Andrew's Sec Sch
G32 .119 A7
St Andrew's Sq G1 .241 B1
St Andrew's St Ayr KA7 .239 A7
Glasgow G1 .241 B1
Kilmarnock KA1 .227 F8
St Andrew's Way ML2 .165 C6
St Andrew's Wlk 2
KA1 .227 F7
St Andrews Ave G71 .141 A1
St Andrews Cres G41 .116 E4
St Andrews Ct
Bellshill ML4 .142 B5
East Kilbride G75 .180 C6
Kirkintilloch G66 .79 D7
Motherwell ML1 .143 A6
St Andrews Dr
Bearsden G61 .75 D7
Bridge of W PA11 .110 C6
Coatbridge ML5 .121 E6
Cumbernauld G68 .62 B6
Gourock PA19 .44 A6
St Andrews Gate ML4 .141 F5
St Andrews La
Alexandria G83 .27 E4
Gourock PA19 .44 A6
St Andrews Path 10
ML9 .185 C1
St Andrews Pl
Beith KA15 .171 A7
10 Falkirk FK1 .42 B4
Kilsyth G65 .36 C1
St Andrews St ML1 .143 A5
St Andrews Way KA12 .224 F8
St Andrews Wynd G84 .16 E3
St Angela's Prim Sch
G53 .135 C3
St Ann's Dr G46 .136 C2
St Ann's RC Prim Sch
ML3 .183 D8
St Anne's Cres FK7 .7 E1
St Anne's Ct ML3 .183 D8
St Anne's Prim Sch
Erskine PA8 .93 C8
Glasgow G40 .118 A5
St Annes Ave PA8 .93 D8
St Annes Wynd PA8 .93 D8
St Anthony's Prim Sch
Glasgow G51 .115 F8
Johnstone PA5 .131 C7
Rutherglen G73 .138 D4
St Anthony's Prim Sch
KA21 .205 E2
St Athanasius' Prim Sch
ML8 .187 F1
St Augustine's Prim Sch
Coatbridge ML5 .121 F6
Glasgow G22 .97 C7
St Barbara's Prim Sch
G69 .100 D7
St Barchan's Rd PA10 .111 B2
St Bartholomew's Prim Sch
ML5 .101 D1
St Benedict's Prim Sch
G34 .100 C1
St Bernadette's Prim Sch
ML1 .163 B8
St Bernadette's RC Prim Sch
FK10 .4 A2
St Bernard's Prim Sch
G53 .135 A5
St Bernard's RC Prim Sch
ML5 .122 B3
St Blane's Dr G73 .137 F6
St Blane's Prim Sch
Glasgow G23 .76 D1
Hamilton G72 .161 C8
St Boswell's Cres PA2 .113 A1
St Boswells Dr ML5 .122 D4
St Brendan's High Sch
PA3 .112 C6
St Brendan's Prim Sch
G13 .94 F7
St Brendan's RC Prim Sch
ML1 .164 B2
St Brennans Ct KA25 .170 A7
St Bride's Ave G71 .141 C7
St Bride's Dr KA23 .190 D5
St Bride's High Sch G74 160 A1
St Bride's Pl KA12 .219 C5
St Bride's Prim Sch
G72 .139 A5
St Bride's RC Prim Sch
G71 .141 A4
St Bride's Rd
Glasgow G43 .136 D6
West Kilbride KA23 .190 D6
St Brides Way G71 .141 A4
St Bridget's Prim Sch
Glasgow G69 .120 D5
Kilbirnie KA25 .170 A8
St Brigid's Prim Sch
Glasgow G42 .137 E8
Wishaw ML2 .166 A5
St Bryde La G74 .159 F2
St Bryde St G74 .159 F2
St Cadoc's Prim Sch
Cambuslang G72 .139 C4
Newton Mearns G77 .156 C5
St Catherine's Prim Sch
PA3 .113 F6
St Catherine's RC Prim Sch
G21 .98 C5
St Catherine's Rd G46 .136 C2
St Catherines Cres ML7 .146 E6
St Catherines Rd KA8 .236 F2
St Charles Prim Sch
Cambuslang G72 .139 F6
Paisley PA2 .113 F2
St Charles' Prim Sch G20 .96 F4
St Clair Ave G46 .136 C3
St Clair St G20 .96 F2
St Clair Terr KA10 .229 C2
St Clare's Prim RC Sch
G15 .75 A4
St Columba Dr G66 .79 E7
St Columba Mews G84 .16 D2
St Columba Pl KA20 .206 F2
St Columba's High Sch
G81 .74 C4
St Columba's High Sch
PA16 .45 A6
St Columba's Prim Sch
KA1 .228 A8
St Columba's RC Prim Sch
G71 .141 C7
St Columba's Sch PA13 .89 C8
St Columbkille's Prim Sch
G73 .138 B7
St Conval's Prim Sch
G43 .136 D8
St Crispin's Pl FK1 .42 B4
St Cuthbert Way ML3 .161 F5
St Cuthbert's Cres
KA9 .236 D6
St Cuthbert's High Sch
PA5 .131 C7
St Cuthbert's Prim Sch
Glasgow G22 .97 B4
Hamilton ML3 .162 A5
St Cuthbert's Rd KA9 .236 C6
St Cyrus Gdns G64 .78 C1
St Cyrus Rd G64 .78 C1
St David's Ct FK5 .23 B1
St David's Pl ML9 .185 A3
St David's Prim Sch
PA5 .111 D1
St David's RC Prim Sch
ML6 .104 A2
St Davids Dr ML6 .123 C4
St Denis Way ML5 .121 F8
St Denis' Prim Sch G31 .118 B7
St Dominic's Prim Sch
G45 .137 F2
St Dominic's RC Prim Sch
ML6 .123 D6
St Edmund's Prim Sch
G53 .115 D1
St Edmunds Gr G62 .55 A3
St Edward's Prim Sch
ML6 .123 C7
St Elizabeth Seton Prim Sch
G33 .119 C8
St Enoch Ave G71 .141 C8
St Enoch Pl G1 .240 C2
St Enoch Sh Ctr G1 .241 A1
St Enoch Sq G1 .240 C1
St Enoch Underground Sta
G1 .240 C1
St Eunan's Prim Sch G81 .74 C2
St Fergus's Prim Sch
PA3 .113 B5
St Fillan's Prim Sch
G44 .137 B6
St Fillan's Prim Sch
PA6 .91 B1
St Fillans Dr PA6 .91 A2
St Fillans Rd G33 .99 C5
St Flanan Rd G65,G66 .59 D2
St Flannan's Prim Sch
G66 .58 F1
St Francis of Assisi Prim Sch
G68 .82 A7
St Francis Prim Sch
PA14 .68 F7
St Francis Xavier Coll
ML5 .122 C4
St Francis Xavier's RC Prim
Sch FK2 .42 A6
St Francis' of Assisi Prim
Sch G69 .119 F3
St Francis' Prim Sch
G5 .117 D4
St Gabriel's Prim Sch
Greenock PA16 .44 D3
Uddingston G71 .141 D8
St George's Cross 10
G3 .97 A2
St George's Ct FK5 .23 B1
St George's Gate PA1 .113 E4
St George's Pl 8 G3 .97 A2
St George's Prim Sch
G52 .114 F5
St George's RC Prim Sch
ML4 .142 A7
St George's Rd Ayr KA8 .236 B3
Glasgow G3 .97 A2
St Germains G61 .75 E4
St Gilbert's RC Prim Sch
G21 .98 C3
St Giles Pk ML3 .162 B2
St Giles Sq FK1 .41 B6
St Giles Way Falkirk FK1 .41 B6
Hamilton ML3 .162 B2
St Gregory's Prim Sch
G20 .96 D6
St Helen's Prim Sch
Bishopbriggs G64 .78 C2
Cumbernauld G67 .82 B7
St Helena Cres G81 .74 C6
St Hilary's Prim Sch
G74 .181 B8
St Ignatius's RC Prim Sch
ML2 .165 B3
St Inan Ave KA12 .219 E3
St Inan's Dr KA15 .150 C1
St Ives Rd G69 .80 F3
St James Ave PA3 .113 C7
St James Bsns Ctr PA1 .112 E4
St James Ct ML5 .121 E3
St James Rd G4 .241 B3
St James Way ML5 .121 E3
St James' Orch FK9 .2 D1
St James' Pl KA20 .206 F2
St James' Prim Sch
Coatbridge ML5 .121 E4
Glasgow G40 .117 E5
Renfrew PA4 .94 C3
St James' St PA1 .113 E5
St James's Prim Sch
PA3 .113 D7
St Jerome's Prim Sch
G51 .115 E7
St Joachim's Prim Sch
G32 .119 C1
St Joan of Arc Sch G22 .97 B7
St Joan's Cres KA13 .207 E2
St John Bosco Prim Sch
PA8 .72 F2
St John Ogilvie Prim Sch
Irvine KA11 .220 B3
Paisley PA1 .114 B4
St John St 6 Ayr KA7 .235 F1
Coatbridge ML5 .122 A7
Prestwick KA9 .236 C8
Stirling FK8 .7 A8
St John The Baptist Prim Sch
G71 .141 A6
St John's Ave FK2 .42 C6
St John's Bvd G71 .141 A6
St John's Ct FK2 .42 C6
St John's Ct G41 .116 E4
St John's Gate FK6 .21 C2
St John's Gdns FK6 .21 C2
St John's Gr FK6 .21 C2
St John's Manor PA19 .44 E8
St John's Pl KA22 .205 C2
St John's Pl KA20 .206 F2
St John's Prim Sch
Alloa FK10 .9 F6
Barrhead G78 .134 C4
Glasgow G5 .117 B5
Hamilton ML3 .162 D3
Port Glasgow PA14 .47 A2
St John's Prim Sch
KA20 .206 F1
St John's Quadrant 1
G41 .116 E4
St John's Rd
Glasgow G41 .116 E4
Gourock PA19 .44 E8
St John's Sch KA8 .236 A1
St Johns Way G65 .59 F3
St Joseph's Acad
(Kilmarnock Campus)
KA3 .223 B2
St Joseph's Ct G21 .97 F1
St Joseph's Pl G21 .97 F1
St Joseph's Prim Sch
Clarkston G76 .157 E5
Clydebank G81 .74 D7
Glasgow G4 .97 B2
St Joseph's Prim Sch
PA16 .45 A4
St Joseph's Prim Sch
Hamilton G72 .161 D8
Milngavie G62 .54 F1
St Joseph's Prim Sch
G33 .99 E5
St Joseph's RC Prim Sch
FK4 .40 B4
St Joseph's View G21 .97 F1
St Josephs Prim Sch G84 .16 F2
St Jude's Prim Sch G33 .119 E6
St Kenneth Dr G51 .115 E8
St Kenneth's Prim Sch
G74 .159 E2
St Kenneth's Prim Sch
PA15 .46 C2
St Kentigerns Rd ML11 .215 B5
St Kessog's Prim Sch
G83 .27 F8
St Kevin's Prim Sch
G69 .121 A5
St Kevin's Sch G21 .97 E2
St Kilda Bank KA11 .220 A2
St Kilda Ct KA11 .220 A2
St Kilda Dr G14 .95 E4
St Kilda Pl KA11 .220 A2
St Kilda Way ML2 .165 E5
St Laurence Cres FK1 .86 B8
St Laurence's Prim Sch
PA15 .46 A3
St Lawrence Pk G75 .159 C1
St Lawrence Pl KA21 .206 A1
St Lawrence St PA15 .46 B4
St Leonard St ML11 .215 B5
St Leonard's Ct KA7 .239 A5
St Leonard's Dr G46 .136 C3
St Leonard's Prim Sch
G74 .160 D3
St Leonard's Rd Ayr KA7 .239 A5
Lanark ML11 .215 B4
St Leonard's Sq G74 .160 C1
St Leonard's Wynd KA7 .239 A6
St Leonards Rd G74 .160 D2
St Leonards Wlk ML5 .122 C3
St Louise's Prim Sch
East Kilbride G75 .180 E6
Glasgow G46 .135 D4
St Lucy's Prim Sch G67 .62 E4
St Luke's Ave ML8 .201 E8
St Luke's Prim Sch
KA13 .207 B2
St Lukes High Sch G78 .155 C8
St Lukes Pl G5 .117 C5
St Lukes Terr G5 .117 C5
St Machan's Prim Sch
G66 .33 D1
St Machan's Way G66 .33 D1
St Machars Rd PA11 .110 E7
St Margaret Ave KA24 .191 B7
St Margaret Mary's Prim Sch
G45 .137 C1
St Margaret Mary's Sec Sch
G45 .137 D2
St Margaret's Ave G65 .37 E3
St Margaret's Ct
Greenock PA16 .45 B5
Paisley PA3 .113 F7
St Margaret's Dr ML2 .164 E1
St Margaret's High Sch
ML6 .123 B8
St Margaret's Pl G1 .241 A1
St Margaret's Prim Sch
PA5 .111 E2
St Margaret's RC Prim Sch
FK7 .12 D7
St Margarets Ct ML4 .142 B5
St Margarets Rd KA22 .205 D4
St Mark Gdns G32 .118 F5
St Mark St G32 .118 E5
St Mark's Ct ML2 .165 C6
St Mark's Prim Sch
Barrhead G78 .134 C1
Glasgow G31 .118 E5
Hamilton ML3 .161 F1
Irvine KA12 .219 E4
Rutherglen G73 .138 B5
St Marnock Pl 10 KA1 .227 F8
St Marnock St
Glasgow G40 .118 A5
Kilmarnock KA1 .227 F8
St Marnock's Prim Sch
G53 .115 C1
St Marnock's Prim Sch
Annexe G53 .115 C1
St Martha's RC Prim Sch
G21 .98 B5
St Martin's Prim Sch
Alexandria G83 .27 E3
Glasgow G45 .137 F2
St Martins Gate ML5 .122 A4
St Mary's (Maryhill) Sch
G20 .96 C7
St Mary's Cres G78 .134 D2
St Mary's Ct ML2 .165 B2
St Mary's La G2 .240 C2
St Mary's Pl KA21 .205 F1
St Mary's Prim Sch
Clydebank G81 .74 A6
Cumbernauld G67 .61 E1
St Mary's Prim Sch
PA16 .45 E6
St Mary's Prim Sch
Hamilton ML3 .162 D4
Lanark ML11 .215 C3
St Mary's Prim Sch
ML9 .184 F2
St Mary's Prim Sch PA1 .113 C3
St Mary's RC Prim Sch
Alexandria G83 .27 E5
Bannockburn FK7 .7 D2
St Mary's RC Prim Sch
ML6 .104 F5
St Mary's RC Prim Sch
Cleland ML1 .144 B1
Coatbridge ML5 .122 A5
Stirling FK8 .1 E2
St Mary's Rd
Bellshill ML4 .141 E5
Bishopbriggs G64 .77 E1
St Mary's Way G82 .49 F3
St Mary's Wynd 5 FK8 .7 A8
St Marys Ct ML11 .215 C4
St Marys Gdns G78 .134 D2
St Matthew's Prim Sch
Bishopbriggs G64 .78 B2
Kilmarnock KA3 .223 C1
St Matthew's RC Prim Sch
ML2 .164 E4
St Maur's Cres KA3 .222 E3
St Maur's Pl KA3 .222 E3
St Maurice's Rdbt G68 .61 A1

Seaforth Rd *continued*
Falkirk FK2 24 C1
Glasgow G52 115 A7
Seaforth Rd N G52 115 A7
Seaforth Rd S G52 115 A7
Seagate Irvine KA12 219 B3
Prestwick KA9 233 C2
Seagrove St G32 118 D6
Seamill Gdns G74 159 D2
Seamill Path G53 134 F5
Seamill St G53 134 F5
Seamore St 4 G20 96 F2
Seath Ave Airdrie ML6 122 E7
Langbank PA14 70 D6
Seath Rd G73 118 A1
Seath St G42 117 C2
Seaton Pl FK1 42 D4
Seaton Terr
Hamilton ML3 162 A4
Irvine KA12 219 C5
Seaview Rd KA21 216 F7
Seaview Terr KA10 230 A4
Seaward La G41,G5 116 E6
Seaward Pl G41 116 F5
Seaward St
6 Glasgow G41 116 E5
Glasgow G5,G41 116 F5
Second Ave
Alexandria G83 27 F5
Auchinloch G66 79 D1
Bearsden G61 76 A3
Clydebank G81 74 A3
Dumbarton G82 50 C2
Glasgow G44 137 B6
Irvine KA12 224 E8
Millerston G33 99 B4
Renfrew PA4 94 C2
Uddingston G71 120 E1
Second Ave La G44 137 B7
Second Gdns G41 116 A4
Second Rd G72 161 E5
Second St G71 140 F8
Seedhill PA1 113 F4
Seedhill Rd PA1 114 A4
Seggielea La G13 95 D6
Seggielea Rd G13 95 D6
Segton Ave KA13 207 C3
Seil Dr G44 137 C4
Selborne Pl 5 G13 95 E5
Selborne Place La 4
G13 95 E5
Selborne Rd G13 95 E5
Selby Gdns G32 119 D5
Selby Pl ML5 101 D2
Selby St ML5 101 D2
Selkirk Ave Glasgow G52 115 C4
Paisley PA2 133 A8
Selkirk Ct 9 PA15 46 B3
Selkirk Dr G73 138 C7
Selkirk Pl
East Kilbride G74 160 D3
Hamilton ML3 162 E2
Selkirk Rd PA14 68 D8
Selkirk St
Hamilton,Blantyre G72 161 D7
Hamilton,Silvertonhill ML3 162 E2
Wishaw ML2 165 C5
Selkirk Way Bellshill ML4 142 B7
Coatbridge ML5 122 E3
Sella Rd G64 78 D2
Selvieland Farm Cotts
PA3 92 D3
Selvieland Rd G52 114 F5
Semphill Gdns G74 160 B2
Sempie St ML3 161 F4
Sempill Ave PA8 72 F2
Semple Ave Bishopton PA7 72 B3
Lochwinnoch PA12 129 C3
Semple Pl PA3 112 B7
Semple Rd KA9 236 D5
Semple View PA9 130 F5
Senate Pl ML1 142 C1
Senga Cres ML4 142 A7
Seres Rd G76 157 D8
Sergeant Law Rd
Paisley G78,PA2 132 E3
Uplawmoor G78 153 B7
Seright Cres KA3 228 D7
Seright Sq KA3 228 D8
Serpentine Wlk PA15 46 C3
Sersley Dr KA25 148 F1
Service St G66 33 C1
Seton Dr FK7 7 C4
Seton La KA22 205 C2
Seton St KA22 205 C2
Seton Terr 3 G31 117 F7
Settle Gdns G69 119 F4
Seven Sisters G66 79 E5
Seventh Ave G71 140 F8
Seventh Rd G72 161 E5
Severn Rd G75 179 F7
Seymour Ave KA13 207 F2
Seymour Gn G75 180 B7
Seyton Ave G46 136 C1
Seyton Ct G46 136 C1
Seyton La G74 159 E3
Shaftesbury Ct G74 160 C5
Shaftesbury St Alloa FK10 10 A7
Clydebank G81 73 F2
Glasgow G3 240 A3
Shafton Pl G13 95 E8
Shafton Rd G13 95 E8
Shaftsbury Ave G81 73 F2
Shaftsbury Cres ML1 143 D3
Shakespeare Ave G81 73 F4
Shakespeare St G20 96 E5
Shalloch Pk KA7 238 C2
Shalloch Pl KA11 220 B2
Shamrock St
Glasgow G4 240 B4
Kirkintilloch G66 79 D8
Shand La ML8 187 F3
Shand St ML2 165 B3
Shandon Brae G83 27 F8
Shandon Cres Balloch G83 27 F8
Bellshill ML4 142 A8
Shandon Pl PA15 46 C2
Shandon Terr ML3 161 F3
Shandwick St G34 120 A8
Shankland Gr PA15 46 F2
Shankland Rd PA15 46 F2
Shanks Ave
Barrhead G78 134 C2
Denny FK6 39 E8
Shanks Cres PA5 111 E2
Shanks Ct KA3 222 F2
Shanks Ind Pk G78 134 C4
Shanks St Airdrie ML6 103 A1
Glasgow G20 96 E5
Shanks Way G78 134 C5
Shannon Dr FK1 41 F4
Shannon St G20 96 F5
Shanter Pl Alloway KA7 238 E1
Kilmarnock KA3 228 C8
Shanter Way KA7 238 E1
Shanter Wynd KA7 238 E1
Shantron Rd G83 27 E6
Shapinsay St G22 97 D8
Sharnothshield Small
Holdings ML2 166 E6
Sharon St KA24 191 B8
Sharp Ave ML5 121 C4
Sharp St Gourock PA19 44 F7
Motherwell ML1 163 B7
Sharpe Ave KA11 220 D1
Sharphill Ind Est KA21 206 A3
Sharphill Rd KA21 216 F8
Shavian Terr KA13 207 E2
Shavin Brae KA7 239 D6
Shaw Ave PA7 72 C3
Shaw Cres ML2 164 D1
Shaw Ct Erskine PA8 72 F3
Newton Mearns G77 156 F4
Shaw Farm Ind Est KA9 233 F1
Shaw Pl Dalry KA24 191 B7
Greenock PA15 45 F5
Linwood PA3 112 B5
Saltcoats KA21 206 A2
Shaw Rd Milngavie G62 76 A8
Newton Mearns G77 156 E4
Prestwick KA9 233 D1
Prestwick KA9 233 E1
Shaw St Glasgow G51 116 A8
Larkhall ML9 199 B8
Shawbank Pl KA1 228 A7
Shawbridge Arc G43 136 C8
Shawbridge Ind Est
G43 136 B7
Shawbridge St G43 136 C7
Shawburn Cres ML3 162 B4
Shawburn St ML3 162 B4
Shawfarm Ct KA9 233 D1
Shawfarm Pl KA9 233 D1
Shawfarm Rd KA9 233 E1
Shawfield Ave KA7 239 A4
Shawfield Cres ML8 186 F6
Shawfield Dr G73 117 F2
Shawfield Ind Est G73 117 F2
Shawfield Rd G73 117 F2
Shawgill Ct ML8 186 F4
Shawhead Ave ML5 122 B4
Shawhead Cotts ML5 122 B3
Shawhead Prim Sch
ML5 122 B3
Shawhill Cres G77 156 E3
Shawhill Rd G43 136 D8
Shawholm Cres G43 136 C7
Shawlands Acad G41 116 E1
Shawlands Arc G41 136 D8
Shawlands Cross 5
G41 116 E1
Shawlands Prim Sch
G41 136 D8
Shawlands Sta G41 136 D8
Shawmoss Rd G41 116 D1
Shawpark St G20 96 E6
Shawrigg Rd ML9 185 C2
Shaws Rd ML9 199 C8
Shawsgate ML9 185 E1
Shawstonfoot Rd ML1 145 A1
Shawwood Cres G77 156 E3
Shearer Dr ML3 183 C7
Shearer Quadrant G83 28 A8
Shearers La PA4 94 C3
Sheena Dr G83 27 F2
Sheepburn Rd G71 140 E7
Sheila St G33 98 E4
Sheildhill 3 G75 180 F7
Sheiling Hill ML3 162 E4
Sheilings The FK10 4 B1
Sheldrake Pl PA5 131 D6
Shellbridge Way KA22 205 C2
Shelley Ct G12 96 A5
Shelley Dr Bothwell G71 141 B2
Clydebank G81 74 A4
Shelley Rd G12 96 A5
Shells Rd G66 58 E1
Sherbrooke Ave G41 116 C3
Sherbrooke Dr G41 116 C4
Sherbrooke Gdns G41 116 C3
Sherbrooke Pl G75 159 C1
Sherburn Gdns G69 119 F3
Sherdale Ave ML6 123 D2
Sheriff Park Ave G73 138 A7
Sheriffmuir Rd FK9 2 D7
Sheriffmuirlands FK9 2 C3
Sherriff La FK5 23 F3
Sherry Ave ML1 143 A5
Sherry Dr ML3 162 A1
Sherry Hts G72 139 A6
Sherwood Ave
Paisley PA1 114 A5
Uddingston G71 141 A5
Sherwood Dr G46 136 A3
Sherwood Pl G15 75 B4
Sherwood Rd
Hurlford KA1 228 F6
Prestwick KA9 236 E8
Shetland Ct FK10 10 B5
Shetland Dr
Glasgow G44 137 C4
Kilmarnock KA3 223 A6
Shettleston Rd G32 119 B5
Shettleston Sheddings
G32 118 E5
Shettleston Sta G32 119 B5
Shewalton Dr KA11 225 D6
Shewalton Moss KA11 225 D6
Shewalton Pits (Nature
Reserve)* KA11 224 F7
Shewalton Rd
Drybridge KA11 225 B6
Irvine KA11 224 F6
Shewalton Rdbt KA11 225 A6
Shewalton Sand Quarry
KA11 224 G7
Shiel Ave G74 159 F3
Shiel Ct G78 134 B5
Shiel Dr ML9 184 F5
Shiel Gdns Falkirk FK2 24 C1
Shotts ML7 147 A3
Shiel Hill KA7 239 B2
Shiel Pl Coatbridge ML5 122 D5
East Kilbride G74 159 F3
Irvine KA12 219 C6
Shiel Rd G64 78 B1
Shiel Terr ML2 165 F6
Shielbridge Gdns G23 76 E1
Shieldaig Dr G73 138 B4
Shieldaig Rd G22 97 B8
Shieldburn Rd G51 115 D7
Shieldhall Gdns G51 115 C7
Shieldhall Rd
Glasgow,Shieldhall G51 115 C7
Glasgow,West Drumoyne
G51 115 E6
Shieldhill Prim Sch FK1 66 D6
Shieldhill Rd
Carluke ML8 201 E8
Shieldhill FK2 66 F7
Shieldmuir St ML2 164 C4
Shieldmuir Sta ML2 164 C3
Shields Ct ML1 164 B3
Shields Dr ML1 164 B3
Shields Holdings PA12 130 B6
Shields Loan ML11 214 F5
Shields Rd
East Kilbride G75 180 B3
Glasgow G41 116 E2
Glasgow G41 116 F3
Glasgow G41 116 F4
Motherwell ML1 164 B3
Shields Road Underground
Sta G5 116 F5
Shields Twr ML1 164 B3
Shielhope Ct KA11 220 A4
Shieling Pk KA7 238 E7
Shierlaw Gdns FK2 14 D4
Shilford Ave G13 95 A7
Shilford Rd G78 132 C1
Shillay St G22 97 E8
Shilliaw Dr KA9 236 D5
Shilliaw Pl KA9 236 D5
Shillinghill FK10 10 B6
Shillingworth Pl PA11 110 D6
Shilton Dr G53 135 C5
Shilton La PA7 72 E4
Shinwell Ave G81 74 D1
Shipbank La G1 241 A1
Shiphaugh Pl FK8 2 C1
Shira Terr G74 160 B1
Shire Way FK10 9 F6
Shirley Quadrant ML1 163 D4
Shirley's Cl ML11 215 A4
Shirra's Brae Rd FK7 7 B4
Shirrel Ave ML4 142 A7
Shirrel Rd ML1 143 B4
Shirva Lea G65 59 F4
Shiskine Dr Glasgow G20 96 C8
Kilmarnock KA3 222 E4
Shiskine Pl Glasgow G20 96 C8
Helensburgh G84 16 F2
Shiskine St G20 96 C7
Sholto Cres ML4 141 D7
Shore Rd Airth FK2 14 D4
Ayr KA8 235 F3
Stevenston KA20 217 D7
Stirling FK8 7 C8
Troon KA10 229 C2
Shore St Glasgow G40 118 A2
Gourock PA19 44 E8
Port Glasgow PA14 47 B2
Shore The FK10 10 A5
Shortlees Cres KA1 227 F3
Shortlees Prim Sch KA1 227 F3
Shortlees Rd KA1 227 F2
Shortridge St G20 96 E5
Shortroods Ave PA3 113 E7
Shortroods Cres PA3 113 D7
Shortroods Rd PA3 113 D7
Shotts Rd ML7 126 E2
Shotts St G33 119 D8
Shotts Sta ML7 146 E4
Shottsburn Rd ML7 126 A3
Shottskirk Rd ML7 146 C6
Shuna Gdns G20 96 F5
Shuna Pl Glasgow G20 96 E5
Newton Mearns G77 156 B6
Shuna St G20 96 E5
Shuttle St Glasgow G1 241 B2
Kilbarchan PA10 111 A3
Kilsyth G65 60 D8
Paisley PA1 113 E4
Sidehead Rd
Harthill ML7 127 E5
Stonehouse ML9 198 E1
Sidland Rd G21 98 C5
Sidlaw Ave Barrhead G78 134 C1
Hamilton ML3 161 F2
Port Glasgow PA14 68 F6
Sidlaw Ct ML5 122 C3
Sidlaw Dr ML2 164 F3
Sidlaw Foot KA11 220 C2
Sidlaw Pl KA1 228 A3
Sidlaw Rd G61 75 B7
Sidlaw Way
Chapelhall ML6 123 F1
Larkhall ML9 184 F5
Sidney St KA21 216 E7
Sielga Pl G34 120 A8
Siemens Pl G21 98 B1
Siemens St G21 98 B1
Sievewright St G73 118 C1
Sighthill Loan 5 ML9 185 B4
Sighthill Prim Sch G21 97 D3
Sighthill Terr ML7 125 B2
Sikeside Pl ML5 122 D5
Sikeside Prim Sch ML5 122 D5
Sikeside St ML5 122 D5
Silk Ho FK1 42 B5
Silk St PA1 113 F5
Silkin Ave G81 74 D1
Sillars Mdw KA12 219 E2
Silvan Pl G76 158 A5
Silver Birch Dr 4 G51 115 D7
Silver Birch Gdns 5
G51 115 D7
Silver Firs ML1 143 C3
Silver Glade G52 115 B4
Silverbirch Gdns ML3 183 F3
Silverbirch Gr ML3 183 F3
Silverburn Cres ML1 143 D3
Silverburn Gdns FK12 5 C7
Silverburn St G33 118 E8
Silverdale G74 159 C3
Silverdale Cres ML11 214 F4
Silverdale Ct ML11 214 F4
Silverdale St G31 118 C4
Silverdale Terr ML6 103 F3
Silverfir St G5 117 D3
Silvergrove St G40 117 E5
Silvermuir Ave ML11 215 F7
Silverton Ave G82 50 B3
Silvertonhill Ave ML3 162 E1
Silvertonhill La G82 50 B3
Silvertonhill Pl ML3 183 D7
Silverwells G71 141 B1
Silverwells Cres G71 141 A1
Silverwood Ct G71 141 B1
Silverwood Prim Sch
KA3 223 C3
Silverwood Rd KA3 228 D8
Sim St KA3 211 C8
Simons Cres
Kilmarnock KA1 227 E4
Renfrew PA4 94 D5
Simonsburn Rd KA1 227 E3
Simpson Ct Clydebank G81 74 A2
Troon KA10 229 G3
Uddingston G71 140 F6
Simpson Dr
East Kilbride G75 180 D7
Saltcoats KA21 205 F3
Simpson Gdns G78 134 B2
Simpson Hts G4 241 C2
Simpson Pl
East Kilbride G75 180 D7
Kilwinning KA13 207 F1
Simpson Quadrant G83 28 A8
Simpson St
Crosshouse KA2 222 A1
Falkirk FK1 41 E6
Glasgow G20 96 F3
Simpson Way ML4 142 C7
Simshill Prim Sch G44 137 B4
Simshill Rd G44 137 C4
Simson Ave KA23 190 E4
Sinclair Ave G61 75 E6
Sinclair Cres FK6 21 D1
Sinclair Ct Bannockburn FK7 7 E1
Kilmarnock KA3 223 C3
Sinclair Dr
Coatbridge ML5 121 D7
Fallin FK7 8 D4
Glasgow G42 136 F7
Glasgow G42 137 A8
Helensburgh G84 16 E3
Sinclair Gdns G64 98 B8
Sinclair Gr ML4 141 F2
Sinclair La G84 16 E4
Sinclair Pk 4 G75 180 F8
Sinclair Pl
East Kilbride G75 180 F8
Falkirk FK2 24 A1
Sinclair St Clydebank G81 94 D8
Greenock PA15 46 D3
Helensburgh G84 16 D2
Milngavie G62 55 A2
Stevenston KA20 206 C1
Singer Rd Clydebank G81 73 F3
East Kilbride G75 180 F6
Singer St G81 74 B3
Singer Sta G81 74 B2
Sir James Clark Bldg
PA1 113 F4
Sir John Graham Ct FK5 23 B1
Sir John Maxwell Prim Sch
G43 136 C7
Sir Michael Ct 10 PA15 45 F5
Sir Michael Pl
Greenock PA15 45 F5
Paisley PA1 113 D4
Sir Michael St PA15 45 F5
Sir William Wallace Ct
FK5 23 B3
Sixth Ave PA4 94 C1
Sixth St G71 120 E1
Skaethorn Rd G20 96 B7
Skaithmuir Ave FK2 24 B3
Skaithmuir Cres FK2 24 B3
Skara Wlk ML2 165 F7
Skaterigg Dr G13 95 F5
Skaterigg Gdns G13 95 F5
Skaterigg La G13 95 E5
Skelbo Path G34 100 D1
Skelbo Pl G34 100 D1
Skellyton Cres ML9 185 B2
Skelmorlie Pl
Kilwinning KA13 207 D3
Stenhousemuir FK5 23 F4
Skene Rd Glasgow G51 116 B5
Kilmarnock KA3 223 C3
Skene St FK4 40 A6
Skerne Gr G75 179 F6
Skernieland Rd KA3 213 A4
Skerray Quadrant G22 97 C8
Skerray St G22 97 C8
Skerryvore Pl G33 119 B8
Skerryvore Rd G33 119 B8
Skibo La G46 135 E3
Skimmers Hill G66 58 B4
Skipness Ave ML8 202 A8
Skipness Dr G51 115 E8
Skirsa Ct G23 97 A8
Skirsa Pl G23 96 F7
Skirsa Sq G23 97 A7
Skirsa St G23 96 F8
Skirving St G41 136 E8
Skovlunde Way G75 180 E6
Skye G74 160 C1
Skye Ave PA4 94 C1
Skye Cres Gourock PA19 44 D6
Old Kilpatrick G60 73 C5
Paisley PA2 133 D8
Skye Ct Cumbernauld G67 82 D8
Irvine KA11 225 C8
Skye Dr Cumbernauld G67 82 D8
Old Kilpatrick G60 73 C5
Skye Gdns Bearsden G61 75 B6
Kilmarnock KA3 223 A6
Skye Pl Airdrie ML6 123 D6
Cumbernauld G67 82 D8
Stevenston KA20 206 F2
Skye Quadrant ML2 165 E5
Skye Rd Cumbernauld G67 82 D8
Port Glasgow PA14 69 B6
Prestwick KA9 233 E1
Rutherglen G73 138 D3
Skye St PA16 45 C4
Skye Wynd ML3 161 F1
Skylands Gr ML3 183 A8
Skylands Pl ML3 183 A7
Skylands Rise ML3 183 A8
Skythorn Way FK1 41 E2
Slaemuir Ave PA14 68 F6
Slaemuir Gdns PA14 68 F6
Slaemuir Prim Sch PA14 69 A6
Slakiewood Ave G69 100 E7
Slamannan Prim Sch
FK1 86 A7
Slamannan Rd
Avonbridge FK1 87 F6
Falkirk FK1 42 A2
Slamannan FK1 86 B2
Slatefield G66 57 D8
Slatefield Ct G31 118 A6
Slatefield St G31 118 A6
Sleaford Ave ML1 163 D4
Slenavon Ave G73 138 D3
Slessor Dr G75 180 F7
Slioch Sq ML1 143 C4
Sloan Ave KA12 219 D2
Sloan Pl Ayr KA8 236 D2
Irvine KA12 219 D2
Sloan St KA8 236 D2
Sloy St Glasgow G22 97 D4
Wishaw ML2 165 A1
Small Cres G72 161 D7
Smart Village Bsns Campus
FK10 9 E7
Smeaton Ave G64 78 B8
Smeaton Ct KA10 229 G4
Smeaton Dr G64 78 A4
Smeaton Gr G20 96 F6
Smeaton St G20 96 F6
Smiddy Ct
Kilmarnock KA1 227 F6
Kilwinning KA13 207 E3
Lanark ML11 215 A4
Smiddy View FK7 6 D6
Smiddy Wynd FK12 5 A6
Smillie Pl KA2 227 C6
Smillie St PA15 46 E2
Smith Art Gallery & Mus*
FK8 7 A8
Smith Ave
Glengarnock KA14 170 D6

Strathleven Pl G82 ....49 F3
Strathmiglo Ct 7 G75 ...179 E8
Strathmiglo Pl FK5 ....23 F4
Strathmore Ave
Blantyre G72 ....140 C1
Paisley PA1 ....114 D4
Strathmore Cres
Airdrie ML6 ....103 A2
Stirling FK9 ....2 A3
Strathmore Ct G14 ....95 F4
Strathmore Dr FK9 ....2 A3
Strathmore Gdns G73 ...138 D4
Strathmore Gr G75 ....179 E8
Strathmore Pk KA11 ...220 B6
Strathmore Pl ML5 ....122 D5
Strathmore Rd
Glasgow G22 ....97 B7
Hamilton ML3 ....162 E3
Strathmore Wlk ML5 ...122 D5
Strathmungo Cres ML6 ..102 F2
Strathnairn Ave G75 ...179 E8
Strathnairn Ct 4 G75 ..179 E8
Strathnairn Dr G75 ....179 E8
Strathnairn Way 5 G75 .179 E8
Strathnaver Cres ML6 ..103 A3
Strathnaver Gdns 6
G75 ....179 E8
Strathord Pl G69 ....81 A4
Strathord St G32 ....119 A3
Strathpeffer Cres ML6 ..103 A2
Strathpeffer Dr 2 G75 ..179 E8
Strathrannoch Way G75 179 E8
Strathspey Ave G75 ....179 E8
Strathspey Cres ML6 ...103 A3
Strathtay Ave
East Kilbride G75 ....158 F1
East Kilbride G75 ....179 E8
Glasgow G44 ....136 E2
Strathtummel Cres ML6 .103 A3
Strathview Gr G44 ....136 E2
Strathview Pk G44 ....136 E2
Strathview Rd ML4 ....141 F3
Strathvithie Gr 10 G75 ..179 E8
Strathy Pl 5 Glasgow G20 .96 D6
Kilmarnock KA1 ....228 B5
Strathyre Ct 11 G75 ....179 E8
Strathyre Gdns
Bearsden G61 ....76 B5
East Kilbride G75 ....179 E8
Glenmavis ML6 ....102 F5
Moodiesburn G69 ....81 A3
Strathyre Rd G72 ....161 F6
Strathyre St G41 ....136 E8
Stratton Dr G46 ....136 B2
Strauss Ave G81 ....74 E1
Stravaig Path PA2 ....133 A7
Stravaig Wlk PA2 ....133 B7
Stravanan Ct G45 ....137 E2
Stravanan Gdns G45 ...137 C1
Stravanan Pl G45 ....137 D2
Stravanan Rd G45 ....137 D2
Stravanan St G45 ....137 D2
Stravanan Terr G45 ....137 D2
Stravenhouse Rd ML8 ...186 F4
Strawberry Field Rd PA6 .91 B1
Strawberrybank Rd
KA3 ....223 A2
Strawhill Ct G76 ....157 F7
Strawhill Rd G76 ....157 F7
Streamfield Gate G33 ...98 D7
Streamfield Gdns G33 ...98 E7
Streamfield Lea G33 ....98 E8
Streamfield Pl G33 ....98 E7
Strenabey Ave G73 ....138 D4
Stripehead 3 FK10 ....10 B6
Striven Cres ML2 ....165 A1
Striven Ct ML5 ....122 B3
Striven Dr FK2 ....24 C1
Striven Gdns G20 ....96 F3
Striven Terr ML3 ....162 A1
Stroma Ave PA14 ....69 B6
Stroma Ct KA11 ....225 C8
Stroma St G21 ....98 B2
Stromness St G5 ....117 A4
Strone Cres PA15 ....46 B3
Strone Gdns G65 ....60 B8
Strone Path ML5 ....101 C6
Strone Pl ML6 ....123 C5
Strone Rd Alexandria G83 ..27 F6
Glasgow G33 ....119 B7
Stronend St G22 ....97 B5
Stronsay Ct KA11 ....220 A2
Stronsay Pl
Bishopbriggs G64 ....78 D2
Kilmarnock KA3 ....223 A5
Stronsay St G21 ....98 B2
Stronsay Way KA11 ....220 A2
Stronvar Dr G14 ....95 B4
Stroud Rd G75 ....180 D6
Strowan Cres G32 ....119 B4
Strowan St G32 ....119 C4
Strowan's Rd G82 ....50 C3
Strowan's Well Rd G82 ..50 C3
Struan Ave G46 ....136 C3
Struan Gdns G44 ....137 A5
Struan House Sch FK10 ..10 A7
Struan Rd G44 ....137 A5
Strude Howe FK12 ....5 B7
Strude Mill FK12 ....5 B7
Strude St FK12 ....5 B7
Struie St G34 ....120 A8
Struma Dr G76 ....157 C8
Struther & Swinhill Rd
ML9 ....199 D6
Struther St ML9 ....199 B8
Strutherhill ML9 ....199 B8
Strutherhill Ind Est
ML9 ....199 C8
Struthers Ave KA3 ....228 D8
Struthers Cres G74 ....160 B4
Struthers Pl KA10 ....229 G8
Struthers Prim Sch
KA10 ....229 G5
Stuart Ave
Old Kilpatrick G60 ....73 B5
Rutherglen G73 ....138 B5
Stuart Dr Bishopbriggs G64 .97 E8
Lanark ML11 ....215 B5
Larkhall ML9 ....185 C1
Stuart Ho G67 ....62 B3
Stuart Pl KA2 ....225 F2
Stuart Quadrant ML2 ...164 E1
Stuart Rd Bishopton PA7 ..72 B3
Carmunnock G76 ....158 D8
Dumbarton G82 ....50 C4
Stuart St
East Kilbride G74 ....159 F2
Old Kilpatrick G60 ....73 B5
Stuarton Pk G74 ....159 E2
Stuckleckie Rd G84 ....17 A1
Sturrock St KA1 ....227 F8
Styles Pl FK1 ....41 F2
Succoth St G13 ....95 F7
Sudbury Cres 2 G75 ...159 B1
Suffolk Rd PA16 ....44 E4
Suffolk St Glasgow G40 ..241 B1
Helensburgh G84 ....16 C2
Sugworth Ave G69 ....120 B5
Suisnish PA4 ....93 C7
Sumburgh St G33 ....119 A7
Summer St G40 ....117 F5
Summerfield Cotts G14 ..95 E2
Summerfield Rd G67 ....82 A6
Summerfield St G40 ....118 B3
Summerford FK1 ....41 D4
Summerford Gdns FK1 ..41 D4
Summerford Rd FK1 ....41 D4
Summerhill & Garngibbock
Rd G67 ....82 D4
Summerhill Ave ML9 ...185 A2
Summerhill Dr G15 ....75 B4
Summerhill Gdns G15 ...75 B4
Summerhill Pl
Clydebank G15 ....75 B4
Shotts ML7 ....166 F8
Summerhill Prim Sch
G15 ....75 B4
Summerhill Rd
Clarkston G76 ....157 F7
Clydebank G15 ....75 B4
Summerhill Way ML4 ...141 F4
Summerlea Rd
Glasgow G46 ....135 F4
West Kilbride KA23 ....190 B4
Summerlee Cotts ML5 ..121 F7
Summerlee Heritage Mus*
ML5 ....121 F8
Summerlee Rd
Larkhall ML9 ....184 F5
Wishaw ML2 ....164 C4
Summerlee St
Coatbridge ML5 ....121 F7
Glasgow G33 ....119 C7
Summerston Sta G20 ...96 D8
Summertown Rd G51 ...116 B7
Suna Path ML7 ....147 B3
Sunart Ave PA4 ....94 B4
Sunart Ct ML3 ....162 A1
Sunart Gdns G64 ....78 C1
Sunart Rd
Bishopbriggs G64 ....78 C1
Glasgow G52 ....115 F5
Sunart St ML2 ....165 A1
Sunbury Ave G76 ....157 C7
Sundale Ave G76 ....157 D6
Sunderland Ave G82 ....49 C4
Sunderland Ct KA25 ...170 A7
Sundrum Pl KA13 ....207 D2
Sunflower Gdns ML1 ...163 D8
Sunningdale Ave
Ayr KA7 ....239 A3
Newton Mearns G77 ....156 F6
Sunningdale Dr PA11 ...110 C6
Sunningdale Pl G84 ....25 B8
Sunningdale Rd G23 ....96 E8
Sunningdale Sq KA13 ...207 C4
Sunningdale Wynd G71 .140 E3
Sunnybank ML7 ....146 F5
Sunnybank Dr G76 ....157 D7
Sunnybank Gr G76 ....157 D6
Sunnybank Rd FK7 ....7 B3
Sunnybank St G40 ....118 B3
Sunnydale Dr EH48 ....107 E3
Sunnydale Rd EH48 ....107 E3
Sunnyhill G65 ....59 F3
Sunnylaw Dr PA2 ....113 B2
Sunnylaw Pl FK1 ....41 F3
Sunnylaw Rd FK9 ....2 A8
Sunnylaw St G22 ....97 B4
Sunnyside Kilmaurs KA3 .222 B7
Stirling FK7 ....7 A4
Sunnyside Ave
Motherwell ML1 ....143 B5
Port Glasgow PA14 ....69 A8
Uddingston G71 ....140 F5
Sunnyside Cres ML1 ...143 A5
Sunnyside Ct FK10 ....10 B7
Sunnyside Dr
Clarkston G76 ....157 D8
Clydebank G15 ....75 A1
Coatbridge G69 ....121 A5
Sunnyside Gate ML1 ...143 A5
Sunnyside Oval PA2 ....113 E1
Sunnyside Pl
Barrhead G78 ....134 B2
Clydebank G15 ....75 A1
Motherwell ML1 ....143 A5
Stirling FK9 ....2 A4
Sunnyside Prim Sch
Alloa FK10 ....10 B7
Glasgow G33 ....99 C3
Sunnyside Rd Alloa FK10 ..10 B7
Cleland ML1 ....165 B8
Coatbridge ML5 ....122 A8
Falkirk FK1 ....41 F5
Kilmarnock KA1 ....227 F2
Kirkfieldbank ML11 ....214 D5
Larkhall ML3,ML9 ....184 C3
Paisley PA2 ....113 D1
Sunnyside Square E
KA1 ....227 F2
Sunnyside Square W
KA1 ....227 F2
Sunnyside St Falkirk FK1 ..41 E6
Larkhall ML9 ....184 F4
Sunnyside Terr ML1 ...143 B5
Surcoat Loan FK7 ....7 E3
Surrey La 1 G5 ....117 B4
Surrey St 3 G5 ....117 B4
Susannah St G83 ....27 E5
Sussex St G41 ....116 E5
Sutcliffe Ct G13 ....95 E7
Sutcliffe Rd G13 ....95 F7
Sutherland Ave
Alloa FK10 ....10 C7
Bearsden G61 ....75 E7
Glasgow G41 ....116 C3
Stirling FK8 ....2 C1
Sutherland Cres ML3 ...162 A4
Sutherland Ct G41 ....116 E4
Sutherland Dr
Airdrie ML6 ....122 F5
Denny FK6 ....39 D8
Dumbarton G82 ....50 C3
Glasgow G46 ....136 D1
Kilmarnock KA3 ....223 D2
Sutherland La G12 ....96 D2
Sutherland Pl
Bellshill ML4 ....141 F2
Helensburgh G84 ....16 B2
Sutherland Rd
Clydebank G81 ....74 B2
Greenock PA16 ....45 A4
Sutherland St
Hamilton G72 ....161 C5
Helensburgh G84 ....16 B2
Paisley PA1 ....113 D5
Sutherland Way G74 ...160 C3
Sutherness Dr G33 ....119 A8
Suttie Way FK9 ....1 F8
Sutton Ct KA13 ....207 B3
Sutton Park Cres FK5 ...23 E3
Sutton Pl FK2 ....42 D5
Swaledale G74 ....159 C3
Swallow Dr PA5 ....131 C7
Swallow Gdns G13 ....94 F7
Swallow Pl KA3 ....228 C7
Swallow Rd
Clydebank G81 ....74 D7
Wishaw ML2 ....165 B3
Swan Pl PA5 ....131 C7
Swan St Clydebank G81 ...73 F3
Glasgow G4 ....241 A4
Swan Way ML8 ....186 F4
Swanson Rd G83 ....27 D7
Swanston St G40 ....118 A2
Sween Ave G44 ....137 A4
Sween Dr ML3 ....162 A1
Sween Path ML4 ....142 C3
Sweethill Terr ML5 ....122 D3
Sweethill Wlk ML4 ....142 C7
Sweethope Gdns G71 ...141 B2
Sweethope Pl G71 ....141 A3
Swift Bank ML3 ....161 E1
Swift Cl ML2 ....165 B3
Swift Cres G13 ....94 F8
Swift Pl East Kilbride G75 .179 F6
Johnstone PA5 ....131 D7
Swinburne Ave G72 ....161 B7
Swinburne Dr FK10 ....5 B1
Swindon St G81 ....73 E3
Swinhill Rd ML9 ....199 C6
Swinstie Rd ML1 ....165 D8
Swinstie View ML1 ....144 C1
Swinton Ave G69 ....120 D5
Swinton Cres
Coatbridge ML5 ....121 B4
Glasgow G69 ....120 D5
Swinton Dr G52 ....115 B5
Swinton Gdns G69 ....120 D5
Swinton Path G69 ....120 D5
Swinton Pl
Coatbridge ML5 ....121 B4
Glasgow G52 ....115 B5
Irvine KA11 ....220 B7
Swinton Prim Sch G69 ..120 C6
Swinton Rd G69 ....120 C5
Swinton View G69 ....120 C5
Swisscot Ave ML3 ....183 B8
Swisscot Wlk ML3 ....183 B8
Switchback Rd G61 ....75 F1
Sword St Airdrie ML6 ...122 F7
Glasgow G31 ....117 F6
Sword's Way FK2 ....24 A1
Swordale Pl G34 ....120 A8
Sycamore Ave
Beith KA15 ....150 B2
Johnstone PA5 ....112 A1
Kirkintilloch G66 ....79 D5
Uddingston G71 ....141 C8
Sycamore Cres
Airdrie ML6 ....123 D6
Ayr KA7 ....239 D6
East Kilbride G75 ....180 D6
Sycamore Ct Beith KA15 .150 B1
East Kilbride G75 ....180 D6
Sycamore Dr
Airdrie ML6 ....123 D6
Clydebank G81 ....74 A4
Hamilton ML3 ....162 F2
Sycamore Gr G72 ....161 C8
Sycamore Pl
East Kilbride G75 ....180 D6
Gourock PA19 ....44 C6
Motherwell ML1 ....143 C3
Stirling FK8 ....6 F5
Sycamore Way
Cambuslang G72 ....139 F4
Carmunnock G76 ....158 D7
Milton Of C G66 ....58 C5
Sycamores The FK10 ....4 B1
Sydenham Ct G12 ....96 B4
Sydenham La G12 ....96 C3
Sydenham Rd G12 ....96 C3
Sydes Brae G72 ....161 B4
Sydney Dr G75 ....180 C8
Sydney Pl 6 G75 ....180 C8
Sydney St Clydebank G81 ..73 D4
Glasgow G31 ....241 C1
Sykehead Ave ML4 ....142 B5
Sykes Terr G78 ....154 F7
Sykeside Rd ML6 ....122 F4
Sylvania Way G81 ....74 B2
Sylvania Way S G81 ....74 B1
Symington Ct 6 KA10 ...229 E5
Symington Dr G81 ....74 B2
Symington Pl Falkirk FK2 ..24 B3
Irvine KA11 ....224 H7
Symington Prim Sch
KA1 ....231 D4
Symington Rd N KA1 ...231 D3
Symington Rd S KA1 ...231 C3
Symington Sq 9 G75 ...180 F8
Symon Twr FK1 ....42 D4
Syms La KA8 ....236 A1
Syriam Pl 1 G21 ....97 F4
Syriam St G21 ....97 F5

T

Tabard Pl G13 ....95 C8
Tabard Rd G13 ....95 C8
Tabernacle La G72 ....139 A5
Tabernacle St G72 ....139 A5
Taggart Rd G65 ....60 F3
Taig Rd G66 ....80 B7
Tain Terr G72 ....161 C3
Tait Ave G78 ....134 D3
Tait Dr FK5 ....41 C8
Tait Wlk ML8 ....201 B1
Tak-Ma-Doon Rd G65 ...36 F3
Takmadoon Rd G65,FK6 ..37 A7
Talbot G74 ....160 C4
Talbot Cres ML5 ....121 E4
Talbot Ct G13 ....95 B5
Talbot Dr G13 ....95 B5
Talbot Pl G13 ....95 B5
Talbot Rd G83 ....28 A8
Talbot Terr Glasgow G13 ..95 B5
Uddingston G71 ....140 E8
Talisker FK10 ....4 B2
Talisman G81 ....74 D2
Talisman Ave G82 ....49 C4
Talisman Cres
Helensburgh G84 ....25 B8
Motherwell ML1 ....142 D2
Talisman Rd Glasgow G13 .95 C6
Paisley PA2 ....132 E7
Talisman Wlk KA21 ....206 A2
Tall Ship The* G3 ....116 C8
Talla Rd G52 ....115 B5
Tallant Rd G15 ....75 B3
Tallant Terr G15 ....75 C3
Tam O'shanter Dr FK7 ...12 D7
Tam O'Shanter Experience*
KA7 ....238 E1
Tam's Brig KA8 ....236 A3
Tamar Dr G75 ....179 F6
Tamarack Cres G71 ....141 C8
Tambowie Ave G62 ....54 F2
Tambowie Cres G62 ....54 F2
Tambowie St G13 ....95 E8
Tamfourhill Ave FK1 ...41 C4
Tamfourhill Ind Est FK1 ..41 C4
Tamfourhill Rd FK1 ....41 C4
Tammy Dale's Rd KA13 ..207 F3
Tamshill St G20 ....96 F5
Tanar Ave PA4 ....94 F1
Tanar Way PA4 ....94 E1
Tandlehill Rd PA10 ....111 B1
Tanera Ave G44 ....137 C4
Tanera Cl FK1 ....42 B2
Tanfield Pl G32 ....119 C7
Tanfield St G32 ....119 C7
Tankerland Rd G44 ....137 A6
Tanna Dr G52 ....115 F3
Tannadice Ave G52 ....115 C4
Tannadice Path G52 ....115 C4
Tannahill Cres
Johnstone PA5 ....111 E1
Johnstone PA5 ....111 F1
Tannahill Dr G74 ....160 C3
Tannahill Rd
Glasgow G43 ....136 F6
Paisley PA3 ....113 B6
Tannahill Terr PA3 ....113 B6
Tanners Rd FK1 ....42 A4
Tannery La FK8 ....2 A1
Tannoch Dr
Cumbernauld G67 ....82 F7
Milngavie G62 ....55 B3
Tannoch Pl G67 ....82 F7
Tannoch Rd G78 ....153 B3
Tannochside Dr G71 ...121 B1
Tannochside Pk
Motherwell G71 ....121 B1
Uddingston G71 ....141 B8
Tannochside Prim Sch
G71 ....141 B8
Tannock St Glasgow G22 ..97 B4
Kilmarnock KA1 ....227 F6
Tantallon Ave PA19 ....43 F5
Tantallon Ct ML8 ....187 E3
Tantallon Dr
Coatbridge ML5 ....101 C2
Falkirk FK2 ....24 A3
Paisley PA2 ....113 A1
Tantallon Pk G74 ....159 D2
Tantallon Rd
2 Bothwell G71 ....141 B3
Glasgow,Baillieston G69 ..120 A3
Glasgow,Langside G41 ...136 E8
Tanzieknowe Ave G72 ..139 B3
Tanzieknowe Dr G72 ...139 B3
Tanzieknowe Pl G72 ...139 A3
Tanzieknowe Rd G72 ...139 B3
Tappoch Pl FK5 ....23 A3
Taransay Ct G22 ....97 E7
Taransay St G51 ....116 A8
Tarbert Ave Blantyre G72 .140 C2
West Kilbride KA23 ....190 E5
Wishaw ML2 ....165 A1
Tarbert Ct ML3 ....162 A1
Tarbert Pl ML8 ....188 A1
Tarbert Way ML5 ....121 E4
Tarbet St PA19 ....44 F7
Tarbolton G74 ....160 D3
Tarbolton Cres ML6 ...123 D1
Tarbolton Dr G81 ....74 C3
Tarbolton Path ML9 ....184 F3
Tarbolton Pl KA3 ....223 C6
Tarbolton Rd
Cumbernauld G67 ....62 B2
Dundonald KA2 ....225 F1
Glasgow G43 ....136 D6
Monkton KA9 ....233 E4
Symington KA1 ....231 F5
Tarbolton Sq G81 ....74 C3
Tarbrax Path ML7 ....147 A3
Tarbrax Way ML3 ....162 A3
Tarduff Pl FK6 ....21 B2
Tarff Ave G76 ....178 E5
Tarfside Ave G52 ....115 C4
Tarfside Gdns G52 ....115 D4
Tarfside Oval G52 ....115 D4
Targe Wynd FK7 ....7 E3
Target Rd ML6 ....123 B6
Tarland St G51 ....115 F6
Tarn Gr G33 ....98 E8
Tarquin Pl ML1 ....163 C8
Tarras Dr PA4 ....94 E1
Tarras Pl G72 ....139 D5
Tarryholme Dr KA12 ...219 D2
Tasker St PA16 ....45 C5
Tasman Dr G75 ....180 B8
Tasmania Quadrant
ML2 ....165 E3
Tassie Pl G74 ....160 A2
Tassie St G41 ....136 D8
Tattershall Rd G33 ....99 C1
Tavistock Dr G43 ....136 D5
Tay Ave PA4 ....94 E3
Tay Cres Bishopbriggs G64 ..78 B1
Glasgow G33 ....98 E1
Tay Ct Alloa FK10 ....10 C6
East Kilbride G75 ....179 E7
Tay Gdns ML3 ....183 B8
Tay Gr G75 ....179 E7
Tay La ML2 ....166 A5
Tay Loan ML1 ....143 A5
Tay Pl Dumbarton G82 ....50 B7
East Kilbride G75 ....179 E7
Johnstone PA5 ....131 C8
Kilmarnock KA1 ....228 A5
Larkhall ML9 ....199 A8
Shotts ML7 ....146 E6
Tay Rd Bearsden G61 ....75 D2
Bishopbriggs G64 ....78 B1
Troon KA10 ....229 G4
Tay St Coatbridge ML5 ...101 C1
Falkirk FK2 ....24 C1
Greenock PA16 ....45 B5
Tay Terr G75 ....179 E7
Tay Wlk 10 G67 ....61 F1
Taybank Dr KA7 ....239 A3
Tayinloan Dr ML8 ....202 B8
Taylor Ave
Kilbarchan PA10 ....110 F3
Motherwell ML1 ....143 D2
Taylor Brown Cl KA3 ...211 E8
Taylor Ct 1 Ayr KA8 ...235 F2
Falkirk FK2 ....42 C7
Taylor High Sch ML1 ...143 A3
Taylor Pl Glasgow G4 ...241 B3
Saltcoats KA21 ....216 F8
Taylor St Alexandria G83 ..27 C7
Ayr KA8 ....235 F2
Clydebank G81 ....94 C8
Glasgow G4 ....241 B3
Taylor's Rd FK5 ....23 C1
Taymouth Dr PA19 ....43 F5
Taymouth St G32 ....119 B3
Taynish Dr G44 ....137 B5
Tayside ML6 ....102 F1
Teak Pl G71 ....121 D1

Towie Pl 2 Glasgow G20 ... 96 D6
Uddingston G71 ... 140 F6
Town Burn FK7 ... 6 F4
Town House St FK6 ... 21 E2
Townend KA3 ... 222 C7
Townend Brae KA1 ... 231 B3
Townend La KA24 ... 191 C7
Townend Pl KA1 ... 231 B3
Townend Rd
Dumbarton G82 ... 50 A5
Kilmarnock KA1 ... 227 E3
Symington KA1 ... 231 C4
Townend St KA24 ... 191 C7
Townend Terr KA1 ... 231 C4
Townfoot KA11 ... 220 C1
Townhead Beith KA15 ... 171 B8
Irvine KA12 ... 219 D2
Kilbirnie KA25 ... 149 B2
Kilmaurs KA3 ... 222 C8
Kilwinning KA13 ... 207 D3
Kirkintilloch G66 ... 79 D7
Kirkintilloch G66 ... 79 D8
Townhead Apartments 9
FK10 ... 10 B6
Townhead Ave ML1 ... 142 E8
Townhead Dr ML1 ... 143 F3
Townhead Gdns KA3 ... 223 A2
Townhead Pl G71 ... 141 A8
Townhead Prim Sch
ML5 ... 101 D2
Townhead Rd
Coatbridge ML5 ... 101 C1
Helensburgh G84 ... 17 A2
Newton Mearns G77 ... 156 D4
Saltcoats KA21 ... 217 A8
Townhead Rdbt G66 ... 79 D8
Townhead St
Hamilton ML3 ... 162 F3
Kilsyth G65 ... 60 D8
Stevenston KA20 ... 206 D1
Stonehouse ML10 ... 198 E2
Townhead Terr PA1 ... 113 D4
Townhill Prim Sch ML3 ... 161 E2
Townhill Rd ML3 ... 161 E3
Townhill Terr ML3 ... 161 E3
Townholm KA3 ... 223 A2
Townmill Rd G31 ... 118 A8
Townsend St G4 ... 97 C2
Traction Bsns Ctr ML1 ... 163 C6
Tradeston Ind Est G5 ... 117 A4
Tradeston St G5 ... 117 A5
Trafalgar Ct G68 ... 61 D6
Trafalgar St
Clydebank G81 ... 73 F2
Glasgow G40 ... 117 F3
Greenock PA15 ... 45 F4
Greenock PA15 ... 45 F5
Trainard Ave G32 ... 118 F4
Tramore Cres KA9 ... 236 C8
Tranchard Ct 6 KA7 ... 235 E1
Tranent Pl Cleland ML1 ... 144 C2
Glasgow G33 ... 118 E8
Traquair Ave Paisley PA2 ... 132 E8
Wishaw ML2 ... 165 C5
Traquair Dr G52 ... 115 B5
Traquair Wynd 10 G72 ... 161 C7
Treebank Cres KA7 ... 239 C5
Treeburn Ave G46 ... 136 B3
Treemain Rd G46 ... 157 A8
Treesbank KA13 ... 207 C2
Treesbank Rd KA1 ... 227 F4
Treespark Ave G78 ... 134 B4
Treeswoodhead Rd
KA1 ... 228 A2
Trefoil Ave G41 ... 136 D8
Trefoil Pl KA7 ... 239 C3
Trelawney Terr KA20 ... 217 E6
Trent Pl G75 ... 179 E6
Trent St ML5 ... 101 D2
Tresta Rd G23 ... 96 F8
Treviot Pl 1 PA15 ... 46 B3
Triangle Sh Ctr The G64 ... 78 A1
Tribboch St ML9 ... 184 F3
Trident Way PA4 ... 94 C1
Trinidad Gn 3 G75 ... 159 A1
Trinidad Way G75 ... 159 A1
Trinity Ave G52 ... 115 C4
Trinity Cres KA15 ... 150 C1
Trinity Dr
Cambuslang G72 ... 139 C3
Dalry KA24 ... 191 B6
Trinity High Sch
Renfrew PA4 ... 94 D3
Rutherglen G73 ... 138 E6
Trinity Pl G82 ... 27 D1
Trinity Way 14 ML9 ... 185 C1
Trinley Rd G13 ... 75 D1
Triton Pl ML4 ... 142 F5
Tron Ct FK10 ... 4 B2
Trondra Gdns KA3 ... 223 A6
Trondra Path G34 ... 119 F8
Trondra Pl G34 ... 119 F7
Trongate Glasgow G1 ... 241 A1
Stonehouse ML9 ... 198 F2
Troon Ave G75 ... 180 A6
Troon Ct G75 ... 180 B6
Troon Dr PA11 ... 110 C7
Troon Gdns G68 ... 61 F6
Troon Pl G77 ... 157 A4
Troon Prim Sch KA10 ... 229 D3
Troon Rd KA10 ... 230 B3
Troon St G40 ... 118 B3
Troon Sta KA10 ... 229 E2
Trossachs Ave ML1 ... 143 A5
Trossachs Ct G20 ... 97 A3
Trossachs Rd G73 ... 138 D2
Trossachs St G20 ... 97 A3
Troubridge Ave PA10 ... 111 B1
Troubridge Cres PA10 ... 111 B2
Trovaig PA8 ... 93 C7
Trows Rd ML2 ... 186 B6
Truce Rd G13 ... 95 B8
Truro Ave G69 ... 80 F3
Tryfield Pl KA8 ... 236 A2
Tryst Pk FK5 ... 23 C5
Tryst Rd Cumbernauld G67 ... 61 F1
Cumbernauld,Carbrain G67 ... 62 A2
Stenhousemuir FK5 ... 23 D2
Stenhousemuir FK5 ... 23 D3
Tryst Wlk
Cumbernauld G67 ... 62 A2
Cumbernauld G67 ... 61 F1
Tudhope Cres G83 ... 27 D7
Tudor La S G14 ... 95 E3
Tudor Rd G14 ... 95 E3
Tudor St G69 ... 119 F3
Tulley Wynd ML1 ... 142 D2
Tulliallan Pl
East Kilbride G74 ... 181 A8
Stenhousemuir FK5 ... 24 A4
Tullibody Rd FK10 ... 9 F8
Tullichewan Cres G83 ... 27 D7
Tullichewan Dr G83 ... 27 D7
Tullichewan Rd G83 ... 27 D8
Tulligarth Pk FK10 ... 10 A7
Tullis Ct G40 ... 117 E4
Tullis St G40 ... 117 F4
Tulloch Gdns ML1 ... 164 B4
Tulloch Rd ML7 ... 147 B3
Tulloch St G44 ... 137 A6
Tullochard Pl G73 ... 138 D3
Tullymet Rd ML3 ... 183 D8
Tummel Dr ML6 ... 102 F2
Tummel Gn G74 ... 159 E3
Tummel Pl FK5 ... 23 E3
Tummel St G33 ... 98 E2
Tummell Way PA2 ... 112 F1
Tunnel St G3 ... 116 E7
Tuphall Rd ML3 ... 162 D2
Turnberry Ave
2 Glasgow G11 ... 96 B3
Gourock PA19 ... 44 B6
Turnberry Cres
Chapelhall ML6 ... 123 E1
Coatbridge ML5 ... 121 E4
Turnberry Ct KA13 ... 207 B3
Turnberry Dr
Bridge of W PA11 ... 110 C6
Hamilton ML3 ... 161 D2
Kilmarnock KA1 ... 227 F4
Newton Mearns G77 ... 157 A5
Rutherglen G73 ... 137 F5
Turnberry Gdns G68 ... 61 F5
Turnberry Pl
Dumbarton G82 ... 49 C8
East Kilbride G75 ... 180 B6
Rutherglen G73 ... 137 F4
Turnberry Rd
Glasgow G11 ... 96 A3
Glasgow G11 ... 96 B3
Turnberry Wynd
Bothwell G71 ... 140 E2
Irvine KA11 ... 224 F8
Turnbull Ave G83 ... 27 D3
Turnbull Cres G83 ... 27 D3
Turnbull High Sch G64 ... 77 E2
Turnbull St G1 ... 241 B1
Turner Pl KA3 ... 223 A3
Turner Rd PA3 ... 113 F8
Turner St ML5 ... 121 F6
Turners Ave PA1 ... 113 B3
Turnhill Ave PA8 ... 93 B7
Turnhill Cres PA8 ... 93 B7
Turnhill Dr PA8 ... 93 B7
Turnhill Gdns PA8 ... 93 B7
Turningshaw Rd PA6 ... 91 E5
Turnlaw G75 ... 180 D5
Turnlaw Rd G72 ... 139 A2
Turnlaw St G5 ... 117 D4
Turnyland Mdws PA8 ... 93 B7
Turnyland Way PA8 ... 93 B7
Turquoise Terr ML4 ... 142 B3
Turret Cres G13 ... 95 D8
Turret Ct FK10 ... 10 C6
Turret Rd G13 ... 95 C8
Turriff St G5 ... 117 B4
TV ML2 ... 186 A8
Twain Ave FK5 ... 24 A3
Twechar Prim Sch G65 ... 60 A3
Tweed Ave PA2 ... 112 F2
Tweed Cres Glasgow G33 ... 98 E1
Kilmarnock KA1 ... 228 A5
Renfrew PA4 ... 94 E2
Wishaw ML2 ... 165 C5
Tweed Ct ML6 ... 123 C5
Tweed Dr G61 ... 75 D3
Tweed La ML1 ... 143 B5
Tweed Pl PA5 ... 131 C8
Tweed St Ayr KA8 ... 236 B3
Coatbridge ML5 ... 122 A3
East Kilbride G75 ... 179 F7
Greenock PA16 ... 45 B5
Larkhall ML9 ... 185 A1
Tweed Wlk G67 ... 61 F2
Tweedmuir Pl ML5 ... 122 D3
Tweedsmuir G64 ... 78 C2
Tweedsmuir Cres G61 ... 75 E7
Tweedsmuir Pk ML3 ... 183 C8
Tweedsmuir Rd G52 ... 115 B5
Tweedvale Ave G14 ... 94 E6
Tweedvale Pl G14 ... 94 E6
Twinlaw St G34 ... 100 D1
Tygetshaugh Ct FK6 ... 21 D4
Tylney Rd PA1 ... 114 D5
Tyndrum Rd G61 ... 76 B5
Tyndrum St G4 ... 241 A4
Tyne Pl G75 ... 179 E6
Tynecastle Cres G32 ... 119 B7
Tynecastle Path G32 ... 119 B7
Tynecastle Pl G32 ... 119 B7
Tynecastle St G32 ... 119 B7
Tynron Ct ML3 ... 161 E1
Tynwald Ave G73 ... 138 D4

U

Uddingston Gram Sch
G71 ... 140 E6
Uddingston Rd G71 ... 141 A3
Uddingston Sta G71 ... 140 E6
Udston Hospl ML3 ... 161 F4
Udston Prim Sch ML3 ... 161 E4
Udston Rd ML3 ... 161 F5
Udston Terr ML3 ... 161 F5
Uig Pl G33 ... 119 E5
Uig Way ML7 ... 147 A3
Uist Ave PA14 ... 69 A7
Uist Cres G33 ... 99 E4
Uist Dr G66 ... 80 A8
Uist La KA3 ... 222 F6
Uist Pl ML6 ... 123 D6
Uist St G51 ... 115 F7
Uist Way ML2 ... 165 E5
Ullswater G75 ... 179 F5
Ulundi Rd PA5 ... 111 E2
Ulva St G52 ... 115 F5
Ulverston Terr ML3 ... 183 D6
Umachan PA4 ... 93 C7
Umberly Rd KA1 ... 227 E3
Underwood KA13 ... 207 D5
Underwood Cotts FK7 ... 6 D5
Underwood Ct PA3 ... 113 D5
Underwood Dr ML2 ... 166 A7
Underwood La PA1 ... 113 D5
Underwood Pl KA1 ... 227 F3
Underwood Rd
Cambusbarron FK7 ... 6 D5
Paisley PA3 ... 113 D5
Prestwick KA9 ... 236 D7
Rutherglen G73 ... 138 C6
Underwood St G41 ... 136 E8
Union Arc KA7 ... 238 F7
Union Ave KA8 ... 236 A3
Union Gdns FK1 ... 41 D5
Union Pl Glasgow G1 ... 240 C2
Larbert FK5 ... 23 B1
Union Rd FK1 ... 41 D5
Union St Alexandria G83 ... 27 F4
4 Alloa FK10 ... 10 B6
Bridge of A FK9 ... 2 A7
Carluke ML8 ... 187 F1
Falkirk FK2 ... 42 B7
Glasgow G1 ... 240 C2
Greenock PA16 ... 45 E6
Hamilton ML3 ... 162 D3
Hurlford KA1 ... 228 E6
Kilmarnock KA3 ... 222 F1
Kirkintilloch G66 ... 79 C8
Larkhall ML9 ... 185 A3
Motherwell ML1 ... 143 A4
Paisley PA2 ... 113 E2
Saltcoats KA21 ... 216 F7
Shotts ML7 ... 146 D5
Stenhousemuir FK5 ... 23 E3
Stirling FK8 ... 2 B1
Stonehouse ML9 ... 198 F2
Troon KA10 ... 229 C3
Union Street La G83 ... 27 F4
Unitas Cres ML8 ... 187 E1
Unitas Rd ML4 ... 142 C5
Unity Pk ML7 ... 146 D4
Unity Pl G4 ... 97 A2
Univ of Glasgow G11,G12 ... 96 D2
Univ of Glasgow (Bearsden
Campus) G61 ... 75 D7
Univ of Glasgow (Kelvin
Campus) G20 ... 76 B1
Univ of Glasgow (St Andrew's
Building) G3 ... 96 E2
Univ of Glasgow (Veterinary
Medicine) G61 ... 96 A8
Univ of Paisley PA1 ... 113 D4
Univ of Paisley (Ayr Campus)
KA8 ... 239 C7
Univ of Stirling FK9 ... 2 D6
Univ of Strathclyde G1,
G4 ... 241 B3
Universal Rd FK2 ... 42 E7
University Ave G12 ... 96 D2
University Gdns G12 ... 96 D2
University Pl G12 ... 96 D2
University Rd W FK9 ... 2 C6
Unsted Pl PA1 ... 114 A4
Unthank Rd ML4 ... 142 C5
UP La G65 ... 60 D8
UP Rd G65 ... 60 D8
Uphall Pl G33 ... 118 E7
Upland La 2 G14 ... 95 C4
Upland Rd G14 ... 95 C4
Uplawmoor Prim Sch
G78 ... 153 B3
Uplawmoor Rd
Neilston G78 ... 154 B6
Uplawmoor G78 ... 153 E4
Upper Adelaide St G84 ... 16 F1
Upper Arthur St G83 ... 27 D4
Upper Bourtree Ct G73 ... 138 C4
Upper Bourtree Dr G73 ... 138 C4
Upper Bridge St
Alexandria G83 ... 27 D4
Upper Bridge St *continued*
Stirling FK8 ... 2 A1
Upper Carman Rd G82 ... 27 D1
Upper Cartsburn St PA15 ... 46 A3
Upper Castlehill 2 FK8 ... 7 A8
Upper Colquhoun St G84 ... 16 D4
Upper Craigs FK8 ... 7 B7
Upper Crofts KA7 ... 238 F1
Upper Glenburn Rd G61 ... 75 D5
Upper Glenfinlas St G84 ... 16 E2
Upper Hall Rd G84 ... 15 D5
Upper Loaning KA7 ... 238 F1
Upper Mill St ML6 ... 123 A8
Upper Mill Street Ind Est
ML6 ... 123 A8
Upper Newmarket St
FK1 ... 42 B5
Upper Smollett St G83 ... 27 D4
Upper Stoneymollan Rd
G83 ... 27 B8
Upper Sutherland Cres
G84 ... 16 B3
Upper Sutherland St G84 ... 16 B3
Upper Torwoodhill Rd
G84 ... 15 F4
Ure Cres FK4 ... 40 A6
Urquhart Cres PA4 ... 94 C2
Urquhart Dr
East Kilbride G74 ... 160 A3
Gourock PA19 ... 43 F5
Urquhart Pl
Gartcosh G69 ... 100 F4
Helensburgh G84 ... 16 D4
Urquhart Rd KA3 ... 223 D2
Urrdale Rd G41 ... 116 B5
Usmore Pl G33 ... 119 E5

V

Vaila Pl G23 ... 97 A7
Vaila St G23 ... 96 F7
Vale Gr FK9 ... 1 F5
Vale Of Bonny View FK4 ... 39 F5
Vale of Leven Acad G83 ... 27 D3
Vale of Leven Hospl
(General) G83 ... 27 C6
Vale of Leven Ind Est
G82 ... 27 E1
Vale Pl FK6 ... 21 E3
Vale Wlk G64 ... 98 C8
Valence Twr G71 ... 140 D4
Valerio Ct G72 ... 161 D8
Valetta Pl G81 ... 73 D3
Valeview FK5 ... 23 D2
Valeview Terr
Dumbarton G82 ... 50 A6
Glasgow G42 ... 137 A8
Vallantine Cres G71 ... 141 A8
Vallay St G22 ... 97 D8
Valley Ct ML3 ... 162 C2
Valley International Pk*
ML8 ... 201 C2
Valley View
Cambuslang G72 ... 139 C6
Motherwell ML1 ... 164 B3
Valleybank G65 ... 37 D3
Valleyfield
East Kilbride G75 ... 159 D1
Milton Of C G66 ... 58 B6
Valleyfield Dr G68 ... 60 E1
Valleyfield Pl FK7 ... 7 C6
Valleyfield St 1 G21 ... 97 E3
Valleyview Dr FK2 ... 42 A8
Valleyview Pl FK2 ... 42 A7
Vancouver Ct 1 G75 ... 159 B1
Vancouver Dr G75 ... 159 B1
Vancouver La
15 Glasgow G14 ... 95 C4
Glasgow G14 ... 95 D4
Vancouver Pl G81 ... 73 D4
Vancouver Rd G14 ... 95 D4
Vanguard St G81 ... 74 D2
Vanguard Way PA4 ... 94 C1
Vardar Ave G76 ... 157 C8
Vardon Lea ML1 ... 143 E1
Varna La G14 ... 95 E3
Varna Rd G14 ... 95 E4
Varnsdorf Way ML6 ... 123 E6
Vasart Pl G20 ... 96 F4
Vatersay Pl KA3 ... 223 A6
Vaults La KA13 ... 207 E3
Veir Terr G82 ... 49 E3
Veitch Pl G66 ... 57 D8
Veitches Ct G81 ... 74 A6
Vennachar St ML7 ... 146 E6
Vennacher Rd PA4 ... 94 B4
Vennard Gdns G41 ... 116 F2
Vennel (Mus) The*
KA12 ... 219 C2
Vennel La KA3 ... 211 E8
Vennel St Dalry KA24 ... 191 B7
Stewarton KA3 ... 211 E8
Vennel The FK6 ... 21 E2
Vermont Ave G73 ... 138 A7
Vermont St G41 ... 116 E5
Vernon Bank G74 ... 159 E3
Vernon Dr PA3 ... 112 A6
Vernon Pl KA2 ... 225 E2
Vernon St KA21 ... 216 F7
Verona Ave G14 ... 95 C4
Verona Gdns 4 G14 ... 95 C4
Verona La G14 ... 95 C4
Verona Pl KA22 ... 205 D1
Vesalius St G32 ... 119 A5
Viaduct Circ KA13 ... 207 E5
Viaduct Rd G76 ... 157 F7
Vicar St FK1 ... 42 B5
Vicarfield St G51 ... 116 B7
Vicarland Pl G72 ... 139 A4
Vicarland Rd G72 ... 139 A5
Vicars Rd ML9 ... 198 E2
Vicars Wlk G72 ... 139 B5
Vickers St ML1 ... 163 B8
Victor St ML6 ... 104 A2
Victoria Ave
Barrhead G78 ... 134 B4
Carluke ML8 ... 187 E1
Victoria Buildings Bsns Ctr
PA1 ... 114 A4
Victoria Cir G12 ... 96 C3
Victoria Cres Airdrie ML6 ... 122 F6
Barrhead G78 ... 134 B4
Clarkston G76 ... 157 F7
Irvine KA12 ... 219 B1
Kilsyth G65 ... 60 B8
Wishaw ML2 ... 164 D4
Victoria Crescent La G12 ... 96 C3
Victoria Crescent Pl 4
G12 ... 96 C3
Victoria Crescent Rd
G12 ... 96 C3
Victoria Cross G42 ... 117 A2
Victoria Ct Larkhall ML9 ... 185 A4
Newton Mearns G77 ... 156 D2
Victoria Dr Barrhead G78 ... 134 B4
Troon KA10 ... 229 E2
Victoria Dr E PA4 ... 94 C2
Victoria Dr W PA4 ... 94 B3
Victoria East Rd KA1 ... 228 A7
Victoria Gdns
Airdrie ML6 ... 122 F7
Barrhead G78 ... 134 B4
Kilmacolm PA13 ... 69 C1
Paisley PA2 ... 113 C2
Victoria Glade G68 ... 61 D6
Victoria Gr G78 ... 134 B4
Victoria Infmy
Glasgow G42 ... 137 A8
Helensburgh G84 ... 16 F1
Victoria La G77 ... 156 D2
Victoria Mans KA7 ... 238 E6
Victoria Meml Cottage Hospl
G65 ... 60 B8
Victoria Park Cnr G14 ... 95 D3
Victoria Park Dr N G14 ... 95 E3
Victoria Park Dr S G14 ... 95 D3
Victoria Park Gdns N
G11 ... 95 F3
Victoria Park Gdns S
G11 ... 95 F3
Victoria Park La N G14 ... 95 D3
Victoria Park La S G14 ... 95 D3
Victoria Park Sch ML8 ... 187 F2
Victoria Park St 7 G14 ... 95 D3
Victoria Pk Ayr KA7 ... 238 E6
* Glasgow G14 ... 95 E3
Kilsyth G65 ... 60 B8
Victoria Pl Airdrie ML6 ... 122 E6
Barrhead G78 ... 134 C4
Bellshill ML4 ... 141 F4
Kilsyth G65 ... 60 C8
Milngavie G62 ... 55 B1
4 Rutherglen G73 ... 138 A8
Stirling FK8 ... 7 A7
Victoria Prim Sch
Airdrie ML6 ... 122 F7
Falkirk FK2 ... 42 D6
Glasgow G42 ... 117 B2
Victoria Quadrant ML1 ... 142 F5
Victoria Rd
Barrhead G78 ... 134 B4
Brookfield PA5 ... 111 D5
Dullatur G68 ... 61 D6
Falkirk FK2 ... 42 C6
Glasgow G42 ... 117 A3
Gourock PA19 ... 44 C7
Harthill ML7 ... 127 E5
Helensburgh G84 ... 16 E2
Kirkintilloch G66 ... 79 C3
Larbert FK5 ... 23 B1
Paisley PA2 ... 113 C2
Rutherglen G73 ... 138 B6
Saltcoats KA21 ... 217 A8
Stepps G33 ... 99 D5
Stirling FK8 ... 7 A8
Victoria Rdbt KA12 ... 219 B2
Victoria Sq
Newton Mearns G77 ... 156 D2
Stirling FK8 ... 7 A7
Victoria St Alexandria G83 ... 27 E4
Alloa FK10 ... 10 A7
Ayr KA8 ... 236 A1
Dumbarton G82 ... 50 A3
Hamilton,Blantyre G72 ... 161 D7
Hamilton,Whitehill ML3 ... 162 B6
Harthill ML7 ... 127 E5
Kirkintilloch G66 ... 79 C8
Larkhall ML9 ... 185 A4
Rutherglen G73 ... 138 B8
Wishaw ML2 ... 166 A4
Victoria Terr Dullatur G68 ... 61 D6
Menstrie FK11 ... 4 B7
Victoria Way KA3 ... 195 F1
Victory Dr PA10 ... 111 A4
Victory Way G69 ... 120 B4
Viewbank G46 ... 136 A3
Viewbank Ave ML6 ... 123 B2
Viewbank St ML5 ... 101 F5
Viewfield Airdrie ML6 ... 122 E7
Moodiesburn G69 ... 80 E4
Viewfield Ave
Bishopbriggs G64 ... 97 E8
Blantyre G72 ... 140 E1
Glasgow G69 ... 119 F5
Kirkintilloch G66 ... 79 C5

Viewfield Ave *continued*
Lochwinnoch PA12 ....129 B2
Milton Of C G66 ....58 B5
Viewfield Bsns Ctr KA8 ..236 A2
Viewfield Dr Alva FK12 ....4 F6
Bishopbriggs G64 ....97 E8
Glasgow G69 ....119 F5
Viewfield La G12 ....96 E2
Viewfield Pl Harthill ML7 .127 F6
3 Stirling FK8 ....7 B8
Viewfield Rd Ayr KA8 ....236 A2
Banknock FK4 ....38 D3
Bellshill ML4 ....141 F3
Bishopbriggs G64 ....97 E8
Coatbridge ML5 ....121 C4
Viewfield St Harthill ML7 .127 F6
4 Stirling FK8 ....7 B8
Viewforth FK8 ....7 B6
Viewglen Ct G45 ....137 D1
Viewmount Dr G20 ....96 D7
Viewpark Beith KA15 ....150 B1
Milngavie G62 ....55 B1
Viewpark Ave G31 ....118 B8
Viewpark Ct G73 ....138 C6
Viewpark Dr G73 ....138 B6
Viewpark Gdns PA4 ....94 B2
Viewpark Pl ML1 ....163 C6
Viewpark Rd ML1 ....163 C6
Viewpark Sh Ctr G71, ML4 ....141 D6
Viewpoint Pl G21 ....97 F6
Viewpoint Rd G21 ....97 F6
Viking Cres PA6 ....111 D8
Viking Rd ML6 ....123 B5
Viking Terr G75 ....180 E6
Viking Way Glasgow G46 .135 F5
Renfrew PA4 ....94 C1
Villabank FK6 ....21 E2
Villafield Ave G64 ....78 A3
Villafield Dr G64 ....78 A3
Villafield Loan G64 ....78 A3
Village Gdns G72 ....140 E1
Village Rd G72 ....139 F5
Vincent Ct ML4 ....142 A4
Vine Park Ave KA3 ....222 B7
Vine Park Dr KA3 ....222 B7
Vine St G11 ....96 B2
Vineburgh Ave KA12 ....219 C4
Vineburgh Ct KA12 ....219 B4
Vines The KA12 ....219 C4
Vinicombe La 3 G12 ....96 D3
Vinicombe St G12 ....96 D3
Vintner St G4 ....97 C2
Viola Pl G64 ....78 C8
Violet Gdns ML8 ....201 E8
Violet Pl ML1 ....143 B6
Violet St PA1 ....114 A4
Virginia Ct G1 ....241 A2
Virginia Gdns Ayr KA8 ...236 A2
Milngavie G62 ....76 C8
Virginia Pl G1 ....241 A2
Virginia St Glasgow G1 ...241 A2
1 Greenock PA15 ....46 A4
Virtue Well View ML6 ...102 E3
Viscount Ave PA4 ....94 C1
Viscount Gate G71 ....140 E5
Vivian Ave G62 ....54 F1
Voil Dr G44 ....137 A4
Voil Rd FK9 ....2 A3
Vorlich Ct G78 ....134 C1
Vorlich Dr FK1 ....66 E7
Vorlich Gdns G61 ....75 C7
Vorlich Pl
Kilmarnock KA1 ....228 A4
Stirling FK9 ....2 A3
Vorlich Wynd ML1 ....143 C4
Vrackie Pl KA1 ....228 A4
Vryburg Cl G75 ....180 A4
Vryburg Cres G75 ....180 A4
Vulcan St 4 Glasgow G21 .97 E4
Motherwell ML1 ....163 E8

W

Waddell Ave ML6 ....102 D4
Waddell Ct Glasgow G5 ..117 D5
Kilmarnock KA3 ....222 F4
Waddell St Airdrie ML6 ...103 A1
Falkirk FK2 ....24 C2
Glasgow G5 ....117 D4
Waggon Rd Ayr KA8 ....235 F2
Falkirk FK2 ....42 B7
Waid Ave G77 ....156 C6
Waldemar Rd G13 ....95 C7
Walden Rd KA1 ....228 E6
Waldo St 3 G13 ....95 F7
Walk The FK10 ....10 A5
Walker Ave
Kilmarnock KA3 ....228 B8
Troon KA10 ....229 E5
Walker Ct Glasgow G11 ....96 B1
Hurlford KA1 ....228 F6
Walker Dr
Bonnybridge FK4 ....39 D5
Elderslie PA5 ....112 C2
Walker Path 2 G71 ....141 A8
Walker Rd KA8 ....236 B2
Walker St Glasgow G11 ....96 B1
Greenock PA16 ....45 C5
5 Kilbirnie KA25 ....149 A1
Paisley PA1 ....113 D4
Walkerburn Dr ML2 ....165 C6
Walkerburn Rd G52 ....115 B4
Walkinshaw Rd PA4 ....93 C3
Walkinshaw St
Glasgow G40 ....118 A4
Johnstone PA5 ....112 A3
Walkinshaw Way PA3 ...113 E7
Walkmill La G81 ....74 B6
Wall Gdns FK1 ....41 C5
Wall St FK1 ....41 C5
Wallace Ave
Bishopton PA7 ....72 B3
Dundonald KA2 ....225 F2
Elderslie PA5 ....112 C2
Stevenston KA20 ....206 D1
Troon KA10 ....229 E6
Wallace Bldgs FK2 ....42 B6
Wallace Cres Denny FK6 ...21 C2
Plean FK7 ....12 D3
Wallace Ct
Kilmarnock KA1 ....228 E6
Prestwick KA9 ....236 D7
Stirling FK8 ....2 B1
Wallace Dr
3 Bishopbriggs G64 ....98 D8
Larkhall ML9 ....185 C2
Wallace Gate
2 Bishopbriggs G64 ....98 D8
Stirling FK8 ....7 B8
Wallace Gdns Stirling FK9 ..2 D3
Torrance G64 ....57 B1
Wallace High Sch FK9 ....2 B3
Wallace Ho G67 ....61 E2
Wallace Monument* FK9 ..2 E4
Wallace Pl
1 Bishopbriggs G64 ....98 D8
Blantyre G72 ....140 E1
Cambusbarron FK7 ....6 D5
Falkirk FK2 ....42 C6
Fallin FK7 ....8 C4
Greenock PA15 ....45 F5
Hamilton ML3 ....163 A2
Wallace Prim Sch PA5 ...112 D2
Wallace Rd Irvine KA12 ..219 C4
Motherwell ML1 ....143 B2
Renfrew PA4 ....94 A1
Wallace St Alloa FK10 ....10 C7
Bannockburn FK7 ....7 E1
Clydebank G81 ....74 B1
Coatbridge ML5 ....122 A5
Dumbarton G82 ....50 A3
Falkirk FK2 ....42 C6
Glasgow G5 ....117 A5
Greenock PA16 ....45 D4
Kilmarnock KA1 ....227 E7
Motherwell ML1 ....163 D7
Paisley PA3 ....113 E6
Plains ML6 ....104 A2
Port Glasgow PA14 ....47 E1
Rutherglen G73 ....138 A7
Stirling FK8 ....2 B1
Wallace View
Kilmarnock KA1 ....227 F5
Shieldhill FK1 ....66 D7
Tullibody FK10 ....4 D3
Wallace Way ML11 ....215 C4
Wallace Wynd
Cambuslang G72 ....139 A3
Law ML8 ....187 A6
Wallacefield Rd KA10 ...229 E3
Wallacehill Rd KA1 ....227 F4
Wallacetown Ave KA3 ...223 B6
Wallacewell Cres G21 ....98 B5
Wallacewell Pl G21 ....98 B5
Wallacewell Quadrant
G21 ....98 C6
Wallacewell Rd G21 ....98 C6
Wallbrae Rd G67 ....82 F8
Wallneuk PA1 ....113 F5
Wallneuk Rd PA3 ....113 F5
Walls St G1 ....241 B2
Wallstale Rd FK7 ....7 A3
Walmer Cres G51 ....116 C5
Walnut Cl G75 ....180 C6
Walnut Cres Glasgow G22 ...97 D5
Johnstone PA5 ....112 B1
Walnut Ct G66 ....58 B5
Walnut Dr G66 ....79 B6
Walnut Gate G72 ....139 F4
Walnut Gr G75 ....180 C6
Walnut Pl Glasgow G22 ....97 D5
Motherwell G71 ....121 C1
Walnut Rd Glasgow G22 ...97 D5
Kilmarnock KA1 ....227 C7
Walpole Pl PA5 ....131 C7
Walter St Glasgow G31 ...118 C7
Wishaw ML2 ....165 D3
Walton Ave G77 ....156 C6
Walton Ct G46 ....136 C2
Walton St Barrhead G78 ..134 C3
Glasgow G41 ....136 E8
Wamba Ave G13 ....95 E8
Wamphray Pl G75 ....179 D7
Wandilla Ave G81 ....74 D2
Wanlock St G51 ....116 A8
Ward Ct KA8 ....236 B4
Ward Rd KA8 ....236 B4
Ward St FK10 ....10 A5
Warden Rd G13 ....95 D7
Wardend Rd G64 ....57 B1
Wardhill Rd G21 ....98 B5
Wardhouse Rd PA2 ....133 C7
Wardie Pl G33 ....119 F7
Wardie Rd G34 ....120 A7
Wardlaw Ave G73 ....138 B7
Wardlaw Cres
East Kilbride G75 ....181 A7
Troon KA10 ....230 A4
Wardlaw Dr G73 ....138 B8
Wardlaw Gdns KA11 ....220 B7
Wardlaw Pl FK2 ....24 C2
Wardlaw Rd Bearsden G61 .75 F1
Kilmarnock KA3 ....223 E5
Wardneuk KA9 ....236 C6
Wardneuk Ct KA11 ....220 A6
Wardneuk Dr KA3 ....223 A4
Wardpark Ct G67 ....62 D6
Wardpark East Ind Est
G68 ....62 E8
Wardpark North Ind Est
G68 ....62 D7
Wardpark Pl G67 ....62 D6
Wardpark Rd G67 ....62 D6
Wardpark Rdbt G68 ....62 D7
Wardpark South Ind Est
G67 ....62 D6
Wardrop Pl G74 ....159 F3
Wardrop St Beith KA15 ...171 C8
2 Glasgow G51 ....116 A8
Paisley PA1 ....113 E4
Wardrop Terr KA15 ....171 C8
Wards Cres ML5 ....121 E5
Wards Pl KA1 ....227 F7
Ware Rd G34 ....120 A7
Warilda Ave G81 ....74 C2
Warlock Dr PA11 ....90 D1
Warlock Rd PA11 ....90 D3
Warly Dr KA2 ....225 F1
Warly Pl KA2 ....225 F1
Warner St KA20 ....217 D7
Warnock Cres ML4 ....142 B4
Warnock Rd G77 ....156 C7
Warnock St G31 ....241 C3
Warren Rd ML3 ....183 D8
Warren St G42 ....117 B1
Warren Wlk G66 ....57 E7
Warriston Cres G33 ....118 D8
Warriston Ct G33 ....118 F8
Warriston Pl G32 ....119 B7
Warriston St G33 ....118 E8
Warriston Way G73 ....138 D4
Warrix Ave KA12 ....219 D2
Warrix Gdns KA10 ....232 E8
Warrix Intc KA11 ....219 E1
Warroch St G3 ....240 A2
Warwick G74 ....160 C4
Warwick Gr ML3 ....161 E5
Warwick Rd PA16 ....44 E4
Warwick Villas G81 ....94 E7
Warwickhill KA11 ....220 B5
Warwickhill Pl KA1 ....222 E2
Warwickhill Rd KA1 ....222 D1
Washington Rd
Kirkintilloch G66 ....79 B8
Paisley PA3 ....113 F8
Washington St G3 ....240 B2
Watchmeal Cres G81 ....74 C7
Water La 8 KA1 ....227 F8
Water Rd G78 ....134 C3
Water Row G51 ....116 A8
Water St PA14 ....47 C2
Waterbank Rd G76 ....158 D5
Watercut Rd Irvine KA13 .218 F8
Irvine KA13 ....219 A8
Waterfoot Ave G53 ....135 C8
Waterfoot Rd
Newton Mearns,Kirkhill
G77 ....157 B3
Newton Mearns,Mearns
G77 ....156 F3
Waterfoot Row G76 ....157 D3
Waterfoot Terr G53 ....135 C8
Waterford Ct G46 ....136 B2
Waterford Rd G46 ....136 B3
Waterfront Way FK9 ....2 A3
Waterfurs Dr FK2 ....42 A8
Waterhaughs Gdns G33 ..98 D7
Waterhaughs Gr G33 ....98 D7
Waterlands Gdns ML8 ...188 A3
Waterlands Pl ML8 ....187 A4
Waterlands Rd ML8 ....187 B6
Waterloo Cl G66 ....58 D1
Waterloo Dr ML11 ....215 A5
Waterloo Gdns 6 G66 ....58 D1
Waterloo La G2 ....240 C2
Waterloo Rd
Lanark ML11 ....215 A5
Prestwick KA9 ....236 B5
Waterloo St G2 ....240 C2
Watermill Ave G66 ....79 D4
Waters End FK2 ....24 B2
Watersaugh Dr ML1 ....144 B2
Watersedge Ct G84 ....15 D4
Waterside Clarkston G76 ..157 F5
Irvine KA12 ....219 B3
Waterside Ave G77 ....156 C4
Waterside Ct
Carmunnock G76 ....158 D7
Kilmarnock KA1 ....227 F8
Waterside Dr G77 ....156 C4
Waterside Gdns
Cambuslang G72 ....139 E3
Carmunnock G76 ....158 D7
Hamilton ML3 ....162 E1
Waterside La PA10 ....111 C2
Waterside Pl G5 ....117 D4
Waterside Rd
Carmunnock G76 ....158 D6
Carmunnock G76 ....158 D8
Kilwinning KA13 ....207 F4
Kirkintilloch G66 ....79 E7
Waterside St
Glasgow G5 ....117 D4
Kilmarnock KA1 ....227 F8
Waterside Terr PA10 ....111 C2
Waterside Way PA10 ....111 C2
Waterslap KA3 ....213 A2
Waterston Way PA12 ....129 C3
Wateryetts Dr PA13 ....69 D1
Watling Ave FK1 ....41 C5
Watling Dr FK1 ....41 D5
Watling Gdns FK1 ....41 D6
Watling Pl 7 G75 ....159 A1
Watling St Falkirk FK1 ....41 C5
Motherwell ML1 ....142 C1
Uddingston G71 ....140 E8
Watson Ave Linwood PA3 .112 B5
Rutherglen G73 ....137 F7
Stonehouse ML9 ....199 A3
Watson Cres G65 ....60 E8
Watson Pl Hamilton G72 ..161 B7
Longcroft FK4 ....39 C4
Watson St Falkirk FK2 ....42 B5
Glasgow G1 ....241 B1
Hamilton G72 ....161 C7
Kilmarnock KA3 ....228 B8
Larkhall ML9 ....184 F3
Motherwell ML1 ....163 E5
Uddingston G71 ....140 F6
Watson Terr KA12 ....219 D2
Watsonville Pk 3 ML1 ..163 E6
Watstone Rd ML9 ....199 A2
Watt Ave G33 ....99 F5
Watt Cres ML4 ....142 B7
Watt Ct Dalry KA24 ....191 C7
Stonehouse ML9 ....198 E1
Watt Gdns FK1 ....41 E6
Watt La PA11 ....110 E7
Watt Low Ave G73 ....137 F6
Watt Pl Greenock PA15 ....46 A5
Hamilton G72 ....161 C4
Milngavie G62 ....54 F3
Watt Rd
Bridge of W PA11 ....110 D7
Glasgow G52 ....115 A7
Watt St Airdrie ML6 ....103 C1
Glasgow G5 ....240 A1
Greenock PA16 ....45 E6
Wattfield Rd KA7 ....238 F6
Waukglen Ave G53 ....135 B2
Waukglen Cres G53 ....135 C3
Waukglen Dr G53 ....135 B3
Waukglen Gdns G53 ....135 B2
Waukglen Path G53 ....135 B3
Waukglen Pl G53 ....135 B3
Waukglen Rd G53 ....135 B3
Waulker St FK8 ....1 F2
Waulking Mill Rd G81 ....74 C7
Waulkmill Ave G78 ....134 D4
Waulkmill Pl KA1 ....228 A7
Waulkmill St G46 ....135 E4
Waulkmill Way G78 ....134 D4
Waverley Clydebank G81 ...74 C2
East Kilbride G74 ....160 D4
Waverley Ave
Helensburgh G84 ....25 C7
Kilmarnock KA1 ....222 C1
Waverley Cres
Bonnybridge FK4 ....40 B3
Cumbernauld G67 ....82 D7
Hamilton ML3 ....161 F4
Kirkintilloch G66 ....79 D8
Lanark ML11 ....215 C4
Stirling FK8 ....2 C1
Waverley Ct
Bothwell G71 ....141 A2
Helensburgh G84 ....16 D2
Waverley Dr Airdrie ML6 .103 B1
Rutherglen G73 ....138 C7
Wishaw ML2 ....165 B4
Waverley Gdns
Elderslie PA5 ....112 D2
Glasgow G41 ....116 E1
Waverley Park Rdbt G66 ..79 E8
Waverley Pk G66 ....79 D8
Waverley Pl KA21 ....205 E1
Waverley Rd Paisley PA2 .132 F8
Stenhousemuir FK5 ....23 C2
Waverley St
Coatbridge ML5 ....102 B1
Falkirk FK2 ....42 B8
Glasgow G41 ....116 E1
Greenock PA16 ....45 C3
Hamilton ML3 ....161 F4
Larkhall ML9 ....199 A8
Waverley Terr
Dumbarton G82 ....49 B4
Hamilton G72 ....161 D5
Stenhousemuir FK5 ....23 C2
Waverley Way PA2 ....132 F7
Weardale La G33 ....119 C8
Weardale St G33 ....119 C8
Weaver Ave G77 ....156 C7
Weaver Cres ML6 ....123 A5
Weaver La PA10 ....111 A4
Weaver Pl G75 ....179 F7
Weaver Row FK7 ....7 A4
Weaver St Ayr KA8 ....235 F2
Glasgow G4 ....241 B2
Weaver Terr PA2 ....114 A3
Weavers Ave PA2 ....113 B3
Weavers Cott* PA10 ....111 A3
Weavers Ct
1 East Kilbride G74 ....159 F2
Kilbarchan PA10 ....111 A3
3 Hamilton ML3 ....162 E2
Weavers Gate PA1 ....113 B3
Weavers Rd PA2 ....113 B3
Weavers Way ML9 ....198 E1
Weavers Wlk ML11 ....215 A3
Webster Ave FK2 ....24 B4
Webster Groves ML2 ....165 D5
Webster St Clydebank G81 .94 E8
Glasgow G40 ....118 A3
Wedderlea Dr G52 ....115 B5
Wee Cl KA15 ....171 B8
Wee Row FK2 ....42 B6
Wee Sunnyside Rd ML9 .184 B2
Weensmoor Rd G53 ....134 F4
Weeple Dr PA3 ....112 A6
Weighhouse Cl PA1 ....113 E4
Weighhouse Rd ML8 ....187 E3
Weir Ave Barrhead G78 ..134 C2
Prestwick KA9 ....233 D1
Weir Dr FK7 ....8 D4
Weir Pl Greenock PA15 ....46 D3
Kilbirnie KA25 ....149 B1
Law ML8 ....186 F4
Weir Rd Ardrossan KA22 ..205 D4
Ayr KA8 ....235 F3
Weir St Coatbridge ML5 ...122 A7
Falkirk FK1 ....42 C5
Greenock PA15 ....46 D2
Paisley PA1,PA3 ....113 F5
Stirling FK8 ....1 F2
Weirston Rd KA13 ....208 A3
Weirwood Ave G69 ....120 A5
Weirwood Gdns G69 ....119 F4
Welbeck Cres KA10 ....229 C2
Welbeck Ct KA10 ....229 C2
Welbeck Rd G53 ....135 B4
Welbeck St
Greenock PA16 ....45 C8
Kilmarnock KA1 ....228 A7
Weldon Pl G65 ....60 F3
Welfare Ave G72 ....139 D4
Well Dr ML11 ....214 E3
Well Gn G43 ....136 C8
Well Gn Ct G43 ....136 C8
Well La G66 ....57 D8
Well Rd Bridge of A FK9 ....2 A8
Falkirk FK1 ....41 F3
Kilbarchan PA10 ....111 A3
Lanark ML11 ....215 B3
Well St Paisley PA1,PA3 ...113 C5
West Kilbride KA23 ....190 C5
Welland Pl G75 ....179 E7
Wellbank Gdns KA23 ....190 C5
Wellbank Pl G71 ....140 F5
Wellbeck Ho 7 G74 ....159 F2
Wellbeck Mews KA10 ....229 C2
Wellbrae Larkhall ML9 ...185 A2
Stonehouse ML9 ....198 E2
Wellbrae Rd ML3 ....162 B1
Wellbrae Terr G69 ....80 F2
Wellbuttslea Dr ML11 ...214 E3
Wellcroft Pl G5 ....117 B4
Wellcroft Rd ML3 ....161 E3
Wellcroft Terr ML3 ....161 E3
Welldale La ML11 ....214 B5
Wellesley Cres
Cumbernauld G68 ....81 E8
East Kilbride G75 ....179 F7
Wellesley Dr
Cumbernauld G68 ....60 D1
East Kilbride G75 ....179 F8
Wellesley Pl G68 ....60 D1
Wellfield Ave G46 ....136 B3
Wellfield St G21 ....97 F4
Wellgate ML11 ....215 A4
Wellgate Ct ML9 ....185 A4
Wellgate Dr FK9 ....2 C7
Wellgate St ML9 ....185 A4
Wellgatehead ML11 ....215 A3
Wellgreen Pl FK8 ....7 B6
Wellgreen Rd FK8 ....7 B7
Wellhall Ct ML3 ....162 B4
Wellhall Rd ML3 ....162 B3
Wellhead Ct ML11 ....215 B4
Wellhouse Cres G33 ....119 F7
Wellhouse Gdns G33 ....119 F7
Wellhouse Gr G33 ....119 F7
Wellhouse Prim Sch
G33 ....119 E7
Wellhouse Rd G33 ....119 F7
Wellington G75 ....180 B7
Wellington Acad PA15 ....45 F4
Wellington Ave KA3 ....228 D8
Wellington La Ayr KA7 ...238 E8
Glasgow G2 ....240 C2
Wellington Path G69 ....120 B4
Wellington Pl
Clydebank G81 ....73 D3
Coatbridge ML5 ....121 C5
Kilmarnock KA3 ....222 F2
Wishaw ML2 ....186 D8
Wellington Rd G64 ....78 B4
Wellington Sch KA7 ....238 E7
Wellington Sq KA7 ....238 E8
Wellington St
Airdrie ML6 ....103 A1
Glasgow G2 ....240 C2
Greenock PA15 ....45 E4
Kilmarnock KA3 ....222 F1
Paisley PA3 ....113 D5
Prestwick KA9 ....236 B5
Wishaw ML2 ....164 C5
Wellington Terr ML11 ...214 F5
Wellington Way
Greenock PA15 ....45 E4
5 Renfrew PA4 ....94 C1
Wellknowe Ave G74 ....158 C2
Wellknowe Pl G74 ....158 C3
Wellknowe Rd G74 ....158 C3
Wellmeadow Annexe (Univ of
Paisley) PA1 ....113 D4
Wellmeadow Cl G77 ....156 D5
Wellmeadow Gn G77 ....156 D5
Wellmeadow Rd G43 ....136 B6
Wellmeadow St PA1 ....113 D4
Wellmeadow Way G77 ....156 D6
Wellmeadows Ct ML3 ....162 A2
Wellmeadows La ML3 ...162 A2
Wellpark KA7 ....238 F2
Wellpark Ave KA3 ....228 C8

Wellpark Bldgs 3 PA15 ..46 A4
Wellpark Cres FK7 ..6 F4
Wellpark Ct
Greenock PA15 ..45 F4
Kilmarnock KA3 ..228 C8
Wellpark Gr KA3 ..228 C8
Wellpark La
Neilston G78 ..154 D6
Saltcoats KA21 ..216 F8
Wellpark Pl KA3 ..228 C8
Wellpark Rd
Banknock FK4 ..38 D2
Motherwell ML1 ..163 C6
Saltcoats KA21 ..216 F8
Wellpark St G31 ..241 C2
Wellpark Terr
Bonnybridge FK4 ..40 A5
Neilston G78 ..154 D6
Wells Quarry Rd G76, G74 ..159 C5
Wells St G81 ..73 F3
Wellsbourne Ho KA7 ..238 E7
Wellshot Dr G72 ..138 F5
Wellshot Prim Sch G32 ..118 F4
Wellshot Rd G32 ..118 F4
Wellside Ave ML6 ..103 A1
Wellside Ct FK1 ..42 A5
Wellside Dr G72 ..139 C4
Wellside La ML6 ..103 B1
Wellside Pl FK1 ..42 A5
Wellside Quadrant ML6 ..103 A1
Wellview Dr ML1 ..163 D6
Wellwood KA13 ..207 C2
Wellwood Ave ML11 ..215 B5
Wellwynd ML6 ..122 F8
Wellwynd Gdns 2 ML6 ..122 F8
Wellyard La PA16 ..44 C3
Wellyard Way PA16 ..44 C2
Wellyard Wynd PA16 ..44 C2
Welsh Dr
Hamilton,Blantyre G72 ..161 D6
Hamilton,Eddlewood ML3 ..183 C7
Welsh Gdns FK9 ..2 A8
Welsh Pl KA21 ..205 E1
Welsh Rd KA9 ..233 D2
Welsh Row ML6 ..123 C3
Wemyss Ave G77 ..156 C7
Wemyss Bay St PA15 ..45 E3
Wemyss Cres KA10 ..229 F1
Wemyss Dr G68 ..60 E1
Wemyss Gdns G69 ..120 A3
Wendur Way PA3 ..113 D8
Wenlock Rd PA2 ..113 F2
Wensleydale G74 ..159 C3
Wentworth Dr 5 G23 ..76 E1
Wentworth Sq KA13 ..207 C4
Wesley St ML6 ..122 F7
West Abercromby St G84 ..16 D3
West Academy St ML2 ..164 E3
West Ave Carluke ML8 ..187 E1
Hamilton G72 ..161 E5
Motherwell ML1 ..143 A2
Paisley PA1 ..112 D4
Plains ML6 ..104 A3
Renfrew PA4 ..94 D3
Stepps G33 ..99 D5
Uddingston G71 ..141 C6
West Balgrochan Rd G64 ..57 B1
West Barmoss Ave PA14 ..68 F7
West Benhar Rd ML7 ..127 B3
West Blackhall St
1 Greenock PA15 ..45 F5
Greenock PA15 ..45 F6
West Boreland Rd FK6 ..21 D2
West Bowhouse Gdns KA11 ..220 A5
West Bowhouse Head KA11 ..220 A5
West Bowhouse Way KA11 ..220 A5
West Bowhouse Workshops KA11 ..220 A5
West Brae PA1 ..113 D4
West Bridge St FK1 ..42 A5
West Bridgend G82 ..49 E4
West Buchanan Pl PA1 ..113 D4
West Burn St PA15 ..45 F5
West Burnside St G65 ..60 D8
West Byrehill Ind Est KA13 ..207 B2
West Campbell St
Glasgow G2 ..240 C3
Paisley PA1 ..113 B4
West Canal St ML5 ..121 F7
West Carmuirs Loan FK5 ..40 F6
West Chapelton Ave G61 ..75 F4
West Chapelton Cres G61 ..75 F4
West Chapelton Dr G61 ..75 F4
West Chapelton La G61 ..75 F4
West Clyde St
Helensburgh G84 ..16 C1
Larkhall ML9 ..185 B2
West Coats Prim Sch G72 ..138 F5
West Coats Rd G72 ..138 F5
West Cres KA10 ..229 G4
West Cross ML2 ..165 A3
West Ct Clydebank G81 ..73 E4
Irvine KA12 ..219 B2
West Dhuhill Dr G84 ..16 D4
West Doura Ave KA21 ..205 F1
West Doura Ct KA13 ..207 B3
West Doura Way KA13 ..207 C3
West Dr Airdrie ML6 ..123 E6
Stenhousemuir FK5 ..23 C1
West End KA24 ..191 B7
West End Dr ML4 ..141 F4
West End Gdns FK10 ..10 A6
West End Pl ML4 ..141 F4
West Fairholm St ML9 ..184 F5
West Faulds Rd ML11 ..215 E5
West Fullarton St KA1 ..222 E1
West Gate ML2 ..165 D3
West George La G2 ..240 C3
West George St
Coatbridge ML5 ..122 A8
Glasgow G2 ..240 C3
Kilmarnock KA1 ..222 F1
West Glebe G76 ..178 F5
West Glebe Terr ML3 ..162 C2
West Glen Gdns PA13 ..69 E1
West Glen Rd PA13,PA14 ..69 E1
West Gr KA10 ..229 G4
West Graham St G3 ..240 B4
West Greenhill Pl G3 ..116 E8
West Hamilton St ML1 ..163 E6
West High St G66 ..58 C1
West James St FK12 ..5 A6
West Johnstone St FK12 ..5 A6
West Kilbride Mus* KA23 ..190 C5
West Kilbride Prim Sch KA23 ..190 C5
West Kilbride Rd KA24 ..191 A7
West Kilbride Sta KA23 ..190 D5
West King St G84 ..16 B2
West Kirk St ML6 ..122 F8
West Kirklands Pl KA24 ..191 B7
West La PA1 ..113 B4
West Langlands St KA1 ..222 E1
West Lennox Dr G84 ..16 D3
West Link Rd FK9 ..2 D5
West Lodge Gdns FK10 ..9 F8
West Lodge Rd PA4 ..94 B4
West Main St ML7 ..127 E5
West Mains Ind Est FK3 ..42 F7
West Mains Rd
East Kilbride G74 ..159 D2
Falkirk FK3 ..42 F7
West Montrose St G84 ..16 C2
West Murrayfield FK7 ..7 D1
West Nemphlar Rd ML11 ..214 C6
West Netherton St KA1 ..227 F7
West Nile St G1 ..241 A3
West of Scotland Science Pk (Todd Campus) G20 ..76 B1
West Park Cres KA3 ..222 B8
West Park Dr KA3 ..222 B8
West Pl ML2 ..166 A5
West Port ML11 ..214 F4
West Portland St KA10 ..229 C2
West Porton Pl PA7 ..71 F4
West Prim Sch PA1 ..113 C4
West Prince's St
6 Glasgow G4 ..96 E2
Glasgow G4 ..96 F2
West Princes St G84 ..16 C2
West Quay PA14 ..47 C2
West Rd Irvine KA12 ..219 B3
Irvine KA12 ..219 B7
Kilbarchan PA10 ..111 A4
Port Glasgow PA14 ..68 E8
Stevenston KA20 ..218 A6
Torrance G64 ..57 B1
West Regent La G2 ..240 C3
West Regent St G2 ..240 C3
West Rossdhu Dr G84 ..16 D3
West Row G63 ..31 A4
West Sanquhar Ave KA8 ..236 B2
West Sanquhar Pl KA8 ..236 B2
West Sanquhar Rd KA8 ..236 B3
West Scott Terr ML3 ..162 D1
West Shaw St
Greenock PA15 ..45 E5
Kilmarnock KA1 ..227 F6
West St Clydebank G81 ..94 E8
Glasgow G5 ..117 A5
Paisley PA1 ..113 C4
West Sta ML3 ..162 C4
West Stewart St
Greenock PA15 ..45 F5
Hamilton ML3 ..162 C4
West Stirling St FK12 ..4 F7
West Street Underground Sta G5 ..117 A5
West Thomson St G81 ..74 B3
West Thornlie St ML2 ..165 A2
West Vennel 6 FK10 ..10 B6
West View KA3 ..213 E4
West View Terr KA3 ..195 B8
West Wellbrae Cres ML3 ..183 B8
West Whitby St G31 ..118 C4
West Woodside Ave PA14 ..68 F6
West Woodstock Ct 3 KA1 ..227 E8
West Woodstock St KA1 ..227 E8
Westacres Rd G77 ..156 B4
Westbank Ct 7 G12 ..96 E2
Westbank La G12 ..96 E2
Westbank Quadrant G12 ..96 E2
Westborne Gdns G84 ..16 C2
Westbourne Ave KA9 ..236 D8
Westbourne Cres G61 ..75 C5
Westbourne Ctr G78 ..134 B2
Westbourne Dr G61 ..75 D5
Westbourne Gardens La 6 G12 ..96 C4
Westbourne Gdns KA9 ..236 D8
Westbourne Gdns N 7 G12 ..96 C4
Westbourne Gdns S G12 ..96 C4
Westbourne Gdns W 8 G12 ..96 C4
Westbourne Rd G12 ..96 B4
Westbourne Terrace La N 9 G12 ..96 C4
Westbourne Terrace La S 3 G12 ..96 B4
Westbrae Dr G13,G14 ..95 E4
Westbrae Rd G77 ..156 F6
Westburn Ave
Cambuslang G72 ..139 D6
Falkirk FK1 ..41 F4
Paisley PA3 ..113 B5
Westburn Bldgs 2 PA15 ..45 F5
Westburn Cres
Clydebank G81 ..74 B7
Rutherglen G73 ..137 F7
Westburn Farm Rd G72 ..139 B6
Westburn Rd
Cambuslang,Newton G72 ..140 B5
Cambuslang,Westburn G72 ..139 D6
Stewarton KA3 ..195 E1
Westcastle Cres G45 ..137 D3
Westcastle Ct G45 ..137 D3
Westcastle Gdns G45 ..137 D3
Westcastle Gr G45 ..137 D3
Westcliff G82 ..49 B4
Westclyffe St 3 G41 ..116 E1
Westcott Pl ML11 ..215 C5
Westcraigs Pk EH48 ..107 C3
Westcraigs Rd
Blackridge EH48 ..107 D2
Harthill ML7 ..127 F6
Westcross Rdbt G77 ..156 A5
Westend G61 ..76 A2
Westend Ct ML8 ..186 F4
Westend Park St G3 ..96 F2
Westend Ret Pk G11 ..96 A2
Wester Boghead G66 ..78 F4
Wester Carriagehill PA2 ..113 E2
Wester Cleddens Prim Sch G64 ..78 A2
Wester Cleddens Rd G64 ..78 C2
Wester Cochno Holdings G81 ..74 A8
Wester Common Dr G22 ..97 A4
Wester Common Rd G22 ..97 A4
Wester Leddriegreen Rd G63 ..31 B4
Wester Mavisbank Ave ML6 ..122 F8
Wester Moffat Ave ML6 ..123 E7
Wester Moffat Cres 2 ML6 ..123 E7
Wester Moffat Hospl ML6 ..123 F8
Wester Myvot Rd G67 ..82 A4
Wester Rd G32 ..119 D3
Westerburn St G32 ..118 F6
Westercommon Prim Sch G22 ..97 A4
Westercraigs G31 ..117 F7
Westerdale G74 ..159 C3
Westerfield Annexe (Univ of Paisley) PA2 ..113 D3
Westerfield Rd G76 ..158 D4
Westergate Sh Ctr G2 ..240 C2
Westergill Ave ML6 ..123 E6
Westerglen Rd FK1 ..42 A2
Westergreens Ave G66 ..79 C6
Westerhill Rd G64 ..78 D3
Westerhouse Ct ML8 ..187 D2
Westerhouse Rd
Glasgow G34 ..119 F8
Glasgow G34 ..120 B8
Westerkirk Dr G23 ..76 E1
Westerlands G12 ..96 A6
Westerlands Dr
Newton Mearns G77 ..156 B4
Stirling FK8 ..7 B5
Westerlands Gdns G77 ..156 B4
Westerlands Gr G77 ..156 B4
Westerlands Pl G77 ..156 B5
Westerlea Ct FK9 ..2 A5
Westerlea Dr FK9 ..2 A5
Westermains Ave G66 ..79 B7
Western Ave Falkirk FK2 ..42 B6
Rutherglen G73 ..137 F8
Western Cres KA25 ..170 A7
Western Ind Est KA3 ..222 E2
Western Infmy G11 ..96 C2
Western Isles Rd G60 ..73 C5
Western Pl KA3 ..223 A4
Western Rd
Cambuslang G72 ..138 F3
Kilmarnock KA1,KA3 ..222 E2
Westerpark Ave G72 ..161 C3
Westerton Cowie FK7 ..12 D8
Lennoxtown G66 ..57 F8
Westerton Ave
Clarkston G76 ..158 A5
Glasgow G61 ..95 F8
Larkhall ML9 ..185 A1
Westerton Ct G76 ..158 A5
Westerton Dr FK9 ..2 A7
Westerton La G76 ..158 A5
Westerton of Mugdock G62 ..55 B6
Westerton Prim Sch G61 ..75 E2
Westerton Rd G68 ..61 D6
Westerton Sta G61 ..75 E1
Westerton Terr FK2 ..24 C3
Westfarm Cres G72 ..139 D6
Westfarm Gr G72 ..139 D7
Westfarm Wynd G72 ..139 D6
Westfield Dumbarton G82 ..49 C4
Kilbirnie KA25 ..170 B8
Westfield Ave G73 ..137 F7
Westfield Cres G61 ..75 E2
Westfield Ct KA21 ..216 E7
Westfield Dr
Bearsden G61 ..75 E2
Cumbernauld G68 ..81 F7
Glasgow G52 ..115 A5
Greenock PA16 ..45 C8
Kilmacolm PA13 ..89 B8
Westfield Ind Area G68 ..81 D6
Westfield Pl
Cumbernauld G68 ..81 D6
Denny FK6 ..21 E1
Westfield Prim Sch G68 ..81 F7
Westfield Rd Ayr KA7 ..238 E6
Cumbernauld G68 ..61 A1
Cumbernauld G68 ..81 E7
Glasgow G46 ..136 A3
Kilmarnock KA3 ..223 C6
Kilsyth G65 ..36 B1
Motherwell ML1 ..143 C7
Port Glasgow PA14 ..68 F8
Westfield Rdbt FK2 ..42 F6
Westfield St FK2 ..42 E5
Westfield Trad Est FK6 ..21 E1
Westfields G64 ..77 E3
Westgarth Pl G74 ..159 A3
Westgate Way ML4 ..141 F5
Westhaugh Cvn Site FK10 ..5 A4
Westhaugh Rd FK9 ..1 F4
Westhorn Dr G32 ..119 A1
Westhouse Ave G73 ..137 E7
Westhouse Gdns G73 ..137 E7
Westknowe Gdns G73 ..138 B5
Westland PA13 ..89 C8
Westland Dr G14 ..95 D4
Westland Drive La 8 G14 ..95 D3
Westlands Gdns PA2 ..113 D2
Westlea Pl ML6 ..123 B6
Westminster Pl FK5 ..23 E4
Westminster Terr 3 G3 ..116 E8
Westmoor Cres KA1 ..227 D7
Westmoreland St G42 ..117 A2
Westmorland Rd PA16 ..44 E4
Westmuir Pl G73 ..137 F8
Westmuir St G31 ..118 D5
Weston Pl KA9 ..236 D6
Weston Terr KA23 ..190 C5
Westpark Ct KA20 ..217 C7
Westpark Dr PA3 ..113 B5
Westpark Wynd KA24 ..191 B8
Westport
East Kilbride G75 ..159 A1
Lanark ML11 ..214 E3
Westport St 10 G65 ..60 D8
Westray Ave
Newton Mearns G77 ..156 C7
Port Glasgow PA14 ..69 B6
Westray Cir G22 ..97 D6
Westray Ct G67 ..82 E8
Westray Dr KA3 ..223 A6
Westray Pl
Bishopbriggs G64 ..78 D2
Glasgow G22 ..97 D7
Westray Rd G67 ..82 E8
Westray Sq G22 ..97 D7
Westray St G22 ..97 C7
Westray Terr FK1 ..42 C2
Westray Wynd 2 ML2 ..165 F6
Westreron Ho
Bridge of A FK9 ..2 A8
Stirling FK9 ..2 A1
Westside Gdns G11 ..96 C2
Westview Cres FK10 ..4 C2
Westward Way KA10 ..229 F7
Westwood Ave Ayr KA8 ..236 E2
Glasgow G46 ..136 B3
Westwood Cres Ayr KA8 ..236 E2
Hamilton ML3 ..162 C2
Westwood Dr ML1 ..144 E1
Westwood Gdns PA3 ..113 B5
Westwood Hill G75 ..180 B7
Westwood Quadrant G81 ..74 D1
Westwood Rd
East Kilbride G75 ..180 B8
Glasgow G43 ..136 B6
Wishaw ML2 ..165 F7
Wishaw ML2 ..166 A5
Westwood Sq G75 ..180 B8
Weymouth Cres PA19 ..44 E5
Weymouth Ct G12 ..96 B6
Weymouth Dr G12 ..96 A6
Whamflet Ave G69 ..120 C7
Whamond Twr ML1 ..163 E5
Whangie The* G63 ..29 A5
Wharf Rd KA12 ..218 D3
Wharry Rd FK12 ..4 E7
Whatriggs Rd KA1 ..228 A4
Wheatfield Rd Ayr KA7 ..238 E7
Bearsden G61 ..75 D2
Wheatholm Cres ML6 ..103 B1
Wheatholm St ML6 ..103 B1
Wheatland Ave G72 ..161 C8
Wheatland Dr ML11 ..214 F5
Wheatlandhead Ct G72 ..161 C8
Wheatlands Ave FK4 ..40 A6
Wheatlands Dr PA10 ..111 A4
Wheatlands Farm Rd PA10 ..111 A4
Wheatlandside ML11 ..214 F5
Wheatley Cres G65 ..60 D7
Wheatley Ct G32 ..119 A5
Wheatley Dr G32 ..119 A5
Wheatley Loan G64 ..98 C8
Wheatley Pl G32 ..119 A5
Wheatley Rd
Saltcoats KA21 ..206 A2
Stevenston KA20 ..206 E1
Wheatpark Pl KA8 ..236 F3
Wheatpark Rd Ayr KA8 ..236 E3
Lanark ML11 ..214 F4
Whifflet Ct ML5 ..122 B5
Whifflet St ML5 ..122 B4
Whifflet Sta ML5 ..122 B5
Whin Ave G78 ..134 B4
Whin Hill G74 ..160 B4
Whin Hill Rd KA7 ..239 B2
Whin Loan G65,G66 ..59 D8
Whin Pl G74 ..160 B5
Whin St G81 ..74 B4
Whinfell Dr G75 ..180 A6
Whinfell Gdns G75 ..180 A6
Whinfield Ave
Cambuslang G72 ..138 E7
Prestwick KA9 ..236 C6
Whinfield Gdns KA9 ..236 C6
Whinfield Rd
Glasgow G53 ..135 A4
Prestwick KA9 ..236 B6
Whinhall Ave ML6 ..102 F1
Whinhall Rd ML6 ..102 E1
Whinhill Cres PA15 ..46 B2
Whinhill Ct 2 PA15 ..45 F4
Whinhill Gdns G53 ..115 A3
Whinhill Pl G53 ..115 A3
Whinhill Rd
Glasgow G53 ..115 A3
Greenock PA15 ..46 A3
Paisley PA2 ..114 B2
Whinhill Sta PA15 ..46 B3
Whinknowe ML9 ..199 F8
Whinney Gr ML2 ..165 E4
Whinnie Knowe ML9 ..184 F1
Whinpark Ave ML4 ..141 F3
Whinriggs ML9 ..198 D1
Whins of Milton Sch FK7 ..7 B1
Whins Rd Alloa FK10 ..10 C7
Glasgow G41 ..116 C1
Stirling FK7 ..7 B2
Troon KA10 ..229 F7
Whinwell Rd FK8 ..2 A1
Whirlie Dr PA6 ..111 B8
Whirlie Rd PA6 ..91 B1
Whirlies Rdbt The G74 ..160 A3
Whirlow Gdns G69 ..120 A5
Whirlow Rd G69 ..120 B5
Whistleberry Cres ML3 ..162 B7
Whistleberry Dr ML3 ..162 B7
Whistleberry Ind Est ML3 ..162 A7
Whistleberry Pk ML3 ..162 A7
Whistleberry Rd ML3 ..162 A7
Whistleberry Ret Pk G72 ..161 F7
Whistlefield Ct G61 ..75 F3
Whitacres Path G53 ..135 A4
Whitacres Rd G53 ..135 A4
Whitburn St G32 ..118 F7
White Ave G82 ..50 B4
White Cart Rd PA3 ..113 E8
White Craig Rd KA22 ..205 D4
White St Ayr KA8 ..236 B4
Clydebank G81 ..94 D7
Glasgow G11 ..96 C2
White's Neuk ML11 ..215 C5
White-Cart Twr G74 ..181 B7
Whiteadder Pl G75 ..179 D7
Whitecraigs Ct G46 ..157 A8
Whitecraigs Pl G23 ..96 E8
Whitecraigs Sta G46 ..157 A8
Whitecrook Bsns Ctr G81 ..74 C1
Whitecrook Prim Sch G81 ..74 C1
Whitecrook St G81 ..74 C1
Whitefield Ave G72 ..139 A4
Whitefield Rd G51 ..116 C6
Whitefield Terr G66 ..33 C1
Whiteford Ave G82 ..50 C5
Whiteford Cres G82 ..50 C5
Whiteford Ct ML3 ..183 C6
Whiteford Pl G82 ..50 C5
Whiteford Rd
Paisley PA2 ..114 A2
Stepps G33 ..100 A5
Whiteford View KA7 ..239 D7
Whitegates G66 ..79 C7
Whitegates Pl FK1 ..41 C4
Whitehall Ave KA9 ..236 D8
Whitehall St G3 ..240 A2
Whitehaugh Ave PA1 ..114 B6
Whitehaugh Cres G53 ..135 A4
Whitehaugh Dr PA1 ..114 B5
Whitehaugh Rd G53 ..135 A4
Whitehill Ave
Airdrie ML6 ..103 A1
Cumbernauld G68 ..61 D2
Kirkintilloch G66 ..58 F1
Stepps G33 ..99 D6
Whitehill Cres
Carluke ML8 ..187 F3
Clydebank G81 ..74 E7
Kirkintilloch G66 ..58 F1
Lanark ML11 ..214 F4

Woodlands Cres *continued*
Bothwell G71 ....141 A3
Falkirk FK1 ....42 A4
Glasgow G46 ....135 F3
Johnstone PA5 ....131 E8
Woodlands Ct
Alexandria G83 ....27 C7
8 Glasgow,Kelvingrove G3 .96 E1
Glasgow,Thornliebank G46 .135 F2
Old Kilpatrick G60 ....73 B5
Woodlands Dr
Coatbridge ML5 ....121 D7
Glasgow G4 ....96 F2
Motherwell ML1 ....142 F5
Woodlands Gate
Glasgow G3 ....240 A4
Glasgow,Thornliebank G46 .135 F3
Woodlands Gdns G71 ...141 A4
Woodlands Gr
Kilmarnock KA3 ....223 B4
Milngavie G62 ....55 A3
Woodlands Pk G46 ......135 F3
Woodlands Pl
Coatbridge ML5 ....121 D7
Kilmarnock KA3 ....223 B4
Woodlands Prim Sch
Cumbernauld G67 ....82 E7
Irvine KA12 ....219 D3
Linwood PA3 ....112 A5
Woodlands Rd
Glasgow G3 ....240 A4
Glasgow,Thornliebank G46 .135 F2
Motherwell ML1 ....163 F4
Motherwell,Holytown ML1 .143 D7
Thornliebank G46 ....136 A2
Woodlands St
Milngavie G62 ....55 A2
Motherwell ML1 ....163 F4
Prestwick KA9 ....236 B8
Woodlands Terr G3 .....240 A4
Woodlands The ML4 ....142 D3
Woodlands View ML9 ...199 A3
Woodlea Ave ML6 ....123 C4
Woodlea Cres KA2 ......221 F2
Woodlea Ct KA2 ....221 F2
Woodlea Dr
Glasgow G46 ....136 D4
Hamilton ML3 ....183 D8
Woodlea Gdns Alloa FK10 ..5 A1
Bonnybridge FK4 ....39 F5
Woodlea La PA19 ....45 A7
Woodlea Pk Alloa FK10 ....10 B8
Sauchie FK10 ....5 A1
Woodlea Pl Airdrie ML6 ..103 C1
Ayr KA7 ....239 B2
Woodlinn Ave G44 ......137 B5
Woodmill KA13 ....207 F1
Woodmill Dr G64 ....57 C1
Woodmill Gdns G67 ......81 F6
Woodneuk La G69 ......100 F5
Woodneuk Rd
Gartcosh G69 ....100 F5
Woodneuk Rd *continued*
Glasgow G53 ....135 B5
Woodneuk St ML6 ......123 D1
Woodneuk Terr G69 .....100 F5
Woodpark KA9 ....236 B5
Woodrow ML1 ....143 B8
Woodrow Ave
Kilmacolm PA13 ....69 D1
Motherwell ML1 ....143 B2
Woodrow Cir G41 ....116 D4
Woodrow Pl G41 ....116 C4
Woodrow Rd G41 ....116 D4
Woodside Houston PA6 ....91 D1
Motherwell ML1 ....142 E8
West Kilbride KA23 ......190 D3
Woodside Ave
Bridge Of W PA11 ....90 D1
Glasgow G46 ....136 A3
5 Hamilton ML3 ....162 E2
Kilmarnock KA1 ....227 D6
Kilsyth G65 ....60 F8
Kirkintilloch G66 ....79 D5
Rutherglen G73 ....138 C7
Woodside Cres
Alexandria G83 ....28 A6
Barrhead G78 ....134 D2
Glasgow G3 ....240 A4
Paisley PA1 ....113 C4
Wishaw ML2 ....166 B6
Woodside Ct
Cambusbarron FK7 ....6 D5
Coatbridge ML5 ....121 D5
Falkirk FK1 ....42 B3
4 Hamilton ML3 ....162 E2
Woodside Dr
Calderbank ML6 ....123 B2
Eaglesham G76 ....157 D2
Woodside Gdns
Carmunnock G76 ....158 D7
Clarkston G76 ....157 D7
Coatbridge ML5 ....121 D4
Woodside Gr Larbert FK5 ..41 D8
Rutherglen G73 ....138 C7
Woodside La PA5 ....111 D6
Woodside Pl Dunlop KA3 .195 C7
Fallin FK7 ....8 C4
Glasgow G3 ....240 A4
Uddingston G71 ....141 C8
Woodside Place La G3 ..240 A4
Woodside Prim Sch
ML3 ....162 E2
Woodside Rd Alloa FK10 ....4 F1
Beith KA15 ....150 B1
Brookfield PA5 ....111 D6
Carmunnock G76 ....158 D7
Forrestfield ML6 ....106 A3
Kilwinning KA13 ....207 C4
Stirling FK8 ....2 A3
Tullibody FK10 ....4 A1
Woodside St
Chapelhall ML6 ....123 D2
Coatbridge ML5 ....121 D4
Motherwell ML1 ....164 B4
Motherwell,New Stevenston
ML1 ....143 A3
Woodside Terr
Clackmannan FK10 ....10 F4
Falkirk FK1 ....42 B3
Glasgow G3 ....240 A4
Woodside Terrace La
G3 ....240 A4
Woodside Twr ML1 ......164 B3
Woodside Wlk ML3 .....162 E2
Woodstock Ave
Glasgow G41 ....116 D1
Kirkintilloch G66 ....79 F8
Lanark ML11 ....215 C4
Paisley PA2 ....132 F8
Woodstock Dr
Lanark ML11 ....215 B4
Wishaw ML2 ....165 C4
Woodstock Pl KA1 ......222 E1
Woodstock Rd
Greenock PA16 ....45 C3
Lanark ML11 ....215 B4
Woodstock Sch KA1 ....227 E8
Woodstock St KA1 ......227 E8
Woodstock Way PA2 ....132 E8
Woodstone Ct G84 ....15 E4
Woodvale Ave
Airdrie ML6 ....123 D4
Bearsden G61 ....76 B2
Rutherglen G46 ....157 B8
Woodvale Dr PA3 ....113 A5
Woodview G71 ....141 D8
Woodview Dr
Airdrie ML6 ....123 A5
Bellshill ML4 ....142 C7
Woodview La ML6 ......123 A5
Woodview Rd ML9 ......199 A8
Woodview Terr ML3 .....162 B4
Woodville Pk G51 ....116 B6
Woodville St G51 ....116 B6
Woodwynd KA13 ....207 E4
Woodyard Rd G82 ....49 E3
Woodyett Pk G76 ....157 F5
Woodyett Rd G76 ....157 F5
Wooer St 4 FK1 ....42 B4
Woolcarders Ct FK7 ....6 D6
Wordle Rd FK7 ....6 F4
Wordsworth Way G71 ...141 B3
Workshop Rd KA20 .....218 B5
Worsley Cres G77 ....156 C7
Wotherspoon Dr KA15 ..150 B2
Wraes Ave G78 ....134 D4
Wraes View G78 ....133 F1
Wraisland Cres PA7 ......71 F4
Wrangholm Cres ML1 ...143 B3
Wrangholm Dr ML1 .....143 B3
Wren Ct ML4 ....141 E8
Wren Pl Johnstone PA5 ..131 D7
Wishaw ML2 ....165 B3
Wren Rd PA16 ....45 A4
Wright Ave G78 ....134 A2
Wright St Falkirk FK2 ......42 B6
Renfrew PA4 ....94 A1
Wright Way ML1 ....143 A3
Wrightfield Pl KA7 ......238 E2
Wrightlands Cres PA8 ....93 E8
Wyburn Pl KA8 ....236 A3
Wye Cres ML5 ....101 D1
Wykeham Pl G13 ....95 C6
Wykeham Rd G13 ....95 C6
Wyler Twr ML3 ....162 E3
Wylie G74 ....160 D5
Wylie Ave Alexandria G83 ..27 D4
Newton Mearns G77 .....156 D7
Wylie Pl Renton G82 ......27 E2
Stewarton KA3 ....195 E1
Wylie St ML3 ....162 D2
Wyllie Rd KA21 ....217 A8
Wynd The Alva FK12 ....5 A7
Cumbernauld G67 ....62 B5
Wyndford Dr G20 ....96 D5
Wyndford Pl 3 G20 ......96 D5
Wyndford Prim Sch G20 ..96 D5
Wyndford Rd
Cumbernauld G68 ....62 D8
Glasgow G20 ....96 D5
Wyndford Terr G71 ......141 B7
Wyndham Ct G12 ....96 D4
Wyndham St G12 ....96 D4
Wynyard Gn G75 ....180 B8
Wyper Pl G31 ....118 A6
Wyvil Ave G13 ....75 E1
Wyvis Ave Bearsden G61 ...75 C7
Glasgow G13 ....94 F8
Wyvis Ct G77 ....156 D2
Wyvis Gdns KA1 ....228 A3
Wyvis Pl Glasgow G13 .....94 F8
Irvine KA11 ....220 A4
Newton Mearns G77 ......156 C2
Shotts ML7 ....147 B3
Wyvis Quadrant G13 .....94 F8
Wyvis Rd KA1 ....228 A3

Y

Yair Dr G52 ....115 A6
Yardley Pl FK2 ....24 A1
Yardside Rd KA3 ....222 B7
Yarrow Cres
Bishopton PA7 ....72 C2
Wishaw ML2 ....165 B4
Yarrow Ct G72 ....139 E5
Yarrow Gardens La 2
G20 ....96 F3
Yarrow Gdns G20 ....96 F3
Yarrow Pk G74 ....160 A1
Yarrow Rd G64 ....78 A4
Yarrow Way G72 ....161 E8
Yate Gr G31 ....118 B5
Yate Rd G31 ....118 B5
Yate St G31 ....118 B5
Yerton Brae KA23 ....190 C4
Yetholm Gdns G74 ......159 F4
Yetholm St G14 ....94 E6
Yetholm Terr ML3 ....161 E3
Yett Rd ML1 ....143 D3
Yetts Ave PA13 ....69 D1
Yetts Cres G66 ....79 F8
Yetts Hole Rd ML6 ......102 B5
Yetts The FK7 ....6 C5
Yew Dr G21 ....98 A3
Yew Pl PA5 ....111 F1
Yews Cres ML3 ....162 B5
Yieldshields Rd ML8 ....189 D3
Yoker Ferry Rd G14 ......94 E6
Yoker Mill Gdns G13 .....94 E7
Yoker Mill Rd G13 ....94 F8
Yoker Prim Sch G14 ......94 F6
Yoker Sta G81 ....94 D7
Yokerburn Pl G13 ....94 E7
Yokerburn Terr G81 ......94 D7
Yonderton Pl KA23 ......190 D4
York Ct KA10 ....229 E3
York Dr Falkirk FK2 ....42 D6
Rutherglen G73 ....138 D5
York Pl Ayr KA8 ....235 F2
Bellshill ML4 ....142 A5
1 Kirkintilloch G66 ....79 C8
York Rd Greenock PA16 ....44 E5
Motherwell ML6 ....143 D8
York St Ayr KA8 ....235 F2
Clydebank G81 ....74 D2
Falkirk FK2 ....42 D6
Glasgow G2 ....240 B2
Wishaw ML2 ....165 B2
York Street La KA8 ......235 F2
York Way PA4 ....94 C1
Yorke Ct KA10 ....229 E2
Yorke Pl KA1 ....222 D1
Yorke Rd KA10 ....229 E2
Yorkhill Par G3 ....96 C1
Yorkhill St G3 ....96 D1
Young Ave KA10 ....229 E6
Young Pl
East Kilbride G75 ....181 A5
1 Uddingston G71 ....141 A8
Wishaw ML2 ....166 B5
Young Rd ML11 ....215 E5
Young St Ardrossan KA22 .205 C2
Clydebank G81 ....74 B4
Prestwick KA8 ....236 B5
Wishaw ML2 ....165 B3
Young Terr G21 ....98 A4
Young Wynd ML4 ....142 A8
Younger Dr KA9 ....233 C3
Younger Quadrant G64 ...78 A1
Yukon Terr G75 ....180 B8
Yvetot Ave ML11 ....215 B4
Yvetot Ct ML8 ....187 E3

Z

Zambesi Dr G72 ....140 C1
Zena Cres G33 ....98 D4
Zena Pl G33 ....98 D4
Zena St G33 ....98 D4
Zetland Pl FK2 ....24 F3
Zetland Rd G52 ....114 F8

Addresses

Name and Address	Telephone	Page	Grid reference

Addresses

Name and Address	Telephone	Page	Grid reference

Any feature in this atlas can be given a unique reference to help you find the same feature on other Ordnance Survey maps of the area, or to help someone else locate you if they do not have a Street Atlas.

The grid squares in this atlas match the Ordnance Survey National Grid and are at 500 metre intervals. The small figures at the bottom and sides of every other grid line are the National Grid kilometre values (**00** to **99** km) and are repeated across the country every 100 km (see left).

To give a unique National Grid reference you need to locate where in the country you are. The country is divided into 100 km squares with each square given a unique two-letter reference. Use the administrative map to determine in which 100 km square a particular page of this atlas falls.

The bold letters and numbers between each grid line (**A** to **F**, **1** to **8**) are for use within a specific Street Atlas only, and when used with the page number, are a convenient way of referencing these grid squares.

Example   The railway bridge over DARLEY GREEN RD in grid square B1

Step 1: Identify the two-letter reference, in this example the page is in **SP**

Eastings (read from left to right along the bottom) come before Northings (read from bottom to top). If you have trouble remembering say to yourself "Along the hall, THEN up the stairs"!

Step 2: Identify the 1 km square in which the railway bridge falls. Use the figures in the southwest corner of this square: Eastings **17**, Northings **74**. This gives a unique reference: **SP 17 74**, accurate to 1 km.

Step 3: To give a more precise reference accurate to 100 m you need to estimate how many tenths along and how many tenths up this 1 km square the feature is (to help with this the 1 km square is divided into four 500 m squares). This makes the bridge about **8** tenths along and about **1** tenth up from the southwest corner.

This gives a unique reference: **SP 178 741**, accurate to 100 m.

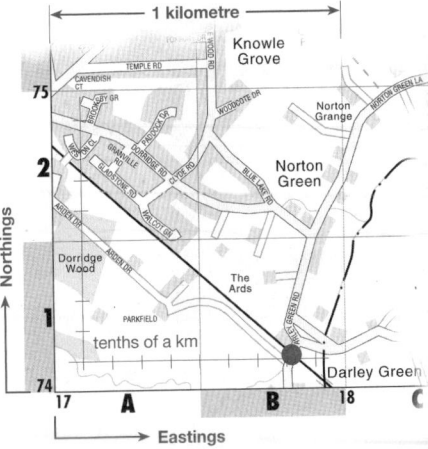